SCIENCE IN THE LAW

SOCIAL AND BEHAVIORAL
SCIENCE ISSUES

By

David L. Faigman
*University of California
Hastings College of the Law*

David H. Kaye
*Arizona State University
College of Law*

Michael J. Saks
*Arizona State University
College of Law*

Joseph Sanders
*University of Houston
Law Center*

AMERICAN CASEBOOK SERIES®

WEST
GROUP

A THOMSON COMPANY

ST. PAUL, MINN., 2002

American Casebook Series, and the West Group symbol
are registered trademarks used herein under license.

COPYRIGHT © 2002 By WEST GROUP
                 610 Opperman Drive
                 P.O. Box 64526
                 St. Paul, MN 55164–0526
                 1–800–328–9352

All Rights Reserved
Printed in the United States of America

ISBN 0–314–26289–X

 TEXT IS PRINTED ON 10% POST CONSUMER RECYCLED PAPER

For Susan
(DLF)

For Miranda
(DHK)

For Roselle
(MJS)

For Mary
(JS)

*

Preface

For the rational study of the law the black
letter man may be the man of the present, but
the man of the future is the man of statistics
and the master of economics.

— Oliver Wendell Holmes[1]

The intellectual life of the whole of western
society is increasingly being split into two
polar groups. . . . Literary intellectuals at one
pole — at the other scientists. . . . Between
the two a gulf of mutual incomprehension.

— C.P. Snow[2]

Judges and lawyers, in general, are not known for expertise in science
and mathematics. Nor is science a subject given significant attention in American law schools. The reasons are manifold. Despite Justice Holmes' prescient
and often-quoted statement, the legal profession has perceived little need for
lawyers to have a grounding in the scientific method. Indeed, law students, as
a group, seem peculiarly averse to math and science. The American educational system is partly at fault, for students routinely divide, or are divided, into two
separate cultures early in their training. Students who display a talent in math
and science typically pursue careers in medicine, engineering, biology, chemistry, computer science, and similar subjects. Students with less inclination
toward quantitative analysis very often go to law school. It is perhaps not surprising that the student who excels in the humanities soon learns that the best
job opportunities for a graduate in Nineteenth Century Russian Literature can
be found through law school. Whatever its origins, the legal profession today is
a particularly salient example of a literary culture that remains largely ignorant
of scientific culture.

Increasingly, however, there are signs that a "third culture" is emerging
in the law.[3] This third culture would be one that integrates a sophisticated
understanding of science into legal decisionmaking. Perhaps the most visible
sign of this emerging integration is the United States Supreme Court's decision

---

1. Oliver Wendell Holmes, Jr., *The Path of the Law,* 10 HARV. L. REV. 457, 469 (1897).
2. C.P. Snow, *The Two Cultures and the Scientific Revolution* 3 (Rede Lecture 1959).
3. Cf. JOHN BROCKMAN, THE THIRD CULTURE (1995) (chronicling the emergence of a
"third culture" in society generally, through the increasing numbers of scientists writing
for a general audience); STEVEN GOLDBERG, CULTURE CLASH: LAW AND SCIENCE IN AMERICA (1994) (exploring the many contexts in which law and science overlap in practice).

in *Daubert v. Merrell Dow Pharmaceuticals, Inc.*[4] The Court, for the first time in its history, considered the standard for evaluating the admissibility of scientific expert testimony. Briefly, the *Daubert* Court held that under the Federal Rules of Evidence, trial court judges must act as "gatekeepers," and evaluate the validity of the basis for proferred scientific expertise before permitting the expert to testify. In two subsequent cases – *General Electric Co. v. Joiner*[5] and *Kumho Tire Ltd. v. Carmichael*[6] – the Court further explicated the obligations that this gatekeeping role demands. These obligations were codified in the Federal Rules of Evidence in 2000. Moreover, states have increasingly followed the Supreme Court's lead, with many adopting *Daubert* outright, and still others incorporating the insights of *Daubert's* validity standard into their preexisting tests for admission of expert testimony.

Application of the *Daubert* standard requires an understanding of scientific research. Whether the Court intended to change the way the law responds to scientific evidence, or had more modest expectations, is impossible to know. Without doubt, however, the many judges, lawyers and scholars who have written on the decision have discovered a revolution of sorts. This revolution is one of perspective, and it affects profoundly not only the judges who guard the gate, but also the lawyers who seek to enter through it.

Until *Daubert,* courts had applied a variety of tests, with most courts being deferential to the scientists in their respective fields of expertise. This role was most closely associated with the general acceptance test articulated in *Frye v. United States.*[7] *Frye* instructed judges to admit scientific evidence only after it had achieved general acceptance in its field. The *Daubert* Court, in contrast, found that the Federal Rules of Evidence require judges themselves to determine the scientific validity of the basis for expert testimony. The shift in perspective is subtle yet profound. Whereas *Frye* required judges to survey the pertinent field to assess the validity of the proferred scientific evidence, *Daubert* calls upon judges to assess the merits of the scientific research supporting an expert's opinion. Implicitly, as well, the *Daubert* standard contemplates that lawyers will have sufficient expertise to explain the science to judges when they make admissibility arguments. The *Daubert* perspective immediately raised the spectre, as Chief Justice Rehnquist decried it, of judges assuming the role of "amateur scientists."[8] The gatekeeping role, he feared, was one most judges were ill-suited to fill.

Daubert has not come to mean that judges must be trained as scientists to carry out admissibility decisions. No one expects judges to join physicists soon in the search for grand unified theories.[9] But there is considerable space between being a trained scientist and being ignorant of science. Although *Daubert* does not expect judges and lawyers to be scientists, it does expect them to be sophisticated consumers of science. This book was formulated with that goal in mind. It is intended to introduce students to the rigors and details

---

4. 509 U.S. 579, 113 S.Ct. 2786, 125 L.Ed.2d 469 (1993).

5. 522 U.S. 136, 118 S.Ct. 512, 139 L.Ed.2d 508 (1997).

6. 526 U.S. 137, 119 S.Ct. 1167, 143 L.Ed.2d 238 (1999).

7. 293 F. 1013 (D.C. Cir. 1923).

8. 113 S.Ct. at 2800 (Rehnquist, C.J., concurring in part and dissenting in part).

9. See generally STEVEN WEINBERG, DREAMS OF A FINAL THEORY: THE SEARCH FOR THE FUNDAMENTAL LAWS OF NATURE (1992).

underlying scientific expert testimony. This book offers an entry point to a host of scientific fields that are highly relevant to the law. It is not intended to provide simple "answers" or final "conclusions." Instead, it is designed and organized to acquaint aspiring lawyers with scientific fields that will be crucial to their practices.

This volume is part of a special student edition of a much larger work intended for a professional audience, our four volume treatise, MODERN SCIENTIFIC EVIDENCE: THE LAW AND SCIENCE OF EXPERT TESTIMONY (2d ed. 2002). There are three volumes in the student edition. The first volume, *Standards, Statistics and Research Issues*, concentrates on the background issues in both law and science that lie behind the sundry contexts in which experts are employed. The second volume, *Social and Behavioral Science Issues*, is organized around substantive topics in the social and behavioral sciences. The third volume, *Forensic Science Issues*, concentrates on an array of important forensic subjects. We hope that the three volumes will be of service either standing alone or as companions to regular texts in a variety of classes, ranging from social science in law to forensic science classes. More fundamentally, we hope that the process of educating lawyers and judges regarding the scientific method will begin in law school. If *Daubert* stands for the proposition that judges and lawyers must henceforth understand science well enough to integrate it successfully into the law, then the educational process that will allow this to occur must begin in law school.

The chapters follow one of two formats. Several chapters provide general overviews of the subject. Most chapters, however, are divided into two sections, one dedicated to the legal relevance of the particular field and the second concerned with the state of the art of the research in that field. The first section is authored by the editors and the second is authored by one or more eminent scientists. The sections on the state of the science are all written largely following a similar organizational scheme. We asked the contributors to discuss the scientific questions or hypotheses posited by the researchers, the methods brought to bear to study these hypotheses, the areas of scientific agreement, the areas of scientific disagreement, and the likely future directions for scientific research in the area. Some scientific topics lend themselves to this scheme better than others. Nonetheless, our guiding objective was to make the science accessible to the non-scientifically trained generalist.

Daubert, perhaps, represents nothing more, *or less,* than that the legal culture must assimilate the scientific culture. As compared to the sciences, the law obviously has different objectives, values, and time tables in which to work. The law should not, nor could it, adopt the scientific perspective wholly and without qualifications. Science is merely a tool that the law can and must use to achieve its own objectives. Science cannot dictate what is fair and just. We can confidently conclude, however, that science has become, and will forever more be, a tool upon which the law must sometimes rely to do justice.

> David L. Faigman
> David H. Kaye
> Michael J. Saks
> Joseph Sanders

February, 2002.

*

Acknowledgments

At the conclusion of THE ADVENTURES OF HUCKLEBERRY FINN, Huck states, ". . . and so there ain't nothing more to write about, and I am rotten glad of it, because if I'd a knowed what a trouble it was to make a book I wouldn't a tackled it and ain't agoing to no more."[1] We, perhaps, suffer Huck's lament more than he, for he never knew the pain of periodic supplements, as are planned for these volumes. However, we have had the immeasurable assistance of a score of colleagues and students who have made our task less trouble. We wish to thank all of the people who contributed so much to both the first and second editions.

At the University of California, Hastings College of the Law, we wish to thank our colleagues Mary Kay Kane, William Schwarzer, Roger Park, and Eileen Scallen for their support, encouragement and comments on various parts of this book. In addition, much is owed the student research assistants who spent innumerable hours on the project, including Tamara Costa, Kathryn Davis, Jamie Tenero, Paula Quintiliani, Amy Wright, Ali Graham, Cliff Hong, Lucia Sciaraffa, Faith Wolinsky and Sara Zalkin. Finally, we owe a considerable debt to Ted Jang and, especially, Barbara Topchov for secretarial support.

At Arizona State University, College of Law, we thank Gail Geer, Sonja Quinones and Rosalind Pearlman for secretarial support and Vivian Chang and James Pack for research assistance.

At the University of Iowa, College of Law, we thank research assistants "Max" Wilkinson, Alec Hillbo, and Patricia Fowler.

At the University of Houston Law Center, we wish to thank the students in the Spring 1996 Scientific Evidence seminar who did much in assisting on the toxic tort sections of the of the first edition: Angela Beavers, Chris Blanton, Armi Easterby, Nellie Fisher, Stephanie Hall, Jim Hildebrandt, Lynn Huston, Preston Hutson, Dino Ioannides, Candice Kaiser, Bill Long, Helen O'Conor, Ruth Piller, Larry Pinsky, John Powell, Jane Starnes, Donna Woodruff, and Kirk Worley. On the second edition, we extend our grateful appreciation to the research assistance of William Campbell, Mary Chapman, Alison Chein, Cynthia DeLaughter, Linda Garza, Linda Glover, Jamie Liner, Laura Moore, Jason Pinkall, Scott Provinse, Amanda Snowden and Angela Williams. Special thanks goes to Bethany Fitch who helped to cite check and proof read the manuscript.

Outside of our respective home institutions, we have had the generous assistance of many colleagues and institutions. At the Federal Judicial Center, we wish to thank Joe Cecil for his support and encouragement of this project. We are also indebted to Bert Black, for both his assistance in identifying authors and his generous sharing of ideas on a variety of topics.

*

---

[1] MARK TWAIN, ADVENTURES OF HUCKLEBERRY FINN 363 (Random House 1996).

ix

List of Contributors

Edith D. Balbach is a postdoctoral fellow at the Institute for Health Policy Studies, University of California at San Francisco, where she studies issues related to youth and tobacco.

Alfred A. Biasotti (1926–1997), M.S. in Criminalistics, U.C. Berkeley, was a criminalist, supervising criminalist, and administrator from 1951 to 1990, retiring as Assistant Chief of the Bureau of Forensic Sciences, California Department of Justice. He helped establish the California Criminalistics Institute; authored numerous articles on firearms and toolmark identification; was a Fellow of the American Academy of Forensic Sciences; and a distinguished member of the Association of Firearm and Toolmark Examiners. He passed away on June 24, 1997, from complications associated with Parkinson's Disease.

Stuart Bondurant received his B.S. in Medicine and his M.D. from Duke University. He interned and completed his residency in Internal Medicine at Duke University Medical Center and the Peter Bent Brigham Hospital in Boston. He served in the United States Air Force as a research internist and chief medical officer in the Acceleration Section of the Aeromedical Laboratory at Wright–Patterson Air Force Base. Dr. Bondurant was a member of the faculty of the School of Medicine at Indiana University Medical Center and was Chief of the Medical Branch of the Artificial Heart–Myocardial Infarction Program at the National Heart Institute. Dr. Bondurant was also Professor and Chair of the Department of Medicine prior to serving as President and Dean of Albany Medical College in Albany, New York. In 1979 he became Professor of Medicine and Dean of the School of Medicine of the University of North Carolina at Chapel Hill. In July 1994 he retired as Dean and on leave of absence from UNC-CH served as Director of the Center for Urban Epidemiologic Studies of the New York Academy of Medicine. He is currently Professor of Medicine and Dean Emeritus at the School of Medicine of the University of North Carolina at Chapel Hill. During his career, Dr. Bondurant has served as an officer of many organizations and societies including President of the American College of Physicians, the Association of American Physicians, and the American Clinical and Climatological Association, Acting President of the Institute of Medicine of the National Academy of Sciences, Vice President of the American Heart Association and of the American Society for Clinical Investigation, Chairman of the Board of the North Carolina Biotechnology Center, Chair of the Council of Deans of the Association of American Medical Colleges, and Chair of the Association of American Medical Colleges. From 1989 to 1995 he served as Chair of the North Carolina Governors Commission on the Reduction of Infant Mortality.

Dr. Bondurant has also served as advisor to the National Institutes of Health, the Veterans Administration, the Department of Defense, and the Department of Health and Human Services. He is a Master of the American College of Physicians, and a Fellow of the Royal College of Physicians of Edinburgh and of the Royal College of Physicians of London. He holds an Honorary Doctor of Science Degree from Indiana University, the Citizen Laureate Award of the Albany (New York) Foundation, and the 1998 Thomas Jefferson Award of the Faculty of the University of North Carolina. He received the David P. Rall Award of the Institute of Medicine of the National Academy of Sciences in 2000.

Eugene Borgida, Ph.D. is Professor of Psychology and Law at the University of Minnesota, Twin Cities. He is also a Morse–Alumni Distinguished Teaching Professor of Psychology. In addition, Borgida is Adjunct Professor of Political Science and serves as Co–Director of the University's Center for the Study of Political Psychology. He has served as Associate Dean of the College of Liberal Arts and as chair of the Psychology Department. Borgida is a Fellow of the APA and APS, and on the Board of Directors for APS and the Social Science Research Council. He has published on a variety of research issues in psychology and law and in social psychology, and his work has been funded by NIMH, NIH, and NSF.

Dr. C. Michael Bowers practices dentistry and law in Ventura, CA. He has been a Deputy Medical Examiner for the Ventura County Coroner's Office since 1988. He is a diplomate of the American Board of Forensic Odontology.

Robert M. Bray is the director of the Substance Abuse Epidemiology, Prevention, and Risk Assessment Program at Research Triangle Institute in Research Triangle Park, North Carolina, where he has been since 1980. Previously, he was a faculty member at the University of Kentucky. He holds B.S. and M.S. degrees in psychology from Brigham Young University and a Ph.D. in social psychology from the University of Illinois, Urbana–Champaign. He is a member of the American Psychological Association and the American Public Health Association. He served on the Committee on Drug Use in the Workplace for the National Research Council, Institute of Medicine. His recent work has focused on substance use epidemiology and related problems in military and civilian populations. He has directed the 1982, 1985, 1988, 1992, 1995, and 1998 Worldwide Surveys of Substance Use and Health Behaviors Among Military Personnel and is currently conducting the 2001 survey in the series. He also was coordinator of analytic reports for the 1988 and 1990 National Household Surveys on Drug Abuse (NHSDAs) and is currently directing the National Analytic Center, a project focused on analyzing data from the NHSDA and other substance abuse datasets. Dr. Bray directed the Washington, DC, Metropolitan Area Drug Study (DC*MADS), a 6-year comprehensive project of the prevalence, correlates, and consequences of drug abuse in household and nonhousehold populations (including people who are homeless or institutionalized, adult and juvenile offenders, clients entering treatment programs, and new mothers). He is the principal editor of a book, published by Sage Publications, based on findings from DC*MADS and titled DRUG USE IN METROPOLITAN AMERICA. Dr. Bray is co-editor of THE PSYCHOLOGY OF THE COURTROOM.

Diana Burgess, Ph.D. is a senior research associate in Strategic Growth Initiatives in the Consumer Insights division of General Mills. She has conducted research on sexual harassment, gender stereotyping and political participation. Currently, she is conducting organizational research on knowledge sharing and knowledge seeking within General Mills. She also is conducting pro bono research for the National Campaign to Prevent Teen Pregnancy.

Stephen J. Ceci, Ph.D., holds a lifetime endowed chair in developmental psychology at Cornell University. He studies the accuracy of children's courtroom testimony, and is the author of over 300 articles, books, and chapters. Ceci's honors include a Senior Fulbright–Hayes fellowship and a Research Career Scientist Award. In 1993 Ceci was named a Master Lecturer of the American Psychological Association. He is currently a member of seven editorial boards and a fellow of six divisions of the APA, and of the American Association of Applied and Preventive Psychology, British Psychological Society, and American Psychological Society. His book (co-written with Maggie Bruck) JEOPARDY IN THE COURTROOM: A SCIENTIFIC ANALYSIS OF CHILDREN'S TESTIMONY (1995) is an American Psychological Association bestseller and winner of the William James Book Award by APA. He is a senior scientific advisor to the Canadian Institute for Advanced Research. Ceci is a member of the National Academy of Sciences Committee on Behavioral, Cognitive, and Sensory Sciences, and a member of the American Psychological Society's Board of Directors. He is past president of Division 1 (General Psychology) of APA. In 2000 Ceci received the Lifetime Distinguished Contribution Award from the American Academy of Forensic Psychology.

Michael R. Chial is Professor of Audiology in the Department of Communicative Disorders at the University of Wisconsin–Madison. His doctorate is from the University of Wisconsin Madison. For 20 years he has worked with the American National Standards Institute and is currently working with the Audio Engineering Society to develop technical standards for forensic applications of audio recordings. He is past associate editor of the JOURNAL OF SPEECH AND HEARING RESEARCH, and Fellow of the American Speech–Language–Hearing Association and the American Academy of Audiology.

Dennis J. Crouch is the interim director at the Center for Human Toxicology, University of Utah, where he has been employed since 1977. He is also a research assistant professor at the University of Utah's College of Pharmacy, Department of Pharmacology and Toxicology He received a B.S. degree from Western Illinois University, Macomb, Illinois, in 1971; received graduate training at the University of Utah, 1980–1981 in biochemistry and pharmacology; and received a M.B.A. degree from Utah State University, Logan, Utah in 1989. From May 1990 through November 1991, he was at the National Institute on Drug Abuse. He was responsible for administrative aspects of the National Laboratory Certification Program for forensic laboratories and research on the impact of occupational drug testing on drug use patterns, transportation safety, and business. He is a member of the California Association of Toxicologists, Society of Forensic Toxicologists, and the International Association of Forensic Toxicologists, as well as a fellow of the American Academy of Forensic Sciences. Mr. Crouch has published over 50 peer-reviewed scientific articles on therapeutic drug monitoring, analytical toxicology, forensic toxicology, drugs and driving, and workplace drug testing. Current research interests include alcohol and other drug use in transportation safety, evaluating the impact of workplace testing programs on businesses, monitoring of laboratories performing workplace testing, GC/MS, LC/MS, and MS/MS analyses of drugs of abuse.

Russellyn S. Carruth is an Adjunct Professor of Law at the University of Pittsburgh School of Law, where she teaches in the environmental law clinic.

She practiced law with the firm of Burr, Pease & Kurtz in Anchorage, Alaska from 1974–1995. Her practice included toxic torts litigation, which involved issues of admissibility of scientific evidence. Since retiring from private practice, she has taught environmental law at the University of Medicine and Dentistry of New Jersey, School of Public Health, where she is an Adjunct Assistant Professor. She has written and spoken on legal/scientific issues, including the admissibility of scientific evidence in litigation. She serves on the Board of the Society of Risk Analysis Section on Risk Law. She received her B.A. degree from University of California at Berkeley in 1966 and J.D. from University of California at Davis in 1974.

Shari Diamond, a social psychologist and attorney, is a Professor of Law and Psychology at the Northwestern University School of Law and a Senior Research Fellow at the American Bar Foundation. She has practiced intellectual property law at Sidley & Austin. She was a member of the Panel on Evaluation of DNA Forensic Evidence and the Panel on Sentencing Research for the National Academy of Sciences. Professor Diamond was President of the American Psychological Association's Division of Psychology and Law, received the APA's Distinguished Contributions to Research in Public Policy Award, and was Editor of the LAW & SOCIETY REVIEW.

Patricia L. Dill completed her Master of Science degree in Social Psychology at Mississippi State University in 1997 and currently is a doctoral student in Health Psychology at University of Missouri–Kansas City. She also is currently a Health Communication Intern at the National Cancer Institute. Her research interests include prevention and intervention of alcohol use (particularly DUI offenders) and tobacco use, treatment of obesity, and health behavior, with a focus on community and public health interventions.

John P. Foreyt, Ph.D., received his Ph.D. in clinical psychology in 1969 from Florida State University and completed his clinical internship at the University of Southern California Medical School. He served on the faculty at Florida State University until 1974 when he moved to Baylor College of Medicine, Houston, Texas. He is currently Professor there in the Department of Medicine and Department of Psychiatry. He is the Director of the DeBakey Heart Center's Behavioral Medicine Research Center, Department of Medicine. He is a member of the Medical Scientist Staff, Internal Medicine Service, The Methodist Hospital, Houston, Texas. Dr. Foreyt is a Fellow of the Society of Behavioral Medicine, a Fellow of the Behavioral Therapy and Research Society, and a Fellow of the Academy of Behavioral Medicine Research and other professional organizations. He also is an honorary member of the American Dietetic Association. Dr. Foreyt is currently a member of the editorial boards of: *Eating Disorders, Obesity Research, Journal of Cardiopulmonary Rehabilitation, American Journal of Health Promotion, Journal of Behavioral Medicine, American Journal of Health Promotion,* and *Diabetes, Obesity and Metabolism*. Dr. Foreyt has published extensively in the areas of diet modification, cardiovascular risk reduction, eating disorders, and obesity. He has published 15 books and more than 230 articles in these areas.

Professor Patricia Frazier received her Ph.D. in Social Psychology and Counseling Psychology in 1988 from the University of Minnesota. She currently is an Associate Professor in the Counseling Psychology and Social Psychology programs at the University of Minnesota. Dr. Frazier is past Associate Editor of LAW AND HUMAN BEHAVIOR and past chair of the Courtwatch Committee of the Society for the Psychological Study of Social Issues. Her research interests include sexual victimization and the interface between psychology and the law, particularly the use of expert testimony in rape trials.

David A. Freedman is Professor of Statistics, University of California, Berkeley, California. He is the author of many works on probability theory and statistics, including a widely used elementary textbook. He is a member of the American Academy of Arts and Sciences.

Gary L. French is Senior Vice President and Director of Litigation and Regulation Practice with Nathan Associates Inc., Arlington, Virginia. He earned his Ph.D. in economics from the University of Houston and then taught economics, finance, and statistics as a member of the faculties at three universities.

James C. Garriott is a toxicology consultant in San Antonio, Texas. He holds a Ph.D. in Toxicology and Pharmacology, and is a diplomat of the American Board of Forensic Toxicology, Inc. He served as the chief toxicologist for Dallas County, Texas from 1970 to 1982, and then held the same position at Bexar County, Texas until retiring in 1997. He was also professor at the University of Texas Health Science Centers of Dallas and San Antonio. Dr. Garriott is the author of over 100 articles and book chapters in the toxicology literature, as well as co-author and editor of two toxicology reference books and is on the editorial review board of four toxicology and forensic journals. He is recognized for his knowledge and expertise in the forensic toxicology of ethyl alcohol, and he edited the text Medicolegal Aspects of Alcohol, now in its third edition. Dr. Garriott was the 1993 recipient of the Alexander O. Gettler award for outstanding achievements in analytical toxicology by the American Academy of Forensic Sciences.

David W. Gjertson, Ph.D., is Associate Professor of Biostatistics and Pathology, UCLA, and chair of the Parentage Testing Unit of the Standards Program Committee of the American Association of Blood Banks.

Stanton A. Glantz, a professor of medicine at the University of California at San Francisco and a member of the Institute faculty. He also served as a consultant to OSHA.

Bernard D. Goldstein is the Dean of the University of Pittsburgh's Graduate School of Public Health. He served as the Director of the Environmental and Occupational Health Sciences Institute, a joint program of Rutgers, The State University of New Jersey and the University of Medicine and Dentistry of New Jersey (UMDNJ)–Robert Wood Johnson Medical School from 1986–2001. He was the Chair of the Department of Environmental and Community Medicine, UMDNJ–Robert Wood Johnson Medical School from 1980–2001. He was the first Principal Investigator of the Consortium of Risk Evaluation with Stakeholder Participation (CRESP). Dr. Goldstein earned his B.S. degree at the University of Wisconsin in 1958 and his M.D. degree at New York University School of Medicine in 1962. He is a physician, board certified in Internal Medicine and Hematology; board certified in Toxicology. Dr. Goldstein's past activities include Member and Chairman of the NIH Toxicology Study Section and EPA's Clean Air Scientific Advisory Committee; Chair of the Institute of Medicine Committee on the Role of the Physician in Occupational and Environmental Medicine, the National Research Council Committees on Biomarkers in Environmental Health Research and Risk Assessment Methodology and the Industry Panel of the World Health Organization Commission on Health and Environment. He is a Member of the Institute of Medicine where he has chaired the Section on Public Health, Biostatistics, and Epidemiology and he has been a Member of the Institute of Medicine Committee on Environmental Justice: Research, Education, and Health Policy Needs. He is the author of over two hundred articles and book chapters related to environmental health sciences and to public policy.

Dr. Grant Harris is a Research Psychologist at the Mental Health Centre, Penetanguishene, Ontario, Canada. He is also an adjunct Associate Professor of Psychology at Queen's University, Kingston. He obtained a B.Sc. from the University of Toronto, and his Ph.D. in Experimental Psychology from McMaster University. He first worked at the Penetanguishene Mental Health Centre in 1974 and rejoined the staff in 1980. He was, for several years, responsible for the development and supervision of behavioral programs on maximum security units for dangerous and assaultive men. Since joining the Research Department in 1988, he has been awarded several research grants and has conducted extensive scientific research on violent and criminal behavior, psychopathy, and sexual aggression and deviance. He is (together with Vernon Quinsey, Marnie Rice and Catherine Cormier) an author of the recent book, *Violent Offenders: Appraising and Managing Risk* published by the American Psychological Association. In 1997, with colleagues from MHCP's Research Department, Dr. Harris received the Amethyst Award for Outstanding Achievement in the Ontario Public Service.

Patricia A. Hastings, Ph.D., York University, is currently on staff at DecisonQuest in Washington, D.C.

Kirk Heilbrun is Professor and Chair, Department of Clinical and Health Psychology, MCP Hahnemann University, and Lecturer in Law, Villanova Law School. He received his A.B. from Brown University in 1975 and his Ph.D. from the University of Texas at Austin in 1980. He is past-president of both the American Psychology–Law Society and the American Board of Forensic Psychology. He is the author of Principles of Forensic Mental Health Assessment (forthcoming, Klumer/Plenum) as well as a number of articles in related areas.

Roger C. Herdman, born in Boston, MA, September 22, 1933; Phillips Exeter Academy, 1951; Yale University, Magna Cum Laude, Phi Beta Kappa, BS, 1955; Yale University School of Medicine, MD, 1958. Interned at the University of Minnesota. Medical Officer, US Navy, 1959–1961. Thereafter, completed a residency in pediatrics and continued with a medical fellowship in immunology/nephrology at Minnesota. Held positions of Assistant Professor and Professor of Pediatrics at the University of Minnesota and the Albany Medical College between 1966–1979. In 1969, appointed Director of the New York State Kidney Disease Institute in Albany. During 1969–1977 served as Deputy Commissioner of the New York State Department of Health responsible for research, departmental health care facilities and the Medicaid program at various times. In 1977, named New York State's Director of Public Health. From 1979 until joining the US Congress's Office of Technology Assessment (OTA) was a Vice President of the Memorial Sloan–Kettering Cancer Center in New York City. In 1983, named Assistant Director of OTA and then Acting Director and Director from January 1993–February 1996. After the closure of OTA, joined the National Academy of Sciences' Institute of Medicine as a Senior Scholar, directed studies on a national trust fund for graduate medical education, medical and ethical issues in organ transplantation, the safety of silicone breast implants, and the VA National Formulary. After completing those studies was appointed Director of the IOM's National Cancer Policy Board in August 2000. He also works on Institute relations with the U.S. Congress and chairs the National Academies' Institutional Review Board.

Professor Charles R. Honts is the Department Head and a Professor of Psychology at Boise State University and Editor of The Journal of Credibility Assessment and Witness Psychology. He is the recipient of grants from the U.S. Office of Naval Research and from the Royal Canadian Mounted Police to conduct research on the psychophysiological detection of deception. He is a Forensic Psychological Consultant to numerous public agencies in the United States in Canada. He has been a licensed polygraph examiner for 25 years.

Herbert Hovenkamp is the Ben V. & Dorothy Willie Professor of Law at the University of Iowa. He is the author of Federal Antitrust Policy: the Law of Competition and its Practice (1994), co-author of Antitrust Law (rev. ed.1995–1999), and many other works on anti-trust law, the law of property, legal history, and the history of law and science and law and economics.

James I. Hudson, M.D. is an Associate Professor of Psychiatry at Harvard Medical School and an Associate Psychiatrist at McLean Hospital, Belmont, Massachusetts. He is an author of more than 150 articles in the areas of eating disorders, fibromyalgia, psychopharmacology, the neurophysiology of sleep, and the issues of trauma and memory. He is currently engaged in studies of the genetic epidemiology of affective spectrum disorder, and of new medications for mood, anxiety and eating disorders.

Jennifer S. Hunt, Ph.D. is an Assistant Professor of Psychology at the University of Nebraska–Lincoln. Her research investigates the ways that pre-existing expectations, including stereotypes, influence people's thoughts and behavior. Her current work is examining the effects of stereotypes on health judgments, as well as the influence of individuating information on stereotype activation. In addition, she is investigating how cultural variations in beliefs about the justice system affect legal participation.

Melissa L. Hyder is currently a doctoral student in the Interdisciplinary Ph.D. program in Clinical Health Psychology at the University of Missouri–Kansas City. She received her B.A. in Psychology from Rockhurst University in 1999. Her research interests include physical activity, sports medicine, and childrens' obesity and nutrition.

William G. Iacono, is Distinguished McKnight University Professor, Professor of Psychology, University of Minnesota, Director, Clinical Science and

Psychopathology Research Training Program, recipient of the American Psychological Association's Distinguished Scientific Award for an Early Career Contribution to Psychology, the Society for Psychophysiological Research's Distinguished Scientific Award for an Early Career Contribution to Psychophysiology, Past–President of the Society for Psychophysiological Research (1996–97) and former Member, Department of Defense Polygraph Institute's Curriculum and Research Guidance Committee.

Kristina Kelly is a doctoral candidate at the University of Minnesota, Twin Cities. Her research interests include the psychology of gender and the study of health judgment and decision-making. She is currently investigating how social and cultural factors affect women's behaviors and cognitions, and in particular, how these factors influence the ways that women explain their own behavior in health and non-health domains.

Raymond D. Kent is Professor of Speech Science in the Department of Communicative Disorders, University of Wisconsin–Madison. His doctorate is from University of Iowa and he did postdoctoral work in speech analysis and synthesis at the Massachusetts Institute of Technology. He has edited or written eleven books, including THE ACOUSTICAL ANALYSIS OF SPEECH (with Charles Read, 1992), and is past editor of the JOURNAL OF SPEECH AND HEARING RESEARCH. He holds an honorary doctorate from the University of Montreal Faculty of Medicine, is a Fellow of the Acoustical Society of America, the International Society of Phonetic Sciences, and the American Speech–Language–Hearing Association, and has earned Honors of the American Speech–Language–Hearing Association.

Professor John C. Kircher is an Associate Professor of Educational Psychology, University of Utah. He specializes in the use of computer, psychometric, and decision theoretic methods for assessing truth and deception from physiological recordings. He pioneered the development of the first computerized polygraph system and has collaborated with David C. Raskin and Charles R. Honts since 1977 on research and development of methods for the physiological detection of deception.

John J. Lentini is a fire investigator and chemist who manages the fire investigation division of Applied Technical Services of Marietta, Georgia. He is a fellow of the American Academy of Forensic Sciences and the American Board of Criminalistics, holds certificates from the National Association of Fire Investigators and the International Association of Arson Investigators. He chairs the ASTM Committee Responsible for developing forensic science standards, and is a principal member of the National Fire Protection Association's Technical Committee on Fire Investigations. Mr. Lentini has investigated more than 1500 fires, and analyzed more than 20,000 samples of fire debris.

Paul S. Lowengrub is a consulting economist and financial expert with Nathan Associates, Arlington, Virginia. He earned his Ph.D. in economics and finance from Arizona State University, and taught economic and finance courses for a year at The American Graduate School of International Management.

David T. Lykken is Professor of Psychology, University of Minnesota, author of A TREMOR IN THE BLOOD: USES AND ABUSES OF THE LIE DETECTOR, (2d ed. 1998), recipient of the American Psychological Association's Award for a *Distinguished Contribution to Psychology in the Public Interest* (1991) and for *Distinguished Scientific Contributions for Applications of Psychology* (2001), Past-President of the Society for Psychophysiological Research (1980–81), and recipient of that Society's *Award for Distinguished Scientific Contributions to Psychophysiology* (1998).

John Monahan, a clinical psychologist, holds the Doherty Chair in law at the University of Virginia, where he is also a Professor of Psychology and of Legal Medicine. He has been a Guggenheim Fellow, a Fellow at Harvard Law School and at the Center for Advanced Study in the Behavioral Sciences, and a Visiting Fellow at All Souls College, Oxford. He was the founding President of the American Psychological Association's Division of Psychology and Law and received an honorary doctorate in law from the City University of New York. Monahan has won the Isaac Ray Award of the American Psychiatric Association, has been elected to membership in the Institute of Medicine of the National Academy of Sciences, has been appointed to the Committee on Law and Justice of the National Research Council, and has directed the MacArthur Research Network on Mental Health and the Law. His work has been cited frequently by courts, including the California Supreme Court in *Tarasoff v. Regents* and the United States Supreme Court in *Barefoot v. Estelle*, in which he was referred to as "the leading thinker on the issue" of violence risk assessment.

Jeffrey W. Morris, M.D., Ph.D., is the former Director, Long Beach Genetics and Clinical Associate Professor of Pathology, University of California, Irvine. He serves as a member of the Parentage Testing Ancillary Committee, College of American Pathologists and is a past Chairman, Committee on Parentage Testing of the American Association of Blood Banks.

John E. Murdock, M.C. in Criminalistics, U.C. Berkeley, is a Senior Firearms and Toolmark Examiner with the Bureau of Alcohol, Tobacco, and Firearms, San Francisco Laboratory Center. Author of a number of articles on firearms and toolmark examination, he is past president of the California Association of Criminalists, an emeritus member of the American Society of Crime Laboratory Directors, and a distinguished member of the Association of Firearm and Toolmark Examiners.

Robert Nadon, Ph.D., is Associate Professor of Psychology at Brock University in St. Catharines, Ontario, Canada. Actively engaged in both research and teaching, Dr. Nadon has published extensively on hypnosis, with particular interest in personality and methodological issues. He is a Fellow of the Society for Clinical and Experimental Hypnosis, a past Research Fellow of the Canadian Social Sciences and Humanities Research Council, an Advisory Editor for the INTERNATIONAL JOURNAL OF CLINICAL AND EXPERIMENTAL HYPNOSIS, and a Consultant Editor, for CONTEMPORARY HYPNOSIS.

Michael Nash, Ph.D., is Associate Professor at the University of Tennessee and is actively engaged in clinical training, research, and teaching. He is Editor in Chief of the INTERNATIONAL JOURNAL OF CLINICAL AND EXPERIMENTAL HYPNOSIS, Past President of Division 30 of the American Psychological Association, Fellow of both the Society for Clinical and Experimental Hypnosis and the

American Psychological Association, and is a Diplomate of the American Board of Professional Psychology. Dr. Nash has published extensively on the effects of sexual abuse, short-term psychotherapy, and hypnosis. Dr. Nash is Co–Editor with Dr. Fromm of the classic text on experimental hypnosis, Contemporary Hypnosis Research, and his research and writing have earned him numerous awards.

Paul Oliva, B.A., M.A. is a former senior clinical research technician in the Biological Psychiatry Laboratory at McLean Hospital, Belmont, Massachusetts.

Joseph L. Peterson, D.Crim., is Professor of Criminal Justice at the University of Illinois at Chicago. His research has tracked the evolution of the forensic sciences over the past thirty years, focusing on the quality of results emanating from crime laboratories, ethical dilemmas facing scientists, and the impact of science on legal decision making. Previously, he served as Executive Director of the Forensic Sciences Foundation and directed the criminal justice research center at John Jay College of Criminal Justice in New York.

Henry Petroski, Ph.D., P.E., is Aleksandar S. Vesic Professor of Civil Engineering and Professor of History, Duke University, Durham, North Carolina.

Harrison G. Pope, Jr., M.D. is a Professor of Psychiatry at Harvard Medical School and Chief of the Biological Psychiatry Laboratory at the McLean Hospital Alcohol and Drug Abuse Research Center in Belmont, Massachusetts. He is an author of more than 300 published papers on a range of topics in psychiatry, including eating disorders, mood disorders, psychiatric diagnosis, substance abuse, psychopharmacology, and the current debate about trauma and memory. Dr. Pope currently devotes most of his time to research and teaching.

Walker S. Carlos Poston II, M.P.H., Ph.D. received his Ph.D. from the University of California-Santa Barbara and an M.P.H. from the University of Texas Houston Health Sciences Center. He is Co–Director of Behavioral Cardiology Research at the Mid America Heart Institute and Assistant Professor in the Clinical Health Psychology Interdisciplinary Ph.D. program at the University of Missouri–Kansas City. His research focuses on understanding genetic and environmental contributions to cardiovascular disease and obesity, particularly in minority populations. Dr. Poston has been the principal or co-investigator on several funded studies examining health outcomes in obesity treatment and the epidemiology of hypertension and obesity in African Americans. He has published nearly 80 articles and book chapters focusing on obesity and cardiovascular disease and has presented his work in national and international scientific forums. Dr. Poston is a fellow of the North American Association for the Study of Obesity and a member of the American Heart Association's Council on Epidemiology and Prevention and the Society of Behavioral Medicine.

Martine Powell, Ph.D. is a Senior Lecturer in the School of Psychology, Deakin University, Melbourne Australia. She has been conducting research in the area of child eyewitness memory, as well as training programs in investigative interviewing, for the past ten years. She has also trained and worked as a clinical psychologist, specializing in the treatment of child abuse and neglect.

Norman Poythress is a Professor in the Department of Mental Health Law & Policy, Florida Mental Health Institute, University of South Florida. He received his A.B. from Indiana University in 1969 and his Ph.D. from the University of Texas at Austin in 1977. He is past-president of the American Psychology–Law Society (Division 41 of the American Psychological Association). In 1990, he received the American Academy of Forensic Psychology's Award for Distinguished Contributions to Forensic Psychology. He is a coauthor of PSYCHOLOGICAL EVALUATIONS FOR THE COURTS: A HANDBOOK FOR MENTAL HEALTH PROFESSIONALS AND LAWYERS, as well as numerous articles on the interaction of mental illness and the criminal justice system.

Gabrielle F. Principe is a National Institute of Mental Health Postdoctoral Fellow at Cornell University. She was educated at Temple University and the University of North Carolina at Chapel Hill, where she received her doctorate in developmental psychology. Her research examines factors affecting the accuracy and retention of young children's memories for salient personal experiences.

Professor David C. Raskin is Professor Emeritus, University of Utah and Editor of Psychological Methods in Criminal Investigation and Evidence and Co–Editor of Electrodermal Activity in Psychological Research. He has been the recipient of numerous grants and contracts from the National Institute of Justice, U.S. Department of Defense, U.S. Secret Service, and U.S. Army Research and Development Command to conduct research and development on psychophysiological detection of deception. He was the Co–Developer of the first computerized polygraph system. He was Past President Rocky Mountain Psychological Association and is an Elected Fellow in the American Psychological Association, American Psychological Society, American Association for Applied and Preventive Psychology. He has served as a Forensic Psychological Consultant to numerous federal and local agencies and legislative bodies in the United States, Canada, Israel, United Kingdom, and Norway. He has been a licensed polygraph examiner for 27 years.

Dr. Marnie Rice is Director of Research of the Mental Health Centre, Penetanguishene, Ontario, Canada. She is Professor of Psychiatry and Behavioural Neurosciences at McMaster University, Associate Professor of Psychology at Queen's University, and Scientific Director of the Centre for the Study of Aggression and Mental Disorder. She has been awarded several research grants and has over eighty publications including three coauthored books on the topics of violent and criminal behavior, sex offenders, psychopaths and arson. Dr. Rice obtained her honours B.A. in Psychology from McMaster University; a Master's Degree from the University of Toronto; and a Ph.D. in Clinical Psychology from York University. She was the 1995 recipient of the American Psychological Association's award for Distinguished Contribution to Research in Public Policy, and the 1997 recipient of a Government of Ontario Amethyst Award for Outstanding Contribution by an Ontario Public Servant.

D. Michael Risinger is a Professor of Law at Seton Hall University School of Law; B.A. Magna Cum Laude, Yale University, 1966, J.D. Cum Laude, Harvard Law School, 1969.

Dr. Victor L. Roggli received a B.A. degree in Biochemistry and Environmental Engineering from Rice University in Houston Texas in 1973, and doctor of medicine degree from Baylor College of Medicine in 1976. He completed residency training in pathology at Baylor Affiliated Hospitals in 1980, and is board certified in Anatomic and Clinical Pathology. Dr. Roggli has published more than 120 articles in peer reviewed journals, approximately half of which deal with asbestos or asbestos-related diseases. He has also published 21 chapters in textbooks and is the author/editor of three books, including Pathology of Asbestos–Associated Diseases.

Daniel L. Rubinfeld is Robert L. Bridges Professor of Law and Professor of Economics at the University of California, Berkeley. He has been a fellow of the National Bureau of Economic Research, the Center for the Advanced Study in the Behavioral Sciences, and the Simon Guggenheim Foundation.

Sara Rzepa is a graduate student in the Psychology Department at York University in Toronto, Ontario, Canada. Her research interests include jury decision making and she is currently involved in research on jury decision making in trials involving battered women who have killed their abusers.

Regina A. Schuller, Ph.D. is Associate Professor of Psychology at York University in Toronto, Ontario, Canada. She is actively engaged in both research and teaching and in 1995 received York's President's Prize for Promising Scholars. Her research interests focus on the impact of social science framework testimony, in particular, expert testimony pertaining to battered women and on juror/jury decision processes. She also serves on the editorial board of LAW & HUMAN BEHAVIOR AND PSYCHOLOGY, PUBLIC POLICY, AND LAW.

George F. Sensabaugh, Jr., is Professor, School of Public Health, University of California at Berkeley. He was a member of the National Academy of Sciences' Committee on DNA Technology in Forensic Science and its subsequent Committee on DNA Forensic Science: An Update.

Christopher Slobogin is Stephen C. O'Connell Professor of Law at the University of Florida Levin College of Law, an affiliate professor with the Department of Psychiatry at the University of Florida, and an adjunct professor at the Florida Mental Health Institute, a department of the University of South Florida. Professor Slobogin received an A.B. from Princeton University, and a J.D. and LL.M. from the University of Virginia. He has served as chair of the American Association of Law Schools Section on Mental Disability and Law, Reporter for the American Bar Association's Standards on Criminal Responsibility, editor or reviewer for Behavioral Science & the Law, Law & Human Behavior, the American Journal of Psychiatry, and Psychology, Public Policy & Law, and as the Director of the University of Virginia's Forensic Psychiatry Clinic. He has authored a casebook and a treatise on mental health law, as well as numerous articles in the area.

John L. Solow is Associate Professor of Economics at The University of Iowa, where he has been a member of the faculty for over twenty years. He received his B.A. in economics from Yale University, and his M.A. and Ph.D. in economics from Stanford University.

Tomika N. Stevens is currently an advanced student in the Law–Psychology Program at Villanova Law School and MCP Hahnemann University, where she is a candidate for Juris Doctorate (2003) and Doctor of Philosophy, Clinical Psychology (2004). She received her A.B. from Princeton University in 1997.

David A. Stoney has a Ph.D. in Forensic Science from the University of California, Berkeley, where he worked on the statistical modeling of fingerprint identifications. He worked for six years at the Institute of Forensic Sciences, Criminalistics Laboratory, in California before joining the faculty of the University of Illinois at Chicago. After serving as Director of Forensic Sciences for eight years he left to become Director of the McCrone Research Institute in Chicago, a not-for-profit corporation dedicated to teaching and research in microscopy and microscopic analysis.

John Thornton, D.Crim., is an Emeritus Professor of Forensic Science at the University of California at Berkeley. He worked in an operational crime laboratory for 15 years and taught at Berkeley for 24 years. He also has taught forensic science in Colombia, Israel, Mexico, India, and the People's Republic of China. He is a past president of the California Association of Criminalists and past chairman of the Criminalistics Section of the American Academy of Forensic Sciences.

Dr. Lawrence M. Tierney, Jr. is a professor of medicine at the University of California at San Francisco. He received his M.D. From the University of Maryland in 1967, and did his residency in internal medicine at Emory University and the University of California at San Francisco. After two years in the U.S. Navy, he joined the faculty at the latter institution, where he is Professor of Medicine. He served as director of the residency training program as well of the third and fourth year medical student clerkships, and is also Associate Chief of the Medical Service at the San Francisco Veterans Affairs Medical Center. He has won over twenty major teaching awards, and has been invited on five separate occasions to address the UCSF medical school's graduating class. He is the senior editor of Current Medical Diagnosis and Treatment, a textbook in its 42nd edition, and has published numerous articles in medical journals, his principal interests being clinical decision-making, medical education, and evidence-based medicine.

Dr. Wartenberg received a Ph.D. degree in Ecology and Evolution from the State University of New York at Stony Brook in 1984 and then was a Fellow in the Interdisciplinary Programs in Public Health at the Harvard School of Public Health. He joined the faculty of the Robert Wood Johnson Medical School of the University of Medicine and Dentistry of New Jersey (UMDNJ) in Piscataway, New Jersey in 1986 where he is currently Professor and Chair of the Doctoral Committee for the UMDNJ School of Public Health. He serves on the New Jersey Commission on Radiation Protection, is a member of the National Council on Radiation Protection and Measurement, and served on both the National Academy of Sciences Committee and the National Institute of Health's Working Group addressing the possible health effects of electric and magnetic fields. Dr. Wartenberg has investigated a variety of methodological issues related to the study of magnetic fields and cancer, and has conducted two meta-analyses of the magnetic field and childhood cancer studies. Currently, he is completing a study of children with unusually high magnetic field exposures that he has identified using geographic information system (GIS) technology. In addition to his work on magnetic fields, he also conducts research on risk assessment, the effects of exposure to toxic chemicals and the investigation of disease clusters.

Noel S. Weiss received an M.D. degree from Stanford University School of Medicine and an M.P.H. and Dr. P.H. from the Harvard School of Public Health. In 1973, after two years at the National Center for Health Statistics, he joined the faculties of the University of Washington School of Public Health and Community Medicine and the Fred Hutchinson Cancer Research Center. He served as Chairman of the Department of Epidemiology at the University of Washington from 1984–1993. While the majority of his research has been in the area of cancer (he was awarded an Outstanding Investigator grant from the National Cancer Institute for the period 1985–1999), he has maintained an interest in and written extensively on epidemiologic methods and clinical epidemiology.

Gary Wells is Professor of Psychology and Distinguished Professor of Liberal Arts and Sciences at Iowa State University, Ames, Iowa. His experiments and papers on eyewitness testimony have appeared in scientific psychology's premiere journals.

Summary of Contents

Table of Contents

---

*

Table of Cases

References are to section and note.

SCIENCE IN THE LAW
SOCIAL AND BEHAVIORAL SCIENCE ISSUES

*

CHAPTER 1

INSANITY AND DIMINISHED CAPACITY

Table of Sections

A. LEGAL ISSUES

Westlaw Electronic Research

See Westlaw Electronic Research Guide preceding the Summary of Contents.

———————

A. LEGAL ISSUES

§ 1–1.0 THE LEGAL RELEVANCE OF RESEARCH ON INSANITY AND DIMINISHED CAPACITY

§ 1–1.1 Introduction

Perhaps more than any other topic in this treatise, scientific information about cognitive and volitional capacities (i.e., "mental competency") at the time of an alleged offense fits awkwardly into the existing legal boxes in which this subject must be placed. The most immediate difficulty concerns the very different philosophical starting points brought by law and psychology[1] to the matter. The legal paradigm is constructed around assumptions of free will and individual responsibility, whereas the psychological paradigm begins with the assumptions of determinism.[2] On a more practical level, the problem of

———————

§ 1–1.0

1. Insanity and diminished capacity are subjects studied by a wide range of professionals, mainly within the domains of psychology and psychiatry. This section uses the word "psychology" to refer to the general fields doing research in this area, since this research is primarily done by psychologists. However, when referring to expert testimony more specifically, it employs the word "psychiatrist,"

since these professionals play a disproportionate role in the courtroom.

2. *See* MICHAEL L. PERLIN, JURISPRUDENCE OF THE INSANITY DEFENSE 32 (1994) ("The insanity defense symbolizes the gap between the aspirations of a theoretically positivist, objective, common law legal system (in which behavior is allegedly animated by free will and is judged and assessed on a conscious level), and the reality of an indeterminate, subjective, psycho-

mental competency in the legal context is complicated by the very different vocabularies that lawyers and scientists bring to the subject. Lawyers speak in terms of insanity and diminished capacity, whereas psychologists employ a rich and expansive vocabulary that attempts to account for the wide variation in behaviors observed.[3] The law, therefore, presumes, and has constructed, a world in which mental competency exists largely in two-dimensional space: a person was insane or sane when he committed a particular act.[4] Psychology, in contrast, presumes, and has constructed, a world in which mental competency varies widely in multi-dimensional space: a person might suffer from a disability with multiple etiologies and with varying effects on his competency.[5]

Yet, the amount of ink spilled and the oratory expended on the insanity defense is out of proportion to the number of cases in which it is claimed and even more so to the number in which it is successful. Few defendants plead insanity and many fewer still prevail in their claims.[6] Nonetheless, understanding the insanity defense is an essential step in appreciating the American system of justice.[7] It provides a Rorschach test of the sensibilities of actors in the criminal justice system, politics and society more generally. More basically, cases in which defendants claim lack of "responsibility" throw needed light on the vast majority of cases in which defendants must accept responsibility. A system defined by individual responsibility thus gains definition from its opposite. Criminal insanity, if it did not already exist, would have to be invented if only to allow us to define criminal culpability.

social universe (in which behavior is determined by a host of biological, psychological, physiological, environmental and sociological factors, and is frequently driven by unconscious forces.")). *Cf.* Alan Stone, *The Insanity Defense on Trial,* 33 HOSP. & COMMUNITY PSYCHIATRY 636, 640 (1982) ("The insanity defense is the exception that proves the rule of free will It demonstrates that all other criminals have free will, the ability to choose between good and evil.").

3. *See generally* Michael Clay Smith, *The Insanity Plea in Mississippi. A Primer and a Proposal,* 10 MISS. C.L. REV. 147, 167 (1990) ("Behavioral science utilizes a relativist approach to human actions and tends to recognize gradations of conduct. Psychiatry is concerned primarily with therapy. The criminal law, on the other hand, must ultimately reduce the analysis to black or white, guilty or innocent.").

4. Even newer standards, such as "guilty but mentally ill," *see infra* § 8–1.2.5, revolve around an essentially categorical conception of mental competency.

5. *See generally* GARY B. MELTON, JOHN PETRILA, NORMAN G. POYTHRESS & CHRISTOPHER SLOBOGIN, PSYCHOLOGICAL EVALUATIONS FOR THE COURTS: A HANDBOOK FOR MENTAL HEALTH PROFESSIONALS AND LAWYERS (1987).

6. *See* Callahan ct al., *The Volume and Characteristics of Insanity Defense Pleas: An Eight–State Study,* 19 BULL. AM. ACAD. PSYCHIATRY & L. 331 (1991) (finding that insanity is claimed in about one percent of all felony cases and is successful only about one-quarter of the time).

7. Unfortunately, a crucial step in understanding and making judgments about the insanity defense—being informed about the current practice—is missing in the law. Lawyers, judges and the public continue to believe sundry myths about the use of the insanity defense. Michael Perlin identified, and refuted, eight such myths: (1) "The insanity defense is overused;" (2) "Use of the insanity defense is limited to murder cases;" (3) "There is no risk to the defendant who pleads insanity;" (4) "[Insanity] acquitees are quickly released from custody;" (5) "[Insanity] acquitees spend much less time in custody than do defendants convicted of the same offenses;" (6) "Criminal defendants who plead insanity are usually faking;" (7) "Most insanity defense trials feature 'battles of the experts;' " (8) "Criminal defense attorneys—perhaps inappropriately—employ the insanity defense plea solely to 'beat the rap.' " M. PERLIN (1994), *supra* note 2, at 108–114.

§ 1–1.2 Legal Tests of Insanity

§ 1–1.2.1 Background

Most commentators place the first successful use of the insanity defense in 1505.[8] But the underlying principle associated with insanity, lack of responsibility for "involuntary"[9] actions, is ancient.[10] Excusing, and then treating, the insane for their antisocial acts and violent propensities is, perhaps, the mark of a civilized society.[11] Through history, however, the believed etiology of insanity, or the accepted psychological state that would qualify a defendant as "insane," changed.[12] In the nineteenth century, for example, a "wild beast" view of the "insane" held sway.[13] Dr. Benjamin Rush's description of the symptoms of "moral derangement" illustrates this perspective: "A wild and ferocious countenance; enlarged and rolling eyes; constant singing; whistling and hallowing; imitations of the voices of different animals; walking with a quick step; or standing still with hands and eyes elevated towards the heavens the madman, or maniac, is in a rage."[14]

The relationship between psychology's definition of mental illness and the law's definition of mental insanity has always been somewhat at odds. In past centuries, there was greater consonance between the two professions' conceptions of mental disability.[15] Whatever the truth about the past, clearly the two

---

8. *See* Allen D. Spiegel & Peter B. Suskind, *A Paroxysmal Insanity Plea in an 1865 Murder Trial*, 16 J. LEGAL MED. 585, 586–87 (1995) (*citing* Y.B. Mich. 21 Hen. 7, pl. 16 (1506)); *see also* Richard Moran, *The Origin of Insanity as a Special Verdict: The Trial for Treason of James Hadfield (1800)*, 19 LAW & SOC'Y. REV. 487 (1985).

9. "Involuntary" is being used here broadly to include both those actions not understood to be wrong by, and were not willed by, the actor. It should be noted, further, that truly involuntary actions are the subject of a separate defense, referred to as automatism. Most defendants found to be "insane" acted "voluntarily," though reality was not what they thought it to be.

10. Aristotle offered the following observation:

> Since virtue is concerned with passions and actions, and on voluntary passions and actions praise and blame are bestowed, on those that are involuntary pardon, and sometimes also pity, to distinguish the voluntary and the involuntary is presumably necessary for those who are studying the nature of virtue, and useful also for legislators with a view to the assigning both of honours and of punishments.

ARISTOTLE, ETHICA NICOMACHEA 1109b (W. Ross trans., 1925); *see generally* Anthony Platt & Bernard L. Diamond, *The Origins of the "Right and Wrong" Test of Criminal Responsibility and Its Subsequent Development in the United States: An Historical Survey*, 54 CAL. L. REV. 1227, 1228–29 (1966) ("The 'knowledge of

right and wrong' test, in the form of its earlier synonym ('knowledge of good and evil') is traceable to the Book of Genesis."); MICHAEL MOORE, LAW AND PSYCHIATRY: RETHINKING THE RELATIONSHIP 64–65 (1984) (same).

11. *See* United States v. Baldi, 344 U.S. 561, 570, 73 S.Ct. 391, 97 L.Ed. 549 (1953) ("Ever since our ancestral common law emerged out of the darkness of its early barbaric days, it has been a postulate of Western civilization that the taking of life by the hand of an insane person is not murder."); *see also* § 8–1.2.6, *infra* (discussing whether the Constitution requires states to offer an insanity defense to criminal defendants).

12. For an excellent review of "pre-dynamic psychiatry," ranging back to "Prince Ptahhotep [who] attempted the first classification of mental illness almost five thousand years ago," *see* M. PERLIN, *supra* note 2, at 37–41; *see also id.* at 41–49 (discussing "dynamic psychiatry").

13. *See* Anthony Platt & Bernard L. Diamond, *The Origins and Development of the "Wild Beast" Concept of Mental Illness and Its Relation to Theories of Criminal Responsibility*, 1 J. HIST. BEHAV. SCI. 355, 360 (1965) (The "wild beast" test consisted of a "medley of legal theories of responsibility mixed with popular superstitions about mental illness.").

14. BENJAMIN RUSH, MEDICAL INQUIRIES AND OBSERVATIONS UPON THE DISEASES OF THE MIND 144 (1812).

15. *See* M. PERLIN, *supra* note 2, at 81 ("Th[e] rigid, cognitive-only responsibility test, ... reflected 'the prevailing intellectual and scientific ideas of the times,' and stemmed

professions no longer speak the same language. "Today, insanity is a legal concept; mental illness is a medical condition."[16] Although psychiatrists clearly play an important role in the criminal justice system, the rules are imposed by courts and legislatures. Hence, culpability is determined by legal concepts of responsibility rather than the theories and observations of psychology. In fact, since the law has largely maintained the *M'Naghten* conception of mental illness, courts require psychiatrists of the twenty-first century to testify using concepts and language of the mid-nineteenth century.[17] This practice is not well-designed to promote communication or trust—or salutary outcomes.

§ 1–1.2.2　The *M'Naghten* Test

In many respects, the circumstances surrounding the trial and acquittal of Daniel M'Naghten[18] mirror the modern debate about the insanity defense.[19] On January 20, 1843, M'Naghten attempted to assassinate Sir Robert Peel, the British Prime Minister, and shot and killed Peel's assistant, Edward Drummond, by mistake.[20] M'Naghten was under the delusion that Peel had been persecuting him; because of this delusion, he was acquitted on the ground of insanity. The British public responded with outrage to the acquittal and Queen Victoria demanded that the House of Lords summon the common-law judges to explain the result. In response to this summons, the judges framed what has come to be known as the *M'Naghten* test. The judges explained that a defendant should be acquitted if he "was labouring under such a defect of reason, from disease of the mind, as not to know the nature and quality of the act he was doing, or, if he did know it, that he did not know he was doing what was wrong."[21] This test is also commonly described as the "right/wrong test."

The *M'Naghten* right/wrong test has been enormously influential in the United States and is employed, though often with significant variations, in

from an 'immutable philosophical and moral concept which assumes an inherent capacity in man to distinguish right from wrong and to make necessary moral decisions.' ") (*quoting* Herbert Hovencamp, *Insanity and Responsibility in Progressive America,* 57 N.D.L. Rev. 541, 551 (1981)).

16. Spiegel & Suskind, *supra* note 8, at 586. The one modern exception to this phenomenon of separating insanity from mental illness is the *Durham* test, discussed *infra* § 8–1.2.3. The *Durham* test, however, was an unmitigated failure.

17. *See* Robert Waelder, *Psychiatry and the Problem of Criminal Responsibility,* 101 U. PA. L. Rev. 378, 381 (1952) (noting that the law's insanity jurisprudence is comparable to requiring a physicist to testify about radioactivity "in the language of Aristotle" or a medical doctor to testify about an injury "in the language of Galen"); *see also* Donald H. J. Hermann & Yvonne S. Sor, *Convicting or Confining? Alternative Directions in Insanity Law Reform: Guilty But Mentally Ill Versus New Rules for Release of Insanity Acquitees,* 1983 B.Y.U. L. Rev. 499, 512–13.

18. Part of the debate surrounding the M'Naghten rule, albeit a trivial part, concerns the correct spelling of the name. *See* Bernard L. Diamond, *On the Spelling of Daniel M'Naghten's Name,* 25 OHIO ST. L.J. 84 (1964) (suggesting that the correct spelling is "McNaughten").

19. *See* Ira Mickenberg, *A Pleasant Surprise: The Guilty but Mentally Ill Verdict Has Both Succeeded in its Own Right and Successfully Preserved the Traditional Role of the Insanity Defense,* 55 U. CIN. L. Rev. 943, 945 (1987) (noting the similarities between the *M'Naghten* acquittal and the *Hinckley* acquittal); Jodie English, *The Light Between Twilight and Dusk: Federal Animal Law and the Volitional Insanity Defense,* 40 HASTINGS L.J. 1, 4–8 (1989) (same).

20. M'Naghten's Case, 1843–60 All E.R. 229 (H.L. 1843); *See generally* Rollin, *Crime and Mental Disorder: Daniel M'Naghten, a Case in Point,* 50 MEDICO-LEGAL J. 102 (1982); Bernard L. Diamond, *Isaac Ray and the Trial of Daniel M'Naghten,* 112 AM.J. OF PSYCHIATRY 651 (1956).

21. M'Naghten's Case, 1843–60 All E.R. at 233.

most jurisdictions today.[22] Indeed, jurisdictions sometimes moved away from this test in favor of a modern reform, only to return to it when the reform had less salutary effects than anticipated.[23] The most dramatic example of this move back to *M'Naghten* was Congress' passage of the Insanity Defense Reform Act,[24] with many states following the federal lead.[25] As the Mississippi Supreme Court noted, although *M'Naghten* "may not be a perfect means to test sanity," it remains true that "no better solution has been offered."[26]

In *United States v. McBroom*,[27] the Third Circuit Court of Appeals considered the question whether the United States Sentencing Guidelines permit downward departures due to volitional incapacity. Congress abolished the volitional prong of the insanity defense in 1984 when it enacted the Insanity Defense Reform Act. This Act returned federal practice to the single cognitive standard of the M'Naghten rule for affirmative claims of insanity. In *McBroom*, the court answered the question whether, in promulgating the guidelines, the Sentencing Commission had intended to similarly abandon the volitional prong for sentencing decisions. The court concluded that it had not:

> We do not believe ... that the Commission intended to preclude district courts from considering volitional impairments during the sentencing phase in the same manner in which Congress precluded consideration of volitional impairments as an affirmative defense.[28]

The pertinent language in the sentencing guidelines comes from section 5K2.13:

> If the defendant committed a non-violent offense while suffering from significantly reduced mental capacity not resulting from voluntary use of drugs or other intoxicants, a lower sentence may be warranted to reflect the extent to which reduced mental capacity contributed to the commission of the offense, provided that the defendant's criminal history does not indicate a need for incarceration to protect the public.[29]

The court determined that the term "reduced mental capacity" encompassed "both a 'cognitive prong' and a 'volitional prong.' "[30] The court reasoned that "[t]he mind is the organ of volition as well as of reflection."[31] Therefore, it concluded, "[a] person who knows what he is doing and that it is wrong but cannot control himself is deficient in mental capacity."[32] The underlying rationale for this conclusion was provided by Judge Easterbrook:

> "The criminal justice system long has meted out lower sentences to persons who, although not technically insane, are not in full command of

22. *See* M. PERLIN, *supra* note 2, at 27–28; *see generally* Michelle Migdal Gee, *Annotation: Modern Status of Test of Criminal Responsibility—State Cases*, 9 ALR 4th, 526 (1981).

23. *See generally* M. PERLIN, *supra* note 2, at 25 ("The legislation ultimately enacted by Congress—legislation that closely comported with the public's moral feelings—returned the insanity defense to 'status quo ante 1843: the year of ... M'Naghten.' ").

24. 18 U.S.C.A. § 17 (1988). The Congressional reform differed from the traditional *M'Naghten* test in several respects, including that it put the burden of proof on the defen-

dant, and required that the mental disease or defect be "severe" to qualify under the test. *Id.*

25. M. PERLIN, *supra* note 2, at 27.

26. Russell v. State, 729 So.2d 781 (Miss. 1997).

27. 124 F.3d 533 (3d Cir.1997).

28. *Id.* at 546.

29. U.S. SENTENCING GUIDELINES MANUAL § 5K2.13.

30. *McBroom*, 124 F.3d at 546.

31. *Id.*

32. *Id.*

their actions.... Persons who find it difficult to control their conduct do not—considerations of dangerousness to one side—deserve as much punishment as those who act maliciously or for gain."[33]

The Easterbrook rationale, however, would apply equally to affirmative defenses based on "insanity." The *McBroom* court never addressed the basis for distinguishing between an affirmative defense and a downward departure in regard to the relevance of having a "reduced mental capacity." The distinction in practice appears, therefore, entirely a product of positive law. Congress intended to abolish the volitional prong and the Sentencing Commission did not. In effect, then, in federal courts following the *McBroom* interpretation of the guidelines, the *M'Naghten* test applies to the trial phase, whereas the ALI test applies to sentencing. But these variances in practice are not easily reconciled in terms of legal theory.

§ 1–1.2.3   The *Durham* "Product" Test

Perhaps the most stunning failure of all of the law reform efforts was the one instituted by the United States Court of Appeals for the District of Columbia Circuit in a 1954 opinion authored by Judge David Bazelon, a highly respected jurist. Judge Bazelon made the not unreasonable attempt to merge the legal concept of insanity with the psychological concept of mental illness. In *Durham v. United States*,[34] Judge Bazelon wrote that "an accused is not criminally responsible if his criminal act was the product of mental disease or mental defect."[35] This rule expanded the scope of the information the jury might consider to encompass extant scientific opinion.[36] Although the *Durham* rule increased the number of insanity acquitees substantially, some researchers believe that these increases came from the ranks of those who would have otherwise been acquitted rather than the ranks of the "guilty."[37] This hypothesis, however, remains only conjecture.

Durham offers a case study of the complications and complexities surrounding the integration of legal and psychological tests of mental competency to commit "crime." Judge Bazelon was enormously influenced by what appeared to be the increasing sophistication and maturity of the sciences of the mind. It seemed logical at that time, and not altogether illogical even today, that if the criminal activity was attributable to mental illness, it should not be subject to criminal sanction. In retrospect, the difficulties with this approach are manifest. Because psychiatrists view all behavior as determined, all criminal acts might, by definition, be the product of mental disease or defect. Even if this observation is exaggerated, defendants would not have

33. *Id.* (*quoting* United States v. Poff, 926 F.2d 588, 595 (7th Cir.1991) (*en banc*) (Easterbrook, J., dissenting)). *Cf.* People v. Coddington, 23 Cal.4th 529, 97 Cal.Rptr.2d 528, 2 P.3d 1081 (Cal.2000).

34. 214 F.2d 862 (D.C.Cir.1954).

35. *Id.* at 874–75. According to the opinion, a mental disease is capable of "improving or deteriorating," whereas a "mental defect" is "not considered capable of either improving or deteriorating and which may be either congenital, or the result of injury, or the residual effect of a physical or mental disease." *Id.* at 875.

36. *See* B. Weiner, *Mental Disability and Criminal Law, in* THE MENTALLY DISABLED AND THE LAW (S. Brakel et al., eds. 3d ed. 1985).

37. *See* RITA SIMON, THE JURY AND THE DEFENSE OF INSANITY 203 (1967); *but see* L. COLEMAN, THE REIGN OF ERROR 49–50 (1984). *See generally* Loftus E. Becker, Jr., Durham *Revisited: Obstacles to the Presentation of Psychiatric Testimony Remain*, 3 PSYCHIATRIC ANNALS 9 (1973) (recounting how the increase in acquittals resulted largely from local psychiatrists deciding that mental disease or defect under *Durham* included sociopathy).

difficulty finding psychiatrists to so testify. Moreover, under the test, once the defendant introduced a psychiatric defense, the prosecutor had the burden to prove that a mental disease or defect did not cause the criminal act. Unfortunately, psychology does not provide answers at the level of specificity demanded by the *Durham* test. Psychology illuminates little more than the shadows of midnight, while the law demands nothing less than the "blaze of noon."[38]

Durham confirmed many lawyers' fears of the dark shadows cast by psychology.[39] The *Durham* test lasted eighteen years and was replaced in the District of Columbia with the ALI standard,[40] a test designed to be more practical than either *Durham* or *M'Naghten*.

§ 1–1.2.4   The ALI Test

In 1962, the American Law Institute put forth its standard for insanity: "A person is not responsible for criminal conduct if at the time of such conduct as a result of mental disease or defect he lacks substantial capacity either to appreciate the criminality [wrongfulness] of his conduct or to conform his conduct to the requirements of law."[41] The ALI test thus integrates the cognitive component of the *M'Naghten* test with a volitional component associated with the irresistible impulse test.[42] The cognitive component of the ALI test is somewhat broader than the one contained in *M'Naghten*, since under ALI the defendant need only show that he lacked "substantial" capacity, not all capacity.

The second component, the volitional prong,[43] has been the subject of substantial debate and criticism in both the legal and psychological communities. Perhaps the principal concern is metaphysical: "there is no objective basis for distinguishing between the impulse that was irresistible and the impulse not resisted."[44] Melton et al. explain the more specific concerns of the two communities as follows:

> Many in the legal community believed that impulsivity could easily be feigned, and feared that the test would lead to numerous invalid insanity acquittals. From the medical side came the criticism that a separate "control" test furthered the mistaken impression that the human psyche is compartmentalized into cognitive and volitional components.[45]

Although the ALI test achieved substantial success, especially in the federal courts, criticisms of its volitional prong led to many revisions in its

38.   John Milton, Paradise Lost, Book IV.

39.   *See* Burt, *Of Mad Dogs and Scientists: The Perils of the "Criminal–Insane,"* 123 U. Pa. L. Rev. 258, 258–59 (1974) ("The *Durham* experiment has succeeded by graphically demonstrating a proposition of considerable social importance: the conjoining of psychiatry and the criminal law frequently (perhaps inevitably) produces mutual misunderstandings and defeats optimistic expectations on all sides.").

40.   *See* United States v. Brawner, 471 F.2d 969, 973 (D.C.Cir.1972).

41.   Model Penal Code § 4.01(1) (1985).

42.   *See* Smith, *supra* note 3, at 158.

43.   The volitional test was well described in *Parsons v. State*, 81 Ala. 577, 2 So. 854 (Ala.1887), by one of the first courts to ever use it:

> [The defendant is not] legally responsible if the two following conditions concur: (1) If, by reason of the duress of . . . mental disease he had so far lost the power to choose between the right and wrong, and to avoid doing the act in question, as that his free agency was at the time destroyed; (2) and if, at the same time, the alleged crime was so connected with such mental disease, in the relation of cause and effect, as to have been the product of it solely.

44.   Melton et al., *supra* note 5, at 124.

45.   *Id.* at 116.

statement and use.[46] Moreover, it became the focus of intense scrutiny in the 1980s, because it was the test under which John Hinckley was acquitted.[47] The Hinckley acquittal led to congressional passage of the Insanity Defense Reform Act, essentially a return to the *M'Naghten*-style right/wrong test.[48] Other jurisdictions pursued alternative formulations or sought to reconceptualize the insanity defense altogether.

In *State v. Wilson*,[49] the Connecticut Supreme Court sought to give content to the term "wrongfulness" in its ALI-based insanity statute.[50] The wrongfulness prong, of course, is also shared by the *M'Naghten* test. The specific question presented to the *Wilson* court concerned defining the moral component that is inherent in the term "wrongfulness." As the court pointed out, "by choosing the term 'wrongfulness' instead of 'criminality,' the legislature intended to import [a] moral element into Connecticut's insanity statute."[51] The difficulty lay in choosing *whose* morality.

The defendant claimed that "morality must be defined in purely personal terms."[52] Under such a reading, "a defendant is not responsible for his criminal acts as long as his mental disease or defect causes him personally to believe that those acts are morally justified, even though he may appreciate that his conduct is wrong in the sense that it is both illegal and contrary to societal standards of morality."[53] In contrast, the state argued that "morality must be defined by societal standards."[54] Under this approach, "a defendant is [] responsible for his criminal acts unless, because of mental disease or defect, he lacks substantial capacity to appreciate that his actions were wrong under society's moral standards."[55]

The court found that the state's view of wrongfulness was tantamount to reading "wrongfulness" as "criminality," since society's moral standards are codified into law.[56] At the same time, the court rejected a purely personal standard of morality. The court would not permit any interpretation that would allow "a defendant who appreciates both the illegality and the societal immorality of his actions [to] be relieved of criminal responsibility due to his purely personal, albeit delusional, moral code."[57]

The Connecticut court, therefore, attempted to find a middle ground between the possibly deluded morality of the individual and the possibly too demanding morality of society. The court offered the following compromise:

46. *See id.* at 118 (summarizing the law in the states).

47. *See* United States v. Hinckley, 525 F.Supp. 1342 (D.D.C.1981).

48. *See supra* § 1–1.2.2.

49. 242 Conn. 605, 700 A.2d 633 (Conn. 1997).

50. The applicable law closely tracks the Model Penal Code test. The Connecticut law provides, in pertinent part, as follows:

Lack of capacity due to mental disease or defect as affirmative defense. (a) In any prosecution for an offense, it shall be an affirmative defense that the defendant, at the time he committed the proscribed act or acts, lacked substantial capacity, as a result of mental disease or defect, either to appreciate the wrongfulness of his conduct or to control his conduct within the requirements of the law.

Conn. Gen. Stat. § 53a–13(a).

51. *Wilson*, 700 A.2d at 639.

52. *Id.*

53. *Id.*

54. *Id.* at 639–40.

55. *Id.* at 640.

56. *Id.* at 642.

57. *Id.* at 640.

We conclude ... that a defendant does not truly "appreciate the wrongfulness of his conduct" ... if a mental disease or defect causes him both to harbor a distorted perception of reality and to believe that, under the circumstances as he honestly perceives them, his actions do not offend societal morality, even though he may also be aware that society, on the basis of the criminal code, does not condone his actions. Thus, a defendant would be entitled to prevail ... if, as a result of his mental disease or defect, he sincerely believes that society would approve of his conduct if it shared his understanding of the circumstances underlying his actions. This formulation appropriately balances the concepts of societal morality that underlie our criminal law with the concepts of moral justification that motivated the legislature's adoption of the term "wrongfulness" in our insanity statute.[58]

§ 1–1.2.5 Guilty but Mentally Ill

The category of "guilty but mentally ill" is not a test of insanity, but rather a net-widening device designed to catch those cases threatening to drop through the traditional insanity "loophole." The insanity defense, therefore, has not been abolished in those states adopting the "guilty but mentally ill" classification. Michigan, for example, uses the ALI test for insanity, but permits juries to find, alternatively, that the defendant is "guilty but mentally ill" if he suffers from "a substantial disorder of thought or mood which significantly impairs judgment, behavior, capacity to recognize reality or ability to cope with the ordinary demands of life."[59] The jury, however, must determine that the defendant was not insane when he committed the act before reaching a guilty but mentally ill verdict.[60] The perceived benefit of this alternative is that it ensures that the convicted person will be segregated from society for a set period of time. In theory, a defendant found guilty but mentally ill is incarcerated in a psychiatric institution for treatment and, if he recovers, is sent to prison for the remainder of his sentence. The practice, however, appears quite different. Many defendants convicted under these provisions receive little or no psychiatric treatment.[61]

In *Neely v. Newton*,[62] the petitioner asked the Tenth Circuit to find that New Mexico's Guilty But Mentally Ill (GBMI) statute violated due process. The petitioner argued that the statute infringes on a defendant's right to a fair trial and undermines an insanity defense by calling upon juries to identify a middle ground between culpability and excuse that does not exist.[63] The court ultimately concluded, however, that the statute did not fail under due process.[64]

The *Neely* court noted at the outset that the GBMI standard, a very new approach to the subject, has become somewhat more popular since John Hinckley was found not guilty by reason of insanity for the attempt on

---

58. *Id.* at 643.

59. Mich. Comp. Laws § 330.1400a (1980); *see also* Ill.Rev.Stat. ch. 38, § 6–2 (1988).

60. *See generally* People v. Ramsey, 422 Mich. 500, 375 N.W.2d 297 (Mich.1985)(upholding the constitutionality of the Michigan rule).

61. *See* M. Perlin, *supra* note 2, at 92–94; *see generally* Christopher Slobogin, *The Guilty But Mentally Ill Verdict: An Idea Whose Time Should Not have Come*, 53 Geo. Wash. L. Rev. 494, 513 (1985).

62. 149 F.3d 1074 (10th Cir.1998).

63. *Id.* at 1080.

64. *Id.* at 1082.

President Reagan's life. It has now been adopted in thirteen states.[65] Although commentators have been generally critical, the court noted, all but one court considering this issue have found GBMI statutes constitutional.[66] The one exception was *People v. Robles*,[67] in which an Illinois appellate court concluded "that the GBMI statute encourages compromise verdicts and that, as a result, the subject statutory scheme deprives a defendant of due process."[68] *Robles*, however, has since been overruled by the Illinois Supreme Court.[69]

The Tenth Circuit found that the GBMI statute advanced legitimate state interests and thus did not violate due process. "[N]ot judg[ing] the wisdom of the legislature's enactment," the *Neely* court found two legitimate bases to support the law. First "[t]he GBMI verdict ... may actually serve to clarify the jury's duty by disclosing gradations of criminal responsibility. A defendant who is mentally ill, but not insane, at the time of the commission of the offense must be held responsible for her conduct."[70] Second, the verdict could identify those individuals in need of treatment for a mental illness.[71]

In *Robles* an intermediate Illinois appellate court had rejected both of these bases in light of the way the GBMI standard was employed in practice. First of all, quoting from a dissenting opinion from Justice Montgomery of the New Mexico Supreme Court when that court had heard *Neely*, the *Robles* court found that "the GBMI verdict 'induces compromise verdicts by seducing jurors into settling on a middle ground between guilty and not guilty, when in fact there is no middle ground.' "[72] As for the second claimed legitimate government interest, the court found that in Illinois "the psychiatric treatment afforded those found GBMI was identical to that of other prisoners."[73] Therefore, "the GBMI statute has no practical effect."[74] The Tenth Circuit in *Neely* did not determine whether there was any practical effect that followed the identification of those in need of psychiatric care in New Mexico.[75]

Robles, however, was overturned by the Illinois Supreme Court in *People v. Lantz*.[76] The *Lantz* court focused primarily on two main contentions: (1) that the statutory scheme places "conflicting burdens of proof on the defense," since under Illinois law insanity and GBMI are mutually exclusive;[77]

65. "These 13 states are Alaska, ALASKA STAT. § 12.47.030; Delaware, DEL. CODE ANN. tit. 11, § 401(b); Georgia, GA. CODE ANN. § 17–7–131; Illinois, 725 ILL. COMP. STAT. ANN. 5/115–3(c), –4(j), Indiana, IND. CODE ANN. § 35–36–2–3; Kentucky, KY. REV. STAT. ANN. §§ 504.120, .130; Michigan, MICH. COMP. LAWS ANN. § 768.36; Nevada, NEV. REV. STAT. § 174.035; New Mexico, N.M. STAT. ANN. §§ 31–9–3 to –4; Pennsylvania, 18 PA. CONS. STAT. ANN. § 314; South Carolina, S.C. CODE ANN. § 17–24–20; South Dakota, S.D. CODIFIED LAWS § 23A–26–14; and Utah, UTAH CODE ANN. §§ 77–16a–103 to –104 ('guilty and mentally ill')." *Id.* at 1079.

66. *Id.* at 1079–80.

67. 288 Ill.App.3d 935, 224 Ill.Dec. 633, 682 N.E.2d 194 (1997).

68. *Id.* at 205.

69. People v. Lantz, 186 Ill.2d 243, 238 Ill.Dec. 592, 712 N.E.2d 314 (Ill.1999).

70. *Neely*, 149 F.3d at 1080.

71. *Id.* at 1081.

72. *Robles*, 682 N.E.2d at 205 (quoting State v. Neely, 112 N.M. 702, 819 P.2d 249, 261 (N.M.1991) (Montgomery, J., concurring in part and dissenting in part)).

73. *Id.* at 204.

74. *Id.*

75. The applicable statute does require the corrections department to "examine the nature, extent, continuance and treatment of the defendant's mental illness." N.M. Stat. Ann. § 31–9–4. A due process analysis should probably inquire into the actual operation of this provision.

76. 186 Ill.2d 243, 238 Ill.Dec. 592, 712 N.E.2d 314 (Ill.1999).

77. *Id.* at 318.

and (2) that the GBMI defense invites jurors to strike a compromise between guilt and insanity.[78]

The *Lantz* court rejected the defendant's claim that "the statutory scheme denies a GBMI offender a fair trial and violates due process by placing conflicting burdens of proof on the defense."[79] The court acknowledged that the statutory definitions were distinct, but disagreed that this fact required "the defense to prove inconsistent propositions at the same time."[80] The court explained that the two constructs were effectively complementary, and related to different degrees of the same underlying phenomenon: "mental illness is a less serious form of psychological functioning than insanity."[81] Therefore, no inconsistency was present, for a defendant could present evidence of insanity which would fully support the alternative GBMI verdict.[82]

The *Lantz* court also rejected the defendant's contention that the GBMI verdict represented "a meaningless option."[83] As noted, a general concern with GBMI is that it offers juries a way to avoid the insanity acquittal, but does not treat offenders convicted under it substantially differently from those found guilty. The court, however, argued to the contrary: "we do not believe that the GBMI verdict represents a meaningless option. The separate verdict helps clarify for the jury the differences between insanity and mental illness that falls short of insanity."[84] Yet, the court also found it to be non-objectionable that the jury is not told of "the consequences of its determination."[85] The court quoted the *Neely* opinion for support:

> "The jury need not be informed of the consequences of a GBMI verdict in order for the verdict to have the effect of signaling to the sentencing court or the corrections department that the defendant may be in need of psychiatric treatment. The jury accomplishes this purpose simply by finding the defendant mentally ill."[86]

And like the Tenth Circuit in *Neely*, the Illinois Supreme Court ignored whether, in fact, there was any practical effect following the identification of those in need of psychiatric care.

The guilty but mentally ill classification gives courts and juries some flexibility in responding to the complexities of mental illness.[87] Although this might appear to be an improvement over the simple dichotomous choice

---

78. *Id.*

79. *Id.*

80. *Id.* at 320. Under the applicable Illinois statutes, insanity is defined as follows:

> an offender is insane if "as a result of mental disease or defect, he lacks substantial capacity either to appreciate the criminality of his conduct or to conform his conduct to the requirements of law."

Id. at 319 (quoting 720 ILCS 5/6–2(a) (West 1994)). Guilty but mentally ill employs the following definition of mental illness:

> "a substantial disorder of thought, mood, or behavior which afflicted a person at the time of the commission of the offense and which impaired that person's judgment, but not to

the extent that he is unable to appreciate the wrongfulness of his behavior or is unable to conform his conduct to the requirements of law."

Id. (quoting ILCS 5/6–2(d) (West 1994)).

81. *Id.* at 320.

82. *Id.*

83. *Id.*

84. *Id.* at 321.

85. *Id.* at 322.

86. *Id.* (*quoting* Neely v. Newton, 149 F.3d 1074, 1081 (10th Cir.1998)).

87. *See generally* Norman J. Finkel & Kevin B. Duff, *The Insanity Defense: Giving Jurors a Third Option*, 2 FORENSIC REP. 235 (1989).

traditionally presented,[88] it remains a fairly blunt instrument for responding to this enormously complex issue.[89] Moreover, there is some reason to fear that this defense widens the net in only one direction, permitting juries to convict mentally ill defendants who otherwise would have prevailed under an insanity defense.[90] It also raises expectations among defendants, lawyers, judges and the public that the mentally ill defendant who is convicted will receive treatment; to the degree he does not, the classification is a sham and should be abolished.[91] The possibility that this reform is built on false pretenses makes the guilty but mentally ill test worse than outright abolition, a course pursued by some states; however barbaric outright abolition might be, at least it has the virtue of honesty.

§ 1–1.2.6   Abolition of the Insanity Defense

Although not a new idea, abolition of the insanity defense gained substantial momentum after the acquittal of John Hinckley.[92] Three states have abolished the insanity defense.[93] Abolition of insanity, however, does not relieve the state of the burden of proving *mens rea*. Hence, a defendant who suffers from a mental disease or defect might still be acquitted if that illness prevented him from forming the requisite intent as defined by the statute. This is, without question, the constitutional minimum required. Whether the Constitution demands more remains an unanswered question. Although the United States Supreme Court has yet to determine whether due process

---

88. See Mickenberg, *supra* note 19

89. See State v. Neely, 112 N.M. 702, 819 P.2d 249, 255 (N.M.1991) (Court upheld distinction between those found not guilty by reason of insanity and those found guilty but mentally ill finding that this classification "is rationally related to a legitimate interest—it allows those mentally ill who did not have the capacity to form the appropriate criminal intent to avoid criminal liability while providing for criminal liability for those guilty because they possessed the criminal intent, yet who are nonetheless mentally ill.").

90. See Robey, *Guilty but Mentally Ill*, 6 BULL. AM. ACAD. PSYCHIATRY & I. 374, 379–80 (1978). More research needs to be done on this issue; but, at this time, juries appear to be applying the new category in an even manner. See C. Roberts, S. Golding & F. Fincham, *Implicit Theories of Criminal Responsibility: Decision Making and the Insanity Defense*, 11 LAW & HUM. BEHAV. 207, 212 (1987); Finkel & Duff, *supra* note 87.

91. Michael Perlin offers the following observation:

The GBMI [guilty but mentally ill] verdict is a perfect exemplar of insanity defense ambivalence and popular attitudes. We rationalize that we are "doing something" for the mentally disabled criminal defendant, but the results of this legislative "reform" are, at best, cosmetic, and, at worst, meretricious. With no meaningful promise of treatment or

rehabilitative services, and with the countenancing of punitive sentencing, the GBMI verdict becomes deceptive and hollow.

M. PERLIN, *supra* note 2, at 95. *Cf.* People v. Scott, 194 Ill.2d 268, 252 Ill.Dec. 37, 742 N.E.2d 287 (Ill.2000) ("[A] person found guilty but mentally ill may be executed."); People v. Crews, 122 Ill.2d 266, 119 Ill.Dec. 308, 522 N.E.2d 1167 (Ill.1988) (same).

92. See, e.g., State v. Herrera, 895 P.2d 359, 361 (Utah 1995)("When John Hinckley was found not guilty by reason of insanity for shooting President Ronald Reagan ... public outrage prompted ... Utah [to] abolish[] the traditional insanity defense."). For more general discussion of the effect of John Hinckley's acquittal, see Michael L. Perlin, *"The Things We Do For Love:" Hinckley's Trial and the Future of the Insanity Defense in the Federal Courts*, 30 N.Y.L. SCH. L. REV. 857 (1985).

An early, and highly respected, academic supporter of abolition is Norval Morris. See NORVAL MORRIS, MADNESS AND THE CRIMINAL LAW (1982); Norval Morris, *Psychiatry and the Dangerous Criminal*, 41 S. CAL. L. REV. 514 (1968); see generally Michael Moore, *Justice, Mercy, and Craziness*, 36 STAN. L. REV. 1485 (1984) (Reviewing MORRIS, MADNESS AND THE CRIMINAL LAW (1982)).

93. 1979 MONT. LAWS 714; UTAH CODE ANN. § 76–2–305 (Supp. 1993); IDAHO CODE § 18–207 (Supp. 1986).

requires the availability of an insanity defense,[94] recent state court decisions have upheld abolition statutes against constitutional attack.[95]

Utah provides a good illustration of the move toward abolishing the insanity defense and constitutional challenges to such efforts. In *State v. Herrera*,[96] the Utah Supreme Court upheld the Utah scheme abolishing the insanity defense. Utah's code provides as follows:

> It is a defense to a prosecution under any statute or ordinance that the defendant, as a result of mental illness, lacked the mental state required as an element of the offense charged. Mental illness is not otherwise a defense.[97]

Utah courts refer to this as the *mens rea* model, since lack of the requisite *mens rea* operates as a complete defense.[98]

In *Herrera,* the defendants[99] challenged the constitutionality of the Utah law on the basis that it violated, among other guarantees, the Due Process and Equal Protection Clauses of the United States Constitution.[100] The Due

---

94. In *Ake v. Oklahoma*, 470 U.S. 68, 105 S.Ct. 1087, 84 L.Ed.2d 53 (1985), Justice (now Chief Justice) Rehnquist observed that "[i]t is highly doubtful that due process requires a State to make available an insanity defense to a criminal defendant." *Id.* at 91. Whether there is substantial agreement on the Court for this view is unknown; Justice Rehnquist was the lone dissenter in *Ake*.

95. In recent times, state courts have uniformly upheld abolition of the insanity defense by statute. *See* State v. Herrera, 895 P.2d 359 (Utah 1995); State v. Cowan, 260 Mont. 510, 861 P.2d 884 (Mont.1993); State v. Beam, 109 Idaho 616, 710 P.2d 526 (Idaho 1985). In the somewhat distant past, however, three state courts invalidated abolition of the insanity defense by statute for constitutional reasons. *See* Sinclair v. Mississippi, 161 Miss. 142, 132 So. 581 (Miss.1931); Louisiana v. Lange, 168 La. 958, 123 So. 639 (La.1929); Washington v. Strasburg, 60 Wash. 106, 110 P. 1020 (Wash. 1910).

96. 895 P.2d 359 (Utah 1995).

97. Utah Code Ann. § 76–2–305(1).

98. *Herrera,* 895 P.2d at 361–62; *see also* Harlow M. Huckabee, *Avoiding the Insanity Defense Straight Jacket: The Mens Rea Route,* 15 Pepp. L. Rev. 1, 25 (1987).

The *Herrera* court provided the following explanation for how the new provision changes the Utah practice:

If A kills B, thinking that he is merely squeezing a grapefruit, A does not have the requisite mens rea for murder and would be acquitted under both the prior and new law. However, if A kills B, thinking that B is an enemy soldier and that the killing is justified as self-defense, then A has the requisite mens rea for murder and could be convicted under the new law but not under the prior

law, because he knowingly and intentionally took another's life. Under the amended provision, it does not matter whether A understood that the act was wrong. The new law does away with the traditional affirmative insanity defense that the killing was perceived to be justifiable and therefore done with innocent intent.

Herrera, 895 P.2d at 362. This is the "lemon squeezer" exception. *See* Wales, *An Analysis of the Proposal to "Abolish" the Insanity Defense in S.1: Squeezing a Lemon,* 124 U. Pa. L. Rev. 687, 687 (1976). Daniel M'Naghten would have been convicted under the Utah scheme. *See supra* notes 18–21 and accompanying text.

99. *Herrera* is a consolidation of two cases in which separate defendants challenged the constitutionality of the Utah law abolishing the insanity defense. Thus, the court refers to "defendants" throughout in the plural.

100. In addition to Due Process and Equal Protection, the *Herrera* Court reviewed the defendants' claims that the Utah statute violated their Fifth Amendment privilege against self-incrimination, because it compelled them to submit to a psychiatric examination by the state. The court rejected the defendants' argument that by abolishing the insanity defense the State had forfeited its right to subject defendants to a mental examination when they raise a mental competency defense. The Court explained: "If the defendants were permitted to rebut the state's case by pleading insanity and then to be shielded from any state psychiatric examination, the state's burden of proving they possessed the requisite mental intent beyond a reasonable doubt would become practically insurmountable." *Id.* at 370. *See also* Estelle v. Smith, 451 U.S. 454, 101 S.Ct. 1866, 68 L.Ed.2d 359 (1981) ("When a defendant asserts the insanity defense and introduces supporting psychiatric testimony, his silence

Process Clause of the Fourteenth Amendment extends to those rights that are so fundamental that they are "implicit in the concept of ordered liberty" and without which "a fair and enlightened system of justice would be impossible."[101] The *Herrera* court found that an affirmative defense for insanity did not qualify as a fundamental right.[102] The court observed that throughout history the content of the insanity defense had changed so significantly as to cast doubt on any such claim. Moreover, the court argued, the Utah scheme, while severely restricting the availability of an insanity-styled defense, still permits insanity claims that negate *mens rea*.[103] Due Process, the court concluded, requires no more.

The court also rejected the defendants' argument that the Utah scheme was arbitrary and capricious and thus unconstitutional under the Equal Protection Clause. The *mens rea* model distinguishes between those who kill intending to take a human life and those who do not. This distinction, the court found, was not irrational:

> The legislature has drawn a line between those who do not comprehend that they are taking a human life and those who do.... The first group makes no moral judgment, while the second group realizes that they are actually killing someone and therefore their actions come closer to the realm of criminality.[104]

Justice Stewart, in a strong dissent, challenged the majority's reading of the history of western civilization (i.e., Due Process) and comprehension of moral philosophy (i.e., Equal Protection). Although the nature of the insanity defense has changed over time, he argued, it has continuously existed in one form or another for the past two centuries.[105] In fact, the core principle underlying the insanity defense reaches back further still.[106] Moreover, the very foundation of a civilized criminal justice system prohibits imposing " 'punishment where it cannot impose blame.' "[107] Justice Stewart categorical-

---

may deprive the State of the only effective means it has of controverting his proof on an issue that he interjected into the case.").

The *Herrera* court declined to review the defendants' claims under the Eighth Amendment's guarantee against cruel and unusual punishments because the cases were before them on interlocutory appeal and the defendants had not been convicted of any crime. See *Herrera*, 895 P.2d at 371.

Finally, the *Herrera* court considered several claims under the State Constitution. *See id.* at 366–71. Because of the general focus of this section, these state concerns are not discussed here.

In *State v. Herrera (Herrera II)*, 993 P.2d 854 (Utah 1999), the Utah Supreme Court again visited the question whether Utah's scheme abolishing the insanity defense was unconstitutional. Whereas *Herrera I* concerned a facial challenge to the Utah law, in *Herrera II* the court rejected the defendant's challenge of the Utah scheme as it was applied to him. The *Herrera II* court concluded that the Utah law does not violate due process, improperly relieve the prosecution of the burden of proof,

contravene equal protection or infringe the Eighth Amendment's guarantees.

101. Palko v. Connecticut, 302 U.S. 319, 325, 58 S.Ct. 149, 82 L.Ed. 288 (1937).

102. *Herrera*, 895 P.2d at 363–64.

103. *Id. See* United States v. Barney, 55 F.Supp.2d 1310 (D.Utah 1999) ("[E]vidence of mental illness may be introduced to show the defendant did not have the requisite mens rea for the offense.").

104. *Herrera*, 895 P.2d at 368–69.

105. *Id.* at 374–75 (Stewart, J., dissenting).

106. Justice Stewart noted as follows:

For over four centuries, Anglo–American law has held that there can be no criminality when there is a total defect of understanding or a loss of the ability to comprehend reality. Long before the rise of psychiatry, the law so held. For there to be criminality, it has been necessary that there be at least some degree of rationality, making possible some degree of free choice.

Id. at 375.

107. *Id.* at 376 (*quoting* Holloway v. United States, 148 F.2d 665, 666–67 (D.C.Cir.1945)).

ly rejected the majority's assertion "that moral culpability is established solely by an intent to kill a human being without regard for a defendant's insanity."[108] Justice Stewart explained as follows:

> [The majority's] argument, in effect, recognizes no difference between human beings and animals. On the Court's [moral] theory, an animal that intentionally kills its prey is guilty of wrongful conduct. The law does not now, and has not for centuries, premised criminality solely on an intent to commit a criminal act when extenuating circumstances justify or excuse the act and negate moral wrongfulness.... An adult who kills intentionally does not commit a criminal act if he acts in self-defense.... Likewise, a person's acts, though intentional and otherwise criminal, are not criminal if the act is done under duress, in defense of habitation or property, or in effectuating an arrest. And from very early territorial days until 1983, when the present statute was enacted, an act done by an insane person as a result of insanity was not criminal.[109]

Therefore, according to Justice Stewart, by allowing conviction and punishment for acts for which the defendant cannot be held morally accountable, the Utah scheme violates the most basic principles of a civilized society.[110]

§ 1–1.3 Diminished Capacity

The *mens rea* model underlying efforts to abolish the insanity defense is also central to any discussion concerning the diminished capacity defense. Although sometimes mistakenly construed as a "mini" insanity defense,[111] diminished capacity claims are directed at negating some or all of the *mens rea* requirement necessary for committing the charged offense.[112] In short, the

---

108. *Id.* at 376.

109. *Id.* at 376–77 (footnotes and citations omitted).

110. *Id.* at 378. *Cf.* People v. Coddington, 23 Cal.4th 529, 97 Cal.Rptr.2d 528, 2 P.3d 1081, 1156 (2000) (Mosk, J., dissenting) ("It is not enough in a case like this, where the [defendant] had a unique concept of morality, to say simply ... that a person is incapable of recognizing that conduct is morally wrong if he or she believes God has commanded that conduct."). *See generally* Peter Arenella, *Convicting the Morally Blameless: Reassessing the Relationship Between Legal and Moral Accountability,* 39 UCLA L. Rev. 1511, 1521 (1992); Stephen J. Morse, *Excusing the Crazy: The Insanity Defense Reconsidered,* 58 S. Cal. L. Rev. 777, 781 (1985); Michael L. Perlin, *Unpacking the Myths: The Symbolism Mythology in Insanity Defense Jurisprudence,* 40 Case W. Res. L. Rev. 599, 658–66 (1990).

111. *See* Arenella, *supra* note 110, at 1615 (pointing out this error).

112. Melton et al. explain the distinction between the *mens rea* model and insanity as follows:

It is ... important to recognize that the *mens rea* inquiry ... is quite distinct from the insanity inquiry. While it may be true that persons who meet the *M'Naghten* test may also be incapable of forming the requisite intent for an offense, it is theoretically and practically possible for persons to have the appropriate *mens rea* and yet still to have been insane. Their reasons for committing acts may be so "crazy" that no jury would be willing to hold them criminally responsible, even though their knowledge of what they were doing was relatively unimpaired.... Daniel M'Naghten probably met the *mens rea* requirements for the crime charged (i.e., knowingly shooting at another with the purpose of killing him), but he was nonetheless found insane.

Melton et al., *supra* note 5, at 128. In *State v. Shaw,* 168 Vt. 412, 721 A.2d 486 (Vt.1998), the Vermont Supreme Court explained as follows:

Voluntary manslaughter may ... be based on a defendant's diminished capacity at the time of the killing.... Diminished capacity is predicated on finding that the defendant suffered from mental disabilities which prevented him from forming the state of mind ... which is an essential element of the greater offense charged.

Id. at 490.

defendant proffers clinical testimony that purports to negate his capacity to form the requisite intent under the law.[113]

Although states vary widely in how they define mental state (e.g., "willful and wanton" or "with a depraved heart"), these practices fall roughly along a spectrum ranging from specific intent to achieve the prohibited result, to a general intent or knowledge of the circumstances surrounding the prohibited result. For example, the Model Penal Code establishes four categories of criminal intent: purpose, knowledge, recklessness and negligence. The "purpose" requirement is met when the offender consciously intends the criminal result; the "knowledge" standard is satisfied when the offender is aware of the circumstances that render the conduct criminal; the "recklessness" test is met when the offender "consciously disregards a substantial and unjustifiable risk" that the conduct will produce the criminal result; and the "negligence" standard is satisfied when the offender "should be aware of a substantial and unjustifiable risk" that the conduct will produce the criminal result.[114]

The diminished capacity defense, therefore, refers straightforwardly to the admission of clinical testimony indicating that the defendant was incapable of forming the requisite mental intent. In particular cases, this might mean that the defendant could not have formed the required "purpose," though he might have sufficiently understood the circumstances to meet the knowledge or recklessness standards. In some cases, clinical testimony might indicate that none of the subjective states of knowledge could have been met by the defendant. Since negligence is an objective standard—querying the response of a "reasonable person"—clinical testimony is not relevant when that standard applies.[115] Therefore, a diminished capacity defense, if successful, might result in the defendant being convicted of a lesser included offense or, in some cases, outright acquittal.

In light of the *mens rea* basis for the defense of diminished capacity, due process might require its availability. Melton et al. made this point in observing that,

> since the prosecution is entitled to an inference that accused persons intend the natural consequences of their acts, denying defendants the opportunity to present competent clinical evidence when such evidence is the only means of overcoming the inference would in effect permit the prosecution to convict the defendants when there is a reasonable doubt as to their guilt.[116]

In fact, several courts have held that due process requires the admission of clinical testimony on diminished capacity.[117] Many states, however, do not permit the introduction of psychiatric testimony as to any issue other than insanity, finding its use to prove diminished capacity too speculative and unreliable.[118] Moreover, it should be noted, despite the obvious relevance of

113. For an excellent, extended, discussion of diminished capacity, *see* MELTON ET AL., *supra* note 5, § 6.03(b), at 127–130.

114. MODEL PENAL CODE § 2.02 (Official Draft 1962); *see* MELTON ET AL., *supra* note 5, at 127.

115. MELTON ET AL., *supra* note 5, at 128–29.

116. *Id.* at 128.

117. *See, e.g.,* State v. Hines, 187 Conn. 199, 445 A.2d 314 (Conn.1982); Commonwealth v. Walzack, 468 Pa. 210, 360 A.2d 914 (Pa.1976).

118. MELTON ET AL., *supra* note 5, at 128–129. *Cf.* Montana v. Egelhoff, 518 U.S. 37, 41–44, 116 S.Ct. 2013, 135 L.Ed.2d 361 (1996) (concluding that the due process clause does

the defense of diminished capacity to *mens rea*, courts have never held that any speculative or unreliable testimony must be admitted. Expert clinical testimony on a defendant's inability to form the requisite mental state should, in all cases, still meet basic standards of scientific validity before it is admitted.

§ 1–1.4 Procedural Safeguards for Insanity Claims

§ 1–1.4.1 Provision of a Psychiatrist

In *Ake v. Oklahoma*,[119] the Court held "that when a defendant has made a preliminary showing that his sanity at the time of the offense is likely to be a significant factor at trial, the Constitution requires that a state provide access to a psychiatrist's assistance on this issue if the defendant cannot otherwise afford one."[120] In reaching this conclusion, the Court evaluated the rights and interests of the individual, the costs to the government, and the benefit that a psychiatrist's services would provide to an indigent defendant who raises a serious claim of insanity.[121] The defendant's interest here was particularly compelling, since the criminal proceeding "places an individual's life or liberty at risk."[122] The government's interest, in contrast, was solely an economic one; and provision of a single psychiatrist is not sufficiently burdensome, "in light of the compelling interest of both the State and the individual in accurate dispositions."[123] Finally, the Court found that a psychiatrist is indispensable to a defense based on insanity.[124]

The *Ake* Court cautioned, however, that the right to a psychiatrist does not extend so far as to include the "right to choose a psychiatrist of [the defendant's] personal liking or to receive funds to hire his own."[125] In fact, the right to a psychiatrist might not necessarily extend to the defendant's right to have his own psychiatrist. In *Granviel v. Lynaugh*,[126] the Fifth Circuit read *Ake* to require no more than an "independent court-appointed psychiatrist whose report would be available to both the prosecution and defense." Justice Marshall (the author of *Ake*), wrote in a dissent to the Court's denial of certiorari in *Granviel,* that "Ake was directed at providing a defendant with the tools necessary to present an effective defense within the context of our adversarial system, in which each party marshals evidence favorable to its side and aggressively challenges the evidence presented by the other side."[127]

---

not require the admission of evidence of the defendant's voluntary intoxication when offered as a defense to the purpose prong of the state's homicide statute).

119. 470 U.S. 68, 105 S.Ct. 1087, 84 L.Ed.2d 53 (1985).

120. *Id.* at 74.

121. *Id.* at 77. Considerations of the individual's interest, the government's costs, and the benefits of the safeguard are derived from the balancing test set forth in Mathews v. Eldridge, 424 U.S. 319, 335, 96 S.Ct. 893, 47 L.Ed.2d 18 (1976) (establishing a three-factor test for procedural due process, requiring courts to balance the individual's private interest, the burdens on government, and the benefits associated with the procedure).

122. *Ake,* 470 U.S. at 78.

123. *Id.* at 79.

124. *Id.* at 82 ("[T]he testimony of psychiatrists can be crucial and 'a virtual necessity if an insanity plea is to have any chance of success.'") (*quoting* Gardner, *The Myth of the Impartial Psychiatric Expert: Some Comments Concerning Criminal Responsibility and the Decline of the Age of Therapy,* 2 LAW & PSYCH. REV. 99, 113–114 (1976)).

125. *Id.* at 83.

126. 881 F.2d 185 (5th Cir.1989).

127. Granviel v. Texas, 495 U.S. 963, 964, 110 S.Ct. 2577, 109 L.Ed.2d 758 (1990)(Marshall, J., dissenting from denial of cert.). Justice Marshall also noted as follows:

Texas' provision of a "disinterested" expert thus does not satisfy *Ake*. Texas may, of

Further eroding the holding of *Ake v. Oklahoma* requiring the provision of a psychiatrist for a defendant who makes a "preliminary showing that his sanity at the time of the offense is likely to be a significant factor at trial,"[128] the Fourth Circuit held in *Wilson v. Greene*[129] that there is no constitutional requirement that this assistance be "effective" or even "adequate."[130] The court explained that "[t]o entertain such claims would immerse federal judges in an endless battle of the experts to determine whether a particular psychiatric examination was appropriate."[131] Moreover, "it would undermine the finality of state criminal convictions, which would constantly be subject to psychiatric reappraisal years after the trial has ended."[132]

Although the Fourth Circuit must certainly be correct that it was not the Court's intention in *Ake* to "guarantee[] a particular substantive result,"[133] the reverse is not obviously correct. The Fourth Circuit is of the view that *Ake* stands merely for the proposition "that the failure to provide *any* evaluation [does] not comport with the Due Process Clause."[134] But if *Ake* stands for nothing more than that the Constitution guarantees merely a breathing psychiatrist, it is a hollow right indeed.

§ 1–1.4.2 The Burdens of Proof for Commitment Following Acquittal by Reason of Insanity[135]

In *Jones v. United States*,[136] the Court held that "the Constitution permits the Government, on the basis of the insanity judgment, to confine [the defendant] to a mental institution until such time as he has regained his sanity or is no longer a danger to himself or society."[137] However, once the individual has regained his sanity or is no longer a danger to himself or society, incarceration must end.[138] In *Foucha v. Louisiana*,[139] for instance, the defendant had been found not guilty by reason of insanity. Subsequently,

course, provide for appointment of such an expert to aid the factfinder in determining the validity of a defendant's insanity defense. Cf. Fed.Rule Evid. 706. Such an appointment, however, must supplement—not take the place of—appointment of a psychiatrist to assist the defendant in preparing his defense.

Id. at 965.

128. *Ake*, 470 U.S. at 74.

129. 155 F.3d 396 (4th Cir.1998).

130. *Id.* at 401.

131. *Id.*

132. *Id.*

133. *Id.*

134. *Id.* (emphasis added).

135. In *Cooper v. Oklahoma*, 517 U.S. 348, 116 S.Ct. 1373, 134 L.Ed.2d 498 (1996), a unanimous Court invalidated an Oklahoma law that presumed a defendant was competent to stand trial and required "that a criminal defendant establish incompetence by clear and convincing evidence." *Id.* at 355. The defendant in *Cooper* demonstrated incompetence by a preponderance of evidence, but could not

meet the higher standard. *Id. See also id.* (*citing* Medina v. California, 505 U.S. 437, 449, 112 S.Ct. 2572, 120 L.Ed.2d 353 (1992)) ("[A] State may presume that the defendant is competent and require him to shoulder the burden of proving his incompetence by a preponderance of the evidence."). Based on historical precedent and a near-consensus of contemporary practice, the Court held that a state cannot "proceed with a criminal trial after the defendant had demonstrated that he is more likely than not incompetent." *Id.*

136. 463 U.S. 354, 103 S.Ct. 3043, 77 L.Ed.2d 694 (1983).

137. *Id.* at 368.

138. *See* Foucha v. Louisiana, 504 U.S. 71, 77, 112 S.Ct. 1780, 118 L.Ed.2d 437 (1992) ("'The committed acquittee is entitled to release when he has recovered his sanity or is no longer dangerous;' i.e., the acquittee may be held as long as he is both mentally ill and dangerous, but no longer.") (*quoting Jones*, 463 U.S. at 368).

139. 504 U.S. 71, 112 S.Ct. 1780, 118 L.Ed.2d 437 (1992).

however, he regained his sanity;[140] but the State sought to keep him incarcerated until he could prove that he was no longer dangerous.[141] Applying the standard adopted in *Addington v. Texas*,[142] the Court held that to continue to incarcerate a person who has been found not guilty by reason of insanity, the State must demonstrate by clear and convincing evidence "that the person sought to be committed is mentally ill and that he requires hospitalization for his own welfare and protection of others."[143]

In *Nagel v. Osborne*,[144] the petitioner had been found not guilty by reason of insanity in the killing of his grandparents in 1981. He was subsequently civilly committed. After ten years of confinement, he sought release from the state courts. At the superior court hearing, two doctors, a psychiatrist and a psychologist, testified that the petitioner was neither mentally ill nor dangerous.[145] In fact, they testified further that he was probably never mentally ill and that the earlier acquittal was an error.[146] No other expert testimony on the petitioner's mental status was introduced. The superior court denied the application for release and the Georgia state courts affirmed. He then filed a habeas corpus petition, which was denied by a federal district court. The Eleventh Circuit in *Nagel* affirmed the denial of the petition.

The Eleventh Circuit's explanation appears to rely primarily on the Georgia presumption that insanity acquitees are insane. Despite the fact that no contrary evidence was presented, all of the courts hearing this matter were left unconvinced that the petitioner was sane and not dangerous. However, the Eleventh Circuit's logic in reaching its decision is, to say the least, twisted and tortured:

> The condition that [petitioner] had at the time of his trial was a condition that was factually, legally and pragmatically a mental illness and insanity sufficient to afford him a defense to murder. Georgia law presumes that condition remains the same unless the acquittee proves that it has changed. In testifying that [petitioner] is not now mentally ill and was never mentally ill, the experts testified that his condition remains unchanged. Therefore, [petitioner] has failed to carry his burden of showing that his condition had changed.[147]

By the court's logic, then, if the petitioner were shown to be mentally ill and dangerous he would have to remain in confinement; and if, as here, he is

---

140. A psychiatrist testified that he had recovered from what was "probably" a "drug induced psychosis." *Id.* at 75.

141. *Id.* The testifying psychiatrist found that the defendant "evidenced no signs" of mental illness, but that he had an "antisocial personality" that *might* make him "a danger to himself or to other people." Id.

142. 441 U.S. 418, 99 S.Ct. 1804, 60 L.Ed.2d 323 (1979).

143. *Foucha,* 504 U.S. at 75–76. This burden does not apply to the initial commitment following a verdict of not guilty by reason of insanity. The Court explained as follows:

> When a person charged with having committed a crime is found not guilty by reason of insanity, a State may commit that person

without satisfying the *Addington* burden with respect to mental illness and dangerousness. Such a verdict . . . "establishes two facts: (i) the defendant committed an act that constitutes a criminal offense, and (ii) he committed the act because of mental illness. . . ." From these two facts, it could be properly inferred that at the time of the verdict, the defendant was still mentally ill and dangerous and hence could be committed.

Id. at 76 (*quoting Jones,* 463 U.S. at 363).

144. 164 F.3d 582 (11th Cir.1999).

145. *Id.* at 583.

146. *Id.*

147. *Id.* at 584.

shown to be not mentally ill or dangerous, then his condition has not changed, and he must remain in confinement.[148] This, as Judge Clark pointed out in dissent, effectively creates an irrebuttable presumption and violates *Foucha v. Louisiana.*[149]

§ 1–1.5 Conclusion

The insanity defense is entangled with many of the most basic and profound issues in the American criminal justice system. Professor George Fletcher captured the importance of the insanity defense in the following observation:

> The issue of insanity requires us to probe our premises for blaming and punishing. In posing the question whether a particular person is responsible for a criminal act, we are forced to resolve our doubts about whether anyone is ever responsible for criminal conduct.[150]

The law's response to criminal insanity has reflected the changing tides of the public toward the concept of criminal responsibility. Jurisdictions have experimented with a wide assortment of insanity tests, ranging from the *M'Naghten* right/wrong test to the *Durham* product rule; still other jurisdictions have experimented by adding categories to the insanity defense, such as not guilty by reason of insanity, or by abolishing the insanity defense altogether.

What is clear from all of these experiments is that more experiments are needed. Perhaps the principal continuing defect is that most law reforms in this area proceed blithely ignorant of any sophisticated understanding of modern psychology. To be sure, as the next section well documents, the state of the art of the psychology of mental illness remains far from perfect. But psychological research need not be perfect to provide valuable insights and information to lawmakers and triers of fact. Clearly, however, perpetuating the current gulf between the state of the art of psychological knowledge and the practice of law will only perpetuate the current incoherent state of legal doctrine. Only through the integration of ideas, values and knowledge can the fields of law and psychology begin to impose rationality on the insanity jurisprudence. For now, insanity doctrine is surely irrational, and perhaps even insane.

---

148. Perhaps anticipating *Nagel*, Lewis Carroll wrote, " 'Contrariwise,' continued Tweedledee, 'if it was so, it might be; and if it were so it would be; but as it isn't, it ain't. That's logic.' " LEWIS CARROLL, THROUGH THE LOOKING-GLASS AND WHAT ALICE FOUND THERE, Ch.4 (1992). Or, more to the point, the Red Queen's statement, "Sentence first—verdict afterwards," captures the spirit of the *Nagel* opinion. LEWIS CARROLL, ALICE'S ADVENTURES IN WONDERLAND, Ch.12 (1992).

149. *Nagel*, 164 F.3d at 584. (Clark, J., dissenting) ("In *Foucha*, the Court stated that it is unconstitutional to confine a person who has a personality disorder but no mental illness, regardless of whether the person presents a danger to society.").

150. GEORGE FLETCHER, RETHINKING CRIMINAL LAW 835 (1978).

B. SCIENTIFIC STATUS

by

Norman Poythress,* Christopher Slobogin,** Tomika N. Stevens*** & Kirk Heilbrun****

§ 1–2.0 THE SCIENTIFIC STATUS OF RESEARCH ON INSANITY AND DIMINISHED CAPACITY

§ 1–2.1 Major Psychoses

§ 1–2.1.1 Introduction

The "major psychoses" are generally thought to include schizophrenia,[1] delusional disorders,[2] major depressive disorder,[3] and the bipolar disorders (formerly, manic-depressive illness).[4] These disorders involve a wide variety of symptoms that reflect disturbance in several different spheres of functioning, including: thinking (errant basic assumptions, illogical thinking, disorganization or confusion of thought or speech), perception (inaccurate input through auditory, visual, or other senses), and mood (extreme dampening or excitation of emotional responding).

When the more extreme forms of these symptoms are present, persons are said to exhibit *impaired reality testing* and to be actively *psychotic*. These terms indicate that some aspect of the person's experience would not be consensually validated by most or all of his peers. Common symptoms of impaired reality testing are *delusions, hallucinations*, and *ideas of reference*.

* Norman Poythress is a Professor in the Department of Mental Health Law & Policy, Florida Mental Health Institute, University of South Florida. He received his A.B. from Indiana University in 1969 and his Ph.D. from the University of Texas at Austin in 1977. He is past-president of the American Psychology–Law Society (Division 41 of the American Psychological Association). In 1990, he received the American Academy of Forensic Psychology's Award for Distinguished Contributions to Forensic Psychology. He is a coauthor of Psychological Evaluations for the Courts: A Handbook for Mental Health Professionals and Lawyers, as well as numerous articles on the interaction of mental illness and the criminal justice system.

** Christopher Slobogin is Stephen C. O'Connell Professor of Law at the University of Florida Levin College of Law, an affiliate professor with the Department of Psychiatry at the University of Florida, and an adjunct professor at the Florida Mental Health Institute, a department of the University of South Florida. Professor Slobogin received an A.B. from Princeton University, and a J.D. and LL.M. from the University of Virginia. He has served as chair of the American Association of Law Schools Section on Mental Disability and Law, Reporter for the American Bar Association's Standards on Criminal Responsibility, editor or reviewer for *Behavioral Science & the Law, Law & Human Behavior, the American Journal of Psychiatry*, and *Psychology, Public Policy & Law*, and as the Director of the University of Virginia's Forensic Psychiatry Clinic. He has authored a casebook and a treatise on mental health law, as well as numerous articles in the area.

*** Tomika N. Stevens is currently an advanced student in the Law–Psychology Program at Villanova Law School and MCP Hahnemann University, where she is a candidate for Juris Doctorate (2003) and Doctor of Philosophy, Clinical Psychology (2004). She received her A.B. from Princeton University in 1997.

**** Kirk Heilbrun is Professor and Chair, Department of Clinical and Health Psychology, MCP Hahnemann University, and Lecturer in Law, Villanova Law School. He received his A.B. from Brown University in 1975 and his Ph.D. from the University of Texas at Austin in 1980. He is past-president of both the American Psychology–Law Society and the American Board of Forensic Psychology. He is the author of Principles of Forensic Mental Health Assessment (forthcoming, Klumer/Plenum) as well as a number of articles in related areas.

§ 1–2.0

1. American Psychiatric Association, Diagnostic and Statistical Manual of Mental Disorders 273–290 (4th ed. 1994)[hereinafter DSM-IV].

2. *Id.* at 296–301.

3. *Id.* at 339–345.

4. *Id.* at 350–363.

Delusions are inaccurate but strongly held beliefs, e.g., the assertion that one is an important government figure (an FBI agent or a Cabinet member) or an important historical figure (Napoleon or Jesus Christ). Hallucinations involve "hearing" voices that others present would not be able to hear or "seeing" visions or objects that would not be visible to others present. The term "ideas of reference" refers to the interpretation of ordinary and innocuous events as if they have highly significant personal meaning (e.g., believing that a blinking traffic light is sending a coded signal).

Some persons who experience psychotic symptoms act on these experiences as if they were real, and some of these actions may constitute violations of the law. A grandiose delusion ("I am the head of the CIA") may convince an individual that he is entitled to commandeer public resources, resulting in the unlawful taking of someone else's automobile; a severely depressed person may respond to the directives of a command auditory hallucination attributed to a beloved but deceased family member ("Bring our children to join me in heaven!"), resulting in a suicide/homicide; misinterpretation of an innocuous event (e.g., seeing someone point a finger in a restaurant) may lead to hostile and preemptive defensive action against the person who "fingered me for assassination."

When such individuals are apprehended, the insanity defense is often asserted. The fact that the defendant's symptoms diminish this ability to "know" or "appreciate" the nature of criminal behavior or "conform" conduct to objective legal mandates provides a potential basis for the judge or jury to determine that the individual should not be held morally responsible. Some types of psychosis may also form the basis for a *mens rea* defense (the "CIA director" may not have had the *mens rea* for larceny, which requires the intent to deprive another of property permanently).

This chapter's treatment of the literature on the major psychoses will be relatively brief, for two reasons. Schizophrenia has been a recognized diagnosis for nearly a century,[5] and the major affective disorders have been well-known for an even longer period; thus the literature on these disorders is massive and precludes comprehensive coverage in the space allotted. Furthermore, the major psychoses are the most commonly accepted basis for the insanity defense; when the insanity defense does succeed, which is rare,[6] the supporting diagnosis in the overwhelming majority of cases is a major psychotic disorder.[7] Accordingly, scientific controversies are less likely to arise in connection with these diagnoses as compared to others addressed in this chapter.

§ 1–2.1.2 Introductory Discussion of the Science

[1] The Scientific Questions

Several different types of studies have been conducted in connection with the major psychoses. First, the scientific community has exerted considerable

5. Marvin Karno & Grayson S. Norquist, *Schizophrenia: Epidemiology, in* 1 COMPREHENSIVE TEXTBOOK OF PSYCHIATRY—V 699 (Harold I. Kaplan & Benjamin J. Sadock, eds., 1989)[hereinafter COMPREHENSIVE TEXTBOOK OF PSYCHIATRY]. Some of the earliest clinical descriptions consistent with schizophrenia appeared in the literature near the turn of the 19th century. IRVING I. GOTTESMAN, SCHIZOPHRENIA GENESIS 5 (1991).

6. The best data suggest that the insanity plea is raised in less than 1% of felony indictments and that it is successful in less than one-quarter of the cases in which it is raised. HENRY J. STEADMAN ET AL., BEFORE AND AFTER HINCKLEY: EVALUATING INSANITY DEFENSE REFORM at 28, Table 2.2 (1993).

7. Data from New York (1982–1987), California (1982–1987), and Georgia (1979–1985)

effort to identifying meaningful subtypes of schizophrenia and affective disorders, and to describing the clinical courses and behavioral and demographic correlates associated with those subtypes. Second, epidemiological studies attempting to establish the incidence and prevalence of these disorders have been conducted. Third, much recent research has sought to, or at least helped to, disentangle competing hypotheses regarding "nature" or "nurture" as the leading etiological source of these conditions. In this vein are genetic and adoption studies, attempts to discover underlying biochemical disturbances and deviant structures or functions in the brain, investigations of the role stressful events play in the etiology and triggering of psychotic episodes, and a wide variety of studies regarding treatment (biological and psychosocial) and treatment outcome. Finally, studies examining the relationship(s) between violence and diagnosis (or specific symptoms of psychosis) have also been reported.

Although definitive studies have not been conducted in some areas, most questions of interest to the law have been studied.

[2] Scientific Methods Applied in the Research

A variety of research methods have been employed in studying the processes and symptoms associated with psychotic behavior. Analogue studies, using sub-clinical populations, of the relationships between symptoms (e.g., depression, rigid/delusional thinking) and irrational beliefs have been conducted. Correlational analyses have been employed in laboratory studies that have compared various clinical groups (persons with schizophrenia, major depression, bipolar disorder) on a variety of outcome measures related to perception, cognition, and emotional functioning. Animal laboratory studies have been conducted that permit researchers to manipulate aspects of the organism's internal environment (loading or depleting certain drugs) or external environment (induced stress) to observe their effect on behaviors in domains analogous to behaviors that are impaired in persons suffering from psychosis (e.g., attentional deficits, information processing).

Behavior geneticists have examined the concordance of diagnoses in family members of cohorts identified as suffering from major psychotic disorders. Of particular value have been comparative studies of monozygotic (MZ) (100% gene sharing) versus dizygotic (DZ) (50% gene sharing) twins, and studies of twins adopted soon after birth (separating out the confounding factor of being raised in highly similar environments) to explore the relative contribution of genetic versus environmental factors in the development of these illnesses. Survey studies based on large epidemiological (unselected) samples have provided estimates of the incidence and prevalence of these disorders in the general population. These studies have also permitted investigation of the associations between diagnoses (or particular symptom complexes) and violent or aggressive behavior. Inpatient clinical trials have been conducted to examine the effects of medications (with or without complementary psychosocial therapies) and to determine empirically the effectiveness of treatments for these disorders.

reveal that major psychoses were diagnosed in 82–97%, 84%, and 85–86% of successful insani- ty cases, respectively. *Id.* at 74–83 (New York), 50–62 (California), 105–119 (Georgia).

§ 1–2.1.3 Areas of Scientific Agreement

There is reasonable consensus in the field regarding certain epidemiological issues and the clinical course of major psychotic disorders. Affective disorders occur much more frequently than does schizophrenia. The lifetime prevalence for major depression is about 6%,[8] and for bipolar disorder is about 1.2%.[9] Lifetime prevalence for schizophrenia is about 1%.[10]

There are some notable differences within mood disorders in terms of demographics, family history, and clinical course. Major depression is more common among women than men, has a modal age of onset in the late 20s, occurs somewhat more frequently in persons of lower socioeconomic status (SES), and frequently follows a precipitating negative life event.[11] In contrast, bipolar disorder is equally prevalent across genders, has a modal age of onset in the early 20s,[12] occurs somewhat more frequently in persons of higher SES, and has no clearly established association with precipitating life events.[13] Schizophrenia occurs with equal frequency among men and women, although the median ages of onset are different between genders.[14] There is also an association between schizophrenia and lower SES, though, as discussed below, there are competing hypotheses about this relationship.[15]

There is strong evidence for a genetic etiology for the major psychoses, with concordance rates among various combinations of family members (MZ twins, DZ twins, first degree relatives, second degree relatives) typically showing a stronger relationship with closer kinship.[16] Studies suggest that

8. Leonard J. Schmidt & Michael R. Lowry, *Prevention of Affective Disorders: A Current Review, in* AFFECTIVE DISORDERS: PERSPECTIVES ON BASIC RESEARCH AND CLINICAL PRACTICE 128 ('Tetsuhiko Kariya & Michio Nakagawara, eds. 1993)[hereinafter AFFECTIVE DISORDERS].

9. Richard F. Mollica, *Mood Disorders: Epidemiology, in* COMPREHENSIVE TEXTBOOK OF PSYCHIATRY *supra* note 5, at 863.

10. GOTTESMAN, *supra* note 5, at 75; Karno & Norquist, *supra* note 5, at 701.

11. Mollica, *supra* note 9, at 864 (Table 17.1–2). The female:male prevalence ratio for all forms of depression (except unipolar mania) is approximately 2:1. Robert M.A. Hirschfield, *The Epidemiology, Classification, and Clinical Course of Depression, in* AFFECTIVE DISORDERS: RECENT RESEARCH AND RELATED DEVELOPMENTS 1, 12 (S.M. Channabasavanna & Saleem Shah, eds. 1987).

12. *Id.* Some authors suggest that the modal age of onset for unipolar depression is in the 40s. *See* EUNICE CORFMAN, NATIONAL INSTITUTE OF MENTAL HEALTH, SCIENCE REPORTS 1: DEPRESSION, MANIC DEPRESSIVE ILLNESS, AND BIOLOGICAL RHYTHMS 9 (1980).

13. "There is fairly general agreement that manic episodes mostly occur spontaneously, that is, independently of external factors such as stressful life events.... In contrast ... life events play a precipitating role in the development of depressive disorder." Kaoru Sakamoto et al., *A Clinical Study on the Precipitation of*

Mania, in AFFECTIVE DISORDERS, *supra* note 8, at 73. In their own study, these authors reported that 17.4% of 403 individual manic episodes were considered to have been precipitated by external events. *Id.* at 74.

14. For males, onset is greatest in the 15–24 age range; for females greatest risk is at 25–34 years. Karno & Norquist, *supra* note 5, at 703. *See also* GOTTESMAN, *supra* note 5, at 68.

15. *See infra* § 8–2.1.4[2].

16. GOTTESMAN, *supra* note 5, at 95–96, summarizes the research regarding concordance in relatives of persons with schizophrenia, including MZ twins (48%), first degree relatives (6–17%), and second degree relatives (2–6%). Karno & Norquist, *supra* note 5, at 702, report concordance rates for schizophrenia among DZ twins at 8–28%, and a 35–40% risk for the development of schizophrenia in children of parents who have a schizophrenia diagnosis. *See also* E. FULLER TORREY ET AL., SCHIZOPHRENIA AND MANIC-DEPRESSIVE DISORDER 11–12 (1994).

Comparable data for bipolar disorder are presented in DAVID ROSENTHAL, GENETICS OF PSYCHOPATHOLOGY (1971). Over six studies, concordance rates for MZ twins range from 50–92%, compared to 2.6–38.5% for DZ twins. When both parents have manic-depressive illness, there is a 20–40% chance for the illness to occur in their children. *Id.* at 119–121, and Table 6–2. A more recent review indicated a median concordance for bipolar disorder in MZ

heritability is a stronger factor in the affective disorders than in schizophrenia. However, even in studies of MZ twins (who share identical genes), concordance for these illnesses is less than 100%, leaving a definite, if uncertain, contribution of the environment to the expression of these illnesses.

§ 1–2.1.4 Areas of Scientific Disagreement

[1] Diagnostic Criteria

For both schizophrenia and affective disorder, researchers and clinicians have long struggled over the diagnostic criteria. Karno and Norquist[17] note the use of at least 15 different sets of diagnostic criteria for schizophrenia in Western psychiatry alone, which has no doubt contributed to variance in the clinical and research outcomes reported in the literature. Recent and regular revisions of the DSM[18] may have helped improve the reliability of diagnostic practice, but evidence concerning validity is mixed.[19] Historically researchers have attempted to grapple with the heterogeneity of schizophrenia by identifying subtypes along varying dimensions (e.g., acute versus insidious onset; paranoid versus non-paranoid). There has also been research regarding "positive versus negative symptoms"[20] and "deficit psychopathology"[21] in schizophrenia, including studies that begin to examine whether heritability coeffi-

---

twins of 67%, versus 15% for DZ twins, and higher concordance rates in bipolar disorder (both manic and depressive features) than in unipolar (depression only); Elliot S. Gershon et al., *Mood Disorders: Genetic Aspects*, in COMPREHENSIVE TEXTBOOK OF PSYCHIATRY, *supra* note 5, at 879.

17. Karno & Norquist, *supra* note 5, at 699.

18. The Diagnostic and Statistical Manual has been revised four times since its initial publication in 1952. DSM–II was published in 1968, DSM–III in 1980, DSM–III–R in 1987, and DSM–IV in 1994.

19. For a good discussion of reliability and validity concerns in the diagnosis of schizophrenia, *see* Ann E. Farmer et al., *The Phenomena of Schizophrenia, in* SCHIZOPHRENIA: THE MAJOR ISSUES 36 (Paul Bebbington & Peter McGuffin eds., 1988).

More recent diagnostic systems (DSM–III–R and International Classification of Diseases, Tenth Revision (ICD–10)) have high predictive validity, and are superior to the ICD. The one-month duration criterion for the diagnosis of schizophrenia under ICD–10 is less restrictive than the six-month criterion for DSM–III–R, but predictive validity and stability remain high for the ICD–10 diagnostic criteria. Peter Mason et al., *The Predictive Validity of a Diagnosis of Schizophrenia: A Report from the International Study of Schizophrenia (IsoS) Coordinated by the World Health Organization and the Department of Psychiatry, University of Nottingham*, 170 BR. J. PSYCHIATRY 321 (1997).

20. The more florid symptoms of schizophrenia, such as hallucinations (hearing voices, seeing visions) and delusions (rigidly held beliefs that are objectively or consensually false) are considered "positive" symptoms that suggest an overly active nervous system; in contrast, "negative" symptoms, such as psychomotor retardation, impoverished speech, flattening or blunting of emotions, etc. suggest reduction or deficit in nervous system functioning. *See generally*, POSITIVE AND NEGATIVE SYMPTOMS IN PSYCHOSIS: DESCRIPTION, RESEARCH AND FUTURE DIRECTIONS (Philip D. Harvey & Elaine F. Walker eds., 1987) [hereinafter POSITIVE AND NEGATIVE SYMPTOMS].

A cluster analysis of the Positive and Negative Syndrome Scale (PANSS) scores of 138 patients suggested the existence of at least four subtypes of schizophrenia: positive, negative, mixed, and disorganized. Sonia Dollfus et al., *Identifying Subtypes of Schizophrenia by Cluster Analyses*, 22 SCHIZOPHRENIA BULL. 545 (1996).

21. Primary, enduring negative symptoms are used to define the deficit syndrome of schizophrenia. The validity of the deficit syndrome has been demonstrated by using brain imaging, neuropsychological testing, illness outcome, and developmental history data. In a study of 43 outpatients with schizophrenia and schizoaffective disorder, there was 83% agreement between initial and blind follow-up categorization of deficit status, and 88% on nondeficit designation, Xavier Amador et al., *Stability of the Diagnosis of Deficit Syndrome in Schizophrenia*, 156 AM. J. PSYCHIATRY 637 (1999).

cients differ for these types of symptoms.[22]

The study of affective disorders has been similarly impeded by definitional issues, because over fourteen different modifiers of the term "depression" have appeared in the literature.[23] Diagnosis of major depression under DSM–IV is based on the presence or absence of antecedent dysthymia (a milder form of depression), whether the episode is single or has been recurrent and, if recurrent, whether there was full recovery between the two most recent episodes.[24] Other recent research, using epidemiologic and twin studies, however, has identified somewhat different forms of depression and associated parameters.[25] This scientific progress in the diagnosis and classification of schizophrenia and affective disorders should result in associated modifications to the diagnostic system in the next version of the *Diagnostic and Statistical Manual* of the American Psychiatric Association.

[2]   Nervous System Etiological Factors

Another question (or set of questions) left unanswered by the genetic studies concerns the specific nervous system or structural deficits that give rise to psychoses. Research into the biological bases of psychosis has proceeded on many fronts; two primary ones are mentioned here briefly.

First, extensive work is underway in an effort to determine whether and how imbalances in brain chemistry (neurotransmitters) account for psychotic symptoms. In the affective disorders, particularly depression, the neurotransmitter serotonin has been implicated. Early theories attributed an etiological role to serotonin deficiency, although recent evidence is not supportive of this theory in its simplest form.[26] Clinical trials have helped to refine the role of

22. Deficit and nondeficit schizophrenia cohorts are different in that deficit patients have less severe delusions, are less likely to abuse substances, are less prone to depression, may be less likely to commit suicide, and exhibit less awareness of their impairments. The deficit syndrome has proven to be reliable, with construct validity as well as predictive validity using biological, treatment, and course of illness variables. William Carpenter et al., *Deficit Psychopathology and a Paradigm Shift in Schizophrenia Research*, 46 BIOLOGICAL PSYCHIATRY 352 (1999).

Howard Berenbaum et al., *A Twin Study Perspective on Positive and Negative Symptoms of Schizophrenia*, in POSITIVE AND NEGATIVE SYMPTOMS, *supra* note 20, at 50–67.

23. The putative types of depression have included: retarded, agitated, endogenous, reactive, psychotic, neurotic, anxious, masked, neurasthenic, involutional, paranoid, puerperal, chronic, and atypical. Max Hamilton, *Mood Disorders: Clinical Features, in* COMPREHENSIVE TEXTBOOK OF PSYCHIATRY, *supra* note 5, at 894.

24. Martin Keller et al., *Summary of the DSM–IV Mood Disorders Field Trial and Issue Overview*, 19 PSYCHIATRIC CLINIC N. AM. 1 (1996).

25. Statistical analysis was applied to 14 different DSM–III–R symptoms of major depression reported over the last year by members of 1,029 female-female twin pairs, resulting in the identification of three depressive syndromes: (1) mild typical depression, (2) atypical depression, and (3) severe typical depression. The prominent components of severe typical depression were comorbid anxiety and panic, long episodes, impairment, and help seeking. Kenneth Kendler et al., *The Identification and Validation of Distinct Depressive Syndromes in a Population–Based Sample of Female Twins*, 53 ARCHIVES GEN. PSYCHIATRY 391 (1996).

Using the administration of different forms of medication in controlled clinical trials, other investigators identified three depressive subtypes similar to those described by Kendler and colleagues: severe depression, mild depressive reaction, and atypical depression. Frederic Quitkin et al., *Letter to the Editor Regarding The Identification and Validation of Distinct Depressive Syndromes in a Population–Based Sample of Female Twins*, 54 ARCHIVES GEN. PSYCHIATRY 970 (1997).

26. Morris H. Aprison & Joseph N. Hingtgen, *A Neurochemist's Perspective on Human Depression and Stress, in* AFFECTIVE DISORDERS, *supra* note 8, at 6. These authors suggest that, based on recent animal studies, some forms of

serotonin in the etiology of affective disorders.[27] A related theory is that affective disturbances result from erratic performance in the internal "pacemaker" or "oscillator," thought to reside in the hypothalamus, that is responsible for the regulation of various biological rhythms (e.g., sleep cycle, activity and rest cycles, secreting activity of hormonal glands, secretion of neurotransmitters).[28]

In the case of schizophrenia the neurotransmitter dopamine has been the leading focus of research efforts.[29] Drugs such as amphetamine and phencyclidine can mimic the symptoms of psychosis and are known to increase dopamine levels in the nervous system. Further, the neuroleptic drugs that are most effective in the treatment of schizophrenia (and may aid in the reduction of drug induced psychoses) are those which block dopamine receptors in the nervous system.[30] Finally, amphetamine and neuroleptic drugs affect behaviors in animals (e.g., attentional abilities, learning) that may be considered analogues of the symptomatology of persons with schizophrenia.[31]

On a second front, medical researchers are employing ever more sophisticated brain imaging techniques (CT–Scan, Magnetic Resonance Imaging (MRI)) to examine the brains of persons with psychoses, in an effort to identify brain anomalies that may be diagnostic of these disorders and provide clues to their underlying causes.[32] Numerous studies have identified structural variations that differentiate the brains of persons with schizophrenia from those of normal persons. Although multiple anomalies have been identified across studies, no particular anomaly appears in the brain of all persons with the diagnosis, and some of these anomalies appear in persons with other disorders or in persons with no psychopathology.[33]

depression may be associated with an excess of serotonin in response to a "psychiatric precipitating factor." *Id.* at 8. Increased specificity regarding the mechanism of serotonin involvement has been seen in recent studies.

One study investigated the role of the serotonin transporter gene (hSERT) and the association of allelle 12 in subjects with bipolar disorder, but not unipolar depression or schizophrenia. David A. Collier et al., *The Serotonin Transporter is a Potential Susceptibility Factor for Bipolar Affective Disorder*, 7 NEUROREPORT 1675 (1996). A second such study involved a meta-analysis of over 1,400 European individuals with bipolar (N=375) or unipolar (N=299) disorder, along with 772 controls; the investigators described a significant association of promotor allelle 2 with both bipolar and unipolar disorders. Robert A. Furlong et al., *Analysis and Meta–Analysis of Two Serotonin Transporter Gene Polymorphisms in Bipolar and Unipolar Affective Disorders*, 81 AM. J. MED. GENETICS 58 (1998). *See generally*, Joseph J. Schildkraut et al., *Mood Disorders: Biochemical Aspects, in* COMPREHENSIVE TEXTBOOK OF PSYCHIATRY, *supra* note 5, at 868–879.

27. A summary of randomized clinical trials (a total of 315) evaluating newer antidepressants such as serotonin reuptake inhibitors and serotonin norepinephrine reuptake inhibitors showed that such medications were more

effective than placebo for major depression and dysthymia. John W. Williams et al., *A Systematic Review of Newer Pharmocotherapies for Depression in Adults: Evidence Report Summary*, 132 ANNAL INTERNAL MED. 743 (2000).

28. CORFMAN, *supra* note 12, at 10–11.

29. *See generally*, J.F.W. Deakin, *The Neurochemistry of Schizophrenia, in* SCHIZOPHRENIA: THE MAJOR ISSUES, *supra* note 19, at 56; Richard Jed Wyatt, Darrell G. Kirch & Lynn E. DeLisi, *Biochemical, Endocrine, and Immunological Studies, in* COMPREHENSIVE TEXTBOOK OF PSYCHIATRY, *supra* note 5, at 717–32.

30. GOTTESMAN, *supra* note 5, at 236.

31. N.R. Swerdlow et al., *A Cross-Species Model of Psychosis: Sensorimotor Gating Deficits in Schizophrenia, in* ANIMAL MODELS OF PSYCHIATRIC DISORDERS, VOL. 2: AN INQUIRY INTO SCHIZOPHRENIA AND DEPRESSION 1–18 (P. Simon, P. Soubrie & D. Widlocher eds. 1988) [hereafter ANIMAL MODELS]; Paul R. Solomon & Andrew Crider, *Toward An Animal Model of Schizophrenia Attention Disorder, in* ANIMAL MODELS, *supra*, at 21–42.

32. CAN SCHIZOPHRENIA BE LOCALIZED IN THE BRAIN? (Nancy C. Andreasen, ed. 1984).

33. Karen Faith Berman & Daniel R. Weinberger, *Schizophrenia: Brain Structure and Function, in* COMPREHENSIVE TEXTBOOK OF PSYCHIATRY, *supra* note 5, at 705–716.

In summary, researchers are fervently searching for biological and structural deficits that may explain psychotic behavior. While much has been learned regarding the role of neurotransmitters in psychopathology, the precise mechanisms of action are not fully understood and much debate (and further research) continues. Brain-imaging research also continues in the search for structural diagnostic indicators and etiological factors, but to date no clear diagnostic indicators have emerged.[34] Given the heterogeneity in the clinical presentation of schizophrenia, some investigators are skeptical that a one-to-one correspondence between cerebral structures and symptoms will be found.[35]

[3]   Etiological Role of the Environment

Although there is general consensus that genetics is a significant etiological factor in the major psychoses, debate remains concerning the role of the environment. As discussed in the section on Posttraumatic Stress Disorder (see § 8–2.4), people vary widely in their responses to adverse life events, and the interaction of stress with underlying psychological (subjective) or biological factors is poorly understood.

As noted above, adverse life events have been associated with the onset of episodes of depression[36] and a major behavioral model, "learned helplessness," has emerged from animal laboratory studies to explain reactive depression.[37] Similarly, some observers, citing the increased frequency of stressors faced by poor or indigent persons, have posited that lower SES contributes to and perhaps even "causes" schizophrenia (the so called "breeder" model).[38] In contrast, the "downward drift" theory suggests just the opposite scenario: persons at all SES levels are vulnerable to schizophrenia but experience a gradual reduction in quality of life and SES due to the progressive deterioration associated with the illness. In between is the "diathesis-stress" model,[39] which relegates environmental factors to the role of triggering psychosis in persons who are predisposed to schizophrenic symptoms because of genetic vulnerability.[40] Although some authorities conclude that the evidence favors

34. "In spite of advances in the technology of biological research, no disease marker or laboratory test is yet available for the identification of schizophrenia, and its diagnosis remains entirely dependent on clinical judgment and convention." A. Jablensky, *Epidemiology of Schizophrenia, in* SCHIZOPHRENIA: THE MAJOR ISSUES, *supra* note 19, at 19. "There is not yet a blood test; urine or cerebrospinal fluid analysis; or CT (computerized tomography), rCBF (regional cerebral blood flow), PET (positron emission tomography), or MRI (magnetic resonance imaging) brain-imaging scan that can establish an unchallenged diagnosis of schizophrenia.... We know that something goes wrong chemically and/or physically in the brain of a schizophrenic, but we do not yet know what." GOTTESMAN, *supra* note 5, at 18–19.

35. "[F]inding a direct, one-on-one correspondence between cerebral structures and symptoms seems unlikely." Mantosh J. De-Wan, *Cerebral Structures and Symptomatology,*

in POSITIVE AND NEGATIVE SYMPTOMS, *supra* note 19, at 216, 241.

36. *See supra* § 1–2.1.3.

37. J. Bruce Overmier & Dirk H. Hellhammer, *The Learned Helplessness Model of Human Depression, in* ANIMAL MODELS, *supra* note 31, at 175–202.

38. A variety of theories have accorded the environment an extensive role in the development of psychopathology, including psychodynamic and family transaction models. For a general discussion of these models, see Thomas H. McGlashan, *Schizophrenia: Psychodynamic Theories, in* COMPREHENSIVE TEXTBOOK OF PSYCHIATRY *supra* note 5, at 745–756.

39. Paul E. Meehl, *Schizotaxia, Schizotypy, Schizophrenia,* 17 AM. PSYCHOL. 1 (1962).

40. "[T]he aetiology of schizophrenia is basically genetic and ... there is no significant environmental contribution." T.J. Crow, *Ae-*

the "downward drift" hypothesis, this remains an active debate in the literature.[41]

[4] Psychosis and Violence

A final issue, and one of particular relevance to the legal system, is the relationship (if any) between psychoses and criminal behavior. Although some general studies are available, most researchers have focused specifically on the relationship of mental disorder and *violence*. The literature is quite diverse, ranging from anecdotal reports, to investigations of the incidence of mental illness among offender populations, to studies of the incidence of criminal activity among persons diagnosed with psychiatric disorders. Many studies have design flaws, such as biased sample selection, questionable diagnostic validity, a limited range of predictors, or inadequate measures of violence (criminality), all of which may contribute to inconsistent results across studies or limit the generalizability of their findings.[42]

More recently, large epidemiological samples have been studied in which investigators systematically gathered information about both diagnosis and aggressive behavior. A number of early studies found that approximately 2% of persons with no psychiatric diagnosis are violent in a one-year period, compared to 10–12% of persons with major psychotic diagnoses, a 5–fold increase.[43] In the most comprehensive study to date on violence and threats among those with mental disorder, however, researchers funded by the MacArthur Foundation found a more complicated association between mental disorder, substance abuse, and violence.[44] That study compared 1136 male and female patients with mental disorders to a group of 519 individuals randomly selected from the same census tract. Outcome behavior was divided into two categories of seriousness: *violence* (battery resulting in physical injury, sexual assaults, and threats with a weapon) and other *aggressive acts* (battery that did not result in a physical injury). Information sources included self-report (every 10 weeks), collateral report (every 10 weeks), and agency records (arrest, hospitalization). The patient group that did not suffer from substance abuse was no more likely to engage in either violent or aggressive acts than those in the community comparison group who were free of substance abuse. However, patients were more likely than the community group to have symptoms of substance abuse (with co-occurrence between substance abuse

tiology of Psychosis: The Way Ahead, in SCHIZO-PHRENIA: THE MAJOR ISSUES, *supra* note 19, at 129.

41. GOTTESMAN, *supra* note 5, at 76–78; Karno & Norquist, *supra* note 5, at 702.

42. *See* Alexander Brooks, *The Constitutionality and Morality of Civilly Committing Violent Sexual Predators,* 15 U. PUGET SOUND L. REV. 709 (1993). *See also* VIOLENCE AND MENTAL DISORDERS: DEVELOPMENTS IN RISK ASSESSMENT 101 (John Monahan & Henry J. Steadman eds., 1994)[hereinafter VIOLENCE AND MENTAL DISORDERS]. See generally Chapter 2.

43. Jeffrey W. Swanson et al., *Violence and Psychiatric Disorder: Evidence from the Epidemiologic Catchment Area Surveys,* 41 HOSP. COMMUNITY PSYCHIATRY 761 (1990). Notably, the

relative risk for violence is substantially higher for persons with alcohol or drug abuse/ dependence diagnoses (25–35% annual prevalence). *Id.* at 765 (Table 2); *see* Jeffrey W. Swanson, *Alcohol Abuse, Mental Disorder and Violent Behavior,* 17 ALCOHOL HEALTH & RES. WORLD 123 (1993); Jeffrey W. Swanson, *Mental Disorder, Substance Abuse and Community Violence: An Epidemiological Approach, in* VIOLENCE AND MENTAL DISORDERS, *supra* note 42.

44. Henry J. Steadman et al., *Violence by People Discharged from Acute Psychiatric Inpatient Facilities and by Others in the Same Neighborhoods,* 55 ARCHIVES GEN. PSYCHIATRY 393 (1998).

and severe major mental disorder in 40 to 50% of the cases). Furthermore, the patient group showed greater risk of violence and other aggressive acts than the community comparison group when both experienced symptoms of substance abuse, particularly during the 10 weeks immediately following hospital discharge. Finally, further analysis of data from one site in the study indicated that concentrated poverty, with associated high unemployment, racial segregation, rapid population turnover, low income levels, single-parent families with children, and an overall lack of economic opportunities, contributed to increased violence risk over and above the effects of individual characteristics.[45]

Research has also tried to pinpoint relationships between violence and the acute symptoms of impaired reality testing discussed at the outset of this chapter. Such research is difficult because of the subjective and temporary nature of these experiences. Nonetheless, researchers have begun to investigate the behavior of clients who report various types of delusional beliefs that may *potentially* give rise to aggressive actions.[46] There is also a small but developing body of literature on the extent to which persons who experience command hallucinations comply with such commands (particularly when exhorted to commit violence).[47]

One promising line of research in this regard may have fizzled, however. A study by Link and associates indicated that persons with severe mental illness were more violent than "normal" citizens only when acute symptoms were present.[48] A subsequent reanalysis of these same data suggested that the increased risk for violent behavior was associated with particular kinds of symptoms, termed "threat/control override" symptoms.[49] Threat symptoms pertain primarily to delusional beliefs by the person that others are plotting or attempting to harm him; control override describes the subjective experience that the control of one's mind has been taken over by another person or entity, thus leaving the person with the feeling of vulnerability and loss of autonomous control. A correlation between these symptoms and violence seemed plausible. However, the aforementioned MacArthur project, a large-

---

45. Eric Silver et al., *Assessing Violence Risk Among Discharged Psychiatric Patients: Toward an Ecological Approach*, 23 L. & Human Behav. 237 (1999).

46. *See generally* Alec Buchanan, *Acting on Delusion: A Review*, 23 Psychol. Med. 123 (1993); Pamela J. Taylor et al., *Delusions and Violence*, in Violence and Mental Disorders, *supra* note 42, at 161. Psychiatry has given specific names to particular types of delusional syndromes: Capgras' syndrome involves the belief that a familiar person has been replaced by a double or an imposter; Fregoli's syndrome involves the belief that one's persecutors have disguised themselves as benign individuals in the person's environment; the delusion of "subjective doubles" involves the belief that there is a precise psychological, or even physical, double of the person. Whether these particular delusional syndromes are associated with an increased risk for violence remains an open empirical question. *See* Stephen H. Dinwiddie & Sean Yutzy, *Dangerous Delusions? Misiden-*

tification *Syndromes and Professional Negligence*, 21 Bull. Am. Acad. Psychiatry & L. 513 (1993).

47. John Junginger, *Predicting Compliance with Command Hallucinations*, 147 Am. J. Psychiatry 245 (1990); Richard Rogers et al., *The Clinical Presentation of Command Hallucinations in a Forensic Population*, 147 Am. J. Psychiatry 1304 (1990); Judith S. Thompson et al., *Command Hallucinations and Legal Insanity*, 5 Forensic Rep. 29 (1992); Dale E. McNiel, *Hallucinations and Violence*, in Violence and Mental Disorders, *supra* note 42, at 183.

48. Bruce G. Link et al., *The Violent and Illegal Behavior of Mental Patients Reconsidered*, 57 Am. Soc. Rev. 275, 287–88 (1992).

49. Bruce G. Link & Ann Stueve, *Psychotic Symptoms and the Violent/Illegal Behavior of Mental Patients Compared to Community Controls*, in Violence and Mental Disorder, *supra* note 42, at 137.

scale, multi-site study, was unable to replicate this relationship, at least for those more than 10 weeks out of the hospital.[50]

Although further research may yield a better understanding of the relationship between violence and psychosis (and its symptoms), controversy is likely to remain with respect to attributing specific criminal acts to "causal" symptoms. Mentally ill persons who commit crimes may be vulnerable to a host of stressors (homelessness, poverty) and factors (greed, drug/alcohol abuse) other than simply the subjective symptoms of their illness. In individual cases, the opinions of clinicians and courts regarding the exculpating effect, if any, of symptoms of psychosis will likely remain a determination based on reasoned judgment rather than a direct inference from scientific studies.

§ 1–2.2 Mental Retardation

§ 1–2.2.1 Introduction

Mental retardation has long been recognized as a significant disorder. It was not until 1962, however, that the current definition of the disorder gained widespread recognition. In that year, the President's Commission on Mental Retardation adopted a three part definition of mental retardation: "[1] subaverage general intellectual functioning which [2] originates in the developmental period and [3] is associated with impairment in adaptive behavior."[51] This definition has survived three decades of debate. With minor editing, it appears in the current Diagnostic and Statistical Manual of Mental Disorders (DSM–IV),[52] which includes as criteria for the disorder [1] "significantly subaverage intellectual functioning [defined as] an IQ of approximately 70 or below;"[53] [2] "onset ... before age 18 years;"[54] and [3] "[c]oncurrent deficits in present adaptive functioning [in at least two areas]."[55] Historical labels such as "moron", "idiot", and "imbecile," now considered largely pejorative in nature, have given way to more neutral terms that parallel graded classifications of measured intelligence, the primary construct that underlies definitions of mental retardation. The DSM–IV speaks to four categories of mental retardation: mild (IQ level 50–55 to approximately 70), moderate (IQ level 35–40 to 50–55), severe (IQ level 20–25 to 35–40), and profound (IQ level below 20–25).[56]

The notion that mental retardation may provide a potential basis for mental state defenses to criminal activity is not particularly controversial. Statutory and case law that provide the definitional framework for the

---

50. Paul S. Appelbaum et al., *Delusions and Violence: Data from the MacArthur Violence Risk Assessment Study*, 157 AM. J. PSYCHIATRY 566 (2000).

51. President's Commission on Mental Retardation, Task Force on Education and Habilitation (GPO, 1962), cited at THOMAS E. JORDAN, THE MENTALLY RETARDED 7 (4th ed., 1976).

52. DSM–IV, *supra* note 1.

53. *Id.* at 46.

54. *Id.*

55. The relevant functional areas include: communications, self-care, home living, social/interpersonal skills, use of community re-

sources, self-direction, functional academic skills, work, leisure, health, and safety. *Id.*

56. *Id.* at 40, 46. These categories also have parallels in the Special Education System in the United States, which classifies persons (roughly) in the 50–70 IQ range as the "educable mentally retarded," persons in the 25–50 IQ ranges as the "trainable mentally retarded," and persons with IQ less than 25 as "profoundly mentally retarded." DAVID L. WESTLING, INTRODUCTION TO MENTAL RETARDATION 23–24 (1986).

insanity defense and other mental state defenses commonly refer to "mental disease" and "mental defect" as the necessary conditions upon which such defenses may be constructed. Although there is no rigorous translation of clinical nosological categories into these legal categories, mental retardation arguably is what drafters had in mind by the term "mental defect." Logically, the insanity defense is more likely applicable in cases involving more significant levels of impairment—those defendants diagnosed with severe or profound retardation. However, relatively few of these individuals live outside of institutional settings; thus, mentally retarded offenders are more likely to come from the moderate and mild categories, for which the applicability of a mental state defense to criminal responsibility may be more difficult to judge.

Any of several impairments associated with mental retardation may give rise to a mental state defense to criminal behavior. These may include, but are not necessarily limited to, impairment in reasoning ability, superficiality of comprehension (limited ability to emotionally appreciate or anticipate the results of actions), or susceptibility to being led or duped into criminal activity by other persons viewed by the mentally retarded individual as authoritative. Additionally, people with mental retardation may lack behavior controls associated with people who are not retarded.

§ 1–2.2.2 Introductory Discussion of the Science

[1] The Scientific Questions

A wide variety of issues concerning mental retardation have been examined by scientists from diverse fields. The issues examined have included epidemiology, etiology and heritability of the disorder; description and measurement of intellectual and adaptive functioning; comparative studies of cognitive, social and developmental abilities of retarded versus non-retarded individuals; outcome studies of "treatment" and "training" of persons with mental retardation; and the relationship between intelligence and delinquency (antisocial behavior).

Of these various areas, perhaps the most legally pertinent scientific studies are those that relate to the measurement of intelligence and adaptive functioning (the primary diagnostic dimensions of mental retardation) and the relationships (if any) between mental retardation and cognitive/decisionmaking abilities presumably related to choices about legally/morally correct behavior. This literature can provide baseline knowledge regarding the type and degree of impairments often found in persons at various levels of intellectual impairment. Of less relevance to legal questions about moral responsibility are those studies of a more theoretical nature (e.g., studies about the nature of intelligence and studies that examine conflicting theories about the etiology of impairments in persons who are mentally retarded). Also of less relevance to criminal responsibility issues is research related to training/education/treatment of persons with mental retardation.

[2] Scientific Methods Applied in the Research

A variety of disciplines, each of which brings its own language and perspective to problems of impaired mental functioning, have been involved in the study of mental retardation.[57] Researchers have made nervous system, metabolic, and chromosomal comparisons of impaired persons and those with normal intellectual functioning utilizing laboratory techniques (e.g., microscopic examination of chromosomes).

Researchers have also conducted correlational studies of the heritability of intelligence in cohorts of family members (parent-child, sibling-sibling) and between identical (100% genetic overlap) and dizygotic (50% shared genes) twins. In the area of training and rehabilitation, some true experiments have been conducted with random assignment of mentally retarded individuals to one or another treatment interventions or control groups.

The studies of most relevance to criminal responsibility are primarily correlational in design. To evaluate the relationship of mental retardation (or intelligence) to dependent variables such as capacity for moral judgment, logical reasoning, or appropriate social functioning, groups of persons varying in terms of intellectual capacity (e.g., retarded versus non-retarded; differing levels within the retarded range) have been compared on a variety of intellectual, moral, and social problem solving tasks. Consumers of this literature should be alerted to weaknesses in some of the research designs employed, however, particularly in earlier research. In some studies comparing persons of normal intelligence with others who are mentally retarded, investigators failed to adequately control for other variables that also differentiated the groups to be compared. For example, some studies contrasted mentally retarded individuals from institutional settings with persons of normal intelligence from community settings, resulting in a confounding of placement with IQ level as independent variables of study.[58] Similarly, some researchers failed to control for differences in motivation or attention seeking that may have contributed to observed differences on outcome measures.[59] A further consideration is that children and adolescents of varying intellectual abilities have often been the subjects of research in the social scientific studies of mental retardation. Thus, generalizing findings to adults who are mentally retarded may not be appropriate.

§ 1–2.2.3　Areas of Scientific Agreement

There seems to be general agreement in the field regarding some epidemiological issues. It is commonly accepted that the prevalence of mental retardation is in the 1–3% range,[60] and that this range represents two relatively distinct subgroups of mentally retarded persons.[61] The higher end of the range (3%) includes both the "familially" retarded, i.e., persons who score below two

57. One author noted at least ten different disciplines involved in the study of mental retardation: education, psychology, sociology, physiology, biology, genetics, cytology, teratology, medicine, and radiology. JORDAN, *supra* note 51, at 65.

58. EDWARD ZIGLER & ROBERT M. HODAPP, UNDERSTANDING MENTAL RETARDATION 34–36 (1986).

59. For instance, some research subjects who are mentally retarded may have experienced relative social deprivation in institutional settings or in lower socioeconomic families.

In research projects in which they are exposed to interested and supportive adults, they may perform below capacity (e.g., become disinterested in tasks, or be more tolerant of boring activities) in order to prolong their contact with the researcher. *Id.* at 117–123.

60. WESTLING, *supra* note 56, at 34; ZIGLER & HODAPP, *supra* note 58, at 94.

61. For a description of the characteristics and associated features of these groups, *see* ZIGLER & HODAPP, *supra* note 58, at 52–54.

standard deviations on a standard intelligence test,[62] but for whom there is no known etiology (representing approximately 2.28% of the general population), and the "organically" retarded persons, whose mental impairment stems from a known cause (an estimated .75%). The lower (1%) figure is based on estimates that as many as two-thirds of the familially retarded make a satisfactory social adjustment after their school years, thus eventually failing to meet the second diagnostic criterion (impaired adaptive behavior).[63]

Scientists are also in agreement about certain etiological issues. Although there are over 500 different causes of mental retardation,[64] among the organically retarded specific nervous system, metabolic, or genetic defects have been identified for a number of syndromes (e.g., Downs syndrome, mucopolylipidosis).[65] There is also little dispute that intelligence is partially genetically determined, and it is generally accepted that familial retardation may result from the influence of multiple genes, although the precise number or combination of contributing genes is not determined.[66]

Not surprisingly, given the criteria for diagnosing mental retardation, the research is also consistent in demonstrating that persons classified as mentally retarded have more deficits in social and cognitive functioning than do non-retarded persons of comparable chronological age. Jordan describes impairments in speech and language among persons with mental retardation, including immature speech, brief auditory memory spans, and reduced use of abstract language.[67] He also notes personality characteristics that may limit behavioral or decision making abilities of mentally retarded persons, including the tendency to go along or acquiesce in ambiguous situations.[68] Similarly, Westling discusses the limited learning abilities of persons at different levels of mental retardation according to Special Education Classifications[69] and the classification system of the American Association on Mental Deficiency.[70] In

62. Researchers appreciate that the "cutoff" is an arbitrary one. In 1961 the diagnosis of mentally retarded included persons who scored below *one* standard deviation, or approximately 32 million people; in 1971 the cutoff changed to *two* standard deviations and the number of potentially retarded persons in this country dropped to 6 million. *Id.* at 90–91.

63. Estimates are also affected by differential detection rates (the organically retarded are more often living in institutions) and mortality rates (organically retarded persons are more vulnerable to early death). Empirical studies yield median prevalence estimates of about 2.25%. *Id.* at 94.

64. Over 500 genetic causes of intellectual disability have been described. J.C. Harris, Developmental Neuropsychiatry 103 (1995). Nearly 100 mental retardation syndromes have been linked to the X chromosome, with the most frequent causes being Down syndrome and fragile X syndrome, accounting for about 40% of X chromosome-linked retardation, and fetal alcohol syndrome. E.J. Feldman, *The Recognition and Investigation of X–Linked Learning Disability Syndromes*, 40 J. Intell. Disability. Res. 400 (1996).

65. For a review and discussion of these syndromes, see L. Crome & J. Stern, The Pathology of Mental Retardation (1967). *See also* Feldman, *supra* note 64.

66. For brief discussions of this literature, *see id.* at 2–4; Irving I. Gottesman, *An Introduction to Behavioral Genetics of Mental Retardation, in* The Role of Genetics in Mental Retardation 49–69 (Robert M. Allen, Arnold D. Cortazzo & Richard P. Toister eds., 1970).

67. Jordan, *supra* note 51, at 228.

68. *Id.* at 230.

69. Persons who are in the "educable" mentally retarded (est. IQ 50–70) range may be capable of some accomplishment in traditional education subjects such as reading, writing, or arithmetic, and may master basic activities of daily living (ADLs); persons who are "trainable" mentally retarded (est. IQ 25–50) may learn some ADLs, such as self-feeding, dressing, or toilet training, but will not likely master academic tasks; "profoundly" mentally retarded persons (est. IQ <25) may not master any of the above. Westling, *supra* note 56, at 23–24.

70. Persons who are mildly retarded (IQ = 50–55 to 70) may be "... capable of daily self care and academic skills up to about fourth or fifth grade level. They can develop acceptable

persons who are mentally retarded, general cognitive deficits have been documented in the areas of attention,[71] memory,[72] organizing information and using logic,[73] and observational learning or modeling.[74] Finally, persons who are learning disabled or have mental retardation may have cognitive deficits in areas such as weighing pros and cons of varying courses of action, generating options, or taking others' perspectives which in turn may create difficulties in making appropriate choices with respect to socially correct or appropriate behavior.[75]

There are also standard assessment instruments that are widely accepted for use in diagnosing mental retardation. Although there are some theoretical disputes and disagreements about the nature of the construct that underlies intelligence tests,[76] these tests, especially the Stanford–Binet and the Wechsler Intelligence Tests, are widely used and accepted measures. General consensus about these tests notwithstanding, there is concern that some tests may result in biased (low) estimates of intellectual function for some ethnic or racial groups[77] and for persons at the lower ranges of intellectual functioning (i.e., those with mental retardation), due to low motivation or to other personality factors not conceived as part of the intelligence construct but which may nevertheless affect test performance.

social skills and, as adults, often participate in competitive, non-sheltered employment." *Id.* at 24–25. Persons who are moderately retarded (IQ = 35–40 to 50–55) "... can usually develop communication skills, fairly good motor coordination, generally acceptable social skills, and basic vocational skills.... [W]ith intense training they can achieve first or second grade level reading, writing, and arithmetic skills." *Id.* at 26. Persons who are severely and profoundly retarded will most likely live in institutional settings and, if placed in the community, will require considerable support. *Id.* at 27. Jordan describes a study of the adaptive skills of 348 severely retarded persons in the community: 18% can read street signs, 14% can take a bus in a familiar area, and 10% can walk unescorted to the corner in the same block. JORDAN, *supra* note 51, at 205–206.

71. Persons who are mentally retarded are less likely to identify and appropriately respond to the relevant dimensions of a stimulus or object or to make appropriate discriminations. WESTLING, *supra* note 56, at 116–117.

72. Persons with mental retardation have deficits in all types of memory, but particularly immediate, short-term recall. *Id.* at 117.

73. Persons with mental retardation do not organize input as well as do persons of normal intelligence. Perhaps related in part to memory deficits, they do not "chunk" or associate elements as well as do persons of normal intelligence and therefore require much extra rehearsal. Studies using games that require the use of logic to solve problems reveal significant deficits among retarded participants. *Id.* at 118.

74. *Id.* at 121.

75. Katherine A. Larson, *A Research Review and Alternative Hypothesis Explaining the Link Between Learning Disability and Delinquency,* 21 J. LEARNING DISABILITIES 357 (1988).

76. For instance, a major debate is whether intelligence should be conceived essentially as a single, general problem solving/coping ability or a compilation of various separate abilities. While this debate is of relatively little import to the criminal law, a related concern that may be more pertinent in legal arenas is the nature of the IQ index itself. Some tests, like the Stanford–Binet, conceive of the Intelligence Quotient as a ratio of a person's true Mental Age to their Chronological Age: IQ = MA/CA (x 100). *See* JORDAN, *supra* note 51, at 360. This construction of IQ invites the comparison of a mentally retarded adult's Mental Age to that of a "normal" person (child/adolescent) of more tender years, which may in turn encourage the unwarranted inference that the retarded adult has social/adaptive skills comparable to those of the chronologically younger individual. Other tests, such as the Wechsler Intelligence Test series, do not use the Mental Age construct, instead discussing IQ level as a deviation score based on the person's abilities relative to the abilities of others in a comparable demographic population. *Id. See generally*, ASSESSMENT IN MENTAL HANDICAP: A GUIDE TO ASSESSMENT PRACTICES, TESTS & CHECKLISTS ch. 1 (James Hogg & Norma V. Raynes eds. 1987) [hereinafter AS-SESSMENT IN MENTAL HANDICAP].

77. ZIGLER & HODAPP, *supra* note 58, at 10–11.

§ 1–2.2.4   Areas of Scientific Disagreement

There is considerable controversy about the measurement of adaptive behavior and its role in the diagnosis of mental retardation. The DSM–IV diagnostic criteria for mental retardation require a finding of impairment in adaptive behavior, but the construct has been difficult to define and measure psychometrically.[78] Although the Vineland Social Maturity Scale and the American Association on Mental Deficiency (AAMD) Adaptive Behavior Scale have achieved status as the instruments of choice,[79] the number of scales purporting to measure adaptive skills exceeded 132 in 1977,[80] and many clinicians diagnose mental retardation almost solely on the basis of impaired intellectual functioning "perhaps because social adaptation is itself undefined and simply too vague to have any utility in a classification system."[81]

The lack of any consistent relationship between impaired intellectual functioning and impairment in adaptive behavior is also problematic.[82] The diagnostic criteria require an association between these factors,[83] yet some researchers have demonstrated correlations ranging from .00 to .90 depending on the samples studied,[84] with the result that " . . . two retarded individuals with exactly the same IQ may differ dramatically in everyday social competence."[85] Further, neither IQ nor adaptive skills, as currently measured, predicts well an individual's behavior in different contexts.[86]

Relatedly, the literature reveals that there are discernable differences across professional disciplines in clinical judgments regarding the diagnosis, prognosis, and adaptive abilities of mentally retarded persons. One study of inter-rater agreement on the level of mental retardation diagnosed by psychiatrists and psychologists found agreement levels below chance.[87] Other studies have documented that psychiatrists, as compared to other health care profes-

---

78. Establishing the validity of measures of adaptive behavior can be difficult because: (1) definitions of adaptive behavior are very general and provide little guidance in clearly defined content areas; (2) adaptive behavior is a function of many complex influences, including the setting, the person's abilities, and social values; and (3) objective criteria of adjustment for the validation of adaptive behavior ratings do not exist. N.V. Raynes, *Adaptive Behavior Scales, in* Assessment in Mental Handicap, *supra* note 76, at 96.

79. *Id.* at 83–98.

80. *Id.* at 82–83.

81. Zigler & Hodapp, *supra* note 58, at 65.

82. "Over the past several years there has been an increased concern about the extent to which narrowly cognitive formulations of mental retardation accurately convey the variability in performance routinely encountered in persons of limited intellect. [E]mpirically, we find that IQ scores for most retarded persons simply do not describe the level of operant and social behavior." Jordan, *supra* note 51, at 207.

83. See *supra* note 41 and accompanying text.

84. See studies cited by Zigler & Hodapp, *supra* note 58, at 11.

85. *Id.* at 65.

86. "Efforts to measure adaptive behavior . . . have focused on the assessment of a person's current abilities as they are manifest in particular social situations. . . . They [adaptive behavior scales] do not predict success or failure in alternative placements." Raynes, *supra* note 78, at 81, 103.

87. Greg M. MacMann & David W. Barnett, *Reliability of Psychiatric and Psychological Diagnoses of Mental Retardation Severity: Judgments under Naturally Occurring Conditions,* 97 Am. J. Mental Retardation 559 (1993). The authors noted that the overall chance-corrected (kappa) level of agreement was .47, considerably lower than the .80 level obtained in validation studies of the DSM, which were conducted using carefully selected, well-coached clinicians in carefully controlled settings. The authors also noted that agreement rates were "fairly consistent" between two psychologists, but that there was much variation in the diagnoses of the psychiatrists.

sionals in the mental retardation community, view mentally retarded persons as having poorer prognoses and greater deficits in adaptive skills.[88]

There is also lack of agreement on the association between mental retardation and delinquency or criminality. Some have reported that the incidence of mental retardation in prisons is significantly higher (9.5%) than in the general population (3%), suggesting a positive association and some increased tendency for persons with mental retardation to commit criminal acts.[89] Others have argued, however, that this apparent relationship may be an administrative artifact caused by such factors as differential detection and apprehension of mentally retarded offenders (they may be less adept at eluding apprehension); fewer diversion programs or community services for mentally retarded offenders, resulting in higher incarceration rates; differences in statutory or parole regulations governing the sentencing and release of persons with mental retardation; and measurement factors (e.g., exclusive reliance on intelligence test scores).[90]

Another issue of considerable debate is the degree to which deprived social conditions can contribute to mental retardation, and whether placing an intellectually impaired individual in an enriched environment can enhance IQ. Zigler and Hodapp indicate that socioeconomic status generally has little effect in terms of suppressing IQ, although IQ may be suppressed for children living in families with "abysmal conditions" if the exposure is long term.[91]

Other controversies of legal relevance focus on the degree of cognitive impairment associated with mental retardation. One issue about which the evidence is inconclusive is whether the cognitive impairments observed in persons of lower intelligence reflect qualitative differences in abilities or simply developmental delays that are, in essence, quantitative in nature.[92] Similarly, beyond the finding that mentally retarded adults do not attain the same levels of cognitive and moral development as non-retarded persons of comparable chronological age, findings relating intellectual ability to moral decision-making are inconsistent.[93] Furthermore, much of this literature has examined the moral decision-making abilities of children and adolescents responding to hypothetical moral dilemmas; studies comparing retarded and normal adults challenged with *in vivo* moral dilemmas were not found.

88. Mark L. Wolraich & Gary N. Siperstein, *Assessing Professionals' Prognostic Impressions in Mental Retardation,* 21 MENTAL RETARDATION 8 (1983); Mark L. Wolraich & Gary N. Siperstein, *Physicians' and Other Professionals' Expectations and Prognoses for Mentally Retarded Individuals,* 91 AM. J. MENTAL DEFICIENCY 244 (1986).

89. Robert L. Marsh, Charles M. Friel & Victor Eissler, *The Adult MR in the Criminal Justice System,* 13 MENTAL RETARDATION 21 (1975).

90. Ann E. MacEachron, *Mentally Retarded Offenders: Prevalence and Characteristics,* 84 AM. J. MENTAL DEFICIENCY 165, 166 (1979).

91. ZIGLER & HODAPP, *supra* note 58, at 83–86. A poorer environment may suppress other factors and traits, including the development of a positive self-concept and motivation, that impact intellectual development. *Id.* at 86.

92. *Id.* at 15–17.

93. James V. Kahn, *Moral and Cognitive Development of Moderately Retarded, Mildly Retarded, and Non-retarded Individuals,* 81 AM. J. MENTAL DEFICIENCY 209 (1976); Jonathan J. Taylor & Thomas M. Achenbach, *Moral and Cognitive Development in Retarded and Non-retarded Children,* 80 AM. MENTAL DEFICIENCY 43 (1975); Marian Sigman et al., *Moral Judgment in Relation to Behavioral and Cognitive Disorders in Adolescents,* 11 J. ABNORMAL CHILD PSYCHOL. 503 (1983).

§ 1–2.3 Epilepsy

§ 1–2.3.1 Introduction

Epilepsy is a neurological disorder that involves a "tendency for recurrent seizures (two or three or more) unprovoked by any known proximate [external] insult,"[94] and discharge of abnormal and uncontrolled electrical impulses across all or some parts of the brain. A number of different conditions fall under this definition. One dimension for the classification of seizures is the locus of origin of the seizure.[95] Seizures are said to be *generalized* if the electrical discharge begins simultaneously throughout the brain; *partial*, or *focal* seizures are those that begin in a relatively circumscribed region, the best known of which are temporal lobe seizures. Another dimension of classification is *simple* versus *complex*. Simple seizures affect motor or sensory functioning but do not involve alterations in the person's consciousness; in contrast, complex seizures involve at least some alteration in consciousness during the seizure event.

Epilepsy is further classified by the cause of the seizure.[96] Seizures are *symptomatic* when the cause of the seizure is a known or suspected brain disease or lesion. Among the category of symptomatic seizures are those for which the cause is unknown but presumed, known as *cryptogenic* seizures. Seizures that are inherited or are not symptomatic and are without identifiable pathologic cause are known as *idiopathic* seizures.

Seizures proceed through stages. The formal seizure event, or period of atypical electrical discharge, is called the *ictus* and typically lasts from a few seconds to one and a half minutes in duration.[97] This ictus is followed by a period of recovery, the *post-ictal* phase, during which the person may often appear confused or disoriented. Upon recovery and stabilization following the seizure, the person is said to be in the *interictal* period.

Further classification of seizures is based on electroencephalograph (EEG) and clinical behavior during the ictal period, which may vary radically. Most dramatic is the *grand mal seizure*, which involves massive, generalized electrical discharge in the brain.[98] The person suffers a complete loss of consciousness during the seizure and displays massive convulsions throughout; thrashing of the limbs and biting of the tongue are not uncommon. In contrast, the least disruptive general class of seizures is *petit mal* or "ab-

94. W. Allen Hauser & Dale C. Hesdorffer, Epilepsy: Frequency, Causes, and Consequences 2 (1990). In the absence of a known or presumed cause, seizures are said to be "idiopathic." If there is a prior event (e.g., head injury, systemic illness) presumed to cause the seizure, the seizure is termed "remote symptomatic or secondary." *Id.* at 3.

95. Eugene J. Rankin et al., *Epilepsy and Nonepileptic Attack Disorder, in* Neuropsychology for Clinical Practice: Etiology, Assessment, and Treatment of Common Neurological Disorders 131–35 (Russell L. Adams et al. eds., 1996) (overviewing the classification of epileptic seizures into partial (or focal) seizures, generalized seizures and unclassified seizures as defined by the Commission on Classification and

Terminology of the International League Against Epilepsy (CCTILAE)).

96. Joseph I. Sirven, *Epilepsy in Older Adults: Causes, Consequences and Treatment*, 46 J. Am. Geriatrics Soc'y 1291, 1291 (1998); Rankin et al., *supra* note 95, at 135 (explaining that the CCTILAE further subdivided seizures into specific epileptic syndromes).

97. Rarely, individuals experience a condition called "status epileptus," in which the seizure state persists from 30 minutes to an hour. Ernst Niedermeyer, *Neurologic Aspects of the Epilepsies, in* Psychiatric Aspects of Epilepsy 99, 123 (Dietrich Blumer, ed., 1984).

98. *Id.* at 104.

sence" seizures.[99] These events are of relatively brief duration and involve little if any abnormal motor movement. The person simply appears to "tune out" for a few moments before resuming normal functioning. A third type of seizure, and one quite common in adults, is the *complex partial seizure* (CPS). With CPS there is only partial disruption in consciousness, and postural functions (ability to sit, stand, etc.) are preserved. CPS

> usually begins with a cessation in verbal and motor activity associated with a motionless stare. The patient may not respond to normal auditory or visual information. Automatisms that are gestural (picking movements with the fingers) or oralalimentary (lip smacking) may be observed. They represent involuntary, automatic movements that occur with an alteration in consciousness.[100]

The ictal and post-ictal stages have characteristic behavioral features. In many cases, particularly with grand mal and complex partial seizures,[101] the person has a conscious subjective experience, called an *aura*,[102] at the beginning of the ictal period.[103] This experience may involve perceptual aberrations, such as hallucinations, or affective disturbances including the sudden onset of fear. Some persons describe the aura as a mixture between reality and dreaming; others report a sense of deja-vu. Post-ictally, persons who suffer grand mal seizures may be quite confused and disoriented, if not drowsy and sleeping. In contrast, the post-ictal phase for petit mal seizures may be clinically unremarkable.[104] Most complex is the post-ictal behavior of persons who suffer from CPS. The post-ictal phase may last several minutes to several hours. Although there is some alteration in consciousness, frequently including confusion and disorientation, these individuals continue to function with varying degrees of efficiency; some rather complex behaviors may be exhibited,[105] although organized and purposeful behavior is rare.[106] Post-ictal behavior in CPS has also been associated with irritability and inappropriate behavior,[107]

---

99. Petit mal seizures usually occur between ages of 4–12 and rarely persist into adulthood. Their duration is usually 5–30 seconds. *Id.* at 105.

100. Gregory D. Cascino, *Complex Partial Seizures: Clinical Features and Differential Diagnosis*, 15 PSYCHIATRIC CLINICS N. AM. 373, 374 (1992); *see* L.F. Quesney, *Clinical and EEG Features of Complex Partial Seizures of Temporal Lobe Origin*, 27 EPILEPSIA 27–45 (Supp. 1986) (describing 19 patients with clinically intractable temporal lobe epilepsy).

101. See *supra* notes 85–87 and accompanying text.

102. MICHAEL R. TRIMBLE, THE PSYCHOSES OF EPILEPSY 80 (1991) (describing two studies with large samples in which 57% and 56% of patients reported auras).

103. Although the aura is typically very brief, one author has described a rare epileptic condition of "continuous aura" in which the aura recurs serially and aura elements (hallucinations, affective states) persist. Such patients are described as being in a confused state manifest by incoherent thought processing and decreased and variable ability to attend to

their environment. They may attempt to act on their hallucinations. Frank D. Benson, *Interictal Behavior Disorder in Epilepsy*, 9 PSYCHIATRIC CLINICS N. AM. 283, 285 (1986).

104. "Absence seizures are usually very brief (10 seconds) and are not preceded by auras. Most patients with absence seizures are unaware of their seizure activity." Cascino, *supra* note 100, at 376.

105. "[S]trikingly complex activities can be performed. A patient may disrobe, may go out for a long walk, may drive a car, may perform household chores, such as washing dishes or cleaning the floor, and so on." BENSON, *supra* note 103, at 285. Such automatisms, however, "always occur out of context with environmental activities, and they have short duration (measured in minutes) during which the victim is recovering orientation." *Id.*

106. "Organized and purposeful behavior is unusual during complex partial seizures ..." Cascino, *supra* note 100, at 374.

107. *Id.*

and there are case reports of severe behavioral disturbances, including psychosis,[108] in some instances.

Several aspects of seizure disorder arguably may be relevant to mental state defenses in the criminal law. Because the law does not hold citizens morally responsible for involuntary actions, an automatism defense might be advanced for criminal behavior reasonably attributable to either (a) the uncontrolled convulsions of an unconscious person experiencing a grand mal seizure (e.g., an assault from a flailing arm or leg) or (b) the automatisms of a partially conscious person experiencing a CPS. Alternatively, the more conventional insanity defense might be advanced on behalf of an individual who allegedly experienced severe cognitive or emotional symptoms as a result of a seizure; it might be alleged that post-ictal confusion, or post-ictal or interictal sequalae involving hallucinations, delusions, or other severe symptoms impaired the person's capacity to distinguish right from wrong or control behavior to the degree required by law. Alternatively, criminal conduct that occurs during the ictal or post-ictal phases may be seen as unintended, in which case epilepsy could form the basis for a *mens rea* (diminished capacity) defense.

§ 1–2.3.2 Introductory Discussion of the Science

[1] The Scientific Questions

Epilepsy is a well-established diagnosis in neurology that has been studied for decades both in the United States and abroad. Aided by laboratory devices such as the EEG, which permits monitoring of electrical activity in various parts of the brain, researchers have been able to begin the classification and description of various types of seizures. Epidemiological studies to establish the incidence and prevalence of the disorder have been conducted, and clinical studies to determine factors that increase the risk for seizures have been reported. There is also a considerable literature on the treatment of epilepsy, primarily with anticonvulsant medications. Because of the diverse, and sometimes dramatic, behavioral presentations of persons who experience seizures, researchers have also investigated the behavioral correlates of different types of seizures and have sought to establish whether, and what kinds of, clinical syndromes may be associated with seizures and seizure histories.

[2] Scientific Methods Applied in the Research

A wide variety of methods have been utilized in the study of seizures and the impact of electrical stimulation of the brain more generally. Animal studies have figured prominently in the research. Models for human behavior, particularly human aggression, have been developed from laboratory studies of animals whose brains have been subjected to electrical stimulation or surgical ablation procedures. Of particular focus has been the limbic area,

---

108. *See* Sidney Levin, *Epileptic Clouded States*, 116 J. Nervous & Mental Disease 215 (1952) (describing 52 cases in which abnormal mental states developed from 24 hours to 7 days post-seizure); S.J. Logsdail & B.K. Toone, *Post-ictal Psychoses*, 152 Br. J. Psychiatry 246 (1988) (describing 14 cases of psychosis or confusion immediately post-seizure or within 1 week of apparent return to normal functioning).

thought to be critical in the control and expression of emotion.[109]

A variety of clinical and research studies with human subjects have also been utilized. Although ethical considerations preclude large scale studies involving the random assignment of human subjects to experimental surgical procedures, scientists have been able to recruit persons planning to undergo surgery, enabling study both of the effects of the surgery and of systematic electrical stimulation of portions of the brain made accessible by the surgery. Patients seeking non-surgical treatment for seizure disorder have also been studied, through both comprehensive case study methods and experimental techniques (e.g., chemically inducing seizures in order to document EEG or behavioral correlates). Finally, scientists have compared persons with seizure disorder to those with other neurological, medical, or psychiatric problems and to "normal" subjects on behavioral measures of interest (e.g., psychiatric symptoms, aggression); these studies involve correlational designs and measurement of dependent variables by both direct observation and retrospective interviewing or archival techniques.

§ 1–2.3.3 Areas of Scientific Agreement

Although figures differ somewhat across studies, the incidence and prevalence of epilepsy have been established within a reasonably narrow range. The annual incidence is 11–54 new cases per 100,000 population,[110] and the prevalence in the general population is about .5%.[111] The prevalence of temporal lobe epilepsy (TLE), which accounts for most of the psychomotor or complex partial seizures (CPS), is about .3%.[112] The incidence of epilepsy is higher in early years but fairly stable until 65 years of age or older,[113] and it is more prevalent in males than in females.[114] Family studies reveal an increased risk for the offspring of persons with epilepsy, particularly if the affected parent had an early age of seizure onset. The risk of epilepsy is twice as high for offspring of affected women as for children of affected males.[115] Genetic heritability is higher for generalized seizures than for partial seizures, although it is present in both.[116] Recent findings have elaborated on this genetic

109. *See, e.g.,* Burr Eichelman, *The Limbic System and Aggression in Humans,* 7 NEUROSCIENCE & BIOBEHAVIORAL REV. 391 (1983); Burr Eichelman, *Bridges From the Animal Laboratory to the Study of Violent or Criminal Individuals, in* MENTAL DISORDER AND CRIME 194 (Sheilah Hodgins ed., 1993).

110. Janusz J. Zielinski, *Epidemiologic Overview of Epilepsy: Morbidity, Mortality and Clinical Implications, in* PSYCHIATRIC ASPECTS OF EPILEPSY, *supra* note 97, at 67, 71 (estimate based on 10 studies from 8 different countries). Hauser and Hesdorffer report a similar range of incidence estimates (28.9–53.1 per 100,000) based on their review of studies. HAUSER & HESDORFFER, *supra* note 94, at 1.

111. Across several studies, estimates range from .15% to 1.9%. Zielinski, *supra* note 110, at 73 (Table 2).

112. David Bear et al., *Behavioral Alterations in Patients with Temporal Lobe Epilepsy, in* PSYCHIATRIC ASPECTS OF EPILEPSY, *supra* note 97, at 197. Some writers have erroneously used

the terms "complex partial seizures," "psychomotor epilepsy," and "temporal lobe epilepsy" interchangeably. These terms are not equivalents. About 20% of patients with temporal lobe EEG focus will never have a seizure, and about 20% of patients who experience a psychomotor seizure will fail to reveal a temporal lobe focus on repeated EEG. Janice R. Stevens, *Psychiatric Implications of Psychomotor Epilepsy,* 14 ARCH. GEN. PSYCHIATRY 461, 461 (1966).

113. Sirven, *supra* note 96, at 1291.

114. *Id.* at 21; Zielinski, *supra* note 110, at 73.

115. Ruth Ottman, *Genetic Epidemiology of Epilepsy,* 19 EPIDEMIOLOGIC REVS. 120, 123–24 (1997) (summarizing studies on maternal transmission of epilepsy).

116. HAUSER & HESDORFFER, *supra* note 94, at 93–105. In twin studies monozygotic twins consistently show higher concordance rates for seizure than do dizygotic twins, regardless of seizure type. *Id.* at 104.

heritability difference by identifying higher familial risk of generalized seizures for parents and siblings, whereas higher risk of partial seizures applies to offspring.[117] A variety of factors have been identified as risk factors associated with higher rates of seizure occurrence, including history of head trauma, alcohol use, mental retardation, lower income/socioeconomic status, encephalitis, meningitis, and stroke.[118]

§ 1–2.3.4 Areas of Scientific Disagreement

One area of controversy in the scientific literature is the relationship between epilepsy and mental disorder. Some researchers have investigated potential links between epilepsy and major psychiatric disorders (e.g., depression, psychosis), while others have sought to determine whether there is a unique personality syndrome characteristic of the interictal period of functioning, particularly for persons with TLE.

There is no doubt that some persons with epilepsy do suffer from depression,[119] schizophrenia,[120] or another major psychiatric disorder.[121] Whether there is a significant association between epilepsy and psychosis is unclear. In studies showing relatively higher rates of psychiatric disorder among persons with epilepsy, the disorders tend not to be significant. Further, many of the epidemiological studies utilize clinical samples of persons with epilepsy, which may lead to overestimation of the prevalence of psychiatric disorders among those with epilepsy because the more severe cases are overrepresented in these types of samples.[122] Studies have also suffered from

117. Ottman, *supra* note 115, at 124–25 (citing Ruth Ottman et al., *Clinical Indicators of Genetic Susceptibility in Epilepsy*, 37 EPILEPSIA 353 (1996)).

118. Cascino, *supra* note 100, at 374–375; HAUSER & HESDORFFER, *supra* note 94, at 53; M. Leone, *Alcohol Use Is a Risk Factor for a First Generalized Tonic–Clonic Seizure*, 48 NEUROLOGY 614, 617 (1997) (presenting findings that a strong association exists between first generalized tonic-clonic seizure and chronic alcoholism in sample of first seizure patients matched to hospital controls).

119. One review reported that 11–16% of patients with epilepsy were also diagnosed with depression, compared to a 2.2 to 3.5% prevalence of depression in random community samples. HAUSER & HESDORFFER, *supra* note 94, at 248–49. A recent study with 76 epileptic patients found support for an association between depression and epilepsy, as 31.6% met the criteria for lifetime major depressive disorder, 9.2% met criteria for current major depressive disorder, 25% were diagnosed with current minor depressive disorders and 1.3% were diagnosed with bipolar disorder. Pam Wiegartz et al., *Co-morbid Psychiatric Disorder in Chronic Epilepsy: Recognition and Etiology of Depression*, 53 NEUROLOGY 3, 5–6 (Supp. 2 1999). The risk for suicide among persons with epilepsy is also higher. Hauser and Hesdorffer estimate the relative risk at 2–7 times that of the general population of the United States. HAUSER & HESDORFFER, *supra* note 94, at 248–

49. Benson reports the relative risk at 5–25 times that of the normal population. Benson, *supra* note 103, at 289. Kanner and Nieto estimate the frequency of suicide attempts for epileptic patients as four times higher than for the general population, with more frequent successful suicides occurring among patients with interictal depression. Andres M. Kanner & Juan Carlos Rivas Neito, *Depressive Disorders in Epilepsy*, 53 NEUROLOGY 26, 27 (Supp. 2 1999).

120. Studies reviewed by Zielinski indicate the prevalence of schizophrenia per 1000 persons with epilepsy to be from 1.0–9.6; similar estimates for any psychosis range from 5.9–44, or for any psychiatric disorder 19.1–140. Zielinski, *supra* note 110, at 85. Sachdev estimates the prevalence of schizophrenic-like psychosis among epileptic patients to be 6–12 times higher than the prevalence in the general population. Perminder Sachdev, *Schizophrenia-Like Psychosis and Epilepsy: The Status of the Association*, 155 AM. J. PSYCHIATRY 325, 329 (1998).

121. For case reports describing various clinical samples of persons with epilepsy who also exhibited significant psychiatric symptoms, *see* Levin, *supra* note 108; Logsdail & Toone, *supra* note 108; Venkat Ramani & Robert J. Gumnit, Intensive Monitoring of Interictal Psychosis in Epilepsy, 11 ANNALS OF NEUROLOGY 613 (1982).

122. HAUSER & HESDORFFER, *supra* note 94, at 247; Stevens, *supra* note 112, at 462.

poorly defined outcome measures (i.e., psychosis)[123] and have inadequately distinguished between seizure disorders and psychiatric disorders associated with a specific type of seizure.[124] Further, a lack of correspondence between psychotic symptoms and EEG abnormality has been observed in some reports,[125] while in others the psychiatric symptoms emerge only during periods when the seizures are controlled.[126] Finally, the psychoses associated with epilepsy may appear qualitatively different from similar psychiatric diagnoses. The appearance of psychoses in persons with epilepsy is typically many years after the onset of seizures.[127] Moreover, persons with epilepsy who manifest cognitive and perceptual symptoms of schizophrenia (e.g., delusions, hallucinations) often retain the capacity for warm, engaging interpersonal relationships.[128] These characteristic historical and clinical features may be of value in differentiating psychiatric symptoms attributable to seizure events from traditional psychiatric symptoms.

Within this literature is a further debate as to whether one particular form of epilepsy, temporal lobe epilepsy (TLE), has a more robust association with psychiatric disorder than do other forms of epilepsy. Again, the scientific evidence is mixed. One author reviewed studies that utilized observational or paper-and-pencil measures of psychopathology (e.g., Minnesota Multiphasic Personality Inventory) and concluded that, although the results have been mixed, the literature as a whole yields some support for the assertion that psychopathology is more likely in TLE patients compared to patients with generalized epilepsy (GE) or controls.[129] Another major review paper, admitting that the subject is "probably the greatest area of controversy" in epilepsy research, concluded that persons with TLE are no more likely than those with other forms of epilepsy to have emotional or behavioral problems.[130] Others have noted the conflicting results and have suggested that methodological

123. "It is the criticism of much of the work in the area of epilepsy and psychosis that the latter term has been used without definition, and little attempt has been made to specify the precise phenomenology of patients examined." TRIMBLE, *supra* note 102, at 130.

124. Thomas M. Hyde & Daniel R. Weinberger, *Seizures and Schizophrenia*, 23 SCHIZOPHRENIA BULL. 611, 611 (1997). Hyde and Weinberger note that the terms *seizure disorder* and *epilepsy* are both cited in the literature, but they point out that "a single seizure disorder" is "distinctly different from a seizure disorder, in which there is a substantial long-term risk for recurrent seizures." Epilepsy is characterized by actual recurrent seizures, while a person suffering from a seizure disorder need not experience recurrent seizures. *Id.*

125. Paul Fedio, *Behavioral Characteristics of Patients with Temporal Lobe Epilepsy*, 9 PSYCHIATRIC CLINICS N. AM. 267, 273 (1986) ("Interictal psychosis may, at times, have no direct relation to seizure activity . . . "). Logsdail & Toone, *supra* note 108, at 249 ("There was no particular association between EEG abnormalities [and psychotic symptom onset].").

126. For case reports of this phenomenon, *see* A. Palkanis et al., *Forced Normalization*, 44 ARCHIVES NEUROLOGY 289 (1987); Stevens,

supra note 112, at 469 (reporting that 10 of 13 patients who decompensated psychiatrically did so as seizures went into relative remission). The phenomenon of psychiatric symptoms appearing only when the seizures are well controlled has been termed "forced normalization" or "alternative psychosis." TRIMBLE, *supra* note 102, at 69–72.

127. Benson reports a median onset of 14 years after the seizure onset. Benson, *supra* note 103, at 290. Trimble notes that the onset of psychosis is usually 11–15 years after the onset of seizures. TRIMBLE, *supra* note 102, at 137.

128. Benson, *supra* note 103, at 290. Trimble commented that affective warmth is retained in many patients diagnosed with both epilepsy and schizophrenia (e.g., 60% in one study) and suggested that this may be the single most discriminating feature between schizophrenia and psychoses associated with epilepsy. TRIMBLE, *supra* note 102, at 134.

129. *Id.* at 113–120.

130. Carl B. Dodrilla & Lawrence W. Batzel, *Interictal Behavioral Features of Patients with Epilepsy*, 27 EPILEPSIA 64, 70 (Supplement, 1986).

problems (biased samples, different definitions of psychopathology) contribute to the conflicting findings.[131]

There have been a few studies using brain-imaging techniques (e.g. MRI, PET, SPECT) that link temporal lobe abnormalities in patients with psychosis and epilepsy, leading some researchers to conclude that there is a robust association between temporal lobe epilepsy and psychopathology.[132] Barr and colleagues compared brain images of first-episode schizophrenic (FES) patients, temporal lobe epilepsy (TLE) patients, and healthy controls, and cited noteworthy differences in various aspects of brain functioning. They found in FES patients significantly diminished volume in the hippocampus, a brain structure that contributes to memory, with a similar degree of reduction in TLE patients whose epilepsy originated in the left hemisphere of the brain.[133] A recent study went further, comparing hippocampal volumes in TLE patients with and without psychosis to schizophrenic patients and healthy controls.[134] For both schizophrenic patients and TLE patients with psychosis, a significant volume reduction was identified in the left hippocampal region of the brain, while no such reduction was found in TLE patients who did not have a co-occurring psychosis. These results suggest "that schizophrenia and [temporal lobe epilepsy concomitant with psychosis] may both be associated with extensive cerebral abnormalities and that the abnormalities in the hippocampus may be a necessary, but not the only, component for psychosis to develop."[135] This conclusion must be considered with particular caution, however, because of the limited number of studies in this area.

As noted, there have also been efforts to investigate whether a unique interictal personality syndrome exists. Clinical observations of epileptic patients have given rise to a number of hypotheses regarding behaviors that may be differentially associated with epilepsy, particularly TLE. Some of the features observed in some persons with TLE include hypergraphia (sudden, excessive writing behavior), reduced sexual drive, increased interest in philo-

131. Hauser & Hesdorffer, *supra* note 94, at 251; Hyde & Weinberger, *supra* note 124, at 613.

132. Hyde & Weinberger, *supra* note 124, at 614 (summarizing findings of neuroimaging studies on schizophrenia and temporal lobe epilepsy); Sachdev, *supra* note 120, at 331 (summarizing findings of neuroimaging and neuropathological studies linking schizophrenia and epilepsy). One PET study compared four groups, each with six patients: (1) those with epilepsy and psychoses who were taking anti-psychotic medication, (2) those with epilepsy and psychoses who were not taking anti-psychotic medication, (3) a matched group of normal patients and (4) a matched group of epileptic patients without psychoses. The cerebral brain flow results of the epilepsy and psychosis group revealed brain abnormalities centralized to the frontotemporal region. Hyde & Weinberger, *supra* note 124, at 614. A SPECT study focused on five patients with schizophrenia and seizures matched to five epileptic controls, and found "significant reductions in the left medial temporal cerebral blood flow." These results may be misleading, how-

ever, as the control group had lower IQs and a higher rate of seizures, and CT scans of the "epilepsy with schizophrenia" group showed signs of "cerebral atrophy." Hyde & Weinberger, *supra* note 124, at 614.

133. W.B. Barr et al., *Brain Morphometric Comparison of First–Episode Schizophrenia and Temporal Lobe Epilepsy*, 170 Br. J. Psychiatry 515, 516–17 (1997). Barr and colleagues also found significant enlargement in lateral ventricular volume in FES and TLE patients compared to controls, but no difference between the FES and TLE groups.

134. M. Maier et al., *Schizophrenia, Temporal Lobe Epilepsy and Psychosis: An In Vivo Magnetic Resonance Spectroscopy and Imaging Study of the Hippocampus/Amygdala Complex*, 30 Psychol. Med. 571, 577 (2000). The study also compared metabolite levels in the four groups, and found significant reductions in left hemisphere hippocampal volume in the temporal lobe epilepsy with psychosis and schizophrenic groups compared with the temporal lobe epilepsy without psychosis and control groups.

135. *Id.*

sophical or religious issues (with multiple religious conversions), and circumstantiality (excessive detail) in speech.[136] Again, the results of empirical studies have been conflicting;[137] as one review noted, "efforts by investigators to relate epilepsy and aberrant behavior have been less successful, and it is not universally accepted that TLE predisposes an individual to specific behavioral changes."[138]

A second area of major controversy, and one of considerable importance to the legal system, is the relationship (if any) between epilepsy and violence. One report noted that

> aggressive behavior has been extensively reported in association with temporal lobe epilepsy.... [I]t would be difficult to cite ... another medical or neurologic illness in which aggressive behavior is described so regularly.[139]

However, assertions of a positive association between epilepsy and violence seem to be based on infrequent and atypical case studies, for most systematic studies and major reviews fail to support such claims. Several lines of evidence have been developed, including studies of epilepsy in offender populations, EEG studies of persons who experience "rage" attacks, and direct observational studies of persons experiencing seizure. Although some studies of prisoner populations have found a higher prevalence of epilepsy than in the general population, suggesting an increased risk for criminal behavior due to seizures, these studies have generally been criticized for failing to control for confounding variables (lower IQ, lower socioeconomic status) that may explain the results obtained.[140] In studies that have used matched-subjects designs, controlling for confounding demographic variables, no differences in dependent measures of violence (e.g., seriousness of index charges, rated violence in index charges, history of violent behavior) have been found.[141] Similarly, studies of persons referred specifically because of episodes of violence, outbursts of anger without provocation, and recurrent aggression have failed to implicate seizure activity as contributory.[142]

The available data suggest that aggression during the seizure proper (ictus) is a particularly remote possibility. Clinicians who have observed large numbers of seizures rarely if ever report the occurrence of directed violent behavior.[143] One investigator photographed 150 patients at an epilepsy clinic

---

136. For a comprehensive discussion of behaviors thought to constitute the "interictal syndrome" of TLE patients, *see* David Bear et al., *Interictal Behavior in Hospitalized Temporal Lobe Epileptics: Relationship to Idiopathic Psychiatric Syndromes*, 45 J. NEUROLOGY, NEUROSURGERY & PSYCHIATRY 481 (1982).

137. Benson, *supra* note 103, at 288.

138. Fedio, *supra* note 125, at 269.

139. Orrin Devinsky & David Bear, *Varieties of Aggressive Behavior in Temporal Lobe Epilepsy*, 141 AM. J. PSYCHIATRY 651, 653 (1984).

140. Fedio, *supra* note 125, at 271; David M. Treiman, *Epilepsy and Violence: Medical and Legal Issues*, 27 EPILEPSIA 77 (Supp. 1986); STEVEN WHITMAN & BRUCE P. HERMANN, PSYCHOPATHOLOGY IN EPILEPSY 288 (1986).

141. *Id.* at 289.

142. Treiman describes a study of 229 EEGs taken on 212 such individuals; only 14 of 212 (6.6%) had minimally or slightly abnormal EEGs, and none of the EEG abnormalities were interpreted as epileptiform. Treiman, *supra* note 140, at 78. Niedermeyer similarly concluded that "[m]ost cases of rage attacks show no EEG evidence of temporal lobe epilepsy." Niedermeyer, *supra* note 97, at 106.

143. WHITMAN & HERMANN, *supra* note 140, at 286–288 (discussing clinicians who have observed 10,000 seizures with automatisms but no reports of "directed exertion of physical force so as to injure, abuse or destroy"); HAUSER & HESDORFFER, *supra* note 94, at 254 (describing a study in which a single incident of violence in 5,400 seizures-.02%-was reported).

during the ictal and post-ictal phases of seizures that were chemically induced in persons treated for epilepsy.[144] Although some of these patients had a history of acting out, there were no incidents of aggression during the ictus or post-ictal stage.[145] In a companion study from the same clinic, 34 patients coded in the clinic files as positive for "destructive-assaultive behavior" did not differ on EEG measures from 34 non-aggressive patients matched on age, gender, and IQ. A study sponsored by the American Epilepsy Foundation involving an international panel of 18 epileptologists noted the "extreme rarity of directed aggression during seizures and the near impossibility of committing murder or manslaughter during random and unsustained automatisms."[146] Similarly, sustained, directed aggression does not commonly occur during the post-ictal phase; when it does occur, it is likely due to confusion, such as the patient misinterpreting as threatening the attempts of others to render medical assistance.[147]

There is relatively more evidence that persons may display sustained, directed aggression toward others during the interictal period, but even this finding is in much dispute. TLE in particular has been suspected of contributing to aggression during the interictal period. Clinically it has been observed that some persons with seizure disorders become testy, argumentative, and combative preceding seizure onset, and that such behaviors tend to diminish after the seizure occurs.[148] However, findings from controlled studies involving persons with seizure disorder and various comparison groups raise doubts about attributing such behavior to epilepsy per se. In one study persons with TLE were compared to groups of persons suffering from other forms of epilepsy, schizophrenia, primary affective disorders, and aggressive character disorders on a variety of behavioral measures.[149] Generally, persons with TLE were no more aggressive, or more prone to angry outbursts, than comparison subjects. In another study that used cluster analysis to identify groups of neurologically impaired patients in terms of violence profiles, the group with the most benign profile (in terms of violence) showed the highest incidence of neurological abnormality, raising further doubts about any direct, positive association between neurological impairment and aggression.[150]

---

144. Ernst A. Rodin, *Psychomotor Epilepsy and Aggressive Behavior*, 28 ARCHIVES GEN. PSYCHIATRY 210 (1973).

145. *Id.* at 211.

146. Antonio V. Delgato-Escueta et al., *The Nature of Aggression During Epileptic Seizures*, 305 NEW ENG. J. MED. 711, 715 (1981). In this study the expert panel viewed videotaped recordings of 33 epileptic attacks involving 19 patients. The attacks "appeared suddenly, without evidence of planning, and lasted an average of 29 seconds.... Aggressive acts were stereotyped, simple, unsustained, and never supported by consecutive series of purposeful movements." *Id.*

147. Bear, Freeman & Greenberg, *supra* note 112, at 201–202.

148. Benson, *supra* note 103, at 287.

149. Bear et al., *supra* note 136, at 482.

150. Dan Mungas, *An Empirical Analysis of Specific Syndromes of Violent Behavior*, 171

J. NERVOUS & MENTAL DISEASE 354, 359 (1983). Also of interest are clinicians' qualitative descriptions of the interictal aggressive episodes of persons with epilepsy. Professor Blumer noted that "[i]t is further remarkable how even during extreme outbursts a measure of control seems to be present; the rage is frightening, furniture is destroyed, a family member is struck, but rarely is someone injured." Dietrich Blumer, *Epilepsy and Violence*, in RAGE/HATE/ASSAULT AND OTHER FORMS OF VIOLENCE 210 (Daniel Madden & John Lion, 1976). Similarly, " ... an aggressive act might be carried out for a clear motive, often following considerable planning in response to an objectively minor provocation. The patient frequently experiences moral concerns or a sense of outrage. The perpetrator generally does not claim amnesia for the event and may recall these actions with considerable regret." Bear et al., *supra* note 136, at 202.

In summary, early writing in the epilepsy literature suggested a positive association between epilepsy and violence. More recent clinical and empirical studies have taken issue with that claim, leading some major reviewers to conclude that "there is no evidence that violence is more common among epileptics than among non-epileptics"[151] and that "there is no remotely persuasive evidence linking epilepsy to violence/aggression."[152]

§ 1–2.4 Posttraumatic Stress Disorder

§ 1–2.4.1 Introduction

The possibility that stressful life events may cause serious psychological symptoms has long been recognized.[153] But the diagnosis of posttraumatic stress disorder (PTSD) is a relatively new one. Prior to 1980 a psychological disturbance attributable to stressful events was labeled a "transient situational disturbance" and included reactions of any severity, including those of psychotic proportions, which represented "an acute reaction to overwhelming environmental stress."[154] PTSD first appeared in the third edition of the Diagnostic and Statistical Manual of Mental Disorders (DSM–III)[155] and has been retained, with modifications, in subsequent editions.

PTSD is somewhat of an anomaly among DSM diagnoses in that the diagnostic criteria include an explicit causal etiology. For most psychiatric disorders, the DSM criteria are silent with respect to specific etiology. In contrast, the PTSD entry in DSM–IV speaks to:

> . . . the development of characteristic symptoms following exposure to an extreme traumatic stressor involving direct personal experience of an event that involves actual or threatened death or serious injury, or other threat to one's physical integrity; or witnessing an event that involves death, injury, or a threat to the physical integrity of another person; or learning about unexpected or violent death, serious harm, or threat of death or injury experienced by a family member or other close associate.[156]

The person's initial reaction to the stressor must be one of "intense fear, helplessness, or horror,"[157] and result in subsequent symptoms lasting more than one month[158] that include persistent re-experiencing of the traumatic event,[159] persistent avoidance of or "numbing" toward stimuli associated with

---

151. Treiman, *supra* note 140, at 77.

152. WHITMAN & HERMANN, *supra* note 143, at 296.

153. The study of stress related disorders has developed primarily in the context of war, including the study of war neurosis (combat related stress) and victims of the holocaust. It has expanded into research on the impact of natural disasters (e.g., hurricanes) and industrial accidents and thence to specific individual experiences (e.g., rape, assault). For a review, *see* Philip A. Saigh, *History, Current Nosology, and Epidemiology, in* POSTTRAUMATIC STRESS DISORDER: A BEHAVIORAL APPROACH TO ASSESSMENT AND TREATMENT 1 (Philip A. Saigh, 1992)[hereinafter POSTTRAUMATIC STRESS DISORDER].

154. AMERICAN PSYCHIATRIC ASSOCIATION, DIAGNOSTIC AND STATISTICAL MANUAL OF MENTAL DISORDERS 48 (2d ed. 1968) [hereinafter DSM-II].

155. AMERICAN PSYCHIATRIC ASSOCIATION, DIAGNOSTIC AND STATISTICAL MANUAL OF MENTAL DISORDERS 236 (3d ed. 1980) [hereinafter DSM-III].

156. DSM–IV, *supra* note 1.

157. *Id.* at 428.

158. *Id.* at 429.

159. These may include distressing recollections (images, thoughts, perceptions), dreams, acting or feeling as if the event were recurring (including hallucinations or dissociative flashbacks), and intense psychological distress or physiological reactivity on exposure to internal or external cues that symbolize or resemble an aspect of the event. *Id.* at 428.

the trauma,[160] and persistent symptoms of increased hypervigilance.[161]

Since its introduction in the DSM, PTSD has achieved considerable popularity in the legal community as a basis for recovery claims in personal injury cases.[162] Moreover, it has achieved some success as an exculpating condition for mental state defenses to criminal behavior such as insanity.[163] Because contemporary legal tests for insanity seem to require impaired reality testing in order for the defense to prevail,[164] those who base an insanity claim on PTSD often emphasize the complex of symptoms associated with "reexperiencing" the trauma; in such cases, the defense asserts that at the time of the offense the defendant experienced a dissociative "flashback" during which the trauma appeared to reoccur and the defendant acted accordingly. Thus, for instance, a Vietnam veteran may claim that a homicide was "justified" given his or her misperception that the victim was an enemy soldier, or a rape victim may claim that an assault occurred because she thought she was fighting off her previous assailant.[165]

The symptom of hypervigilance may also contribute to such reliving scenarios. Re-experiencing phenomena may result from exposure to external cues that symbolize or resemble an aspect of the traumatic event (e.g., a Vietnam vet who hears helicopter noises and gunshot-like sounds).[166] Thus, persons with PTSD who vigilantly scan and defensively construe their environment in terms of threat cues may be at increased risk to trigger re-experiencing symptoms.[167]

The evaluation for a possible insanity defense based on PTSD poses several difficulties for the forensic examiner, however. Most fundamental are problems establishing the diagnosis. Although a number of structured measures have been developed to assess PTSD,[168] most are based on direct

---

160. Symptoms include efforts to avoid thoughts, feelings or conversations about the trauma; efforts to avoid activities, places, or people who arouse recollections of the trauma; inability to recall important aspects of the trauma; diminished interest or participation in significant activities; feeling detached or estranged from others; restricted affect; or sense of foreshortened future. *Id.*

161. These include difficulty falling or staying asleep, irritability or outbursts of anger, difficulty concentrating, hypervigilance, and exaggerated startle response. *Id.*

162. Because the traumatic stressor and presumed causal relationship to emotional disorder are inherent in the diagnosis, PTSD has become particularly popular in civil litigation. *See* Alan A. Stone, *Post-traumatic Stress Disorder and the Law: Critical Review of the New Frontier*, 21 BULL. AM. ACAD. PSYCHIATRY & L. 23 (1993).

163. *Id.*; *see* Landy F. Sparr et al., *Military Combat, Posttraumatic Stress Disorder; Criminal Behavior in Vietnam Veterans*, 15 BULL. AM. ACAD. PSYCHIATRY & L. 141 (1987); Anthony S. Higgins, *Post-traumatic Stress Disorder and Its Role in the Defense of Vietnam Veterans*, 15 L. & PSYCHOL. REV. 259 (1991).

164. The large majority of persons acquitted NGRI suffer from major psychoses (schizo-

phrenia or major affective disorder) with which hallucinations (false perceptions such as seeing visions or hearing imaginary voices) or delusions (mistaken beliefs, often bizarre and of a persecutory nature) are often associated. *See* HENRY J. STEADMAN ET AL., BEFORE AND AFTER HINCKLEY: EVALUATING INSANITY DEFENSE REFORM 56 (1993) (84% of NGRI acquittals in California were diagnosed with a major mental illness), at 70 (90% in Georgia), and at 78 (97% in New York).

165. On their face, among all the PTSD symptoms, only the reliving experiences (particularly "flashbacks"), appear to involve a level of reality distortion comparable to that in schizophrenia and major affective disorders. *See supra* 137–39 and accompanying text; *see* Higgins, *supra* note 163, at 270; Sparr et al., *supra* note 163, at 157.

166. *Cf. supra* note 137.

167. Brett T. Litz et al., *Assessment of Posttraumatic Stress Disorder, in* POSTTRAUMATIC STRESS DISORDER: A BEHAVIORAL APPROACH TO ASSESSMENT AND TREATMENT 50, 57 (Philip A. Saigh, ed. 1992).

168. *See infra* notes 176, 177 and 234 and accompanying text.

symptom endorsement by the respondent (self-report) and are therefore susceptible to manipulation or malingering by the defendant. Further, establishing retrospectively that a reliving "flashback" occurred is difficult because flashbacks are thought to be unconscious occurrences; the individual does not make a deliberate decision to "relive" the past trauma, nor does he later have memory of the flashback episode.[169] Thus, obtaining reliable accounts of the defendant's thoughts, feelings and perceptions during the episode, particularly in the absence of detailed third-party accounts of his actions, may be difficult.[170]

Second, viability of the claimed flashback may hinge in part on the ability to identify triggering stimuli in the current (crime scene) environment that are reminiscent of the features of the original trauma. These stimuli may be difficult to ascertain both because information regarding the specifics of the original trauma is sparse, and because (theoretically) the stimuli need only be *symbolic* of the original trauma.[171] The clinician who is not careful may be lured into forcing a PTSD interpretation on behavior that is merely erratic.[172] Finally, one investigator found that, at least among Vietnam veterans, flashbacks with disorientation for people with PTSD were more common among those who were also suffering from alcoholism (72%) than among non-alcoholics (16%).[173] These data suggest that clinicians and courts may further have to wrestle with the possibility (and certainly the prosecution's assertions) that the effects of voluntarily consumed alcohol, commonly proscribed as a basis for an insanity defense, may have played a prominent role in producing the defendant's flashback.

A second criminal law arena in which PTSD has played a role concerns defendants charged with rape who concede they had intercourse with the complainant but assert it was consensual. In such cases, the prosecution might attempt to rebut the consent defense with proof that the complainant's current condition could only have been caused by the trauma of forcible sexual contact. Although some of the research described here is relevant to the "rape-trauma syndrome," this topic is treated at length in another chapter of this treatise and thus is not focused upon here.

169. Flashback experiences among Vietnam veterans have been described as " . . . sudden, discrete experience(s), leading to actions where the manifest psychic content is only indirectly related to the war; in addition the veteran does not have conscious awareness of reliving events in Vietnam." Herbert J. Cross, *Social Factors Associated with Post-traumatic Stress Disorder in Vietnam Veterans,* in Post-Traumatic Stress Disorder: Assessment, Differential Diagnosis and Forensic Evaluation 73, 85 (Carroll L. Meek ed., 1990).

170. Because of the psychogenic nature of the amnesia, special interviewing techniques such as hypnosis or sodium brevital may be helpful in cases of suspected Vietnam flashback. A case report of a successful NGRI defense in which such procedures were employed is described in Gary B. Melton, John Petrila, Norman G. Poythress & Christopher Slobogin, Psychological Evaluations for the Courts: A Handbook for Mental Health Professionals and Lawyers 382 (1987).

171. Anecdotal reports reveal how ordinary, innocuous events may have symbolic associations for victims of trauma. One author recited the case of a concentration camp survivor experiencing discomfort after "seeing a person stretching his arms and associating this with his fellow prisoners hung up by their arms under torture." Posttraumatic Stress Disorder, *supra* note 153, at 3.

172. T. Ayllon et al., *Interpretations of Symptoms: Fact or Fiction,* 3 Behav. Research & Therapy 1 (1965). *See generally,* Stephen Morse, *Failed Explanations and Criminal Responsibility: Experts and the Unconscious,* 68 Va. L. Rev. 971 (1982).

173. David Behar, *Flashbacks and Post-traumatic Stress Symptoms in Combat Veterans,* 28 Comprehensive Psychiatry 459, 463 (1987).

§ 1–2.4.2 Introductory Discussion of the Science

[1] The Scientific Questions

[a] Questions Studied

Several factors limit the nature and progress to date in the scientific study of PTSD. First, PTSD as a diagnostic entity has been in existence for fewer than 15 years. Thus, the research published prior to 1980 focused only on the relationship of stressful events to general emotional reactions, not to PTSD per se; the degree to which findings and relationships from that literature generalize to PTSD varies depending on study population and design. Second, problems with the definition of the stressor criterion for PTSD have played havoc with research design and interpretation; until 1994, the DSM required that the traumatic event be one that is "generally outside the realm of human experience,"[174] a requirement about which no normative consensus exists. Thus, some researchers have investigated the impact of stressful life events uncertain as to whether their independent variable was truly "PTSD" or merely some bastardized version of it.

Additionally, optimal research regarding PTSD confronts enormous practical difficulties. Many of the qualifying events (e.g., rape, tornadoes, toxic spills) cannot be predicted in advance. Thus, having an adequate research infrastructure in place, ready to study reactions to traumatic events when they occur, is virtually impossible. As a consequence, many studies have been limited to retrospective investigations of events that affect large numbers of people (e.g., war, natural disasters, concentration camp survivors),[175] and others must rely on self-reports of the traumatic occurrence (e.g., studies of rape trauma).

Within these constraints, researchers have addressed diverse issues related to PTSD. One fundamental issue has been the measurement of PTSD, and a variety of survey, self-report, and rating measures have been developed for both descriptive research and clinical use.[176] Many of these measures have reasonably good reliability and validity with respect to the measurement of PTSD symptoms.[177] Epidemiological studies have attempted to establish the

174. DSM–III, *supra* note 154, at 236.

175. An exception is the study of rape and assault victims, made possible by the advent of rape crisis centers and other victim assistance programs.

176. Litz et al., *supra* note 167; *see also* Alan E. Brooker et al., *Conceptualizing a Better Understanding of Diagnosing and Treating Posttraumatic Stress Disorder: A Review of Two Case Studies*, 89 PERCEPTUAL MOTOR SKILLS 607, 611–612 (describing four measures including special scales from conventional tests, such as the Minnesota Multiphasic Personality Inventory, and special instruments focused on traumatic events); Thomas W. Miller et al., *Assessment of Life Stress Events: The Etiology and Measurement of Traumatic Stress Disorder*, 38 INT'L J. SOC. PSYCHIATRY 215 (1992) (describing 10 measures including special scales from conventional tests, such as the

Minnesota Multiphasic Personality Inventory, and special instruments focused on combat-related or civilian accident/disaster events).

177. *See, e.g.,* E.J. Costello et al., *Life Events and Post–Traumatic Stress: The Development of a New Measure for Children and Adolescents*, 28 PSYCHOL. MED. 1275, 1283–85 (1998) (finding reliability for reports of life events, individual events, PTSD screening symptoms and symptoms and diagnosis of PTSD, as well as discriminant validity for the Child and Adolescent Psychiatric Assessment); Jonathan R. T. Davidson et al., *Assessment of a New Self–Rating Scale for Post–Traumatic Stress Disorder*, 27 PSYCHOL. MED. 153, 155–58 (1997) (finding high test-retest reliability, internal consistency, factorial validity, concurrent validity, convergent and discriminant validity and predictive validity for the Davidson Trauma Scale); Edward S. Kubany et al., *Vali-*

incidence and prevalence of PTSD,[178] as well as the relationship of stressor characteristics (severity, duration) to the probability of developing PTSD. The co-morbidity of PTSD with other diagnoses has also been documented.

A related area of inquiry has been the extent to which individual characteristics influence a post-traumatic response. Noting that many persons exposed to severe stressors do not develop PTSD, some researchers have sought to examine the role of factors that mediate the stress-response relationship, such as individual vulnerability (e.g., heritability, personality traits, prior experiences); in this same vein, some investigators have questioned whether the objective parameters of the stressor are as important as an individual's phenomenological interpretation of the traumatic event. With certain samples (primarily persons exposed to combat), researchers have even confronted individuals with trauma-related stimuli in a laboratory setting and measured their physiological reaction as part of the validation of the PTSD construct.

[b]   Questions Not Yet Studied

There are a number of key issues that have not been adequately addressed or resolved in the scientific study of PTSD. These include: (a) problems with the definition of the qualifying stressor; (b) comparability of features across stressors; and (c) the relative "causal" effects of exposure to traumatic stress, the development of PTSD, and other events following exposure to trauma on the individual's subsequent adjustment.

Even with the removal from DSM–IV of the "outside the realm of human experience" requirement, concerns about the definition and characteristics of the stressor remain.[179] Qualifying events include those that involve "actual or threatened death or serious injury, or a threat to the physical integrity of self or others."[180] While some extreme traumas that easily meet this definition may be identified (e.g., war, some natural disasters), science has not developed techniques for judging and classifying other, more ambiguous events. For instance, whether a person's subjective fears about having worked in a building with asbestos in the roof or the effect of long-term exposure to passive smoking constitute a clear "threat to physical integrity of self or others" is not agreed upon.

Presently there is no good typology of traumatic events that permits confidence in comparisons of individuals' or groups' reactions to trauma of

---

dation of a Brief Measure of Posttraumatic Stress Disorder: The Distressing Event Questionnaire (DEQ), 12 PSYCHOL. ASSESSMENT 197, 201–07 (finding high internal consistency, good temporal stability and discriminative validity and strong convergent validity for DEQ); Caron Zlotnick & Teri Pearlstein, Validation of the Structured Interview for Disorders of Extreme Stress, 38 COMPREHENSIVE PSYCHIATRY 243, 245–46 (1997) (finding good construct validity and divergent validity for Structured Interview for Disorders of Extreme Stress).

178. See infra, § 1–2.4.4.

179. See, e.g., Naomi Breslau & Glenn C. Davis, Posttraumatic Stress Disorder: The

Stressor Criterion, 150 J. NERVOUS & MENTAL DISEASE 255 (1987); Jonathan R. Davidson & Edna B. Foa, Diagnostic Issues in Posttraumatic Stress Disorder: Considerations for the DSM–IV, 100 J. ABNORMAL PSYCHOL. 346 (1991); Jonathan R. Davidson & Edna B. Foa, Refining Criteria for Posttraumatic Stress Disorder, 42 HOSP. & COMMUNITY PSYCHIATRY 259 (1991) [hereinafter Refining Criteria]; Anthony Feinstein & Ray Dolan, Predictors of Post-traumatic Stress Disorder Following Physical Trauma: An Examination of the Stressor Criterion, 21 PSYCHOL. MED. 85 (1991).

180. DSM–IV, supra note 1, at 427.

different types. Some stressors are human-caused (e.g., arson, torture) while others are caused by nature (e.g., hurricanes, floods). There are also potentially important qualitative differences, such as duration and intensity of the stressor; some stressors involve lengthy and intense exposure (e.g., lengthy assignment in a combat zone or a concentration camp), while with others the exposure is brief and vicarious (e.g., being told of a loved one's death from automobile accident).[181] The occurrence of some stressful events can be anticipated (e.g., a hurricane; combat), thus allowing psychological preparation but also possibly increasing anticipatory anxiety; other traumatic events occur spontaneously, eliminating any anticipatory reaction (e.g., rape, automobile wrecks). Difficulty determining the comparability of stressors raises significant concerns about the generalizability of findings from one PTSD population to another; for example, the degree to which the experiences of concentration camp survivors or rape victims inform judgments about the probable psychological reactions of persons to death of a loved one or a hostile work environment is not clear.

A third problem relates to causal inferences about the impact of the stressor and resulting PTSD symptoms on subsequent adjustment. There has been relatively little systematic research on the contribution of other, ongoing life events to the continuing functional difficulties of PTSD sufferers. Some researchers have noted, however, that exposure to trauma may increase the likelihood that the individual will experience other stressors. For example, an individual whose uninsured home and business have been destroyed in a natural disaster is likely to suffer a variety of economic setbacks. Efforts to tease apart the contribution of these "secondary disasters" to subsequent adjustment from the effects of the original stressor have been limited.[182] Relatedly, with those individuals who develop PTSD only six months or more after the trauma (a group diagnosed as suffering from *delayed onset* PTSD[183]), the role of events subsequent to the traumatic stressor appears to have received relatively little research attention.[184]

[2]   Scientific Methods Applied in the Research

Ethical considerations prevent researchers from randomly exposing people to severe trauma (e.g., rape, toxic chemicals); thus, correlational designs and animal laboratory analogues have played significant roles in PTSD research. Animal laboratory studies have been found useful in developing theories about PTSD based on classical conditioning principles. These models hold that the traumatic event creates a strong, permanent representation in memory that can subsequently activate both the cognitive and physiological

181. The PTSD research has focused overwhelmingly on persons who actually experienced or witnessed trauma; there has been relatively little study of PTSD as a function of "learning about" qualifying stressful events, although this vicarious experiencing is also included in the diagnostic criteria. *Id.*

182. Susan D. Solomon & Glorisa J. Canino, *Appropriateness of DSM–III–R Criteria for Posttraumatic Stress Disorder*, 31 COMPREHENSIVE PSYCHIATRY 227 (1990).

183. DSM–IV, *supra* note 1, at 425.

184. One interesting study finding no symptomatic differences between persons reporting delayed vs. undelayed onset, and therefore questioning the value of separate subtypes of the disorder, is reported in Charles G. Watson et al., *Differences Between Posttraumatic Stress Disorder with Delayed and Undelayed Onsets*, 176 J. NERVOUS & MENTAL DISEASE 568 (1988).

symptoms in response to cues or stimuli associated with the trauma. Similarities between the reactions of laboratory animals exposed to "experimental neurosis" paradigms[185] and some PTSD symptoms have been noted; disturbances in animals have included alterations between sudden outbursts and agitated behavior ("increased arousal") on the one hand and lethargy, passivity and withdrawal ("avoidance and numbing of general responsiveness") on the other.[186] Animals exposed to laboratory stressors can also be sacrificed in order to study associated changes in their underlying biochemical systems that mediate behavioral responding, thus contributing to hypotheses about the action of neurological and physiological mechanisms in humans exposed to trauma.[187]

Some laboratory designs have also been used with voluntary human subjects. Persons diagnosed with PTSD following exposure to a particular trauma have been exposed systematically to stimuli that replicate some aspect of the trauma experience; for example, Vietnam veterans with PTSD may agree to experience audio or video tapes of combat action and permit researchers to gather self-report or psychophysiological measures (e.g., changes in heart rate or blood pressure) at different points in the research protocol. Their responses may be compared to those of one or more control groups of subjects (e.g., Vietnam veterans who did not develop PTSD, persons exposed to civilian but not combat trauma, persons with other diagnoses) to determine the degree to which increased physiological reactivity is associated with trauma related cues.

By far the most common studies involve correlational designs in which investigators obtain dependent measures (e.g., self-report symptom endorsements, psychological test results) on persons differentially exposed to a particular type of traumatic event (e.g., combat or rape). More often than not these studies have involved clinical samples rather than random selection of persons exposed to the trauma and thus results are potentially affected by sampling bias.

For purposes of this chapter, it is important to note that our review revealed a paucity of studies examining the relationship of PTSD to criminal behavior or to impairment in cognitive and emotional functioning of a type that might be relevant to mental state defenses for criminal defendants. Preoccupied with studying the role of stressors in symptom development, developing PTSD measures, and establishing the construct validity of PTSD, few researchers have moved beyond these concerns to treat PTSD as an independent variable and examine its impact on behaviors of relevance to the criminal justice system.

185. One example of an "experimental neurosis" paradigm is when an animal is exposed to experimenter controlled electric shock from which the animal may (or may not) be able to escape. This is thought to share features common with PTSD situations because "environmental events of vital importance to the organism become unpredictable, uncontrollable, or both." Edna B. Foa et al., *Uncontrollability and Unpredictability in Post-traumatic Stress Disorder: An Animal Model*, 112 PSYCHOL. BULL. 218, 220 (1992).

186. Of course, animal studies are of little use in studying the subjective symptoms of PTSD, such as nightmares or intrusive recollections of the traumatic event. *Id.* at 218.

187. Dennis S. Charney et al., *Psychobiological Mechanisms of Posttraumatic Stress Disorder*, 50 ARCHIVES GEN. PSYCHIATRY 294 (1993).

§ 1–2.4.3   Areas of Scientific Agreement

One consistent finding in the literature is that persons who suffer from PTSD often qualify for other DSM diagnoses as well. Other diagnoses frequently found in PTSD subjects include anxiety disorders, depression, substance abuse/dependence disorders, and personality disorders.[188]

There is general agreement, based on findings of reactions to a variety of different stressors, that stress reaction to trauma is dose dependent: the more prolonged and intense the person's exposure to the trauma, the greater the likelihood of severe stress responses such as PTSD.[189] This relationship has been reliably replicated in a number of studies of combat veterans,[190] rape/assault victims,[191] and with victims of other trauma.[192]

There is also agreement that a variety of other factors may mediate the trauma-stress reaction relationship. For example, studies of combat veterans have revealed that soldiers may be at increased risk for combat related PTSD as a function of such factors as genetic makeup,[193] family history of mental illness,[194] negative life experiences during the three months prior to combat trauma,[195] or dispositional variables such as attribution style.[196] Thus, individ-

---

188. *See, e.g.,* Steven M. Southwick et al., *Abnormal Noradrenergic Function in Posttraumatic Stress Disorder*, 50 Archives Gen. Psychiatry 266, 267 (1993) (80% of PTSD subjects met criteria for lifetime diagnosis of depression; 85% met criteria for alcohol dependence); Behar, *supra* note 173, at 461 (reporting that of 37 veterans referred to an outpatient clinic for PTSD, 95.4% met criteria for one or more additional psychiatric disorders). *See generally,* Litz et al., *supra* note 167, at 58 (studies reviewed suggest 60–100% of PTSD victims have secondary diagnoses, commonly substance abuse or dependence); Terence M. Keane & Danny G. Kaloupek, *Comorbid Psychiatric Disorders in PTSD: Implications for Research*, 821 Annals N.Y. Acad. Sci. 24, 24–28 (1997) (reviewing studies finding high rates of comorbidity of Antisocial Personality Disorder and Borderline Personality Disorder among persons with PTSD).

189. A meta-analysis of 52 published studies (limited to civilian disasters of natural origin and affecting large groups of people) found a reliable increase in pathology with severity of the disaster (as measured by death rate). Anthony V. Rubonis & Leonard Bickman, *Psychological Impairment in the Wake of Disaster: The Disaster–Psychopathology Relationship*, 109 Psychol. Bull. 384, 396 (1991).

190. Branachey L. Buydens et al., *Duration and Intensity of Combat Exposure and Posttraumatic Stress Disorder in Vietnam Veterans*, 178 J. Nervous & Mental Dis. 582 (1990); William R. True et al., *A Twin Study of Genetic and Environmental Contributions to Liability for Posttraumatic Stress Symptoms*, 50 Archives Gen. Psychiatry 257 (1993) [hereinafter *Twin Study*].

191. David W. Foy et al., *Etiology of Posttraumatic Stress Disorder, in* Posttraumatic Stress Disorder, *supra* note 153, at 28–49 (re-

views of rape/assault studies reveal that PTSD reaction is highest when rape included physical injury and threat to the life of the victim).

192. *But see* Alexander C. McFarlane, *The Aetiology of Post-traumatic Stress Disorders Following a Natural Disaster*, 152 Brit. J. Psychiatry 116, 118–119 (1988) (finding no dose-response effect among firefighters differentially exposed to huge bushfires in Australia).

193. *Twin Study, supra* note 190; *see also* Jack Goldberg et al., *A Twin Study of the Effects of the Vietnam War on Posttraumatic Stress Disorder*, 263 JAMA 1227 (1990); William R. True & Michael J. Lyons, *Genetic Risk Factors for PTSD: A Twin Study, in* Risk Factors for Posttraumatic Stress Disorder 61–78 (Rachel Yehuda ed., 1999).

194. Foy et al., *supra* note 191, at 32 (studies of combat veterans suggest that soldiers with high exposure to combat are at increased risk regardless of family history of mental illness; only soldiers with positive family history of mental illness are disproportionately at risk under low combat exposure); Jonathan R. T. Davidson & Kathryn M. O'Connor, *Family Studies of PTSD: A Review, in* Risk Factors for Posttraumatic Stress Disorder 81–82 (Rachel Yehuda ed., 1999) (summarizing study results of familial psychopathology and risk of PTSD with combat veterans); Kathryn M. O'Connor & Jonathan R. T. Davidson, *Familial Risk Factors in Posttraumatic Stress Disorder*, 821 Annals N.Y. Acad. Sci. 35, 37–46 (1997) (summarizing studies on familial aspects of combat neurosis and family data from studies of PTSD).

195. Foy et al., *supra* note 191, at 34.

196. *Id. See generally* Paula P. Schnurr & Melanie J. Vielhauer, *Personality as a Risk Factor for PTSD, in* Risk Factors for Posttrau-

ual factors and prior experience contribute to individuals' reactivity to trauma exposure.[197]

Another replicated finding important for the construct validity of PTSD comes from laboratory studies of the physiological reactivity of persons exposed to cues related to their prior trauma experiences. In studies of Vietnam veterans exposed to various combat related stimuli, heightened reactivity (compared to controls, and compared to non-combat stimuli) has been reliably demonstrated by researchers using a wide variety of dependent measures.[198] These studies lend support to the notion of a fundamental and more or less permanent change in the underlying neurochemical environment of PTSD sufferers, one that accounts for increased arousal and susceptibility to "reliving" symptoms.

In this regard, a study by Professor Southwick and colleagues[199] merits brief discussion. Twenty Vietnam veterans with PTSD and 18 healthy male controls received a ten minute infusion of either a stress inducing drug[200] or placebo (saline solution). Dependent measures included both physiological measures (blood samples, blood pressure) and self-report measures taken at designated intervals over a three-hour period post injection. For purposes of this chapter, the most important finding was that exposure to the central nervous system stressor induced panic attacks in 70% of the PTSD subjects and combat related flashbacks in 40% of the PTSD subjects.[201] The authors discuss possible links between traumatic memories and biochemical states and suggest that "reproducing a neurobiological state . . . similar to the one that existed at the time of the memory encoding can elicit the traumatic memory."[202] This study suggests that not only cues symbolic of the prior trauma, but also exposure to a new stressful life event, might activate a particular neurochemical response that in turn activates a reliving (e.g., intrusive memories, flashback) experience in an individual with PTSD.[203]

MATIC STRESS DISORDER 191–222 (Rachel Yehuda ed., 1999) (summarizing results of studies on relationship between personality factors and personality disorders and PTSD risk).

197. In some studies, stress response has been more strongly associated with individuals' subjective experience of the trauma than with the severity of the stressor, raising questions about the primary etiological role assigned to the stressful event. *See* Feinstein & Dolan, *supra* note 179, at 90. *See generally* Breslau & Davis, *supra* note 179.

198. Roger K. Pittman et al., *Psychophysiologic Assessment of Posttraumatic Stress Disorder Imagery in Vietnam Combat Veterans*, 44 ARCHIVES GEN. PSYCHIATRY 970 (1987) (confirming predicted increases in PTSD subjects for measures of heart rate, skin conductance, and muscle tension in response to combat related stimuli, but not to neutral stimuli); Miles E. McFall et al., *Autonomic Responses to Stress in Vietnam Combat Veterans with Posttraumatic Stress Disorder*, 27 BIOLOGICAL PSYCHIATRY 1165 (1990) (confirming predicted increases in measures of heart rate, blood pressure, and plasma epinephrine). *See generally*, Litz et al., *supra* note 167, at 72–74.

199. *See supra* note 165.

200. Yohimbine hydrochloride is a chemical that activates noradrenergic neurons, producing a variety of biochemical, behavioral, and cardiovascular effects. It has been used in a variety of research studies to induce "stress" in the central nervous system. Higgins, *supra* note 163.

201. For purposes of the experiment, "flashback" was defined as the patient reporting a re-experiencing of a past traumatic event via one or more sensory modalities (e.g., hearing, smelling, tasting), in a way that was similar to prior, naturally occurring flashbacks. It is important to note that none of the subjects in this study (Vietnam veterans) became physically aggressive or disruptive during these reported "flashbacks." On the other hand, these experimentally induced flashbacks clearly were of limited scope. *Id.* at 267.

202. *Id.* at 272.

203. The authors are careful to note, however, that these findings may not generalize to non-combat traumatized populations or to persons suffering from acute (versus chronic) PTSD. *Id.* at 273.

As noted above, empirical studies relating exposure to trauma to increased propensity for criminal behavior and, in particular, to the subsequent development of more severe symptoms that might provide a basis for an insanity defense are relatively few in number. With this caveat, the research shows only a tenuous link between PTSD and criminal behavior. One study of Vietnam veterans found that those suffering with PTSD were significantly more likely to endorse dissociative symptoms (e.g., feelings of disconnection, misperception of reality) during structured diagnostic interviews,[204] but there was no association reported between these symptom endorsements and criminal activity. Another study compared the responses of Vietnam veterans suffering from PTSD to both clinical (i.e., people with other psychiatric diagnoses) and normal controls on standardized measures of cognitive thinking and irrational beliefs,[205] finding no significant impairment in persons with PTSD relative to controls.[206]

Two recent studies have found some support for a relationship between PTSD and interpersonal violence. The first compared combat veterans with PTSD to combat veterans without PTSD and found higher rates of violence toward others.[207] Among the factors significantly related to interpersonal violence among the former group were PTSD diagnosis and combat exposure (level of wartime stressors).[208] The second study sought variables associated with interpersonal violence among combat veterans with PTSD seeking outpatient care. A majority of the sample reported six or more violent acts, with interpersonal violence significantly related to three variables (lower SES, greater PTSD severity, and higher aggressive responding).[209] The researchers concluded that "these results show for the first time that PTSD severity within a group of PTSD combat veterans was related to violence."[210] Nevertheless, the small sample size of the first study, the absence of comparative analysis in the second study, and the possible impact of alcohol use and substance abuse all suggest that these results be considered cautiously.[211]

Some investigators have examined arrest rates among Vietnam veterans,[212] and others have looked at the frequency of violent crimes in the index offenses of inmates with and without combat-related (Vietnam) PTSD.[213] The latter study found no difference in the frequency of conviction for violent offenses.[214] Among the inmate group with PTSD, there was no claim of any

204. J. Douglas Bremner et al., *Use of the Structured Clinical Interview for DSM–IV Dissociative Disorders for Systematic Assessment of Dissociative Symptoms in Posttraumatic Stress Disorder*, 150 Am. J. Psychiatry 1011 (1993).

205. Elizabeth M. Muran & Robert W. Motta, *Cognitive Distortions and Irrational Beliefs in Post-traumatic Stress, Anxiety, and Depressive Disorders*, 49 J. Clinical Psychol. 166 (1993).

206. *Id.* at 168.

207. Jean C. Beckham et al., *Interpersonal Violence and Its Correlates in Vietnam Veterans with Chronic Posttraumatic Stress Disorder*, 53 J. Clinical Psychol. 859, 862 (1997).

208. *See id.* at 862.

209. *See id.* at 864–65.

210. *Id.* at 865.

211. *See id.* at 866.

212. For a review, *see* Adela Beckerman & Leonard Fontana, *Vietnam Veterans and the Criminal Justice System: A Selected Review*, 16 Crim. Just. & Behav. 412 (1989).

213. Donna M. Shaw et al., *Criminal Behavior and Post-traumatic Stress Disorder in Vietnam Veterans*, 28 Comprehensive Psychiatry 403 (1987).

214. *Id.* at 408. Further, in comparison to Vietnam veterans in the community, PTSD was not significantly more prevalent among inmates (39%) than among community controls (37%). *Id.* at 403.

association between the offense and combat related experiences or symptoms (e.g., flashbacks or altered states of consciousness).[215] To our knowledge, investigations of the criminogenic role of PTSD in other PTSD populations (e.g., victims of toxic spills, tornadoes, refugee camps, etc.) are not available. Finally, one multi-state study examined the prevalence of PTSD as a diagnosis among those raising an insanity defense, finding no differences in terms of type of offense, type of victim, or success rate between those who pled NGRI on the basis of PTSD and those who based their defense on some other diagnosis.[216]

§ 1–2.4.4   Areas of Scientific Disagreement

Despite the periodic revisions to and continued presence of PTSD in the DSM, there is continued debate about the viability of this disorder in the literature. At a conceptual level, some have commented that the trauma-stress reaction paradigm represents normal, as opposed to pathological functioning. Some have observed that humans should respond emotionally to traumatic events and thus some level of reactive symptomatology is appropriate.[217] Consistent with this interpretation others have noted that most persons affected by stressful experiences recover relatively quickly,[218] suggesting that a gradual return to normal emotional functioning further challenges the wisdom of pathologizing the initial emotional responses. At an empirical level, others have questioned the integrity of the specific symptom complex that constitutes PTSD in light of the significant correlation between PTSD and global pathology measures[219] and the frequent co-morbidity with other disorders.[220]

In response, defenders of the diagnosis have discussed trauma reaction as normally distributed in the general population and have asserted that the more intense post-traumatic stress disorder, like mental retardation, is pathological in the sense of representing the extreme tail of the distribution.[221] Others have tendered suggestions that the diagnosis not be made until

---

215. *Id.* at 409.

216. Paul S. Appelbaum et al., *Use of Post-traumatic Stress Disorder to Support an Insanity Defense*, 150 Am. J. Psychiatry 229 (1993). In terms of frequency, NGRI offenses were neither more violent, gender related, nor victimless for persons with PTSD than for those with other diagnoses. *Id.* at 231. There was a nonsignificant trend for PTSD defendants' cases to be tried by a jury and to result in a guilty finding (reflecting, perhaps, some skepticism about claims of legal insanity based on PTSD). *Id.* at 232.

217. A paper discussing the work of the DSM–IV work group on Anxiety disorders noted that "acute PTSD symptoms . . . could be viewed as a normal response to an abnormal event. [A]n acute PTSD reaction may well be an expected response to trauma and should not be uncritically applied as a psychiatric diagnosis." *Refining Criteria, supra* note 182, at 260. The "normality" of PTSD symptoms has also been challenged in terms of their comparability to emotional reactions to lesser life stresses. *See, e.g.,* Solomon & Canino, *supra* note 182.

218. *See* Behar, *supra* note 173, at 459 (citing 15 studies of disaster victims in which little or no symptomatology remained after a few months time had passed, and studies of Cambodian concentration camp victims revealing significant recovery after one year's time).

219. Measures of general or global psychopathology correlate in the .50–.60 range with PTSD, suggesting that general psychological stress, and not simply a tight set of PTSD symptoms, define the syndrome. Foy et al., *supra* note 194, at 34.

220. *See supra* note 165.

221. "Like mental retardation, posttraumatic stress disorder appears to be the extreme end of a normal distribution. Everybody who experiences adverse events responds to them emotionally." Lee N. Robins, *Steps Toward Evaluating Post-traumatic Stress Reaction as a Psychiatric Disorder*, 20 J. Applied Soc. Psychol. 1674, 1675 (1990).

symptoms have been present for at least three months.[222] However, the recently promulgated DSM–IV requires only one month of symptom duration for the diagnosis, and also adds a new diagnostic category (Acute Stress Disorder) for persons whose symptoms last up to one month.[223] Because of a variety of conceptual and design problems, the data are mixed regarding the prevalence of PTSD. A major epidemiological study conducted in the United States estimated the lifetime prevalence for PTSD at 1% for the general population, 3.5% in victims of physical attack, and 20% in Vietnam veterans who were wounded in combat.[224] A more recent study using DSM–IV criteria (which estimated the lifetime prevalence of exposure to one or more traumatic events as 89.6%[225]), estimated the probability of developing PTSD as a result of a traumatic exposure was 9.2% for women and 6.2% for men, which may be explained by the higher risk for PTSD for women following exposure to assaultive violence.[226] Major reviews have summarized prevalence data from studies of war, refugee, abuse, and disaster groups,[227] but rates from various studies are discordant for a variety of reasons, leading reviewers to conclude that "epidemiologists have failed to reach a consensus about the prevalence of the disorder."[228]

There has been increased attention to the neuroanatomical features of PTSD, including studies on structural brain changes in persons with PTSD and the impact of neurotransmitters, particularly norepinephrine release.[229] A review of studies on PTSD found support for decreased hippocampal volume (size of the brain structure associated with memory and possibly to emotional expression),[230] but there is currently no agreement regarding the dominant area of the hippocampus where reduction is significant.[231] Other researchers

---

222. When this suggestion was made during the revision process for the DSM, it was rejected in part due to concern that a three-month requirement "might make access to treatment more difficult." *Refining Criteria*, *supra* note 182, at 260. Because access to treatment is significantly related to access to third party reimbursement for mental health service providers, the latter position may illustrate how economic and social policy considerations can influence otherwise "scientific" decisions about whether or not something gets labeled a disorder.

223. DSM–IV, *supra* note 1, at 429.

224. James E. Helzer et al., *Post-traumatic Stress Disorder in the General Population: Findings of the Epidemiologic Catchment Area Survey*, 87 New Eng. J. Med. 1630 (1987).

225. Naomi Breslau et al., *Trauma and Posttraumatic Stress Disorder in the Community: The 1996 Detroit Area Survey of Trauma*, 55 Arch. Gen. Psychiatry 626, 627 (1996).

226. *See id.* at 817.

227. Posttraumatic Stress Disorder, *supra* note 153, at 22.

228. *Id.* at 13.

229. *See generally* J. Douglas Bremner et al., *Positron Emission Tomography Measurement of Cerebral Metabolic Correlates of Yohimbine Administration in Combat–Related*

Posttraumatic Stress Disorder, 54 Archives Gen. Psychiatry 246 (1997) (finding that administration of yohumbine, an adrenergic antagonist, resulted in increased anxiety in PTSD patients compared to healthy controls, and generated significantly different metabolic responses in various brain regions for PTSD patients); Scott L. Rauch & Lisa M. Shin, *Functional Neuroimaging Studies in Posttraumatic Stress Disorder*, 821 Annals N.Y. Acad. Sci. 83 (1997) (reviewing studies using neuroimaging techniques on the brain structure and function for persons with numerous psychiatric disorders, including PTSD).

230. Scott P. Orr & Roger K. Pitman, *Neurocognitive Risk Factors for PTSD*, in Risk Factors for Posttraumatic Stress Disorder 131–34 (Rachel Yehuda ed., 1999) (summarizing study findings on hippocampal reductions and concluding that findings "thus far supports a relationship between smaller hippocampal volume and severity of trauma exposure and/or PTSD symptomatology").

231. Murray B. Stein et al., *Structural Brain Changes in PTSD: Does Trauma Alter Neuroanatomy*, 821 Annals N.Y. Acad. Sci. 76, 77–78 (1997) (describing results of various studies with combat veterans showing that they have significantly reduced hippocampal volume bilaterally, left-sided or right-sided depending on the study, while studies with wom-

have suggested structural changes in the brains of persons with PTSD, including the presence of focal lesions.[232] Nevertheless, these findings are not yet conclusive because of the high rate of co-occurrence of PTSD with other disorders, and the associated difficulty in isolating the impact of PTSD alone. Further research must address the possibility that preexisting or otherwise co-occurring psychiatric or neurological disorders account for such structural brain changes, rather than the traumatic exposure or PTSD alone.[233]

There is also concern in the field that measures developed to diagnose PTSD either for research purposes or for treatment may not be adequate for forensic assessments. As noted, most of the structured measures developed to date are self-report scales and questionnaires.[234] Many have not been examined in terms of their susceptibility to feigning, while others have been found vulnerable to malingering.[235] These concerns have led some to suggest that psychophysiologic testing be an integral part of forensic assessments as a way of establishing evidence for the disorder that is less susceptible to the client's conscious manipulations.[236]

§ 1–2.5 Multiple Personality Disorder (Also Called Dissociative Identity Disorder)

§ 1–2.5.1 Introduction

The notion that an individual might have more than one personality capable of exerting autonomous control over the individual's behavior has considerable longevity. Clinical literature in the early nineteenth century discussed such notions as trance states, possession, and double consciousness,[237] and popular writings since then have described the same traits.[238] But it was not until 1980, with the publication of the third edition of the

en subjected to severe childhood trauma reduction found significant reductions limited to the left side of the hippocampus).

232. Jose M. Canive et al., *MRI Reveals Gross Structural Abnormalities in PTSD*, 821 ANNALS N.Y. ACAD. SCI. 512, 512–13 (1997) (comparing MRI results of forty-two outpatients with combat-related PTSD to twenty healthy controls and finding white matter disease present in eight PTSD patients and cortical atrophy in two PTSD patients).

233. *See id.* at 514.

234. *See supra* § 1–2.4.2[1][a].

235. One of the initially more promising diagnostic scales was an MMPI subscale: T.M. Keane et al., *The Empirical Development of an MMPI Subscale for the Assessment of Combat-related Post-traumatic Stress Disorder*, 52 J. CONSULTING & CLINICAL PSYCHOL. 888 (1984). However, several limitations of the scale have since been revealed in studies: (a) finding questionable utility with persons exposed to other traumatic events—Robert J. McCaffrey, Edward J. Hickling & Martin J. Marrazo, *Civilian-related Post-traumatic Stress Disorder: Assessment Related Issues*, 45 J. CLINICAL PSYCHOL. 72 (1989); (b) showing that feigned PTSD could not be adequately detected—Stephen T.

Perconte & Anthony J. Goreczny, *Failure to Detect Fabricated Posttraumatic Stress Disorder with the Use of the MMPI in a Clinical Population*, 147 AM. J. PSYCHIATRY 1057 (1990); and (c) failing to replicate the original findings regarding diagnostic validity—William F. Gayton et al., *An Investigation of the Utility of an MMPI Posttraumatic Stress Disorder Subscale*, 42 J. CLINICAL PSYCHOL. 916 (1986); Rodney D. Vanderploeg et al., *A Reevaluation of the Use of the MMPI in the Assessment of Combat-related Posttraumatic Stress Disorder*, 51 J. PERSONALITY ASSESSMENT 140 (1987).

236. Roger K. Pitman & Scott P. Orr, *Psychophysiologic Testing for Post-traumatic Stress Disorder: Forensic Psychiatric Application*, 21 BULL. AM. ACAD. PSYCHIATRY & L. 37 (1993); *see* Scott P. Orr & Roger K. Pitman, *Psychophysiologic Assessment of Attempts to Simulate Posttraumatic Stress Disorder*, 33 BIOLOGICAL PSYCHIATRY 127 (1993) (demonstrating difficulty feigning psychophysiological responses in a laboratory study).

237. Ian Hacking, *Double Consciousness in Britain 1815–1875*, 4 DISSOCIATION: PROGRESS IN THE DISSOCIATIVE DISORDERS 134 (1991).

238. CORBETT H. THIGPEN & HERVEY M. CLECKLEY, THE THREE FACES OF EVE (1957).

Diagnostic and Statistical Manual of Mental Disorders,[239] that organized psychiatry formally recognized multiple personality disorder. The recently published DSM–IV continues to recognize the disorder,[240] although the name has been changed to Dissociative Identity Disorder. This review will use the more widely known term multiple personality disorder (MPD).

MPD comes under the rubric of dissociative disorders. DSM–IV states that "[t]he essential feature of these disorders is a disruption in the usually integrated functions of consciousness, memory, identity, or perception of the environment. The disturbance may be sudden or gradual, transient or chronic."[241] Although MPD is only one of five dissociative disorders in the DSM–IV,[242] it will be the focus of this review because research on the other four disorders is almost non-existent. The DSM–IV lists four criteria for this diagnosis:

A.   The presence of two or more distinct identities or personality states (each with its own relatively enduring pattern of perceiving, relating to, and thinking about the environment and self).

B.   At least two of these identities or personality states recurrently take control of the person's behavior.

C.   Inability to recall important personal information that is too extensive to be explained by ordinary forgetfulness.

D.   The disturbance is not due to the direct physiological effects of a substance (e.g., blackouts or chaotic behavior during Alcohol Intoxication) or a general medical condition (e.g., complex partial seizures).[243]

In clinical parlance, the individual's birth identity is most commonly referred to as the "host" and other identities or personality states are referred to as "alters." The alters are usually, but not always, other human identities.[244]

It is hypothesized that alter personalities are created during childhood as mechanisms for coping with extreme trauma (e.g., physical or sexual abuse)

---

239.   DSM–III, *supra* note 155.

240.   DSM–IV, *supra* note 1. Despite the recent change in nomenclature, in this chapter we will utilize the more familiar term Multiple Personality Disorder (MPD), because it is more frequently found in the scientific literature.

241.   *Id.* at 477.

242.   The four other dissociative disorders and DSM–IV descriptions are as follows:

Dissociative Amnesia is characterized by an inability to recall important personal information, usually of a traumatic or stressful nature, that is too extensive to be explained by ordinary forgetfulness.

Dissociative Fugue is characterized by sudden, unexpected travel away from home or one's customary place of work, accompanied by an inability to recall one's past and confusion about personal identity or the assumption of a new identity.

Depersonalization Disorder is characterized by a persistent or recurrent feeling of being detached from one's mental processes or body that is accompanied by intact reality testing.

The remaining DSM–IV dissociative disorder is **Dissociative Disorder Not Otherwise Specified**, for classification of individuals with a prominent dissociative symptom who do not meet criteria for MPD (Dissociative Identity Disorder) or the other three specific diagnoses noted above.

Id.

243.   *Id.* An additional exclusion criterion regarding the diagnosis in children includes a finding that symptoms are not attributable to imaginary playmates or other fantasy play.

244.   Some MPD individuals manifest one or more animal alters. *See, e.g.,* Kate M. Hendrickson, *Teresita McCarty & Jean M. Goodwin, Animal Alters: Case Reports,* 3 DISSOCIATION: PROGRESS IN THE DISSOCIATIVE DISORDERS 218 (1990).

when other, less radical mechanisms fail to deal with the stress.[245] Alter personality states represent a compartmentalization of experience that isolates the host from the emotional trauma of the abuse (thus explaining the amnesia frequently reported by the hosts). Because alters are created as a defense to trauma and reappear later in life, some have argued that MPD should be considered a variant of post-traumatic stress disorder (PTSD),[246] discussed in the previous section.

A finding of multiple personality disorder has several implications for mental state defenses such as insanity and diminished capacity.[247] The first concern is an important conceptual one: do the host and various alters constitute distinct personalities residing within the same body, or do they simply represent different aspects of a fragmented whole? If distinct personalities exist, then the question arises whether one personality (e.g., the host) can be held morally responsible for actions under control of another (e.g., an alter); if, on the other hand, the host and alters are viewed as different aspects of the same personality, then arguably only a single entity exists for purposes of legal responsibility. A second important issue is the nature of the justification. Is exculpation warranted simply by the fact that the person's behavior was under the control of an alter (i.e., the host could not conform conduct because the alter was "in control"), or must whatever personality (host or alter) that was "in control" at the time of the offense be shown to have specific deficits described in the relevant insanity formulation (e.g., the alter couldn't distinguish right-from-wrong at the time of the offense)? These considerations challenge mental health professionals to untangle, in a retrospective evaluation, the power relationship between the host and alter personalities and the cognitive and volitional capacities and impairments of each personality state.

§ 1–2.5.2 Introductory Discussion of the Science

[1] The Scientific Questions

[a] Questions Studied

Efforts to study MPD scientifically are relatively recent; virtually all of the important studies have been published in the past 20 years. Further, progress has been hampered by the lack of systematic methods for making the diagnosis. Nonetheless, researchers have addressed diverse issues, including the epidemiology of MPD and the characteristics of persons who suffer from MPD. Further, efforts to standardize criteria for diagnosing MPD have led to

245. Richard P. Kluft, *Treatment of Multiple Personality Disorder: A Study of 33 Cases*, 7 PSYCHIATRIC CLINICS N. AM. 9, 14 (1984)[hereinafter *Treatment*]; Richard P. Kluft, *An Update on Multiple Personality Disorder*, 38 HOSPITAL & COMMUNITY PSYCHIATRY 363, 366 (1987)[hereinafter, *Update*].

246. *Id.*

247. For discussions of the potential legal aspects of MPD, *see* Stephen H. Dinwiddie et al., *Multiple Personality Disorder: Scientific and Medicolegal Issues*, 21 BULL. AM. ACAD.

PSYCHIATRY & L. 69 (1993); Dorothy O. Lewis & Jennifer S. Bard, *Multiple Personality and Forensic Issues*, 14 PSYCHIATRY CLINICS OF NORTH AMERICA 741 (1991); Jill O. Radwin, *The Multiple Personality Disorder: Has this Trendy Alibi Lost Its Way?*, 15 L. & PSYCHOL. REV. 351 (1991); Irwin N. Perr, *Crime and Multiple Personality Disorder: A Case History and Discussion*, 19 BULL. AM. ACAD. PSYCHIATRY & L. 203 (1991). Professor Perr also discusses a number of appellate cases dealing with MPD and criminal responsibility. *Id.* at 209–213.

the development of a number of scales and structured interviews that may facilitate such research in the future. The most promising screening measure is the Dissociative Experiences Survey (DES).[248] Although not intended as a diagnostic instrument, a meta-analysis of 100 studies suggests that the DES has good discriminant validity (distinguishing MPD from other diagnostic groups),[249] and may also have some utility as a screening device.[250] Comprehensive diagnostic interview instruments have also been developed,[251] although there are relatively few reports of their use in the literature.[252]

The literature also reflects a number of attempts to identify psychophysiological correlates of MPD. Researchers in these studies typically obtain a sample of persons diagnosed with MPD who are judged clinically capable of "producing" the host personality or any of several alter personality states at the request of the investigator. The host and one or more alters are then tested and compared on any of several psychophysiological measures such as EEG[253] or ophthalmological responses.[254] The theoretical basis for such studies is the supposition that dissociation involves a fundamental psychophysiological process that produces alterations of consciousness.[255] Discovery and documentation of specific psychophysiological correlates would provide evidence to support the construct of MPD as a "disease" and provide objective laboratory indices to aid in diagnosis.

Finally, some clinicians have looked at treatment of MPD. However, the literature on this subject is almost completely anecdotal, consisting of case reports and theoretical or descriptive papers from individual clinicians who have worked with large numbers of persons suffering from MPD. Most often mentioned as the treatment approach of choice is long term, dynamic therapy, which usually must be highly individualized because of concomitant disorders. The goal of therapy is the fusion of the fragmented personality states into a

---

248. Eve M. Bernstein & Frank W. Putnam, *Development, Reliability, and Validity of a Dissociation Scale*, 174 J. NERVOUS & MENTAL DISEASE 727 (1986). Another brief measure is the Questionnaire of Experiences of Dissociation, described in Kevin C. Riley, *Measurement of Dissociation*, 176 J. NERVOUS & MENTAL DISEASE 449 (1988).

249. COLIN A. ROSS, DISSOCIATIVE IDENTITY DISORDER: DIAGNOSIS, CLINICAL FEATURES, AND TREATMENT OF MULTIPLE PERSONALITY 173 (2d ed. 1997) [hereinafter DISSOCIATIVE IDENTITY].

250. Eve B. Carlson et al., *Validity of the Dissociative Experiences Scale in Screening for Multiple Personality Disorder: A Multicenter Study*, 150 AM. J. PSYCHIATRY 1030 (1993).

251. Richard J. Lowenstein, *An Office Mental Status Examination for Complex Chronic Dissociative Symptoms and Multiple Personality Disorder*, 14 PSYCHIATRY CLINICS N. AM. 567 (1991); Colin A. Ross et al., *The Dissociative Disorders Interview Schedule: A Structured Interview*, 2 DISSOCIATION: PROGRESS IN THE DISSOCIATIVE DISORDERS 169 (1989); Marlene Steinberg et al., *The Structured Clinical Interview for DSM–III Dissociative Disorders: Preliminary Report on a New Diagnostic Instrument*, 147 AM. J. PSYCHIATRY 76 (1990). Ross provides a

general overview of the validity and reliability of various structured interviews and self-report measures of dissociation, including the Dissociative Experiences Scale, the Dissociative Questionnaire, the Dissociative Disorders Interview Schedule and the Structured Clinical Interview for DSM–IV Dissociative Disorders, and emphasizes that further research is necessary for each of these instruments. DISSOCIATIVE IDENTITY, *supra* note 249, at 167–77.

252. Colin A. Ross et al., *Differences Between Multiple Personality Disorder and Other Diagnostic Groups on Structured Interview*, 177 J. NERVOUS & MENTAL DISEASE 487 (1989) [hereinafter *Differences*].

253. Philip M. Coons et al., *Multiple Personality Disorder: A Clinical Investigation of 50 Cases*, 176 J. NERVOUS & MENTAL DISEASE 519, 523 (1988) (reporting that only 7 of 30 persons with MPD had abnormal EEGs).

254. Scott D. Miller, *Optical Differences in Cases of Multiple Personality Disorder*, 177 J. NERVOUS & MENTAL DISEASE 480 (1989).

255. Jean Franklin, *The Diagnosis of Multiple Personality Disorder Based on Subtle Dissociative Signs*, 178 J. NERVOUS & MENTAL DISEASE 4, 5 (1990).

single, integrated personality.[256] Rigorous, controlled treatment studies with random assignment of MPD clients to different forms of therapy have not been reported.[257]

[b] Questions Not Yet Studied

Several questions about MPD that are of considerable interest to both science and the law have not been studied to date. For example, science has yet to develop operational definitions that permit the objective measurement of basic MPD processes. MPD experts assert that various alters may "take control" of the person's functioning from time to time—indeed this phenomenon must occur to meet the DSM–IV diagnostic criteria. However, there is no objective measure to verify when, whether, and to what degree a person with MPD has passed control from one personality state to another. Rather the degree of control is assumed based on relatively subjective measures such as whether the person begins behaving differently, announces the emergence of a different alter, or responds only to a different name. These indicators permit an inference, or a professional judgment, that some basic change in the underlying executive function of personality has occurred, but preclude direct measurement of the presumed/inferred changes in personality "control."

Similarly, there are no scientific techniques for measuring the impact or influence of one personality state upon another. Clinical case reports reveal that some hosts are unaware of the presence or activities of at least some of their alters; when the host personality is questioned about the emergence or behavior of certain alters, the host denies any knowledge of the alter or its activities, but may acknowledge a break in the stream of consciousness and amnesia for that period when the alter was "in control." However, other case reports suggest that the alters may communicate with one another and "listen in" on the experiences of each other or those of the host. Some suggest that the alters may subtly influence the host or one another without fully taking control.[258] All accounts of this type are clinical anecdotes and reflect the judgments and inferences of mental health professionals about what may be going on inside the person with MPD.

Also of interest to the law might be studies of the cognitive abilities and moral/legal decision-making abilities of the host and different alter personalities. Individuals might be tested in their different personality states on tasks of logical or abstract reasoning, rational thinking, level of moral development, and so forth. Such findings might arguably be relevant to judgments about the legal responsibility of persons with MPD. Comparisons among the host

---

256. *Update, supra* note 245, 370–371.

257. "Several treatment approaches have been described, but none has been assessed with rigorous methodologies or along objective dimensions. There are no studies comparing the efficacy of one approach with that of another." *Treatment, supra* note 245, at 9. "[C]ontrolled outcome studies have not been conducted ..." Colin Ross et al., *Multiple Personality Disorder: An Analysis of 236 Cases*, 34 CAN. J. PSYCHIATRY 413, 417 (1989).

258. Alters " ... suggest their presence by partly emerging, subtly switching, rapidly fluc-

tuating in and out, or influencing each other by transferring personality elements (behaviors, sensations, affects, thoughts, and memories) from one to another. These changes represent the camouflaged, indirect expressions of their multiple identities." *Id.* at 5. *See also* Jean Franklin, *Diagnosis of Covert and Subtle Forms of Multiple Personality Disorder Through Dissociative Signs*, 1 DISSOCIATION: PROGRESS IN THE DISSOCIATIVE DISORDERS 27 (1988).

and various alter personalities have been attempted using general psychological tests (e.g., intelligence tests, personality tests),[259] but the literature is relatively barren with respect to examinations of the specific cognitive and moral/legal abilities of hosts and various alters.

[2] Scientific Methods Applied in the Research

Research on MPD has been limited to human subjects. The important issues in MPD are closely tied to individuals' phenomenology, and research measures are largely limited to verbal report. Thus, the study of MPD does not lend itself easily to animal analogue studies.

Much of the early literature regarding MPD consists of descriptive case reports of individual cases or small samples. In recent years large sample descriptive studies that report historical and behavioral features of persons with MPD have been undertaken, although some of these studies fail to use the control groups that are needed to compare the performance of MPD subjects on outcome measures (e.g., those with other psychiatric diagnoses or no diagnosis). In those that do have controls, the research has been primarily correlational in nature; between-groups differences have been attributed to differences in diagnoses that define the groups, but other ways in which the groups might differ have not been measured or controlled to rule out potential competing explanations.

Research on the etiology of MPD is particularly difficult to conduct. Obviously, ethical considerations preclude experimental manipulations that would expose infants or children to differential levels of trauma in order to study whether dissociative symptoms develop. Similarly, ethical and therapeutic consideration preclude withholding treatment from abused children in an effort to investigate the development and course of MPD or other trauma-related disturbances. Therefore, research concerning the role of childhood trauma in the development of MPD is necessarily correlational in nature and relies considerably on retrospective reports of persons diagnosed with MPD later in life.[260]

---

259. *See, e.g.*, Susan M. Labott et al., *Rorschach Indicators of Multiple Personality Disorder*, 75 PERCEPTUAL AND MOTOR SKILLS 147 (1992) (failing to validate proposed diagnostic signs for MPD on the Rorschach Inkblot Test); Judith G. Armstrong & Richard J. Lowenstein, *Characteristics of Patients with Multiple Personality and Dissociative Disorders on Psychological Testing*, 178 J. NERVOUS & MENTAL DISEASE 448 (1990). Much of the literature on use of psychological testing of MPDs to establish the presence of valid and distinct alter personality states is methodologically weak. Rorschach studies reviewed by Armstrong & Lowenstein, *id.* at 449, reported on extremely small numbers of subjects (1 to 4) which precludes meaningful statistical analysis; the authors' own study examined 14 subjects with MPD, which they indicate is well below the recommended number of 75 per group for adequate statistical power, and they had no control group. They also failed to specify in advance the specific indicators on the Rorschach that would confirm or disconfirm their hypotheses about the testing behavior of persons with MPD.

260. Frank Putnam et al., *The Clinical Phenomenology of Multiple Personality Disorder: Review of 100 Cases*, 47 J. CLIN. PSYCHIATRY 285, 289 (1986) (89% of adult MPDs reported that their alter appeared before age 12). *See also* Barbara Sanders & Marina H. Giolas, *Dissociation and Childhood Trauma in Psychologically Disturbed Adolescents*, 148 AM. J. PSYCHIATRY 50 (1991) (in a sample of 47 adolescents, a significant, positive correlation was found between self-reported dissociative symptoms and self-reported childhood abuse/trauma; no significant association was found, however, when level of abuse/trauma was measured using staff ratings based on review of historical and chart information).

More generally, progress in research on MPD suffers from the same inherent problem that plagues research on psychodynamic formulations—the defining aspects of the disorder are virtually all covert entities and internal processes[261] that have thus far defied objective measurement. As one group of critics noted,

> we are left with a syndrome that clinicians ultimately diagnose based on their beliefs about an underlying "intrapsychic structure" rather than observable, overt phenomena, an approach that historically has hardly lent itself . . . to rigorous investigation.[262]

§ 1–2.5.3 Areas of Scientific Agreement

Only one epidemiological study of MPD has apparently been conducted to date; it suggests that the lifetime prevalence of MPD is about 1% of persons in the general population.[263] However, a review of other studies in the literature, which use selected populations (e.g., hospital or clinical samples) indicates that other researchers have estimated a higher prevalence rate for MPD, ranging from 3% to 11%,[264] and about 5% for general psychiatric patients.[265] The disorder is more prevalent among women than among men,[266] and the typical person with MPD has multiple alters.[267] The overwhelming majority of persons with MPD report a history of physical or sexual abuse during childhood.[268] Co-morbidity with other psychiatric disorders is quite common, particularly depressive disorders, borderline personality disorder, and somatization disorder.[269]

261. "The irreducible core of MPD is a persistent form of intrapsychic structure rather than overt behavioral manifestations. . . ." Richard P. Kluft, *Clinical Presentations of Multiple Personality Disorder*, 14 PSYCHIATRIC CLINICS N. AM. 605, 609 (1991).

262. Dinwiddie, et al., *supra* note 247, at 73.

263. Colin A. Ross, *Epidemiology of Multiple Personality Disorder and Dissociation*, 14 PSYCHIATRIC CLINICS N. AM. 503, 509 (1991) (about 10% of the persons surveyed met DSM–III–R criteria for dissociative disorder of some kind). Ross cautions that the 1% estimate is a "conservative interpretation of the data," as some respondents endorsed dissociative criteria but were not classified as Dissociative Identify Disorder for a variety of reasons, including their failure to endorse a history of trauma. DISSOCIATIVE IDENTITY, *supra* note 249, at 109.

264. *Id.* at 114.

265. *Id.* at 112 (noting that a review of the literature places prevalence of undiagnosed MPD among general psychiatric patients between 4% and 6%); Colin A. Ross et al., *The Frequency of Multiple Personality Disorder Among Psychiatric Patients*, 148 AM. J. PSYCHIATRY 1717 (1990). Ross and colleagues found 5.4% of 299 inpatients met diagnostic criteria for MPD. *Id.* at 1719. Several studies reviewed by these authors yielded estimates from 1%–5%, with a single study reporting an outlier estimate of 16%. *Id.* at 1717.

266. The ratio of women to men *diagnosed* with MPD is about 9:1. Coons et al., *supra* note 253, at 520 (reporting 92% women in the sample); *Differences*, *supra* note 252, at 414 (reporting 87.7% women in the sample); Colin A. Ross et al., *Structured Interview Data on 102 Cases of Multiple Personality Disorder from Four Centers*, 147 AM. J. PSYCHIATRY 596, 598 (1990) [hereinafter *Structured Interview*] (reporting 90.2% women in the sample).

267. In one study of 236 cases, the mean number of alters at the time of reporting was 15.7. *Differences*, *supra* note 252, at 415. The distribution of reported number of alters is positively skewed. Another study reported the mean number of alters was 13.3, but the median was only 9 and the mode (most commonly occurring frequency) was 3. Putnam et al., *supra* note 260, at 288.

268. In a study by Ross and colleagues, 79.2% of MPD subjects reported extensive sexual abuse and 74.9% reported extensive physical abuse. *Differences*, *supra* note 256, at 416. In another sample of 100 MPDs, 97% reported overwhelming and abusive experiences, Putnam et al., *supra* note 260, at 290. *See also* Coons et al., *supra* note 253, at 521 (96% of the sample reported physical or sexual abuse in childhood).

269. DISSOCIATIVE IDENTITY, *supra* note 249, at 178–215 (reviewing literature on comorbidity of MPD and other psychiatric disorders with a focus on borderline personality disorder and

Although limited, the data on the intellectual functioning of persons with MPD is uniform. Persons at all levels of intelligence may develop MPD and as a group MPDs do not have significant intellectual deficits.[270] Descriptive studies also note that persons with MPD frequently endorse some symptoms associated with schizophrenia, particularly auditory hallucinations.[271] However, some experts distinguish between the "voices" heard by persons with schizophrenia, which are typically described as originating "outside" the person's head, from those described by persons with MPD, which often take the form of commentaries or conversations inside the head; the latter are construed as commentaries by or conversations among alters.[272]

Significant controversy about the lack of psychophysiological substrata for MPD is also absent. Despite some suggestive studies, major reviews suggest that findings to date are mixed and inconclusive and that the research is limited due to weak methodology.[273] Currently there are no psychophysiological indicators that are clearly diagnostic of MPD.

§ 1–2.5.4 Areas of Scientific Disagreement

Although mental health professionals have long recognized that a variety of patients present one or more symptoms of dissociation, skepticism about MPD as a legitimate and distinct diagnoses persists, for a number of reasons.[274] First, as an historical matter, MPD has been characterized as a rare disorder.[275] Thus, contemporary skepticism is attributable in part to the exponential rate of the diagnosis in the literature between 1980 and 1986.[276]

schizophrenia). In one study that included 20 MPD patients, 7 (35%) met criteria for somatization disorder. Colin A. Ross et al., *Somatic Symptoms in Multiple Personality Disorder*, 30 PSYCHOSOMATICS 154, 157 (1989). A major review paper cited studies reporting co-morbidity for borderline personality at 15% and 70% in two studies. *Update, supra* note 245, at 368. Another study reported that 91% of 102 MPD subjects met criteria for major depression and 64% had borderline personality disorder. *Structured Interview, supra* note 266, at 598–99. MPD subjects also endorse symptoms thought to be primarily associated with schizophrenia, more frequently than do persons suffering from schizophrenia. Colin A. Ross et al., *Schneiderian Symptoms in Multiple Personality Disorder and Schizophrenia*, 31 COMPREHENSIVE PSYCHIATRY 111, 115 (1990) [hereinafter *Schneiderian*].

270. In a sample of 21 persons with MPD, the mean full scale IQ score on the Wechsler Adult Intelligence Scale was 101.8, with a range of 77–123. Coons et al., *supra* note 253, at 523.

271. *See Schneiderian, supra* note 269.

272. *Id.*

273. Scott D. Miller & Patrick J. Triggiano, *The Psychophysiological Investigation of Multiple Personality Disorder: Review and Update*, 35 AM. J. CLINICAL HYPNOSIS 47 (1992); Philip M. Coons, *Psychophysiologic Aspects of Multiple Personality Disorder: A Review*, 1 DISSOCIATION: PROGRESS IN THE DISSOCIATIVE DISORDERS 47 (1988).

274. Ross identifies twenty-five errors in "logic, argument and scholarship" in the criticisms of MPD. For example, Ross observes that the reported increase in the frequency of MPD diagnosis in the 1980s does not undermine the validity of MPD, as the rate is "neutral concerning the validity of the disorder." DISSOCIATIVE IDENTITY, *supra* note 249, at 226–44.

275. Compare "The disorder is apparently extremely rare." DSM–III, *supra* note 155, at 258; "Recent reports suggest that this disorder is not nearly so rare as it has commonly been thought to be." DIAGNOSTIC AND STATISTICAL MANUAL OF MENTAL DISORDERS 271 (3d ed. rev. 1987); "The sharp rise in reported cases of Dissociative Identity Disorder in the United States in recent years has been subject to very different interpretations." DSM–IV, *supra* note 1, at 486. One prominent researcher has asserted that pathologic dissociation appears to be about as common as anxiety, mood, and substance abuse disorders. Ross, *supra* note 263, at 503.

276. Ross and colleagues cited studies estimating that a total of 200 cases had been reported worldwide up until 1980, but that by 1986 more than 6000 cases had been diagnosed. *Differences, supra* note 252, at 487; *see* Martin T. Orne et al., *On the Differential Diagnosis of Multiple Personality in the Forensic Context*, 32 INT. J. CLINICAL & EXP. HYPNOSIS 118,

Second, skeptics are aware that, as noted above, subjective professional judgments play a significant role in the diagnosis of MPD.[277] Experienced psychiatrists working outside of major medical teaching centers where many of the large sample studies have been conducted have expressed concerns about the validity of the diagnosis,[278] and clinicians who work in the area of multiple personality disorder report frequent, and sometimes extreme expressions of skepticism from colleagues.[279] Finally, the frequent finding of other conditions co-morbid with MPD[280] suggests that it may not be a distinct diagnostic entity. Some have suggested that MPD really represents attention seeking behavior by persons suffering from hysteria,[281] or learned behavior that is reinforced by western media and culture.[282]

There is also controversy about how the diagnosis can or should be made. Some experts assert that the diagnosis usually cannot be made through routine psychiatric mental status interviews because most MPD patients initially try to hide their dissociative experiences.[283] Therefore, it is asserted, prolonged and even stressful interviewing may be needed to make the accurate diagnosis in some cases,[284] while prolonged observation over the course of therapy may be necessary in others.[285] However, these assertions are not based on findings from controlled studies, and they are complicated by other clinical warnings that "new" alter personalities may result from certain

119 (1984) (noting a variety of factors, e.g., increase in true prevalence, change in diagnostic criteria, shift in tendency to report, etc.).

277. *See supra* § 1–2.5.2[1][a].

278. Paul Chodoff, *Comment*, 144 Am. J. Psychiatry 124 (1987) (reporting having observed only one "very doubtful case" in forty years of practicing psychiatry, and informal polling of colleagues in private practice who report no, or at most 1–2 cases); Corbett H. Thigpen & Hervey M. Cleckley, *On the Incidence of Multiple Personality Disorder: A Brief Communication*, 32 Int. J. Clinical & Experimental Hypnosis 63 (1984) (reporting having seen only 1 case of MPD in "tens of thousands" of patients in over three decades of practicing psychiatry).

279. Paul F. Dell, *Professional Skepticism About Multiple Personality*, 176 J. Nervous & Mental Disease 528, 528–29 (1988) (reporting a mail survey of 120 members of the International Society for the Study of Multiple Personality Disorder. Of the 62 respondents, 83.2% reported having experienced "moderate to extreme" skepticism from colleagues; 52% had been told by one or more colleagues that "there is no such thing as multiple personality").

280. *See* John Lauer et al., *Multiple Personality Disorder and Borderline Personality Disorder: Distinct Entities or Variations on a Common Theme*, 5 Annals Clinical Psychiatry 129 (1993) (concluding that MPD may not be a valid diagnosis after finding that 14 persons with MPD and 13 with a diagnosis of borderline personality disorder showed few differences and many similarities on a variety of

clinical and demographic measures). Other investigators have found that MPD and borderline subjects are not distinguishable on conventional clinical measures such as the Brief Psychiatric Rating Scale and Minnesota Multiphasic Personality Inventory. Kristen Kemp et al., *Differential Diagnosis of Multiple Personality Disorder from Borderline Personality Disorder*, 1 Dissociation: Progress in the Dissociative Disorders 41 (1988). The negative findings of this study should be qualified by noting the small number of subjects (N=10) in each group being studied.

281. Thomas A. Fahy, *The Diagnosis of Multiple Personality Disorder: A Critical Review*, 153 Br. J. Psychiatry 597 (1988). Thigpen & Cleckley, *supra* note 278, at 64.

282. Nicholas P. Spanos et al., *Multiple Personality: A Social Psychological Perspective*, 94 J. Abnormal Psychol. 362 (1985).

283. Richard P. Kluft, *The Natural History of Multiple Personality Disorder, in* Childhood Antecedents of Multiple Personality 197, 211 (Richard P. Kluft, ed. 1985).

284. Richard P. Kluft, *The Simulation and Dissimulation of Multiple Personality Disorder*, 30 Am. J. Clinical Hypnosis 104 (1987) [hereinafter *Simulation*]; Richard P. Kluft, *Making the Diagnosis of Multiple Personality Disorder, in* Diagnosis and Psychopathology 207 (Frederic Flack, ed., 1987).

285. Philip M. Coons, *Iatrogenic Factors in the Misdiagnosis of Multiple Personality Disorder*, 2 Dissociation: Progress in the Dissociative Disorders 70 (1989).

interviewing techniques (e.g., leading questions)[286] or the traumatic impact of treatment or errors by the therapist.[287]

The literature also reflects a concern about the malingering of MPD,[288] particularly in the forensic context,[289] as well as disagreement about the clinical strategies to evaluate it.[290] Clinicians' impressions suggest that persons with MPD commonly present many of the behaviors thought to indicate malingering,[291] and at least one analogue study suggests that normal persons instructed to "fake bad" are able to feign MPD on common self-report measures of dissociation.[292] One study did describe evidence for MPD in a small sample of those who had committed homicide, finding evidence in clinical records, corroborated by third-party sources, for reported amnesia and underreporting of severe childhood or adulthood abuse in 11 of the 12 individuals studied.[293] Because of methodological limitations of the study (e.g., small sample size, selected population, absence of a comparison group or quantitative analysis), however, these results and their generalizability must be regarded with great caution.

§ 1–2.6 Selected Impulse Disorders: Pyromania, Kleptomania, and Pathological Gambling

§ 1–2.6.1 Introduction

A subset of mental disorders that could form the basis for an insanity defense, particularly in jurisdictions that retain a volitional (e.g., "irresistible impulse") test, are those characterized in the mental health field as impulse control disorders. In this section we review three such disorders: pyromania, kleptomania, and pathological gambling. In the contemporary psychiatric nosology found in the fourth edition of the Diagnostic and Statistical Manual of Mental Disorders (DSM–IV) these disorders are listed as "Impulse–Control Disorders Not Elsewhere Classified."[294] Although discrete criteria for each disorder are provided, the unifying characteristic of those disorders is "the

---

286. Philip M. Coons, *Iatrogenesis and Malingering of Multiple Personality Disorder in the Forensic Evaluation of Homicide Defendants*, 14 Psychiatric Clinics of North America 757 (1991).

287. Richard P. Kluft, *Iatrogenic Creation of New Alter Personalities*, 2 Dissociation: Progress in the Dissociative Disorders 83 (1991).

288. Susan S. Brick & James A. Chu, *The Simulation of Multiple Personalities: A Case Report*, 28 Psychotherapy 267 (1991) (describing a 15 year old patient who successfully feigned MPD for over 3 months).

289. "[I]t is extremely difficult-if not impossible-to be sure that a defendant who has not been in psychotherapy for the disorder really has multiple personality syndrome, since we have no firm criteria against which to measure him." Ralph B. Allison, *Difficulties Diagnosing the Multiple Personality Syndrome in a Death Penalty Case*, 32 Int. J. Clinical & Experimental Hypnosis 101, 115 (1984) (discussing

the controversy over the diagnosis of MPD in the famous Hillside Strangler case).

290. Renowned experts in the area of MPD disagree on the validity of strategies to detect malingering of MPD. *Compare* Orne et al., *supra* note 276, *with Simulation, supra* note 284.

291. *Simulation, supra* note 284.

292. Alan D. Gilbertson et al., *Susceptibility of Common Self-Report Measures of Dissociation to Malingering*, 5 Dissociation: Progress in the Dissociative Disorders 216 (1992).

293. Dorothy Otnow Lewis et al., *Objective Documentation of Child Abuse and Dissociation in 12 Murderers with Dissociative Identity Disorder*, 154 Am. J. Psychiatry 1703, 1705–07 (1997).

294. DSM–IV, *supra* note 1. Additional diagnoses in this category not covered in this review include Intermittent Explosive Disorder and Trichotillomania (compulsive hair pulling).

failure to resist an impulse, drive, or temptation to perform an act that is harmful to the person or to others."[295]

In the instances of pyromania and kleptomania, diagnostic criteria require the clinician to rule out other more common or "rational" motives for the problem behavior. The criteria for pyromania require a conclusion that "fire setting is not done for monetary gain, as an expression of sociopolitical ideology, to conceal criminal activity, to express anger or vengeance, to improve one's living circumstances."[296] Similarly, the diagnosis of kleptomania may only be made if the stolen objects "are not needed for personal use or their monetary value"[297] and the stealing "is not committed to express anger or vengeance."[298] Nor can these behaviors be in response to major cognitive or perceptual symptoms,[299] or "better accounted for by Conduct Disorder, a Manic Episode, or Antisocial Personality Disorder."[300] Rather, internal motivations involving arousal and reduction of tension are required for these diagnoses.[301]

Pathological gambling also involves affective components of this type. To fit this diagnosis, the person must gamble "in order to achieve the desired excitement," and must be "restless or irritable when attempting to cut down or stop gambling," or gamble "as a way of . . . relieving a dysphoric mood (e.g., feelings of helplessness, guilt, anxiety, depression)."[302] The subjective experience of the pathological gambler includes obsessive/compulsive features, in the sense that the individual "is preoccupied with gambling" and "has repeated unsuccessful efforts to control, cut back, or stop gambling."[303] The diagnosis also involves ruling out gambling behavior attributable to a Manic Episode.[304]

Further, none of these diagnoses are appropriate if the person's misconduct stems from significant cognitive or perceptual distortions (delusions, hallucinations). Persons who have kleptomania "know" that stealing is illegal and do not feel justified in their actions, just as persons who suffer from pyromania "know" that it is illegal and wrong to set fires that destroy property or harm others. Persons who suffer from pathological gambling and who become involved in illegal acts such as forgery, fraud, theft, or embezzlement in order to finance their gambling habit also "know" that such activities are in violation of the law. Thus, to the degree that these disorders may be asserted as the basis for the insanity defense, the focus is on the issue of volition rather than cognizance of "right or wrong" in a cognitive or moral sense.

295. *Id.*

296. *Id.* at 615.

297. *Id.* at 613.

298. *Id.*

299. *Id.* at 613, 615.

300. *Id.*

301. For kleptomania the person experiences an "[i]ncreasing sense of tension immediately before committing the theft" and "[p]leasure, gratification, or relief at the time of committing the theft." *Id.* at 613. For pyromania the person experiences "[t]ension or affective arousal before the act" and "[p]leasure, gratification, or relief when setting fires, or when witnessing or participating in their aftermath." *Id.* at 615.

302. *Id.* at 618.

303. *Id.*

304. *Id.*

§ 1–2.6.2 Introductory Discussion of the Science

[1] The Scientific Questions

[a] Questions Studied

There has been little systematic, scientific study of any of the impulse disorders considered in this section.[305] Pathological gambling has been studied more than either kleptomania and pyromania, despite the fact that it was the last of the three to be recognized as a disorder (in the 1980 edition of the DSM (DSM–III)). There have been efforts to develop interview guides or assessment instruments to aid in the diagnosis of pathological gambling,[306] as well as some preliminary epidemiological studies.[307] As described below, other research efforts have been directed at identifying (1) personality features (e.g., proneness to boredom, sensation seeking) hypothesized to characterize persons diagnosed with pathological gambling and (2) other diagnoses that are common among people who are in treatment for pathological gambling ("psychiatric co-morbidity").

With respect to pyromania and kleptomania, a wealth of clinical anecdotes, self-descriptions and psychoanalytic speculations about unconscious motives exist, but little rigorous research can be found. In part, this paucity of data is probably due to the rarity of these disorders. One recent article reported that a comprehensive review of the English language literature on kleptomania yielded a total of 26 case reports of persons diagnosed with this disorder,[308] a more extensive review that scanned literature published in English, German and French languages yielded a total of 56 case reports.[309] Similarly, recent efforts to examine the prevalence of fire setting in the histories of persons hospitalized for psychiatric disorder have yielded few if any cases that meet operational criteria for pyromania.[310]

---

305. Two of the better reviews of the disorders discussed in this section are Michael J. Popkin, *Impulse Control Disorders Not Elsewhere Classified, in* 2 COMPREHENSIVE TEXTBOOK OF PSYCHIATRY-V, 1145–1154 (Benjamin J. Sadock ed., 1989), Susan L. McElroy et al., *The DSM-III Impulse Control Disorders Not Elsewhere Classified: Clinical Characterization and Relationship to Other Psychiatric Disorders,* 149 AM. J. PSYCHIATRY 318 (1992) [hereinafter *Clinical Characteristics*]. Professor Popkin noted that these disorders " . . . have been the subject of much theorizing and speculation but distressingly little systematic study." Popkin, *supra,* at 1145. McElroy and colleagues echoed this appraisal, noting that " . . . as a group [these disorders] remain poorly studied." McElroy et al., *supra,* at 319.

306. Henry R. Lesieur & Sheila B. Blume, *The South Oaks Gambling Screen (SOGS): A New Instrument for the Identification of Pathological Gamblers,* 144 AM. J. PSYCHIATRY 1184 (1987); Edward E. Johnson et al., *The Lie/Bet Questionnaire for Screening Pathological Gamblers: A Follow–Up Study,* 83 PSYCHOL. REP.

1219, 1219–24 (1998), Jeffrey I. Kassinove, *Development of the Gambling Attitude Scales: Preliminary* Findings, 54 J. CLINICAL PSYCH. 763, 763–71 (1998); Rachel A. Volberg & Steven M. Banks, *A Review of Two Measures of Pathological Gambling in the United States,* 6 J. GAMBLING STUDIES 153 (1990).

307. Robert Ladouceur, *Prevalence Estimates of Pathological Gambling in Quebec,* 36 CAN. J. PSYCHIATRY 732 (1991); R.C. Bland et al., *Epidemiology of Pathological Gambling in Edmonton,* 38 CAN. J. PSYCHIATRY 108 (1993).

308. Marcus J. Goldman, *Kleptomania: Making Sense of the Non-sensical,* 148 AM. J. PSYCHIATRY 986 (1991).

309. Susan L. McElroy et al., *Kleptomania: Clinical Characteristics and Associated Psychopathology,* 21 PSYCHOL. MED. 93 (1991).

310. *See e.g.,* Jeffrey L. Geller, *Firesetting in the Adult Psychiatric Population,* 38 HOSPITAL & COMMUNITY PSYCHIATRY 501 (1987); Jeffrey L. Geller et al., *Adult Lifetime Prevalence of Firesetting Behaviors in a State Hospital Population,* 63 PSYCHIATRIC Q. 129 (1992).

[b]   Questions Not Yet Studied

As suggested in the previous section, in connection with kleptomania and pyromania, no controlled studies of age of onset, family history, heritability, treatability, or psychiatric co-morbidity exist. With the exceptions noted above and below, much the same is true regarding pathological gambling.

[2]   Scientific Methods Applied in the Research

The scientific literature on kleptomania is limited almost exclusively to case studies.[311] Due to the small number of cases reported,[312] neither experimental nor correlational studies involving control groups have been published. Similarly, the literature on pyromania is largely limited to case reports and a few surveys of the incidence of firesetting in the histories of persons in psychiatric hospitals.[313]

The literature on pathological gambling is somewhat more extensive. The availability of potential research subjects through self-help (e.g., Gamblers Anonymous) or other (i.e., professional) treatment programs has permitted some studies with appropriate control groups (e.g., "problem gamblers," normals). These studies involve primarily correlational designs, contrasting groups on dependent measures of personality or psychopathology. Even with pathological gambling, however, the availability of controlled studies with rigorous experimental designs is quite limited.

§ 1–2.6.3   Areas of Scientific Agreement

Kleptomania

As noted, there are few "scientific" findings regarding kleptomania. One study reporting data on a modest size sample (n=20) found a mean age of 36 years and a mean frequency of 27–33 episodes per month of stealing.[314] Interestingly, however, 100% of this sample also met diagnostic criteria for mood disorder. Among reported cases the disorder is more prevalent among women than men.[315] Few persons arrested for shoplifting meet diagnostic criteria for this disorder.[316]

Pyromania

With respect to pyromania, two separate studies on the lifetime prevalence of fire-setting in the histories of state hospital psychiatric patients have

311.   "In our recent review of the literature, we found no systematic studies of a series of rigorously diagnosed kleptomanic individuals." Susan L. McElroy et al., *Kleptomania: A Report of 20 Cases*, 148 AM. J. PSYCHIATRY 652 (1991) [hereinafter *Kleptomania*].

312.   The largest reported sample of persons with diagnosed kleptomania consists of 20 individuals. *Id.*

313.   *See supra* § 1–2.6.2[1][a].

314.   *Kleptomania, supra* note 311, at 653.

315.   One review reported that women constituted 81% of reported cases. Marcus J. Goldman, *Kleptomania: An Overview*, 22 PSYCHIATRIC ANNALS 68 (1992). Women constituted 75% of the 20 cases described by McElroy and colleagues. *Kleptomania, supra* note 311.

316.   "Although shoplifting is rampant, kleptomania is unlikely to explain more than a tiny fraction of such 'offenses.' Fewer than 5% of arrested shoplifters give a history that is consistent with kleptomania." Popkin, *supra* note 305, at 1148.

been conducted, obtaining figures of 26%[317] and 27.2%.[318] However, these figures are *not* prevalence figures for pyromania. For many of these individuals the occurrence of illegal fire-setting was limited to a single event[319] and the diagnosis of pyromania was therefore rare within the sample.[320] Fire-setting among psychiatric patients appears to cut across a wide variety of diagnoses, and "there appear to be no data on the salient features that would distinguish psychiatric patients with a history of fire-setting from those without such a history."[321] Despite the proliferation of articles with titles suggesting the existence of discrete psychological profiles for fire-setters,[322] the consensus of contemporary writers suggests agreement that no distinct profiles or syndromes exist.[323]

Pathological Gambling

In contrast, prevalence data are available for pathological gambling. More recent research has identified a prevalence rate in the U.S. as high as 5.4%,[324] but results from the St. Louis Epidemiologic Catchment Area Study reflected a low prevalence rate among St. Louis household samples (0.9%). Studies from Canada have yielded lower estimates, from .42% to 1.2%.[325] Estimated prevalence rates of pathological gambling among adolescents are higher, however, with a recent meta-analysis of Canadian and U.S. studies identifying the rate of "problem gambling" among adolescents as 14.8% and "pathological gambling" as 5.8%.[326]

Pathological gambling appears more commonly among males.[327] However,

---

317. Jeffrey L. Geller & Gregory Bertsch, *Fire-setting Behavior in the Histories of a State Hospital Population*, 142 Am. J. Psychiatry 464 (1985).

318. Geller et al., *supra* note 310, at 129.

319. Geller & Bertsch, *supra* note 317 (half the group of fire setters had a history limited to a single episode).

320. In one study of 191 non-geriatric inpatients, none of those who had set illegal fires had a diagnosis of pyromania. *Id.* at 466.

321. *Id.* at 464.

322. Louis H. Gold, *Psychiatric Profile of the Firesetter*, 7 J. Forensic Sci. 404 (1962). Lee R. Macht & John E. Mack, *The Firesetter Syndrome*, 31 Psychiatry 277 (1968).

323. "Though much has been written on firesetting behavior, the literature provides little practical information . . . beyond a multiplicity of diverse and arbitrary classification systems, a variety of motivational factors, and a number of narrowly defined profiles or composites of arsonists." Anthony Olen Rider, *The Firesetter: A Psychological Profile*, FBI Law Enforcement Bull. (Jun.-Aug., 1980). "There is no adequate description of the typical arsonist, for there is not now, nor has there ever been, such a character." Jeffrey L. Geller, *Arson in Review: From Profit to Pathology*, 15 Psychiatry Clinics N. Am. 623 (1992).

324. Nancy M. Petry & Christopher Armentano, *Prevalence, Assessment, and Treatment of Pathological Gambling: A Review*, 50

Psychiatric Services 1021, 1022 (1998) (citing R.A. Volberg, *Prevalence Studies of Problem Gambling in the United States*, 12 J. Gambling Studies 111 (1996)).

325. Bland et al., *supra* note 307, at 108 (reporting lower prevalence estimate); Robert Ladouceur, *Prevalence Estimates of Pathological Gambling in Quebec*, 36 Can. J. Psychiatry 732, 733 (1991) (reporting higher prevalence estimate). The variability in prevalence estimates may be attributable to site differences or to methodological differences (e.g., the studies used different diagnostic instruments and different administration procedures, i.e., telephone versus face-to-face interviews).

326. James R. Westphal et al., *Gambling Behavior of Louisiana Students in Grades 6 Through 12*, 51 Psychiatric Services 96, 96 (2000) (citing H.J. Shaffer, *Estimating the Prevalence of Adolescent Gambling Disorders: A Quantitative Synthesis and Guide Toward Standard Gambling Nomenclature*, 12 J. Gambling Studies 193 (1996)).

327. Concetta M. DeCaria et al., *Diagnosis, Neurobiology, and Treatment of Pathological Gambling*, 57 J. Clinical Psychiatry 80, 81 (Supp. 1998). Among the St. Louis household sample in the Epidemiologic Catchment Area Study, the great majority of problem gamblers and recreational gamblers were male (61.7% and 78.2%, respectively), while the majority of non-gamblers were female (70.5%). Renee Cunningham–Williams et al., *Taking Chances: Problem Gamblers and Mental Health Disor-*

females remain an under-studied population.[328] It would be useful for future investigators to assess the familial influence of pathological gambling, as research to date has revealed that 14% of female gamblers' fathers and 4% of female gamblers' mothers met diagnostic criteria for pathological gambling.[329]

Co-morbidity of pathological gambling with several other disorders has been reported. Such disorders include alcohol abuse/dependence, nicotine abuse/dependence, obsessive compulsive disorders, depressive disorders, anxiety disorders and antisocial personality.[330] A recent study of pathological gambling among cocaine-dependent outpatients found a higher rate of pathological gambling within this population compared to the general population.[331]

Few studies have focused on the etiological development of pathological gambling. Researchers have investigated a possible familial vulnerability to gambling behavior using structured measures of gambling behavior and focusing on genetic differences in persons suffering from addictive gambling.[332] A recent twin study estimated the impact of genetic and environmental determinants of pathological gambling among monozygotic and dizygotic male twin pairs.[333] Concordance rates were highest for monozygotic twins, suggesting that genes do contribute to pathological gambling risk.[334] Genetic influence explained a large portion of the findings for a range of gambling behaviors, including 35% of reports of gambling 25 times in a year without developing a gambling disorder, 48% of reports of one or more pathological gambling symptoms, 54% of reports of two or more pathological gambling symptoms and 46% to 55% of reports of five pathological gambling symptoms.[335]

A review of the literature between 1996 and 2000 did not yield any relevant studies on the neurobiogical features of pathological gambling. Theories of neurotransmitter functioning for pathological gambling have been developed based on studies of disorders associated with impulse control; these suggest that certain characteristics of neurotransmitter functioning (e.g., low MAO activity and diminished serotonergic functioning) are associated with

---

ders: Results from the St. Louis Epidemiologic Catchment Area Study, 7 *Am. J. Public Health* 1093, 1094 (1998).

328. DeCaria et al., *supra* note 327, at 81.

329. *Id.* (noting that "familial influence may be an important predictor of the development of pathological gambling").

330. *Id.* at 80–81 (summarizing study results revealing commodity rates between pathological gambling and depressive symptoms and substance abuse); Cunningham–Williams et al., *supra* note 327, at 1094–95 (reporting results from St. Louis Epidemiologic Catchment Area Study in which recreational and problem gamblers reportedly met more psychiatric criteria for Axis I diagnoses (e.g., depression) and antisocial personality disorder compared to non-gamblers).

In a study reviewed by McElroy and colleagues, 72% of a treatment group of 25 persons diagnosed with pathological gambling experienced an episode of major depression after attempting to quit gambling. *Clinical Characteristics*, *supra* note 305, at 320. Bland and colleagues reported that of their sample of per-

sons meeting criteria for pathological gambling 40% also met criteria for antisocial personality disorder, 63.3% met criteria for alcohol abuse or dependence, and 33% met criteria for affective disorder. Bland et al., *supra* note 307, at 109.

331. Gladys W. Hall et al., *Pathological Gambling Among Cocaine–Dependent Outpatients*, 157 AM. J. PSYCHIATRY 1127, 1131 (2000).

332. Seth A. Eisen et al., *Familial Influences on Gambling Behavior: An Analysis of 3359 Twin Pairs*, 93 ADDICTION 1375, 1376 (1998) (*citing* H.R. Lesieur et al., *Gambling and Pathological Gambling Among University Students*, 16 ADDICTIVE BEHAVIORS 517 (1991) and H.R. Lesieur et al., *Alcoholism, Drug Abuse, and Gambling*, 10 ALCOHOLISM: CLINICAL AND EXPERIMENTAL RESEARCH 33 (1986)).

333. Eisen et al., *supra* note 332, at 1376.

334. *Id.* at 1380.

335. *Id.* (noting that the remaining variance accounted for environmental influences and measurement error).

impulsivity.[336] Nevertheless, these theories need significantly more research before firm conclusions can be drawn regarding pathological gambling.

Diagnostic studies of persons with pathological gambling have failed to reveal significant cognitive or functional impairment apart from the gambling behavior itself. IQ estimates of pathological gamblers in treatment have yielded above average mean scores.[337]

Although more a matter of opinion than of science, a consensus seems to be emerging in the psychiatric literature that the use of pathological gambling as a basis for an insanity defense to property crimes committed in furtherance of one's gambling habit is inappropriate.[338]

§ 1–2.6.4 Areas of Scientific Disagreement

Given the lack of solid research on the three impulse disorders considered here, much remains unknown about them. Much of the early writing about kleptomania and pyromania utilized a psychoanalytic framework for analysis.[339] However, the constructs of psychoanalytic theory are difficult to test empirically because of the unconscious and unobservable nature of the key elements. At the same time, the adequacy of the medical model of pathological gambling (positing some organic cause) has also been challenged.[340] As a result, other theoretical models have been set forth to try to capture these diverse impulse disorders. Noting the co-morbidity of some of these disorders with alcohol abuse/dependence, some have postulated a general "addictive personality" notion.[341] Others, noting the obsessive/compulsive qualities of these disorders and their co-morbidity with mood disorders, particularly depression, have hypothesized an "affective disorder spectrum" meant to incorporate them.[342] Beyond differences in theoretical approach, there remain

336. DeCaria et al., *supra* note 327, at 81–82.

337. D.W. Bolen et al., *Personality Traits of Pathological Gamblers*, paper presented at the Second Annual Conference on Gambling, Lake Tahoe, Nevada, 1975 (reporting a mean IQ of 112.7 for ten persons in therapy for pathological gambling). [This paper is cited in Jule D. Moravec & Patrick H. Munley, *Psychological Test Findings on Pathological Gamblers in Treatment*, 18 INT'L. J. ADDICTIONS 1003, 1004 (1983). In their own study Moravec and Munley obtained a mean IQ estimate of 116.78 in 23 veterans in a V.A. pathological treatment program. *Id.* at 1006.]

338. A. Louis McGarry, *Pathological Gambling: A New Insanity Defense*, 11 BULL. AM. ACAD. PSYCHIATRY & L. 301 (1983); Alan J. Cunnien, *Pathological Gambling as an Insanity Defense*, 3 BEHAV. SCI. & L. 85 (1985); *see also* Richard Bonnie, *The Moral Basis of the Insanity Defense*, 69 A.B.A. J. 194, 197 (1983); American Psychiatric Association, *Statement on the Insanity Defense* 12 (1983) (an insanity defense should be based only on "those severely abnormal mental conditions that grossly and demonstrably impair a person's perception or understanding of reality and that are not attributable primarily to the voluntary ingestion of alcohol or other psychoactive substances").

339. "The tendency to incendiarism is linked with urethral eroticism through the desire to urinate while watching the flames (a regression to psychosexual infantilism, a masturbation equivalent)." Gold, *supra* note 322, at 406.

340. Alex P. Blaszczynski & Neil McConaghy, *The Medical Model of Pathological Gambling: Current Shortcomings*, 5 J. GAMBLING BEHAV. 42 (1989). Most research on pathological gambling, including the derivation of current assessment measures, is based on a mental disorder approach (relying on DSM–IV criteria). *See* Mark Dickerson & Ellen Baron, *Contemporary Issues and Future Directions for Research into Pathological Gambling*, 95 ADDICTION 1145, 1146 (2000). This approach has been criticized on two fronts: (1) the validity of the diagnosis is weakened by overinclusive criteria, and (2) the heterogeneity of the diagnostic criteria diminish the orthogonal nature of the research variables. *See id.*

341. For a discussion of this notion, see Blaszczynski & McConaghy, *supra* note 340, at 45–46.

342. *Clinical Characteristics*, *supra* note 305, at 323–325. The authors are quick to note, however, that "this hypothesis does *not* argue that impulse disorders are caused by affective

concerns about the validity of the diagnoses themselves.[343]

spectrum disorder, but rather, that they may share the same underlying physiologic abnormality as other forms." *Id.* at 324.

343. "[T]heir diagnostic validity, individually and as a category, remains in question." *Id.* at 323.

CHAPTER 2

CLINICAL AND ACTUARIAL PREDICTIONS OF VIOLENCE

Table of Sections

A. LEGAL ISSUES

Westlaw Electronic Research

See Westlaw Electronic Research Guide preceding the Summary of Contents.

A. LEGAL ISSUES

§ 2–1.0 THE LEGAL RELEVANCE OF RESEARCH ON CLINICAL AND ACTUARIAL PREDICTIONS OF VIOLENCE

§ 2–1.1 Introduction

The central legal issue for virtually all of the topics in this book concerns the evidentiary standards for the admissibility of scientific expert testimony.

Although the admissibility standard is obviously pertinent in the many legal contexts in which expert witnesses propose to testify on a person's future violence, it has not occupied center stage in the case law. In fact, only in rare cases do appellate courts discuss the admissibility rules for expert testimony in any depth, and most courts ignore it entirely. Yet, at the same time, expert testimony predicting violence has been, and remains, an extraordinarily controverted use of science in the trial process. In fact, courts regularly remark that predicting future behavior is inherently difficult and most research indicates that psychiatrists and psychologists do not do it well.[1] This area of the law thus presents a paradox in which judges seemingly take the most lenient approach toward scientific evidence involving some of the most controversial science to enter the courtroom.[2]

The struggle over expert testimony predicting violence focuses instead on constitutional matters. In particular, courts focus on the question whether expert testimony predicting future violence violates constitutional guarantees of due process. In fact, any evidentiary analysis offered usually blends seamlessly into this constitutional assessment. The evidentiary standard thus becomes coterminous with due process. But this assessment, whatever its ultimate legal basis, nearly invariably glosses over inadequacies in the scientific foundation for predictions of violence.

The initial difficulty with bringing order to expert testimony concerning future behavior is the large number and wide variety of legal contexts in which this testimony is relevant. Some of the most prominent contexts include ordinary civil commitment hearings,[3] capital sentencing cases,[4] commitment hearings following a verdict of not guilty by reason of insanity,[5] commitment hearings following a determination of incompetency to stand trial,[6] parole and probation hearings,[7] and hearings established under the recent sexual predator laws concerning community notification.[8] This section

---

§ 2–1.0

1. *See, e.g.*, Heller v. Doe, 509 U.S. 312, 113 S.Ct. 2637, 125 L.Ed.2d 257 (1993) (noting "that psychiatric predictions of future violent behavior by the mentally ill are inaccurate"); Barefoot v. Estelle, 463 U.S. 880, 901, 103 S.Ct. 3383, 77 L.Ed.2d 1090 (1983) (accepting that two out of three predictions of dangerousness are wrong); Addington v. Texas, 441 U.S. 418, 429, 99 S.Ct. 1804, 60 L.Ed.2d 323 (1979) (noting "the fallibility of psychiatric diagnosis"); *see also*, Warren v. Harvey, 632 F.2d 925, 931 (2d Cir.1980); Benham v. Ledbetter, 785 F.2d 1480, 1486 (11th Cir.1986); Carlisle v. State, 512 So.2d 150, 159 (Ala.Crim.App.1987); People v. Murtishaw, 29 Cal.3d 733, 175 Cal. Rptr. 738, 631 P.2d 446, 470 (1981); People v. Stevens, 761 P.2d 768 (Colo.1988); In re Stephenson, 67 Ill.2d 544, 10 Ill.Dec. 507, 367 N.E.2d 1273, 1277 (1977); *In re* Mohr, 383 N.W.2d 539, 542 (Iowa 1986); Taylor v. Commissioner of Mental Health & Mental Retardation, 481 A.2d 139, 146 (Me.1984); Commonwealth v. Helms, 352 Pa.Super. 65, 506 A.2d 1384, 1389 (1986); Hatcher v. Wachtel, 165 W.Va. 489, 269 S.E.2d 849, 851 (W.Va.1980).

2. An area closely related to the subject of this Chapter and arguably a subcategory of it—predictions of violence in the context of sexual aggressors—is considered at length in Chapter 10, *infra*.

3. *E.g.*, CA WELF. & INST. CODE § 5256.4 (West 1998); KY REV. STAT. ANN. § 202A (Banks–Balwin 1988); TEX. HEALTH AND SAFETY CODE ANN. § 574.031 (Vernon 1990); IA Code § 229.12 (2000).

4. *E.g.*, TEX. CRIM. PROC. CODE ANN. ART. 37.071 (Vernon 1981).

5. *E.g.*, WASH. REV. CODE ANN. § 10.77.110 (West 1990); NY CRIM. PROC. § 330.20 (McKinney 1994).

6. *E.g.*, TEX. CRIM. PROC. Code Art. 46.02 (Vernon 1979).

7. *See generally* JOHN MONAHAN & LAURENS WALKER, SOCIAL SCIENCE IN LAW 315–318 (3d ed. 1994).

8. *See generally* Doe v. Poritz, 142 N.J. 1, 662 A.2d 367 (N.J.1995) (evaluating the constitutional validity of the New Jersey law that requires community notification of certain classes of convicted sex offenders). *See* Chapter 10.

cannot hope to exhaustively cover these sundry contexts and, instead, ventures to provide a broad overview of the issue of the legal uses for predictions of violence.[9] Despite the widely divergent contexts in which this expertise is offered, the case law displays a remarkable similarity in its approach to the subject. This approach moves quickly from evidentiary standards to the minimum standard guaranteed by the Constitution.

§ 2–1.2   Evidentiary Standards of Admissibility

Most courts either entirely ignore evidentiary standards for expert testimony concerning future violence, or give it scant attention. A variety of explanations might account for this seeming oversight. Foremost, in many states, predictions of violence are offered in settings in which, explicitly and as a matter of statute, the rules of evidence are modified or suspended.[10] In other cases, in which the statutes are silent, courts sometimes find that the admissibility requirements do not apply to predictions of violence.[11] For example, in *Doe v. Poritz*,[12] the New Jersey Supreme Court recently upheld a community notification law for sexual offenders who, the legislature feared, might pose a continuing danger to society. In upholding the law, however, the court ruled that the state's decision regarding the level of notification imposed on an offender returning to the community was subject to judicial review.[13] In describing the requisite proceeding, the court stated that "[t]he rules of evidence shall not apply and the court may rely on documentary presentations, including expert opinions, on all issues."[14] The New Jersey court did not document the constitutional basis for the procedural aspects of the required hearing.

In a large number of cases, however, statutes do not explicitly suspend the evidence rules, or do so only in part, and courts fail to explicitly find that the expert testimony rules do not apply. Instead, courts ignore evidence rules that would otherwise exclude testimony on future violence because of a sense

---

9. *See also* Christopher Slobogin, *Dangerousness and Expertise*, 133 U. Pa. L. Rev. 97 (1984) (surveying four areas: civil commitment hearings, "criminal" commitment hearings, noncapital sentencing hearings and capital sentencing hearings).

10. E.g., Cal. Welf. Inst. Code § 5256.4 (West 1998) (At civil commitment hearings, the person conducting the hearing is not bound by the rules of procedure or evidence applicable in judicial hearings.); Iowa Code § 229.12 (2000) (At hospitalization hearing, court shall receive all relevant and material evidence which may be offered and need not be bound by rules of evidence.); Tex. Crim. Proc. Code Ann. 37.071 (Vernon 1981) (At sentencing for a capital case, all relevant evidence may be presented, including evidence of the defendant's background and character.).

11. *See e.g.*, State v. Mahone, 127 Wis.2d 364, 379 N.W.2d 878, 882–83 (Wis.App.1985) ("[W]e see no reason to graft the formal rules of evidence upon a recommitment proceeding.").

12. 142 N.J. 1, 662 A.2d 367 (N.J.1995).

13. The three levels of notification created by the New Jersey statute, popularly known as "Megan's Law," are as follows:

"(1) If risk of reoffense is low, law enforcement agencies likely to encounter the person registered shall be notified;

(2) If risk of reoffense is moderate, organizations in the community including schools, religious and youth organizations shall be notified in accordance with the Attorney General's Guidelines, in addition to the notice required by paragraph (1) of the subsection;

(3) If risk of reoffense is high, the public shall be notified through means in accordance with the Attorney General's Guidelines designed to reach members of the public likely to encounter the person registered, in addition to the notice required by paragraphs (1) and (2) of this subsection."

Doe, 662 A.2d at 378 (citing Community Notification, N.J. Stat. Ann. § 2C:7–8c (West 1995)).

14. *Id.* at 383.

of imperative created by the substantive law in these areas. In short, when the law mandates clinical assessments of violence, courts are reluctant to rule that the only experts who offer such opinions are incompetent to testify.

§ 2–1.2.1 Qualifications

The initial question courts ordinarily address concerns an expert's "qualifications" to testify. In the context of expert predictions of violence, courts do not state whether this qualifications assessment is mandated by evidentiary standards or constitutional requirements. Whatever its basis, however, the qualifications requirement has not operated as a bar to experts testifying on the likelihood that some individual will, or will not, be violent in the future.

The types of qualifications necessary to be permitted to testify are not well-defined in the case law. Courts uniformly assume that psychiatrists and psychologists are qualified to predict future dangerousness. For example, in *Addington v. Texas*,[15] the Supreme Court observed as follows:

> There may be factual issues to resolve in a commitment proceeding, but the factual aspects represent only the beginning of the inquiry. Whether the individual is mentally ill and dangerous to either himself or others and is in need of confined therapy turns on the meaning of the facts which must be interpreted by expert psychiatrists and psychologists.[16]

Moreover, courts ordinarily do not require mental health experts to specialize in predicting violent behavior.[17] Instead, they assume that all psychologists and psychiatrists are capable of making this determination and that triers of fact will be able to determine what weight to attribute to a particular expert's testimony. Finally, courts sometimes permit mental health professionals other than psychiatrists and psychologists to testify.[18]

§ 2–1.2.2 The [Missing] Evidentiary Requirements

Frequently, statutes do not specify whether the general evidentiary rules regarding expert testimony apply to predictions of violence.[19] Courts typically assume that they do not. The reasons behind this assumption can be found in a decision in which the court did not make this assumption, but, nonetheless, reached this conclusion.

In *In re Melton*,[20] the District of Columbia Court of Appeals, on rehearing *en banc*, reversed a panel decision which had excluded expert testimony concerning the likelihood that Melton would be violent in the future on the evidentiary ground that the foundation for such expertise was not "sufficiently established."[21] Melton, frequently hospitalized for paranoid schizophrenia, was tried before a jury under a District of Columbia commitment statute for

---

15. 441 U.S. 418, 99 S.Ct. 1804, 60 L.Ed.2d 323 (1979).

16. *Id.* at 429.

17. *See, e.g.,* In re Melton, 597 A.2d 892 (D.C.1991); Chambers v. State, 568 S.W.2d 313, 324 (Tex.Crim.App.1978).

18. *See, e.g.,* Schmidt v. Goddin, 224 Va. 474, 297 S.E.2d 701, 703 (Va.1982) (noting that, in addition to psychiatric testimony, the

trial court heard from a licensed practical nurse and a recreational therapist).

19. *But see In re D.H.*, 507 N.W.2d 314, 315 (N.D.1993), *citing* N.D. CENT. CODE § 25–03.1–19 ("Evidentiary matters at involuntary treatment hearings are governed by the North Dakota Rules of Evidence.").

20. 597 A.2d 892 (D.C.1991).

21. *Id.* at 894.

being "likely to injure himself or others."[22] The District of Columbia introduced several psychiatrists who testified that "when Melton did not adhere to his regimen of medication, he constituted a danger to others."[23] The jury agreed, and the trial judge committed Melton to a psychiatric hospital "for an indefinite period."[24]

Melton claimed on appeal that "the trial judge abused his discretion by 'refusing to consider Melton's counsel's objection to the psychiatrists' qualifications to predict his client's dangerousness.' "[25] Courts in the District of Columbia ordinarily apply the three-part *Dyas* test[26] to expert testimony:

> (1) the subject matter "must be so distinctively related to some science, profession, business or occupation as to be beyond the ken of the average [lay person]"; (2) "the witness must have sufficient skill, knowledge, or experience in that field or calling as to make it appear that his [or her] opinion or inference will probably aid the trier in his [or her] search for truth"; and (3) expert testimony is inadmissible if "the state of the pertinent art or scientific knowledge does not permit a reasonable opinion to be asserted even by an expert."[27]

The Court of Appeals found that the District's experts were clearly "qualified" to testify.[28] In addition, the court stated that these experts must surely be able to assist the trier of fact. "It defies common sense to suggest that a lay juror knows as much as a qualified psychiatrist does about what is likely to happen if a schizophrenic patient does not receive Prolixin shots."[29] Moreover, the court ruled, the proffered experts, as psychiatrists, had sufficient knowledge so as to assist the jury in its "search for truth," as required by the second prong of the *Dyas* test.[30]

In addressing the third prong of the *Dyas* test, the state of knowledge in the pertinent field, the court turned to the Supreme Court's decision in *Barefoot v. Estelle*.[31] In *Barefoot*, the Court rejected the defendant's argument, supported by the American Psychiatric Association, that psychiatric predictions of dangerousness are so unreliable that they should not be admitted. As the Court of Appeals recognized, *Barefoot* was set in constitutional terms and

---

22. Melton was tried under the ERVIN ACT, D.C. CODE ANN. §§ 21–501 to 21–592 (1989); the quoted language comes from D.C. CODE ANN. § 21–521 (1989).

23. *Melton*, 597 A.2d at 894.

24. *Id.*

25. *Id.* at 897 *quoting In re Melton*, 565 A.2d 635 (D.C.App.1989) (*Melton I*), *rehearing. granted and opinion vacated* 581 A.2d 788 (D.C.1990).

26. Dyas v. United States, 376 A.2d 827 (D.C.1977).

27. *Dyas*, 376 A.2d at 832 (*quoting* EDWARD W. CLEARY, McCORMICK ON EVIDENCE § 13, at 29–31 (2d ed. 1972)) (emphasis omitted).

28. *Melton*, 597 A.2d at 897–98. *See infra* § 9–1.2.1 for discussion of the qualifications test in this area.

29. *Id.* at 898.

30. *Id.* (*citing Dyas*, 376 A.2d at 832). The court put it this way:

[T]he judge did not abuse his discretion in permitting [the psychiatrists] to express expert opinions as to the probable consequences for Melton of not requiring him to report for medication. When an oncologist testifies that a malignancy, unless properly treated, is likely to metastasize and cause danger to the patient, he too is predicting the future. Nevertheless, such a cancer specialist need not demonstrate expertise with a crystal ball as well as in medicine in order to render his prognosis receivable in evidence. The same holds true for a psychiatrist.

Id.

31. 463 U.S. 880, 103 S.Ct. 3383, 77 L.Ed.2d 1090 (1983). *Barefoot* is discussed *infra* § 2–1.3.

involved capital sentencing hearings. The court found, nonetheless, that *Barefoot's* analysis applied equally to the evidentiary issue before it.

Although the District of Columbia's commitment statute does not directly suspend the evidentiary rules for expert testimony, the court found that it did so indirectly. As the court explained, the statute "explicitly contemplates that [dangerousness] determinations will be made by psychiatrists."[32] Quoting the District's statutory scheme, the court noted that "[i]n proceedings to determine whether a person acquitted of an offense by reason of insanity should be released, psychiatric testimony may be submitted on the issue whether such person 'has recovered his sanity' and 'will not in the reasonable future be dangerous to himself or others.'"[33] Therefore, because the statute mandates psychiatric predictions of violence as a matter of substantive law, the procedural rules of evidence cannot be interpreted to frustrate the legislative scheme. The court was explicit in this judgment:

> We therefore agree with the District that to accept appellant's theory that psychiatrists cannot predict dangerousness, and therefore should not be permitted to testify on this issue, would nullify the entire legislative scheme for treatment of mentally ill persons in the District of Columbia. The legislature has effectively decided that " 'the state of the pertinent art or scientific knowledge [permits] a reasonable opinion to be asserted . . . by an expert,' " and we would be impermissibly intruding upon a legislative prerogative if we were to challenge that judgment.[34]

Although other courts do not devote the same attention to evidentiary matters involving the scientific basis for predictions of violence as did the District of Columbia Court of Appeals, it appears that most courts follow the District's logic.[35] This logic effectively nullifies the core principles of both *Frye* and *Daubert*. Psychiatric predictions of violence thus are admissible on the basis of substantive law, and neither lack of general acceptance nor lack of scientific validity effects this conclusion. Therefore, the evidentiary determination in the sundry contexts in which predictions of violence are relevant is limited to assessing the qualifications of the proffered experts.[36]

§ 2–1.3 Constitutional Standards: Admissibility

Predictions of violence have been challenged on constitutional grounds in a variety of legal contexts. However, these various challenges were largely resolved when the Supreme Court found, in *Barefoot v. Estelle*,[37] that such

32. *Melton*, 597 A.2d at 899.

33. *Id.* at 899–900, *citing* D.C. CODE ANN. § 24–301(e)(1)–(2) (1981). The quoted language, of course, comes from the statutory provisions regarding commitment hearings following an acquittal by reason of insanity. The statutory language relevant to ordinary civil commitment hearings is somewhat less clear. *See id.*, citing D.C. CODE ANN. §§ 21–522, 21–544 (1981).

34. *Id.* at 900, *quoting Dyas*, 376 A.2d at 832 (citation omitted).

35. In *People v. Murtishaw*, 29 Cal.3d 733, 175 Cal.Rptr. 738, 631 P.2d 446, 469 (1981), for example, the California Supreme Court noted that in most cases in which prediction testi-

mony is upheld, the judge or jury is required by statute to determine whether the defendant is "dangerous." "In such cases expert prediction, unreliable though it may be, is often the only evidence available to assist the trier of fact." *Id. See also* People v. Stevens, 761 P.2d 768, 771 (Colo.1988) (noting that "predictions of future behavior are inherent in showing that medical intervention is mandated").

36. The issue of qualifications in the context of predictions of dangerousness is discussed *supra* § 2–1.2.1.

37. 463 U.S. 880, 103 S.Ct. 3383, 77 L.Ed.2d 1090 (1983).

predictions were constitutional when introduced at the sentencing stage of capital trials.[38] In *Barefoot*, the Court found that admission of expert testimony in capital sentencing hearings concerning the likelihood the defendant will commit future criminal acts does not violate the Eighth Amendment.

Although the *Barefoot* Court cited "the rules of evidence generally extant at the federal and state levels" to buttress its opinion,[39] it explicitly rested its decision on the Constitution.[40] The Court began its analysis by noting that it had previously accepted lay persons' ability to predict dangerousness in *Jurek v. Texas*.[41] Therefore, the Court observed, "it makes little sense, if any, to submit that psychiatrists, out of the entire universe of persons who might have an opinion on the issue, would know so little about the subject that they should not be permitted to testify."[42] This argument, however, contains several assumptions. First, it assumes that *Jurek* was "correctly" decided and that lay persons can predict violence; or, alternatively, that the Court will not consider *Jurek's* continuing vitality.[43] The argument also assumes that expert witnesses are on the same constitutional plain as lay-person-jurors in regard to predicting violence. Even if future violence is a constitutionally allowable matter for juries to consider in deciding whether to impose the death penalty, it is not obvious that experts should be constitutionally permitted to testify on this matter. There are many factual matters juries decide that are not inevitably accompanied by expert testimony.[44] Under most evidence codes, for example, expert testimony must provide some assistance beyond what jurors can do on their own. It is not clear why this usual prerequisite is not part of the constitutional analysis.

Much of the Court's constitutional analysis appears to flow less from a belief that accurate predictions are possible than a recognition that they are

38. Prior to *Barefoot*, courts made the distinction between ordinary civil cases and capital cases, finding unreliable predictions of dangerousness particularly problematic in the latter. *See, e.g.*, People v Murtishaw, 29 Cal.3d 733, 175 Cal.Rptr. 738, 631 P.2d 446, 448 (1981) ("In short, evidence which is barely reliable enough to justify a civil judgment or a limited commitment is not reliable enough to utilize in determining whether a man should be executed.").

39. *Barefoot*, 463 U.S. at 898. The Court noted that most state and federal evidence rules "anticipate that relevant unprivileged evidence should be admitted and its weight left to the fact finder, who would have the benefit of cross examination and contrary evidence by the opposing party." *Id. Barefoot*, however, predated *Daubert v. Merrell Dow Pharmaceuticals, Inc.*, 509 U.S. 579, 113 S.Ct. 2786, 125 L.Ed.2d 469 (1993), which held that scientific evidence must also be "valid." For discussion of the implications of *Daubert* for capital sentencing cases generally, *see infra* § 9–1.5.

40. *Barefoot*, 463 U.S. at 899 n.6 (rejecting the dissent's citations to case law contrary to the majority's holding, because they "are not constitutional decisions, but decisions of federal evidence law").

41. *Barefoot*, 463 U.S. at 896–97 (*citing* Jurek v. Texas, 428 U.S. 262, 96 S.Ct. 2950, 49 L.Ed.2d 929 (1976)).

42. *Id.* at 897.

43. *Id.* at 896 ("The suggestion that no psychiatrist's testimony may be presented with respect to a defendant's future dangerousness is somewhat like asking us to disinvent the wheel.")

44. Some observers argue that substantial dangers are associated with experts whose aura of scientific infallibility might overwhelm the common sense of the jury. *See, e.g.*, United States v. Addison, 498 F.2d 741, 744 (D.C.Cir.1974) (scientific evidence may "assume a posture of mystic infallibility in the eyes of a jury of laymen"). Research, however, does not yet support this hypothesis. The relationship between expert testimony and jury decisionmaking is complex and still awaits substantial research to understand. *See* Edward Imwinkelried, *The Standard for Admitting Scientific Evidence: A Critique from the Perspective of Juror Psychology*, 28 VILL. L. REV. 554 (1982–83) (concluding that jurors can usually understand scientific evidence). Whatever the reality, the Court should not ignore the issue or hastily discount the dangers possibly attending this testimony.

an integral and necessary part of many legal contexts.[45] The *Barefoot* Court quoted the following language from Justice Stevens' opinion in *Jurek*:

> It is, of course, not easy to predict future behavior. The fact that such a determination is difficult, however, does not mean that it cannot be made. Indeed, prediction of future criminal conduct is an essential element in many of the decisions rendered throughout our criminal justice system. . . . The task that a Texas jury must perform in answering the statutory question in issue is thus basically no different from the task performed countless times each day throughout the American system of justice.[46]

Of course, that the legal system regularly predicts future behavior says nothing about the accuracy of those predictions. Moreover, admitting experts who are unable to make these predictions reliably does not follow naturally from Justice Stevens' statement. In neither *Barefoot* nor in *Jurek* did the Court specifically explain why unreliable expert testimony was admissible to assist the jury make what, concededly, might be a "necessary" judgment. Presumably, the Court assumed that experts are better than lay jurors at predicting violence. If they are not, then this testimony has no probative value and should be excluded on that basis alone. Researchers, however, have yet to study this question.

In fact, the Court appears to have largely accepted the insight that expert predictions of future violence are not reliable.[47] However, in a turn of logic vehemently criticized by commentators, the Court placed its faith in the adversarial process.[48] First, the Court noted that "[n]either petitioner nor the [American Psychiatric] Association suggests that psychiatrists are always wrong with respect to future dangerousness, only most of the time."[49] And, despite the Association's statement that psychiatrists cannot distinguish accurate from inaccurate predictions, the Court believed juries could do so. "We are unconvinced . . . that the adversary process cannot be trusted to sort out the reliable from the unreliable evidence and opinion about future dangerousness, particularly when the convicted felon has the opportunity to present his own side of the case."[50] Finally, the Court found that expert testimony predicting violence did not have to be based on personal observation or an interview of the defendant.[51] Experts are permitted to draw conclusions on the ultimate issue exclusively from the facts of a hypothetical question.[52]

---

45. This substantive law imperative is similar to the force motivating the District of Columbia Court of Appeals in *In re Melton*, discussed *supra* § 9–1.2.2.

46. *Id.* at 897 (*quoting Jurek*, 428 U.S. at 274–76).

47. *See id.* at 917 (Blackmun, J., dissenting) ("The Court holds that psychiatric testimony about a defendant's future dangerousness is admissible, despite the fact that such testimony is wrong two times out of three.").

48. *See generally* Robyn Dawes et al., *Clinical Versus Actuarial Judgment*, 243 SCIENCE 1668 (1989); Thomas Grisso & Paul Appelbaum, *Is it Unethical to Offer Predictions of*

Future Violence?, 16 LAW & HUM. BEH. 621 (1992).

49. *Id.* at 901.

50. *Id.*

51. *Id.* at 904–905.

52. *Id.* One doctor testified for the state, without benefit of meeting the defendant, that " 'within a reasonable psychiatr[ic] certainty,' [he is] a 'criminal sociopath.' " *Id.* at 918 (Blackmun, J., dissenting). The state's second expert, also without having met the defendant, agreed, and added that "there was a 'one hundred percent and absolute' chance that Barefoot would commit future acts of criminal violence." *Id.* at 919 (Blackmun, J., dissenting).

The *Barefoot* Court's decision does not specifically address, and wholly fails to resolve, the basic tension between unreliable or invalid science and legal policy. In the evidentiary context, the statutory direction that predictions of violence are an integral part of the legislative scheme naturally supersedes a procedural rule that might dictate a different result. Thus, as was true in *In re Melton*,[53] statutes might explicitly or implicitly suspend the critical application of the rules of evidence regarding expert testimony, because of a legislatively defined special need. But this "need" for predicting violence does not explain the relaxed admission standard found to be tolerated by the Constitution.[54] The Court should explain more clearly why the constitutional right to reliable evidence, as guaranteed by due process, does not outweigh the legislative decision to make "dangerousness" an aggravating factor that supports imposition of the death penalty.[55]

§ 2–1.4 Constitutional Standards: Burdens of Proof

The burdens of proof applied to expert predictions of future criminal activity vary by legal context.[56] Given the wide variety of contexts in which this testimony is relevant, this section does not attempt an exhaustive summary.[57] Instead, it focuses on the burden of proof in civil commitment hearings in order to illustrate the multiplicity of factors that support adoption of one standard rather than another.

In *Addington v. Texas*,[58] the Court held that the Constitution requires a "clear and convincing" standard of proof when a state seeks to involuntarily commit a person to a mental hospital for an indefinite period. In so holding, the Court rejected the more lenient "preponderance" standard as well as the stricter standard applied in criminal cases of proof "beyond a reasonable

---

53. *See supra* § 2–1.2.2.

54. *See Barefoot*, 463 U.S. at 923 (Blackmun, J., dissenting) ("It is impossible to square admission of this purportedly scientific but actually baseless testimony with the Constitution's paramount concern for reliability in capital sentencing.").

55. In *Schall v. Martin*, 467 U.S. 253, 104 S.Ct. 2403, 81 L.Ed.2d 207 (1984), the Court upheld the pretrial detention of juveniles upon a finding that there is a "serious risk" that if released the juvenile would commit a crime before his next court appearance. Responding to the argument that such predictions could not be made reliably, the Court said that "our cases indicate, however, that from a legal point of view there is nothing inherently unattainable about a prediction of future criminal conduct." *Id.* at 278. The Court did not elaborate.

56. For example, as discussed in this section, the Supreme Court held that in ordinary civil commitment hearings the state must bear the burden of proof by at least clear and convincing evidence; in *Jones v. United States*, 463 U.S. 354, 103 S.Ct. 3043, 77 L.Ed.2d 694 (1983), however, the Court upheld a statute placing a preponderance of the evidence burden on defendants in commitment hearings following acquittal on the ground of insanity.

57. The Wisconsin Supreme Court conveniently summarized the range of burdens of proof under current doctrine:

> [T]he Supreme Court has found the following to be constitutionally permissible: civil and criminal insanity acquittees may be treated differently with regard to the burden of proof required for the initial commitment—commitment following an insanity acquittal may be based on a preponderance of the evidence, whereas in a civil commitment the state must establish its burden of proof by clear and convincing evidence; automatic commitment following an insanity acquittal does not violate due process; the length of commitment for both civil and criminal committees may be indefinite; the term of commitment for an insanity acquittee may exceed the length of the maximum sentence the acquittee could have been subjected to had a sentence been imposed; and, following the initial commitment of an insanity acquittee, the burden of proof at a subsequent hearing for reexamination and release may be borne by the acquittee.

State v. Randall, 192 Wis.2d 800, 532 N.W.2d 94 (Wis.1995).

58. 441 U.S. 418, 99 S.Ct. 1804, 60 L.Ed.2d 323 (1979).

doubt." The Court first explained that the function of a standard of proof "is to instruct the factfinder concerning the degree of confidence our society thinks he should have in the correctness of factual conclusions for a particular type of adjudication."[59] The Court found that commitment hearings, which pose "a significant deprivation of liberty,"[60] require a standard greater than a preponderance of the evidence, which is typically employed in "monetary dispute[s] between private parties."[61] At the same time, however, the Court refused to require proof beyond a reasonable doubt. The Court offered a variety of reasons for choosing this lighter burden. First, following an involuntary commitment, the continuing involvement of professionals, family and friends in the person's treatment provides opportunities for errors to be corrected. Second, making an error that permits a mentally ill person to live in the general community is not necessarily good for that person; "[i]t cannot be said . . . that it is much better for a mentally ill person to 'go free' than for a mentally normal person to be committed."[62] Finally, the Court observed, "[g]iven the lack of certainty and the fallibility of psychiatric diagnosis, there is a serious question as to whether a state could ever prove beyond a reasonable doubt that an individual is both mentally ill and likely to be violent."[63]

Although the last premise the Court cites for supporting an intermediate standard of proof flows logically from the recognition of the fallibility of evaluations of future violence,[64] a later case appears to reject it. In *Heller v. Doe*,[65] the Court considered an equal protection challenge to Kentucky's statutory scheme which applied a clear and convincing evidence standard at commitment hearings involving mentally retarded defendants and a beyond a

---

59. *Id.* at 423 (*quoting In re* Winship, 397 U.S. 358, 370, 90 S.Ct. 1068, 25 L.Ed.2d 368 (1970) (Harlan, J., concurring)).

60. *Id.* at 425.

61. *Id.* at 423.

62. *Id.* at 430. *See also* In re Binkley, 178 Ind.App. 301, 382 N.E.2d 952, 955 (Ind.Ct.App. 1978) ("[T]he situation would be an unfortunate one should a person in need of care be deprived of aid because he is mentally incapable of knowing his needs and the medical profession can not meet a too strict burden.").

63. In an important paragraph that sheds light on the Court's understanding of the law's employment of "psychiatric science," the Court observed as follows:

The subtleties and nuances of psychiatric diagnosis render certainties virtually beyond reach in most situations. The reasonable-doubt standard of criminal law functions in its realm because there the standard is addressed to specific, knowable facts. Psychiatric diagnosis, in contrast, is to a large extent based on medical "impressions" drawn from subjective analysis and filtered through the experience of the diagnostician. This process often makes it very difficult for the expert physician to offer definite conclusions about any particular patient. . . . If a trained psychiatrist has difficulty with the categorical "beyond a reasonable doubt" standard, the untrained lay juror—or indeed even a trained judge—who is required to rely upon expert opinion could be forced by the criminal law standard of proof to reject commitment for many patients desperately in need of institutionalized psychiatric care. Such "freedom" for a mentally ill person would be purchased at a high price.

Addington, 441 U.S. at 430.

64. *See In re* Stephenson, 67 Ill.2d 544, 10 Ill.Dec. 507, 367 N.E.2d 1273, 1277 (1977) ("Predictions of dangerousness can hardly be beyond a reasonable doubt in the undeveloped framework of psychiatric diagnosis and prediction, for the subjective determinations therein involved are incapable of meeting objective certainty."); Taylor v. Comm'r. of Mental Health & Mental Retardation, 481 A.2d 139, 146 (Me. 1984) ("The ability of the State to establish the elements of a crime beyond a reasonable doubt does not give any assurance that this standard of proof is attainable in predicting the future conduct of a patient after release from a mental institution."); Commonwealth v. Helms, 352 Pa.Super. 65, 506 A.2d 1384, 1389 (1986) ("The term 'reasonable probability' [adopted by the court] underscores the impossibility of demanding total accuracy in predictions of future dangerousness.").

65. 509 U.S. 312, 113 S.Ct. 2637, 125 L.Ed.2d 257 (1993).

reasonable doubt standard for mentally ill defendants.[66] Applying rational basis review,[67] the Court found that "Kentucky has proffered more than adequate justifications for the differences in treatment between the mentally retarded and the mentally ill."[68] Yet the Court cited in support of Kentucky's judgment the inherent unreliability of psychiatric predictions of dangerousness for the mentally ill as compared to the mentally retarded.[69] "[It was] plausible for Kentucky to conclude that the dangerous determination was more accurate as to the mentally retarded than the mentally ill."[70] But Kentucky's justification exactly contradicts the logic of *Addington*. In *Addington*, the fallibility of behavioral predictions supported a ***lesser*** standard of proof, whereas in *Heller* this fallibility supported a ***greater*** standard of proof.[71] Following the *Addington* logic, the standard of proof should be the same or greater for commitment of mentally retarded persons who are potentially dangerous; in Kentucky it is less. It is difficult to reconcile *Heller* and *Addington*.[72]

In *United States v. Muhammad*,[73] the Fifth Circuit considered whether the civil commitment of a federal prisoner pursuant to a preponderance standard was unconstitutional. Under 18 U.S.C.A. § 4245(d), a federal prisoner can be involuntarily committed

> [i]f, after the hearing, the court finds by a *preponderance of the evidence* that the person is presently suffering from a mental disease of defect for the treatment of which he is in need of custody for care or treatment in a suitable facility.[74]

The *Muhammad* court distinguished *Addington*, explaining that "it dealt with the civil commitment of an ordinary citizen, not a prisoner."[75] The *Muhammad* court found support for the preponderance standard in *Jones v.*

---

66. *Id.* at 315.

67. The Court applied rational basis review to Kentucky's classification based on type of mental handicap, because that was the standard by which the parties had litigated the case below. Although on appeal the respondents argued for heightened scrutiny, the Court refused to consider this issue given the lateness of the hour when it was raised. *Id.* at 319.

68. *Id.* at 321.

69. *Id.* at 322–23. The Court explained as follows:

> Mental retardation is a permanent, relatively static condition, so a determination of dangerousness may be made with some accuracy based on previous behavior.... This is not so with the mentally ill. Manifestations of mental illness may be sudden, and past behavior may not be an adequate predictor of future actions ... It is thus no surprise that psychiatric predictions of future violent behavior by the mentally ill are inaccurate.

Id. (citations omitted).

70. *Id.* at 324.

71. It should be noted that the Court found an additional "rationale justifying the different burdens of proof: The prevailing methods of treatment for the mentally retarded, as a gen-

eral rule, are much less invasive than are those given the mentally ill." *Id.* at 325.

72. One possible explanation is that in *Addington* the Court believed that higher error rates in psychiatric predictions should produce lower standards of proof and thus supported the constitutional holding there. In *Heller*, the Court merely accepted that Kentucky might rationally find the opposite to be true and thus the Court upheld this justification under the permissive rational basis test. The difficulty in accepting this explanation is that the relationship between error rates and standards of review is not the kind of issue ordinarily subject to deferential review. It is not a factual matter with which reasonable people might disagree. Rather, as made clear in *Addington*, it is a constitutional value judgment to be made as a matter of constitutional interpretation. The fallibility of psychiatric science is thus a "constitutional fact" that is pertinent to the interpretation of the Constitution and should be reviewed *de novo*, not deferentially as occurred in *Heller*.

73. 165 F.3d 327 (5th Cir.1999).

74. 18 U.S.C.A. § 4245(d) (2000) (emphasis added).

75. *Muhammad*, 165 F.3d at 333.

United States.[76] In *Jones*, the Court upheld the use of the preponderance standard in commitments of criminal defendants who had been found not guilty by reason of insanity. The *Jones* Court distinguished *Addington*, finding that "there were 'important differences between the class of potential civil-commitment candidates and the class of insanity acquittees that justify differing standards of proof.' "[77] In *Muhammad*, the court also found support in *Vitek v. Jones*,[78] in which the Supreme Court had suggested that "involuntary commitment of convicted felons, who are already confined in prison, is less a curtailment of liberty than the involuntary commitment of ordinary citizens."[79] The *Muhammad* court concluded, therefore, that Congress had used a constitutionally adequate burden of proof.

§ 2–1.5 *Barefoot* in the World of *Daubert*

To date, no court has evaluated the admissibility of expert testimony regarding future violence under the Court's *Daubert* decision.[80] In light of the very few cases preceding *Daubert* which engaged in any evidentiary analysis whatsoever, this state of affairs is unlikely to change soon.

Although *Daubert* changed the evidentiary focus from counting noses in order to determine general acceptance to evaluating the scientific basis for the expert testimony, this change of perspective is not likely to affect courts' evidentiary analyses in this context. First of all, to the extent courts used a *Frye*-style general acceptance test, the American Psychiatric Association's participation on behalf of the defendant in *Barefoot* should have undermined

---

76. 463 U.S. 354, 103 S.Ct. 3043, 77 L.Ed.2d 694 (1983).

77. *Muhammad*, 165 F.3d at 334 (*quoting Jones*, 463 U.S. at 367). In *United States v. Wattleton*, 110 F. Supp. 2d 1380 (N.D.Ga.2000), the defendant was found not guilty by reason of insanity at trial. The court held that a federal statute that places the burden of proof on the defendant to show, at the statutorily required commitment hearing, that he is not dangerous does not violate due process. *Id.* at 1381. The court held further that this was true despite the fact that it was the government who sought the insanity verdict. (The defendant at trial had claimed that his mental disease had made it impossible for him to form the requisite intent.) *Id.*

78. 445 U.S. 480, 100 S.Ct. 1254, 63 L.Ed.2d 552 (1980).

79. *Muhammad*, 165 F.3d at 334.

80. Although no court has specifically considered the *Barefoot* Court's approach to predictions of violence after *Daubert*, several courts and commentators have pointed out the tension between *Daubert's* gatekeeping requirement and the open-gate standard reflected in *Barefoot*. Perhaps the most forceful and considered response to this tension was written by Judge Garza in a specially concurring opinion in *Flores v. Johnson*, 210 F.3d 456 (5th Cir.2000). Judge Garza wrote separately to question the consistency and, indeed, constitutionality of the Supreme Court's allowance of psychiatric predictions of violence in its death

penalty jurisprudence. *Id.* at 458. Based on a review of the scientific authority, Judge Garza concluded "that the use of psychiatric evidence to predict a murderer's 'future dangerousness' fails all five *Daubert* factors." *Id.* at 464 (The fifth factor Judge Garza considered, in addition to the usually-cited four of testing, peer review and publication, error rate and general acceptance, was the existence of standards controlling the operation of the technique.). Judge Garza concluded as follows:

> [W]hat separates the executioner from the murderer is the legal process by which the state ascertains and condemns those guilty of heinous crimes. If that process is flawed because it allows evidence without any scientific validity to push the jury toward condemning the accused, the legitimacy of our legal process is threatened.

Id. at 469–70. Many commentators have also questioned whether the rule in *Barefoot* can be squared with the approach adopted in *Daubert*. *See* Erica Beecher–Monas & Edgar Garcia–Rill, *The Law and The Brain: Judging Scientific Evidence of Intent*, 1 J. App. Prac. & Process 243, (1999); Michael H. Gottesman, *From Barefoot to Daubert to Joiner: Triple Play or Double Error*, 40 Ariz. L. Rev. 753 (1998); Randy Oto, *On the Ability of Mental Health Professionals to "Predict Dangerousness" Literature*, 18 Law & Psychol. Rev. 43 (1994); Paul C. Giannelli, *"Junk Science": The Criminal Cases*, 84 J. Crim. L. & Criminology 105 (1993).

any belief that psychiatric predictions of violence enjoyed "general acceptance."[81] Indeed, on cross-examination, one of the state's experts observed that the studies which indicate the unreliability of psychiatric predictions "were accepted by only a 'small minority group' of psychiatrists—'[i]t's not the American Psychiatric Association that believes that.'"[82] Yet the American Psychiatric Association filed an *amicus curiae* brief that found the conclusion of unreliability to be "an established fact."[83] But this "fact" has not impressed itself upon either the Supreme Court or lower courts more generally.

Still, it is possible that *Daubert* heralds a new perspective that will transcend its evidentiary birthplace.[84] Specifically, *Daubert* indicates a change in perspective regarding scientific evidence, moving the judge from being a casual bystander to an informed observer of the scientific enterprise. *Daubert* marks a new awareness of the sum and substance of science among lawyers and judges. It anticipates, indeed requires, that they have a sophisticated understanding of the scientific process and this new and vigorous appreciation should be expected to have an effect outside the evidentiary context. This increased sophistication should be brought to bear in other contexts, such as constitutional law, in which empirical research plays (or should play) a significant role.[85]

Indeed, the category of expert predictions of future violence offers a vehicle for this change. This testimony ostensibly raises evidentiary concerns, but swiftly rises to constitutional dimensions. An appreciation for the subtleties of the scientific research regarding future violence should better inform courts' constitutional judgments. In fact, this appreciation gains in importance as research increasingly indicates that the psychological community's rate of success is improving. One of the hallmarks of science is its changing, or evolutionary, character. As Dr. Monahan's chapter indicates, the state of the art of predictions of violence has changed since the time of *Barefoot*. Scientists are gaining increased confidence in the accuracy of these predictions. Still, predictions of future behavior will never be perfected, so judges cannot escape their responsibility to decide what degree of error is constitutionally acceptable.

Some success in predicting violence is unlikely, alone, to be sufficient to meet critics' concerns about this testimony. Under both rules of evidence and the Constitution, modestly valid predictions will still face substantial objections. Under evidentiary principles, experts might still be challenged on one or both of two bases. First, experts should be expected to show that they used the techniques that have been shown by research to be effective.[86] Second,

---

81. In fact, Justice White thought it significant that some psychiatrists believe they can predict dangerousness, as evidenced by the two experts who testified for the state. *Barefoot*, 463 U.S. at 900–901. This turns *Frye* on its head, changing the analysis from whether the scientific basis for testimony is generally accepted to whether anyone with sufficient credentials can be found who accepts it.

82. *Id.* at 919.

83. *Id.* at 920.

84. Laurens Walker & John Monahan, Daubert *and the Reference Manual: An Essay on the Future of Science in the Law*, 82 VA. L.REV. 837 (1996).

85. *See generally* David L. Faigman, *"Normative Constitutional Fact–Finding": Exploring the Empirical Component of Constitutional Interpretation*, 139 PA. L. REV. 541, 581–84 (1991) (discussing the role of empirically testable facts in constitutional law from *Marbury* to *McCleskey*, with stops along the way at *Plessy, Brown, Roe* and others).

86. *Cf.* State v. Davee, 558 S.W.2d 335, 339 (Mo.Ct.App.1977) ("[The expert's] testimony consisted of his conclusions as a psychiatrist.

courts must find that the probative value of the evidence is not substantially outweighed by unfair prejudice. Under constitutional principles, of course, mere probative value, though of great significance, has never been sufficient. The reliability and validity of this sort of testimony must be evaluated together with constitutional guarantees.[87]

§ 2–1.6 Conclusion

The scientific study of predictions of violence presents substantial challenges to the courts. Although courts appear to uniformly accept the inherent difficulty in predicting future behavior, they have, nonetheless, liberally permitted expert testimony on this issue. In the evidentiary context, this permissiveness stems from statutory schemes that make future violence a principal question and which presuppose that someone must have the capacity to answer it. Thus, courts, usually implicitly, discard any evidentiary roadblocks to the accomplishment of the statutory scheme. In the constitutional context courts appear to follow this same logic, however inappropriate it is to the matter of constitutional interpretation. Although the result might be the same—a permissive stance toward this form of expert testimony—courts have yet to explain fully the constitutional basis for permitting admittedly unreliable evidence when a person's liberty or life is at risk. Possibly, as judges become more comfortable with the complexity and subtlety of the scientific method as the *Daubert* era progresses, their constitutional analysis in this area will also grow more complex and subtle.

B. SCIENTIFIC STATUS

by

John Monahan*

§ 2–2.0 THE SCIENTIFIC STATUS OF RESEARCH ON CLINICAL AND ACTUARIAL PREDICTIONS OF VIOLENCE

§ 2–2.1 Introductory Discussion of the Science

§ 2–2.1.1 The Scientific Questions

Behavioral scientists have concentrated their energies on providing answers to two questions on the topic of risk assessment of violence: (1) **Is**

His testimony was devoid of objective facts, test results, detailed observations or examinations from which his conclusions could be evaluated.'').

87. The New Jersey Supreme Court explained the "delicate balance" between science and policy as follows:

It should be emphasized that while courts in determining dangerousness should take full advantage of expert testimony presented by the state and by defendant, the decision is not one that can be left wholly to the technical expertise of the psychiatrists and psychol-

ogists. The determination of dangerousness involves a delicate balancing of society's interest in protection from harmful conduct against the individual's interest in personal liberty and autonomy. This decision, while requiring the court to make use of the assistance which medical testimony may provide, is ultimately a legal one, not a medical one.

State v. Krol, 68 N.J. 236, 344 A.2d 289, 302 (N.J.1975).

* John Monahan, a clinical psychologist, holds the Doherty Chair in law at the University of Virginia, where he is also a Professor of

mental disorder a risk factor for violence? and (2) **How valid are clinical predictions of violence?**

[1] Mental Disorder and Violence

There are two ways to determine whether a relationship exists between mental disorder and violent behavior and, if it does, to estimate the strength of that relationship. If being mentally disordered raises the likelihood that a person will commit a violent act—that is, if mental disorder is a "risk factor" for the occurrence of violent behavior—then the actual (or "true") prevalence rate for violence should be higher among disordered than among non-disordered populations. And to the extent that mental disorder is a contributing cause to the occurrence of violence, the true prevalence rate of mental disorder should be higher among people who commit violent acts than among people who do not.

Within each generic category, two types of research exist. The first seeks to estimate the relationship between mental disorder and violence by studying people who are being *treated* either for mental disorder (in hospitals), or for violent behavior (in jails and prisons). The second seeks to estimate the relationship between mental disorder and violence by studying people *unselected* for treatment status in the open community. Both types of studies are valuable in themselves, but both have limitations taken in isolation.

[a] Violence Among the Disordered

Three types of studies provide data from hospitalized mental patients that can be used to estimate the relationship between mental disorder and violence. One type looks at the prevalence of violent acts committed by patients *before* they entered the hospital. A second type looks at the prevalence of violent incidents committed by mental patients *during* their hospital stay. A final type of study addresses the prevalence of violent behavior among mental patients *after* they have been released from the hospital.[1]

I have reviewed research of each type elsewhere.[2] I found 11 published studies that provide data on the prevalence of violent behavior among persons

---

Psychology and of Legal Medicine. He has been a Guggenheim Fellow, a Fellow at Harvard Law School and at the Center for Advanced Study in the Behavioral Sciences, and a Visiting Fellow at All Souls College, Oxford. He was the founding President of the American Psychological Association's Division of Psychology and Law and received an honorary doctorate in law from the City University of New York. Monahan has won the Isaac Ray Award of the American Psychiatric Association, has been elected to membership in the Institute of Medicine of the National Academy of Sciences, has been appointed to the Committee on Law and Justice of the National Research Council, and has directed the MacArthur Research Network on Mental Health and the Law. His work has been cited frequently by courts, including the California Supreme Court in *Tarasoff v. Regents* and the United States Supreme Court in

Barefoot v. Estelle, in which he was referred to as "the leading thinker on the issue" of violence risk assessment.

§ 2–2.0

1. I restrict myself here to remarking upon findings on violent behavior toward others, and exclude violence toward self, verbal threats of violence, and property damage. By "mental disorder," I refer, unless otherwise noted, to those "major" disorders of thought or affect that form a subset of Axis I of the Fourth Edition (1994) of the Diagnostic and Statistical Manual of the American Psychiatric Association ("DSM–IV").

2. John Monahan, *Mental Disorder and Violent Behavior: Perceptions and Evidence*, 47 AM. PSYCHOLOGIST 511 (1992). For other reviews reaching largely the same empirical conclu-

who eventually became mental patients. The time period investigated was typically the two weeks prior to hospital admission. The findings across the various studies vary considerably: between approximately 10 and 40 percent of the patient samples (with a median rate of 15 percent) committed a physically assaultive act against another shortly before they were hospitalized. Twelve studies with data on the prevalence of violence by patients on mental hospital wards are also available. The periods studied varied from a few days to a year. The findings here also range from about 10 to 40 percent (with a median rate of 25 percent).

There is a very large literature, going back to the 1920's, on violent behavior by mental patients after they have been discharged from civil hospitals.[3] Klassen and O'Connor found that approximately 25–30 percent of male patients with at least one violent incident in their past—a very relevant, but highly selective sample of patients—are violent within a year of release from the hospital.[4] Tardiff and colleagues followed patients by telephone for two weeks after their discharge from a civil psychiatric hospital and found that 3.7 percent were violent during that period.[5] "Patients who were violent in the month before admission were nine times more likely to be violent in the two weeks after discharge, compared with patients who were not violent just before admission. Patients with a personality disorder were four times more likely than patients without a personality disorder to be violent after discharge."[6]

In the MacArthur Violence Risk Assessment Study,[7] the largest research of this kind yet conducted, Steadman et al. studied the epidemiology of violence among patients discharged from short-term mental health facilities.[8] They monitored violence to others every 10 weeks during the first year after discharge for 1,136 male and female civil patients between 18 and 40 years old, at three sites in the United States (Pittsburgh, PA, Worcester, MA, and

sions, see Simon C. Wessely and Pamela J. Taylor, *Madness and Crime: Criminology versus Psychiatry*, 1 CRIM. BEHAV. & MENTAL HEALTH 193 (1991); Edward P. Mulvey, *Assessing the Evidence of a Link Between Mental Illness and Violence*, 45 HOSPITAL & COMMUNITY PSYCHIATRY 663 (1994); E. Fuller Torrey, *Violent Behavior by Individuals With Serious Mental Illness*, 45 HOSPITAL & COMMUNITY PSYCHIATRY 653 (1994); James Beck, *Epidemiology of Mental Disorder and Violence: Beliefs and Research Findings*, 2 HARV. REV. PSYCHIATRY 1 (1994); Sheilagh Hodgins, *Major Mental Disorder and Crime: An Overview*, 2 PSYCHOL., CRIME & LAW 5(1995); Bruce Link & Ann Stueve, *Evidence Bearing on Mental Illness as a Possible Cause of Violent Behavior*, 17 EPIDEMIOLOGICAL REVIEWS 1 (1995); Pamela Taylor & John Monahan, *Dangerous Patients or Dangerous Diseases?* 312 BRIT. MED. J. 967 (1996).

3. Judith A. Rabkin, *Criminal Behavior of Discharged Mental Patients: A Critical Appraisal of the Research*, 86 PSYCHOLOGICAL BULL. 1 (1979).

4. Deidre Klassen & William A. O'Connor, *Crime, Inpatient Admissions, and Violence Among Male Mental Patients*, 11 INT'L. J. L. &

PSYCHIATRY 305 (1988); Deidre Klassen & William A. O'Connor, *Assessing the Risk of Violence in Released Mental Patients: A Cross-Validation Study*, 1 PSYCHOLOGICAL ASSESSMENT: J. CONSULTING & CLINICAL PSYCHOL. 75 (1990).

5. Kenneth Tardiff et al., *A Prospective Study of Violence by Psychiatric Patients After Hospital Discharge*, 48 PSYCHIATRIC SERVICES 678 (1997). *See also* Kenneth Tardiff et al., *Violence by Patients Admitted to a Private Psychiatric Hospital*, 154 AM. J. PSYCHIATRY 88 (1997).

6. Tardiff et al., *A Prospective Study*, *supra* note 5, at 678.

7. Henry Steadman et al., *Designing a New Generation of Risk Assessment Research*, in VIOLENCE AND MENTAL DISORDER: DEVELOPMENTS IN RISK ASSESSMENT (J. Monahan and H. Steadman eds., 1994).

8. Henry Steadman et al., *Violence by People Discharged from Acute Psychiatric Inpatient Facilities and by Others in the Same Neighborhoods*, 55 ARCHIVES GEN. PSYCHIATRY 1 (1998).

Kansas City, MO). Patient self-reports of violence were augmented by reports from collaterals (usually family members) and by police and hospital records.

Findings suggest that it is crucial for future studies to use multiple measures of violence rather than the single measures that have characterized most prior research. Relying solely on agency records, Steadman et al. reported a one-year violence rate for all discharged patients of 4.5%. By using three independent information sources, they reported a rate six times higher: 27.5%. Steadman et al. found the presence of a co-occurring substance abuse disorder to be a key factor in violence: the 1–year prevalence of violence was 17.9% for patients with an Axis I mental disorder (i.e., schizophrenia, major depression, or bipolar disorder) and without a substance abuse diagnosis, 31.1% for patients with an Axis I mental disorder and a substance abuse diagnosis, and 43.0% for patients with some other form of mental disorder (primarily Axis II diagnoses of personality or adjustment disorder) and a substance abuse diagnosis.[9]

At one site (Pittsburgh), Steadman et al. obtained a general-population comparison group, consisting of 519 people living in the neighborhoods in which the patients resided after hospital discharge. They found the prevalence of violence among patients without symptoms of substance abuse to be statistically indistinguishable from the prevalence of violence among others in their neighborhoods without symptoms of substance abuse. Substance abuse significantly raised the prevalence of violence in both patient and community samples. Among those who reported symptoms of substance abuse, the prevalence of violence among patients was significantly higher than the prevalence of violence among others in their neighborhoods during the first follow-up (i.e., the first 10 weeks after discharge from the hospital). The patient sample also was significantly more likely to report such symptoms of substance abuse than was the community sample.

As will be discussed below, these studies of institutionalized populations of mental patients, while valuable for many purposes, have serious biases when used to draw inferences about the fundamental relationship between violence and mental disorder. For that purpose, data on unselected samples of people from the open community are needed to augment the findings based on the behavior of identified mental patients. Fortunately, a seminal study by Swanson, Holzer, Ganju, and Jono provides this essential epidemiological information. Swanson and his colleagues drew their data from the National Institute of Mental Health's Epidemiological Catchment Area (ECA) study.[10] Representative weighted samples of adult household residents of Baltimore, Durham, and Los Angeles were pooled to form a data base of approximately 10,000 people. The Diagnostic Interview Schedule (DIS), a structured interview designed for use by trained lay persons, was used to establish mental disorder according to the criteria established in the American Psychiatric

---

9. *See also* Marvin Swartz et al., *Violence and Severe Mental Illness: The Effects of Substance Abuse and Nonadherence to Medication*, 155 Am. J. Psychiatry 226 (1998); Jeffrey Swanson et al., *Violent Behavior Preceding Hospitalization Among Persons with Severe Mental Illness*, 23 Law & Hum. Behav. 185 (1999); Barbara Havassy & Paul Arns, *Relationship of Cocaine and Other Substance Dependence to Well–Being* of High–Risk Psychiatric Patients, 49 Psychiatric Services 935 (1998).

10. Jeffrey W. Swanson et al., *Violence and Psychiatric Disorder in the Community: Evidence from the Epidemiologic Catchment Area Surveys*, 41 Hospital & Community Psychiatry 761 (1990).

Association's official Diagnostic and Statistical Manual (3d)—known as DSM III. Five items on the DIS—four embedded among the criteria for antisocial personality disorder and one that formed part of the diagnosis of alcohol abuse/dependence—were used to indicate violent behavior.[11] A respondent was counted as positive for violence if he endorsed at least one of these items and reported that the act occurred during the year preceding the interview. This index of violent behavior, as Swanson et al. note, is a "blunt measure": it is based on self-report without corroboration, the questions overlap considerably, and it does not differentiate in terms of the frequency or the severity of violence. Yet there is little doubt that each of the target behaviors is indeed "violent," and I believe that the measure is a reasonable estimate of the prevalence of violent behavior.

Confidence in the Swanson et al. findings is increased by their conformity to the demographic correlates of violence known from the criminological literature. Violence in the ECA study was seven times as prevalent among the young as among the old, twice as prevalent among males as among females, and three times as prevalent among persons of the lowest social class as among persons of the highest social class.

But it is the clinical findings that are of direct interest here. Three findings are noteworthy: (1) the prevalence of violence is over five times higher among people who meet criteria for a DSM–III Axis I diagnosis (11–13 percent) than among people who are not diagnosable (2 percent); (2) the prevalence of violence among persons who meet criteria for a diagnosis of schizophrenia, major depression, or mania/bi-polar disorder is remarkably similar (between 11 and 13 percent); and (3) the prevalence of violence among persons who meet criteria for a diagnosis of alcoholism (25 percent) is twelve times that of persons who receive no diagnosis, and the prevalence of violence among persons who meet criteria for being diagnosed as abusing drugs (35 percent) is sixteen times that of persons who receive no diagnosis.

When both demographic and clinical factors were combined in a regression equation to predict the occurrence of violence, several significant predictors emerged. Violence was most likely to occur among young, lower class males, among those with a substance abuse diagnosis, and among those with a diagnosis of major mental disorder.[12]

Another equally notable study not only corroborates the ECA data but takes them a significant step further. Link, Andrews, and Cullen analyzed data from a larger study conducted using the Psychiatric Epidemiology Research Interview (PERI) to measure symptoms and life events.[13] Link et al. compared rates of arrest and of self-reported violence (including hitting, fighting, weapon use, and "hurting someone badly") in a sample of approxi-

---

11. The items were: "(1) Did you ever hit or throw things at your wife/husband/partner? [If so] Were you ever the one who threw things first, regardless of who started the argument? Did you hit or throw things first on more than one occasion? (2) Have you ever spanked or hit a child (yours or anyone else's) hard enough so that he or she had bruises or had to stay in bed or see a doctor? (3) Since age 18, have you been in more than one fight that came to swapping blows, other than fights with your hus-band/wife/partner? (4) Have you ever used a weapon like a stick, knife, or gun in a fight since you were 18? (5) Have you ever gotten into physical fights while drinking?"

12. Jeffrey W. Swanson & Charles E. Holzer, *Violence and The ECA Data*, 42 HOSPITAL & COMMUNITY PSYCHIATRY 79 (1991).

13. Bruce G. Link et al., *The Violent and Illegal Behavior of Mental Patients Reconsidered*, 57 AM. SOCIOLOGICAL REV. 275 (1992).

mately 400 adults from the Washington Heights area of New York City who had never been in a mental hospital or sought help from a mental health professional with rates of arrest and self-reported violence in several samples of former mental patients from the same area. To eliminate alternative explanations of their data, the researchers controlled, in various analyses, for an extraordinary number of factors: age, gender, educational level, ethnicity (African–American, white, and Hispanic), socioeconomic status, family composition (e.g., married with children), homicide rate of the census tract in which a subject lived, and the subject's "need for approval." This last variable was included to control for the possibility that patients might be more willing to report socially undesirable behavior (such as violence) than non-patients.

The study found that the patient groups were almost always more violent than the never-treated community sample, often two to three times as violent. As in the ECA study, demographic factors clearly related to violence (e.g., males, the less educated, and those from high-crime neighborhoods were more likely to be violent). But even when all the demographic and personal factors, such as social desirability, were taken into account, significant differences between the patients and the never-treated community residents remained. The association between mental patient status and violent behavior, as the authors noted, was "remarkably robust" and could not be explained away as an artifact.

Most importantly, Link et al. then controlled for "current symptomatology." They did this by using the psychotic symptoms scale of the PERI (e.g., "During the past year, how often have you heard things that other people say they can't hear?"). Remarkably, not a single difference in rates of recent violent behavior between patients and never-treated community residents remained significant when current psychotic symptoms were controlled. The psychotic symptomatology scale, on the other hand, was significantly and strongly related to most indices of recent violent behavior, even when additional factors, such as alcohol and drug use, were taken into account. Finally, Link et al. also found that the psychotic symptomatology scale significantly predicted violent behavior among the never-treated community residents. Even among people who had never been formally treated for mental disorder, actively experiencing psychotic symptoms was associated with the commission of violent acts.

Link and Stueve[14] re-analyzed the data used in Link et al.[15] to allow for a more precise specification of *what kind* of "psychotic symptoms" are most related to violence. They found that three symptoms on the psychotic symptoms scale largely explained the relationship between mental disorder and violence.[16] The authors refer to these as "threat/control-override symptoms," because they either involve the overriding of internal self-controls by external factors (items 1 and 2) or imply a specific threat of harm from others (item 3).

14. Bruce Link & Ann Stueve, *Psychotic Symptoms and the Violent/Illegal Behavior of Mental Patients Compared to Community Controls, in* VIOLENCE AND MENTAL DISORDER: DEVELOPMENTS IN RISK ASSESSMENT (J. Monahan and H. Steadman eds., 1994).

15. Link et al., *supra* note 13.

16. The items were: During the past year ... (1) "How often have you felt that your mind was dominated by forces beyond your control?"; (2) "How often have you felt that thoughts were put into your head that were not your own?"; and (3) "How often have you felt that there were people who wished to do you harm?"

Swanson et al. replicated Link and Stueve's finding with data from the Epidemiological Catchment Area (ECA) study.[17] However, Appelbaum et al., using data from the prospective MacArthur Violence Risk Assessment Study,[18] failed to replicate this finding. They stated that any connection between threat/control-override symptoms and violence "may be accounted for by an association between a generally suspicious attitude towards others—with associated anger and impulsiveness—and violent behavior,"[19] rather than by "delusional" thinking.

Several major European studies have been published that employ a "birth cohort" methodology that lies somewhere between the institutional and open community strategies just described.[20] Hodgins and her colleagues[21] studied everyone born in Denmark between 1943 and 1947, a sample of over 350,000 people. Data on psychiatric admissions and on criminal convictions up to age 43 were obtained. Among both men and women, all diagnostic groups (except organic disorder) were found to be at increased risk of criminality in general, and of violent crime in particular. Depending on the time period studied, men with a major mental disorder were 2–4 times more likely to have a conviction for a violent crime than men with no disorder, and women with a major mental disorder were 6–9 times more likely to have a conviction for a violent crime than women without a major mental disorder.

Belfrage studied all patients diagnosed with schizophrenia, affective psychosis, and paranoia who were discharged from mental hospitals in Stockholm in 1986, and followed them for 10 years in the national police register to see who was sentenced for a criminal conviction.[22] The rate of criminality among this sample during the 10 years after discharge was 14 percent.[23] This 28 percent lifetime figure compares with a lifetime rate of criminal conviction and sentencing in the general Swedish population of 10 percent. Close to half of the crimes that the patients committed were violent. Persons diagnosed

17. Jeffrey Swanson et al., *Psychotic Symptoms and Disorders and the Risk of Violent Behaviour in the Community*, 6 CRIM. BEHAV. & MENTAL HEALTH 317 (1996).

18. Paul Appelbaum et al., *Violence and Delusions: Data from the MacArthur Violence Risk Assessment Study*, 157 AM. J. PSYCHIATRY 566 (2000).

19. *Id*. at 571.

20. *See also* Paul Mullen et al., *Community Care and Criminal Offending in Schizophrenia*, 355 THE LANCET 614 (2000). Using the Victorian Psychiatric Case Register in Australia, these researchers concluded that "Compared with controls, significantly more of those with schizophrenia were convicted at least once for all categories of criminal offending except sexual offenses." *Id*. at 614. Similar results have been found in New Zealand; Louise Arseneault et al., *Mental Disorders and Violence in a Total Birth Cohort: Results from the Dunedin Study,* 57 ARCHIVES GEN. PSYCHIATRY 979 (2000); and in Israel, Ann Stueve & Bruce Link, *Violence and Psychiatric Disorders: Results from an Epidemiological Study of Young Adults in Israel*, 68 PSYCHIATRIC Q. 327 (1997).

21. Sheilagh Hodgins et al., *Mental Disorder and Crime: Evidence from a Danish Birth*

Cohort, 53 ARCHIVES GEN. PSYCHIATRY 489 (1996). In further work with this sample, the researchers concluded, "Individuals hospitalized for schizophrenia and men hospitalized with organic psychosis have higher rates of arrest for violence than those never hospitalized. This relationship cannot be fully explained by demographic factors or comorbid substance abuse." Patricia Brennan et al., *Major Mental Disorders and Criminal Violence in a Danish Birth Cohort*, 57 ARCHIVES GEN. PSYCHIATRY 494, 494 (2000).

22. Henrik Belfrage, *A Ten–Year Follow–Up of Criminality in Stockholm Mental Patients: New Evidence for a Relationship Between Mental Disorder and Crime*, 38 BRIT. J. CRIMINOLOGY 145 (1998). Compare Per Lindqvist & Peter Allebeck, *Criminality Among Stockholm Mental Patients*, 39 BRIT. J. CRIMINOLOGY 450 (1999).

23. That is, 28 percent of the patients had a criminal conviction and sentence during their lifetime, and for half of these that conviction and sentence occurred in the 10 years *after* discharge.

with schizophrenia had a significantly higher rate of crime in general than persons with other diagnoses, but not a higher rate of violent crime.

Tiihonen and colleagues performed a longitudinal, 26–year prospective study on an unselected birth cohort of 12,058 individuals born in Northern Finland in 1966.[24] Information on mental hospitalization was obtained from the Finnish Hospital Discharge Register and information from criminal records was obtained from the Ministry of Justice. The researchers concluded that people diagnosed with schizophrenia were 7 times more likely to have a conviction for a violent crime, and people with an affective disorder were 9 times more likely to have a violent conviction, than people with no disorder.

"It must be emphasized," these researchers noted, "that alcohol abuse accounts for most of the criminal behavior among schizophrenic subjects." They also caution, as did Hodgins et al., that "these data may be generalizable to other industrialized Western countries that have relatively low crime rates (e.g., Sweden, Denmark, Norway, United Kingdom, and Canada) but not to countries with high crime rates such as the United States."[25]

Wessely reported findings from a longitudinal study based on the Camberwell Cumulative Psychiatric Case Register in England.[26] The subjects were all persons from Camberwell who had their first contact with psychiatric services between 1965 and 1984. He summarized the results:

> Overall, we conclude that men with clinically defined schizophrenia do not have an overall increased risk of criminality compared with other mental disorders.... However, the risk of being convicted for violent offenses is at least twice that of men with other mental disorders.... In contrast, women with schizophrenia have an overall increased rate of convictions compared with all other mental illnesses, found across several offense categories, including violence.[27]

Wessely noted that "the strongest predictors of criminal behavior in people with schizophrenia were gender, ethnicity, age of onset and previous offending. No amount of psychiatric care and supervision can alter these associations."[28]

[b]   Disorder Among the Violent

Recall that there is a second empirical tack that might be taken to determine whether a fundamental relationship between mental disorder and violence exists and to estimate what the magnitude of that relationship might be. If mental disorder is in fact a contributing cause to the occurrence of violence, then the prevalence of mental disorder should be higher among people who commit violent acts than among people who do not. As before, there are two ways to ascertain the existence of such a relationship: by

---

24. Jari Tiihonen et al., *Specific Major Mental Disorders and Criminality: A 26–Year Prospective Study of the 1966 Northern Finland Birth Cohort*, 154 AM. J. PSYCHIATRY 840 (1997).

25. *Id.* at 844.

26. Simon Wessely, *The Epidemiology of Crime, Violence and Schizophrenia*, 170 BRIT. J.

PSYCHIATRY 8 (1997). *See also* Simon Wessely et al., *The Criminal Careers of Incident Cases of Schizophrenia*, 24 PSYCHOLOGICAL MED. 483 (1994).

27. Wessely (1997), *supra* note 26, at 11.

28. *Id.*

studying treated cases—in this instance, people "treated" for violence by being institutionalized in local jails and state prisons—and determining their rates of mental disorder, and by studying untreated cases—people in the open community who are violent but not institutionalized for it—and determining their rates of mental disorder.

A large number of studies exist that estimate the prevalence of mental disorder among jail and prison inmates. Of course, not all jail and prison inmates have been convicted of a violent crime. Yet 66 percent of state prisoners have a current or past conviction for violence,[29] and there is no evidence that the rates of disorder of jail inmates charged with violent offenses differ from those of jail inmates charged with non-violent offenses. So I believe that data on the prevalence of disorder among inmates in general also apply reasonably well to violent inmates in particular.

Teplin reviewed 18 studies of mental disorder among jail samples.[30] Most of the studies were conducted on inmates referred for a mental health evaluation, and thus present obviously inflated rates of disorder. Among those few studies that randomly sampled jail inmates, rates of mental disorder varied widely, from 5 to 16 percent psychotic. Roth, in reviewing the literature on the prevalence of mental disorder among prison inmates, concluded that the rate of psychosis was "on the order of 5 percent or less of the total prison population",[31] and the rate of any form of disorder was in the 15–20 percent range. More recent studies have reported somewhat higher rates of serious mental disorder. Steadman, Fabisiak, Dvoskin, and Holohean, in a "level of care" survey of over 3,000 prisoners in New York State, concluded that 8 percent had "severe mental disabilities" and another 16 percent had "significant mental disabilities."[32]

While the rates of mental disorder among jail and prison inmates appears very high, comparison data for similarly defined mental disorder among the general non-institutionalized population were typically not available. As well, the methods of diagnosing mental disorder in the jail and prison studies often consisted of unstandardized clinical interviews or the use of proxy variables such as prior mental hospitalization.[33]

Recently, however, several studies using jail inmates and prisoners as subjects have become available that use the Diagnostic Interview Schedule (DIS) as their diagnostic instrument. This not only allows for a standardized method of assessing disorder independent of previous hospitalization, it permits comparison across the studies and between these institutionalized populations and the random community samples of the ECA research.

In the first study, Teplin administered the DIS to a stratified random sample—half misdemeanants and half felons—of 728 males from the Cook

29. BUREAU OF JUSTICE STATISTICS, VIOLENT CRIME IN THE UNITED STATES, REPORT NO. NCJ 127855 (1991).

30. Linda A. Teplin, *The Prevalence of Severe Mental Disorder among Male Urban Jail Detainees: Comparison with the Epidemiologic Catchment Area Program,* 80 AM. J. PUB. HEALTH 663 (1990).

31. Loren Roth, *Correctional Psychiatry, in* MODERN LEGAL MEDICINE, PSYCHIATRY AND FORENSIC SCIENCE 688 (W. Curran, A. McGarry, and C. Petty eds., 1980).

32. Henry Steadman et al., *A Survey of Mental Disability Among State Prison Inmates,* 38 HOSPITAL AND COMMUNITY PSYCHIATRY 1086 (1987).

33. Henry Steadman et al., *The Impact of State Mental Hospital Deinstitutionalization on United States Prison Populations, 1968–1978,* 75 J. CRIM. L. & CRIMINOLOGY 474 (1984).

County (Chicago) jail.[34] In the most comparable of the prison studies, the California Department of Corrections commissioned a consortium of research organizations to administer the DIS to a stratified random sample of 362 male inmates in California prisons. Comparative data from the ECA study for male respondents were provided by Teplin.[35]

These studies reveal, for example, that the prevalence of schizophrenia (3 percent) is approximately three times higher in the jail and prison samples than in the general population samples (1 percent), and the prevalence of major depression (4 percent) is four times higher than in the general population (1 percent). Overall, the prevalence of any severe disorder (6–8 percent) was 3–4 times higher than in the general population (2 percent). Although no controls for demographic factors existed in the prison study, Teplin controlled for race and age in the jail study, and the jail-general population differences persisted. While these studies all relied on male inmates, even more dramatic data for female prisoners have been reported in two studies.[36]

These findings on the comparatively high prevalence of mental disorder among jail and prison inmates have enormous policy implications for mental health screening of admissions to these facilities and for the need for mental health treatment in correctional institutions.[37] But given the systematic bias inherent in the use of identified criminal offenders, they cannot fully address the issue of whether there is a fundamental relationship between mental disorder and violence. Mentally disordered offenders may be more or less likely to be arrested and imprisoned than non-disordered offenders. On the one hand, Robertson found that offenders who were schizophrenic were much more likely than non-disordered offenders to be arrested at the scene of the crime or to give themselves up to the police.[38] Teplin, in the only actual field study in this area, found the police more likely to arrest disordered than non-disordered suspects.[39] On the other hand, Klassen and O'Connor found that released mental patients whose violence in the community evoked an official response were twice as likely to be re-hospitalized—and thereby to avoid going to jail—than they were to be arrested.[40] An individual's status as a jail or prison inmate, in short, is not independent of the presence of mental disorder.

As before, complementary data on the prevalence of mental disorder among unselected samples of people in the open community who commit violent acts are necessary to fully address this issue. And, as before, the analysis of the ECA data by Swanson et al. provides the required information.[41]

---

34. Teplin, *supra* note 30.

35. CALIFORNIA DEPARTMENT OF CORRECTIONS, OFFICE OF HEALTH CARE SERVICES, CURRENT DESCRIPTION, EVALUATION, AND RECOMMENDATIONS FOR TREATMENT OF MENTALLY DISORDERED CRIMINAL OFFENDERS (1989).

36. A.E. Daniel et al., *Lifetime and Six–Month Prevalence of Psychiatric Disorders Among Sentenced Female Offenders*, 16 BULL. AM. ACAD. PSYCHIATRY & L. 333 (1988); Linda Teplin et al., *The Prevalence of Psychiatric Disorder Among Incarcerated Women: I. Pretrial Detainees,* 53 ARCHIVES GEN. PSYCHIATRY 505 (1996).

37. HENRY STEADMAN ET AL., THE MENTALLY ILL IN JAIL: PLANNING FOR ESSENTIAL SERVICES (1989).

38. Graham Robertson, *Arrest Patterns Among Mentally Disordered Offenders*, 153 BRIT. J. PSYCHIATRY 313 (1988).

39. Linda A. Teplin, *The Criminality of the Mentally Ill: A Dangerous Misconception*, 142 AM. J. PSYCHIATRY 676 (1985).

40. Klassen & O'Connor (1990), *supra* note 4.

41. Swanson et al., *supra* note 10.

The prevalence of schizophrenia among male respondents who endorsed at least one of the five questions indicating violent behavior in the past year (4 percent) was approximately four times higher than among respondents who did not report violence (1 percent), the prevalence of affective disorder (9 percent) was three times higher (3 percent), the prevalence of substance abuse (either alcohol or other drugs) (42 percent) was eight times higher (5 percent) among persons who reported violence than among persons who did not report violence.

Several studies of the rates of disorder among women in American jails have recently been published by Teplin.[42] She found that over 80 percent of a sample of jail detainees met criteria for one or more lifetime psychiatric disorders, and 70 percent had been symptomatic within six months of the jail interview. Substance abuse and post-traumatic stress disorder were the most common diagnoses. The most common of the major mental illnesses was major depression. Rates for all mental disorders (except schizophrenia) were higher in jailed women than in women in the general population.

In addition to these studies conducted in the United States, two non-American studies of rates of mental disorder among criminal or violent populations are available. Wallace et al. used a psychiatric case register to ascertain the rate of contact with the mental health system by all persons convicted in the Higher Courts of Victoria, Australia, between 1993 and 1995.[43] Approximately one-quarter of those convicted of any offense, and one-third of males convicted of a violent offense, had prior contact with the mental health system.

Eronen et al. studied the forensic psychiatric records of persons arrested for homicide in Finland from 1984 through 1991. (Finish courts had ordered a forensic psychiatric evaluation for 70 percent of all persons charged with homicide).[44] They compared rates of offender diagnosis with estimated diagnostic rates in the general population. They found that 6 percent of the homicide offenders were diagnosed with schizophrenia, compared with a general population rate of less than 1 percent. Personality disorders were diagnosed in 35 percent of the offenders, and 5 percent of the general population. Alcoholism was diagnosed in 39 percent of the male offenders, compared to 6 percent of the male population, and 32 percent of the female offenders, compared to 1 percent of the female population.

Research on the prevalence of mental disorder among persons who are violent, therefore, complements research on the prevalence of violence among persons with mental disorder. Both strands of research are consistent with

42. Linda Teplin et al., *The Prevalence of Psychiatric Disorder Among Incarcerated Women: Pretrial Jail Detainees*, 53 ARCHIVES GEN. PSYCHIATRY 505 (1996); Linda Teplin et al., *Mentally Disordered Women in Jail: Who Receives Services?*, 87 AM. J. PUB. HEALTH 604 (1997). For a self-report survey of mental illness among both male and female American prisoners, see Paula Ditton, *Bureau of Justice Statistics Special Report: Mental Health and Treatment of Inmates and Probationers* (1999). Prisoners were defined as mentally ill in this study if "they reported a current mental or

emotional condition, or they reported an overnight stay in a mental hospital or treatment program." *Id.* at 2. Overall 16% of all persons in prisons or jails were estimated to be mentally ill by this definition.

43. Cameron Wallace et al., *Serious Criminal Offending and Mental Disorder: Case Linkage Study*, 172 BRIT. J. PSYCHIATRY 477 (1998).

44. Markku Eronen et al., *Mental Disorders and Homicidal Behavior in Finland*, 53 ARCHIVES GEN. PSYCHIATRY 497 (1996).

the proposition that mental disorder is a risk factor of modest magnitude for the occurrence of violence.

[2] The Validity of Clinical Predictions

I reviewed research on the accuracy of clinical judgments at predicting the criterion of violent behavior toward others in 1981, concluding that "psychiatrists and psychologists are accurate in no more than one out of three predictions of violent behavior over a several-year period among institutionalized populations that had both committed violence in the past (and thus had high base rates for it) and who were diagnosed as mentally ill."[45] Remarkably, only one study of the validity of clinicians at predicting violence in the community was published between 1979 and 1993. This was a study conducted in 1978 of court-ordered pretrial mental health assessments.[46] Thirty-nine percent of the defendants rated by clinicians as having a "medium" or "high" likelihood for being dangerous to others were reported to have committed "dangerous" acts during a two-year follow-up compared to 26% of the defendants predicted to have a "low" likelihood of violence, a statistically significant difference, but not a large one in absolute terms.[47]

More recently, researchers have shown a renewed interest in the topic of clinical prediction. For example, Lidz, Mulvey, and Gardner, in what is surely the most sophisticated study published on the clinical prediction of violence, took as their subjects male and female patients being examined in the acute psychiatric emergency room of a large civil hospital.[48] Psychiatrists and nurses were asked to assess potential patient violence toward others over the next six-month period. Violence was measured by official records, by patient self-report, and by the report of a collateral informant in the community (e.g., a family member). Patients who elicited professional concern regarding future violence were found to be significantly more likely to be violent after release (53%) than were patients who had not elicited such concern (36%). The accuracy of clinical prediction did not vary as a function of the patient's age or race. The accuracy of clinicians' predictions of male violence substantially exceeded chance levels, both for patients with and without a prior history of violent behavior. In contrast, the accuracy of clinicians' predictions of female violence did not differ from chance. While the actual rate of violent incidents among released female patients (46%) was higher than the rate among released male patients (42%), the clinicians had predicted that only 22 percent of the women would be violent, compared with predicting that 45 percent of the men would commit a violent act. The inaccuracy of clinicians at predicting violence among women appeared to be a function of the clinicians' serious underestimation of the base-rate of violence among mentally disordered women (perhaps due to an inappropriate extrapolation from the great gender differences in rates of violence among persons without mental disorder).[49]

45. John Monahan, The Clinical Prediction of Violent Behavior 47–49 (1981).

46. Diana S. Sepejak et al., *Clinical Predictions of Dangerousness: Two Year Follow-up of 408 Pre-trial Forensic Cases*, 11 Bull. Am. Acad. Psychiatry & L. 171 (1983).

47. *Id.* at 181 n.12.

48. Charles Lidz et al., *The Accuracy of Predictions of Violence to Others*, 269 J. Am. Med. Assoc. 1007 (1993).

49. Close to 90 percent of all persons arrested for violent crime in the United States are men, and "there is no place in the world where men make up less than 80 percent of the people arrested for violence, now or at any

McNiel and Binder illustrate research predicting inpatient violence (rather than violence in the community). They studied clinical predictions that patients would be violent during the first week of hospitalization.[50] Of the patients whom nurses had estimated had a 0% to 33% probability of being violent on the ward, 10% were later rated by the nurses as having committed a violent act; of the patients whom nurses had estimated had a 34% to 66% chance of being violent, 24% were later rated as having committed a violent act; and of the patients whom nurses had estimated had a 67% to 100% chance of being violent, 40% were later rated as having acted violently.

The field of "violence risk assessment" has seen a dramatic shift in the past several years away from studies attempting to validate the accuracy of clinical predictions and toward studies attempting to isolate specific risk factors[51] that are actuarially (meaning statistically) associated with violence.[52] Borum has noted that a wide range of procedures can be subsumed under the rubric of "actuarial" prediction:

> At a minimum, these devices can serve as a checklist for clinicians to ensure that essential areas of inquiry are recalled and evaluated. At best, they may be able to provide hard actuarial data on the probability of violence among people (and environments) with a given set of characteristics, circumstances, or both.[53]

There is a long tradition in criminology of using actuarial techniques to combine risk factors in predicting recidivism by released prisoners.[54] Actuarial techniques have only recently been applied in earnest to predicting violence among people with mental disorder, however.[55] For example, Klassen and

time in history." JOHN MONAHAN, *Causes of Violence, in* DRUGS AND VIOLENCE IN AMERICA 79 (U.S. Sentencing Commission ed., 1993); *see also* Dale McNiel & Renee Binder, *Correlates of Accuracy in the Assessment of Psychiatric Inpatients' Risk of Violence,* 152 AM. J. PSYCHIATRY 901, 901 (1995) ("Clinical judgments emphasizing gender and race/ethnicity were associated with predictive errors.").

50. Dale McNiel & Renée Binder, *Clinical Assessment of the Risk of Violence Among Psychiatric Inpatients,* 148 AM. J. PSYCHIATRY 1317 (1991).

51. On terminology, see Helena Kraemer et al., *Coming to Terms With the Terms of Risk,* 54 ARCHIVES GEN. PSYCHIATRY 337 (1997). To say that a variable is a "risk factor" for violence means two things and only two things: (1) the variable correlates with the outcome (in this case, violence), and (2) the variable precedes the outcome. To call a variable a risk factor does not imply that its relationship to the outcome is "causal."

52. An excellent brief guide for clinicians doing violence risk assessment is Dale McNiel, *Empirically Based Clinical Evaluation and Management of the Potentially Violent Patient, in* EMERGENCIES IN MENTAL HEALTH PRACTICE: EVALUATION AND MANAGEMENT 95–116 (P. Kleespies ed., 1998). *See also* Dale McNiel et al., *The Relationship Between Confidence and Accuracy in Clinical Assessment of Psychiatric*

Patients' Potential for Violence, 22 LAW & HUM. BEHAV. 655 (1998). Clinical risk assessment is also very well treated in GARY MELTON, JOHN PETRILA, NORMAN POYTHRESS, & CHRISTOPHER SLOBOGIN, PSYCHOLOGICAL EVALUATIONS FOR THE COURTS: A HANDBOOK FOR MENTAL HEALTH PROFESSIONALS AND LAWYERS (2d ed, 1997). Clinical and actuarial approaches are considered in depth in an important book, VERNON QUINSEY, GRANT HARRIS, MARNIE RICE, & CATHERINE CORMIER, VIOLENT OFFENDERS: APPRAISING AND MANAGING RISK (1998).

53. Randy Borum, *Improving the Clinical Practice of Violence Risk Assessment: Technology, Guidelines, and Training,* 51 AM. PSYCHOLOGIST 945, 948 (1996).

54. For a strong argument for the superiority of actuarial over clinical prediction, *see* William Gove & Paul Meehl, *Comparative Efficiency of Informal (Subjective, Impressionistic) and Formal (Mechanical, Algorithmic) Prediction Procedures: The Clinical–Statistical Controversy,* 2 PSYCHOL., PUB. POL., & L. 293 (1996); John Swets et al., *Psychological Science Can Improve Diagnostic Decisions,* 1 PSYCHOLOGICAL SCI. PUB. INTEREST 1 (2000).

55. A strong move to actuarially assess risk of recidivism among sexual offenders is also taking place. *See* P. Randall Kropp & Stephen Hart, *The Spousal Assault Risk Assessment (SARA) Guide: Reliability and Validity in*

O'Connor found that, among males released from a mental hospital, a diagnosis of substance abuse, prior arrests for violent crime, and age (young) were significantly associated with arrests for violent crime after release into the community.[56] Several actuarial tools have been studied in the past several years. A well-established instrument that has been associated with violence in many studies is the Hare Psychopathy Checklist–Revised (the Hare PCL–R). Hare has argued that "psychopathy is the single most important clinical construct in the criminal justice system, with particularly strong implications for the assessment of risk for recidivism and violence."[57]

A noteworthy advance in the development of actuarial risk assessment to predict violence in the community was reported by Harris, Rice, and Quinsey.[58] A sample of 618 men who were either treated or administered a pre-trial assessment at a maximum security forensic hospital in Canada served as subjects. All had been charged with a serious criminal offense. A wide variety of predictive variables were coded from institutional files. The criterion variable was any new criminal charge for a violent offense, or return to the institution for an act that would otherwise have resulted in such a charge. The average time at risk after release was almost 7 years. Twelve variables were identified for inclusion in the final statistical prediction instrument, the Violence Risk Appraisal Guide (VRAG).[59] If the scores on this instrument were dichotomized into "high" and "low," the results indicated that 55 percent of the "high scoring" subjects committed violent recidivism, compared with 19 percent of the "low scoring" group.[60]

Adult Male Offenders, 24 LAW & HUM. BEHAV. 101 (2000); R. Karl Hanson & David Thornton, *Improving Risk Assessments for Sex Offenders: A Comparison of Three Actuarial Scales*, 24 LAW & HUM. BEHAV. 119 (2000).

56. Deidre Klassen & William O'Connor, *A Prospective Study of Predictors of Violence in Adult Male Mental Patients*, 12 LAW & HUM. BEHAV. 143 (1988).

57. Robert Hare, *The Hare PCL–R: Some Issues Concerning its Use and Misuse*, 3 LEGAL & CRIMINOLOGICAL PSYCHOL. 99 (1998); Anders Tengstrom et al., *Psychopathy (PCL–R) as a Predictor of Violent Recidivism Among Criminal Offenders with Schizophrenia*, 24 LAW & HUM. BEHAV. 45 (2000). For a review of the extensive research on psychopathy and violence, see Robert Hare, *Psychopathy: A Clinical Construct Whose Time Has Come*, 23 CRIM. JUST. & BEHAV. 25 (1996).

58. Grant T. Harris et al., *Violent Recidivism of Mentally Disordered Offenders: The Development of a Statistical Prediction Instrument*, 20 CRIM. JUST. & BEHAV. 315 (1993); see also Vernon Quinsey et al., *Actuarial Prediction of Sexual Recidivism*, 10 J. INTERPERSONAL VIOLENCE 85 (1995); David Villeneuve & Vernon Quinsey, *Predictors of General and Violent Recidivism Among Mentally Disordered Inmates*, 22 CRIM. JUST. & BEHAV. 397 (1995); Marnie Rice & Grant Harris, *Violent Recidivism: Assessing Predictive Validity*, 63 J. CONSULTING & CLINICAL PSYCHOL. 737 (1995); Marnie Rice & Grant Harris, *Cross-Validation and Extension of the Vio-*

lence Risk Appraisal Guide for Child Molesters and Rapists, 21 LAW & HUM. BEHAV. 231 (1997); see also Grant Harris & Marnie Rice, *Risk Appraisal and Management of Violent Behavior*, 48 PSYCHIATRIC SERVICES 1168 (1997); Marnie Rice, *Violent Offender Research and Implications for the Criminal Justice System*, 52 AM. PSYCHOLOGIST 414 (1997); Marnie Rice & Grant Harris, *The Treatment of Mentally Disordered Offenders*, 3 PSYCHOL., PUB. POL. & L. 126 (1997).

59. The variables were (1) score on the Psychopathy Checklist, (2) separation from parents under age 16, (3) victim injury in index offense, (4) DSM–III schizophrenia, (5) never married, (6) elementary school maladjustment, (7) female victim in index offense, (8) failure on prior conditional release, (9) property offense history, (10) age at index offense, (11) alcohol abuse history, and (12) DSM–III personality disorder. For all variables except numbers 3, 4, 7, and 10 the nature of the relationship to subsequent violence was positive. (That is to say, subjects who injured a victim in the index offense, who were diagnosed as schizophrenic, who chose a female victim for the index offense, or who were older, were significantly *less* likely to be violent recidivists than other subjects.)

60. Computed from CHRISTOPHER D. WEBSTER, GRANT T. HARRIS, MARNIE E. RICE, CATHERINE CORMIER, & VERNON L. QUINSEY, THE VIOLENCE PREDICTION SCHEME: ASSESSING DANGEROUSNESS IN HIGH RISK MEN 33 (1994).

Douglas and Webster[61] reviewed research on a new actuarial instrument to assess risk of violence, the "HCR–20," which consists of 20 ratings addressing *H*istorical, *C*linical, or *R*isk management variables.[62] Douglas and Webster also reported data from a retrospective study with prisoners, finding that "scores above the median on the HCR–20 increased the odds of the presence of various measures of past violence and antisocial behavior by an average of four times."

Gardner, Lidz, Mulvey, and Shaw made an important methodological contribution to the use of actuarial information in predicting violence by civil patients in the community.[63] They contrast the usual "regression equation" model—in which points for various risk factors are summed to yield a prediction score, to which cut-offs are applied—with newer "regression tree" methods.[64] This regression tree identified a small group of patients (3% of the patient population) who committed violent acts at the high rate of 2.75 incidents per month.

The most recent development in this area is the publication of the work of the MacArthur Violence Risk Assessment Study.[65] Here, the researchers developed what they called an "Iterative Classification Tree," or ICT. They sought to increase the utility of this actuarial method for real-world clinical decision making by applying the method to a set of violence risk factors commonly available in clinical records or capable of being routinely assessed in clinical practice. Results showed that the ICT partitioned three-quarters of a sample of psychiatric patients into one of two categories with regard to their risk of violence to others during the first 20 weeks after discharge. One

61. Kevin Douglas & Christopher Webster, *The HCR–20 Violence Risk Assessment Scheme: Concurrent Validity in a Sample of Incarcerated Offenders*, 26 CRIM. JUST. & BEHAV. 3 (1999). *See also* Kevin Douglas et al., *Assessing Risk for Violence Among Psychiatric Patients: The HCR–20 Violence Risk Assessment Scheme and the Psychopathy Checklist; Screening Version*, 67 J. CONSULTING & CLINICAL PSYCHOL. 917 (1999); Martin Grann et al., *Actuarial Assessment of Risk for Violence: Predictive Validity of the VRAG and the Historical Part of the HCR–20*, 27 CRIM. JUST. & BEHAV. 97 (2000).

62. Christopher Webster et al., *HCR–20: Assessing Risk for Violence (version 2)*, Vancouver: Simon Fraser University (1995).

63. William Gardner et al., *A Comparison of Actuarial Methods for Identifying Repetitively Violent Patients with Mental Illness*, 20 LAW & HUM. BEHAV. 35 (1996); *see also* William Gardner et al., *Clinical Versus Actuarial Predictions of Violence in Patients with Mental Illnesses*, 64 J. CONSULTING & CLINICAL PSYCHOL. 602 (1996); Edward Mulvey & Charles Lidz, *The Clinical Prediction of Violence as a Conditional Judgment*, 33 SOC. PSYCHIATRY & PSYCHIATRIC EPIDEMIOLOGY S107 (1998).

64. A regression tree is "a structured sequence of yes/no questions that lead to the classification of a case." Gardner et al., *A Comparison*, *supra* note 63, at 36. The four Yes/No questions contained in the Gardner et al. re-

gression tree were: "Is BSI Hostility greater than 2?," [i.e., is the patient's score on the Hostility subscale of the Brief Symptom Inventory greater than 2?], "Is age less than 18?," "Is the patient a heavy drug user?," and "Are there more than 3 prior violent acts?"

65. Henry Steadman et al., *A Classification Tree Approach to the Development of Actuarial Violence Risk Assessment Tools*, 24 LAW & HUM. BEHAV. 83 (2000); John Monahan et al., *Developing a Clinically Useful Actuarial Tool for Assessing Violence Risk*, 176 BRIT. J. PSYCHIATRY 312 (2000); Eric Silver et al., *Assessing Violence Risk Among Discharged Psychiatric Patients: Toward an Ecological Approach*, 23 LAW & HUM. BEHAV. 235 (1999); Paul Appelbaum et al., *Violence and Delusions: Data from the MacArthur Violence Risk Assessment Study*, 157 AM. J. PSYCHIATRY 566 (2000); Thomas Grisso et al., *Violent Thoughts and Violent Behavior Following Hospitalization for Mental Disorder*, 68 J. CONSULTING & CLINICAL PSYCHOL. 388 (2000); Steven Banks et al., *A Multiple Models Approach to Violence Risk Assessment among People with Mental Disorder*, CRIM. JUST. & BEHAV. (forthcoming 2001). The entire study is described in JOHN MONAHAN, HENRY STEADMAN, ERIC SILVER, PAUL APPELBAUM, PAMELA ROBBINS, EDWARD MULVEY, LOREN ROTH, THOMAS GRISSO, & STEVEN BANKS, RETHINKING RISK ASSESSMENT: THE MACARTHUR STUDY OF MENTAL DISORDER AND VIOLENCE (2001).

category consisted of groups whose rates of violence were *no more than half* the baserate of the total patient sample (i.e., equal to or less than 9% violent). The other category consisted of groups whose rates of violence were *at least twice* the baserate of the total patient sample (i.e., equal to or greater than 37% violent). The prevalence of violence within individual Risk Groups varied from 3% to 53%.

§ 2–2.1.2 The Scientific Methods Applied in the Research

Different scientific methods have been applied in the research on whether mental disorder is a risk factor for violence and in the research on the validity of clinical predictions of violence.[66]

[1] Mental Disorder and Violence

As mentioned above, three types of studies provide data from hospitalized mental patients that can be used to estimate the relationship between mental disorder and violence. One type looks at the prevalence of violent acts committed by patients *before* they entered the hospital. A second type looks at the prevalence of violent incidents committed by mental patients *during* their hospital stay. A final type of study addresses the prevalence of violent behavior among mental patients *after* they have been released from the hospital.

Each of these three types of research has important policy and practice implications. Studies of violence before hospitalization supply data on the workings of civil commitment laws and the interaction between the mental health and criminal justice systems.[67] Studies of violence during hospitalization have significance for the level of security required in mental health facilities and the need for staff training in managing aggressive incidents. Studies of violence after hospitalization provide essential base-rate information for use in the risk assessments involved in release decision making and in after-care planning.

For the purpose of determining whether there is a fundamental relationship between mental disorder and violent behavior, however, each of these three types of research is unavailing. Only rarely do the studies provide any comparative data on the prevalence of similarly-defined violence among non-hospitalized groups. While the rates of violence by mental patients before, during, or after hospitalization reported in the other studies certainly appear much higher than would be expected by chance, the general lack of data from non-patients makes comparison speculative. But even if such data were available, several sources of systematic bias would make their use for epidemiological purposes highly suspect. Since these studies dealt with persons who were subsequently, simultaneously, or previously institutionalized as mental

---

66. There has been an increasing awareness of the role played by the legal context in which violence risk assessment takes place. *See* Kirk Heilbrun, *Prediction Versus Management Models Relevant to Risk Assessment: The Importance of Legal Decision–Making Context*, 21 LAW & HUM. BEHAV. 347 (1997); David Carson, *A Risk Management Approach to Legal Decision–Making About "Dangerous" People, in* LAW AND UNCERTAINTY: RISKS AND LEGAL PROCESSES 255–269 (R. Baldwin ed., 1997).

67. John Monahan & Henry Steadman, *Crime and Mental Disorder: An Epidemiological Approach, in* CRIME AND JUSTICE: AN ANNUAL REVIEW OF RESEARCH 145–189 (M. Tonry & N. Morris eds., vol. 4 1983).

patients, none of them can distinguish between the *participation* of the mentally disordered in violence—the topic of interest here—and the *selection* of that sub-set of the mentally disordered persons who are violent for treatment in the public sector inpatient settings in which the research was carried out. Further, studies of violence after hospitalization suffer from the additional selection bias that only those patients clinically predicted to be non-violent were released. Nor can the studies of violence during and after hospitalization distinguish the effect of the *treatment* of potentially violent patients in the hospital from the existence of a prior relationship between mental disorder and violence.

For example, to use the prevalence of violence before hospitalization as an index of the fundamental relationship between mental disorder and violence would be to thoroughly confound rates of violence with the legal criteria for hospitalization. Given the rise of the "dangerousness standard" for civil commitment in the United States and throughout the world,[68] it would be amazing if many patients were not violent before they were hospitalized: violent behavior is one of the *reasons* that these disordered people were selected out of the total disordered population for hospitalization. Likewise, the level of violent behavior exhibited on the ward during hospitalization is determined not only by the differential selection of violent people for hospitalization (or, within the hospital, the further selection of "violence prone" patients for placement in the locked wards that were often the sites of the research), but by the skill of ward staff in defusing potentially violent incidents and by the efficacy of treatment in mitigating disorder (or by the effect of medication in sedating patients).

Since the prevalence of violence after hospitalization may be a function of the type of patients selected for hospitalization, of the nature and duration of the treatment administered during hospitalization, and of the risk assessment cut-offs used in determining eligibility for discharge, these data, too, tell us little about whether a basic relationship between mental disorder and violence exists.

Only by augmenting studies of the prevalence of violence among *treated* (i.e., hospitalized) samples of the mentally disordered with studies of the prevalence of violence among samples of disordered people *unselected* for treatment status in the community can population estimates free of selection and treatment biases be offered. This is precisely what was done in the epidemiological studies by Swanson et al. and by Link et al., described above.

[2] The Validity of Clinical Predictions

Since patients whom clinicians assess as having a very high likelihood of imminent violence are, for that reason, unlikely to be released (and thus are unavailable for community follow-up), research validating clinical assessments of high likelihood of community violence upon release can be done only when those discharge predictions are overridden by a judge or other decision maker.

---

68. John Monahan & Saleem A. Shah, *Dangerousness and Commitment of the Mentally Disordered in the United States*, 15 SCHIZO-PHRENIA BULL. 541 (1989); *Principles for the* *Protection of Persons with Mental Illness and for the Improvement of Mental Health Care*, G.A.Res. 119, U.N., 46th Sess. (1991).

This can occur either if the judge substantively disagrees with the clinician's prediction in a given case and orders the person released, or if a court holds that a legal basis for detaining a class of persons is lacking and orders the class released.[69]

The studies by Lidz et al.,[70] and the MacArthur Risk Assessment Study,[71] employed a different methodology. Clinicians were asked to make risk assessments of violence on persons who had been admitted to an acute inpatient psychiatric ward. The patients were then treated in the usual manner and released whenever the staff chose to discharge them (rather than having a judge release the patients over staff objection). Presumably, the staff believed that the risk of violence at the time of discharge was less than the risk of violence at the time of admission—or else the patient would not be being discharged. The subsequent violence of these patients in the community was then measured. While the effect of treatment received in the hospital may well have reduced the amount of violence that was later observed in the community, the fact that these were acute patients, hospitalized only briefly, lessened this methodological problem.

As noted above, existing actuarial risk assessment research employs one of two methodologies. One type of study attempts to identify factors that predict violence *in the hospital*, the other to identify factors that predict violence *in the community*.

One obvious difficulty with trying to predict violence in the hospital is that the structured milieu of the institution and the therapeutic (or at least sedative) effects of medication seriously suppress the base rate of violence. The National Institute of Mental Health's National Plan of Research to Improve Services endorses research on inpatient violence, but with an important annotation: "It is much easier and cheaper to do research on inpatient violence than on violence by mental patients in the community. It should, however, be undertaken with certain goals in mind. Its highest priority should be on discerning types of interaction that are likely to be present in patient violence in the community as well."[72]

Validating risk assessments in the community presents different issues than validating risk assessments in the hospital. As noted, actuarial research on community violence uses as subjects patients released from the hospital with staff concurrence. Since staff are unlikely to recommend someone for release that they view as likely to be imminently violent, the association that is found between valid predictors and violence will, to the extent that clinicians base their release decisions on those cues, be attenuated. Under these conditions, in order to obtain a sufficient level of violence during the follow-up, researchers often limit themselves to enrolling only subjects assumed to have a high base-rate of violence (e.g., males with a prior history of violence). While assuring a base-rate of follow-up violence sufficient to permit statistical validation of the predictor variables is indeed a necessity, restrict-

69. *See* John Monahan & Henry Steadman, *Toward the Rejuvenation of Risk Research, in* Violence and Mental Disorder: Developments in Risk Assessment 1–17 (J. Monahan and H. Steadman eds., 1994).

70. Lidz et al., *supra* note 48.

71. *Supra* note 65.

72. National Institute of Mental Health, Caring for People with Severe Mental Disorders: A National Plan of Research to Improve Services 44 (1991).

ing the sample to only one gender obviously eliminates any chance of uncovering associations between risk factors and violence in the other, and therefore also eliminates the possibility of discovering interactions between gender and the risk factors being studied. Given that several recent studies have reported that, among acutely disordered populations, the level of violence committed by women is as high as that committed by men, the restriction of actuarial risk research to male samples seems ill advised.[73] And given that the predictors of violence among persons who have already committed a violent act—that is, the predictors of repeat violence—may be different than the predictors of initial violence,[74] making prior violence a criterion for inclusion in actuarial risk assessment research may yield findings inapplicable to persons who have not yet been violent. The use of large sample sizes would allow fewer constraints to be placed on subject recruitment while providing a sufficient amount of follow-up violence to permit the statistical validation of risk factors. By obtaining basic descriptive data on subjects *not* selected for the research, one could extrapolate results from the study sample back to the entire population from which the sample was drawn.

§ 2–2.2 Areas of Scientific Agreement

There is a widespread and growing consensus on two propositions in the area we are considering: (1) **Acute mental disorder is a modest risk factor for the occurrence of violence**, and (2) **Clinical predictions of violence have more than chance validity.**

§ 2–2.2.1 Mental Disorder and Violence

The data reviewed above, which have only become available since 1990, fairly read, suggest that whether the measure is the prevalence of violence among the disordered or the prevalence of disorder among the violent, whether the sample is people who are selected for treatment as inmates or patients in institutions or people randomly chosen from the open community, and no matter how many social and demographic factors are statistically taken into account, there appears to be a greater-than-chance relationship between mental disorder and violent behavior. Mental disorder may be a statistically significant risk factor for the occurrence of violence.

However, demonstrating the existence of a statistically significant relationship between mental disorder and violence is one thing, demonstrating the legal and policy significance of the magnitude of that relationship is another. By all indications, the great majority of people who are currently disordered—approximately 90 percent from the Swanson et al. study—are not violent. None of the data give any support to the sensationalized caricature of the mentally disordered served up by the media, the shunning of former patients by employers and neighbors in the community, or "lock 'em all up" laws proposed by politicians pandering to public fears. The policy implications of mental disorder as a risk factor for violent behavior can be understood only in relative terms. Compared to the magnitude of risk associated with the

---

73. Lidz et al., *supra* note 48; Steadman et al., *supra* note 8.

74. *See* Edward P. Mulvey et al., *Reframing the Research Question of Mental Patient* *Criminality,* 9 INT'L. J. L. & PSYCHIATRY 57 (1986), on the distinction between predicting the prevalence and predicting the incidence of violence.

combination of male gender, young age, and lower socioeconomic status, for example, the risk of violence presented by mental disorder is modest. Compared to the magnitude of risk associated with alcoholism and other drug abuse, the risk associated with "major" mental disorders such as schizophrenia and affective disorder is modest indeed. Clearly, mental health status makes at best a trivial contribution to the overall level of violence in society.[75]

These conclusions are in accord with those reached by Mulvey.[76] He concluded that on the basis of the available literature, six statements could be made about the relationship between violence and mental disorder:

(1) Mental illness appears to be a risk factor for violence in the community. A body of research, taken as a whole, supports the idea that an association exists between mental illness and violence in the general population.

(2) The size of the association between mental illness and violence, while statistically significant, does not appear to be very large. Also, the absolute risk for violence posed by mental illness is small.

(3) The combination of a serious mental illness and a substance abuse disorder probably significantly increases the risk of involvement in a violent act.

(4) The association between mental illness and violence is probably significant even when demographic characteristics are taken into account. However, no sizeable body of evidence clearly indicates the relative strength of mental illness as a risk factor for violence compared with other characteristics such as socioeconomic status or history of violence.

(5) Active symptoms are probably more important as a risk factor than is simply the presence of an identifiable disorder.

(6) No clear information about the causal paths that produce the association between mental illness and violence is available.[77]

The MacArthur Research Network on Mental Health and the Law collaborated with the National Stigma Clearinghouse, a family and consumer-oriented advocacy group, to produce a "Consensus Statement" that has been endorsed by a large number of researchers and advocates, and may serve as a point of agreement in an area that lends itself to political controversy.

"Mental disorder" and violence are closely linked in the public mind. A combination of factors promotes this perception: sensationalized reporting by the media whenever a violent act is committed by "a former mental patient," popular misuse of psychiatric terms (such as "psychotic" and "psychopathic"), and exploitation of stock formulas and narrow stereotypes by the

75. *But see* Note, *Developments in the Law: Civil Commitment of the Mentally Ill*, 87 HARV. L. REV. 1190, 1233 (1974), on the legal justification—"because [the mentally disordered] are . . . unable to make autonomous decisions"—for preventively intervening in the lives of disordered people in situations where we do not intervene with non-disordered people, even when the non-disordered people present a higher risk of violence. On the issue of the decisionmaking competence of people with mental disorder, *see* Thomas Grisso & Paul S. Appelbaum, *The MacArthur Treatment Competence Study: III. Abilities of Patients to Consent to Psychiatric and Medical Treatment*, 19 LAW & HUM. BEHAV. 149 (1995).

76. Edward P. Mulvey, *Assessing the Evidence of a Link Between Mental Illness and Violence*, 45 HOSPITAL & COMMUNITY PSYCHIATRY 663 (1994).

77. *Id.* at 663–65.

entertainment industry. The public justifies its fear and rejection of people labeled "mentally ill," and attempts to segregate them in the community, by this assumption of "dangerousness."

The experience of people with psychiatric conditions and of their family members paints a picture dramatically different from the stereotype. The results of several recent large-scale research projects conclude that only a weak association between mental disorders and violence exists in the community. Serious violence by people with major mental disorders appears concentrated in a small fraction of the total number, and especially in those who use alcohol and other drugs. Mental disorders—in sharp contrast to alcohol and drug abuse—account for a minuscule portion of the violence that afflicts American society.

The conclusions of those who use mental health services and of their family members, and the observations of researchers, suggest that the way to reduce whatever relationship exists between violence and mental disorder is to make accessible a range of quality treatments including peer-based programs, and to eliminate the stigma and discrimination that discourage, sometimes provoke, and penalize those who seek and receive help for disabling conditions.[78]

Mullen has reviewed the literature on mental disorder and violence and reached conclusions in line with those of others: "Recent research appears to have established a modest association between having a mental illness and an increased propensity to violence."[79] Likewise, Eronen et al. concluded that "recent evidence suggests that there are several subgroups of mentally disordered persons who may behave violently.[80] The clinical features of these groups are a previous history of violent behavior, non-compliance with medications, and importantly, comorbidity of substance abuse. Compared with the magnitude of risk associated with the combination of personality disorders, male gender, and substance abuse, the risk, in general, associated with major mental disorders such as schizophrenia is moderate."[81]

This risk is substantially less than that assumed by the American public.[82]

§ 2–2.2.2   The Validity of Clinical Predictions

Four brief quotations are representative of a growing consensus among researchers[83] on risk assessment of violence. The most advanced study of the validity of clinical predictions of violence, Lidz et al., concluded:

> What this study [shows] is that clinical judgment has been undervalued in previous research. Not only did the clinicians pick out a statistically

78. John Monahan & Jean Arnold, *Violence By People with Mental Illness: A Consensus Statement by Advocates and Researchers*, 19 PSYCHIATRIC REHABILITATION J. 67 (1996).

79. Paul Mullen, *A Reassessment of the Link Between Mental Disorder and Violent Behaviour, and Its Implications for Clinical Practice*, 31 AUSTRALIAN & NEW ZEALAND J. PSYCHIATRY 31 (1997).

80. Markku Eronen et al., *Psychiatric Disorders and Violent Behavior*, 1 INT'L. J. PSYCHIATRY CLINICAL PRAC. 1 (1997).

81. *Id.* at 9.

82. Bernice Pescosolido et al., *The Public's View of the Competence, Dangerousness and Need for Legal Coercion Among Persons with Mental Illness*, 89 AM. J. PUB. HEALTH 1339 (1999).

83. *See* John Monahan, *Violence Risk Assessment: Scientific Validity and Evidentiary Admissibility*, 57 WASH. & LEE L. REV. 901 (2000).

more violent group, but the violence that the predicted group committed was more serious than the acts of the comparison group.[84]

Likewise, a recent critical analysis of existing risk assessment research reached this judgment:

> This article's reevaluation of representative data from the past 2 decades suggests that clinicians are able to distinguish violent from nonviolent patients with a modest, better-than-chance level of accuracy.[85]

Douglas, Cox, and Webster, leading researchers in this area, have stated:

> Until fairly recently, it may have been argued that the state of knowledge did not provide any sort of reliable or trustworthy direction on violence risk assessment. This position seems no longer tenable.[86]

Finally, the most recent international scientific review of violence risk assessment, published in England in 2000, concluded

> Risk assessment has steadily increased in importance since [the 1960's], and this has been accompanied by methodological improvements, particularly in the last decade.... It is relatively recently that the science of risk assessment has developed sufficiently to claim a level of accuracy which makes it useful.[87]

As the field has moved in a more actuarial direction, professional consensus has shifted from the question of "how accurate are clinicians in general at predicting violence?" to "how valid are specific risk factors, or specific instruments, for predicting violence?" In a recent major meta-analysis of actuarial risk factors for crime and violence among mentally disordered offenders, Bonta, Law, and Hanson found those risk factors to be remarkably similar to well-known risk factors among the general offender population:

> Criminal history, antisocial personality, substance abuse, and family dysfunction are important for mentally disordered offenders as they are for general offenders. In fact, the results support the theoretical perspective that the major correlates of crime are the same, regardless of race, gender, class, and the presence or absence of mental illness. Clinical or psychopathological variables were either unrelated to recidivism or negatively related.[88]

§ 2–2.3   Areas of Scientific Disagreement

Scientific disagreement in this area has of late been more of degree than of kind. On the one hand, one rarely now sees statements being made that were once routine—statements such as those of the National Mental Health Association that "people with mental illnesses pose no more of a crime threat

84. Lidz et al., *supra* note 48, at 1010.

85. Douglas Mossman, *Assessing Predictions of Violence: Being Accurate About Accuracy*, 62 J. Consulting & Clinical Psychol. 783, 790 (1994). *See also* Douglas Mossman, *Further Comments on Portraying the Accuracy of Violence Predictions*, 18 Law & Hum. Behav. 587 (1994).

86. Kevin Douglas et al., *Violence Risk Assessment: Science and Practice*, 4 Legal & Criminological Psychol. 149, 149 (1999).

87. Stephen Blumenthal & Tony Lavender, Violence and Mental Disorder: A Critical Aid to the Assessment and Management of Risk (2000), 1–2, 14.

88. J. Bonta et al., *The Prediction of Criminal and Violent Recidivism Among Mentally Disordered Offenders: A Meta–Analysis*, 123 Psychological Bull. 123, 139 (1998).

than do other members of the general population"[89] or of the American Civil Liberties Union that "mental health professionals have no expertise in prediction of future dangerous behavior."[90] On the other hand, no one claims that mental disorder *per se* is a dominating risk factor for the occurrence of violence, or that clinical predictions are anywhere near perfection. In general, the sober conclusion that clinicians are "modestly better than chance" at predicting violence appears to be becoming the consensus view.

§ 2–2.4 Future Directions

The future is likely to see more precise depictions of which risk factors are associated with violence in which specific types of people. Violence risk assessment is likely to continue to move strongly in an actuarial direction, including the introduction of violence risk assessment software.[91] Increased attention is likely to be given to how estimates of risk are best communicated to those who have to make decisions based on them.[92]

89. NATIONAL MENTAL HEALTH ASSOCIATION, STIGMA: A LACK OF AWARENESS AND UNDERSTANDING 2 (1987).

90. BRUCE J. ENNIS & RICHARD D. EMERY, THE RIGHTS OF MENTAL PATIENTS—AN AMERICAN CIVIL LIBERTIES UNION HANDBOOK 20 (1978).

91. John Monahan et al., *Developing a Clinically Useful Actuarial Tool for Assessing Violence Risk*, 176 BRIT. J. PSYCHIATRY 312 (2000).

92. John Monahan & Henry Steadman, *Violent Storms and Violent People: How Meteorology Can Inform Risk Communication in Mental Health Law*, 51 AM. PSYCHOLOGIST, 931–938 (1996); Paul Slovic et al., *Violence Risk Assessment and Risk Communication: The Effects of Using Actual Cases, Providing Instruction, and Employing Probability Versus Frequency Formats*, 24 LAW & HUM. BEHAV. 271 (2000).

CHAPTER 3

SEXUAL AGGRESSORS

Table of Sections

A. LEGAL ISSUES

Westlaw Electronic Research

See Westlaw Electronic Research Guide preceding the Summary of Contents.

A.   LEGAL ISSUES

§ 3–1.0   THE LEGAL RELEVANCE OF RESEARCH ON SEXUAL AGGRESSORS

§ 3–1.1   Introduction

     Legislatures and courts have reacted with great vehemence toward perpetrators of sexual assaults, especially when children are their victims. This response can be seen across a wide legal spectrum. For instance, the Federal Rules of Evidence were amended in 1994 to permit the admission of evidence of allegations of past sexual offenses to prove conduct in conformity with the defendant's "character."[1] These amendments suggest, implicitly at least, that crimes involving sexual aggressiveness are different than other crimes, not simply in the egregiousness of their consequences but also in the supposition that they are more likely to recur. In short, there is a popular belief among lawmakers that sexual aggressiveness is an enduring trait that is susceptible to ready identification.[2] This belief is manifest in two other areas which are

---

§ 3–1.0
1. *See* FED.R.EVID. 413, 414 and 415.

2. The view that sexual predation is an inherent trait that leads inexorably to future

the principal concern of this section, civil commitment statutes directed at "sexual predators" and community registration and notification laws. Section 2.0, which surveys the scientific research on sexual aggression, provides some insights about whether sexual aggressiveness is as constant a "trait" as the law supposes and what research is available to identify those who present a substantial danger. This section focuses on the legal framework that has been built to deal with the individuals who are thought to present a special threat to the community, a framework that has so far been largely unconcerned with the empirical research available about these people.

§ 3–1.2 Commitment Statutes

States have enacted a variety of regulatory schemes to achieve the goal of protecting society from so-called "sexual predators." These statutes are not easily categorized, since they differ in so many ways from one another. This section, however, attempts to bring some order to these differences by identifying the basic points at which these regulatory schemes converge or diverge. It should be noted at the outset, however, that since the Supreme Court upheld the Kansas commitment statute in *Kansas v. Hendricks* (discussed in detail *infra* § 10–1.3), the Kansas scheme might emerge as the model in the future.

The Kansas statute itself was modeled on the Washington statute.[3] However, since the *Hendricks* Court used the Kansas statute[4] in its constitutional assessment, we will refer to this approach as the Kansas model, with our apologies to the state of Washington. The Kansas model defines a "sexually violent predator" as "any person who has been convicted of or charged with a crime of sexual violence and who suffers from a mental abnormality or personality disorder which makes the person likely to engage in predatory acts of sexual violence if not confined in a secure facility."[5]

The Kansas model offers a baseline by which other state frameworks can be considered. First of all, although perhaps cosmetic, many states prefer the more neutral term "sexually violent person," thus eschewing the more disturbing connotations associated with the word "predator."[6] Nonetheless,

---

behavior consistent with this trait is illustrated by the following statement of the California Legislature which accompanied the passage of its sexual predator commitment statute:

> The Legislature finds and declares that a small but extremely dangerous group of sexually violent predators that have diagnosable mental disorders can be identified while they are incarcerated. These persons are not safe to be at large and if released represent a danger to the health and safety of others in that they are likely to engage in acts of sexual violence.... The Legislature further finds and declares that while these individuals have been duly punished for their criminal acts, they are, if adjudicated sexually violent predators, a continuing threat to society.

1995 CAL. LEGIS. SERV. 4611 (West). Community notification laws are motivated by a similar view that sexual crimes are more likely to be repeated than other crimes. In enacting the widely copied Megan's law, for example, the New Jersey Legislature observed as follows:

> Sex offenders' recidivism compounds the problem. As a group, sex offenders are significantly more likely than other repeat offenders to reoffend with sex crimes or other violent crimes, and that tendency persists over time.

N.J. STAT. ANN. § 2C:7–1 (West 1994).

3. WASH. REV. CODE ANN. § 71.09.01 et seq.

4. KAN. STAT. ANN. § 59–29a01 et seq. (1994).

5. KAN. STAT. ANN. § 59–29a02(b).

6. *See e.g.*, WISC. § 980.01 et seq.; MASS. CH. 123A; Ill. ch. 725, § 205 et seq. Other terms commonly used are Sexual Psychopathic Personality (SPP) and Sexually Dangerous Person (SDP). *See* MINN. STAT. § 253B.18, subds. 2,3 (Supp. 1997).

we refer to these state schemes collectively as "sexual predator" laws, since this colorful term reflects the strong motivations that lie behind them.[7] As the Kansas law illustrates, commitment requires three factors to be met: the person must (1) have committed a sexual offense sometime in the past;[8] (2) be mentally abnormal (or defective, disordered etc.); and (3) be likely to commit a sexual offense in the future.

The Kansas model focuses primarily on confinement of individuals thought to pose a substantial threat to the community. In enacting its legislative plan, an approach that would later be adopted by Kansas, the Washington legislature expressly found "that the prognosis for curing sexually violent offenders is poor, the treatment needs of this population are very long term, and the treatment modalities for this population are very different" than those appropriate for individuals confined under the general commitment laws.[9] In contrast, many states have designed their state schemes around treatment alternatives. Nebraska, for example, requires the Department of Health and Human Services to conduct "an evaluation of the offender for purposes of determining whether treatment in a treatment program operated by the Department . . . is appropriate for the offender."[10]

Most sexual predator statutes share the requirement of a showing of "dangerousness." The state statutes also share the characteristic that they do not specify "how dangerous" the defendant must be to be committed. Kansas, for instance, defines dangerousness simply as "likely to engage in the predatory acts of sexual violence."[11] Illinois describes this dangerousness component as a person "with criminal propensities to the commission of sex offenses." State statutes, and judicial interpretations of those statutes, range from the "propensity" language of Illinois to the "highly likely" language of Minnesota. It is disconcerting that legislatures do not insist, and courts have not insisted, that states define with more precision the quantitative likelihood that must be demonstrated in these commitment hearings. No court or legislature has attempted to quantify the risk necessary for civil confinement.[12]

The other major factor typically coupled with dangerousness is some mental health condition, variously termed illness, abnormality, defect or disorder. States, however, do not typically separate the prediction of violence component from the mental condition aspect. Kansas, as quoted above, makes the prediction of violence a product of the mental disorder. Arizona defines "mental disorder" as "either a paraphilia or personality disorder that predisposes a person to commit sexual acts to such a degree as to render the person a danger to the health and safety of others."[13] Wisconsin similarly provides for

---

7. *See, e.g.,* Standard Jury Instructions–Criminal Cases, 777 So.2d 366 (Fla.2000) (discussing and approving "sexually violent predator" term despite its inflammatory nature).

8. While all states require a prior sexual offense as a prerequisite to commitment, states divide on whether the offense had to result in a conviction.

9. WASH. § 71.09.010.

10. NEB. § 29–2923 et seq. & § 29–2925. The constitutional aspects of treatment in these cases is discussed *infra* § 10–1.3.

11. KAN. STAT. ANN., § 59–29a02(b).

12. For a full discussion concerning the issue of specifying probabilities more exactly, *see infra* § 10–1.5.

13. ARIZ. STAT. ANN. § 13–4601. Before 1997, Arizona employed the term "mental abnormality" which it defined as "a congenital or acquired condition that affects the emotional or volitional capacity of a person and that predisposes the person to commit criminal sexual acts to such a degree as to render the person a menace to the health and safety of others."

the commitment of a person who is "dangerous because he or she suffers from a mental disorder that makes it substantially probable that the person will engage in acts of sexual violence."[14]

§ 3–1.3   Constitutional Issues Surrounding Commitment of "Sexual Predators"

§ 3–1.3.1   *Kansas v. Hendricks* and Its Progeny

In 1997, in *Kansas v. Hendricks*,[15] the Supreme Court held that the Kansas law which provides for the civil commitment of a person who is "mentally abnormal" and "dangerous" is not unconstitutional. The law was challenged on the basis that it violated three separate provisions of the Constitution, substantive due process, the guarantee against double jeopardy and the *Ex Post Facto* clause.[16] The Kansas Supreme Court had invalidated the statute on the basis that it failed to require that the person being civilly committed be found to suffer from a "mental illness" and thus violated substantive due process.[17] The Kansas Court had found in *Foucha v. Louisiana*[18] a constitutional due process requirement that a person be both mentally ill and dangerous before being civilly committed. Because of the importance of this decision, both for the present context as well as civil commitment law generally, this section provides a detailed analysis of the Court's *Hendricks* opinion. Although *Hendricks* was only concerned with a narrowly drawn statute directed at "a limited subclass of dangerous persons,"[19] the Court's reasoning is less narrowly tailored. The opinion might prove to have far-reaching ramifications well beyond the relatively narrow context of "sexual predators."

Justice Thomas wrote for the Court, with Justices Breyer, Stevens, Souter and Ginsburg dissenting from the holding and various parts of the reasoning. At least eight of the Justices agreed that the Kansas law satisfies "substantive due process" requirements under the Fourteenth Amendment.[20] Five members of the Court found that the law did not violate either the Double Jeopardy or *Ex Post Facto* Clauses, a conclusion with which the four dissenting Justices disagreed.

[1]   Substantive Due Process

/a/   *The Framework of* Kansas v. Hendricks

Although the Court readily dismissed Hendricks' substantive due process claim, this holding is likely to have the most far-reaching consequences for

---

14. Wis. Stat. § 980.01.

15. 521 U.S. 346, 117 S.Ct. 2072, 138 L.Ed.2d 501 (1997).

16. Subsequent cases have also raised Equal Protection Clause challenges. They have, however, met a similar fate. *See In re* Hay, 263 Kan. 822, 953 P.2d 666 (Kan.1998).

17. *In re* Hendricks, 259 Kan. 246, 912 P.2d 129, 138 (Kan.1996).

18. 504 U.S. 71, 112 S.Ct. 1780, 118 L.Ed.2d 437 (1992).

19. *Hendricks*, 521 U.S. at 357.

20. We note that only eight agreed that the law satisfies substantive due process because Justice Ginsburg's position on this issue is unclear. Part I of Justice Breyer's dissenting opinion, in which he stated his reasons for agreeing that the law does not violate due process, was not joined by Justice Ginsburg. She did, however, join the rest of his dissent and none of the majority opinion. This suggests several possibilities: (1) she believes the law violates due process, but was not inclined to explain why; (2) she believes the law does not violate due process for reasons other than Justice Breyer stated; or (3) she believes the Court did not have to reach the issue, since there were two other grounds for invalidating the law, and, therefore, she felt no need to commit to any one position at this time.

subsequent cases. The Kansas Supreme Court rested its invalidation of the statute on this basis, and all of the Court's prior commitment-area cases were premised on either procedural or substantive due process, or a combination of the two. The Court did not expressly overrule *Foucha*. However, *Foucha's* continuing precedential value is in some doubt.

In *Foucha*, the Court held that due process allows an insanity acquittee to be incarcerated only " 'as long as he is both mentally ill and dangerous, but no longer.' "[21] In *Hendricks*, Justice Thomas, who had dissented in *Foucha*, wrote for the Court and found that *Foucha* had established no categorical requirement that commitment be premised on both mental illness and dangerousness. Instead, the Court maintained, *Foucha* stood for no more than that proof of dangerousness must be coupled "with the proof of some additional factor."[22] The Court concluded that "mental abnormality" could suffice, because "it narrows the class of persons eligible for confinement to those who are unable to control their dangerousness."[23]

"Dangerousness," or a prediction of violence, therefore, is the foundational premise of the decision as well as the key to satisfying substantive due process. Surprisingly, however, the Court gave it little attention. And the Court said nothing *at all* concerning the uncertainties associated with predictions of violence.[24] Instead, the Court noted the fact that the Kansas statute requires that the person "has been convicted of or charged with a sexually violent offense"[25] and thus, in the Court's words, "requires evidence of past sexually violent behaviour."[26] Of course, since the statute applies also to those who have only been "charged with" a sexually violent offense, proof of "past sexually violent behaviour" will likely be by less than beyond a reasonable doubt.[27] The Court did not indicate what level of proof might be constitution-

---

21. *Foucha*, 504 U.S. at 77 (*quoting* Jones v. United States, 463 U.S. 354, 368, 103 S.Ct. 3043, 77 L.Ed.2d 694, (1983)).

22. *Hendricks*, 521 U.S. at 358.

23. *Id.* It should be noted that the logic of *Hendricks* might extend to any "mental abnormality," not simply those associated with sexual predators. *See, e.g.*, People v. Robinson, 63 Cal.App.4th 348, 74 Cal.Rptr.2d 52 (Cal.App. 1998) (civil commitment of mentally disordered offender who had been convicted of involuntary manslaughter).

24. The reliability of predictions of future violence is an issue that has virtually disappeared from case analysis. Most courts, including the United States Supreme Court, do not even see any need to raise it. And when courts do consider it, they dismiss it in a conclusory fashion, or simply assume that such predictions are possible. The California Supreme Court, for instance, recently swept this issue under the rug in the following way:

Notwithstanding the nuances of psychiatric diagnosis and the difficulties inherent in predicting human behavior, the United States Supreme Court has consistently upheld com-

mitment schemes authorizing the use of prior dangerous behavior to establish both present mental impairment and the likelihood of future harm. . . .

[T]he Legislature could reasonably conclude that the evidentiary methods contemplated by the Act are sufficiently reliable and accurate to accomplish its narrow and important purpose—confining and treating mentally disordered individuals who have demonstrated their inability to control specific sexually violent behavior through the commission of similar prior crimes.

Hubbert, 81 Cal.Rptr.2d at 508–509 (citations omitted).

25. Kan. Stat. Ann. § 59–29a02(a) (1994).

26. *Hendricks*, 521 U.S. at 357.

27. *See, e.g., In re* Hay, 263 Kan. 822, 953 P.2d 666, 678 (Kan.1998). Under the Kansas statute, a person is civilly committed only if a jury finds that he is mentally abnormal and dangerous by proof beyond a reasonable doubt. (This standard is considered in detail *infra* § 10–1.5.) This standard of proof, however,

ally required, since Hendricks had been convicted of past sexually violent acts.[28] It is worth emphasizing, however, that prior convictions apparently are not required by due process. Actually, a prior conviction requirement would be theoretically inconsistent with the Court's conclusion that the Kansas statute does not violate the Double Jeopardy and *Ex Post Facto* Clauses. Committing only those previously convicted might suggest that the legislature's intent was punitive.[29]

As a substantive requirement beyond dangerousness, "mental abnormality" is not very well defined. First of all, like "insanity," it is a term of legal convenience, employed by the Kansas Legislature, that does not correspond to any psychological construct or specific diagnosis. The Court, however, noted that it had never required correspondence between the nomenclature of state legislatures and that of the mental health community: "[W]e have traditionally left to legislators the task of defining terms of a medical nature that have legal significance."[30] Justice Breyer's dissent agreed, noting that "the psychiatric profession itself classifies the kind of problem from which Hendricks suffers as a serious mental disorder."[31]

The second reason advanced by the Court for finding "mental abnormality" a satisfactory "additional factor" was similarly analogous to insanity: Hendricks' mental abnormality meant that he lacked "volitional control."[32] The Court emphasized the fact that the Act "requires a finding of future dangerousness, and then links that finding to the existence of a 'mental abnormality' or 'personality disorder' that makes it difficult, if not impossible, for the person to control his dangerous behavior."[33] Justice Breyer, agreeing with the majority on this issue, summarized the Court's reasoning:

> Hendricks' abnormality does not consist simply of a long course of antisocial behavior, but rather it includes a specific, serious, and highly unusual inability to control his action. (For example, Hendricks testified that, when he gets "stressed out," he cannot "control the urge" to molest children.) The law traditionally has considered this kind of abnormality akin to insanity for purposes of confinement.[34]

Whether this component of the decision, the lack of "volitional control," will prove to be a limiting principle may be doubted.[35] Taken at face value, the

---

must be clearly distinguished from what standard applies to evidence concerning the extrinsic offenses that might be admitted to prove that the person is dangerous. This evidentiary question is considered *infra* note 28.

28. Under the Federal Rules of Evidence, the standard for this sort of "preliminary fact" is very slight: if a reasonable trier of fact could find that the offense occurred, then it is admissible unless another Rule would exclude it. *See* Huddleston v. United States, 485 U.S. 681, 108 S.Ct. 1496, 99 L.Ed.2d 771 (1988). It would be surprising if the Court required a more substantial standard in civil commitment cases than it finds mandated by the Federal Rules of Evidence, and which is applied in criminal prosecutions.

29. Justice Breyer made this point in reaching his conclusion that the Kansas statute was in fact criminal punishment: "[T]he

Act, like criminal punishment, imposes its confinement (or sanction) only upon an individual who has previously committed a criminal offense." *Hendricks*, 521 U.S. at 380 (Breyer, J., dissenting).

30. *Id.* at 359.

31. *Id.* at 375 (Breyer, J., dissenting).

32. *Id.* at 360.

33. *Id.* at 358.

34. *Id.* at 375 (Breyer, J., dissenting).

35. The issue whether the United States Constitution requires "a showing of utter lack of control of sexual impulses for commitment" is considered *infra* § 1.3.1[1][b]. The Supreme Court is expected to decide this issue during its 2001–2002 term. Kansas v. Crane, ___ U.S. ___, 121 S.Ct. 1483, 149 L.Ed.2d 372 (2001).

Court's interpretation of "mental abnormality" as synonymous with "lack of volitional control" or "irresistible impulse," might actually render *Hendricks* much more restrictive than anything contemplated under *Foucha*. One of the principal reasons states abandoned the irresistible impulse test of insanity was the inherent difficulty in distinguishing between an irresistible impulse and an impulse not resisted. States might find it exceedingly embarrassing, and practically difficult, to reject a volitional test as unprovable in the criminal context and then embrace it in the civil context. *Hendricks*, by this standard, was a relatively easy case. Hendricks himself testified that "when he 'get[s] stressed out,' he 'can't control the urge' to molest children."[36] States are unlikely to find many cases as easy as *Hendricks* to prove that a person has no volitional control.

Given the general tenor of the decision, however, there is good reason to doubt that lower courts will enthusiastically conclude that the "additional factor" of mental abnormality requires proof that defendants lack volitional control.[37] Most state statutes, in fact, are similar to the Kansas model and do not explicitly require a separate "irresistible impulse" determination. Indeed, it is anything but clear that Justice Thomas and the Court believed that if Hendricks committed another offense that his lack of control meant that he should be able to successfully assert an insanity claim.

Despite Justice Breyer's observation to the contrary, the Court's commitment jurisprudence is at odds with how most jurisdictions approach insanity. On the criminal docket, most jurisdictions, including federal law, presume free will and require defendants claiming insanity to prove they could not distinguish right from wrong at the time of the act. A criminal defendant who could distinguish right from wrong at the time of the offense, but could not control his behavior, goes to prison. This fate befalls the volitionally impaired offender despite the fact, as the *Hendricks'* Court explained it, prison offers neither retribution nor deterrence to someone who cannot control his behavior. Yet, on the civil side under *Hendricks*, that same person is deemed "mentally abnormal" and is committed. Although *Hendricks* exemplifies a striking discontinuity between the criminal and civil dockets in terms of philosophies of human behavior, the legal result is consistent at a base practical level: on either side of the docket, these people get locked up.

Upon reflection, however, lack of volitional control might indeed be a constitutional necessity, for without it there appears to be no "additional factor" beyond dangerousness. The Kansas statute mandates "mental abnormality" as this additional factor. The question is, what does this term mean? Without the volitional component, the "additional factor" of mental abnormality appears to have no content. It is whatever the legislature says it is. The Kansas statute illustrates this concern well. The statute defines mental abnormality as "[a] congenital or acquired condition affecting the emotional or volitional capacity which predisposes the person to commit sexually violent offenses in a degree constituting such person a menace to the health and safety of others."[38] In effect, a person is mentally abnormal because he is dangerous.[39] Upon close analysis, then, under the Kansas statute a person can

---

36. *Hendricks*, 521 U.S. at 355 (*quoting* App. at 172).

37. *See infra* note 39.

38. KAN. STAT. ANN. § 59–29a02(b) (1994).

39. A good illustration of the circular reasoning occurring in these cases comes from the

be committed if he is both dangerous and dangerous.[40] Thus, there may be no "additional factor" after all.[41]

The great challenge now before lower courts and state legislatures is to define what content this "additional factor" has in these sexual predator cases. While Justice Thomas might accept a contentless "additional factor," there appears to be five votes for the proposition that there must be something more than dangerousness. Justice Breyer and the other dissenters especially urged the irresistible impulse test. Justice Kennedy, who joined the majority, wrote separately to warn that "if it were shown that mental abnormality is too imprecise a category to offer a solid basis for concluding that civil detention is justified, our precedents would not suffice to validate it."[42] To date, lower courts have split on their definitions of the meaning of mental abnormality and how, if at all, it incorporates "lack of volitional control" on the part of the defendant.

[b]   *The "Lack of Volitional Control" Test After* Hendricks

The controversy surrounding the meaning of the Constitution is often greater after the Supreme Court decides a case than it was before. In the case of the constitutionality of sexual predator laws, this has certainly proved true. In *Kansas v. Hendricks*,[43] the Court held that the relatively straight-forward two-fold requirement articulated in *Foucha v. Louisiana*[44] for civil commitments—(1) mental illness and (2) dangerousness—was not specifically mandated by the Constitution. Instead, the *Hendricks* Court held that dangerousness must be coupled "with the proof of some additional factor."[45] Under the Kansas statute at issue in *Hendricks*, this additional factor was "mental abnormality." Mental abnormality was sufficient, according to the Court, because "it narrows the class of persons eligible for confinement to those who are *unable to control their dangerousness.*"[46] As anticipated, the identification of a volitional test as a required factor presented a potentially serious obstacle to the employment of sexual predator statutes. Specifically, given the unwieldy nature of the volitional test, state attorneys found proving this element quite difficult indeed. In light of the fact that the tenor of *Hendricks* indicated an intention to make it easier, not harder, to incarcerate sexual predators, we

---

California legislature's description of the additional factor its law joined with the dangerousness component: "The continuing danger posed by these individuals and the continuing basis for their judicial commitment is a currently diagnosed mental disorder which predisposes them to engage in sexually violent criminal behavior." *Hubbart*, 81 Cal.Rptr.2d at 495 (*quoting* Stats.1995, ch. 763, § 1). Hence, sexual predators are dangerous because they have a mental disorder and they have a mental disorder because they are dangerous.

40. Dr. Befort, the state's own expert, testified in *Hendricks* that mental abnormality is "circular in that certain behavior defines the condition which is used to predict behavior." *In re Hendricks*, 259 Kan. 246, 912 P.2d 129 (1996).

41. *See generally* Stephen J. Morse, *Blame and Danger: An Essay on Preventive Detention*, 76 B.U.L. Rev. 113, 137 (1996) ("But if anyone who has a tendency to engage in sexual vio-

lence is abnormal, then the term 'mental abnormality' is circularly defined and does no independent conceptual or causal work. Moreover, such a definition collapses all badness into madness.").

42. *Hendricks*, 521 U.S. at 373 (Kennedy, J., concurring).

43. 521 U.S. 346, 117 S.Ct. 2072, 138 L.Ed.2d 501.

44. 504 U.S. 71, 112 S.Ct. 1780, 118 L.Ed.2d 437.

45. *Hendricks*, 521 U.S. at 357.

46. *Id.* (emphasis added). Under the Kansas statute, "mental abnormality" is "[a] congenital or acquired condition affecting the emotional or volitional capacity which predisposes the person to commit sexually violent offenses in a degree constituting such person a menace to the health and safety of others." Kan.Stat. Ann. § 59–29a02(b) (1994).

predicted in the first edition of this Chapter that "there is reason to believe that lower courts will not read the 'additional factor' of mental abnormality as requiring proof that the defendant lacks volitional control." We correctly predicted developments in Minnesota, but have been surprised by the Kansas Supreme Court.

[i] The Weak Volitional Control Test

The Minnesota Supreme Court in *In re Linehan*[47] (*Linehan IV*) held that the Supreme Court did not intend to create a constitutionally based "absolute" or "total" volitional requirement. Linehan had a long history of sexual aggression, including having killed a fourteen year-old while trying to sexually assault her in 1965. Shortly before he was to be released in 1992, the state sought to commit him under the Psychopathic Personality Commitment Act (PPC Act). The PPC Act specifically required that, to be committed, the person "must evidence an 'utter lack of power to control [his or her] sexual impulses.' "[48] In *Linehan I*,[49] however, the Minnesota Supreme Court overturned Linehan's commitment, finding that "the state failed to present 'clear and convincing evidence that appellant has an utter lack of power to control his sexual impulses.' "[50]

After Linehan's release, Minnesota passed the Sexually Dangerous Person Act (SDP Act).[51] The language of the SDP Act closely paralleled that of the Kansas law upheld in *Hendricks*.[52] The SDP Act specifically provided that "it is not necessary to prove that the person has an inability to control the person's sexual impulses."[53] In light of the *Hendricks* Court's statements concerning the importance of "lack of volitional control" as constituting the "additional factor" beyond dangerousness that supported the constitutionality of the Kansas law, Linehan attacked the Minnesota act for failing to contain this, or any other, "additional factor." In *Linehan IV*, he argued, "the SDP Act does not sufficiently narrow the class of targeted persons because it dispenses with the need to prove that a person has an utter inability to control his or her sexual impulses before allowing indeterminate civil commitment."[54]

The Minnesota Supreme Court phrased the question presented as follows:

[D]oes Hendricks require a complete or, at a minimum, a partial lack of volitional control over sexual impulses in order to narrowly tailor a civil commitment law to meet substantive due process standards.[55]

The Minnesota court found no categorical statement that a sexual predator law would fail "substantive due process without a volitional impairment element."[56] Rather, the *Linehan IV* court found that the Supreme Court's reasoning establishes that "*some* lack of volitional control is necessary to

---

47. 594 N.W.2d 867 (Minn.1999).

48. *Linehan IV*, 594 N.W.2d at 869 (*quoting* Pearson v. Probate Court of Ramsey County, 205 Minn. 545, 287 N.W. 297, 302 (Minn. 1939)).

49. *In re Linehan*, 518 N.W.2d 609 (Minn. 1994).

50. *Linehan IV*, 594 N.W.2d at 869 (*quoting Linehan I*, 518 N.W.2d at 614).

51. MINN.STAT. § 253B.02, subd. 18c (1998).

52. *Linehan IV*, 594 N.W.2d at 871.

53. MINN.STAT. § 253B.02, subd. 18c.

54. *Linehan IV*, 594 N.W.2d at 872.

55. *Id.*

56. *Id.* at 873.

narrow the scope of civil commitment statutes."[57] The Minnesota court explained that the issue concerns whether *Hendricks* created a "total lack of control" requirement or merely a "some" lack of control test. As it summarized its conclusion, "Hendricks states that a person may be civilly committed if he suffers from a mental abnormality or personality disorder 'that makes it difficult, if not impossible, for the person to control his dangerous behavior.' Clearly this language does not require an utter lack of control over harmful behavior, but rather a lack of adequate control over harmful behavior."[58]

[ii] The Strong Volitional Control Test

In *In re Crane*,[59] the Kansas Supreme Court considered "whether it is constitutionally permissible to commit Crane as a sexual predator absent a showing that he was unable to control his dangerous behavior."[60] Crane had been originally convicted of kidnaping and assorted sexual assaults arising out of an incident involving a clerk at a video store.[61] His conviction, however, was later overturned on appeal.[62] On remand, the defendant and state entered into a plea agreement in which Crane pled guilty to the single offense of aggravat ed sexual battery.[63] According to the video store clerk's testimony at Crane's commitment hearing, the state intended to follow the plea agreement with a petition to commit him under the state's sexual predator law.[64]

57. *Id.* (emphasis added).

58. *Id.* at 873n.3 (*quoting Hendricks*, 521 U.S. at 358). The court in *In re Detention of Brooks* agreed with the *Linehan IV* court's interpretation of *Brooks*, 94 Wash.App. 716, 973 P.2d 486 (1999). The petitioner there argued that *Hendricks* requires the state to "show that the person lacks volitional control." *Id.* at 492. The Washington appellate court disagreed. It observed that "the Supreme Court found that the statutory requirements limited 'involuntary civil confinement to those who suffer from a volitional impairment rendering them dangerous beyond their control.' " *Id.* (*quoting Hendricks*, 521 U.S. at 358). Hence, the court stated, "[t]he Court did not require . . . a showing of a total lack of control." Instead, the court concluded, "the person's mental abnormality or personality disorder must make it 'difficult, if not impossible, for the person to control his dangerous behavior.' " *Id.* (*quoting Hendricks*, 521 U.S. at 358). Like the *Linehan IV* court's statement of the rule, this explanation helps little. It may be that *Hendricks* does not mandate "total" lack of control. But the courts ought to provide some guidance on the meaning of the statement in *Hendricks* that limits "involuntary civil confinement to those who suffer from a volitional impairment rendering them dangerous beyond their control." *Hendricks*, 521 U.S. at 358.

59. 269 Kan. 578, 7 P.3d 285 (Kan.2000), cert. granted, ___ U.S. ___, 121 S.Ct. 1483, 149 L.Ed.2d 372 (2001).

60. *Id.* at 287.

61. *Id.* at 292.

62. State v. Crane, 260 Kan. 208, 918 P.2d 1256 (Kan.1996). In this decision, however, the court affirmed Crane's conviction of lewd and lascivious behavior for exposing himself in another incident at a tanning salon

63. *In re Crane*, 7 P.3d at 292.

64. *Id.* In regard to the State's revealed intention to prolong the defendant's incarceration using the civil commitment statute, the court found that this case appeared to present exactly the concern registered by Justice Kennedy in his *Hendricks'* concurrence. In *Hendricks*, Kennedy had stated as follows:

Notwithstanding its civil attributes, the practical effect of the Kansas law may be to impose confinement for life. . . .

A common response to this may be, "A life term is exactly what the sentence should have been anyway," or, in the words of a Kansas task force member, "SO BE IT." [Citation omitted.] The point, however, is not how long Hendricks and others like him should serve a criminal sentence. With his criminal record, after all, a life term may well have been the only sentence appropriate to protect society and vindicate the wrong. The concern instead is whether it is the criminal system or the civil system which should make the decision in the first place. *If the civil system is used simply to impose punishment after the State makes an improvident plea bargain on the criminal side, then it is not performing its proper function.*

Id. (*quoting Hendricks*, 521 U.S. at 371–73) (emphasis supplied).

At the commitment hearing, Crane argued that his diagnosis was a personality disorder, and that his actions were willful, so that he did not lack volitional control. Under *Hendricks*, therefore, he could not be committed unless the jury found otherwise. The court below disagreed, and found no such requirement in *Hendricks*. It held that "the State must only prove the existence of a mental disorder that makes [Crane] likely to reoffend."[65] The Kansas Supreme Court reversed, finding that *Hendricks* requires a factual determination that the defendant lacks volitional control over his sexually violent proclivities.[66]

The court explained that "[t]here is no question that the majority opinion is replete with references to the commitment of persons who cannot control their own behavior."[67] Yet, Kansas' statutory scheme provides no express requirement of such a showing and, in fact, "gives the opposite impression."[68] *Hendricks,* the court found, cast considerable doubt on the constitutionality of the Kansas scheme. The court summarized its conclusion as follows:

> A fair reading of the majority opinion in Hendricks leads us to the inescapable conclusion that commitment under the Act is unconstitutional absent a finding that the defendant cannot control his dangerous behavior. To conclude otherwise would require that we ignore the plain language of the majority opinion in *Hendricks.*[69]

In support of this conclusion, the court quoted the many times Justice Thomas repeated that "to be constitutional, a civil commitment must limit involuntary confinement to those 'who suffer from a volitional impairment rendering them dangerous beyond their control.' "[70]

Moreover, the *Crane* court pointed out, "Hendricks' admitted inability to control his behavior figured heavily in the Supreme Court's classifying the Act as nonpunitive."[71] Commitment does not serve the criminal law objectives of retribution and deterrence, so long as it is limited to those who cannot control their behavior.[72] If, as applied below, commitment statutes extend to willful conduct, they potentially run afoul of the *Ex Post Facto* Clause, because they constitute punishment. The *Crane* court observed that five justices, including Justice Kennedy and the four dissenters, agreed "that factual circumstances different from those of *Hendricks* might warrant independent consideration of an *ex post facto* claim."[73]

[iii]   An Analysis of the Weak and Strong Tests

The difficulty with the Minnesota court's approach in *Linehan IV* is that it establishes a false dichotomy in which neither of the two choices is

65. *Id.* at 287–88 (quoting lower court decision).

66. *Id.* at 290.

67. *Id.* at 288.

68. *Id.* at 289. Kansas allows the commitment of those diagnosed as mentally abnormal who suffer from either a volitional or emotional impairment. In addition, the Act provides alternatively for those suffering from a personality disorder, though it fails to define the term, or specify whether those suffering such a disorder must lack volitional control before they can be committed. The statute thus contemplates commitments for "bad behavior other than inability to control behavior." *Id.*

69. *Id.* at 290.

70. *Id.* (quoting *Hendricks*, 521 U.S. at 358).

71. *Id.* at 291.

72. *Id.*

73. *Id.*

particularly well defined. On the one hand, the "utter lack of control" standard is a strawman, since no one seriously expects the law to apply a "total" lack of control test. Our knowledge of human behavior hardly allows us to make such definitive statements.[74] Moreover, even if the legal conclusion were "total" lack of control, this factual finding would be accompanied by the dramatically less certain burden of proof of clear and convincing evidence. On the other hand, the "some degree of volitional impairment" standard is largely meaningless or, at least, not meaningfully defined by the court. How much is "some"? It would be hard to articulate a more vapid standard than the one the Minnesota court selected.[75]

In the absence of any substantial lack of control requirement, the *Linehan IV* approach effectively permits indefinite incarceration on the basis of dangerousness alone. This appears to destroy any distinction between criminal liability and civil commitment.[76] Justice Page, in a strong dissent, explained that to maintain this distinction, "something more than a finding of dangerousness is required."[77] He asserted that "[w]hat is required is a finding that the individual suffers from a mental illness or mental abnormality that causes a volitional impairment rendering them dangerous beyond their control."[78] In fact, nowhere in the opinion does the *Linehan IV* court cite evidence supporting *any* lack of control on Linehan's part, other than the lower court's finding that it was concerned that he would "reoffend."[79] Presumably, this is what made him dangerous.[80]

It should be remembered that a principal reason for the Court's not finding that the sexual predator law violated the Double Jeopardy or *Ex Post Facto* Clauses was the fact that the Act was not designed to, and did not in fact, punish the person committed under it. This conclusion followed from the

---

74. It is worth comparing the volitional test in the civil commitment area to the language of the volitional test that is incorporated in the Model Penal Code, § 4.01, which excuses responsibility for mental disease or defect: "A person is not responsible for criminal conduct if at the time of such conduct as a result of mental disease or defect he lacks *substantial capacity ... to conform his conduct to the requirements of law*." (Emphasis added.)

75. The dissent made this very point: "The court provides no definition because 'lack of adequate control' is not capable of definition." *Linehan IV*, 594 N.W.2d at 881. The dissent supported this insight by relying on the court's own jurisprudence of human behavior:

It is interesting to note that in the criminal setting, we have rejected the doctrine of diminished capacity because it "inevitably opens the door to variable or sliding scales of criminal responsibility[, but] [t]he law recognizes no degree of sanity.... For the purposes of conviction there is no twilight zone between abnormality and insanity. An offender is wholly sane or wholly insane." ... Yet while this court does not allow a defendant to use diminished capacity to avoid criminal responsibility, by its decision today it will allow the state to use diminished capacity's mirror opposite, "lack of adequate

control," to civilly commit an individual. If there is "no twilight zone between abnormality and insanity" and an "offender is wholly sane or wholly insane," then what does "lack of adequate control" mean?

Linehan IV, 594 N.W.2d at 881 n.5 (Page, J., dissenting).

76. *Id.* at 882.

77. *Id.*

78. *Id.*

79. *See id.* at 882 n.10.

80. The *Linehan IV* court had a further difficulty, since the Minnesota statute explicitly stated that "it is not necessary to prove that the person has an inability to control the person's sexual impulses," and thus appeared to run afoul of *Hendricks*. The court interpreted this requirement to mean that it is not necessary to prove that the person has an "utter" inability to control his sexual impulses. Despite the Act's seemingly plain statement to the contrary, the court concluded that the SDP Act still requires the state to prove that "the person's disorder or dysfunction does not allow the person to adequately control his or her behavior such that the person is highly likely to commit harmful sexual acts in the future." *Id.* at 876 n.4.

Court's finding that the Act did not further the objective of deterrence, a core principle of the criminal law. It did not seek to deter, because these offenders could not control their behavior.[81]

Taken too literally, a volitional requirement might too severely narrow the class of committable sexual offenders. Moreover, as experience in the criminal law demonstrates, proving lack of volitional control might be difficult for states and would at least greatly exacerbate their task in these cases. At the same time, courts are disinclined to find that these laws "punish," and thus violate the Double Jeopardy and *Ex Post Facto* Clauses. But, as the volitional prong is increasingly discounted, the confinement begins to assume qualities of criminal punishment.

However challenging it might appear to be, courts must face the problem of defining with greater specificity the meaning of the volitional prong. While it is not unreasonable to reject a "total" lack of volitional control test, courts are constitutionally obligated to define *how much* lack of control the state must prove, together with proof of dangerousness, to involuntarily commit someone under a sexual predator act. Otherwise, there is no "additional factor" operating in these cases and, under both *Foucha* and *Hendricks*, these laws should be declared unconstitutional.

[2] The Double Jeopardy and *Ex Post Facto* Clauses

[a] On Defining Criminal Proceedings and Punishment

The key to analyzing whether the Kansas statute violated the Double Jeopardy or *Ex Post Facto* Clauses was the determination whether the commitment proceeding was civil or criminal in nature. It was on this point that the majority and the dissenters most sharply disagreed. The Court began its opinion on this issue by noting that the Kansas Legislature labelled the law "civil" and there was a strong presumption favoring the legislative characterization: "[W]e will reject the legislature's manifest intent only where a party challenging the statute provides 'the clearest proof' that 'the statutory scheme [is] so punitive either in purpose or effect as to negate [the State's] intention' to deem it 'civil.' "[82]

In order to assess the "punitive purpose or effect," the Court began by examining whether the Kansas commitment statute shared the objectives of criminal punishment: retribution or deterrence.[83] The Act was not retributive, according to the Court, since it "did not affix culpability for prior criminal conduct."[84] The requirement that the defendant have been "charged with or convicted of a sexually violent offense" was merely evidence of dangerousness, and not the basis for incarceration. As noted above, this suggests that there is no constitutional requirement that persons subject to these laws must have committed a sexually violent offense. In fact, such a requirement is somewhat inconsistent with the necessary finding that these statutes have a non-punitive purpose. So long as there is sufficient evidence to find that the

---

81. *Hendricks*, 521 U.S. at 361.

82. *Hendricks*, 521 U.S. at 361 (*quoting* United States v. Ward, 448 U.S. 242, 248–49, 100 S.Ct. 2636, 65 L.Ed.2d 742 (1980)).

83. *Id.* at 361–62.

84. *Id.* at 362.

person is dangerous, the Constitution does not bar civil commitment.[85]

In addition, the Court found no support for the view that the legislature "intended the Act to function as a deterrent."[86] The principal reason for this conclusion, the Court explained, is the mental abnormality requirement:

> Those persons committed under the Act are, by definition, suffering from a "mental abnormality" or "personality disorder" that prevents them from exercising adequate control over their behaviour. Such persons are therefore unlikely to be deterred by the threat of confinement.[87]

Although it haunts subsequent cases, the volitional component once again played a dominant role in the Court's analysis.

Finally, the Court concluded, neither incarceration itself[88] nor its indefinite nature[89] cause commitment to be punitive.[90] In what became the most contentious issue between the majority and the dissent, the Court held that Kansas' failure to provide treatment did not make confinement punitive.[91] Although there were conflicting statements both about Hendricks' treatability and the availability of treatment if Hendricks was treatable, the Court made clear that treatment, *per se*, was not constitutionally mandated.[92] First, if Hendricks is not treatable, the Court maintained, "it would be of little value to require treatment as a precondition for civil confinement of the dangerous-

---

85. The Court also noted that there was no scienter requirement in the law, which is "customarily an important element in distinguishing criminal from civil statutes." *Id.*

86. *Id.*

87. *Id.*

88. The Court observed: "Although the civil commitment scheme at issue here does involve an affirmative restraint, 'the mere fact that a person is detained does not inexorably lead to the conclusion that the government has imposed punishment.'" *Id.* at 2083 (*quoting* United States v. Salerno, 481 U.S. 739, 746, 107 S.Ct. 2095, 95 L.Ed.2d 697 (1987)).

89. Under the Kansas statute, a confined person can be released at any time if he is adjudged "safe to be at large." KAN. STAT. ANN. § 59a07 (1994). In addition, those incarcerated are entitled to annual proceedings at which they must be found to present a continuing danger beyond a reasonable doubt, or they are released. *Hendricks*, 521 U.S. at 364 (*citing* § 59–29a08). *But see* In the Matter of the Detention of Petersen, 138 Wash.2d 70, 980 P.2d 1204, 1209 (1999) (Court stated that the Kansas statute does not require annual proceedings and that the Supreme Court was "simply wrong about this." Moreover, the court held, due process does not require annual *de novo* evaluations.)

90. Justice Kennedy, who joined the entire majority opinion, wrote separately to warn that there were limits to states' use of civil commitment to confine "sexual predators." He stated as follows:

> On the record before us, the Kansas civil statute conforms to our precedents. If, however, civil confinement were to become a

mechanism for retribution or general deterrence, or if it were shown that mental abnormality is too imprecise a category to offer a solid basis for concluding that civil detention is justified, our precedents would not suffice to validate it.

Kansas v. Hendricks, 521 U.S. 346, 373, 117 S.Ct. 2072, 138 L.Ed.2d 501 (1997) (Kennedy, J., concurring).

91. Most states appear to at least suggest that treatment comprises some part of their purpose for civil commitment. These suggestions, however, might be little more than cosmetic. *See, e.g.,* People v. Putney, 67 Cal. Rptr.2d 283, 290 (1997), *rev. granted, opinion superseded* 71 Cal.Rptr.2d 212, 950 P.2d 56 (Cal.1997) ("the California Legislature's statement of purpose clearly indicates that treatment is at least an ancillary purpose of the Act."). In *Hubbert*, the California Supreme Court unambiguously "rejected" the "suggestion that the Legislature cannot constitutionally provide for the civil confinement of dangerous mentally impaired sexual predators unless the statutory scheme guarantees and provides 'effective' treatment." *Hubbert*, 81 Cal.Rptr.2d at 509.

92. On a related issue, the Minnesota Supreme Court found that its statutory scheme did not create a right to receive treatment in the program that is the least restrictive alternative. *In re* Senty–Haugen, 583 N.W.2d 266, 269–70 (Minn.1998). Since neither side argued it, the Court did not reach the constitutional question posed by this issue. *Id.* at 270.

ly insane when no acceptable treatment existed."[93] Second, if Hendricks is treatable, then the statute itself recommends treatment.[94] The Constitution, however, apparently guarantees no more treatment than what might be "available," and "States enjoy wide latitude in developing treatment regimes."[95]

[b] Double Jeopardy

The Double Jeopardy Clause provides as follows:

[N]or shall any person be subject for the same offense to be twice put in jeopardy of life or limb.

Hendricks argued that this Clause was violated in his case because his commitment operated as a second punishment for the offense for which he was originally convicted. The Court dismissed this claim on the ground already determined that civil commitment is not "punishment." The Court concluded simply: "Because we have determined that the Kansas Act is civil in nature, initiation of its commitment proceedings does not constitute a second prosecution."[96]

[c] The Ex Post Facto Clause

The *Ex Post Facto* Clause " 'forbids the application of any new punitive measure to a crime already consummated.' "[97] Once again, since "the Act does not impose punishment ... its application does not raise *ex post facto* concerns." The Act, according to the Court, did not operate to lengthen the sentence already imposed, but rather instituted a new set of proceedings that led to confinement that was non-criminal and non-punitive in nature. The Court reiterated and emphasized that the prior offense provision was non-substantive:

To the extent that past behavior is taken into account, it is used ... solely for evidentiary purposes. Because the Act does not criminalize conduct legal before its enactment, nor deprive Hendricks of any defense that was available to him at the time of his crimes, the Act does not violate the *Ex Post Facto* Clause.[98]

---

93. *Hendricks*, 521 U.S. at 366.

94. *Id.* at 367

95. *Id.* at 368 n.4. The Court's position on the relevance of treatment for the constitutional analysis is unclear. Justice Thomas, for example, went beyond the record to find that Hendricks' early "meager" treatment had become somewhat more substantial. *Id.* at 368. At oral argument, the state assured the Court that Hendricks was receiving "in the neighborhood of '31.5 hours of treatment per week.' " *Id.* (*quoting* Tr. of Oral Arg. 14–15, 16). Justice Breyer strongly criticized the Court for going beyond the record to reject the lower court's factual finding that "treatment was not a particularly important objective of the Act." *Id.* at 386 (Breyer, J., dissenting). Moreover, Justice Breyer quoted the commitment program's director who stated that Hendricks was receiving

"essentially no treatment." *Id.* at 384 (Breyer, J., dissenting).

96. *Hendricks*, 521 U.S. at 348.

97. *Id.* (*quoting* Lindsey v. Washington, 301 U.S. 397, 401, 57 S.Ct. 797, 81 L.Ed. 1182 (1937) (internal quotation marks excluded)).

98. *Id.* at 371. In a somewhat different legal context than presented in *Hendricks*, a Washington appellate court examined whether sexual predators were denied equal protection because state law provided that they be committed pending consideration of "less restrictive alternatives to total confinement," whereas persons suffering from mental illness could not be confined until after this determination had been made. *In re Detention of Brooks*, 94 Wash.App. 716, 973 P.2d 486, 488 (Wash.Ct. App.1999). Although the court ruled that the

[d]   Conditions of Confinement

In *Seling v. Young*,[99] the Supreme Court considered a habeas petitioner's claim that Washington State's sexual predator law was unconstitutional as applied to him, and that his continued confinement was illegal.[100] Although the law had been deemed civil by the Washington Supreme Court and upheld as constitutional,[101] The Ninth Circuit held that Young could challenge the law as applied to him. The Ninth Circuit found that Young had alleged facts that, if true, would indicate that the statute was being applied in a punitive way in violation of the Double Jeopardy and *Ex Post Facto* Clauses.[102] The Ninth Circuit remanded for an evidentiary hearing and the State appealed.

Although the Court recognized the "serious" allegations made by Young,[103] it concluded that the *Ex Post Facto* and Double Jeopardy Clauses did not permit an as-applied challenge to a law previously deemed civil by the state's supreme court.[104] The Court explained that allowing as-applied challenges "would prove unworkable."[105] Because confinement is not a fixed event, and its features change over time, the Court stated, an as-applied analysis "would never conclusively resolve whether a particular scheme is punitive and would thereby prevent a final determination of the scheme's validity under the Double Jeopardy and *Ex Post Facto* Clauses."[106] The Court recognized that under applicable law, if a challenger presents "the clearest proof that the statutory scheme [is] so punitive either in purpose *or effect* as to negate [the State's] intention that the proceeding be civil, it must be considered criminal."[107] However, this language, the Court held, is limited to challenges of *the Act* as punitive, not its application to particular detainees. "Permitting [Young's] as-applied challenge," the Court argued, "would invite an end run around the Washington Supreme Court's decision that the Act is civil in circumstances where a direct attack on that decision is not before this Court."[108] Therefore, the "effects of a putatively civil commitment scheme are

state need only show a rational basis for the different treatment, it found that the "state's interest in treating sex predators and in protecting society from their actions is ... irrefutably compelling." *Id.* at 489

99. 531 U.S. 250, 121 S.Ct. 727, 148 L.Ed.2d 734 (2001).

100. *Id.* at 732.

101. *In re* Young, 122 Wash.2d 1, 857 P.2d 989 (Wash.1993) (*en banc*).

102. Young v. Weston, 192 F.3d 870 (9th Cir.1999).

103. The Court summarized Young's allegations regarding the conditions of his confinement as follows:

Young alleged that for seven years, he had been subject to conditions more restrictive than those placed on true civil commitment detainees, and even state prisoners. The Center, located wholly within the perimeter of a larger Department of Corrections (DOC) facility, relied on the DOC for a host of essential services, including library services, medical care, food, and security. More recently, Young claimed, the role of the DOC had increased to include daily security "walk-throughs." Young contended that the conditions and restrictions at the Center were not reasonably related to a legitimate non-punitive goal, as residents were abused, confined to their rooms, subjected to random searches of their rooms and unit, and placed under excessive security.

Young, 121 S.Ct. at 733.

104. *Id.* at 735. The Court also noted that it had found a nearly identical statute to be civil on its face in *Hendricks*. *Id.* at 730.

105. *Id.* at 735.

106. *Id.*

107. *Id.* at 741 (Stevens, J., dissenting) (internal quotation marks omitted); *see* majority opinion in accord, *id.* at 735.

108. *Id.*

relevant, if at all, in the initial challenge of a law on its face."[109]

§ 3–1.4 Community Registration and Notification Statutes

Laws requiring registration of sexual offenders and notification of their presence to the local communities are today strongly associated with New Jersey's enactment of "Megan's law."[110] Although most states, and the federal government, have passed registration laws, New Jersey's Megan's law remains the model upon which these laws are largely based. Because of this, as well as the fact that the New Jersey Supreme Court exhaustively considered the challenges to Megan's law, we will use it to ground our exploration of the legal issues surrounding registration of sex offenders and community notification of their whereabouts. The text and notes will also consider other state laws and the court opinions evaluating their constitutionality.

§ 3–1.4.1 Introduction: The Law's Particulars

Megan's law is comprised of several provisions, the most important two of which "require registration with law enforcement authorities of certain convicted sex offenders" and, "[s]econd, . . . provide for notice of the presence of such offenders in the community."[111] We will generally refer to the two provisions of the New Jersey Act as together comprising Megan's law. For those offenders convicted prior to the law's effective date, the following crimes trigger the registration and notification procedures: aggravated sexual assault, sexual assault, aggravated criminal sexual contact, and kidnapping pursuant to a sexual assault.[112] Megan's Law also adds a host of more minor offenses for those convicted after the statute's effective date.[113]

109. *Id.* It should be noted that the Court observed that this case gave it "no occasion to consider the extent to which a court may look to actual conditions of confinement and implementation of the statute to determine in the first instance whether a confinement scheme is civil in nature." *Id.* at 736–37. Justice Scalia, joined by Justice Souter, wrote a concurring opinion in which he argued that courts can never consider actual conditions to determine whether a confinement scheme is civil in nature. *Id.* at 737–38 (Scalia, J., concurring). Justice Thomas, concurring, went even further, arguing that implementation-based challenges were precluded "at any time." *Id.* at 740 (Thomas, J., concurring). Justice Stevens, dissenting, strongly disagreed. He stated as follows: "If conditions of confinement are such that a detainee has been punished twice in violation of the Double Jeopardy Clause, it is irrelevant that the scheme has been previously labeled as civil without full knowledge of the effects of the statute." *Id.* at 742 (Stevens, J., dissenting).

110. As summarized in *Lannie v. Engler*, the facts underlying the passage of Megan's law are profoundly disturbing:

On July 29, 1994, seven-year-old Megan Kanka was abducted, raped, and murdered near her home in New Jersey. The man who confessed to her murder lived across the street from the Kanka family and had twice been convicted of sex offenses involving young girls. Neither Megan, her parents, local police, or members of the community were aware of the confessed murderer's criminal history. Nor were they aware that he shared his house with two other men previously convicted of sex crimes. Public outcry, led by Megan Kanka's parents, prompted legislatures around the country to quickly enact sex offender registration laws in an effort to protect the public.

Lanni v. Engler, 994 F.Supp. 849, 851 (E.D.Mich.1998).

111. *Poritz*, 662 A.2d at 373 (*citing* L.1994, c.133 (Registration Law, N.J.S.A. 2C:7–1 to – 5); and L.1994, c.133 (Community Notification, N.J.S.A. 2C:7–6 to –11)).

112. *Id.* at 377.

113. *Id.* (These include "various laws concerning endangering the welfare of a child, luring or enticing, criminal sexual contact if the victim is a minor, and kidnapping, criminal restraint, or false imprisonment if the victim is a minor and the offender not the parent; and in all cases an attempt to commit any of the foregoing.").

Once Megan's Law is triggered, offenders must register with local authorities,[114] and the local police must notify interested institutions of the offender's presence in the area.[115] Institutions' interest is defined by the Act in accordance with three levels of risk of reoffense, low, moderate and high. Megan's law provides as follows:

(1) If risk of reoffense is low, law enforcement agencies likely to encounter the person registered shall be notified;

(2) If risk of reoffense is moderate, organizations in the community including schools, religious and youth organizations shall be notified in accordance with the Attorney General's Guidelines, in addition to the notice required by paragraph (1) of this subsection;

(3) If risk of reoffense is high, the public shall be notified through means in accordance with the Attorney General's Guidelines designed to reach members of the public likely to encounter the person registered in addition to the notice required by paragraphs (1) and (2) of this subsection.[116]

There are several noteworthy aspects of this tiered approach to notification. Initially, it is admirable that the New Jersey Legislature sought a measured response to the matter. Still, it assumes that "risk of reoffense" *is* subject to measurement, an empirical conclusion baldly asserted by the Legislature and assumed by the *Poritz* court.[117] In addition, as interpreted by the *Poritz* court, "all registrants will be subjected at the very least to Tier One Notification."[118] This fact reflects the apparent assumption that *all* sex offenders present at least a low risk of reoffense. This failsafe over-inclusive ness is inconsistent with the New Jersey Legislature's, and the court's, belief that risk can be measured. Surely, some individuals pose no continuing risk. The only question is whether they can be reliably identified. Of course, the other side of this question concerns the state's ability to reliably identify offenders who pose more than a low risk.

Under the original terms of Megan's law, the prosecutor of the county of conviction had the responsibility of assigning the category of risk to the offender.[119] The *Poritz* court held that this procedure was constitutionally inadequate. The court found that because "the statute sufficiently impinges on liberty interests," procedural due process required that sex offenders were "entitled to the protection of procedures designed to assure that the risk of reoffense and the extent of notification are fairly evaluated before Tier Two or Tier Three notification is implemented."[120] These procedures require the following guarantees and definitional aspects:

---

114. The *Poritz* court explained that [r]egistration requires ... appearance at a local police station for fingerprinting, photography, and providing information for a registration form that will include a physical description, the offense involved, home address, employment or school address, vehicle used, and license plate number. *Id.* at 377.

115. Failure to register is a "fourth-degree crime." N.J. STAT. ANN. § 2C:7–2a.

116. N.J. STAT. ANN. § 2C:7–8c

117. *Poritz*, 662 A.2d at 380 ("Our Legislature could reasonably conclude that risk of reoffense can be fairly measured, and that knowledge of the presence of offenders provides increased defense against them.").

118. *Id.* at 378.

119. *Id.*

120. *Id.* at 382.

(1) Written notice to the offender "of the proposed level and specific manner and details of notification;"

(2) The right to counsel, which will be provided to the offender if he cannot afford it;

(3) The right to a hearing at which the court controls the proceeding and either affirms or reverses the prosecutor's assessment;

(4) The rules of evidence do not apply;

(5) Expert testimony is admissible to assist the court;

(6) The burdens of proof shift as follows: "the State shall have the burden of going forward, that burden satisfied by the presentation of evidence that prima facie justifies the proposed level and manner of notification. Upon such proof, the offender shall have the burden of persuasion on both issues, that burden to remain with the offender. In other words, the court, assuming the State has satisfied its burden of going forward, shall affirm the prosecutor's determination unless it is persuaded by a preponderance of the evidence that it does not conform to the laws and Guidelines."[121]

§ 3–1.4.2 Constitutional Challenges

Because most of the constitutional challenges to registration and notification statutes were discussed in the generally more troubling context of civil commitment, this section only briefly summarizes these issues. Our focus lies on those constitutional issues special to registration and notification provisions.

[1] Constitutional Issues Based on Claims that Registration and Notification Laws *Punish*

As was true in the civil commitment issue decided in *Hendricks*, a key constitutional concern involves whether notification laws "punish." Challengers who claim that they constitute punishment assert that these laws consequently violate the following clauses: double jeopardy, *ex post facto*, bills of attainder and cruel and unusual punishment. However, courts have generally found that the respective legislatures passing these laws did not intend to punish.[122] Absent such an intent, a court will find that a law punishes only where "the statutory scheme was so punitive either in purpose or effect to transform what was clearly intended as a civil remedy into a criminal penalty."[123]

In most instances, legislatures make clear the regulatory and non-punitive intention behind their enactment of notification statutes. But even when they fail to include this prefatory savings language, courts find it to be implicit in these laws.[124] The New Jersey Supreme Court in *Poritz* explained the legislative purpose behind notification statutes as follows:

---

121. *Id.* at 383.

122. The test for determining whether a law "punishes" comes from *United States v. Ward*, 448 U.S. 242, 100 S.Ct. 2636, 65 L.Ed.2d 742 (1980); *see also* Hudson v. United States,

522 U.S. 93, 118 S.Ct. 488, 139 L.Ed.2d 450 (1997).

123. *Hudson*, 522 U.S. at 99 (citations omitted).

124. *See, e.g.*, Lanni v. Engler, 994 F.Supp. 849, 853 (E.D.Mich.1998) (upholding the Mich-

They were designed simply and solely to enable the public to protect itself from the danger posed by sex offenders, such offenders widely regarded as having the highest risk of recidivism. Unarguably, as the Supreme Court pointed out in *Salerno*, . . . , "There is no doubt that preventing danger to the community is a legitimate regulatory goal."[125]

Similarly, in *Meinders v. Weber*,[126] the South Dakota Supreme Court rejected the claim that the State's offender registration statute was cruel and unusual punishment when applied retroactively. The court put it this way:

> The Legislature's intention in requiring registration was to accomplish the regulatory purpose of assisting law enforcement in identifying and tracking sex offenders to prevent future sex offenses, especially those against children. Furthermore, the purpose of the public access to registrant information . . . was to alert the public in the interest of community safety, and to prevent and promptly resolve incidents involving sexual offenses. These are remedial measures akin to warning communities of potential health hazards.[127]

[2] Privacy and Procedural Due Process

In *Poritz*, the court stated that privacy is "[g]rounded in the Fourteenth Amendment's concept of personal liberty."[128] This liberty interest comprises both matters of "confidentiality" and "autonomy." As the Supreme Court explained in *Whalen v. Roe*, the first strand encompasses "the individual interest in avoiding disclosure of personal matters," and the second, "the interest in making certain kinds of important decisions."[129] The registration and notification laws implicate the confidentiality aspects of the privacy right.[130]

In *Poritz*, the court held that the registration component of Megan's law did not violate the privacy guarantee, since the information required therein is already publicly available.[131] Offenders, therefore, can have no "reasonable expectation of privacy" over this information. Similarly, the court held as regards the notification component that "[m]atters of public record, such as criminal background, may be disclosed without impinging on privacy interests."[132] However, the court found that its "analysis [was] altered . . . by the disclosure of [an offender's] home address, and more importantly, by the totality of the information disclosed to the public."[133] Thus infringed, the court proceeded to evaluate whether the State's interest in community notification outweighed offenders' interest in privacy.

igan Act, concluding that "[t]he text and structure reveal no intent to punish."); State v. Williams, 88 Ohio St.3d 513, 728 N.E.2d 342, 357 (Ohio 2000) (same).

125. *Poritz*, 662 A.2d at 404 (*quoting Salerno*, 481 U.S. at 747).

126. 604 N.W.2d 248 (S.D.2000).

127. *Id.* at 255.

128. *Poritz*, 662 A.2d at 406.

129. Whalen v. Roe, 429 U.S. 589, 598 n. 23, 599–600, 97 S.Ct. 869, 51 L.Ed.2d 64 (1977).

130. This confidentiality prong also has two aspects: It includes "the right to be free from the government disclosing private facts about its citizens and from the government inquiring into matters in which it does not have a legitimate and proper concern." ACLU v. Mississippi, 911 F.2d 1066, 1069–70 (5th Cir.1990) (emphasis omitted).

131. *Poritz*, 662 A.2d at 406.

132. *Id.* at 408.

133. *Id.*

The court concluded that it did, finding that the information involved here was "not deserving of a particularly high degree of protection."[134] The information was not of an intimate nature. "Counterbalanced against [an offender's] diminished privacy interest," the court pointed out, "is a strong state interest in public disclosure."[135] The court, in fact, found that the "state interest in protecting the safety of members of the public from sex offenders is clear and compelling."[136] Moreover, "the degree and scope of disclosure is carefully calibrated to the need for disclosure: the risk of reoffense: The greater the risk of reoffense, the greater is the scope of disclosure."[137] Buttressing this conclusion is the court's requirement, discussed *supra*, that due process requires judicial oversight of the classification and disclosure provisions of the law.

[3] Equal Protection

The Equal Protection Clause provides that no state shall "deny to any persons within its jurisdiction the equal protection of the laws."[138] In *Doe v. Poritz*, the plaintiff argued that Megan's Law classified him as a sex offender for purposes of the law, and failed to treat him as an individual as dictated by the principle of equality.[139] In particular, he pointed out, unlike the more general class, he had been released from custody after being "determined to be no longer dangerous."[140]

The *Poritz* court, however, found that Megan's Law did not violate the plaintiff's right to equal protection of the laws. It noted, first, that "[a] classification that does not impact a suspect class or impinge upon a fundamental constitutional right will be upheld if it is rationally related to a legitimate government interest."[141] Here, the legislature had the "unquestionable" interest in "protecting the public from recidivistic sex offenders."[142] Under the rational basis test, it does not matter that the law is not narrowly tailored to reach this interest. The equality guarantee requires only that "the classifications do not discriminate arbitrarily between persons who are similarly situated."[143]

---

134. *Id.* at 411.

135. *Id.* at 412.

136. *Id.*

137. *Id.* The court summarized its holding as follows:

> [W]e find that a hearing is required prior to notification under Tiers Two and Three. First, the private interests in privacy and reputation are significant. Second, additional safeguards would ensure that deprivations of those interests occur only when justified by the risk posed by the offender. Last, the State interest in prompt classification and notification will not seriously be burdened by additional safeguards, and any resulting burden is justified by the benefits of ensuring accurate classification.

Id. at 421.

138. U.S. Const. Amend. XIV.

139. *Poritz*, 662 A.2d at 413.

140. *Id.*

141. *Id.*

142. *Id.* at 414.

143. *Id. See also* State v. Williams, 88 Ohio St.3d 513, 728 N.E.2d 342, 359 (Ohio 2000) (rejecting an Equal Protection challenge). The *Poritz* court also determined that Megan's Law did not violate the New Jersey Constitution:

> To determine whether the Registration and Notification Laws violate equal protection under the New Jersey Constitution, we apply a balancing test which considers the nature of the right affected, the extent to which the government action interferes with that right, and the public need for such interference.... We conclude that the public need for information about dangerous sex offenders greatly outweighs plaintiff's right to privacy and the intrusion of that right associated with registration and notification.

Poritz, 662 A.2d at 414.

§ 3–1.5   Burdens of Proof in Predicting Sexual Predation

Courts that have considered the issue of predicting violent behavior have been remarkably, and lamentably, reluctant to confront the uncertainties endemic in this enterprise. This reluctance extends to virtually every legal context in which predictions of violence are employed.[144] The Supreme Court, indeed, has distinguished the legal practice of predicting violence from the empirical capacity to make such predictions. This is reflected in its retort to the evidence proffered in *Barefoot v. Estelle* that psychiatric predictions of violence are wrong two out of three times. The Court responded, "[n]either petitioner nor the [American Psychiatric] Association suggests that psychiatrists are always wrong with respect to future dangerousness, only most of the time."[145] In permitting experts to testify regarding dangerousness, the Court follows the maxim first articulated in *Schall v. Martin*: "[O]ur cases indicate, however, that from a legal point of view there is nothing inherently unattainable about a prediction of future criminal conduct."[146] In what way the empirical world of law differs from the world studied by researchers remains unexplained by the Court.

It is clear enough that the Court's empirical jurisprudence is being driven largely, if not entirely, by normative considerations. The Court has sought to regulate the effect of psychiatric predictions of violence by manipulating the burdens of proof employed in different contexts. As the Court explained in *Addington v. Texas*,[147] standards of proof are used "to instruct the factfinder concerning the degree of confidence our society thinks he should have in the correctness of factual conclusions for a particular type of adjudication."[148] In *Addington*, the Court settled on the standard of "clear and convincing evidence" for civil commitment hearings. This choice represented a compromise between the relatively slight preponderance standard of ordinary civil disputes and the demanding beyond a reasonable doubt standard of criminal prosecutions. This compromise was suggested by a variety of considerations present in civil commitments. First, following an involuntary commitment, the continuing involvement of professionals, family and friends in the person's treatment allows errors to be corrected. Second, making an error that permits a mentally ill person to live in the general community is not necessarily good for that person: "[i]t cannot be said . . . that it is much better for a mentally ill person to 'go free' than for a mentally normal person to be committed."[149] Finally, the Court observed, "[g]iven the lack of certainty and the fallibility of psychiatric diagnosis, there is a serious question as to whether a state could ever prove beyond a reasonable doubt that an individual is both mentally ill and likely to be violent."[150]

In *Hendricks*, the Court was not presented with the question of what standard of proof is required to involuntarily commit sexual predators. Under the Kansas statute, the state had the burden of demonstrating mental

---

144. *See, e.g.,* Barefoot v. Estelle, 463 U.S. 880, 103 S.Ct. 3383, 77 L.Ed.2d 1090 (1983) (capital sentencing; *see* § 7–1.4); Schall v. Martin, 467 U.S. 253, 104 S.Ct. 2403, 81 L.Ed.2d 207 (1984) (pretrial detention of juveniles); United States v. Salerno, 481 U.S. 739, 107 S.Ct. 2095, 95 L.Ed.2d 697 (1987) (bail hearings).

145. *Barefoot*, 463 U.S. at 901.

146. *Schall*, 467 U.S. at 278.

147. 441 U.S. 418, 99 S.Ct. 1804, 60 L.Ed.2d 323 (1979).

148. *Id.* at 423.

149. *Id.* at 430.

150. *Id.*

abnormality and dangerousness by proof beyond a reasonable doubt. We might presume that, because of its civil nature, *Addington* would permit the lower clear and convincing standard to be employed in sexual predator commitments. But there are important differences between the case of sexual predators and the commitments contemplated in *Addington*. First of all, the *Hendricks* Court found that treatment was not constitutionally mandated and, indeed, might not even be available for some of these committees. It is thus rather more difficult to suggest that the detainee necessarily gains from incarceration, or that errors will likely be discovered in a timely fashion. Unlike the commitment of the mentally ill, then, committing mentally abnormal sexual predators is based largely on the need to protect society, rather than any benevolent desire to cure the "patient." This alternative objective might require a heightened standard of proof.

There is little explicit discussion in the caselaw concerning what quantitative standards the various burdens of proof correspond to. In both the commitment cases and the registration and notification cases, courts readily maintain that violence predictions can be made with more or less certainty. The legal consequences, in fact, often turn on this very judgment. Thus, the higher the likelihood of violence associated with a person, the more dire the legal consequences. Yet courts have resolutely avoided the task of articulating what statistical figures correspond to such terms as "likely," "substantially probable," or "moderate versus high risk."

Wisconsin v. Kienitz[151] offers a nice illustration of courts' reluctance to become mired in quantitative standards for dangerous determinations. *Kienitz* is by no means unusual in this regard.[152] Wisconsin law permits the civil commitment of someone if he is found, by proof beyond a reasonable doubt, to be "substantially probable" to commit acts of sexual violence.[153] The court explicitly refrained from defining " 'substantially probable' with a minimum percentage."[154] The court concluded "that 'substantially probable' means 'considerably more likely to occur than not to occur.' "[155] The court made no attempt to provide a ballpark range for this nomenclature. Presumably, it is well above 50%, but well below 100%. Despite the wideness of the range, the court found that this standard did not render the statute ambiguous.[156]

---

151. 221 Wis.2d 275, 585 N.W.2d 609 (Wis. App.1998).

152. Most courts ignore the issue altogether. *See, e.g.*, Kansas v. Hendricks 521 U.S. 346, 117 S.Ct. 2072, 138 L.Ed.2d 501 (1997), in which the Court never even mentioned the matter.

153. *Kienitz* 585 N.W.2d at 611. The phraseology used by the *Kienitz* court should be highlighted. Some courts and commentators have speculated about the quantitative meaning of legal standards such as preponderance, clear and convincing and beyond a reasonable doubt. A more recent, and salutary, trend is to apply these legal standards to the probability estimations that social scientists employ. This approach was first suggested by John Monahan and David Wexler, *A Definite Maybe: Proof and Probability in Civil Commitment*, 2 LAW & HUM. BEHAV. 37, 37 (1978). It goes a long way toward solving the difficulty cited by the Supreme Court in *Addington* that "[g]iven the lack of certainty and the fallibility of psychiatric diagnosis, there is a serious question as to whether a state could ever prove beyond a reasonable doubt that an individual is both mentally ill and likely to be violent." *Addington*, 441 U.S. at 430. It is well within the psychiatric profession's ability to demonstrate by proof beyond a reasonable doubt that someone is "substantially probable" to commit violent acts. Whether this is sufficient to incarcerate someone is a legal policy judgment, not an empirical question. *See* Monahan & Wexler, *supra*.

154. *Kienitz*, 585 N.W.2d at 612.

155. *Id.*

156. *Id.*

Courts' fear of quantitative certainty also is found throughout the cases evaluating registration and community notification statutes. In *Doe v. Poritz*, for example, the New Jersey Supreme Court required a judicial proceeding to determine which past offenders posed a "moderate" risk, and which a "high" risk. The court, however, had some difficulty articulating the manner by which this categorization was to occur. All it could say was that the risk had to be "substantially higher" for the latter categories:

> [G]iven the unavoidable uncertainties in this entire area, we do not believe it is realistic to impose requirements of proof of some statistical differentiation of the risk of reoffense between the classes or between the offender before the court and the typical offender of the other classes. We can say no more about the meaning of "substantially higher" other than that it is intended to portray a difference in risk so significant as to warrant the conclusion that the Legislature intended this most substantial difference in the level and therefore the manner of notification.[157]

§ 3–1.6　Conclusion

The outrage associated with the crimes of "sexual predators" has had a distorting influence on courts' judgments. Courts have been extraordinarily cavalier in their scrutiny of state laws committing these offenders, or which require them to register and notify communities of their presence. In particular, the commitment cases reflect a lack of considered judgment. The courts uncritically accept that state statutes incorporate two factors, dangerousness and mental abnormality, with little reflection on the content of them. They appear to be both theoretically and practically indistinguishable. Compounding this error, courts give little or no attention to the dependability of dangerousness predictions. Despite the substantial doubt that swirls around the question of the accuracy of predictions of violence, courts blithely assert that they are reliable enough. They make no effort to explain this conclusion.

Without question, society's vehement response to sexual aggressors, especially when their victims are children, is understandable. Sexual predators are not a group deserving of much sympathy. Still, the Constitution is tested most when its protections might appear to shield those individuals whom we most despise. By this measure, the Constitution has failed us. The California Supreme Court, for example, after concluding that treatment is not constitutionally mandated for those committed under the applicable California law, so discounted the defendants in these cases as to observe that "the maximum length of each commitment term is relatively brief–two years."[158] It is hard to imagine any court saying such a thing in any other context.

---

157. *Poritz*, 662 A.2d at 384.　　　　**158.** *Hubbert*, 81 Cal.Rptr.2d at 511.

B. SCIENTIFIC STATUS

by

Marnie E. Rice* & Grant T. Harris**

§ 3–2.0   THE SCIENTIFIC STATUS OF RESEARCH ON SEXUAL AGGRESSORS

§ 3–2.1   Introduction: Terminology

In this section, "sexual aggressors" refers to persons who are the subject of sex offender registration, community notification, and special civil commitment laws. The term also includes all those who have engaged in sexual acts involving physical contact with a child or nonconsensual sexually violent acts against adults (i.e., offenses involving the use of force in such a way that the sexual integrity of the victim was violated). Although under the law, a child (or "minor") may be someone under the age of 18, in most of the scientific and professional literature on sex offenders, a child is usually defined as someone who has not yet completed puberty,[1] which, for females especially, occurs considerably younger than 18.[2]

The overwhelming majority of sexual aggressors are men,[3] although there is an emerging literature on female sexual aggressors[4] and there are at least two women who have been committed under the sexual predator statutes as

* Dr. Marnie Rice is Director of Research of the Mental Health Centre, Penetanguishene, Ontario, Canada. She is Professor of Psychiatry and Behavioural Neurosciences at McMaster University, Associate Professor of Psychology at Queen's University, and Scientific Director of the Centre for the Study of Aggression and Mental Disorder. She has been awarded several research grants and has over eighty publications including three coauthored books on the topics of violent and criminal behavior, sex offenders, psychopaths and arson.

She obtained her honours B.A. in Psychology from McMaster University; a Master's Degree from the University of Toronto; and a Ph.D. in Clinical Psychology from York University. She began working at Oak Ridge in 1975 as the psychologist on a behavioural unit. She was the 1995 recipient of the American Psychological Association's award for Distinguished Contribution to Research in Public Policy, and the 1997 recipient of a Government of Ontario Amethyst Award for Outstanding Contribution by an Ontario Public Servant.

** Dr. Grant Harris is a Research Psychologist at the Mental Health Centre, Penetanguishene, Ontario, Canada. He is also an adjunct Associate Professor of Psychology at Queen's University, Kingston. He obtained a B.Sc. from the University of Toronto, and his Ph.D. in Experimental Psychology from McMaster University. He first worked at the Penetanguishene Mental Health Centre in 1974 and rejoined the staff in 1980. He was, for several years, responsible for the development and supervision of behavioral programs on maximum security units for dangerous and assaultive men. Since joining the Research Department in 1988, he has been awarded several research grants and has conducted extensive scientific research on violent and criminal behavior, psychopathy, and sexual aggression and deviance. He is (together with Vernon Quinsey, Marnie Rice and Catherine Cormier) an author of the recent book, *Violent Offenders: Appraising and Managing Risk* published by the American Psychological Association. In 1997, with colleagues from MHCP's Research Department, Dr. Harris received the Amethyst Award for Outstanding Achievement in the Ontario Public Service.

§ 3–2.0

1. American Psychiatric Association, Diagnostic And Statistical Manual Of Mental Disorders (4th ed. 1994); Vernon L. Quinsey, *Men Who Have Sex with Children, in* Law & Mental Health: International Perspectives 140–172 (D.N. Weisstub ed., 1986).

2. J.M. Tanner, *Sequence, Tempo, and Individual Variation in the Growth and Development of Boys and Girls Aged 12 to 16*, 100 Daedaulus 907, 930 (1971).

3. Gene Abel et al., *Sexually Aggressive Behavior, in* Forensic Psychology & Psychiatry: Perspectives & Standards For Interdisciplinary Practice (J. Curran et al. eds., 1986).

4. Ruth A. Mathews et al., *Juvenile Female Sexual Offenders: Clinical Characteristics and Treatment Issues*, 9 Sexual Abuse: A Journal Of Research & Treatment 187, 199 (1997); Art O'Connor, *Female Sex Offenders*, 150 British Journal Of Psychiatry 615, 620 (1987).

"sexually violent predators."[5] Among incarcerated sex offenders, most are rapists (i.e., men who have assaulted adult women), and a smaller percentage are child molesters.[6] There is also a sizeable proportion of incarcerated sex offenders who have offended against both adults and children.[7] Under the "sexual psychopath" laws enacted between 1937 and the early 1970s, the vast majority of offenders who qualified were men who had offended against children—or children and adults—because the diagnosis that most often led to the designation was sexual deviation or paraphilia (almost always pedophilia or sexual sadism) in the Diagnostic and Statistical Manual of Mental Disorders.[8] Because most rapists did not qualify for such diagnoses, they were included much less often. However, under the new sexually violent predator laws, "personality disorders," which are much more common among rapists than paraphilias, are explicitly recognized as sufficient to qualify for designation as a "predator." Thus, under the sexually violent predator commitment laws, rapists will likely be much more commonly committed than under the older laws. Data from California, Minnesota and Washington suggest that at least one third of the current sexually violent predators have convictions for offending exclusively against adults.[9]

§ 3–2.2 The Scientific Questions

§ 3–2.2.1 How Well Can Recidivism Among Sexual Aggressors Be Predicted?

Although risk assessment among sexual aggressors has been studied for many years, progress was slow until the last decade. A similar statement can be made with regard to research on prediction of violence in general.[10] Research on risk assessment among sexual aggressors has burgeoned in the past decade. For example, a search on PsycINFO, a database that contains journal articles pertaining to the social sciences over the period since 1890, identified just 27 papers on the prediction of recidivism among sex offenders before 1980, 47 during the 1980's and 114 during the 1990s.[11] In a 1984 review of the literature on sexual aggressors against women, Quinsey summarized the recidivism studies up to that time.[12] He found tremendous variation

5. One in Minnesota and one in Washington, Personal Communication from Roxanne Lieb (January 30, 2001).

6. Frank Porporino & Larry Motiuk, *Preliminary Results of National Sex Offender Census*, 29 RESEARCH REPORT CORRECTIONAL SERVICES CANADA (1991).

7. *Id.* (Porporino and Motiuk reported 28%).

8. AMERICAN PSYCHIATRIC ASSOCIATION, DIAGNOSTIC AND STATISTICAL MANUAL OF MENTAL DISORDERS (1ST ED. 1952); AMERICAN PSYCHIATRIC ASSOCIATION, DIAGNOSTIC AND STATISTICAL MANUAL OF MENTAL DISORDERS (2nd ed. 1968); AMERICAN PSYCHIATRIC ASSOCIATION, DIAGNOSTIC AND STATISTICAL MANUAL OF MENTAL DISORDERS (3rd ed. 1980); AMERICAN PSYCHIATRIC ASSOCIATION, TREATMENTS OF PSYCHIATRIC DISORDERS (3rd ed.—revised 1987); AMERICAN PSYCHIATRIC ASSOCIATION, DIAGNOSTIC AND STATISTICAL MANUAL OF MENTAL DISORDERS (4th ed. 1994).

9. Personal Communication from Lucy Berliner (August 7, 1997); Eric S. Janus & Nancy Walbek, *Sexual Offender Commitments in Minnesota: A Descriptive Study of Second Generation Commitments* 18 BEHAV. SCI. & L. 343 (2000); Personal Communication from Janice Marques (August 6, 1997).

10. *See* John Monahan, *Clinical and Actuarial Predictions of Violence, in* MODERN SCIENTIFIC EVIDENCE 283–314 (D. Faigman et al., eds., 1997).

11. The search of PsycINFO was done January 23, 2001 using Journal Articles as the database and searching for the words (predict* or recidiv*) AND (sex offenders) in the abstract.

12. Vernon L. Quinsey, *Sexual Aggression: Studies of Offenders Against Women, in* LAW & MENTAL HEALTH: INTERNATIONAL PERSPECTIVES 84–121 (D. Weisstub ed., 1984).

in the reported recidivism rates and noted that there was marked heterogeneity among the offenders, a point also emphasized by investigators who have developed typologies of rapists.[13] Nevertheless, there were subgroups of offenders who were at high risk of committing new acts of sexual violence upon release. Frisbie and Dondis followed 70 men who had committed sexual acts accompanied by threats or force on women and found that 36% committed a new sexual offense within 5 years of their release from an institution where they had been judged to be sexually dangerous.[14] In an era where one of the most common arguments about why the prediction of violence was so difficult was that the base rate of violence was low, this was a high rate of recidivism. More recent studies have obtained rates of violent recidivism over 50%, at least among some subgroups.[15] Moreover, among mixed groups of offenders, sex offenders exhibit higher risk than other offenders.[16] There is also evidence that sex offenders show considerable risk for sexual or violent recidivism for very long periods of time.[17]

In a 1986 review of the literature on child molesters, Quinsey found three consistent predictors of sexual recidivism: the number of previous sexual offenses, the selection of male victims (either exclusively or in addition to female victims), and the selection of unrelated victims. Perhaps the best of the early follow up studies of child molesters was that of Frisbie and Dondis who studied 1509 child molesters, all "sexual psychopaths" treated at Atascadero in California, discharged to the court as improved, and released.[18] In addition to the three predictors mentioned above, this study also showed that recidivists were younger and more frequently diagnosed as sociopathic.

Since these reviews, the number of studies of the predictors of violent and sexual recidivism among sex offenders has increased dramatically. Hanson and Bussière conducted a meta-analysis (see *infra* § 3–2.3.7, for a discussion of meta-analysis) of studies available by the end of 1995 that examined the predictors of sexual recidivism among a total of 28,972 sex offenders in 87 articles based on 61 data sets; half of the reports had been produced since 1989.[19] The median sample size was 198, and the median follow-up period was four years. The strongest predictor of sexual recidivism was deviant sexual preferences measured phallometrically (see *infra* § 3–2.3.6, for a discussion of phallometry). Other important predictors included prior sexual offenses, and early onset of sexual offending. Two other important predictors were also

13. Robert A. Prentky & Raymond A. Knight, *Identifying Critical Dimensions for Discriminating Among Rapists*, 59 J. OF CONSULTING & CLINICAL PSYCHOL. 643, 661 (1991).

14. Louise V. Frisbie & Ernest H. Dondis, *Recidivism Among Treated Sex Offenders*, 5 MENTAL HEALTH RESEARCH MONOGRAPH, California Department of Mental Hygiene (1965).

15. Vernon L. Quinsey et al., *A Retrospective Evaluation of the Regional Treatment Centre Sex Offender Treatment Program*, 13 J. OF INTERPERSONAL VIOLENCE, 621, 644 (1998); Marnie E. Rice & Grant T. Harris, *Cross Validation and Extension of the Violence Risk Appraisal Guide for Child Molesters and Rapists*, 21 LAW & HUMAN BEHAV. 399, 412 (1997).

16. Grant T. Harris et al., *Violent Recidivism of Mentally Disordered Offenders: The*

Development of a Statistical Prediction Instrument, 20 CRIM. JUST. & BEHAV. 315, 335 (1993).

17. Karl Hanson et al., *Long-term Recidivism of Child Molesters*, 61 J.CONSULTING & CLINICAL PSYCHOL. 646, 652 (1993); Robert A. Prentky et al., *Recidivism Rates Among Child Molesters and Rapists: A Methodological Analysis*, 21 LAW & HUM. BEHAV. 635 (1997); Frisbie & Dondis, *supra* note 14; Rice & Harris, *supra* note 15.

18. Frisbie & Dondis, *supra* note 14.

19. Karl R. Hanson & Monique T. Bussière, *Predicting Relapse: A Meta–Analysis of Sexual Offender Recidivism Studies*, 66 J. CONSULTING & CLINICAL PSYCHOL. 348 (1998).

important predictors of criminal recidivism among offenders in general: age (negatively related) and never having been married. Of less importance, but still significantly related to sexual recidivism were having a male victim and having a victim who was a stranger.[20] Thus, the meta-analytic data confirmed the importance of the variables reported by Quinsey and identified additional variables, especially deviant sexual arousal.

Although several individual factors have been related to recidivism, the relationships have tended to be modest. Thus, several investigators have examined how well recidivism could be predicted by additive combinations of risk factors. As has been conclusively demonstrated in every prediction situation in which it has been examined,[21] statistical (or actuarial) methods of combining variables out-perform judgments in which clinicians (or other practitioners) use intuition and experience in deciding which factors to include and how to combine them.[22] Hanson has also examined seven studies that used statistical techniques to identify the best combination of variables to predict sexual aggression.[23] Although the various combinations worked quite well on the samples used to construct them (the median correlation of scores with sexual recidivism was .44),[24] some of the samples were not very large so that predictive validity would be expected to shrink upon cross-validation (testing with new samples). Using data from the meta-analysis, Hanson developed a brief actuarial risk scale called the Rapid Risk Assessment for Sex Offender Recidivism (RRASOR) and then tested it on an additional independent sample. The scale contained four items: prior sexual offenses, age, any extrafamilial victims, and any boy victims, and showed moderate predictive accuracy in the prediction of sexual recidivism.

20. Because there were so many subjects included in this meta-analysis, it was also possible to identify some factors that were not related to sexual recidivism. Having a history of being sexually abused as a child, substance abuse, and general psychological problems (including anxiety, low self-esteem, and depression) were unrelated to sexual recidivism. Although having deviant sexual preferences was related to sexual recidivism in the entire sample of sex offenders (comprising both rapists and child molesters), the strongest results were obtained for child molesters separately. Hanson and Bussière found no significant relationship between phallometric preferences for rape and sexual recidivism.

21. William M. Grove & Paul E. Meehl, *Comparative Rehabilitation Efficiency of Informal (Subjective, Impressionistic) and Formal (Mechanical, Algorithmic) Prediction Procedures: The Clinical–Statistical Controversy*, 2 PSYCHOL., PUB. POL. & L. 293, 323 (1996).

22. Hanson & Bussière, *supra* note 19.

23. Karl R. Hanson, *The Development of a Brief Actuarial Risk Scale for Sexual Offense Recidivism* (User Report No. 1997–04), Ottawa Department of the Solicitor General.

24. This is the Pearson correlation coefficient described in SCIENCE IN THE LAW: STANDARDS, STATISTICS AND RESEARCH ISSUES, Chapter 5, *Statistical Proof*. Also, as explained there, the correlation coefficient is an imperfect measure of association, or predictive accuracy in this case, when the base rate or proportion of violent recidivists is not close to 50%. This means that predictive correlations from studies with different base rates cannot be compared directly. In that chapter, the binomial effect size display is shown as a solution to the problems inherent in the correlation coefficient. As we have shown elsewhere (Marnie E. Rice & Grant T. Harris, *Violent Recidivism: Assessing Predictive Validity*, 63 J. CONSULTING & CLIN. PSYCHOL. 737 (1995)), predictive accuracy really has two components: sensitivity (or hit rate) which is the probability that violent recidivists will be identified, and specificity (or avoiding false alarms) which is the probability that nonrecidivists will not be misclassified. It is a basic principle of prediction that the sensitivity of a prediction system cannot be improved without a concomitant decrease in specificity and *vice versa*. Consequently, the best indexes of predictive accuracy indicate effect sizes and incorporate this sensitivity-specificity tradeoff as in the *relative operating characteristic* or ROC which effectively ranges from .5 (no accuracy) to 1.0 (perfect). *See also* John Swets et al., *Psychological Science Can Improve Diagnostic Decisions* 1 PSYCHOLOGICAL SCIENCE IN THE PUBLIC INTEREST 1 (2000) for another discussion of how the use of ROC can enhance diagnostic decisions and prediction.

[1] Questions Addressed by Scientists Versus Information Relevant to Legal Issues

One problem in the juncture between science and the law is that the questions addressed by scientists are often not precisely the same as those most relevant to the law. For example, the concern of sexually violent predator laws is the prevention, presumably for the remainder of the offender's life, of further sexual predation, defined as the sexual victimization of strangers (or persons with whom a relationship has been formed for the specific purpose of sexual victimization). Researchers, however, have not studied sexual recidivism only as it involves such types of victims. Although it seems reasonable to assume that the predictors of sexual offending against strangers are the same as those that predict sexual recidivism in general, there are few data to corroborate that assumption. (However, data discussed below showing that among violent offenders in general, the same instrument that predicts all violent offenses also predicts more serious offenses considered separately might provide some preliminary evidence for the reasonableness of such an assumption.) Furthermore, researchers have only followed offenders for finite followup periods, usually for periods averaging less than ten years, and never for the rest of offenders' lives. Also, there are many studies of recidivism of sex offenders that have examined subsequent arrests or convictions for sexual offenses, and many others have examined subsequent arrests or convictions for all violent (including all sexual) offenses. It is unclear at this point in time which of these outcome measures is closer to a measure of "sexual predation" as specified in the law.

There are, however, subgroups of sex offenders whose rates of sexual recidivism are so high that, for all intents and purposes, they could be considered to meet the legal criteria for sexual predators. For example, in one study, we used survival analyses to show that 80% of sexually deviant psychopaths had been reconvicted of a sexual offense within six years of release.[25] Other recent studies have confirmed the high recidivism rates for sexually deviant psychopaths, although not necessarily for sexual recidivism specifically.[26] Thus, there is reason to believe that current techniques can identify at least some persons who would meet strictly-interpreted legal criteria for sexual predator designation.

[2] The Outcome Measure

It is likely that at least part of the reason for the limited success in developing a specific prediction instrument for sexual recidivism lies in the

---

25. *See* Marnie Rice & Grant Harris, *Cross-validation and Extension of the Violence Risk Appraisal Guide for Child Molesters and Rapists* 21 LAW & HUMAN BEHAV. 231 (1997). Sexual deviance was defined as a preference for violent or pedophilic material in a phallometric assessment (described later) and psychopaths were those offenders who scored at least 25 on the Hare Psychopathy Checklist. ROBERT D. HARE, THE HARE PSYCHOPATHY CHECKLIST-REVISED (1991). These sexually deviant psychopaths comprised only 7% of the total sample of sex offenders in that study. Research suggests that strangers are much more often among the victims of psychopathic than nonpsychopathic offenders. Sherri Williamson et al., *Violence: Criminal Psychopaths and Their Victims*, 19 CANADIAN J. BEHAV. SCI. 454 (1987).

26. Heather Gretton et al., *Psychopathy and Recidivism in Adolescent Sex Offenders*, CRIMINAL JUSTICE & BEHAV. (forthcoming 2001); Grant Harris et al., *A Multi-site Comparison of Actuarial Risk Instruments for Sex Offenders* (Manuscript submitted for publication 2001).

validity of the outcome measure. Sexual recidivism has variously been defined as any new arrest, conviction, or, less often, hospital readmission for what was known to be a sexual offense. Official criminal records often constitute the only available information. Of course, all official records are an underestimate of the actual rates of re-offending. Moreover, there is extra cause for concern in the case of sex offenses because of the tendency for the "sexual" component of the offense to be eliminated from the arrest or conviction charge (e.g., sexual assault becomes simply "assault") due to lack of sufficient evidence of the sexual component or through a plea bargaining agreement.[27] The names of some offenses (e.g., murder, kidnaping) recorded in official police data carry no sexual connotation even though they are often sexually motivated. Thus, "sexual recidivism" as it is usually defined is a gross underestimate of actual sexual reoffending.

Violent recidivism has been defined as any arrest, conviction or readmission to hospital for any violent offense (defined as offenses ranging from assault or armed robbery through murder and including all assaultive sexual offenses).[28] Although overinclusive, violent recidivism is likely to capture significantly more sexual reoffenses than "sexual recidivism" as commonly measured because it captures many offenses that are actually sexually motivated, but that have been changed to violent but nonsexual offenses through such things as plea bargaining. The prediction of violent recidivism in general has received much more attention than the prediction of sexual recidivism specifically,[29] and the accuracy of prediction of violence in general has been higher than the prediction of sexual recidivism specifically.[30]

[3]　Instruments for the Prediction of Recidivism Among Sex Offenders

Harris, Rice, and Quinsey developed the Violence Risk Appraisal Guide, or VRAG, for the prediction of violent recidivism among mentally disordered and non-mentally disordered offenders.[31] The instrument was developed on a sample of 618 offenders, of whom 28% had committed at least one sex offense. Several steps were taken to ensure that the VRAG would generalize to a new population. For example, although multiple regression procedures were used to select the best combination of variables to include, the weighting procedure did not rely on those obtained from the multiple regression analyses, but used a much simpler method. The instrument yielded a correlation with violent recidivism of .44 in a seven-year average followup (and a ROC area of .76), indicating good predictive accuracy. In another study that included the original subjects plus additional subjects for a total sample size of 799 (288 of whom were sex offenders), the accuracy of the VRAG was robust with respect

---

27. Alexander Brooks, *The Incapacitation by Civil Commitment of Pathologically Violent Sex Offenders, in* LAW. MENTAL HEALTH & MENTAL DISORDER 384–396 (B.D. Sales & D.W. Shuman eds., 1996).

28. Rice & Harris, *supra* note 25

29. *See* JOHN MONAHAN, PREDICTING VIOLENT BEHAVIOR: AN ASSESSMENT OF CLINICAL TECHNIQUES (1981), Douglas Mossman, *Assessing Predictions of Violence: Being Accurate About Accura-*

cy, 62 J. OF CONSULTING & CLINICAL PSYCHOLOGY 783 (1994).

30. *See* Vernon L. Quinsey et al., *Actuarial Prediction of Sexual Recidivism*, 10 J. INTERPERSONAL VIOL. 85 (1995).

31. Grant Harris et al., *Violent Recidivism of Mentally Disordered Offenders: The Development of a Statistical Prediction Instrument* 20 CRIM. JUST. & BEHAV. 315 (1993).

both to the length of the prediction interval (intervals from 3.5 to 10 years), and the severity of the offense being predicted (more serious violent offenses were predicted just as well as all violent offenses).[32] The VRAG was cross-validated by testing its predictions of violent and sexual recidivism for 159 sex offenders not used in the construction of the instrument and where the follow up averaged 10 years. The violent recidivism rate was 58%.[33] The VRAG predicted violent recidivism at least as well in this new sex offender sample as it had originally. It did not perform nearly as well, however, in predicting sexual recidivism exclusively. In the same report, an instrument that had been developed on a sample of 178 sex offenders[34] for the prediction of sexual recidivism was also tested with a new sample. Although the instrument had yielded a significant correlation with sexual recidivism in its construction, its correlation with sexual recidivism on the new sample was poorer than that of the VRAG. This study illustrated the importance of cross-validating an instrument to show that the instrument would generalize to new samples.

Since the development of the VRAG, there have been a few other actuarial prediction instruments developed for the prediction of recidivism among sex offenders. One instrument is the RRASOR described earlier.[35] The Sex Offender Risk Appraisal Guide or SORAG was developed by using the sample of 288 sex offenders described in an earlier study.[36] Starting with the VRAG variables, certain other variables (such as deviant sexual preferences and sex offense history) were added and some of the original VRAG variables were altered or deleted according to the same procedures used in the development of the VRAG. The resulting instrument contained 14 variables and norms were developed for sex offender samples.[37] Highly correlated with the VRAG (as would be expected because of the high overlap in items), the SORAG was similar to VRAG in showing high predictive accuracy for violent recidivism and moderate predictive accuracy for sexual recidivism.

The MnSOST–R was developed on sex offenders in Minnesota using methods similar to those used to develop the VRAG. The instrument showed high accuracy for the prediction of sexual recidivism on both the development sample and a cross-validation sample.[38]

The Static–99 was developed by combining variables from the RRASOR and from a nonactuarial instrument called the Structured Anchored Clinical Judgment. Actuarial tables were produced for sexual recidivism at three different followup periods. The Static–99 showed a higher degree of accuracy than either of the two original instruments, although the improvement was small.[39]

32. Marnie Rice & Grant Harris, *Violent Recidivism: Assessing Predictive Validity* 63 J. CONSULTING & CLINICAL PSYCHOL. 737 (1995).

33. Rice & Harris, *supra* note 25.

34. Quinsey et al., *supra* note 30.

35. Hanson, *supra* note 23.

36. Rice & Harris, *supra* note 25.

37. The SORAG development is described and norms and percentile scores are presented in VERNON QUINSEY ET AL., VIOLENT OFFENDERS: APPRAISING AND MANAGING RISK (1998).

38. The MnSOST–R and the research supporting it are unpublished but are available on the internet at the following site: http://psych-server.iastate.edu/faculty/epperson/mnsost_download.htm

39. Karl Hanson & David Thornton, *Improving Risk Assessments for Sex Offenders: A Comparison of Three Actuarial Scales* 24 LAW & HUM. BEHAV. 129 (2000).

Are the available actuarial instruments ready for application in legal decision-making? Although one commentator has said no,[40] others are more positive.[41] The VRAG has undoubtedly the heaviest weight of empirical evidence behind it inasmuch as it has been replicated in at least 20 studies, 5 with sex offenders and 8 that have appeared or are in press in the peer-reviewed literature.[42] The evidence supporting each instrument has been summarized in two recent reports.[43] Most recently, there have been two studies comparing the performance of several of the instruments on the same sample of sex offenders. One study compared the VRAG, SORAG, RRASOR,

40. Terrence Campbell, *Sexual Predator Evaluations and Phrenology,* 18 BEHAV. SCI. & L. 111 (2000). Campbell reviewed the criteria set out in *Daubert v. Merrill Dow Pharmaceuticals* and asserted that standards for "widespread acceptance" are equivalent to standards for educational and psychological testing promulgated by the American Psychological Association. No basis for this claimed equivalence between risk assessment and psychological testing was provided. Especially odd was the assumption that the courts would bind all professions to the standards of one. Nevertheless, Campbell asserted that no means currently used to assess the risk of sex offenders met more than one of the A.P.A. standards for psychological testing and there is, therefore, no available expert testimony about the recidivism risk of convicted sex offenders.

41. Dennis Doren, *Being Accurate About the Accuracy of Commonly Used Risk Assessment Instruments,* 19th Annual Association for the Treatment of Sexual Abusers Research and Treatment Conference, November, 2000, San Diego; Susan Sachsenmaier & James Peters, *Sexual Offender Risk Assessment Methods and Admissibility as Expert Witness Evidence, in* ASSESSMENT & MANAGEMENT OF SEX OFFENDERS: WHAT PROSECUTORS NEED TO KNOW (J. Peters ed., forthcoming 2001).

42. Howard Barbaree et al., *Evaluating the Accuracy of Six Risk Assessment Instruments for Adult Sex Offenders* CRIM. JUST. & BEHAV. (forthcoming); Rebecca Dempster, *Prediction of Sexually Violent Recidivism: A Comparison of Risk Assessment Instruments.* Doctoral Dissertation, Simon Fraser University (1999); Anthony Glover et al., *A Comparison of Predictors of General and Violent Recidivism Among High Risk Federal Offenders,* CRIMINAL JUSTICE & BEHAV. (forthcoming); Martin Grann et al., *Actuarial Assessment of Risk For Violence: Predictive Validity of the VRAG and Historical Part of the HCR-20,* 27 CRIMINAL JUST. & BEHAV. 97 (2000); Martin Grann & Ingela Wedin, *Risk Factors for Recidivism Among Spousal Assault and Spousal Homicide Offenders* PSYCHOL., CRIME & L. (in press); Karl Hanson & Andrew Harris, *Where Should We Intervene? Dynamic Predictors of Sex Offense Recidivism* 27 CRIM. JUST. & BEHAV. 6 (2000); Zoe Hilton & Janet Simmons, *Actuarial and Clinical Risk Assessment in Decisions to Release Mentally Disordered Offenders from Maximum Security.* Manuscript submitted for publication (2000); Zoe Hilton et al., *Predicting Violence by Serious Wife Assaulters* J. INTERPERSONAL VIOL. (forthcoming); Daryl Kroner & Jeremy Mills, *The Relative Efficacy of Predicting Criminal Behavior: A Comparison of Five Instruments,* CRIM. JUST. & BEHAV. (forthcoming); Wagdy Loza & Amel Loza–Fanous, *The Effectiveness of the Self-appraisal Questionnaire in Predicting Offenders' Postrelease Outcome* 28 CRIM. JUST. & BEHAV. 105 (2001); Michelle McBride, *Predicting Violence Among Federal Inmates,* Paper presented at the Correctional Research Forum, Toronto, 1999; J. Nadeau et al., *The PCL-R and VRAG as Predictors of Institutional Behavior.* Paper presented at Risk Assessment and Risk Management: Implications for the Prevention of Violence Conference, Vancouver, B.C. (1999); T. Nichols et al., *Assessing Risk of Inpatient Violence in a Sample of Forensic Psychiatric Patients: Comparing the PCLISV, HCR-20, and VRAG.* Paper presented at the Risk Assessment and Risk Management: Implications for the Prevention of Violence Conference, Vancouver, B.C., 1999; Patricia Nugent, *The Use of Detention Legislation: Factors Affecting Detention Decisions and Recidivism Among High Risk Federal Offenders in Ontario.* Doctoral Dissertation, Queen's University (1999); Nathalie Polvi, *The Prediction of Violence in Pretrial Forensic Patients: The Relative Efficacy of Statistical Versus Clinical Predictions of Dangerousness.* Doctoral Dissertation, Simon Fraser University (1999); Vernon Quinsey et al., *A Followup of Deinstitutionalized Developmentally Handicapped Men with Histories of Antisocial Behavior,* Unpublished manuscript (2000); Vernon Quinsey et al., *Proximal Antecedents of Eloping and Reoffending Among Mentally Disordered Offenders* 12 J. INTERPERSONAL VIOL. 794 (1997); Rice & Harris, *supra* note 25; Rice & Harris, *supra* note 32; Gabriella Sjöstedt & Niklas Langström, *Assessment of Risk for Criminal Recidivism Among Rapists: A Comparison of Four Different Measures* PSYCHOL., CRIME & L. (in press). For an updated list of replications *see* http://www.mhcva.on.ca./Research/ragreps.htm

43. Doren, *supra* note 41, Sachsenmaier, *supra* note 41.

Static–99, Mn–SOST–R and a nonactuarial "guided clinical" assessment instrument in predicting violent and sexual recidivism in a sample of 215 sex offenders released from a Canadian federal prison for an average of 4.5 years.[44] The first four instruments all significantly predicted both outcomes, and the latter two did not. Another study compared the VRAG, SORAG, RRASOR and Static–99 in predicting violent and sexual recidivism in four different samples of Canadian sex offenders.[45]

[4] Cautionary Remarks About "Expert" Predictions

As we have reviewed, actuarial (statistical) methods of prediction outperform unaided clinical judgment. As discussed above, this is not in dispute. "Unaided clinical judgment" refers to statements by professionals (usually parole, correctional, or mental health clinicians) based on case-by-case experience, clinical training, general familiarity with the research and professional literature, and intuition. Though clinical judgments sometimes show better-than-chance predictions, in hundreds of tests they have very rarely performed better than actuarial methods and are most often less accurate.[46] Even when clinical judgments have been shown to exhibit better-than-chance accuracy, they have never been shown to exceed the accuracy exhibited by laypeople.[47] In the preceding section, we described several actuarial instruments for the prediction of recidivism among sexual aggressors. It is a scientific certainty that predictions made by these actuarial instruments are superior to those based on unaided clinical judgment. The accuracies achieved by current actuarial methods for the prediction of violent recidivism compare favorably to those regarded as useful in other areas; for example, with those achieved by meteorologists in the prediction of tornadoes and hurricanes.[48]

However, *not every checklist or scale is an actuarial instrument.* "Actuarial" refers to the methods used to create a decision tool and actuarial instruments are, by definition, derived through the empirical (i.e., specifically tested) relationships between potential predictor variables (and their specific combination) and the outcome in question (violent or sexual recidivism for our purposes). That is, an actuarial instrument can only be developed by testing combinations of predictor variables in samples whose outcome is known. A structured list of variables for clinicians to attend to based on surveys of the follow up literature does not make an actuarial instrument, even if it also includes a means to derive an overall score. A hallmark of such nonactuarial tools is the absence of probability estimates for various cutoff scores. Since the actual statistical relationships were not part of the develop-

---

44. Barbaree et al., *supra* note 42

45. Harris et al., *supra* note 26.

46. ROBYN DAWES, HOUSE OF CARDS: PSYCHOLOGY AND PSYCHOTHERAPY BUILT ON MYTH (1994); Robyn Dawes et al., *Clinical Versus Actuarial Judgment*, 243 SCI. 1668 (1989); Douglas Mossman, *Assessing Predictions of Violence: Being Accurate About Accuracy*, 62 J. CONSULTING & CLINICAL PSYCHOL. 783 (1994); *see generally* discussion at *supra* note 21.

47. Ziskin and Faust argue that accuracy significantly better than that achieved by laypeople ought to be the primary criterion for

expertise in the legal sense. David Faust & Jay Ziskin, *The Expert Witness in Psychology and Psychiatry*, 241 SCI. 501 (1988); Vernon L. Quinsey & Rudolph Ambtman, *Variables Affecting Psychiatrists' and Teachers' Assessments of the Dangerousness of Mentally Ill Offenders*, 47 J. CONSULTING & CLINICAL PSYCHOL. 353 (1979); JAY ZISKIN & DAVID FAUST, COPING WITH PSYCHIATRIC & PSYCHOLOGICAL TESTIMONY (4th ed. 1988).

48. John Swets, *Measuring the Accuracy of Diagnostic Systems*, 240 SCI. 1285 (1988); John Swets et al., *supra* note 24.

ment, they cannot be provided. Giving such lists to clinicians might result in improved *aided* clinical judgments about the risk of recidivism, but there are few data on this.[49]

Second, *the independent contribution of predictor variables is an empirical question and cannot be assumed.* A common criticism of actuarial methods is that they entail only static (stable and unalterable) historical predictors and, therefore, cannot give an accurate appraisal of risk because situational and contextual variables are obviously also essential. It stands to reason that variables representing offenders' post-discharge environment would make an independent contribution to the accuracy of actuarial prediction. However, in science (as in life) what stands to reason often turns out to be false.[50] It is *possible* that such contextual variables would improve prediction, but it is just as possible that they would not. This might occur, for example, if static variables were good predictors of post-release situational variables (e.g., if psychopaths were very much more likely to seek out and maintain criminal associates, or very much less likely to comply with post-release therapy contacts). Under such circumstances, a post-release contextual variable (though itself statistically related to recidivism) might provide no improvement upon predictions based on historical predictors.

Third, *an actuarial instrument in the hands of a clinician does not guarantee an actuarial prediction.* For example, although it has been stated that recent research indicates that clinical judgment is improved by the addition of actuarial methods (we have even said so ourselves),[51] it is much more accurate to say, "Recent research indicates that decisions are more accurate when clinical judgment is replaced by actuarial methods." Available research indicates that the blending of static historical predictors with clinical judgments yields poorer accuracy compared to static predictors alone.[52] As another example, we have seen a clinician write, "While I did not compute the Violence Risk Appraisal Guide for this man, it is my clinical opinion that he would receive a very high score." Obviously, no matter what the superficial appearance, this is not the use of actuarial methods.

§ 3–2.2.2　Does Treatment, Supervision, Or Community Notification Reduce The Risk Of Recidivism Among Sex Offenders?

Because the risk posed by sex offenders released from custody has been shown to be considerable and to last for a long time, it is surprising that little well-controlled research exists on treatment efficacy. Treatments for sex offenders have been of three main types (although there is overlap and the

49. Christopher Webster et al., *Assessing Risk of Violence to Others*, *in* IMPULSIVITY: THEORY, ASSESSMENT, & TREATMENT 251–277 (C.D. Webster & M.A. Jackson eds., 1997). A structured clinical assessment instrument was evaluated along with several actuarial instruments in a study by Barbaree et al., *supra* note 42. The instrument was found to predict general recidivism for sex offenders, but not violent or sexual recidivism. The instrument showed much poorer predictive accuracy than the actuarial instruments. The authors concluded that actuarial approaches were to be recommended over structured clinical approaches.

50. Scientists have many times demonstrated that things that stood to reason (the flatness of the earth, the geocentrality of the solar system) were actually false.

51. CHRISTOPHER WEBSTER ET AL., THE VIOLENCE PREDICTION SCHEME: ASSESSING DANGEROUSNESS IN HIGH RISK MEN (1994).

52. *See* discussion *supra* note 49. *See also* Hilton & Simmons, *supra* note 42.

distinctions have not always been clear-cut): nonbehavioral psychotherapy, pharmacological and surgical treatments, and cognitive-behavioral treatments.

[1] Nonbehavioral Psychotherapy

Although, until recently at least, nonbehavioral therapy was the most common treatment for sex offenders, the few programs that have been subjected to controlled evaluation have provided no evidence that they reduce the likelihood of future sex offenses by child molesters or rapists. Frisbie[53] and Frisbie and Dondis[54] studied "sexual psychopaths" treated in a maximum security psychiatric hospital in California and compared their outcomes with those of untreated sex offenders. The overriding philosophy behind the therapy program was humanistic, and group therapy was combined with recreation, school, and leisure activities. The treated and untreated groups were neither matched nor randomly assigned; nevertheless, the rate of new sex offenses was higher among the treated than the untreated men.

Sturgeon and Taylor followed a later group of 260 men treated in the same institution as the Frisbie and Dondis subjects, but released in 1973.[55] The sexual and nonsexual violent re-offending of these men was again compared to that of a group of 122 untreated sex offenders who were released from prison in the same year. The untreated group included more rapists than the treated group. The treated sex offenders had fewer re-convictions for sex offenses, but there were no differences for nonsexual violent offenses. Furthermore, when rapists and child molesters were considered separately, there were no differences for either sexual or nonsexual violent reoffenses.

Undoubtedly, the most rigorous outcome study for nonbehavioral treatments was of 231 men treated at the J.J. Peters Institute.[56] In this study, probationers (over 80% of whom were rapists or child molesters) were randomly assigned to either intensive probation or to psychodynamically-oriented group psychotherapy plus probation. Those men assigned to the group psychotherapy had higher rates of rearrest for sexual offenses (though not significantly) than those assigned to intensive supervision alone. Moreover, among just those men who completed over 40 weeks of treatment (thought by the providers of the group psychotherapy to be optimal), the treated subjects were significantly more likely to be rearrested for a sexual offense. Similar to findings for offenders in general,[57] then, humanistic and psychodynamic treatments apparently do not reduce sexual or generally violent reoffending by rapists and child molesters. Even more sobering is evidence that they may even increase the likelihood of new sexual offenses.

53. Louise Frisbie, *Another Look At Sex Offenders In California,* 5 MENTAL HEALTH RES. MONOGRAPH, California Department of Mental Hygiene (1969).

54. Frisbee & Dondis, *supra* note 14.

55. Vikki Sturgeon & John Taylor, *Report of a Five–Year Followup Study of Mentally Disordered Sex Offenders Released from Atascadero State Hospital,* 4 CRIM. JUST. J. 31 (1980).

56. Joseph Romero & Linda Williams, *Group Psychotherapy and Intensive Probation Supervision with Sex Offenders,* 47 FED. PROBATION 36 (1983).

57. Donald Andrews et al., *Does Correctional Treatment Work? A Clinically Relevant and Psychologically Informed Meta-analysis,* 28 CRIMINOLOGY 369 (1990).

[2]   Pharmacological and Surgical Treatments

The second broad category of treatments that have been used are surgical and pharmacological therapies. Although rarely used on humans in North America, castration (surgical removal of the gonads) has been studied in animals and has been used extensively in Europe to reduce sex drive and sexual recidivism. Most of the human studies of the effects of castration have been completely uncontrolled, and many have included men who are not now considered to be sex offenders (for example, homosexuals who prefer adult male partners). Freund reviewed the uncontrolled and some partially controlled studies of castration.[58] In general, the sexual recidivism rates among castrated offenders were very low even though many offenders considered for castration were at high risk for reoffending. Freund stated that despite the absence of well-controlled studies, it was safe to conclude that castration could virtually abolish sexual reoffending in non-psychotic offenders whose offenses were limited to sexual ones, whose offenses were likely to be related to hormone levels (as evidenced by high initial hormone levels, unwanted sexual fantasies and the lack of nonsexual crimes), and who freely consented to the procedure.

Castration cannot, however, provide a solution to the problem of sexual recidivism among the majority of sexual aggressors until the issue of consent is resolved, especially for institutionalized offenders or offenders who are given a choice between castration and institutionalization. Offenders castrated under coercion might, for example, later illicitly obtain testosterone or other anabolic steroids and thereby reverse the effects of castration. Although this has not been much of a problem to date according to the literature,[59] anabolic steroids are now easily available from the illicit market and they are commonly used by body builders and other athletes.[60] In any event, castration likely is not appropriate for the large proportion of offenders who have a history of diverse nonsexual violent offenses in addition to their sexual ones.

Recently, pharmacological treatments for sex offenders have been much more popular than surgery, especially in North America. Cyproterone acetate (CPA) and medroxyprogesterone acetate (MPA) are the two most common drugs used for the reduction of deviant sexual behavior. Both are used to achieve, through pharmacological means, the same sex drive reducing effects as surgical castration but with fewer ethical problems because surgery is not required and because the effects are completely (and apparently quickly) reversible upon their withdrawal. Both drugs have unpleasant side effects in addition to reducing sexual desire, and most men dislike taking them. Common complaints include weight gain, fatigue, headaches, reduced body hair, depression, and gastrointestinal problems. These pharmacologic treatments are viewed by sex offenders as one of the least desired therapies.[61]

58. Kurt Freund, *Therapeutic Sex Drive Reduction*, 62 Acta Psychiatrica Scandinavica 5 (1980).

59. Stürup reports that one rapist in his study obtained testosterone. George Stürup, *Treatment of Sexual Offenders in Herstedvester*

Denmark, 44 Acta Psychiatrica Scandinvica 5 (1968).

60. Kirk Brower, *Anabolic Steroids*, 16 Psychiatric Clinics Of N. Am. 117 (1993).

61. Ronald Langevin et al., *What Treatment Do Sex Offenders Want?* 1 Annals Of Sex Res. 353 (1988).

There have been very few controlled outcome studies of the effectiveness of either CPA or MPA in reducing sexual reoffending among child molesters or rapists. In one study, 40 men treated with MPA were compared with 21 men who were offered drug treatment but refused.[62] Most of the subjects in the study were child molesters and the remainder were rapists, exhibitionists, and voyeurs. Both groups were treated as outpatients and received group therapy, individual therapy, and sometimes family therapy. All of the men admitted their offenses, and admitted to having overwhelming deviant fantasies. Most men were self-referred or referred by their family physicians, although a few (mostly in the comparison group) were referred by their lawyers. Men who admitted their offenses but blamed alcohol or drugs were excluded, as were men who had histories of serious antisocial behavior. Although all men who started MPA treatment remained on it for at least six months, the expectation was that men would remain on the medication for much longer (three to five years). However, 29 of the 40 men started on MPA dropped out of the drug treatment prematurely, and 10 of these later reoffended. Of the 40 patients started on MPA, 7 reoffended while taking the drug—43% of the men started on MPA reoffended. By comparison, 12 of the 21 or 58% of the men who refused MPA treatment reoffended while receiving other therapies. The recidivism rates (which included both self-reported and official arrests for sex offenses) were not significantly different, and recidivism rates for all groups were surprisingly high considering that they were a relatively low risk, and highly motivated group from the start.

In another study, 46 paraphiliacs (including 29 pedophiles) were treated on an outpatient basis for 5 years with either group therapy alone or group therapy plus MPA.[63] The rate of relapse among those who received MPA was 15%, whereas the relapse rate of those not receiving MPA was significantly higher at 68%. Among the pedophiles specifically, there was also a statistically significant effect inasmuch as only one who received MPA relapsed, whereas 9 who did not receive MPA relapsed. However, an additional 88 patients were excluded from the study because they refused MPA treatment and another 38 were excluded because they were arrested before completing 5 years of treatment (it is not reported how many of those 38 were on MPA). This study supports the conclusion that among child molesters who remained in long-term psychotherapy, those who also received MPA were less likely to re-offend. The authors are very cautious in their conclusions and point out a number of methodological limitations. The subjects were not randomly assigned to receive MPA. Therapists were not blind as to whether subjects were receiving MPA. Perhaps most seriously, however, was the fact that men in the MPA plus psychotherapy condition may have been more highly motivated to refrain from sex offending by virtue of their willingness to volunteer for MPA treatment in the first place.

Langevin et al. attempted a study in which exhibitionists were to be randomly assigned to either MPA alone, assertion training alone, or MPA plus

62. Evangeline Emory et al., *The Texas Experience with Depo Provera: 1980–1990*, 18 J. OFFENDER REHABILITATION 125 (1992); Walter Meyer et al., *Depo Provera Treatment for Sex Offending Behavior: An Evaluation of Outcome*, 20 BULL. AM. ACAD. PSYCHIATRY & L. 249 (1992).

63. Paul Fedoroff et al., *Medroxyprogesterone Acetate in the Treatment of Paraphilic Sexual Disorders*, 18 J. OFFENDER REHAB. 109 (1992).

assertion training.[64] So many of the men assigned to the MPA alone condition dropped out that the condition had to be dropped. Also, 67% of the men in the MPA plus assertion training condition also dropped out—significantly more than the 29% drop-out rate in the assertion training only condition. Recidivism rates in a two-year follow up did not differ between the two groups despite the high dropout rates in the MPA conditions.

Finally, Hucker, Langevin and Bain studied child molesters randomly assigned to either an MPA treatment group or to a placebo group.[65] Of 100 eligible offenders approached to participate, only 48 agreed to complete the initial assessment battery. Eighteen agreed to take part in the study. Only 11 completed a 3 month trial, 5 MPA subjects and 6 controls. Although there was good evidence that those on MPA had reduced testosterone levels compared to subjects receiving placebo, there was no evidence that MPA changed sexual behavior.

In summary, the evidence so far suggests that few offenders will voluntarily accept currently available drugs to reduce testosterone levels, and even fewer will remain on them for extended periods. However, the limited available evidence suggests that re-offense rates are low among those few child molesters who do stay in treatment that includes such drugs. It is important to note, however, that there is, as yet, no convincing reason to believe that the drugs themselves are responsible for reducing reoffending. Just as plausible is the hypothesis that the few sex offenders who remain in long term drug treatment are highly motivated to avoid re-offending so that participating in such treatment is a good predictor of success. It is also important to note that currently there is no reason to believe that such drugs will reduce sexual recidivism among men who are coerced into taking them. Hanson and Harris showed convincingly that being compelled to take antiandrogens as a condition of parole had no beneficial effect on sexual recidivism.[66] As is the case with castration, the sex-drive reducing effects of the drugs can be reversed by stopping treatment or (for MPA) by taking testosterone or other anabolic steroids. Moreover, men who are coerced to take the drugs may be particularly at risk for obtaining such substances.

There are other drugs that block testosterone that, like CPA, have not yet been subjected to controlled evaluation (e.g., leuprolide acetate).[67] There are also recent reports of serotonergic medications in the treatment of sexual deviance with the suggestion that these medications may decrease deviant sexual interests without impairing non-deviant interests.[68] There is also reason to believe, given the general popularity of certain serotonergic drugs (e.g., fluoxetine) that compliance might be less of a problem. Nevertheless, there have been no controlled outcome studies of these drugs.

64. R. Langevin et al., *The Effect of Assertiveness Training, Provera and Sex of Therapists in the Treatment of Genital Exhibitionism*, 10 J. BEHAV. THERAPY & EXPERIMENTAL PSYCHIATRY 275 (1979).

65. Stephen Hucker et al., *A Double Blind Trial of Sex Drive Reducing Medication in Pedophiles*, 1 ANNALS OF SEX RES. 227 (1988).

66. Hanson & Harris, *supra* note 42.

67. Robert Dickey, *The Management of a Case of Treatment–Resistant Paraphilia with a Long Acting LHRH Agonist*, 37 CANADIAN JOURNAL OF PSYCHIATRY 567 (1992).

68. Paul Fedoroff, *Serotonergic Drug Treatment of Deviant Sexual Interests*, 6 ANNALS OF SEX RES. 105 (1993).

[3] Cognitive–Behavioral Treatments

The third broad category of sex offender treatment comprises behavioral and cognitive-behavioral therapies. Almost every published evaluation of behavioral or cognitive behavioral treatment shares one common treatment component—behavioral techniques to normalize deviant sexual preferences.[69] Most published reports indicate that training in social competence is a key treatment component.[70] Many contain a wide variety of such other components as sex education,[71] anger management,[72] nonspecific counselling,[73] family systems therapy,[74] and relapse prevention.[75]

We have reviewed the controlled-evaluation literature on the efficacy of behavioral and cognitive-behavioral treatments for sexual aggressors in detail elsewhere.[76] This literature includes several individual studies,[77] as well as a small meta-analysis (twelve studies) that included some of the above research as well as studies of other forms of treatment.[78] There is now a larger meta-analysis that included approximately 40 studies of psychological treatment, most of them cognitive-behavioral and many of them unpublished.[79] In our earlier review, we concluded that the number of studies was too small to permit an informative meta-analysis, especially considering the serious methodological weaknesses of all but one of the studies (the study described by Marques and her colleagues). We concluded, as had Furby, Weinrott, &

69. Gene Abel et al., *Predicting Child Molesters' Response to Treatment, in* HUMAN SEXUAL AGGRESSION: CURRENT PERSPECTIVES 223–243 (R. Prentky & V.L. Quinsey eds., 1988); Paul Davidson, *Recidivism In Sex Offenders: Who Are The Bad Risks?*, Paper presented at the 2nd national Conference on the Evaluation and Treatment of Sexual Aggressors (1979); Paul Davidson, *Behavioral Treatment For Incarcerated Sex Offenders: Post–Release Outcome*, Paper presented at the Conference on the Assessment and Treatment of the Sex Offender (1984); Diane Hildebran & William Pithers, *Relapse Prevention: Application and Outcome, in* THE SEXUAL ABUSE OF CHILDREN: CLINICAL ISSUES 365–393 (O. O'Donohue & J.H. Geer eds., 1992); Rice et al., *Treating the Mentally Disordered Sex Offender, in* TREATING ADULT AND JUVENILE OFFENDERS WITH SPECIAL NEEDS (J.B. Ashford et al. eds., 2001); BARRY MALETZKY, TREATING THE SEXUAL OFFENDER (1991); William Marshall & Howard Barbaree, *The Long–Term Evaluation of a Behavioral Treatment Program for Child Molesters*, 26 BEHAV. RES. & THERAPY 499 (1988); Janice Marques et al., *Effects of Cognitive–Behavioral Treatment on Sex Offender Recidivism*, 21 CRIM. JUST. & BEHAV. 28 (1994); Marnie Rice et al., *Sexual Recidivism Among Child Molesters Released from a Maximum Security Psychiatric Institution*, 59 J. CONSULTING & CLINICAL PSYCHOL. 381 (1991); *see also* Louise Furby et al., *Sex Offender Recidivism: A Review*, 105 PSYCHOLOGICAL BULL. 3 (1989); William Marshall et al., *The Treatment of Exhibitionists: A Focus on Sexual Deviance Versus Cognitive and Relationship Features*, 29 BEHAV. RES. & THERAPY 129 (1991).

70. *See* citations *supra* note 69; Rice et al., *id.*; Janice Marques et al., *Findings and Recommendations from California's Experimental Treatment Program, in* SEXUAL AGGRESSION: ISSUES IN ETIOLOGY, ASSESSMENT AND TREATMENT 197–214 (C.G.N. Hall et al. eds., 1993).

71. *See* citations *supra* note 69.

72. *Id.*

73. Rice et al., *supra* note 69.

74. Charles Borduin et al., *Multisystemic Treatment of Adolescent Sexual Offenders*, INT'L J. OF OFFENDER THERAPY & COMPARATIVE CRIMINOLOGY 105 (1990).

75. *See* citations *supra* note 69.

76. Rice et al., *supra* note 69.

77. *See* citations *supra* notes 69, 70, and 74.

78. Gordon Hall, *Sexual Offender Recidivism Revisited: A Meta-analysis of Recent Treatment Studies*, 63 J. CONSULTING & CLINICAL PSYCHOL. 802 (1995).

79. Karl Hanson, *The Effectiveness of Treatment for Sexual Offenders*. Report of the Association for the Treatment of Sexual Abusers Collaborative Data Research Committee. Presented at the 19th Annual 2000 Research and Treatment Conference, San Diego, November 2000; *See also* Catherine Gallagher et al., *A Quantitative Review of the Effects of Sex Offender Treatment on Sexual Reoffending* 3(4) CORRECTIONS MGMT. Q. 19 (1999).

Blackshaw[80] about therapies in general, and Quinsey, Harris, Rice, and Lalumière[81] about cognitive-behavioral treatment in particular, that the effectiveness of sex offender treatment has yet to be demonstrated. Although there have been some studies that have reported positive results (mostly these have been with offenders in the low to moderate risk levels), the existing data provide no evidence about what might have been responsible for any reduction in recidivism. Just as was the case with drug treatments, the data so far are consistent with the conclusion that agreeing to and persisting with treatment over the long term serves as a filter detecting those offenders who are least likely to re-offend, and that the nature of the treatment (so long as it is not exclusively humanistic or psychodynamic) has little or no specific effect on outcome.

The field of sex offender treatment awaits the outcome evaluation of the Marques et al. (1994) program.[82] It is without question a superbly designed study. The treatment program was multifaceted, targeting those aspects of sexual offenders for which there existed any evidence linking them to sexual offending and sexual recidivism. Each treatment component was linked to pre-, post-, and follow up assessments ultimately enabling conclusions about which changes wrought by therapy were responsible for reductions in recidivism. From a pool of sex offenders who volunteered for treatment, some were randomly selected to receive it. In addition, subjects who refused treatment were included and matched to treated and untreated volunteers. Also, treatment dropouts were followed. This powerful design will permit the evaluation of the specific effects of treatment versus the effects of motivation to desist from sexual offending on recidivism. Officially recorded rates of violent, sexual and general criminal recidivism are gathered separately. This minimizes the effects of plea bargaining, and police and offender expectancies on conclusions about the effectiveness of treatment.

Sadly, after over two decades of therapeutic effort, this study in progress appears to be one of very few methodologically sophisticated evaluations of any treatment for sex offenders. Its methodological power notwithstanding, the Marques et al. project is but a single study.[83] It appears that the question of the effectiveness of cognitive behavioral or behavioral treatment of sex offenders will go without a scientifically definitive answer for many years to come.[84]

There is no literature available on the ability of either supervision or community notification, to reduce the recidivism of sex offenders. The literature on the effects of "intermediate punishments" upon criminals in general is of some relevance, however. This literature suggests that although intensive supervision programs run the risk of "widening the net" by including low risk offenders, supervision that is limited to offenders of moderate to high risk and that includes rehabilitation components can reduce the risk of recidivism.[85]

80. Furby et al., *supra* note 69.

81. Vernon L. Quinsey et al., *Assessing Treatment Efficacy in Outcome Studies of Sex Offenders*, 8 J. Interpersonal Violence 512 (1993).

82. *See supra* note 70. The final results from this study should be available late in 2001

(Marques, Personal Communication, January, 2001).

83. Marques et al., *supra* note 69.

84. *See also* Rice et al., *supra* note 69.

85. Paul Gendreau et al., *Intensive Rehabilitation Supervision: The Next Generation in*

Such supervision might include the use of technologies such as cellular telephones, electronic monitoring, and drug testing. However, there is as yet little evidence that these technologies do anything to reduce recidivism.[86] In addition, it is important to note that few violent offenders have been assigned to electronic monitoring or home confinement programs, let alone sex offenders.[87] Also, most candidates for electronic monitoring to date have been persons assigned to it instead of, rather than after, prison.[88] It has been shown that such technologies are certainly not infallible.[89] Because pathological lying and use of deceit are among the distinguishing characteristics of psychopaths (who form a sizeable proportion of high risk sex offenders), it is obvious that great care would have to be taken by those charged with supervision to ensure that conditions of supervision were being followed. We are aware of no data about the effectiveness of intensive supervision (which might include technological aids) for sex offenders (or sexually violent predators specifically). On the other hand, there is some evidence that there are signs that indicate when an offender is at higher risk to reoffend.[90]

In summary, the empirical data to date suggest that antiandrogen drugs and cognitive-behavioral treatments are valuable in the prevention of future sexual offenses if only in the sense that they may provide a "dynamic" risk predictor—that is, although we have no evidence to date that they reduce the likelihood of recidivism, they do at least serve as a "filter" to identify those offenders who are most likely to fail upon release. Whether dropping out of or refusing these treatments adds anything beyond the "static" actuarial prediction provided by instruments such as the VRAG remains to be seen.

§ 3–2.2.3 Do Sexual Aggressors Have A Mental Disorder?

The idea that sex offenders, or many of them, at least, suffer from a mental disorder has been debated at length. It is generally agreed that only a minority of sex offenders held in either prisons or psychiatric settings suffer from such major disorders as schizophrenia or other psychoses,[91] and most sex offender treatment programs specifically exclude acutely psychotic offenders.[92] As we mentioned earlier, under the old sexual psychopath laws, the diagnosis most commonly responsible for a designation as a "mentally disordered" sex offender was a sexual deviation or paraphilia (almost always pedophilia or

Community Corrections?, 58 PROBATION 72 (1994).

86. Terry Baumer & Robert Mendelsohn, *Electronically Monitored Home Confinement: Does It Work?*, in SMART SENTENCING: THE EMERGENCE OF INTERMEDIATE SANCTIONS 54–67 (J.M. Byrne & J. Petersilia eds., 1992); James Byrne & April Pattavina, *The Effective Issue: Assessing What Works in the Adult Community Corrections System*, in SMART SENTENCING: THE EMERGENCE OF INTERMEDIATE SANCTIONS 281–303 (J.M. Byrne & J. Petersilia eds., 1992); Francis Cullen et al., *Control in the Community: The Limits of Reform?*, in CHOOSING CORRECTIONAL OPTIONS THAT WORK 69–116 (A.T. Harland ed., 1996).

87. Marc Renzema, *Home Confinement Programs: Development, Implementation and Impact*, in SMART SENTENCING: THE EMERGENCE OF INTERMEDIATE SANCTIONS 41–53 (J.M. Byrne, A.J. Lurigio & J. Petersilia eds., 1992).

88. *Supra* note 86.

89. Ronald Corbett & Gary Marx, *Emerging Technofallacies in the Electronic Monitoring Movement*, in SMART SENTENCING: THE EMERGENCE OF INTERMEDIATE SANCTIONS 85–102 (J.M. Byrne et al. eds., 1992).

90. Hanson & Harris, *supra* note 42; Quinsey et al., *supra* note 42.

91. Romero & Williams, *supra* note 56.

92. *See* citations at *supra* note 69; William Pithers et al., *Vermont Treatment for Sexual Aggressors*, in RELAPSE PREVENTION WITH SEX OFFENDERS 292–310 (D.R. Laws ed., 1989).

sexual sadism) in the Diagnostic and Statistical Manual of Mental Disorders.[93] Although there has been considerable disagreement as to whether paraphilias satisfy what has traditionally met the legal requirement of mental illness,[94] there is general agreement within the mental health professions that paraphilias (especially pedophilia and sadism) are serious mental disorders.[95] The term "mental abnormality" used in the legal definition of a sexually violent predator is not commonly used by mental health professionals, but there seems little doubt that a diagnosis of pedophilia or sexual sadism is sufficient to meet the legal definition.[96]

Of course, not all child molesters are pedophiles, nor are all pedophiles child molesters. A person with pedophilia must be sexually attracted to children, either exclusively, or in addition to, adults. There are occasions, however, when individuals choose partners from a nonpreferred category because of the unavailability of persons with the preferred attributes or other special circumstances.[97] Although there is some evidence that incest offenders are less likely to exhibit sexual arousal to children than other offenders,[98] there is also evidence that many incest offenders do exhibit deviant preferences.[99] More important than whether the offender has offended against children inside or outside the family is the number of victims.[100] Thus, with incest offenders as well as with other sex offenders, it is extremely important to obtain good information about all past offenses, as well as the results of sexual preference testing. Obviously, information about past offenses cannot be obtained simply by asking the offender. Police records and other sources such as family members, must be obtained.

It is also important to note that not all pedophiles engage in the hands-on molestation of children. Although they likely do not volunteer to take part in studies of sexual preferences, there are undoubtedly some pedophiles whose deviant arousal, though very distressing, is confined to fantasies or at least to hands-off offenses such as exposing themselves to or masturbating in front of children.

Considerably more controversial among mental health professionals is the inclusion of "personality disorder" as a condition that qualifies for designation as a sexually violent predator. Although a diagnosis of personality disorder (typically "antisocial" personality disorder) is very common among sex offenders (particularly among rapists), it was not often sufficient to qualify for a classification as a "mentally disordered" sex offender under the

---

93. *Supra* note 8; AMERICAN PSYCHIATRIC ASSOCIATION, DIAGNOSTIC AND STATISTICAL MANUAL OF MENTAL DISORDERS (3rd ed. 1980).

94. Robert Schopp & Barbara Sturgis, *Sexual Predators and Legal Mental Illness for Civil Commitment*, 13 BEHAV. SCI. & L. 437 (1995).

95. Gene Abel & Joanne Rouleau, *Male Sex Offenders*, in HANDBOOK OF OUTPATIENT TREATMENT OF ADULTS (M. Thase, B. Edelstein & M. Hersen eds., 1990).

96. Brooks, *supra* note 27.

97. American Psychiatric Association, *supra* note 1.

98. Vernon L. Quinsey et al., *Sexual Preferences Among Incestuous and Non–Incestuous Child Molesters*, 10 BEHAV. THERAPY 562 (1979).

99. Gene Abel et al., *Identifying Dangerous Child Molesters*, in VIOLENT BEHAVIOR: SOCIAL LEARNING APPROACHES TO PREDICTION MANAGEMENT AND TREATMENT 116–137 (R.B. Stuart ed., 1981); Marnie E. Rice & Grant T. Harris, *Why Do Men Commit Incest?*, Paper presented at the 11th Annual Forensic Conference (June 1997); Michael Seto et al., *The Sexual Age Preferences of Incest Offenders*, 108 J. OF ABNORMAL PSYCHOL. 267 (1999).

100. *Id.*

older sexual psychopath laws.[101] Under the new sexual predator laws, however, the term "personality disorder" is mentioned specifically as a qualifying condition, and it is clear that antisocial personality disorder (as well as other personality disorders) as defined in DSM–IV will satisfy the legal criteria.

The term "psychopath" although sometimes used synonymously with antisocial personality disorder,[102] and although correlated with antisocial personality disorder, is actually much more restrictive.[103] Psychopathy has been defined as "a socially devastating disorder defined by a constellation of affective, interpersonal, and behavioral characteristics, including egocentricity; impulsivity; irresponsibility; shallow emotions; lack of empathy, guilt or remorse; pathological lying; manipulativeness; and the persistent violation of social norms and expectations."[104] The measure of psychopathy with the most scientific validity is the Psychopathy Checklist–Revised, or PCL–R.[105] Among forensic populations, the prevalence of psychopathy is much lower (15% to 25%) than the prevalence of antisocial personality disorder or APD (50% to 75%). Most psychopaths also meet the criteria for APD, but most of those with APD are not psychopaths. Psychopathy also has a smaller amount of overlap with narcissistic and borderline personality disorders. There has been some preliminary evidence that psychopathy may not constitute a "disorder" in the sense that the term is usually used in the medical literature, but rather is better conceived as an evolutionary adaptation. We and others have put forth the idea that psychopaths might have evolved a "cheating" life strategy that is highly functional inasmuch as it allows them to succeed in passing on their genes into succeeding generations.[106] Preliminary data provide stronger support for the "adaptation" hypothesis than for the "disorder" hypothesis,[107] but many more data will be required to settle the issue.

This question of mental disorders among sex offenders approaches a logical conundrum. To provide a full scientific answer, one would need a scientific definition of mental disorder. Unfortunately, the most influential nomenclature for mental disorders, the fourth edition of the American Psychiatric Association's Diagnostic and Statistical Manual (DSM–IV) is not yet a completely scientific classification system. Almost all of the diagnoses and disorders listed there are based on the preferences and customary practices of clinicians and are based on few scientific data about the nosological entities described. As a result, the DSM–IV contains such a vast array of aberrations and peculiarities (as but a few examples: mathematics disorder, vascular dementia, pain disorder, caffeine induced sleep disorder, nicotine withdrawal

101. John Monahan & S.K. Davis, *Mentally Disordered Sex Offenders, in* MENTALLY DISORDERED OFFENDERS: PERSPECTIVES FROM LAW & SOCIAL SCIENCE, 191–204 (J. Monahan & H.J. Steadman eds., 1983).

102. American Psychiatric Association, *supra* note 1.

103. Robert Hare, *Psychopathy: A Clinical Construct Whose Time Has Come*, 23 CRIM. JUST. & BEHAV. 25 (1996).

104. *Id.* at 25.

105. *See supra* note 25.

106. Grant T. Harris et al., *Psychopathy as a Taxon: Evidence that Psychopaths are a Discrete Class*, 62 J. CONSULTING & CLINICAL PSYCHOL. 387 (1994); Linda Mealey, *The Sociobiology of Sociopathy: An Integrated Evolutionary Model*, 18 BEHAV. & BRAIN SCIENCES 523 (1995); Marnie E. Rice, *Violent Offender Research and Implications for the Criminal Justice System*, 52 AM. PSYCHOLOGIST 414 (1997).

107. Grant Harris et al., *Criminal Violence: The Roles of Psychopathy, Neurodevelopmental Insults and Antisocial Parenting*, CRIM. JUST. & BEHAV. (forthcoming).

disorder, sleepwalking disorder, factitious disorder) that the association of each with sex offending is entirely moot.

Indeed, we argue that this list of "mental" disorders illustrates the current impossibility of a sensible scientific definition of mental disorder. Science is, by definition, the study of the natural, material world. To the extent that "mental" implies nonmaterial events and causes, "mental" events and disorders are difficult to approach scientifically. Some psychologists have endeavored to provide material, scientific definitions of mental phenomena, but it is clear that such efforts are not reflected in everyday use and legal terminology. Most people think of human action as flowing from (and caused by) such nonmaterial mental ideas and intentions. Scientifically, and as illustrated by the DSM–IV, the distinction between mental and physical (and the concept of mental disorder as distinct from physical disorder) has little meaning. In the end, the legal question of whether a sex offender has a mental disorder (distinct from some other form of disorder, or as opposed to being different from other men in some nonmental way) holds little scientific interest. In practice, the legal question usually boils down to two other practical questions: "Shall the offender be held morally responsible (blamed and punished) for his actions? What shall be done with him?" The question of moral responsibility cannot be answered scientifically and the question about disposition should be addressed, in our view, according to risk level and treatment needs.[108]

§ 3–2.3　Scientific Methods Applied to Sexual Aggression

There are two complementary aspects to scientific research—theorizing and data collection. Though in any single study, one aspect can predominate, both aspects are always present. The two are, of course, intimately associated: a theory gives an explanation of the data already collected about known phenomena, and predicts what will be observed when data are collected about phenomena yet to be observed. The variables and measures researchers use, at least implicitly, always reflect prior theoretical decisions. Any body of data is consistent with many different theories, so that no single study can provide the "true explanation." Consequently, science is an incremental and cooperative process. Progress occurs only when researchers build upon the work of others. The popular conception of scientists locked in competition with one another for ground breaking discoveries is much more the exception than the rule. Certainly, all sciences make fitful progress with many wrong turns, but in general, scientists should agree with one another about the current state of knowledge and about the important questions. Indeed, it is fair to say that, no matter how forcefully individuals might assert their knowledge, a research field with very high levels of disagreement so that every question is controversial indicates an "immature" science not ready to be applied to public policy questions.

---

108. The question, "How wrong is this crime?" is one purely of values and, therefore, cannot be answered scientifically. However, "How wrong do people perceive this crime to be?" and "How much would people blame the perpetrator of this crime?" *are* questions that can be (and have been) addressed scientifically—by asking people's opinions in a systematic research study. *See* Marvin Wolfgang et al., Bureau of Justice Statistics, THE NATIONAL SURVEY OF CRIME SEVERITY (1985).

All research involves procedural compromises of many different kinds. For example, many theoretically interesting concepts must be measured indirectly or with imprecision. As well, it is often impossible to subject humans to experiments in which all extraneous variables (those not directly relevant to the question at hand) are controlled. Without experiments, there are always other possible explanations for the observations obtained. Many successful scientific fields involve indirect measurement without the possibility of experimentation (astronomy, for example). It is neither the experimental method alone nor the precise measurement of physical entities that defines science. Again, the point here is that scientific progress is always cumulative, halting, and usually slow. Nevertheless, modern medical, transportation and information technologies are all clear evidence of the tremendous power of scientific methods. What scientific methods have been applied to sexual aggressors?

§ 3–2.3.1 Case Studies

Probably the most common publications about sex offenders are reports of a single case (or a small number of cases) encountered in clinical practice. By definition, such reports are usually concerned with bizarre or unique features of the case. Unusual cases often stimulate interesting hypotheses, but otherwise have no scientific value and, consequently have not been reviewed in this chapter.

§ 3–2.3.2 Clinical Sample Studies

In their simplest forms, clinical sample studies (often called postdiction studies) merely report in a systematic way on a sample of sexual aggressors. A classic study of this type would report on the psychological test scores (or scores on measures of attitudes, reports of childhood experiences, and so on) of a group of sexual aggressors all admitted for assessment to a particular clinic. Important here are sufficiently large samples to permit generalization to sexual aggressors in general, clear statements about how the subjects came to be assessed, evidence that the variables were measured reliably, statistical or methodological control for multiple comparisons, and the inclusion of comparison groups. The use of comparison groups is crucial to guard against the risk that findings, taken to be particular to sex offenders, are instead just as true of other violent offenders, offenders in general, or even men in general. The choice of comparison groups depends on the particular theoretical questions addressed, but without a comparison group, clinical sample studies can be of very limited scientific value.

Other features of clinical sample studies are noteworthy. First are the problems of bias. Sampling bias is an important problem. All clinical (or offender) samples are biased to some degree—all members of a clinical sample have come to the attention of a professional. Often little is known about the characteristics of individuals who engage in the behavior but who never come to professional attention. The best clinical sample studies address this form of bias in some way—by using very large samples or using samples from multiple sources, as examples. Because clinical samples are usually being evaluated for some non-research purpose (before therapy, pre-trial assessment, etc.), there is always a real danger that the data collected reflect conscious or unconscious wishes by the participant to present himself in favorable ways (or ways consistent with his own beliefs about why he did what he did). This is called response bias. Another pernicious form of bias occurs in measurement: all other things being equal, observations tend (unconsciously) to confirm our expectations and scientists are not immune to this bias. Thus, the best clinical sample studies include some means to control for the inadvertent effects of such expectations (e.g., using objective measures that are less prone to biasing the judgements of raters, or raters/coders who are "blind" to experimental hypotheses and to subject group membership).

Second, clinical sample studies can be highly sophisticated. For example, attempts to produce stable, universal typologies of sexual aggressors are clinical sample studies.[109] The measurement of a number of physiological variables among sexual aggressors are also clinical sample studies. Such physiological variables have included sexual arousal patterns (discussed below under a separate heading), brain images, electroencephalograms, and various assays for neurotransmitters and hormones. Regardless of the technical sophistication involved, the important considerations about measurement reliability, comparison groups and avoiding bias are at least as important as in the more typical clinical sample studies using standard psychological tests and "variables of convenience."

§ 3–2.3.3　Survey or Epidemiological Studies

Survey studies collect data from large samples that are usually much less selected and often are designed to be representative of the population at large. Gathering data from large numbers of relatively unselected subjects avoids some of the biases inherent in clinical samples. To the extent that the samples are truly representative of the population of interest, sampling bias can be eliminated. Survey studies often collect data anonymously hoping to avoid problems of response bias—subjects are presumably less eager (than clinical cases) to create favorable impressions. Of course, anonymity cannot eliminate all forms of response bias. A typical survey study would ask subjects about whether and how often they had engaged in various forms of sexual aggression and would also have them complete several measures of earlier experiences, attitudes, personality and psychopathology. The inter-relationships of all the measures are then subjected to sophisticated analyses of correlations in order to "predict" sexual aggression from the other measures. Of course, this sense of prediction is only statistical—all the measures are collected on a single occasion and there is no guarantee that the predictive relationships so discovered are the true ones.

Survey studies have other risks. First, many surveys do not use representative samples, relying heavily on college undergraduates, for example. Second, many surveys rely on self report, though it is clear that self reports of violence perpetration are very inaccurate.[110] If the accuracy that exists varies as a function of other research variables (and that is quite possible), the statistical models generated can only explain the reports (as opposed to actual

109. Raymond Knight & Robert Prentky, *A Taxonomic Analysis of Child Molesters, in* Human Sexual Aggression: Current Perspectives 2–20 (R.A. Prentky & V.L. Quinsey eds., 1988).

110. N. Zoe Hilton et al., *On the Validity of Self–Reported Rates of Interpersonal Violence,* 13 J. Interpersonal Viol. 58 (1998).

events). Officially recorded violent crime is also known to be inaccurate, of course, but the nature of this inaccuracy is better understood. Relatedly, it is very unclear how officially reported crime relates to self-reported criminal activity.[111] Third, surveys are almost always restricted to variables that can be easily measured in a paper-and-pencil format. This appears to lead researchers to abandon more powerful (but technically difficult) measures in favor of those that are easier to gather.[112] Some sources of bias can still operate in survey studies. For example, men who believe that being sexually abused in childhood causes adult sexual aggression might be more likely to "remember" childhood sexual abuse if they also report adult sexual aggression. A correlation between the two in a survey might be entirely the spurious result of such an unconscious expectation.

As with clinical sample studies, surveys can do little to answer questions about individual risk or the effects of treatment. They are valuable in testing theories about sexual aggression (assuming some veridicality to the self reports). It is, however, difficult to see many direct applications of this to legal proceedings.

§ 3–2.3.4 Prediction Studies

Prediction studies solve some of the problems of clinical sample studies and surveys by gathering data at truly distinct times (as opposed to asking participants on one occasion to report about different times). For example, data gathered at the time sexual aggressors were assessed at a clinic could be used to truly predict which men actually commit new offenses later (a follow up study). As another example, data collected about the attitudes and personalities of college freshmen could be used to truly predict which would later engage in "date rape" during their college careers (a panel design). The key to true prediction studies is that events that occur later in time cannot cause earlier ones, permitting stronger causal inferences. Clearly, many of the risks to valid inference outlined for clinical sample studies and surveys are just as crucial for prediction studies.

Thus, establishing that the study variables are measured reliably is just as important as in the other scientific methods. The inclusion of appropriate comparison groups is a key consideration. The benefits of true prediction studies would be squandered if the researchers who scored and coded the earlier data did so with knowledge of the later-occurring outcome; the unconscious effects of bias would be given an opportunity to operate. The representativeness of the subjects studied is just as important a concern in prediction studies, especially if subjects disappear from the study (refuse to participate later, cannot be found for follow up, are in jail and cannot be contacted). In follow up studies, only those offenders released can be studied because those not released do not have the opportunity to engage in the behavior of interest.

111. Delbert Elliot et al., *The Identification and Prediction of Career Offenders Utilizing Self–Reported Official Data*, in PREVENTION OF DELINQUENT BEHAVIOR 90–121 (J.D. Burchard & S.N. Burchard eds., 1987).

112. Neil Malamuth, *Predictors of Naturalistic Sexual Aggression*, 50 J. PERSONALITY & SOC. PSYCHOL. 953 (1986).

For all research studies, there is the risk that the predictive relationships (or more seriously their size) discovered are heavily inflated by chance. We discuss this issue now because it is most often raised in connection with follow up studies. Researchers can take several steps to reduce this risk. For example, they should keep the ratio of variables to subjects small (below 1:30), and they should use large numbers of subjects. Most importantly, they should conduct replications or cross-validations (repetitions of the study with new samples) of their findings. As discussed at length in the earlier section, follow up studies can identify characteristics of offenders that could be used to reduce uncertainty about which ones will commit further offenses. Some follow up studies go on to construct an actuarial system by identifying the smallest set of variables that, when combined mathematically, produces the most accurate prediction of recidivism.

Clearly, replicated prediction studies have their greatest value in legal proceedings where the questions concern the risk that individual sexual aggressors will commit new offenses if given the opportunity to do so.

§ 3–2.3.5   Treatment Outcome Studies

Treatment outcome studies are usually a form of prediction study, but we discuss them separately because they have generated a distinct literature. Typically in this field, a treatment outcome study compares the re-offenses of a group of sexual aggressors who received some therapy to the re-offenses of a group who received no treatment. Sometimes two treatments are compared (instead of having an untreated control group). Given that some therapies are known to cause harm,[113] neither discovering that one group has a better outcome nor that the two are equal can help provide a scientifically sound answer to whether treatment was effective. Sometimes two groups are not compared; rather, the rate of offending of a single group before treatment is compared to the rate after treatment. For sexual aggression, this research design is extremely weak—so weak that studies using it were not included in the earlier section summarizing the existing literature on treatment effectiveness.

Obviously, several forms of bias can operate in treatment outcome studies. Most clear is the possibility that researchers will inadvertently be more assiduous in discovering the re-offenses of the untreated subjects than those who received therapy. Tests of reliability and blind coding (the coder is unaware of subjects' group membership) are key tools in the fight against such bias. The most worrisome form of bias concerns the assignment of subjects to treatment versus no treatment. An obvious concern arises when the untreated group is comprised of men offered therapy but who refused or quit shortly after beginning. Such refusers might give many reasons for declining (travel difficulties, handling the problem sufficiently without help, innocent of the charges in the first place), but such refusal must at least partly reflect the motivation to refrain from offending. If the groups differ in motivation at the outset (or in any other risk factor), differences in outcome cannot be unambiguously attributed to the specific effects of the therapy. The

113. Grant T. Harris et al., *Psychopaths: Is a Therapeutic Community Therapeutic?*, 15 THERAPEUTIC COMMUNITIES 283 (1994); Marnie E. Rice et al., *Evaluation of a Maximum Security Therapeutic Community for Psychopaths and Other Mentally Disordered Offenders*, 16 LAW & HUM. BEHAV. 399 (1992).

classic and best cure for this problem is to assign subjects to treatment at random and keep track of any who withdraw from therapy.

The legal import of treatment outcome studies lies in whether, for example, an offender can be compelled to partake of a therapy for which there exists little evidence of effectiveness. As well, these data might be relevant to whether it is appropriate to detain offenders until they are judged no longer likely to commit a new sexually predatory offense when no treatments exist that have been shown to reduce that risk.

§ 3–2.3.6 Phallometric Studies

As mentioned above, phallometric studies are a type of clinical sample study, but we tackle them separately because of their specialized literature. Phallometry involves the measurement of sexual arousal, monitoring changes in penis size, while stimuli are presented to the subject in a controlled fashion. In most studies, variations in the characteristics of the stimuli are used to test theories about how the sexual interests of sexual aggressors differ from those of normal men (or nonsexual aggressors). Phallometric studies most often come closest, compared to the other research methods described here, to true experimental research.

There is reason to believe from studies comparing the sexual preferences of sex offenders (rapists or child molesters) and non-sex offenders that assessments with more graphic and brutal stimuli have higher discriminative and predictive validity than others.[114] Studies using stimuli describing brutal and graphic aggression have found relative arousal to sexual or nonsexual violence to be a good predictor of sexual recidivism among rapists.[115]

It is also important to note that, as used clinically in forensic situations, phallometry shows higher specificity than sensitivity. That is, whereas a lack of a deviant pattern does not necessarily imply normal sexual preferences, a deviant-looking pattern is strong evidence of deviant preferences.[116] It is also quite clear that, even though they might wish to, few men spontaneously successfully fake their phallometric responses during initial testing. Repeated testing (or training in faking) however, can result in invalid profiles. There are, however, methods to detect and interfere with faking strategies.[117] It is also important to note that although there is some laboratory evidence that deviant sexual arousal patterns can be altered with treatment, unfortunately

114. Terry C. Chaplin et al., *Salient Victim Suffering and the Sexual Responses of Child Molesters*, 163 J. CONSULTING & CLINICAL PSYCHOL. 249 (1995); Grant T. Harris et al., *Maximizing the Discriminant Validity of Phallometric Assessment*, 4 PSYCHOLOGICAL ASSESSMENT 502 (1992); Martin Lalumière & Vernon L. Quinsey, *The Sensitivity of Phallometric Measures With Rapists*, 6 ANNALS OF SEX RESEARCH 123 (1993); Marnie E. Rice et al., *Empathy for the Victim and Sexual Arousal Among Rapists and Nonrapists*, 9 J. OF INTERPERSONAL VIOLENCE 435 (1994).

115. Marnie E. Rice et al., *A Followup of Rapists Assessed in a Maximum Security Psy-*

chiatric Facility, 5 J. OF INTERPERSONAL VIOL. 435 (1990).

116. Grant T. Harris & Marnie E. Rice, *Risk Appraisal and Management of Violent Behavior*, 48 PSYCHIATRIC SERVICES 1168 (1997); VERNON L. QUINSEY & MARTIN LALUMIÈRE, ASSESSMENT OF SEXUAL OFFENDERS AGAINST CHILDREN (1996).

117. Vernon L. Quinsey & Terry C. Chaplin, *Preventing Faking in Phallometric Assessment of Sexual Preference*, 528 ANNALS OF THE NEW YORK ACADEMY SCI. 49 (1988); Grant T. Harris et al., *Dissimulation in Phallometric Testing of Rapists' Sexual Preferences* 28 ARCHIVES OF SEXUAL BEHAV. 223 (1999).

only pre-treatment arousal patterns have been shown to be predictive of future violent or sexual offending.[118]

We have addressed the scientific value of phallometry in detail elsewhere.[119] Here, we summarize those discussions by saying that, under limited circumstances, phallometric tests can be valid and reliable scientific procedures. Many clinicians who employ phallometric tests fall outside those limits and, therefore, provide assessments that are, at best, of unknown scientific value. Even within those limits, phallometric testing can answer only a few legally relevant questions. Phallometric testing provides evidence about whether a subject has an identifiable problem that might be amenable to treatment. Phallometric testing might provide evidence about an offender's motivation for committing a particular offense. However, phallometric testing could not be used to determine whether a particular offender was likely to be guilty of a particular offense in the first place.

§ 3–2.3.7   Conclusions

Clearly, a research study could fall into more than one category—for example, a study examining the ability of phallometric test results to predict recidivism among previously identified sexual aggressors.[120] No study can be free of all methodological weaknesses, but to the extent that any one study exhibits weaknesses, its findings need to be accepted with greater caution. Whenever a researcher attempts a narrative review of a particular field (as we do here), there is an almost inevitable result: some researchers find result X and some do not, and some even find the opposite. Having identified methodological problems with every study and then computed that "box score," the narrative reviewer is always left implying that the field is controversial and fraught with disagreement. In reality, however, apparently contradictory findings are inevitable, especially when researchers are forced to use indirect and imprecise measurement and when full-fledged experiments are impossible. A solution to these contradictions lies in meta-analysis—a means to combine the findings, whatever their direction, from all available studies.[121] Meta-analysis provides a more definitive answer to the original question, "Does effect X occur?" More, importantly, meta-analysis gives information about when effect X occurs and why.

Meta-analysis is not a separate research method itself, but is, rather, a numerical means to combine results from other research methods. Thus, meta-analysis can be applied to clinical sample studies, surveys and prediction studies alike and even permits combination across study types. Meta-analyses have established the validity of phallometric testing,[122] the predictors of recidivism among sexual aggressors,[123] and have been applied to treatment

---

118. *See* citations at *supra* note 69.

119. Martin Lalumière & Grant T. Harris, *Common Questions About The Use Of Phallometric Assessment*, 10 SEXUAL ABUSE: J. OF RES. & TREATMENT 227 (1998); Grant T. Harris, & Marnie E. Rice, *The Science in Phallometric Measurement of Male Sexual Interest*, 5 CURRENT DIRECTIONS IN PSYCHOLOGICAL SCI. 156 (1996).

120. *See* Rice, Quinsey, & Harris, *supra* note 69; Rice et al., *supra* note 115.

121. Martin L. Lalumière & Vernon L. Quinsey, *The Discriminability of Rapists from Non–Sex Offenders Using Phallometric Measures: A Meta–Analysis*, 21 CRIM. JUST. & BEHAV. 150 (1994).

122. *Id.*

123. Hanson & Bussière, *supra* note 19.

research.[124] Meta-analysis is not a panacea, of course. Meta-analyses require that there be some competently done studies in the first place. And of course, when the characteristics of individual studies are examined in a meta-analysis, steps must be taken to avoid inaccuracy and bias in scoring and coding those characteristics (as must be done in individual studies).[125] Nevertheless, meta-analysis can remove much apparent noise and controversy in a particular scientific field and serves to remind all researchers that the accumulation of scientific knowledge is collaborative and incremental.

§ 3–2.4 Issues About Which There Is Scientific Consensus

§ 3–2.4.1 The Recidivism of Sexual Aggressors Can Be Predicted

It is beyond scientific doubt that certain characteristics of sex offenders, when measured objectively, are correlated with subsequent violent recidivism including sexual re-offending. These characteristics include measures of psychopathy, phallometrically-determined sexual deviance, the frequency and severity of prior sexual, violent and criminal history, the sex offender's history of victim choice, as well as substance abuse, age and marital status. Although less frequently investigated, the sex offender's history of conduct disorder and childhood aggression have also been shown to be related to recidivism. Furthermore, it is well established that, when individual predictor variables are selected and combined based on their actual empirical relationships with recidivism, the resulting combination (called an actuarial instrument or method) renders usefully accurate statements about the likelihood of violent (including sexual) recidivism in many populations.

§ 3–2.4.2 Actuarial Methods Out–Perform Clinical Judgment

In literally hundreds of comparisons over many domains including the prediction of recidivism, clinical judgment has almost never been found superior while the converse has most often been demonstrated.[126] Though some studies have shown that clinicians' unaided judgments were better than chance (i.e., outperformed blind guess work), many studies have not.[127] No studies have demonstrated that clinicians' unaided judgments were more accurate than those of laypersons.

§ 3–2.4.3 Sexual Aggressors Who Voluntarily Complete Certain Treatments Have Been Shown To Be Of Lower Risk

In the most methodologically sophisticated studies, all other things being equal, those sexual offenders who refuse, begin and then quit, or are ejected from pharmacological or cognitive-behavioral treatment exhibit considerably higher rates of violent recidivism than sex offenders in general.[128] By defini-

---

124. Hall, *supra* note 78; Hanson, *supra* note 79.

125. Marnie E. Rice & Grant T. Harris, *The Treatment of Adult Offenders, in* HANDBOOK OF ANTISOCIAL BEHAVIOR 425–435 (D.M. Stoff et al. eds., 1997).

126. *See supra* note 21.

127. *See id.*

128. *Supra*, note 59.

tion, this finding means that volunteering for and persisting with such treatment is a positive prognostic sign.

§ 3–2.4.4   Some Interventions Cause Harm By Producing An Increase In Recidivism

In the fields of treatment for offenders, therapy for violent offenders, and treatment for sex offenders specifically, there have been demonstrations that some well-intentioned interventions have made antisocial conduct, violent crime and sexual offending more likely compared to doing nothing.[129]

§ 3–2.4.5   Sexual Aggressors Are Sexually Deviant

On average and compared to men who are not sex offenders, child molesters exhibit greater arousal to children relative to their arousal to adults.[130] Similarly, on average and compared to men who are not sexual aggressors, rapists exhibit greater arousal to coercive sex and violence compared to their responses to consenting sexual activity.[131] Also, sexual aggressors are more likely to endorse value statements supportive of sex offending, justifying it and excusing the behavior on various grounds.[132]

§ 3–2.5   Issues About Which There Is Scientific Controversy (or Ignorance)

§ 3–2.5.1   How Exactly Should Risk Appraisals Be Conducted?

Which actuarial instrument should be used in giving expert evidence about a particular sex offender? Under what circumstances are clinically based adjustments (or overrides) to actuarial estimates scientifically justified? How should risk appraisal be accomplished when no relevant actuarial tools exist (for example, for female sex offenders)?

§ 3–2.5.2   Do Any Treatments Have Specific Effects in Reducing Recidivism?

So far, no data permit any scientifically valid statements about whether any therapeutic activities or drugs reduce the risk of sexual aggressors. If any treatments ever are demonstrated to lower risk, would the completion of treatment make an independent contribution to the prediction of recidivism? Do community notification and registration have benefits? While it is entirely possible that notification and registration have salutary effects, it is also possible that these measures (or some ways of implementing these interventions, at least) could increase the risk of sexual aggression compared to doing nothing. Moreover, such social policies could have other untoward negative effects by, for example, increasing the fear and suspicion (resulting in vigilan-

129. Joan McCord, *A Thirty-year Followup of Treatment Effects,* 33 Am. Psychologist 284 (1978); Frisbie & Dondis, *supra* note 13; Andrews et al., *supra* note 46. *See also* Nathaniel McConaghy, *Methodological Issues Concerning Evaluation of Treatment for Sexual Offenders: Randomization, Treatment Dropouts, Untreated Controls, and Within–Treatment Studies* 11 Sexual Abuse: J. Res. & Treatment 183 (1999).

130. Marnie Rice et al., *Sexual Recidivism Among Child Molesters Released From a Maxi-*

mum Security Psychiatric Institution, 59 J. Consulting & Clinical Psychol. 381 (1991).

131. Martin Lalumière & Vernon Quinsey, *The Discriminability of Rapists from Non-sex Offenders Using Phallometric Measures: A Meta-analysis,* 21 Crim. Just. & Behav. 150 (1994).

132. *Id.*

teism perhaps) of sexual aggression out of proportion to the actual risk. States that have examined the incidence of effects such as vigilanteism have reported very low rates,[133] but there are few data on the topic.

§ 3–2.5.3 What Proportion of Sexual Aggressors are Sexually Deviant?

Some investigators find huge differences in sexual deviance between sexual aggressors and other men, while other researchers find only small differences or differences that appear only in group data. Undoubtedly some of this apparent discrepancy is due to the use of suboptimal assessment and research methods, but how much? So far little is known, for example, about the sexual deviance of sexually coercive men who offend against acquaintances without being charged with criminal offenses. Another criticism of phallometric studies to date is that few normal males are represented in all the research on men's sexual preferences.[134]

§ 3–2.6 New Research Directions on Sexual Aggressors

§ 3–2.6.1 Prediction of Recidivism

Promising and useful avenues of research lie in attempts to improve actuarial methods. For example, new theoretically motivated variables (e.g., serotonin levels, neuropsychological test scores) might improve prediction. More valid, less expensive ways to assess psychopathy, the severity of criminal history, and sexual deviance are all being pursued. As well, the empirical contribution of contextual and situational variables (e.g., post release social supports, criminal associates) are being evaluated. In addition, actuarial prediction instruments have so far included only additive relationships among their constituent predictors, despite theoretical reasons to expect multiplicative relationships and empirical evidence of their existence. For example, as described earlier, we found a significant interaction between psychopathy and sexual deviance such that those men who were both psychopaths and exhibited deviant phallometric preferences failed at an extremely high rate and significantly sooner than all other men.[135] In fact, over half of those men with both risk factors had committed a new sexual offense within three years at risk, and three quarters had committed a new sexual offense within six years. Additionally, our previous research suggests that age, alcohol abuse and sexual deviance all have different relationships with violent recidivism depending on whether the offender is (or is not) also a psychopath. Thus, there is good reason to believe that instruments that include multiplicative effects will yield higher accuracies than have been attained using instruments that do not include such effects.

There is also evidence, as mentioned earlier, that some predictors do predict sexual recidivism (even defined in the relatively crude manner used in most studies) better than they predict violent recidivism in general. Past history of sexual offenses and deviant sexual preferences are the most robust

133. Roxanne Lieb et al., *Sexual Predators and Social Policy*, 23 CRIME & JUST.: A REVIEW OF RESEARCH 43 (M. Tonry ed., 1998).

134. Gordon Hall et al., *Sexual Arousal and Arousability to Pedophilic Stimuli in a* *Community Sample of Normal Men*, 26 BEHAV. THERAPY 681 (1995).

135. Rice & Harris, *supra* note 25. *See also* Harris et al., *supra* note 26.

of these predictors, although, of course, they have not been tested in offenders who were not sex offenders. Thus, it is quite likely that future studies will go to greater effort than previously to determine which new offenses are actually sexually motivated or involve a sexual component in order to attain higher predictive accuracy for sexual recidivism than has been achieved to date. The use of survival analyses and the combination of additional predictor variables might well improve the empirical identification of sexual aggressors that meet the legal criteria as sexual predators.

§ 3–2.6.2 Treatment and Management

The preferred or recommended treatment for sex offenders continues to evolve but the evolution is not based on an empirical foundation of effective treatment and has little chance to be so grounded.[136] If any specific treatment effects have so far been achieved, all scientists would agree that the magnitudes have been small at best, and limited to child molesters. If therapy is to play a large role in protecting society from new offenses committed by identified sex offenders in general or sexual predators in particular, moderate to large treatment effects are required. Although the long term effects of cognitive behavior treatment are still being evaluated, there are sensible grounds to consider other modalities. For example, few drug treatments or treatments that combine behavioral methods to alter sexual preferences with drugs or with other cognitive-behavioral treatments have received methodologically sound outcome evaluations.

Distinct from therapy are several interventions designed to reduce the opportunity for sexual aggression while an offender is in the community. Sex offender registration, community notification, intensive supervision, and physical castration are all possibilities in various jurisdictions. Data on their effectiveness are even more scarce than data on the effectiveness of therapy. Social policy would be well served by methodologically sound empirical evaluations of such services.

§ 3–2.6.3 The Causal Role of Other Psychological Constructs

As mentioned above, there are many individual differences among men in the ways they approach sexual behavior, and sexual aggression in particular. Sexual aggressors have been reported to endorse "rape myths," traditional (as opposed to enlightened) sex roles, interpersonal violence, hostility to women, adversarial sexual beliefs, sensation seeking, and generally right-wing beliefs. In addition, sexual aggression has been reported to be related to general antisociality (juvenile delinquency, generally violent conduct), social isolation and, as already mentioned, to psychopathy and sexual deviance. What are the causal and explanatory relationships here and which are epiphenomena? For example, do attitudes hostile to women cause a man to engage in sexual aggression, or are they merely the result of sexual aggression—rationaliza-

136. Gordon Hall et al., *Conceptually Derived Treatments for Sexual Aggressors*, 24 PROFESSIONAL PSYCHOL.: RES. & PRAC. 62 (1993); William Marshall, *A Revised Approach to the Treatment of Men who Sexually Assault Adult Females, in* SEXUAL AGGRESSION: ISSUES IN ETIOLOGY, ASSESSMENT AND TREATMENT 143–166 (G.C. Nagayama Hall et al. eds., 1993); William Marshall, *Treatment Effects on Denial and Minimization in Incarcerated Sex Offenders*, 32 BEHAV. RES. & THERAPY 559 (1994); William Pithers, *Treatment of Rapists: Reinterpretation of Early Outcome Data and Exploratory Constructs to Enhance Therapeutic Efficacy, in* SEXUAL AGGRESSION: ISSUES IN ETIOLOGY, ASSESSMENT & TREATMENT 167–196 (G.C.N. Hall et al. eds., 1993).

tions adduced to justify behavior actually caused by something else? Many theories of sexual aggression posit a causal role for such constructs. This is consistent with everyday understandings of behavior—internal mental states (intentions, beliefs, attitudes, etc.) cause external actions. Many scientists question this way of thinking about the bases for behavior, pointing out that attributing an action to a hypothetical internal state does nothing to explain the action until the necessary and sufficient conditions for the occurrence of the internal state are also specified. Once those conditions are specified, positing the internal state adds nothing of scientific value. In any case, we anticipate future research on the attitudes, beliefs, and personalities of sexual aggressors in attempts to build more complete models (i.e., explanations) of sexual aggression.

§ 3–2.6.4 Ontogeny and Etiology

A full scientific explanation of sexual aggression has yet to be provided. Nevertheless, ongoing research suggests that sexual aggression might have several independent causes. For example, there is considerable variation in men's sexual strategies. That is, some men have relatively few sexual partners and invest considerably in each relationship. Other men invest their efforts, not in relationships, but in having as much uncommitted sexual activity with as many sexual partners as possible (sometimes referred to as high mating effort), and among the tactics such men employ is sexual coercion. High mating effort males, especially those who employ sexually coercive tactics, would be expected to be relatively uninfluenced by the reproductive interests of their sexual partners. Specifically, their sexual arousal (in real life and in phallometric testing) would be less inhibited by the suffering of a "sexual partner" than that of other men. Some of this latter high mating effort group would, of course, be psychopaths, and members of this subgroup are at much higher risk for sexual coercion. Future research is required to elucidate the factors responsible for the "selection" between these strategies and how men might be influenced to switch.

More or less independent of the sexual strategy of an offender is sexual deviance. It is clear that in addition to a general tendency (or lack thereof) to be concerned about the interests and welfare of others, some men are sexually interested in and attracted to anomalous activities and targets. Some atypical sexual interests are, of course, in and of themselves, innocuous—a sexual interest in adult members of the same sex, for example. On the other hand, some anomalous sexual preferences represent risk to others—sexual interest in children, sexual attraction to the pain and suffering of others, as examples. Until very recently, almost nothing has been known about how such sexual deviance could develop. Many investigators have theorized that while normal sexual preferences (sexual attraction to fertile members of the opposite sex), must be inborn to a large extent, sexual deviance arises through a process of conditioning to deviant material and fantasies, perhaps during a critical period around the time of puberty. Such a conditioning hypothesis has run into problems, however. Sexual deviance, no matter how defined, is very much less common in women than in men. No one has been able to get good evidence of any conditioning of sexual interests in the laboratory. And, in many cases, it is very clear that some homosexual preferences, at least, occur long before puberty and without any apparent conditioning history.[137]

Very recent work suggests quite a different basis for men's sexual deviance and other anomalous sexual interests. That is, there have been reports of a genetic link to homosexuality.[138] There are reports that male homosexuals exhibit a variety of differences in their brain structures compared to heterosexual men. These brain structures are also those in which men and women show similar differences.[139] Homosexual men have more older brothers, but not more older sisters nor younger siblings, compared to heterosexual men.[140] Finally, sexual deviance among sex offenders (rapists and child molesters) is related in the same way to older brothers but not younger brothers or sisters.[141] These findings all imply a similar, non-psychosocial basis for sexual deviance and other anomalous sexual preferences.

Finally, evaluation of theories implied by these results is hampered by lack of knowledge of the normal, unperturbed development of sexuality. For example, sexologists do not know whether prepubertal males are most sexually attracted to persons their own age or to adults. Without such knowledge, the apparently deviant sexual interests of young adolescent sex offenders cannot easily be interpreted theoretically or clinically. All of these considerations and early findings point to an increasing scientific interest in sexual aggression and sexual deviance as biological phenomena.

§ 3–2.6.5   Screening Potential Sex Offenders

All of these research directions, in addition to answering theoretically interesting questions about sexuality and how it can go wrong, have some applications with practical and legal relevance: How can schools, churches, recreational organizations, and professional groups ensure that men who apply to work with vulnerable populations are not motivated by inappropriate sexual interests? Now the issue is not the prediction of recidivism, since identified sex offenders are unlikely to be considered for such roles, but the prediction of a first offense. Would the differences already discovered between sex offenders and normal men be useful here? Would a combination of phallometric test results (or some other measure of sexual preferences), combined with measures of attitudes, accurately discriminate potential sex offenders from other men? Obviously, such a notion entails much more than a simple empirical question about accuracy. As discussed above, any selection process can achieve a high hit rate (sensitivity, i.e., correctly identifying deviant men) only at the cost of some (and sometimes, many) false alarms (falsely identifying safe men as deviant; i.e., lack of specificity). There is no

137. Chandler Burr, A Separate Creation (1996).

138. Stella Hu et al., *Linkage Between Sexual Orientation and Chromosome Xq28 in Males But Not In Females*, 11 Nature Genetics 248 (1995);

139. Simon Levay, *A Difference in Hypothalamic Structure Between Heterosexual and Homosexual Men*, 253 Science 1034 (1991); Simon Levay & Dean Hamer, *Evidence for a Biological Influence in Male Homosexuality*, 270 Sci. Am. 44 (1994).

140. Raymond Blanchard & Anthony Bogaert, *Additive Effects of Older Brothers and Homosexual Brothers in the Prediction of Marriage and Cohabitation*, 27 Behav. Genetics 45 (1997).

141. Martin L. Lalumière et al., *Sexual Deviance and Number of Older Brothers Among Sexual Offenders*, 10 Sexual Abuse: J. Res. & Treatment 5 (1998).

simple way to resolve this inevitable tradeoff. Resolution depends on the human costs one attaches to sexual victimization versus denying an innocent person vocational opportunities. In legal fora, these costs and values are often expressed in terms of the importance of individual civil rights versus the state's duty to protect vulnerable citizens from avoidable harm. Although answers to these moral and legal dilemmas do not exist, we anticipate that researchers will increasingly tackle the scientific questions in the near future.[142]

142. Gene Abel et al., *Screening Tests for Pedophilia*, 221 CRIM. JUST. & BEHAV. 115 (1994); Grant T. Harris et al., *Viewing Time as a Measure of Sexual Interest Among Child Molesters and Normal Heterosexual Men*, 34 BEHAV. RES. & THERAPY 389 (1996).

CHAPTER 4

THE BATTERED WOMAN SYNDROME AND OTHER PSYCHOLOGICAL EFFECTS OF DOMESTIC VIOLENCE AGAINST WOMEN

Table of Sections

A. LEGAL ISSUES

171

Sec.

4–2.4   Future Directions.

Westlaw Electronic Research

See Westlaw Electronic Research Guide preceding the Summary of Contents.

A. LEGAL ISSUES

§ 4–1.0 THE LEGAL RELEVANCE OF RESEARCH ON DOMESTIC VIOLENCE AGAINST WOMEN

The battered woman syndrome has received more attention from, and greater acceptance by, courts than perhaps any other area of psychological research. The reasons for this positive reception lie in the policies and values implicit and explicit in the law, rather than the quality or force of the science. In particular, courts have been justly outraged at the rate of domestic violence and the very poor record of the legal system in responding to this violence.[1] Moreover, anecdotal stories of the nature of the abuse illustrate compellingly the depth and horror of the problem. Courts, and policymakers generally,[2] became aware of the matter and were amenable to, or actively sought, solutions to it.

Yet, both the legal and empirical pillars that define the battered woman syndrome rest on less than sound foundations.[3] These weaknesses lead some courts to completely exclude expert testimony on battered woman syndrome and other courts to express an unwillingness to follow syndrome theory everywhere it might lead. Moreover, many courts apply the syndrome in ways

----

§ 4–1.0

1. *See* Schuller & Rzepa, *infra*.

2. It should be noted that a number of states provide for the admission of the battered woman syndrome through legislation. Ohio passed legislation declaring that the syndrome "is a matter of commonly accepted scientific knowledge" and "not within the general understanding of experience of a person who is a member of the general populace." OHIO REV. CODE ANN. § 2901.06(A) (Baldwin 1994). The statute provides that defendants who contend that they used force against another in self-defense "*may* introduce expert testimony of the 'battered woman syndrome.'" *Id.* § 2901.06(B) (emphasis supplied). Ohio's statute further requires that expert testimony introduced pursuant to the statute must "be in accordance with the Ohio Rules of Evidence." *Id. See also* Mass.Gen.Laws Ann. ch. 233, § 23E (West Supp. 1995); MD.CODE ANN., Cts. & Jud. Proc. § 10–916 (1995); MO.ANN.STAT. § 563.033(1) (Vernon Supp. 1994); WYO. STAT. § 6–1–203(b) (Supp. 1994). Of course, to the extent that a state statute mandates admission of battered woman syndrome expert testimony, many of the evidentiary issues discussed in this

section do not apply. *See, e.g.,* State v. Williams, 787 S.W.2d 308, 311 (Mo.Ct.App. 1990) (The court concluded that the Missouri legislature's passage of section 563.033 made it unnecessary for the court "to engage in ... [an] examination ... [of] the scientific validity of the syndrome or its admissibility where self-defense is raised."). However, legislation does not solve the problems associated with poor research methodology or advocacy masquerading as science; in fact, it exacerbates it. If legislators believe that the values represented by battered woman syndrome advocates are substantively correct, they should create an exception that reflects this judgment. By carving the exception in terms of the admissibility of research having doubtful scientific validity, legislators send exactly the wrong message to social scientists about the kind of research they should be doing and an entirely convoluted message to the public about the values reflected in the legislation. It is a cowardly approach to a profound social problem that is in need of courageous solutions.

3. *See generally* David L. Faigman, *Note, The Battered Woman Syndrome and Self-Defense: A Legal and Empirical Dissent,* 72 VA. L. REV. 619 (1986).

inconsistent with its theoretical premises. Finally, most courts ignore other psychological theories that have significantly better empirical support and, in some cases, greater legal relevance.

Advocates of the battered woman syndrome deserve substantial credit for bringing the important problem of domestic violence to the attention of courts and the public. Indeed, publicity concerning the depth and severity of the problem was accompanied by a proposed, albeit partial, solution. In 1979, Lenore Walker, a clinical researcher, proposed the psychological condition she termed the "battered woman syndrome."[4] According to Walker, the syndrome, discussed more fully below, explains why battered women sometimes kill their abusers under circumstances that do not mirror traditional cases of self-defense. Specifically, syndrome advocates seek to explain why battered women sometimes resort to deadly force when, seemingly, they are not confronted by an imminent harm. The syndrome also speaks to a common question believed to be uttered in response to domestic violence: Why don't women simply leave violent relationships? The syndrome closely parallels the requirements of self-defense and thus provides courts with a ready solution to undeniably compelling and sympathetic cases in which an abused woman has killed her abuser.

Although expert testimony on the battered woman syndrome made its debut in self-defense cases, this testimony is now offered in a wide assortment of contexts. In criminal cases, the syndrome is sometimes proffered by defendants claiming duress and, increasingly, it has become a tool for prosecutors in a variety of settings. The syndrome is also sometimes offered in civil cases.[5] The most typical use of battered woman syndrome evidence, however, is by defendants claiming self-defense in homicide prosecutions. This section begins by describing the syndrome as it was developed for use in self-defense cases and then considers extensions and generalizations of the syndrome to other contexts.[6]

§ 4–1.1   Self–Defense

§ 4–1.1.1   Legal Theory

Although practice varies widely, most jurisdictions begin their analyses with the four traditional requirements of self-defense. First, at the time of the act, a defender must have believed that he was in *imminent danger* of *unlawful bodily harm*.[7] Second, he must have used a reasonable amount of force to respond to the threatened danger.[8] Third, he cannot have been the

---

4. Lenore Walker, The Battered Woman (1979) [hereinafter cited as L. Walker (1979)]. Walker developed and expanded her theory in later research. Lenore Walker, The Battered Woman Syndrome (1984) [hereinafter cited as L. Walker (1984)].

5. *See infra* § 4–1.4.

6. Perhaps the most legally accepted extension of the battered woman syndrome is to abused children who kill their abuser. This use is considered separately. *See* Chapter 5.

7. Wayne R. LaFave & Austin W. Scott, Jr., Handbook on Criminal Law § 53, at 391 (1972).

The imminence requirement contemplates an element of necessity; the threatened actor had no choice but to defend himself. *See also* George Fletcher, Rethinking Criminal Law 856 (1978) ("[s]tressing the element of involuntariness is but our way of making the moral claim that [the actor] is not to be blamed for the kind of choice that other people would make under the same circumstances").

8. W. LaFave & A. Scott, *supra* note 7, at 391. An actor is limited to the use of nondeadly force against a nondeadly attack, but he can respond to deadly force with deadly force of his own. *Id.* at 392. LaFave and Scott define dead-

aggressor.[9] Fourth, under some circumstances he must have had no opportunity to retreat safely.[10] Although courts and commentators sometimes view the four elements of self-defense categorically,[11] the essential premise of self-defense doctrine should not be lost: where an individual cannot resort to the law in response to aggression, he may use reasonable force to protect himself from physical harm.

In many cases in which women kill their batterers, however, the traditional criteria of self-defense are not met, or are met imperfectly. Typically, the defensive act occurs during a lull in the violence and, sometimes, when the batterer is sleeping. A battered woman may have used a knife or gun, while the abuser did not. In addition, though most jurisdictions impose no formal duty to retreat, the "defensive" act usually follows a long history and pattern of violence in the relationship, thus possibly raising the question, "why didn't the woman just leave?" Proponents of the battered woman syndrome maintain that these departures from the traditional expectations of self-defense law can be explained by the psychological concomitants associated with violence in intimate relationships.

§ 4–1.1.2 The Theory of the Battered Woman Syndrome

The battered woman syndrome was first offered in 1979 and again in 1984 as an empirical description of the "typical" battering relationship. Since that time it has metamorphosized into a variety of forms. Some courts remain faithful to the original formulation that the syndrome merely describes a contextual framework in which a particular battered woman's actions might be understood. Other courts, however, understand the syndrome in more diagnostic terms, and as a subcategory of post-traumatic stress disorder

ly force as "force (a) which its user uses with the intent to cause death or serious bodily injury to another or (b) which he knows creates a substantial risk of death or serious bodily injury to the other." *Id.* (footnote omitted).

9. *Id.* at 394–95.

10. *Id.* at 391. The law's attitude toward the duty to retreat reflects the tensions underlying self-defense doctrine generally. On one hand, an individual should be encouraged to retreat in order to avoid injury to himself or the aggressor. At the same time, one who is attacked should not be required to adopt a cowardly or humiliating posture. The majority of American jurisdictions impose no duty to retreat if the aggressor employs deadly force and the defender reasonably believes that he is in danger of death or serious bodily injury. A substantial minority of states, however, require the defending party to retreat if he can do so in complete safety. *Id.* at 395–96.

An individual has no duty to retreat if attacked by an intruder in his home. Courts are divided, though, on whether there is an obligation to retreat when the assailant is a co-occupant of the dwelling. *See id.* at 396 n.36; Annot., 26 A.L.R.3d 1296 (1969). A majority of jurisdictions do not require retreat when the assault occurs within the home and the assailant is a co-occupant. *See, e.g.*, Robinson v.

State, 308 S.C. 74, 417 S.E.2d 88, 92 (S.C.1992) (A battered woman could "claim the inapplicability of this element of self-defense because she [often] acts while on her own premises, and has no duty to retreat."). The rationale for this position apparently is that the defender has no safer place to which he can escape. Nevertheless, some jurisdictions ignore this logic and impose a duty to retreat in this situation. *See, e.g.*, State v. Ordway, 619 A.2d 819, 823–24 (R.I.1992) (" 'a person assailed in his or her own residence by a co-occupant is not entitled under the guise of self-defense to employ deadly force and kill his or her assailant.' "); *see also* Elizabeth Schneider, *Equal Rights to Trial for Women: Sex Bias in the Law of Self–Defense,* 15 Harv. C.R.–C.L. L. Rev. 623, 633 (1980); Sandra F. Williams, Note, *Limits on the Use of Defensive Force to Prevent Intramarital Assaults,* 10 Rut.-Cam. L.J. 643, 654 (1979).

11. W. LaFave & A. Scott, *supra* note 7, at 392 ("On the question of what is reasonable, the law of self-defense has tended 'to ossify into specific rules,' not always fixed with regard to reason.") (*quoting* Brown v. United States, 256 U.S. 335, 343, 41 S.Ct. 501, 65 L.Ed. 961 (1921) (Holmes, J.)).

(PTSD).[12] Some courts consider it a combination of the two. Moreover, the syndrome is routinely extended to men and children with little or no explanation.[13] These different approaches parallel the evolution of the syndrome from the time it was first introduced. Lenore Walker, the originator of the concept, has increasingly moved to describing the syndrome as a manifestation of trauma.[14] This is undoubtedly attributable to the perceived legal efficacy of such a move rather than any body of research that would support it. Nonetheless, at least as compared to the research behind the original formulation, the risk of PTSD for women in violent relationships has some support behind it. The specific legal relevance of PTSD, however, is less clear. It is not obviously pertinent to a claim of justification and the research done so far has not tied it to a specific theory of excuse. Instead, courts seem satisfied to note the general support for this concept (at least among clinicians who specialize in this area and courts), and allow the testimony for what it is worth.[15] The syndrome has proved to be elastic enough to fit virtually any legal theory.[16]

As § 2.0 makes abundantly clear, psychological research on domestic violence against women can no longer be limited to "syndrome" research. Yet, expert witnesses and courts continue to approach this matter primarily, if not exclusively, from the syndrome perspective. In fact, the psychology has nearly merged with the law to form a hybrid self-defense—battered woman syndrome defense.[17] This result has led to an interdependence that is not unusual in the law and science connection, however unfortunate it might be. The law does not simply borrow the social science, it shapes the type of social science that is done and the conclusions the researchers draw from their studies. And the law has become myopic; once having accepted the syndrome perspective it fails to even inquire about the latest developments in the field. Therefore, although other perspectives have been offered,[18] the syndrome approach continues to predominate.

12. *See, e.g.*, State v. Grecinger, 569 N.W.2d 189, 193 (Minn.1997).

13. *See, e.g.*, Freeman v. State, 269 Ga. 337, 496 S.E.2d 716 (Ga.1998) (extending the theory to men).

14. *See, e.g.*, Lenore A. Walker, *Post-Traumatic Stress Disorder in Women: Diagnosis and Treatment of Battered Woman Syndrome*, 28 Psychotherapy 21, 22 (1991).

15. It should be noted that in many jurisdictions the admission of the battered woman syndrome is mandated by statute. *See* discussion *supra* note 2.

16. *See, e.g.*, Riley, 500 S.E.2d at 530 n.6 (Court explained that in West Virginia the syndrome has been allowed to (1) "determine the defendant's mental state where self-defense is asserted," (2) "negate criminal intent" and (3) "establish either the lack of malice, intention, or awareness, and thus negate or tend to negate a necessary element of one or the other offenses charged.").

17. Although courts sometimes confuse the issue, proponents of syndrome theory insist that they do not intend to create a new legal category of defense. Instead, they believe that the syndrome explains apparent inconsistencies between the factual circumstances of some cases in which battered women kill and traditional notions of self-defense. *Compare* Elizabeth Vaughn & Maureen L. Moore, *The Battered Spouse Defense in Kentucky*, 10 N. Ky. L. Rev. 399, 399 (1983) ("The defense of battered women who kill their mates is slowly developing a distinct style or technique called the abused spouse defense. This defense emerges as akin to, but separate from, the more familiar and established defenses of self-defense and diminished capacity.") *with* Roberta K. Thyfault, *Comment, Self-defense: Battered Woman Syndrome on Trial*, 20 Cal. W.L. Rev. 485, 495 (1984) ("The battered woman syndrome is not in of itself a defense. The defense which is asserted is self-defense, not that the woman was a battered woman.").

18. *See* Schuller and Rzepa, *infra*, § 2.0. Professor Charles Ewing offers an alternative that has, yet, gained no adherents among courts and which has been severely criticized by commentators. Charles Patrick Ewing, Battered Women Who Kill: Psychological Self-Defense as Legal Justification (1987); *contra* David L. Faigman, *Discerning Justice When Battered Women Kill*, 39 Hastings L.J. 207

Battered woman syndrome researchers posit two theories that address the discrepancies between the paradigm of self-defense and the facts of many battered women cases.[19] The first is the "Walker cycle theory," used to demonstrate that, although the "defensive" act may have occurred during a period of relative calm, the defendant was reasonable in her belief, at the time of the act, that the man presented her with a threat of imminent harm.[20] Second, researchers extend the psychological theory of learned helplessness, coupled with the cycle theory, to explain the incapacity of the battered woman to leave the abusive relationship.[21]

[1] The Cycle Theory

The cycle theory[22] forms the conceptual bridge that spans the time gap between the batterer's threat of death or serious bodily harm and the defendant's act.[23] According to proponents, there are three distinct phases of the typical battering relationship. A "tension building phase" erupts into an "acute battering incident," which is in turn followed by "loving contrition."[24] The first phase is marked by verbal bickering and increasing tension between the man and woman.[25] In the second phase, the batterer explodes into an uncontrollable and violent rage.[26] In the final phase, the batterer typically expresses regret and profusely apologizes, usually promising never to batter the woman again.[27] Despite the man's promises during this third phase, the cycle eventually begins anew.[28]

According to the cycle theory, the battered woman is reduced to a state of fear and anxiety during the first two phases of the cycle,[29] and her perception of danger extends beyond the time of the battering episodes themselves. A "cumulative terror" consumes the woman and holds her in constant fear of

(1987); Stephen Morse, *The Misbegotten Marriage of Soft Psychology and Bad Law*, 14 LAW & HUM. BEHAV. 595 (1990).

19. Walker defines a battered woman as any woman "18 years of age or over, who is or has been in an intimate relationship with a man who repeatedly subjects or subjected her to forceful physical and/or psychological abuse." L. WALKER (1984), *supra* note 4, at 203. Walker's definition is expansive. She defines an intimate relationship as one "having a romantic, affectionate, or sexual component." *Id.* "Repeatedly" merely means "more than once." *Id.* Finally, "abuse" includes, in addition to physical assaults, "extreme verbal harassment and expressing comments of a derogatory nature with negative value judgments." *Id.*

20. *See, e.g.*, Ibn–Tamas v. United States, 407 A.2d 626, 634 (D.C.1979) (expert would provide "a basis from which the jury could understand why [the defendant] perceived herself in imminent danger at the time of the shooting"); State v. Kelly, 97 N.J. 178, 478 A.2d 364, 377 (N.J.1984) ("expert's testimony, if accepted by the jury, would have aided it in determining whether, under the circumstances, a reasonable person would have believed there

was imminent danger to her life"); State v. Kelly, 102 Wash.2d 188, 685 P.2d 564, 570 (Wash.1984) (expert testimony "offered to aid the jury in understanding the reasonableness of [the defendant's] apprehension of imminent death or bodily injury").

21. *See, e.g.*, State v. Kelly, 97 N.J. 178, 478 A.2d 364, 372 (N.J.1984).

22. *See* L. WALKER (1984), *supra* note 4, at 95–104; L. WALKER (1979), supra note 4, at 55–70.

23. For further discussion of the cycle theory and consideration of the research underlying it, *see infra* § 2.1.2.

24. *See* L. WALKER (1984), *supra* note 4, at 95–96; L. WALKER (1979), *supra* note 4, at 55–70.

25. L. WALKER (1984), *supra* note 4, at 95.

26. *Id.* at 96.

27. *Id.*

28. *Id.*

29. *See* Loraine Patricia Eber, Note, *The Battered Wife's Dilemma: To Kill or To Be Killed*, 32 HASTINGS L.J. 895, 928 (1981).

harm.[30] This fear of harm continues even during the peaceful interlude between episodes of abuse.[31] It is during this lull in the violence that the woman may seize the opportunity to strike back at the batterer.[32] Thus, according to the cycle theory, the woman experiences the growing tension of phase one, develops a fear of death or serious bodily harm during phase two, and, perceiving that she will be unable to defend herself when the next attack comes, finally "defends" herself at her only opportunity.[33]

The cycle theory addresses primarily two essential aspects of the law of self defense: the defendant's knowledge of the aggressor's history of violence and the defendant's physical inability to protect herself. First, according to the theory, the battered woman's knowledge of the batterer's history of violence shapes her perception of harm. A woman's experience in the recurring cycles of violence puts her in constant fear of what appears to her as imminent harm. This factor goes to the first element of the battered woman's self-defense claim, the reasonableness of her belief in the necessity for self-defensive action. If the court allows the defendant to introduce evidence on the implications of the cycle theory, the defendant may be able to convince the jury that a reasonable person in her position would have perceived imminent danger and responded accordingly.

Second, battered woman cases typically involve women who cannot easily defend themselves against the attacks of a larger and stronger man. Here the cycle theory speaks to the second element of the self-defense claim, the reasonableness of the amount of force used to repel the aggression. If a woman perceives herself to be trapped in a cycle of potentially deadly violence, she may reasonably feel compelled to resort to deadly force in preempting the aggression of the unarmed but more powerful man.[34]

[2] Learned Helplessness

The cycle theory, in itself, may be insufficient to convince a jury that the battered woman acted in self-defense. Some states require the defendant to

---

30. *See, e.g.,* In re Appeal in Maricopa County, Juvenile Action No. JV–506561, 182 Ariz. 60, 893 P.2d 60, 63 (Ariz.App.1994) (referring to the state of mind resulting from BWS (here a child) as a "sustained 'heat of passion'" that was "sufficient to deprive a reasonable person of self-control."); *see generally Comment, Battered Wives Who Kill: Double Standard Out of Court, Single Standard In?* 2 LAW & HUM. BEHAV. 133, 164 (1978).

31. *See, e.g.,* Robinson v. State, 308 S.C. 74, 417 S.E.2d 88, 91 (S.C. 1992) (Because battered women suffer from a "perpetual terror of physical and mental abuse . . . [that] does not wane," a sense of imminent danger could exist "even when the batterer is absent or asleep."). *See generally* Michael A. Buda & Teresa L. Butler, *The Battered Wife Syndrome: A Backdoor Assault on Domestic Violence,* 23 FAM.L. 359, 375 (1984–85).

32. Walker argues that "sometimes, [the battered woman] strikes back during a calm period, knowing that the tension is building towards another acute battering incident, where this time she may die." L. WALKER

(1984), *supra* note 4, at 142. *But see,* State v. Reid, 155 Ariz. 399, 747 P.2d 560, 562 (Ariz. 1987) (rejecting use of the battered woman syndrome where defendant killed the batterer when he was asleep).

33. *See* Lumpkin v. Ray, 977 F.2d 508, 509 (10th Cir.1992) (asserting an Equal Protection claim [*see infra* § 4–1.3.2], the defendant argued "that the cyclical trap of the 'battered woman syndrome' sets the battered woman apart from others who have the financial and other resources and support, including reasonable access to police and courts, to supplement their smaller size and lack of ability to defend themselves").

34. *See generally* Catherine Mackinnon, *Toward Feminist Jurisprudence,* 34 STAN. L. REV. 703, 732 (1982) ("[W]omen thus perceive the need and do need to resort to deadly force, [and] are more threatened than they would be if they were trained the way men are trained.").

show that she could not have retreated from the threat of harm. More generally, Walker has argued that, even in jurisdictions that do not formally impose a duty to retreat, jurors will assume the defendant was unreasonable in failing to leave the abusive relationship.[35] According to Walker, jurors subscribe to "popular myths" regarding women who remain in violent relationships. These myths include "the belief that battered women are masochistic, that they stay with their mates because they like beatings, that the violence fulfills a deep-seated need within each partner, or that they are free to leave such relationships if that is what they really want."[36] Courts readily accept Walker's view that jurors, if not specially instructed, will believe the battered woman somehow consented to the beatings inflicted upon her.[37]

To explain why a woman in a "constant state of fear" does not simply leave the battering relationship, Walker invoked Martin Seligman's "learned helplessness" theory.[38] Seligman and his colleagues found that laboratory dogs, after being subjected to repeated shocks over which they had no control,

---

35. Lenore Walker, Roberta K. Thyfault & Angela Browne, *Beyond the Jurors' Ken: Battered Women*, 7 Vt. L. Rev. 1, 5 (1982).

The basic relevance of learned helplessness in self-defense cases comes from the real or perceived obligation that a victim of violence has a duty to retreat before acting defensively. In the context of domestic violence, most jurisdictions do not impose such a duty, though many fear that jurors will misunderstand a woman's "decision to stay in a violent relationship." In Weiand v. State, 732 So.2d 1044 (Fla.1999), the Florida Supreme Court joined this majority view: "We join the majority of jurisdictions that do not impose a duty to retreat from the residence when a defendant uses deadly force in self-defense, if that force is necessary to prevent death or great bodily harm from a cooccupant." *Id.* at 1051. This conclusion was supported, in part, by research indicating "that forty-five percent of the murders of women 'were generated by the man's rage over the actual or impending estrangement from his partner.' " *Id.* at 1053 (*quoting* Donald G. Dutton, The Batterer: A Psychological Profile 15 (1995) (additional internal quotation marks omitted)).

36. Walker et al., *supra* note 35, at 1–2.

37. In *State v. Kelly*, 97 N.J. 178, 478 A.2d 364 (N.J.1984), the court held that a jury must consider the factors restraining a battered woman before it can evaluate her conduct. The court stated that "[o]nly by understanding these unique pressures that force battered women to remain with their mates, despite their long-standing and reasonable fear of severe bodily harm and the isolation that being a battered woman creates, can a battered woman's state of mind be accurately and fairly understood." *Id.* at 372; *see also* State v. Borrelli, 227 Conn. 153, 629 A.2d 1105, 1112 (Conn.1993) (citing "research" that " 'indicate[s] that potential jurors may hold beliefs and attitudes about abused women at variance with the views of experts who have studied . . .

abused women' "); State v. Hodges, 239 Kan. 63, 716 P.2d 563, 566 (Kan.1986) ("The expert evidence would counter any 'common sense' conclusions by the jury that if the beatings were really that bad the woman would have left her husband much earlier.").

The courts frequently voice their assumption that most lay people—and hence most jurors—believe battered women enjoy or participate in the abuse. *See, e.g. id.* at 370. Indeed, this proposition seems to have taken on mythical proportions itself. The source the courts most often cite to buttress their assumption is Walker's 1979 book, The Battered Woman, which contains no empirical research on this question. L. Walker (1979), *supra* note 4, at 20. Walker merely alludes (without providing a reference) to a twenty-year-old study on abused wives suggesting that some women might enjoy the abuse because of masochistic tendencies. *Id.* Perhaps Walker is referring to a 1964 study that characterized battered women as "aggressive, efficient, masculine, and sexually frigid" and suggested the beatings provided "apparent masochistic gratification." Snell, Rosenwald & Robey, *The Wifebeater's Wife: A Study of Family Interaction*, 11 Archives Gen. Psychiatry 107, 111 (1964). At most, this severely outdated study shows only that some psychologists or psychiatrists believe that some women enjoy beatings; it cannot be taken to show that the general public holds this view. *See* James R. Acker & Hans Toch, *Battered Women, Straw Men, and Expert Testimony: A Comment on State v. Kelly*, 21 Crim.L.Bull. 125, 138–41 (1985) (noting that many jurors may be sympathetic to the woman's failure to *leave*). *See generally* P. Caplan, The Myth of Women's Masochism (1985) (exploring the psychoanalytic evidence regarding the masochism of women and questioning its validity).

38. *See* L. Walker (1984), *supra* note 4, at 86.

"learned" that they were helpless.[39] When subsequently placed in an escapable situation, the dogs failed to escape.[40] Seligman generalized this phenomenon to depression in humans.[41] Walker, applying this theory to the problem of battered women, explains that "the women's experiences ... of their attempts to control the violence would, over time, produce learned helplessness and depression as the 'repeated batterings, like electrical shocks, diminish the woman's motivation to respond.' "[42] The court in State v. Kelly[43] embraced this view, asserting that some women "become so demoralized and degraded by the fact that they cannot predict or control the violence that they sink into a state of psychological paralysis and become unable to take any action at all to improve or alter the situation."[44]

In addition, the third phase of the cycle theory—the loving contrition phase—is invoked to explain why battered women fail to leave violent relationships. According to Walker, the batterer's "extremely loving, kind, and contrite behavior"[45] operates as a "positive reinforcement for remaining in the relationship."[46] This loving and contrite behavior follows the acute battering incident and softens the woman's response to the extremely negative preceding phase. Therefore, a woman suffers the paralysis of learned helplessness due to the uncontrollable beatings, and, additionally, is lured into staying by that hope that things will be different in the future.

§ 4–1.1.3 Judicial Responses to the Battered Woman Syndrome in Self–Defense Cases

In general, courts have been sympathetic toward defense use of the battered woman syndrome in homicide prosecutions and most admit expert

39. *See* Martin Seligman, Steven Maier & James Geer, *Alleviation of Learned Helplessness in the Dog*, 73 J. ABNORMAL PSYCHOLOGY 256 (1968). Seligman and his associates placed the dogs in harnesses and subjected them to electrical shocks at random intervals. After initial attempts to escape proved futile, the dogs began to submit to the shocks without resistance. When the procedure was changed to present the dogs with an opportunity to escape, the "helpless" dogs failed to respond.

40. Many dogs overcame their helplessness after the experimenter physically dragged them from their confinement; other dogs, though, never learned to escape. *Id.* at 260–61.

41. See MARTIN SELIGMAN, HELPLESSNESS: ON DEPRESSION, DEVELOPMENT, AND DEATH (1975); Lyn Y. Abramson, Martin Seligman & John D. Teasdale, *Learned Helplessness in Humans: Critique and Reformulation*, 87 J. ABNORMAL PSYCHOLOGY 49, 50 (1978).

42. L. WALKER (1984), *supra* note 4, at 87 (quoting L. WALKER (1979), *supra* note 4, at 49).

43. 97 N.J. 178, 478 A.2d 364 (N.J.1984).

44. *Id.* at 372. The concept of learned helplessness is sometimes used outside of the traditional self-defense context. For example, in Parrish v. State, 237 Ga.App. 274, 514 S.E.2d 458 (Ga.App.1999), the defendant appealed his conviction for raping his ex-fiancee. After brutally beating her over an extended period of time, the defendant raped her at knifepoint. Defendant's counsel attempted to undermine the victim's credibility by questioning her failure to seek help during the long ordeal before the rape. The prosecution introduced the concept of learned helplessness from the battered woman syndrome in order to explain this failure. The appellate court found this to be proper, stating that "testimony regarding the 'learned helplessness' of women in abusive relationships was relevant to explain the victim's behavior." *Id.* at 463. The court, however, did not review the research supporting the learned helplessness phenomenon, and made no effort to determine whether the available research fit this novel use of it. In the usual self-defense case in which learned helplessness is posited, the phenomenon is said to be a product of the long period of abuse, typically lasting many years. In *Parrish*, however, the court did not mention a history of abuse prior to the brutal day of the attack and rape. In light of the theory regarding how learned helplessness develops over time, it does not seem to fit the facts of this case. A more prosaic explanation might have been that she was too fearful of the consequences if she had unsuccessfully sought help.

45. L. WALKER (1979), *supra* note 4, at 65.

46. L. WALKER (1984), *supra* note 4, at 96.

testimony concerning this issue. This sympathetic approach, however, has not been entirely uncritical.[47] This section surveys the major issues that arise when battered women defendants proffer expert testimony to support claims of self-defense.

[1] Legal Issues Surrounding the Battered Woman Syndrome

The battered woman syndrome is a multifaceted construct that addresses a wide assortment of legal issues ranging from implicit concerns over why the woman did not escape the violence to explicit concerns over the application of self-defense doctrine. Inextricably linked to these multifarious issues lies a basic query common to all admissibility standards for expert testimony: is expert testimony on the battered woman syndrome helpful to the trier of fact? In each of the contexts discussed below, courts evaluate the legal doctrine at two levels. First, they consider the parameters and integrity of the legal doctrine itself. Second, courts consider whether the expertise will assist triers of fact in applying the pertinent doctrine to the facts of the case before them.

The proponent of the battered woman syndrome must lay an adequate factual foundation to support its use. In *People v. Gomez*,[48] a prosecution of an alleged batterer for battery, the court found expert testimony on the battered woman syndrome to be "irrelevant," since there was no evidence that the victim had suffered prolonged abuse, that the defendant was a "batterer" or that the two lived in a "battering relationship."[49] Although *Gomez* involved prosecutorial use of the syndrome, it should be expected that a factual foundation would be required in all contexts in which the syndrome is used.[50]

[a] Failure to Leave the Abusive Relationship

Although not a component of self-defense doctrine in most jurisdictions, many courts and commentators express concern that triers of fact will misconstrue a woman's failure to leave a violent relationship.[51] Courts and commentators hypothesize that jurors will believe that the woman actively participated in the violence, enjoyed the abuse, or the violence was not that bad. These lay conjectures, many worry, will undermine a battered woman's claim of self-defense.[52] Moreover, the need to dispel "common myths" is

---

47. *See, e.g.,* State v. Norman, 324 N.C. 253, 378 S.E.2d 8, 12–14 (N.C.1989).

48. 72 Cal.App.4th 405, 85 Cal.Rptr.2d 101 (Cal.App.1999).

49. *Id.* at 108.

50. In *Duran v. State*, 990 P.2d 1005 (Wyo. 1999), the court upheld a trial court's exclusion of battered woman syndrome expert testimony because the underlying facts did not support a claim of self-defense. The court explained that the "battered woman syndrome statute does not create a separate defense; it permits the introduction of expert testimony on the battered woman syndrome when the affirmative defense of self-defense is raised." *Id.* at 1009 (internal quotations omitted). Accordingly, "[o]nce the trial court determined that self-

defense was not an appropriate defense in this case[,] . . . reliance on the statute was misplaced." *Id.*

51. Many jurisdictions require that the expert testimony be "beyond the ken of the average layperson" for admission. The Federal Rules of Evidence require that the expert evidence "assist the trier of fact," a standard generally thought to be more liberal than the "beyond the ken" standard. FED. R. EVID. 702; *see* Chapter 1, *Legal Standards*. Still, many courts use these standards interchangeably. *See, e.g.,* State v. Hennum, 441 N.W.2d 793, 798 (Minn.1989).

52. The "common myths" believed to be held by triers of fact regarding the reasons why a battered woman might fail to leave an abusive relationship are discussed *supra* note 37.

especially urgent, courts find, when those myths are relied upon by the prosecution in making its case.[53]

In practice, however, courts do little more than cite the recurring fear that juries hold these "common myths" about battered women.[54] They do not cite any research indicating that such myths are commonly held, nor do they express chagrin that such research does not exist. In addition, courts rarely take the trouble to determine the fit between explanations such as learned helplessness and the facts of a particular case. Indeed, learned helplessness, as a psychological construct, is fundamentally at odds with a situation in which a woman has exercised the degree of control reflected in the act of self-defense.[55] Finally, in many cases, non-psychological factors, such as threats or economic dependence, might fully explain the woman's failure to escape the violence. The need for expert testimony on the syndrome is not obvious where such factors are present.

It should be noted that using the syndrome as an explanation for why the woman did not leave the abusive relationship might open the door to prosecutorial attacks on the defendant's character that would tend to prove otherwise. For example, in *State v. Daws*,[56] the court held as follows:

> Because [the defendant] claimed to be suffering from the Battered Woman Syndrome, we believe the State was entitled to present evidence in rebuttal that [she] was not afraid of her husband and had engaged in prior violent acts against him ..., all of which cast doubt on her proclaimed status as a victim.[57]

This suggests that a cost that must be factored into the defense's decision whether to rely on battered woman syndrome expert testimony is opening the door to the defendant's past bad acts.[58]

[b]   Imminent Harm

In self-defense cases in which the battered woman syndrome is introduced, courts and defendants alike typically struggle to wrench the facts of their cases into the traditional framework. In the paradigm case of self-defense, a person is confronted with no choice but to kill; using a proportional amount of force, this defender kills out of necessity. Proponents of the

---

53. *See, e.g.*, People v. Day, 2 Cal.App.4th 405, 2 Cal.Rptr.2d 916, 922–24 (Cal.App.1992) (court found that defense counsel's failure to proffer battered woman syndrome expert testimony constituted ineffective assistance of counsel, because of the misconceptions relied upon by the prosecution regarding the battered woman's role in the violence and her failure to escape it).

54. *See, e.g.*, State v. Hodges, 239 Kan. 63, 716 P.2d 563, 567 (Kan.1986) ("Expert testimony on the battered woman syndrome would help dispel the ordinary lay person's perception that a woman in a battering relationship is free to leave at any time.").

55. Faigman, *supra* note 3, at 641 ("[F]rom a theoretical perspective one would predict that if battered women suffered from learned helplessness they would not assert control over their environment; certainly, one would not predict such a positive assertion of control as killing the batterer.").

56. 1997 WL 736502 (Ohio App.1997); *see also* State v. Free, 1998 WL 57373 *15–16 (Ohio App.1998) (allowing questions about the defendant's "previous miscarriage and who she was dating" after she "opened the door" by claiming that she suffered from the battered woman syndrome).

57. *Id.* at 11.

58. The *Daws* court held that the state could only offer character evidence regarding the defendant in rebuttal, and not in its case-in-chief.

battered woman syndrome have been successful in showing that primarily male notions of self-defense inform this paradigmatic scenario, a scenario that bears little resemblance to the circumstances and necessities confronting women in violent relationships. The syndrome specifically targets the insight associated with the imminence requirement by indicating that even when not confronting a specific overt act threatening immediate harm, a woman can honestly and reasonably believe she must kill in self-defense.[59] This Part begins by examining the parameters of self-defense doctrine and, in particular, how courts have struggled to define the acceptable limits of these parameters, both before and after the fatal act. It then goes on to examine the honesty and reasonableness factors intrinsic to the defense. Finally, this part briefly examines the philosophical bases for the defense and the syndrome's convergence with this foundation.

[i] Incongruence Between Battered Women Cases and Traditional Notions of Self–Defense

The perceived need to educate triers of fact sometimes depends on the specific circumstances of the case. For example, in *People v. Minnis*,[60] the defendant testified that her husband died after she kicked him off her while he was raping her.[61] After she ascertained that he was dead, she decided to dismember the body and deposit various sections of the corpse in different dumpsters.[62] At trial, the defendant proffered the battered woman syndrome to explain this bizarre act. The trial court excluded the evidence; the Illinois appellate court reversed. The trial court had "arrived at the fixed and immutable conclusion that the syndrome applies only to explain the woman's conduct at the time of the victim's death, *not to events which transpire afterwards.*"[63] The appellate court disagreed with the trial court's limited perspective, noting that the "defendant clearly has the right to introduce evidence [on the battered woman syndrome] to rebut the State's evidence of consciousness of guilt."[64] In light of the relevance of the testimony, "the defendant had a right to present evidence relevant to her explanation of her conduct, no matter how far-fetched it might appear to the average individual."[65]

In contrast, in *Lentz v. State*,[66] the Mississippi Supreme Court upheld the trial court's exclusion of battered woman syndrome expert testimony because the circumstances surrounding the killing were inconsistent with the defendant's theory of self-defense.[67] In *Lentz*, the defendant had shot her boyfriend twice, at two different points in time.[68] After the first shot, the evidence indicated that the victim tried to retreat, but the defendant followed him and

59. *See* Bechtel v. State, 840 P.2d 1, 12 (Okla.Crim.App.1992) ("[T]he meaning of imminent must necessarily envelope the battered woman's perceptions based on all the facts and circumstances of ... her relationship with the victim.").

60. 118 Ill.App.3d 345, 74 Ill.Dec. 179, 455 N.E.2d 209 (1983).

61. *Id.* at 215.

62. *Id.*

63. *Id.* at 217 (emphasis supplied).

64. *Id.*

65. *Id.*

66. 604 So.2d 243 (Miss.1992).

67. *See also* Fultz v. State, 439 N.E.2d 659, 662 (Ind.Ct.App.1982) (excluding expert testimony on BWS, "because the victim had not committed an aggressive act sufficient for [the defendant] to form a reasonable belief that an imminent use of force was necessary").

68. 604 So.2d at 247.

shot him again in the back.[69] According to the court, evidence on the battered woman syndrome was irrelevant: "upon these facts ... neither the evidence nor the issue of whether [the defendant] acted as a reasonable person would in similar circumstances have been made clearer by expert testimony."[70]

Perhaps the most extraordinary use of the syndrome in self-defense cases is in response to a homicide charge arising out of the defendant's hiring of a "hit-man" to do the killing. Courts uniformly exclude expert testimony in these kinds of cases.[71] In *People v. Yaklich*,[72] for example, the defendant hired a man to kill her husband, and paid him $4,200 to commit the offense.[73] At her trial, the defendant was acquitted of murder after presenting a self-defense claim based on her status as a battered woman; however, the jury convicted her of conspiracy to commit first-degree murder.[74] The state appealed this verdict and argued that the trial court had erroneously instructed the jury on self-defense.[75]

At the outset, the Court of Appeals noted that no Colorado court had yet decided whether women who kill their batterers during a lull in the violence were entitled to a self-defense instruction.[76] Next, the court reviewed the general characteristics of the battered woman syndrome and observed that "numerous cases across the country have held that the battered woman syndrome is 'a recognized phenomenon in the psychiatric profession and is defined as a technical term of art in professional diagnostic textbooks.' "[77] After examining several other battered women cases that included "murder-for-hire" situations, the court concluded that a self-defense instruction should not be provided in "contract-for-hire" cases.[78] The court explained that no other jurisdictions allowed such an instruction under similar circumstances.[79] In addition, the court declared that "a self-defense instruction in a murder-for-hire situation would undermine ancient notions of self-defense which

---

69. *Id.*

70. *Id. See also* State v. Norman, 324 N.C. 253, 378 S.E.2d 8, 12-15 (N.C.1989) (The court concluded that a self-defense instruction was inappropriate where the battered woman was not abused immediately prior to the shooting and where the defendant retrieved a gun from her mother's house and, after the gun jammed the first time she tried shooting it, she fixed it and then shot her husband three times in the head.)

71. *See* People v. Yaklich, 833 P.2d 758 (Colo.Ct.App.1991); *see also* State v. Martin, 666 S.W.2d 895, 899 (Mo.Ct.App.1984) (concluding that "the evidence here falls woefully short of establishing an issue of justifiable self-defense"); State v. Anderson, 785 S.W.2d 596, 600 (Mo.Ct.App.1990) (finding that the defendant had failed to raise the issue of self-defense adequately).

The situation of a battered woman who hired a "hit-man" provided the background for a challenge, ultimately rejected, to the imposition of a capital sentence in *Ex Parte Haney*. 603 So.2d 412 (Ala.1992). In *Haney*, the defendant argued that her status as a battered woman should have precluded the court from im-

posing the death penalty as a punishment for her husband's murder. *Id.* at 413. Haney and two family members plotted to kill Haney's husband after Haney fled her home to escape from her husband's abuse. *Id.* at 416. The murder was committed by Haney's brother-in-law, and Haney paid him $3,000 for the killing. *Id.* at 417. The conspirators eluded detection for nearly four years, until Haney's sister finally confessed to the crime. *Id.* The Alabama Supreme Court did not find that these circumstances counseled leniency. *Id.* at 418. The court observed that the "record discloses a continuous pattern of lies told by Haney ... and reveals a cold and calculating attitude toward the murder." *Id.* at 417.

72. 833 P.2d 758 (Colo.Ct.App.1991).

73. *Id.* at 759.

74. *Id.*

75. *Id.* at 760.

76. *Id.* at 762.

77. *Id.* at 760 (*quoting* State v. Allery, 101 Wash.2d 591, 682 P.2d 312 (Wash.1984)).

78. *Id.* at 762.

79. *Id.*

originated in the common law and were later codified in Colorado law."[80] Finally, the defendant's active role in the crime precluded a self-defense instruction: "[W]e would be establishing poor public policy if [the defendant] were to escape punishment by virtue of an unprecedented application of self-defense while the . . . [contract killers] were convicted of murder."[81]

[ii] Honesty of Belief in Need to Use Deadly Force

Most American courts require juries evaluating a self-defense claim to focus on the *objective* reasonableness of the defendant's belief that he was in imminent danger.[82] Under this objective test, the defendant must in fact have believed self-defense was necessary, and this belief must also be reasonable by the standards of the ordinary person. By contrast, the subjective test followed in some jurisdictions requires only that the defendant have honestly believed that self-defensive action was necessary; that this belief was unreasonable will not defeat the defendant's claim.[83] The distinction between the objective and subjective tests can be elusive.[84] A court nominally applying the objective test

80. *Id.*

81. *Id.*

82. *See* W. LaFave & A. Scott, *supra* note 7, at 393–94.

83. *See, e.g.,* State v. Leidholm, 334 N.W.2d 811, 818 (N.D.1983) (Trial court erred in not instructing the jury to "assume the physical and psychological properties peculiar to the accused . . ., to place itself as best it can in the shoes of the accused, before deciding whether the circumstances surrounding the incident were sufficient to create a sincere and reasonable belief in the need to use force."). *See generally* Wayne R. LaFave & Austin W. Scott, Jr., § 5.7(c) Criminal Law 457 (2d ed. 1986 & 1995 Supp.). The Model Penal Code adopts the subjective test: "[T]he use of force upon or toward another person is justifiable when the actor believes that such force is immediately necessary for the purpose of protecting himself against the use of unlawful force by such other person on the present occasion." Model Penal Code § 3.04(1) (Proposed Official Draft 1962). Under the Model Penal Code, "deadly force is not justifiable . . . unless the actor believes that such force is necessary to protect himself against death, serious bodily harm, kidnaping or sexual intercourse by force or threat. . . ." *Id.* § 3.02(2)(b).

84. In a widely quoted passage, the Kansas Supreme Court observed as follows regarding the mental state of the defendant in syndrome cases:

> Battered women are terror-stricken people whose mental state is distorted and bears a marked resemblance to that of a hostage or a prisoner of war. The horrible beatings they are subjected to brainwash them into believing there is nothing they can do. . . . Under the facts of this case, after ten years of abuse, [the defendant] finally became so desperate in her terror . . . [of the decedent] she

fled. Her escape was to no avail; he followed her. Her fear was justified. . . . The objective test is how a reasonably prudent battered wife would perceive . . . [the decedent's] demeanor. Expert testimony is admissible to prove the standard mental state of hostages, prisoners of war, and others under long-term life-threatening conditions.

State v. Hundley, 236 Kan. 461, 693 P.2d 475, 479 (Kan.1985). *Hundley* entirely blurs any distinction between the objective and the subjective. In Bechtel v. State, 840 P.2d 1 (Okla. Crim.App.1992), the court similarly had difficulty keeping the standards clear. The Oklahoma standard for determining the reasonableness of the defendant's action is as follows:

> A person is justified in using deadly force in self-defense if that person reasonably believed that use of deadly force was necessary to protect herself from imminent danger of death or great bodily harm. Self-defense is a defense although the danger to life or personal security may not have been real, *if a reasonable person, in the circumstances and from the viewpoint of the defendant, would reasonably have believed that she was in imminent danger of death or great bodily harm.*

Id. at 11 (emphasis supplied). The court referred to this standard as a "hybrid," "combining both the objective and subjective standards" of reasonableness. *Id.* While the jury was to "assume the viewpoint and circumstances of the defendant in assessing her reasonableness," the standard also requires "the defendant's viewpoint to be that of a reasonable person." *Id.* In order to accommodate its decision to allow syndrome expert testimony, the court decided to modify the self-defense instruction in cases involving self-defense claims by battered women. The modified instruction consisted of the following language:

may allow the jury to consider so many of the defendant's unique circumstances that the hypothetical "reasonable person" assumes most of the fears and weaknesses of the defendant.[85] The jury may thus come close to evaluating the necessity of self-defensive action as the defendant saw it.[86]

The defendant's honest belief in the need to use deadly force is generally relevant whether the jurisdiction applies an objective test or a subjective test in self-defense cases. Given the psychological etiology of the defense, courts readily find syndrome evidence to be relevant to the subjective aspects of the defendant's perception and thus the honesty of her belief. The New Jersey Supreme Court explained that the expert's testimony "would have helped the jury understand that [the defendant] could have honestly feared that she would suffer serious bodily harm from her husband's attacks, yet still remain with him."[87] The use of the battered woman syndrome to bolster a defendant's claim of honesty is closely linked to the unusual circumstances of these cases, and especially the duration of the abuse, which might suggest to jurors a lack of good faith.

Similarly, in *Ibn-Tamas,* the District of Columbia Court of Appeals held that the defendant's credibility should be supported by expert evidence on the battered woman syndrome.[88] The court concluded that the expert's testimony "would have supplied an interpretation of the facts which differed from the ordinary lay perception . . . advocated by the government."[89] Since the government had implied that "the logical reaction of a woman who was truly frightened by her husband . . . would have been to call the police . . . or to leave him," the defense needed to offer evidence to rebut this assumption.[90] By proffering expert testimony on battered women's characteristics, the defense would have "enhanced [the defendant's] general credibility" and

---

A person is justified in using deadly force in self-defense if that person believed that use of deadly force was necessary to protect herself from imminent danger of death or great bodily harm. Self-defense is a defense although the danger to life or personal security may not have been real, if a person, in the circumstances and from the viewpoint of the defendant, would have believed that she was in imminent danger of death or great bodily harm.

Id. Thus, the court omitted all references to "reasonable" beliefs or behavior in this modified instruction. The court also decided to state explicitly that under this new standard, "the meaning of imminent must necessarily envelope the battered woman's perceptions based on all the facts and circumstances of . . . her relationship with the victim." *Id.* at 7.

85. In *State v. Hodges,* 239 Kan. 63, 716 P.2d 563 (Kan.1986), the Kansas Supreme Court stated that the battered woman syndrome was relevant under both subjective and objective interpretations of self-defense:

In a state that follows the subjective standard, an evaluation of defendant's actions is made in light of her subjective impressions and the facts and circumstances known to her. . . . In states following the objective standard, the jury must determine whether

the defendant's belief in the need to defend one's self was reasonable and the expert's testimony, if accepted by the jury, would aid it in determining whether, under the circumstances, a reasonable person in the defendant's position would have believed her life to be in imminent danger.

Id. at 569; *but see* Lentz v. State, 604 So.2d 243, 246–47 (Miss.1992) (ruling that BWS was "irrelevant" under state's objective standard).

86. *See, e.g.,* People v. Goetz, 68 N.Y.2d 96, 506 N.Y.S.2d 18, 497 N.E.2d 41 (N.Y.1986) (The court, though maintaining an "objective standard," permitted the defendant to introduce "any prior experiences he had which could provide a reasonable basis for [his] belief" that he would be "maimed" by his attackers.); *see generally* GEORGE FLETCHER, A CRIME OF SELF-DEFENSE (1988).

87. *Kelly,* 478 A.2d at 375.

88. *Ibn-Tamas,* 407 A.2d at 633–34.

89. *Id.* at 635; *see also* State v. Allery, 101 Wash.2d 591, 682 P.2d 312, 316 (Wash.1984) (Court found that syndrome testimony would assist the "jury in understanding a phenomenon not within the competence of an ordinary lay person.").

90. *Ibn-Tamas,* 407 A.2d at 634.

bolstered her assertion that "her husband's actions had provoked a state of fear which led her to believe she was in imminent danger."[91]

[iii]   Reasonableness of Belief in Need to Use Deadly Force

A somewhat more controversial application of the battered woman syndrome concerns its use to support the defendant's contention that her employment of deadly force was *reasonable*. Courts that permit the expert evidence to show reasonableness approach the question in one of two ways. First, some courts accept that the history of abuse and, in particular, the nature of that abuse, is pertinent to the reasonableness of the defendant's belief in the need to use deadly force. Alternatively, many courts appear to adopt a quasi-subjective reasonableness standard, by establishing the relevant comparison to be a reasonable battered woman rather than the ordinary reasonable person.

In *State v. Kelly*,[92] the New Jersey Supreme Court found expert testimony on the syndrome, with its description of the nature of the abuse suffered by the defendant, to be relevant to the reasonableness of the defendant's deadly action. The court observed as follows:

> At the heart of the claim of self-defense was defendant's story that she had been repeatedly subjected to "beatings" over the course of her marriage.... [A] juror could infer from ... the detail given concerning some of these events (the choking, the biting, the use of fists), that these physical assaults posed a risk of serious injury or death. When that regular pattern of serious physical abuse is combined with defendant's claim that the decedent sometimes threatened to kill her, defendant's statement that on this occasion she thought she might be killed ... could be found to reflect a reasonable fear; that is, it could so be found if the jury believed [the defendant's] story of the prior beatings ... and, of course, if it believed her story of the events of that particular day.[93]

In contrast, many courts appear to adopt a quasi-subjective standard for reasonableness by changing the comparison group from ordinary reasonable persons to ordinary battered women. In *State v. Hundley*, for example, the court declared that "[t]he objective test is how a reasonably prudent battered wife would perceive ... [the decedent's] demeanor."[94] This expansion of the objective test of reasonableness poses the danger of becoming so broad that it metamorphosizes into the subjective test. At some point, identification with the defendant's situation and circumstances can become so specific that, given her experience, whatever is honestly believed must also be reasonable.

[c]   *Use of the Battered Woman Syndrome to Provide Context or a "Social Framework"*

In 1987, Professors Walker and Monahan described an emerging use of social science in law in which research could be used to provide a background

---

91. *Id.*; *see also* State v. Koss, 49 Ohio St.3d 213, 551 N.E.2d 970, 973 (Ohio 1990) (Applying a subjective standard, the court found expert testimony to be admissible "to help the jury understand the battered woman syndrome ... [and] also to determine whether the defendant had reasonable grounds for an honest belief that she was in imminent danger when considering the issue of self-defense.").

92. 97 N.J. 178, 478 A.2d 364 (N.J.1984).

93. *Id.* at 377; *see also* Robinson v. State, 308 S.C. 74, 417 S.E.2d 88, 91 (S.C.1992) ("where torture appears interminable and escape impossible, the belief that only the death of the batterer can provide relief may be reasonable in the mind of a person of ordinary firmness").

94. *Hundley*, 693 P.2d at 479.

context for deciding factual issues crucial to the resolution of a specific case.[95] Some scholars have argued that battered woman syndrome research is especially suited for this use.[96] Under this approach, the research could provide jurors with contextual information in which they could understand the battered woman's behavior. The testimony would give jurors general information about domestic violence and its victims, without necessarily speaking to the particular woman's actions. The subsequent admissibility of clinical expert testimony about whether the battered woman is typical of the group characteristics, or is "suffering" from a syndrome, would be separately considered.

Minnesota has effectively limited expert testimony on the battered woman syndrome to this framework use. In *State v. Ritt*,[97] the Minnesota Supreme Court stated that "[e]xpert testimony is helpful and admissible if it explains a behavioral phenomenon not within the understanding of an ordinary lay jury, such as battered woman syndrome or the behavior of sexually abused children."[98] The court explained that "[t]estimony on battered woman syndrome is limited to a description of the syndrome's general nature and the expert is not allowed to testify whether a particular defendant or witness suffers from the syndrome because the expert testimony may be perceived as evidence on the ultimate issue of guilt or innocence, or as an unwarranted 'stamp of scientific legitimacy' to the testimony."[99]

[d] Justification or Excuse?

Substantial confusion attends the battered woman syndrome concerning the jurisprudential bases for the defense. Specifically, many courts approach these claims as based on excuse, rather than justification, or, alternatively, create some hybrid of the two. Claims of self-defense, however, are based entirely on a theory of justification. Thus, someone who kills in self-defense is not morally culpable because society considers the act to be justified. The action is one that, upon sober reflection, society considers to have been correct under the circumstances. The theory of the battered woman syndrome adheres closely to this justification rationale; in fact, the syndrome so closely parallels the law of self-defense that its basic parameters appear dictated more by legal convenience than psychological observation or theory.

Many courts construe the defense when battered woman syndrome testimony is offered as partly or wholly based on principles of excuse. Hence, some courts place syndrome testimony in such legal categories as diminished

---

95. Laurens Walker & John Monahan, *Social Frameworks: A New Use of Social Science in Law*, 73 VA.L.REV. 559, 563–70 (1987).

96. *See* Robert P. Mosteller, *Syndromes and Politics in Criminal Trials and Evidence Law*, 46 DUKE L.J. 461 (1996) (preferring the term "group character" evidence); *see also* Robert P. Mosteller, *Legal Doctrines Governing the Admissibility of Expert Testimony Concerning Social Framework Evidence*, 52 LAW & CON-

TEMP. PROBS. 85 (Autumn 1989); Neil Vidmar & Regina A. Schuller, *Juries and Expert Evidence: Social Framework Testimony*, 52 LAW & CONTEMP. PROBS. 133 (Autumn 1989).

97. 599 N.W.2d 802 (Minn.1999).

98. *Id.* at 811.

99. *Id.* (internal citations omitted).

capacity or insanity.[100] And even when courts correctly interpret the theory as one based on justification, they invariably describe the defendant as "suffering" from the *syndrome,* as though it were a medical malady. This "mental disability" perspective has important ramifications for the law as well as battered women defendants.

Louisiana perhaps best illustrates the extreme interpretation of the theory as indicating that the woman suffers from a psychological infirmity that is offered to excuse her conduct. In *State v. Necaise,*[101] for example, the defendant claimed self-defense in the shooting death of her husband. She was convicted of manslaughter and appealed, arguing that she should have been permitted to introduce expert testimony about the battered woman syndrome.[102] Relying on case law, the appellate court affirmed the conviction.[103] The court expressed its reluctance to allow any evidence of the syndrome to be admitted in homicide prosecutions:

> We believe that allowing testimony which would attempt to prove the defendant a victim of "battered woman syndrome" and which would seek to establish her "state of mind" at the time of the shooting, absent a plea of "not guilty and not guilty by reason of insanity," would be, in effect, condoning the concept of "partial responsibility"—the allowing of proof of mental derangement short of insanity as evidence of lack of "deliberate or premeditated design." The concept of partial or impaired responsibility has been rejected in this State in favor of an "all or nothing" (i.e., sane or insane) approach.[104]

Clearly, in light of the theoretical underpinnings of the defense, the Louisiana courts have misunderstood the nature of the defense. Proponents of the syndrome have always maintained that the basis for the defense is the reasonableness of the woman's actions given the circumstances of her life; the basis does not rest on any claimed psychological incapacity inflicted upon the woman by these circumstances.[105] In *Hawthorne v. State,*[106] for example, the court specifically cautioned that expert testimony on the battered woman

100. *See, e.g.,* State v. Mott, 183 Ariz. 191, 901 P.2d 1221 (Ariz.App.1995) (The court reversed the trial court's exclusion of the battered woman syndrome in a child abuse case, rejecting the state's argument that the defendant was "essentially raising the defense of diminished capacity, a defense not permitted in Arizona."); Anderson v. Goeke, 44 F.3d 675, 681 (8th Cir.1995) (Eighth Circuit held that trial court had not violated due process by admitting the battered woman syndrome "only as evidence of diminished capacity (by which to negate the mens rea element), and not as an affirmative defense."); *see also* Cathryn Jo Rosen, *The Excuse of Self–Defense: Correcting A Historical Accident on Behalf of Battered Women Who Kill,* 36 Am.U.L.Rev. 44 (1986).

101. 466 So.2d 660 (La.Ct.App.1985).

102. *Id.* at 663.

103. *Id.* at 664 (*citing* State v. Edwards, 420 So.2d 663, 677 (La.1982)). The *Edwards* court had categorized the battered woman syndrome as a diminished capacity defense and noted that Louisiana law prohibits "evidence of a mental condition or defect ... when the defendant failed to plead not guilty and not guilty by reason of insanity." *Edwards,* 420 So.2d at 678.

104. *Necaise,* 466 So.2d at 665. *See also* State v. Moore, 568 So.2d 612, 617 (La.Ct.App. 1990) (defendant had asserted an insanity defense based on the battered woman syndrome, but had failed to demonstrate insanity "by a preponderance of the evidence").

105. *See* People v. Torres, 128 Misc.2d 129, 488 N.Y.S.2d 358, 361–62 (Sup.Ct.1985) (The court observed that the syndrome was not "intended to establish that ... [it] was a mental disease or defect relieving defendant of criminal responsibility." Instead, the court asserted that "the syndrome is best understood as being descriptive of an identifiable group of symptoms that characterize the behavior and state of mind of abused women rather than being disease-like in character.").

106. 408 So.2d 801 (Fla.Dist.Ct.App.1982).

syndrome should not be categorized as an attempt to establish the defendant's diminished capacity and lack of responsibility for the shooting.[107] Instead, such testimony "would be offered to show that because ... [the defendant] suffered from the syndrome, it was reasonable for her to have remained in the home and ... to have believed that her life and the lives of her children were in imminent danger."[108] Thus, this expert testimony spoke directly to the self-defense doctrine's requirement that the defendant "reasonably believed it was necessary to use deadly force to prevent imminent death or great bodily harm."[109]

Much of the blame for judicial confusion over the legal relevance of syndrome theory lies with proponents of the theory. Foremost, the choice of the label "syndrome" suggests a medical/biological genesis for the condition, rather than a social or behavioral basis. Undoubtedly, advocates believe that likening the phenomenon to a medical condition or malady enhances its credibility. While this may have occurred, this gain has been achieved at significant cost. In addition to doctrinal confusion, courts may be simply accepting traditional stereotypes of women in adopting a defense based on a "cycle of violence" that results in "helplessness."[110] What began as an attempt to educate the law on the realities and necessities of domestic violence has evolved into an excuse-based defense founded on the helplessness of the woman defendant. Moreover, the medical linkage makes the action "understandable" rather than "reasonable," and thus fails to explain why a battered woman kills with justification; instead, the syndrome defense merely makes triers of fact sympathetic to the woman's plight. This might explain why syndrome testimony has been mainly effective in reducing the severity of the offenses for which these defendants are convicted, instead of winning outright acquittals.[111]

One particularly salient consequence of the courts' medical model approach to battered women cases is the likelihood that they will require defendants to undergo psychiatric examinations by the prosecution. This was the issue presented in *State v. Hickson*.[112] In *Hickson*, in response to the defendant's proffer of expert testimony on the battered woman syndrome, the state filed a motion to require the defendant to submit to a psychiatric examination by the state's expert.[113] On appeal, the Florida Supreme Court held that the defendant would have to submit to a state psychiatric hearing, unless she did not apply the syndrome evidence to her case.[114] Specifically, the

107. *Id.* at 807.

108. *Id.*

109. *Id.* at 806. In *Pugh v. State*, 191 Ga. App. 394, 382 S.E.2d 143 (Ga.App.1989), the trial court had excluded all expert testimony regarding the battered woman syndrome because the defendant had failed to comply with a court rule entitled, "Notice of Intention of Defense to Raise Issue of Insanity, Mental Illness or Mental Incompetency." *Id.* at 143. The Court of Appeals held that this decision was clear error since "the Supreme Court [of Georgia] has specifically held that evidence of the battered woman syndrome is independently admissible in conjunction with a claim of self-defense." *Id.* at 144.

110. *See* Elizabeth M. Schneider, *Describing and Changing Women's Self-Defense Work and the Problem of Expert Testimony*, 9 WOMEN'S RIGHTS LAW REPORTER 195 (1986).

111. *See* C. Ewing, *supra* note 18, at 55–56.

112. 630 So.2d 172 (Fla.1993).

113. *Id.* at 173.

114. *Id.* at 175–76; *see also* State v. Manning, 74 Ohio App.3d 19, 598 N.E.2d 25 (Ohio App.1991) (The court held that the defendant has "introduce[d] psychiatric evidence and place[d] her state of mind directly at issue ... [thus,] she can be compelled to submit to a [sic] independent examination by a state psychiatrist."); Bechtel v. State, 840 P.2d 1, 7–9

court held that as long as the defense's expert does not provide an opinion on whether the defendant herself suffers from the battered woman syndrome, no examination of the defendant can be conducted by the opposing side's expert.[115] However, if the defendant chooses to proffer expert testimony that links the syndrome to the facts of her case, then "she waives her right to refuse to submit to an examination by the state's expert."[116] The court reasoned that "if a defendant were able to rely on her statements being presented to a trier of fact through an expert's testimony, she would, in effect, be able to testify without taking the stand and subjecting herself to the state's questions."[117]

Similarly, *People v. Rossakis*[118] offers a particularly illuminating example of courts' difficulty in understanding the jurisprudential basis for the defense and the concomitant dangers this creates for women employing the defense. In this murder case, the prosecution sought to preclude the defendant from offering battered woman syndrome expert testimony or, in the alternative, sought an order compelling the defendant to give notice of her intent to offer psychiatric or psychological evidence to support her claim of justification. The defendant planned to enter a claim of "justification" in response to the People's murder charges and contended that the introduction of the battered woman syndrome did not "give rise to a . . . [statutory] notice requirement and the . . . obligation of subjecting herself to a psychiatric/psychological examination."[119]

The trial court held that expert testimony regarding the syndrome was admissible because it had "a substantial bearing on the defendant's state of mind at the time of the shooting . . . and is probative of the reasonableness of defendant's apprehension of danger at the time of the shooting."[120] However, the court also decided that such evidence fell within New York's statutory definition of "psychiatric evidence," thus requiring the defendant to provide written notice of her intent to present the evidence. The court asserted that the "defendant seeks to escape punishment for the shooting by reason of her claimed mental condition at the time of the commission of the acts charged."[121] Thus, the court declared that "fundamental fairness requires that notice pursuant to CPL 250.10 be served and the People be permitted to conduct a psychiatric/psychological examination of her."[122]

(Okla.Crim.App.1992) (Despite finding that the battered woman syndrome is not a "mental disease," the court concluded that, "at the discretion of the trial court, . . . [defendants must] submit to an examination by the State's expert witness.").

115. *Hickson,* 630 So.2d at 175; *see also* State v. Schaller, 199 Wis.2d 23, 544 N.W.2d 247 (Wis.App.1995) (compelled psychiatric examination is not required where the woman's experts testify only to general characteristics of battering relationships).

116. *Hickson* 630 So.2d at 176.

117. *Id. See also* State v. Briand, 130 N.H. 650, 547 A.2d 235, 238–40 (N.H.1988) (The court held that requiring the defendant to sub-mit to a psychiatric examination does not violate her Fifth Amendment right against self-incrimination, since the defendant waives this right by introducing expert testimony on the battered woman syndrome. Therefore, a defendant who decides to undergo an examination by a mental health professional of her own choosing and "evinces the intention to rely on that testimony at trial" must submit to a court-ordered psychiatric examination.).

118. 159 Misc.2d 611, 605 N.Y.S.2d 825 (Sup.Ct.1993).

119. *Id.* at 827.

120. *Id.*

121. *Id.* at 828.

122. *Id.*

§ 4–1.1.4 Judicial Responses to the Battered Woman Syndrome in Other Criminal Contexts

[1] The Defense of Duress

The battered woman syndrome is increasingly being used by defendants for crimes committed seemingly in complicity with their abusers, but for which they claim duress. Most of the legal issues in duress cases are similar to those in self-defense cases, including, in particular, the specific relevance of the expert testimony to the elements of a duress defense and general concerns over the objective versus subjective nature of the defense.

In *United States v. Homick*,[123] the Ninth Circuit, in a case involving a battered woman, held that the defendant claiming duress must show that she: (1) was suffering an "immediate threat of death or serious bodily injury;" (2) had "a well-grounded fear that the threat will be carried out;" and (3) had "no reasonable opportunity to escape the threatened harm."[124] These elements bear a close resemblance to those of self-defense and syndrome testimony similarly is offered as relevant to all three elements of the defense.

The courts that have considered the syndrome in duress cases vary in their receptivity to this evidence.[125] In *United States v. Willis*,[126] the Fifth Circuit gave this evidence a cool reception.[127] In *Willis*, the defendant admitted that she and her male companion had planned to sell marijuana to an undercover officer; however, she contended that the gun found in her purse at the time of her arrest was her companion's gun.[128] The defendant testified that she was extremely fearful of her companion and allowed him to put the gun in her purse immediately before their apprehension because she believed that if she objected to carrying the gun, he would have beaten her.[129] Accordingly, she argued, she had not "knowingly, intentionally, or voluntarily" carried the gun and "did so only under duress."[130]

---

123. 964 F.2d 899 (9th Cir.1992).

124. *Id.* at 906.

125. Sometimes, courts' receptivity depends on whether the specific facts of the case support the defense. For example, in People v. Herrera, 219 A.D.2d 511, 631 N.Y.S.2d 660 (App.Div.1995), the defendant appealed her conviction, arguing that her proffered testimony regarding the syndrome should have been admitted by the trial court. She alleged that her accomplice and co-defendant "had abused and coerced her into committing the crime." *Id.* at 662. The court affirmed the trial court's decision, noting that there was no testimony "laying a foundation regarding the co-defendant's alleged abusive behavior toward [the defendant]." *Id.* Thus, the psychologist's proffered testimony "would not have been based on admissible evidence." *Id.*

126. 38 F.3d 170 (5th Cir.1994).

127. The Ninth Circuit also gives syndrome evidence a chilly reception in duress cases. *See* United States v. Johnson, 956 F.2d 894 (9th Cir.1992); United States v. Homick, 964 F.2d 899 (9th Cir.1992). Many other courts follow suit. *See* United States v. Morton, 153 F.3d 724 (4th Cir.1998); United States v. Madoch, 149 F.3d 596 (7th Cir.1998); Maestas v. State, 963 S.W.2d 151 (Tex.App.1998); State v. Lucus, 87 Wash.App. 1084 (1997). *See also* Foster v. Commonwealth, 827 S.W.2d 670, 682–83 (Ky. 1991) (Kentucky Supreme Court found that the trial court erroneously admitted syndrome testimony in a duress case in which the alleged abuser was another woman: "the syndrome by its own definition is inapplicable to the relationship these co-defendants may have had with each other."); Cox v. State, 843 S.W.2d 750, 754–56 (Tex.App.1992) (Court rejected use of syndrome evidence where the woman "was able to exert herself and could control her husband's action to some extent when she deemed it necessary.").

128. *Willis*, 38 F.3d at 173.

129. *Id.* at 174.

130. *Id.*

On appeal, the defendant argued that the trial court had erroneously excluded expert psychological testimony concerning the battered woman syndrome.[131] Applying an abuse of discretion standard, the court reviewed the elements of a successful duress defense, emphasizing that the "requirements are addressed to the impact of a threat on a *reasonable* person."[132] According to the court, since syndrome testimony was "inherently subjective," it did not provide any insight into "whether a person of reasonable firmness would have succumbed to the level of coercion present in a given set of circumstances."[133] Rather, such testimony would merely establish that the defendant's psychological condition rendered her "unusually susceptible to ... coercion."[134] Because this testimony fails to address the objective components which comprise a duress defense, the court concluded that the evidence was not relevant.[135] The court explained as follows:

> To consider battered woman syndrome evidence in applying ... [the] test ... would be to turn the objective inquiry that duress has always required into a subjective one. The question would no longer be whether a person of ordinary firmness could have resisted. Instead, the question would change to whether this individual woman, in light of the psychological condition from which she suffers, could have resisted.[136]

The Ninth Circuit held similarly in *United States v. Johnson,*[137] observing that courts are reluctant to "vary legal norms with the individual's capacity to meet the standards they prescribe, absent a disability that is both gross and verifiable."[138] In *Johnson,* however, the court concluded that syndrome testimony was relevant at sentencing.[139] The court noted that federal sentencing guidelines allow courts to reduce a sentence if the defendant "committed the offense because of serious coercion, blackmail or duress, under circumstances not amounting to a complete defense."[140] Furthermore, the guidelines state that courts should consider "the reasonableness of the defendant's actions" as well as "the circumstances as the defendant believed them to be."[141] Therefore, although battered woman syndrome testimony could not be taken into

131. *Id.*

132. *Id.* at 175 (emphasis supplied). The *Willis* court summarized the elements of duress as follows:

(1) The defendant was under an unlawful and present, imminent, and impending threat of such a nature as to induce a well-grounded apprehension of death or serious bodily injury; (2) that the defendant had not recklessly or negligently placed herself in a situation in which it was probable that she would be forced to choose the criminal conduct; (3) that the defendant had no reasonable legal alternative to violating the law, a chance both to refuse to do the criminal act and also to avoid the threatened harm; and (4) that a direct causal relationship may be reasonably anticipated between the criminal action taken and the avoidance of the threatened harm.

Id.

133. *Id.*

134. *Id.*; *See also* State v. Riker, 123 Wash.2d 351, 869 P.2d 43, 51 (Wash.1994) (In a duress defense, the defendant sought admission of syndrome testimony, even though she was not battered by the claimed source of the duress, but had merely once been in a battering relationship. The court observed that "[w]ithout requiring a foundation which would distinguish [the defendant's] fear from that of every other citizen who has a troubled past, there is a danger that the evidentiary doors will be thrown open to every conceivable emotional trauma.").

135. *Willis,* 38 F.3d at 176.

136. *Id.*

137. 956 F.2d 894 (9th Cir.1992).

138. *Id.* at 898.

139. *Id.*

140. *Id.*

141. *Id.*

account when determining a woman's criminal liability, it could be considered in setting her sentence.

The application of the battered woman syndrome to the defense of duress has been received more warmly by the Tenth Circuit. In *Dunn v. Roberts,*[142] the court held that the district court's refusal to provide expert witness funds to a defendant claiming a duress defense infringed her due process rights.[143] The defendant was charged with aiding and abetting felony murder, kidnaping, and aggravated battery.[144] The charges stemmed from a long trip to Florida the defendant took with Daniel Remeta.[145] During the trip, Remeta repeatedly physically abused the defendant, threatened her with a gun, and told her that he would hurt her or her family if she tried to leave him.[146] The violent threats culminated in a crime spree, during which Remeta shot a police officer and another man, then killed two hostages.[147] The defendant sought to introduce syndrome testimony to demonstrate that she lacked the necessary intent to aid and abet any of these crimes.[148] The trial court denied the defendant's request for funds to hire an expert witness, and she was convicted.[149] After the Kansas Supreme Court affirmed her conviction, the defendant petitioned for a writ of habeas corpus, and the district court granted the writ. The district court held that the defendant was unable to present an effective defense as a result of the trial court's refusal to grant expert witness fees and granted her a new trial.[150] The state appealed.

The Tenth Circuit observed that one of the "basic tools of an adequate defense" was expert psychiatric assistance when "a defendant makes a threshold showing that her mental condition at the time of an offense is likely to be a 'significant factor' at trial."[151] Finding that the case "rested on [the defendant's] ... ability to show that she lacked the requisite intent," the court concluded that the trial court's denial of expert witness funds "precluded Petitioner from presenting an effective defense."[152] Because expert testimony could have explained "why a defendant suffering from the battered woman syndrome wouldn't leave her batterer," the court stated that "such evidence could have provided an alternative reason for Petitioner's continued presence with Daniel Remeta."[153]

In cases in which battered women defendants claim duress, therefore, syndrome testimony closely parallels its use in self-defense cases. Its relevance comes from its purported power to explain why a battered woman might believe she was in "imminent harm" and why she failed to leave the abuser before the perpetration of criminal acts.[154] Moreover, the syndrome is purportedly relevant to whether the defendant had the requisite intent, especially when specific intent is required.[155] However, as in its application to self-

---

142. 963 F.2d 308 (10th Cir.1992).

143. *Id.* at 309–310. The issue of a defendant's right to state supported expert witness testimony concerning the battered woman syndrome is discussed *infra* § 11–1.3.1.

144. *Id.*

145. *Id.* at 310.

146. *Id.*

147. *Id.*

148. *Id.* at 311.

149. *Id.*

150. *Id.*

151. *Id.*

152. *Id.*

153. *Id.* at 314.

154. *But see* State v. Riker, 123 Wash.2d 351, 869 P.2d 43, 51 (Wash.1994) (holding that duress requires "immediate" harm, while self-defense requires "imminent" harm).

155. *See Dunn,* 963 F.2d at 313 (holding that the battered woman syndrome is relevant as to whether the defendant had specific intent to assist the crimes).

defense doctrine, courts are confused regarding the exact import of the evidence. Some courts interpret the syndrome as an excuse-type defense, relevant to the subjective state of mind or mental disability of the defendant, rather than the objective reasonableness of her decision to comply with a threat of imminent harm.[156]

[2] Miscellaneous Defenses

In addition to self-defense and duress, battered woman syndrome testimony has been offered in a variety of other contexts. These cases typically raise questions concerning the state of mind of the defendant at the time of the alleged crime.[157] For example, in *Clenney v. State*,[158] the Georgia Supreme Court considered whether syndrome testimony was admissible to determine the "voluntariness" of the defendant's pretrial statements.[159] At trial, defense counsel proffered expert testimony in order to "rebut the state's contention that the appellant was not remorseful and had lied in her statements, and to explain her post-arrest state of mind."[160] The court determined that the testimony was not admissible for this purpose since the "jury could decide the issue as to the appellant's remorse or lack of it without the aid of expert-witness testimony, this not being a conclusion 'beyond the ken of the average layman.' "[161]

In contrast, in *State v. Mott*,[162] the Arizona Court of Appeals reversed a trial court's exclusion of battered woman syndrome in a child abuse case. In *Mott,* the defendant had left her two-year-old daughter with her boyfriend.[163] When she returned approximately an hour later, she found her daughter unconscious.[164] Her boyfriend said her daughter had hit her head when she fell off the toilet.[165] Although a friend offered to transport the child to a hospital several times that evening, the boyfriend refused and would not allow the defendant to accept the friend's offer.[166] The next morning, paramedics were summoned when her daughter began having seizures.[167] Medical tests revealed that the child had suffered a brain hemorrhage; she died a week later.[168]

---

156. *See* United States v. Sebresos, 972 F.2d 1347 (9th Cir.1992) [Unpublished Disposition], in which the court held that the district court had not erred in rejecting the defendant's expert testimony on "spouse abuse syndrome." *Id.* at *3. The defendant was attempting to establish a duress defense; however, the proffered testimony would have focused on the expert's diagnosis that the defendant was suffering from depression and "dependent personality disorder" and could not act voluntarily. *Id.* at *2. The court declared that such testimony was at odds with a duress defense, which acknowledges that the defendant acted voluntarily, but claims no other choice was possible. *Id.* The court concluded that "individual psychological incapacity cannot be the basis for a duress defense." *Id.*

157. *See generally* McMaugh v. State, 612 A.2d 725, 728–34 (R.I.1992) (Court granted the defendant post-conviction relief after she intro-

duced creditable evidence that she implicated herself in a murder because of her husband's abuse directed at attempting to have her exonerate him.).

158. 256 Ga. 123, 344 S.E.2d 216 (Ga. 1986).

159. *Id.* at 218.

160. *Id.*

161. *Id.*

162. 183 Ariz. 191, 901 P.2d 1221 (Ariz. App.1995).

163. *Id.* at 1222.

164. *Id.*

165. *Id.*

166. *Id.*

167. *Id.*

168. *Id.*

The trial court denied the defendant's proffer of syndrome testimony, finding that "it was not relevant to any recognized defense."[169] According to the state, the defendant was "essentially raising the defense of diminished capacity, a defense not permitted in Arizona."[170] The Court of Appeals rejected this argument, citing earlier Arizona cases that permitted "character evidence" to be introduced when it was intended to negate "the mental element of the offense charged," rather than "relieve the defendant of responsibility."[171] Since the Arizona statute under which the defendant was charged required that she "intentionally or knowingly" permitted a child to suffer physical injury, the court reasoned that syndrome testimony was admissible "to negate the state's contention that [the defendant] acted with intent or knowledge when she temporarily left [her daughter] with [her boyfriend], and when she failed to promptly take [her daughter] to the hospital."[172] The trial court's exclusion of the expert testimony constituted a denial of due process because the defendant had been denied "the opportunity to present evidence essential to her defense."[173]

In a somewhat unusual use for the battered woman syndrome, the court in *Commonwealth v. Crawford*,[174] found that the trial court committed reversible error in excluding syndrome expert testimony regarding the voluntariness of the defendant's confession. The defendant claimed that she was a battered woman and was suffering from post-traumatic stress disorder when she confessed to being involved in the killing of the victim. The trial court had apparently excluded the psychological evidence because the judge had been previously exposed to it and he thought it was "within the common experience of the ordinary juror."[175] The appellate court disagreed, and found that he should have heard the testimony before ruling and that the psychological testimony was relevant, and should have been permitted, to assist the jury in determining the voluntariness of the confession.[176]

§ 4–1.2   Prosecution Use of the Battered Woman Syndrome

Prosecutorial use of the syndrome raises different issues—some posing a greater chance of unfair prejudice to the opposing party— than when employed by defendants. Prosecutors typically offer the syndrome to support or bolster the credibility of battered women who testify in prosecutions of their batterers. Battered women witnesses occasionally change their testimony in favor of the defendant, and thus prosecutors use the syndrome to explain this

---

169. *Id.* at 1224.

170. *Id.*

171. *Id.*

172. *Id.* at 1225.

173. *Id. See also* Rice v. State, 113 Nev. 1300, 949 P.2d 262, 277 (Nev.1997) (Springer, J., concurring in part and dissenting in part) ("The battered woman syndrome is often accepted by the courts to explain and justify the actions of women who are accused of crimes. The theory amply explains why [the defendant] may have delayed her decision to call in professional care until the baby's back started to blister."). In re Glenn G., 154 Misc.2d 677, 587 N.Y.S.2d 464, 470 (Fam.Ct.1992) (The court dropped child abuse charges brought against a mother who, because of the battered woman syndrome, could not "be said to have 'allowed' the abuse within the meaning" of the statute. A finding of "neglect" was entered against the mother since that statute imposed "strict liability."); *but see* Campbell v. State, 999 P.2d 649, 659–60 (Wyo.2000) (Court stated that the statute allowing expert evidence of battered woman syndrome "expressly limits its reach to the affirmative defense of self-defense. Self-defense does not apply when charged with child endangerment.").

174. 429 Mass. 60, 706 N.E.2d 289 (Mass. Sup.Jud.Ct. 1999).

175. *Id.* at 294.

176. *Id.* at 294–95.

otherwise inexplicable behavior. Yet, introduction of the syndrome against defendants raises substantial questions of fairness under both specific rules against character evidence and general principles reflected in evidence rules that exclude evidence when its probative value is substantially outweighed by unfair prejudice.

Arcoren v. United States[177] offers a typical illustration of the prosecutorial use of the syndrome.[178] The defendant was charged with, among other things, aggravated sexual abuse.[179] The defendant's spouse provided details of the sexual and physical abuse that she suffered to the grand jury; but she later recanted this testimony at trial.[180] In order to explain her reversal, the prosecutor offered battered woman syndrome expert testimony from a psychologist. The trial court found that the testimony met the requirements of Rule 702 and admitted it. However, the trial court limited the scope of this testimony by prohibiting the expert from offering an opinion about whether " 'a particular party in this case ... actually suffers from battered women syndrome.' "[181]

On appeal, the Eighth Circuit observed that the jury was confronted with a "bizarre situation."[182] According to the court, "a jury naturally would be puzzled at the complete about-face ... [the victim] made, and would have great difficulty in determining which version ... it should believe."[183] The court concluded that the "expert testimony regarding the battered woman syndrome provided the explanation."[184] The defendant, however, argued that

---

177. 929 F.2d 1235 (8th Cir.1991).

178. For a nearly identical factual pattern to *Arcoren*, *see* State v. Borrelli, 227 Conn. 153, 629 A.2d 1105 (Conn.1993); *see also* Thompson v. State, 203 Ga.App. 339, 416 S.E.2d 755, 757 (Ga.App.1992); State v. Cababag, 9 Haw.App. 496, 850 P.2d 716, 719 (Haw.App.1993); People v. Christel, 449 Mich. 578, 537 N.W.2d 194 (Mich.1995); State v. Frost, 242 N.J.Super. 601, 577 A.2d 1282, 1287 (App.Div.1990); People v. Morgan, 58 Cal.App.4th 1210, 68 Cal. Rptr.2d 772, 775 (Cal.App.1997) (allowing the syndrome "to explain or offer a motive for [the witness'] recantation and thereby reconcile inconsistencies in her testimony"); State v. Grecinger, 569 N.W.2d 189, 193 (Minn.1997) (Court held that the expert would help "the jury understand the delay in reporting and the inconsistencies in the victim's testimony."); State v. Bahn, 578 N.W.2d 208, 208 (Wis.App. 1998) ("A psychotherapist testified regarding the features of this syndrome and the 'cycle of violence' which can include the victim's recantation of her accusations and delays in reporting episodes of abuse."); Odom v. State, 711 N.E.2d 71, 76 (Ind.Ct.App.1999) ("[A]n expert ... who was undisputably qualified as an expert in domestic violence, is able to offer those additional reasons which may aid the jury in determining the witness' credibility. Therefore, we cannot conclude that because a victim/witness provides an explanation for her recantation, expert testimony which also tends to explain the witness' recantation is necessarily irrelevant.").

179. 929 F.2d at 1237.

180. *Id.* at 1238.

181. *Id.* The expert testified that "a 'battered woman' is one who assumes responsibility for a cycle of violence occurring in a relationship." *Id.* The expert also described the "general characteristics of the syndrome," including the victim's belief that the violence is her fault, an inability to attribute responsibility for abuse to the batterer, fear for both her life and her children's and "an irrational belief that the abuser is omnipresent and omniscient." *Id.*

182. *Id.* at 1240.

183. *Id. See also* State v. Ciskie, 110 Wash.2d 263, 751 P.2d 1165, 1173 (Wash.1988) (Court allowed syndrome testimony in a rape prosecution where the "defense challenged [the victim's] ... credibility and attempted to persuade the jury that her failure to leave the relationship, or to complain earlier to a doctor or police, was inconsistent with ... [the behavior] of a rape victim.").

184. *Arcoren*, 929 F.2d at 1240. *See also* People v. Hryckewicz, 221 A.D.2d 990, 634 N.Y.S.2d 297, 298 (1995) (In upholding prosecutorial use of the syndrome, the court observed that it " 'explain[ed] behavior on the part of the complainant that might seem unusual to a lay jury unfamiliar with the patterns of response exhibited' by a person who has been physically and sexually abused over a period of time.").

the battered woman syndrome should not be permitted outside the context of defense use in self-defense claims.[185] The Eighth Circuit disagreed, stating that "the standard under Rule 702 ... is whether the 'evidence will assist the trier of fact to understand the evidence or determine a fact in issue.' ... [I]t is immaterial whether the testimony is presented by the prosecution or by the defense."[186]

The Eighth Circuit is not entirely accurate in its conclusion that the identity of the proponent of expert syndrome testimony is irrelevant. A battered woman defendant to a homicide charge offers syndrome testimony for very different purposes than a prosecutor might in an assault or homicide prosecution. In both, however, the evidence raises concerns over the use of character to prove conduct. Although syndrome testimony is typically portrayed as a description of the victim, it is actually defined by the pattern of violence practiced by the abuser.[187] Inevitably, therefore, prior bad acts committed by the abuser will be presented to the trier of fact.[188] Most evidence codes, however, draw sharp distinctions concerning the admissibility of prior bad acts depending on whether the alleged perpetrator of those acts is the defendant.[189]

To be sure, the prosecution does not proffer the battered woman syndrome to prove the character of the defendant; instead it is offered to explain the behavior of the battered woman witness. The structure of all rules of evidence is such that one relevant use of the evidence is sufficient to allow introduction of the evidence. As in other contexts, however, the defendant is probably entitled to an instruction concerning the limited scope of the testimony. Moreover, given the little attention such instructions probably receive, the danger that juries will be prejudiced by the evidence must be factored into a Rule 403 balance.

The Rule 403 balance does not obviously favor admission of the syndrome to authenticate the prior statements of a prosecution witness who has

---

185. *Arcoren*, 929 F.2d at 1241.

186. *Id.* (*quoting* Fed.R.Evid. 702); *see also* State v. Frost, 242 N.J.Super. 601, 577 A.2d 1282, 1287 (App.Div.1990) ("[I]t would seem anomalous to allow a battered woman, where she is a criminal defendant, to offer this type of expert testimony in order to help the jury understand the actions she took, yet deny her that same opportunity when she is the complaining witness ... and her abuser is the criminal defendant.").

187. In *Parrish v. State*, 237 Ga.App. 274, 514 S.E.2d 458 (Ga.Ct.App.1999), the court held that in a rape prosecution it was error to allow the state's expert to testify "regarding the typical characteristics of an abuser." *Id.* at 463. The court concluded that the expert's "testimony regarding the typical batterer's drug and alcohol abuse" had "improperly placed [the defendant's] character in issue." *Id. See also* State v. Pargeon, 64 Ohio App.3d 679, 582 N.E.2d 665 (Ohio App. 1991) (The prosecution's use of the syndrome "really serves as evidence of the prior bad acts of the appellant from which the inference may be drawn that appellant has the propensity to beat his wife and that he beat her on this particular occasion."); Ryan v. State, 988 P.2d 46, 57 (Wyo.1999) ("After showing that [batterers] tended to commit homicide when faced with the prospect of separation, [the expert] impliedly invited the jury to group [the defendant] among those subjects and by this method determine conduct."). *See generally* Mosteller (1989), *supra* note 96, at 109–12.

188. *See, e.g.*, Thompson v. State, 203 Ga. App. 339, 416 S.E.2d 755, 757–58 (Ga.App. 1992) (The court rejected defendant's complaint that the expert's testimony had exceeded its scope because the expert alluded to "certain acts committed by the defendant." The court declared that these references "were necessary and reasonable" to the expert's testimony concerning the syndrome.).

189. *See* Chapman v. State, 258 Ga. 214, 367 S.E.2d 541, 542–43 (Ga.1988) (When the "defendant makes a prima facie showing that the victim was the aggressor ... and ... the defendant was honestly trying to defend himself," then a defendant may introduce evidence about the victim's violent propensities.).

changed her testimony. Foremost, this use comes perilously close to testimony affirming the credibility of a witness, a use generally prohibited by courts.[190] Moreover, the syndrome was not designed with this use in mind and no research whatsoever supports the conclusion that battered women are more likely than any other complainant to change their testimony at trial.[191] In fact, since there is no research on the likelihood that battered women are more likely to change their testimony than other witnesses, Rule 702 should exclude the testimony; there is no "fit" between the research and the expert opinion on this matter.

Indeed, the relevance of the syndrome research that has been done, when proffered to bolster battered woman's testimony against her alleged abuser, is not altogether obvious. None of the dependent (outcome) measures used in the original or subsequent research indicates that battered women are likely to be inconsistent witnesses. Moreover, the witness who changes her story fearing retribution, possesses a motive that is readily understandable by the average lay-juror. The admissibility of past occurrences of violence should be evaluated separately to determine their relevance and their possible prejudicial effect. Courts confronting expert testimony on the battered woman syndrome do not always carefully evaluate the true relevance of the research supporting the expert testimony.[192] As courts come to better understand the

190. In a somewhat novel use of the battered woman syndrome, in *People v. Howard*, 305 Ill.App.3d 300, 238 Ill.Dec. 658, 712 N.E.2d 380 (Ill.App.1999), the prosecutor introduced a syndrome expert to buttress the credibility of the state's main witness. The defendant was accused of murdering Carrie Gaines, the victim. The state's only witness was the victim's mother who had apparently witnessed the death and subsequent surreptitious burial of her daughter. She then continued to live with the defendant for five years. *Id.* at 380–81. In order to help explain this bizarre behavior on the part of the victim's mother, the state introduced syndrome testimony to account for it. On appeal, the court found that the defendant's conviction had to be overturned because of the use of this evidence. *Id.* at 385. The court found that the only relevance of this evidence was to support the credibility of the state's witness. "[T]rial courts should reject the State's attempts to use expert testimony to bolster the credibility of witnesses, as these are matters best left to the trier of fact." *Id.* at 384. The court concluded that permitting evidence of the defendant's abusive behavior after the victim's death substantially prejudiced him. *Id.* at 385–86. The court remanded for a new trial.

191. In *State v. Bednarz*, 179 Wis.2d 460, 507 N.W.2d 168 (Wis.App.1993), the court concluded that because "an untrained lay person does not know that recantation can be suggestive of post traumatic stress [disorder] in the form of 'battered woman syndrome,' expert testimony provided by the prosecution allows the jury to assess an additional explanation for the victim's actions that would have been unavailable without expert testimony." *Id.* at

172. The court cited no support for this proposition and did not explain its basis for believing in its validity.

192. In *State v. Baker*, 120 N.H. 773, 424 A.2d 171 (N.H.1980), the prosecution introduced the battered woman syndrome for a highly unusual purpose. The defendant was charged with attempted murder of his wife, and he entered a plea of not guilty by reason of insanity. After the defendant's experts completed their testimony indicating that the defendant was insane at the time of the crime, the prosecution introduced testimony from an expert on the battered woman syndrome. The prosecution's expert testified that "current research does not indicate that mental illness is an important cause of wife-beating." *Id.* at 172. Moreover, the expert concluded that the defendant's marriage "probably f[e]ll within the contours of the 'battered woman syndrome.' " *Id.* On appeal, the defendant argued that the prosecution's expert's testimony was "only marginally relevant" and was "highly prejudicial." *Id.* The New Hampshire Supreme Court disagreed, noting that "when the proffered evidence is relevant and otherwise unobjectionable, we will uphold the court's decision to admit evidence claimed to be prejudicial unless it is so inherently prejudicial as to constitute an abuse of discretion." *Id.* Because the battered woman syndrome testimony supplied "an alternative explanation for the defendant's assault on his wife," it was relevant to the "determination of the defendant's mental condition at the time of the offense." *Id.*

Unfortunately, the court failed to note that none of the research studying the battered

research measures used to study this issue, they should become more careful in their legal balancing of probative value and prejudicial effect.

§ 4–1.3   Constitutional Issues Raised in Battered Women Cases

Two constitutional guarantees, in particular, have been addressed at length in battered women cases involving defenses to homicide prosecutions. The first concerns the Fifth and Fourteenth Amendment guaranties of effective representation by counsel. The second concerns an Equal Protection challenge to a state's law of self-defense that, assertedly, discriminates against women. These issues are considered in turn.

§ 4–1.3.1   Due Process and Effective Counsel

The matter of the minimum standard of representation guaranteed by the Constitution to battered women claiming self-defense in homicide prosecutions is manifested in two contexts. First, several courts have examined whether due process requires governments to provide funds for expert testimony on the battered woman syndrome. In addition, courts have considered whether counsel's failure to assert a defense premised on the battered woman syndrome constitutes ineffectiveness of counsel.

The most important decision to hold that due process requires governmental support of defendant's expert witnesses is *Dunn v. Roberts*,[193] In *Dunn*, the Tenth Circuit granted the petitioner's writ of habeas corpus from her conviction following the trial court's refusal, later affirmed by the Kansas Supreme Court, to grant her expert witness funds. The court observed that one of the "basic tools of an adequate defense" was expert psychiatric assistance when "a defendant makes a threshold showing that her mental condition at the time of the offense is likely to be a 'significant factor' at trial."[194] The court concluded that the trial court's denial of expert witness funds "precluded Petitioner from presenting an effective defense"[195] and thus she was "deprived of the fair trial due process demands."[196]

Similarly, in *People v. Evans*,[197] the Illinois Appellate Court reversed the trial court's denial of an indigent defendant's request for funds to hire an expert on the battered woman syndrome.[198] The defendant had hired the

woman syndrome has studied the abusers as subjects. Although psychologists have studied abusers, the court did not cite any of this research, or otherwise explain the connection between syndrome research on victims of abuse and conclusions drawn about the mental state of abusers. Thus, the primary, if not exclusive, significance of the prosecution's use of syndrome expertise was to introduce past bad acts of the defendant. The court did not consider the possible prejudice of this evidence and, indeed found it to be a virtue. The court observed that this evidence supported the prosecution's theory that the defendant's attempted murder was only a "single episode in a recurring pattern of domestic violence," which was similar to prosecutorial arguments in child abuse prosecutions in which admission of battered child syndrome expert testimony is sought to prove that pediatric injuries are "not

accidental but rather ... consistent with a pattern of physical abuse." *Id*. These reasons reverberate with the sounds of character evidence.

193. 963 F.2d 308 (10th Cir.1992); the facts and general analysis of *Dunn* are discussed *supra* notes 142–153 and accompanying text.

194. 963 F.2d at 312.

195. *Id*. at 313.

196. *Id*. at 314.

197. 271 Ill.App.3d 495, 208 Ill.Dec. 42, 648 N.E.2d 964 (Ill.App.1995).

198. *Id*. at 965. In State v. Dannels, 226 Mont. 80, 734 P.2d 188 (Mont.1987), the Montana Supreme Court affirmed the lower court's denial of defendant's request for expert witness funds. Dannels is somewhat unusual,

expert before petitioning the court for the necessary funds, and the court refused to authorize funds to pay the expert, finding that the "hours are padded" and "the amount of money is excessive."[199] The appellate court stated that if the defendant's case would be prejudiced without the expert and the expert's services are needed "to prove a crucial issue in the case," then the expert is "necessary."[200] The court found that in this case the expert's services were needed to address the "defendant's state of mind at the time of the killing."[201] According to the court, without the expert's testimony, the "evidence at trial would tend to belie the conclusion that ... [the defendant] reasonably believed that deadly force was necessary ... and thus undermine her claim of self-defense."[202] The court remanded the matter to the trial court to determine a reasonable fee for the defendant's expert witness.[203]

Courts have also considered the parameters of due process in determining whether a defense counsel's failure to rely on syndrome testimony in a homicide prosecution of a battered woman constituted ineffective assistance of counsel.[204] Courts have shown great reluctance to find that defense counsel's failure to employ the battered woman syndrome constituted ineffective assistance of counsel. Courts typically rule that the decision to forego use of the syndrome was a matter of trial tactics and within the broad discretion of counsel.[205] There are, however, exceptions to this usual outcome. For example, in *People v. Day*,[206] the court held that the defendant was denied effective assistance of counsel because her attorney failed to "investigate or present evidence of Battered Woman Syndrome."[207] The court ruled that syndrome testimony should have been proffered to rebut the prosecution's argument

however, since the defendant sought expert assistance to "buttress her credibility." *Id.* at 192–93. The court stated that, since the defendant "did not seek to prove that she suffered from abused spouse syndrome [sic] and ... did not have the necessary state of mind to commit the homicide," her expert testimony was inadmissible. *Id.* at 192. The court referred to a Montana statute that allows evidence of a defendant's "mental disease or defect" to be admitted if "it is relevant to prove that the defendant did or did not have a state of mind which is an element of the offense." *Id.* (*citing* Mont.Code.Ann. § 46–14–102). Presumably, however, if the defendant had offered "abused spouse syndrome" to prove a "mental disease or defect" and presuming that such evidence is relevant to this issue, expert witness funds would be made available in Montana.

199. *Evans,* 648 N.E.2d at 966.

200. *Id.* In *State v. Aucoin,* 756 S.W.2d 705 (Tenn.Crim.App.1988), the court rejected the defendant's claim that she was entitled to receive funds to hire a private psychologist to testify on the syndrome. The trial court had provided enough funds to hire a psychiatrist who testified on her behalf; this was sufficient, according to the court. *Id.* at 714.

201. *Evans,* 648 N.E.2d at 969.

202. *Id.*

203. *Id.* at 971.

204. In *Commonwealth v. Stonehouse,* 521 Pa. 41, 555 A.2d 772 (Pa.1989), although de-

fendant's appellate counsel informed the court during oral argument that "battered woman syndrome is not implicated in the case," a plurality of the court concluded otherwise. *Id.* at 774. The plurality declared that "there was no reasonable basis for trial counsel not to call an expert witness to counter the erroneous battered woman myths upon which the Commonwealth built its case." *Id.* at 784–85. Two other justices joined the plurality's conclusion that trial counsel was ineffective, but they protested the plurality's decision to address the syndrome. *Id.* at 785.

205. *See, e.g.,* United States v. Nelson, 141 F.3d 1186 (10th Cir.1998); United States v. Valdez, 125 F.3d 860 (9th Cir.1997); Foreshaw v. Commissioner of Correction, 48 Conn.App. 122, 708 A.2d 600 (Conn.App.1998); Brown v. State, 698 N.E.2d 1132 (Ind.1998); State v. Sallie, 81 Ohio St.3d 673, 693 N.E.2d 267 (Ohio 1998).

206. 2 Cal.App.4th 405, 2 Cal.Rptr.2d 916 (1992).

207. *Id.* at 925. *But see* People v. Ransome, 207 A.D.2d 504, 615 N.Y.S.2d 911, 911 (App. Div.1994) (Court rejected appellant's ineffective assistance of counsel claim where the defense counsel "made appropriate motions and objections, vigorously cross-examined the People's witnesses, and strenuously argued the defendant's position to the jury.").

that the defendant's conduct was inconsistent with self-defense.[208] The court explained that "[battered woman syndrome] evidence would have deflected the prosecutor's challenge to appellant's credibility. Such evidence would have assisted the jury in objectively analyzing appellant's claim of self-defense by dispelling many of the commonly held misconceptions about battered women."[209] Since the failure to present such evidence may have led "to a conclusion based on misconceptions," the court held that defense counsel's oversight was prejudicial.[210] Furthermore, the court noted that the jury had deliberated for a lengthy period of time, had requested clarification on self-defense law, and had reviewed the testimony, indicating that the "case was close."[211] Thus, the defendant was entitled to a new trial.[212]

§ 4–1.3.2 Equal Protection

In a novel challenge to traditional self-defense law, the defendant in *Lumpkin v. Ray*[213] argued that she was "deprived by Oklahoma law of a reasonable opportunity to present ... evidence [concerning the battered woman syndrome] because of the imminence requirement of the Oklahoma statute defining self-defense."[214] In addition, the defendant claimed "that the cyclical trap of the 'battered woman syndrome' sets the battered woman apart from others who have the financial and other resources and support, including reasonable access to police and courts, to supplement their smaller physical size and lack of ability to defend themselves."[215] The Tenth Circuit rejected this argument, finding that the defendant failed to produce evidence at trial of "the existence or characteristics of the discrete group of women suffering from 'battered woman syndrome.' "[216]

The court's analysis emphasized that the defendant had failed to articulate clearly "whether the basis of her equal protection claim was that the Oklahoma self-defense statute discriminated against her because she was a woman or because she was a *battered* woman."[217] The court explained that if the defendant sought to challenge the statute because it discriminated against *all* women, she would not have to define the class, "nor would she be required to prove her inclusion in that class."[218] However, the defendant would have to prove "why the class of all women is disadvantaged by the statute."[219] On the other hand, if the defendant claimed that the statute discriminated specifical-

---

208. *Day,* 2 Cal.Rptr.2d at 921–22.

209. *Id.* at 922.

210. *Id.*

211. *Id.*

212. *Id.* In a consistent holding, in *State v. Scott,* 1989 WL 90613 (Del.Super.Ct.1989), the court granted the defendant's motion to withdraw her guilty plea to a manslaughter charge after determining that the defendant received ineffective assistance of counsel. The defendant's attorney urged her to plead guilty, telling her that the "battered woman's defense" was "relatively novel" in Delaware, and expressed "reservations as to its applicability." *Id.* Interpreting Delaware's self-defense statute, the court found that deadly force is justifiable if the *defendant,* rather than a reasonable person, believes that it is necessary to employ

such force to protect herself from death or serious bodily harm. DEL.CODE.ANN. Tit. 11, § 464(c)(1994). Since the statute uses a subjective test to determine whether deadly force was justified, the court reasoned that the defendant's own perceptions about the danger posed by the victim were relevant. 1989 WL 90613 at *2. Thus, the court concluded that it was "not open to doubt that a colorable claim of self-defense was available to [the defendant]." *Id.*

213. 977 F.2d 508 (10th Cir.1992).

214. *Id.* at 509.

215. *Id.*

216. *Id.* at 510.

217. *Id.* (emphasis supplied).

218. *Id.*

219. *Id.*

ly against *battered* women, then "she would be required at trial to define the class of those with 'battered woman syndrome,' to prove her inclusion in that class, and to show why the class of those with battered woman syndrome is disadvantaged by strict application of the statute."[220] The Tenth Circuit concluded that the defendant had failed to provide sufficient "discrete group evidence" at trial to support her equal protection challenge to the Oklahoma statute.[221]

§ 4–1.4 Civil Cases

In the civil context, expert testimony on the battered woman syndrome is typically offered in divorce or child custody cases. It is introduced for many of the same reasons it is employed in criminal cases including, especially, to explain behavior on the part of the woman that appears inconsistent with supposed expectations of laypersons. In *Pratt v. Wood*,[222] for example, a child's maternal grandparents filed a petition to obtain custody. The child's mother had been arrested on charges relating to the death of another child. The grandparents offered evidence that the child's father had abused the child and the child's mother. Following their daughter's testimony about the abuse she had suffered, the grandparents attempted to introduce expert testimony regarding the battered woman syndrome, and the trial court excluded the evidence and ultimately awarded custody to the father. The appellate court held that the trial court's exclusion of this evidence was error: "[I]t has come to be recognized that expert testimony in the field of domestic violence is admissible since the psychological and behavioral characteristics typically shared by victims of abuse in a familial setting are not generally known by the average person."[223] The appellate court found the trial court's exclusion of syndrome testimony especially prejudicial since the trial court had "found [the mother's] ... testimony [regarding domestic violence] to be incredible because she never went to a hospital or sought treatment."[224]

Similarly, the battered woman syndrome is sometimes considered relevant to the circumstances surrounding the dissolution of a marriage and the attending property settlement.[225] In *Blair v. Blair*,[226] for example, the wife

220. *Id.*

221. *Id.*

222. 210 A.D.2d 741, 620 N.Y.S.2d 551 (App.Div.1994).

223. *Id.* at 553.

224. *Id. See also* In re Victoria C. v. Higinio C., 165 Misc.2d 702, 630 N.Y.S.2d 470, 471 (Fam.Ct.1995) (In seeking a protective order against her husband, the petitioner sought to introduce syndrome testimony to explain her reaction to the abuse and her failure to escape it. The family court judge ruled that syndrome expert testimony "has found acceptance in the courts of New York" and was *"presumptively admissible* in this family offense proceeding.") (emphasis supplied). Knock v. Knock, 224 Conn. 776, 621 A.2d 267, 270–72 (Conn.1993) (The court permitted battered woman syndrome expert testimony in a hearing to determine child custody.); Cusseaux v. Pickett, 279 N.J.Super. 335, 652 A.2d 789, 791–93 (Law Div.1994) (The court, applying New Jersey's Prevention of Domestic Violence Act, declared that an abused domestic partner can maintain a cause of action against his or her partner for "battered woman's syndrome." The court treated the syndrome as a "continuing tort," and held that it applied to all abused partners, regardless of sexual orientation, so long as the plaintiff had "go[ne] through the battering cycle at least twice."). For an example in which this evidence was excluded from civil cases, *see* Morrison v. Bradley, 622 P.2d 81, 82 (Colo. App.1980), rev'd on other grounds, 655 P.2d 385 (Colo.1982) (The court excluded syndrome testimony offered by the defendant, a battered woman, in a wrongful death action brought by the decedent's children after the defendant killed her boyfriend following a long history of abuse.).

225. *See, e.g.*, Quebodeaux v. Quebodeaux, 102 Ohio App.3d 502, 657 N.E.2d 539, 541 (Ohio App.1995) (The appellate court upheld

contested a divorce order, claiming that the court's property distribution award was an abuse of discretion. At trial, the wife had introduced evidence of the physical abuse she had endured during her four-year marriage.[227] The Vermont Supreme Court found the lower court's reaction to the abuse testimony troubling. Specifically, the family court judge stated as follows:

> The marital misdeeds that have been attributed to [the husband], most of them, we don't believe.... [T]here may be these temper tantrums, ... but the strangling ... and violence and threats that were described by [the wife] have been blown way out of proportion as evidenced by the fact that she stayed throughout the four years of marriage. The children were in the house and don't relate any corroboration at all regarding these things.... I think that they're blown up by her own hurt with what happened to the marriage.[228]

The Supreme Court noted that the court's belief that the allegations were inflated because the woman had not left the marriage was a myth about abusive relationships.[229] The Supreme Court concluded that "the findings were inadequate to afford meaningful review ... given defendant's extensive testimony which dovetailed [with] the profile of a battered woman."[230] The Court remanded for a new trial.

In *Labow v. Labow*,[231] the defendant counterclaimed for intentional infliction of emotional distress in a suit distantly related to the parties' divorce twenty years before. The defendant claimed to be suffering from the battered woman syndrome which she argued sufficed to satisfy a claim of intentional infliction of emotional distress.[232] The court rejected this claim on two grounds. "First, the court reject[ed] the defendant's reasoning that all persons suffering from battered woman's syndrome also have a cause of action for intentional infliction of emotional distress."[233] Simply put, the court explained, the elements of the syndrome are different than the legal requirements for intentional infliction of emotional distress.[234] Second, the court held that the defendant's expert's "testimony is insufficient to establish that the defendant suffered from battered woman syndrome."[235] The expert had relied on unreliable information provided by the defendant, and had failed to review pertinent medical records.[236]

§ 4–1.5 Conclusion

No court or commentator has defended the methodology used to develop the syndrome or has suggested that adequate research methods were employed in its development. Unfortunately, courts have almost uniformly failed

the trial court's reliance on battered woman syndrome expert testimony to dissolve an earlier dissolution agreement that the lower court had found to be the product of duress.); Soutiere v. Soutiere, 163 Vt. 265, 657 A.2d 206, 208–209 (Vt.1995) (Concerning the relevance of battered woman syndrome expert testimony on the fair distribution of property, the court stated that "the severity and long-lasting effects of defendant's abuse on plaintiff's emotional health, her future counseling needs, and her potential employability were at issue during the trial.").

226. 154 Vt. 201, 575 A.2d 191 (Vt.1990).

227. *Id.* at 192.
228. *Id.* at 192–93.
229. *Id.* at 193.
230. *Id.* (citation omitted).
231. 1999 WL 185150 (Conn.Super.1999).
232. *Id.* at *6.
233. *Id.*
234. *Id.*
235. *Id.*
236. *Id.*

to examine in any detail whatsoever the empirical support, or lack thereof, for the battered woman syndrome.[237] As the next section discusses in detail, the battered woman syndrome remains little more than an unsubstantiated hypotheses that, despite being extant for over fifteen years, has yet to be tested adequately or has failed to be corroborated when adequately tested.

As the validity test in *Daubert*, and the lessons it teaches, are brought to bear in cases in which battered woman syndrome expertise is proffered, the thin empirical pillars supporting the evidence are likely to become increasingly apparent. In *Fowler v. State*,[238] a Texas appellate court considered the question so far wholly ignored by other courts: is the battered woman syndrome scientifically valid enough to support expert testimony?[239] Texas is a *Daubert* state.[240] The case involved the prosecution's use of the expertise, though this fact appears not to be relevant to the court's analysis. The court began by rejecting the state's claim that psychological testimony is "specialized," and therefore not subject to a validity test. In an analysis anticipating the Supreme Court's decision in *Kumho*, the court observed:

> In considering whether *Daubert* applies to the soft sciences, a look at pre-Daubert decisions shows that the United States Supreme Court made no distinction between soft and hard scientific evidence.[241]

In addition, the court noted that Rule 702 does not create different standards for different forms of expertise[242] and that psychology is no less amenable to a reliability assessment than the so-called "hard sciences."[243] The court concluded:

> We believe that [Rule 702] extends the responsibility of the trial court as "gatekeeper" to screening evidence from the soft sciences for reliability. Whether such evidence will assist the jury in making an intelligent evaluation of the facts rather than obfuscating them depends largely on the reliability of the testimony.[244]

After reviewing the record, the court concluded that "the State failed to present sufficient evidence of the validity of the scientific theories underlying [the expert's] testimony and the validity of the techniques used to apply the theories."[245]

Still, courts and commentators, quite understandably, are likely to remain sympathetic to the situation of battered women who kill. This sympathy might take two forms upon the recognition of the scientific inadequacy of the basis for most aspects of the expert testimony. Some proponents might suggest that expert testimony on the battered woman syndrome should not be

---

237. For example, in *State v. Riley*, 201 W.Va. 708, 500 S.E.2d 524 (W.Va.1997), the expert below had "explained that 'a battered spouse syndrome is a cluster of types of thinking and feeling and acting by women, 99.9 percent of the time, in which they repeatedly get into bad relationships.' " The doctor "testified that such women 'feel unable to break free from that abuse.' " *Id.* at 528 n.3. The court accepted this testimony without blinking an eye.

238.   958 S.W.2d 853 (Tex.App.1997).

239.   *Id.* at 862.

240.   *See* E.I. du Pont de Nemours and Co., Inc. v. Robinson, 923 S.W.2d 549, 556 (Tex. 1995).

241.   *Fowler*, 958 S.W.2d at 862n.6.

242.   *Id.* at 864.

243.   *Id.* at 863–64.

244.   *Id.* at 864 (citations omitted).

245.   *Id.*

held to the usual standards for scientific evidence.[246] The principal reason given for this stance is that, as a product of the "soft sciences," battered woman syndrome expert testimony can be critically assessed by juries. Jurors, according to this view, are unlikely to be overwhelmed by the aura of certainty believed to be cast by, at least, "hard" science. The problems with this argument are manifold. First, little, if any, research supports the belief that jurors are better able to critically assess the soft sciences as compared to the hard sciences. Second, one reason testimony on battered woman syndrome continues to be so soft is courts' failure to demand more rigorous methods. Finally, the potential unfair prejudice of admitting this expert testimony is not limited to the possibility that jurors will be overwhelmed by it. A large component of this testimony is character in nature, with all of the attendant concerns this evidence produces.

Alternatively, courts and, more likely, legislatures might consider interpreting or altering the substantive law to make it more inclusive of the battered woman's perspective. As many courts and commentators have pointed out, the imminence and proportional force requirements of self-defense doctrine embrace an essentially male perspective regarding the proper and justifiable uses of force. When women are physically beaten, isolated from friends and family and given little hope from the institutions of society designed to serve and protect them, it is not difficult to understand and, perhaps, justify, their use of deadly force to defend themselves.

Finally, although the battered woman syndrome remains little more than a poorly substantiated hypothesis, rigorous research has been and continues to be carried out on multiple aspects of battered women's lives. Yet, courts have focused on a syndrome model to the exclusion of other research that, though less legally convenient, more accurately depicts the social and psychological consequences of domestic violence. In time, this research will do much to advance our understanding and will mold our responses to this important and disturbing problem. A good faith application of admissibility standards should lead courts to move from the simple solutions embodied in syndrome-based defenses to a greater appreciation of the complex circumstances surrounding these cases. For example, in attempting to explain why women do not leave violent relationships, courts can be expected to reject opinions on learned helplessness that are now offered with virtually no research basis to support them. Such rejection of facile expert opinion, however, will not leave battered women with no explanation for their conduct, for good research indicates that many factors conspire to trap women in violent relationships.[247] In the end, battered women, and society in general, will benefit from a more discriminating evaluation of ostensibly scientific research in this area. Good research should make clear the factual picture from which legal policy should be made. To date, the research has only muddied that picture. Courts should expect, indeed demand, more from social science.

---

246. *See, e.g.,* State v. Borrelli, 227 Conn. 153, 629 A.2d 1105, 1110–1111 (Conn.1993) (The court held that expert testimony on the general effects of domestic violence was not subject to the *Frye* test, since "the method is accessible to the jury, and not dependent on familiarity with highly technical or obscure scientific theories.").

247. *See infra* § 11–2.0.

B. SCIENTIFIC STATUS

by

Regina Schuller* & Sara Rzepa**

§ 4–2.0 THE SCIENTIFIC STATUS OF RESEARCH ON DOMESTIC VIOLENCE AGAINST WOMEN

§ 4–2.1 Introductory Discussion of the Science

§ 4–2.1.1 The General Questions

The scientific research on male violence against women in intimate relationships and its impact on women was initiated in the early 1970s.[1] It was during this time that researchers began to document systematically the pervasiveness and severity of the problem of violence in intimate relationships.[2] Since this time, national surveys and crime statistics continue to document the widespread scope and severity of the problem. In addition to documenting the scope of wife abuse, researchers have primarily directed their attention to delineating the dynamics of abusive relationships and to

* Regina A. Schuller, Ph.D. is Associate Professor of Psychology at York University in Toronto, Ontario, Canada. She is actively engaged in both research and teaching and in 1995 received York's President's Prize for Promising Scholars. Her research interests focus on the impact of social science framework testimony, in particular, expert testimony pertaining to battered women and on juror/jury decision processes. She also serves on the editorial board of LAW & HUMAN BEHAVIOR and PSYCHOLOGY, PUBLIC POLICY, AND LAW.

** Sara Rzepa is a graduate student in the Psychology Department at York University in Toronto, Ontario, Canada. Her research interests include jury decision making and she is currently involved in research on jury decision making in trials involving battered women who have killed their abusers.

The authors would like to acknowledge the significant contributions of Patricia A. Hastings to an earlier publication of this chapter and to thank the Social Sciences and Humanities Research Council of Canada for their support in the form of a research grant to the first author.

§ 4–2.0

1. It should be acknowledged that the Women's Movement and grassroots activism were largely responsible for increasing public awareness of the social problem of battering. *See* SUSAN SCHECHTER, WOMEN AND MALE VIOLENCE (1982).

2. The focus of this chapter is woman abuse within a heterosexual relationship. The term wife is used to refer to both married and co-habiting women in intimate heterosexual re-

lationships. Although battering within same-sex relationships has been documented, traditionally, domestic violence research has focused almost exclusively on battering within heterosexual relationships. Only more recently has attention begun to focus on same-sex partner abuse. In describing the dynamics of abuse within gay and lesbian relationships, researchers note both similarities and differences between battered heterosexual women and battered gay men and lesbian women. *See* Leslie K. Burke & Diane R. Follingstad, *Violence in Lesbian and Gay Relationships: Theory, Prevalence, and Correlational Factors,* 19 CLINICAL PSYCHOL. REV. 487 (1999); *see also* Claire M. Renzetti, *Violence in Lesbian and Gay Relationships, in* INTERDISCIPLINARY PERSPECTIVES 285 (Laura L. O. Toole & Jessica Schiffman eds., 1997); Claire M. Renzetti, *Violence and Abuse in Lesbian Relationships: Theoretical and Empirical Issues, in* ISSUES IN INTIMATE VIOLENCE 117 (Raquel K. Bergen ed.,1998); Gregory S. Merrill, *Understanding Domestic Violence Among Gay and Bisexual Men, in* ISSUES IN INTIMATE VIOLENCE, *supra* at 129; Carolyn M. West, *Leaving a Second Closet: Outing Partner Violence in Same–Sex Couples, in* PARTNER VIOLENCE: A COMPREHENSIVE REVIEW OF 20 YEARS OF RESEARCH 163 (Jana L. Jasinski et al. eds., 1998); Valerie E. Coleman, *Lesbian Battering: The Relationship Between Personality and the Perpetration of Violence,* 9 VIOLENCE & VICTIMS 139 (1994); Patrick Letellier, *Gay and Bi-sexual Male Domestic Violence Victimization: Challenges to Feminist Theory and Responses to Violence,* 9 VIOLENCE & VICTIMS 95 (1994); Denise Bricker, *Fatal Defense: An Analysis of Battered Woman's Syndrome Expert Testimony for Gay Men and Lesbians Who Kill Abusive Partners,* 58 BROOK. L. REV. 1379 (1993).

understanding women's experience of and reactions to male violence.[3] This body of research consistently documents the myriad obstacles battered women confront in their attempts to end the violence, as well as the profound emotional and psychological impact that the violence can have on a woman.

[1] The Scope of the Problem

Depending upon the way in which violence is measured and on the particular sample studied, varying estimates of the incidence of domestic violence have been found.[4] Although domestic violence has been noted in all segments of the population, a number of variables have been identified as risk markers for women's victimization: age,[5] income,[6] pregnancy,[7] separation,[8]

---

3. This chapter focuses exclusively on research examining battered women's experiences in abusive relationships. For research examining the male batterer more specifically, see Daniel G. Saunders, *A Typology of Men Who Batter: Three Types Derived From Cluster Analysis,* 62 AM. J. OF ORTHOPSYCHIATRY 264 (1992); see also Donald G. Dutton, *The Origin and Structure of the Abusive Personality,* 8 J. OF PERSONALITY DISORDERS 181 (1994); Donald G. Dutton, *Traumatic Origins of Intimate Rage,* 4 AGGRESSION & VIOLENT BEHAV. 431 (1999); DONALD G. DUTTON, THE ABUSIVE PERSONALITY: VIOLENCE AND CONTROL IN INTIMATE RELATIONSHIPS (1998); Edward W. Gondolf, *MCMI III Results for Batterer Program Participants in Four Cities: Less "Pathological" Than Expected,* 14 J. OF FAM. VIOLENCE 1 (1999); Amy Holtzworth–Munroe et al., *A Typology of Male Batterers: An Initial Examination, in* VIOLENCE IN INTIMATE RELATIONSHIPS 45 (Ximena B. Arriaga & Stuart Oskamp eds., 1999); L. Kevin Hamberger & James E. Hastings, *Personality Correlates of Men Who Batter and Nonviolent Men: Some Continuities and Discontinuities,* 6 J. OF FAM. VIOLENCE 131 (1991).

4. See Richard J. Gelles, *Estimating the Incidence and Prevalence of Violence Against Women: National Data Systems and Sources,* 6 VIOLENCE AGAINST WOMEN 784, 797 (2000).

5. Higher levels of violence have been found for women who are younger, see RICHARD J. GELLES, INTIMATE VIOLENCE IN FAMILIES 82 (3rd ed., 1997); see also Ronet Bachman & Linda E. Saltzman, *Violence Against Women: Estimates From the Redesigned Survey,* Washington, DC: U.S. DEPARTMENT OF JUSTICE, BUREAU OF JUSTICE STATISTICS (1995); HOLLY JOHNSON, DANGEROUS DOMAIN, VIOLENCE AGAINST WOMEN IN CANADA (1996).

6. Although wife abuse is not confined to low income families, it is more likely to be reported in these households. For example, Kaplan found that, compared to women living in households with higher incomes, women in households with incomes of less than $10,000 per year were four times more likely to be attacked by their partners. See A. Kaplan, *Domestic Violence and Welfare Reform,* I(8) WEL-

FARE INFORMATION NETWORK: ISSUES NOTES 1 (1997). Wolfner and Gelles also found higher rates of abuse for women living below the poverty line. See G. D. Wolfner & R. J. Gelles, *A Profile of Violence Toward Children: A National Study,* 17 CHILD ABUSE & NEGLECT 197 (1993). Hotaling and Sugarman found that while women from all socioeconomic levels encountered similar rates of minor assaults, women whose partners were less financially secure, or unemployed, were at greater risk of severe assaults. See G. T. Hotaling & D. B. Sugarman, *A Risk Marker Analysis of Assaulted Wives,* 5 J. OF FAM. VIOLENCE 1 (1990); see also RICHARD J. GELLES (1997), supra note 5, at 82–83; Daniel G. Saunders, *Prediction of Wife Assault, in* ASSESSING DANGEROUSNESS, VIOLENCE BY SEXUAL OFFENDERS, BATTERERS AND CHILD ABUSERS (Jacquelyn C. Campbell ed., 1995); Bachman & Saltzman (1995), supra note 5; JOHNSON (1996) supra note 5.

7. Estimates of the prevalence of violence during pregnancy range from 7% to 20%. Although some evidence suggests that violence escalates during pregnancy, other research suggests that pregnant women may be at no greater risk for abuse than women who are not pregnant, and that the increase in reporting of violence during pregnancy may be accounted for by age (younger women are more likely to be pregnant than older women). See Glenda Kaufman Kantor & Jana. L. Jasinski, *Dynamics and Risk Factors in Partner Violence, in* PARTNER VIOLENCE, supra note 2, at 31–33. See also Terri J. Ballard et al., *Violence During Pregnancy: Measurement Issues,* 88 AM. J. OF PUBLIC HEALTH 274 (1998); Mary Ann Dutton et al., *Impact of Violence on Women's Health, in* HEALTH CARE FOR WOMEN, PSYCHOLOGICAL, SOCIAL, AND BEHAVIORAL INFLUENCES 43, 44–45 (Sheryle J. Gallant et al. eds., 1997).

8. See infra notes 107–111 and accompanying text. See also GELLES (1997), supra note 5; JOHNSON, supra note 5; Desmond Ellis, *Post-Separation Woman Abuse: The Contribution of Lawyers as "Barracudas," "Advocates" and "Counsellors,"* 10 INT'L J. OF L. & PSYCHIATRY 403 (1987); Leslie W. Kennedy & Donald G.

alcohol consumption on the part of the batterer,[9] and witnessing wife battering in childhood.[10]

Perhaps the most cited work documenting the pervasiveness of wife abuse involves a series of national surveys conducted by a group of sociologists at the Family Research Laboratory.[11] In 1975 these researchers conducted in-person interviews with over 2,000 individual family members (men and women married or co-habiting with a partner of the opposite sex).[12] Overall, they found that one of every six wives reported that she was struck during the course of her marriage and approximately 12 percent of the women were physically attacked during the year of the survey, with 4 percent of these attacks involving severe violence.[13] Ten years later the study was replicated,

Dutton, *The Incident of Wife Assault in Alberta,* 21 CANADIAN J. OF BEHAV. SCIENCE 40 (1989).

9. Although alcohol is neither necessary nor sufficient for the occurrence of violence, the association between the batterer's alcohol use and his violence has been demonstrated in a number of studies. Despite this link, the contribution of alcohol to interpersonal violence is controversial and various theories have been posited to account for the association. *See* W. Vernon Lee & Stephan P. Weinstein, *How Far Have We Come? A Critical Review of the Research on Men who Batter, in* 13 RECENT DEVELOPMENTS IN ALCOHOLISM: ALCOHOL AND VIOLENCE 337–56 (Marc Galanter ed., 1997); JOHNSON, *supra* note 5, at 155–58; Christine Wekerle & Anne–Marie Wall, *The Overlap Between Relationship Violence and Substance Abuse, in* THE VIOLENCE AND ADDICTION EQUATION: THEORETICAL AND CLINICAL ISSUES IN SUBSTANCE ABUSE AND RELATIONSHIP VIOLENCE (Christine Wekerle & Anne–Marie Wall eds., in press); Conner & Ackerley, *Alcohol-Related Battering: Developing Treatment Strategies,* 9 J. OF FAM. VIOLENCE 144 (1994); Roberts, *Substance Abuse Among Men Who Batter Their Mates,* 5 J. SUBSTANCE ABUSE & TREATMENT 83 (1988); Theresa M. Zubretsky & Karla M. Digirotama, *False Connection Between Domestic Violence and Alcohol* (1996), *in* HELPING BATTERED WOMEN, NEW PERSPECTIVES & REMEDIES 222–228 (Albert R. Roberts ed., 1995); Susan Ehrlick Martin & Ronet Bachman, *The Relationship of Alcohol to Injury in Assault Cases, in* RECENT DEVELOPMENTS IN ALCOHOLICS, *supra,* at 41–56; Kenneth E. Leonard, *Alcohol Use and Marital Aggression Among Newlywed Couples, in* VIOLENCE IN INTIMATE RELATIONSHIPS, *supra* note 3, at 113–35. The association between the woman's alcohol consumption and the violence is less consistent and it appears that the batterer's, as opposed to the victim's, use of alcohol is more proximally associated with the violence. *See* Wekerle & Wall, *supra; see also* G. Kaufman Kantor & N. N. Asdigian, *When Women Are Under the Influence: Does Drinking or Drug Use by Women Provoke Beatings by Men?, in* 13 RECENT DEVELOPMENTS IN ALCOHOLISM, *supra,* at 315–36; Mary Ann Dutton, *Necessary Issues for Understanding Battered Women,* 2 DOMESTIC VIOLENCE REP. 33, 42–43 (1997); Ira W. Hutchison, *Alcohol,*

Fear, and Woman Abuse, 40 SEX ROLES 893 (1999).

10. The elevated risk of becoming a victim or perpetrator of intimate violence associated with witnessing violence in childhood has been well documented in the literature. *See* David A. Wolfe et al., *Interrupting the Cycle of Violence, in* CHILD ABUSE, NEW DIRECTIONS IN PREVENTION AND TREATMENT ACROSS THE LIFESPAN 102–29 (David Wolfe et al. eds., 1997). As researchers have pointed out (*e.g.,* GELLES, 1997, *supra* note 5), although exposure to violence as a child may increase the likelihood of becoming a victim or batterer, this relationship is far from predetermined. Not all men exposed to such violence in their childhood grow up to be abusers and, conversely, men not exposed to such violence in their childhood may become violent in their marital relationships.

11. MURRAY A. STRAUS ET AL., BEHIND CLOSED DOORS: VIOLENCE IN THE AMERICAN FAMILY (1980); RICHARD J. GELLES & MURRAY A. STRAUS, INTIMATE VIOLENCE: THE CAUSES AND CONSEQUENCES OF ABUSE IN THE AMERICAN FAMILY (1988). For these surveys a "Conflict Tactics Scale" was developed. In addition to measuring the use of rational discussion and agreement, this measure assesses both "verbal or non-verbal expressions of anger or hostility (e.g., insulted or swore; sulked or refused to talk; ... threatened to hit or throw something; threw, smashed, or hit something)" and "physical force or violence (e.g., threw something at the other person; pushed, grabbed or shoved; slapped or spanked; kicked, bit or hit with a fist; hit or tried to hit with something; beat up; choked, threatened or used a knife or gun)." GELLES & STRAUS, *supra,* at 207. Using this scale, respondents merely indicate which of the various conflict tactics they have engaged in during the previous year.

12. STRAUS et al., *supra* note 11.

13. Comparable rates were found for wife-to-husband abuse. As the Conflict Tactics Scale merely notes the occurrence of a violent act (e.g., slap, hit) with no information regarding the context in which the event occurs, the meaning of these data have been vigorously

this time, however, with the interviews conducted over the telephone.[14] A nationally representative sample of over 6,000 individuals was interviewed (the spouse abuse data were based on a smaller sample of 3,520). Again, a substantial, albeit somewhat lower, rate of husband-to-wife violence was found (an 11 percent annual incident rate, with 3 percent representing severe violence). Murray Straus and Richard Gelles estimated from these survey results that, over the one year period, more than 1.8 million women were severely assaulted by a male partner.[15] More recently, Straus and Kantor conducted a third study in which approximately 2000 respondents were interviewed by telephone. Comparing the results of this survey to the previous two surveys, it was found that the rate of "minor violence"[16] declined from "100 per 1,000 women in 1975 to about 80 per 1,000 in 1985, and then rose to 91 per 1,000 in 1992."[17] More serious acts of violence[18] "declined from 38 per 1,000 in 1975 to 19 per 1,000 in 1992."[19]

A host of other studies both within[20] and outside the U.S.[21] provide further confirmation of the scope and severity of the problem of husband-to-

debated and heavily critiqued as "misleading and flawed." Demie Kurz, *Physical Assaults By Husbands: A Major Social Problem, in* CURRENT CONTROVERSIES ON FAMILY VIOLENCE 94 (Richard J. Gelles & Donileen R. Loseke eds., 1993). For instance, husband-to-wife abuse, compared to wife-to-husband abuse, is more likely to result in serious injury. Moreover, the woman's violent acts are more likely to be a defensive response to the husband's initial assault. *See* Daniel G. Saunders, *Wife Abuse, Husband Abuse, or Mutual Combat?, in* FEMINIST PERSPECTIVES ON WIFE ABUSE 90 (Kersti Yllo & Michele Bograd eds., 1988); *see also* E. Pleck et al., *The Battered Data Syndrome: A Comment on Steinmetz's Article,* 2 VICTIMOLOGY 260 (1977–78); Russell P. Dobash et al., *The Myth of Sexual Symmetry in Marital Violence,* 39 SOC. PROBLEMS 71 (1992); Angela Browne, *Violence Against Women by Male Partners: Prevalence, Outcomes, and Policy Implications,* 48 AM. PSYCHOL. 1077 (1993); Walter S. DeKeseredy, *Tactics of the Antifeminist Backlash Against Canadian National Woman Abuse Surveys,* 5 VIOLENCE AGAINST WOMEN 1258 (1999). In response to these critiques, *see* Murray Straus, *Physical Assaults by Wives: A Major Social Problem, in* CURRENT CONTROVERSIES ON FAMILY VIOLENCE, *supra,* at 67; Marilyn J. Kwong et al., *Gender Differences in Patterns of Relationship Violence in Alberta,* 31 CANADIAN J. OF BEHAV. SCIENCE 150 (1999).

14. GELLES AND STRAUS, *supra* note 11.

15. Murray A. Straus & Richard J. Gelles, *How Violent are American Families? Estimates from the National Family Violence Resurvey and Other Studies, in* FAMILY ABUSE AND ITS CONSEQUENCES: NEW DIRECTIONS IN RESEARCH 14–36 (Gerald T. Hotaling & David Finkelhor eds., 1988).

16. Minor violence was described as "violence that had a low probability of causing a

physical injury," Gelles (2000), *supra* note 4, at 797.

17. *Id.*

18. Acts "labeled *severe assaults* or *wife beating* by the investigators." *Id.*

19. *Id.*

20. For instance, on the basis of the National Crime Victimization Survey, which employs a stratified, multistage cluster sample (hence representing a nationally representative sample), it is estimated that approximately one million women within the U.S. experience violence at the hands of an intimate partner annually, Bachman & Saltzman (1995), *supra* note 5. *See also* Ronet Bachman & Bruce M. Taylor *The Measurement of Family Violence and Rape by the Redesigned National Crime Victimization Survey,* 3 JUST. Q. 499 (1994). And, on the basis of a nationally representative cross-sectional survey of adult women and men residing in the U.S., it was found that 8% (N=1,334) of the married or co-habiting women between the ages of 18 and 64 reported experiencing physical abuse from their partner in the past two years, with 3.2% reporting suffering severe forms of abuse *See* Stacey B. Plichta, *Violence and Abuse, Implications for Women's Health, in* WOMEN'S HEALTH, THE COMMONWEALTH FUND SURVEY 237, at 244 (Marilyn M. Falik & Karen Scott Collins eds., 1996). For estimates provided by official case records (e.g., police incident reports, hospital emergency records, homicide rates), *see* GELLES (2000), *supra* note 4; Daniel G. Saunders & Angela Browne, *Domestic Homicide, in* CASE STUDIES IN FAMILY VIOLENCE 379 (Robert T. Ammerman & Michel Hersen eds., 1991).

21. The results of a large national survey conducted north of the U.S. border provides data that paints a similar portrait of the battering context to that found in U.S. *See* JOHNSON (1996), *supra* note 5.

wife assault. Although traditionally much of the early research focused primarily on the physical aspects of violence, it is equally important to recognize the nonphysical forms of abuse to which battered women may be subjected.[22] Along these lines, researchers have now documented a range of psychological and emotional abuse that battered women commonly experience and various measures to assess the psychological maltreatment experienced by battered women have emerged.[23] Through surveys and interviews with battered women, researchers find that, along with physical and sexual abuse, the following are common in battered women's lives: restriction of economic finances, threats of harm (to both self and others), destruction of property and pets, ridicule, social isolation and restriction of the woman's behavior.[24]

Taken in their entirety, the results of these surveys document a range of violent and abusive behaviors that women may experience at the hands of an intimate male partner. Although we must be mindful of the retrospective self-report nature of the information collected through the surveys,[25] the sampling techniques employed in the research increase our confidence that the responses are likely to be fairly representative of the population of assaulted women in general.[26] Moreover, given the private and hidden nature of intimate violence, as well as the social stigma and embarrassment attached to disclosure of violence at the hands of a partner, under (as opposed to over)

22. "Emotional abuse is the ongoing backdrop against which physical abuse occurs." Mary Ann Dutton et al. (1997), *supra* note 7, at 43. *See also* Mary Ann Dutton, *Understanding Women's Response to Domestic Violence: A Redefinition of Battered Woman Syndrome*, 21 HOFSTRA L. REV. 1191, 1204–07 (1993); Karla Fischer et al., *The Culture of Battering and the Role of Mediation in Domestic Violence Cases*, 46 S.M.U. L. REV. 2117, 2120–21 (1993).

23. *See* Richard M. Tolman, *The Validation of the Psychological Maltreatment of Women Inventory*, 14 VIOLENCE & VICTIMS 25 (1999); *see also* Richard M. Tolman, *The Development of a Measure of Psychological Maltreatment of Women by Their Male Partners*, 4 VIOLENCE & VICTIMS 3 (1989); Linda L. Marshall, *Psychological Abuse of Women: Six Distinct Clusters*, 11 J. OF FAM. VIOLENCE 379 (1996); Leslie A. Sackett & Daniel G. Saunders, *The Impact of Different Forms of Psychological Abuse on Battered Women*, 14 VIOLENCE & VICTIMS 105 (1999). For a review of the reliability and validity of the construct of psychological aggression, *see* K. Daniel O'Leary, *Psychological Abuse: A Variable Deserving Critical Attention in Domestic Violence*, 14 VIOLENCE & VICTIMS 3 (1999).

24. *E.g.*, Tolman (1999), *id.*, at 29 (documenting higher levels of psychological abuse in physically abusive as compared to dissatisfied but nonabusive or satisfied relationships); Russell P. Dobash et al., *Separate and Intersecting Realities, A Comparison of Men's and Women's Accounts of Violence Against Women*, 4 VIOLENCE AGAINST WOMEN 382, 404 (1998) (a substantial portion of their sample reported that "continuous, repetitive controlling and coercive

acts" on the part of the batterer formed "an integral part of their relationships"); ANGELA BROWNE, WHEN BATTERED WOMEN KILL 100, 70 (1987) (71% of women who had killed their abusers reported physical or sexual abuse of the children by the batterer, compared to 51% of battered women who had not killed); Fischer et al., *supra* note 22, at 2122 n.25 & 2121, n.18 (reporting that 36% of her sample indicate that abusers had threatened family or friends, 30% reported batterer's abused pets, 70% reported batterer's destroyed property); Diane R. Follingstad et al., *The Role of Emotional Abuse in Physically Abusive Relationships*, 5 J. OF FAMILY VIOLENCE 107 (1990) (documenting six types of abuse (threats, ridicule, jealousy, restriction, threats to change the marriage, property damage), with more than half of their sample reporting restriction, batterer jealousy, and ridicule occurring at least once a week or more frequently).

25. *See* Bachman & Saltzman, *supra* note 5. For discussions of critiques of such surveys, *see* Holly Johnson, *Response to Allegations About the Violence Against Women Survey*, in WIFE ASSAULT & THE CANADIAN CRIMINAL JUSTICE SYSTEM 148 (Mariana Valverde et al. eds., 1995); *see also* Anthony Doob, *Understanding the Attacks on Statistics Canada's Violence Against Women Survey*, in WIFE ASSAULT, *supra*, at 157.

26. It must be noted, however, that important segments of the population are not reached in these surveys (e.g., those lacking telephones, those who do not speak English fluently, etc.).

reporting is more likely to occur. In short, figures derived from these surveys may actually underestimate the severity of the problem.[27]

[2] Dynamics of Abusive Relationships

The most influential research in this area was pioneered by Dr. Lenore Walker and considerable attention, especially within the courtroom, has been given to her work. In 1979, Walker published *The Battered Woman*[28] in which she first described observations she derived from interviews with over one-hundred battered women, who were either self-referred volunteers or drawn from her clinical practice.[29] These women were predominately white and middle class. In collaboration with her colleagues, Walker subsequently conducted a more extensive study in which in-depth interviews were conducted with over 400 battered women.[30] These women were self-referred and no claims to the representativeness of the sample can be made. In the interviews, a 200 page questionnaire, taking approximately six to eight hours to complete, was administered. In addition to obtaining demographic information, attitudes, and psychological functioning of the women, the women were also asked to describe four battering episodes they had experienced: the first, the second, one of the worst, and the last.

It was through this research that Walker developed the two key theoretical constructs underlying the "battered woman syndrome:" the Cycle Theory of Violence and Learned Helplessness. We examine the former first. Basically, on the basis of the interviews, Walker discerned that the violence was not constant, but rather was characterized by a three stage, repetitive cycle, with no specific time frame defining either the length of the cycle or the phases within it. As described by Walker, in the first or "tension building" phase there is a build up of "minor" abusive incidents (e.g., emotional threats, verbal outbursts) in which the woman is hyper-vigilant to her spouses cues and moods, modifying her behavior in an effort to calm and placate the batterer. The tension eventually escalates, however, and the woman is subjected to a severe battering incident ("acute battering" phase). This phase is then followed by a third or "loving contrition" phase in which the batterer is remorseful, promising never to harm the woman again.[31] According to Walker, this repetitive three stage cycle of violence is key to understanding the psychological impact of the abuse on the woman and why she remains in the relationship. Specifically, the third or contrition stage in which the husband is loving and remorseful provides initial hope to the woman and reinforces her for staying. Believing his promises, the woman gives him another chance, hoping he will change.[32] Eventually, however, the cycle begins again and the woman is subjected to further violence at the hands of her partner. Given this cyclical pattern, however, the woman never feels completely out of danger and is reduced to a perpetual state of fear.

To assess the validity of the cycle theory, interviewers in Walker's research solicited both open-ended descriptions of the abusive incidents, as

27. *See* Gelles (2000), *supra* note 4, at 796; *see also* Browne (1993), *supra* note 13, at 1078.

28. *See* Lenore Walker, The Battered Woman (1979).

29. *See id.* at xiii.

30. *See* Lenore Walker, The Battered Woman Syndrome (1984, 2000 2nd ed.).

31. *Id.* at 95.

32. *See id.* at 65–70.

well as asked the women whether the abuser's behavior prior to the beating was "irritable, provocative, aggressive, hostile, threatening"[33] and whether the batterer's behavior following the abusive incident was "nice, loving, contrite?"[34] For each of these adjectives the women provided a rating on a five point scale. On the basis of the woman's open-ended description and her responses to the series of close-ended questions, the interviewer recorded whether there was "evidence of tension building and/or loving contrition." Although no data regarding the percentage of cases in which all three phases of the cycle occurred were reported, in approximately two-thirds of the episodes there was "evidence of a tension-building phase prior to the battering"[35] and "in 58 percent of all cases there was evidence of loving contrition afterward."[36] Walker also noted that over the course of the relationship, tension building increased while contrition declined.[37]

On the basis of these findings, Walker concluded that the data provide "support for the cycle theory of violence in a majority of battering incidents."[38] Given that almost half of the cases did not conform to the three stage pattern,[39] commentators question this conclusion.[40] Since no psychological theory purports to account for total variability in behavior, these findings do not completely invalidate the theory;[41] at the very least, however, they place limits on the universality of the cycle. On a more basic level, however, the methodology of the study itself has also been criticized.[42] These concerns stem from the interview format employed, specifically the inclusion of "leading" questions. That is, it is possible that the questions used by the interviewers conveyed the hypotheses to the women and thus provided them with responses that they might otherwise not have given. As well, since the interviewers were aware of the hypotheses under investigation, they may have interpreted more consistency with the hypotheses than the responses in fact warranted (i.e., experimenter expectancy effects).[43]

A second study addressing the cycle theory of violence was conducted by Angela Browne.[44] Using a similar interview format to that employed by Walker, Browne interviewed 42 battered women who had been charged with

---

33. WALKER (1984), *supra* note 30, at 96.

34. *Id.*

35. *Id.*

36. *Id.*

37. *See id.* at 97.

38. *Id.*

39. The percentage of cases in which all three stages of the cycle were identified is not provided, but given the findings that are reported, this value could not exceed 58%.

40. *See* David L. Faigman, *The Battered Woman Syndrome and Self Defense: A Legal and Empirical Dissent,* 73 VA. L. REV. 619 (1986); *see also* Marilyn McMahon, *Battered Women and Bad Science: The Limited Validity and Utility of Battered Woman Syndrome,* 6 PSYCHIATRY, PSYCHOL. & L. 23, 33 (1999).

41. *See* Regina A. Schuller & Neil Vidmar, *Battered Woman Syndrome Evidence in the Courtroom,* 16 L. & HUMAN BEHAV. 273, 280 (1992).

42. *See* Faigman, *supra* note 40; McMahon, *supra* note 40, at 32–33.

43. Walker provides too little information to completely rule out these possibilities and little information attesting to the reliability of the assessments is provided. Open-and close-ended questions, however, have complementary strengths and weaknesses and an interview format that incorporates open-ended questions, followed by a series of detailed items that serve as probes, is a common research approach. *See* CHARLES M. JUDD ET AL., RESEARCH METHODS IN SOCIAL RELATIONS 241 (6th ed. 1991). The former does not restrict or provide any preconceived notions or categories, while the latter "ensures that all aspects of the violent event [are] covered in the same manner for each respondent." R. Emerson Dobash & Russell P. Dobash, *The Nature and Antecedents of Violent Events,* 24 CRIT. J. CRIMINOL. 269, 272 (1984).

44. *See* BROWNE, *supra* note 24.

the murder or attempted murder of their partner. Her contact with these women was initiated by the women's attorneys' requests for psychological assessments, and, again, no claims to the representativeness of the sample can be made. The women in this sample were asked to describe the first, most typical, worst, and last violent incident they had experienced. Although Browne does not report data for each stage of the cycle, some data regarding the final or contrition phase are provided. Initially, the men expressed contrition (87 percent for the first violent incident),[45] but this behavior dropped drastically over the course of the relationship (73 percent after the second or a typical violent incident and 58 percent after the worst).[46] Thus, for these women there was also evidence of a more variable pattern than was initially articulated by Walker in the three phase cycle of violence.

Dobash and Dobash, on the basis of in-depth interviews with 109 battered women drawn from shelters, further questioned whether contrition is demonstrated by the husband even in the early stages of a relationship.[47] Similar to Browne's study, the women in this research described the first, most typical, worst, and last violent incident. For each incident, Dobash and Dobash asked the women to "tell me exactly what happened during the . . . assault?" This was then followed by a series of detailed, systematic questions about the incidents. On the basis of these interviews, a somewhat different pattern from the three phase cycle of violence emerged. Immediately following the most typical incident of abuse, only 8 percent of the women reported that the husband apologized or expressed regret. This was somewhat higher, albeit still low (22 percent), for the first incidence of violence.[48]

Taken in their entirety, these studies indicate that the cycle does not characterize all battering relationships and that the pattern is not necessarily an invariable cycle with three clear and distinct phases. In her later work, Walker indicates that a more detailed analysis of the research data reveals that not all relationships follow the common cycle pattern and that variations in the pattern can be found.[49] Similarly, Mary Ann Dutton concludes that not all violent relationships follow the cycle and other patterns are evidenced.[50] The sequence of physical, sexual, psychological, and property assaults to which women are subjected seems to "deny a characteristic cycle of violence."[51] As such, Dutton conceptualizes the violence more as a "single and continuing entity."[52]

---

45. *See id.* at 62.

46. *See id.* at 64.

47. *See* Dobash & Dobash (1984), *supra* note 43.

48. *See id.* at 280.

49. Four of the common patterns described are: (A) stable long term battering; (B) the acute battering is less severe, but the stage of contrition is often minimal or missing; (C) lethal, acute battering incidents followed by stages of loving contrition, with the contrition eventually disappearing; (D) once acute battering is reached, it remains at lethal levels. *See* Lenore E. A. Walker, *Psychology and Law, Symposium: Women and the Law,* 20 Pepp. L. Rev. 1170, 1184 (1993).

50. Such as ones in which the violence "appears to come out of the blue or when there is no contrition only the transient absence of abuse." Mary Ann Dutton, Empowering and Healing the Battered Woman a Model for Assessment and Intervention 27, 29 (1992).

51. *Id.*

52. "Several physically and sexually violent assaults may recur over a period of time with periods of psychological abuse interspersed between them. Fitting this pattern of abuse to the cycle of violence suggests that the acute battering phase may involve repeated occurrences of violence over an extended period of time, which are not separated by the other phases of the cycle." *Id.* at 29. *See also* Mary Ann Dutton (1993), *supra* note 22, at 1208.

Another central aspect of Walker's initial research involved the theory of learned helplessness and its application to the battered woman's situation. This theory was first developed through experiments in which dogs were trapped in cages and administered a set of random shocks from which they could not escape.[53] The experimenters noted that, over time, the dogs would not attempt to leave the cage when shocks were administered, even when escape routes were made possible. The dogs, learning that they had no control over the shocks, eventually lost any motivation to alter their situation; they remained submissive and passive.

Drawing on this research, Walker analogized the battered woman's situation to that of the dogs.

> It was hypothesized that the women's experiences of the noncontingent nature of their attempts to control the violence would, over time, produce helplessness and depression as the "repeated beatings, like electrical shocks, diminish the woman's motivation to respond."[54]

In short, the women learn, as the cycle of violence repeats itself, that they have no control over the violence and, eventually, lose any motivation to escape the situation. It should be noted that in Walker's more recent descriptions of the concept of learned helplessness, she emphasizes the battered woman's limited repertoire of behaviors as opposed to the notion of passivity.[55] Indeed, in a revised edition of her 1984 book, she notes that its "original intended meaning" is not that of being "helpless" but rather of *"having lost the ability to predict that what you do will make a particular outcome occur."*[56] According to Walker, the theory of learned helplessness as applied to battered women helps to explain how battered women become psychologically victimized in the relationship, utilizing "survival techniques" as opposed to "escape skills."[57]

To assess whether battered women in fact exhibit learned helplessness, Walker compared the responses of women who were still in battering relationships to those of women who had left the relationship.[58] Other forms of comparison groups (e.g., women not in battering relationships or women terminating non-abusive relationships) were not included.[59] Walker reasoned that battered women who were still in abusive relationships should report more "fear, anxiety, and depression" and less "anger, disgust, and hostility" over the course of the relationship than women who had escaped the relationship. Although Walker concluded that the results were "compatible with learned helplessness theory,"[60] no statistical tests of the differences between the groups were provided. Moreover, the pattern of responses across the three battering incidents reported by the women did not conform to the pattern

---

53. *See* MARTIN SELIGMAN, HELPLESSNESS: ON DEPRESSION, DEVELOPMENT AND DEATH (1975).

54. WALKER (1984), *supra* note 30, at 87.

55. *See* Lenore E. A. Walker, *Assessment of Abusive Spousal Relationships*, *in* HANDBOOK OF RELATIONAL DIAGNOSIS AND DYSFUNCTIONAL FAMILY THERAPY 343 (Florence W. Kaslow ed., 1996). *See also* McMahon , *supra* note 40, at 28–29.

56. WALKER (2000), *supra* note 30, at 116.

57. WALKER (1984), *supra* note 30, at 87 ("[F]or example, becoming angry rather than depressed and self-blaming; active rather than passive; and more realistic about the relationship continuing on its adverse course rather than improving").

58. *See id.*

59. *See* Faigman, *supra* note 40, at 642; *see also* McMahon, *supra* note 40, at 31.

60. WALKER (1984), *supra* note 30, at 89.

articulated by Walker.[61] Other responses of the women also were not consistent with this interpretation.[62] Even if the hypothesized pattern had been found, it is questionable whether it provides support for the theory of learned helplessness, since the indices collected focused only on the affective responses of the women and completely ignored actual behavioral responses women may exhibit.[63]

Along these lines, a host of researchers take exception to the passive characterization of battered women conveyed through the theory of learned helplessness, arguing that the data pertaining to behavioral responses do not support this portrayal.[64] Lee Bowker addressed the issue of battered women's helplessness in two separate studies. The first involved in-depth interviews with 146 formerly battered women,[65] while the second involved a sample of 1,000 battered or formerly battered women who responded to a questionnaire in a women's magazine.[66] For both studies the women were asked to describe the ways in which they attempted to stop the abuse. Similar to Walker's study, they were asked this question with respect to a number of abusive incidents (first, second, third, worst, and last). In the 1986 study, Bowker found that the women used a wide range of strategies[67] and help sources[68] in

---

61. See id. at 88.

62. For instance, data pertaining to the women's level of self-esteem were relatively mixed. Walker found the women's self-reported level of self-esteem to be high compared to their ratings of either a man or a woman in general (although no statistical tests of this difference are provided), a finding she suggests may be due to having survived a violent relationship. Id. at 80–82. Moreover, in her earlier sample, the women reported attempting to control people and events in their environment to keep the batterer from losing his temper. See WALKER (1979), supra note 28, at 34. In fairness to Walker, she describes the complexity of the woman's response as neither "extremely passive or mutually combative. Rather these data suggest that battered women develop survival or coping strategies that keep them alive with minimal injuries." Id. at 33. With respect to levels of self-esteem, some research, however, provides support for battered women's low self-esteem. Aguilar and Nightingale, for instance, administered the Barksdale Self-esteem Evaluation to 49 battered women identified through various social agencies and found their responses to be significantly lower than those of a control group of 49 non-battered women selected from a university and the general community. In addition, this study investigated the impact of specific types of battering experiences on self-esteem and found "Controlling/Emotional" type abuse to be most strongly related to low self-esteem. See Rudy J. Aguilar & Narina Nunez Nightingale, The Impact of Specific Battering Experiences on the Self–Esteem of Abused Women, 9 J. OF FAM. VIOLENCE 35 (1994). A recent study confirms these results, as a sample of abused women were found to have lower levels of self-esteem compared to a sample of non-abused women. Additionally, it

was found that women who experienced higher levels of abuse had lower self-esteem. See Stephanie J. Woods, Normative Beliefs Regarding the Maintenance of Intimate Relationships Among Abused and Nonabused Women, 14 J. OF INTERPERSONAL VIOLENCE 479 (1999).

63. Faigman has similarly argued that there is "little theoretical basis for Walker's selection of these factors as the variables representing learned helplessness." Faigman, supra note 40, at 641.

64. It has been suggested that the choice of the term "learned helplessness" may have been a poor one and a misnomer, as "battered women are often resourceful and active in their efforts to avoid violence." JULIE BLACKMAN, INTIMATE VIOLENCE: A STUDY OF INJUSTICE 192 (1989). See N. Nancy R. Rhodes & Eva Baranoff McKenzie, Why Do Battered Women Stay?: Three Decades of Research, 3 AGGRESSION AND VIOLENT BEHAV. 391, 402 (1998) ("[D]ata suggest that the concept of learned helplessness may not be as pertinent to battered women as once thought.").

65. LEE H. BOWKER, BEATING WIFE BEATING (1983).

66. This sample consisted of the 146 in-depth interviews with formerly battered wives plus 854 questionnaires sent in by women throughout the U.S. in response to an ad in Women's Day Magazine. See LEE H. BOWKER, ENDING THE VIOLENCE (1986).

67. Seven personal strategies were identified by Bowker: talking, extracting promises, nonviolent threatening, hiding, passive defense, avoidance, and counterviolence. See BOWKER, supra note 66, at 62.

68. Both informal (turning to family, in-laws, neighbours, friends, and shelter services),

their attempt to end the violence in their lives. Although no statistical tests are provided, Bowker noted an increase, not a decrease, in the frequency of women's help-seeking behavior over time.[69] In light of these findings, Bowker concluded that the difficulty women have in freeing themselves from violent relationships had more to do with "the intransigence of their husbands' penchant for domination and the lack of support from traditional institutions," than passivity or helplessness.[70]

Relying on their survey methodology, Richard Gelles and Murray Straus found that, although the notion of learned helplessness applied to some battered women, the vast majority of woman surveyed also engaged in a variety of responses in an attempt to end the abuse.[71] Similarly, Dobash and Dobash, in the interviews they conducted with battered women, also found that the women employed a range of behaviors throughout the course of their relationship that were inconsistent with the notion of learned helplessness.[72] Fischer et al., in her interviews with battered women, found that the women employed an average of 13 different strategies in an attempt to end the abuse.[73] Further, rather than decreasing over time, the frequency and variety of these strategies increased over time.[74] Edward Gondolf and Ellen Fisher refer to this pattern of increased help seeking as the "survivor hypothesis."[75]

Another theory posited to explain the dynamics involved in battering relationships involves the notion of "traumatic bonding."[76] This term describes "the development and course of strong emotional ties" that develop "between two persons where one person intermittently harasses, beats, threatens, abuses or intimidates the other."[77] The phenomenon is not unique to battered women, but can develop in a variety of contexts (e.g., between hostages and their captors, abused children and their parents) that share two common features: (1) a power imbalance in which the abused individual perceives himself to be dominated by the other and (2) intermittent exposure to abuse.[78] Dutton and Painter argue that it is the intermittency of the abuse, "not a battering cycle per se, [that] is a major determinant of the battered woman syndrome."[79]

Basically, according to this theory, as the power imbalance increases between two parties, the people in the low power position begin to feel more

and formal help sources (turning to police, social-service agencies, lawyers/district attorneys, clergy, women's groups) were identified. *See id.* at 75, 87.

69. *See id.* at 71–72.

70. Lee H. Bowker, *Battered Women's Problems are Social, Not Psychological, in* CURRENT CONTROVERSIES ON FAMILY VIOLENCE 154, *supra* note 13, at 155.

71. *See* GELLES & STRAUS (1988), *supra* note 11, at 149.

72. *See* Dobash & Dobash (1984), *supra* note 43, at 281; *see also* EDWARD W. GONDOLF & ELLEN R. FISHER, BATTERED WOMEN AS SURVIVORS: AN ALTERNATIVE TO TREATING LEARNED HELPLESSNESS (1988); Ira W. Hutchison & J. David Hirschel, *Abused Women, Help–Seeking Strategies and Police Utilization*, 4 VIOLENCE AGAINST WOMEN 436 (1998).

73. Reported in Fischer et al., *supra* note 22, at 2136.

74. *See id.* Walker's own data provided some evidence for this as well. She indicated that as the violence increased over time so did the probability that the woman would seek help. *See* WALKER (1984), *supra* note 30, at 26.

75. GONDOLF & FISHER, *supra* note 72.

76. Donald G. Dutton & Susan L. Painter, *Traumatic Bonding: The Development of Emotional Attachments in Battered Women and Other Relationships of Intermittent Abuse*, 6 VICTIMOLOGY: AN INT'L J. 139 (1981). *See also* DEE L.R. GRAHAM, LOVING TO SURVIVE SEXUAL TERROR, MEN'S VIOLENCE AND WOMEN'S LIVES (1994).

77. Dutton & Painter, *id.* at 146–47.

78. *See id.* at 147.

79. *Id.* at 212.

"negative in their self-appraisal, more incapable of fending for themselves, and thus more in need of the high power person."[80] What develops is a cycle of dependency and lowered self-esteem on the part of the low power person that, eventually, results in a strong affective bond to the high power person. The other feature, "periodicity of abuse," involves the intermittent nature of the abuse. That is, the abuse is not constant but rather is characterized by bouts between maltreatment and "more normal and acceptable social behavior." Using Walker's cycle theory of violence, Dutton and Painter describe a range of cognitive and affective alterations that occur in the woman as the relationship progresses through the various phases of the cycle. The arousal the woman experiences during the battering, which is followed by a collapse "accompanied by inactivity, depression, self-blame and feelings of helplessness," leaves the woman extremely vulnerable and dependent after the battering incident.[81] The contrition and remorse on the part of the husband, which follows the abusive incident, provides reinforcement for the woman to remain in the relationship, with the intermittent nature of this reinforcement further strengthening the woman's bond to the husband.[82]

In support of their theory, Dutton and Painter draw heavily on naturalistic and laboratory animal studies. To apply the theory to battered women they turn to the work of others, most notably, Walker's book, *The Battered Woman*.[83] While the application of the theory of traumatic bonding to battered women still remains empirically untested,[84] indirect support for the notion that attachment, as predicted by the theory, would be strongly related to the relationship variables of abuse intermittency and power imbalance has been found. For instance, Dutton and Painter[85] assessed 50 physically abused and 25 emotionally-only-abused[86] women at two points in time, immediately after separation from an abusive partner and again six months following separation. Although the emotionally abused-only women are referred to as a control sample,[87] the researchers do not treat them as a comparison group, but rather assess the variables underlying the theory within the entire sample. In line with the theory, the researchers found that a woman's attachment to her abuser was negatively related to her sense of self esteem and positively related to trauma symptomology at both points of assessment. Also in line with the theory, the intermittency of the abuse and perceived changes in power were strong predictors of the woman's post-separation attachment. Although the study focused only on post-relationship functioning and provides only a static examination of these variables at one point in time, it does demonstrate the powerful and lasting relationship between these variables and attachment within abusive relationships (both physical and emotional).[88]

80. *Id.* at 147.

81. *Id.* at 150.

82. *See id.*

83. *See* WALKER (1979), *supra* note 28.

84. *See* P. Lynn McDonald, *Helping With the Termination of an Assaultive Relationship,* in INTERVENING WITH ASSAULTED WOMEN: CURRENT THEORY, RESEARCH, & PRACTICE 99 (Barabara Pressman et al. eds., 1989).

85. *See* Donald G. Dutton & Susan Painter, *Emotional Attachments in Abusive Relationships: A Test of Traumatic Bonding Theory,* 8 VIOLENCE AND VICTIMS 105 (1993); *see also* DON-

ALD G. DUTTON, THE DOMESTIC ASSAULT OF WOMEN: PSYCHOLOGICAL & CRIMINAL PERSPECTIVES 207–13 (1995 revised and expanded edition).

86. Although some of the women in this group were also physically battered, women in this group had experienced less than two incidents of physical abuse and no instances of severe physical violence.

87. *See id.* at 110.

88. Although not directly assessing the theory of traumatic bonding, Dutton and Haring have conducted research in which they find "relationship" dynamics (i.e., physical abuse,

More general descriptions of the dynamics of battering relationships focus on the batterer's domination and control of the woman's behavior.[89] Indeed, a number of researchers view the batterer's attempts at domination and control as key to understanding the battering relationship.[90] Along these lines, Karla Fischer describes four elements that are characteristic of battering relationships that underlie the batterers' domination and control.[91] The first element involves the abuser's definition of himself as the "rule-maker" and everyone else as "the ones who follow the rules."[92] His domination may range from control over household rules to control over each family member's behavior and activities.[93] The second element involves the battered woman's internalization of the batterer's rules or what Fischer refers to as the process of self-censorship. In response to fears of violence, the woman censors her behavior, and eventually, as time goes on, the batterer needs to do less and less to control his family's behavior. This process is further reinforced by the woman's feelings of responsibility for the marriage and its success[94] and by the abuser's constant denigration of the woman for everything that goes wrong.[95]

Eventually, these rules become established in a pattern and are enforced through the use of punishment (third element); "batterers may either simply respond with abuse when a rule is broken, or they may make it clear that the abuse is punishment for violations."[96] Throughout this process "the batterer's behavior forms a cohesive pattern of coercive control."[97] In some cases, the pattern of control extends to "virtually every aspect of a woman's life, including money, food, sexuality, friendships, transportation, personal appearance, and access to supports including children, extended family members,

the abuser's domination/isolation and emotional abuse) to be related to women's attachment, trauma symptoms, and self-esteem, assessed 6 months following termination of the relationship. They also document the relationship between characteristics of the abuser's personality (e.g., borderline personality disorder) and the dynamics of the relationship. *See* Donald G. Dutton & Michelle Haring, *Perpetrator Personality Effects on Post–Separation Victim Reactions in Abusive Relationships*, 14 J. OF FAMILY VIOLENCE 193 (1999).

89. The context of coercion and control is also central to Walker's work. *See* WALKER (1984, 2000), *supra* note 30.

90. *See, e.g.*, Martha R. Mahoney, *Legal Images of Battered Women: Redefining the Issue of Separation*, 90 MICH. L. REV. 1, 53–60 (1991); Fischer et al., *supra* note 22, at 2126; R. EMERSON DOBASH & RUSSELL P. DOBASH, VIOLENCE AGAINST WIVES: A CASE AGAINST PATRIARCHY (1979); R. EMERSON DOBASH & RUSSELL P. DOBASH, WOMAN, VIOLENCE AND SOCIAL CHANGE 232 (1992); DEL MARTIN, BATTERED WIVES (1976); Kersti A. Yllo, *Through a Feminist Lens: Gender, Power, and Violence, in* CURRENT CONTROVERSIES ON FAMILY VIOLENCE, *supra* note 13; Evan Stark, *Representing Woman Battering: From Battered Woman Syndrome to Coercive Control*, 58 ALB. L. REV. 973; Sally A. Lloyd, *The Interpersonal and Communication Dynamics of Wife Batter-*

ing, in VIOLENCE IN INTIMATE RELATIONSHIPS, *supra* note 3, at 91–111. These approaches to wife assault further contextualize the domination and control of the batterer within a broader explanatory framework that emphasizes the "gendered expectations about family relationships and dynamics, and the patriarchal ideology and structure of society within which individuals and relationships are embedded." *Id.* at 47. In short, according to this view, cultural norms and sexual inequality within society grant men both the right and the ability to control women.

91. *See* Fischer et al., *supra* note 22.

92. *Id.* at 2126.

93. *See id.* at 2126–29.

94. These feelings of responsibility have been noted by a number of researchers and have been attributed to the woman's internalization of societal norms regarding sex roles. It should be noted, however, that rigid sex role socialization has not been observed in battered women as a group. *See* MARY ANN DUTTON (1992), *supra* note 50, at 82–84.

95. *See* Fischer et al., *supra* note 22, at 2129–30.

96. *Id.* at 2131.

97. Donald G. Dutton (1994), *supra* note 3, at 220.

and helping sources."[98] Emotional and abusive controlling acts on the part of the batterer forms the ongoing backdrop against which the physical abuse occurs.[99] At the core of the batterers' control, however, is the woman's fear of future violence (fourth element).[100] This fear may stem from past abuse or from threats of future physical or sexual abuse. Moreover, the woman's fear can be further intensified by the batterer's threats against other family members, his use of emotional or financial abuse, and the woman's social isolation.[101] Finally, the fear itself may also be triggered indirectly as the result of some verbal or non-verbal symbolic action of the batterer that is associated with the onset of an abusive incident.[102] Along these lines, Wilson, Johnson, and Daly found that the severity and recurrence of violence on the part of the batterer was positively related to both his psychological control of the woman (i.e., his attempts to limit her autonomy) and the woman's reported feelings of fear.[103]

In their attempts to end the abuse, battered women may employ a variety of strategies (e.g., trying to change the man's behavior, attempting to leave, protecting themselves and other members of the family).[104] These acts of "rebellion or resistance" to the man's control may be met with increased control and violence by the batterer. For instance, a woman may be physically and violently restrained from leaving, she may be held prisoner in her own home, her savings may be taken away, or she may be threatened with custody battles.[105] Martha Mahoney has described and labeled this form of assault on a woman's attempt to separate as "separation assault": "a specific type of attack that occurs at or after the moment she decides on a separation or begins to prepare for one."[106] Indeed, attempts at separation are not without risk. Empirical research suggests an elevated risk of violence for battered women when they separate from their abusers.[107] Data collected from the Canadian national survey found that 19 percent of women who had separated from a violent partner indicated that the violence continued after the separation, with one-third of these women reporting that the assaults actually

---

98. Evan Stark, *Framing and Reframing Battered Women, in* DOMESTIC VIOLENCE: THE CHANGING CRIMINAL JUSTICE RESPONSE 271, 282 (Eve S. Buzawa & Carl G. Buzawa eds., 1992).

99. *See* Fischer et al., *supra* note 22. For recent measures and conceptualizations of the battering context that attempt to capture the dynamic, ongoing and continuous nature of intimate violence within the measures used to assess the experience of violence in battered women's lives, *see* Paige Hall Smith et al., *Beyond the Measurement Trap: A Reconstructed Conceptualization and Measurement of Woman Battering,* 23 PSYCHOL. OF WOMEN Q. 177 (1999); *see also* Mary Ann Dutton, *Multidimensional Assessment of Woman Battering: Commentary on Smith, Smith, and Earp,* 23 PSYCHOL. OF WOMEN Q. 195 (1999); Jody Brown, *Working Toward Freedom From Violence,* 3 VIOLENCE AGAINST WOMEN 5 (1997).

100. *See* Fischer et al., *supra* note 22, at 2131.

101. *See id.* at 2121–32; *see also supra* note 24 and accompanying text.

102. *See id.*

103. *See* Margo Wilson et al., *Lethal and Nonlethal Violence Against Wives,* CANADIAN J. CRIMINOLOGY 331, 341 (1995).

104. *See supra* notes 66–77, and accompanying text.

105. *See* Mahoney, *supra* note 90, at 63.

106. *Id.* Mahoney notes the pragmatic recognition of the dangers of separation through the use of shelters with unlisted telephone numbers and addresses, and court issued protective orders. *Id.* at 65.

107. *See supra* note 8; *see also* WALTER S. DEKESEREDY & LINDA MACLEOD, WOMAN ABUSE: A SOCIOLOGICAL STORY (1997); Desmond Ellis & Walter S. DeKeseredy *Rethinking Estrangement, Interventions, and Intimate Femicide,* 3 VIOLENCE AGAINST WOMEN 590 (1997); Emma Morton et al., *Partner Homicide–Suicide Involving Female Homicide Victims: A Population–Based Study in North Carolina, 1988–1992,* 13 VIOLENCE & VICTIMS 91 (1998).

increased in severity. Wilson and Daly using police records investigated the frequency of homicides for co-habiting and estranged women in three samples (Canada; New South Wales, Australia; and Chicago). In all three samples women incurred substantially elevated risks when separated as compared to when living together with their partner.[108] Examining the motivation behind male-perpetrated partner homicide, another team of researchers, using an interview format, found that the most frequent precipitating event cited by men who had killed their partners was some form of perceived rejection on the part of the woman, her separation, or threat of separation.[109]

Coupled with the batterer's domination and control is a social reality that provides these women with few easy or viable options and it is against this backdrop that the battered woman's actions must be understood. Most prominent among the factors that further entrap women within the relationship is the woman's financial or economic dependence on the batterer, which as described earlier, may be exacerbated by the batterer's financial control of the woman.[110] Although wife battery is not confined to low socio-economic status families, research has consistently documented that violence is more likely to be reported in low-income households and in which the man is unemployed.[111] In one of the first studies that addressed the issue of economic dependence, it was found that women who remained in abusive relationships were more likely to be unemployed and were less educated than women who had left abusive relationships.[112] Since this study, other researchers, using a variety of methodologies, have similarly found that women who lack the financial means are less likely to leave violent partners or, if they do leave, are more likely to return.[113] A recent review of the research examining the relationship between battering and women's employment suggests that battering can have both a direct (e.g., batterer's negative interference) and an indirect (e.g., via its impact on a woman's health) impact on a women's job stability.[114] Lynn McDonald, in a review of the research examining the various

108. *See* Margo Wilson & Martin Daly, *Spousal Homicide Risk and Estrangement*, 8 VIOLENCE & VICTIMS 3 (1993). It is not necessarily the case that separation is causally linked to increased risk. An alternative explanation might be that women leave at a time when the violence is already escalating. Other case descriptions, however, suggest that there is a link between separation and murder. *See* Saunders & Browne, *supra* note 20, at 384–87.

109. *See* George W. Barnard et al., *'Til Death Do Us Part: A Study of Spouse Murder*, 10 BULL. OF THE ACAD. OF PSYCHIATRY & L. 271 (1982); *see* Morton et al., *supra* note 107.

110. *See* Follingstad et al. (1990), *supra* note 24.

111. *See supra* note 6.

112. *See* Richard J. Gelles, *Abused Wives: Why Do They Stay?* 38 J. OF MARRIAGE & THE FAM. 659 (1976).

113. *See* GONDOLF & FISHER, *supra* note 72; *see also* Michael J. Strube & Linda S. Barbour, *The Decision to Leave an Abusive Relationship: Economic Dependence and Psychological Commitment*, 45 J. OF MARRIAGE & THE FAM. 785

(1983); Michael J. Strube & Linda S. Barbour, *Factors Related to the Decision to Leave an Abusive Relationship*, 46 J. OF MARRIAGE & THE FAM. 837 (1984); B. E. Aguirre, *Why Do They Return? Abused Wives in Shelters*, 30 SOCIAL WORK 350 (1985). For reviews, *see* Michael J. Strube, *The Decision to Leave an Abusive Relationship: Empirical and Theoretical Issues*, 104 PSYCHOL. BULL. 236 (1988); MILDRED DALEY PAGELOW, FAMILY VIOLENCE 309–13 (1984).

114. *See* Richard M. Tolman & Jody Raphael, *A Review On Welfare and Domestic Violence*, 56 J. OF SOC. ISSUES 655 (2000). For example, Raphael found that women in abusive relationships faced many obstacles to both obtaining and maintaining employment. These obstacles included, "sabotage (e.g., destroying work, educational materials, or clothing, or bruising the woman's face), stalking, menacing the work site, traumatic aftereffects of violence, and even two documented murders when battered women neared financial independence." J. RAPHAEL, PRISONERS OF ABUSE: DOMESTIC VIOLENCE AND WELFARE RECEIPT. A SECOND REPORT OF THE WOMEN, WELFARE, AND ABUSE PROJECT 397(1996). Brown et al. found that women

resources available to assist battered women, concludes that there is indeed empirical support for the economic dependency hypothesis.[115]

Empirical support also exists for the claim that traditional social services provide limited assistance to battered women attempting to end the abuse.[116] For instance, in a review of this work, McDonald notes that medical personnel typically fail to ask about the abuse, are unlikely to identify abused women, and are evaluated by abused women as one of the least helpful resource groups.[117] Similarly, research has documented the unwillingness on the part of the police to respond to domestic disputes and to provide women with legal action.[118] In response to police minimization of the problem, several jurisdictions have implemented mandatory arrest or no-drop prosecution policies.[119] The findings in the literature, however, are fairly mixed with respect to the impact of mandatory arrest in terms of deterring the batterers' subsequent abuse.[120] Moreover, the extent to which these new laws and policies have

who had experienced recent physical aggression (i.e., in the past 12 months) had only "one third the odds of working at least 30 hours per week for 6 months or more during the following year as did women who had not experienced such aggression." Angela Browne et al., *The Impact of Recent Partner Violence on Poor Women's Capacity to Maintain Work*, 5 VIOLENCE AGAINST WOMEN 393, 417 (1999).

115. *See* McDonald, *supra* note 84, at 103.

116. For a review of studies that have examined the types of community and professional services contacted by battered women and women's perceptions of their usefulness, *see* Judith S. Gordon, *Community Services for Abused Women: A Review of Perceived Usefulness and Efficacy*, 11 J. OF FAM. VIOLENCE 315 (1996).

117. *See* McDonald, *supra* note 84, at 104.

118. For example, in one study, 58% of victims called the police and less than 25% of the batterers were arrested. *See* Martha L. Coulter et al., *Police-Reporting Behavior and Victim–Police Interactions as Described by Women in a Domestic Violence Shelter*, 14 J. OF INTERPERSONAL VIOLENCE 1290 (1999). Another study found that police arrested suspected batterers in only 21% of cases reported, even with clear evidence of abuse. DONALD G. DUTTON, THE DOMESTIC ASSAULT OF WOMEN: PSYCHOLOGICAL & CRIMINAL PERSPECTIVES (1988). This is comparable to data reported in the interview study conducted by Bowker, *supra* note 65 (1983). Police arrested batterers in only 15% of incidents. Moreover, in this study the women reported that the police refused to arrest the batterer arguing that no case existed (31%) and in 46% of the incidents the police recommended reconciliation. *Id.* at 88. Similarly, in another study researchers reported that of 53% of the women who called for police assistance, only 15% resulted in the arrest of the batterer and 32% reported incidents in which the police did nothing. Furthermore, this research discovered the police response, as is the case in many contexts, to be more influenced by the antiso-

cial nature of the batterer's behavior (e.g., a previous arrest was found to be the most influential) rather than the actual nature of the wife abuse. *Id.* at 67–73. GONDOLF & FISHER, *supra* note 72. For police attitudes, *see* Pam Waaland & Stuart Keeley, *Police Decision Making in Wife Abuse: The Impact of Legal and Extralegal Factors*, 9 L. & HUM. BEHAV. 355 (1985).

119. *See* Lynette Feder, *Police Handling of Domestic Violence Calls: An Overview and Further Investigation*, 10 WOMEN & CRIM. JUST. 49 (1999); *see also* Linda G. Mills, *Mandatory Arrest and Prosecution Policies for Domestic Violence: A Critical Literature Review and the Case for More Research to Test Victim Empowerment Approaches*, 25 CRIM. JUST. & BEHAV. 306 (1998). For research examining women's experiences in the prosecution of battering partners, *see* Mary Ann Dutton et al., *Court-Involved Battered Women's Responses to Violence: The Role of Psychological, Physical, and Sexual Abuse*, 14 VIOLENCE & VICTIMS 89 (1999); Lauren Bennett et al., *Systematic Obstacles to the Criminal Prosecution of a Battering Partner*, 14 J. OF INTERPERSONAL VIOLENCE 761 (1999).

120. *See* L. W. Sherman, *The Influence of Criminality on Criminal Law: Evaluating Arrest for Misdemeanor Domestic Violence*, 85 J. OF CRIM. L. & CRIMINOLOGY 901 (1992). For instance, the initial Minneapolis Domestic Violence Experiment concluded that arrest was the most effective response in deterring subsequent abuse. Lawrence W. Sherman & Richard A. Berk, *The Specific Deterrent Effects of Arrest for Domestic Assault*, 49 AM. SOC. REV. 261 (1984). In contrast, replications of this study have reported no differences in recidivism across different types of police responses. *See* Franklyn W. Dunford et al., *The Role of Arrest in Domestic Assault: The Omaha Police Experiment*, 28 CRIMINOLOGY 183 (1990); *see also* J. David Hirschel & Ira W. Hutchison, *Female Spouse Abuse and the Police Response: The Charlotte, North Carolina Experiment*, 83 J. OF

altered the actual behavior of the police has been questioned.[121] Thus, it is not surprising that battered women may not always call or turn to the police for help. A recent U.S. study explored the extent to which a sample of 137 women (African American or White), recruited from a battered women's shelter, called the police over a six–month period.[122] Sixty-seven percent of the sample had contacted the police and the majority of women reported that they had not had as much contact as they felt they needed. A range of situational barriers such as being physically prevented from calling, lacking a telephone, the ineffectiveness of the police response on a previous contact, and fear for their physical safety were cited for not calling the police.[123] Through interviews with 146 formerly battered women, Lee Bowker found that, over the course of five incidents of abuse, the police were contacted only 9 percent to 38 percent of the time.[124] Further, when asked to rate the success of the police intervention, only 34 percent of the interventions were viewed by the women as successful.[125]

More recently, investigators have turned their attention to delineating the dynamics of violence within intimate relationships in more ethnically and racially diverse couples. Such investigations have typically involved in-depth interviews with small select samples of battered women drawn from non-white populations,[126] but also includes national survey data.[127] This research

CRIM. L. & CRIMINOLOGY 73 (1992). Further, research has reported that a number of variables (e.g., marital status, employment status) may moderate the effectiveness of arrest as a deterrent. For example, using data collected in the Dade County replication study, the authors found that arrest had a significant deterring effect among employed batterers, whereas arrest led to a significant increase in subsequent assaults among unemployed batterers. Antony M. Pate & Edwin E. Hamilton, *Formal and Informal Deterrents to Domestic Violence: The Dade County Spouse Assault Experiment*, 57 AM. SOC. REV. 691 (1992). *See also* Lawrence W. Sherman et al., *The Variable Effects of Arrest on Criminal Careers: The Milwaukee Domestic Violence Experiment*, 83 J. OF CRIM. L. & CRIMINOLOGY 137 (1992).

121. *See* Feder (1999), *supra* note 119, at 52.

122. *See* Ruth E. Fleury et al., *"Why Don't They Just Call the Cops?": Reasons for Differential Police Contact Among Women with Abusive Partners*, 13 VIOLENCE & VICTIMS 333 (1998).

123. *See id.*

124. *See* LEE H. BOWKER (1983), *supra* note 65, at 87. Recently, in a sample of over 300 abused pregnant Hispanic women, only 23% had used the police during the past year. *See* William H. Wiist & Judith McFarlane, *Utilization of Police by Abused Pregnant Hispanic Women*, 4 VIOLENCE AGAINST WOMEN 677 (1998). Johnson found that women were "unlikely to call the police until they [had] been beaten up, and that well over half of all women who had been beaten up or choked . . . did not report the abuse to the police." JOHNSON (1996), *supra* note 5, at 205. Moreover, the women who

reported turning to the police reported experiencing more severe violence (e.g., multiple instances of violent episodes, use of a weapon, injury, presence of children). *Id.* at 205–08.

125. *See* BOWKER (1983), *supra* note 65, at 89.

126. *See e.g.,* Jenet R. Brice–Baker, *Domestic Violence in African–American and African–Caribbean Families*, 3 J. SOC. DISTRESS & THE HOMELESS 23 (1994); Kimberly A. Huisman, *Wife Battering in Asian American Communities*, 2 VIOLENCE AGAINST WOMEN 260 (1996); Catherine So–Kum Tang, *Psychological Impact of Wife Abuse, Experiences of Chinese Women and Their Children*,12 J. INTERPERSONAL VIOLENCE 466 (1997); Shamita Das Dasgupta & Sujata Warrier, *In the footsteps of "Arundhati" Asian Indian Women's Experiences of Domestic Violence in the United States*, 2 VIOLENCE AGAINST WOMEN 238 (1996); YOUNG I. SONG, BATTERED WOMEN IN KOREAN IMMIGRANT FAMILIES, THE SILENT SCREAM (1996). Carolyn M. West, *Lifting the "Political Gag Order" Breaking the Silence Around Partner Violence in Ethnic Minority Families, in* PARTNER VIOLENCE: A COMPREHENSIVE REVIEW OF 20 YEARS OF RESEARCH 184–209 (Jana L. Jasinski & Linda M. Williams eds., 1998); Meeta Mehrotra, *The Social Construction of Wife Abuse, Experiences of Indian Women in the United States*, 5 VIOLENCE AGAINST WOMEN 619 (1999); Hoan N. Bui & Marry Morash, *Domestic Violence in the Vietnamese Immigrant Community, An Exploratory Analysis*, 5 VIOLENCE AGAINST WOMEN 769 (1999); Satya P. Krishnan et al., *Documenting Domestic Violence among Ethnically Diverse Populations: Results from a Preliminary Study*, 20 FAM. COMMUNITY HEALTH 32 (1997).

increasingly documents a range of unique structural and cultural constraints (e.g., institutionalized racism, language barriers, familial norms, cultural acceptance and silence on issues of male violence, lack of knowledge about legal rights, lack of social support, immigration status, etc.) that further limit these women's options.

Finally, in the culmination of some battering relationships a battered woman may kill her batterer, ultimately ending the abuse she suffers. A number of studies, involving in-depth interviews with battered women who have killed, have attempted to examine the dynamics of violent relationships more specifically within these fatal relationships.[128] In the earliest of these studies, Browne compared battered women charged with the death or attempted death of their partners to a sample of battered women who had not killed.[129] No differences between these groups were found as a function of the women's characteristics or behavior. In contrast, the features that distinguished the experiences of women in these two groups were specific to the batterers' behavior. When compared to the comparison group, men in the homicide group were more likely to use drugs, were intoxicated more often, threatened and engaged in more frequent and harmful abuse of their partner, and were more likely to have abused a child or children.[130] Similar findings have been found in more recent investigations that have compared the responses of incarcerated battered women who have killed their abusers to battered women who have not killed (the comparison groups involved either battered women incarcerated for other crimes,[131] battered women drawn from community samples,[132] or battered women drawn from battered women's shelters[133]). Specifically, factors such as the frequency and severity of the violence, the severity of the woman's injuries, and the batterer's threats to kill or harm have been found to distinguish battered women who had resorted to lethal violence from those who had not.[134] In addition, in comparison to battered women who have not killed, greater alcohol involvement—on the part of both the women[135] and their partners[136]—has been found in some of the

127. *See e.g.*, Carolyn M. West et al., *Sociodemographic Predictors and Cultural Barriers to Help–Seeking Behavior by Latina and Anglo American Battered Women*, 13 VIOLENCE & VICTIMS 361 (1998); Juanita M. Firestone et al., *Intimate Violence Among Women of Mexican Origin: Correlates of Abuse*, 4 J. OF GENDER, CULTURE & HEALTH, 119 (1999); Mieko Yoshihama, *Domestic Violence Against Women of Japanese Descent in Los Angeles: Two Methods of Estimating Prevalence*, 5 VIOLENCE AGAINST WOMEN 869 (1999).

128. *See* BROWNE (1987), *supra* note 24; *see also* Maura O'Keefe, *Incarcerated Battered Women: A Comparison of Battered Women Who Killed Their Abusers and Those Incarcerated for Other Offences*, 12 J. FAM. VIOLENCE 1 (1997); Albert R. Roberts, *Battered Women Who Kill: A Comparative Study of Incarcerated Participants with a Community Sample of Battered Women*, 11 J. FAM. VIOLENCE 291 (1996); Gloria Hamilton & Tammy Sutterfield, *Comparison Study of Women Who Have and Have Not Murdered Their Abusive Partners*, in BREAKING THE RULES: WOMEN IN PRISON AND FEMI-

NIST THERAPY 45–55 (Judy Harden & Marcia Hill eds., 1998); William R. Blount et al., *Alcohol and Drug Use Among Abused Women Who Kill, Abused Women Who Don't, and Their Abusers*, 24 J. DRUG ISSUES 165 (1994); Mary Ann Dutton et al., *Traumatic Responses Among Battered Women Who Kill*, 7 J. TRAUMATIC STRESS 549 (1994); Joanne Hattendorf et al., *Type and Severity of Abuse and Posttraumatic Stress Disorder Symptoms Reported by Women Who Killed Abusive Partners*, 5 VIOLENCE AGAINST WOMEN 292 (1999).

129. *See* BROWNE (1987), *supra* note 24.

130. *See id.*

131. *See* O'Keefe, *supra* note 128.

132. *See* Roberts, *supra* note 128.

133. *See* Hamilton & Sutterfield, *supra* note 128; *see also* Blount et al., *supra* note 128.

134. *See* Roberts, *supra* note 128, at 297–98; *see also* O'Keefe, *supra* note 128, at 10–13; Dutton et al. (1994), *supra* note 128, at 553.

135. *See* Roberts, *supra* note 128, at 297; *see also* Blount et al., *supra* note 128, at 173.

samples of the women who had killed. Also noteworthy, in the majority of these samples, high rates of reported childhood experiences with sexual abuse or exposure to violence were evident.[137]

[3] The Impact of Abuse on a Woman—Battered Woman Syndrome and Psychological Sequelae

The term that the courts are perhaps most familiar with in terms of expert testimony pertaining to battered women is the "battered woman syndrome." Definition and use of this term, however, is far from clear.[138] Examination of the term in the legal literature indicates that it has been used loosely to refer to a wide range of phenomena.[139] Within the psychological literature there is also considerable variation. For instance, Bowker views it not as a psychological construct, but as a "shorthand term for a variety of conditions that hold battered women captive in violent" relationships.[140] For Lenore Walker, who first coined the term in 1979, the term takes on a more specific and clinical meaning.[141] "Battered woman syndrome" describes "a group of usually transient psychological symptoms that are frequently observed in a particular recognizable pattern in women who report having been physically, sexually, and/or psychologically abused."[142]

Although still somewhat imprecise in her definition,[143] since this initial description, Walker has devoted considerable attention to the delineation of the syndrome. In a book chapter, she notes that the "diagnostic term 'battered woman syndrome' may be used as a subcategory of Post Traumatic Stress Disorder (PTSD),"[144] but also indicates that "the collection of psychological symptoms that make up the Battered Woman Syndrome are very similar but not identical to those that comprise the diagnosis of Post-Traumatic Stress Disorder."[145] It should be noted that BWS is not a mental disorder, but rather refers to reactions that any normal person exposed to a traumatic event might develop.

To determine whether exposure to a trauma results in PTSD, two threshold criteria must first be met: presence of a stressor that could cause a traumatic response (i.e., the battering) and the symptoms must persist for

136. For example, only 34% of the women in the shelter group reported that their partners used alcohol on a daily basis compared to 62% of the women from the homicide sample. *See* Blount et al., *supra* note 128, at 172. At the same time, however, another study revealed no differences in the spouse's alcohol use. High rates of alcohol abuse were reported for the woman's partner in both the sample of women who had killed their abuser and those who had not. *See* O'Keefe, *supra* note 128.

137. *See* Roberts, *supra* note 128, at 298–99.

138. *See* Mary Ann Dutton (1993), *supra* note 22, at 1193–96.

139. It has been used to refer to both the pattern of violence battered women experience as well as the psychological effects of the violence on women. *Id.* at 1195 n.14; McMahon *supra* note 40, at 26. Similarly, Walker notes

that "the legal system uses BWS to describe both the clinical syndrome and the dynamics of the battering relationship." Lenore A. Walker, *Understanding the Battered Woman Syndrome*, 31 TRIAL 30, 32 (1995).

140. BOWKER (1983), *supra* note 65, at 154. For conditions that this would encompass, *see supra* notes 112 to 129 and accompanying text.

141. *See* Walker (1995), *supra* note 139, at 32.

142. Walker (1993), *supra* note 49, at 135.

143. *See* McMahon (1999), *supra* note 40, at 36–37.

144. PTSD is a diagnostic category listed in the DIAGNOSTIC AND STATISTICAL MANUAL OF MENTAL DISORDERS (4th ed.) (DSM–IV). BWS is not explicitly listed by name, but no subcategories are listed.

145. *Id.* at 344.

more than one month.[146] In addition to these two criteria, three different symptom clusters of PTSD must be identified in the individual: arousal symptoms, intrusive symptoms, and avoidance symptoms.[147] In the battered woman's case, the high arousal of the woman's physical and mental systems result in such symptoms as pervasive anxiety, panic attacks, phobias, and hypervigilance to cues of further harm.[148] The woman becomes "hypervigilant to cues of any potential danger, recognizing the little things that signal an impending incident, and often acts as though she is nervous, jumpy, and highly anxious."[149] The second set of symptoms refers to the woman's re-experiencing of the traumatic event through nightmares, repetitive intrusive memories, flashbacks, dissociative states and intense fear of recurrence of the trauma.[150] Given the woman's exposure to the violence in the past, "certain behaviors such as specific verbal responses (e.g., yelling obscenities that had previously been paired with violence) or gestures (e.g., pounding fist on table) may trigger a PTSD reaction, even when there is no actual danger."[151] In such an instance, these intrusive symptoms "may lead a battered woman to believe that she must take immediate action to protect herself."[152]

Finally, the third cluster of symptoms, avoidance symptoms, involve the woman's "denial, minimization and repression" of the abuse.[153] These symptoms are employed as survival "techniques . . . to avoid having to deal with the dangerousness of the situation,"[154] and explain why battered women may not respond to the violence in a way in which one might expect—for instance, with denial and minimization of the abuse, "she is less likely to acknowledge the abuse to herself, name it for others, or seek help in responding to it."[155] The woman with PTSD, it is contended, alternates between phases of the intrusion and the avoidance symptoms,[156] which can help explain what appears on the surface to be contradictory behaviors.[157]

Walker claims most battered women easily meet PTSD criteria, "usually with more symptoms observed than is needed for diagnosis."[158] Although she provides no data pertaining to the reliability or validity of this diagnosis, a number of investigators have now examined this issue directly by assessing the extent to which battered women are at risk for developing PTSD. For instance, using self-report measures that included PTSD indicators, Anita

---

146. Two factors must be present for a positive diagnosis: "(1) the person experienced, witnessed, or was confronted with an event or events that involved actual or threatened death or serious injury, or a threat to the physical integrity of self or others, (2) the person's response involved intense fear, helplessness, or horror." This criterion requires that the symptoms cause "clinically significant distress or impairment in social, occupational, or other important areas of functioning." *Id.* at 427–29.

147. *See id.*

148. *See* Walker (1996), *supra* note 55, at 217.

149. Lenore E. A. Walker, *Battered Women Syndrome and Self–Defense,* 6 Notre Dame J. of L. Ethics & Pub. Pol'y 321, 328 (1992).

150. *Id.* at 327–328; Walker (1996), *supra* note 57 at 345.

151. *See* Mary A. Dutton & Lisa A. Goodman, *Posttraumatic Stress Disorder Among Battered Women: Analysis of Legal Implications,* 12 Behav. Sci. & L. 215, 225 (1994).

152. *Id.*

153. Walker (1992), *supra* note 149, at 328; Walker (1996), *supra* note 55, at 344–45.

154. Walker (1992), *supra* note 149, at 328.

155. Dutton & Goodman (1994), *supra* note 151, at 225.

156. The length and timing of these particular phases within the individual, however, are not specified.

157. *See* Dutton & Goodman (1994), *supra* note 151, at 217.

158. Walker (1993), *supra* note 49, at 329.

Kemp and her colleagues[159] found that approximately 85 percent of a sample of 77 battered women drawn from a shelter residence were diagnosed with PTSD.[160] Houskamp and Foy,[161] using both self-report measures and a Structured Interview for PTSD,[162] found that 45 percent of a sample of 26 women who had contacted a domestic violence clinic met full criteria for PTSD. Moreover, in both of these studies the presence of PTSD symptomology was positively related to the frequency and severity of the violence. Another study conducted by Kemp and her colleagues[163] found that 81 percent of a sample of 179 battered women[164] were diagnosed with PTSD. And again, the severity of the abuse was related to the severity of symptomatology; battered women with PTSD "experienced more physical abuse, more verbal abuse, more injuries, a greater sense of threat, and more forced sex" than battered women without PTSD. This study also included a control group of nonbattered but verbally abused women.[165] Sixty-two percent of this sample was also diagnosed with PTSD. It should be noted, however, that, as in the sample of battered women, high rates of past abuse were reported in this latter sample.[166]

Astin and her colleagues[167] assessed the prevalence of diagnosable PTSD in a sample of 53 battered women who were either shelter residents or clients of a community counselling center. Participants in this study were administered two standardized self-report measures of PTSD symptomology.[168] Overall, both measures yielded prevalence rates in the mid-fifties.[169] The two measures, however, were only moderately related,[170] and a more conservative classification system in which a positive PTSD diagnosis on both measures had to be obtained, yielded a 33 percent prevalence rate for PTSD. Similar to

159. *See* Anita Kemp et al., *Post-Traumatic Stress Disorder (PTSD) in Battered Women: A Shelter Sample*, 4 J. OF TRAUMATIC STRESS 137 (1991).

160. The criteria set out in the DSM–III–R for PTSD was used: one re-experiencing symptom, three avoidance symptoms, and two persistent symptoms of increased arousal. Also, in an effort to examine the validity of the self-report measures, 20 of the women were additionally interviewed face to face following completion of the self-report questionnaire. Similar results were found using the interview method. *See id.* at 140.

161. *See* Beth M. Houskamp & David W. Foy, *The Assessment of Posttraumatic Stress Disorder in Battered Women*, 6 J. OF INTERPERSONAL VIOLENCE 367 (1991).

162. *See id.* at 370–71.

163. *See* Anita Kemp et al., *Incidence and Correlates of Posttraumatic Stress Disorder in Battered Women*, 10 J. OF INTERPERSONAL VIOLENCE 43 (1995).

164. Women were recruited from shelters, support groups, therapist referrals, and newspaper advertisements Eighty-two percent were Caucasian and 14% were African American. *See id.*

165. Women were recruited primarily from newspaper advertisements. Eighty-five percent were Caucasian and 10% were African American. *Id.*

166. Ninety-six percent of the verbally abused women reported being abused as a child, 31% reported experiencing unwanted sexual contact by a family member as a child, 21% reported being raped as an adult, and 15% reported experiencing other physically abusive relationships in the past. The rates for the physical abuse group were 71%, 26%, 50%, and 41%, respectively. *See id.* at 45.

167. *See* Millie C. Astin et al., *Posttraumatic Stress Disorder Among Battered Women: Risk and Resiliency Factors*, 8 VIOLENCE & VICTIMS 17 (1993).

168. These measures included the Impact Event Scale and a 47 item Symptom Checklist of which 17 were related to PTSD criteria. *See id.* at 20.

169. With respect to the Impact of Event Scale (IES), the researchers diagnosed a woman as PTSD positive if she obtained a score equal to or greater than the mean on one of the two subscales of the IES (i.e., Intrusion). The validity of this is questionable since the IES measures only two of the three PTSD criteria (Intrusion, Avoidance). Moreover, as the mean of a sample will fluctuate depending upon the sample participants involved, the choice of the mean as a cutoff for diagnosis is inappropriate as it is entirely dependent upon the sample employed.

170. Astin et al., *supra* note 167, at 22.

the other studies, a positive relationship between the intensity of the symptomology and the frequency of the violence was found. In a second study Astin and her colleagues[171] compared a sample of 50 battered women seeking assistance with a community sample of 37 women in distressed relationships who had not experienced battering.[172] Using a structured clinical interview to assess PTSD, it was found that more of the battered women (55 percent) than the maritally distressed women (19 percent) were diagnosed with PTSD.[173] Within both samples, a prior history of childhood sexual abuse distinguished those women who were diagnosed with PTSD from those who did not develop PTSD.[174]

Saunders[175] compared two groups of battered women on three different self-report measures of post-traumatic stress.[176] Reasoning that battered women seeking help at domestic violence agencies would experience more severe violence than battered women seeking help at non-domestic violence programs (e.g., mental health centers, private practitioners), he hypothesized that the former group of women would experience higher levels of PTSD. In total, 159 women comprised the sample of women seeking assistance from domestic violence programs and 33 women comprised the sample of women seeking help from other types of agencies. For assessment of PTSD, the study employed nine PTSD relevant items from the Diagnostic Interview Schedule, a 263–item interview schedule originally developed to determine the incidence and prevalence of mental disorders in the U.S.[177] Women were classified as PTSD positive if four of the nine symptoms were met.[178] Overall, approximately 60 percent of the women within each group met this diagnostic criteria.[179] Using the same instrument, another researcher[180] reported a prevalence rate of 40 percent for a sample of 30 women who were shelter residents and a rate of 31 percent for a sample of 32 women living at home (some with and some

---

171. *See* Millie C. Astin et al., *Posttraumatic Stress Disorder and Childhood Abuse in Battered Women: Comparisons with Maritally Distressed Women,* 63 J. CONSULTING & CLINICAL PSYCHOL. 308 (1995).

172. On the basis of the Conflict Tactics Scale, 19 of the 56 women recruited for the maritally distressed sample were excluded because they also indicated exposure to violence in their relationship. The investigators report that of these women, half were subsequently diagnosed as PTSD positive (a rate similar to that evidenced in the sample of battered women). A number of researchers have noted the difficulty of obtaining comparison groups of women in distressed but nonviolent relationships. *See* Linda L. Marshall, *Physical and Psychological Abuse, in* THE DARK SIDE OF INTERPERSONAL COMMUNICATION 281, 291 (Brian H. Spitzberg ed., 1994).

173. *See* Astin et al. (1995), *supra* note 171, at 310. Although the two samples were found to be different on a range of demographics (e.g., age, education, socioeconomic status), only age was related to PTSD status. Moreover, additional analyses indicated that age did not account for the differential rates of PTSD within the samples.

174. In contrast, childhood physical abuse did not predict PTSD-status within either sample. *See id.* at 310.

175. *See* Daniel G. Saunders, *Posttraumatic Stress Symptom Profiles of Battered Women: A Comparison of Survivors in Two Settings,* 9 VIOLENCE & VICTIMS 31 (1994).

176. These included the Impact of Event Scale, a 17 item Posttraumatic Stress Scale, and 9 symptoms from the Diagnostic Interview Schedule. *See id.* at 35.

177. This instrument has been employed in large epidemiological studies of mental disorders and employs DSM–III diagnoses. *See id.*

178. *See id.* at 38. Note that this diagnosis is not as stringent as the criteria employed in the DSM–III–R.

179. Women who sought assistance from a domestic violence program displayed a greater frequency of PTSD symptoms compared to those seeking help elsewhere. These differences were eliminated, however, when statistically controlling for injury, abuse frequency and length of time since the relationship. *See id.* at 39.

180. *See* Walter J. Gleason, *Mental Disorders in Battered Women: An Empirical Study,* 8 VIOLENCE & VICTIMS 53 (1993).

without the batterer) who were receiving assistance from the same shelter agency.[181] A comparison group of 10,953 women from a national epidemiological study reported a prevalence rate of only one percent.[182]

In a series of studies, Dutton and her colleagues explored PTSD symptomology in various samples of battered women. In one such study, a sample of 33 battered women charged with actual or attempted homicide of their abusive partners[183] were compared to a group of 30 battered women matched for age and ethnicity (drawn from a mental health clinic). Two variables believed to mediate the effects of the violence on the women—the severity of the violence and the woman's perceived level of social support—were also measured. The study did not assess for a full clinical diagnosis of PTSD, but rather assessed the level of post-traumatic indicators. Overall, more women in the forensic sample reported greater levels of post-traumatic stress (on both general and specific indicators), more severe violence and less social support, than did the comparison group.[184] When group differences in terms of social support and severity of violence were statistically controlled for, however, group differences in general levels of post-traumatic stress were eliminated.[185] In contrast, even after controlling for these group differences, battered women who had killed their abusers still reported more intrusion and avoidance symptoms than did the comparison sample.[186]

In yet another study, Dutton and her colleagues examined the role played by the meaning women attached to the violence in their lives.[187] To this end, 72 battered women, drawn from a family violence outpatient clinic, were administered measures to assess their cognitive schemata[188] regarding such issues as safety, trust, self-esteem, and intimacy. Cognitions or beliefs about the violence (e.g., attributions regarding its cause, appraisals of past severity, expectations of severe violence), as well as five measures of post-traumatic stress were obtained. The purpose of the study was to assess the relation between the meaning women ascribed to the violence and their cognitive schemata, and, further, the relation of this latter variable to indicators of psychological distress. Overall, the study revealed that the women's cognitive schemata (e.g., regarding issues of safety and fear) were related to the meaning women assigned to the violence. More specifically, the women's expectation of some form of violence in the future was the most important variable to explain women's negative schemata. As predicted, negative cognitive schemata also co-occurred with indicators of post-traumatic stress. Also noteworthy in the study, a significant relationship was found between measures of intrusive symptoms and the women's perceptions of safety, suggest-

---

181. *See id.* at 57.

182. *See id.*

183. *See* Dutton et al. (1994), *supra* note 128.

184. *See id.* at 554–56.

185. *See id.*

186. A number of possible explanations for this finding are offered: (1) the groups may have differed in terms of their expectations of lethal violence, a variable not measured in the study, (2) the forensic sample may have been exposed to a greater number of traumatic events unrelated to the battering, and (3) social support may offer less of a buffer for these particular symptoms. *See id.* at 560–61.

187. *See* Mary Ann Dutton et al., *Battered Women's Cognitive Schemata*, 7 J. TRAUMATIC STRESS 237 (1994).

188. Cognitive schemata is a psychological term referring to an individual's organized knowledge structure about some type of concept or stimulus (e.g., events, people). *See id.* at 238.

ing to the authors "that the 'recollections' of trauma ... may function to maintain generalized fear structures."[189]

More recently, Dutton and her colleagues explored the psychological impact that battering can have on women (i.e., depression, PTSD symptomatology, acute stress), with particular attention given to the component of psychological abuse that battered women experience.[190] This investigation examined court-involved battered women's responses to intimate violence (i.e., using the criminal justice system, terminating the relationship) and included separate measures of physical, psychological, and sexual abuse.[191] Consistent with other research, more severe violence lead to greater help-seeking behavior and more severe psychological stress symptoms. Moreover, the measures of physical abuse were more important determinants of the women's use of the legal system and their decisions to leave the relationship, while the measure of psychological abuse played a greater role in predicting the women's traumatic responses (acute and posttraumatic stress). Dutton and colleagues concluded that in the context of physical assault, it is the "psychological abuse that is more determinant of stress disorder symptoms."[192]

In an attempt to differentiate the effects of psychological abuse from those associated with physical violence, Vitanza and colleagues[193] examined levels of emotional distress and PTSD symptomology in a sample of 93 psychologically abused women (predominantly white and middle class)[194] who differed in terms of the level of physical violence they had sustained at the hands of their male partner (none, moderate, severe).[195] The women were recruited through advertisements that were targeted for "women in long-term 'bad' or 'stressful' relationships."[196] Although the researchers found that the severity of violence was positively related to PTSD symptoms, high levels of emotional distress symptoms were evidenced across all three groups.[197] Higher reports of suicide attempts were also found for the women who experienced severe violence.[198]

---

189. *Id.* at 250–51. Although the results are certainly consistent with this interpretation, the direction of causality between these variables, as the authors note, cannot be ascertained given the methodology employed. *Id.* at 252.

190. *See* Dutton et al. (1999), *supra* note 119.

191. The sample consisted of 149 women seeking assistance from a domestic violence intake center that was located in the court. Participants were predominately African American (91%). *See id.*

192. *Id.* at 102.

193. *See* Stephanie Vitanza et al., *Distress and Symptoms of Posttraumatic Stress Disorder in Abused Women*, 10 VIOLENCE & VICTIMS 21 (1995).

194. Eighty-nine percent were white and 70% were middle class. *See id.* at 26.

195. The women were first screened to ensure that they had been subjected to high levels of psychological abuse from their part-

ner. A second level of screening, based on the women's responses to a 46 item measure assessing the male's level of violence, resulted in three groups of women: (1) those that had not sustained any level of violence, (2) those that had sustained a moderate level of violence, and (3) those that had sustained high levels of violence in the relationship. *See id.* at 26–27.

196. *Id.* at 26.

197. The PTSD subscale employed identified approximately 56% of the sample as having PTSD. Using a more conservative score on the measure, approximately 33% of the sample was classified with PTSD. Breakdowns for the three groups are not provided. *See id.* at 31.

198. Forty-three percent of women in the severe group had attempted suicide compared to 23% in the psychological abuse group. Those experiencing moderate levels of violence reported the lowest level of attempted suicide (13%). *See id.* at 28. Consistent with this finding, Evan Stark & Anne Flitcraft, *Killing the Beast Within: Woman Battering and Female Suicidality*, 25 INT'L J. HEALTH SERVICES 43

Similar to Vitanza and colleagues, Arias and Pape attempted to examine the role of psychological abuse on women's psychological adjustment "above and beyond the effects of their physical abuse."[199] Their study also looked at the relationship between psychological abuse and a woman's decision to terminate the relationship, again controlling for the effects of physical abuse. To this end, 68 women[200] recruited from battered women's shelters were administered a range of self-report measures that assessed the frequency and severity of physical and psychological violence in their lives, as well as coping strategies, and psychological symptomatology. High levels of physical violence, psychological abuse, and PTSD symptomatology, were reported by the women (88 percent of the sample reaching the cutoff score of suspected PTSD).[201] And, as expected there was a strong association between physical and psychological abuse. Of particular note, however, was the finding that, while physical abuse was not predictive of PTSD symptomatology or a woman's intention to end the relationship, psychological abuse was predictive of these two variables, even after controlling for the effects of physical abuse. The more extreme the psychological abuse reported, the more extreme the PTSD symptomatology exhibited and the stronger the woman's resolve to leave the batterer. Moreover, the researchers found that PTSD symptomatology moderated the relationship between the abuse experienced and a woman's intention to leave. That is, the severity of abuse was only predictive of a woman's intention to leave when PTSD symptomatology was low, thus leading the researchers to conclude that "women were able to conceive of termination of the abusive relationship as a viable option and were committed to that option in response to abuse only if they were not hampered by psychological distress."[202]

Taken in their entirety, the studies indicate that battered women are indeed at risk for developing PTSD with estimates ranging from 31 percent to 88 percent. Moreover, across the majority of studies, the severity of the

---

(1995), investigated the association between abuse and attempted suicide by examining the medical records of 176 women who presented to an emergency hospital during a 1–year period. Using a conservative estimate of battering (documented injury requiring medical attention), they found evidence of abuse in approximately 29% of the women (with black women and those pregnant over represented in the group of women). Moreover, "over a third of the battered women visited the hospital with an abuse-related injury or complaint *on the same day* as their suicide attempt." *Id.* at 53. Also of note was the finding that the medical response to the women identified as battered neglected the issue of their abuse history. These women were more likely to be sent home or receive no referrals for mental health or social services. Another recent study examined the association between partner abuse and suicidal behavior in a sample of low income, African–American women. The sample consisted of 119 women presenting to a hospital following a non-fatal suicide attempt. These women were compared to a control group of 85 women who presented to the hospital for non-emergency medical problems. Women who had attempted

suicide were about "three times more likely to report both physical and nonphysical partner abuse, and three times more likely to meet criteria for PTSD than women with no history of suicide behavior." *Id.* at 67. Analyses also indicated that the relationship between physical abuse and suicidal behavior was mediated by PTSD symptomatology. *See id.* at 66–67. Martie P. Tompson et al., *Partner Abuse and Posttraumatic Stress Disorder as Risk Factors for Suicide Attempts in a Sample of Low–Income, Inner City Women,* 12 J. Traumatic Stress 59 (1999).

199. Ileana Arias & Karen T. Pape, *Psychological Abuse: Implications for Adjustment and Commitment to Leave Violent Partners,* 14 Violence & Victims 55, 57; *see also* Ileana Arias, *Women's Responses to Physical and Psychological Abuse, in* Violence in Intimate Relationships, *supra* note 3, at 139–61.

200. Forty-eight percent were White American, 43% were African American, 3% were Latino American, and 6% were Native American. Arias & Pape, *see id.* at 58.

201. *See id.* at 60.

202. *Id.* at 64.

violence experienced was positively related to PTSD diagnosis and symptomology. The criteria employed across the studies have varied widely, with the majority primarily relying on self-report measures, which, in turn, have employed different criteria for a positive diagnosis. The studies also vary in terms of the stage in the woman's relationship at which the assessment occurs. All of these variables can affect the prevalence rates reported. For instance, measures administered shortly after arrival at a shelter may yield inflated estimates as the symptomology evidenced may reflect a temporary crisis rather than PTSD symptomology.[203] Moreover, the samples have varied in terms of the extent to which the women have suffered other forms of trauma in their lives (both past and present). It was not uncommon for battered women to have experienced multiple traumatic stressors in their lives (e.g., prior history of abusive relationships), thus rendering explanations for the elevated level of risk of PTSD difficult to disentangle.[204]

The more recent studies also point to the profound impact of the verbal and emotional abuse that women experience within battering relationships. Indeed, the impact of emotional abuse is typically described by battered women as severe, and sometimes more devastating, than the physical abuse they sustain.[205] The inclusion of control or comparison groups, typically involving women in conflictual or distressful relationships, however, indicates that PTSD is present, albeit not to the same degree, in women in non-violent relationships as well. If this finding is due to the verbal abuse in these relationship alone, the results pose "an issue for the present version of the diagnosis"[206] as the presence of a trauma involving "a physical threat to one's life or physical integrity, to family, to home or the witnessing of violence" is required for a positive diagnosis of PTSD.[207]

In addition to PTSD, researchers report that a host of other physical, emotional, and psychological problems can occur as a result of the violence. Indeed, through interviews and observation of battered women, researchers have identified symptoms such as multiple somatic complaints, agitation, anxiety, insomnia (frequented by violent nightmares), depression and suicidal behavior.[208]

203. *See* Astin et al. (1993), *supra* note 167, at 18.

204. For instance, the association between PTSD and history of past abuse (primarily sexual abuse) is well documented in the literature. *See* Christine Wekerle & David A. Wolfe, *Child Maltreatment, in* CHILD PSYCHOPATHOLOGY (Eric J. Mash & Russell A. Barkle eds., 1996).

205. *See* Follingstad et al., *supra* note 24; *see also* O'Leary (1999), *supra* note 23.

206. Kemp et al. suggest that if verbal abuse alone predicts PTSD, the trauma criterion for diagnosis is questionable and "either the trauma needs to be more broadly and more psychologically defined, or the diagnosis needs to be refined." *See* Kemp et al., *supra* note 163, at 53.

207. The DSM–IV, as did its predecessor the DSM–III–R, requires that the stressor "involved actual or threatened death or serious injury, or a threat to the physical integrity of self or others," for a positive diagnosis of PTSD.

208. For example, Rounsaville and Weissman interviewed 31 battered women (drawn from emergency services and a mental health center) and found that 60% of the women exhibited moderate depressive symptoms, 20% revealed levels similar to hospitalized patients and 20% were asymptomatic. Using a more stringent criteria (DSM–II) 52% were diagnosed with depression. *See* Bruce Rounsaville & Myrna Weissman, *Battered Women: A Medical Problem Requiring Detection*, 8 INT'L J. PSYCHIATRY IN MED. 191 (1978). Similar rates were found by Cascardi & O'Leary, *Depressive Symptomatogy, Self-esteem, and Self Blame in Battered Women*, 7 J. FAM. VIOLENCE 99 (1992). Suzanne Kerouac et al. examined the psychological health of 130 women seeking help from a shelter; scores on measures of depression, anxiety, and somatization were higher than those of a comparison group of 170 women

In one of the more representative studies, Gelles and Harrup[209] examined 3,002 currently or previously (within the last year) coupled women respondents interviewed for the Second National Family Violence Survey.[210] Women were divided into three groups depending on the level of reported violence (no violence, minor, and severe violence). In general, the higher the level of violence experienced, the greater the proportion of women reporting some form of psychological distress (e.g., these women reported feeling nervous or stressed, bad/worthless, unable to cope, hopeless, and considered taking their own lives). Similarly, Follingstad et al.[211] found that women experiencing more severe types of violence were more likely to report a greater number of symptoms. In addition, these authors measured the women's subjective reports of their emotional health during five stages in their lives (childhood, before abusive relationship, early in the relationship prior to abuse, during the abuse, and since the abuse ended). Results indicated that the periods prior to the abuse were typically healthier emotionally than during the abuse, followed by improved health after the abuse ended. Although these findings must be interpreted with caution since they are retrospective in nature and therefore susceptible to bias, the findings are supported by a recent longitudinal study that involved in-depth interviews with 98 battered women who were interviewed at three points in time over a three-year period.[212] The sample

taken from the general population. These differences were only statistically significant, however, for the depression and anxiety dimensions. *See* Kerouac et al., *Dimensions of Health in Violent Families,* 7 HEALTH CARE FOR WOMEN INT'L 413 (1986). In a similar study, 40 battered women admitted to a shelter were compared with 40 women from the community. Battered women displayed greater distress on a number of measures and scored higher on the Beck Depression Inventory. *See* Christina Christopoulos et al., *Children of Abused Women: Adjustment at Time of Shelter Residence,* 49 J. MARRIAGE & THE FAM. 611 (1987). Mitchell and Hodson, examining 60 battered women seeking assistance from one of six shelters, also found these women to be characterized by higher rates of depression when compared to nonpatient females (but, were close to scores for psychiatric outpatients). *See* Roger E. Mitchell & Christine A. Hodson, *Coping With Domestic Violence: Social Support and Psychological Health Among Battered Women,* 11 AM. J. COMM. PSYCH. 629 (1983). Bergman and Brismar examined diagnosis in psychiatric inpatient care received by 117 battered women seeking assistance at a hospital emergency room during a fifteen year period. These women were compared to a control group selected from the population register and matched for age and geographic area. Diagnosis of depression (16%), psychoses (9%), alcoholism (23%), drug addiction (9%), and suicide attempts (15%) were significantly higher for the battered women group. *See* Bo Bergman & Bo Brismar, *A 5–Year Follow-up Study of 117 Battered Women,* 81 AM. J. PUB. HEALTH 1486 (1991). Similarly, Hilberman and Munson examined 60 battered women seeking assistance

at a health clinic and through interviews observed a range of symptoms, such as somatic concerns, anxiety and depression. *See* Elaine Hilberman & Kit Munson, *Sixty Battered Women,* 2 VICTIMOLOGY 460 (1977). With a sample of 141 battered women (predominantly African American) drawn from the community, Campbell and Soeken found evidence for both a direct and indirect effect of battering on women's health (e.g., depression, physical health), with the latter relationship mediated by women's "self care agency" (perceived care of self). *See* Jacquelyn C. Campbell & Karen L. Soeken, *Women's Responses to Battering: A Test of the Model,* 22 RES. IN NURSING & HEALTH 49 (1999); *see also* Phyllis W. Sharps & Jacqueline Campbell, *Health Consequences for Victims of Violence in Intimate Relationships, in* VIOLENCE IN INTIMATE RELATIONSHIPS, *supra* note 3, at 162–80; Nancy R. Rhodes & Eva Baranoff McKenzie, *Why Do Battered Women Stay?: Three Decades of Research,* 3 AGGRESSION & VIOLENCE 391–406 (1998).

209. *See* Richard J. Gelles & John W. Harrup, *Violence, Battering, and Psychological Distress Among Women,* 4 J. INTERPERSONAL VIOLENCE 400 (1989).

210. *See* GELLES & STRAUS, *supra* note 11.

211. *See* Diane R. Follingstad, et al., *Factors Moderating Physical and Psychological Symptoms of Battered Women,* 6 J. FAM. VIOLENCE 81, 88 (1991).

212. *See* Jacquelyn C. Campbell & Karen L. Soeken, *Women's Responses to Battering Over Time, An Analysis of Change,* 14 J. INTERPERSONAL VIOLENCE 21 (1999).

was divided into three groups: those abused only at Time 1 (n=28); those abused at Times 1 and 2 (n=22); and those abused at all three times of assessment (n=39). Women who were abused at all three time periods evidenced a deterioration in their mental health (e.g., self-esteem, depression), whereas the other two groups evidenced improvements over time (e.g., improvements in self-esteem, depression). The only identifiable difference across the three groups at Time 1, in terms of the demographic and abuse related variables that were measured, involved an index of the woman's assessment of danger, with those abused at all three time periods significantly higher in terms of their assessment of danger, compared to the other two groups.[213]

Recently, Golding,[214] using meta-analytic techniques, reviewed the literature on the prevalence of mental health problems among women who have been physically abused by an intimate male partner.[215] Her analyses document the high prevalence rates of depression,[216] suicidality,[217] PTSD,[218] alcohol abuse or dependence,[219] and drug abuse or dependence found among battered women.[220] When compared to female rates in general population studies and control groups (for those studies that included them), the prevalence rates in all cases were substantially higher for battered women. Golding also found that the variation in rates evidenced across the studies was largely due to the methodological differences in the research such as the samples employed (e.g., high prevalence rates for depression observed in shelter residents; the highest rates for suicidality found among psychiatric patients) or the methods of data collection (e.g., higher rates of PTSD were evidenced in studies that used self-administered measures of PTSD as opposed to structured interviews). Finally, with respect to depression and PTSD, the prevalence rate was also related to the severity or duration of the violence experienced, with greater abuse associated with more elevated levels of depression and PTSD.

In sum, a range of studies document the profound impact that intimate violence can have on women's physical and mental health, with a host of psychological problems or symptomology identified among battered women. There does not, however, appear to be overwhelming support for a single profile that captures the impact of abuse on a woman. On the contrary, the research demonstrates that "battered women's diverse psychological realities are not limited to one particular profile."[221] As such, Dutton, in a review of the range of psychological sequelae that can follow physical and sexual violence,

213. *See id.* at 30.

214. *See* Jacqueline M. Golding, *Intimate Partner Violence as a Risk Factor for Mental Disorders: A Meta–Analysis*, 14 J. Fam. Violence 99 (1999).

215. In her review she includes only those studies that have provided specific prevalence rates of mental health. *Id.* at 103.

216. Across the 18 studies that included measures of depression, the weighted mean prevalence of depression was 47.6% (with rates ranging from 15% to 83% across the studies). A weighted mean gives greater weight to the estimates associated with greater precision (i.e., smaller variability). *See id.* at 106.

217. The weighted mean prevalence across the 13 studies that included suicidality was

17.9% (ranging from 4.6% to 77% across the studies). *See id.* at 112.

218. Across the 11 studies that assessed PTSD the mean prevalence rate was 63.8% (with rates varying from 31% to 84.4%). *See id.* at 116.

219. For the 10 studies that included assessments of alcohol abuse or dependence the weighted mean was 18.5% (6.6% to 44%). *See id.* at 120.

220. For drug abuse or dependence, the weighted mean across the four studies was 8.9% (ranged from 7% to 25%). *See id.* at 124.

221. Dutton (1993), *supra* note 22, at 1195.

argues that it is much broader than is generally considered.[222] Although some women clearly meet the full criteria for a diagnosis of PTSD, this diagnosis characterizes only a subset of some battered women's experiences.[223]

§ 4–2.1.2 The Scientific Methods Applied in the Research

The scope and dynamics of violence within intimate relationships and its impact on a woman have been studied using a variety of methods. These include clinical observations, social surveys, psychological tests and question-naires, and in-depth interviews. Each of these methods is associated with various strengths and limitations. For example, the national surveys docu-ment the prevalence of abuse utilizing large representative samples, but typically fail to get at the complex nature of the abuse experienced and its impact on a woman. On the other hand, the in-depth interviews provide a rich and detailed description of battered women's experiences, but typically employ small and select samples, making claims to representativeness difficult.

As is apparent from this review, the research strategy of choice has been primarily the in-depth interview, often accompanied by pencil and paper type questionnaires. One of the most cited limitations to this work involves the relatively small and select nature of the samples studied.[224] This brings into question the representativeness, and hence, the generalizability of the re-search to the broader population of battered women. White and middle class women appear to be over-represented in the research—poor and ethnically diverse women have been largely ignored.[225] While this is true for research that has drawn its samples primarily from therapy seeking populations, poor and minority women are represented in research examining legal responses to male violence (e.g., police responses).[226] On the whole, however, little attention has been paid to the issue of male violence experienced by minority women (e.g., Native, women of color, immigrants). A number of researchers are now examining the dynamics of male violence in intimate relationships in these populations[227] and continued work along these lines is essential since defini-tions of what is abusive, as well as women's perceived and actual levels of safety and their alternatives from violence, may differ across cultural and other groupings.[228]

---

222. See id. at 1226. Judith Herman also contends that the symptoms that result from prolonged and repeated abuse are not fully accounted for in the classic diagnosis of PTSD. She has expanded upon the official diagnosis of PTSD and identified three symptom categories ranging from a brief stress reaction that may improve without intervention, to the classic PTSD, to the complex syndrome of prolonged, repeated trauma. See JUDITH L. HERMAN, TRAUMA AND RECOVERY 119 (1992).

223. See Dutton (1993), supra note 22, at 1221.

224. See Strube (1988), supra note 113, at 238; Faigman, supra note 40, at 642.

225. See Browne (1993), supra note 13, at 1082.

226. Karla Fischer (personal communica-tion, March 1996); see Lisa Goodman et al., Obstacles to Victims' Cooperation With the

Criminal Prosecution of Their Abusers: The Role of Social Support, 14 VIOLENCE & VICTIMS 427 (1999); Bennett et al. (1999), supra note 119; West et al. (1998), supra note 127.

227. See, e.g., James W. Zion & Elsie B. Zion, Hozho' Sokee'—Stay Together Nicely: Do-mestic Violence Under Navajo Common Law, 25 ARIZ. ST. L. J. 407 (1993); BETH E. RICHIE, COMPELLED TO CRIME: THE GENDER ENTRAPMENT OF BATTERED BLACK WOMEN (1996); Soraya M. Coley & Joyce O. Beckett, Black Battered Women: Practice Issues, 69 SOC. CASEWORK 483 (1988); Jenny Rivera, Domestic Violence Against Lati-nas by Latino Males: An Analysis of Race, National Origin, and Gender Differentials, 14 B.C. THIRD WORLD L. J. 231 (1994).

228. See id. See also Coley & Beckett, su-pra note 227, at 490.

Also at issue in this research is the fact that the women typically assessed or interviewed have been identified when seeking assistance from various social agencies (e.g., shelters, police, hospitals), thus limiting the generalizability of the findings. The practicality of such a criticism must be considered, however, within the context of battered women research. Do the responses of women who have failed to seek assistance differ from those who have not? Given the private and hidden nature of male violence in intimate relationships, this question may ultimately be unanswerable. Indeed, because some women may not actually think of themselves as victims (i.e., do not recognize the violence as such),[229] or may be afraid to report the abuse or may not seek help for it, the population itself is difficult, if not impossible to identify.[230] The extent of psychiatric problems identified in these studies, in particular those that have relied on clinical samples, however, must be treated with caution as their results might be specific to the type of sample employed (e.g., women identified in psychiatric settings). Given such concerns, Strube contends that researchers need to "define their samples more carefully and take steps to determine ... their representativeness,"[231] suggesting that this is possible through examination of the national surveys (e.g., Straus and Gelles).[232]

The other major concern raised regarding research in this area involves the lack of control or comparison groups,[233] what is often viewed as a hallmark of scientific methodology. If the researchers' goal is to assess trauma symptomology in battered women, then comparisons with other samples may be warranted. For example, if the researcher wishes to determine whether depression is a reaction specific to the fear experienced in an abusive situation, a control group of women provides useful insights. The failure to include such a comparison can limit the conclusions that can be drawn from such a study and raises questions regarding the specificity of the findings to the population of interest. In some cases, because there are national norms available on these trauma symptoms, the researcher can employ these for comparison purposes. If, however, the researchers' goal is to identify the features unique to the use of violence in a relationship or to assess the relationship between these features (e.g., form, severity, pattern) and its impact on a woman, the need for a comparison group is not readily apparent. Thus, as in any area of research, the necessity of a comparison group depends upon the researchers' question. In the early research, few studies employed comparison or control groups.[234] In contrast, the more recent investigations include comparisons samples such as women distressed for other reasons, for example trauma victims, women who are maritally distressed, or emotionally but not physically abused.[235]

Another limitation to this area of research that has been raised in the literature, specifically in reference to the work examining the factors related

229. *See* Dutton & Goodman (1994), *supra* note 151, at 225.

230. Karla Fischer (personal communication, March 1996).

231. Strube (1988), *supra* note 113, at 239.

232. Caveats, however, are associated with such comparisons as certain segments of the population may not be well represented in these surveys (e.g., non-English speakers, poor).

233. *See id.*

234. *See* Aguilar & Nightingale, *supra* note 62; *see also* Gleason, *supra* note 180; Christopoulos et al., *supra* note 208; Kerouac et al., *supra* note 208.

235. *See* Diane R. Follingstad et al., *Reactions to Victimization and Coping Strategies of Battered Women: The Ties That Bind*, 8 CLINICAL PSYCHOL. REV. 373, 387 (1988).

to relationship maintenance or termination, concerns the retrospective and self-report nature of the research.[236] While many of the interview studies attempt to obtain women's accounts of the relationship and its impact upon them throughout the course of the relationship, the potential biases inherent in these data limit both the reliability and validity of the findings. For example, as most of the studies that report the percentage of women who return to an abusive relationship used brief follow-up periods, the findings are likely an underestimation of the return rate.[237] Similarly, battered women's tendencies towards denial and minimization of the violence would suggest that women's reports may underestimate[238] their actual experiences of the violence. For models attempting to explain the dynamics of why a woman remains in an abusive relationship (e.g., learned helplessness, traumatic bonding), the retrospective nature of the research also poses interpretive problems since the direction of causality cannot be ascertained. Given the ethical considerations involved in research in this area, prospective studies of the effects of violence are extremely difficult, if not impossible, since such examination would be precluded by the inherent impact or intervention of the research process itself.[239] Despite this difficulty, researchers are now adopting longitudinal designs and results of such research will undoubtedly increase our understanding of the dynamics and impact of abuse on women.[240]

In addition, across the studies there is considerable variability in the measures that have been employed, making comparisons across them difficult.[241] While the early research tended to focus their attention on objective measures of violence (e.g., degree, frequency), greater attention is now given to the subjective meaning that the violence has for the woman. As well, incorporation of contextual variables such as the battered woman's expectation of lethal violence by her partner, which may be based on such factors as timing (e.g., imminent threat vs. potential threat sometime in the future), recent events (e.g., verbal threats to kill the battered woman, a battered woman's escalation of resistance to abuser's control or violence), setting in which violence occurred and so forth, would provide greater insight into the severity of the violence to which the woman responds.[242] Some research along these lines can now be found in the literature and more work in this area holds considerable promise.[243]

§ 4–2.2   Areas of Scientific Agreement

Despite the difficulties of conducting this research, researchers have gained considerable knowledge about the dynamics of male violence against women within intimate relationships and consistency in findings across the studies can be found. An area in which there is considerable agreement among researchers involves the pervasive nature and scope of woman abuse in

---

236. *See* Strube (1988), *supra* note 113, at 238, 239–40.

237. *See id.* at 238. Further, Strube notes that the variability in findings across the research may be due to the variability in time frames used in the research—decisions to remain or leave may be unstable and change over time. *See id.* at 240.

238. *See* Dutton & Goodman (1994), *supra* note 151, at 225.

239. *See id.* at 252.

240. *See, e.g.*, Campbell & Soeken (1999), *supra* note 212.

241. *See* Strube, *supra* note 113, at 240.

242. *See id.* at 558.

243. *See* Dutton et al. (1994), *supra* note 187.

intimate relationships. The domineering and controlling behavior on the part of the batterer has also been well documented. Co-occurring with the batterer's physical violence is a range of psychological and emotional abuse including threats to the woman or members of her family, restrictions on her finances and behavior, destruction of property, and the potential for fatal violence when attempts to separate from the abuser are made. Researchers also consistently cite numerous external and social barriers women face when trying to end the abuse, documenting the lack of social resources available to assist battered women in their attempts to terminate the violence. Using the term "entrapment" to characterize the battering experience, Evan Stark argues that a woman's failure to leave the relationship has less to do with learned helplessness than with the "actual level of control enforced through violence, cultural restraints, and institutional collusion with the batterer."[244]

Researchers in the area have also documented the profound psychological impact that the violence has on a woman, viewing these reactions not as pathologies, but rather as a response to the violence the woman experiences. In addition to PTSD, a range of indicators of distress and dysfunction have been identified in battered women in the literature:

> fear and terror, depression and grief, nightmares and flashbacks, avoidance, and/or physiological reactivity to violence related stimuli, anxiety, anger and rage, difficulty concentrating or memory problems including amnesia and dissociation, hypervigilance or suspiciousness, feelings of shame, lowered self esteem, somatic complaints, sexual dysfunction, morbid hatred, addictive behaviors, and other forms of impaired functioning.[245]

With the exception of intrusion, avoidance, and physiological arousal symptoms, "few of these indicators ... are specific only to trauma or victimization,"[246] thus pointing to the varied responses battered women may exhibit.

§ 4–2.3 Areas of Scientific Disagreement

As the earlier discussion highlights, little support for the universality of Walker's cycle theory of violence or the development of learned helplessness can be found in the literature. Although the cycle of violence may characterize some battering relationships, not all follow this pattern. Further, throughout the relationship the pattern may change. Considerable research also documents the wide range of responses taken by battered women in violent relationships. Moreover, given the reality and inherent danger that some of these actions may provoke, these behaviors have been viewed more as a response to a realistic appraisal of the situation as opposed to a helpless reaction to the violence. The research demonstrates the inadequacy of using a "single profile," for example "battered woman syndrome" or PTSD, as the criterion for defining the experiences of battered women.

Considerable disagreement in the scientific literature pertaining to male violence against women in intimate relationships can be located in the conflicting approaches and interpretations adopted by the various researchers. This is most clearly illustrated when one examines definitions of the "bat-

---

244. Stark, *supra* note 98, at 280.   **246.** *Id.*
245. Dutton (1993), *supra* note 22, at 1222.

tered woman syndrome." For instance, Bowker argues that the battered woman syndrome is merely a "summary term for the many social, psychological, economic, and physical variables that tend to hold battered women in abusive relationships," rather than "a property of the personalities of battered women."[247] Further, Bowker argues that resorting to clinical diagnoses, such as PTSD, is inappropriate to explain battered women's behaviors: "battered women's problems are social, not psychological."[248] Others argue that the battered woman syndrome, with its focus on incapacity and learned helplessness, conveys an image of disorder or pathology on the part of the woman.[249] In response, Walker contends that she has never stated that battered women have personality disorders nor that battered woman syndrome is part of the women's personalities:[250]

> Rather ... there are psychological effects to being battered, ... such effects are predictable and have a name, BWS, and ... they may be temporary and may abate with safety, or may be more long-lasting and need special intervention.[251]

If we turn to the scientific evidence, research supports both the contention that violence in an intimate relationship has a profound psychological impact upon a woman (although a single psychological profile does not emerge), and documents the constrictive social realities confronting a battered woman's attempts to end the violence. Although issues in conceptualization across fields might invariably lead to disagreements, the experiences of battered women appear to be quite varied and it is possible that, as Dutton suggests, some of the confusion may be alleviated if a singular term or profile is not employed to characterize this body of research.[252]

Of concern in any psychological diagnosis is also the problem of false positives and false negatives. For example, with respect to the battered woman syndrome, as defined by PTSD, a woman might exhibit identifiable psychological reactions to the violence that help explain her behavior and responses and not exhibit the symptoms (false negative). Thus, the experiences of many battered women, since they do not fit this "singular" profile, will not be captured if "battered woman syndrome is defined exclusively as PTSD."[253] Alternatively, she might be suffering from some other trauma and be classified falsely as suffering from the battered woman syndrome (false positive). Misclassification is of particular concern since the diagnostic category of PTSD for battered women overlaps with several other disorders (e.g., depression and anxiety disorders).[254] Thus, although the profound impact of abuse on a woman is generally agreed upon, the discriminate validity of any specific diagnosis has not been adequately addressed in the literature. At

247. Bowker (1993), *supra* note 70, at 164.

248. *Id.* at 154.

249. *See* Elizabeth M. Schneider, *Describing and Changing Women's Self–Defense Work and the Problem of Expert Testimony,* 9 Women's Rts. L. Rep. 195 (1986); *see also* Cynthia K. Gillespie, Justifiable Homicide (1989).

250. *See* Lenore E. Walker, *The Battered Woman Syndrome is a Psychological Consequence of Abuse, in* Current Controversies on Family Violence, *supra* note 13, at 133.

251. *Id.* at 150.

252. *See* Dutton (1993), *supra* note 22.

253. Dutton (1993), *supra* note 22, at 1198.

254. *See* Dutton & Goodman, *supra* note 151, at 217. For other findings that highlight the diagnostic errors that can occur with the population, *see* Lynne Bravo Rosewater, *Battered or Schizophrenic? Psychological Tests Can't Tell, in* Feminist Perspectives on Wife Abuse 200 (Kersti Yllo & Michele Bograd eds., 1988).

present, it is also difficult to determine why a battered woman responds one way as opposed to another. Investigations are now beginning to explore the potential mediating variables that may explain the observed heterogeneity of battered women's responses.

§ 4–2.4 Future Directions

As research in the area continues to accumulate, it appears that the reactions of battered women can be quite varied and a host of psychological sequelae may result as a function of the violence. There does not appear to be a single profile of the battered woman and although there is certainly a large subset of battered women who meet the criteria for PTSD, battered women's

> reactions to violence and abuse vary; they include emotional reactions (e.g., fear, anger, sadness); changes in beliefs and attitudes about self, others, and the world (e.g., self-blame, distrust, generalized belief that the world is unsafe); and symptoms of psychological distress or dysfunction (e.g., depression, flashback, anxiety, sleep problems, substance abuse). A particular battered women's reactions may or may not meet criteria to warrant a clinical diagnosis.[255]

As such, Dutton argues that defining battered woman syndrome "as a specific type of psychological reaction ... fails to account for the other possible psychological reactions to battering recognized in the scientific literature."[256] Moreover, utilizing a narrow definition or treatment of this large body of research is problematic as it fails to include many other "relevant aspects of the ecological context that may be central" to understanding a battered woman's reactions and responses.[257] Accordingly, Dutton argues that the term "battering and its effects" may more "accurately represent the current state of knowledge in the area."[258]

---

255. Mary Ann Dutton, *Critique of the "Battered Woman Syndrome" Model,* Unpublished manuscript (on file).

256. Mary Ann Dutton, *Relevance of the Psychological Effects of Battering for Understanding a Battered Person's Behavior or State of Mind: Implications for Criminal and Civil Cases* (1995).

257. Dutton (1993), *supra* note 22, at 1198; Mary Ann Dutton, *Forensic Evaluation and Testimony Related to Domestic Violence, in* 16 INNOVATIONS IN CLINICAL PRACTICE: A SOURCE BOOK 306 (Leon Vandecreek et al. eds., 1998).

258. Thus, rather than adopting the term "battered woman syndrome," Dutton argues that "descriptive references should be made to 'expert testimony concerning battered woman's experiences.' Second, the scope of the testimony should be framed within the overall social context that is essential for explaining battered women's responses to violence. Third, evaluation and testimony concerning battered women's psychological reactions to violence should incorporate the diverse range of traumatic reactions described in the scientific literature." Dutton (1998), *id.* at 307.

CHAPTER 5

BATTERED CHILD SYNDROME AND OTHER PSYCHOLOGICAL EFFECTS OF SEXUAL AND PHYSICAL ABUSE OF CHILDREN

Table of Sections

Westlaw Electronic Research

See Westlaw Electronic Research Guide preceding the Summary of Contents.

A. LEGAL ISSUES

§ 5–1.0 THE LEGAL RELEVANCE OF RESEARCH ON THE SEXUAL AND PHYSICAL ABUSE OF CHILDREN

§ 5–1.1 Introduction

This section focuses on the psychological effects associated with child abuse and the relevance of that research to the law. To this end, the research and its legal relevance closely parallels that of domestic violence against women. Therefore, this section does not repeat the discussion of the basic standards applied in the various legal contexts in which this research is introduced, such as self-defense and duress, and instead concentrates on the particular application of the psychological constructs to children in these legal contexts.

In addition, it should be noted at the outset that the primary focus of this section is on the psychological effects of abuse rather than the medical markers that indicate abuse. The term "battered child syndrome" is employed to refer to both medically-oriented and psychologically-oriented expert testimony in this area.[1] This confusion of terms is unfortunate.[2] The medical and psychological forms of expert testimony are wholly unrelated, and whereas the former has not been a major source of controversy concerning its scientific merit, the latter has limited scientific grounding. This section begins with a brief tour of the medical version of battered child syndrome and then devotes most of its space to the psychological version.

§ 5–1.2　The Battered Child Syndrome: The Medical Model

A near consensus of courts permit the use of the medical version of battered child syndrome.[3] This evidence typically involves a clinical description of the injuries sustained by the child, both presently and historically, and the opinion that these injuries are inconsistent with accidental or natural causes.[4] Courts generally find that this evidence is relevant to the nonaccidental causes of the injuries (or death).[5] Moreover, courts find this evidence to be relevant to intent. This view was articulated by the Fifth Circuit in *United States v. Bowers*, as follows:

> [E]vidence that the victim was a battered child, coupled with proof that the child was in the sole custody of the parent, may well permit the jury to infer not only that the child's injuries were not accidental but that they

§ 5–1.0

1. *See generally* State v. Miller, 204 W.Va. 374, 513 S.E.2d 147, 160 n. 8 (W.Va.1998) (discussing and citing literature regarding the fact "that the 'battered child syndrome' has come to describe both the physiological and psychological effects of a prolonged pattern of physical, emotional and sexual abuse").

2. Battered child syndrome is sometimes also used by courts to describe a third purported phenomenon, a profile that purportedly identifies whether a particular child's behavior is consistent with having been physically or sexually abused. *See, e.g.,* Commonwealth v. Federico, 425 Mass. 844, 683 N.E.2d 1035, 1038 (Mass.1997) (Describing battered child syndrome as "a description of the general or typical characteristics shared by child victims of sexual abuse."). This third use is more akin to rape trauma syndrome (or child abuse accommodation syndrome), and is considered in Chapter 13. Unfortunately, the looseness of the nomenclature affects the degree of rigor brought to analyses of the legal relevance and scientific validity of expert testimony based on these ideas.

3. *See* State v. Dumlao, 3 Conn.App. 607, 491 A.2d 404, 409 (Conn.App.1985) (noting that "battered child syndrome has become a

well established medical diagnosis" and "has consistently been held admissible in other jurisdictions").

4. *See* People v. DeJesus, 71 Ill.App.3d 235, 27 Ill.Dec. 448, 389 N.E.2d 260 (Ill.App.1979) (finding that expert testimony was admissible since it was "merely descriptive of the nature of the injuries observed by the physician"); *see also* State v. Clarke, 738 A.2d 1233, 1235 (Me. 1999) (describing injuries associated with syndrome).

5. *See, e.g.,* United States v. Bowers, 660 F.2d 527, 529 (5th Cir.1981) (relevant to show that "the child's injuries were not accidental"); *see also* United States v. Boise, 916 F.2d 497, 503 (9th Cir.1990); Bell v. State, 435 So.2d 772, 776 (Ala.Crim.App.1983); People v. Jackson, 18 Cal.App.3d 504, 95 Cal.Rptr. 919, 921 (1971); People v. Gordon, 738 P.2d 404, 406 (Colo.Ct. App.1987); State v. Dumlao, 3 Conn.App. 607, 491 A.2d 404, 409 (Conn.App.1985); People v. Platter, 89 Ill.App.3d 803, 45 Ill.Dec. 48, 412 N.E.2d 181, 193 (Ill.App.1980); State v. McKowen, 447 N.W.2d 546, 548 (Iowa Ct.App. 1989); Bell v. Commonwealth, 684 S.W.2d 282, 283 (Ky.Ct.App.1984); People v. Barnard, 93 Mich.App. 590, 286 N.W.2d 870, 871 (Mich. App.1979); State v. Durfee, 322 N.W.2d 778 (Minn.1982).

occurred deliberately, at the hands of the parent.[6]

In *State v. Heath*,[7] the Kansas Supreme Court explained that the battered child syndrome diagnosis is admissible "to show that the child died at the hands of another rather than by accident and that the other person inflicted the injuries intentionally."[8]

However, courts do not permit the expert to testify about the identity of the perpetrator.[9] At the same time, if evidence ties the defendant to the other injuries subsumed by the diagnosis, then Rule 404(b) potentially permits their introduction against him.[10]

In a notable departure from other jurisdictions, in *State v. Guyette*,[11] the New Hampshire Supreme Court excluded expert testimony regarding an abused child's prior injuries. The court concluded that the evidence was irrelevant.[12] The trial court had permitted expert medical testimony concerning battered child syndrome, ruling that "when offered to show that certain injuries are a product of child abuse, rather than accident, evidence of prior injuries is relevant even though it does not purport to prove who might have inflicted those injuries."[13] The State Supreme Court rejected this reasoning. The court argued that "the inferential jump from ... [the child's] prior intentional injuries to the conclusion that the defendant scalded him ... is seductive, but not logically permissible in the absence of evidence connecting

---

6. *Bowers*, 660 F.2d at 529; *see also* State v. McKowen, 447 N.W.2d 546, 549 (Iowa Ct.App. 1989) ("[T]estimony on battered child syndrome in a case such as ... [this one]—where the victim is an infant, incapable of communication, and possesses fractures of various ages—is highly relevant evidence when the jury is asked to decide the mens rea element of the offense of child endangerment."); People v. Barnard, 93 Mich.App. 590, 286 N.W.2d 870, 871 (Mich.Ct.App.1979) (concluding that "the evidence was highly relevant to the material issues of intent and nonaccident").

7. 264 Kan. 557, 957 P.2d 449 (Kan.1998).

8. *Id.* at 463. *See also* State v. Atkins, 349 N.C. 62, 505 S.E.2d 97, 120 (N.C.1998) ("Concerning the circumstances of the offense, the evidence was relevant to demonstrate premeditation and deliberation. The State presented evidence that [the victim] suffered extensive injuries over a four-week period, leading to his ultimate death. This evidence supported the State's contention that defendant did not simply 'snap' and 'lose control.' "); State v. Koon, 730 So.2d 503, 511 (La.App. 2d Cir.1999) ("The evidence demonstrating battered-child syndrome assisted in proving that the child died at the hands of another and not by falling off of a bed, and this evidence also tends to show that the person inflicted the injuries intentionally."); State v. Wright, 593 N.W.2d 792, 801 (S.D.1999) (" 'The prosecution's burden to prove every element of the crime is not relieved by a defendant's tactical decision not to contest an element of the offense.... The evidence of battered child syndrome was relevant to show intent, and nothing in the Due Process Clause of the Fourteenth Amendment

requires the State to refrain from introducing relevant evidence simply because the defense chooses not to contest the point.' ") (quoting Estelle v. McGuire, 502 U.S. 62, 69–70, 112 S.Ct. 475, 116 L.Ed.2d 385 (1991)).

9. *See* People v. DeJesus, 71 Ill.App.3d 235, 27 Ill.Dec. 448, 389 N.E.2d 260 (Ill.App.1979) (finding that expert testimony was admissible since it was "merely descriptive of the nature of the injuries observed by the physician" and did not conclude that any particular person caused the injuries); People v. Barnard, 93 Mich.App. 590, 286 N.W.2d 870, 871 (Mich.Ct. App.1979) (Court held that expert testimony on battered child syndrome was admissible since "the diagnosis indicates only lack of accident and does not suggest whether a particular person injured the child."); State v. Durfee, 322 N.W.2d 778 (Minn.1982) (concluding that battered child syndrome evidence was admissible since expert did not attempt to name the defendant as the child's assailant).

10. *See, e.g.*, State v. Norlin, 134 Wash.2d 570, 951 P.2d 1131, 1133 (Wash.1998). It is worth noting that under Washington's evidence rules, these prior acts must be proved by "a preponderance of the evidence." *Id.* Under the Federal Rules of Evidence, prior bad acts under 404(b) are merely a matter of conditional relevance under Rule 104(b). *See* Huddleston v. United States, 485 U.S. 681, 108 S.Ct. 1496, 99 L.Ed.2d 771 (1988).

11. 139 N.H. 526, 658 A.2d 1204 (N.H. 1995).

12. *Id.* at 1207.

13. *Id.* at 1206.

the defendant to the prior injuries."[14] In its concluding remarks, the court acknowledged that its decision contradicted the majority trend; however, it concluded, "we are not persuaded by the logic [of other jurisdictions' opinions]."[15]

§ 5–1.3　The Battered Child Syndrome: The Psychological Model

Contrary to some courts' understanding, the psychologically-based battered child syndrome is an extension of the battered woman syndrome, *not* the medically-based battered child syndrome.[16] This is true both as a matter of the empirical research brought to bear on the psychology of child abuse and the legal relevance of the expert testimony offered on the psychologically based battered child syndrome. Section 2.0 make this fact plain. In the courtroom, the two forms of battered child syndrome are offered in entirely different sorts of cases. As the previous section indicates, the medical version is typically offered to show the nonaccidental (and thus intentional) cause of injuries in a prosecution of an alleged child abuser. The psychological version, in contrast, is typically offered by the defense to support a claim of self-defense where a child who has suffered abuse has killed his abuser. This use fully parallels that of the battered woman syndrome.

Like the battered woman syndrome, the battered child syndrome is used in claims of self-defense under circumstances in which the traditional factors of the defense do not seem to be met.[17] Specifically, in many of these cases, the defendant killed when not confronting "imminent" harm or used a disproportional amount of force.[18] For example, in *State v. Nemeth*,[19] the Ohio Supreme Court considered whether the battered child syndrome was admissible to support a defense of self-defense. The facts of *Nemeth* present a very hard case indeed. *Nemeth* also provides particularly compelling evidence for Holmes' general observation in this regard: "Great cases like hard cases make bad law."[20] The defendant was a sixteen year-old who had killed his mother by

14. *Id.* at 1207.

15. *Id.*

16. The ambiguity over the scientific identity of the psychologically-based battered child syndrome appears to have confused the Arizona Court of Appeals in *In re Appeal in Maricopa County*, 182 Ariz. 60, 893 P.2d 60 (Ariz. Ct.App.1994). The court observed that early cases had only described the medical elements of a battered child syndrome diagnosis, but that the syndrome had "since been expanded to include psychological components." Id. at 63.

17. For a full discussion of the elements of a self-defense defense, see Chapter 4.

18. In *In re Appeal in Maricopa County, Juvenile Action No. JV–506561*, 182 Ariz. 60, 893 P.2d 60 (Ariz.Ct.App.1994), the 12–year old defendant introduced battered child syndrome to establish that she acted in a "heat of passion" resulting from "adequate provocation" when she shot and killed her sleeping mother. *Id.* at 63. The expert's testimony indicated that the victim's abuse of the defendant

"was worsening in intensity and severity to the point of possible death." *Id.* The defendant, therefore, "believed that, particularly given the lack of response from adult authorities from whom she repeatedly had sought help, shooting her mother was her only option to protect herself and her younger sister from further peril and death." *Id.* The court characterized this state of mind as a "sustained 'heat of passion'" that was "sufficient to deprive a reasonable person of 'self-control.'" *Id.* According to the court, therefore, the lower court correctly concluded that the defendant's actions fell within the parameters of manslaughter. *Id.*

19. 82 Oh.St.3d 202, 694 N.E.2d 1332 (Ohio 1998).

20. The full quote follows:

Great cases like hard cases make bad law. For great cases are called great, not by reason of their real importance in shaping the law of the future, but because of some accident of immediate overwhelming interest

shooting her five times using a bow and arrows as she lay in a drunken stupor on a couch. He had been the victim of incessant physical and emotional abuse for many years. On the night before the killing, his mother had dragged him home from a friend's house where he had earlier sought refuge. The court provided a detailed and lengthy summary of the abuse he suffered.[21]

The court began by noting that the original use of the term "battered child syndrome" was for medical diagnosis and was used by experts in court to identify the existence of physical abuse. The court noted, however, that the term had recently undergone an expansion to include certain psychological aspects of abuse. This expansion has gone in two distinct directions. The first is analogous to the medical version, and is used to identify victims of abuse by the psychological characteristics of the alleged victim. The second is analogous to the battered woman syndrome, and is used to describe the psychological effects of abuse. The former, the court observed, was extremely controversial, while the latter was not. In *Nemeth*, the court emphasized, battered child syndrome referred to a set of symptoms suffered by children in abusive relationships that were analogous to the battered woman syndrome and consistent with the diagnostic criteria of post traumatic stress disorder (PTSD).

The court sought to assess both the legal relevance of the battered child syndrome as well as its scientific validity. The court found that it was relevant for four purposes, including whether the defendant

> (1) had acted with prior calculation and design as charged in the indictment, (2) had acted with purpose as required for the lesser included offense of murder, (3) had created the confrontation or initiated the aggression, and (4) had an honest belief that he was in imminent danger, a necessary element in the affirmative defense of self-defense.[22]

The court then proceeded to conduct a *Daubert*-styled reliability assessment of the proffered expert testimony. The court offered uncritical observations about the general acceptance of the syndrome in children and seemed particularly impressed by its empirical link to PTSD. However, other than a surplus of conclusory statements based on a lamentable number of law review articles and too few scientific citations, the court never actually considered the research available to support its conclusion that

> [t]he psychiatric and legal communities have clearly accepted that despite any minor differences in the degree of power differentials between the batterer and the abused, the psychological effects of family violence are legally indistinguishable whether suffered by children or adults.[23]

Finally, the court offered no analysis whatsoever regarding the "fit" between the psychological theory and its asserted legal relevance. The relevance of

---

which appeals to the feelings and distorts the judgment. These immediate interests exercise a kind of hydraulic pressure which makes what previously was clear seem doubtful, and before which even well settled principles of law will bend.

Northern Securities Co. v. United States, 193 U.S. 197, 400, 24 S.Ct. 436, 48 L.Ed. 679 (1904) (Holmes, J., dissenting).

21. *Nemeth*, 694 N.E.2d at 1333–35.

22. *Id.* at 1336. It should be noted that in this context courts are more amenable to expert testimony on "credibility" than in analogous contexts, such as rape trauma syndrome, so long as the expert does not comment directly on the witness's veracity. *See id.*

23. *Id.* at 1340.

PTSD to the four purposes posited for this evidence is far from obvious. The court never explained in what way PTSD made it more likely that the defendant had not acted with prior calculation, had not acted with purpose, had not created the confrontation and was honest in his belief that he was in imminent harm.

The facts of battered child cases like those presented in *Nemeth* pose significant challenges for courts. It is difficult to argue that the defendant there does not deserve our fullest sympathy. But, even more than in the context of battered women, it is clear that admissibility decisions regarding expert testimony in these cases is a product of substantive legal policy, not evidentiary principles. These decisions do not depend on the underlying validity of the science, or its fit with the traditional substantive law of self defense. The experts are advocates that offer testimonial support to very sympathetic defendants. Courts should be more honest in recognizing this fact.

As a general matter, jurisdictions respond to a proffer of the battered child syndrome very similarly to their response to the battered woman syndrome. Louisiana, for example, is particularly unsympathetic to the use of the battered woman syndrome in self-defense cases[24] and this disdain is similarly displayed in battered child syndrome claims. Louisiana courts consider the question to be one of sanity versus insanity and do not permit expert testimony on the battered woman syndrome to establish what they consider to be a "partial or impaired responsibility" defense.[25] *State v. Gachot*,[26] illustrates the Louisiana court's response to battered child syndrome. In *Gachot*, the defendant had killed both of his parents when he was fifteen years-old. The defendant apparently had suffered extreme verbal abuse from both parents, but no physical abuse.[27] According to the defendant's testimony, the homicides were triggered by a fierce argument between his parents, which included a verbal attack upon the defendant by his father.[28] During this dispute, the defendant claimed that "he lost awareness of his actions until after he had shot both his father and mother."[29] The trial court permitted evidence of the father's past acts of verbal abuse to be admitted, but excluded all mention of the mother's past actions.[30] The defendant was convicted of manslaughter for the killing of his father and murder for the death of his mother.[31]

On appeal, the defendant claimed that the trial court erred in excluding the mother's verbal abuse and that Louisiana law recognizes a "battered child defense."[32] The Court of Appeal, however, not only agreed that evidence of the mother's past acts were properly excluded, but expressed the view that the evidence of the father's past actions were improperly admitted since the "defendant's blood had an opportunity to cool" before he killed his parents.[33] The court further rejected the "battered child defense," stating that, unless the defendant pled "not guilty and not guilty by reason of insanity," he

24. *See, e.g.*, State v. Necaise, 466 So.2d 660 (La.Ct.App.1985) (discussed in Chapter 4, § 8–1.1.3[c]).

25. *Id.* at 665.

26. 609 So.2d 269 (La.Ct.App.1992).

27. *Id.* at 271.

28. *Id.* at 272.

29. *Id.*

30. *Id.* at 276.

31. *Id.* at 272.

32. *Id.* at 276, 278.

33. *Id.*

should not be permitted to present *any* evidence concerning his mental abuse.[31] Therefore, the defendant's attempt to rely on a "battered child defense" was misguided, since this strategy would not allow the defendant "to introduce . . . psychological evidence of defendant's emotional differences from that of a reasonable adult male."[35]

In contrast to Louisiana, Washington courts are sympathetic to the battered woman syndrome and respond similarly to the battered child syndrome. In *State v. Janes*,[36] the defendant, a 17–year-old male, shot and killed his mother's boyfriend. Abundant testimony established that the victim was physically and verbally abusive to the defendant's mother, the defendant, and other children in the family during the ten years that he lived at their residence.[37] On the night before the shooting, the victim became verbally abusive towards the defendant's mother.[38] The next day, the defendant told several of his friends that he was going to kill the victim. He produced a shotgun before leaving for school and loaded it.[39] When he returned home, he drank alcohol and smoked marijuana, then retrieved the gun that he had loaded earlier.[40] He then recorded a statement in a tape recorder, stating, among other things, that "I declare war on [the victim] and whoever else. I feel that what I am doing is right."[41] When the victim returned home, the defendant shot him as he walked through the front door.[42]

In response to the defendant's claim of self-defense,[43] the Washington Supreme Court likened the battered child syndrome to the battered woman syndrome. The court explained that the battered child syndrome had "come to describe both the physiological and psychological effects of a prolonged pattern of physical, emotional and sexual abuse."[44] According to the court, children suffering from this syndrome display traits of learned helplessness and hypervigilance.[45] Battered children are "acutely aware" of their surroundings and are constantly "on the alert for any signs of danger."[46] The court found that the battered child syndrome was remarkably similar to the battered woman syndrome, since "both syndromes find their basis in abuse-induced PTSD and elicit a similar response from the abuse victim."[47] Accordingly, the court concluded that "the same reasons that justify admission of battered woman syndrome . . . apply with equal force to . . . the battered child syndrome."[48]

Consequently, the court next considered whether the evidence here was sufficient to require a self-defense instruction. The trial court indicated that

34. *Id.*

35. *Id.*

36. 121 Wash.2d 220, 850 P.2d 495 (Wash. 1993).

37. *Id.* at 496.

38. *Id.*

39. *Id.*

40. *Id.* at 497.

41. *Id.*

42. *Id.* The defendant also shot at the police when they arrived, wounding one officer and a bystander. *Id.*

43. At trial, the court allowed the defendant to introduce testimony that he suffered from post traumatic stress disorder, allegedly caused by the victim's abuse, but refused to instruct the jury on self-defense. The discussion in this section is limited to the Supreme Court's discussion of the availability of the battered child syndrome in a claim of self-defense.

44. *Jones*, 850 P.2d at 501.

45. *Id.* at 502.

46. *Id.*

47. *Id.*

48. *Id.*

the victim's last contact with the defendant was "too far removed and lacked sufficient aggressiveness to constitute imminent danger" to the defendant.[49] However, the Supreme Court determined that the trial court gave "undue consideration to the length of time between the alleged threat and the homicide."[50] Since Washington courts employ a hybrid standard for determining the presence of imminent danger, juries were "to consider the defendant's actions in light of all the facts and circumstances known to the defendant, even those substantially predating the killing."[51] If a "reasonably prudent person, knowing all the defendant knows and seeing all the defendant sees," would believe that imminent danger existed, then a self-defense instruction would be warranted.[52] Although the existence of a syndrome diagnosis, by itself, is not sufficient to require a self-defense instruction, a lone threat could support the self-defense theory "when there is a reasonable belief that the threat will be carried out."[53] Therefore, the court held that the trial court must consider the defendant's "subjective knowledge and perceptions" in weighing the adequacy of the evidence intended to show that the defendant acted in self-defense.[54]

§ 5–1.4 Conclusion

Battered child syndrome comes to court in two versions; and these versions differ significantly in both scientific genealogy and legal relevance. The medical version is based on medical opinion concerning the source of multiple injuries and is introduced to show the nonaccidental and, thus, intentional cause of those injuries. The medical version of battered child syndrome is not controversial scientifically and most courts find the expert testimony to be relevant.

The psychological version of battered child syndrome closely parallels and, indeed, is largely based on the battered woman syndrome. Numerous difficulties, however, attend the extension of battered woman syndrome research to cases in which children kill. Foremost, the research on battered woman syndrome itself is not the model of scientific rigor and only weakly supports the syndrome as applied to adults. Second, little research has been carried out on children who are victims of abuse, so the hypothesis that they respond the way adult women do is entirely speculative. For this reason, also, generalizing from battered women to battered children is problematic. There are few reasons to believe that children victims respond similarly to adult victims of abuse and many reasons to believe otherwise. Clearly, in both areas, more research needs to be done.

49. *Id.* at 503.

50. *Id.* at 506.

51. *Id.* at 504.

52. *Id.*

53. *Id.* at 506.

54. *Id.*

B. SCIENTIFIC STATUS

by
Regina Schuller* & Patricia A. Hastings**

§ 5–2.0 THE SCIENTIFIC STATUS OF RESEARCH ON THE SEXUAL AND PHYSICAL ABUSE OF CHILDREN

§ 5–2.1 Introductory Discussion of the Science

§ 5–2.1.1 The General Questions

Similar to research in the area of woman assault,[1] the study of child abuse has focused attention on the prevalence of physical abuse, as well as its impact on a child. Although child abuse is certainly not a recent phenomenon,[2] its recognition as an important social concern is fairly new. The initial impetus of interest in the area has been largely attributed to a pediatric physician named Dr. Henry Kempe, who, in the early sixties, alarmed at the large number of children arriving at his clinic with non-accidental injuries, turned his attention to the problem. In 1961, under Dr. Kempe's direction, the American Academy of Pediatrics held a symposium specifically addressing the issue of child abuse.[3] The following year, the term "battered child syndrome" was coined in a study published by Dr. Kempe and a group of physicians.[4] Specifically, battered child syndrome was used to refer to a clinical condition found in young children who had received serious physical abuse, typically from a parent or foster parent. Although the syndrome was described as occurring at any age, in general, the majority of children examined by the researchers were below the age of 3 years.[5] Characteristics of the syndrome noted by these authors involved a range of physical symptoms (e.g., subdural hematoma, fracture of the long bones, multiple soft tissue injuries) coupled with discrepancies between the historical data supplied by the parents and the observed clinical findings, as well as an absence of lesions when the child was placed in a protective environment.[6] In essence, Kempe et al. presented the battered child syndrome as a series of physical symptoms that could be identified by a physician and that could demonstrate that a child has been physically abused.[7]

* Regina A. Schuller, Ph.D. is Associate Professor of Psychology at York University in Toronto, Ontario, Canada. She is actively engaged in both research and teaching and in 1995 received York's President's Prize for Promising Scholars. Her research interests focus on the impact of social science framework testimony, in particular, expert testimony pertaining to battered women and on juror/jury decision processes. She also serves on the editorial boards of LAW & HUMAN BEHAVIOR and PSYCHOLOGY, PUBLIC POLICY & LAW.

** Patricia A. Hastings, Ph.D., York University, is currently on staff at DecisonQuest in Washington, D.C.

§ 5–2.0

1. *See* Regina Schuller & Sara Rzepa, § 11–2.0.

2. For a review, *see* Raymond H. Starr, *Physical Abuse of Children, in* HANDBOOK OF FAMILY VIOLENCE, 119, 119–122 (Vincent B. Van Hasselt et al. eds., 1988).

3. Samuel X. Radbill, *A History of Child Abuse and Infanticide, in* THE BATTERED CHILD 3, 18–19 (Ray E. Helfer & C. Henry Kempe eds. 1974). *See* Starr (1988), *supra* note 2, at 121–122.

4. C. Henry Kempe et al., *The Battered Child Syndrome* 181 JAMA 17 (1962).

5. *Id.*

6. *Id.* at 18.

7. This work increased public awareness of the problem of child abuse and by 1967 all states had enacted child protection laws, *see* Radbill (1974), *supra* note 3. Given the resultant impact of this early research, it is not surprising that, in a recent study, a sample of experts and professionals working within the

In a chapter reviewing judicial responses to child abuse and neglect,[8] Catherine Brooks similarly described the battered child syndrome as a medical diagnosis that indicates that a child has been physically abused by a caregiver. Thus, in contrast to the "battered woman syndrome," which focuses on the psychological impact of abuse on a woman,[9] the "battered child syndrome" was derived from purely medical research,[10] with the focus largely on the physical aspects of child abuse and its detection. In contrast to this more restricted use of the term, however, several legal scholars have argued that the psychological effects experienced by a battered child mirror those experienced by a battered woman, and, as such, like battered women who kill their partners, battered children who commit parricide should be allowed to present evidence to explain the effects.[11] Jamie Sacks notes that "because of its medical origins ... battered child's syndrome has not been officially recognized as a psychological syndrome,"[12] but that "because modern medicine treats battered child's syndrome as a valid psychological syndrome, courts should recognize it in the interests of fairness when battered children are on trial for killing their abusers."[13] In fact, some courts have acknowledged parallels between women and children who kill their abusers after years of family violence.[14] Moreover, based on the premise that both syndromes are analogous and should, therefore, be treated similarly, some scholars have suggested the use of a more generic term, "the Battered Person Syndrome," to encompass both the "battered woman syndrome" and the "battered child syndrome."[15]

Within the scientific psychological literature, however, the term battered child syndrome has not been widely adopted nor has the concept been developed in the manner suggested in the legal literature. No community of scholars specifically focuses on battered child syndrome as a psychological construct. The research addressing the impact of abuse and its relevance to parricide is still in its infancy and thus quite fragmented, addressing only aspects of child abuse rather than providing a unified theory. In the following section, we review the observations drawn by those writing on the topic of

area of child protection ranked the article by Dr. Kempe and his colleagues as the most influential paper in the field of child abuse. R. Kim Oates & Anne Cohn Donnelly, *Influential Papers in Child Abuse* 21(3) Child Abuse & Neglect 319 (1997).

8. Catherine M. Brooks, *The Law's Response to Child Abuse and Neglect, in* Law, Mental Health, And Mental Disorder 464–86 (Bruce D. Sales & Daniel.W. Shuman eds., 1996).

9. *See* Schuller & Rzepa, *supra* note 1.

10. The courts have shown greater acceptance of expert testimony regarding the "battered child syndrome" when the testimony has been used in its original medical form to help demonstrate that a child's injuries are not accidental. *See* § 1.0, *supra*.

11. Steven R. Hicks, *Admissibility of Expert Testimony on the Psychology of the Battered Child,* 11 Law & Psychol. Rev. 103, 105–106 (1987); Jamie Heather Sacks, *A New Age

of Understanding: Allowing Self–Defense Claims for Battered Children Who Kill Their Abusers,* 10 J. of Contemp. Health L. & Pol. 349, 351 (1994); Paul Mones, *When the Innocent Strike Back,* 8 J. Interpersonal Violence 297, 298–299 (1993).

12. Sacks, *supra* note 11, at 354. *See also* Hicks, *supra* note 11, at 105. In Kempe et al.'s 1962 article on battered child syndrome, *supra* note 4, a section called "Psychiatric Aspects" was included. This section, however, focused solely on the characteristics of the abusive parent, not on the effects or impact to the child victim.

13. Sacks, *supra* note 11; *see also* Hicks, *supra* note 11, at 105.

14. *See, e.g.,* State v. Janes, 121 Wash.2d 220, 850 P.2d 495, 503 (Wash.1993) (en banc) (concluding that "battered child syndrome is the functional and legal equivalent of the battered woman syndrome").

15. Hicks, *supra* note 11.

parricide and then examine the social science research addressing the claims that have been made.

[1] Parricide

Estimates of parricide, defined as the killing of one's parent (mother, father, or both), indicate that this accounts for approximately 2% of all homicides committed in the United States.[16] Although there seems to be little systematic research carried out on this subject, those who have investigated this phenomenon report two common themes. Several authors note that children who kill a parent have generally been severely victimized by that parent,[17] and further, that the violence within these families is often widespread involving both sibling and spousal abuse.[18]

The work in this area is perhaps best characterized as case studies of adolescent homicide, typically involving small samples that are not systematically analyzed in any fashion. For instance, based on clinical observations of eight cases of parricide in which he provided assessments, Emanuel Tanay, a psychiatrist, described what he called "reactive parricide." To Tanay "reactive parricide" is viewed as a last-resort effort of self-preservation.[19] In describing the dynamics of the family situation, he concluded that the dead parent was sadistic (with the parent's behavior often focused on the perpetrator); the family lived in fear of this parent; the surviving parent was passive and dependent; the family relationships and the relationship between the parents were highly dysfunctional; during the problem years responses from outside the family were ineffective, making the adolescent feel powerless; and finally, the death of the parent resulted in an overall improvement in family life, and, for the perpetrator in particular.[20]

Similarly, Paul Mones, a defense attorney, drawing on a range of cases in which he was involved,[21] concludes that the child's act of killing is an "act of ... self-preservation."[22] In addition, he reports that these adolescents were often victims of two types of trauma: being abused themselves and witnessing the abuse of other family members.[23] Mones further describes these youths as "unique among teenage killers," and notes a number of common characteris-

16. CHARLES PATRICK EWING, WHEN CHILDREN KILL: THE DYNAMICS OF JUVENILE HOMICIDE 32 (1990); *see also* Paul Mones, *Battered Child Syndrome: Understanding Parricide,* 30 TRIAL 24, 24 (1994), CHARLES PATRICK EWING, FATAL FAMILIES: THE DYNAMICS OF INTRAFAMILIAL HOMICIDE (1997).

17. Mones, *supra* note 16, at 24–26; GREGORY W. MORRIS, THE KIDS NEXT DOOR 293 (1985); Emanuel Tanay, *Reactive Parricide,* 21 J. FORENSIC SCI. 76, 80–81 (1976); KATHLEEN M. HEIDE, WHY KIDS KILL PARENTS: CHILD ABUSE AND ADOLESCENT HOMICIDE 6–7 (1992); Paul Mones, *The Relationship Between Child Abuse and Parricide: An Overview, in* UNHAPPY FAMILIES 34–35 (Eli H. Newberger & Richard Bourne eds. 1985); EWING, *supra* note 16.

18. Shelley Post, *Adolescent Parricide in Abusive Families,* 7 CHILD WELFARE 445, 449

(1982); Douglas Sargent, *Children Who Kill—A Family Conspiracy?* 7 SOCIAL WORK 35, 38 (1962); PAUL MONES, WHEN A CHILD KILLS 12–13 (1991).

19. Tanay, *supra* note 17, at 76.

20. *Id.* at 80.

21. Specifically, his observations were drawn from trial notes, court transcripts and depositions, personal interviews with children, family members, friends, neighbours, interviews with defense attorneys, detectives, prosecutors, judges and press reports. *See* Mones, *supra* note 18, at xv.

22. Mones, *supra* note 16; Mones, *supra* note 17, at 36.

23. Mones, *supra* note 16, at 26; MONES, *supra* note 18, at 12–13.

tics:[24] the majority are males, 17 to 18 years old, Caucasian, and from a middle to upper socioeconomic class; they appear to be respectful, loners, anxious to please their peers, overly polite to adults and average to above average students with rarely any significant history of delinquency.[25] Mones does not report the frequency of these characteristics within the group of adolescents who committed parricide nor does he compare them with other relevant groups (e.g., adolescents who have committed homicide). Thus, similar to Tanay, Mones' conclusions and observations are, at best, impressions gleaned from his experiences with these cases. Several other similar case analyses have been reported in the literature.[26]

Another approach used by researchers to examine the dynamics involved in parricide involves comparisons of juvenile homicide on the basis of the victim-offender relationship. Billie Corder et al.[27] reviewed hospital records (collected over a fourteen-year period) of adolescents charged with murder who were admitted for observation during a fourteen-year period.[28] Ten adolescents were identified as cases of parricide[29] and matched[30] with two other samples of adolescents who had killed (10 who had killed close acquaintances, 10 who had killed strangers). Evidence of wife battering within the home and physical abuse of the adolescent by parents was found among a greater number of the adolescents charged with parricide compared to the other two groups.[31] Further, fewer of the adolescents charged with parricide had a history of aggressive behavior.[32]

In another retrospective study, Dewey Cornell et al. examined 72 adolescents charged with homicide and seen for pretrial evaluation (over a nine-year period).[33] Of these, 21% involved the murder of a family member, 47% the murder of an acquaintance and 32% the murder of a stranger. These researchers reported that family members were most often murdered with a gun and killed by a single perpetrator when compared to the acquaintance and stranger homicides. In addition, through individual case analysis of the family homicides, the authors reported a history of extended interpersonal conflict between the offender and the victim. They reported that the typical family

24. Mones, *supra* note 16, at 24; MONES, *supra* note 18, at 12.

25. Mones, *supra* note 16, at 24; MONES, *supra* note 18, at 12. Other case studies of adolescent parricide also note little or no prior criminal behavior in adolescents who commit parricide; Tanay, *supra* note 17; Robert L. Sadoff, *Clinical Observations on Parricide*, 45 PSYCHIATRIC Q. 65 (1971).

26. *See* MORRIS, *supra* note 17; POST, *supra* note 18; Douglas Sargent, *supra* note 18.

27. Billie F. Corder et al., *Adolescent Parricide: A Comparison with Other Adolescent Murder*, 133 AM. J. PSYCHIATRY 957 (1976).

28. The total group of adolescents ranged in age from 13 to 18.

29. This group of ten included nine males and one female.

30. Adolescents were matched "as closely as possible" on age, sex, IQ, socioeconomic status, and date of admission. A complete breakdown of demographics for each group, however, was not reported by these authors.

31. Evidence of wife battering was found in families of five of the ten adolescents committing parricide, compared to no cases in the two comparison groups. Abuse toward the adolescent was evidenced in seven of the ten parricide cases, compared to three in the acquaintance group and two in the stranger group. Corder et al., *supra* note 27, at 959.

32. Three of the adolescents in the parricide group, compared to six of the adolescents in the acquaintance group, and all of the adolescents in the stranger group, evidenced a history of aggressive behavior.

33. Dewey G. Cornell et al., *Characteristics of Adolescents Charged with Homicide: Review of 72 Cases*, 5 BEHAV. SCI. & L. 11 (1987).

homicide case involved an adolescent who murdered an abusive father after years of physical abuse and witnessing abuse of other family members.[34]

A review by Marc Hillbrand et al.,[35] which relies on much of the earlier research reviewed, concluded that perpetrators of parricide are typically male, White, middle-class, and have no prior history of violence. Victims of parricide are more likely to be fathers than mothers. In addition, child abuse frequently precedes parricides,[36] but the authors caution that "reliable estimates of the prevalence of child maltreatment in parricides" is not possible because studies have "lumped together mild and severe physical abuse, sexual abuse, verbal abuse, psychological abuse, and in some cases physical and psychological neglect."[37] Hillbrand et al. also note the association between serious mental disorders, conduct disorder or antisocial personality, and parricide by youths.[38]

In summary, the work in this area indicates a theme of violence within the homes of adolescents who kill their parents, as well as differences between children who kill parents as opposed to strangers. The information collected regarding parricide at this point, however, is somewhat limited. Much of this work relies on retrospective analyses of court records that identify differences between children who kill parents as opposed to strangers, or on case histories that attempt to describe the dynamics underlying parricide, with the latter typically based on observations drawn from an author's clinical practice. In both instances, this involves examinations of extremely small and select samples. While comparison groups have been used in some of the studies, other appropriate control groups (e.g., children who are abused, but who do not kill) have not been used. Furthermore, those studies positing "self-preservation" explanations for the parricide are based only on the authors' clinical impressions, which do not appear to be assessed in any systematic fashion.[39]

[2] Impact of Physical Abuse on the Child

At this point, we turn to the more general psychological literature examining the impact of abuse on children, focusing on those aspects that have been linked to battered child syndrome by some in the legal community. Specifically, legal scholars have equated the "battered child syndrome" with the "battered woman syndrome," positing that abused children, like battered women, suffer from Post Traumatic Stress Disorder (PTSD), exhibit signs of hypervigilance, and experience learned helplessness.

---

34. *Id.* at 20–21.

35. Marc Hillbrand et al., *Parricides: Characteristics of Offenders and Victims, Legal Factor, and Treatment Issues*, 4 AGGRESSION & VIOLENT BEHAV. 179 (1998).

36. *Id.* at 182.

37. *Id.*

38. *Id.* at 182–183.

39. In contrast to this work, Dutton and Yamini present an innovative theoretical model that links chronic abuse and parricide based on comparisons with suicide and other forms of catathymic violence (e.g., sudden acts precip-

itated by anger). They view parricide, like suicide, as "an attempt to escape unbearable aversiveness," with the circumstances in the case of parricide including severe and unrelenting abuse. Donald G. Dutton and Sanaz Yamini, *Adolescent Parricide: An Integration of Social Cognitive Theory and Clinical Views of Projected–Introjective Cycling*, 65(1) AM. J. ORTHOPSYCHIATRY 39, 42 (1993). While the model provides a conceptualization of the role of abuse in cases of parricide, it still requires considerable development and empirical validation.

[a] Post–Traumatic Stress Disorder

In analogizing the battered child syndrome to the battered woman syndrome, legal writers have discussed the occurrence of PTSD in abused children.[40] A number of psychological studies have now investigated the prevalence of post-traumatic stress disorder,[41] as well as other psychiatric disorders, in abused children, and thus it is possible to assess the validity of this claim. As will be evident from this review, however, the forms and definitions of abuse (physical, sexual, neglect) that have been employed in the research have varied widely, rendering comparisons across the studies difficult. With this caveat in mind, however, we have loosely grouped the research in terms of the type of abuse under investigation in the research: physical, sexual, or both.

In a study focusing solely on victims of physical abuse, David Pelcovitz et al. examined 27 adolescent victims of intrafamilial physical abuse who reported to a New York city registrar for child abuse.[42] The physically abused adolescents were compared to 27 controls (comparable on age, sex, and socioeconomic status).[43] Only three of the physically abused children received a diagnosis of PTSD (as measured by the PTSD module of the Structured Clinical Interview for Diagnosis) and these children also reported extrafamilial sexual assaults (there was no history of sexual abuse in the remaining 24 abused children who did not receive a diagnosis of PTSD). No cases of PTSD were found in the comparison group. Based on these findings, the authors concluded that PTSD was not evident in higher proportions in physically abused adolescents when compared to a group of normal controls.

In a much larger study, Alan Flisher et al.[44] drew on a community probability sample of children to compare the psychosocial characteristics (i.e., psychiatric diagnoses, global functioning impairment, social competence, academic performance and language ability) of children who had been physically abused with those who had not.[45] Controlling for several variables including family environment, family psychiatric history, perinatal problems, current physical health and experiences of sexual abuse, they found a wide range of psychopathology (e.g., major depression, conduct disorder, etc.) associated with physical abuse. The authors concluded, however, that "there is not one specific syndrome or diagnosis that is uniquely associated with physical abuse."[46]

---

40. *See* Sacks, *supra* note 11, at 356.

41. For a full description of PTSD, *see* Schuller & Rzepa, *supra* note 1; *see also* Chapter 1.

42. David Pelcovitz et al., *Post-Traumatic Stress Disorder in Physically Abused Adolescents*, 33 J. Am. Acad. Child & Adolescent Psychiatry 305 (1994).

43. *Id.* The control group was recruited using a random-digit dialing procedure. The mean age of both groups was 15.1 years, and 55.6% of the abused children and 59.3% of the control group were female.

44. Alan J. Flisher et al., *Psychosocial Characteristics of Physically Abused Children*

and Adolescents, 36(1) J. Am. Acad. Child & Adolescent Psychiatry 123 (1997).

45. The sample involved a random selection of 665 children between 9 to 17 years old, from New York and Puerto Rico. Approximately 26% of the sample reported a history of physical abuse (17% represented abuse that involved more than "having been hit very hard on fewer than five occasions"). *Id.* at 126.

46. *Id.* at 129. They also found physical abuse to be associated with functional impairment, but not with academic achievement or language ability. In contrast to previous studies, they did not find a higher rate of suicide in

Richard Famularo and his colleagues[47] examined the relationship between physical abuse and PTSD in a sample of "severely" maltreated children[48] and found that 62 of the 156 children evaluated met the criteria for PTSD.[49] Two years later, a reexamination of 52 of the children who met the criteria for PTSD indicated that approximately 33% of the children had retained the diagnosis.[50] The authors concluded that there is a high rate of PTSD persistence in "substantially traumatized children."[51] In an earlier study Famularo et al.[52] examined the prevalence of PTSD in 61 abused children drawn from a juvenile court and hospital and compared them to 35 patient controls recruited from the same hospital.[53] A significantly greater incidence of PTSD in the abused children compared to the control group was found (39% as measured by a structured psychiatric interview for children, 21% as measured by a parallel parent version of the interview vs. no cases in the control group).[54] The authors again concluded that there is a strong link between child abuse and the incidence of PTSD. Unfortunately, in this study the researchers did not distinguish between the different types of abuse, or victim-offender relationship, thus rendering interpretation difficult. They did, however, describe their abused sample as "severely" abused, suggesting, again, a possible link between severity of abuse and the incidence of PTSD.

Some of the studies investigating the psychological impact of child abuse have focused strictly on sexual abuse and its impact. For example, to determine the frequency of PTSD and associated symptoms, Susan McLeer et al.[55] examined 31 sexually abused children recruited from an outpatient child psychiatry unit.[56] Children and their guardians were interviewed using a structured interview developed by the investigators. Interviews were scored according to a PTSD symptom checklist developed from DSM–III–R criteria for PTSD. Of the abused children, approximately 49% met DSM–III–R criteria for PTSD (75% of those were abused by their father; 25% were abused by a trusted adult).[57] In addition, these authors reported that a large number of children not meeting full PTSD criteria, nonetheless, exhibited symptoms in the PTSD subcategories. One or more symptoms of re-experiencing behaviors

the abused sub-sample even though these children suffered from more depression.

47. Richard Famularo et al., *Persistence of Pediatric Post Traumatic Stress Disorder After Two Years*, 20(12) CHILD ABUSE & NEGLECT 1245 (1996).

48. All children in the study had been removed from their parents' custody because of severe child maltreatment or neglect. *Id.* at 1246.

49. PTSD was assessed using a structured clinical interview that assesses a range of pediatric psychological problems (Diagnostic Interview for Children and Adolescents). *Id.* at 1246.

50. *Id.* at 1247.

51. *Id.* at 1248.

52. Richard Famularo et al., *Psychiatric Diagnoses of Maltreated Children: Preliminary Findings*, 31 J. AM. ACAD. CHILD & ADOLESCENT PSYCHIATRY 863 (1992).

53. Children in the control group were similar to the abused children in age, gender, race and family income. The mean age of children in both groups was 7.8 years, with ages ranging from 5 to 10 years. Fifty-six percent of the abused group and 57% of the control group were female. In the abused group 48% of the children were White, 35% Black, 8% Hispanic and 8% other. Similarly in the control group 40% were White, 43% were Black, 11% were Hispanic and 6% were other. *Id.* at 865.

54. *Id.* at 864.

55. Susan V. McLeer et al., *Post-Traumatic Stress Disorder in Sexually Abused Children*, 27 J. AM. ACAD. CHILD & ADOLESCENT PSYCHIATRY 650 (1988).

56. *Id.* There were 25 females, and 6 males and the mean age was 8.4 years.

57. There were only 3 children abused by a stranger, 2 of them met PTSD criteria; however, due to the small number, no comparisons were made with the other groups.

was exhibited by 81% of the sample, 48% reported experiencing three or more avoidant behaviors and 65% demonstrated two or more symptoms of autonomic hyperarousal. Similarly, in a subsequent study[58] that examined 26 sexually abused children and 23 nonabused controls,[59] McLeer et al. found that 42% were diagnosed with PTSD compared to only 9% in the control group.[60] In addition, the abused group displayed a "clustering" of psychological problems.[61] Whether these other psychological disorders suggest risk factors for the development of PTSD, however, cannot be discerned from the data. As the authors note, it is difficult to interpret the finding given the correlational nature of the data. Moreover, the presence of comorbidity in this sample may be especially elevated because of the sampling procedures employed; those children exhibiting the more severe problems are likely to be the ones targeted to receive mental health services.

A comparable rate of PTSD was found in a study that evaluated 90 children referred to a child witness preparation program.[62] Approximately half of the children in this sample[63] exhibited PTSD symptomatology.[64] In their analyses, the researchers incorporated several variables such as the severity and duration of the abuse, the victim's relationship to the offender, the perpetrator's use of violence, as well as the victim's level of guilt and self blame. They found that age and gender were significantly associated with PTSD, with more girls and older children more likely to be diagnosed with PTSD.[65] Moreover, the abuse reported by those diagnosed with PTSD occurred over a longer period of time and was more likely to involve the use of threats or coercion.[66] In contrast, the child's relationship to the offender and the frequency of the abuse did not appear to differ between the groups. Finally, the group of children who fit the PTSD criteria, compared to those who did not, were more likely to report abuse-related fears, anxiety, depression, and guilt.[67]

In contrast to the above studies, which have relied primarily on samples recruited from clinical or legal settings, McLeer and her colleagues[68] recently investigated the prevalence of psychiatric symptoms, including PTSD, in a sample of 80 non-clinically referred, sexually abused children.[69] These children

58. Susan McLeer et al., *Psychiatric Disorders in Sexually Abused Children,* 33 J. Am. Acad. Child & Adolescent Psychiatry 313 (1994).

59. The control sample was recruited from an outpatient psychiatric center. *Id.*

60. PTSD was the second most common diagnosis among the abused group. The most frequent diagnosis in both groups was Attention Deficit Hyperactive Disorder. *Id.* at 316.

61. Twenty-three percent suffered PTSD and ADHD, 15 suffered PTSD and conduct disorders and 12% suffered all three. *Id.* at 317.

62. David A. Wolfe et al., *Factors Associated with the Development of Posttraumatic Stress Disorder Among Child Victims of Sexual Abuse,* 18 Child Abuse & Neglect 37 (1994).

63. The sample was comprised of 69 girls and 21 boys with an average age of 12.4 years. In all cases, charges of abuse had been laid and the child was to testify in court. In approxi-

mately half (54%) of the cases, the abuser was a non-family member, in 26% the abuser was a parent or stepparent, in 11% the abuser was an extended family member, and in the remainder the abuser was a stranger. *Id.* at 40.

64. *Id.* at 43.

65. *Id.* at 43–44.

66. *Id.* at 44.

67. *Id.* at 43–44.

68. Susan V. McLeer et al., *Psychopathology in Non–Clinically Referred Sexually Abused Children,* 37 J. Am. Acad. Child & Adolescent Psychiatry 1326 (1998).

69. The children were selected from 142 children between the ages of 6 and 16 referred to the Philadelphia Human Services. Selection was not based on need for clinical intervention but rather on the following criteria: "the child had been sexually abused, the abuse had been disclosed and terminated within the preceding

were compared with clinical and non-clinical samples of nonabused children.[70] Although the rate of PTSD found in the sexually abused group was somewhat lower than that evidenced in the previous studies, a substantial number of the children in this group (36%) were diagnosed with PTSD. Moreover, in comparison to both of the control groups, the sexually abused children evidenced greater PTSD, anxiety and depression.[71] Also, in marked contrast to the two control groups, the majority of sexually abused children exhibited threshold symptoms of PTSD.[72]

Finally, we turn to some of the research that has included both physically and sexually abused children in the samples assessed. For instance, Laurel Kiser et al. examined 163 adolescent patients admitted to a day treatment program.[73] Of these patients, 89 were identified as victims of sexual abuse, physical abuse, or both.[74] Through diagnostic interviews, these patients were further classified into one of two groups, those displaying clinical symptoms characteristic of PTSD (55%), and those exhibiting depression, and externalizing behaviors including delinquency and aggression (45%). The researchers found that a classification of PTSD was associated with more severe physical abuse (greater than 5 years),[75] more perpetrators per physical abuse victim, a longer duration of sexual abuse,[76] and exposure to a combination of both physical and sexual abuse.[77] On the basis of these results the authors suggest two separate and distinct reactions to abuse and an association between severity of abuse and the development of PTSD. Although the results do suggest, at least within this clinical sample, a link between severity of abuse and the development of PTSD, it is difficult to draw precise conclusions since these authors fail to report the nature of the victim-offender relationship, exact break down by type of abuse in each of the two categories, or child gender.

Other researchers have attempted to differentiate the potential impact of the two forms of abuse. In a retrospective study, Esther Deblinger et al. examined the medical records of 155 children admitted to a child inpatient hospital unit during a one year period.[78] From this group, 29 children were identified as sexually/physically abused (20 of the 29 were both physically and sexually abused), 29 as physically abused only and 29 as nonabused (samples

30 to 60 days, and age and perpetrator criteria were met." *Id.* at 1327.

70. The control groups were comprised of 77 nonabused children clinically referred for psychiatric outpatient evaluation and 73 non-clinically referred school children. *Id.*

71. One child in the psychiatric group was diagnosed with PTSD. *Id.* at 1329.

72. Sixty-five of the sexually abused children reported one or more re-experiencing symptoms, 44% had three of more avoidant behaviors, and 58% reported one or more symptoms of autonomic hyperarousal. The rates found in the psychiatric and nonabused control groups were as follows: 3%, 9%, & 13% and 1%, 8%, & 8%, respectively. *Id.*

73. Laurel J. Kiser et al., *Physical and Sexual Abuse in Childhood: Relationship with Post-Traumatic Stress Disorder*, 30 J. Am. Acad. Child & Adolescent Psychiatry 776 (1991).

74. Forty victims were physically abused, 25 were sexually abused and 24 were both physically and sexually abused. *Id.* at 777–778.

75. A full 90% of the participants identified as physically abused for greater than five years were classified in the PTSD group. *Id.* at 780.

76. Two-thirds of those severely sexually abused were classified in the PTSD group. *Id.* at 780.

77. Seventy-one percent of the abused patients who had been both physically and sexually abused were classified in the PTSD group. *Id.* at 780.

78. Esther Deblinger et al., *Post-Traumatic Stress in Sexually Abused, Physically Abused, and Nonabused Children*, 13 Child Abuse & Neglect 403 (1989).

were matched on age, sex, and socioeconomic status).[79] A review of the medical chart records revealed that, overall, approximately 21% of the sexually/physically abused, 10% of the nonabused and 7% of the physically abused only children met diagnostic criteria for PTSD (as measured by a symptom checklist).[80] While these differences were not significant, it was the sexually/physically abused children who were most likely, and the physically abused who were the least likely, to meet the criteria for PTSD, suggesting a lower incidence rate of PTSD in children who are only physically abused. However, a number of interpretive difficulties attend the results of this study. The overlap of physical and sexual abuse in the sexual abuse sample, for instance, renders it impossible to determine whether the type of abuse accounts for the differences between this group and the physical abuse group or whether it is due to other characteristics that differ between the two groups (e.g., abuse severity rather than type of abuse). Moreover, differences existed between the groups in terms of perpetrator-victim relationship, with 86% of the physically abused children abused by a parent compared to only 14% of the children in the sexually/physically abused group.

Lamenting the lack of clarity regarding the relationship between child sexual abuse, physical abuse, and PTSD, Alison Dubner and Robert Motta[81] set out to assess PTSD in three different samples of children: physically abused only, sexually abused only, and nonabused.[82] The researchers hypothesized that the majority of children who experienced sexual abuse would exhibit PTSD, with a greater number of sexually abused children diagnosed with PTSD compared to the other two groups. They expected more of the physically abused children would be diagnosed with PTSD compared to the nonabused control group. As predicted, substantial rates of PTSD were found in both of the abused groups of children, with more children in the sample of the sexually abused group (64%) with PTSD compared to the physically abused group (42%) (18% of the children in the nonabused group exhibited PTSD).[88] In contrast to other studies, however, no relationship was found between the duration and severity of sexual abuse and PTSD.

Peggy Ackerman and her colleagues,[84] similarly investigated the "characteristics of abused children who do and do not develop PTSD and other

---

79. The mean age of the children was 8.8 years, with ages ranging from 3 to 13 years. There were 41 females and 46 males. *Id.* at 404.

80. *Id.* The symptom checklist was developed using seventeen items taken from the DSM–III–R PTSD criteria and grouped into three subcategories (re-experiencing phenomena, avoidance/dissociative phenomena and symptoms of autonomic hyperarousal). As the authors note, the retrospective analysis of medical records and diagnosis of PTSD using only a checklist rather than a structured interview may account for the low rate of PTSD observed in the abused groups.

81. Allison E. Dubner & Robert W. Motta, *Sexually and Physically Abused Foster Care Children and Posttraumatic Stress Disorder*, 67 J. Consulting & Clinical Psychol. 367 (1999).

82. The children (50 in each group) were evaluated within 6 months of their placement within a foster care agency. The children were between the ages of 8 to 19 and primarily boys (82%). The majority of the girls in the study, however, were in the sexually abused group (67%). Children who reported a history of both sexual and physical abuse were excluded from the study. *Id.* at 368.

83. *Id.* at 370. The authors note that the relatively high percentage of PTSD evidenced among the nonabused sample may be due to other traumas experienced by the children (e.g., the majority of children reported multiple instances of trauma such as witnessing family violence). *Id.* at 371.

84. Peggy Ackerman et al., *Prevalence of Post Traumatic Stress Disorder and Other Psychiatric Diagnoses in Three Groups of Abused Children (Sexual, Physical, and Both)*, 22 Child Abuse & Neglect 759 (1998).

psychiatric disorders," in three groups of children: sexually abused, physically abused, or both.[85] The children were recruited from hospital inpatient and outpatient evaluation and treatment centers. They found that boys were more frequently referred for physical abuse and girls for sexual abuse.[86] As well, black children were over represented in the physically abused and under represented in the sexually abused samples.[87] In terms of PTSD, depending on the criteria employed for diagnoses,[88] just over 30% of the children met criteria for PTSD, with the diagnosis of PTSD comorbid with other anxiety disorders and mood disorders.[89] A higher rate of PTSD was found for the children who experienced both forms of abuse (55%) compared to the sexual abuse only group (32%) and the physical abuse only group (26%), leading the researchers to conclude that "children who have been jointly physically and sexually abused are at greatest risk for psychiatric disorders."[90]

Finally, Boney–McCoy and Finkelhor[91] conducted a national survey to assess the psychological effects of "victimization."[92] One third of their respondents reported that they had been the victim of an assault at some point in their lives. The results demonstrated that those who had been victimized exhibited more psychological and behavioral problems, compared to the non-victimized group, with sexual assault associated with the most severe problems. When the researchers looked specifically at physical assault by a parent, which was reported by just over 2% of their sample, they found that "parental physical violence was associated with marked post traumatic stress disorder symptomatology."[93] Comparisons with sexual assault victimizations yielded comparable rates of PTSD-related symptomatology.[94] The researchers also assessed whether the link between psychopathology (e.g., PTSD) and victimization was moderated by family environment. Since the children in the study were assessed at two points in time (separated by a 15 month interim), the researchers were able to test the strength of the relationship between victimization in the interim and psychopathology at Time 2, after controlling for the effects of the prior symptoms and family variables (assessed at Time 1). Evidence for the independent effect of the interim victimization on psychopathology was found, especially in the case of sexual abuse, parental assault, and

---

85. The children were between the ages of 7 to 13; 127 were classified as sexually abused, 43 as physically abused, and 43 as both sexually and physically abused. *Id.* at 761.

86. *Id.* at 762.

87. *Id.*

88. The child and parent (caregiver) forms of the Diagnostic Interview for Children and Adolescents was administered; overall, children endorsed fewer diagnoses than caregivers. *Id.* at 764.

89. *Id.* at 765.

90. *Id.* at 771.

91. Sue Boney–McCoy & David Finkelhor, *Psychosocial Sequelae of Violent Victimization in a National Youth Sample*, 63(5) J. CONSULTING & CLINICAL PSYCHOL. 726 (1995).

92. Telephone interviews were conducted with 1042 boys and 958 girls between the ages of 10 and 16. The respondents were selected

randomly and constitute a representative sample of the adolescent population as a whole. Forms of victimization included aggravated and simple assault by a nonfamily member, physical assault by a parent or other family member, attempted/completed kidnaping and sexual assault. *Id.*

93. Boney–McCoy & Finkelhor, *supra* note 91, at 730. To assess PTSD symptomatology respondents were asked to indicate how often (i.e., "not at all," "only a bit," "quite a bit") within the past week, they had experienced each of 10 symptoms that were taken from the "Symptom Checklist–90–R." *Id.* at 727.

94. Since sexual assault is "so widely recognized as an extremely serious form of child trauma" the authors consider it to be a "benchmark" against which the other types of victimizations can be compared. With the exception of nonparental family assault and simple assault by a nonfamily member, all other forms of victimization evidenced similar associations with the symptom measures. *Id.* at 733.

kidnaping. Given the small number of intrafamilial sexual abuse sampled in the study, however, the researchers' ability to assess adequately the hypothesis that family environment moderates the impact of sexual abuse has been questioned.[95]

Taken together, the above studies have produced mixed results, revealing a great deal of variability in the prevalence of PTSD in abused children (ranging from as low as 7% to over 60%). In general, lower prevalence rates have been reported in children who have been physically abused only and higher levels have been reported in children who have been victims of sexual abuse (i.e., sexual abuse alone or in conjunction with physical abuse). Given these findings, some researchers have concluded that sexual abuse/assault is associated with the most adverse psychological effects.[96] There appears to be some agreement among researchers that abuse and family functioning play a role in the development of psychopathology, although researchers view the relative importance of context differently.[97] Some of the investigations have explored the intervening variables, that is, the factors that may predispose certain children to develop PTSD or other mental health problems by examining the role played by such variables as the abuse history of the child's mother,[98] family environment,[99] characteristics of both the victim[100] and the abuse.[101] A recent review of research in the area of sexual abuse and its impact

---

95. Michael R. Nash et al., *Psychopathology Associated With Sexual Abuse: The Importance of Complementary Designs and Common Ground*, 66 CONSULTING & CLINICAL PSYCHOL. 568 (1988) Nash et. al. also take exception to Boney–McCoy and Finkelhor's characterization of their research, arguing that Boney–McCoy and Finkelhor misrepresent their findings as supportive of the hypothesis that the "effects of victimization are 'cancelled out' by the inclusion of family relationship measures." They also note their finding that they "found and reported effects for abuse per se, even after controlling for context."

96. *See* Boney–McCoy & Finkelhor, *supra* note 91 at 377.

97. *See* Nash et al., *supra* note 95; Sue Boney–McCoy & David Finkelhor, *Psychopathology Associated with Sexual Abuse: A Reply to Nash, Neimeyer, Hulsey, and Lambert*, 66 CONSULTING & CLINICAL PSYCHOL. 572, 573 (1998).

98. For example, Timmons–Mitchell et al. investigated whether or not the abuse history of a child's mother was associated with PTSD in a sample of 28 children who had recently disclosed that they had been abused. Although a substantial number of the children displayed PTSD symptomatology (over half the sample), the diagnosis of PTSD did not differ as a function of the mother's abuse history. Jane Timmons–Mitchell et al., *Post-Traumatic Stress Disorder Symptoms in Child Sexual Abuse Victims and Their Mothers*, 6(4) J. CHILD SEXUAL ABUSE 6 (1997).

99. *See generally* Nash et al., *supra* note 95; Boney–McCoy & Finkelhor, *supra* note 97.

100. For example, Feiring et al. examined how individual differences such as the victim's age, gender, and cognitive processes (e.g., attributional style, self-evaluations of shame) impact upon children's adaptation to sexual abuse. Candice Feiring et al., *Age and Gender Differences in Children's and Adolescents' Adaptation to Sexual Abuse*, 23 CHILD ABUSE & NEGLECT 115 (1998); Candice Feiring et al., *The Role of Shame and Attributional Style in Children's and Adolescents' Adaptation to Sexual Abuse*, 3 CHILD MALTREATMENT 129 (1998). The role of mediating variables has also been explored in examinations of physical abuse. *See, e.g.*, Steve Spaccarelli, *Stress, Appraisal, and Coping in Child Sexual Abuse: A Theoretical and Empirical Review*, 116(2) PSYCHOLOGICAL BULL. 340 (1994). Scerbo and Kolko propose an interactional model, in which they contend that, although physically abused children are more overtly aggressive than other children, the relationship between physical abuse and aggression interacts with the characteristics of the child. They investigated this hypothesis in a small sample of children (predominately boys) who were attending a treatment program for behavioral disorders. Consistent with their hypothesis, they found a higher rate of aggressive behavior among children who had been both physically abused and internalized their problems. Angela Scarpa Scerbo & David Kolko, *Child Physical Abuse and Aggression: Preliminary Findings on the Role of Internalizing Problems*, 34(8) J. AM. ACAD. CHILD & ADOLESCENT PSYCHIATRY 1060.

101. For instance, while not investigating PTSD specifically, Mennen and Meadow studied how several variables (type and duration of

on children suggests that "the variables most consistently associated with more adverse impact are longer duration of abuse, force or violence accompanying the abuse, and father or father-figure as the perpetrator."[102] In a recent review of the research pertaining to physical abuse, Sandra Kaplan et al.[103] conclude that although PTSD "may be present in cases of extreme physical abuse, it does not appear to be commonly associated with mild physical maltreatment."[104]

[b] Hypervigilance

One of the major behavioral characteristics or symptoms of child abuse frequently discussed in the legal literature with respect to the battered child syndrome is hypervigilance.[105] For instance, Hicks describes battered children in the following way:

> acutely aware of his or her environment and remains on alert for any signs of danger, events to which the unabused child may not attend.[106]

In essence, given the child's history of abuse, the child eventually develops the ability to perceive danger in subtle changes in a parent's expressions or mannerisms and becomes sensitized to these changes.[107]

Support for the presence of hypervigilance in abused children primarily comes from clinical studies. For example, in a case study observing the behavior of 50 children (ages 2–13 years), Harold Martin and Patricia Beezley noted commonly occurring characteristics including hypervigilance.[108] Along similar lines, some clinical studies observing mother and child interactions, describe the presence of "frozen watchfulness" in abused children.[109] The researchers describe these children as being in a state of constant uncertainty resulting from intermittent abuse. The children sat passively, but were alert and hypervigilant so as to detect possible danger in the environment.

Since hypervigilance is one of the possible (but not necessary) symptoms required for a diagnosis of PTSD, some support for the presence of hypervigi-

---

abuse, use of force, relationship of perpetrator, age, age at onset of abuse and race) impact upon depression, anxiety and self worth. They found that the most powerful variable associated with psychological problems was the type of abuse. Girls who experienced penetration suffered more depression and anxiety and had lower levels of self esteem. Ferol E. Mennen & Diane Meadow, *The Relationship of Abuse Characteristics to Symptoms in Sexually Abused Girls*, 10 J. INTERPERSONAL VIOLENCE 259 (1995).

102. Penelope K. Trickett & Frank W. Putman, *Developmental Consequences of Child Sexual Abuse, in* VIOLENCE AGAINST CHILDREN IN THE FAMILY AND THE COMMUNITY 49 (Penelope K. Trickett & Cynthia J. Schellenbach, eds., 1998).

103. Sandra J. Kaplan et al., *Child and Adolescent Abuse and Neglect Research: A Review of the Past 10 Years. Part I: Physical and Emotional Abuse and Neglect*, 38 J. AM. ACAD. CHILD & ADOLESCENT PSYCHIATRY 1214 (1999).

104. *Id.* at 1217.

105. *See, e.g.*, Hicks, *supra* note 11, at 103–104; Mones, *supra* note 16, at 26; Sacks, *supra* note 11, at 356; Joelle A. Moreno, *Killing Daddy: Developing a Self–Defense Strategy for the Abused Child*, 137 U. PA. L. REV. 1281, 1287 (1989); State v. Janes, 121 Wash.2d 220, 850 P.2d 495, 503 (Wash.1993) (en banc).

106. Hicks, *supra* note 11, at 103–104.

107. *Id.*

108. Harold P. Martin & Patricia Beezley, *Behavioral Observations of Abused Children*, 19 DEVELOPMENTAL MED. & CHILD NEUROLOGY 373 (1977).

109. Arthur H. Green, *Child Abuse: Dimension of Psychological Trauma in Abused Children*, 22 J. AM. ACAD. CHILD & ADOLESCENT PSYCHIATRY 231 (1983); Christopher Ounsted et al., *Aspects of Bonding Failure: The Psychotherapeutic Treatment of Families of Battered Children*, 16 DEVELOPMENTAL MED. OF CHILD NEUROLOGY 446 (1974).

lance in abused children comes from studies investigating PTSD (discussed in the previous section). Although some of the more recent studies examining PTSD in abused children have found elevated levels of hyperarousal and hypervigilance,[110] unfortunately, the majority of studies did not always report the occurrence of actual symptoms, thus rendering it difficult to determine the actual prevalence of this symptom in this population.

[c] Learned Helplessness

The theory of learned helplessness, which has been used to explain the impact of abuse on battered women, has similarly been linked to abused children, particularly in the legal literature.[111] When learned helplessness is raised in the psychological research, it tends to occur in investigations examining the incidence of depression and low self-esteem in abused children. Because these children live in environments that are adversive, punitive, and noncontingent in nature, it is contended that depressive symptoms will develop.[112] Indeed, a number of studies provide support for the existence of depressive symptomatology in abused children.

Alan Kazdin et al. evaluated 79 children selected from hospital admissions to an inpatient psychiatric facility (children were admitted due to acute disorders not directly related to abuse).[113] Thirty-three of these children were identified as physically abused[114] and compared to the remaining 46 non-abused children.[115] Compared to the nonabused children, self-evaluations of depression and hopelessness were significantly higher and self-evaluations of self-esteem significantly lower in the sample of children who had been physically abused.[116] These differences, however, were not found on the parent versions of these same measures. The authors note that this finding is consistent with previous research showing little or no relationship between child and parent evaluations of the children's depression. Further, they report that child and parent ratings are correlated with different aspects of dysfunction. Parent reports of the child's depression are related to overt social behavior and affective expression, while child ratings of depression are related to self-evaluations and expectancies about the future.

In addition, these researchers looked at the impact that the "history of abuse" had on the children's level of depression, hopelessness, and self-esteem. Children who had a protracted history of abuse (greater than one year) were significantly higher in depression and hopelessness and lower in self-esteem compared to abused children with a shorter duration of abuse or

110. For example, see McLeer et al., *supra* note 68; Deblinger et al., *supra* note 78.

111. Hicks, *supra* note 11, at 123–124; Sacks, *supra* note 11, at 355–356.

112. Alan E. Kazdin et al., *Depressive Symptoms Among Physically Abused and Psychiatrically Disturbed Children*, 94 J. ABNORMAL PSYCHOL. 298 (1985); Amy B. Gross & Harold R. Keller, *Long-Term Consequences of Childhood Physical and Psychological Maltreatment*, 18 AGGRESSIVE BEHAV. 171 (1992).

113. Kazdin et al., *supra* note 112. The mean age of these children was 10.4 years.

114. There was not enough evidence, however, to meet state legal criteria for filing an abuse report. *Id.*

115. *Id.* There were no differences between groups on age, gender, race, IQ, mother's age, mother's race, welfare status, diagnosis, and social class.

116. Depression was measured using the Children's Depression Inventory (CDI) and the Bellevue Index of Depression. Hopelessness was measured using the Hopelessness Scale for Children (HPLS) and self-esteem was measured using the Self–Esteem Inventory (SEI).

"past" abuse only (i.e., no abuse within the past year). Children with "past" abuse were the least depressed of the abused groups, the least hopeless and highest in self-esteem of the abused groups, but tended to be slightly worse off than the control group (although this was not a significant difference). Once again, these differences were not apparent in the parents' ratings of their children. These findings of lower self esteem or self concept[117] and depressive symptomology[118] in abused samples is consistent with other findings in the area.

Other studies investigating depression in abused children have assessed the prevalence of diagnosable Major Depressive Disorder as opposed to only depressive symptomology. For example, Joan Kaufman studied 56 abused children and their mothers who were referred to the study by social workers working for a youth services agency.[119] Each child was assessed for experiences of physical abuse, neglect, emotional maltreatment and sexual abuse. Eighteen percent of these children were found to meet diagnostic criteria for Major Depressive Disorder (as measured by a semi-structured clinical interview) and 25% met criteria for a less severe pattern of depression. Comparing the depressed group to the nondepressed group, depressed children were more likely to receive more severe scores on physical abuse and emotional maltreatment than nondepressed children.[120] Depressed children revealed fewer social supports, more conflictual relationships, and perceived their social supports to care less for them than nondepressed children. In addition, the depressed children revealed a more maladaptive attributional style, attributing the outcome of positive events to external factors and the outcome of negative events to themselves.[121] Six variables were found to significantly distinguish

117. For example, Oates et al. matched 37 abused children (abused for an average of 5.5 years) to a group of nonabused children and found that, compared to the nonabused group, the abused children have fewer friends, lower ambitions (determined during a short structured interview) and lower self-esteem (as measured by the Piers–Harris Self–Concept Scale). In this study children were matched on age, sex, ethnic group, school and social class. The mean age of these children was 8.9 years. R. Kim Oates et al., *Self-Esteem of Abused Children,* 9 CHILD ABUSE & NEGLECT 159 (1985).

118. Cerezo and Frias investigated the differences between 19 abused children referred for psychological evaluation (16 boys, 3 girls, average age 10.3 years, who had suffered at least two years of physical and emotional abuse) and 26 nonabused children (14 boys, 12 girls, average age 9.4 years, with no history of parental abuse) coming from the same community on depressive symptomatology (as measured by the CDI children's self-report). Abused children revealed significantly higher depressive symptomatology and displayed a more negative affective state (e.g., self/concept, health/illness, death worries, social relationships and enjoyment experiences). Angeles Cerezo & Dolores Frias, *Emotional and Cognitive Adjustment in Abused Children,* 18 CHILD ABUSE & NEGLECT 923 (1994). Looking only at

sexually abused adolescents, Huguette Sansonnet–Hayden et al. reported significantly more depressive symptoms (as measured using the Diagnostic Interview Schedule for Children) in a group of 17 sexually abused adolescents compared to 37 non-sexually abused controls. Huguette Sansonnet–Hayden et al., *Sexual Abuse and Psychopathology in Hospitalized Adolescents,* 26 J. AM. ACAD. CHILD & ADOLESCENT PSYCHIATRY 753 (1987). *See also* Flisher et al., *supra* note 44.

119. Joan Kaufman, *Depressive Disorders in Maltreated Children,* 30 J. AM. ACAD. CHILD & ADOLESCENT PSYCHIATRY 257 (1991). The sample consisted of 29 girls and 27 boys with an average age of 9.7 years; 64% of the sample were White, 17% were Black and 19% Hispanic.

120. No differences were found between the depressed and nondepressed group on race, sex, family status, and welfare status, but the depressed children were slightly older than the nondepressed children.

121. Robert Barahal et al., measuring internal vs. external locus of control (to both positive and negative situations), found that abused children compared to controls were more likely to feel that outcomes were determined by external factors particularly when referring to negative situations. Robert M. Bar-

between the non-depressed children and the children who either met the criteria for Major Depressive Disorder or who exhibited the less severe pattern of depression (number of out-of-home placements, attributional style, conflictual relations, physical abuse, and perceived affection from social supports and emotional maltreatment).

Further support for the link between child abuse, in particular physical abuse, and the incidence of major depression has been demonstrated in a study conducted by Pelcovitz and his colleagues.[122] Their examination of 27 adolescent victims of physical abuse identified through a social agency found significantly higher incidence of major depression in this sample of children (40%) compared to a community-based nonabused control group (3.7%).

In a study comparing sexually abused, physically abused and nonabused children for major depression, Richard Livingston administered the Diagnostic Interview for Children and Adolescents (DICA) to 28 victims of abuse selected from 100 children consecutively admitted to an inpatient child psychiatric unit.[123] The abuse victims (13 sexual abuse victims and 15 physical abuse victims) were compared to 72 psychiatric patients who were not abused.[124] A greater percentage of the sexually abused victims were diagnosed with Major Depression (77%) compared to both the physically abused victims (33%) and the nonabused controls (10%).[125] The physically abused victims did, however, reveal a significantly higher incidence of major depression than the controls.[126]

In sum, studies examining abused children reveal elevated levels of depressive symptomatology (as measured by both self reports and interviews) when compared to both clinical and nonclinical controls. Across these studies, rates of Major Depressive Disorder in abused children range from 18 to 77%. Kaplan et al.[127] in a review of the research on physical abuse concluded that "approximately 8% of children and adolescents documented as physically abused have current diagnoses of major depressive disorder, and at least 30% have lifetime disruptive disorder diagnoses."[128] Typically the highest incidence rates have been reported in children who were psychiatric patients and sexually abused.

As with the research dealing with the application of learned helplessness to battered women, however, the examination of learned helplessness in abused children has been limited to potential correlates of learned helplessness and little attention has been devoted to broader assessments of learned

ahal et al., *The Social Cognitive Development of Abused Children*, 49 J. CONSULTING & CLINICAL PSYCHOL. 508 (1981).

122. Pelcovitz et al., *supra* note 42.

123. Richard Livingston, *Sexually and Physically Abused Children*, 26 J. AM. ACAD. CHILD & ADOLESCENT PSYCHIATRY 413 (1987). These children ranged in age from 6 to 12 years.

124. Thirteen of the 15 physically abused children and 4 of the 13 sexually abused children were male.

125. Similarly, a high rate of major depression (as measured by the DICA) was also noted

in a study by Huguette Sansonnet–Hayden et al. when looking at a group of sexually abused adolescents (71%). No differences in frequency of diagnosis were found, however, between this group and a psychiatric control group (57%). Thus, the high incidence of major depression diagnoses in this study may be due to the clinical sample evaluated. Sanonnet–Hayden et al., *supra* note 118, at 755.

126. Compared to population prevalence rates, the rate for Major Depression was also much higher in the abused samples studied by Ackerman et al., *supra* note 84.

127. Kaplan et al., *supra* note 103.

128. *Id.* at 1217.

helplessness that capture behavioral as well as affective and cognitive components of the theory.[129]

§ 5–2.2   The Scientific Methods Applied in the Research

In general, the research addressing the areas reviewed above is quite fragmented and limited by both conceptual and methodological problems. The studies examining parricide have been primarily limited to case studies in which the researcher has had to rely on retrospective accounts of events surrounding the killings. Since this information is not systematically collected, such an approach limits the researcher to the type of information available, and hence to the conclusions that can be drawn. Further, much of this work has failed to include appropriate comparison or control groups and those studies that have incorporated a control group rely on very small samples, making it difficult to reliably assess any differences between the groups. It should be noted, however, that some of the above difficulties, particularly small sample sizes, may be an inherent problem in this type of research, since the population of children who commit parricide is itself quite small.

For the most part, the research investigating PTSD in abused children is still in its infancy.[130] Issues related to the operational definitions of different subtypes of abuse are still being formulated, and, to date, researchers have reached no consensus.[131] Further, many of the early studies do not even attempt to report the definitions of abuse that were employed, failing to differentiate or report clearly the exact type of abuse being assessed. As a result, any differences that may be associated with different aspects of abuse or that may contribute to inconsistencies noted in the findings are obscured.[132] The studies conducted also vary in their definition and measurement of PTSD (e.g., some look at symptomatology, others at the actual diagnosis), with little attention directed to the adequacy of the instruments used to assess PTSD.[133] For instance, recent work examining the validity of the Child Behavior Checklist, a measure typically used to assess PTSD in children, raises some serious concerns regarding the discriminant validity of the instrument.[134] Although differences between a sample of sexually abused children and nonabused school children were found in terms of the overall PTSD scores derived from this measure, the sexually abused children did not differ when compared to a sample of nonabused psychiatric outpatients.[135] The overlap between symptoms of PTSD and other psychiatric disorders, as well as the comorbidity in PTSD patients,[136] clearly presents problems of classification and diagnosis, which have yet to be resolved.

129. *See* Schuller & Rzepa, *supra* note 1.

130. Richard J. McNally, *Stressors that Produce Posttraumatic Stress Disorder in Children, in* POSTTRAUMATIC STRESS DISORDER: DSM-IV AND BEYOND 57 (Jonathan R. T. Davidson & Edna B. Foa eds. 1993).

131. Jody Todd Manly et al., *The Impact of Subtype, Frequency, Chronicity, and Severity of Child Maltreatment on Social Competence and Behavior Problems,* 6 DEVELOPMENT & PSYCHOPATHOLOGY 121, 122 (1994). For a discussion of definitional issues in terms of sexual abuse, *see* Bruce Rind & Philip Tromovitch, *A Meta–Analytic Review of Findings from National Samples on Psychological Correlates of Child Sexual Abuse,* 34 J. SEX RES. 237 (1997).

132. David Finkelhor, *Sexual Abuse and Physical Abuse: Some Critical Differences, in* UNHAPPY FAMILIES 21 (Eli H. Newberger & Richard Bourne eds. 1985).

133. Kenneth J. Ruggiero & Susan V. McLeer, *PTSD Scale of the Child Behavior Checklist: Concurrent and Discriminant Validity with Non–Clinic–Referred Sexually Abuse Children,* 13 J. TRAUMATIC STRESS 287, 287–289.

134. *Id.*

135. *Id.* at 294–298.

136. Dan Weinstein et al., *Attention-Deficit Hyperactivity Disorder and Posttraumatic Stress Disorder: Differential Diagnosis in*

Although the situation is improving, most studies involve investigations of fairly small samples, with children representing a wide range of age levels (e.g., 4 to 14), different types of abuse, and various victim-perpetrator (e.g., intrafamilial vs. extrafamilial) relationships. Without properly controlling for these confounding variables, their relationship to PTSD cannot be clearly determined. For instance, in physical abuse cases the offender is almost always a member of the immediate family; this is not the case for sexual abuse. Failure to note the nature of the relationship is problematic, as a number of studies suggest a possible relationship between the victim-perpetrator relationship and the level of trauma experienced by the victim.[137]

Also of concern in the research is the sampling that has been employed. In particular, the samples investigated in the studies have typically been based on children admitted to hospitals for treatment or whose abuse has been officially reported. As a consequence, the generalizability of the findings from these studies to battered and abused children more generally may be challenged. Indeed, within the context of sexual abuse, the more general body of research that associates adult psychological maladjustment with childhood sexual abuse[138] has recently come under heavy criticism precisely on these same grounds. In particular, Bruce Rind and his colleagues assert that previous reviews of the literature have relied primarily on studies that have employed clinical and legal samples and as a result are "vulnerable to several biases that threaten their validity."[139] To address these concerns, Rind and his colleagues conducted quantitative reviews (i.e., utilizing meta-analytic techniques) of the research literature examining the psychological correlates of child sexual abuse, relying on nonclinical and nonlegal samples (e.g., national probability samples, college students).[140] Their results question the very claim that victims of childhood sexual abuse necessarily experience negative psychological sequelae.[141] In contrast to the qualitative reviews, their results indicate

---

Childhood Sexual Abuse, 20 CLINICAL PSYCHOLOGICAL REV. 359, 366–367.

137. McLeer et al., *supra* note 55; William N. Friedrich et al., *Behavior Problems in Sexually Abused Young Children*, 11 J. PEDIATRIC PSYCHOL. 47 (1986); Elizabeth Ann Sirles et al., *Psychiatric Status of Intrafamilial Child Sexual Abuse Victims*, 28 J. AM. ACAD. CHILD & ADOLESCENT PSYCHIATRY 225 (1989).

138. This research focuses on the long term effects of sexual abuse in adult survivors, noting the association of PTSD, as well as other psychological problems and disorders in this population. *See, e.g.,* Melissa A. Polusny & Victoria M. Follette, *Long-term Correlate of Child Sexual Abuse: Theory and Review of the Empirical Literature*, 4 APPLIED & PREVENTIVE PSYCHOL. 143 (1995); Ned Rodriguez et al., *Post Traumatic Stress Disorder in Adult Female Survivors of Child Sexual Abuse: A Comparison Study*, 65(1) J. CONSULTING & CLINICAL PSYCHOL. 53 (1997); Lynn Briggs & Peter R. Joyce, *What Determines Post–Traumatic Stress Disorder Symptomatology for Survivors of Childhood Sexual Abuse?*, 21(6) CHILD ABUSE AND

NEGLECT 575 (1997); Kristin K. Schaaf & Thomas R. McCanne, *Relationship of Childhood Sexual, Physical, and Combined Sexual and Physical Abuse to Adult Victimization and Posttraumatic Stress Disorder*, 22 CHILD ABUSE & NEGLECT 1119 (1998), Cathy Spatz Widom, *Posttraumatic Stress Disorder in Abused and Neglected Children Grown Up*, 156 AM. J. PSYCHIATRY 1223 (1999).

139. Bruce Rind et al., *A Meta–Analytic Examination of Assumed Properties of Child Sexual Abuse Using College Samples*, 124 PSYCHOLOGICAL BULL. 22, 24 (1998); Rind & Tromovitch, *supra* note 131.

140. Rind & Tromovitch question the claim that "child sexual abuse (CSA) causes intense harm, regardless of gender, pervasively in the general population." Specifically, the researchers address the following four issues: "(a) CSA causes harm, (b) this harm is pervasive in the population of persons with a history of CSA, (c) this harm is likely too intense, and (d) CSA is an equivalent experience for boys and girls." *Id.* at 22.

141. *Id.* at 22–23.

that in the "entire population of persons with a history of CSA, the magnitude of the CSA-adjustment relation is small."[142]

On more conceptual grounds, David Finkelhor criticizes PTSD as a framework for understanding sexual abuse trauma and many of his criticisms are applicable to research in the area of child abuse more generally.[143] He argues that the conceptualization is far too narrow,[144] concentrates only on the affective realm (ignoring the cognitive realm), and fails to adequately account for victims of sexual abuse who do not show symptoms of PTSD.[145] Finkelhor concludes that while "PTSD has added insight to the understanding of trauma of some sexual abuse victims it is not in itself an adequate conceptualization."[146] Other clinicians and researchers have similarly argued that the complexity of chronic, long term childhood trauma and the resultant symptom patterns that ensue in children are not well captured in the diagnosis of PTSD and have proposed alternative diagnoses that describe symptoms inadequately characterized by PTSD.[147]

§ 5–2.3   Areas of Scientific Agreement and Disagreement

Some agreement in the area is found regarding the psychological impact that abuse can have on a child,[148] but as to the existence of a specific syndrome or profile, the literature remains silent. Therefore, attempting to identify agreement and disagreement regarding battered child syndrome in the scientific literature is premature. The parallel between battered child syndrome and battered woman syndrome that has been drawn is, at this point, not based on an empirical body of work. There is a small body of research documenting the existence of some of the symptoms associated with battered woman syndrome in a proportion of abused children, but as this review of the research indicates, these areas are not yet well developed. Further, no studies have attempted to assess what group of symptoms constitute a reliable and valid battered child syndrome and how well it

---

142. *Id.* at 26.

143. *See* David Finkelhor, *The Trauma of Child Sexual Abuse,* 2 J. INTERPERSONAL VIOLENCE 348 (1987); David Finkelhor, *Early and Long–Term Effects of Child Sexual Abuse: An Update,* 21 PROF. PSYCHOL.: RES. & PRAC. 325, 328–329 (1990).

144. *Id.* at 328.

145. *Id.*

146. *Id.* at 329.

147. *See* Judith L. Herman, *Complex PTSD: A Syndrome in Survivors of Prolonged and Repeated Trauma,* 5 J. TRAUMATIC STRESS 377 (1992); Lenore Terr, based on clinical evaluations of over 150 children, argued for a broadening of the PTSD diagnostic criteria to include "type I" trauma (resulting from a sudden event) and "type II" trauma (resulting from long standing or repeated abuse). Terr described four symptoms characteristic of all PTSD patients (visualization, reenactment, trauma specific fears and futurelessness), but postulates that children suffering from these two traumas differ on several dimensions. Specifically, when exposed to repeated trauma

(type II) the child in attempting to defend himself against ongoing stresses may develop additional problems (e.g., leading to one of a number of psychiatric problems). Lenore C. Terr, *Childhood Traumas: An Outline and Overview,* 148 AM. J. PSYCHIATRY 10 (1991). Empirical examination of this type of classification construct, as applied to abused children can be found in a study conducted by Darlene Hall, *"Complex" Posttraumatic Stress Disorder/Disorders of Extreme Stress (CP1/DES) in Sexually Abused Children: An Exploratory Study,* 8 J. CHILD SEXUAL ABUSE 51.

148. *See, e.g.,* Kathleen A. Kendall–Tackett et al., *Impact of Sexual Abuse on Children: A Review and Synthesis of Recent Empirical Studies,* 13 PSYCHOLOGICAL BULL. 165 (1993); Cathy Spatz Widom & Ashley Ames, *Criminal Consequences of Childhood Sexual Victimization,* 18 CHILD ABUSE & NEGLECT 303 (1994); Alan A. Cavaiola & Matthew Schiff, *Behavioral Sequelae of Physical and/or Sexual Abuse in Adolescents,* 12 CHILD ABUSE & NEGLECT 181 (1988); Howard Dubowitz et al., *A Follow-up Study of Behavior Problems Associated with Child Sexual Abuse,* 17 CHILD ABUSE & NEGLECT 743 (1993).

captures the impact of abuse in this population. The heterogeneity of children's responses to abuse suggests, however, that, as is the case with battered women, a single profile is unlikely to adequately capture the impact of abuse on a child.

In summary, the applicability of the research findings on battered women to battered children still needs to be demonstrated. Certainly the impact of the violence on these two populations will result in some similar effects, but generalizing from battered women to battered children, two very different populations, is only speculative until the effects can be demonstrated in the latter population. While there is evidence to suggest that PTSD is associated with abuse (sexual and physical), there is also considerable variability in children's responses. In a comprehensive review of the research pertaining to child sexual abuse, Wekerle and Wolfe describe a range of symptoms associated with abuse (e.g., PTSD, ADD and hyperactivity, hypervigilance and dissociation).[149] In addition, the psychiatric and psychological effects associated with physical abuse are extremely varied.[150] There appears to be no single profile of the "abused" or "battered child" and the general conclusions drawn by Kendall–Tackett et al. still appear to hold for this area of research more generally. Although children who have been abused exhibit more symptomatic and pathological behaviors compared to nonabused children, "findings suggest the absence of any specific syndrome in children who have been sexually abused and no single traumatizing process."[151]

§ 5–2.4 Future Directions

Research investigating the impact of abuse on children has described a wide variety of symptoms with no clear pattern emerging. At this point in time, the research examining the symptomatology of abused children has been limited in scope and often the observed effects are attributed to abuse in a very global sense. Researchers are just beginning to distinguish more systematically between the type, intensity and frequency of the abusive experience and it is essential that research continues in this direction. David Wolfe and Peter Jaffe also point out the importance of recognizing the child's developmental level,[152] as well as the child's full stress experience. Given that symptomatology will vary by age, the effects of abuse on a child must be examined with an awareness of the child's ongoing developmental stages.[153] Researchers in the area of child abuse have also begun to examine co-occurring risk factors (e.g., poverty, substance abuse, domestic violence) that may exist in addition to the abuse.[154] Since other risk factors are associated with the same negative outcomes, it is not always clear what role the abuse played and thus continued efforts to disentangle these variables is important.

149. Christine Wekerle & David Wolfe, *Child Maltreatment, in* CHILD PSYCHOPATHOLOGY 492 (Eric J. Mash & Russell A. Barkley, eds., 1996).

150. Kaplan et al., *supra* note 103, at 1216–1217.

151. Kathleen A. Kendall–Tackett et al., *Impact of Sexual Abuse on Children: A Review and Synthesis of Recent Empirical Studies*, 113(1) PSYCHOL. BULL. 164 (1996).

152. David Wolfe & Peter Jaffe, *Child Abuse and Family Violence as Determinants of Child Psychopathology*, 23 CANADIAN J. BEHAV. SCI. 282 (1991).

153. *Id.* at 293.

154. *See, e.g.*, Alexander Okun et al., *Distinct and Interactive Contributions of Physical Abuse, Socioeconomic Disadvantage, and Negative Life Events to Children's Social, Cognitive, and Affective Adjustment*, 6 DEV. & PSYCHOPATHOLOGY 77 (1994).

Finally, researchers in the area have turned their attention to the notion of "resilience" in an attempt to understand the wide range of outcomes in abused children.[155] By examining "theoretically relevant compensatory and debilitating factors that may attenuate or accentuate the effects of the abuse" (e.g., IQ, family support) researchers may more fully account for the wide range of phenomena experienced by abused children and help to explain why some children show particular signs of distress (e.g., PTSD), while others do not.[156] Such developments suggest that the research is moving away from the narrow focus of specific symptoms in isolation toward an understanding of the broader circumstances involved in abuse and its impact.

155. *See, e.g.*, Joan Kaufman et al., *Problems Defining Resiliency: Illustrations From the Study of Maltreated Children*, 6 DEV. & PSYCHOPATHOLOGY 215 (1994).

156. Similarly, Cicchetti has noted that this style of research should lead to a more "comprehensive understanding of the occurrence and sequelae of child maltreatment." Dante Cicchetti, *Advances and Challenges in the Study of the Sequelae of Child Maltreatment*, 6 DEV. & PSYCHOPATHOLOGY 1, 2 (1994).

CHAPTER 6

RAPE TRAUMA SYNDROME

Table of Sections

A. LEGAL ISSUES

Westlaw Electronic Research

See Westlaw Electronic Research Guide preceding the Summary of Contents.

A. LEGAL ISSUES

§ 6–1.0 THE LEGAL RELEVANCE OF SCIENTIFIC RESEARCH ON RAPE TRAUMA SYNDROME*

§ 6–1.1 Introduction

Rape trauma syndrome (RTS) is a general term used to describe common responses to a sexual assault. Although the term is regularly used in legal decision-making, it can cause confusion because courts give it a variety of meanings. The term "rape trauma syndrome" was coined by Burgess and Holmstrom to describe a two-stage model of recovery from rape among adult women.[1] However, subsequent research has conceptualized rape trauma in terms of specific symptoms rather than a syndrome or stages of recovery. Moreover, rape is an example of a traumatic event that can lead to the development of a Post–Traumatic Stress Disorder (PTSD). PTSD was first defined by the American Psychiatric Association in 1980 in the third edition of their Diagnostic and Statistical Manual (DSM–III).[2] Thus, RTS often is described as a specific type of PTSD.[3] This can be misleading because the symptoms listed in the psychiatric diagnostic manuals are not the same as those described by Burgess and Holmstrom or those studied in most research on rape. In sum, RTS has been used to refer to the stage model of recovery described by Burgess and Holmstrom, general post-rape symptoms, and rape-related PTSD, none of which are synonymous with each other. In this Chapter, therefore, we use the designation RTS to refer to the entire body of research on the effects of rape, including the early research by Burgess and

---

* The editors gratefully acknowledge the assistance of Professors Patricia Frazier and Eugene Borgida in the preparation of this section.

§ 6–1.0

1. Ann Burgess & Linda Holmstrom, *Rape Trauma Syndrome*, 131 Am. J. Psychiatry 981 (1974); *see also* People v. Taylor, 75 N.Y.2d 277, 552 N.Y.S.2d 883, 552 N.E.2d 131, 133 (N.Y.1990) ("[T]he Burgess and Holmstrom identification of two separate phases in a rape victim's recovery has proven enormously influential.").

2. American Psychiatric Association, Diagnostic and Statistical Manual of Mental Disorders (3d ed. 1980); American Psychiatric Association, Diagnostic and Statistical Manual of Mental Disorders (3d ed. revised 1987); American Psychiatric Association, Diagnostic and Statistical Manual of Mental Disorders (4th ed. 1994).

3. *See, e.g.*, Chapman v. State, 18 P.3d 1164, 1170 (Wyo.2001).

Holmstrom, more recent research on specific post-rape symptoms, and research on rape-related PTSD.[4]

Expert testimony on RTS typically consists of a description of the common after-effects of rape and an opinion that a particular complainant's behavior is consistent with, or not inconsistent with, having been raped. This testimony is used predominantly in criminal cases to corroborate the prosecution's claim that intercourse was not consensual. In other words, if the intercourse had been consensual, the complainant would not be experiencing symptoms of trauma. Although not yet common, defendants sometimes seek to admit evidence regarding RTS to support their version of the facts.[5]

§ 6–1.2   Relevance of RTS in Consent Defense Cases

Rape trauma syndrome evidence and its variants have been offered for a variety of purposes in cases in which the defendant asserts that the alleged victim consented. There is striking agreement in what courts find RTS to be *prohibited* to prove, but some disagreement concerning what RTS might be *permitted* to prove.

Courts generally hold that RTS cannot be used to support or bolster the credibility of the alleged witness.[6] In *State v. Alberico*,[7] for example, although the court was otherwise sympathetic to the admission of PTSD, it objected to its use in support of a witness' credibility: "[PTSD] may not be offered to establish that the alleged victim is telling the truth; that is for the jury to decide."[8]

§ 6–1.2.1   Using RTS to Demonstrate That a "Rape" Occurred

Most courts stress in unequivocal terms that RTS cannot be used to prove that a rape occurred. Courts divide this restriction into two testimonial prohibitions. First, experts are usually prohibited from offering an opinion about the "ultimate issue" that a rape occurred.[9] Although the Federal Rules, and most state codes, permit such testimony, courts find it too intrusive on the jury function in RTS cases. The second, and related, prohibition precludes experts from commenting on the credibility of the alleged victim or the veracity of similarly situated people.[10] Such testimony, courts find, invades the province of the jury.

---

4. Individual courts sometimes strongly prefer one designation over the others. As discussed in more detail below, many courts find the term Rape Trauma Syndrome to be too prejudicial and prefer PTSD. *See infra* § 13–1.3.3. In *State v. Alberico*, 116 N.M. 156, 861 P.2d 192, 212 (N.M.1993), the court rejected RTS, "mainly because it is not part of the specialized manual DSM–III–R like PTSD is...."

5. Expert testimony on sexual abuse also is used in cases involving child victims. These cases are not reviewed here because the testimony is based on a different body of research and because cases involving child victims typically involve different legal issues. For example, consent is not a defense in cases involving child victims.

6. *See, e.g.*, State v. Taylor, 663 S.W.2d 235, 241 (Mo.1984) ("Clearly, the psychiatrist's

specific statement that the victim did not fantasize the rape was an express opinion about her credibility, and his entire testimony that the victim suffered from rape trauma syndrome carried with it an implied opinion that the victim had told the truth in describing the rape."); State v. Chul Yun Kim, 318 N.C. 614, 350 S.E.2d 347, 350–51 (N.C.1986) (Expert could not testify that the alleged victim has "never been untruthful with me about it.").

7. 116 N.M. 156, 861 P.2d 192 (N.M.1993).

8. *Id.* at 210.

9. *See* Commonwealth v. Federico, 425 Mass. 844, 683 N.E.2d 1035, 1040 (Mass.1997); People v. Seaman, 239 A.D.2d 681, 657 N.Y.S.2d 242, 244 (1997).

10. *See* United States v. Funds Held in the Name or For the Benefit of John Hugh Wetterer, 991 F.Supp. 112, 120 (E.D.N.Y.1998); Fed-

Yet, the line between the use of RTS to prove that a rape occurred and its use to disprove consent is not very bright. In *State v. McCoy*,[11] the court sought to allow RTS for the limited purpose of countering the defense claim of consent.[12] The court stated as follows:

> We ... must draw a distinction between an expert's testimony that an alleged victim exhibits post-rape behavior consistent with rape trauma syndrome and expert opinion that bolsters the credibility of the alleged victim by indicating that she was indeed raped.[13]

The distinction drawn by the *McCoy* court, however, is not obvious. Indeed, the closer it is examined the harder it is to see. In *State v. Alberico*,[14] the court inspected this distinction closely and found it to be ephemeral:

> Allowing an expert to testify that PTSD symptoms are a common reaction to sexual assault for the purpose of rebutting the defense that the victim's reactions to the alleged incident are inconsistent with sexual assault is no different from allowing the expert to testify that the alleged victim's symptoms are consistent with sexual abuse. Although ... some ... courts maintain a bright-line distinction between these two purposes ... , we see no logical difference. Both of these purposes for which PTSD evidence is offered rest on the valid scientific premise that victims of sexual abuse exhibit identifiable symptoms. Either PTSD diagnosis is a valid scientific technique for identifying certain symptoms of sexual abuse or it is not.[15]

The *Alberico* court directly addressed the logic of using RTS to prove nonconsent but not to prove that a rape occurred (i.e., in most cases, to prove nonconsent). However, the above quote encompasses two additional issues that may prove troubling. First, PTSD depends substantially on verbal reports from the alleged victim and is, in this sense, self-referential. Second, contrary to the *Alberico* court's characterization, PTSD does not presume to be a "scientific technique for identifying certain symptoms of *sexual abuse*."[16]

---

erico, 683 N.E.2d at 1039. *See also* State v. Kinney, 171 Vt. 239, 762 A.2d 833, 844 (Vt. 2000) (Court excluded expert testimony that 98% of rape complaints are true, because it "was tantamount to an expert opinion that the victim was telling the truth."); Commonwealth v. Balodis, 560 Pa. 567, 747 A.2d 341, 345 (Pa.2000) ("[E]xpert testimony as to the veracity of a particular class of people, of which the victim is a member, is inadmissible.").

11. 179 W.Va. 223, 366 S.E.2d 731 (W.Va. 1988).

12. *Id.* at 736–37 (" ... in a prosecution for rape where consent is the defense, qualified expert testimony regarding the existence of symptoms consistent with rape trauma syndrome is relevant and admissible").

13. *Id.* at 737. *See also* State v. Martens, 90 Ohio App.3d 338, 629 N.E.2d 462, 467 (Ohio Ct.App.1993) ("[E]xpert testimony on RTS was admissible to explain the victim's reactions after the incident, but not admissible to prove that a rape had occurred.") (citing People v.

Taylor, 75 N.Y.2d 277, 552 N.Y.S.2d 883, 552 N.E.2d 131 (N.Y.1990)).

14. 116 N.M. 156, 861 P.2d 192 (N.M. 1993).

15. *Id.* at 210. In *People v. Graham*, 251 A.D.2d 426, 674 N.Y.S.2d 120 (1998), RTS was offered for the more general purpose, but the court held that it had crossed the line into a statement commenting on the specific case:

> At trial, the People's case consisted primarily of the testimony of the complainant and of an expert who testified about "rape trauma syndrome." The testimony of the expert was admitted for the clearly improper purpose of showing that the symptoms exhibited by the complainant were consistent with patterns of response exhibited by proven rape victims and to demonstrate that she had been raped and sodomized.

Id. at 120.

16. *Alberico,* 861 P.2d at 210 (emphasis added).

Some courts have expressed concern with the self-referential aspects of PTSD. In particular, a necessary prerequisite to a finding of PTSD, by definition, is the experiencing of "an event that is outside the range of normal human experience that would be distressing to almost anyone."[17] That the alleged victim suffered such an experience, of course, is what the criminal prosecution is intended to determine. Hence, there is a circularity to reasoning from a diagnosis of PTSD, which accepts that the traumatic experience occurred if the individual says it did, to the judgment that the traumatic experience occurred.[18] This fact, however, does not render psychological testimony irrelevant; indeed, quite the contrary is true. The relevant consideration, as discussed in § 2.0 *infra*, concerns psychological responses that are testable and, through testing, have been shown to be consistent with rape complainants' behavior.

The diagnosis of PTSD is also problematic, some courts maintain, for it makes no pretense of distinguishing between traumatic events that are sexual and those that are not. Although rape is clearly so traumatic that it can lead to psychological injury, specific symptoms of such injury are not connected to sexual assaults through the diagnosis of PTSD. PTSD thus cannot distinguish between victims of rape and victims of other traumas. Although the nature of the trauma is manifest in the content of the intrusive recollection's characteristic of PTSD, the verity of the claimed trauma still depends on the testimonial statements of the alleged victim. This is, of course, the ultimate question before the trier of fact. Still, this insight does not compel the conclusion that evidence of generic psychological injury is irrelevant. Evidence that the alleged victim has symptoms consistent with severe trauma is *relevant* in a case in which the defendant claims consent.[19] "Tests" like DNA profiling or fingerprinting might be desirable (and possibly more probative), but each piece of the evidence puzzle does not need to prove the case; that is the task of the completed puzzle. A court that excludes psychological testimony because it cannot show that the trauma indicated is associated specifically with a rape should similarly exclude evidence that the perpetrator had blonde hair (a characteristic the defendant shares) because many people have blonde hair.[20] Evidence must only be probative to be admitted, it need not be dispositive.

§ 6–1.2.2 Using RTS to Inform the Fact Finder About Typical—or Not Atypical—Post–Rape Behavior

By far the most accepted use of RTS in rape prosecutions in which the defense is consent is to show that the alleged victim's behavior is consistent, or not inconsistent, with that of rape victims. Post-rape behavior is the focus of much of the courtroom use of RTS.[21] On the one hand, courts generally find

17. *See* § 2.2.1, *infra.*

18. *See* Hutton v. Maryland, 339 Md. 480, 663 A.2d 1289, 1300 (Md.1995).

19. *See* State v. Gettier, 438 N.W.2d 1, 6 (Iowa 1989) (" ... the evidence was relevant as tending to show that she had been traumatized").

20. The danger, however, following recognition of the limited power of the psychological testimony, is that defendants will scour the claimant's past for other traumas that might

explain the psychological condition. This would undermine the reforms instituted by rape shield statutes. *See infra* § 6–1.5.

21. It has also been used in the sentencing context to enhance a sentence for a crime that resulted in the " 'protracted impairment of ... [the victim's] mental facult[ies].' " United States v. Vazquez–Rivera, 135 F.3d 172, 178 (1st Cir.1998) (*quoting* 18 U.S.C.A. § 1365(g)(3)(D)).

that the witness's behavior after the alleged rape is relevant. Behavior consistent with having suffered a traumatic event has obvious probative value. Expert testimony regarding RTS is considered to have special relevance in explaining behavior that appears inconsistent with such an experience.[22] As the court in *Rynning* explained, experts are permitted to testify "about behavioral characteristics or behavioral patterns of an alleged sexual abuse victim, 'especially where that behavior would seem to be counterintuitive.' "[23] This is especially so if the defendant has raised the witness's behavior as indicative of having given consent.[24] In many cases, this testimony is offered to provide context so that jurors can appreciate the range of responses to such traumatic experiences.[25] However, a wide range of behaviors potentially fall within this category and courts have not always closely evaluated the empirical support for the evidence offered by experts who testify on these matters.

It must be noted, first, that virtually all courts, even those most critical of RTS, permit lay testimony concerning the alleged victim's behavior after the incident.[26] This indicates that, in fact, relevance is not the principal barrier to post-incident descriptions of the alleged victim that indicate a traumatic event. For example, in *State v. Black*,[27] the court specifically noted that lay testimony concerning the alleged victim's behavior, presumably consistent with a traumatic event, was admissible.[28]

Although many courts are reluctant to allow RTS to show that the alleged victim acted in a way characteristic of a rape victim, they generally accept the strong probative value of evidence that indicates that the alleged victim acted in a way not inconsistent with being a victim of rape.[29] The relevant distinction is between expert testimony that states that the complainant's behavior is consistent with suffering the trauma of rape and expert testimony that indicates that the complainant's behavior is not inconsistent with having suffered such trauma.[30] If followed generally and faithfully, this standard

---

22. *See* United States v. Rynning, 47 M.J. 420, 421 (C.M.A.1998).

23. *Id.* at 422 (*quoting* United States v. Pagel, 45 M.J. 64, 68 (1996)). *See also* Chapman v. State, 18 P.3d 1164, 1171 (Wyo.2001).

24. *See* Houser v. Lowe, 1996 WL 560232 *4 (D.Kan.1996); United States v. Halford, 50 M.J. 402, 404 (C.M.A.1999).

25. *See, e.g.,* United States v. Smith, 142 F.3d 438 (Table) (6th Cir.1998); People v. Thompson, 267 A.D.2d 602, 699 N.Y.S.2d 770, 772 (N.Y.App.Div.1999).

26. *See, e.g.,* Terrence v. Senkowski, 1999 WL 301690 *5 (S.D.N.Y. 1999); State v. Black, 109 Wash.2d 336, 745 P.2d 12, 19 (Wash.1987); People v. Bledsoe, 36 Cal.3d 236, 203 Cal.Rptr. 450, 681 P.2d 291, 301 (Cal.1984); *but see* State v. Alexander, 303 S.C. 377, 401 S.E.2d 146 (S.C.1991) (Because of the special circumstances presented in the instant case, the court excluded lay testimony concerning post-rape behavior as too prejudicial.).

27. 109 Wash.2d 336, 745 P.2d 12 (Wash. 1987).

28. *Id.* at 19.

29. State v. Moran, 151 Ariz. 378, 728 P.2d 248, 254 (Ariz.1986); State v. Huey, 145 Ariz. 59, 699 P.2d 1290, 1294 (Ariz.1985); People v. Bledsoe, 36 Cal.3d 236, 203 Cal.Rptr. 450, 681 P.2d 291, 298 (Cal.1984); People v. Fasy, 829 P.2d 1314, 1317 (Colo.1992); State v. Spigarolo, 210 Conn. 359, 556 A.2d 112, 123 (Conn.1989); State v. Batangan, 71 Haw. 552, 799 P.2d 48, 52 (Haw.1990); Commonwealth v. Mamay, 407 Mass. 412, 553 N.E.2d 945, 951 (Mass.1990); People v. Beckley, 434 Mich. 691, 456 N.W.2d 391, 405 (Mich.1990); State v. Cressey, 137 N.H. 402, 628 A.2d 696, 703 (N.H.1993); State v. J.Q., 130 N.J. 554, 617 A.2d 1196, 1201 (N.J.1993); State v. Alberico, 116 N.M. 156, 861 P.2d 192, 198 (N.M.1993); People v. Taylor, 75 N.Y.2d 277, 552 N.Y.S.2d 883, 552 N.E.2d 131 (N.Y.1990); Townsend v. State, 103 Nev. 113, 734 P.2d 705, 708 (Nev.1987); State v. Hall, 330 N.C. 808, 412 S.E.2d 883, 890 (N.C.1992); State v. Middleton, 294 Or. 427, 657 P.2d 1215, 1221 (Or.1983); State v. Kinney, 171 Vt. 239, 762 A.2d 833, 840–41 (Vt. 2000); State v. Jensen, 147 Wis.2d 240, 432 N.W.2d 913, 923 (Wis.1988).

30. *See, e.g.,* Commonwealth v. Trowbridge, 419 Mass. 750, 647 N.E.2d 413 (Mass.

would exclude virtually all clinical expert testimony that is consistent with having been raped, and admit only general research that describes the range of behaviors exhibited by women who have been raped—research illustrating the wide variation in responses to this crime.[31]

§ 6–1.3 Judicial Views Regarding Scientific Reliability/Validity and General Acceptance of RTS

Courts considering the scientific merit of RTS for courtroom use are divided, with some courts finding it valid[32] and others believing it to be invalid.[33] Although much of the case law concerning RTS predates *Daubert,* the specific standard of admission, general acceptance or scientific validity, does not appear to alter the conclusion.[34] In fact, few courts have seriously evaluated the underlying scientific foundation for expert testimony based on RTS research; instead, courts focus primarily on the courtroom use of the evidence.

A significant validity concern for some courts involves the clinical genesis of RTS. As the court in *State v. Saldana*[35] succinctly complained, "[r]ape trauma syndrome is not a fact-finding tool, but a therapeutic tool useful in counseling."[36] In *State v. Rimmasch,*[37] a case involving child sexual abuse, the court offered the following observation:

> It should not be surprising that those who undertake to treat persons who may have suffered sexual abuse have no peculiar competence to judge the credibility of their patients Working hypotheses relied upon by therapists may be useful for treatment purposes; however, that does not mean that they are reliable enough to be used for forensic purposes.[38]

However, that the genesis of RTS was "therapeutic" does not alone disqualify expert testimony based upon it. If current research has sufficiently built upon this clinical foundation in ways that fit its courtroom use, then expert testimony should be admitted.

§ 6–1.3.1 Qualifications

Courts permitting the use of RTS for one or another purpose have generally not questioned the professional qualifications of the proffered ex-

1995) ("Although expert testimony on the general behavioral characteristics of sexually abused children is permissible, an expert may not refer or compare the child to those general characteristics.").

31. *See* People v. McGuinness, 245 A.D.2d 701, 665 N.Y.S.2d 752, 754 (3d Dept.1997).

32. *See, e.g.,* State v. Marks, 231 Kan. 645, 647 P.2d 1292, 1299 (Kan.1982) ("An examination of the [scientific] literature clearly demonstrates that the so-called 'rape trauma syndrome' is generally accepted to be a common reaction to sexual assault."); State v. Liddell, 211 Mont. 180, 685 P.2d 918, 923 (Mont.1984) (finding RTS to be "reliable as evidence that a forcible assault did take place"); State v. Huey, 145 Ariz. 59, 699 P.2d 1290, 1294 (Ariz.1985) (finding that RTS is generally accepted).

33. *See, e.g.,* Spencer v. General Electric Co., 688 F.Supp. 1072, 1073 (E.D.Va.1988);

People v. Bledsoe, 36 Cal.3d 236, 203 Cal.Rptr. 450, 681 P.2d 291, 301 (Cal.1984) (not reliable to prove that a rape occurred), State v. Black, 537 A.2d 1154, 1156–57 (Me.1988); People v. Beckley, 434 Mich. 691, 456 N.W.2d 391, 404–08 (Mich.1990); State v. Saldana, 324 N.W.2d 227, 229 (Minn.1982) ("Rape trauma is not the type of scientific test that accurately and reliably determines whether a rape has occurred."); State v. Cressey, 137 N.H. 402, 628 A.2d 696, 699–702 (N.H.1993) (not reliable).

34. *See infra* § 1.4.3.

35. 324 N.W.2d 227 (Minn.1982).

36. *Id.* at 230.

37. 775 P.2d 388 (Utah 1989).

38. *Id.* at 407.

perts. Some courts permit experts with master's degrees and some clinical experience to testify.[39] Other courts demand greater expertise.[40] Qualification requirements depend on the content of the testimony. For example, in *State v. Willis*,[41] the Kansas Supreme Court held that an expert who proposes to testify on RTS or PTSD must be a psychiatrist.[42] The court distinguished an earlier Kansas case, *State v. Reser*,[43] in which the expert was not a psychiatrist, on the basis that in the latter the expert only testified to general research findings, not a diagnosis of RTS.[44] The Kansas court thus tied the level of qualifications required to the scope and depth of the proposed testimony.[45] Most courts, however, approach qualifications in a more lackadaisical manner.[46]

§ 6–1.3.2 Frye v. Daubert

The particular standard of admissibility used does not appear to determine whether the testimony is deemed admissible. Cases that have evaluated the testimony in terms of *Frye* have found the testimony both to be scientifically reliable[47] and scientifically unreliable.[48] Similarly, decisions that cite Rule 702 or similar state rules, and do not rely on *Frye*, have ruled both in favor of[49] and against the reliability of the testimony.[50]

Thus, the determining issue does not appear to be which standard is used. Rather, the key issue concerns the purpose of the testimony. Specifically, in every case in which the testimony has been found to be scientifically unreliable, it is because the court has ruled that the testimony cannot reliably determine, or *prove*, that a rape occurred.[51] For example, as stated in the *Saldana* decision, upon which many other decisions rely, "[r]ape trauma symdrome [sic] is not the type of scientific test that accurately and reliably

39. *See, e.g.*, State v. McCoy, 179 W.Va. 223, 366 S.E.2d 731, 733 (W.Va.1988) (expert had master's degree in community agency counseling and extensive clinical experience with victims of sexual abuse and sexual assault).

40. In a case from the Court of Appeals for the Armed Forces, the court excluded the defendant's expert on RTS because his 40 years of experience as a police officer did not qualify him as an expert. United States v. Cauley, 45 M.J. 353, 357 (C.M.A.1996). The court also added that the defendant's expert's proposed testimony "would amount to a comment on the credibility of the government's witness." *Id.*

41. 256 Kan. 837, 888 P.2d 839 (Kan.1995).

42. *Id.* at 844.

43. 244 Kan. 306, 767 P.2d 1277 (Kan. 1989).

44. *Willis*, 888 P.2d at 844; *see Reser*, 767 P.2d at 1279.

45. The DSM–IV and its earlier versions do not have a qualifications standard and is used by a wide variety of mental health professionals.

46. *See* State v. Henry, 329 S.C. 266, 495 S.E.2d 463, 468–69 (S.C.App.1997); *see also* People v. Abrams, 232 A.D.2d 240, 649

N.Y.S.2d 5, 6 (1st Dept.1996) (qualifying emergency room physician to testify about "common reactions" to rape).

47. *See, e.g.*, People v. Taylor, 75 N.Y.2d 277, 552 N.Y.S.2d 883, 552 N.E.2d 131 (N.Y. 1990); State v. Marks, 231 Kan. 645, 647 P.2d 1292 (Kan.1982); State v. Martens, 90 Ohio App.3d 338, 629 N.E.2d 462 (Ohio App.1993); State v. Taylor, 663 S.W.2d 235 (Mo.1984).

48. *See, e.g.*, People v. Bledsoe, 36 Cal.3d 236, 203 Cal.Rptr. 450, 681 P.2d 291 (Cal. 1984); State v. Black, 109 Wash.2d 336, 745 P.2d 12 (Wash.1987).

49. *See, e.g.*, State v. Alberico, 116 N.M. 156, 861 P.2d 192 (N.M.1993); *see also* State v. Kinney, 171 Vt. 239, 762 A.2d 833, 842 (Vt. 2000).

50. *See, e.g.*, State v. Saldana, 324 N.W.2d 227 (Minn.1982).

51. Commonwealth v. Zamarripa, 379 Pa.Super. 208, 549 A.2d 980 (Pa.Super.1988); People v. Bledsoe, 36 Cal.3d 236, 203 Cal.Rptr. 450, 681 P.2d 291 (Cal.1984); State v. Black, 109 Wash.2d 336, 745 P.2d 12 (Wash.1987); State v. Saldana, 324 N.W.2d 227 (Minn.1982); Spencer v. GE, 688 F.Supp. 1072 (E.D.Va. 1988).

determines whether a rape has occurred."[52] In contrast, courts that have found the testimony reliable focus on whether RTS is a generally accepted response to a sexual assault. For example, in *State v. Marks*,[53] another early decision, the Kansas Supreme Court stated, "An examination of the literature demonstrates that the so-called 'rape trauma syndrome' is generally accepted to be a common reaction to sexual assault."[54] This and other decisions note that flaws in the testimony should go to its weight rather than its admissibility.[55] Some of these flaws include the findings that not all victims respond in the same way and that many symptoms of RTS (e.g., depression) are not unique to rape.[56]

Very few cases have considered the admissibility of RTS under *Daubert's* validity test and none have done so in a rigorous or serious manner. In *State v. Alberico*, the New Mexico Supreme Court ostensibly relied on a *Daubert*-styled analysis.[57] The *Alberico* court specifically rejected the use of the *Frye* test arguing that the focus should be on the validity of the scientific method rather than on general acceptance. The court began by explicitly rejecting the argument that PTSD evidence must "prove" that a rape occurred in order to be reliable.[58] Relying on *Daubert*, the court noted that there is no requirement that a scientific technique prove an issue conclusively. Rather, the question is whether the evidence is probative, in this case, of whether a rape occurred. The court concluded that testimony on Posttraumatic Stress Disorder (PTSD) is "grounded in valid scientific principles ... [and that] PTSD is generally accepted by psychologists and psychiatrists as a valid technique for evaluating patients with mental disorders."[59]

Despite its stated reliance on *Daubert*, the *Alberico* court did not seriously evaluate the validity of the research supporting PTSD and did not cite any peer reviewed and published studies. Instead, the court relied on PTSD's presence in the DSMIII–R,[60] court citations,[61] and a single law review article[62] to support its decision. In effect, although the court rejected *Frye*, it applied a diluted general acceptance test to the science. *Daubert* requires more.[63]

52. *Saldana*, 324 N.W.2d at 229.

53. 231 Kan. 645, 647 P.2d 1292 (Kan. 1982).

54. *Id.* at 1299.

55. State v. Hampton, 746 P.2d 947 (Colo. 1987).

56. *See generally* Patricia A. Frazier & Eugene Borgida, *Rape Trauma Syndrome: A Review of Case Law and Psychological Research,* 16 LAW & HUM. BEHAV. 293 (1992).

57. 116 N.M. 156, 861 P.2d 192 (N.M. 1993). *See also* State v. Martens, 90 Ohio App.3d 338, 629 N.E.2d 462 (Ohio Ct.App. 1993).

58. *Alberico*, 861 P.2d at 208. *Cf.* State v. Black, 109 Wash.2d 336, 745 P.2d 12 (Wash. 1987).

59. *Alberico*, 861 P.2d at 208.

60. *Id.* at 209.

61. *Id.* at 208.

62. *Id.* at 209 (citing David McCord, *The Admissibility of Expert Testimony Regarding Rape Trauma Syndrome in Rape Prosecution,* 26 B.C. L. REV. 1143, 1187 (1985)). Although Professor McCord's article is a fine piece of work, it is not a literature review of the science in this area. In *State v. Kinney*, 171 Vt. 239, 762 A.2d 833, 842–43 (Vt.2000), the court applied a very similar analysis, noting the applicability of *Daubert* and then immediately ignoring it.

63. Another decision, *Isely v. Capuchin Province*, 877 F.Supp. 1055 (E.D.Mich.1995), applied *Daubert* to PTSD; unfortunately, the court misunderstood the most basic aspects of that ruling. In *Isely*, the plaintiff brought suit to recover damages for alleged sexual abuse that occurred at a seminary. The defendants filed a motion *in limine* to exclude or limit expert testimony on PTSD and repressed memory. The court observed that "[i]t is not within the province of this Court to decide the ultimate issues of this case." *Id.* at 1066. Instead, the court stated, "under *Daubert* the Court perceives its role with respect to the admissibility of expert testimony as being a 'screener'

§ 6–1.3.3 Courts' Understanding of the Research

As the above discussion suggests, evaluation of the scientific reliability of RTS evidence typically focuses on the purpose of the testimony rather than on the quality of the science. Since the focus of *Daubert* is on the quality of the science, it is important to examine how well-informed courts are about the scientific status of RTS evidence. A review of the case law suggests that courts do not critically assess proffered expert testimony on RTS.[64] One clear indication that courts and some experts may not be well-informed about the scientific data base on RTS is that the expert testimony admitted in court often is not supported by research data. Although appellate decisions do not contain an entire transcript of the testimony, errors in the testimony that is described are noteworthy. For example, expert testimony in *People v. Bledsoe*[65] described RTS as the "umbrella terminology for what a rape victim experiences and it basically describes parameters that ... 99.9 percent of rape victims are going to fall within."[66] This statement does not accurately describe the research literature, and creates unrealistic expectations about what the evidence can show. Other cases describe RTS in terms of *stages* of symptoms,[67] although these stages have not been well-documented in the literature. Other testimony is supported by the research literature but the description of the behavior as part of "RTS" is questionable. An example of this is delays in reporting.[68]

There is general agreement, based on sound scientific data, regarding several aspects of rape trauma that can form the basis of expert testimony. This testimony can describe the symptoms of PTSD and various other symptoms (e.g., depression, fear, anxiety) that are common among rape victims. Unfortunately, however, expert testimony at times does not accurately reflect the scientific literature. Several examples were previously presented, including describing rape trauma in terms of stages, describing symptoms that have not been documented in research, and inappropriately generalizing research on adults to children. It is incumbent upon experts to be familiar with the existing research and only to describe victim behaviors that have been reliably established in the literature. If testimony is not research-based, then it is very important that the basis of the testimony be stated clearly.

of expert testimony, similar to its role under Fed.R.Evid. 104(b) of screening conditionally relevant evidence." *Id.* This perception, however, is incorrect. The *Daubert* Court expressly stated that the gatekeeping function requires trial courts to use Rule 104(a). *Daubert,* 113 S.Ct. at 2796 n.10. The *Isely* court, therefore, used the wrong legal standard in deciding that the expert testimony on PTSD and repressed memory was admissible.

64. Although conducted before *Daubert,* a 1992 study by Frazier and Borgida found that courts are not scientifically well informed on RTS. *Supra* note 57. For example, although the decisions reviewed were published between 1985 and 1990, the most recent research article cited was published in 1983. A 1974 study by Burgess and Holmstrom, in which the term "rape trauma syndrome" was coined, was by far the most frequently cited. The diagnostic

manuals of the American Psychiatric Association—DSM–III (APA, 1980) and DSM–III–R (APA, 1987)—also were cited frequently.

65. 36 Cal.3d 236, 203 Cal.Rptr. 450, 681 P.2d 291 (Cal.1984).

66. *Id.* at 294.

67. *See, e.g.,* People v. Davis, 223 Ill.App.3d 580, 165 Ill.Dec. 818, 585 N.E.2d 214 (Ill.App. 1992); People v. Douglas, 183 Ill.App.3d 241, 131 Ill.Dec. 779, 538 N.E.2d 1335 (Ill.App. 1989); State v. Martens, 90 Ohio App.3d 338, 629 N.E.2d 462 (Ohio Ct.App.1993).

68. *See, e.g.,* Commonwealth v. Mamay, 407 Mass. 412, 553 N.E.2d 945 (Mass.1990); People v. Maymi, 198 A.D.2d 153, 603 N.Y.S.2d 862 (1993); People v. Story, 176 A.D.2d 1080, 575 N.Y.S.2d 589 (1991); State v. Martens, 90 Ohio App.3d 338, 629 N.E.2d 462 (Ohio Ct. App.1993).

Another way in which expert testimony does not accurately describe the research literature concerns the terminology used to describe the after-effects of rape. As mentioned, use of the term "rape trauma syndrome" in legal decision-making has been confusing because it has no clear referent. It has been used to refer to the stage model of recovery described by Burgess and Holmstrom,[69] general post-rape symptoms, and rape-related PTSD, none of which are synonymous with each other. Although the term "PTSD" generally is preferred in legal decisions, this term has both advantages and disadvantages. One advantage is that it is viewed as less prejudicial because it does not equate symptoms exclusively with rape.[70] Another advantage is that PTSD is an officially recognized disorder with clearly defined features. For these reasons, it may be prudent for experts to testify only regarding the criteria for PTSD, and whether a particular victim meets those criteria. On the other hand, limiting testimony to the symptoms of PTSD excludes research on other symptoms common among rape victims (e.g., depression) that are not necessarily part of the diagnostic criteria for PTSD. This research can also be very useful to a jury. However, research on these symptoms can be discussed without using the term "rape trauma syndrome," which implies that there is a particular *pattern* of symptoms that occurs in most victims.

In regard to terminology, it also is important to note that neither RTS nor PTSD are accurately described as "tests" or "techniques," which are terms that sometimes arise in legal decisions. For example, the court in *State v. Saldana* argued that "Rape trauma symdrome (sic) is not the type of scientific *test* that accurately and reliably determines whether a rape has occurred."[71] In *State v. Alberico*,[72] the court ruled that "PTSD is generally accepted by psychologists and psychiatrists as a valid *technique* for evaluating patients with mental disorders." RTS is a general term for the after-effects of rape whereas PTSD is a diagnostic category. To refer to them as tests or techniques is both inaccurate and misleading.

§ 6-1.4 The Potential for Unfair Prejudice of RTS

A common objection to RTS is that the evidence is unduly prejudicial because it invades the province of the jury by improperly bolstering the credibility of the complainant. Courts that admit RTS counter this concern with the argument that the expert evidence is necessary to educate jurors. Although there is little empirical evidence to support the observation, many courts believe jurors hold stereotyped and incorrect views of a person's reactions to a sexual assault. Courts insist, however, that the jury is the ultimate judge of the alleged victim's credibility. The dynamic between the potential for prejudice due to the jury's relative ignorance and the probative power attributable to that same lack of knowledge is difficult to resolve.

§ 6-1.5 Defense Use of RTS

In light of the extent to which prosecutors have used expert testimony on RTS to increase conviction rates, it is not surprising that defendants have

---

69. Burgess & Holmstrom, *supra* note 1.

70. *See, e.g.*, State v. Martens, 90 Ohio App.3d 338, 629 N.E.2d 462 (Ohio Ct.App. 1993).

71. State v. Saldana, 324 N.W.2d 227, 229 (Minn.1982) (emphasis added).

72. State v. Alberico, 116 N.M. 156, 861 P.2d 192, 208 (N.M.1993).

begun to see the utility in this form of expert testimony.[73] In theory, the probative value of RTS is potentially available to any party, depending on the facts of the case. The relevance of prosecution use depends on the alleged victim exhibiting symptoms that rape victims exhibit with greater frequency than others. The relevance associated with defense use depends on the alleged rape victim failing to exhibit symptoms that rape victims typically exhibit. Although theoretically RTS is available to prosecutors and defendants alike, the rules of evidence do not apply similarly to both.

Ironically, prosecutors employ RTS to overcome a structural preference for defendants that exists in virtually all evidence codes. Thus, under general principles of evidence law, defense use of RTS might not only be expected, but it might be considered more likely than use by prosecutors. Nonetheless, as the above discussion indicates, prosecutors have overcome structural objections to expert testimony on RTS on the basis of a combination of a perceived need for the evidence and a belief in the validity of the substance of that testimony.

Under general evidence principles alone, prosecution use of RTS would almost certainly mandate allowance of defense use of the evidence. In fact, in *Henson v. State*,[74] the Indiana Supreme Court held that the defense could introduce expert testimony that the complainant had acted inconsistently with having been raped largely on this basis: "It would be fundamentally unfair to allow the use of such testimony by the State ... and then deny its use by a defendant here."[75]

However, the legal framework is somewhat more complicated than any simple *quid pro quo* approach would suggest. Most evidence codes today provide special protection for alleged victims of sexual assault in what are commonly called "rape shield statutes." These provisions, enacted to remedy the historical abuses surrounding the examination of complainants, severely restrict defense inquiries into the personal histories of alleged victims. To the extent that defense use of RTS raises the possibility that the alleged victim's personal history will be put in issue, contrary to a rape shield statute, some control over defense use should be exerted.[76] Otherwise, unrestricted defense use of RTS could lead to the evisceration of the safeguards enacted in rape shield statutes.[77]

---

73. *See generally*, Susan Stefan, *The Protection Racket: Rape Trauma Syndrome, Psychiatric Labeling, and Law*, 88 Nw. U. L. Rev. 1222, 1324–25 (1994); Jennifer J. Hackman, Comment, Henson v. State: *Rape Trauma Syndrome Used by the Defendant as Well as the Victim*, 19 Am. J. Trial Advoc. 453 (1995).

74. 535 N.E.2d 1189 (Ind.1989).

75. *Id.* at 1193. *But see* State v. Jones, 83 Ohio App.3d 723, 615 N.E.2d 713 (Ohio Ct. App.1992).

76. Defense use of RTS inevitably implicates the core principle of rape shield statutes: such rules restrict defense examination of the complainant's past sexual history. For example, an alleged victim's prior traumatic experiences, sexual or otherwise, are pertinent to whether the symptoms exhibited are attribut-

able to the act for which the defendant is on trial. In addition, an alleged victim's medical records might be discoverable so that the defense expert can conduct an adequate assessment. *See* Hackman, *supra* note 73, at 464.

77. In *State v. Allewalt*, 308 Md. 89, 517 A.2d 741 (Md.Ct.App.1986), the Maryland Court of Appeals offered the following observations:

When a trial judge admits PTSD evidence because he believes that the existence of the disorder coupled with the absence of any triggering trauma, other than the evidence of rape, will aid the jury, the ruling necessarily carries certain baggage with it. Cross-examination can include not only cross-examining the expert about PTSD in general, but also cross-examining the expert and the

How courts strike the balance regarding defense use of RTS depends on both the values embodied in evidence codes and the Constitution,[78] together with the validity of the science associated with testimony on RTS. Unrestricted prosecutorial use of this evidence, while, at the same time, complete foreclosure of defense use, would violate basic precepts of fairness.[79] This is particularly true given the criminal justice system's commitment to guaranteeing defendants due process. At the same time, most jurisdictions are committed to protecting alleged victims from the kinds of abuse that were commonplace prior to enactment of protective legislation. These considerations might lead courts to strike a balance whereby defense use of RTS is limited to rebuttal of prosecution use of this evidence. In particular cases, therefore, if the state opens the door to the "psychological state" of the alleged victim, the defense would be permitted to rigorously test and rebut this claim.

In *Clark v. Commonwealth*,[80] the defendant appealed from a statutory rape conviction, arguing that the trial court had erred in not permitting an independent medical examination of the complaining witness. The trial court had found that it did not have the authority to order a medical examination, "and that to do so would place a tremendous chill on reporting and prosecution of such criminal activity."[81] After conducting a useful review of the practice in other jurisdictions, since this was a case of first impression in Virginia, the court concluded "that a trial court had discretion to require a complaining witness to submit to an independent physical examination, provided the defendant makes a threshold showing of a compelling need or reason."[82] In making this determination, the trial court should consider, among other things, the following factors:

> "(1) the nature of the examination requested and the intrusiveness inherent in that examination; (2) the victim's age; (3) the resulting physical and/or emotional effects of the examination on the victim; (4) the probative value of the examination to the issue before the court; (5) the remoteness in time of the examination to the alleged criminal act; and (6) the evidence already available for the defendant's use."[83]

Finally, it is worth noting that there is no reason to believe that good science will systematically benefit particular causes. Defense use of RTS is a

---

prosecutrix about possible causes of the disorder other than the assault charged in the criminal case. In addition, we can foresee cases where the defendant will seek to counter the State's PTSD evidence with his own expert testimony. That can, in turn, lead to issues concerning compulsory psychiatric examination of the complainant by an expert for the defense. Lurking in the background is the nice question of whether the absence of PTSD is provable by the accused in defense of a rape charge, as tending to prove that there was consent.
Id. at 751 (*quoted in* Chapman v. State, 18 P.3d 1164, 1173–74 (Wyo.2001)).

78. *See* U.S. Const. amend VI.

79. *See Henson*, 535 N.E.2d at 1194 ("[T]o bar the defendant from presenting such evidence exceeds the discretion of the trial court;

and, in this case, the trial court's ruling impinged upon the substantial rights of appellant to present a defense and was reversible error.").

80. 31 Va.App. 96, 521 S.E.2d 313 (Va.Ct. App.1999).

81. *Id.* at 314.

82. *Id.* at 319. Judge Benton, concurring in the holding, strongly disagreed with the requirement that the defendant show "a compelling need or reason." He argued the defendant should only have to show "materiality." *Id.* at 320 (Benton, J., concurring).

83. *Id.* at 320 (quoting State v. Delaney, 187 W.Va. 212, 417 S.E.2d 903, 907 (W.Va. 1992) (en banc)).

particularly good example of this point. Specifically, a psychological concept with origins in the desire to aid victims of sexual abuse may now be employed to subject those victims to compelled psychological examinations,[84] and searching cross-examination regarding past sexual history. This would be an unfortunate result of a well-intentioned policy. Perhaps the best lesson that can be drawn from defense use of RTS is that courts should assume greater responsibility in scrutinizing the research, whoever the proponent might be. This, of course, is a basic lesson of *Daubert*.

§ 6–1.6 Conclusion

Rape Trauma Syndrome has proved to be an enormously controversial form of expert testimony. It is likely to continue to be controversial in the future. The first difficulty is the term itself, since it is used to describe a wide range of hypotheses, some of which are not consistent with one another. Precision has not been the forte of courts and experts in this context. Secondly, courts attempt to draw a distinction between prohibiting RTS to prove that a rape occurred and allowing it to prove that the alleged victim did not consent. Since a principal aspect of defining rape as rape is lack of consent, this line is very blurry indeed. However, courts are mostly in agreement that expert testimony can be offered to show that the alleged victim's behavior is not inconsistent with being raped, especially including a diagnosis of PTSD. But this agreement leads to several additional complications. PTSD itself depends on the existence of a traumatic stressor, such as rape, which usually is the very issue before the court. The PTSD diagnosis also creates opportunity for possible abuse, since defendants might seek to put complainants on trial by exploring other stressors that could have caused the PTSD. This result, which might be compelled by the prosecution's opening the door to the issue of the complainant's psychological health, could undermine the protections of legislative reforms such as rape shield statutes.

Finally, courts have displayed a disappointing lack of curiosity regarding the scientific bases for RTS. Even courts applying *Daubert's* validity test, though ostensibly obligated to evaluate the basis for proffered expert testimony, have failed to closely scrutinize the evidence. Courts' focus has been on the legal uses to which the evidence is put—its relevance—and they have so far completely failed to consider its reliability. This is unfortunate, especially if, as can be expected, defendants begin using this theory to put complainants' psychological health on trial. As the next section discusses, there is much that psychologists know—and much that they still do not know—about the aftereffects of rape. The courts should begin paying attention to this research, for much of what passes as expert testimony today is not supported in the research literature. Their responsibility as gatekeepers, and their duty to do justice, require courts to critically assess the bases for expert testimony on RTS.

---

84. *See, e.g.,* People v. Wheeler, 151 Ill.2d 298, 176 Ill.Dec. 880, 602 N.E.2d 826, 833 (Ill.1992) ("[U]nless the victim consents to an examination by an expert chosen by the defendant, the State may not introduce testimony from an examining expert that the victim of an alleged sexual assault suffers from a 'recognized and accepted form of post-traumatic stress syndrome.' ").

B. SCIENTIFIC STATUS

by
Patricia A. Frazier*

§ 6–2.0 THE SCIENTIFIC STATUS OF RESEARCH ON RAPE TRAUMA SYNDROME

§ 6–2.1 Introduction

Prior to evaluating the scientific research on the effects of rape, it is important to discuss similarities and differences between the questions asked by scientists and the questions asked in legal decision-making, as well as to discuss some of the methodological issues that arise in doing research on rape trauma.

§ 6–2.1.1 Scientific vs. Legal Questions

Scientific research has addressed many questions concerning rape, including the prevalence of rape, attitudes and beliefs about rape, the characteristics of rapists, the effects of rape on victims, factors that predict higher levels of post-rape distress, rape prevention, and treatment of rape trauma. The scientific research most relevant to legal decision-making on the admissibility of Rape Trauma Syndrome (RTS) evidence concerns the effects of rape on victims. As discussed in the following sections, this research assesses the prevalence of various symptoms among victims, often comparing symptom levels among victims to those among non-victim comparison groups. Thus, the key scientific questions are: "What symptoms do victims experience?" and "Do rape victims differ from non-victims in terms of symptomatology?"

In legal proceedings, experts typically are called to testify about a particular complainant's behavior and the common after-effects of rape in order to support the prosecution's theory of nonconsent. The relevant legal question is framed either in terms of (a) whether specific behaviors are consistent with having been raped or (b) whether specific behaviors *prove* that a rape occurred. When the question is framed in terms of "consistency," the questions asked by scientists and in legal proceedings are quite similar. However, there is less convergence when the legal question is framed in terms of whether the evidence can "prove" that a rape occurred. Scientific research identifies victims through various methods and assesses symptomatology among them; it does not seek to establish that research participants were in fact raped. It should be stressed, however, that this latter standard for assessing reliability has been strongly criticized.[1]

Although the "consistency" standard is more widely accepted, it should be mentioned that there is a difference between effects being described as

---

* Professor Patricia Frazier received her Ph.D. in Social Psychology and Counseling Psychology in 1988 from the University of Minnesota. She currently is an Associate Professor in the Counseling Psychology and Social Psychology programs at the University of Minnesota. Dr. Frazier is past Associate Editor of LAW AND HUMAN BEHAVIOR and past chair of the Courtwatch Committee of the Society for the Psychological Study of Social Issues. Her research interests include sexual victimization and the interface between psychology and the law, particularly the use of expert testimony in rape trials.

§ 6–2.0

1. State v. Alberico, 116 N.M. 156, 861 P.2d 192 (N.M.1993).

common among rape victims and effects being described as *consistent* with having been raped. Effects that are common are those that occur in a majority of victims. Effects that are consistent with having been raped are those that are *possible* consequences of rape. Evidence that a symptom is consistent with having been raped implies merely that the probability of this symptom occurring among rape victims is greater than zero. Whether this is relevant depends on the probability of the symptom occurring in nonvictims. Lyon and Koehler argue that symptoms that are *more* common among victims than nonvictims are relevant to whether a rape occurred.[2] Thus, even common symptoms are not necessarily relevant if they are equally common in nonvictims. On the other hand, evidence that a particular symptom is consistent with having been raped is relevant if the defense has argued that it is inconsistent with rape. In addition, a symptom that is uncommon in victims can be relevant if it is even less common in nonvictims. Finally, evidence that a very common symptom is not present also can be relevant. Courts have been divided regarding the admissibility of evidence of lack of symptoms, with some arguing that evidence of the lack of symptoms is relevant[3] and some arguing that it is not relevant. Although scientific studies generally focus on the presence rather than the absence of symptoms, scientific research on the frequency of symptoms provides data on both the presence and absence of symptoms. In summary, to the extent that expert testimony on RTS focuses on the frequency of various post-rape symptoms, the scientific and legal questions converge, with the relevance of the evidence depending on the frequency of symptoms in victims in comparison to nonvictims.

§ 6–2.1.2 Methodological Issues

Prior to reviewing the research on the effects of rape, it is important to acknowledge some of the difficulties of doing research in this area. One such difficulty concerns recruiting victims to participate in the research. Several different methods have been used and each has its strengths and limitations. One method is to recruit participants from clients seen at rape crisis centers. Investigators that recruit victims through rape crisis centers are able to assess immediate reactions and assess symptoms longitudinally over time. However, because many women do not seek help at such centers, those that do may not be representative of most victims.[4] To further compound the problem, of the minority that do report, often a small percentage participate in the research.[5] Another recruitment method is to advertise for research participants who have been sexually assaulted. Sample representativeness also is a concern in studies that rely on this method because research volunteers may differ in various ways from other victims. A third method is to identify rape victims through screening questions in surveys of larger samples. The validity of studies that identify victims in this manner depends in large part on the screening questions used to assess sexual assault. Because many women do

---

2. Thomas Lyon & Jonathan Koehler, *The Relevance Ratio: Evaluating the Probative Value of Expert Testimony in Child Sexual Abuse Cases*, 82 CORNELL L. REV. 43 (1996).

3. *See, e.g.*, Henson v. Indiana, 535 N.E.2d 1189 (Ind.1989); State v. Jones, 83 Ohio App.3d 723, 615 N.E.2d 713 (Ohio Ct.App. 1992). *See generally* § 1.0, *infra*.

4. Women who seek help at rape crisis centers may, however, be representative of victims whose cases go to trial because both groups have sought help.

5. *See, e.g.*, B. M. Atkeson et al., *Victims of Rape: Repeated Assessment of Depressive Symptoms*, 50 J. CONSULTING & CLINICAL PSYCHOL. 96 (1982).

not define experiences as "rape," even if they meet the legal definition, many victims will be undetected if that terminology is used.[6] Questions that describe rape in behavioral terms are much more likely to identify victimization experiences.

Another difficulty of doing research in this area is obtaining assessments of functioning prior to the victimization that are not retrospective. Information on pre-rape functioning is important to show that post-rape symptoms were not present prior to the rape. One way to get this information is to administer measures of symptoms and victimization experiences at several points in time among samples of women who are known to be at risk of being assaulted. Comparisons can then be made between victims and non-victims and between pre-rape and post-rape functioning among victims. Although this obviously is difficult to carry out, at least one such study has been done using a sample of female undergraduate students.[7] Similar community-based studies of prevalence, risk factors, and pre-and post-rape symptoms also would be very useful.

Other limitations are not inherent in doing research on sexual assault but nonetheless sometimes are present. For example, some studies use unstandardized measures of symptomatology with unknown reliability and validity, even though standardized measures are widely available. In addition, information on symptoms and functioning is obtained almost exclusively through the self-report of the victim on questionnaires or in interviews rather than through more objective methods.[8] Another problem is that investigators, particularly those who have recruited victims through rape crisis centers, often do not include the definition of sexual assault used in their studies. Alternatively, studies that identify victims through screening questions often use very broad definitions of sexual assault (e.g., from unwanted kissing to forced intercourse). Although this is not necessarily a problem, it complicates the comparison of findings across studies. Studies that recruit victims through advertisements or surveys do not always specify the time since the rape occurred, which also makes comparisons across studies difficult. Finally, because many victims do not want to participate in research, samples often are small, which reduces the power of statistical analyses.

§ 6-2.2 Review of the Scientific Research on Rape Trauma

The purpose of this section is to review the scientific research on the after-effects of rape. Relevant research was identified through searches of psychological and medical databases of articles published through December 2000. Additional articles were identified through the reference lists of those articles. Only articles published in peer-reviewed journals were reviewed;

6. Mary P. Koss, *The Underdetection of Rape: Methodological Choices Influence Incidence Estimates*, 48 J. Soc. Issues 61 (1992).

7. Christine A. Gidycz et al., *Sexual Assault Experience in Adulthood and Prior Victimization Experiences: A Prospective Analysis*, 17 Psychol. of Women Q. 151 (1993).

8. The following articles are exceptions: M. Jenkins et al., *Attentional Dysfunction Associated with PTSD Among Rape Survivors*, 14

The Clinical Neuropsychologist 7 (2000); M. Jenkins et al., *Learning and Memory in Rape Victims with Posttraumatic Stress Disorder*, 155 Am. J. Psychiatry 278 (1998); M. G. Griffin et al., *Objective Assessment of Peritraumatic Dissociation: Psychophysiological Indicators*, 154 Am. J. Psychiatry 1081 (1997); Morgan & Grillon, *Abnormal Mismatch Negativity in Women with Sexual Assault–Related PTSD*, 45 Biological Psychiatry 827 (1999).

unpublished papers, conference presentations, and book chapters were excluded. Even if peer-reviewed, studies were excluded if they were conducted outside of the United States, if they included only male victims, if they were treatment studies that reported only post-treatment symptoms, if they focused exclusively on the effects of childhood sexual victimization, or if they combined victims of sexual assault with victims of other traumas (e.g., physical assault).

Research on the prevalence of Post–Traumatic Stress Disorder (PTSD) among rape victims is described first because some courts explicitly prohibit the use of the term RTS in favor of PTSD because the latter is viewed as less prejudicial.[9] Research on the prevalence of various other symptoms among women who have been raped are then reviewed, including depression, fear, anxiety, social adjustment problems, health problems, and substance abuse. Results obtained using standardized symptom measures are emphasized.[10] Studies are organized in terms of whether they employed a comparison group of non-victims, given Lyon and Koehler's argument that symptoms are relevant to the extent that they are more common among victims than non-victims.[11] Studies that assess short-term (within one year post-rape) symptoms are distinguished from those that assess long-term (more than one year post-rape) symptoms. Because most cases go to trial within one year of the assault, research on short-term symptoms may be more relevant. This review is followed by a discussion of areas of agreement and disagreement across studies and future research directions.

§ 6–2.2.1   Posttraumatic Stress Disorder

The essential feature of PTSD is the development of characteristic symptoms following a psychologically distressing event. Although the criteria differ somewhat in the various editions of the diagnostic manual of the American Psychiatric Association[12] the basic elements of the PTSD diagnosis are (a) experiencing a traumatic event, (b) reexperiencing the trauma (e.g., intrusive recollections, nightmares), (c) avoidance and numbing (e.g., avoiding thoughts or feelings about the trauma, feelings of detachment from others), and (d) increased arousal (e.g., difficulty concentrating, hypervigilance, exaggerated startle response).

[1]   Studies Using Comparison Groups

Short-term symptoms. No studies were located that compared recent victims to non-victims in terms of the prevalence of a diagnosis of PTSD or symptoms of PTSD.

9. *See, e.g.,* State v. Martens, 90 Ohio App.3d 338, 629 N.E.2d 462 (Ohio Ct.App. 1993).

10. For example, I have not included a series of studies by Ruch and her colleagues that assess trauma through a 1–item stress scale completed by a crisis worker. *See, e.g.,* Libby O. Ruch & Susan M. Chandler, *The Crisis Impact of Sexual Assault on Three Victim Groups: Adult Rape Victims, Child Rape Victims, and Incest Victims,* 5 J. Soc. Service Res. 83 (1982); Libby O. Ruch et al., *Life Change and Rape Impact,* 21 J. Health & Soc. Behav. 248 (1980).

11. Lyon & Koehler, *supra* note 2.

12. American Psychiatric Association, Diagnostic and Statistical Manual of Mental Disorders (3d ed. 1980); American Psychiatric Association, Diagnostic and Statistical Manual of Mental Disorders (3d ed. revised 1987); American Psychiatric Association, Diagnostic and Statistical Manual of Mental Disorders (4th ed. 1994).

Long-term symptoms. Approximately ten studies have assessed the prevalence of PTSD diagnoses among non-recent victims of sexual assault in comparison to victims of other traumas.[13] The current and lifetime PTSD prevalence rates for victims of sexual assault differ widely across these studies as a function of the nature of the sample and the way in which sexual assault is defined. Three studies assessed PTSD among large representative samples of women and used behaviorally-specific questions to assess completed rape (i.e., experiences involving nonconsent, force or threat of force, and penetration).[14] Across these three studies the lifetime prevalence of PTSD ranged from 32% to 57% and the current PTSD prevalence rates ranged from 12% to 17% for victims of rape. Two additional studies used behaviorally specific questions, but did not use representative samples. Specifically, Cloitre et al.[15] reported a higher current PTSD prevalence rate (70%) among a sample of rape victims offered free treatment in exchange for participation in the study whereas Layman et al.[16] reported a much lower current PTSD prevalence rate (3%) among a sample of college women who had been raped. Three of the above studies reported that the current and lifetime rates of PTSD following rape were higher than the PTSD rates associated with other traumatic events.[17] Studies in which women have been asked whether they have been "raped" report high lifetime PTSD prevalence rates, ranging from 49%[18] to 80%.[19] Studies that have used broader definitions of sexual assault (e.g., unwanted sexual contact as children or adults) generally report lower rates of lifetime PTSD (4% to 14%).[20] However, the PTSD prevalence rates in the latter studies still were higher than those associated with other traumas.

Other investigators have assessed the severity of PTSD symptoms among nonrecent victims in comparison to non-victims without determining whether all criteria for the diagnosis are met.[21] The measures used to assess PTSD symptoms include the Crime–Related PTSD scale of the SCL–90–R,[22] the

---

13. PTSD prevalence rates are typically compared across traumatic events, rather than between victims and non-victims, because the symptoms of PTSD make reference to having experienced a traumatic event, such as avoiding reminders of the trauma.

14. H. S. Resnick et al., *Prevalence of Civilian Trauma and Posttraumatic Stress Disorder in a Representative National Sample of Women*, 61 J. CONSULTING & CLINICAL PSYCHOL. 984 (1993); Ronald C. Kessler et al., *Posttraumatic Stress Disorder in the National Comorbidity Survey*, 52 ARCHIVES GEN. PSYCHIATRY 1048 (1995); D. Kilpatrick et al., *Criminal Victimization: Lifetime Prevalence, Reporting to Police, and Psychological Impact*, 33 CRIME & DELINQUENCY 479 (1987).

15. M. Cloitre et al., *Posttraumatic Stress Disorder, Self-and Interpersonal Dysfunction Among Sexually Retraumatized Women*, 10 J. TRAUMATIC STRESS 437 (1997).

16. M. J. Layman et al., *Unacknowledged Versus Acknowledged Rape Victims: Situational Factors and Posttraumatic Stress*, 105 J. ABNORMAL PSYCHOL. 124 (1997).

17. Resnick et al., *supra* note 14; Kessler et al., *supra* note 14; Kilpatrick et al., *supra* note 14.

18. N. Breslau et al., *Trauma and Posttraumatic Stress Disorder in the Community: The 1996 Detroit Area Survey of Trauma*, 55 ARCHIVES GEN. PSYCHIATRY 626 (1998).

19. Naomi Breslau et al., *Traumatic Events and Post-traumatic Stress Disorder in an Urban Population of Young Adults*, 48 ARCHIVES GEN. PSYCHIATRY 216 (1991).

20. F. H. Norris, *Epidemiology of Trauma: Frequency and Impact of Different Potentially Traumatic Events on Different Demographic Groups*, 60 J. CONSULTING & CLINICAL PSYCHOL. 409 (1992); I. Winfield et al., *Sexual Assault and Psychiatric Disorders Among a Community Sample of Women*, 147 AM. J. PSYCHIATRY 335 (1990).

21. Victims can be compared to non-victims on these measures because the symptoms are not linked to a traumatic event.

22. B. Saunders et al., *Development of a Crime–Related Posttraumatic Stress Disorder Scale for Women Within the Symptom Check-*

Impact of Event Scale (IES),[23] the Trauma Symptom Checklist,[24] the Trauma Symptom Inventory,[25] and the Mississippi Scale for PTSD.[26] Using a variety of samples, symptom measures, and definitions of sexual assault, these studies consistently show that victims of sexual assault report more symptoms of PTSD than do non-victims.[27] For example, in a study of female college students,[28] victims of molestation, attempted rape, coerced rape, and forcible rape all reported more PTSD symptoms than non-victims on the Crime–Related PTSD scale. Women in the victimized groups (34%) also were more likely to meet the clinical cutoff for PTSD on this measure than were non-victims (22%). Other studies have found that sexual assault victims generally report more symptoms of PTSD than do victims of other traumas.[29] For example, rape victims had higher scores on the IES than victims of other events such as natural disasters.[30]

[2] Studies With No Comparison Groups

Short-term symptoms. Six published studies have reported data on the prevalence of PTSD diagnoses among rape victims without using a comparison group. In two studies by Foa and her colleagues, PTSD symptoms were assessed weekly for 12 weeks among recent victims of rape and attempted rape.[31] In the first study, 94% of the victims met the criteria for PTSD at 2 weeks post-assault.[32] This figure dropped to 65% at 1 month and to 47% at 3 months post-assault. The corresponding figures in the second study were 90%, 60%, and 51%.[33] Other studies assessing PTSD among recent rape victims

list–90–Revised, 3 J. TRAUMATIC STRESS 439 (1990).

23. Mardi J. Horowitz et al., *Impact of Event Scale: A Measure of Subjective Distress*, 41 PSYCHOSOMATIC MEDICINE 209 (1979).

24. J. Briere & M. Runtz, *The Trauma Symptom Checklist (TSC–33): Early Data on a New Scale*, 4 J. INTERPERSONAL VIOLENCE 151 (1989).

25. J. Briere, TRAUMA SYMPTOM INVENTORY PROFESSIONAL MANUAL (1995).

26. T. M. Keane et al., *Mississippi Scale for Combat–Related Posttraumatic Stress Disorder: Three Studies in Reliability and Validity*, 56 J. CONSULTING & CLINICAL PSYCHOL. 85 (1988).

27. Hutchings & Dutton, *Symptom Severity and Diagnoses Related to Sexual Assault History*, 11 J. ANXIETY DISORDERS 607 (1997); C. M. Arata & B. R. Burkhart, *Post-Traumatic Stress Disorder Among College Student Victims of Acquaintance Assault*, 8 J. PSYCHOL. & HUMAN SEXUALITY 79 (1996); Briere et al., *Trauma Symptom Inventory: Psychometrics and Association With Childhood and Adult Victimization in Clinical Samples*, 10 J. INTERPERSONAL VIOLENCE 387 (1995); J. R. T. Davidson, et al., *The Association of Sexual Assault and Attempted Suicide Within the Community*, 53 ARCHIVES GEN. PSYCHIATRY 550 (1996); Wolfe et al., *Sexual Harassment and Assault as Predictors of PTSD Symptomatology Among U.S. Female Persian Gulf War Military Personnel*, 13 J. INTERPERSON-

AL VIOLENCE 40 (1998); Layman et al., *supra* note 16; V. Gil–Rivas et al., *Sexual Abuse, Physical Abuse, and Posttraumatic Stress Disorder Among Women Participating in Outpatient Drug Abuse Treatment*, 28 J. PSYCHOACTIVE DRUGS 95 (1996).

28. Arata & Burkhart, *supra* note 27.

29. S. B. Ullman & J. M Siegel, *Predictors of Exposure to Traumatic Events and Posttraumatic Stress Sequelae*, 22 J. COMMUNITY PSYCHOL. 328 (1994); S.E. Ullman, *Adult Trauma Survivors and Post–Traumatic Stress Sequelae: An Analysis of Reexperiencing, Avoidance, and Arousal Criteria*, 8 J. TRAUMATIC STRESS 179 (1995); S. Vrana & D. Lauterbach, *Prevalence of Traumatic Events and Post–Traumatic Psychological Symptoms in a Nonclinical Sample of College Students*, 7 J. TRAUMATIC STRESS 289 (1994).

30. Vrana & Lauterbach, *supra* note 29.

31. Edna B. Foa & David S. Riggs, *Post-traumatic Stress Disorder Following Assault: Theoretical Considerations and Empirical Findings*, 4 CURRENT DIRECTIONS PSYCHOL. SCI. 61 (1995); Barbara O. Rothbaum et al., *A Prospective Examination of Post–Traumatic Stress Disorder in Rape Victims*, 5 J. TRAUMATIC STRESS 455 (1992).

32. Rothbaum et al., *supra* note 31.

33. Foa & Riggs, *supra* note 31.

report prevalence rates of between 51% and 73%.[34] For example, Kramer and Green assessed PTSD symptoms among 30 sexual assault victims at 6 to 8 weeks post-rape.[35] Seventy-three percent were diagnosed with PTSD using DSM–III criteria and 67% met the DSM–III–R criteria. The most common symptoms, each reported by 80% of the sample, were efforts to avoid thoughts/feelings about the event, exaggerated startle response, and hypervigilance.

Investigators also have measured symptoms of PTSD (without assessing whether victims meet the diagnostic criteria for the disorder) in studies that do not use comparison groups.[36] Most of these studies have used the IES, which measures intrusive and avoidance symptoms related to a traumatic event.[37] Higher scores on both scales are positively correlated with receiving a diagnosis of PTSD.[38] Across these studies, victims scored more than one standard deviation above the mean scores of female medical students and within one standard deviation of the mean scores of female outpatients.[39] A very recent study used a self-report measure of PTSD symptoms developed by Foa and her colleagues[40] and found that the average score for rape victims was above the cutoff for severe PTSD.[41]

Long-term symptoms. Studies assessing the prevalence of PTSD among non-recent sexual assault victims without comparison to non-victim groups have yielded PTSD prevalence rates ranging from 23% to 77%.[42] Specifically, Santello and Leitenberg assessed PTSD among undergraduate women who had experienced unwanted sexual contact an average of 2 years previously; 59% met the DSM–III–R criteria for a diagnosis of PTSD.[43] Deykin and Buka assessed trauma experiences and PTSD in a sample of chemically dependent adolescents.[44] Forty percent of the female adolescents had been raped and 77% of those met lifetime criteria for PTSD, which was the highest rate of any trauma assessed. Finally, Blanchard et al. reported data on 13 women who

34. J. R. Freedy et al., *The Psychological Adjustment of Recent Crime Victims in the Criminal Justice System,* 9 J. INTERPERSONAL VIOLENCE 450 (1994); Teresa Kramer & Bonnie Green, *Post-traumatic Stress Disorder as an Early Response to Sexual Assault,* 6 J. INTERPERSONAL VIOLENCE 1660 (1991); H. S. Resnick et al., *Effect of Previous Trauma on Acute Plasma Cortisol Level Following Rape,* 151 AM. J. PSYCHIATRY 1675 (1995); Griffin et al., *supra* note 8.

35. Kramer & Green, *supra* note 34.

36. Sandra K. Burge, *Post-traumatic Stress Disorder in Victims of Rape,* 1 J. TRAUMATIC STRESS 193 (1988); Kramer & Green, *supra* note 34; Debra Popiel & Edwin Susskind, *The Impact of Rape: Social Support as a Moderator of Stress,* 13 AM. J. COMMUNITY PSYCHOL. 645 (1985); Patricia A. Resick et al., *A Comparative Outcome Study of Behavioral Group Therapy for Sexual Assault Victims,* 19 BEHAV. THERAPY 385 (1988); Rothbaum et al., *supra* note 31.

37. Mardi J. Horowitz et al., *supra* note 23.

38. Matisyohu Weisenberg et al., *Assessing the Severity of Posttraumatic Stress Disorder: Relation Between Dichotomous and Continuous Measures,* 55 J. CONSULTING & CLINICAL PSYCHOL. 432 (1987)

39. Kramer & Green, *supra* note 34; Popiel & Susskind, *supra* note 36; Rothbaum et al., *supra* note 31.

40. E. B. Foa et al., *Reliability and Validity of a Brief Instrument for Assessing Post-Traumatic Stress Disorder,* 6 J. TRAUMATIC STRESS, 459 (1993).

41. P. Nisith et al., *Prior Interpersonal Trauma: The Contribution to Current PTSD Symptoms in Female Rape Victims,* 109 J. ABNORMAL PSYCHOL. 20 (2000).

42. M. D. Santello & H. Leitenberg, *Sexual Aggression by an Acquaintance: Methods of Coping and Later Psychological Adjustment,* 8 VIOLENCE & VICTIMS 91 (1993); Deykin & Buka, *Prevalence and Risk Factors for Posttraumatic Stress Disorder Among Chemically Dependent Adolescents,* AM. J. PSYCHIATRY 752 (1997); Blanchard et al., *Psychometric Properties of the PTSD Checklist (PCL),* BEHAV. RES. AND THERAPY 669 (1996).

43. Santello & Leitenberg, *supra* note 42.

44. Deykin & Buka, *supra* note 42.

had been sexually assaulted several years previously, 23% of whom met criteria for a diagnosis of PTSD.[45]

Studies using the IES to assess PTSD symptoms among non-recent victims also report higher scores among victims than among non-patient norm groups.[46] The only study that explicitly compared victims' scores to those of norm groups found that victims scored significantly higher than both male and female medical students on intrusion and avoidance and higher than male stress patients on avoidance.[47]

[3] Summary

Studies that have assessed the prevalence of PTSD among recent victims report that the vast majority meet the criteria for PTSD immediately post-rape and that approximately 50% continue to meet the criteria at one year post-rape. Studies that have assessed the prevalence of PTSD several years post-rape report lifetime PTSD prevalence rates ranging from 4% to 80%. This variability is partly a function of differences in the way in which sexual assault has been defined. Studies that use legal definitions of rape, without requiring participants to label their experiences as rape, report lifetime prevalence rates of 32% and 57%. Studies that use broader definitions (e.g., unwanted sexual contact) report lower rates (4%) whereas those that require rape victims to label themselves as such report higher rates (80%). Current PTSD prevalence rates among victims raped several years previously are fairly consistent in large representative samples, ranging from 12% to 17% across three studies. Because the symptoms of PTSD refer to a traumatic event, it is difficult to assess PTSD among comparison groups who have not experienced a trauma. However, several studies have found that rates of PTSD were higher among rape victims than among victims of other traumas, and that victims score higher than non-victims and victims of other traumas on measures of PTSD symptoms.

§ 6–2.2.2 Depression

Depression is another commonly studied after-effect of rape. Typically, symptoms of depression are assessed through self-report measures of depressive symptoms, such as the Beck Depression Inventory (BDI),[48] the Center for Epidemiological Studies Depression Scale (CES–D)[49] or the depression sub-scale of the Symptom Checklist 90–R (SCL–90–R)[50] or the Brief Symptom Inventory (BSI).[51] Other studies have assessed whether victims meet the criteria for a diagnosis of Major Depressive Disorder (MDD) as outlined in the DSM. Symptoms of depression, which overlap somewhat with the symptoms

45. Blanchard et al., *supra* note 42.

46. Burge, *supra* note 36; Resick et al., *supra* note 36; D. Riggs et al., *Long-term Psychological Distress Associated with Marital Rape and Aggravated Assault: A Comparison to Other Crime Victims*, 7 J. FAM. VIOLENCE 283 (1992).

47. Burge, *supra* note 36.

48. A. T. Beck et al., *An Inventory for Measuring Depression*, 4 ARCHIVES GEN. PSYCHIATRY 561 (1961).

49. L. Radloff, *The CES–D Scale: A Self–Report Depression Scale for Research in the General Population*, 1 APPLIED PSYCHOLOGICAL MEASUREMENT 385 (1977).

50. L. R. Derogatis, MANUAL FOR THE SCL–90, Baltimore, MD: Johns Hopkins School of Medicine (1977).

51. L. R. Derogatis & N. Melisaratos, *The Brief Symptom Inventory: An Introductory Report*, 13 PSYCHOLOGICAL MED. 595 (1983).

of PTSD, include depressed mood, diminished interest or pleasure in activities, weight loss or gain, sleep disturbances, feelings of worthlessness, inability to concentrate, and suicidal thoughts.

[1]　Studies Using Comparison Groups

Short-term symptoms. Approximately seven studies have assessed the prevalence of depression among victims and non-victims within one year of the assault. These studies consistently find higher rates of diagnoses of depression and depressive symptoms among victims than non-victims. For example, Frank and Anderson reported that 38% of a sample of victims from a rape crisis center met the criteria for MDD 6 months post-rape, in comparison to 16% of a matched comparison group.[52] Using the CES–D, Sorenson and Golding reported that 33% of the participants who had experienced forced sexual contact within the past 6 months met the cutoff for depression (in comparison to 11% of the comparison group).[53] Longitudinal studies of rape victims seen at rape crisis centers have found that victims differ from non-victims until about 2 months post-rape.[54] Moss et al.[55] also reported much higher BDI scores among victims recruited from rape crisis centers than among non-victims. The one exception to this trend occurs in studies assessing depression among female undergraduate students who have experienced unwanted sexual contact within the past year. Using student samples, one study found that victims scored higher than non-victims on the BDI[56] and one study found no differences between victims and non-victims.[57]

Long-term symptoms. Several studies have compared the prevalence of depressive diagnoses among non-victims and victims assaulted more than one year previously. These studies also very consistently show higher rates of MDD among victims than non-victims. For example, five studies have used structured interviews to assess MDD according to some version of the DSM. All five show that victims of sexual assault (variously defined) have higher rates of MDD than non-victims.[58] The rates of MDD for victims in these studies range from 12% to 30% (versus 0% to 6% for non-victims). The 30% rate is from a study in which victims were offered free treatment for rape-related difficulties.[59] Hutchings and Dutton[60] assessed the prevalence of various mood disorders (including Major Depression, Bipolar Disorder and Dys-

52. Ellen Frank & Barbara Anderson, *Psychiatric Disorders in Rape Victims: Past History and Current Symptomatology*, 28 COMPREHENSIVE PSYCHIATRY 77 (1987).

53. Susan B. Sorenson & Jacqueline M. Golding, *Depressive Sequelae of Recent Criminal Victimization*, 3 J. TRAUMATIC STRESS 337 (1990).

54. Atkeson et al., *supra* note 5; D. Kilpatrick et al., *The Aftermath of Rape: Recent Empirical Findings*, 49 AM. J. ORTHOPSYCHIATRY 658 (1979); D. Kilpatrick et al., *Effects of a Rape Experience: A Longitudinal Study*, 37 J. SOC. ISSUES 105 (1981).

55. M. Moss et al., *The Effects of Marital Status and Partner Support on Rape Trauma*, 60 AM. J. ORTHOPSYCHIATRY 379 (1990).

56. Gidycz et al., *supra* note 7.

57. M. Larimer et al., *Male and Female Recipients of Unwanted Sexual Contact in a College Student Sample: Prevalence Rates, Alcohol Use, and Depression Symptoms*, 40 SEX ROLES 295 (1999).

58. D. G. Kilpatrick et al., *Rape in Marriage and in Dating Relationships: How Bad Is It for Mental Health?*, 528 ANNALS NEW YORK ACAD. SCIENCES 335 (1988); M. A. Burnam et al., *Sexual Assault and Mental Disorders in a Community Population*, 56 J. CONSULTING & CLINICAL PSYCHOL. 843 (1988); Winfield et al., *supra* note 20; Cloitre et al., *supra* note 15; Davidson et al., *supra* note 27.

59. Cloitre et al., *supra* note 15.

60. Hutchings & Dutton, *supra* note 27.

thymia) and found higher rates among abused (48%) than among nonabused females (27%). Studies that have assessed depressive symptoms using methods other than structured interviews also report higher rates of depressive diagnoses among victims than non-victims. For example, Briere and colleagues interviewed women seen in an urban psychiatric emergency room regarding lifetime victimization history and gathered data on previous psychiatric diagnoses through hospital charts.[61] Rape victims were more likely (41%) to have had a diagnosis of depressive disorder than women who had not been raped (29%). Studies of female veteran outpatients[62] and homeless women[63] also find higher rates of depression (using the CESD) among victims (60% to 70%) than non-victims (33% to 46%).

Other studies have compared non-recent victims to non-victims using standardized self-report measures of depression such as the BDI, SCL–90R, and Trauma Symptom Checklist. All of these studies find that victims score significantly higher than non-victims on these measures of depressive symptoms.[64] In studies using the BDI, between 19% and 45% of the victims were moderately to severely depressed compared to between 4% and 23% of non-victims.[65] For example, in the Becker et al. study, 19% of the rape victims were classified as severely depressed in comparison to none of the non-victims.[66] The only exception is a study that found no differences on the BDI between battered women who had been sexually assaulted and those who had not.[67] Both groups reported mild to moderate levels of depression.

Several studies also have reported data on suicidal thoughts and attempts, which are symptoms of depression. In the Cloitre et al. study, 45% of those who had been victimized as both children and adults (i.e., the retraumatized group) had attempted suicide, which was a higher rate than the adult assault only group (13%) or the no assault group (0%).[68] The suicide attempts in the adult assault group all had occurred after the assaults. Davidson et al. also found that the prevalence of suicide attempts was higher in the victimized group (15%) than in the non-victim group (1%).[69] In the chart review

61. Briere et al., *Lifetime Victimization History, Demographics, and Clinical Status in Female Psychiatric Emergency Room Patients*, J. Nervous & Mental Disease 95 (1997).

62. C. Hankin et al., *Prevalence of Depressive and Alcohol Abuse Symptoms Among Women VA Outpatients Who Report Experiencing Sexual Assault While in the Military*, 12 J. Traumatic Stress 601 (1999).

63. S. Wenzel et al., *Health of Homeless Women with Recent Experience of Rape*, 15 J. Gen. Internal Medicine 265 (2000).

64. J. Becker et al., *Depressive Symptoms Associated with Sexual Assault*, 10 J. Sex & Marital Therapy 185 (1984); E. Ellis et al., *An Assessment of Long-term Reaction to Rape*, 90 J. Abnormal Psychol. 263 (1981); C. A. Gidycz & M. P. Koss, *Predictors of Long-term Sexual Assault Trauma Among a National Sample of Victimized College Women*, 6 Violence & Victims 175 (1991); V. Rickert et al., *Ethnic Differences in Depressive Symptomatology Among Young Women*, 95 Obstetrics & Gynecology 55 (2000);

J. Surrey, et al., *Reported History of Physical and Sexual Abuse and Severity of Symptomatology in Women Psychiatric Outpatients*, 60 Am. J. Orthopsychiatry 412 (1990); S. Gold et al., *A Cross-validation Study of the Trauma Symptom Checklist*, 9 J. Interpersonal Violence 12 (1994); J. Santiago et al., *Long-term Psychological Effects of Rape in 35 Rape Victims*, 142 Am. J. Psychiatry 1338 (1985); Briere et al., *supra* note 27; Shapiro & Schwarz, *Date Rape: Its Relationship to Trauma Symptoms and Sexual Self–Esteem*, 12 J. Interpersonal Violence, 407 (1997); Vrana & Lauterbach, *supra* note 29.

65. Becker et al., *supra* note 64; Ellis et al., *supra* note 64; Gidycz & Koss, *supra* note 64.

66. Becker et al., *supra* note 64.

67. Campbell & Soeken, *Forced Sex and Intimate Partner Violence*, 5 Violence Against Women 1017 (1999).

68. Cloitre et al., *supra* note 15.

69. Davidson et al., *supra* note 27.

study by Briere et al.,[70] suicidal ideation and attempts (62% and 68%, respectively) were higher among women who had been raped versus those who had not been raped (39% and 34%, respectively). Finally, in two samples of college students, women who had been raped were more likely to have had serious thoughts about suicide[71] and to have engaged in suicidal acts[72] than non-victims.

[2] Studies With No Comparison Groups

Short-term symptoms. Several additional studies provide information on levels of depression within rape victims without comparing victims to non-victims. Several papers by Frank and her colleagues described data from victims recruited from rape crisis centers participating in a treatment research project.[73] Across these studies, 1 month post-rape BDI scores were in the moderately depressed range, and 12 month BDI scores were in the nondepressed range. Approximately half (45% to 56%) of the victims scored in the moderately to severely depressed range at 1 month post-rape. Rothbaum and her colleagues also recruited participants from a rape crisis program.[74] One month BDI scores were in the moderately depressed range and 12 month BDI scores were in the mildly depressed range. In a study by Griffin et al., mean BDI scores were in the moderately depressed range and one-third (34%) of the sample met diagnostic criteria for Depressive Disorder (although the specific disorder was not specified).[75]

Long-term symptoms. Studies assessing depression among victims more than one year post-rape also report significant levels of depression. For example, victims score higher than non-patient norm groups[76] and similar to outpatient norm groups[77] on the SCL–90R depression scale. Another study reported that rape victims scored higher than victims of other traumas on the BSI depression scale.[78] Mackey et al.[79] reported that 60% of their sample were mildly to severely depressed according to their scores on the BDI. Others report mean BDI scores in the mild or moderate range.[80]

70. Briere et al., *supra* note 61.

71. Brener et al., *Forced Sexual Intercourse and Associated Health–Risk Behaviors Among Female College Students*, 67 J. Consulting & Clinical Psychol. 252 (1999).

72. Stepakoff, *Effects of Sexual Victimization on Suicidal Ideation and Behavior in U.S. College Women*, 28 Suicide & Life-Threatening Behav. 107 (1998).

73. Patricia A. Cluss et al., *The Rape Victim: Psychological Correlates of Participation in the Legal Process*, 10 Crim. Just. & Behav. 342 (1983); Ellen Frank & Barbara D. Stewart, *Depressive Symptoms in Rape Victims: A Revisit*, 7 J. Affective Disorders 77 (1984); Ellen Frank et al., *Depressive Symptoms in Rape Victims*, 1 J. Affective Disorders 269 (1979); Ellen Frank et al., *Efficacy of Cognitive Behavior Therapy and Systematic Desensitization in the Treatment of Rape Trauma*, 19 Behav. Therapy 403 (1988); Barbara D. Stewart et al., *The Aftermath of Rape: Profiles of Immediate*

and Delayed Treatment Seekers, 175 J. Nervous & Mental Disease 90 (1987).

74. Rothbaum et al., *supra* note 01.

75. Griffin et al., *supra* note 8.

76. Burge, *supra* note 36; Lawrence Cohen & Susan Roth, *The Psychological Aftermath of Rape: Long-term Effects and Individual Differences in Recovery*, 5 J. Soc. & Clinical Psychol. 525 (1987).

77. Burge, *supra* note 36; Resick et al., *supra* note 36.

78. Patricia Frazier & Laura Schauben, *Causal Attributions and Recovery from Rape and Other Stressful Life Events*, 13 J. Soc. & Clinical Psychol. 1 (1994).

79. T. Mackey et al., *Factors Associated with Long-term Depressive Symptoms of Sexual Assault Victims*, 6 Archives of Psychiatric Nursing 10 (1992).

80. J. Becker et al., *Time Limited Therapy with Sexually Dysfunctional Sexually Assault-*

Finally, three studies assessed depression among victims using non-standardized measures. In a large-scale study in Los Angeles, 50% of the female sexual assault victims reported feeling "sad, blue, or depressed" as a result of the assault.[81] Norris and Feldman–Summers[82] recruited 179 victims through rape crisis centers and media ads who had been raped an average of three years previously. Thirty percent reported being depressed prior to the rape and 80% reported being depressed in the 6 months following the rape. Nadelson et al. interviewed 41 women who had been seen at an emergency room rape crisis program at least 1 year previously.[83] Seventy-eight percent reported that they had experienced depression since the rape and 41% reported that they were still depressed. Finally, in a study by Burgess and Holmstrom, 11% of the victims reported a suicide attempt.[84]

[3] Summary

Despite differences in the measurement of depression, sample characteristics, definition of sexual assault, and time since the assault occurred, the results of many studies yield very consistent evidence that victims are more likely to be diagnosed with depressive disorders and to report more symptoms of depression than non-victims. In addition, several studies that do not use comparison groups reveal that many victims are moderately to severely depressed initially and remain at least mildly depressed for a substantial period of time post-rape. When asked directly, between 50% and 80% of victims reported feeling depressed as a result of the rape.

§ 6–2.2.3 Fear

Fear is another common symptom among rape victims. These fears can either relate specifically to the rape (e.g., fear of men) or involve more general fears. Most studies have assessed fear through self-report measures such as the Veronen–Kilpatrick Modified Fear Survey (MFS), which is a well-validated measure yielding an overall fear score and scores on several subscales, including a rape fears subscale.[85]

[1] Studies Using Comparison Groups

Short-term symptoms. Studies that have assessed short-term reactions to rape have found differences between victims and non-victims on the MFS for up to one year post-rape. Resick et al. reported data from 296 victims who had participated in two large scale studies of reactions to rape.[86] In this combined

ed Women, 3 J. Soc. Work & Hum. Sexuality 97 (1984); E. Foa et al., *Evaluation of a Brief Cognitive–Behavioral Program for the Prevention of Chronic PTSD in Recent Assault Victims*, 63 J. Consulting & Clinical Psychol. 948 (1995).

81. Judith Siegel et al., *Reactions to Sexual Assault: A Community Study*, 5 J. Interpersonal Violence 229 (1990).

82. Jeanette Norris & Shirley Feldman–Summers, *Factors Related to the Psychological Impact of Rape on the Victim*, 90 J. Abnormal Psychol. 562 (1981).

83. Carol Nadelson et al., *A Follow-up Study of Rape Victims*, 139 Am. J. Psychiatry 1266 (1982).

84. A. W. Burgess & L. L. Holmstrom, *Adaptive Strategies and Recovery from Rape*, 136 Am. J. Psychiatry 1278 (1979).

85. L. J. Veronen & D. G. Kilpatrick, *Self-reported Fears of Rape Victims: A Preliminary Investigation*, 4 Behav. Modification 383 (1980).

86. Patricia A. Resick et al., *Assessment of Fear Reactions in Sexual Assault Victims: A Factor Analytic Study of the Veronen–Kilpa-*

sample, victims differed from non-victims at two to eight months post-rape on six out of eight MFS subscales. Other articles report longitudinal data from these two studies. In one of the studies, the MFS was administered to 115 victims and 87 non-victims at 6 points from 2 weeks to 12 months post-rape.[87] Combining across time periods, victims scored higher than non-victims on the total MFS scale and five of six subscales. Differences between groups were still evident at the 12 month assessment for the total scale and the rape and classical fears subscales. In the other study, 46 victims and 35 non-victims were compared on the MFS from 1 week to 12 months post-rape.[88] Victims differed from non-victims at 12 months post-rape on the overall and rape fears scales. Wirtz and Harrell compared rape victims to victims of four other crimes (i.e., domestic assault, nondomestic assault, robbery, and burglary) using 12 of the 120 items from the MFS.[89] Rape victims reported higher levels of fear than victims of any other crimes at both 1 and 6 months postcrime.

Long-term symptoms. Although these studies yield consistent evidence that victims differ from non-victims for up to one year post-rape, three studies assessing long-term reactions using the MFS have yielded inconsistent results. For example, Santiago et al. found that victims who had been assaulted from 2 to 46 years previously differed from non-victims on the total MFS score and four of the MFS subscales.[90] On the other hand, neither Ellis et al.[91] nor Roth et al.[92] found differences between victims and non-victims on MFS scores several years post-rape, although Ellis et al. noted that virtually all victims reported extreme fearfulness soon after the assault.

[2] Studies With No Comparison Groups

Short term symptoms. Frank et al.[93] made no explicit comparisons to MFS norms, although reported scores were similar to victims' scores in other studies[94] and much higher than non-victim scores.[95] Moss et al. reported higher scores on the MFS among victims than non-victims although no statistical comparisons were made.[96]

Using a non-standardized measure, Becker et al. assessed symptoms among 20 completed rape victims within a year following the assault.[97] At the acute stage, 80% reported general fear, 80% reported fear of physical violence, and 70% reported fear of death. At one year post-rape, 80% reported fear of

trick Modified Fear Survey, 8 Behav. Assessment 271 (1986).

87. Karen Calhoun et al., *A Longitudinal Examination of Fear Reactions in Victims of Rape*, 29 J. Counseling Psychol. 655 (1982).

88. Kilpatrick et al. (1979), *supra* note 54; Kilpatrick et al. (1981), *supra* note 54.

89. Philip W. Wirtz & Adele V. Harrell, *Victim and Crime Characteristics, Coping Responses, and Short and Long Term Recovery from Victimization*, 60 J. Consulting & Clinical Psychol. 167 (1987).

90. Santiago et al., *supra* note 64.

91. Ellis et al., *supra* note 64.

92. Susan Roth et al., *Victimization History and Victim–Assailant Relationship as Factors*

in Recovery from Sexual Assault, 3 J. Traumatic Stress 169 (1990).

93. Frank et al., *supra* note 73.

94. *See* Becker et al., *supra* note 64; Moss et al., *supra* note 55; Kilpatrick et al. (1979), *supra* note 54; Kilpatrick et al. (1981), *supra* note 54.

95. *See* Moss et al., *supra* note 55; Kilpatrick et al. (1979), *supra* note 54; Kilpatrick et al. (1981), *supra* note 54.

96. Moss et al., *supra* note 55.

97. Judith Becker et al., *The Effects of Sexual Assault on Rape and Attempted Rape Victims*, 7 Victimology: An Int'l J. 106 (1982).

being alone, 75% reported fear of being indoors/outdoors/crowds, and 55% reported fear of people behind them.

Long-term symptoms. Studies also have compared MFS scores among non-recent rape victims to published norms. For example, Cohen and Roth reported that victims scored higher than non-victims on total MFS scores and the rape subscale several years post-rape.[98] Resick et al. presented scores for 37 victims seeking treatment an average of 5 years post-rape.[99] Pretreatment scores on two of the three MFS scales used in the study were more than one standard deviation above non-victim norm group means. Becker et al. reported similar results.[100]

Finally, two studies assessed fear among victims more than one year post-rape using non-standardized measures. In the Los Angeles study mentioned previously, 55% of the women who had been assaulted reported feeling fearful as a result of the assault, and 31% reported fear of being alone.[101] In the study by Nadelson et al., 83% of victims reported that they had experienced fear of being alone since the rape and 49% reported that they were still fearful.[102]

[3] Summary

There is consistent evidence that victims are more fearful than non-victims for up to one year post-rape, especially in regard to rape-related fears. One study also has shown that recent rape victims are more fearful than victims of other crimes. In studies that have not used comparison groups, means for victim groups are higher than norm group means, particularly among victims of recent assaults. Evidence regarding the duration of fear is mixed, however, with some studies reporting differences several years post-rape and others reporting no differences. Studies using non-standardized measures provide evidence that fear is common, with up to 83% of victims reporting various fears as a result of the assault.

§ 6–2.2.4 Anxiety

Anxiety also is common among rape victims. Several symptoms of anxiety overlap with the diagnosis of PTSD (e.g., difficulty concentrating, avoiding situations due to anxiety), which is not surprising because PTSD is itself an anxiety disorder. Most studies have assessed anxiety through self-report measures, such as State–Trait Anxiety Inventory (STAI),[103] which measures both state (present level) and trait (general level) anxiety; the anxiety and phobic anxiety subscales of the SCL90–R or the BSI;[104] the Beck Anxiety Inventory;[105] or the anxiety subscales of the Trauma Symptom Checklist[106] or the Trauma Symptom Inventory.[107] Other investigators have assessed whether victims meet the criteria for anxiety-related disorders other than PTSD, such

98. Cohen & Roth, *supra* note 76.

99. Resick et al., *supra* note 36.

100. Becker et al., *supra* note 64.

101. Siegel et al., *supra* note 81.

102. Nadelson et al., *supra* note 83.

103. CHARLES D. SPIELBERGER, RICHARD L. GORSUCH & ROBERT E. LUSHENE, THE STATE-TRAIT ANXIETY INVENTORY (1970).

104. Derogatis, *supra* note 50; Derogatis & Melisaratos, *supra* note 51.

105. Aaron Beck et al., *An Inventory for Measuring Clinical Anxiety: Psychometric Properties*, 56 J. CONSULTING & CLINICAL PSYCHOL. 893 (1988).

106. Briere & Runtz, *supra* note 24.

107. Briere, *supra* note 25.

as Generalized Anxiety Disorder, Panic Disorder, Phobic Disorder, and Obsessive Compulsive Disorder.

[1]   Studies Using Comparison Groups

Short-term symptoms. Three studies have compared recent victims and non-victims on self-report measures of anxiety. Using the STAI, victims differ from non-victims[108] and from other crime victims[109] in state anxiety until one-month post-rape. Victims differ from non-victims in terms of trait anxiety through twelve months post-rape.[110] Gidycz et al.[111] also reported differences between recent victims (assaulted within the past 9 weeks) and non-victims on the Beck Anxiety Inventory. Finally, on the SCL–90 anxiety subscales, victims differed from non-victims for up to twelve months post-rape.[112]

Only one study has assessed the prevalence of diagnosable anxiety disorders (other than PTSD) among recent victims in comparison to non-victims. Specifically, Frank and Anderson found higher rates of Generalized Anxiety Disorder in victims (82%) versus non-victims (32%).[113] There were no differences between victim and non-victim groups in the prevalence of Phobic Disorder.

Long-term symptoms. Studies assessing differences between non-recent victims and non-victims have yielded somewhat mixed results. Several studies have found differences between victims and non-victims on various self-report measures of anxiety.[114] In another study, abused women scored higher than non-abused women on the Anxiety scale of the Brief Symptom Inventory, although whether the difference was statistically significant was not reported.[115] However, several other studies have found no differences between victims and non-victims on self-report anxiety measures.[116] Frazier and Schauben also found no differences between victims of rape and other stressors on the BSI anxiety subscales.[117]

Studies assessing the prevalence of various diagnosable anxiety disorders among non-recent victims and non-victims also have yielded mixed results. For example, in terms of Panic Disorder, two studies found that victims were more likely than non-victims to meet the criteria for the disorder several years post-rape[118] and two studies found no differences between victims and non-victims.[119] In regard to Generalized Anxiety Disorder (GAD), Winfield et al.[120] found no differences in prevalence between victims and non-victims and

108. Kilpatrick et al. (1979), *supra* note 54; Kilpatrick et al. (1981), *supra* note 54.

109. Wirtz & Harrell, *supra* note 89.

110. Kilpatrick et al. (1979), *supra* note 54; Kilpatrick et al. (1981), *supra* note 54.

111. Gidycz et al., *supra* note 7.

112. Kilpatrick et al. (1979), *supra* note 54; Kilpatrick et al. (1981), *supra* note 54.

113. Frank & Anderson, *supra* note 52.

114. Gidycz & Koss, *supra* note 64; Santiago et al., *supra* note 64; Gold et al., *supra* note 64; Briere et al., *supra* note 27; Shapiro & Schwarz, *supra* note 64.

115. Hutchings & Dutton, *supra* note 27.

116. Santiago et al., *supra* note 64; Vrana & Lauterbach, *supra* note 29; Riggs et al., *supra* note 46; Surrey et al., *supra* note 64.

117. Frazier & Schauben, *supra* note 78.

118. Burnam et al., *supra* note 58; Winfield et al., *supra* note 20.

119. Davidson et al., *supra* note 27; Cloitre et al., *supra* note 15.

120. Winfield et al., *supra* note 20.

Cloitre et al.[121] found differences only between women who had been victimized as both children and adults (i.e., revictimized group) and non-victims. Women who had been sexually assaulted only as adults did not differ from non-victims. Two studies found differences between victims and non-victims in the prevalence of various Phobic Disorders.[122] However, Cloitre et al. only found differences in the prevalence of Social Phobia and Simple Phobia between the revictimized group and the non-victim group.[123] In regard to Obsessive Compulsive Disorder, two studies found differences between victims and non-victims[124] and one study found no differences.[125] Hutchings and Dutton reported a much higher rate of anxiety disorders (76%) among women who had been sexually assaulted or abused in comparison to non-victims (21%).[126] However, they included PTSD in this category, along with Panic Disorder, Simple Phobia, and Generalized Anxiety Disorder. Finally, in the Briere et al. study in which data were gathered on previous psychiatric diagnoses through hospital charts, rape victims actually were less likely (0%) to have had a diagnosis of an anxiety disorder than women who had not been raped (19%).[127] Whether this was a statistically significant difference was not reported.

[2]   Studies With No Comparison Groups

Short-term symptoms. Investigators also have administered the STAI to groups of recent victims without comparing victims' scores either to those of a comparison group or to non-victim norms.[128] Means on the state and trait anxiety scales ranged from 48 to 57 across these studies. In comparison, norms from studies that have included comparison groups range from 34 to 40.

Long-term symptoms. Three additional studies report scores on the anxiety or phobic anxiety subscale of the SCL90–R or the BSI. All three studies compared victims' scores either to non-patient or outpatient norms. In general, victims scored higher than non-patient norm groups[129] and similar to outpatient norm groups.[130] Finally, 53% of the victims in another study reported being tense, nervous, or anxious as a result of the assault.[131]

[3]   Summary

Studies consistently have found that victims report more anxiety than do non-victims for the first year post-rape. In one study, 82% of the sample met the criteria for Generalized Anxiety Disorder one month post-rape. The evidence regarding long-term anxiety is more mixed, although slightly more studies find differences between victims and non-victims in terms of self-

---

121.   Cloitre et al., *supra* note 15.

122.   Burnam et al., *supra* note 58; Kilpatrick et al., *supra* note 58.

123.   Cloitre et al, *supra* note 15.

124.   Burnam et al., *supra* note 58; Winfield et al., *supra* note 20.

125.   Kilpatrick et al., *supra* note 58.

126.   Hutchings & Dutton, *supra* note 27.

127.   Briere et al., *supra* note 61.

128.   Frank et al., *supra* note 73; Moss et al., *supra* note 55; Rothbaum et al., *supra* note 31.

129.   Burge, *supra* note 36; Cohen & Roth, *supra* note 76.

130.   Burge, *supra* note 36; Resick et al., *supra* note 36.

131.   Siegel et al., *supra* note 81.

reported anxiety and the prevalence of various anxiety disorders than find no differences. Studies that have not employed comparison groups report means among victims that are higher than scores of non-victims in other studies.

§ 6–2.2.5   Social Adjustment and Interpersonal Functioning

The impact of sexual assault on social adjustment and interpersonal functioning also has received some research attention. The areas of social adjustment assessed include work adjustment, interpersonal relationships, and social and leisure activities. Investigators have assessed social adjustment through self-report measures and structured interviews.

[1]   Studies Using Comparison Groups

Short-term symptoms. Two studies have examined social adjustment among victims and non-victim comparison groups within one year post-rape. The first used the Social Adjustment Scale—Self Report Form (SAS–SR)[132] which assesses role performance in several major areas of interpersonal functioning: work, economic, social and leisure activities, relationships with extended family members, and roles as a spouse, parent, and family member. Specifically, Resick et al. administered the SAS–SR to victims at 6 points, from 2 weeks to 12 months post-rape and found that victims reported more adjustment problems (collapsing across role areas) than non-victims for the first 2 months post-rape.[133] At 4 months post-rape, victims showed more impairment in extended family relationships than did the comparison group. The other study assessed social adjustment among victims and non-victims using a measure of self-esteem in eight life domains (i.e., self, others, children, authority, work, reality, parents, and hope).[134] Assessments were made at seven time points, from 2 weeks to 2 years post-rape. On the total scale, victims reported lower self-esteem than non-victims through the 6 month assessment. The only domain in which victims differed from non-victims at 2 years post-rape was family relationship problems (i.e., quality of relationships with parents).

Long-term symptoms. Two other studies have assessed longer-term impairment among rape victims in comparison to non-victims. Roth et al. assessed post-assault functioning in a sample of university women and reported no significant differences between victims and non-victims on global adjustment.[135] Administering the SAS–SR to a sample of victims raped an average of three years previously, Ellis et al. found significant differences between victims and non-victims only in terms of family problems.[136]

132. Myrna Weissman & Sallye Bothwell, *Assessment of Social Adjustment by Patient Self-report*, 33 Archives Gen. Psychiatry 1111 (1976); Myrna Weissman et al., *Social Adjustment by Self-report in a Community Sample and in Psychiatric Outpatients*, 166 J. Nervous & Mental Disease 317 (1978).

133. Patricia Resick et al., *Social Adjustment in Victims of Sexual Assault*, 49 J. Consulting & Clinical Psychol. 705 (1981).

134. S. M. Murphy et al., *Rape Victims' Self-esteem: A Longitudinal Analysis*, 3 J. Interpersonal Violence 355 (1988).

135. Roth et al., *supra* note 92.

136. Ellis et al., *supra* note 64.

[2] Studies With No Comparison Groups

Short-term symptoms. Frank and her colleagues assessed social adjustment among three overlapping samples of victims recruited from rape crisis centers.[137] These studies used the SAS–II which is a structured interview developed from the SAS–SR to assess functioning in four specific role areas (i.e., work, household, external family, and social/leisure activities) as well as overall social functioning.[138] The most relevant finding was that victims who actually were able to prosecute their case in court had lower work adjustment scores at 6 months post-rape than those who wanted, but were unable, to prosecute.[139]

Long-term symptoms. Cohen and Roth administered the SAS–SR to a sample of sexual assault victims who had been raped an average of eight years prior to their participation in the study.[140] Across all the subscales and the global measure, victims scored significantly below standardized norms for women. Using non-standardized measures, Burgess and Holmstrom reported that 59% of the victims in their sample, who had been raped an average of 4 to 6 years previously, reported disruptions in their relationships after the rape.[141]

[3] Summary

Studies that have assessed short-term symptoms have found that victims generally report more social adjustment problems than non-victims for 2 to 6 months post-rape. Studies that have assessed longer-term social adjustment have yielded inconsistent results, with one finding no differences between victims and non-victims, one finding differences only in family adjustment, and one finding differences between victims and norm group means in all areas of social adjustment. The most consistent finding is that family relationships appear to be the domain in which victims are most likely to differ from non-victims.

§ 6–2.2.6 Health Problems

A growing body of research suggests that a history of sexual assault is associated with poorer physical, as well as mental, health. Most of these studies have focused on long-term health problems, including perceptions of poor health, various health problems, and medical service utilization.

[1] Studies Using Comparison Groups

Short-term symptoms. Very few studies have assessed short-term health problems in victims in comparison to non-victims. In the only longitudinal study conducted to date, victims and non-victims were compared from two weeks to one year post-rape in terms of physical symptoms, perceived health, and physician visits.[142] Victims differed from non-victims on all three mea-

---

137. Frank et al., *supra* note 73; Stewart et al., *supra* note 73; Cluss et al., *supra* note 73.

138. Nina R. Schooler et al., *Prevention of Relapse in Schizophrenia: An Evaluation of Fluphenazine Deconoate*, 37 ARCHIVES GEN. PSYCHIATRY 16 (1980).

139. Cluss et al., *supra* note 73.

140. Cohen & Roth, *supra* note 76.

141. Burgess & Holmstrom, *supra* note 84.

142. Rachel Kimerling & Karen S. Calhoun, *Somatic Symptoms, Social Support, and Treatment Seeking Among Sexual Assault Victims*, 2 J. CONSULTING & CLINICAL PSYCHOL. 333 (1994).

sures at 4 months post-rape. At one year post-rape, victims still reported more physician visits than non-victims. The most common physical symptoms reported by victims were tension headaches, stomachache or nausea, and back pain. Another study examined physical health status among homeless women who had been raped in the past year in comparison to homeless women who had not been raped.[143] Compared to non-victims, homeless women who had been raped were more likely to report fair or poor health, at least one current physical health limitation, and at least two gynecological symptoms and two serious physical health symptoms in the past year.

Long-term symptoms. Golding and her colleagues have published several papers comparing victims and non-victims, identified through large-scale population surveys, on various indicators of physical health. In these studies sexual assault generally is defined as pressured or forced sexual contact as a child or adult. These studies indicate that, in comparison to non-victims, victims report poorer health,[144] more physical symptoms of various kinds,[145] more physical limitations,[146] more chronic diseases,[147] and more physician visits.[148] In regard to particular symptoms, victims report more headaches,[149] reproductive and sexual health problems,[150] pain,[151] premenstrual distress[152] and gastrointestinal, cardiopulmonary, and neurological problems.[153]

In another large scale study, Brener et al.[154] examined the association between forced sexual intercourse and health risk behaviors in a large, nationally representative sample of female college students. After controlling for demographic factors (i.e., age, parents' education, race, sorority membership), having had a history of forced sexual intercourse was associated with all nine health risk behaviors, including driving after drinking, smoking, heavy drinking, marijuana use, and having two or more current sexual partners. The odds of engaging in these behaviors were 1.5 to 2.7 times higher among women who had been raped.

These findings have been replicated in studies that compare victims and non-victims recruited in various clinical settings. For example, Leserman and her colleagues have published several papers based on data from a clinical sample of 239 women seen at a gastroenterology clinic.[155] In comparison to

143. Wenzel et al., *supra* note 63.

144. J. M. Golding et al., *Sexual Assault History and Health Perceptions: Seven General Population Studies*, 16 HEALTH PSYCHOL. 417 (1997); J. M. Golding, *Sexual Assault History and Physical Health in Randomly Selected Los Angeles Women*, 13 HEALTH PSYCHOL. 130 (1994).

145. J. M. Golding, *Sexual Assault History and Women's Reproductive and Sexual Health*, 20 PSYCHOL. WOMEN Q. 101 (1996); Golding, *supra* note 144; Golding et al., *Prevalence of Sexual Assault History Among Women with Common Gynecologic Symptoms*, AM J. OBSTET. GYNECOL. 1013 (1998); J. Golding, *Sexual Assault History and Headaches: Five General Population Studies*, 187 J. NERVOUS & MENTAL DISORDERS 624 (1999).

146. Golding, *supra* note 144; J. Golding, *Sexual Assault History and Limitations in Physical Functioning in Two General Popula-*tion Samples, 19 RES. IN NURSING & HEALTH 33 (1996).

147. Golding, *supra* note 144.

148. Golding et al., *supra* note 145.

149. Golding (1999), *supra* note 145.

150. Golding (1996), *supra* note 145; Golding, *supra* note 144.

151. Golding, *supra* note 144.

152. J. Golding & D. Taylor, *Sexual Assault History and Premenstrual Distress in Two General Population Samples*, 5 J. WOMEN'S HEALTH 143 (1996).

153. Golding, *supra* note 144.

154. Brener et al., *supra* note 71.

155. *See, e.g.,* Leserman et al., *Sexual and Physical Abuse History in Gastroenterology Practice: How Types of Abuse Impact Health Status*, PSYCHOSOMATIC MED. 4 (1996); Leserman

women who had not been raped, women who had been raped in adulthood reported more pain, more non-gastrointestinal symptoms, more days in bed because of illness, more surgeries, and more functional disability.[156] Other studies also reveal that victims report more health problems in general,[157] more gynecological problems,[158] more physician visits,[159] and more health risk behaviors[160] than non-victims.

Finally, other studies have assessed the prevalence of victimization experiences among women who have a specific medical problem in comparison to women who do not have the medical problem (i.e., in contrast to comparing victims and non-victims in terms of the prevalence of a specific medical problem). For example, two studies have found a higher prevalence of rape among women who are HIV-positive than among women who are not HIV positive.[161] Another study found higher rates of sexual assault (48%) among women with gynecological or breast problems than among women seeking routine care (24%).[162] A final study used data from a clinical sample of 100 women scheduled for laparoscopy.[163] Half of the women had chronic medically unexplained pelvic pain. They were compared to women referred for laparoscopy for other reasons (i.e., tubal ligation, infertility evaluation). Both child and adult sexual abuse were more common in the chronic pain group than in the comparison group.

[2] Studies With No Comparison Groups

Short-term symptoms. A few studies have examined short-term physical health symptoms among victims using non-standardized measures. For example, the physical effects documented in the immediate post-rape period have included physical trauma (e.g., general soreness and bruising), skeletal muscle tension (e.g., headaches), gastrointestinal problems (e.g., stomach pains), and genitourinary problems (e.g., vaginal discharge).[164] Percentages of victims experiencing each symptom were not reported. Norris and Feldman–Summers asked women who had been raped an average of three years previously about the symptoms that they had experienced within the 6 months following the

et al., *Impact of Sexual and Physical Abuse Dimensions on Health Status: Development of an Abuse Severity Measure*, Psychosomatic Med. 152 (1997).

156. Leserman et al. (1996), *supra* note 155.

157. Campbell & Soeken, *supra* note 67; M. P. Koss et al., *Deleterious Effects of Criminal Victimization on Women's Health and Medical Utilization*, 151 Archives of Internal Med. 342 (1991); A. Sadler et al., *Health-related Consequences of Physical and Sexual Violence: Women in the Military*, 96 Obstetrics & Gynecology 473 (2000); A. Waigandt et al., *The Impact of Sexual Assault on Physical Health Status*, 3 J. Traumatic Stress 93 (1990).

158. Campbell & Soeken, *supra* note 67; Waigandt et al., *supra* note 157.

159. Koss et al., *supra* note 157; Waigandt et al., *supra* note 157.

160. Waigandt et al., *supra* note 157.

161. R. Kimerling et al., *Victimization Experiences and HIV Infection in Women: Associations with Serostatus, Psychological Symptoms, and Health Status*, 12 J. Traumatic Stress 41 (1999); S. Zierler, et al., *Sexual Violence Against Women Living with or at Risk for HIV*, 12 Am. J. Preventive Med. 304 (1996).

162. Read et al., *Use of a Screening Instrument in Women's Health Care: Detecting Relationships Among Victimization History, Psychological Distress, and Medical Complaints*, Women & Health 1 (1997).

163. Walker et al., *Psychiatric Diagnoses and Sexual Victimization in Women with Chronic Pelvic Pain*, Psychosomatics 531 (1995).

164. A. Burgess & L. Holmstrom, *Rape Trauma Syndrome*, 131 Am. J. Psychiatry 981 (1974).

rape.[165] In regard to physical symptoms, 18% reported cystitis, 29% reported menstrual irregularity, and 40% reported headaches.

[3]　Summary

Results of these studies consistently show that women who have been sexually assaulted are at greater risk for physical health problems, including perceptions of poorer health, chronic pain, disability, and reproductive health problems, than are non-victims. In addition, women with various medical problems (e.g., women who are HIV-positive) report higher rates of sexual assault than women without those medical problems.

§ 6–2.2.7　Substance Abuse

Several studies have assessed the prevalence of alcohol and drug abuse among victims, typically in comparison to non-victims. Some use structured diagnostic interviews to assess whether victims and non-victims meet the criteria for substance abuse disorders outlined in the DSM (i.e., Substance Abuse and Substance Dependence). A key feature of these disorders is a maladaptive pattern of substance abuse leading to clinically significant impairment or distress. Other investigators compare victims and non-victims on self-report measures of alcohol and drug use.

[1]　Studies Using Comparison Groups

Short-term symptoms. Approximately four studies have compared victims and non-victims in terms of substance abuse within one year postassault. The four studies have used very different kinds of samples. In the earliest study, Frank and Anderson recruited victims from a rape crisis center.[166] There were no differences between victims and a matched comparison group in terms of previous diagnoses of alcohol or drug abuse. There also was no difference between victims and non-victims in terms of alcohol abuse after the assault. However, victims were more likely to have met the diagnostic criteria for drug abuse after the assault (28%) than were non-victims (3%). Similarly, among a sample of homeless women, when several demographic variables were controlled, victims were more likely to report a lifetime diagnosis of drug abuse/dependence and reported more current drug use but did not differ from non-victims in terms of lifetime alcohol abuse/dependence or current alcohol use.[167] Larimer et al. assessed the relations among unwanted sexual experiences and alcohol use among a sample of female sorority members on a college campus.[168] Women who had had unwanted sexual experiences scored higher than non-victims on measures of alcohol use, alcohol-related negative consequences, and symptoms of alcohol dependence. Whether the alcohol problems came before or after the assault was unclear.

Kilpatrick et al. specifically addressed this issue of the timing of substance abuse relative to sexual assaults using data from the National Women's Study, which involved phone interviews (two years apart) with a national

165. Norris & Feldman–Summers, *supra* note 82.

166. Frank & Anderson, *supra* note 52.

167. Wenzel et al., *supra* note 63.

168. Larimer et al., *supra* note 57.

household probability sample of over 4000 women.[169] They found that using drugs or drugs and alcohol was associated with increased risk of assault over a two-year time span and that having experienced an assault during the two-year time span increased the risk of alcohol and drug abuse, after controlling for the effects of age, education, race, previous assaults, and previous substance abuse. In other words, abusing drugs appeared to lead to subsequent assaults and assaults appeared to lead to drug abuse in a reciprocal relationship. Alcohol abuse, on the other hand, appeared to result from having been assaulted sexually or physically.

Long-term symptoms. More studies have assessed the prevalence of substance abuse in non-recent victims in comparison to non-victims. Two of these studies have used large representative community samples and both of them tried to assess the timing of substance abuse relative to the assault. One study found that the prevalence of alcohol abuse/dependence and substance abuse/dependence were both higher among victims than non-victims and that the onset was either at the same time as, or after, the assault.[170] The other study, which assessed forced sexual contact among both men and women, reported higher rates of alcohol and drug abuse/dependence in victims than non-victims both before and after the sexual assault.[171] However, the onset of the substance abuse diagnosis typically occurred after the sexual assault in the victim group. In a nationally representative sample of college women, Brener et al. found that a history of forced intercourse was associated with various behaviors associated with substance abuse such as driving after drinking, heavy drinking, and marijuana use.[172] The timing of those behaviors relative to the assault was not assessed. Studies that have used various nonrepresentative samples also report higher rates of substance use and abuse among victims than non-victims. These include studies in which investigators have placed advertisements for research participants who have been sexually assaulted[173] or recruited participants from women seeking help at outpatient clinics.[174] A final study found a relation between forced sex and alcohol/drug use among women at risk for HIV.[175]

[2] Studies with No Comparison Groups

Short-term symptoms. No studies were located that assessed substance abuse in recent victims without the use of a comparison group.

Long-term symptoms. Consistent with the association between sexual assault and substance abuse revealed in the above studies, Dansky et al. reported that a very high percentage (59%) of women in treatment for substance abuse had a history of completed rape.[176]

169. Kilpatrick et al., *A 2–year Longitudinal Analysis of the Relationships Between Violent Assault and Substance Abuse in Women,* 65 J. CONSULTING & CLINICAL PSYCHOL. 834 (1997).

170. Winfield et al., *supra* note 20.

171. Burnam et al., *supra* note 58.

172. Brener et al., *supra* note 71.

173. Waigandt et al., *supra* note 157.

174. Hutchings & Dutton, *supra* note 27; Hankin et al., *supra* note 62; C. Swett et al., *High Rates of Alcohol Use and History of Phys-ical and Sexual Abuse Among Women Outpatients,* 17 AM. J. DRUG & ALCOHOL ABUSE 49 (1991).

175. Zierler et al., *supra* note 161.

176. B. S. Dansky et al., *Victimization and PTSD in Individuals with Substance Use Disorders: Gender and Racial Differences,* 22 AM. J. DRUG & ALCOHOL ABUSE 75 (1996).

[3] Summary

The results of these studies very consistently indicate that victims report more substance abuse than do non-victims. This includes both alcohol and drug abuse and dependence. Studies that attempt to assess the timing of the substance abuse relative to the sexual assault generally indicate that the abuse occurred after the assault. However, in many studies, the timing of the substance abuse relative to the assault is unclear.

§ 6–2.3 Areas of Scientific Agreement and Disagreement

In this section, areas of agreement and disagreement within the scientific research on rape trauma are summarized.

§ 6–2.3.1 Areas of Agreement

On the most general level, there is considerable agreement across studies that victims report more psychological distress than do non-victims, particularly in the first year following the assault. Victims report more symptoms of PTSD, depression, fear, and anxiety; more social adjustment and health problems; and more substance abuse than do non-victims, and more symptoms of PTSD than victims of other traumatic events. In terms of prevalence, these symptoms also are common among victims of rape. For example, the majority of victims (over 90%) meet the symptom criteria for PTSD in the first two weeks post-rape. About one-half of rape victims report moderate to severe depression at one month post-rape, although when asked directly up to 80% report having been depressed following the rape. Similarly, up to 80% of victims report feeling fearful post-rape. A recent meta-analysis of research on psychological distress associated with interpersonal violence reported an effect size of .21 for the effects of rape across 38 studies. This indicates that, on average, there is a 21% increase in the prevalence of psychological distress in rape victims compared to non-victims.[177]

§ 6–2.3.2 Areas of Disagreement

There are, however, some areas of disagreement in the research literature that also need to be mentioned. First, studies that have assessed the lifetime prevalence of PTSD among rape victims report estimates varying from 4% to 80%. Part of this variability may be due to differences in how rape/sexual assault is defined. As mentioned, studies that use strict definitions of rape tend to produce higher estimates of PTSD while those that use broader definitions produce lower PTSD estimates. Given the importance of the PTSD diagnosis in legal decision-making, more research is needed on the prevalence of PTSD among rape victims using the legal definition of rape and behaviorally-specific measures.

Second, although there is agreement across studies that victims report more depressive symptoms, social adjustment problems, and health problems than do non-victims, cross-sectional and longitudinal studies tend to produce different results in terms of the duration of these differences. For example,

177. Terri L. Weaver & George A. Clum, *personal Violence: A Meta–Analysis,* 15 Clinical
Psychological Distress Associated with Inter- Psychol. Rev. 115 (1995).

although several studies have found that victims report more depressive symptoms several years post-rape than do non-victims, longitudinal studies have found that victims do not differ from non-victims past two months post-rape. Similarly, the one longitudinal study of health problems found differences between victims and non-victims only through 4 months post-rape on most measures, although numerous other studies have found higher rates of health problems in victims than in non-victims for up to several years post-rape. This may be partly because victims in longitudinal studies improve more rapidly than other victims. To address this issue, Atkeson et al.[178] compared victims who participated in one assessment with victims who completed repeated assessments and found that those in the repeated assessment group improved more quickly. It may also be the case that individuals who volunteer to participate in a research study several years post-rape are those who continue to be distressed; thus these studies of long-term effects show significant differences between victims and non-victims.

Third, although longitudinal studies of both fear and anxiety tend to show differences between victims and non-victims through one year post-rape, studies of more long-term effects are less consistent. Some studies report differences between victims and non-victims several years post-rape, whereas others do not. Research on the long-term effects of an assault on social adjustment also is mixed.

§ 6–2.4 Future Directions

In this section some current developments in the field are discussed that may have implications for the use of RTS evidence in future legal cases. These include changes in the diagnostic criteria for PTSD and the development of a new diagnostic category, as well as a new area of research emphasis.

§ 6–2.4.1 Changes in Diagnostic Categories

One important development is that the criteria for the diagnosis of PTSD have changed slightly in the fourth edition of the diagnostic manual (DSM–IV) of the American Psychiatric Association. Although the DSM–IV was published in 1994, most research published to date has not used DSM–IV criteria. The first change in the criteria is that the individual's response to the stressor event must involve "intense fear, helplessness, or horror."[179] This response was not necessary for a diagnosis of PTSD in DSM–III or DSM–III–R. In addition, although the primary symptoms of PTSD are the same, they now must "cause clinically significant distress or impairment in social, occupational, or other important areas of functioning."[180]

In addition to these two changes in the criteria for a diagnosis of PTSD, a new diagnostic category of Acute Stress Disorder (ASD) has been added in DSM–IV.[181] The primary difference between PTSD and ASD is that, to meet the criteria for ASD, symptoms have to be present for a minimum of two days and a maximum of one month and occur within one month of the traumatic event. (For a diagnosis of PTSD the symptoms have to be present for at least one month). The individual also must experience at least three dissociative

---

178. Atkeson et al., *supra* note 5.

179. APA DSM–IV, *supra* note 12, at 428.

180. *Id.* at 429.

181. APA DSM–IV, *supra* note 12.

symptoms either during or following the trauma (e.g., depersonalization), which is not a part of the diagnosis of PTSD. Although the re-experiencing, avoidance, and arousal symptoms are the same in PTSD and ASD, an individual must experience persistent re-experiencing, marked avoidance, and marked symptoms of anxiety or increased arousal to be diagnosed with ASD. In contrast, the diagnostic criteria for PTSD outline the *numbers* of symptoms that must be reported. As in PTSD, the trauma must evoke intense fear, helplessness, or horror and cause clinically significant impairment in functioning for a diagnosis of ASD.

These changes have implications both for research and for expert testimony. In regard to research, investigators must now assess whether the response to the stressor involved "intense fear, helplessness, or horror" and whether the trauma caused clinically significant impairment in order to determine whether research participants meet the criteria for the diagnosis of PTSD or ASD. These changes may make research more difficult because these features are not clearly defined and are thus harder to assess than checklists of symptoms. In addition, to assess ASD, victims must be assessed within one month of the trauma. This may be problematic because it in effect restricts the samples that can be used to recent victims who have sought help. In regard to expert testimony, to the extent that experts actually make a *diagnosis* of PTSD, these added features might make it more difficult for victims to meet the diagnostic criteria.

§ 6–2.4.2　New Areas of Research Emphasis

One area of current research that may have implications for legal proceedings is research on positive life changes following a sexual assault. This focus on positive change among rape victims reflects a general trend to examine "post-traumatic growth" among trauma survivors.[182] To date, two published studies have systematically assessed positive changes among rape victims. In a study of immediate post-rape symptoms, Frazier and Burnett found that 57% of a sample of victims reported that the rape had caused some positive change in their life.[183] These included being more cautious, appreciating life more, positive changes in relationships, and re-evaluating life and goals. Burt and Katz also reported positive changes among rape victims, including more positive feelings about themselves, positive changes in relationships, and positive changes in behaviors (e.g., becoming more politically involved).[184] This research is important because it might be argued that positive changes are inconsistent with having been raped, whereas they actually are quite common.

182. *See, e.g.*, POSTTRAUMATIC GROWTH: POSITIVE CHANGES IN THE AFTERMATH OF CRISIS (R. Tedeschi et al. eds., 1998).

183. P. Frazier & J. Burnett, *Immediate Coping Strategies Among Rape Victims*, 72 J. COUNSELING & DEV. 633 (1994).

184. Martha Burt & Bonnie Katz, *Dimensions of Recovery from Rape: Focus on Growth Outcomes*, 2 J. INTERPERSONAL VIOLENCE 57 (1987).

CHAPTER 7

CHILDREN'S MEMORY AND TESTIMONY

Table of Sections

A. LEGAL ISSUES

Westlaw Electronic Research

See Westlaw Electronic Research Guide preceding the Summary of Contents.

A.   LEGAL ISSUES

§ 7–1.0 THE LEGAL RELEVANCE OF RESEARCH ON CHILDREN'S MEMORY AND TESTIMONY

§ 7–1.1 Introduction

Perhaps more than any other area of evidence law, in prosecutions for child sexual abuse, courts explicitly contemplate the balance between the reliability or trustworthiness of the children's testimony, on the one hand, and the need for this evidence, on the other. This basic theme is repeated in a wide variety of evidentiary situations arising in these cases. Whether the child's statements occurred out of court or in court, judges struggle with the question of just how reliable this evidence is, in light of the oftentimes great need for it. Unfortunately, as § 2.0 describes, there is no simple or straightforward answer to this important empirical matter. The uncertainty surrounding children witnesses is compounded by the difficulties surrounding prosecution of child sexual abuse cases. Given the nature of the offense, there are rarely witnesses other than the victims. Also, physical evidence is often ambiguous or fails to point to any particular individual and, in many cases, it is lost through the passage of time. The child's statements, therefore, are usually the best evidence available. But it can also be the worst evidence available. The challenge confronting courts has concerned the need to maneuver this rocky shoal.[1]

The subject of children's memory and testimony arises in two distinct, though closely associated, legal contexts. First, substantial evidentiary issues arise regarding children's out of court statements that are offered in court against criminal defendants. Second, a myriad of issues are associated with in-court testimony of children, including especially the employment of experts to comment on the credibility or accuracy of children witnesses and the use of closed circuit video or similar technical devices that physically separate child witnesses from defendants. The unifying issue driving much of the law in this area involves the difficulties surrounding children as witnesses. This concern has two aspects. First, children are believed to have greater difficulty distinguishing fact from fiction and, especially among younger children, might not

---

§ 7–1.0

1. *See generally* Swan v. Peterson, 6 F.3d 1373, 1377 (9th Cir.1993) ("When the crime is child sexual abuse, one of the more difficult to detect and prosecute, a conviction hinges often on the words of children.").

appreciate the obligation to tell the truth.[2] And second, it is supposed that children are not as capable as adults in handling the rigors of testifying and that they, in particular, will suffer serious psychological damage from the experience.

Although the evidentiary reforms that are the subject of this section have been largely driven by the recognition that children are different from adults, the basic rules of competency of witnesses typically do not draw such categorical distinctions. For example, the Federal Rules treat all witnesses as competent.[3] Some state codes, however, place limitations on child witnesses or place the burden on the proponent of the evidence to demonstrate competency when the witness is below a certain age.[4] But, in general, rules of evidence are not finely crafted for the situations where children might testify. This area of the law, then, largely involves the courts' attempts to tailor the evidence rules for this special group. This typically involves a fine balancing of the needs of children against the evidentiary and constitutional protections accorded criminal defendants.[5]

§ 7–1.2 Out-of-Court Statements of Child Witnesses

§ 7–1.2.1 Introductory Background: Hearsay and the Confrontation Clause

Most evidence codes prohibit witnesses from testifying to hearsay.[6] At the same time, these codes also provide a dizzying array of exclusions and

2. On occasion, a psychological malady, such as child-abuse accommodation syndrome (CAAS) will be cited to explain the failure of a child witness to testify "truthfully." For example, in *Department of Health and Rehab. Services v. M.B.*, 701 So.2d 1155 (Fla.1997), the court found that the Florida rule that permitted prior statements of child victims also applied to inconsistent statements. Subsequent to identifying her stepfather as her abuser, the child told investigators that she could no longer identify who had abused her. Although not offered as evidence at trial, a psychologist attributed this inconsistency to CAAS. As the court explained, "[u]nder that theory, a child sexual abuse victim, whose story is distrusted by the non-offending parent ... eventually retracts the accusation in order to restore the family system to its pre-accusation status." *Id.* at 1156. We discuss the psychological effects of child abuse in more detail in Chapters 12 (Battered Child Syndrome) and 13 (Rape Trauma Syndrome).

3. Rule 601 provides as follows:

Every person is competent to be a witness except as otherwise provided in these rules. However, in civil actions and proceedings, with respect to an element of a claim or defense as to which State law supplies the rule of decision, the competency of a witness shall be determined in accordance with State law.

Fed.R.Evid. 601.

4. In *Ryan v. State*, 988 P.2d 46 (Wyo. 1999), the Wyoming Supreme Court described

a five part test that should guide a trial court's determination of the competency of a child witness. According to the court, the child must demonstrate

(1) an understanding of the obligation to speak the truth on the witness stand; (2) the mental capacity at the time of the occurrence concerning which he is to testify, to receive an accurate impression of it; (3) a memory sufficient to retain an independent recollection of the occurrence; (4) the capacity to express in words his memory of the occurrence; and (5) the capacity to understand simple questions about it.

Id. at 57. The court pointed out further that " '[i]ntelligence, not age, is the guiding criteria [sic] in determining the competency of a witness.' " *Id.* at 58 (*quoting* Baum v. State, 745 P.2d 877, 879 (Wyo.1987)).

5. Indeed, a common phenomenon in these cases is that a court will determine that a child is not competent to testify, but that his or her hearsay statements are sufficiently reliable to be admitted. *See, e.g.*, Swan v. Peterson, 6 F.3d 1373, 1378 & 1382 (9th Cir.1993) ("The trial court recognized the distinction between [the child's] ability to testify in a courtroom setting and to tell the truth at the time of the declarations. It clearly considered her incompetent only as to the former."); *see also* Gross v. Greer, 773 F.2d 116, 120 (7th Cir.1985).

6. The Federal Rules of Evidence define hearsay as follows:

(a) Statement. A "statement" is (1) an oral or written assertion or (2) nonverbal conduct

exceptions to their rule proscribing hearsay. These exclusions and exceptions are based on a combination of factors. The principal concern in this section is what the Federal Rules label exceptions, which are premised on the twin pillars of trustworthiness and special need.[7] Under the Federal Rules, for example, Rule 803 exceptions are generally considered to be particularly trustworthy. Since these statements are considered to have been made under circumstances that make them reliable, Rule 803 does not require that the declarant be shown to be unavailable. Cross-examination, it is presumed, would add little to their evidentiary value. In comparison, Rule 804 requires that the declarant be shown to be unavailable. Rule 804 exceptions are made under circumstances that also make them trustworthy, but, because they are somewhat less reliable than Rule 803 exceptions, a special need of unavailability must be present before they can be employed at trial. In Rule 804, necessity combines with trustworthiness to support admission of statements that, in a more perfect world, would have been subject to cross-examination when they were made.

In principle, a child's hearsay statements are no different than an adult's. In practice, however, children's hearsay presents special problems for the courts. Three inter-related issues recur around children's hearsay. First, many jurisdictions have enacted special exceptions that specifically control the use of children's hearsay in child sexual abuse prosecutions. Second, where special exceptions have not been promulgated, many courts turn to residual, "catch-all," exceptions to govern this evidence. Finally, third, and supplying the background against which all hearsay exceptions must be measured in the criminal context, is the Confrontation Clause of the Sixth Amendment. Because of its importance to all of the discussion that follows, we begin with the Confrontation Clause.

§ 7–1.2.2 The Confrontation Clause

The Confrontation Clause of the Sixth Amendment provides as follows: "In all criminal prosecutions, the accused shall enjoy the right ... to be confronted with the witnesses against him."[8] Despite the apparent import of these words, the Court has never taken the position that the clause prohibits

of a person, if it is intended by him as an assertion.

(b) Declarant. A "declarant" is a person who makes a statement.

(c) Hearsay. "Hearsay" is a statement, other than one made by a declarant while testifying at the trial or hearing, offered in evidence to prove the truth of the matter asserted.

Fed.R.Evid. 801.

7. The Federal Rules also have a category of hearsay exclusions, which is premised on one of two principles. The first is responsibility and the second is that the hearsay evidence is invaluable evidence that should be permitted to buttress in-court testimony. Rule 801(d)(2) incorporates the responsibility principle. Exclusions are allowed under this rule when a party's opponent offers the party's own statement (801(d)(2)(a)), one which he adopted

(801(d)(2)(b)), one which he authorized to be made or was made by his agent (801(d)(2)(C) & (D)), or a statement which was made by a coconspirator during and in furtherance of the conspiracy (801(d)(2)(D)). Rule 801(d)(1), on the other hand, illustrates the drafters' recognition that sometimes hearsay statements have independent value, at least insofar as the declarant also testifies at trial and is subject to cross-examination regarding the statement. Exclusions under this rule include prior inconsistent statements given under oath (801(d)(1)(A)), prior consistent statements that rebut a charge of recent fabrication (801(d)(1)(B)), and statements of identification made close to the time of the event (801(d)(1)(C)).

8. U.S. Const. Amend. XI.

the use of all hearsay against criminal defendants.[9] Instead, the modern Court has sought to maneuver a middle course that permits use of reliable hearsay, but which protects criminal defendants and vindicates the values implicit in the Sixth Amendment.[10] The Court has sought to define the constitutional test independently of the evidentiary standards, despite the fact that the two serve similar values. In theory, then, the Confrontation Clause "bars the admission of some evidence that would otherwise be admissible under an exception to the hearsay rule."[11] In practice, however, the two doctrines tend to track one another very closely.

In *Ohio v. Roberts*, the Court set forth "a general approach" to establishing when hearsay statements run afoul of the Confrontation Clause.[12] The Court noted, first, that the Clause reflects "the Framers' preference for face-to-face accusation." This preference means that "[i]n the usual case . . . , the prosecution must either produce, or demonstrate the unavailability of the declarant whose statement it wishes to use against the defendant."[13] Once a declarant has been shown to be unavailable, the *Roberts* Court held, it "is admissible only if it bears adequate 'indicia of reliability.' "[14] The Court noted that "[r]eliability can be inferred without more in a case where the evidence falls within a firmly rooted hearsay exception. In other cases, the evidence must be excluded, at least absent a showing of particularized guarantees of trustworthiness."[15]

In subsequent cases, however, the Court relaxed the requirement that the prosecution ordinarily must "demonstrate the unavailability of the declarant." Specifically, in several contexts in which the rules of evidence do not require unavailability, the Court has determined that the Constitution similarly does not require it. In *United States v. Inadi*,[16] for instance, the Court held that the Constitution does not require proof that a non-testifying coconspirator is unavailable before his out of court statements are admitted under the pertinent hearsay exclusion.[17] Since *Inadi*, the Court has consistently towed this line, finding that "firmly rooted" hearsay exceptions "carry

---

9. In *Bourjaily v. United States*, 483 U.S. 171, 182, 107 S.Ct. 2775, 97 L.Ed.2d 144 (1987), the Court stated that "[w]hile a literal interpretation of the Confrontation Clause could bar the use of any out-of-court statements when the declarant is unavailable, this Court has rejected that view as 'unintended and too extreme.' " *Id.* (*quoting* Ohio v. Roberts, 448 U.S. 56, 63, 100 S.Ct. 2531, 65 L.Ed.2d 597 (1980)).

10. *See* Ohio v. Roberts, 448 U.S. 56, 100 S.Ct. 2531, 65 L.Ed.2d 597 (1980).

11. Idaho v. Wright, 497 U.S. 805, 814, 110 S.Ct. 3139, 111 L.Ed.2d 638 (1990).

12. *Roberts*, 448 U.S. at 65.

13. *Id.*

14. *Id.*

15. *Id.* at 66. *See, e.g.,* State v. Anderson, 608 N.W.2d 644, 656–59 (S.D.2000) (The court allowed the "excited utterances" of a 3–year old kidnaping victim made several hours after she was released, because "she was still under

stress caused by the event."); *but see* Reed v. Thalacker, 198 F.3d 1058, 1060 (8th Cir.1999) (holding that statements made days after the event did not qualify as excited utterances).

16. 475 U.S. 387, 106 S.Ct. 1121, 89 L.Ed.2d 390 (1986).

17. *Id.* at 394–400. Although the Court has found symmetry between the Constitution and the evidence rule that excludes coconspirator statements from the hearsay rule, it appears that the underlying principles supporting the two differ. The Court observed that the basis for relying on the coconspirator exception lay in the fact that it was a "firmly rooted" exception. Therefore, according to the Court, sufficient "indicia of reliability" could be assumed. However, the coconspirator exception, though surely firmly rooted, is not primarily based on "reliability." Instead, it is based, as are the other exclusions in Rule 801(d)(2), on a theory of responsibility. Like statements made by agents, coconspirators are presumed to be *responsible* for statements made by their partners in crime.

sufficient indicia of reliability to satisfy the reliability posed by the Confrontation Clause."[18] *Inadi* initiated a trend in the modern Court's Confrontation Clause jurisprudence in which the constitutional requirements of confrontation closely resemble the dictates of the Federal Rules of Evidence.

In *White v. Illinois*,[19] for example, the Court held that the prosecution did not have to demonstrate the unavailability of the four-year-old victim of a sexual assault, because her statements fell within the hearsay exceptions for spontaneous declarations and statements made for the purpose of a medical examination. The Court noted that statements that are offered under these "firmly rooted" exceptions are especially trustworthy. Spontaneous declarations can be relied upon because they are made without reflection and thus with no time to manufacture a falsehood.[20] Similarly, statements made pursuant to medical treatment carry guarantees of reliability since medical care depends on them.[21] Moreover, the Court asserted, statements that fall within "firmly rooted" hearsay exceptions are "so trustworthy that adversarial testing can be expected to add little to its reliability."[22] As the *White* court made clear, the values underlying the Confrontation Clause and the Federal Rules were similar. Although the Court regularly insisted that the two are not coterminous, it was clear by *White* that they were very close.

The places at which the Constitution and the Federal Rules should most likely part company are where the exceptions are not "firmly rooted." In the

---

18   White v. Illinois, 502 U.S. 346, 355 n. 8, 112 S.Ct. 736, 116 L.Ed.2d 848 (1992).

19.   *Id.*

20.   *Id.* at 355.

21.   *Id.* at 356 ("[A] statement made in the course of procuring medical services, where the declarant knows that a false statement may cause misdiagnosis or mistreatment, carries special guarantees of credibility.").

An issue that arises repeatedly when the medical services exception to the hearsay rule is used in child sexual abuse cases concerns whether statements regarding the identity of the perpetrator are admissible. The better approach requires that the identity of the perpetrator must be " 'reasonably pertinent' to the victim's proper treatment." United States v. Joe, 8 F.3d 1488, 1495 (10th Cir.1993). The court in *Joe* explained what this means in the domestic violence context as follows:

> All victims of domestic sexual abuse suffer emotional and psychological injuries, the exact nature and extent of which depend on the identity of the abuser. The physician generally must know who the abuser was in order to render proper treatment because the physician's treatment will necessarily differ when the abuser is a member of the victim's family or household. In the domestic sexual abuse case, for example, the treating physician may recommend special therapy or counseling and instruct the victim to remove herself from the dangerous environment by

leaving the home and seeking shelter elsewhere.

Id. at 1494–95 (footnote omitted) (quoted in United States v. Tome, 61 F.3d 1446, 1450 (10th Cir.1995) (extending the analysis to cases "in which the victim is a child")); *see also* United States v. Cherry, 938 F.2d 748, 757 (7th Cir.1991) ("[T]he task of the physician treating the victim of such an attack requires attention not only to the physical manifestations of trauma but to the psychological ones as well.").

22.   *Id.* at 357. Many courts do not uncritically accept the Supreme Court's diminished view of cross-examination even in the presence of a firmly rooted hearsay exception. For example, the Ohio Supreme Court found this argument "not obvious" to "many who have litigated such cases." The Ohio Court explained as follows:

> A common practice in prosecution of child abuse cases is to take the child to a medical practitioner, at least in part to obtain evidence for purposes of subsequent prosecution. In certain circumstances, the interaction between the child and physician borders on detective-witness....
>
> Cross-examination of a child making a statement to a physician could in fact enlighten the trier of fact in many circumstances.... Knowing why the child made the statement and the circumstances surrounding the giving of the statement could be extremely important and would in most circumstances assist the trier of fact.

area of children's hearsay, there are two contexts, in particular, in which the statements fall outside firmly rooted hearsay exceptions, but jurisdictions have sought to use them against criminal defendants. The first concerns the residual exception to the hearsay rule, and the second involves rules promulgated to apply specifically to children's hearsay.

§ 7–1.2.3 The Residual Exception to the Hearsay Rule

Most evidence codes include a "catch-all" provision, commonly referred to as a residual exception, for statements not covered by a specific exception to the hearsay rule, but which have "equivalent circumstantial guarantees of trustworthiness" and for which there is special need.[23] There are two aspects of residual exceptions worthy of attention. The first concerns their evidentiary usefulness[24] and, the second, their constitutionality under the Confrontation Clause. As the following discussion makes clear, these two aspects are not easily separated, since constitutionality largely depends on the same values that underlie the evidence rules. We begin, therefore, with the Confrontation Clause, but will consider below several purely evidentiary matters.

The Supreme Court had occasion to consider the constitutionality of admitting certain kinds of evidence under residual provisions in child sexual abuse cases in *Idaho v. Wright*.[25] At trial, the court had admitted statements that a three-year-old victim of sexual abuse had made to an examining physician. The statements did not fit within the medical treatment exception. Further, following a *voir dire* examination, the court determined that the child was "not capable of communicating to the jury."[26] The trial court admitted the doctor's testimony regarding the child's statements under the state's residual exception.[27] On appeal, the Supreme Court of Idaho reversed, finding that the admission of the child's out-of-court statements violated the Confrontation Clause.[28] The Supreme Court affirmed this reversal.

The Court began by noting that the first consideration presented by

---

Storch, 612 N.E.2d at 313.

23. The residual exception of the Federal Rules of Evidence provides as follows:

A statement not specifically covered by Rule 803 or 804 but having equivalent circumstantial guarantees of trustworthiness, is not excluded by the hearsay rule, if the court determines that (A) the statement is offered as evidence of a material fact; (B) the statement is more probative on the point for which it is offered than any other evidence which the proponent can procure through reasonable efforts; and (C) the general purposes of these rules and the interests of justice will best be served by admission of the statement into evidence. However, a statement may not be admitted under this exception unless the proponent of it makes known to the adverse party sufficiently in advance of the trial or hearing to provide the adverse party with a fair opportunity to prepare to meet it, the proponent's intention to offer the statement and the particulars of it,

including the name and address of the declarant.

FED. R. EVID. 807. *See generally* United States v. Grooms, 978 F.2d 425, 427–28 (8th Cir.1992).

24. It is worth emphasizing at the outset of this discussion that "[c]ourts must use caution when admitting evidence under [the residual exception], for an expansive interpretation of [it] would threaten to swallow the entirety of the hearsay rule." *Tome*, 61 F.3d at 1452.

25. 497 U.S. at 816.

26. *Id.* at 809.

27. *Id.* at 812 (*citing* Idaho Rule Evid. 803(24)).

28. 116 Idaho 382, 775 P.2d 1224 (Idaho 1989). It is worth noting that the Idaho Supreme Court rejected the claim, arising in a companion case, that the trial court had erred in admitting the evidence under the residual exception. State v. Giles, 115 Idaho 984, 772 P.2d 191 (Idaho 1989). Given the court's conclusion, then, the evidentiary rule in Idaho is more permissive than the U.S. Constitution.

Roberts, unavailability of the declarant, was not at issue in *Wright*.[29] Defense counsel accepted the trial court's determination that the three-year-old was incapable of communicating with the jury. The Court thus assumed, without deciding, that the unavailability requirement was satisfied, and focused its attention on the "indicia of reliability" of the statement. However, since the statements had been admitted under the residual exception, it did not benefit from the presumption of trustworthiness that is associated with "firmly rooted" hearsay exceptions. As a result, the statements were " 'presumptively unreliable and inadmissible for Confrontation Clause purposes.' "[30] Consequently, they " 'must be excluded, at least absent a showing of particularized guarantees of trustworthiness.' "[31]

The tricky aspect of the Confrontation Clause analysis lay in the evaluation of whether certain hearsay possesses "particularized guarantees of trustworthiness." The Idaho Supreme Court had been especially troubled by the doctor's failure to follow procedural safeguards when interviewing the young child.[32] The Court, however, held that while possibly of some benefit, the Sixth Amendment imposed no rigorous requirement to follow a set of procedural guidelines in these cases. Instead, the Court held, " 'particularized guarantees of trustworthiness' must be shown from the totality of the circumstances."[33] The Court noted that it offered no "mechanical test" by which to measure trustworthiness, though it suggested that factors such as spontaneity, motive to lie and age-inappropriate use of language might be considered.[34]

---

29. In *State v. Castaneda*, 621 N.W.2d 435 (Iowa 2001), the court examined the unavailability requirement of the residual exception for out of court statements made by child witnesses. It referred to this unavailability as "psychological unavailability." *Id.* at 447. It observed that the United States Supreme Court had not set specific requirements for this unavailability, but thought that, "given the serious constitutional implication of the potential loss of a fundamental right, that the standard must necessarily be high." *Id.* At the same time, the court stated, "one cannot dispute that it is extremely difficult to accurately predict a person's response to psychological trauma." *Id.* "Therefore," the court concluded, "while we must closely guard a defendant's rights, we must carefully balance those rights against the real potential for harm to tender, and as yet not fully developed, psyches." *Id.* The *Castaneda* court adopted the standard set forth in *People v. Gomez*, 26 Cal.App.3d 225, 103 Cal.Rptr. 80, 83–84 (1972), that "psychological unavailability must exist to such a degree as to render the witness' attendance, or his testifying, relatively impossible and not merely inconvenient." And borrowing from *Warren v. United States*, 436 A.2d 821, 830n.18 (D.C.Ct.App.1981), the *Castaneda* court held that trial courts should examine four factors when determining "psychological unavailability." These include

(1) the probability of psychological injury as a result of testifying, (2) the degree of anticipated injury, (3) the expected duration of the injury, and (4) whether the expected psycho-

logical injury is substantially greater than the reaction of the average victim of a rape, kidnaping or terrorist act . . . The factors should be weighed in the context of each other, as well as in the context of the nature of the crime and the pre-existing psychological history of the witness.

Castaneda, 621 N.W.2d at 447 (*quoting Warren*, 436 A.2d at 830n.18 (1981)). *See also* J.L.W.W. v. Clarke Cty. Dept. of Hum. Serv., 759 So.2d 1183, 1186 (Miss 2000) (Under Mississippi's tender years exception to the hearsay rule, "[the chancellor] must require evidence and determine whether the children would be traumatized by having to testify in front of their parents, that the trauma would be more than mere nervousness, and that there are not other means of testifying that would eliminate that trauma.").

30. *Wright*, 497 U.S. at 818 (*quoting* Lee v. Illinois, 476 U.S. 530, 106 S.Ct. 2056, 90 L.Ed.2d 514 (1986)).

31. *Id.* (*quoting Roberts*, 448 U.S. at 66).

32. *Id.*

33. *Id.* at 819.

34. *See infra* note 47, in which the Ohio Rule permitting child hearsay statements, and which is largely modeled on *Wright*, suggests a longer list of factors that courts might consider when determining trustworthiness. The Florida Supreme Court offered this useful non-exclusive list of factors:

[A] consideration of the statement's spontaneity; whether the statement was made at

A persistent concern regarding trustworthiness in these cases involves the influence adult questioners might have on the children.[35] In the past, authorities have not been particularly attentive to the sensitivity of child victims and, in particular, their predilection for providing answers that investigators expect to hear. The several sensational cases in which child witnesses were apparently manipulated into making detailed accusations, however, have had a sobering influence. Courts today regularly identify interview tactics as a source of possible error.

The most important holding of *Wright*, and the point of greatest disagreement between the majority and the four dissenting Justices, was the conclusion that "corroborating evidence" could not be used to support the trustworthiness of hearsay for Confrontation Clause purposes. As the Court explained, "the use of corroborating evidence to support a hearsay statement's 'particularized guarantees of trustworthiness' would permit admission of a presumptively unreliable statement by bootstrapping on the trustworthiness of other evidence at trial."[36] This result would be "at odds with the requirement that hearsay evidence admitted under the Confrontation Clause be so trustworthy that cross-examination of the declarant would be of marginal utility."[37] The Court concluded, "[t]o be admissible under the Confrontation Clause, hearsay evidence used to convict a defendant must possess indicia of reliability by virtue of its inherent trustworthiness, not by reference to other evidence at trial."[38]

As noted above, a persistent question in this area concerns what standards distinguish the hearsay exceptions from the requirements of the Confrontation Clause. Both require a showing of some special need together with particularized guarantees of trustworthiness. The Court has long insisted that the evidence rules and the Constitution are not coterminous. "[W]ere we to agree that the admission of hearsay statements under the residual exception

the first available opportunity following the alleged incident; whether the statement was elicited in response to questions from adults; the mental state of the child when the abuse was reported; whether the statement consisted of a child-like description of the act; whether the child used terminology unexpected of a child of similar age; the motive or lack thereof to fabricate the statement; the ability of the child to distinguish between reality and fantasy; the vagueness of the accusations; the possibility of any improper influence on the child by participants involved in a domestic dispute; and contradictions in the accusation. State v. Townsend, 635 So.2d 949, 957–58 (Fla. 1994).

35. *See, e.g.*, Quimby v. State, 604 So.2d 741, 743 (Miss.1992) (Although "loath to reverse," the court found error in the admission of a child's answers to the over-zealous questioning of a police detective.).

36. *Wright*, 497 U.S. at 822. Justice Kennedy strenuously disagreed with the Court's view of corroborating evidence. Joined by Chief Justice Rehnquist, and Justices White and Blackmun, Justice Kennedy argued as follows:

I see no constitutional justification for this decision to prescind corroborating evidence from consideration of the question whether a child's statements are reliable. It is a matter of common sense for most people that one of the best ways to determine whether what someone says is trustworthy is to see if it is corroborated by other evidence.... [W]hatever doubt the Court has with the weight to be given the corroborating evidence found in this case is no justification for rejecting the considered wisdom of virtually the entire legal community that corroborating evidence is relevant to reliability and trustworthiness.

37. *Id.*

38. *Id. See, e.g., Swan*, 6 F.3d at 1380 (Court held that it was "impermissible bootstrapping" to reference "other evidence in finding cross-corroboration of each child's statements."). In an apparent violation of *Wright*, the court in *In re Katherine S.*, 271 A.D.2d 538, 705 N.Y.S.2d 670 (App.Div.2000), upheld the admission of two children's out of court statements because they were corroborated by "their in-court testimony and the medical evidence." *Id.* at 671.

automatically passed Confrontation Clause scrutiny, virtually every codified hearsay exception would assume constitutional stature, a step this Court has repeatedly declined to take."[39] One significant difference is that the Constitution does not permit reliance on corroborating evidence to support reliability. This is an important lesson explicitly contemplated in *Wright.*

A second difference between evidence rules and constitutional guarantees, though one only implicitly maintained in *Wright,* is the standard of appellate review. The ordinary standard for evidentiary determinations is the very deferential abuse of discretion standard. Because the preliminary factual determination under the Confrontation Clause has constitutional import, appellate courts are likely to be less deferential to trial courts. Still, appellate courts reviewing these constitutional facts are likely to remain somewhat deferential, since the lower courts are better able to assess credibility of the witnesses before them. In practice, the standard is probably akin to a "hard look," rather than the somewhat more rigorous *de novo* standard.[40] This hard-look standard appears to be roughly what the Court applied in *Wright.* The Court affirmed the factual findings of the Idaho Supreme Court after closely reviewing the premises upon which it stood. The Court did not remand for consideration of this preliminary factual determination, as might have been expected if they were applying an abuse of discretion standard. Instead, they effectively "found" these constitutional facts on appeal.

§ 7–1.2.4 Hearsay Exceptions for Child Statements in Abuse Cases

The various exceptions to the hearsay rule apply in the same way to all out of court statements, whether made by child or adult.[41] Some trial courts appear to read the requirements for exceptions to the hearsay rule more liberally when a child was the declarant. Appellate courts, however, have resisted a loosening of standards, and do not differentiate—positively or negatively—between children and adult declarants. In *United States v. Sumner,*[42] for example, the Eighth Circuit held that the admission of a child victim's statements made to a clinical psychologist did not meet the requirements for the exception for statements made for the purpose of obtaining medical treatment.[43] The court explained that the statements did not meet the rule's requirements because the doctor "did not discuss with [the victim] the need for truthful revelations or emphasize that the identification of her abuser was important to [the doctor's] attempts to help her overcome any emotional trauma resulting from the abuse to which she had been subjected."[44] Many other appellate courts have similarly enforced the rules evenly as between children and adult declarants.[45]

In addition to relying on the traditional hearsay exceptions, states have increasingly adopted specific hearsay exceptions that apply to children's statements in abuse cases.[46] In effect, these statutes codify the practice that

39. *Wright,* 497 U.S. at 817–818.

40. *See id.* at 825–27.

41. *See* FED.R.EVID. 803 & 804.

42. 204 F.3d 1182 (8th Cir.2000).

43. *Id.* at 1185 (*citing* FED.R.EVID. 803(4)).

44. *Id.*

45. *See, e.g.,* State v. Waddell, 351 N.C. 413, 527 S.E.2d 644, 648 (N.C.2000) (Rule 803(4)); State v. Hinnant, 351 N.C. 277, 523 S.E.2d 663, 671–72 (N.C.2000) (Rule 803(4)).

46. In *Department of Health and Rehab. Services v. M.B.,* 701 So.2d 1155, 1157–58 (Fla. 1997), the Florida Supreme Court interpreted

had developed pursuant to state residual exceptions, discussed *infra*. These provisions generally track the language of the Court's Confrontation Clause cases and present few serious constitutional concerns.[47] They place the burden on the state to show both need and particular guarantees of trustworthiness. They also do not permit the use of other evidence to corroborate the child's statements. However, to the extent that they fail to follow the Court's Sixth Amendment analysis, they are vulnerable to attack or are likely to be interpreted in accordance with that case law.[48]

the state's rule permitting statements of child victims to encompass prior inconsistent statements as well.

47. A good example of this type is Ohio Rule 807. It is clearly modeled on the Court's recent Confrontation Clause cases. It provides as follows:

Rule 807. Hearsay Exceptions; Child Statements in Abuse Cases

(A) An out-of-court statement made by a child who is under twelve years of age at the time of trial or hearing describing any sexual act performed by, with, or on the child or describing any act of physical violence directed against the child is not excluded as hearsay under Evid.R. 802 if all of the following apply:

(1) The court finds that the totality of the circumstances surrounding the making of the statement provides particularized guarantees of trustworthiness that make the statement at least as reliable as statements admitted pursuant to Evid.R. 803 and 804. The circumstances must establish that the child was particularly likely to be telling the truth when the statement was made and that the test of cross-examination would add little to the reliability of the statement. In making its determination of the reliability of the statement, the court shall consider all of the circumstances surrounding the making of the statement, including but not limited to spontaneity, the internal consistency of the statement, the mental state of the child, the child's motive or lack of motive to fabricate, the child's use of terminology unexpected of a child of similar age, the means by which the statement was elicited, and the lapse of time between the act and the statement. In making this determination, the court shall not consider whether there is independent proof of the sexual act or act of physical violence.

(2) The child's testimony is not reasonably obtainable by the proponent of the statement.

(3) There is independent proof of the sexual act or act of physical violence.

(4) At least ten days before the trial or hearing, a proponent of the statement has notified all other parties in writing of the content of the statement, the time and place at which the statement was made, the identity of the witness who is to testify about the statement, and the circumstances surrounding the statements that are claimed to indicate its trustworthiness.

(B) The child's testimony is "not reasonably obtainable by the proponent of the statement" under division (A)(2) of this rule only if one or more of the following apply:

(1) The child refuses to testify concerning the subject matter or claims a lack of memory of the subject matter of the statement after a person trusted by the child, in the presence of the court, urges the child to both describe the acts described by the statement and to testify.

(2) The court finds all of the following:

(a) the child is absent from the trial or hearing;

(b) the proponent of the statement has been unable to procure the child's attendance or testimony by process or other reasonable means despite a good faith effort to do so;

(c) it is probable that the proponent would be unable to procure the child's testimony or attendance if the trial or hearing were delayed for a reasonable time.

(3) The court finds both of the following:

(a) the child is unable to testify at the trial or hearing because of death or then existing physical or mental illness or infirmity;

(b) the illness or infirmity would not improve sufficiently to permit the child to testify if the trial or hearing were delayed for a reasonable time. The proponent of the statement has not established that the child's testimony or attendance is not reasonably obtainable if the child's refusal, claim of lack of memory, inability, or absence is due to the procurement or wrongdoing of the proponent of the statement for the purpose of preventing the child from attending or testifying.

(C) The court shall make the findings required by this rule on the basis of a hearing conducted outside the presence of the jury and shall make findings of fact, on the record, as to the bases for its ruling.

48. The Florida exception for statements of child victims, for instance, states that "[u]nless the source of information or the method or circumstances by which the statement is re-

Statutory requirements and constitutional mandates are often inextricably interwoven in this area. In *Ex Parte R.D.W.*,[49] for example, the defendant was convicted of first-degree sexual abuse. On appeal, he argued that the trial court's failure to instruct the jury that the alleged victim's out-of-court statements were obtained without his being afforded the opportunity to cross-examine her violated his right to confrontation.[50] The Alabama Supreme Court agreed. The court found that the lower court's failure, first of all, violated the plain words of a statute that required such a jury instruction.[51] Moreover, the court held, the failure to give the jury instruction "probably injuriously affected [defendant's] substantial rights of confrontation and cross-examination."[52]

§ 7–1.3 "In–Court" Testimony of Child Witnesses

Children, especially young children, do not always make ideal witnesses. They are prone to be traumatized by their surroundings and mesmerized by the proceedings. They might have difficulty understanding the questions they are asked, and courts sometimes have difficulty understanding the answers they provide. Younger children do not always fully appreciate the gravity of the proceedings or the need to be entirely truthful in their responses. The child's world also sometimes appears to veer seamlessly between reality and fantasy. Not surprisingly, then, the courts have had to face a panoply of issues when children are the principal witnesses for the prosecution.

§ 7–1.3.1 The "Opportunity" to Confront Children Witnesses

The Rules of Evidence and the Confrontation Clause do not guarantee defendants the right to an "effective" cross-examination, only the "opportunity" to cross-examine their accusers. In *United States v. Owens*,[53] the Supreme Court held that the Confrontation Clause was not violated by the government's use of "a prior, out-of-court identification when the identifying witness is unable, because of memory loss, to explain the basis for the identification."[54] At trial, the government had introduced the testimony of the victim, a correctional counselor at a federal prison, who had been brutally beaten with a metal pipe. At his first interview in the hospital with an F.B.I. agent, the witness could not recall any of the details of the attack. At a second hospital interview, however, he identified the defendant as his attacker from an array of photographs. At trial, he could no longer remember the details of the attack

---

ported indicates a lack of trustworthiness, an out-of-court statement made by a child victim with a physical, mental, emotional, or developmental age of 11 or less describing any act of child abuse or neglect, ... [that is] not otherwise admissible, is admissible in evidence in any civil or criminal proceeding" if certain conditions are met. FLORIDA STATUTES, § 90.803(23). To the extent that this language appears to place the burden of proof regarding trustworthiness on the criminal defendant, it probably violates the Confrontation Clause. *See Tome*, 61 F.3d at 1453 (Under *Wright*, "we must find that [the child] 'was particularly likely to be telling the truth when the statement was made.' It is not enough merely to find an absence of evidence that the statement

was unreliable.") (quoting *Wright*, 497 U.S. at 822)).

49. 773 So.2d 426 (Ala.2000).

50. *Id.* at 427–28.

51. *Id.* at 428 (The statute, ALA. CODE 1975, § 15–25–36, provided that "[t]he court shall inform the jury that the out-of-court statement was taken without the defendant being afforded cross examination of such out-of-court statement.").

52. *Id.* at 430 (internal quotation marks omitted).

53. 484 U.S. 554, 108 S.Ct. 838, 98 L.Ed.2d 951 (1988).

54. *Id.* at 555.

or identify his attacker. He did clearly recall identifying the defendant during the second interview, and at trial he testified to that earlier identification.

The *Owens* Court, with Justice Scalia writing, found no constitutional error in the trial court's admission of the hospital-room identification. The Court began by pointing out the limits of the Sixth Amendment right: " '[T]he Confrontation Clause guarantees only an opportunity for effective cross-examination, not cross-examination that is effective in whatever way, and to whatever extent, the defense might wish.' "[55] The Court explained that cross-examination permits the opponent to demonstrate such things as "the witness' bias, his lack of care and attentiveness, his poor eyesight, and even (what is often a prime objective of cross-examination) the very fact that he has a bad memory."[56] For the Court, there was no difference between a witness' contemporary identification and expression of no memory (i.e., "I believe this to be the man who assaulted me, but can't remember why"), and a witness' statement of previous identification and expression of no memory (i.e., "I don't know whether this is the man who assaulted me, but I told the police I believed so earlier").[57]

One obvious difference, recognized by the Court, is that the latter is hearsay. Justice Scalia, however, summarily dismissed this point, finding no need to discover, as the lower appellate court thought it needed to find, adequate indicia of reliability to support the statement under traditional Confrontation Clause analysis.[58] When "the hearsay declarant is present at trial and subject to unrestricted cross-examination," the Court explained, "the traditional protections of the oath, cross-examination, and opportunity for the jury to observe the witness' demeanor satisfy the constitutional requirements."[59] Finally, the *Owens* Court also held that the prior identification was admissible under the Federal Rule that excludes from the hearsay rule prior statements " 'of identification of a person made after perceiving the person,' if the declarant 'testifies at the trial or hearing and is subject to cross-examination concerning the statement.' "[60] The Court reached the conclusion that the witness was "subject to cross-examination" despite the fact that he would have been deemed "unavailable" under the Rules due to his "memory loss."[61]

In light of the variability among child witnesses, it is not unusual to find analogous cases to *Owens* in child sexual abuse prosecutions. In *Walters v. McCormick*,[62] for instance, the defendant claimed that permitting the child-victim's wildly vacillating testimony and her inability to appreciate the duty to testify truthfully, denied him the right to confront witnesses.[63] The court recognized the fact that the child "was not an ideal witness."[64] The court observed in this regard as follows:

55. *Id.* at 559 (*quoting* Kentucky v. Stincer, 482 U.S. 730, 739, 107 S.Ct. 2658, 96 L.Ed.2d 631 (1987)) (internal quotation marks omitted).

56. *Id.* (internal citation omitted).

57. *Id.*

58. *Id.* at 560.

59. *Id. See also* State v. Clark, 139 Wash.2d 152, 985 P.2d 377, 381 (Wash.1999) ("Under *Owens* and *Green* the admission of hearsay statements will not violate the confrontation clause if the hearsay declarant is a witness at trial, is asked about the event and the hearsay statement, and the defendant is provided an opportunity for full cross-examination.").

60. *Owens,* 484 U.S. at 561 (*quoting* FED. R.EVID. 801(d)(1)(C)).

61. *Id.*

62. 122 F.3d 1172 (9th Cir.1997).

63. *Id.* at 1175.

64. *Id.*

Her descriptions of events varied, depending primarily on who was questioning her. She testified both that [the defendant] had molested her, and that her mother had invented the story. She testified that God smiles when you tell the truth, but that sometimes he wants you to lie.[65]

The court also accepted the fact that this less-than-ideal witness did not have the capacity "to understand the duty to testify truthfully."[66]

The court concluded that neither the huge inconsistencies in the child's testimony nor her inability to appreciate the duty to tell the truth constituted a constitutional violation. As it explained, " 'the Confrontation Clause is generally satisfied when the defense is given a full and fair opportunity to probe and expose these infirmities through cross-examination.' "[67] The defendant had that opportunity. Moreover, the court emphasized, the right to confrontation is not absolute: "Even the right to confront one's accuser face-to-face may 'give way to considerations of public policy and the necessities of the case' where the testimony of a young child abuse victim is concerned."[68] Because the defendant had the opportunity to make the jury aware of the child's failings, admission of her testimony did not violate the Sixth Amendment.[69]

§ 7–1.3.2   Expert Testimony Buttressing the "Credibility" of Child Witnesses

Given the concerns associated with the reliability of child witness testimony, it is not surprising to find that both proponents and opponents of this evidence seek to introduce experts who might offer opinions regarding its trustworthiness. More surprising is just how complex courts have made this issue. The first issue courts usually confront is the matter of whether the expert intends to attack or support credibility. A second, and closely related concern, involves the import of the expert's testimony. Specifically, some experts seek to comment on a witness' specific testimony, some on the witness' background and some on the credibility of witnesses with similar backgrounds. Expert testimony regarding credibility, then, primarily comprises these two issues, the identity of the sponsor of the expert (opponent or proponent of the child's testimony), and the level of generality (particular to the testimony, particular to the witness, or general).[70] This section examines these two issues.

65. *Id.*

66. *Id.*

67. *Id.*

68. *Id.* at 1176 (*quoting* Maryland v. Craig, 497 U.S. 836, 849, 110 S.Ct. 3157, 111 L.Ed.2d 666 (1990)).

69. *Id.* The court also found that admission of the child's testimony did not violate the defendant's right to due process. *Id.* at 1176–77.

70. A third concern sometimes identified in the case law involves whether admissibility of expert testimony on credibility should turn on the distinction between truth-telling and fantasizing. For example, in *State v. Heath*, 316 N.C. 337, 341 S.E.2d 565 (N.C.1986), the North

Carolina Supreme Court distinguished between "lying" and "fantasizing," with the latter involving moral considerations and the latter nonmoral considerations. *Id.* at 568. The court observed as follows:

> It is one thing to ask an expert in psychology or psychiatry whether a victim fantasizes, but it is another thing altogether to ask whether a witness has made up a story or lied. One who fantasizes can honestly and subjectively believe in the reality of the fantasized-about occurrence, but "making up a story," or lying, denotes an affirmative or conscious intent to deceive, invent, or not tell the truth.

Id. Other courts, including lower courts in North Carolina, have ignored this distinction

[1] Attacking and Supporting Credibility

Courts generally state that expert testimony cannot be introduced for the purpose of attacking or supporting the credibility of a witness. Credibility assessments, pursuant to this general statement, are for the jury to make.[71] However, the reality is rather more complicated. Rule 608 of the Federal Rules of Evidence permits testimony regarding credibility under certain circumstances. Rule 608(a) permits the use of opinion or reputation evidence so long as it is limited to "character for truthfulness or untruthfulness" of the witness, but evidence of truthful character is allowed only after the witness' credibility has been attacked by the opponent.[72] Rule 608(b) allows the use of specific instances of conduct, if probative of truthfulness, to be inquired into only upon cross-examination.[73] They cannot be proved by extrinsic evidence.[74] Under Rule 608, therefore, expert testimony, as extrinsic evidence, is not permitted regarding specific instances of conduct. Therefore, under that rule's provisions, experts can testify for the opponent in order to attack credibility of a witness, but can testify for the proponent only when the other side has "opened the door" to the question of the witness' character for truthfulness.[75]

Rule 608(b) specifically includes "opinion" as a source of support or attack on a witness' credibility. This implies that expert opinion might fit within the rule. In fact, the commentary to a closely analogous rule, Rule 405, indicates that the drafters intended to include expert opinion in these contexts:

> Traditionally character has been regarded primarily in moral overtones of good and bad: chaste, peaceable, truthful, honest. Nevertheless, on occasion nonmoral considerations crop up, as in the case of the incompetent

between lying and fantasy. *See* Schutz v. State, 957 S.W.2d 52, 64 (Tex.Crim.App.1997), on remand, 998 S.W.2d 903 (Tex.App.2000), reversed, ___ S.W.2d ___, 2001 WL 1623303 (Tex. Crim.App.2001). In *United States v. Wertis*, 505 F.2d 683 (5th Cir.1974), the court summed up the value of distinguishing lying and fantasy: "Peeled of its thin veneer of jargon, it amounts to no more than an inquiry whether the witness is to be believed by the jury or not." *Id.* at 685.

71. *See* Washington v. Schriver, 90 F.Supp.2d 384, 389 (S.D.N.Y.2000) (excluding expert testimony on the "suggestibility" of children); *Schutz*, 957 S.W.2d at 68. ("[T]he credibility of witness' or declarant's allegations has generally been considered an issue within the exclusive province of the jury.").

72. Rule 608(a) provides as follows:

(a) Opinion and reputation evidence of character. The credibility of a witness may be attacked or supported by evidence in the form of opinion or reputation, but subject to these limitations: (1) the evidence may refer only to character for truthfulness or untruthfulness, and (2) evidence of truthful character is admissible only after the character of the witness for truthfulness has been attacked by opinion or reputation evidence or otherwise.

FED.R.EVID. 608(a).

73. Rule 608(b) provides, in pertinent part, as follows:

(b) Specific instances of conduct. Specific instances of the conduct of a witness, for the purpose of attacking or supporting his credibility, other than conviction of crime as provided in rule 609, may not be proved by extrinsic evidence. They may, however, in the discretion of the court, if probative of truthfulness, be inquired into on cross-examination of the witness (1) concerning his character for truthfulness or untruthfulness, or (2) concerning the character for truthfulness or untruthfulness of another witness as to which character the witness being cross-examined has testified.

FED.R.EVID. 608(b).

74. Extrinsic evidence is allowed when the specific instances of conduct constituted a crime, as provided by Rule 609. FED.R.EVID. 609.

75. Two key questions, then, are when has the opponent opened the door and, if the door has not been opened, does the proponent's expert evidence comment on "credibility" specifically, or some other matter allowable outside Rule 608? *See infra* §§ 14–1.3.1[2] & [3]. *See* Metzger v. State, 4 P.3d 901 (Wyo.2000).

driver, and this is bound to happen increasingly. If character is defined as the kind of person one is, the account must be taken at varying ways of arriving at the estimate. These may range from the opinion of the employer who has found the man honest to the opinion of a psychiatrist based upon examination and testing. No effective dividing line exists between character and mental capacity, and the latter has traditionally been provable by opinion.[76]

This commentary has been related specifically to the opinion provision of Rule 608(a).[77] Some courts, accordingly, have permitted expert opinion regarding capacity when it might shed light on the witness' truthfulness.[78] Most courts, however, severely restrict the use of expert testimony regarding a specific witness' credibility. As regards capacity, most courts consider this a preliminary matter of competency of the witness to testify, rather than whether some specific testimony is to be believed.[79] Nonetheless, as the next section makes clear, this has not resulted in the wholesale exclusion of experts on credibility, it has only affected the scope of what they might comment upon.

[2] Limiting the Scope of Expert Testimony Regarding Credibility

As regards whether a child witness is telling the truth, expert testimony on this matter might come in a variety of forms. An expert might offer to testify on the specific statements of the witness, the witness' general proclivity for telling the truth, or children who are similarly situated to the witness, so that the fact finder might draw inferences regarding the reliability of the child's statements.

Courts nearly uniformly prohibit experts (or any witness) from offering an opinion regarding the trustworthiness of a witness' specific allegations.[80] In *State v. Lindsey*,[81] for instance, the court stated summarily that "experts should not be allowed to give their opinion of the accuracy, reliability, or credibility of a particular witness in the case being tried."[82] Experts are proscribed from commenting on the accuracy of a witness' testimony primari-

---

76. Notes of Advisory Committee, Fed. R.Evid. 405.

77. *See* United States v. Shay, 57 F.3d 126, 131 (1st Cir.1995).

78. *See id.* at 132 (allowing expert testimony on whether defendant suffered a mental disorder that would lead him to make false statements against his interest); United States v. Butt, 955 F.2d 77, 82–84 (1st Cir.1992) (relevance of mental disorder to truthfulness); United States v. Hall, 93 F.3d 1337, 1344 (7th Cir.1996) (same); United States v. Smith, 77 F.3d 511, 516 (D.C.Cir.1996) (same); *but see* United States v. Lindstrom, 698 F.2d 1154, 1162 n. 6 (11th Cir.1983) (finding that Rule 608 involves only moral inducements for truthfulness, not mental capacity).

79. *See, e.g.*, United States v. Wertis, 505 F.2d 683, 685 (5th Cir.1974); United States v. Binder, 769 F.2d 595, 602 (9th Cir.1985);

Hoult v. Hoult, 57 F.3d 1, 7 (1st Cir.1995); United States v. Cecil, 836 F.2d 1431, 1441 (4th Cir.1988); United States v. Pino, 827 F.2d 1429, 1430 (10th Cir.1987); United States v. Beasley, 72 F.3d 1518, 1528 (11th Cir.1996). State v. Fairweather, 116 N.M. 456, 863 P.2d 1077, 1081 (N.M.1993); Roberson v. State, 214 Ga.App. 208, 447 S.E.2d 640, 643 (Ga.App. 1994).

80. Montana is an exception to this general approach and allows an expert to comment on a child's specific testimony if (1) the child testifies, (2) the child's credibility is first attacked, and (3) the expert is qualified. State v. Scheffelman, 250 Mont. 334, 820 P.2d 1293, 1298 (Mont.1991). The Montana view is premised on the belief that children witnesses require special consideration.

81. 149 Ariz. 472, 720 P.2d 73 (Ariz.1986).

82. *Id.* at 76.

ly because it "would invade the exclusive province of the jury to determine the credibility of the witnesses."[83] In addition, some courts exclude specific psychological assessments of particular testimony on the basis that the state of the art of the science does not permit it. One court explained its "rejection of expert testimony on truthfulness" as partly based on its "belief that psychology is not an exact science but involves much uncertainty and is often subjective."[84]

Although courts adamantly reject attempts to comment on specific testimony, they have been far more accommodating in allowing testimony that concerns specific witnesses. Ordinarily, this kind of expert testimony involves some defining characteristics of the witness that are believed to be associated with truthfulness or reliability more generally. For example, as noted above, courts express substantial concern with the possible influence adults might have had on child witnesses. In *Schutz v. State*, the Court of Criminal Appeals of Texas held that although psychologists could not testify about the truthfulness of a child witness, they could testify regarding possible manipulation of the child.[85] The court, however, was careful to note that expert testimony on manipulation cannot reach whether the witness was or was not manipulated.

Finally, a third strategy for attacking or supporting the credibility of a witness is through expert testimony about child witnesses in general. This approach seeks to provide a framework or context within which a child's statements can be understood. This general framework evidence provides an educational function, and the fact finders are left to apply its lessons to the case before them. This commentary, because it is fixed on a level of generality well beyond what the jury must decide, is thought to present little unfair prejudice. But this very generality tends to reduce its probative value as well.

It is somewhat unclear whether general framework evidence about child witnesses is subject to the strictures of Rule 608 at all.[86] More likely, this information should be evaluated under the general relevancy rules of evidence. This is the way the Federal Rules manage evidence regarding bias.[87] Like bias, framework evidence about children's capacities or responses to abuse is pertinent to credibility assessments, but does not speak to it directly. It is also akin to expert testimony on the reliability of eyewitness identifications. By providing background information, experts allow fact finders to

83. *See* Shumate v. Newland, 75 F.Supp.2d 1076, 1088 (N.D.Cal.1999); *see also* State v. Raymond, 540 N.W.2d 407, 409–10 (S.D.1995); State v. Walters, 120 Idaho 46, 813 P.2d 857, 866 (Idaho 1990); State v. Rice, 261 Kan. 567, 932 P.2d 981, 997–98 (Kan.1997).

84. *Schutz*, 957 S.W.2d at 69.

85. The *Schutz* Court explained as follows:

[A] party may attack the credibility of a witness or other declarant by offering the following kinds of manipulation evidence: (a) evidence that the person is, in general, the kind of person who is easily manipulated, (b) common signs or symptoms of manipulation and evidence that the person displays some or all of these signs or symptoms, and (c) evidence of third person acts or words designed to manipulate. The other party may respond to such attacks with (a) evidence that the person is not, in general, the kind of person who is easily manipulated, (b) common signs or symptoms of manipulation and evidence that the person does not display these signs or symptoms, and (c) evidence rebutting the existence of third person acts or words of manipulation.

Schutz, 957 S.W.2d at 70.

86. *See supra* notes 72–73, for the text of Rule 608.

87. *See* United States v. Abel, 469 U.S. 45, 105 S.Ct. 465, 83 L.Ed.2d 450 (1984) ("[I]t is permissible to impeach a witness by showing his bias under the Federal Rules of Evidence just as it was permissible to do so before their adoption.").

understand what is generally known among specialists, thus combating popular misconceptions or possible stereotypes. This educational function poses little danger of invading the province of the jury. At the same time, courts generally perceive this sort of framework evidence to have relatively low probative value. Its admissibility thus depends on the need, if any, to educate fact finders about children witnesses, balanced against concerns of wasted time or possible confusion of the issues.

§ 7–1.3.3 Physically Separating the Child Witness from the Defendant

As noted above, in most jurisdictions the competency of children to testify as witnesses is measured by ordinary rules of evidence. Many jurisdictions, however, seek to protect children from the perceived psychological harm associated with testifying in court. These attempts have ranged from the placement of screens between the defendant and child witness[88] to the currently predominant practice of one-way closed circuit television. Because these devices physically divide the witness from the defendant, they have been challenged as violations of the Confrontation Clause.[89]

Although the Court at first adopted a categorical, rules-based, methodology to Confrontation Clause matters in child sexual abuse cases, it did not maintain this approach for long.[90] In *Coy v. Iowa*, in which the Court invalidated the practice of placing a screen between the child witness and the defendant, Justice Scalia wrote for the Court. He concluded emphatically that the Clause guaranteed a face-to-face meeting of witness and accused. Justice O'Connor concurred in the result, but urged that confrontation "rights are not absolute but rather may give way in an appropriate case to other competing interests so as to permit the use of certain procedural devices designed to shield a child witness from the trauma of courtroom testimony."[91] In *Maryland v. Craig*,[92] the Court adopted O'Connor's balancing formulation, holding that " 'the Confrontation Clause reflects a preference for face-to-face confrontation at trial,' " but that preference " 'must occasionally give way to considerations of public policy and the necessities of the case.' "[93] In child sex abuse cases, the public policy involved is the "compelling one" of "the protection of minor victims of sex crimes from further trauma and embarrassment."[94]

In *Craig*, the defendant had been charged with an assortment of sexual offenses arising out of incidents that occurred in a prekindergarten and

---

88. In *Coy v. Iowa*, 487 U.S. 1012, 108 S.Ct. 2798, 101 L.Ed.2d 857 (1988), the Court held that placing a screen between the defendant and child witness violated the defendant's right to face-to-face confrontation under the Sixth Amendment.

89. *See also* Kentucky v. Stincer, 482 U.S. 730, 107 S.Ct. 2658, 96 L.Ed.2d 631 (1987) (not a violation of the Confrontation Clause to exclude defendant from the competency hearing of two child witnesses).

90. *Coy*, 487 U.S. at 1019–21.

91. *Id.* at 1022 (O'Connor, J., concurring). As discussed in the text, O'Connor's balancing approach would later prevail when she wrote the opinion in *Maryland v. Craig*. Justice Scalia dissented in *Craig*.

92. 497 U.S. 836, 110 S.Ct. 3157, 111 L.Ed.2d 666 (1990).

93. *Craig*, 497 U.S. at 849 (*quoting Robert*, 448 U.S. at 63 (first quote) and Mattox v. United States, 156 U.S. 237, 243, 15 S.Ct. 337, 39 L.Ed. 409 (1895) (second quote)).

94. *Id.* at 852 (*quoting* Globe Newspaper Co. v. Superior Court of Norfolk County, 457 U.S. 596, 607, 102 S.Ct. 2613, 73 L.Ed.2d 248 (1982)).

kindergarten center at which the six-year-old victim attended. At trial, the judge invoked a Maryland law that permitted the court to receive the child's testimony by one-way closed circuit television. Under the law, the trial judge had to " 'determin[e] that testimony by the child victim in the courtroom will result in the child suffering serious emotional distress such that the child cannot reasonably communicate.' "[95] Applying this statute, the trial court found the six-year-old victim (as well as three other children) competent to testify but likely to suffer " 'serious emotional distress ... such that [she] cannot reasonably communicate.' "[96]

The *Craig* Court began by identifying "[t]he central concern of the Confrontation Clause": "to ensure the reliability of the evidence against a criminal defendant by subjecting it to rigorous testing in the context of an adversary proceeding before the trier of fact."[97] According to the Court, the Clause did not absolutely guarantee the right to a face-to-face encounter between witness and accused.[98] This explains why the many exceptions to the hearsay rule do not run afoul of the Constitution. The Court explained that, "in certain narrow circumstances, 'competing interests, if "closely examined," may warrant dispensing with confrontation at trial.' "[99] The Clause merely creates "a preference for face-to-face confrontation at trial."[100] This preference, however, can give way if the state has a sufficiently important interest.[101] In *Craig*, the Court concluded that "a State's interest in the physical and psychological well-being of child abuse victims may be sufficiently important to outweigh, at least in some cases, a defendant's right to face his or her accusers in court."[102]

In applying its balancing test to the statute before it, the Court emphasized that the video approach "preserves all of the other elements of the confrontation right."[103] In addition, the Maryland statute here "specifically

95. *Id.* at 836 (*quoting* Md.Cts. & Jud.Proc. Code Ann. § 9–102(a)(1)(ii) (1989)). It should be noted that unlike some statutes protecting child witnesses, the Maryland statute requires the psychological trauma to the child to be such that it interferes with the child's ability to "communicate" to the jury. This standard should be distinguished from the more common type that considers psychological harm more generally. *See, e.g.*, Mississippi Rule of Evid. 804(a)(6) (A declarant is unavailable if "[i]n the case of a child, [there is] the substantial likelihood that the emotional or psychological health of the witness would be substantially impaired if the child had to testify in the physical presence of the accused."). As the discussion in the text suggests, both approaches are probably constitutional under *Craig*.

96. *Id.* at 842–843.

97. *Id.* at 845.

98. *Id.*

99. *Id.* at 848 (*quoting Roberts*, 448 U.S. at 64).

100. *Id.* at 849 (*quoting Roberts*, 448 U.S. at 63). The Court, however, did emphasize that face-to-face confrontation, though not required,

should not "easily be dispensed with." The Court explained:

> [O]ur precedents confirm that a defendant's right to confront accusatory witnesses may be satisfied absent a physical, face-to-face confrontation at trial only where denial of such confrontation is necessary to further an important public policy and only where the reliability of the testimony is otherwise assured.

Id. at 850.

101. *Id.* at 852.

102. *Id.* at 853.

103. *Id.* at 851. The Court identified these "other elements" as follows:

> The child witness must be competent to testify and must testify under oath; the defendant retains full opportunity for contemporaneous cross-examination; and the judge, jury, and defendant are able to view (albeit by video monitor) the demeanor (and body) of the witness as he or she testifies.

Id.

intended 'to safeguard the physical and psychological well-being of child victims by avoiding, or at least minimizing, the emotional trauma produced by testifying.' "[104] Ultimately, however, the constitutional inquiry must be conducted case-by-case: "The trial court must hear evidence and determine whether use of the one-way closed circuit television procedure is necessary to protect the welfare of the particular child witness who seeks to testify."[105] This case-specific determination must ensure that the trauma would result because of the defendant's presence, rather than any trauma induced by the formal courtroom setting, and that any likely trauma "is more than de minimis."[106] The Court remanded the case so that the lower court could make the necessary determination.[107]

§ 7–1.4 Conclusion

In what is almost certainly the most distressing area of scientific evidence, courts have struggled mightily in child abuse prosecutions to formulate doctrine that will treat child witnesses kindly, but which will guarantee constitutional safeguards to those accused. The empirical issues surrounding children's memory and testimony implicate a wide range of legal doctrine, from the rules of evidence to a defendant's constitutional right to confront witnesses who testify against him. For the most part, courts have struck a principled balance in the doctrine that applies in these cases, allowing children certain latitude not provided adults. Although in the abstract this balance accords with principles of fairness and due process, courts must be vigilant not to allow their concern for the welfare of child witnesses to blur their judgment of the rights of those accused.

Society is tested most in these kinds of cases. The proof in many of them constitutes little more than the word of a child. But the enormity of the crime does not allow complacency. The challenge to do justice in a just fashion is great. The law must zealously pursue those who have committed unspeakable acts of evil, while, at the same time, providing the utmost of procedural protection to guarantee all defendants a fair trial.

104. *Id.* at 854 (*quoting* Wildermuth v. State, 310 Md. 496, 530 A.2d 275, 286 (Md. 1987)).

105. *Id.* at 855.

106. *Id.* at 856. *See, e.g.,* United States v. Weekley, 130 F.3d 747, 752 (6th Cir.1997) (applying *Craig* balancing and upholding lower court's use of closed circuit television testimony); *see generally* United States v. Withorn, 204 F.3d 790 (8th Cir.2000); Smith v. State, 340 Ark. 116, 8 S.W.3d 534 (Ark.2000); State v. Welch, 760 So.2d 317 (La.2000).

107. *Craig,* 497 U.S. at 860. The trial court had found that the requisite degree of trauma would result to the child if she testified, but the Maryland Court of Appeal had reversed in part because the lower court had failed to observe the child's behavior in the defendant's presence. The *Craig* Court concluded that this sort of evidentiary requirement was not mandated by federal constitutional law. The Court observed that the trial court here, "could well have found, on the basis of the expert testimony before it, that testimony by the child witnesses in the courtroom in the defendant's presence 'will result in [the] child suffering serious emotional distress such that [she] cannot reasonably communicate.' " *Id.* (*quoting* § 9–102(a)(1)(ii), *supra* note 95.

B.　SCIENTIFIC STATUS

by

Stephen J. Ceci,* Martine B. Powell,** & Gabrielle F. Principe***

§ 7–2.0　THE SCIENTIFIC STATUS OF CHILDREN'S MEMORY AND TESTIMONY

§ 7–2.1　Introduction

In the *State of New Jersey v. D.G.*,[1] the defendant married a woman who had two children by a previous marriage. Her youngest child, Michelle, was four and a half years old at the time of the alleged abuse. Michelle claims that her stepfather asked her to accompany him on an errand one day, and during it he took her to an empty house that the family was planning to move into:

> Michelle stated that the defendant ... laid down next to her and proceeded to place his hands under her shirt. Defendant touched and squeezed her breasts, fondled her vagina, and kissed her on the mouth. He then pulled off her shirt and pants, removed his own pants and climbed on top of her. Michelle testified that the defendant put his "dinky" into her and then that he cleaned up the "wet stuff" on the bed with a towel. He then told her to clean herself up and get dressed. The pair then proceeded to a pizza place and then returned to the great-grandmother's house.[2]

Three weeks later while Michelle was playing with two cousins, her aunt found her lying on the bed with these girls who had their pants down to their knees and one of them had her hand down Michelle's pants. The aunt testified that she "freaked out" and called the girls names. She ordered Michelle to sit alone and told her she was very upset with her. The aunt

* Stephen J. Ceci, Ph.D., holds a lifetime endowed chair in developmental psychology at Cornell University. He studies the accuracy of children's courtroom testimony, and is the author of over 300 articles, books, and chapters. Ceci's honors include a Senior Fulbright–Hayes fellowship and a Research Career Scientist Award. In 1993 Ceci was named a Master Lecturer of the American Psychological Association. He is currently a member of seven editorial boards and a fellow of six divisions of the APA, and of the American Association of Applied and Preventive Psychology, British Psychological Society, and American Psychological Society. His book (co-written with Maggie Bruck) JEOPARDY·IN THE COURTROOM: A SCIENTIFIC ANALYSIS OF CHILDREN'S TESTIMONY (1995) is an American Psychological Association bestseller and winner of the William James Book Award by APA. He is a senior scientific advisor to the Canadian Institute for Advanced Research. Ceci is a member of the National Academy of Sciences Committee on Behavioral, Cognitive, and Sensory Sciences, and a member of the American Psychological Society's Board of Directors. He is past president of Division 1 (General Psychology) of APA. In 2000 Ceci received the Lifetime Distinguished Contribution Award from the American Academy of Forensic Psychology.

Please address queries to any of the authors at the Dept. of Human Development, Cornell University, Ithaca, NY 14853. Email: sjc9@cornell.edu.

** Martine Powell, Ph.D. is a Senior Lecturer in the School of Psychology, Deakin University, Melbourne Australia. She has been conducting research in the area of child eyewitness memory, as well as training programs in investigative interviewing, for the past ten years. She has also trained and worked as a clinical psychologist, specializing in the treatment of child abuse and neglect.

*** Gabrielle F. Principe is a National Institute of Mental Health Postdoctoral Fellow at Cornell University. She was educated at Temple University and the University of North Carolina at Chapel Hill, where she received her doctorate in developmental psychology. Her research examines factors affecting the accuracy and retention of young children's memories for salient personal experiences.

§ 7–2.0

1.　157 N.J. 112, 723 A.2d 588 (N.J.1999).

2.　*Id.*

further testified that she took her daughters to the bathroom, washed them, and attempted to "deprogram" them. One of these girls told her that Michelle wanted to "lick her pee-pee."[3]

Forty-five minutes after being scolded and isolated, the aunt questioned Michelle. Although she purported to have calmed down by then, she said that Michelle still seemed nervous. At first, Michelle allegedly blamed the behavior on her two cousins. However, after more questioning, she stated that her stepfather did those things to her. Michelle testified that her aunt asked her: "What made you do this? Did anybody ever do anything like this to you to make you do this?" Michelle replied that her stepfather stuck his "thing" in her and then "peed on the bed," wiping it up with a towel. Michelle begged her aunt not to tell her mother. (Michelle's mother testified for the prosecution that the stepfather was "a fanatic about toweling himself off after intercourse even after ejaculating inside her."[4])

Several days after the incident with her two cousins, Michelle was interviewed by a female detective trained to conduct sex abuse investigations. Her aunt accompanied her to this interview. During this interview, however, Michelle failed to make a disclosure about her stepfather, saying only that he touched her "boobies." After frequent failed attempts to get Michelle to talk, the detective sensed that she was scared and was holding back. She stopped the videotaped interview because Michelle's nose began to bleed and brought her to a bathroom to stop the bleeding. Then the detective asked the aunt to reassure Michelle about talking to her. She put Michelle on her lap and told her to tell the detective the truth. Approximately seven minutes later, the videotape was turned back on and the interview proceeded. Now on video Michelle proceeded to claim the stepfather had put his penis into her vagina.

The following week, Michelle was examined by a pediatrician who specialized in sexual abuse. Although he found no physical evidence that was diagnostic of sexual trauma to Michelle's genitalia (not unusual even in cases of known sexual penetration), this pediatrician did report that Michelle demonstrated with an anatomically detailed doll that she had been raped, plus told him that the stepfather had rubbed his penis against her "private."[5] Based on Michelle's doll use and her oral description of events, the pediatrician concluded there was a "high likelihood that sexual abuse had occurred."

Michelle alleged that her mother beat her in an attempt to get her to recant her allegations. She was sent to live out of state with her biological father. When Michelle returned from his home, however, she accused him of raping her in a similar manner (e.g., including the wiping off with a towel). When examined again by the pediatrician, Michelle recanted her allegation against her stepfather but made three different allegations of sexual abuse against her biological father. In the following six months, Michelle told her aunt, a social worker, and an investigator that she had been lying about her stepfather. To confuse matters even more, Michelle recanted her recantations at various times.

Just before the case came to court, Michelle met with the prosecutor and detective and told them her stepfather did not rape her, but after further

3. *Id.*   5. *Id.*
4. *Id.*

questioning she told them that her mother had urged her to deny the rape. During the trial, Michelle's testimony changed somewhat from her prior statements. A child abuse expert testified that it is not unusual for abused children to change their statements, especially when they believe that others will not believe them or will criticize them. The jury convicted the stepfather; he was sentenced to a seven year term of imprisonment.

This case illustrates many of the challenges facing those who must interview alleged child victims. For example, Michelle was repeatedly interviewed, often by powerful adult authority figures, and her story changed substantially over time. Should her claims of abuse be believed or should we believe her recantations? Was her behavior with anatomical dolls diagnostic of abuse? Are children her age more suggestible than older children and adults? Are there precautions that interviewers can take to minimize suggestibility of children her age? These are a few of the questions that courts turn to psychological research for answers. Below we will briefly review the relevant scientific research from the field of children's testimonial competence. We will address the following topics: the suggestibility of child witnesses, recent trends in suggestibility research, the constructive nature of memory, the use of anatomical dolls in interviewing, interviewing preschoolers, videotaping interviews, and future research.

§ 7–2.2 Suggestibility of Child Witnesses

The issue of childhood suggestibility became prominent in the wake of a series of acquittals and reversals of convictions in child sexual abuse cases. For example, in one of the earliest cases, the *McMartin Preschool* case, none of the seven accused individuals was convicted of child sexual abuse, despite seven indictments on 208 different sexual abuse and exploitation charges, two trials, and expenditures by the State of California in excess of $15 million.[6] A number of the jurors claimed during a press conference after the trial that they believed that some of the children had been abused, but that they were unable to reach a guilty verdict because of the highly suggestive (videotaped) interviews of the child witnesses.

In the *Little Rascals Day Care* case, the Court of Appeals of North Carolina unanimously reversed the child sexual abuse convictions of both Bob Kelly and Dawn Wilson, again due to the suggestive questioning of child witnesses.[7]

Finally, *Wee Care Nursery School* teacher Margaret Kelly Michaels won her freedom after her conviction on 115 counts of sexual abuse against 20 preschool children was overturned by the New Jersey Supreme Court.[8] The Court ruled that if the State wished to retry Michaels, it would have to conduct a pre-trial hearing to show that, despite the suggestive and coercive interviewing techniques used with the child witnesses, their testimony was

---

6. For a discussion of the facts underlying the McMartin preschool case, see McMartin v. Children's Institute Int'l, 212 Cal.App.3d 1393, 261 Cal.Rptr. 437 (1989).

7. *See* State v. Wilson, 118 N.C.App. 616, 456 S.E.2d 870 (N.C.App.1995); State v. Kelly,

118 N.C.App. 589, 456 S.E.2d 861 (N.C.App. 1995).

8. State v. Michaels, 136 N.J. 299, 642 A.2d 1372 (N.J.1994).

still sufficiently reliable to admit them as witnesses at trial. Similar acquittals and reversals are occurring all across America.

In view of these recent decisions, it is vital for legal professionals to have some understanding of the phenomenon of *suggestibility* and its potential impact on children's memory and testimony. Hence, we begin this section with a definition of suggestibility and then discuss a range of issues related to children's suggestibility, including the parameters of the phenomenon and situations that seem especially likely to capitalize on children's heightened vulnerability to suggestion.

§ 7–2.2.1   Defining Suggestibility

The traditional definition of suggestibility, which is "the extent to which individuals come to accept and subsequently incorporate post-event information into their memory recollections," is too restrictive in its scope to be of much help in court cases involving children's suggestibility.[9] There are myriad reasons for this, including the fact that some of the most potent forms of suggestions occur before an event actually occurs, as opposed to after, or post-event. Another limitation of the traditional definition is that some powerful examples of suggestibility do not reflect actual changes in children's memories; that is, some children may acquiesce to suggestions made to them by interviewers while their original event memories remain unaltered.

Because of such limitations, a broader and more applicable definition of children's suggestibility was put forward by Ceci and Bruck to refer to "the degree to which children's encoding, storage, retrieval, and reporting of events can be influenced by a range of social and psychological factors."[10] This broadened definition of suggestibility allows for the possibility of a child accepting inaccurate information suggested by an interviewer while being fully conscious of its divergence from his or her memory of the original event. Such a situation occurs when a child lies to please loved ones, complies with a threat, or acquiesces to an interviewer's social demands. This broadened definition of suggestibility does not set limits on the timing of erroneous suggestions, but rather allows that they may be provided before or after an event. Finally, as was noted above, this broadened definition does not necessarily imply the alteration of the child's underlying memory as a consequence of being exposed to the suggestions; a child may still recall what actually happened, but choose not to report it for motivational reasons.

On the other hand, this broader conceptualization of suggestibility also connotes how easily a child could be influenced by subtle suggestions, leading questions, expectations, and stereotypes which could unconsciously alter their original event memories. Hence, the definition allows for suggestibility resulting from both cognitive (i.e., memory-altering) and social or motivational (e.g., compliance) factors. We explore numerous social and psychological factors

9. Gisli H. Gudjonsson, *The Relationship Between Interrogative Suggestibility and Acquiescence: Empirical Findings and Theoretical Implications*, 7 PERSONALITY & INDIVIDUAL DIFFERENCES 195, 195 (1986); *see also* Peter A. Powers et al., *Eyewitness Accounts of Females and Males*, 64 J. APPLIED PSYCHOL. 339 (1979).

10. Stephen J. Ceci & Maggie Bruck, *The Suggestibility of the Child Witness: A Historical Review and Synthesis*, 113 PSYCHOLOGICAL BULL. 403, 404 (1993).

that can influence children's memory for, and reporting of, events in the sections that follow.

§ 7–2.2.2 The Constructive Nature of Memory

One important implication of the literature on memory for discussions of children's suggestibility is that what is remembered during the course of an interview is the result of constructive processes, rather than an exact replica of the original event. When both children and adults attempt to understand and remember experiences, they condense, modify, and embellish information based on personal knowledge and expectations.[11] Consequently, what is remembered contains more and different information than that present in the "objective" event. Evidence for constructive processing comes from studies that show that when asked to recall prose passages verbatim, both children and adults transform, omit, and add information. Such inaccuracies are not accidental, rather they are guided by existing knowledge. For example, by age 6 or 7, children omit information that is illogical or does not fit with prior expectations, add information that would help explain incongruous passages, change details that are inconsistent with their personal knowledge, and reorder the sequence of events to make it more logical.[12] Also, event memory research has shown that children engage in constructive processing when reporting personal experiences. For example, repeated experience with similar episodes increases the amount of recall, but also results in more memory distortions in the direction of general knowledge as compared with memory for novel events.[13]

Extrapolating these findings to legal contexts, one would expect that correct recall is facilitated in situations where children can use existing knowledge to interpret and encode a personal experience. However, when experiences are not well understood or inconsistent with expectations, the risk of inaccurate memory is heightened. This point is particularly relevant for the testimony of very young witnesses, especially in sexual abuse cases. When child abuse victims are young enough to have almost no sexual knowledge, they may be unable to interpret and accurately remember what has occurred. For example, such a child who experiences "milder" forms of abuse (e.g., "accidental" genital touching) may not even be aware of the inappropriateness of genital fondling versus everyday hygiene and, as a result, construct a very different memory than an older child who has learned the impropriety of certain behaviors.

§ 7–2.2.3 Boundaries of Suggestibility? Salient Events, Actions, and Children's Bodies

The common wisdom in recent decades has been that children's memories for personal experiences, especially those involving their own bodies and those

---

11. *See* F. C. BARTLETT, REMEMBERING: A STUDY IN EXPERIMENTAL AND SOCIAL PSYCHOLOGY (1932).

12. *See* Sharon Bischofshausen, *Developmental Differences in Schema Dependency for Temporally Ordered Story Events*, 14 J. PSYCHOLINGUISTIC RES. 543 (1985); Daniel J. Christie & Gary M. Schumacher, *Developmental Trends in the Abstraction and Recall of Relevant Versus Irrelevant Thematic Information from Connected Verbal Materials*, 46 CHILD DEV. 598 (1975); J. M. MANDLER, STORIES, SCRIPTS, AND SCENES: ASPECTS OF SCHEMA THEORY (1984).

13. *See* Judith A. Hudson, *Constructive Processing in Children's Event Memory*, 26 DEVELOPMENTAL PSYCHOL. 180 (1990).

that are stressful, are too personally meaningful to be vulnerable to the interfering effects of suggestion. As such, one of the greatest challenges for modern researchers has been to develop ethically permissible research paradigms that allow for the study of children's responses to questions concerning the occurrence of bodily touching during personally experienced, stressful situations. The move towards examining children's recall of more forensically relevant events represents an important methodological shift because early studies of suggestibility have been criticized for their limited legal relevance regarding the reliability of child witnesses. For example, the majority of early investigations have focused on children's memories for peripheral details rather than central events, for witnessed episodes rather than actual experiences, and for neutral occurrences rather than salient events involving bodily contact. Most of these studies have examined children's suggestibility for details witnessed in brief stories, slide sequences, or staged events, such as what a fictitious child had for breakfast or the color of a man's beard.

To address these issues regarding the generalizability of memory research to forensic settings, a number of investigators have focused on children's recall of various medical events, such as pediatric examinations, urinary catheterizations, and emergency room visits. Indeed, these experiences are to some extent similar to events about which children are called on to testify. For example, during these salient and often stressful medical procedures, children are handled by adults while partially or entirely undressed. To illustrate, in one study of children's reports of a well-child checkup, 5–and 7–year-old children rarely made false reports in response to abuse-related suggestive questions (e.g., "How many times did the doctor kiss you?").[14] Other research by Ornstein and his colleagues of children's retention of an invasive radiological procedure involving urinary catheterization has demonstrated that 3– to 7–year-olds are highly resistant to false suggestions and can provide accurate accounts of distressful experiences where there is bodily contact.[15]

Although the Saywitz and Ornstein findings illustrate that stressful events involving bodily touching can be reported accurately by preschool children, the suggestive questions used in these studies were embedded in a single unbiased interview that was otherwise maximally supportive of correct recall. As such, these data may have limited value for assessing the veracity of young witnesses' statements when they are obtained under the more suggestive interviewing conditions that have occurred in some criminal investigations. For example, in contrast to a number of child witnesses involved in actual legal cases, the participants in the Saywitz and Ornstein studies were not questioned by biased interviewers, suggestive questions were not repeated within and across interviews, nor were the participants persuaded or encouraged to reply in a certain way. In response to these concerns regarding generalizability to legal situations, other investigators have directed their attention to examining the mnemonic consequences of a range of suggestive techniques that have been observed in actual investigative and therapeutic

14. *See* Karen J. Saywitz et al., *Children's Memory of a Physical Examination Involving Genital Touch: Implications for Reports of Child Sexual Abuse*, 59 J. Consulting & Clinical Psychol. 682 (1991).

15. *See* Kathy Ann Merritt et al., *Children's Memory for a Salient Medical Procedure: Implications for Testimony*, 94 Pediatrics 17 (1994).

interviews with young witnesses. We will discuss these methods below and their possible impact on young children's memory.

§ 7–2.3   Child Witness Interviews and Suggestibility

Because child witnesses typically undergo a barrage of questioning from a wide variety of professionals and nonprofessionals, such as parents, therapists, child protective service workers, police officers, and attorneys, nearly all recent studies of suggestibility have focused on the effects of various interviewing practices. In contrast to the researchers, discussed above, who have emphasized the analogous nature of medical procedures to situations involving abuse, this second group of investigators have stressed the importance of interview structure, rather than that of medical contexts, in designing research paradigms relevant to forensic settings.

Interviews are, at a minimum, verbal interactions between at least two people in which one person (the interviewer) is attempting to obtain specific information from another person (the interviewee). Hence, interviews are a type of conversation that can be carried out by a variety of individuals, including therapists, social workers, police officers, attorneys, and parents. Adult interviewers, however, often find that child interviewees are not especially forthcoming in terms of their event reports, at least not without a certain amount of prompting from the interviewer. For instance, when parents ask their young children open-ended questions about what happened at school, they typically receive uninformative answers such as "nothing" or "we played." In order to elicit more elaborate narration, parents and other interviewers often employ a variety of conversational and interview strategies to structure the discussions and encourage the children into providing more information. In addition to these techniques, there are a variety of subtle emotional and interpersonal dynamics present in interviews with children that have proven to be worthy of investigation. We discuss several of these strategies and dynamics and their implications for children's suggestibility below.

§ 7–2.3.1   Repeated Interviews

In actual court cases, child witnesses often are called upon to tell and retell their stories of what happened many times, to many different people. Although authorities estimate that the average child witness may be questioned 12 times during a forensic investigation,[16] this figure does not take into account the number of times that these children may discuss the alleged event with relatives, friends, teachers, or therapists.[17] Importantly, there are a number of reasons why children commonly are interviewed on multiple occasions. First, given the legal structure of our society, a witness may have to recount his story to a number of different parties in a legal dispute. Second, if additional case details emerge, the witness may be questioned about the veridicality of new information that was unanticipated at the time of an earlier interview.

---

16. *See* DEBRA WITCOMB, WHEN THE CHILD IS A VICTIM (2d ed. 1992).

17. *See* STEPHEN J. CECI & MAGGIE BRUCK, JEOPARDY IN THE COURTROOM: A SCIENTIFIC ANALYSIS OF CHILDREN'S TESTIMONY (1995).

A third reason for repeated questioning is that multiple interviews provide the witness additional opportunities to add previously unreported details. This is an important point for discussions of very young witnesses because longitudinal research has demonstrated that young children's event reports are surprisingly inconsistent, such that a high proportion of information that is recounted during subsequent interviews is not reported initially. For example, in an investigation of 2.5–year-olds' memory for earlier experienced events, 76% of the information recalled during a second interview was new and different from that recounted during an initial memory assessment 6 weeks earlier. Further, at a third interview 14 months after the second memory test (when the participants were almost 4 years old), 74% of the information reported had not been recalled at either prior interview.[18]

The Fivush data demonstrate that young children's event reports are highly inconsistent; but do new details provided at subsequent interviews tend to be accurate? Research by Pipe and her colleagues indicates that new information reported for the first time after lengthy delays (i.e., 1 or 2 years) is substantially less accurate than information repeated across interviews.[19] For example, when children were reinterviewed about an event that they had participated in 2 years earlier when they were 6 years old, more than 30% of the new information reported in free recall and approximately 50% of the new information provided in response to specific prompts was inaccurate. In contrast, information repeated across interviews in both free and prompted recall was very accurate up to 2 years later.[20] Thus, because multiple interviews in legal settings often are conducted in the hope that new information will be recalled, these data call into question the benefits of this practice with very young witnesses.

Notwithstanding high error rates for newly reported information, the classic laboratory–based literature on long term retention provides ample evidence that repetition and rehearsal strengthen memory.[21] On the basis of this work, some professionals and researchers have argued that repeated interviews provide multiple opportunities to rehearse information, and as such, may serve to maintain memory. However, when investigators move outside of the laboratory into contexts that are more analogous to legal situations, the benefits of multiple interviews are not universally obtained. Some studies of event recall have shown that repeated neutral interviews can preserve memory over time.[22] Even children as young as 18 months have been

18. See Robyn Fivush & Nina R. Hamond, *Autobiographical Memory Across the Preschool Years: Toward Reconceptualizing Childhood Amnesia, in* KNOWING AND REMEMBERING IN YOUNG CHILDREN 223 (Robyn Fivush & Judith A Hudson eds., 1990).

19. See Karen Salmon & Margaret–Ellen Pipe, *Recalling an Event One Year Late: The Impact of Props, Drawing and a Prior Interview,* 14 APPLIED COGNITIVE PSYCHOL. 99 (2000).

20. See Margaret–Ellen Pipe et al., *Children's Recall 1 or 2 Years After an Event,* 35 DEVELOPMENTAL PSYCHOL. 781 (1999).

21. See ROBERT G. CROWDER, PRINCIPLES OF LEARNING AND MEMORY (1976); ALAN D. BADDELEY, HUMAN MEMORY: THEORY AND PRACTICE (1990).

22. See Lynne Baker–Ward et al., *The Effects of Involvement of Children's Memory for Events,* 5 COGNITIVE DEVELOPMENT 55 (1990); Robyn Fivush & Nina R. Hamond, *Time and Again: Effects of Repetition and Retention Interval on 2 Year Olds' Event Recall,* 47 J. EXPERIMENTAL CHILD PSYCHOL. 259 (1989); Martine B. Powell & Donald M. Thomson, *The Effect of an Intervening Interview on Children's Ability to Remember an Occurrence of a Repeated Event,* 2 LEGAL & CRIMINOLOGICAL PSYCHOL. 247 (1997); S. E. Martin & Donald M. Thomson, *Videotapes and Multiple Interviews: The Effects on the Child Witness,* 1 PSYCHIATRY, PSYCHOL., & L. 119 (1994); Gabrielle F. Principe et al., *The Effects of Intervening Experiences on Children's Memory for a Physical Examina-*

shown to benefit from intervening memory tests that elicit reenactment of the to-be-recalled activities.[23] In contrast, other investigations have detected no facilitative effects of intervening interviews.[24]

Several factors may explain these inconsistent results. First, there likely exists a critical window of time in which intervening interviews have the potential to facilitate memory. Repeated interviews inevitably occur over time, and as time increases, the memory for the original event decays. As a result, information about the event becomes increasingly difficult to recall[25] and especially prone to suggestive influences.[26] Consequently, when an intervening interview occurs after a substantial delay, its potential benefits may wane presumably because too much memory decay has already occurred. Similarly, because younger children generally construct weaker memories than older children,[27] and because memory decay rates decrease with age,[28] the impact of multiple interviews likely varies developmentally. Second, the adequacy of early interviews seems to affect the potential for enhancement. This factor may be particularly relevant for younger children as they may need a higher level of support to benefit from interpolated interviews than older children. To illustrate, one study showed that children who were given a cognitive interview—an interview that provides a range of highly supportive memory cues—reported substantially more after a 5–month delay compared to children who were given either a standard interview or no interview at all.[29] Thus, the reminding potential of an intervening interview may be in part a function of the extent to which it successfully cues or reactivates relevant information in memory that otherwise may have been forgotten.

There also exists a range of internal processes that may impede the facilitative potential of repeated interviews. For example, memory may change over time as the result of constructive processes that serve to fill in the gaps that occur as the original memory weakens. To illustrate, preschool children have been shown to incorporate information from their general knowledge of what typically happens during a day at nursery school when their memory for details of the actual episode fades.[30] Further, demonstrations of "autosuggestibility" have shown that stored memories can be modified by a child's own reasoning.[31] For instance, when asked to draw the length of the final line in a

tion, 14 APPLIED COGNITIVE PSYCHOL. 59 (2000); Alison Tucker et al., *The Effect of a Repeated Interview on Young Children's Eyewitness Testimony*, 23 AUSTRALIAN AND NEW ZEALAND J. CRIMINOLOGY 117 (1990).

23. *See* Judith A. Hudson & Ellyn G. Sheffield, *Déjà Vu All Over Again: Effects of Reenactment on Toddlers' Event Memory*, 69 CHILD DEV. 51 (1998).

24. *See* Gail S. Goodman et al., *Children's Testimony About a Stressful Event: Improving Children's Reports*, 1. NARRATIVE & LIFE HISTORY 69 (1991); Lynne Baker–Ward et al., *Young Children's Long–Term Retention of a Pediatric Examination*, 64 CHILD DEV. 1519 (1993).

25. *See* Mark L. Howe & Charles J. Brainerd, *Development of Children's Long–Term Retention*, 9 DEVELOPMENTAL REV. 301 (1989).

26. *See* Gabrielle F. Principe, Children's Suggestibility: A Trace Strength Interpretation

(unpublished Ph.D. dissertation, University of North Carolina, Chapel Hill) (manuscript on file with authors).

27. *See* Randall H. Bender et al., *Age Differences in Encoding and Retrieving Details of a Pediatric Examination*, 3 PSYCHONOMIC BULL. & REV. 188 (1996).

28. *See* Howe & Brainerd, *supra* note 25.

29. *See* Rhona Flin et al., *The Effect of a Five–Month Delay on Children's and Adults' Eyewitness memory*, 83 BRITISH J. PSYCHOL. 323 (1992).

30. *See* Marina Myles–Worsley et al., *Children's Preschool Script Reconstruction: Reliance on General Knowledge As Memory Fades*, 22 DEVELOPMENTAL PSYCHOL. 22 (1986).

31. *See* Charles J. Brainerd & Valerie F. Reyna, *Autosuggestibility in Memory Development*, 28 COGNITIVE PSYCHOL. 65 (1995).

previously viewed sequence of lines of increasing length, children's reproductions tend to be longer than the line's objective length, although objective length tends to be reported accurately when the ascending sequence is not observed.[32] Thus, these findings suggest that once memory for an experience is altered as the result of constructive processing, the possible benefits of additional interviews may be nullified.

Some have argued that the most important benefits of repeated interviews are the maintenance of children's free narratives.[33] This is an important point because the legal system has assumed traditionally that spontaneous disclosures are diagnostic of accuracy.[34] However, with additional interviews, there is an increase in both accurate and inaccurate information in both children's and adults' free recall.[35] Other research by Ornstein and his colleagues further demonstrates that even under maximally supportive interviewing conditions, errors can occur in children's free reports.[36] In this investigation, 4– and 6–year-old children's memory was assessed for a mock physical examination that included some highly-expected medical features (e.g., measuring weight), while omitting others, and incorporated several atypical, unexpected features (e.g., collecting a sputum sample). After a 12–week delay, the children exhibited a relatively high frequency of spontaneous intrusions of typical, but not atypical, medical features that had not been included in their checkups. In fact, 42% of the 4–year-olds and 72% of the 6–year-olds made at least one such intrusion, whereas essentially none of the children reported in their free recall any of the atypical procedures that had not taken place during their examinations. Further, the children who were interviewed immediately and after a 12–week delay committed as many spontaneous intrusions of expected-but-omitted features as those who were questioned only at the delayed assessment. Thus, the equivalent error patterns of the two groups at the final interview demonstrate that individual difference factors, such as prior knowledge, may nullify the facilitative effects of repeated interviews on children's free narratives.

Thus far we have focused on the potential effects of multiple neutral interviews. However, as discussed above, some forensic interviews include suggestive questioning and various pressures to report certain types of erroneous information. When these techniques are repeated across multiple interviews, the accuracy of children's reports may be seriously hindered. Indeed, investigations have demonstrated that repeated suggestive interviews can influence children to fabricate entire events, including those that involve bodily touching.[37] The risk of eliciting inaccurate reports from children

32. *See* ALFRED BINET, LA SUGGESTIBILITE (1900).

33. *See* Robyn Fivush, *Developmental Perspectives on Autobiographical Recall, in* CHILD VICTIMS, CHILD WITNESSES: UNDERSTANDING AND IMPROVING TESTIMONY 1 (Gail S. Goodman & Bette L. Bottoms eds., 1993); Debra A. Poole & Lawrence T. White, *Two Years Later: Effects of Question Repetition and Retention Interval on the Eyewitness Testimony of Children and Adults*, 29 DEVELOPMENTAL PSYCHOL. 844 (1993).

34. *See* Ronald P. Fisher & Brian L. Cutler, *The Relation Between Consistency and Accuracy of Eyewitness Testimony, in* PSYCHOLOGY, LAW, AND CRIMINAL JUSTICE: INTERNATIONAL DEVELOPMENTS IN RESEARCH AND PRACTICE 21 (Graham Davies et al. eds., 1995).

35. *See* Poole & White, *supra* note 33.

36. *See* Peter A. Ornstein et al., *Children's Knowledge, Expectation, and Long-term Retention*, 12 APPLIED COGNITIVE PSYCHOL. 387 (1998).

37. *See* Maggie Bruck et al., *"I Hardly Cried When I Got My Shot!": Influencing Children's Reports About a Visit to Their Pediatrician*, 66 CHILD DEV. 193 (1995).

increases as the number of suggestive interviews increases.[38] Further, it has been shown that even repeated interviews that are not overtly suggestive may have a detrimental effect on children's event reports. For example, simply asking children to repeatedly think about or imagine a fictional event can result in nearly 60% of children assenting to the occurrence of that event.[39] Importantly, erroneous reports elicited under such conditions can be highly credible in terms of structure and content.

Bruck, Ceci, and Hembrooke, for example, examined children's reports across multiple suggestive interviews for two false events (helping a lady in the park find her lost monkey and seeing a thief steal food from the daycare facility) and two true events (helping a lady who injured her leg and a recent punishment).[40] The children were interviewed on five different occasions about the four events. Across all five interviews, the children consistently assented to the true helping event. Beginning at the initial interview, however, many of the children were reluctant to talk about the punishment event and all of the children denied the two false events. However, following subsequent interviews that included a combination of suggestive techniques, including peer pressure, guided imagery, repeated misinformation, and selective reinforcement, all of the children agreed that the punishment had taken place and assented to both of the false events. Thus, this study illustrates that the very same repeated suggestive procedures can serve both to facilitate and hinder accurate reporting. For children who seemed reluctant to talk about the true-but-unpleasant event (i.e., the punishment), exposure to multiple suggestive interviews prompted them to recall this previously unreported event. However, the use of these very same procedures resulted in high assent rates for the false events, one of which was a criminal act (i.e., witnessing a thief steal food from the daycare center).

In summary, this line of research demonstrates that repeated interviewing is neither a harmless procedure for eliciting new information nor an inherently suggestive technique to be universally avoided. Memory reconstructions due to the passage of time or exposure to suggestive influences, rather than multiple interviews per se, produce inaccuracies in children's reports. Although factors such as delay and age may decrease the facilitative potential of intervening interviews, only when one or more sources of suggestibility are present do repeated interviews have a negative effect on memory. However, because many real-life interviews contain a range of both subtle and overt suggestive influences, these findings highlight the problems associated with diagnosing the accuracy of young witnesses' reports following repeated interviews. In particular, these data suggest that professionals who work with child witnesses should be cautious about the validity of new details that emerge for the first time after multiple interviews.

38. *See* Bruck et al., *Children's Reports of Pleasant and Unpleasant Events, in* RECOLLECTIONS OF TRAUMA: SCIENTIFIC RESEARCH & CLINICAL PRACTICE (Don J. Read & D. Stephen Lindsay eds., 1998); Ceci & Bruck, *supra* note 10; Michelle D. Leichtman & Stephen J. Ceci, *The Effects of Stereotypes and Suggestions on Pres-*

choolers Reports, 31 DEVELOPMENTAL PSYCHOL. 568 (1995).

39. *See* Stephen J. Ceci et al., *The Role of Source Misattributions in the Creation of False Beliefs among Preschoolers*, 62 INT'L. J. CLINICAL & EXPERIMENTAL HYPNOSIS 304 (1994).

40. *See id.*

§ 7–2.3.2 Stereotype Induction

Another technique that may be used by interviewers when children are reluctant to disclose is that of stereotype induction. This subtle, but powerful interviewing technique involves an interviewer's attempts to communicate to a child a negative characterization of a person or an event, whether it be true or false. For instance, telling a child that the suspect "does bad things" or "tries to scare children" is an attempt at stereotype induction. (Stereotypes can also be positive in nature; however, negative stereotypes are particularly relevant in abuse-related contexts).

Some interviewers justify their use of stereotype induction on the grounds that it helps to provide a supportive environment for children to disclose abuse, thereby increasing the likelihood that a frightened or reluctant child will share his or her experiences. However, there is evidence that stereotype induction can also have powerful negative effects on the accuracy of children's accounts. In fact, interviewers' stereotypes may taint and become incorporated into children's reports.

In one study, for example, a group of preschoolers was told about a fictional person named Sam Stone.[41] Sam was described as clumsy in a series of vignettes presented to some of the children once a week for a month (e.g., "Last night, Sam Stone came to my house and borrowed my Barbie doll and accidentally broke her leg."). The researchers then exposed all of the children to a character they introduced as Sam Stone. He visited their nursery schools during a story reading exercise. Sam Stone smiled amiably at the children, commented that the book they were reading had been his favorite book when he was their age, walked around the classroom and then left. At no time did he do anything clumsy while he was in the room.

Following Sam Stone's two-minute visit to their classroom, control group children were interviewed about his visit four times over the following ten weeks, using non-suggestive techniques (e.g., "Tell me what happened.") (Control group children had not heard the vignettes and thus had no stereotyped expectations about Sam Stone). During the fifth and final interview, these children were first asked for a free narrative ("Tell me everything that happened the day Sam Stone visited your classroom.") and were then asked about two non-events involving a book and a teddy bear (e.g., "Did Sam Stone rip a book?" and "Did he spill anything on a teddy bear?").

The control group children performed very well, correctly recalling most of what actually transpired during Sam Stone's visit and refraining from assenting to the misleading, non-event questions. Only 10% of the youngest children (3–4–year-olds) assented to these false events and only 5% continued to assent when asked if they actually *saw* him do these things as opposed to hearing about it. None of the older preschoolers (5–6–year-olds) said they had seen Sam Stone do anything to a book or a teddy bear.

A second group of preschoolers was interviewed in the same way the control group had been: four times over the ten weeks following Sam Stone's visit, in a non-suggestive manner. However, these children had heard the stereotype-inducing vignettes before Sam's visit. In the fifth and final interview, 42% of the younger children in this group assented to the false events

41. *See* Leichtman & Ceci, *supra* note 38.

(Sam Stone ripping a book and soiling a teddy bear) and 19% claimed they had actually seen them happen. Only 11% of these 3–4–year-olds maintained their false claims when gently challenged ("Tell me what he really did, OK?"). Again, the older preschoolers were more resistant, with error rates about half as high as those of the younger children.

A third group of children, not given the stereotype about Sam Stone, was interviewed four times over ten weeks in a highly suggestive manner (e.g., "Remember that time Sam Stone visited your classroom and spilled chocolate on that white teddy bear? Did he do it on purpose or was it an accident;" "When Sam Stone ripped that book, was he being silly or was he angry?"). During the fifth and final interview, 52% of the younger children and 38% of the older children in this group claimed that Sam Stone had either ripped the book or soiled the teddy bear. Even when gently challenged, 10% of the youngest preschoolers continued to insist that they had actually observed him doing this. The false claim rate for the older children was 8%.

The final group of children was given *both* a stereotype about Sam Stone's clumsiness and was interviewed in a highly suggestive manner during the ten weeks following his visit. During the final interview, 72% of the younger children in this group stated that Sam had done things to the book and teddy bear. This figure dropped to 44% when they were asked if they had *seen* Sam do these things. Even after being challenged, 20% of the younger preschoolers and 11% of the older ones maintained that they saw Sam Stone do the misdeeds, even though he had not.

To assess whether the children's claims might be viewed as convincing to experts, 1,000 researchers and clinicians (psychiatrists and psychologists) were shown videotapes of the final interviews and asked to judge which of the events had actually transpired as well as to rate each child's credibility. Overall, most of the professionals were inaccurate. Despite their confidence in their judgments, experts could not reliably determine the accuracy of the children's testimony. The overall credibility ratings were significantly lower than chance, indicating that the experts consistently applied invalid indicia (e.g., child avoids eye contact) to make their decisions. As a rule, the least accurate children were considered to be the most accurate by the experts. This shows how difficult it is to separate fact from fiction, even for trained professionals, after children have been repeatedly, suggestively interviewed, especially when accompanied by the induction of congruent stereotypes.

The Sam Stone study demonstrates that prior expectations about the personality of a particular person can have a dramatic effect on remembering. But what happens when expectations about an individual change over time? This may be a particularly important issue for understanding young children's memory abilities because their impressions of other people tend to be quite unstable and malleable.[42] Greenhoot explored this issue by manipulating kindergartners' knowledge of a fictional child before and after they were read a series of stories.[43] The stories described the fictional child's involvement in a series of ambiguous events in which his or her behavior could be interpreted

42. *See* Barbara H. Peevers & Paul F. Secord, *Developmental Changes in Attribution of Descriptive Concepts to Persons*, 27 J. PERSONALITY & SOC. PSYCHOL. 120 (1973).

43. *See* Andrea Follmer Greenhoot, *Remembering and Understanding: The Effects of Changes In Underlying Knowledge on Children's Recollections*, 71 CHILD DEV. 1309 (2000).

in a variety of ways. For example, in one story, a puzzle is destroyed while the main character is standing nearby. Before hearing the stories, the participants were told that the protagonist was either a prosocial child (positive) or a bully (negative). When later asked to recall the stories, the children who had been exposed to positive information about the protagonist were more likely than their peers to report positive behaviors, whereas the children who had been given negative orienting information recalled more negative behaviors.

In the second phase of the study, a second knowledge manipulation took place that provided some of the children a new view of the protagonist. Specifically, the children received information that was designed to convince them that the protagonist was either prosocial and well-liked or aggressive and disliked. For some of the children, this new information (either positive or negative) was consistent with their earlier impressions of the protagonist, whereas for others it (again, either positive or negative) was inconsistent with their initial views. Following this second knowledge manipulation, the children's memory for the protagonist's behavior changed in ways that were consistent with the newly acquired information. Regardless of the information provided during the first phase of the study, the children who were given positive information during the second knowledge manipulation tended to recall positive actions, whereas those who were provided with negative information were likely to report negative behaviors. Thus, these data demonstrate that changes over time in a child's general impression of a particular person can result in corresponding changes to what is remembered about the actions of that individual.

§ 7–2.3.3   Influence of Interviewer Status on Suggestibility

Numerous studies reviewed by Ceci and Bruck show that the accuracy and detail of a child's report about an event is mediated in part by the status of the interviewer.[44] Older, more knowledgeable interviewers are able to mislead children more than low status adults or peers. For example, an adult interviewer, who provides false information, compromises the accuracy of a child interviewees' report more than a child interviewer who provides the same information.[45] Also, children are more easily misled by suggestions that are introduced by strangers than those presented by their parents.[46] In this sense, children are no different from adults who also are influenced by the status of their interviewers. For example, an interviewer pretending to be an attorney is viewed with more suspicion by adult bystanders to an automobile accident than if the same individual is introduced as a neutral party.[47]

Research does not imply, however, that children are more likely to provide accurate reports to interviewers who are dressed in civilian clothes compared to uniform. One of the only studies to directly examine the effect of police uniform on children's reports (while controlling for other variables), revealed that officers in full uniform elicited less accurate *and inaccurate* information from children about an event compared to officers in civilian

---

44. Ceci & Bruck, *supra* note 10.

45. *See* Stephen J. Ceci et al., *Age Differences in Suggestibility: Psycholegal Implications,* 117 J. EXPERIMENTAL PSYCHOL.: GENERAL 38 (1987).

46. *See* Shelly Jackson & Susan Crockenberg, *A Comparison of Suggestibility in 4–Year–Old Girls in Response to Parental or Stranger Misinformation,* 19 J. APPLIED DEVELOPMENTAL PSYCHOL. 527 (1998).

47. *See generally* Ceci et al., *supra* note 45.

clothes.[48] It could be that children find police uniforms intimidating and distracting, and thus uniforms are detrimental to the establishment of interviewer-child rapport. Increased interviewer-child rapport could be associated with a higher number of accurate as well as inaccurate details, because the more friendly and trusting an interviewer is, the more eager the child may be to provide answers that the interviewer wants to hear.[49] Alternatively, the children may have perceived a greater sense of the need to tell the truth to the officers in uniform. A fear of providing inaccurate information would have inhibited the overall amount of information (accurate as well as inaccurate recall). This is supported by studies that have shown that training children to report only what they "truly" remember reduces correct information as well as errors.[50] With either explanation, the implication is that the clothing worn by the interviewer (or any other overt sign of interviewer status) is unlikely to outweigh the importance of a neutral, non-leading interview style.

§ 7–2.3.4 Interviewer Bias

An interview with a young child should be an exercise in hypothesis-testing. Just as scientists try to arrive at the truth by ruling out rival hypotheses or by falsifying a favored hypothesis,[51] child interviewers should also attempt to rule out alternative hypotheses, rather than simply trying to confirm their primary ones. Recently, White, Leichtman and Ceci examined how an interviewer's favored hypothesis can influence the accuracy of young children's reports.[52]

Preschoolers were exposed to a game-like event and were interviewed about that event one month later. Prior to the interviews, the interviewer was given information about things that *might* have happened during the event; some of the information was accurate and some of the information was inaccurate. The interviewer was told to interview each child and to use whatever strategies she felt were necessary to elicit the most factually accurate report possible from each child.

The information provided to the interviewer helped her construct her hypotheses about what had transpired during the game. This had a powerful influence on the dynamics of the interview, with the interviewer eventually shaping some of the children's reports to be consistent with her hypotheses about what had happened. When the interviewer was accurately informed, the children correctly recalled 93% of the events that had transpired. The children made *no* false accusations when the interviewer was correctly informed; that is, they only made "errors of omission," leaving out of their reports events

48. *See* Martine B. Powell et al., *The Effect of Uniform and Prior Knowledge on Children's Event Reports and Disclosure of Secrets,* J. POLICE & CRIMINOLOGICAL PSYCHOL. (forthcoming 2001).

49. Karen Saywitz et al., *Effects of Cognitive Interviewing and Practice on Children's Recall Performance*, 77 J. APPLIED COGNITIVE PSYCHOL. 744 (1992).

50. *See* DEBORAH POOLE & MICHAEL LAMB, INVESTIGATIVE INTERVIEWS OF CHILDREN (1998).

51. *See* Stephen J. Ceci & Urie Bronfenbrenner, *On the Demise of Everyday Memory:* *The Rumors of My Death are Greatly Exaggerated*, 46 AM. PSYCHOLOGIST 27 (1991); R. Dawes, *The Importance of Alternative Hypothesis and Hypothetical Counterfactuals in General Social Science,* [Spring] THE GENERAL PSYCHOLOGIST 2 (1992); KARL R. POPPER, CONJECTURES & REFLECTIONS (1962).

52. *See* Tara L. White et al., *The Good, the Bad and the Ugly: Accuracy, Inaccuracy and Elaboration in Preschoolers' Reports About a Past Event*, 11 APPLIED COGNITIVE PSYCHOL. 37 (1997).

that had actually happened. However, when the interviewer was misinformed, 34% of the 3– to 4–year-olds and 18% of the 5– to 6–year-olds corroborated one or more false events that the interviewer erroneously believed had taken place. So, when the interviewer was misinformed, the children made "errors of commission." Additionally, the children seemed to become more credible as the interview unfolded. Many children initially stated details inconsistently or with reluctance or even denied them, but as the interviewer persisted in asking about nonevents, some of the children abandoned their hesitancy and denials to endorse the false information.

A review of the materials from some of the well-publicized child sexual abuse cases, such as *Little Rascals*, reveals that professional interviewers in these cases often steadfastly adhered to one hypothesis even when children continued to deny that the hypothesized events had ever occurred.[53]

§ 7–2.3.5 Peer Pressure and Peer Interaction

To date, there has been relatively little research on the effects of letting children know what their friends have already reported. This is an important issue for legal cases involving young witnesses because some investigators have used peer pressure to elicit disclosures from children. For example, in the *Kelly Michaels* case, one interviewer tried to persuade the children to disclose by telling them that their friends had already revealed the details of the alleged abuse: "All the other friends I talked to told me everything that happened. Randy told me. Charlie told me, Connie told me . . . . And now it's your turn to tell. You don't want to be left out, do you?" Later, in response to a child who did not disclose, the investigator said, "Boy, I'd hate having to tell your friends that you didn't want to help them."

Studies addressing peer pressure have demonstrated that the overheard responses of other children can have a negative influence on the accuracy of memory. Perhaps the most widely cited study regarding peer pressure is Binet's examination of suggestibility in children ages 7 to 14.[54] In this investigation, Binet showed children, who were in groups of three, a series of objects, such as a button glued onto a poster board. Next, the children were asked several misleading questions (e.g., "What was the color of the thread that attached the button to the board?") and told to call out the answer to each question as quickly as possible. Binet found that the children who replied second and third often gave the same answer as the first respondent, even if the answer was erroneous. In contrast, other research has shown that interviewing peers together facilitates disclosures from children who have actually experienced the event in question. For example, in one study, 7–year-olds who witnessed a staged classroom incident were less suggestible and provided more accurate reports when a friend accompanied them to the interview than when they were questioned alone.[55] Importantly, the results of these investigations indicate that the presence of a friend may enhance correct recall, but only under conditions in which children have something relevant to disclose. Otherwise, using peers to elicit disclosures may hinder the accuracy of children's accounts.

53. *See* Ceci & Bruck, *supra* note 10.

54. *See* BINET, *supra* note 32.

55. *See* Stephen Moston & Terry Engelberg, *The Effects of Social Support on Chil-*

dren's Eyewitness Testimony, 6 APPLIED COGNITIVE PSYCHOL. 61 (1992).

An issue related to peer pressure concerns peer interaction, or the extent to which children will fabricate false reports of events that they did not witness or experience but have found out about from peers. Concerns about peer interaction are relevant to children's testimonial abilities because, in naturally occurring situations, child witnesses presumably talk with friends about the incidents in question. Over time, such discussions may cause children within a peer group to hold increasingly similar hypotheses about what happened. In support of this account, Pynoos and Nader found that a number of children who were absent on the day of an actual sniper attack on their school later reported rather detailed memories of the event.[56] Presumably, these children heard about the event from their peers who were present during the sniper attack and later incorporated their friends' accounts into their own reports.

Peer interaction has special relevance to legal cases involving allegations of abuse in settings that involve groups of children (e.g., daycare programs, summer camp, organized trips) because witnesses caught up in these types of investigations frequently spend hours together daily. Further, child witnesses in daycare abuse cases often undergo group therapy sessions with their classmates, thus providing children additional opportunities to hear and be influenced by the perspectives of their peers. A key question is whether children who initially had different experiences will shape their reports to be in line with the peer group but inconsistent with their own experiences. We are currently exploring this issue in a study in which children are repeatedly questioned about non-witnessed events that their classmates either witnessed or overheard.

§ 7–2.3.6 Emotional Tone and Reinforcement of the Child's Behavior and Responses

Most practitioners believe that when questioning a child about a traumatic or embarrassing event, it is important to adopt a supportive and accepting approach while offering the child clear instructions and reinforcement for engaging in the interview process. Generally, the more at ease the child feels,[57] and the more he or she understands the purpose and "ground rules" of the interview, the more likely the child is to provide information that is accurate, detailed, and relevant.[58] Young children, in particular, are usually inexperienced in interviewing, and do not appreciate the intent or purpose of the interviewer's questions and the type of interaction that is expected. They cannot learn these aspects from someone other than the interviewer, as the purpose and ground rules of interviews in the home and classroom are likely to be very different from those in forensic interviews.[59] For example, in a discussion between a child and a teacher, it is generally accepted that the teacher knows more about the topic than the child. It is also generally acceptable for the child to attempt to provide the best answer he or she can to

56. *See* Robert S. Pynoos & Kathleen Nader, *Children's Memory and Proximity to Violence*, 28 J. Am. Acad. Child & Adolescent Psychiatry 236 (1989).

57. Goodman, et al., *supra* note 24.

58. Michael Siegal, *A Clash of Conversational Worlds: Interpreting Cognitive Development Through Communication*, *in* Perspectives on Socially Shared Cognition 23 (Lauren B. Resnick, John M. Levine & Stephanie D. Teasley eds., 1991).

59. J. Clare Wilson & Martine Powell, A Guide to Interviewing Children (forthcoming 2001).

questions, even if the answer is not correct. These principles, however, do not generalize to forensic interviews where the goal is to obtain the most accurate account about an event that the interviewer knows little or nothing about.

A distinction must be made, however, between an interviewer who encourages the child to engage appropriately in the *interview process* and an interviewer who uses selective reinforcement to guide *certain types of answers*. As outlined above, research has demonstrated that children can be led to believe or report false information, even when they have no initial memory of an event occurring. This is particularly likely to occur when an interviewer displays strong beliefs about the event in question, uses threats, bribes, or rewards to encourage the child to talk about the event, and reinforces only those responses that are consistent with the interviewer's beliefs about what occurred.[60] Under these circumstances, children may accept an interviewer's inaccurate suggestions, no matter how bizarre or incongruent, merely because they trust the interviewer and want to please him or her. While an interviewer may need to help a frightened and inexperienced child to engage in the interview process, such guidelines and reinforcements should not be contingent on the *quality* or *content* of the child's answers. Further, any display of attitudes or beliefs about the child, event, or perpetrator in question should be avoided.

§ 7–2.3.7 Type of Questioning Technique

Much empirical memory research has focused on how various questioning techniques affect the quality and accuracy of children's recall of events. Although this is a broad and complex area of research, several clear and consistent findings have emerged. These findings are discussed separately as they relate to two main styles of questioning; general or open-ended, non-specific questioning versus more focused, specific questioning.

General or open-ended, non specific questioning. Responses to general or open-ended non-specific questions typically are referred to as free narrative or free recall. Free narrative is obtained when interviewees are encouraged to provide an account of the event or situation in their own words, at their own pace, and without interruption. The account generally proceeds with the interviewer providing a general instruction or open-ended question, for example "Tell me everything you can remember about.... Start at the beginning. What was the first thing that happened." The interviewer then uses minimal nonverbal encouragers (e.g., head nods, pauses, "Mmmm," silence, "Uh–Huh") or further open-ended questions (e.g., "Tell me more about that," "What happened then?," "What else can you remember about . . . ?") to steer the interviewee to the next point in the story, or to gently encourage the interviewee to provide further narrative information. The importance of these prompts is that they are general; while they may focus the child on a particular part of the account, they do not dictate what specific information is required. Once specific questioning has begun, the child's responses are considered to be cued or guided rather than "free" narrative.

The benefits of eliciting a free narrative compared to more focused or brief responses are fourfold. First, responses to open-ended questions are

---

60. Leichtman & Ceci, *supra* note 38.

usually more accurate compared to more specific or focused questions. This is provided the child has not been subjected previously to multiple interviews involving persistent and erroneous suggestions.[61] Open-ended, non-specific questions tend to elicit more accurate information from children because when details requested in a specific question are not available in the child's memory, the child may attempt to answer the question anyway. Second, responses to specific questions mask poor comprehension as children can adopt strategies to cover up their limitations, such as repeating back phrases or words used by the interviewer, providing a stereotypical response, or providing affirmative answers to yes/no questions even if they do not understand them.[62] Third, swift questioning does not allow the interviewee and interviewer time to collect their thoughts, and as a consequence, does not lend itself to elaborate memory retrieval.[63] Finally, when the interviewer imposes his or her language and framework of the event, there is greater potential for confusion or misunderstanding.[64]

While a child's initial free narrative is regarded as the most reliable and accurate account, it is often "needlessly rushed" by interviewers.[65] One likely reason for this is that children provide relatively little information during free recall, particularly young children (i.e., preschoolers). Further, even if professionals are aware of the importance of such questions, they may not be able to use them effectively in their everyday practice.[66] Eliciting a free narrative from the child requires special training and quality control evaluation, not merely an understanding of the vulnerabilities of child interviewees and an awareness of the techniques that may be used to overcome these.

Focused or Specific Questioning. Although the free reports of cooperative interviewees typically provide the most accurate information, they do not provide all the information that is critical to an investigation. More focused questions usually are required at some point in the interview to elicit contextual features about the event for investigative purposes (e.g., details about where and when the event took place, precisely what happened, and where other people were). As indicated earlier, the problem with specific questioning is that error rates increase compared to spontaneously generated information. Therefore, it is essential that this phase of the interview is withheld until *after* the child's initial free narrative is exhausted.

Choosing questions carefully, however, can control the degree of error when eliciting specific details about an event. Generally the less restricted the answer to a question, or the less the interviewer imposes his or her view of

---

61. *See* Stephen J. Ceci et al., *Repeatedly Thinking about Non–Events*, 3 CONSCIOUSNESS & COGNITION 388 (1994); Leichtman & Ceci, *supra* note 38; C. B. Colo, & Elizabeth Loftus, *The Memory of Children, in* CHILDREN'S EYEWITNESS MEMORY 178 (Stephen J. Ceci, Michael P. Toglia & David F. Ross eds., 1987); Helen Dent & Geoffrey Stephenson, *An Experimental Study of the Effectiveness of Different Techniques of Interviewing Child Witnesses* 18 BRITISH J. SOC. & CLINICAL PSYCHOL. 41 (1979).

62. MICHELLE ALDRIDGE & JOANNE WOOD, INTERVIEWING CHILDREN: A GUIDE FOR CHILD CARE AND FORENSIC PRACTITIONERS (1998).

63. Michael E. Lamb et al., *Effects of Investigative Utterance Types on Israeli Children's Response*, 19 INT'L. J. BEHAV DEV 627 (1996).

64. MARK BRENNAN & ROSLYN BRENNAN, STRANGE LANGUAGE (1988).

65. *See* GRAHAM DAVIES ET AL., VIDEOTAPING CHILDREN'S EVIDENCE: AN EVALUATION (1995).

66. *See* Ron Fisher et al., *Critical Analysis of Police Interview Techniques* 15 J. POLICE SCI. & ADMIN. 177 (1987).

what happened, the lower the potential for errors or misunderstanding.[67] Closed questions that require a one or two word answer (e.g., "Was he wearing a shirt?") increase the likelihood of obtaining contaminated, inconsistent, or ambiguous answers compared to open-ended questions that require more elaborate responses (e.g., "What was he wearing?").[68] This is because child interviewees may acquiesce to or choose a response to a closed question merely to please the interviewer or to get the interview over with quickly, or they may believe that the interviewer's assumptions are correct.[69] Unless closed questions are followed with an open question that seeks further clarification, it may be difficult to determine whether the child actually has understood the question or provided a genuine response.

Leading and suggestive questions are the most problematic types of questions, as children are particularly vulnerable to accepting or assenting to false information suggested by an interviewer, regardless of its truth value.[70] Leading questions are those questions that suggest a certain answer is desired or assume the existence of disputed facts or facts that have not already been mentioned by the child. Suggestive questions include anything in the interviewer's tone, manner, or phrasing that suggests that a particular answer is desired or expected. Researchers have consistently demonstrated that children may agree with or take on false information reported by the interviewer, even when they do not understand the question, or when the information is not consistent with their recollection of the event. For instance, repeatedly asking a child about an alleged perpetrator in an accusatory fashion may subtly communicate to the child that the interviewer wants to hear bad things about this individual. Under these conditions, the child may comply simply to please the interviewer, whether or not he or she knows of any actual wrongdoing.[71]

The implication of these findings for investigating officers is that they should keep their questions as open as possible, while balancing the need for a full and detailed account against the need to minimize the potential for error. Asking a large number of specific questions may result in higher error rates, yet the potential benefits of obtaining more correct details may, in some cases, outweigh the risk of increased errors. For example, the details obtained from a child's responses to specific questions may offer investigating officers more leads to follow and more opportunities to obtain additional evidence to help corroborate the child's report. Indeed, if corroborative evidence is sufficiently strong, a conviction may be secured in some cases on the basis of this evidence and the child would not be required to testify in court.

§ 7–2.3.8 Visualization and Sociodramatic Play

Disclosures of child sexual abuse sometimes occur within the context of therapy sessions involving the use of fantasy, imagery inductions, visualiza-

67. Ceci & Bruck, *supra* note 10.

68. *See* Stephen Moston, *The Suggestibility of Children in Interview Studies*, 7 First Language 67 (1987); Debra A. Poole & Lawrence T. White, *Effects of Question Repetition on the Eyewitness Testimony of Children and Adults*, 27 Developmental Psychol. 975 (1991).

69. *See* Debra A. Poole & D. Stephen Lindsay, *Interviewing Preschoolers: Effects of Non-suggestive Techniques, Parental Coaching, and Leading Questions on Reports of Nonexperienced Events*, 60 J. Experimental Child Psychol. 129 (1995).

70. Ceci & Bruck, *supra* note 10.

71. Leichman & Ceci, *supra* note 38.

tion, and sociodramatic play.[72] For example, therapists may encourage children to regain control of their victimization by demonstrating with dolls and figurines what they would do if they saw the defendant again, or a therapist may use "homework" techniques that involve the child going home and thinking very hard about some of the things that were difficult to think about in therapy. Some investigative interviewing techniques advocate the use of visualization and imagery as a method of facilitating the child's recollection of an event. For example, the widely heralded cognitive interview, developed by Geiselman and colleagues, asks the witness to visualize how a scene might appear from the perspective of other persons or objects that were in the room.[73] Another component of the cognitive interview, mental reinstatement, instructs the witness to "close your eyes and take your mind back to the room.... Try to think about what the room was like. Think about things like what was around you; any smells there? Was it light or dark? Was any one else there? ... Tell me about that person." This is an important issue for studies of children's suggestibility because, for example, the adult memory literature has demonstrated that, under conditions highly supportive of recall of early experiences, when asked to think back to the day after they were born, a high proportion of adults report false day-after-birth experiences.[74]

Ceci and his colleagues have conducted a series of studies to examine whether asking preschool children to repeatedly think about events, constructing mental images each time they did so, would influence them to fabricate false memories.[75] The situations that the children were asked to think about were events that they experienced in the distant past (e.g., visiting an emergency room to get stitches) and fictitious episodes that never occurred (e.g., getting their hand caught in a mousetrap). Each week for 10 consecutive weeks, the children were asked to think about both actual and fictitious events and were offered prompts to help them visualize the scenes (e.g., "I want you to think about who was with you. What were they wearing? How did you feel?"). After 10 weeks of thinking about both real and fictitious experiences, the children were questioned by a new interviewer who provided specific and open ended prompts about both the true and false episodes (e.g., "Did you ever get your finger caught in a mousetrap and have to go to the hospital to get the trap off? ... Can you tell me more? What happened next?"). Over half of the children produced erroneous narratives for at least one of the fictitious events, with one quarter of the children reporting false memories for the majority of the nonexperienced events. Indeed, many of the accounts provided during the final week were highly detailed, plausible narratives. For instance, one child stated:

> My brother Colin was trying to get *Blowtorch* [an action figure] from me, and I wouldn't let him take it from me, so he pushed me into the wood pile where the mousetrap was. And then my finger got caught in it. And then we went to the hospital, and my mommy, daddy, and Colin drove me

72. *See* Ceci & Bruck, *supra* note 10.

73. *See* R. Edward Geiselman et al., *Enhancement of Eyewitness Memory: An Empirical Evaluation of the Cognitive Interview*, 12 J. POLICE SCI. & ADMIN. 74 (1984); R. Edward Geiselman et al., *Enhancement of Eyewitness Memory with the Cognitive Interview*, 99 AM. J. PSYCHOL. 385 (1986).

74. *See* Cheryl A. Terrance et al., *The Role of Expectation and Memory–Retrieval Techniques in the Construction of Beliefs About Past Events*, 14 APPLIED COGNITIVE PSYCHOL. 361 (2000).

75. *See* Ceci et al., *supra* note 61; Bruck et al., *supra* note 38; Ceci et al., *supra* note 39.

there, to the hospital in our van, because it was far away. And the doctor put a bandage on this finger.[76]

During their initial interviews, the children typically denied participating in the false events. Yet, false assent rates increased across the interviews, while the children's inaccurate reports became increasingly credible and elaborate (i.e., mean length of descriptions, confidence ratings, and amount of perceptual detail increased over time). After several interviews, these reports were indistinguishable from children's reports of true events both in terms of content and structure.[77] Further, many of the children continued to maintain these beliefs even in the face of considerable challenge. For example, 27% of the children in one study initially refused to accept debriefing at the completion of the study, with some insisting to both the researchers and their parents that they truly remembered the events happening.[78]

One explanation for the high rate of false reporting may be that the children were confused about the origins of their memories for the fictitious events and consequently misremembered the sources of these recollections as something that they actually experienced. Young children have particular difficulty separating the sources of memories based on actually experienced versus imagined events, often mistaking the familiarity of imagined episodes for real ones.[79] Thus, preschoolers appear to be especially susceptible to source misattributions when they are repeatedly encouraged to think about or visualize events that never occurred. This finding has real world implications for the reports of a child who has been in a certain type of therapy for a long time, engaging in imagery inductions and "memory work" techniques. Similarly, the above-described cognitive interview creates the risk that imagined events will be misattributed later as real events. Because repeatedly creating mental images is a pale version of what can take place in therapy when a variety of suggestive techniques may be used, these studies provide a fairly conservative test of the hypothesis that repeatedly thinking about a fictional event can lead to false beliefs about its reality.

§ 7–2.4 Additional Issues in Children's Memory and Testimony

Although most of the discussion so far has focused on children's suggestibility and the dynamics present in interviews conducted by biased interviewers, there are additional issues of concern. The following section addresses two such issues, the first being the pitfalls involved with the use of tools, such as anatomical dolls, in interviews with children and the other being children's ability to discriminate events in time.

§ 7–2.4.1 Dolls and Props

Dolls and props are used frequently by professionals who conduct investigative interviews with children.[80] There are several rationales behind the use

76. Ceci et al., *supra* note 61, at 399.

77. *See* Bruck et al., *supra* note 38.

78. *See* Ceci et al., *supra* note 61.

79. *See* Mary Ann Foley et al., *Discriminating Between Memories: Evidence for Children's Spontaneous Elaborations*, 48 J. EXPERIMENTAL CHILD PSYCHOL. 146 (1989).

80. *See* Lizette Peterson & Robyn Ridley–Johnson, *Pediatric Hospital Response to Survey on Prehospital Preparation for Children*, 5 J. PEDIATRIC PSYCHOL. 1 (1980); Jon R. Conte et al., *Evaluating Children's Reports of Sexual Abuse: Results from a Survey of Professionals*, 78 AM. J. ORTHOPSYCHIATRY 428 (1991).

of such tools. First, dolls and props are thought to lessen the language demands of verbal interviews and as such facilitate the expression of young children who are unable to describe their experiences in words. A related rationale is that doll and prop manipulation may serve as reminders of the alleged event and thereby cue recall. In addition, doll and prop enactment is thought to help children overcome certain motivational problems, such as embarrassment and shyness, that may be associated with being asked to talk about abusive events. Finally, some professionals have argued that particular behaviors, such as avoidance of the dolls and preoccupation with the dolls' genitalia, are diagnostic of abuse.

Despite the widespread use of anatomically detailed dolls in assessments of alleged child abuse (the rate of doll use in some jurisdictions may be as high as 90%),[81] some researchers and professionals have expressed skepticism about their usefulness as a diagnostic tool. Two concerns have frequently been raised. The first is that, by their very nature, anatomical dolls are suggestive. That is, dolls may encourage sexual play even when abuse has not occurred.[82] For example, a child may insert her finger into a female doll's vagina because of its novelty or simply because it is there. A related criticism of dolls is that judgments about past abuse should not be made on the basis of doll play because research has demonstrated that dolls do not meet the traditional standards of a reliable assessment instrument.[83] Because of these concerns, the use of anatomically detailed dolls for the purposes of providing legal evidence has been banned in a few jurisdictions until research supports their validity.

At the present time, there are at least 20 studies that have explored the diagnostic utility of dolls as an assessment tool. In general, these studies have focused on three related issues. The first deals with whether abused children interact with dolls differently than nonabused children. The second involves examining how normal children interact with dolls. The third concerns the degree to which dolls facilitate children's reporting of personally experienced events.

First, doll play is not a good indicator of abuse status. Generally, there are few differences in doll play of abused and nonabused children. Second, normative studies of doll play indicate that both avoidance of dolls and preoccupation with dolls' genitalia are fairly common among nonabused children, thus suggesting that these behaviors cannot be considered diagnostic of sexual abuse. For example, in Everson and Boat's observations of more than 200 nonabused preschool children at play with dolls, between 3 and 18% of the older preschoolers showed suggestive or clear intercourse positioning.[84]

A third line of study has examined whether manipulating dolls during memory interviews influences the accuracy and completeness of children's

---

81. *See* Barbara W. Boat & Mark D. Everson, *Use of Anatomical Dolls Among Professionals in Sexual Abuse Investigations*, 12 CHILD ABUSE & NEGLECT 171 (1988); Conte et al., *supra* note 80.

82. *See* Lenore C. Terr, *Anatomically Correct Dolls: Should They Be Used As a Basis for Expert Testimony?* 27 J. AM. ACAD. CHILD & ADOLESCENT PSYCHIATRY 245 (1988).

83. *See* Linda J. Skinner & Kenneth K. Berry, *Anatomically Detailed Dolls and the Evaluations of Child Sexual Abuse Investigations: Psychometric Considerations*, 17 LAW & HUM. BEHAV. 399 (1993); Glenn Wolfner et al., *The Use of Anatomical Dolls in Sexual Abuse Evaluations: The State of the Science*, 2 APPLIED & PREVENTATIVE PSYCHOL. 1 (1993).

84. *See* Boat & Everson, *supra* note 81.

accounts. For example, Gordon and her colleagues compared the effectiveness of a verbal interview with two alternate protocols that involved the use of a doll as a means to assess 3– and 5–year-olds' recall of a pediatric examination.[85] The children's memory was assessed three weeks after their checkups in one of three interview conditions. The children in the verbal interview condition were questioned about the details of their examination using a verbal protocol, whereas those in the representational and role play conditions were provided a doll and interviewed with modified protocols. The children in the representational condition were asked to view the doll as a model of the self and to use it to demonstrate what happened during their checkup. In contrast, the children in the role play condition were asked to pretend that the doll was another child who was going to receive a checkup and to show the doll what happened during their recent visit to the doctor. The dolls were dressed only in their underwear and were not sexually detailed. Although the dolls enhanced the recall of the 5–year-olds, the use of dolls did not improve the reports of the 3–year-olds. In fact, in the role play condition, the provision of dolls increased the proportion of errors made by the younger children.

Because anatomically detailed dolls are believed to provide children a tool that will help them overcome their shyness and embarrassment when asked to talk about sexual matters, perhaps dolls would facilitate young children's reports of embarrassing events of a sexual nature. To address this issue, Bruck and her colleagues examined 3–year-old children's memories of a routine pediatric checkup involving genital touching.[86] Half of the children received a genital examination in which the pediatrician touched their buttocks and genitals, and the other half of the children were not touched in these areas. Immediately after the checkup, an experimenter pointed to the genitalia or buttocks of an anatomically detailed doll and asked the children, "Did the doctor touch you here?" Only 47% of the children who received the genital examination correctly said "yes," a figure approximating that obtained by others for errors of omissions (i.e., denying the occurrence of something that really did take place). In contrast, 50% of the children who did not receive a genital examination incorrectly replied "yes" to this question. When the children were asked to "show on the doll" how the doctor had touched their buttocks or genitalia, recall accuracy did not improve. Only 25% of the children who received a genital examination correctly showed how the pediatrician had touched their genitalia and buttocks. Accuracy decreased in part because a significant number of the female children inserted their fingers into the doll's vagina or anus, something that the pediatrician never did. When the children who did not receive a genital examination were asked to demonstrate on the doll how the doctor had touched their genitals and buttocks, only 50% of the children correctly showed no touching; 50% of the children who did not receive genital examinations incorrectly showed either genital or anal touching when given the dolls. This study was repeated with a group of 4–year-olds and obtained quite similar results.[87]

85. *See* Betty N. Gordon et al., *Does the Use of Dolls Facilitate Children' s Memory of Visits to the Doctor?* 7 APPLIED COGNITIVE PSYCHOL. 459 (1993).

86. *See* Maggie Bruck et al., *Anatomically Detailed Dolls Do Not Facilitate Preschoolers'* *Reports of a Pediatric Examination Involving Genital Touching*, 1 J. EXPERIMENTAL PSYCHOL.: APPLIED 95 (1995).

87. *See* Maggie Bruck et al., *Children's Use of Anatomically Detailed Dolls To Report on Genital Touching in a Medical Examination:*

Perhaps dolls do not enhance the performance of young children because a doll alone does not provide enough contextual support for recall. Indeed, it seems possible that the performance of young children may improve if they are provided both dolls and props that are similar to objects used in the original event. That is, props may serve as additional memory cues and encourage demonstration to a greater extent than a doll alone. Further facilitation may be observed if children are interviewed in a setting that resembles the environment in which the to-be-remembered experience occurred. To address these issues, Greenhoot and her colleagues compared children's reports of a recent pediatric examination under verbal and enactment conditions.[88] Half of the children were interviewed using a verbal protocol, whereas the others were interviewed in a room that resembled a pediatric examining room, enabling them to enact as well as report the details of their doctor visit. The simulated examining room contained a variety of props, including replicas of instruments that had actually been used during the children's checkups (e.g., a stethoscope) as well as medically relevant props that were not involved in the actual event (e.g., a thermometer). The children in the enactment condition provided more information in response to general probes and more elaboration than those in the verbal interview condition, with the 3–year-olds showing greater enhancement in the supportive context than the 5–year-olds. However, the children in the enactment condition generated more spontaneous false reports of actions that did not occur during the checkup than those in the verbal interview condition, and this difference was more pronounced among the 3– than the 5–year-olds. Thus, these data suggest that enactment with dolls and props can enhance the recall of young children, but that it does so at the price of a substantial increase in incorrect responding.

These findings regarding the negative mnemonic effects of doll use are incongruous with the widely held belief that children who have not been sexually touched will not demonstrate sexual events on dolls.[89] These results, however, are consistent with research by DeLoache that suggests that children younger than 3 years of age lack the cognitive sophistication to appreciate symbolic relationships in which an object stands for something other than itself.[90] This is an important point because to use dolls accurately during interviews, children must be able to recognize simultaneously that the doll is both a toy and a symbol representing the self. A study by DeLoache and Marzolf illustrates young children's difficulty using dolls to represent themselves.[91] When 2.5– to 4–year-olds were asked to place stickers on a doll in the same places that stickers had been placed on their own bodies, many of the children did not realize that they were supposed to treat the doll as a representation of themselves. In fact, several children rejected the suggestion

Developmental and Gender Comparisons, J. EXPERIMENTAL PSYCHOL.: APPLIED (forthcoming 2001).

88. *See* Andrea Follmer Greenhoot et al., *Acting Out the Details of a Pediatric Check-up: The Impact of Interview Condition and Behavioral Style on Children's Memory Reports*, 70 CHILD DEVELOPMENT 363 (1999).

89. *See* Gail S. Goodman & Christine Aman, *Children's Use of Anatomically Detailed*

Dolls to Recount an Event, 61 CHILD DEV. 1859 (1990).

90. *See* Judy S. DeLoache, *Young Children's Understanding of Models*, in KNOWING AND REMEMBERING IN YOUNG CHILDREN 94 (Robyn Fivush & Judith A. Hudson eds., 1990).

91. *See* Judy S. DeLoache & Donald P. Marzolf, *The Use of Dolls to Interview Young Children: Issues of Symbolic Representation*, 60 J. EXPERIMENTAL CHILD PSYCHOL. 155 (1995).

that they "pretend that this doll is you." This is a noteworthy finding because an unwillingness to play with dolls in therapeutic and forensic settings is in some cases thought to be an indicator of abuse.[92]

§ 7–2.5 Children's Ability to Recall a Single Occurrence of a Repeated Event

Children's recall of a single occurrence of a repeated event is an important issue for the legal system. For an alleged offender to be charged and convicted in relation to a repeated offense (e.g., acts of sexual abuse that occurred on more than one occasion), at least one specific occurrence must be identified with reasonable precision with reference to time and place.[93] The act of remembering an occurrence of a repeated event after a delay in time is a difficult task, especially for child witnesses whose knowledge of time and sequencing ability is not as sophisticated as that of adults.[94] There are two aspects that witnesses may find difficult when recalling an occurrence of a repeated event. A witness may find it difficult to *identify* a particular occurrence of the alleged offense and pinpoint exactly when it occurred in time. Further, a witness may find it difficult to *recall* details that were included in a particular occurrence of the event. Research to date has focused on the latter aspect.

Repeated experience of an event has been shown to have both beneficial and baleful effects on children's memory, depending on the nature of the event-details being recalled. After multiple occurrences of an event, details that are fixed (experienced exactly the same way during each occurrence) are strengthened in memory and are therefore well remembered over time compared to details of an event that was experienced only one time.[95] The better items are remembered the less likely they are to be contaminated or altered by an interviewer's false suggestions.[96] However, with regards to children's recall of details that *vary* across occurrences (e.g., remembering what clothing was worn by a person the last time the event was experienced when the items of clothing differed each time), repeated experience has detrimental effects on children's ability to remember a particular occurrence. Specifically, the number of correct details reported about a *particular* occurrence is lower than when recalling a one-time event, as intrusions of details from other occurrences (referred to as internal intrusion errors) are common.[97] While details that are not included in *any* occurrence are less likely to be reported by children who have experienced a repeated versus a one-time event, the number of internal intrusion errors outweighs the number of false details reported by children who have experienced a one-time event. The high number of internal intrusions arise because recalling an occurrence of a

92. *See* Mary A. Mason, *A Judicial Dilemma: Expert Witness Testimony in Child Sexual Abuse Cases*, J. Psychiatry & Law 185 (Winter 1991).

93. *See* S vs. R, 89 A.L.R., 321 (1989).

94. William Friedman, *The Development of Children's Memory for the Time of Past Events*, 62 Child Dev. 139 (1991).

95. *See* Martine B. Powell & Donald M. Thomson, *Children's Recall of an Occurrence of a Repeated Event: Effects of Age, Retention Interval and Question Type*, 67 Child Dev. 1988 (1996); Kathy Pezdek & Chantal Roe, *The Effect of Memory Trace Strength on Suggestibility*, 60 J. Experimental Child Psychol. 116 (1995).

96. *See* Martine Powell et al., *The Effects of Repeated Experience on Children's Suggestibility*, 35 Developmental Psychol. 1462 (1999).

97. *See* Hudson, *supra* note 13; Powell & Thomson, *supra* note 95.

repeated event involves memory of *content* (i.e., remembering which details were experienced in the event per se) as well as the capacity to remember the source or *temporal location* of details (i.e., remembering precisely which details were included in the target occurrence while keeping this occurrence distinct from others in time). While memory for both the content and temporal source of details weakens over time, the decline is more rapid for temporal information.[98]

The problems associated with children's recall of variable details of an occurrence of a repeated event are accentuated under certain conditions. The more frequently events are experienced, the longer the time delay between the event and the interview, and the greater the similarity between the events, the more difficult it is to keep track of which details were included in a particular occurrence.[99] Young children (i.e., 4–5 year olds) have greater difficulties in discriminating between occurrences of a repeated event than older children.[100] Further, the accuracy of children's recall of an occurrence of a repeated event is shaped by the manner in which memory is tested. When children are asked to freely report what happened in an occurrence of a repeated event, they provide few specific features that discriminate one occurrence from others in the series. In contrast, when questions are asked which focus the child on specific aspects of the event that were likely to have varied, confusion between the occurrences is more evident.[101] However, children's difficulty in remembering an occurrence of a repeated event does not necessarily make them more suggestible compared to children who have experienced a one-time event. If children are asked to generate a response about an occurrence in their own words (e.g.,"What color shirt did he wear the last time?"), they are no more likely to report suggestions that were previously offered by the interviewer as compared to children who experienced a one-time event. However, in response to "yes/no" questions (e.g., "Was the man's shirt red that day?"), repeated experience with an event *increases* children's susceptibility to acquiesce to false suggestions.[102] Further, when false details are suggested about a repeated event that are not linked to any target occurrence of the event (i.e., they are merely suggested as occurring in the event per se), the detrimental effect on children's reports is reduced considerably.[103]

The implication of these findings is that the presence of errors in a child witness' account about a specific occurrence should not be taken to mean that other details of the child's account have been fabricated. However, there is no

---

98. *See* Martine Powell & Donald Thomson, *Contrasting Memory for Temporal–Source and Memory for Content in Children's Discrimination of Repeated Events*, 11 APPLIED COGNITIVE PSYCHOL. 339 (1997).

99. Stephen Lindsay et al., *Developmental Changes in Memory Source Monitoring*, 52 J. EXPERIMENTAL CHILD PSYCHOL. 297 (1991).

100. Michael Farrar & Gail Goodman, *Developmental Changes in Event Memory*, 73 CHILD DEV. 173 (1992).

101. Powell & Thomson, *supra* note 22.

102. Deborah Connolly & Stephen Lindsay, *The Influence of Suggestions on Children's Reports of a Unique Experience Versus Reporting*

of a Repeated Experience, APPLIED COGNITIVE PSYCHOL. (forthcoming 2001); Martine Powell & Kim Roberts, *The Effect of Repeated Experience on Children's Suggestibility Across Two Question Types (manuscript submitted for publication)*; Martine Powell et al., *The Effects of Repeated Experience on Children's Suggestibility*, 35 DEVELOPMENTAL PSYCHOL., 1462 (1999).

103. Martine B. Powell et al., *The Effect of a Suggestive Interview on Children's Memory of a Repeated Event: Does It Matter Whether Suggestions are Linked to a Particular Incident? in* PSYCHIATRY, PSYCHOL. & L. (forthcoming 2001).

clear basis for distinguishing errors intruding from other occurrences from errors relating to details that were not experienced in any occurrence of the event. As with non-repeated events, memory performance is improved when specific cues are used to help children access distinctive information. However, specific questions also increase the rate of intrusion errors, and increase the likelihood that children will acquiesce to false suggestions. Conducting repeated non-leading interviews may be one way to minimize the loss of information over time, rather than simply relying on a single, delayed interview.[104] However, the effective use of repeated interviews requires careful consideration of factors related to children's suggestibility and of the stress that additional interviews impose on the child.[105]

§ 7–2.6 Memory and Development

Thus far, we have discussed several critical issues in children's memory without stating any definitive conclusions about differences in performance across age. The following section outlines the areas where there are clear age differences in performance that may influence the degree of accuracy of a child's account. It is important to keep in mind, however, that age differences are differences in degree only. Children of all ages can provide information that is forensically relevant and accurate, while no particular age group is immune to suggestion.

§ 7–2.6.1 Age Differences in Suggestibility

Contrary to the claims made by some authors,[106] there is sufficient empirical evidence to conclude that preschool aged children are proportionally more vulnerable to suggestion than are older children and adults. In a recent review of the suggestibility literature, 15 of 18 studies supported this conclusion.[107] However, the research also suggests that age differences in errors are reduced in cases where misleading and suggestive questions are avoided. In other words, if an interviewer uses a neutral tone, limits the use of misleading questions, and has no strong bias or motive for the child to make a false report, young children (i.e., three-to five-year-olds) can provide highly accurate accounts, even though their reports may include few details. On the other hand, these conditions do not necessarily make children immune to suggestion. In rare cases, young children may still make spontaneous, bizarre, and unfounded allegations even when questioned by a neutral interviewer who asks few leading and suggestive questions.[108]

There are a number of possible cognitive mechanisms and social factors that might account for the greater suggestibility of young children. These include weaker memory skills, smaller general knowledge bases, lesser developed language and reality monitoring skills, and a desire to please an

104. Powell & Thomson, *supra* note 22.

105. *See* J. E. B. Myers, *The Literature of the Backlash, in* THE BACKLASH: CHILD PROTECTION UNDER FIRE, (J. E. B. Myers ed., 1994).

106. *See* Gary B. Melton, *Children as Partners for Justice: Next Steps for Developmentalists,* 57 (Serial No. 229) MONOGRAPHS OF THE SOCIETY FOR RESEARCH IN CHILD DEVELOPMENT 153 (1992).

107. *See* Ceci & Bruck, *supra* note 10 (Table 2).

108. Saywitz et al., *supra* note 14; Gail S. Goodman et al., *Testifying in Criminal Court: Emotional Effects on Child Sexual Assault Victims,* 57 (Serial No. 229) MONOGRAPHS OF THE SOCIETY FOR RESEARCH IN CHILD DEVELOPMENT (1992).

authoritative interviewer or gain material or social rewards. Indeed, preschooler's susceptibility to suggestion has been found to be predicted by factors such as IQ and memory performance.[109] In the future, research is likely to focus more on understanding the role of individual difference variables (i.e., cognitive, social *and* personality variables) in suggestibility effects with children, rather than global differences across development.

§ 7–2.6.2 Age Differences in Memory

One factor that has been proposed to underlie age differences in suggestibility concerns developmental changes in memory itself. In this view, younger children's heightened vulnerability to suggestion is a direct consequence of their weaker ability to encode, store, and retrieve information in memory over time. This position is based on a fairly large literature that indicates that with increases in age, there are associated changes in a variety of basic information-processing skills (e.g., knowledge, memory strategies, processing speed)[110] that affect what gets into memory, what happens to it during storage, and its subsequent retrievability.[111] It also comes from a theoretical position that suggestibility occurs as a function of the strength of the original memory, with weak memories being especially susceptible to suggestion.[112] Thus, if information about an experience is encoded inadequately, deteriorates in storage, or becomes difficult to retrieve, suggestions are more likely to interfere than if the memory is strongly encoded, well maintained, and easily retrievable.

To explore the link between memory strength and suggestibility, Principe manipulated the degree to which 4–year-olds were able to encode a specific experience.[113] The children participated in a shopping event in which they were read aloud a list of six items needed to bake cookies and asked to buy them from a specially constructed grocery store. Half of the children received a single presentation of the list (one-trial learning), whereas the remaining half received successive presentations until they learned the items to a strict recall criterion (criterion learning). Following the grocery shopping event, the children were interviewed in either a neutral or suggestive manner on three different occasions spread out over a 3–week time period. The suggestive interviews contained strongly worded suggestions that certain items had been on the list, when in fact they were not. One week later, all of the children were questioned in a neutral manner by a new interviewer. Compared to the children in the other three groups, those in the one-trial suggestive group were more likely to report buying the suggested items, indicating that weak memories are more susceptible than strong memories to suggestive questioning. Moreover, the largest degradations in accuracy among the children in the one-trial suggestive condition were observed in their free recall, that is, in the production of intrusions of suggested items. Indeed, 93% of the children in the

---

109. Felicity McFarlane, An Examination of the Validity and Usefulness of the Video Suggestibility Scale for Children (unpublished Ph.D. dissertation, Deakin University, Australia) (on file with authors).

110. *See* ROBERT V. KAIL, THE DEVELOPMENT OF MEMORY IN CHILDREN (2d ed. 1989).

111. *See* Peter A. Ornstein et al., *Understanding Children's Testimony: Implications of Research on the Development of Memory, in* ANNALS OF CHILD DEVELOPMENT 145 (Ross Vasta ed., 1991).

112. *See* C. J. Brainerd & V. F. Reyna, *Memory Loci of Suggestibility Development: Comment on Ceci, Ross, & Toglia (1987)*, 117 J. EXPERIMENTAL PSYCHOL.: GENERAL 197 (1988).

113. *See* Principe, *supra* note 26.

one-trial suggestive group produced at least one intrusion, in contrast to 0 to 14% of the children in the other three groups. Further, many of these children embellished their free narratives with a large number of fabricated details that had not been provided during, but were nonetheless consistent with, the suggestive interviews.

Taken together, the Principe results indicate that the impact of suggestive questioning is dependent in part on memory strength. Many of the children in the criterion suggestive group maintained highly accurate free recall during the final interview, despite repeated erroneous suggestions. However, the same request for free recall, following the same set of suggestive interviews, led to highly inaccurate reports among the children in the one-trial condition, indicating the powerful effect of suggestive questioning when memory for the event in question is weak. Thus, these findings suggest that if a child does not have a clear memory of a particular event (e.g., an experience that occurred several months or years earlier at his or her daycare center), it may be easier to implant a false suggestion than it would be with another child who has a strong memory of the event in question. From a legal point of view, these results are important because they suggest one condition under which children's accounts are especially vulnerable to suggestive questioning.

One implication of a memory strength framework is that age differences in suggestibility occur because younger children encode weaker memories and forget more rapidly than do older children.[114] In addition to making a priori predictions about age trends in suggestibility, memory strength theory provides a rich source of hypotheses about the conditions under which even very young children may be resistant to suggestion. For example, in situations where younger children are more knowledgeable than older children, the latter might be expected to establish more enduring memories that are more resistant to the interfering effects of suggestion. Further, memories that become exceptionally strong as the result of repeated practice and reinforcement, such as a child's own name or birthday, should be extremely difficult to influence.

§ 7-2.6.3 Age Differences in Knowledge

Various research traditions dealing with different types of knowledge, such as semantic knowledge[115] and scripted knowledge[116] have provided ample evidence that what children know affects how information is encoded, stored, and retrieved. Under most conditions, prior knowledge facilitates remembering. For example, child chess experts have been shown to recall the board positions of earlier games better than do non-expert adults.[117] In addition to amount of knowledge, the way that knowledge is structured affects the extent to which memory for an event is enriched during encoding and storage by mnemonic strategies such as elaboration, imagery, and inference. For instance, investigations of story recall have demonstrated that, with age, children become increasingly likely to draw upon their general knowledge to

114. *See* Bender et al., *supra* note 27; Brainerd & Reyna, *supra* note 112.

115. *See* Michelene T. H. Chi, *Knowledge Structures and Memory Development, in* CHILDREN'S THINKING: WHAT DEVELOPS (Robert S. Siegler ed., 1978).

116. *See* KATHERINE NELSON, EVENT KNOWLEDGE: STRUCTURE AND FUNCTION IN DEVELOPMENT (1986).

117. *See* Chi, *supra* note 115.

generate inferences that are consistent with but not included in the actual text.[118] However, when knowledge is inconsistent with what actually occurred, it can interfere with reporting accuracy. To illustrate, kindergarten children have been shown to incorrectly recall the sex of the actor of gender-incongruent tasks after being shown pictures of males and females engaging in gender-stereotypic tasks.[119]

Thus, age-related differences in the amount and structure of knowledge may lead older children to take in more relevant information regarding an experience and to construct more elaborate and enduring memories than younger children. Because of their relatively impoverished knowledge base, children may be more susceptible than older children and adults to misleading information. Developmental differences may be especially pronounced in situations in which a suggestion holds no meaning to the child given his or her lack of understanding of the subject matter, but is absurd or discrepant with the older child's or adult's knowledge base. This point has particular relevance to sexual abuse investigations where young children with fairly limited sexual knowledge may permit the incorporation of false suggestions that, because of their implausibility, likely would be rejected by older children and adults.

Scripted knowledge also has been shown to affect memory and suggestibility. Scripts are temporally and causally organized general memories of routine, repeated events.[120] For example, a child's script of a birthday party might include making a wish, blowing out candles, eating cake, opening presents, and playing games. Although scripts become more elaborate and complex with age, even very young children develop scripts for familiar routines and use expectations generated by scripts to fill in gaps in memory. For example, preschool age children have been shown to report information from their scripts of what happens at daycare when they forget the details of a particular episode.[121] However, when expectations run counter to what actually occurred, scripts can lead to the generation of erroneous memories for the actual event.[122]

Research on scripts reveal that age-related changes in scripted knowledge may contribute to developmental differences in memory and suggestibility. Once young children have developed a script for an event, they rely heavily on it for guiding their recall of events. For example, when 2 ½-year-olds were asked to tell what happened during recent special events, like a trip to the beach or a camping trip, they were more apt to report familiar routines, such as waking up, eating, and going to bed, rather than the novel aspects of these special events.[123] Researchers have speculated that younger children focus on the repeated aspects of events because they are actively working to establish what is common across multiple experiences. Thus, because young children are still in the process of acquiring and modifying event knowledge with each

118. *See* Teresa Nezworksi et al., *Story Structure Versus Content in Children's Recall,* 21 J. VERBAL LEARNING & VERBAL BEHAVIOR 196 (1982); Scott G. Paris & Laurence R. Upton, *Children's Memory for Inferential Relationships in Prose,* 47 CHILD DEV. 660 (1976).

119. *See* Carol L. Martin & Charles F. Halverson, *The Effects of Sex–Typing Schemas on Young Children's Memory,* 54 CHILD DEV. 563 (1983).

120. *See* NELSON, *supra* note 116.

121. *See* Myles–Worsley et al., *supra* note 30.

122. *See* Ornstein et al., *supra* note 36.

123. *See* Fivush & Hamond, *supra* note 18.

new experience, they have difficulty distinguishing special events from typical events.[124] As a result, younger children's scripts are more likely to absorb both one-time and repeated episodes, whereas older children are better able to tag one-time events as unique and establish separate, nonscript memories for such experiences. Thus, age differences in suggestibility may be due to, at least in part, younger children's dependence on scripted knowledge and their tendency to incorporate novel events (such as a false suggestion) into their scripts.

Under certain conditions, however, older children's more elaborate scripts may lead to the generation of false inferences about events that were not witnessed but are nonetheless consistent with an existing script. For example, when participants were erroneously told that a film depicted cheating, older but not younger children were likely to report witnessing cheating based on innocent acts such as one student asking another for the time.[125] Presumably, because younger children's scripts did not include asking for the time as a method of cheating, they were less likely than older children to succumb to the erroneous suggestion.

Thus, the relationship between age, scripted knowledge, and suggestibility is rather complex. When misleading information is consistent with an existing script, it should be easier to implant in memory than if it is incongruent with scripted knowledge. Further, because young children rely heavily on scripts to organize their recall, their memories may be more easily influenced by script congruent suggestions than those of older children whose recall is less dependent on scripts. Also, because younger children tend to fuse both repeated and one-time information into their early scripts, they are more likely than older children to incorporate suggested information into their developing scripts. However, in situations where young children have not yet established a script for an event, older children may be more prone to incorporate suggestions into their subsequent reports. Further, it is possible that children may acquire event scripts simply as the result of repeated questioning about an alleged occurrence.

§ 7–2.6.4   Age Differences in Source Monitoring

An abundance of research has examined children's ability to identify the sources of their memories (e.g., to judge whether they actually saw something or merely imagined it, whether they learned information from one person as opposed to another, or had experienced an event as opposed to simply observing it on television).[126] Source monitoring errors occur when a memory derived from one source is misattributed to another source. Source confusions can be the basis of suggestibility effects, at least in some situations. For example, if one recalls a suggested detail but does not remember the source of that information, then one could misidentify the source of that suggested detail as actually experienced.

124. *See* Farrar & Goodman, *supra* note 100.

125. *See* Marc Lindberg, *An Interactive Approach to Assessing Suggestibility and Testimony of Eyewitnesses, in* THE SUGGESTIBILITY OF CHILDREN'S RECOLLECTIONS: IMPLICATIONS FOR EYEWITNESS TESTIMONY 47 (John Doris ed., 1991).

126. Kim P. Roberts & Mark Blades, *Discriminating Between Memories of Television and Real–Life, in* CHILDREN'S SOURCE MONITORING (Kim P. Roberts & Mark Blades eds., 2000).

An experiment by Poole and Lindsay shows how even subtle interventions, such as parents' reading a book to their child, can cause source monitoring confusions.[127] In this study, preschoolers participated in activities (e.g., folding paper airplanes) with Mr. Science. Four months later, the children's parents were mailed a specially constructed storybook that described both experienced and nonexperienced activities. The parents read this story to their children three times. When later interviewed about what happened during their visit with Mr. Science, a high proportion of the children reported that Mr. Science had done things that were mentioned only in the story. For example, more than half of children agreed that Mr. Science put something "yucky" in their mouths, and many of these children provided details about this nonexperienced event. When asked, "Did Mr. Science put something yuckie in your mouth or did your Mom just read you this in a story," 71% of the children said that it really happened. This occurred despite warnings that some things in the story may not have happened and prior training to say "no" to nonexperienced events. Thus, this study demonstrates that even subtle exposure to misleading information (i.e., when children are never explicitly told that the suggested events happened to them or pressured to report these events) can lead to source monitoring errors about events that could be construed by adults as sexual in nature.

Although source monitoring errors occur at all ages, developmental research indicates that, under most conditions, younger children are more vulnerable to source confusions than are older children and adults.[128] Age differences tend to be greater when the sources to be discriminated are perceptually and semantically similar (e.g., when distinguishing between two female speakers that had spoken a word than distinguishing between words spoken by a male speaker and a female speaker),[129] and when distinguishing events that occurred a long time rather than a short time previously.[130] Further, even though participants of all ages are likely to continue to make source monitoring errors even after being warned not to believe anything that was said to them about the to-be-remembered event, preschoolers are especially likely to do so.[131]

The most likely explanation of developmental differences in source monitoring ability is that younger children are less likely than older children and adults to search memory methodically for additional information when confused about the particular source of a recollection.[132] Indeed, this age related trend may partly explain the fact that preschool age children are more suggestible than older children. For example, if an interviewer suggests details that did not occur in an event, younger children would be expected to have greater difficulty remembering whether they had experienced or merely heard about those details of the event. Overall, these results suggest that it

127. *See* Poole & Lindsay, *supra* note 69.

128. *See* Jennifer K. Ackil & Maria S. Zaragoza, *Developmental Differences In Eyewitness Suggestibility and Memory for Source,* 60 J. EXPERIMENTAL CHILD PSYCHOL. 57 (1995); D. Stephen Lindsay et al., *Aware and Unaware Uses of Memories of Postevent Suggestions, in* MEMORY AND TESTIMONY IN THE CHILD WITNESS (Maria S. Zaragoza et al. eds., 1995).

129. *See* Lindsay et al., *supra* note 99.

130. Robyn Holliday et al., *Children's Eyewitness Suggestibility: Memory Trace Strength Revisited,* 14 COGNITIVE DEV. 443 (1999).

131. *See* Lindsay et al., *supra* note 99.

132. *See* Brian P. Ackerman, *Children's Retrieval Deficit, in* BASIC PROCESSES IN MEMORY DEVELOPMENT: PROGRESS IN COGNITIVE DEVELOPMENT RESEARCH (Charles J. Brainerd & Michael Pressley eds., 1985).

may be particularly important to conduct interviews as early as possible with preschool children compared to older children, and to avoid the use of suggestive and misleading interview techniques. In addition, minimizing the performance demands made on young children for highly specific details (such as temporal information) may reduce the rate of errors.

§ 7–2.6.5 Individual Differences in Children's Memory and Suggestibility

While a child's age has a large impact on memory performance and the degree to which that child is suggestible, age is not the only factor to account for differences in eyewitness performance. Within any age-matched group of children, there is large variability in memory and suggestibility. Given this variability, researchers have recently directed their attention to understanding the precise role of individual difference variables (i.e., cognitive, social and personality variables) in determining memory performance and suggestibility effects, rather than investigating global differences in performance across development. One of the most robust findings in this area is that intelligence (i.e., IQ test performance) negatively relates to suggestibility when a broad range of test scores is obtained. That is, participants with lower intelligence are more suggestible than participants with higher intelligence.[133] While the specific mechanisms underlying this relationship are yet to be determined, it is likely that individuals with lower intelligence also have weaker memory capacity, language ability, and poorer knowledge of the event, which in turn increases their susceptibility to suggestion. Indeed, research has shown that there is a high interrelationship between IQ and these other variables and that in combination these variables account for more of the variance in suggestibility than IQ alone.[134] Note however, that memory of the event and IQ have also been shown to make a small but significant independent contribution to suggestibility.[135]

In addition to cognitive factors, children's memory of an event and their suggestibility has also been shown to relate to social, personality and demo graphic factors. Although research in this area is still in its infancy (and the proposed relationships are largely speculative), higher levels of self-esteem and parental socio-economic status and greater quality of the parent-child relationship and communication style have all been shown to reduce the child's vulnerability to reporting false information.[136] Given that children's cognitive abilities and memory performance is integrally connected with their social and emotional functioning; investigators should attempt to include a variety of factors from various domains in their research designs. It is

133. Gudbjorg Danielsdottir et al., *Interrogative Suggestibility in Children and Its Relationship with Memory and Vocabulary*, 14 PERSONALITY & INDIVIDUAL DIFFERENCES 499 (1993); G H. GUDJONSSON, THE PSYCHOLOGY OF INTERROGATIONS, CONFESSIONS AND TESTIMONY (1992); McFarlane, *supra* note 109.

134. Lane Geddie et al., *Child Characteristics Which Impact Accuracy of Recall and Suggestibility in Preschoolers: Is Age the Best Predictor?*, 24 CHILD ABUSE & NEGLECT 223 (2000).

135. McFarlane, *supra* note 109.

136. Maggie Bruck et al., *External and Internal Sources of Variation in the Creation of False Reports in Children*, 9 LEARNING & INDIVIDUAL DIFFERENCES 289 (1997); Margaret–Ellen Pipe & Karen Salmon, *What Children Bring to the Interview Situation: Individual Differences in Children's Event Reports*, in MEMORY AND SUGGESTIBILITY IN THE FORENSIC INTERVIEW (M. Eisen et al. eds., forthcoming 2001); J. Quas et al., *Individual Differences in Children's and Adults' Suggestibility and False Event Memory*, 9 LEARNING & INDIVIDUAL DIFFERENCES 350 (1997).

important to note, however, that no matter how complex the statistical designs employed are, the results of this new area of research will not allow practitioners to *predict* with absolute certainty whether or not a child has accurately recalled an alleged offence. Nevertheless, this research does have the potential to offer a greater understanding of children's vulnerabilities, which in turn can assist practitioners in tailoring their questioning style to better accommodate the needs and capabilities of individual children.

§ 7–2.7 Issues With Testimony and the Courtroom

Research on children's memory and suggestibility pertaining to the investigation and accurate documentation of child abuse is very important. However, for those cases that progress beyond the investigatory phase, research related to children's testimony is also important. Several issues that are particularly relevant to children's testimony and legal participation are considered below. Recently, Ceci and Friedman provided an extrapolation from this corpus of suggestibility research to courtroom verdicts, under varying assumptions about the strength of proof required to meet the prosecutorial burden.[137]

§ 7–2.7.1 Age Differences in Children's Linguistic Processes and Conversational Issues

Children's linguistic abilities have a direct impact on their understanding of questions and their susceptibility to suggestion in investigative interviews as well as in court. When young children are questioned about events, their reports may be inaccurate because they fail to understand the questions, regardless of whether or not the questions are misleading. In fact, young children often attempt to answer questions they don't understand, rather than stating "I don't know." For example, in one study, some three-year-old children inaccurately answered yes to the question, "Did he (the experimenter) touch your private parts?," whereas, upon further examination, the authors learned that the children simply did not know the meaning of the phrase "private parts."[138]

Similarly, a child's report could be misinterpreted by an adult due to limitations in the child's vocabulary and differences in the ways adults and children describe events. For example, in the case of one sexual abuse allegation, a child reported that her stepfather had "put his pee-pee in my pee-pee." When finally asked, after charges had been brought, what she had meant, the child explained that she had gone to the bathroom without flushing the toilet and her stepfather had gone in and urinated afterwards, literally adding his "pee-pee" to hers. It is important, therefore, for interviewers to assume responsibility for establishing a common vocabulary, for ensuring a child's understanding of their questions and for clarifying inconsistencies or confusing details in a child's account.[139] This may be particularly

---

137. Stephen J. Ceci & Richard D. Friedman, *The Suggestibility of Children: Scientific Research and Legal Implications.* 86 CORNELL L. REV. (2000).

138. Goodman & Aman, *supra* note 89.

139. *See generally* BRENNAN & BRENNAN, *supra* note 64; Anne G. Walker & Amye R. Warren, *The Language of the Child Abuse Interview: Asking the Questions, Understanding the Answers, in* TRUE AND FALSE ALLEGATIONS OF CHILD SEXUAL ABUSE: ASSESSMENT AND CASE MANAGEMENT (T. Ney ed., 1997).

important in courtrooms, where the goal of one of the attorneys, if allowed to do so by the judge, might be to confuse or mislead a child witness using inappropriately complex and difficult language. (Of course, this could also occur when an attorney is simply inexperienced with children and is unaware of the need for developmentally appropriate language for effective communication).[140]

Young children's inexperience with conversation and misunderstandings of the intent or purpose of an interviewer's questions may also lead to errors in children's reports.[141] Young children may not yet fully understand the conventions of narration and, obviously, they do not understand the rules of evidence. Hence, they may perceive important information as irrelevant and omit it from their memory reports. As a consequence, some children may fail to reveal the extent of their relevant knowledge. In addition, when a question or part of a question is repeated within the same interview, children seem to perceive this as a signal that their initial answer was wrong and new information needs to be given.[142] In order to avoid any potential misunderstanding of the task, it is important for interviewers to stress that anything the child remembers may be important and that the interviewer genuinely has no knowledge of what occurred. Further, the child's role and the purpose of the interview should be clearly stated, including the purpose of any repeated questions or any new stage in the interview.

§ 7–2.7.2   Videotaped Evidence

Concern over children's suggestibility has led to a variety of proposed reforms of child abuse investigation procedures. In particular, concerns associated with the repeated interviewing of young children have given rise to recommendations that the number of times a child is interviewed be limited. For instance, a recommendation was made in England to limit the number of times a child is interviewed to one occasion. It was proposed that as soon as possible after the matter becomes known to authorities, an interview would take place whereby the child would be questioned by the prosecution as well as by the opposing counsel. The interview would be videotaped and presented at trial in the place of both the direct and cross-examination of the child.[143] Many jurisdictions, including many in this country, have since adopted videotaped evidence, although it is often the case that a videotaped interview is presented as direct testimony, while the child witness is still made available for cross-examination at trial.[144]

There are several possible advantages to the use of videotaped evidence. First, videotapes provide an incentive for interviewers to conduct proper

---

140. *See* Nancy Walker Perry et al., *When Lawyers Question Children: Is Justice Served?*, 19 LAW & HUM. BEHAV. 609 (1995).

141. *See* Michael Siegal et al., *Misleading Children: Causal Attributions for Inconsistency Under Repeated Questioning*, 45 J. EXPERIMENTAL CHILD PSYCHOL. 438 (1988).

142. *See* Debra A. Poole & Lawrence T. White, *Effects of Question Repetition on the Eyewitness Testimony of Children and Adults*, 27 DEVELOPMENTAL PSYCHOL. 975 (1991); William S. Cassel & David F. Bjorklund, *Developmental Patterns of Eyewitness Memory and Suggesti-*

bility: An Ecologically Based Short–Term Longitudinal Study, 19 LAW & HUM. BEHAV. 507 (1995).

143. *See* J. R. Spencer, *Reforming the Law on Children's Evidence in England: The Pigot Committee and After, in* CHILDREN AS WITNESSES (Helen Dent & Rhona Flin eds., 1992).

144. *See* LUCY S. MCGOUGH, FRAGILE VOICES: THE CHILD WITNESS IN AMERICAN COURTS (1994) (discussing the legal implications of such a reform in the United States).

interviews since the tapes may be scrutinized by the defense. In the United Kingdom, the introduction of children's videotaped evidence was associated with more focused training of police officers and a dramatic increase in the standard of police interviewing techniques.[145] Second, cost is minimized and the stress of the child is reduced because a single taped interview can substitute, at times, for multiple interviews.[146] Third, videotapes provide an accurate record of the child's report and demeanor during the interviews, which may be particularly important if there are lengthy delays between disclosure and trial. Research shows that interviewers often cannot remember exactly what the child told them, even when they attempt to refresh their memory with notes.[147] Both parents and professional interviewers frequently forget the atmospherics of their conversations with children, such as how suggestive their questioning was, how often a child denied an allegation before finally assenting to it, how pressurized the questioning was. In some instances, the existence of an evidentiary videotape may eliminate the need for a child to confront his or her accuser during live testimony, which is the most stressful aspect of testifying for many children.[148] Finally, videotapes may encourage defendants to confess.

However, there are also a number of disadvantages of videotaping raised by its opponents. For instance, combining the investigative and evidentiary interviews may restrict the process of investigation.[149] The financial cost of setting up video suites and training personnel is significant. There is also some concern that children feel inhibited by the videotaping, although most state they prefer making statements on video as they see the recording as an indication that they are being taken seriously.[150] In addition, since initial interviews with children are of the utmost importance, videotaping can be problematic if it does not begin with the first interview, allowing for potential contamination in earlier interviews. This is particularly important since a trial judge must be satisfied that the evidence presented is uncontaminated for a videotaped interview to be admitted in court. Finally, some opponents have argued that videotaping may allow the defense to exaggerate inconsistencies in a child's statements or unreasonably magnify and distort the interviewing practices shown. However, this is a possibility irrespective of whether the statements are written or videotaped, and it does not appear to occur frequently. Of 869 trials involving children's evidence in the United Kingdom, only two included the defense showing the video.[151]

Although there are limited data to address the conflicting arguments in this debate, survey data from a pilot project on the taping of investigative interviews suggest that the benefits of videotaping may outweigh the drawbacks.[152] These data are based on professionals' ratings of the pros and cons of

145. GRAHAM DAVIES et al., VIDEOTAPING CHILDREN'S EVIDENCE: AN EVALUATION (1995).

146. *Id.*

147. M. Bruck, S. J. Ceci, & E. Francouer, *The Accuracy of Mothers' Memories of Conversations with their Preschool Children*, 5 J. EXPERIMENTAL PSYCHOL. APPLIED 1 (1999).

148. Gail Goodman et al., THE EMOTIONAL EFFECTS OF CHILD SEXUAL ASSAULT VICTIMS OF TESTIFYING IN CRIMINAL COURT: FINAL REPORT TO THE NATIONAL INSTITUTE OF JUSTICE (1989).

149. Clare Wilson et al., *Videotaping Children's Evidence: The Costs and Benefits*, 53 AUSTRALIAN POLICE J. 246 (1999).

150. DAVIES et al., *supra* note 145.

151. *Id.*

152. *See* Child Victim Witness Investigative Pilot Projects, *Research and Evaluation Final Report*, California Attorney General's Office, Sacramento, California (July 1994).

videotaping and do not indicate the degree to which videotaping influences jurors. Most of the professionals surveyed (law enforcement agents, district attorneys, and social service workers) were enthusiastic about the continued use of videotaping. However, the extent to which such proposals are implemented across this country remains to be seen, as does their actual effectiveness and acceptability in the courtroom.

§ 7–2.7.3   Children's Lying and Truth–Telling

Historically, young children were considered incapable of lying since it was believed that they lacked the requisite cognitive sophistication to deceive.[153] However, with increased understanding of the definition and development of lying, it has become clear that even children as young as three years of age are quite capable of intentional deception.[154] Children will lie to avoid embarrassment, to keep secrets for loved ones (and even for strangers), to gain personal rewards, to sustain a game and, as most parents know, children will lie to avoid punishment.[155] Although there is support for all of these claims, there is no reliable evidence that young children are more active or vivid liars than older children and adults. They will lie on occasion, as will older individuals.

The existence of the capacity for deception does not mean, however, that children are prone to lying, any more than adults. In fact, because young children are "novice liars," their lies are frequently easily detected, particularly by experts. They have not yet learned to use their faces to mask their deception and are consequently poor liars.[156] Yet, with respect to sexual abuse reports, it seems as though few of the false reports of abuse that have been made can be described as children's deliberate and malicious attempts to distort the truth. In fact, of those few that were categorized as blatant lies, most were initiated by adults and not by the children involved.[157] False reports that result from repeated suggestive techniques over long periods of time seem to be much more problematic. If they are based on children's false beliefs, even trained adults cannot reliably detect them since the children themselves believe that they are telling the truth.

In terms of children's testimony, generally speaking, children know that lying is wrong. Their definition of a lie, however, may be worthy of investigation as it may not always comport with the adult definition.[158] Since children will lie to avoid punishment, McGough suggests that children be reminded that lying in court is a punishable offense, while receiving assurance that they are safe in the face of any threats, because children may lie for a variety of reasons, not all of which will be readily apparent.[159] In actual legal proceedings, however, researchers simply do not know how honest young children

153. *See* Jean Piaget, The Language & Thought of The Child (1926).

154. *See* Cognitive & Social Factors In Early Deception (S.J. Ceci et al. eds., 1992).

155. *See* Ceci & Bruck, *supra* note 17.

156. *See* Carol S. Tate et al., *Adults' Liability for Children's "Lie–Ability": Can Adults Coach Children to Lie Successfully?, in* Cognitive & Social Factors In Early Deception 69 (S. J. Ceci et al. eds., 1992); Ceci & Bruck, *supra* note 10.

157. *See id.*

158. Jeffrey J. Haugaard & N. Dickon Reppucci, *Children and the Truth, in* Cognitive & Social Factors In Early Deception 29 (S. J. Ceci et al. eds., 1992).

159. Lucy S. McGough, *Commentary: The Occasions of Perjury, in* Cognitive & Social Factors In Early Deception 147 (S. J. Ceci et al. eds., 1992).

tend to be. Yet, it is likely that most children truthfully report what they recall and believe to be the truth, given the chance, whether it is accurate or not.

§ 7–2.8 Future Directions and Conclusions

In this chapter, we have discussed a variety of issues related to children's memory and testimony. One of the most prominent concerns that we addressed was children's suggestibility. Despite what may at times appear to be inconsistencies, research on children's suggestibility is in fact quite consistent. Although some studies have found that children are not suggestible when asked abuse-related, leading questions, other studies have routinely found that preschool-aged children are disproportionately more suggestible when such questions are asked repeatedly by a powerful adult authority figure and asked in the context of an accusatory or stereotyped interview. The bottom line of this research is that when strong forms of suggestions are made (this entails repeated questioning, invoking stereotypes, and encouraging imagination) then preschool-aged children are more likely to succumb to erroneous suggestions than older children and adults. Recently, Ceci and Friedman reviewed the evidence for this assertion.[160]

The most unsettling aspect of the research on children's suggestibility is the inability of professionals to correctly detect false statements if a child has been repeatedly exposed to suggestive techniques. Apparently, some children in such circumstances actually come to believe the false suggestions. Hence, they are not lying to interviewers, but really believe what they are saying. As seen in the Sam Stone study above, when young children have been exposed to repeated false suggestions and stereotypes, professionals cannot reliably discriminate actual memories from false memories.[161] Additional support for this assertion comes from the study by Ceci et al. in which professionals were shown videotapes of children after they were encouraged to imagine fictitious events repeatedly for 8–11 weeks. Professionals were little better than chance at distinguishing between true and false statements.[162]

In the future, we expect a great deal of research to focus upon the mechanisms underlying suggestibility. Studies will seek to explore the mechanisms by which false memories are created. Given the multi-determined nature of suggestibility, models to explain it will necessarily be multi-dimensional, including cognitive, social and even biological factors. More specifically, we expect the most active area of research in the coming decade to be "individual differences" in suggestibility. Variations among children's personalities (e.g., compliance, field independence, self-esteem, source monitoring ability), task factors (e.g., whether a task is retrieval-intensive, number of exposures to misinformation) and perhaps demographic factors (e.g., we have reported elsewhere large social class differences in suggestibility[163]) may help to determine a particular child's level of vulnerability to suggestion. If so, this information may some day prove useful in the prevention or detection of false memories among child witnesses.

160. *See* Ceci & Friedman, *supra* note 137.

161. *See* Leichtman & Ceci, *supra* note 38; *see also* Ceci et al., *supra* note 39; Ceci et al., *supra* note 61.

162. Ceci et al., *supra* note 39.

163. *See id.*

To end at the beginning, we repeat that children have tremendous strengths in recollecting their pasts, *with the proviso that the adults in their lives do not in any way usurp their memories through the use of strong suggestions.* While this chapter has focused, in part, on the negative consequences of exposing preschoolers to a variety of suggestive procedures, it should be clear that even very young children can recount their past with high degrees of accuracy and vividness. Respect for and understanding of children's strengths and weaknesses will go a long way toward protecting children's memories and their testimony.

CHAPTER 8

EYEWITNESS IDENTIFICATIONS

Table of Sections

A. LEGAL ISSUES

Westlaw Electronic Research

See Westlaw Electronic Research Guide preceding the Summary of Contents.

A.   LEGAL ISSUES

§ 8–1.0   THE LEGAL RELEVANCE OF RESEARCH ON EYEWITNESS IDENTIFICATIONS

§ 8–1.1   Introduction

As is true with the other topics covered in this treatise, cases reviewed here on the admissibility of expert testimony concerning the reliability of eyewitness identifications have been decided under both the *Frye* and *Daubert* tests. Unlike most of these other topics, however, the key issues presented in eyewitness expert testimony cases generally do not implicate standards that are different under *Frye* and *Daubert*.[1] Instead, the focus in most of these cases is on an admissibility standard that is common to both tests. Specifically, courts focus on whether the accuracy of eyewitness identifications is a matter in which jurors need assistance. Under both *Frye* and *Daubert*, expert testimony is excluded if it will not assist the trier of fact.

Nonetheless, a trend is developing in which courts increasingly recognize a value to eyewitness identification expertise, and, as this trend continues, there will be a greater need to evaluate the validity of the research. A couple of factors, in particular, appear to have contributed to this trend. First, as in so many other contexts involving expert testimony, *Daubert* has caused courts to rethink their preconceptions about eyewitness identification research. The more they delve into the details of the data, the more counter-intuitive insights they are likely to find that will assist triers of fact. Second, the dangers of eyewitness identification have become increasingly obvious. In the great publicity surrounding cases in which DNA was used to exonerate convicted felons, eyewitness evidence played a disproportionate role in the original convictions. In addition, in 1999, relying on several decades of eyewitness research, the Department of Justice published guidelines that are intended to reduce the number of misidentifications made by eyewitnesses by employing procedures that reduce the suggestiveness of lineups and which avoid other common errors in this process.[2] The Justice Department has thus put its imprimatur on much of the research routinely offered in court.

---

§ 8–1.0

1. *See* United States v. Hall, 165 F.3d 1095, 1106 (7th Cir.1999) ("*Daubert* does not undermine our prior analysis of the admissibility of expert scientific testimony under Rule 702.").

2. Eyewitness Working Group, *Eyewitness Evidence: A Guide for Law Enforcement*. Alex-

This section begins with a general overview of the admissibility standards courts apply to expert testimony on eyewitness identifications under both *Frye* and *Daubert*,[3] as well as the specific criteria courts use under these tests. It then turns to the most substantial area of discussion and disagreement among courts, whether experts in this area are needed to assist triers of fact, an issue that in most cases constitutes a Rule 403 evaluation. We next discuss appellate standards of review. Finally, this section considers defendants' claims that excluding the testimony of eyewitness experts violates certain constitutional guarantees.

§ 8–1.2   Overview of Admissibility Standards

The eyewitness expert area has seen a variety of admissibility tests, most of which are hybrid forms of the *Frye* and *Daubert* tests. Most jurisdictions leave to the trial court's discretion whether to admit eyewitness expert testimony.[4] In exercising this discretion, judges use *Daubert* and the other decision rules that have been spun out of Rule 702 and its state equivalents. The main two variations on this theme of deference involve the few jurisdictions that apply a per se rule excluding expert testimony regarding eyewitness reliability[5] and the few jurisdictions that require the allowance of such expert testimony when the only proof at trial is the eyewitness identifications.[6] In this section, we consider a variety of admissibility standards, ranging from multi-part tests to per se exclusion.

andria, VA: U.S. Department of Justice Programs (1999).

3. *See generally Special Theme: Witness Memory and Law*, 1 PSYCHOL. PUB. POL'Y & L. 726 (1995).

It should be noted at the outset that the cases present a somewhat distorted picture of the state of affairs present in the area of expert testimony on the reliability of eyewitness identifications. Virtually all of the cases reported arise from a trial court's exclusion of expert testimony and the appellate court's review of that decision. Thus, the cases do not present the portion of the picture in which the court permitted eyewitness expert testimony and no objection was made at trial and no error was claimed on appeal. The frequency with which eyewitness experts are permitted to testify is difficult to estimate. It appears that eyewitness experts are offered in a large number of cases, but are challenged and excluded in most, leaving a fairly small number of trials in which they actually testify.

4. *See, e.g.*, United States v. Hall, 165 F.3d 1095, 1107 (7th Cir.1999) (After noting that eyewitness expert testimony is strongly disfavored, the court rejected the petitioner's claims that the lower court had applied a *per se* rule of exclusion. The lower court had applied sound discretion in excluding the expert testimony.); United States v. Smith, 156 F.3d 1046, 1052–53 (10th Cir.1998) (" 'Until fairly recently, most, if not all, courts excluded expert psychological testimony on the validity of eyewit-

ness identification. But, there has been a trend in recent years to allow such testimony under circumstances described as narrow.' ") (*quoting* United States v. Harris, 995 F.2d 532, 534 (4th Cir.1993)); Johnson v. State, 272 Ga. 254, 526 S.E.2d 549, 552–53 (Ga.2000) ("Where eyewitness identification of the defendant is a key element of the State's case and there is no substantial corroboration of that identification by other evidence, trial courts may not exclude expert testimony without carefully weighing whether the evidence would assist the jury in assessing whether the reliability of eyewitness testimony is the only effective way to reveal any weakness in an eyewitness identification."); State v. Miles, 585 N.W.2d 368, 371–72 (Minn.1998) (Court noted that "[i]f the expert testimony will be helpful to the jury in fulfilling its responsibilities, the evidence may be admitted." At the same time, however, the court emphasized, "a defendant's right to a fair trial is not automatically impaired by excluding expert eyewitness testimony.").

5. *See* United States v. Holloway, 971 F.2d 675 (11th Cir.1992); State v. Goldsby, 59 Or. App. 66, 650 P.2d 952 (Or.App.1982); Commonwealth v. Simmons, 541 Pa. 211, 662 A.2d 621 (Pa.1995); State v. Wooden, 658 S.W.2d 553 (Tenn.Crim.App.1983).

6. *See* United States v. Downing, 753 F.2d 1224 (3d Cir.1985); People v. McDonald, 37 Cal.3d 351, 208 Cal.Rptr. 236, 690 P.2d 709 (Cal.1984); *see also* Commonwealth v. Santoli, 424 Mass. 837, 680 N.E.2d 1116 (Mass.1997).

In *United States v. Smithers*,[7] the Sixth Circuit made it clear that *Daubert* applies to eyewitness identification experts, and held that district courts have an obligation to consider the scientific basis for the proffered testimony. The defendant had been convicted of bank robbery on the basis of the testimony of three eyewitnesses, two of whom had failed to pick him out of a lineup but later testified that he was the perpetrator.[8] The defendant proffered an expert who would have testified to a number of factors that indicated that the identifications here were not reliable. The district court heard oral argument on the issue, but refused to hold a *Daubert* hearing to consider the scientific basis for the testimony. The district court displayed unusual ignorance in responding to the proffer. The Sixth Circuit summarized the lower court's reactions as follows:

> [The expert's] testimony was "not a scientifically valid opinion," "a jury can fully understand that its [sic] got an obligation to be somewhat skeptical of eyewitness testimony," and "admission of [the expert's] testimony is in this case almost tantamount to the Court declaring the defendant not guilty as a matter of law.... [A]bsent the eyewitness testimony I don't think there's enough here to go to the jury." Finally, the district court remarked, "I'm also interested in seeing what a jury will do absent that expert testimony. It makes it a more interesting case. I recognize it's the defendant's fate that's at stake, but you can always argue for a new trial if he's convicted."[9]

The Sixth Circuit granted him a new trial. It held that *Daubert* places an affirmative obligation on trial courts to evaluate the relevance and the scientific basis for proffered expert testimony.[10] The lower court abused its discretion in failing to conduct this evaluation. The court noted that this does not mean that eyewitness expert testimony is always admissible, or even that it is always necessary to provide a *Daubert* hearing to consider it. In this case, however, no other evidence linked the defendant to the crime. Moreover, the court found the attitude and the comments made by the district court especially disturbing. The comment that excluding the expert testimony will make the case more interesting, the court said, was "gamesmanship at its worst and reveals a troubling disregard for this Defendant's rights, relegating those rights to mere abstractions."[11] The court also observed that the lower court's conclusion that juries understand the limitations of eyewitness identifications was not correct. "Today, there is no question that many aspects of perception and memory are not within the common experience of most jurors, and in fact, many factors that affect memory are counter-intuitive."[12]

The Ninth Circuit in *United States v. Rincon*[13] applied the *Daubert* test, holding that the expert testimony must be based on (1) scientific knowledge[14] that (2) will assist the trier of fact in understanding or determining a fact at issue. Although the *Rincon* court upheld the trial court's exclusion of expert

7. 212 F.3d 306 (6th Cir.2000).

8. *Id.* at 309–310.

9. *Id.* at 310.

10. *Id.* at 312–15.

11. *Id.* at 315.

12. *Id.* at 316.

13. 28 F.3d 921 (9th Cir.1994).

14. *See* SCIENCE IN THE LAW: STANDARDS, STATISTICS AND RESEARCH ISSUES, Chapter 1, *Legal Standards for the Admissibility of Scientific Evidence* (discussing the four factors—testability, error rate, peer review and publication, and general acceptance—that the *Daubert* Court recommended, among others, that lower courts use to determine scientific validity).

testimony on eyewitness identifications under the test, it did not reach any definitive conclusion regarding the scientific validity of eyewitness identification research. Defense counsel in *Rincon* did not introduce any studies demonstrating the scientific basis for the testimony, and this failure supported the trial court's exclusion of the evidence.[15] However, other aspects of the *Rincon* decision, discussed below, might affect later cases more substantially.[16]

Closely related to the *Daubert* test, and indeed influential in the construction of that test, is the standard articulated in 1985 by the Third Circuit in *United States v. Downing.*[17] In *Downing*, the court found that the trial court had erred in excluding expert testimony regarding the reliability of eyewitness identifications on the ground that it could "never meet the 'helpfulness' standard of Fed. R. Evid. 702."[18] Judge Becker, writing for the court, articulated several factors that trial courts must consider in determining the admissibility of expert testimony, including: (1) the reliability of the scientific principles upon which the expert testimony rests; (2) the assistance the testimony gives to the jury in deciding a disputed fact question (i.e., the "fit"); and (3) the likelihood that the testimony might overwhelm or mislead the jury.[19] The court explained that "scientific reliability" does not require the "explicit identification of a relevant scientific community and an express determination of a particular degree of acceptance within that community."[20] Rather, a trial court attempting to assess reliability could consider the "novelty" of the scientific evidence, the existence, if any, of literature concerning the evidence, the "qualifications and professional stature of expert witnesses," and the "non-judicial uses to which the scientific technique are put."[21] The court further explained that the proponent of the expert testimony bears the burden of showing how the evidence "fit" the particular case.[22] This proffer should include "an explanation of precisely how the expert's testimony is relevant to the eyewitness identifications under consideration."[23] Finally, even reliable expert testimony that "fits" the case might be excluded under Rule 403 if it would substantially confuse or mislead the jury.[24]

Another influential test developed in the context of eyewitness expert testimony is the one articulated by the Ninth Circuit in *United States v.*

---

15. The *Rincon* court objected to the fact that the defense only submitted one article in support of its expert, which discussed the views of 63 eyewitness identification experts on the scientific acceptance of eyewitness identification research. *Rincon*, 28 F.3d at 924. (The article submitted by the defense was Kassin, Ellsworth & Smith, *The "General Acceptance" of Psychological Research on Eyewitness Testimony,* AM. PSYCHOLOGIST 1089 (1989).) Oddly, the defense based its motion on the *Frye* general acceptance test, while the trial court was applying the *Daubert* validity test. Not surprisingly, the court upheld exclusion of the evidence, observing that the one article "did not discuss the research in sufficient detail that the district court could determine if the research was scientifically valid." *Rincon*, 28 F.3d at 924.

16. The *Rincon* Court found that the expert testimony would not assist triers of fact

and would likely mislead them. *Rincon*, 28 F.3d at 926. This analysis, however, was premised primarily on Rule 403's balance of probative value and prejudicial effect. *Id.* As the court itself emphasized, this assessment must be calibrated to the particular context and might change from case to case. *Id. See infra* § 8–1.3.4.

17. 753 F.2d 1224 (3d Cir.1985).

18. *Id.* at 1226.

19. *Id.*

20. *Id.* at 1238.

21. *Id.* at 1238–39.

22. *Id.* at 1224.

23. *Id.* at 1242.

24. *Id.* at 1239.

Amaral.[25] The *Amaral* test contains four factors: (1) was the proposed testimony to be given by a qualified expert; (2) was the testimony a proper subject; (3) did the testimony conform to a generally accepted explanatory theory; and (4) was the probative value of the testimony not substantially outweighed by unfair prejudice.[26] In its decision, however, the *Amaral* court provided little guidance on how trial courts should apply the test. Instead, in excluding the proffered eyewitness expert testimony, the court cited the effectiveness of cross-examination as sufficient to "reveal any inconsistencies or deficiencies in . . . eyewitness testimony."[27]

The *Amaral* test was more fully developed, and given real bite, by the Arizona Supreme Court in the celebrated case of *State v. Chapple.*[28] In *Chapple,* the court used the *Amaral* test to reverse a trial court's exclusion of an eyewitness expert, finding such exclusion to be an abuse of discretion.[29] The *Chapple* court concentrated its analysis on two of the four *Amaral* factors, whether the testimony was a proper subject and whether the lower court had correctly balanced probative value and prejudicial effect.[30] First, the *Chapple* court rejected the trial court's conclusion that the testimony was within jurors' common experience and could be adequately presented through cross-examination and closing arguments.[31] Moreover, the court rejected the lower court's 403 balancing, in which it had discounted the probative value of testimony about "general" factors that might interfere with eyewitness accuracy and had inflated the prejudice from the expert's extraordinary qualifications.[32] Although later cases have not equaled *Chapple's* rigor, it remains a symbol of the strict review available under *Amaral* and similar standards of admissibility.

In *United States v. Holloway,*[33] the Eleventh Circuit adopted a *per se* rule of exclusion for expert testimony regarding the reliability of eyewitnesses.[34] In *United States v. Smith,*[35] it was asked to reevaluate this rule in light of *Daubert.* Ultimately, the court found that it did not have to reach the question whether *Daubert* had undermined the use of a *per se* rule. The court held that it did not have to decide whether its "*per se* inadmissibility rule . . . conflict[s] with *Daubert*" because the trial judge "held that expert testimony regarding

---

25. 488 F.2d 1148 (9th Cir.1973). The *Amaral* test is discussed here, despite the Ninth Circuit's more recent application of *Daubert* to eyewitness experts, *see supra* notes 5–8 and accompanying text, because other courts now apply it. *See e.g.,* United States v. Smith, 736 F.2d 1103, 1105 (6th Cir.1984); State v. Chapple, 135 Ariz. 281, 660 P.2d 1208 (Ariz.1983); Echavarria v. State, 108 Nev. 734, 839 P.2d 589 (Nev.1992); State v. Hill, 463 N.W.2d 674 (S.D.1990); Pierce v. State, 777 S.W.2d 399 (Tex.Crim.App.1989).

26. *Id.* at 1153.

27. *Id.*

28. 135 Ariz. 281, 660 P.2d 1208 (Ariz. 1983).

29. *Id.* at 1224.

30. The court did not find the other two *Amaral* factors to be in serious dispute. The expert, Dr. Elizabeth Loftus, was clearly qualified and, as the court observed, "wrote the book" on the topic. 660 P.2d at 1218. Indeed,

the prosecution advanced the unusual argument that she was too qualified, *Id.* at 1219, and thus should have been excluded under a Rule 403 analysis. The general acceptance of the explanatory theory, an issue often a main source of contention in other cases, was "not raised and appears not to be a question in this case." *Id. See infra* § 8–1.3.3.

31. *Id.* at 1223. For a full discussion of the question whether eyewitness expert testimony is within the common experience of jurors, *see infra* § 8–1.3.1.

32. *Id.* at 1220. For a full discussion of the Rule 403 balancing test in eyewitness expert cases, *see infra* § 8–1.3.4.

33. 971 F.2d 675 (11th Cir.1992).

34. *Id.* at 679; *see also* United States v. Benitez, 741 F.2d 1312, 1315 (11th Cir.1984).

35. 122 F.3d 1355 (11th Cir.1997).

eyewitness reliability does not assist the jury.''[36] The court concluded: ''it is as true after *Daubert* as it was before that a district court does not abuse its discretion in excluding such testimony.''[37]

The Eleventh Circuit, in time, might decide to reevaluate its *per se* rule. First of all, it is not employed by any other federal circuit. In addition, the Eleventh Circuit has never explained why it has such a rule. The most recent case, *Smith* from 1997, depends on *Holloway*, a 1992 decision. The *Holloway* opinion simply followed the ''established rule in this circuit . . . that such testimony is not admissible,''[38] and cited *United States v. Benitez*. The *Benitez* court, however, explicitly refused to discuss the expert testimony claim, since ''such testimony is not admissible in this circuit.''[39] *Benitez* cited *United States v. Thevis*[40] in support of its conclusion. The *Thevis* court, however, never held that eyewitness expert testimony is subject to a *per se* rule of exclusion. Indeed, the court explicitly abided by what was then, and what remains, the majority rule: ''As with all evidentiary rulings, the admission of such testimony is addressed to the sound discretion of the trial court.''[41] The *Thevis* court concluded that the trial judge's finding that the expert's testimony about the unreliability of eyewitnesses would not assist the trier of fact was not an abuse of discretion. The Eleventh Circuit appears to be applying a rule that has no foundation in any of the Circuit's own precedents.

Daubert, it should be noted, does not preclude the use of *per se* rules regarding scientific evidence. In fact, its requirement that scientific evidence be supported by valid research might even lend itself to the use of *per se* rules. If an area of scientific evidence generally has little research supporting it, or the research contravenes claims made by some experts, *Daubert* might even recommend creation of a *per se* rule. Such a rule would create consistency across the jurisdiction. In *United States v. Scheffer*,[42] the Court itself upheld a *per se* rule excluding polygraph evidence against constitutional attack. There, as discussed in detail in Chapter 19, the Court found that the extreme division in opinion among scientists could support a *per se* rule excluding the evidence.[43] *Daubert* presumably permits similar judgments to be made.

The Eleventh Circuit's *per se* rule, however, is somewhat different. It is ultimately based on a determination that the expert testimony is not sufficiently helpful. But this is exactly the sort of determination that is likely to change from case to case. Unlike the question of the scientific reliability of expert testimony regarding eyewitnesses—a matter that transcends individual cases—the helpfulness inquiry seems especially suited to individualized determinations. And this has been the overwhelming consensus in other jurisdictions. In fact, Iowa just recently overturned its *per se* rule in favor of the more

---

36. *Id.* at 1358–59.

37. *Id.* at 1359.

38. 971 F.2d at 679.

39. 741 F.2d at 1315.

40. 665 F.2d 616, 641 (5th Cir. Unit B 1982).

41. *Id.*

42. 523 U.S. 303, 118 S.Ct. 1261, 140 L.Ed.2d 413 (1998).

43. It should be noted that five justices in *Scheffer* expressed the belief that *Daubert* was inconsistent with the use of a *per se* rule. This belief is based on the great deference paid to trial courts concerning the admissibility of proffered expert testimony. Despite this deference, inevitably some expert testimony fails *Daubert* as a matter of law, and thus is ripe for a *per se* rule of exclusion.

flexible abuse of discretion standard.[44] Although not compelled by *Daubert*, Rules 702 and 403 appear to recommend a similar result in the Eleventh Circuit.

§ 8–1.3　Specific Admissibility Considerations

§ 8–1.3.1　Assisting the Trier of Fact

By far the principal reason courts give for excluding eyewitness expert testimony is that it will not assist the trier of fact. This conclusion is based on a variety of factors and concerns. Foremost, many courts believe that jurors are well able to evaluate an eyewitness' credibility by virtue of their common knowledge and everyday experience.[45] In addition, to the extent that jurors are

44. Iowa v. Schutz, 579 N.W.2d 317, 320 (Iowa 1998), (*overruling* State v. Galloway, 275 N.W.2d 736 (Iowa 1979)).

45. *See* United States v. Fosher, 590 F.2d 381, 382–83 (1st Cir.1979) (defendant failed to address how the expert testimony would assist the jury in analyzing the eyewitnesses' individual capacities of perception and recall); United States v. Serna, 799 F.2d 842, 850 (2d Cir.1986)(expert "acknowledged that many of his conclusions coincided with common sense"), United States v. Larkin, 978 F.2d 964, 971 (7th Cir.1992) ("[E]xpert testimony regarding the potential hazards of eyewitness identification ... 'will not aid the jury because it addresses an issue of which the jury already generally is aware.' "); United States v. Purham, 725 F.2d 450, 454 (8th Cir.1984)(The proposed eyewitness identification testimony was not "sufficiently beyond the understanding of lay jurors to satisfy Fed.R.Evid. 702."). *See also* State v. Poland, 144 Ariz. 388, 698 P.2d 183, 193 (Ariz.1985) ("[E]xpert testimony on eyewitness identification is usually precluded because it invades the province of the jury ... [and] is usually not a proper subject for testimony."); Utley v. State, 308 Ark. 622, 826 S.W.2d 268, 271 (Ark.1992) (testimony was properly excluded because it addressed a "matter of common understanding and would not assist the trier of fact"); People v. Plasencia, 168 Cal.App.3d 546, 223 Cal.Rptr. 786, 791 (Cal.Ct.App.1985) ("[T]he jury did not need edification on the obvious fact that an unprovoked gang attack is a stressful event or that the passage of time frequently effects [sic] one's memory."); State v. Kemp, 199 Conn. 473, 507 A.2d 1387, 1389 (Conn.1986)(the proffered testimony was "within the realm of common experience and can be evaluated without expert assistance"); Brooks v. United States, 448 A.2d 253, 258 (D.C.1982) (eyewitness expert testimony was not "beyond the ken of jurors"); Johnson v. State, 438 So.2d 774, 777 (Fla.1983) ("[A] jury is fully capable of assessing a witness' ability to perceive and remember ... without the aid of expert testimony."); Norris v. State, 258 Ga. 889, 376 S.E.2d 653, 654 (Ga.1989) (eyewitness expert testimony was "within the exclusive province of the ju-

rors"); People v. Brown, 100 Ill.App.3d 57, 55 Ill.Dec. 429, 426 N.E.2d 575, 585 (Ill.App.1981) ("[W]e find little in the circumstances of this case differing from the usual problems of identification which historically have been within the province of the jury") (*cited* in People v. Enis, 139 Ill.2d 264, 151 Ill.Dec. 493, 564 N.E.2d 1155, 1163 (Ill.1990)); State v. Galloway, 275 N.W.2d 736, 741 (Iowa 1979) ("Explanation of the scientifically identified mechanisms which bring about memory decay may be of academic interest, but it is of little aid to the jury in judging reliability of the particular eyewitness identification before them."); State v. Stucke, 419 So.2d 939, 945 (La.1982) ("such testimony invades the province of the jury and usurps its function"); State v. Fernald, 397 A.2d 194 (Me.1979) (expert testimony is not beyond the "common knowledge" of jurors); Commonwealth v. Francis, 390 Mass. 89, 453 N.E.2d 1204, 1210 (Mass.1983)(juries can understand, without expert assistance, the general factors associated with inaccurate identifications); People v. Hill, 84 Mich.App. 90, 269 N.W.2d 492, 494 (Mich.Ct.App.1978) (subject matter was "within the experiences of ordinary laymen"); State v. Lawhorn, 762 S.W.2d 820 (Mo.1988) ("such matters are within the general realm of common experience of members of a jury"); State v. Ammons, 208 Neb. 797, 305 N.W.2d 812, 814 (Neb.1981) ("the accuracy or inaccuracy of eyewitness observation is a common experience of daily life"); State v. Long, 119 N.J. 439, 575 A.2d 435, 463 (N.J.1990)(using the Third Circuit's *Downing* test, court found that the expert assistance was not "clearly helpful" to the jury); People v. Gibbs, 157 A.D.2d 799, 550 N.Y.S.2d 400 (1990) (expert testimony addressed "matters of common knowledge" and was not "beyond the ken of lay jurors"); State v. Cotton, 99 N.C.App. 615, 394 S.E.2d 456, 459 (N.C.Ct. App.1990) (the jury had sufficient knowledge about the elements that could affect eyewitness identifications); State v. Calia, 15 Or.App. 110, 514 P.2d 1354, 1356 (Or.Ct.App.1973) (experience, not expertise, should be used to assess eyewitness accuracy); State v. Ward, 712 S.W.2d 485 (Tenn.Crim.App.1986) (expert tes-

unfamiliar with specific dangers to eyewitness accuracy, these courts maintain, other traditional methods, such as cross-examination and closing arguments, permit a party sufficient opportunity to articulate variables that might interfere with the accuracy of eyewitness identifications.[46] For example, as the *Amaral* court emphasized, "our legal system places primary reliance for the ascertainment of truth on the 'test of cross-examination.' "[47] Finally, some courts that exclude eyewitness experts see jury instructions as a means to bring to jurors' attention those factors that might interfere with eyewitness identifications.[48] But the accuracy of this empirical judgment should not be too quickly assumed. Research has yet to determine whether jury instructions are as effective as live expert testimony for conveying information to jurors.[49]

Some courts identify an important exception to their more general determination that jurors' common sense is sufficient for evaluating the accuracy of eyewitness identifications. These courts accept the need for eyewitness experts in cases in which the witness is suffering from a mental or psychological disorder that might affect his ability to provide credible or truthful testimony.[50] Yet, scientists have not studied this issue in any depth, so experts might not be able to offer jurors substantial assistance on the effects mental and physical disabilities have on eyewitness identifications. Ironically, then, in the one area in which courts perceive a need for expert

timony would invade the province of the jury); Pierce v. State, 777 S.W.2d 399 (Tex.Crim.App. 1989) ("a jury is amply qualified to make a determination on the credibility of eyewitnesses"); State v. Onorato, 142 Vt. 99, 453 A.2d 393, 396 (Vt.1982) (expert testimony would not be of "real help" to the jury); Rodriguez v. Commonwealth, 20 Va.App. 122, 455 S.E.2d 724, 727 (Va.Ct.App.1995) (the issues addressed by the typical eyewitness expert were issues that " 'men of ordinary intelligence' are capable of understanding"); Hampton v. State, 92 Wis.2d 450, 285 N.W.2d 868, 873 (Wis.1979)("[A]ll people, including those serving on a jury, recognize at least to some extent the difficulties involved in attempting to accurately perceive and remember events in stressful situations.").

46. *See e.g.,* United States v. Fred Smith, 122 F.3d 1355 (11th Cir.1997); United States v. Kime, 99 F.3d 870 (8th Cir.1996); United States v. Hicks, 103 F.3d 837 (9th Cir.1996); United States v. Harris, 995 F.2d 532, 536 (4th Cir.1993) (discrepancies in eyewitness identifications can be "brought out on cross-examination"); United States v. Larkin, 978 F.2d 964, 971 (7th Cir.1992) (the defense was granted "ample opportunity" to discuss the pitfalls of eyewitness identifications and "cast doubt" upon the eyewitness testimony during trial); State v. Kemp, 199 Conn. 473, 507 A.2d 1387, 1390 (Conn.1986) ("The weaknesses of identifications can be explored on cross-examination and during counsel's final arguments to the jury."); State v. Lawhorn, 762 S.W.2d 820, 823 (Mo.1988)(asserting that cross-examination and closing arguments are sufficient to highlight the dangers of eyewitness identifications).

47. *Amaral,* 488 F.2d at 1153.

48. *See e.g.,* *Hicks,* 103 F.3d at 847 ("The district court in this case did not abuse its discretion by excluding the defendant's proffered expert and charging the jury with a comprehensive instruction on the evaluation of eyewitness testimony."); United States v. Rincon, 28 F.3d 921, 925–26 (9th Cir.1994) (observing that "the district court conveyed [the] same information [as that offered by the excluded expert] by providing a comprehensive jury instruction to guide the jury's deliberations"); State v. Cotton, 99 N.C.App. 615, 394 S.E.2d 456, 460 (N.C.App.1990) (trial court's jury instruction was sufficient to instruct jurors on the factors that could affect the accuracy of eyewitness identifications).

49. *Cf.* Neil Vidmar, *Are Juries Competent to Decide Liability in Tort Cases Involving Scientific/Medical Issues? Some Data From Medical Malpractice,* 43 Emory L.J. 885 (1994).

50. *See* Jones v. State, 232 Ga. 762, 208 S.E.2d 850, 853 (Ga.1974) (Expert testimony about a witness' credibility was only admissible if the witness was suffering from a disorder that impeded his "mental or physical faculties."); State v. Buell, 22 Ohio St.3d 124, 489 N.E.2d 795, 804 (Ohio 1986) (Expert testimony addressing the credibility of a particular eyewitness is not allowed unless the witness suffered from a mental or physical impairment.); State v. Lewisohn, 379 A.2d 1192, 1203 (Me. 1977) (Unless the witness, a child, suffered from a medical or psychiatric illness that impaired his ability to serve as a credible witness, the expert testimony was inadmissible.).

assistance, the expert might be barred from testifying for lack of an adequate research foundation; whereas, at the same time, the areas in which the bulk of research is done is perceived as being of no real assistance to jurors.

Not all courts agree with the observation that eyewitness expert testimony is a matter of common sense and thus of little help to triers of fact. In *United States v. Moore*,[51] for example, the Fifth Circuit accepted "the modern conclusion that the admission of expert testimony regarding eyewitness identifications is proper."[52] The court explained that "the conclusions of the psychological studies are largely counter-intuitive and serve to 'explode' common myths about an individual's capacities for perception."[53] One of the strongest statements supporting the need for expert testimony to assist jurors with eyewitness testimony comes from Judge Kaye in dissent. In *People v. Mooney*,[54] the trial court had held that the testimony was not beyond the common knowledge of the jurors and would infringe upon the jury's role of weighing the credibility of the witnesses.[55] Judge Kaye disagreed, arguing that the "notion that jurors are generally aware from their everyday experience of the factors relevant to the reliability of eyewitness observation ... has been refuted by research demonstrating a number of common ... misconceptions on the subject among laypersons."[56] In addition, she noted, the court of appeals had "repeatedly upheld the admission of expert testimony for the purpose of clarifying an area of which the jurors have a general awareness."[57] Since the expert testimony in *Mooney* was similarly designed to dispel common myths and clarify the jury's knowledge, Judge Kaye contended that the trial court erred in excluding the testimony.[58]

Judge Gertner, in *United States v. Hines*, shared many of the same sentiments voiced by Judge Kaye. Judge Gertner explained as follows:

51. 786 F.2d 1308 (5th Cir.1986).

52. *Id.* at 1312.

53. *Id.* The *Moore* court, however, found no abuse of discretion in the trial court's exclusion of the evidence, since "the other evidence of guilt is overwhelming." *Id.* at 1313; *see infra* notes 106–115 and accompanying text for a full discussion of this conclusion.

See also Reed v. State, 687 N.E.2d 209 (Ind. Ct.App.1997); Weatherred v. State, 963 S.W.2d 115 (Tex.App.1998), vacated, 975 S.W.2d 323 (Tex.Crim.App.1998); Nations v. State, 944 S.W.2d 795 (Tex.App.1997). In *Reed* the court stated as follows:

We are not thoroughly convinced that the average juror is conversant with the likelihood or frequency with which misidentifications are made by seemingly unequivocal eyewitnesses.... Accordingly, we suggest that trial courts might be well advised to permit such expert testimony in order to assist the jury in its evaluation of the evidence.

Reed, 687 N.E.2d at 213.

54. 76 N.Y.2d 827, 560 N.Y.S.2d 115, 559 N.E.2d 1274 (N.Y.1990).

55. *Id.* at 1277.

56. *Id.* (*citing* John C. Brigham & Robert K. Bothwell, *The Ability of Prospective Jurors to Estimate the Accuracy of Eyewitness Identifications*, 7 LAW & HUM. BEHAV 19 (1983); Kenneth Deffenbacher & Elizabeth Loftus, *Do Jurors Share a Common Understanding Concerning Eyewitness Behavior?*, 6 LAW & HUM. BEHAV. 15 (1982)).

57. *Id.* As an example, Judge Kaye cited the court's holding on the admissibility of testimony concerning rape trauma syndrome. *Id.*

58. *Id.* Judge Kaye concluded by stating that she did not wish to "suggest that a trial court must permit expert testimony on eyewitness identification in every case, or even most cases, in which it is offered." *Id.* Rather, the trial court could weigh elements such as "the centrality of the identification issue to the particular facts, the existence of other evidence corroborating the identifications, the relevance of the proposed testimony to specific facts of the case [and] the trial court's power to limit the amount and type of evidence presented." *Id.* However, since the trial court in *Mooney* had excluded such testimony "based on a mistake and entirely general legal analysis," Judge

Nor do I agree that this testimony somehow usurps the function of the jury. The function of the expert here is not to say to the jury—"you should believe or not believe the eyewitness." (Indeed, it has far fewer pretensions to conclusions than does handwriting analysis, with far more science attached to it.) All that the expert does is provide the jury with more information with which the jury can then make a more informed decision. And only the expert can do so. In the absence of an expert, a defense lawyer, for example, may try to argue that cross racial identifications between members of the same race, or that stress may undermine accuracy, but his voice necessarily lacks the authority of the scientific studies.[59]

A significant concern for many courts is their frustration that while this research might identify factors that generally interfere with eyewitness accuracy, it does not permit statements to be made about the accuracy of a witness in a particular case.[60] These courts impose what might be termed a "medical model" on eyewitness experts. Specifically, as with much medical and psychological/psychiatric forms of testimony, courts expect not only testimony on the phenomenon at the population level,[61] but demand that the expert offer an opinion on the applicability of the phenomenon to the individual eyewitness. Thus, a number of courts complain that the expert was unfamiliar with the facts of the case and had failed to interview or examine the eyewitness.[62]

Kaye determined that its decision should have been reversed. *Id.* at 119.

59. *United States v. Hines*, 55 F.Supp.2d 62, 72 (D.Mass.1999); *but see* State v. McClendon, 248 Conn. 572, 730 A.2d 1107 (Conn. 1999) (Court upheld exclusion of eyewitness identification expertise, finding that his opinions "should come as no surprise to the average person.").

60. *See e.g.*, State v. Ward, 712 S.W.2d 485, 487 (Tenn.Crim.App.1986) ("[T]here are too many variables involved [in eyewitness identifications] including power of observation, individual reaction to stress ... as well as a number of general, common factors unamenable to charting and categorizing.").

In an interesting about-face, the leading case on eyewitness experts in Ohio until 1986 was State v. Sims, 3 Ohio App.3d 321, 445 N.E.2d 235 (Ohio Ct.App.1981). In *Sims,* the court observed that "the statistical likelihood of eyewitnesses to err would seem analogous to the statistical likelihood of a paid informant to lie." *Id.* at 240. The court explained that "[s]uch evidence would not assist the trier of fact to determine whether a particular eyewitness ... is telling the truth." *Id.* In *State v. Buell,* however, the Ohio Supreme Court adopted exactly the opposite stance toward eyewitness experts. 22 Ohio St.3d 124, 489 N.E.2d 795, 803 (Ohio 1986). The court held first that an expert could testify on the factors "that may impair the accuracy of a typical eyewitness identification." *Id.* But evidence that addressed the credibility of a particular eyewit-

ness' testimony did not comport with Rule 702. *Id.* at 804.

61. Professors Monahan and Walker refer to this use as an example of "social frameworks." *See* Laurens Walker & John Monahan, *Social Frameworks: A New Use of Social Science in Law,* 73 VA. L. REV. 559, 563–67 (1987). The essence of the social framework concept is that some issue in a particular dispute is claimed to be an instance of a social scientific finding or theory of general import. *Id.* They discuss several examples of the use of social science research as social frameworks, including eyewitness identification research. *Id.* They also include assessments of dangerousness, the battered woman syndrome, and sexual victimization in the social framework category. In each of these examples, general scientific findings are sought to be applied in individual cases to assist the trier of fact to determine some fact in issue. *Id.*

62. *See* Williams v. State, 594 So.2d 1225, 1227 (Ala.1992)(Court held that since the expert was unfamiliar with the facts of the case and "had no personal contact with the victim," the trial court had properly excluded the testimony.); Lewis v. State, 572 So.2d 908, 911 (Fla.1990) (Court criticized the expert's intention to offer only "general comments" about eyewitness testimony rather than testifying about the "reliability of any specific witness."); People v. Hill, 84 Mich.App. 90, 269 N.W.2d 492, 495 (Mich.Ct.App.1978)(The eyewitness expert was properly excluded, since the expert

Other courts hold exactly the opposite view. They assert that the generality of the expert's statements makes the testimony less invasive of the jury's province.[63] By limiting the expert's testimony to factors that generally interfere with eyewitness perception and recall, these courts point out, the expert can assist the jurors to appreciate the limitations of eyewitness identifications. The expert thus avoids offering an opinion on the accuracy of a specific witness, an opinion within the province of the trier of fact, and which the research could not support in any case. Finally, under virtually all state evidence codes as well as the Federal Rules of Evidence, expert testimony is not limited to opinions about case-specific matters, but can extend to general matters that are relevant to the case and that will assist the trier of fact.[64]

Under both the *Downing* and *Daubert* tests, the question of "fit" between the science and the factual matters in dispute implicates the "assist the trier of fact" requirement of Rule 702. In general, eyewitness experts limit their testimony to only those research findings that pertain to issues presented in the case at hand. For instance, only in cases in which weapons were used would an expert discuss the effect of the phenomenon known as "weapons focus." Another sense of fit is also important. Because of the difficulty of testing eyewitness identifications under "real-life" conditions, research will sometimes not "fit" the facts presented in particular cases. For example, research on forgetting and memory that permits subjects only a few seconds or minutes to observe the perpetrator might have little or no relevance where the perpetrator was observed over several hours. Courts, of course, must ensure that eyewitness experts limit their testimony to the research that fits the case and is thus relevant.[65]

§ 8–1.3.2 Reliability/Validity of the Science

No cases could be found that specifically evaluated the scientific validity of research on the accuracy of eyewitness identifications. Several courts, however, exclude eyewitness expert testimony when the offering party fails to produce the research that would support the claim of a scientific foundation.[66] This basis, of course, does not impugn the validity of the science, only the lawyer's success in meeting the rigors of the adversarial process. In *United States v. Kime*, for example, defense counsel submitted only the expert's

had not "interviewed or questioned any of the eyewitnesses.").

63. *See e.g.*, State v. Chapple, 135 Ariz. 281, 660 P.2d 1208 (Ariz.1983)("[W]itnesses are permitted to express opinions on ultimate issues but are not required to testify to an opinion on the precise questions before the trier of fact."); *see also* State v. Buell, 22 Ohio St.3d 124, 489 N.E.2d 795, 803 (Ohio 1986), discussed *supra* note 60.

64. The Advisory Committee's Note to Rule 702 is explicit on this issue:

Most of the literature assumes that experts testify only in the form of opinions. The assumption is logically unfounded. The rule accordingly recognizes that an expert on the stand may give a dissertation or exposition of scientific or other principles relevant to the

case, leaving the trier of fact to apply them to the facts.

FED. R. EVID. 702, Advisory Committee Notes.

65. *See e.g.*, Pierce v. State, 777 S.W.2d 399 (Tex.Crim.App.1989) (in upholding lower court's exclusion of eyewitness expert, court found that expert who did not have knowledge of the eyewitness' testimony could not "fit" his testimony to the facts of the case); Rousseau v. State, 855 S.W.2d 666, 686 (Tex.Crim.App. 1993) (same).

66. *See e.g.*, United States v. Kime, 99 F.3d 870 (8th Cir.1996); United States v. Fosher, 590 F.2d 381, 382 (1st Cir.1979) (finding that the defendant had offered no proof that the expert's testimony was based "upon a mode of scientific analysis that meets any of the standards of reliability applicable to scientific evidence"); Jordan v. State, 950 S.W.2d 210 (Tex.

preliminary opinion, his curriculum vitae and one coauthored article in support of his testimony.[67] These materials, the court explained, were "utterly deficient in regard to determining whether his views constitute 'scientific knowledge' within the meaning of *Daubert*."[68]

It might be that defense counsel is so used to losing this particular battle on the "helpfulness" prong that they have abandoned any effort to demonstrate its scientific validity. And, in fact, in *Kime* itself the court stated that the evidence also should be excluded on the ground that "the layman juror would be able to make a common sense determination of the issue without the technical aid of such an expert."[69] We have trouble blaming counsel in *Kime* for not expending the effort and money to make a scientific showing when the court was predisposed to exclude the evidence on alternative grounds in any case. It is, however, somewhat disingenuous of the court to ask for such expenditures when it intends to exclude the evidence no matter what the science shows.

In an interesting and thoughtful opinion, Judge Gertner, in *United States v. Hines*,[70] compared psychological research on eyewitnesses to the basis for handwriting analysis—both subjects before her in the case. She found that the issue for handwriting was whether there was any substantial research, whereas on the subject of eyewitness reliability the matter concerned whether the substantial body of experimental research was generalizeable to the real world. She explained:

> Unlike handwriting analysis, there is no question as to the scientific underpinnings of the [defense] testimony. They are based on experimental studies, testing the acquisition of memory, retention, and retrieval of memory under different conditions. Indeed, the central debate before the jury, eloquently articulated by . . . the government's expert, is the polar opposite of the debate in the handwriting field—whether conclusions obtained in an experimental, academic, setting with college students should be applied to a real life setting.[71]

Finally, even when courts reach the question of scientific validity of eyewitness research fully, some have suggested that as social science it need not meet the rigors of *Daubert*.[72]

Although courts have yet to truly examine the underlying research supporting expert testimony on eyewitness identifications, some scientists have criticized this research on scientific grounds.[73] Courts applying *Daubert* will soon have to confront this matter.

App.1997); Forte v. State, 935 S.W.2d 172 (Tex.App.1996).

67. *Kime*, 99 F.3d at 883.

68. *Id.*

69. *Id.* at 884.

70. 55 F.Supp.2d 62 (D.Mass.1999).

71. *Id.* at 72.

72. *See generally* Weatherred v. State, 985 S.W.2d 234, 236–37 (Tex.App.1999) (The court discussed the admissibility of eyewitness expert testimony in light of the Texas rule in *Nenno v. State*, 970 S.W.2d 549 (Tex.Crim.App.1998) requiring a reliability test for the social sciences,

but one not as rigorous as is applied to the "hard sciences.").

73. For an overview of the scientific basis of eyewitness expert testimony, *see infra* § 15–2.0. The most vehement critic of scientific research on human perception and memory and, particularly, its application to eyewitness testimony, is Professor Rogers Elliott of Dartmouth College. *See* Rogers Elliott, *Expert Testimony About Eyewitness Identification: A Critique,* 17 LAW & HUM. BEHAV. 423, 423 (1993)(concluding that "the scientific basis [to support expert testimony on eyewitness identification] is generally inadequate and that the more we have

§ 8–1.3.3 General Acceptance

Under *Frye,* general acceptance is the *sine qua non* of admissibility; under *Daubert,* it is one of several factors that courts should evaluate when determining scientific validity. Several courts conclude that there remains substantial disagreement in the pertinent field regarding the validity of research on eyewitness identifications. Much of the disagreement identified by these courts can be traced to a 1983 article written by Professors McCloskey and Egeth.[74] But Professors McCloskey and Egeth primarily questioned whether, given the limited scope of the research so far conducted, eyewitness experts could sufficiently assist triers of fact. For example, in a widely quoted statement, they asserted that "there is virtually no empirical evidence that [jurors] are unaware of the problems with eyewitness testimony."[75] However, McCloskey and Egeth did not specifically attack the validity of the research. Instead, they doubted whether the valid research available could be of significant assistance. Their essential argument concerns the relevance or "fit" of the research—i.e., whether expert psychological testimony on memory and perception can assist triers of fact—and thus is a legal matter not a scientific one.[76] The McCloskey and Egeth criticism, therefore, should be consulted in the debate whether eyewitness expert testimony will be "helpful,"[77] not whether its validity is generally accepted. Although the percentage of a field that is required to constitute "general" acceptance is difficult to gauge, few areas of social science can match the level of acceptance of many of the research findings in human memory and perception that eyewitness experts relate in their testimony.[78]

§ 8–1.3.4 Rule 403: Weighing Probative Value and Unfair Prejudice

As noted above, most courts believe that eyewitness expert testimony will provide little or no assistance to triers of fact and thus has little or no probative value. But, if this testimony has even slight probative value, most rules of evidence direct that it should be admitted unless substantial unfair prejudice or waste of time would result.[79] Thus, when affirming a trial court's

learned about various aspects of eyewitness identification, the more inadequate it appears."); *see generally* Rogers Elliott, *On the Reliability of Eyewitness Testimony: A Retrospective Review,* 57 Psychological Reports 219 (1985); Rogers Elliott, et al., *Eyewitness Credible and Discredible,* 18 J. of Applied Social Psychology 1411 (1988).

74. Michael McCloskey & Howard Egeth, *Eyewitness Identification: What Can a Psychologist Tell a Jury?* 38 Am. Psychologist 550, 551 (May 1983).

75. *Id.* at 553, *quoted in* United States v. Christophe, 833 F.2d 1296, 1299 (9th Cir. 1987).

76. *See* People v. Mooney, 76 N.Y.2d 827, 560 N.Y.S.2d 115, 559 N.E.2d 1274, 1275 (N.Y. 1990) (Kaye, J., dissenting).

77. For alternative views on the question whether jurors need assistance, *see* Kenneth Deffenbacher & Elizabeth Loftus, *Do Jurors*

Share a Common Understanding Concerning Eyewitness Behavior? 6 Law & Hum. Behav. 15 (1982); Gary Wells, et al., *Effects of Expert Psychological Advice on Human Performance in Judging the Validity of Eyewitness Testimony,* 4 Law & Hum. Behav. 275, 278 (1980). *See also infra* § 8–1.6.

78. Saul Kassin, et al., *On the "General Acceptance" of Eyewitness Testimony Research: A New Survey of the Experts,* 56 Am. Psychologist 405 (2001).

79. Under the Federal Rules of Evidence, Rule 402 directs that "[a]ll relevant evidence is admissible, except as otherwise provided." Rule 403 provides that "although relevant, evidence may be excluded if its probative value is substantially outweighed by the danger of unfair prejudice, confusion of the issues, or misleading the jury, or by considerations of undue delay, waste of time, or needless presentation of cumulative evidence."

exclusion of eyewitness expert testimony, the balance of probative value and prejudicial effect often figures prominently in the analysis. Appellate courts generally agree that this is a balance to be struck by trial courts and should not be disturbed unless the lower court abused its discretion.

Courts offer a wide array of reasons for believing that the dangers associated with eyewitness experts are too great. Consistent with the view that this testimony will be of little assistance to jurors,[80] many courts find that admitting it would be a waste of time,[81] or cause confusion.[82] In addition, courts find that eyewitness expert testimony will have deleterious effects on the trial process, either by invading the province of the jury[83] or overwhelming the jury by the "aura of infallibility" thought to surround scientific evidence.[84]

In an unusual use of the traditional evidentiary balance of probative value and prejudicial effect, some courts hold that when the other evidence admitted is sufficient to demonstrate guilt, trial courts have discretion to exclude eyewitness expert testimony.[85] This approach—which might be termed the "overwhelming evidence of guilt principle"—is a variation of two themes that recur in these cases. First, appellate courts sometimes find that the trial court abused its discretion, but that this error constitutes "harmless error."[86]

---

80. *See* State v. McClendon, 248 Conn. 572, 730 A.2d 1107 (Conn.1999) (Court upheld exclusion of eyewitness identification expertise, finding that his opinions "should come as no surprise to the average person.").

81. *See e.g.*, People v. Kemp, 885 P.2d 260, 263 (Colo.Ct.App.1994) (citing undue delay to support exclusion of testimony); State v. Barry, 25 Wash.App. 751, 611 P.2d 1262, 1267 (Wash. Ct.App.1980) (asserting that the expert's testimony "raised the possibility of creating a time-consuming side issue as to the testimony's reliability"); Hampton v. State, 92 Wis.2d 450, 285 N.W.2d 868, 873 (Wis.1979) (allowing expert testimony would "lengthen the time and increase the cost of trials").

82. *See e.g.*, United States v. Serna, 799 F.2d 842, 850 (2d Cir.1986)(the expert's testimony "would [not] have done anything other than to muddy the waters"); People v. Kemp, 885 P.2d 260, 263 (Colo.Ct.App.1994) (the expert testimony will confuse the issues and confuse the jury); Bloodsworth v. State, 307 Md. 164, 512 A.2d 1056, 1063 (1986) (expert testimony would tend to confuse jury); State v. Gardiner, 636 A.2d 710, 713 (R.I.1994) (expert testimony will "mislead the jury").

83. *See e.g.*, State v. Stucke, 419 So.2d 939, 945 (La.1982) (expert testimony "invades the province of the jury and usurps its functions"); Porter v. State, 94 Nev. 142, 576 P.2d 275, 278–79 (Nev.1978) (the expert's testimony "would have had a greater influence on the jury than the evidence presented at trial, thereby interfering with the province of the jury"); State v. Barry, 25 Wash.App. 751, 611 P.2d 1262, 1267 (Wash.App.1980) (the testimony "posed the risk of interfering with the jury's role as the factfinder"); Hampton v. State, 92 Wis.2d 450, 285 N.W.2d 868, 873

(Wis.1979) (the testimony might "cause [jurors] to abdicate their role as the 'lie-detector' in the courtroom").

84. *See e.g.*, United States v. Fosher, 590 F.2d 381, 383 (1st Cir.1979) (the testimony would "create a substantial danger of undue prejudice and confusion because of its aura of special reliability and trustworthiness"); United States v. Purham, 725 F.2d 450, 454 (8th Cir.1984) (same); State v. Stucke, 419 So.2d 939, 945 (La.1982)(same); State v. Hill, 463 N.W.2d 674, 678 (S.D.1990) (same).

85. The clearest example of this practice is *United States v. Moore*, 786 F.2d 1308, 1313 (5th Cir.1986), in which the court accepted the value of eyewitness expert testimony. The court observed that "the conclusions of the psychological studies are largely counter-intuitive and serve to 'explode common myths about an individual's capacities for perception.' " The court, however, did not find that the trial court's exclusion of the expert testimony was an abuse of discretion. *Id.* The court explained, "Even if the eyewitness identifications of [the eyewitnesses] are completely disregarded, the other evidence of guilt is overwhelming." *Id.* According to the court, a trial judge does not abuse his discretion if he excludes eyewitness expert testimony because the other evidence overwhelmingly demonstrates guilt. *Id. See also* United States v. Curry, 977 F.2d 1042, 1052 (7th Cir.1992) (the eyewitness testimony against the defendants was "far from the only evidence" against them).

86. *See e.g.*, People v. Walker, 185 Cal. App.3d 155, 229 Cal.Rptr. 591, 598 (Cal.Ct. App.1986) (trial court abused its discretion in excluding eyewitness expert testimony, but this error was harmless).

Second, many courts find the most compelling need for expert testimony when the only evidence consists of eyewitness identifications.[87] But these two unremarkable principles do not fully support the "overwhelming evidence of guilt principle." Especially the first, "harmless error," is not generalizable to the trial level admissibility determination. It is an appellate device that permits courts to correct lower court errors without wasting judicial resources when those errors did not affect the outcome. The harmless error rule effectively gives appellate courts the power to weigh evidence, ordinarily a task for triers of fact. In effect, the "overwhelming evidence of guilt principle" gives similar power to trial courts. To be sure, this is not entirely inconsistent with the fact that courts regularly find a special need for the eyewitness expert when the prosecution's evidence relies principally, or exclusively, on eyewitnesses. This special need analysis illustrates how the general context and evidence of the case affects the probative value of proffered expert testimony. Trial courts, however, should be wary of weighing the evidence too finely under Rule 403 and, in doing so, excluding testimony offered by the defendant on the basis that he will be convicted with it or without it.

§ 8–1.3.5 Procedural Challenges to Eyewitness Identifications

It is important to note an issue that has not been given sufficient attention by courts. There are two qualitatively different kinds of expert testimony that eyewitness experts can give. One type focuses on the *reliability of eyewitnesses* and the other type focuses on the *reliability of the procedures or methods* used to secure the eyewitness evidence. An example of the eyewitness-reliability type would be when an expert states, for instance, that "the confidence of an eyewitness in his identification is not highly correlated to the accuracy of the identification." The focus is on the eyewitness and the expert serves to challenge eyewitness testimony in a general way. An alternative to this approach considers the reliability of the methods used to secure the eyewitness' statements. Such expert testimony, for example, might state that "lineups in which the suspect is the only one who matches the prior description of the culprit are more likely to produce false identifications than lineups in which several people resemble the description of the perpetrator." The expert's focus is thus on the procedure used to secure the identification, one freely chosen by the police investigators in the case.[88]

The difference between the eyewitness-reliability type and the method-reliability type of expert testimony is significant. The method-reliability type is analogous to having a DNA expert testify about the reliability of a particular banding procedure, or a forensics firearms expert testify about the reliability of a particular method of matching bullets to guns. When evidence is presented against a defendant in which some specific method was used by the police or by a lab, the method used inevitably becomes an issue. Calling

---

87. *See e.g.,* State v. Chapple, 135 Ariz. 281, 660 P.2d 1208, 1222 (Ariz.1983)(One factor in determining whether the trial court abused its discretion is if the identification of the defendant was the key factual dispute in the case and excluding expert testimony would "undercut the entire evidentiary basis" for the defense.).

88. *See, e.g.,* State v. Kelly, 752 A.2d 188, 192 (Me.2000) (Court described two-step process to challenges regarding identification procedures: (1) defendant must prove by preponderance of evidence that the procedures were suggestive and (2) if the defendant meets his burden of proof, the state must show by clear and convincing evidence that the identification is nonetheless reliable.).

into question a specific method does not invade the province of the jury and does not call into question the general reliability of the evidence (whether it be DNA evidence, firearms tests or eyewitness identifications). Instead, the testimony suggests limitations and dangers associated with methods that might be changed and improved. Such testimony is likely to be of considerable assistance to the trier of fact and, in the long term, should improve police practices.

In *State v. Morris*,[89] the defendant appealed from a trial court ruling refusing to suppress an eyewitness identification. The defendant claimed that both the photographic array and the subsequent lineup that led to the identification had been "unduly suggestive."[90] On appeal, the defendant argued that the photo array was suggestive because "his photograph appeared to be the only 'black and white' one in the array."[91] Applying a clearly erroneous standard, and viewing the ruling under a totality of the circumstances test, the Rhode Island Supreme Court concluded that the lower court had not erred in denying the defendant's motion to suppress. It explained the rule regarding suggestive arrays as follows:

> "In determining whether the photographic array poses a substantial risk of misidentification, we must compare the physical characteristics of each individual featured in the display to the general description of the suspect given to the police by the victim.... If we conclude that the array was unnecessarily suggestive, we must then consider whether in the totality of circumstances [the witness's] out-of-court identification of defendant was nonetheless reliable."[92]

The defendant also claimed that the subsequent physical lineup was tainted because the witness expected to see the defendant, since he had been in the photographic array, and, moreover, was the only participant wearing an orange shirt. The court found these assertions to "have no merit."[93] Again applying a clearly erroneous standard, the court reviewed the trial court's reasons for refusing to suppress the identification. The lower court had found that the lineup participants were very similar in appearance and that other factors supported the accuracy of the identification. In particular, the lower court explained that the witness had been "face to face" with the defendant for an extended period of time, affording him an ample opportunity to identify him later.

§ 8–1.4 Jury Instructions

In *State v. Cromedy*,[94] the New Jersey Supreme Court reversed and remanded the defendant's conviction because the trial court had failed to give the jury an instruction on the unreliability of cross-racial identifications. In most jurisdictions, the question whether a jury instruction is proper is left to the discretion of the trial court.[95] Some jurisdictions have held it improper to

---

89. 744 A.2d 850 (R.I.2000).

90. *Id.* at 856–57. See also Brooks v. State, 748 So.2d 736, 742–43 (Miss.1999) (finding the fact that the defendant had longer hair than any of the other participants in the lineup did not unduly taint the identification).

91. *Morris*, 744 A.2d at 856.

92. *Id.* (*quoting* State v. Gatone, 698 A.2d 230, 235–36 (R.I.1997) (internal quotation marks omitted).

93. *Id.* at 857.

94. 158 N.J. 112, 727 A.2d 457 (N.J.1999).

95. *See, e.g.*, United States v. Thompson, 31 M.J. 125 (C.M.A.1990); Commonwealth v.

give such an instructions at all.[96] The *Cromedy* court attempted to steer a middle course, recognizing that research and common experience indicate certain difficulties in cross-racial identifications, but that allusions to cross-racial identifications could incite racial prejudices. The court observed that

> the empirical data encapsulate much of the ordinary human experience and provide an appropriate frame of reference for requiring a cross-racial identification jury instruction. Under the jurisprudence of this Court, in a prosecution "in which race by definition is a patent factor[, race] must be taken into account to assure a fair trial."[97]

Nonetheless, the court cautioned, the

> unrestricted use of cross-racial identification instructions could be counter-productive. Consequently, care must be taken to insulate criminal trials from base appeals to racial prejudice. An appropriate jury instruction should carefully delineate the context in which the jury is permitted to consider racial differences. The simple fact pattern of a white victim of a violent crime at the hands of a black assailant would not automatically give rise to the need for a cross-racial identification charge. More is required.[98]

The court concluded, therefore, that such a charge should be given only when special circumstances required it. But when those circumstances were present, as was true in *Cromedy*, failure to give an instruction was error: "A cross-racial instruction should be given only when, as in the present case, identification is a critical issue in the case, and an eyewitness's cross-racial identification is not corroborated by other evidence giving it independent reliability."[99]

§ 8–1.5　Standards of Appellate Review

In *General Electric Co. v. Joiner*,[100] the Supreme Court held that the standard of appellate review for decisions regarding the admissibility of all expert testimony is the "abuse of discretion" standard.[101] Prior to *Joiner*, in both federal and state cases, the nearly unanimous standard of review that applied to trial courts' decisions to exclude eyewitness expert testimony was the abuse of discretion (or "manifestly erroneous") standard.[102] The abuse of

Hyatt, 419 Mass. 815, 647 N.E.2d 1168 (Mass. 1995).

96. *See, e.g.*, State v. Hadrick, 523 A.2d 441, 444 (R.I.1987); People v. Bias, 131 Ill. App.3d 98, 86 Ill.Dec. 256, 475 N.E.2d 253, 257 (Ill.App.1985).

97. *Cromedy*, 727 A.2d at 467 (*quoting* State v. Harris, 156 N.J. 122, 716 A.2d 458 (N.J.1998) (Handler, J., dissenting)).

98. *Id.*

99. *Id.* Interestingly, although the *Cromedy* court held that sometimes cross-racial instructions must be given, expert testimony on the subject was not proper: "Because of the 'widely held commonsense view that members of one race have greater difficulty in accurately identifying members of a different race,' expert testimony on this issue would not assist a jury." *Id.* at 467–68 (*quoting* United States v.

Telfaire, 469 F.2d 552, 559 (D.C.Cir.1972)) (internal citations omitted).

100. 522 U.S. 136, 118 S.Ct. 512, 139 L.Ed.2d 508 (1997).

101. *Id.* at 143–44.

102. *See e.g.*, United States v. Blade, 811 F.2d 461, 465 (8th Cir.1987) (applying manifestly erroneous standard to trial court's exclusion of expert testimony on the accuracy of eyewitness identifications); Bradley v. Brown, 42 F.3d 434 (7th Cir.1994) (applying manifestly erroneous standard to trial court's exclusion of medical testimony on multiple chemical sensitivity disorder); Rosado v. Deters, 5 F.3d 119, 124 (5th Cir.1993) ("[A] trial court's ruling regarding admissibility of expert testimony is protected by an ambit of discretion and must be sustained unless 'manifestly erroneous.' ");

discretion standard is lenient in theory and indulgent in fact.[103] It is easier to document the use of the abuse of discretion standard than the reasons behind its use in various contexts. Courts rarely explain the basis for this test and they indiscriminately apply it to all of the threshold admissibility factors. The ostensible basis for the standard is that admission of expert testimony is principally a preliminary fact question, a category on which appellate courts traditionally deferred to trial courts. The reason for this deference lies in the lower court's proximity to the witnesses who establish the preliminary fact.[104] But in the context of eyewitness experts, the trial court is not necessarily better situated as to all of the factors typically considered when evaluating the admissibility of scientific evidence. In particular, validity and general acceptance of the scientific research upon which the expert bases his testimony is amenable to close and effective appellate review.[105]

Although the vast majority of courts who use the abuse of discretion standard when reviewing the decision whether to admit eyewitness expert testimony uphold the lower court's decision, several courts have found abuses.[106] In *State v. Chapple*, for example, the Arizona Supreme Court found that the lower court erred when it excluded an eyewitness expert.[107] The *Chapple* court identified the following factors as determinative in whether a trial court has committed an abuse of discretion in excluding an eyewitness expert: (1) identification of the defendant was the key factual dispute in the case and excluding expert testimony "undercut the entire evidentiary basis for the defense"; (2) the expert testimony was limited to explaining the factors

United States v. Jones, 24 F.3d 1177 (9th Cir. 1994) (applying the abuse of discretion standard to affirm the trial court's exclusion of the defendant's expert voice identification evidence).

103. Our apologies to Professor Gerald Gunther, who observed that the constitutional standard of review known as strict scrutiny was "strict in theory and fatal in fact." Gerald Gunther, *Foreward: In Search of Evolving Doctrine on a Changing Court: A Model for a Newer Equal Protection*, 86 Harv. L. Rev. 1 (1972).

104. *See* 3 J. Weinstein & M. Berger, Weinstein's Evidence ¶ 702(2) at 22–23 (1993).

105. For a full discussion of appellate review of trial court admissibility decisions regarding scientific evidence, *see* Chapter 1, *Legal Standards for the Admissibility of Scientific Evidence*.

106. *See e.g.*, United States v. Stevens, 935 F.2d 1380, 1400–1401 (3d Cir.1991) (concluding that the trial court's exclusion of eyewitness expert testimony was an abuse of discretion because the expert testimony "fit" the facts of the case); Skamarocius v. State, 731 P.2d 63, 66 (Alaska Ct.App.1987) (finding that the trial court had abused its discretion when it excluded eyewitness expert testimony since such testimony would have addressed the crucial issue of whether the victim's identification was accurate); People v. McDonald, 37 Cal.3d

351, 208 Cal.Rptr. 236, 690 P.2d 709 (Cal. 1984) (applying *Amaral's* four-part test and concluding that the trial court's refusal to allow eyewitness expert testimony was an abuse of discretion); People v. Campbell, 847 P.2d 228, 232–233 (Colo.Ct.App.1992) (holding that eyewitness expert testimony should have been admitted at trial since there was "no indication ... that it would overwhelm or mislead the jury," the proffered testimony "fit" the particular circumstances surrounding the identification, and would assist the jury because it was "contrary to common wisdom"); State v. Whaley, 305 S.C. 138, 406 S.E.2d 369, 372 (S.C.1991) (concluding that trial court's decision to bar eyewitness expert testimony constituted an abuse of discretion since the sole evidence against the defendant was eyewitness testimony, the defendant's identification was the crucial issue at trial, and no other evidence "substantially corroborated" the victim's testimony); State v. Moon, 45 Wash.App. 692, 726 P.2d 1263, 1266–1267 (Wash.App.1986) (ruling that the trial court erred in excluding eyewitness expert testimony for several reasons, including (1) the defendant's identification was the principal issue at trial; (2) the defendant presented an alibi defense; (3) little or no other evidence linked the defendant to the crime; and (4) the victim's description varied significantly from the defendant's actual appearance).

107. State v. Chapple, 135 Ariz. 281, 660 P.2d 1208, 1224 (Ariz.1983).

affecting reliability of eyewitness testimony, and the expert did not try to proffer an opinion on the actual accuracy of the eyewitnesses who gave testimony in the case; (3) there was no "significant prejudice" to the prosecution in admitting the testimony and no waste of time, since the issue was such a crucial one in the trial; (4) all of the *Amaral* criteria had been fulfilled.[108] The court concluded that since there were "a number of substantive issues of ultimate fact on which the expert's testimony would have been of significant assistance," the trial court's decision to preclude the testimony was "legally incorrect and unsupported by the record."[109]

The *Chapple* court, however, emphasized that it did not intend by its decision to subject state courts to a "flood of expert evidence."[110] In fact, since *Chapple,* no appellate court in Arizona has reversed a trial court's decision to exclude expert testimony on eyewitness identification.[111] The same reluctance to overturn lower courts' admissibility decisions is evident in the several other jurisdictions in which courts have found an abuse of discretion.[112] Moreover, of the few courts in which an abuse of discretion has been found, many determine that the error was harmless, because the other evidence sufficiently demonstrated guilt.[113]

Not all courts, however, adhere to the deferential view reflected by the abuse of discretion standard. The Third Circuit's decision in *United States v. Downing,*[114] for example, departs significantly from the prevailing reluctance

108. *Id.* at 1222.

109. *Id.* at 1222, 1224.

110. The *Chapple* court stated as follows:

The rule in Arizona will continue to be that in the usual case we will support the trial court's discretionary ruling on admissibility of expert testimony on eyewitness identification. Nor do we invite opinion testimony in even the most extraordinary case on the likelihood that a particular witness is correct or mistaken in identification or that eyewitness identification in general has a certain percentage of accuracy or inaccuracy.

Id. at 1224.

111. *See e.g.,* State v. Rodriquez, 145 Ariz. 157, 700 P.2d 855, 866 (Ariz.Ct.App.1984) (distinguishing *Chapple,* and finding that this was one of the "usual cases" in which the trial court's broad discretion should not be disturbed, found no abuse of discretion in the trial court's exclusion of eyewitness expert testimony); State v. Poland, 144 Ariz. 388, 698 P.2d 183, 193 (Ariz.1985)(same; and emphasizing that "expert testimony on eyewitness identification is usually precluded because it invades the province of the jury ... [and] is usually not a proper subject for testimony"); State v. McCutcheon, 162 Ariz. 54, 781 P.2d 31, 35 (Ariz.1989)(distinguishing *Chapple* on factual grounds and finding that the trial court had not abused its discretion in excluding the expert testimony).

112. California offers perhaps the best example of appellate courts' reluctance to disturb

lower courts exclusion of eyewitness expert testimony In *People v. McDonald,* 37 Cal.3d 351, 208 Cal.Rptr. 236, 690 P.2d 709, 726 (Cal. 1984), the California Supreme Court found that the trial court had abused its discretion in excluding expert testimony on the accuracy of eyewitness identification. The *McDonald* court cited extensively and approvingly the Arizona Supreme Court's decision in *Chapple.* In several cases after *McDonald,* California courts held that trial courts had abused their discretion in prohibiting eyewitness expert testimony; but all of these courts found such exclusion to be harmless error. *See* People v. Jackson, 164 Cal.App.3d 224, 210 Cal.Rptr. 680 (Cal.Ct.App. 1985); People v. Walker, 185 Cal.App.3d 155, 229 Cal.Rptr. 591, 598 (Cal.App.1986). However, in most of the cases decided after *McDonald,* no abuse of discretion was found. *See e.g.,* People v. Plasencia, 168 Cal.App.3d 546, 223 Cal.Rptr. 786, 791 (Cal.Ct.App.1985); People v. Sanders, 51 Cal.3d 471, 273 Cal.Rptr. 537, 797 P.2d 561 (Cal.1990); People v. Walker, 47 Cal.3d 605, 253 Cal.Rptr. 863, 765 P.2d 70, 82 (Cal.1988).

113. *See* People v. Jackson, 164 Cal.App.3d 224, 210 Cal.Rptr. 680 (Cal.Ct.App.1985); People v. Walker, 185 Cal.App.3d 155, 229 Cal. Rptr. 591, 598 (Cal.Ct.App.1986); State v. Alger, 115 Idaho 42, 764 P.2d 119, 125–27 (Idaho Ct.App.1988); Echavarria v. State, 108 Nev. 734, 839 P.2d 589 (Nev.1992); State v. Hamm, 146 Wis.2d 130, 430 N.W.2d 584 (Wis.Ct.App. 1988).

114. 753 F.2d 1224 (3d Cir.1985).

among appellate courts to interfere in lower courts' discretion concerning the admissibility of expert testimony.[115] Since *Downing*, however, the Supreme Court decided *Joiner*, as noted above, mandating an abuse of discretion standard for appellate review of admissibility determinations of expert testimony.

§ 8–1.6 Constitutional Claims

§ 8–1.6.1 Right to Call Witnesses

Several courts have considered, and all have rejected, claims that the exclusion of eyewitness expert testimony violates a defendant's right to call witnesses on his behalf under the Sixth or Fourteenth Amendments of the Constitution.[116] The compulsory process claim is rejected, as the Eleventh Circuit held in *Johnson v. Wainwright*, not because such testimony is "considered *per se* incompetent, but rather because the content of the testimony was found to be inadmissible."[117] A substantive basis for excluding testimony, the *Johnson* court asserted, is sufficient to meet the requirements of the compulsory process clause.[118] A similar analysis was used by the Connecticut Supreme Court in *State v. Kemp*.[119] The *Kemp* court stressed that the Sixth Amendment does not give defendants the right to call any witness they choose.[120] Instead, defendants must "comply with the established rules of procedure and evidence."[121] The court concluded that since the trial court's exclusion of the expert testimony did not offend the Connecticut standard for determining the admissibility of such evidence, the defendant's constitutional rights were not violated.[122]

The Eleventh Circuit in *Johnson* also considered the defendant's contention that failure to permit eyewitness expert testimony violated due process.[123] In order to prevail in a due process claim, the court observed, the defendant

115. The *Downing* court did not specifically hold that the trial court abused its discretion in excluding expert testimony on eyewitness identification. Instead, the Court found that the trial court had mistakenly ruled that expert testimony on eyewitness identification could never meet the standard for admissibility under Federal Rule of Evidence 702. *Downing*, 753 F.2d at 1226. Not until *United States v. Stevens* did the Third Circuit take this step. In *Stevens*, the court determined that the trial court had abused its discretion in excluding certain facets of expert testimony on eyewitness identification. 935 F.2d 1380 (3d Cir. 1991).

116. The Sixth Amendment provides, in pertinent part:

In all criminal prosecutions, the accused shall enjoy the right ... to have compulsory process for obtaining witnesses in his favor.

U.S. Const. amend. VI. This section of the Sixth Amendment has been incorporated into the due process clause of the Fourteenth Amendment and thus applies to the states. Washington v. Texas, 388 U.S. 14, 18, 87 S.Ct. 1920, 18 L.Ed.2d 1019, *on remand*, 417 S.W.2d 278 (Tex.Crim.App.1967).

117. Johnson v. Wainwright, 806 F.2d 1479, 1485 (11th Cir.1986) (*citing* Phillips v. Wainwright, 624 F.2d 585 (5th Cir.1980)).

118. *Id.*

119. 199 Conn. 473, 507 A.2d 1387 (Conn. 1986).

120. *Id.* at 1390.

121. *Id.*; *see also* Washington v. Schriver, 90 F.Supp.2d 384, 388 (S.D.N.Y.2000) ("[A] defendant's right to present expert testimony is limited by the requirements of relevancy and by the trial court's traditional discretion to prevent prejudicial or confusing testimony."); State v. Percy, 156 Vt. 468, 595 A.2d 248, 253 (Vt.1990) (holding that the accused's right to present witnesses does not allow him to bypass "established rules of procedure and evidence").

122. *Kemp*, 507 A.2d at 1390.

123. *Johnson*, 806 F.2d at 1485; *see also* People v. Wong, 150 Misc.2d 554, 568 N.Y.S.2d 1020, 1023 (1991)(rejecting the defendant's claim of a due process violation because he failed to show a compelling need for such testimony given the facts of his case).

would "have to demonstrate that exclusion of the expert testimony rendered his trial fundamentally unfair because the testimony was material to a crucial, critical, and highly significant matter."[124] But, the court found, exclusion of expert assistance concerning eyewitness identifications was not fundamentally unfair, because this testimony is "merely" a matter of common sense, "well within the ordinary experience of a jury."[125]

In the future, constitutional claims under the Sixth and Fourteenth Amendments will likely be evaluated in light of *United States v. Scheffer*. In *Scheffer*, the Court rejected such a claim in regard to polygraph evidence finding that the lack of consensus on polygraph validity was a reasonable basis upon which to rest a *per se* rule of exclusion.[126] A possible distinction between eyewitness experts and polygraph experts is the ground upon which the exclusion occurs. In *Scheffer*, the *per se* rule was based on the determination that the evidence was not sufficiently reliable. In eyewitness expert cases the basis usually is that the evidence will not assist the trier of fact enough. It is possible that the right to present witnesses is constitutionally stronger in the eyewitness context. A defendant clearly does not have a right to introduce unreliable evidence. In contrast, in eyewitness cases the assertion is that eyewitnesses are less reliable than jurors think and the expert can help them appreciate this fact. Courts excluding these experts generally disagree that jurors need this help, or offer instructions as an alternative way to alert jurors to the dangers. The constitutional analysis might be somewhat more congenial to defendants' claims that relevant and reliable evidence should not be withheld from them because it might waste time or jurors are presumed to already know about the problems of eyewitness identifications.

§ 8–1.6.2 Due Process

Another constitutional concern—though more in the realm of criminal procedure than evidence—is the due process guarantee that a criminal defendant should not be subjected to police identification procedures that create a "very substantial likelihood of irreparable misidentification."[127] Although the procedure must be "unnecessarily suggestive," the "central question" in a due process challenge is "whether under the 'totality of the circumstances' the identification was reliable even though the confrontation procedure was suggestive."[128] The Supreme Court has identified five factors, routinely referred to as the "Biggers factors," to be considered in evaluating the reliability of suggestive procedures, including

124. *Johnson,* 806 F.2d at 1485 (citation omitted).

125. *Id.* at 1486. In State v. Broom, 40 Ohio St.3d 277, 533 N.E.2d 682 (Ohio 1988), the defense contended that the court's refusal to appoint an eyewitness expert resulted in a violation of the defendant's due process rights. The Ohio Supreme Court agreed that experts must be provided to indigent defendants when "the services are reasonably necessary for the proper representation of a defendant charged with aggravated murder." *Id.* at 691. Here, however, the defendant failed to make a showing of demonstrable prejudice, such as the "need to impeach an eyewitness with physical or mental impairment." *Id.* (*relying on* State v.

Buell, 22 Ohio St.3d 124, 489 N.E.2d 795 (Ohio 1986)). *But see* People v. Richardson, 189 Ill.2d 401, 245 Ill.Dec. 109, 727 N.E.2d 362, 374–75 (Ill.2000) ("Where no constitutional right is implicated, the decision to appoint an expert, or to authorize funds to hire an expert, rests within the sound discretion of the circuit court.").

126. *Scheffer* is considered in detail in Chapter 12.

127. Manson v. Brathwaite, 432 U.S. 98, 116, 97 S.Ct. 2243, 53 L.Ed.2d 140 (1977).

128. Neil v. Biggers, 409 U.S. 188, 199, 93 S.Ct. 375, 34 L.Ed.2d 401 (1972).

the opportunity of the witness to view the criminal at the time of the crime, the witness' degree of attention, the accuracy of his prior description of the criminal, the level of certainty demonstrated at the confrontation, and the time between the crime and the confrontation.[129]

Courts typically apply these factors in a straightforward manner to determine whether the identification was constitutionally defective.[130]

§ 8–1.7 Conclusion

Psychologists who are interested in legal issues consider research on the reliability of eyewitness identifications to be one of the great successes of their endeavors over the last twenty-five years. The main claim for success is the great volume of work on the subject, and the many clear empirical findings that appear to be compelled by the research. The law, however, has been much less enthusiastic about these claimed successes. This, however, appears to be changing.

In 1999, the United States Department of Justice published guidelines for the collection and preservation of eyewitness evidence.[131] This report recognized many of the shortcomings of current procedures, and recommended a host of reforms that would reduce the number of misidentifications. Although it remains too early to gauge the influence the guidelines will have on police practices, their very existence is a quantum leap beyond the previous status quo.

Much of the current general recognition of the problems associated with eyewitness identifications comes from another area of scientific evidence. In the well-publicized DNA exoneration cases, a large proportion of these miscarriages of justice were attributable to unreliable eyewitness identifications. In all likelihood, expert testimony on the factors that sometimes interfere with reliable identifications probably would not have avoided all, or even most, of these errors. However, these errors are certainly suggestive that current procedures are error-prone, and that jurors are not adept at screening out identification errors when they are made. Courts should be amenable to the research psychologists have to offer. If police identification procedures can be made more reliable, courts should insist that this be done, either as a matter of constitutional principle or evidentiary requirements. Finally, if researchers can offer insights regarding the limitations inherent in eyewitness identifications, experts should be permitted to testify about these limitations in appropriate cases.

129. *Brathwaite*, 432 U.S. at 114 (*citing Biggers*, 409 U.S. at 199–200); *see also* Abdur–Raheem v. Kelly, 98 F.Supp.2d 295, 305 (E.D.N.Y.2000) (suggesting a sixth factor, the amount of corroborating evidence).

130. *See, e.g.*, Cossel v. Miller, 229 F.3d 649 (7th Cir.2000); Carter v. Bell, 218 F.3d 581 (6th Cir.2000).

131. *See supra* note 2 and accompanying text.

B. SCIENTIFIC STATUS

by

Gary L. Wells*

§ 8–2.0 THE SCIENTIFIC STATUS OF RESEARCH ON EYEWITNESS IDENTIFICATION

§ 8–2.1 Introductory Discussion of the Science

The identification of a defendant at trial by an eyewitness can be a dramatic event when the defense theory is that the offense in question was committed by someone else. Identification testimony seems to have its greatest impact when the eyewitness has no plausible reason to lie and seems certain of the correctness of his identification. Over approximately the last 20 years, psychological scientists have taken considerable interest in eyewitness identification. What is the cause of this interest by scientific psychologists in eyewitness identification? It is always difficult to know why scientists focus their attention and efforts at one question versus another at some point in time, but it appears that there have been three principal reasons for the development of a scientific literature on eyewitness identification. First, some critical empirical reports began to surface in the psychological literature in the 1970s indicating that false identifications were commonplace occurrences when crimes were staged for unsuspecting eyewitnesses. Human errors of all types are interesting to psychological theorists because human error can reveal important flaws in the mental system. Second, scientific psychologists from a variety of sub-areas, primarily cognitive psychology and experimental social psychology, quickly recognized the power of their scientific tools and methods (especially controlled procedures, measurement, and experimental design) to bring answers to an important practical question about the reliability of eyewitness identification. Third, the kinds of psychological processes encompassed by questioning the reliability of eyewitnesses are relevant to a long and distinguished history of basic theory and research in the discipline of psychology on memory, perception, and social influence. Considered together, there were empirical, methodological, and theoretical reasons for a subset of scientific psychologists to develop research programs aimed at issues related directly and indirectly to eyewitness identification. The result has been an accumulation of knowledge that could be useful to police and courts.

This chapter is intended to summarize and generalize the accumulated knowledge in the scientific psychology literature on questions about eyewitness identification. This literature is now large enough that this chapter could not list all empirical studies, let alone describe all such studies. Nevertheless, the questions addressed by the scientific literature can be categorized in

* Gary Wells is Professor of Psychology and Distinguished Professor of Liberal Arts and Sciences at Iowa State University, Ames, Iowa. His experiments and papers on eyewitness testimony have appeared in scientific psychology's premiere journals. He has given expert testimony on lineup and photospread identifications, especially with regard to system variable issues, in numerous cases in the United States and Canada. Portions of this Chapter were supported by National Science Foundation grants awarded to Professor Wells. For additional information on this topic see Professor Wells' home page at http://psych-server.iastate.edu/faculty/gwells/.

various ways, thereby allowing a framework for describing what we know at this point and what we do not know without the need to describe each individual empirical study.

As often happens when scientists pursue a problem area, the questions asked by the scientists are not always the ones that consumers of this new-found knowledge would themselves ask. The following section of this chapter describes the questions that eyewitness scientists have asked and gives a rationale for why these questions are interesting or useful. The next section, Methods of Research, describes how eyewitness scientists have studied the questions. This section is critical to understanding the scientific eyewitness literature. One can be neither a good proponent nor an effective critic of scientific conclusions without first understanding the methods that were used by the scientists to reach those conclusions. This is followed by a section describing some conclusions that are generally accepted (areas of agreement) and then a section that describes some levels of analysis and issues that are not fully resolved (areas of disagreement). A future directions section attempts to articulate what the research agenda is likely to be over the next few years.

§ 8–2.1.1   Questions Asked by Scientists

[1]   Introduction

A good question for a scientist has two necessary properties. First, it has to be an answerable question based on the application of scientific tools. Second, there must be some value, either applied or theoretical, to knowing the answer. When a question does not have one or the other of these properties, the question is abandoned, or changed, or qualified in some way that allows it to capture these two essential properties. In the scientific eyewitness research area, two categories of questions characterize the accumulated knowledge: How accurate are eyewitness identifications from lineups and photospreads? How can the accuracy of eyewitness identifications be increased? I call these *categories* of questions rather than questions because both are far too general to have the property of being answerable in such a general form. Consider the question of the accuracy or inaccuracy of eyewitness identifications. The only way to answer this question is to say "it depends." Hence, the question has to be changed or qualified to something like "Under what conditions is eyewitness identification most likely to be accurate and under what conditions is it most likely to be inaccurate?" In other words, on what does it depend?

Any given research project, of course, must carve out a more specific question than the "on what does it depend" question and instead entertain the role of a *specific* variable either alone or in combination with other variables. As discussed in the next section, Methods of Research, scientific eyewitness research involves the isolation and control of specific variables. Hence, a more typical question would be quite specific such as "Are other-race identifications more likely to yield false identifications than are within-race identifications?" An accumulation of knowledge on specific questions of this sort can yield a body of knowledge that can address the general question of eyewitness accuracy. But, the person who asks about the reliability of eyewitness identification in general needs to recognize that the answers are necessarily much more complex, conditional, and specific than the question posed.

[2] Classification of Variables

Eyewitness researchers classify the variables they study in a number of ways. One important classification scheme distinguishes between variables that are under the control of the criminal justice system versus those that are not under control of the system.[1] This is known in the scientific eyewitness literature as the system variable versus estimator variable distinction. *System variables* are under the control (or potentially can be controlled) by the justice system and examples include the methods used to question eyewitnesses or how lineups are constructed. *Estimator variables* are not under the control of the justice system and examples include eyewitness arousal at the time of eyewitnessing or the race of the eyewitness in relation to that of the culprit. All of these variables can affect the likelihood of obtaining an accurate versus false identification, but the justice system could at best only *estimate* the impact of variables such as race and arousal whereas the system *controls* variables such as how eyewitnesses are questioned and how lineups are constructed.

A second way to classify the variables that are studied by eyewitness scientists is in terms of the psychological process presumed to underlie the variable. Two general processing categories can be identified. First there are variables that affect *perception and memory*. The difficulty that people have with identifying people of another race, for instance, seems to be largely a problem of perception and memory.[2] When a white person observes a black person, the white observer tends to notice features that might serve well for later recognizing a white person among other white people (e.g., hair color, eye color), but fails to notice features that would serve well for recognizing a black person among other black people (e.g., skin shading, size of facial features). Hence, perception and resultant memory are relatively less diagnostic in other-race cases than in same-race cases. The second general category of variables can be described as *social influence* variables. If a police officer were to suggest to an eyewitness which member of a lineup was the suspect, for instance, this would be a social influence variable rather than a perception and memory variable.

These two ways of classifying the scientific eyewitness literature serve somewhat different purposes. The purpose of the system versus estimator variable dichotomy is to distinguish between variables that the justice system can control and those it cannot control. The purpose of the perception and memory versus social influence dichotomy is to describe the cognitive processes that are encompassed by those variables. For purposes of this section, the system versus estimator variable distinction seems more useful and, therefore,

§ 8–2.0

1. Gary L. Wells, *Applied Eyewitness Testimony Research: System Variables and Estimator Variables*, 36 J. PERSONALITY & SOC. PSYCHOL. 1546 (1978).

2. A summary of multiple studies can be found in an article by Robert K. Bothwell et al., *Cross Racial Identification*, 15 PERSONALITY & SOC. PSYCHOL. BULL. 19 (1989).

will be the organizing framework for describing the questions that have been studied.[3]

[a] Estimator Variable Questions

Generally, variables that operate before or during an eyewitnessed event are estimator variables because, until the system (e.g., police, attorneys) begins to interact with the eyewitness, it has no control over the perceptions and memories formed by the eyewitness. A few questions have tended to dominate the estimator variable literature.

[I] GENERAL BACKGROUND

Before addressing these questions, it is important to note that there is an extant literature on human perception and memory that goes well beyond the eyewitness domain and has a rich and distinguished history in scientific psychology.[4] From this voluminous scientific literature that has accumulated for over 100 years, certain general principles have been established. It is useful to mention some of these principles before turning attention to the more specific questions concerning eyewitnesses.

[A] Limited Processing Capacity

There are limits to the brain's capacity to process and store information. Some of these limits are "pre-brain." For example, there are acuity limits for the eyes, decibel limits for the ears, and so on. But even when stimuli fall within the processing range for the sense organs, the brain is limited in its processing capacity. Memory for a single presentation string of random digits, for instance, is limited to about seven unless the person can perceive a pattern or meaning to the numbers or somehow "chunk" the string into meaningful

---

3. It should not go unnoticed by legal scholars and practitioners that the system versus estimator distinction has implications for trial strategy. If defense counsel challenges the accuracy of an eyewitness identification based on system variables, it is the system that is under attack (e.g., an argument that a lineup was constructed or conducted in a way that was biased against the defendant). To the extent that there were significantly better methods that could have been used to obtain an identification, due process considerations may become relevant. This is not the case when the credibility of an eyewitness identification is attacked on the basis of estimator variables (e.g., arguing that an identification is questionable because the eyewitness and defendant are of different races). A focus on estimator variables is not likely to raise due process concerns, does not inform the system about how it should have obtained the evidence, and has little or no chance of convincing a judge to suppress the evidence. Practitioners should also note that many eyewitness scientists, myself included, typically will not proffer expert opinion testimony based purely on estimator variables. In-stead, we are more comfortable and certain about our ability to assess the potential deficiencies of the *procedures* used to obtain an identification than we are in assessing variables that are beyond the control of police and courts. My approach to inquiries regarding whether I am willing to proffer expert opinion is fairly common among my colleagues, namely, I want to know if someone (typically the police investigators) used procedures that unduly increased the risk of mistaken identification.

4. The first laboratory in psychology was devoted to the study of human memory and some of the most sophisticated and influential theories in psychology are theories of memory. This long tradition of memory research in psychology has drawn a large share of psychology's best thinkers, best methodologists, and most productive scholars. Nearly all major psychology departments have several memory researchers and more than one graduate level course devoted to memory. Human memory is an essential part of a curriculum in psychological science, even at the level of introductory psychology.

bits.[5]

[B] *Stimulus & Storage*

What is stored in the human brain is not a *direct* representation of the external stimulus. Many of the stimuli impinging on our senses, for instance, are not stored. Those that are stored are stored incompletely or are stored for gist or meaning rather than verbatim. It is not the exact stimulus that enters long-term memory but rather a psychological transformation of that stimulus. Because it generally is gist rather than verbatim that people recall, people's ability to recognize a sentence that they had recently heard from among sentences of the same gist can reach almost chance levels within one to two minutes.[6] The notion that a stimulus and the stored memory of that stimulus are not identical can be demonstrated to an audience rather easily. Ask each person to recall an event of some significance that they themselves experienced. Some might recall a birthday party, a chance encounter that led to a friendship, a funeral, or whatever. Ask the person to picture the scene in his or her mind and then ask, "Can you see yourself in the scene?" People invariably report "yes." This illustrates an important principle of recollection, namely that it is not a direct representation of the stimuli that impinged on the senses. Clearly, they could not see themselves at the time of the event owing to a rather unfortunate location of eyes in a fixed socket of the skull rather than, say, a more flexible location at the end of the finger.

[C] *Forgetting*

It might seem peculiar to non-psychologists that one of the oldest and most fundamental principles of memory, namely forgetting, remains unresolved in some very important ways. If, by forgetting, we simply mean that a previously experienced event is generally less available for recall with the passage of time, there is little debate. The ability to recall or recognize previously encountered stimuli tends to decline with the passage of time and generally follows a negatively decelerating curve. A negatively decelerating curve indicates that there is more forgetting in the first minute (or hour, or day, or week) than in the second minute (or second hour, or second day, or second week) and more forgetting in the second time frame than in the third, and so on. This "shape" of the forgetting curve is easy to comprehend if we use an extreme example. Consider, for instance, the amount of information you might forget in the first 24 hours about a movie that you saw. Now, consider how much of that same movie you might forget in an equal 24–hour period 6–months later. Clearly, you will lose more information in the first 24 hours than in the 24–hour period 6–months later. The fact that forgetting occurs and generally follows a negatively decelerating curve is not particularly debatable. The question of *how* and *why* forgetting occurs, on the other hand, is more controversial and generally unresolved. Some theorists believe that

5. *See* George A. Miller, *The Magical Number Seven Plus or Minus Two: Some Limits On Our Capacity for Processing Information*, 63 PSYCHOLOG. REV. 81 (1956); *see generally* DANIEL KAHNEMAN & ANNE TRIESMAN, ATTENTION AND EFFORT (1973).

6. *See* John S. Sachs, *Recognition Memory for Syntactic and Semantic Aspects of Connected Discourse*, 2 PERCEPTION & PSYCHOPHYSICS 437 (1967).

memories decay or otherwise change over time whereas other theorists posit that long-term memories are permanent and forgetting is actually a reduction in our ability to "find" the memory.[7] Suffice to note that psychological science has not yet reached a definitive conclusion as to whether forgetting is a result of trace decay or can be explained solely on the basis of an inability to "find" the trace. Trace decay theorists posit a process akin to drawing a picture in the sand. The sand picture may remain for a fairly long time, but is gradually faded by natural elements to the point of functional erasure. Theorists who argue that forgetting is merely an increased difficulty in finding the trace, on the other hand, posit a process akin to drawing a picture with indelible ink and then burying the picture below ground. The picture remains well preserved and intact, but at a later time the person who buried the picture cannot find the location where it was buried. In both cases there is a decline over time in the person's ability to retrieve the picture (i.e., forgetting occurs), but the cognitive processes giving rise to the forgetting are quite different.

[II] THE SPECIFIC QUESTIONS ASKED BY EYEWITNESS RESEARCHERS

Having discussed a few general principles about memory, I now turn to discussing some of the specific questions addressed by eyewitness researchers in the estimator variable category. It seems useful to divide these estimator variables into two domains, characteristics of the eyewitness and characteristics of the event.

[A] Characteristics of the Eyewitness

Three characteristics of eyewitnesses have received considerable attention by eyewitness researchers, namely gender, race, and age. These three variables have some properties that make them distinct and dictate a unique approach to each one. Gender, for example, is a dichotomous (two "levels") variable whereas age is a continuous variable. Hence, there is little practical ambiguity to what is meant by asking whether males are more or less accurate than females. The question of whether children are less accurate than adults, however, leads to a need to further specify the variable level (12–year olds versus adults? 6–year olds versus adults?). Race poses yet another complexity. The question about race is not whether people of one race are better eyewitnesses than are people of another race. Instead, the role of race is typically framed as an *interaction* question. For example, are white eyewitnesses better able to recognize whites than blacks and is the reverse true for black eyewitnesses?

[B] Characteristics of the Event

Events to which eyewitnesses are exposed vary along so many dimensions that it is impossible to research every slight variation. Hence, eyewitness researchers have tended to focus on a few variables that seem to be the most important. Particularly captivating has been the issue of "weapon focus." The

---

7. *See generally* Elizabeth F. Loftus & Geoffrey R. Loftus *On The Permanence of*   *Stored Information in the Human Brain,* 35 Am. Psychologist 409 (1980).

presence versus absence of a weapon is a variable that could impair an eyewitness's ability to identify a culprit through one or both of two processes. First, as the term *weapon focus* implies, the use of a weapon might lead an eyewitness to direct his attention primarily at the weapon, thereby diminishing the time or quality of attention given to the perpetrator's face. A second possibility, not exclusive of the first, is that a weapon might enhance arousal (or anxiety or fear) to a level that interferes with information processing. Other characteristics of the event that have received some research attention include the amount of time that the perpetrator is in view, lighting, distance, and so on.

[b] System Variable Questions

Generally, system variables come into play only after the event in question has occurred and the eyewitness is beginning to interact with police. At this point, there exists some form of trace memory in the mind of the eyewitness. This memory is not perfect or complete and the eyewitness's recollection can easily be made less perfect or distorted by the methods used to obtain information from the eyewitness. Indeed, it seems peculiar to eyewitness scientists that when dealing with physical evidence at a crime scene police commonly summon a forensics team to deal with trace evidence, yet show little or no concern about asking poorly thought out questions of eyewitnesses whose memory traces might be fragile or malleable.

Eyewitness researchers have focused primarily on four types of system variable questions in relation to eyewitness identification. First, can the questions asked of eyewitnesses affect the eyewitness's recollections of the perpetrator? Second, can instructions given to the eyewitness by investigators prior to viewing a lineup or photospread affect the likelihood that the eyewitness will make a false identification? Third, can the structure of the lineup or photospread affect the likelihood of a mistaken identification? Finally, does the eyewitness's certainty or confidence in his or her identification serve as a useful index of whether or not the identification was accurate?[8]

§ 8–2.1.2   Eyewitness Research Methods

Psychological science borrows heavily from the methods of the physical and biological sciences, as well as from statistics, in its quest to discover new knowledge.[9] Five basic elements of scientific methods are essential to eyewitness research. First, control is gained over a target variable so that it can be manipulated systematically. This is commonly called the *independent variable*. Second, variables that are not specifically controlled are either measured or, more commonly, *randomized*. Third, the independent variable is manipulated according to some schedule that is carried out over a large number of *repeated*

---

8. The latter question traditionally has been treated as an estimator variable question rather than a system variable question. Recent experiments, however, show that the diagnostic utility of eyewitness certainty or confidence is heavily affected by what police investigators might tell the eyewitness at this point. Hence, it has taken on a system-variable status. *See infra* notes 39–40 and accompanying text.

9. Readers who are interested in more detailed descriptions of scientific methods in psychological research can consult a variety of texts. See generally ROBERT ROSENTHAL & RALPH ROSNOW, ESSENTIALS OF BEHAVIORAL RESEARCH (1991); MCGUIGAN, EXPERIMENTAL PSYCHOLOGY: METHODS OF RESEARCH (1993).

instances. Fourth, the effect of the independent variable is measured by a *standardized procedure*. Fifth, the results are subjected to statistical analyses that *rule out chance* as an interpretation for the effects observed. In a proper experiment, numerous other assurances are put in place, such as *keeping experimenters blind* as to which level of the independent variable an eyewitness was exposed.

An example of an eyewitness experiment testing a specific hypothesis may be useful in helping to understand the type of methods used in the scientific study of eyewitness identification. The following description of such an experiment is a simplification of the actual study but captures the essential aspects. The hypothesis tested in this study was that an innocent person in a lineup will be more likely to be falsely identified as the culprit if he is the only one in the lineup or photospread who matches the description given by the eyewitness than if all members in the lineup match the description.[10] In order to test this hypothesis, there was a need to establish a target event in which there was a "culprit" and the actual identity of this culprit was known with certainty by the researchers. The solution was to *create* the event using people known to the researchers and following a script that could be repeated as many times as necessary in order to have a large number of eyewitnesses. In this study, the researchers scripted a staged theft of a cash box. People in a waiting room faced a doorway from which a "thief" burst out carrying a cash box. The box was dropped and cash fell out in full view of the people in the waiting room. The thief hurriedly gathered the cash and exited, leaving the box behind. A researcher then entered the room, "noticed" the theft of the cash, and only then were the people in the waiting room informed that the theft was not real. This staged theft was repeated over and over until there were 252 eyewitnesses to the theft. Seven different thieves, varying in gender and race, were used in the experiment in order to increase the generality of the study's findings. Following each staging of the theft, individual eyewitnesses were separated and asked to give a verbal description of the thief. These descriptions were then given to another researcher who built a photospread that included one person who fit the general verbal description (but was not the actual thief) along with five other "filler" photos that either fit this same general description or did not fit the description. These photos were then shown to the eyewitness who was told that the actual thief might or might not be in the photospread and that if the thief was among the photos, the eyewitness should identify him/her. Numerous precautions were taken to ensure that the results would have scientific merit. For example, people in the waiting room were assigned randomly[11] to the condition of viewing one or the other type of photospread. Also, sufficient numbers of eyewitnesses to the

---

10. Readers who are interested in a more thorough description of the full design, procedure, and results should see the original article. *See* Gary L. Wells et al., *The Selection of Distractors for Eyewitness Lineups* 78 J. AP-PLIED PSYCHOL., 835 (1993). The study actually tested several hypotheses. This particular hypothesis is a replication of prior work that had already corroborated this hypothesis.

11. The term "random assignment" has a specific and important meaning in scientific experiments. Many lay people think that the term random is synonymous with the term "haphazard," but almost nothing could be further from the truth. Random assignment means that each and every person in the study (in this case each eyewitness) has an equal chance of being in one condition of the experiment or the other regardless of other considerations such as how good or poor that person's view of the event was or how good or poor that person's memory is in general.

theft were generated with this procedure to ensure that proper statistical analyses could be conducted so that any differences that were due merely to chance could be ruled out. The results showed that there were large differences in false identification rates as a function of how the "fillers" in the lineup were selected. When the fillers who were selected did not match the description given by the eyewitness, the eyewitness falsely identified the one person who did match the description nearly 45% of the time. When all six people in the photospread matched the description, this same person was falsely identified as the thief only about 10% of the time. According to accepted statistical procedures, a difference of 10% or 15% in this study would not allow the researcher to be confident in ruling out interpretations based on chance. In this case, however, the difference was nearly 35%, which allows for the conclusion that the selection of photospread fillers who do not match the eyewitness's description of the culprit can produce a significant increase in the risk of false identification. The fact that this directional difference (false identifications being higher when the fillers do not match the description than when they match the description) was consistent across all seven "thieves" indicates that this effect is likely to be generalizable across lineups and photospreads rather than being specifically true for only some situations. Moreover, this type of result has been obtained from other experiments that used somewhat different methods, which indicates a convergence of empirical evidence and further suggests that this is a generalizable finding.

The staged-crime method is not the only method used in eyewitness research. In some studies, filmed enactments serve as the eyewitnessed events and in a few cases eyewitnesses to actual crimes are used to study eyewitness memory.[12] It is usually the case that, whatever method is used, the eyewitnesses are unaware at the time of the eyewitnessed event that they will have to try to identify the culprit or that they will be asked to report on their memory for other aspects of the event except as might occur to them naturally (e.g., recognizing that there is a crime in view and that it might prove useful later to be able to recall what they are viewing). In some experiments, the ruse (i.e., the deception over the fact that the eyewitnessed event is not a real crime) is maintained throughout the identification task[13] whereas in most experiments the eyewitness is apprized after the "crime" and prior to the identification attempt that the crime was not real. It appears to make little or no difference to the results of such experiments whether the eyewitness thinks it was a real crime at the time of the identification attempt, as long as they thought it was real when they eyewitnessed it.[14]

Earlier, I stated that one can be neither an effective proponent nor critic of a scientific conclusion unless one knows and understands the methods that were used to reach the conclusion in question. Consider, for example, the

---

12. For an example of the use of a filmed event, *see* Thomas H. Kramer et al., *Weapon Focus, Arousal, and Eyewitness Memory*, 14 LAW & HUM. BEHAV. 167 (1990). For an example of the analysis of an actual crime, *see* John Yuille & Judith L. Cutshall, *A Case Study of Eyewitnesses' Memory of a Crime*, 71 J. OF APPLIED PSYCHOL. 291 (1986).

13. *See* C. A. Elizabeth Luus, & Gary L. Wells, *The Malleability of Eyewitness Confi-*

dence: Co–Witness and Perseverance Effects, 79 J. OF APPLIED PSYCHOL. 714 (1994) (An example of an experiment that maintains the ruse of reality for the eyewitnesses throughout the act of identification.).

14. *See* Donna M. Murray & Gary L. Wells, *Does Knowledge That a Crime was Staged Affect Eyewitness Performance?* 12 J. APPLIED SOC. PSYCHOL. 42 (1982).

forgoing conclusion, i.e., that a lineup in which the fillers do not match the eyewitness's previous description of the culprit is biased against the defendant. A proper attack on this conclusion would generally require that one criticize the methods themselves, such as arguing that the eyewitnessed event was not significant enough to the eyewitness to draw their attention and yield a deep and lasting memory. This particular criticism, however, fails to account for why the rate of false identifications was quite low in the condition in which all fillers matched the verbal description because these eyewitnesses viewed the same event as did those in the other conditions. Furthermore, there is little evidence to support the view that some events are so significant that they create "flashbulb" memories that are immune to errors of recall. Research studies concerning "flashbulb" memory for events such as the space shuttle *Challenger* explosion, for example, show that people believe that their recollections are accurate (e.g., where were you when you heard the news?), but in fact such recollections are highly prone to error.[15]

The overriding point about eyewitness research methods is that they follow the typical rules imposed on behavioral science and are subject to peer review. Eyewitness research results have been published in the top scientific journals in psychology, such as *Journal of Personality and Social Psychology, Journal of Experimental Psychology: General, Journal of Applied Psychology, Psychological Bulletin*, and so on. Most research reports submitted to these journals are rejected following peer review in which the reviewers comb the work for any flaws that might threaten the validity of the conclusions. Articles on eyewitnessing that survive this scrutiny to the point of being published can be trusted within the limitations of the peer review process that characterizes the scientific literature. This is not to say that faulty conclusions never make their way into the scientific journals of psychology. Faulty conclusions can and do appear in all scientific journals at certain times and the eyewitness research literature is no exception. Over time, however, seeing that similar conclusions have been reached by different researchers using different methods should result in greater confidence and thus greater acceptance of the hypothesis.

Another way in which the validity of a conclusion can be assessed is to consider the conclusion in light of other things that are already known to be true. If a finding conflicts with this prior knowledge, then it may be questioned on those grounds. For example, if a researcher found that young children recalled much more detail from a staged crime than did adults, such a finding would conflict with things that we generally know about the cognitive capabilities of young children based on general studies of performance using a variety of tasks. On the other hand, so-called "common intuition" is not generally considered to be a criterion for evaluating the truth value of a scientific observation. Common intuition frequently conflicts with scientific fact, such as the intuition that the sun revolves around the earth, and eyewitness scientists, like scientists in general, do not consider a result to

---

15. This is another example of the general problem with using apparent vividness and ease of recall to infer that a memory is accurate. *See* Ulric Neisser & Nichole Harsch, *Phantom Flashbulbs: False Recollections of Hearing the News About Challenger, in* AFFECT AND ACCURACY IN RECALL: STUDIES OF *"FLASHBULB"* MEMORIES 9–31 (Eugene Winograd & Ulric Neisser eds., 1992) (finding considerable inaccuracy in persons' recollections of the space shuttle explosion).

be suspect merely on grounds that it conflicts with our intuition about the issue at hand. This does not mean that all conclusions that are based on empirical methods are accepted without question. If a result conflicts with matters that we already know to be true based on accepted theory or based on other empirical evidence, or if the conclusion is based on flawed methods, then the validity of that conclusion is called into question or perhaps even rejected.

Case studies represent a more recent body of evidence that eyewitness scientists have found useful to augment their experimental findings. The development of a larger body of case studies of mistaken identification has been made possible in recent years by the advent of forensic DNA. Beginning the in the early 1990s, forensic DNA tests of previously-convicted persons began to uncover many cases in which persons found guilty by juries were in fact innocent of the offense for which they convicted. A 1996 report of an initial 28 cases of DNA-based post-conviction exoneration showed that 24 of the 28 cases were attributable largely to mistaken eyewitness identification.[16] A 1998 article showed that 36 of the first 40 DNA exonerations involved mistaken identifications.[17] In January 2000, Scheck, Neufeld, and Dwyer reported that there were 63 definitive DNA-based exoneration cases in the U.S. and that mistaken eyewitness identification was involved in 84% of these wrongful convictions.[18]

Case study methods do not, in and of themselves, constitute scientific proof at the level that eyewitness scientists find appropriately persuasive. Nevertheless, the DNA exoneration cases corroborate several aspects of what eyewitness scientists had previously concluded from their experiments, as described in later sections of this chapter. For instance, experiments show that eyewitnesses can be both absolutely certain and absolutely mistaken about their identification from lineup.[19] Likewise, DNA-exoneration cases show that eyewitness identification testimony in these cases was delivered by highly certain eyewitnesses who were in fact mistaken.

Eyewitness scientists are probably less persuaded by the case studies than they are by the controlled research experiments; the reverse might be the case for actors in the legal system. The retrospective-DNA methodology for studying eyewitness identification evidence has some advantages and some disadvantages over the experimental research methods used by eyewitness scientists. Among the advantages are the fact that these instances come from the "real world" rather than the laboratory. Hence, the common criticisms of laboratory eyewitness research, such as the contention that the eyewitnesses don't take the studies seriously or that the events witnessed are not important to the eyewitness, do not apply to these real cases. Relatedly, these DNA cases involved types of witnessing experiences that eyewitness scientists could not ethically simulate in experiments, particularly sexual assault. On the other hand, there are limits to what can be learned from these DNA cases. First, virtually all of these DNA cases are sexual assault cases. The reason

---

16. E. Connors et al., *Convicted by Juries, Exonerated by Science: Case Studies in the Use of DNA Evidence to Establish Innocence After Trial*. Alexandria, VA: National Institute of Justice (1996).

17. Gary Wells et al., *Eyewitness Identification Procedures: Recommendations for Lineups*

and *Photospreads*, 22 LAW & HUM. BEHAV. 603 (1998).

18. *See generally* BARRY SCHECK, PETER NEUFELD, & J. DWYER, ACTUAL INNOCENCE (2000).

19. Gary Wells et al., *Accuracy, Confidence, and Juror Perceptions in Eyewitness Identification*, 64 J. OF APPLIED PSYCHOL. 440 (1979).

that most DNA cases involve sexual assault is because, unlike the drug store robbery or the drive-by shooting, sexual assault can leave trace evidence (semen) that is directly attributable to the perpetrator. Clearly, sexual assault cases are over-represented in the area of DNA-exoneration. Perhaps there is something about sexual assault cases that makes them unique in their propensities to produce mistaken identifications, leading to some difficulties in generalizing to other crimes. Traditionally, however, sexual assault has been considered by prosecutors to be the least likely crime to involve the risk of mistaken identification because the victim is the witness and has a closer and longer view of the perpetrator than is typical of many other crimes. A second weakness of the retrospective-DNA methodology is that it is scientifically impossible to establish cause-effect relations among the critical variables. For instance, we know that many of the lineups and photospreads that were used in these cases had biases in their structures that made the innocent suspect stand out to the eyewitness. We know that the agents who administered the lineups and photospreads had knowledge of which person was the suspect (i.e., there was no blind testing), and that all the eyewitnesses were stressed by their witnessing experience. However, there is no scientific way to determine which of these factors, or some other factor, caused the false identification to occur. This is a classic problem with the case-study methodology in science. Finally, there are some things that cannot be determined about these cases, such as exactly how the eyewitness was instructed prior to viewing the lineup or photospread, what kinds of nonverbal information might have been conveyed by the agent who administered the lineup or photospread, and so on. These details are not determinable because no video or audio recordings were made of the identification sessions and trial discovery questions were not asked, were asked too late, or were not asked in a way that would effectively establish these facts.

As in all areas of science, it is the convergence of findings from different methods that enables more confident conclusions to be drawn. The significance of the recent DNA studies is that their results converge nicely with the experimental findings. For instance, the experimental finding that eyewitnesses can make false identifications from lineups and photospreads and yet express very high certainty in their identifications converges nicely with the retrospective-DNA studies showing that each eyewitness was extremely certain in his identification even while being absolutely mistaken. Similarly, the finding in experimental studies that eyewitnesses often identify the same innocent person (i.e., agree on their mistake) is corroborated in the DNA cases. In many cases the innocent suspect was mistakenly identified by more than one eyewitness, sometimes as many as six.

§ 8–2.2   Issues of General Agreement

§ 8–2.2.1   Introduction

There are two meanings of "agreement" in the scientific study of eyewitness identification. First, there is agreement in the sense that there are data bearing directly on an issue and the foundation of those data (i.e., the experiment itself) has survived rigorous peer review and has been published in a scientific journal. A second meaning of general agreement is that the phenomenon under consideration is well founded in certain psychological principles of memory, perception, and social influence. Although much of what we know about eyewitness identification has both empirical and theoretical foundations, some areas of agreement are more heavily grounded in one or the other.

Consider, for instance, the relatively weak statistical relation between eyewitness identification accuracy and the confidence or certainty with which the eyewitness holds to the identification. Principles of perception and memory are not the basic foundation of this phenomenon even though scientific psychology has come to largely accept this premise. Instead, the weak accuracy/certainty relation is based almost exclusively on empirical observations. Nothing in psychological theory could have predicted this state of affairs. This does not mean that theoretical accounts have been ignored in an attempt to understand this phenomenon. As described later in this section, there is now a reasonable theoretical understanding of why the certainty/accuracy relation is a precarious one, but it is not our theoretical understanding *per se* or general principles of memory that have produced a general agreement on this point, but rather the overwhelming accumulation of a wealth of empirical evidence that has produced some general agreement.

Consider, on the other hand, general agreement that extremely high levels of arousal will interfere with information processing by eyewitnesses. Agreement on this point tends to come more from general principles of information processing where it is reasonably well accepted that arousal and memory performance follow a curvilinear relation such that a very low level of arousal and a very high level of arousal harm performance on most tasks. With regard to the arousal question, the tendency to rely more on general principles of what we already know about memory and performance rather than relying on experimental data is not purely accidental or a matter of convenience. Instead, reliance on general theory stems in large part from the fact that extremely high levels of arousal are difficult to achieve through ethical means in an experiment (e.g., drawing a gun on research eyewitnesses is not acceptable to research ethics committees) in conjunction with the fact that already a body of knowledge exists that shows curvilinear relations across a variety of tasks and there is no reason to believe that eyewitness tasks would be an exception to the rule.

§ 8–2.2.2 Estimator Variables

As noted earlier, one of the organizational schemes for classifying eyewitness identification variables takes consideration of the question of whether the variable is controllable in actual cases (a system variable) or is not under control of the justice system (estimator variables). The distinction is important because system variables have the potential to raise issues of due process whereas estimator variables do not. Estimator variables include such things as the race of the eyewitness relative to the suspect, the amount of time that the eyewitness had the perpetrator in view, or the lighting conditions that existed at the time of the event in question. Although these variables can be scientifically studied and controlled in experiments, the system cannot control the levels of these variables. I join the eyewitness researchers who caution against using findings in experiments to estimate the likelihood of accuracy in actual cases and instead have argued that one can only use the findings to specify the direction of the effect (rather than the magnitude of the effect) of the variable in question. With regard to the direction of the effect of estimator variables, there is general agreement at this time that such factors as race, opportunity to view, disguises, the visibility of a weapon, retention interval, and eyewitness age are reliably related to the likelihood of obtaining an accurate identification.

[1] Race

There is little debate over the fact that people have more difficulty recognizing people of another race than they do people of their own race.[20] Most of this work has been restricted to the study of black versus white faces and black versus white eyewitnesses. However, there is more recent evidence that the problem also applies to other ethnic and racial groups as well. Scientists tend to attribute this effect to subjects' lack of experience in dealing with faces of another race compared to faces of their own race. Nevertheless, the effect is surprisingly resistant to training or mere practice, and simply having friends of another race or living in an integrated neighborhood appear to be insufficient to eliminate the other-race effect. The precise psychological mechanisms involved in the other-race effect are not fully known. One line of hypothesizing that has been commonly questioned is the role of racial attitudes.[21] Although it might be tempting to think that the other-race effect is related to racial attitudes, empirical data thus far have given little support to such a hypothesis.[22]

[2] Opportunity to View

The amount of time that a person is in view affects the quality of the eyewitness's memory of the person and, consequently, the accuracy of the identification attempt.[23] This is not surprising, of course, because the cognitive system requires processing time to perform various mental operations on visual stimuli. Two interesting observations, however, deserve note. First, somewhat surprisingly, opportunity to view has little effect on the likelihood that an eyewitness will attempt an identification.[24] A second concern about the opportunity-to-view variable is that it is often difficult in real cases to obtain reliable information about the eyewitness's opportunity to view, because one must rely on reports from the very eyewitness whose judgment is being called into question.[25] Research indicates, for instance, that eyewit-

20. *See* Chris Meissner & John C. Brigham, *A Meta-analysis of the Other–Race Effect in Eyewitness Identification*, PSYCHOL., PUB. POL'Y., & LAW (forthcoming 2001).

21. John C. Brigham & Paul Barkowitz, *Do They All "Look Alike"? The Effect of Race, Sex, Experience and Attitudes on the Ability to Recognize Faces*, 8 J. APPLIED PSYCHOL. 306 (1978).

22. *Id.*

23. *See* Brian L. Cutler et al., *Improving the Reliability of Eyewitness Identifications: Putting Context into Context*, 72 J. APPLIED PSYCHOL. 629 (1987).

24. One might expect, for instance, that an eyewitness who had a poor view of the culprit would be cognizant of that fact and not attempt an identification in the first place. Unfortunately, the tendency to attempt an identification does not diminish at the same rate as does the opportunity to view and the result is an increased propensity to make a false identification as viewing conditions get worse. *See* R. C. L. Lindsay, Gary L. Wells & Carolyn M. Rumpel, *Can People Detect Eyewitness Identification Accuracy Within and Between Situations?* 66 J. APPLIED PSYCHOL. 79 (1981).

25. *See* Gary L. Wells & Donna M. Murray, *What Can Psychology Say About the* Neil vs. Biggers *Criteria for Judging Eyewitness Identi-*

nesses tend to overestimate short temporal durations and this tendency is especially pronounced when the eyewitness is feeling stress or anxiety.[26] Hence, the eyewitness who describes his or her view of a culprit as lasting 2 or 3 minutes may in fact have had the culprit in view for 30–45 seconds.

Recent evidence from eyewitness experiments shows that eyewitnesses' estimates of their opportunity to view the face of the perpetrator can be distorted by feedback suggesting to them that they identified the correct person. After eyewitnesses are told that they identified the "actual suspect" in the case, they begin to recall their view as having been very good even when they had a rather poor opportunity to view the face of the perpetrator.[27]

[3] Weapon Focus

A common question in many cases is what role, if any, a weapon might play in affecting the eyewitness's memory for a perpetrator. Weapons can have several effects, each of which tend to diminish the ability of the eyewitness to later identify the perpetrator. The two principal effects are arousal, which is discussed below, and focus of attention. A number of studies now converge on the conclusion that the presence of a weapon tends to diminish the likelihood of an accurate identification.[28] Given the way in which several of these studies were conducted, arousal or fear clearly is not necessary to get the effect and the presence of the weapon can exert its influence simply by drawing the attention of the eyewitness.

[4] Retention Interval

The longer the time that has elapsed between an eyewitnessed event and a test of one's memory for that event the greater the likelihood of the memory being inaccurate or inaccessible. There certainly is nothing surprising about this observation and it is one of the oldest findings in scientific psychology. Nevertheless, many characteristics and issues surrounding this classic concept of "forgetting" are useful to address. First, it should be noted that the relation between retention interval and information loss ("forgetting") is not linear. In statistical terminology, the relation between retention interval and information loss is a negatively decelerating curve. This means that the amount of information in memory that is lost in the first unit of time is

fication Accuracy? 68 J. APPLIED PSYCHOL. 347 (1983).

26. *See, e.g,* Harvey R. Schiffman & Douglas J. Bobko, *Effects of Stimulus Complexity on the Perception of Short Temporal Durations,* 103 J. EXPERIMENTAL PSYCHOL. 156 (1974); Irwin Sarason & Robert Stroops, *Test Anxiety and The Passage of Time* 46 J. CONSULTING & CLINICAL PSYCHOL. 102 (1978).

27. Gary L. Wells & Amy L. Bradfield, *"Good, you identified the suspect:" Feedback to Eyewitnesses Distorts Their Reports of the Witnessing Experience* 86 J. OF APPLIED PSYCHOL. 360 (1998); Gary L. Wells & A. L. Bradfield, *Distortions in Eyewitnesses' Recollections: Can the Postidentification Feedback Effect be Moderated?* 10 PSYCHOLOG. SCI. 138 (1999).

28. *See* Brian L. Cutler et al., *The Reliability of Eyewitness Identification: The Role of System and Estimator Variables,* 11 LAW & HUM. BEHAV. 233 (1987); Helen R. Dent, *Stress as a Factor Influencing Person Recognition in Identification Parades,* 30 BULL. BRIT. PSYCHOL. 339 (1977); Thomas H. Kramer et al., *Weapon Focus, Arousal, and Eyewitness Memory,* 14 LAW & HUM. BEHAV. 167 (1990); Elizabeth F. Loftus et al., *Some Facts About "Weapon Focus,"* 11 LAW & HUM. BEHAV. 55 (1987); Anne Maass & Gunther Kohnken, *Eyewitness Identification: Simulating the "Weapon Effect,"* 13 LAW & HUM. BEHAV. 397 (1989); Vaughn Tooley et al., *Facial Recognition: Weapon Effect and Attentional Focus,* 17 J. APPLIED SOC. PSYCHOL. 845 (1987).

greater than the amount lost in a second unit of the same amount of time which, in turn, is greater than that lost in the third unit of time and so on. This pattern is true for any size time unit. Hence, for instance, the amount of information about the eyewitnessed event that is lost in the first day is greater than the amount lost in the second day, the amount lost in the first week is greater than that lost in the second week, the amount lost in the first month is greater than that lost in the second month, and so on. Although scientists agree about the "shape" of this forgetting curve, too many variables are involved to specify a precise rate of information loss that would generalize over all eyewitnessed events. Hence, under some conditions the amount of information lost in the first 24 hours after the event might be equivalent to the amount lost in the next 48 hours whereas under some other conditions the amount lost in the first 24 hours might be equivalent to the amount lost in the next 24 days. In other words, the rate of the negatively decelerating curve is variable but the fact that the curve is negatively decelerating is not considered to be variable.

It is important to note, for current purposes of discussing the retention interval, that the issue of the passage of time might not be nearly as important as the issue of what events occur during the retention interval. Regardless of whether the original memory remains intact in the brain or undergoes change, the fact is that people's reports of what they remember are very much a function of events that can occur between the time of eyewitnessing and the time of test. The provocative work of Elizabeth Loftus and her colleagues is particularly instructive about this point. In a series of experiments, Loftus and colleagues have shown that people will incorporate *postevent* information (i.e., information acquired during the retention interval) into their reports of what the eyewitnesses had observed. Following the eyewitnessing of a staged argument, for instance, some eyewitnesses were asked, "Was the mustache worn by the tall intruder light or dark brown?" when in fact the person had no mustache. Later, when asked if the intruder had a mustache, those who had previously been asked the critical misleading question were six times more likely to report a nonexistent mustache than were those who had not been asked the misleading question. The main point for current purposes is that an equal amount of time had passed for all eyewitnesses between the eyewitnessed event and the test of whether the intruder had a mustache. Hence, the dramatic introduction of error in the one group of eyewitnesses was not due to the passage of time *per se* but rather to the occurrence of a critical event (i.e., the misleading question) during the retention interval.

[5] Age of Eyewitness

Much of the empirical work on the role of age in eyewitness memory performance has centered on children, with a particular emphasis on the issue of suggestibility.[29] A general conclusion from this research is that children tend to be more suggestible than adults. Hence, for example, a question such as "Did you see the man with the black briefcase?" (when in fact there was no

---

29. *See* CHILDREN'S EYEWITNESS MEMORY (Stephen J. Ceci et al. eds., 1987); CHILDREN AS WITNESSES (Helen Dent & Rhona Flin eds. 1992); THE SUGGESTIBILITY OF CHILDREN'S RECOLLECTIONS (John Doris ed. 1991). See Chapter 14.

briefcase) will tend to yield a greater number of "yes" responses in a child than in an adult. Another general conclusion from this research is that children tend to give less complete accounts of an event that they eyewitnessed than do adults. Interestingly, however, under conditions of free recall, children do not generally make more errors than adults. Instead, error rate differences between adults and children begin to emerge when questions become more specific or when misleading questions are introduced. Eyewitness identification from photospreads and lineups can present special problems for young children when the actual culprit is not present in the photospread or lineup. As noted below, the absence of the actual culprit in a lineup or photospread is a significant problem for all eyewitnesses, but the problem seems especially difficult for young children.[30] In general, it is a more difficult task to recognize that the culprit is absent from a lineup or photospread than it is to recognize the presence of the culprit in a lineup or photospread. Hence, task difficulty might account for some of the special problems that children have with a culprit-absent lineup. In addition, the presentation of a lineup or photospread involves some level of demand or pressure on an eyewitness to select someone even when the eyewitness is clearly informed that the culprit might or might not be present in the lineup or photospread. The greater tendency of children than adults to be susceptible to demands, pressures, and suggestions, especially when those suggestions come from adults, results in a particularly high likelihood that a child will make an identification of someone from a lineup or photospread even though the actual culprit is not among the members of the lineup or photospread. Even without explicit pressures to select someone from a lineup or photospread, children make more false identifications than adults with culprit-absent lineups. Interestingly, when the actual culprit is present in the photospread or lineup, children are approximately equal to adults in their ability to identify the culprit. Unfortunately, in actual cases it is not known whether the true culprit is in the lineup or photospread. Hence, eyewitness experts are more skeptical of the identification decisions of children than they are of the identification decisions of adults.

§ 8–2.2.3 System Variables

As noted above, system variables are in a somewhat different class than are estimator variables. Although both system and estimator variables are related to the likelihood of accurate identification, system variables have the characteristic of being under the control (or potentially under the control) of the justice system. Hence, system variables can raise issues of due process. Consider, for example, the variations that might exist regarding how an eyewitness is instructed by detectives prior to viewing a lineup or photospread. Research shows that when eyewitnesses are told to try to identify the culprit, they tend to show a high rate of identifying someone even when the culprit is not present in the lineup or photospread. When eyewitnesses are explicitly warned that the actual culprit might or might not be present, however, they are much less likely to identify someone when the culprit is in

30. *See* Janet F. Parker & Lourdes E. Carranza, *Eyewitness Testimony of Children in Target–Present and Target–Absent Lineups,* 13 LAW & HUM. BEHAV. 133 (1989); Mary A. King & John Yuille, *Suggestibility and the Child Witness, in* CHILDREN'S EYEWITNESS MEMORY 24–35 (Stephen J. Ceci et al. eds., 1987).

fact not present in the lineup. Ultimately, the courts will need to decide whether failure to warn the eyewitness that the culprit might not be present in the lineup or photospread violates due process or creates an unnecessary risk of mistaken identification. Regardless of how courts treat this issue, however, there is consensus among eyewitness experts that instructional variations of this sort have a large effect on the likelihood of false identification and that such instructions are under the control of the legal system. The remainder of this section describes some system variables for which there is agreement regarding the role that they can play in contributing to the likelihood of false identification.

In general, system variables come into play only after the eyewitnessed event has occurred. Once the eyewitnessed event has occurred, police can begin to exert an influence on the eventual testimony given by any eyewitness. The following organization of system variables follows roughly an ordinal time sequence in which various system variables can exert their influence.

[1]   Initial Questioning of Eyewitnesses

Among the first events that an eyewitness might experience following the eyewitnessing of a crime is questioning by a police officer. At this point it is possible for a number of mistakes to be made by an officer that can have serious consequences for the ability of an eyewitness to accurately describe and later identify the culprit. One of the most consistent and oldest findings in the eyewitness research literature is that people tend to make relatively few errors if they are allowed to use their own words to freely describe, without interruption, what they have observed.[31] This research shows that errors tend to increase as the questioner begins to ask specific questions. Why an officer might ask specific questions is readily understandable, since free narrative reports by eyewitnesses tend to be incomplete. Unfortunately, officers rarely make clear notes as to which statements by the eyewitnesses came from an initial free narrative and which were obtained from the asking of specific questions. Hence, an officer's report that merely notes that the eyewitness described the culprit as about 6 feet tall, dark curly hair, heavy set, no facial hair, and eyeglasses is rendered much less useful by not having information as to which parts of the description were freely reported and which were the result of specific questions. If we knew, for example, that the statement "no facial hair" was in response to the specific question of whether the culprit had facial hair, we would know to trust that statement much less than we trust the height estimate. Eyewitness researchers express considerable concern that officers are too quick to insert specific questions (e.g., "Was he tall or short?") before allowing the eyewitness to complete his or her natural, narrative recollection. Interruption of the natural process of recall not only confuses the issue of which bits of information came from free recall

---

31.   *See, e.g.,* Harold M. Cady, *On the Psychology of Testimony,* 35 AM. J. PSYCHOL. 110 (1924); Brian R. Clifford & Jane Scott, *Individual and Situational Factors in Eyewitness Testimony,* 63 J. APPLIED PSYCHOL. 352 (1978); Jack P. Lipton, *On the Psychology of Eyewitness Testimony,* 66 J. APPLIED PSYCHOL. 79 (1977);

Kent H. Marquis et al., *Testimony Validity as a Function of Question Form, Atmosphere, and Item Difficulty,* 2 J. OF APPLIED SOC. PSYCHOL. 167 (1972); T. Snee & D. Lush, *Interaction of the Narrative and Interrogatory Methods of Obtaining Testimony,* 11 J. OF PSYCHOL. 229 (1941).

and which were solicited, but also disrupts natural recall and can confuse the eyewitness as to what he knew and what was a guess. Hence, the initial questioning of a eyewitness is one of the first junctures at which the system itself is contributing to error in eyewitness accounts.

[2]   The Use of Loaded Questions

The work of Elizabeth Loftus and her colleagues provides considerable evidence that memory reports are influenced by the wording of a question.[32] Although some controversy remains over the issue of whether such factors as misleading questions serve to alter the original memory trace of eyewitnesses or whether misleading questions serve merely to increase the likelihood of a faulty eyewitness report while keeping intact the original memory trace, scientists do not disagree that misleading questions alter the overt reports subsequently obtained from eyewitnesses. Consider a few examples of this phenomenon. It would be misleading to ask the question "How long did the man with the mustache stay in the store before he pulled the gun on the clerk?" if the man did not have a mustache. This misleading question is likely to increase the tendency of the eyewitness to later report that the man had a mustache. Or, consider the question, "Did you notice the color of the man's mustache?" Again, assuming that there was no mustache, this wording of the question assumes the existence of a mustache and leads to an increased tendency to report that the man had a mustache. It is important to note some critical implications of this phenomenon. First, the phenomenon most likely becomes problematic when the police questioners have a particular suspect in mind when they question the eyewitness(es). This can occur under a variety of circumstances. Consider, for example, that someone had noted a license tag number and police ran a check on the tags prior to obtaining a description of the culprit from the eyewitness. This might have led investigators to suspect a particular person. A leading set of questions might then lead to a description that fits the suspect. Another way in which leading questions might become incorporated into the investigator's questions is from interviewing eyewitnesses serially and incorporating one eyewitness's account into the questions asked of a subsequent eyewitness. Under such conditions, eyewitnesses might tend to show agreement in their accounts that is much greater than if they had been questioned separately by different officers. The concept of independence of eyewitnesses is often a critical issue, because people who evaluate eyewitness accounts are generally impressed by agreement among eyewitnesses. In fact, however, the system usually obtains eyewitness accounts in ways that fail to make certain that the accounts are truly independent. This is compounded when investigators fail to note verbatim the questions asked and instead make only scattered summary-notes of the statements of the eyewitnesses.

[3]   Lineup Identification Instructions Given to the Eyewitness

Consistent and robust findings in eyewitness research show that the greatest risk of mistaken identification exists when the actual culprit is not present in the lineup (or photospread). In general, eyewitness identification

---

32. *See* ELIZABETH F. LOFTUS, EYEWITNESS TESTIMONY (1979).

from a lineup is a "relative judgment" in the sense that eyewitnesses tend to select the person who most looks like the culprit relative to the other people in the lineup.[33] This is called a relative judgment process and it has profound implications for how a lineup should be conducted. Note that the relative judgment process is not particularly problematic when the actual culprit is present in the lineup because generally we can expect that the person who looks the most like the culprit is the culprit himself. When the culprit is not in the lineup, however, the relative judgment process leads to the selection of someone nevertheless; after all, there remains someone who looks more like the culprit than do the others in the lineup even when the culprit is not in the lineup. One partial remedy is to specifically instruct the eyewitness prior to the viewing that the culprit might or might not be present. It is important to note that the "might or might not be present" instructions reduce identifications when the culprit is absent but have relatively little effect on rates at which the culprit is identified when the culprit is present.[34] Eyewitness researchers agree that some instructions (e.g., "Try to identify the person who robbed you") lead to an increased likelihood of false identification owing to the already strong tendency for eyewitnesses to select the person who most looks like the culprit and to not consider carefully the possibility that the actual culprit might not be in the lineup at all. In general, those instructing an eyewitness must make salient to the eyewitness that the culprit might not be among the people in the lineup and thereby legitimize the selection of no one as an acceptable response for the eyewitness to make. The dangers of failing to explicitly state that the culprit might not be in the lineup are compounded when other certain characteristics of the lineup are present (as discussed in the next section), but the presence of an error of this sort during prelineup instructions is sufficient to lead most experts to conclude that any resultant identification has been made much less trustworthy by the instructions.

[4] The Selection of Distractors

Scientists generally agree that the characteristics of the distractors in a lineup have serious implications for the risk of false identification. Distractors are the known-innocent foils (or fillers) who are selected by the lineup constructor to stand in the lineup with the suspect. Theory and experimental data converge on the conclusion that risk of false identification increases when the distractors fail to match the description of the culprit that the eyewitness had given verbally to police during the initial questioning.[35] A

33. *See* Gary L. Wells, *The Psychology of Lineup Identifications,* 14 J. APPLIED SOC. PSYCHOL. 89 (1984).

34. *See* Roy S. Malpass & Patricia G. Devine, *Eyewitness Identification: Lineup Instructions and the Absence of the Offender,* 66 J. APPLIED PSYCHOL. 482 (1981); GARY L. WELLS, EYEWITNESS IDENTIFICATION: A SYSTEM HANDBOOK (1988).

35. *See, e.g.,* Anthony N. Doob & H. Kirshenbaum, *Bias in Police Lineups—Partial Remembering,* 1 J. POLICE SCI. & ADMIN. 287 (1973); R. C. L. Lindsay & Gary L. Wells, *What Price*

Justice? Exploring the Relationship Between Lineup Fairness and Identification Accuracy, 4 LAW & HUM. BEHAV. 303 (1980); C. A. Elizabeth Luus & Gary L. Wells, *Eyewitness Identification and the Selection of Distracters for Lineups,* 15 LAW & HUM. BEHAV. 43 (1991); GARY L. WELLS (1988), *supra* note 34; Gary L. Wells, *What Do We Know About Eyewitness Identification?* 48 AM. PSYCHOLOG. 553 (1993); Gary L. Wells, Michael R. Leippe & Thomas M. Ostrom, *Guidelines for Empirically Assessing the Fairness of a Lineup,* 3 LAW & HUM. BEHAV. 285 (1979); Gary L. Wells & C. A. Elizabeth Luus, *Police Lineups as Experiments: Social Method-*

simple test can determine whether a lineup's distractors can be expected to serve as a fair test of the eyewitness's recognition memory. People who are given only the verbal description of the culprit should not be able to select the suspect based on this description at a rate greater than would be expected by chance. When this general rule for selecting distractors is violated in the extreme (i.e., the suspect is the only person in the lineup who matches the eyewitness's description of the culprit), experts will conclude routinely that the lineup is biased against the suspect in a way that leads to a heightened tendency to identify the suspect as the culprit even if the suspect is not the culprit.[36]

The question of how lineup constructors should select distractors becomes increasingly complex to the extent that the suspect himself does not match the description of the culprit. In such cases, police might be ill advised to select distractors who match the description because the suspect might then stand out as unique owing to the suspect being the only one who does not match the description. The general point, however, is that the lineup ought to be a test of the eyewitness's ability to recognize the culprit rather than merely test the eyewitness's ability to figure out (e.g., by method of deduction or inference) which person is the suspect.

[5] Method of Lineup Presentation

Considerable empirical evidence over the last decade indicates that the traditional lineup or photospread procedure, called a simultaneous procedure, is more likely to produce a false identification than is an alternative procedure that operates sequentially.[37] Originally proposed and tested by R.C.L. Lindsay and Gary Wells, a sequential lineup is one in which the eyewitness is shown one person at a time and required to make a "yes" or "no" decision on each one prior to viewing the next person in the sequence. Recall the earlier discussion of the problem of relative judgment processes. The advantage of the sequential over the simultaneous lineup procedure seems to be due to the fact that the sequential procedure largely eliminates the eyewitness's use of a mere relative-judgment strategy for identifying someone. A simultaneous lineup, where all the alternatives are presented at once, allows the eyewitness to reason that one person is the "best" choice among the alternatives. The sequential procedure, however, blocks this crude strategy because the eyewitness cannot be certain that the next person that they will be shown is even more similar to the culprit than the one being viewed at the moment. Hence, the eyewitness must decide with the sequential procedure whether or not the

ology as a Framework for Properly–Conducted Lineups, 16 PERSONALITY & SOC. PSYCHOL. BULL. 117 (1990); Gary L. Wells et al., *On the Selection of Distractors for Eyewitness Lineups,* 78 J. APPLIED PSYCHOL. 835 (1993); Gary L. Wells et al., *Recommendations for Conducting Lineups,* in ADULT EYEWITNESS TESTIMONY: CURRENT TRENDS AND DEVELOPMENTS 223–244 (David F. Ross et al. eds., 1994).

36. *See generally* GARY L. WELLS, *supra* note 34; Luus & Wells, *supra* note 35.

37. *See* Brian L. Cutler & Steven D. Penrod, *Improving the Reliability of Eyewitness*

Identification: Lineup Construction and Presentation, 73 J. APPLIED PSYCHOL. 281 (1988); R. C. L. Lindsay et al., *Sequential Lineup Presentation: Technique Matters,* 76 J. APPLIED PSYCHOL. 741 (1991); R. C. L. Lindsay et al., *Biased Lineups: Sequential Presentation Reduces the Problem,* 76 J. APPLIED PSYCHOL. 796 (1991); R. C. L. Lindsay & Gary L. Wells, *Improving Eyewitness Identification From Lineups: Simultaneous Versus Sequential Lineup Presentations,* 70 J. APPLIED PSYCHOL. 556 (1985).

person being viewed (at any particular time in the sequence) is the actual culprit rather than that the person is the closest match among the alternatives.

[6] Post–Identification Certainty

Scientists generally agree that the certainty an eyewitness expresses in his identification can be a misleading indicator of the identification's accuracy.[38] Experimental data indicate that false identifications are frequently made with very high levels of certainty. This is not to say that there is an absence of statistical relation between eyewitness certainty and accuracy. The magnitude of this relation is still being debated (see following section on areas of disagreement). Nevertheless, scientists do not debate two general conclusions regarding eyewitness certainty. First, false certainty (i.e., high certainty expressed by an eyewitness who has in fact made a false identification) seems to be indistinguishable from true certainty (i.e., the certainty held by an eyewitness who has made an accurate identification). Indications are that certainty in a false identification is "genuine" in the sense that it is felt by the eyewitness the same way that true certainty is felt. As a result, false certainty is no more likely to be shaken by cross-examination than is true certainty. A second feature of eyewitness identification certainty is that it is susceptible to manipulation by such factors as giving the eyewitness information about the identification after the identification has been made.[39] Consider, for example, an eyewitness who has made an identification of the suspect from a lineup and later in court makes a statement such as "I am absolutely certain that this person is the gunman that I saw that night." Courts seem to interpret this as a statement akin to "This person looks so much like the culprit that I can conclude only that this person is in fact the culprit." Eyewitness researchers, however, find that such statements need not reflect a statement about similarity between the suspect and the eyewitness's memory of the suspect, but instead may reflect certainty that arises from the eyewitness's assumptions about or understanding of other evidence that might exist against the suspect. Eyewitnesses who have identified an innocent person can later become highly certain in their identification if they are led to believe that there is other evidence against the accused, such as other eyewitnesses who have identified the suspect, some physical evidence implicating the suspect, or simply learn that they have identified the person who was suspected in the crime.[40] Because the certainty of the eyewitness seems to be the major factor that people use to judge the accuracy of an eyewitness,

38. *See* Robert K. Bothwell et al., *Correlation of Eyewitness Accuracy and Confidence: Optimality Hypothesis Revisited,* 72 J. APPLIED PSYCHOL. 691 (1987); Kenneth A. Deffenbacher, *Eyewitness Accuracy and Confidence: Can We Infer Anything About Their Relationship?* 4 LAW & HUM. BEHAV. 243 (1980); Sigfried Sporer et al., *Gaining Confidence in Confidence: A New Meta–Analysis on the Confidence–Accuracy Relationship in Eyewitness Identification Studies,* Unpublished paper, Aberdeen University (1994); Gary L. Wells & Donna M. Murray, *Eyewitness Confidence, in* EYEWITNESS TESTIMONY: PSYCHOLOGICAL PERSPECTIVES (Gary L. Wells & Elizabeth F. Loftus eds., 1984).

39. *See* Michael R. Leippe, *Effect of Integrative Memorial and Cognitive Processes on the Correspondence of Eyewitness Accuracy and Confidence,* 4 LAW & HUM. BEHAV. 261 (1980); C. A. Elizabeth Luus & Gary L. Wells, *Determinants of Eyewitness Confidence, in* ADULT EYEWITNESS TESTIMONY: CURRENT TRENDS AND DEVELOPMENTS 348–362 (David F. Ross et al. eds., 1994); Gary L. Wells et al., *The Tractability of Eyewitness Confidence and Its Implication for Triers of Fact,* 66 J. APPLIED PSYCHOL. 688 (1981).

40. Wells & Bradfield, *supra* note 27; Gary L. Wells & Amy L. Bradfield, *Distortions in Eyewitnesses' Recollections: Can the Postidenti-*

certainty inflation is a serious problem. Complicating this problem is the fact that photo-lineup identification procedures are almost always conducted by a detective who knows which photo is the suspect's, and it is not yet a prohibited practice to give immediate feedback to the witness (e.g., "good, you identified the suspect"). Feedback of this sort will not become a prohibited practice until courts rule that it taints the evidence and thereby suppress some or all of that testimony.

Eyewitness researchers find it peculiar that current policies and practices in the legal system do not attempt to deal with the certainty malleability problem. Simple solutions include videotaping the lineup and asking the eyewitness at the time of identification to indicate how certain he is in the identification. It is at this point (at the time of identification) that the eyewitness's certainty is likely to be "clean" of other influences that can occur "off camera" later and influence the certainty of the eyewitness's trial testimony.

The certainty that an eyewitness expresses in his identification seems to be the principal determinant of how jurors perceive the accuracy of the eyewitness's identification.[41] Accordingly, the idea that certainty is malleable after the identification (depending on what the eyewitness might be told or otherwise learn later) ought to be a serious issue for the courts.[42] At this point, however, the courts seem to restrict their interest to possible eyewitness biasing influences only up to the point of the identification and seem to show little or no concern for what the eyewitness might be told immediately after making a pick from a lineup. This feedback, in turn, can lead to certain in-court testimony in which the certainty comes not from the strength of the eyewitness's recollection but from the eyewitness's assumptions (right or wrong) about other evidence that might exist against the defendant. The United States Supreme Court probably did not have in mind the problem of certainty malleability when they listed the certainty of the eyewitness's identification as one of five factors to consider when trying to decide whether or not an eyewitness's identification was reliable. Instead, the Court was probably assuming that the certainty statement of the eyewitness would be taken free of taint from the eyewitness. In fact, the potential usefulness of eyewitness certainty receives some support from eyewitness experts as long as it is assumed that the certainty of the eyewitness was carefully measured and recorded at the time of identification, prior to the chance that the eyewitness might be exposed to other evidence regarding the accused.

§ 8–2.3 Issues of Disagreement

Issues of disagreement among eyewitness experts tend to take the form of questioning how the findings should be used and the extent to which the

fication Feedback Effect be Moderated? 10 PSY-CHOLOGICAL SCIENCE 138 (1999).

41. Michael R. Leippe et al., *Eyewitness Persuasion: How and How Well Do Fact Finders Judge the Accuracy of Adults' and Children's Memory Reports?* 63 J. PERSONALITY & SOC. PSYCHOL. 181 (1992); Michael R. Leippe & Ann Romanczyk, *Children on the Witness Stand: A Communication/Persuasion Analysis of Jurors' Reactions to Child Witnesses,* in CHILDREN'S EYEWITNESS MEMORY 155–177 (Ste-

phen J. Ceci et al. eds., 1987); Michael R. Leippe & Ann Romanczyk, *Reactions to Child (Versus Adult) Eyewitnesses: The Influence of Juror's Preconceptions and Witness Behavior* 13 LAW & HUM. BEHAV. 103 (1989); R. C. L. Lindsay et al., *Can People Detect Eyewitness Identification Accuracy Within and Between Situations?* 66 J. APPLIED PSYCHOL. 79 (1981); Wells & Murray, *supra* note 38.

42. *See* Luus & Wells, *supra* note 13.

findings are applicable to the courts rather than disagreement over the nature of the findings themselves. Much of the disagreement can be placed into two broad categories. The first concerns the question of whether it is appropriate to use the experimental method to generalize to actual cases. The second concerns the question of the effects, if any, expert testimony on these issues has on the triers of fact. In other words, scientists generally disagree little over what the research shows but disagree somewhat on the question of how the research findings should be used.

§ 8–2.3.1 Generalizability of the Findings

Generalization from eyewitness experiments to specific cases that reach trial is a somewhat more complex issue than it might at first appear. One level of analysis, for example, could call into question the applicability of the findings based on the nature of the subject populations on which the research experiments are based. It can be noted, for example, that the majority of the data on which eyewitness experts rely is from studies conducted with college students as eyewitnesses. Although some commentators argue that this raises questions of generalizability to other eyewitness populations, arguably, this is not a problem for two reasons. First, critics offer no credible reasons to believe that the variables that influence college student eyewitnesses are any different from those that affect people in general. In fact, no data suggest any real differences between college student eyewitnesses and other populations in terms of how they react to variables in these experiments.[43] Second, to the extent that college student eyewitnesses differ from other populations, such as elderly eyewitnesses or child eyewitness, they do so in the direction of college students being superior to these other populations.[44] Hence, using college students as eyewitnesses in experimental research might actually tend to overestimate the accuracy of eyewitnesses in general.

Somewhat more problematic for purposes of generalization is the question of whether the effects of certain variables, such as those already discussed, are large or small.[45] The concern here is that an expert might testify about the role of a particular variable (such as the inferiority of other-race identifications relative to within-race identifications) and inadvertently ascribe too much weight to that variable. The issue here is partly statistical because it requires an understanding of the distinction between the concept of statistical significance and the concept of effect size. Statistical significance is the basic statistical test that must be passed in order to conclude that two variables are related at a level that exceeds chance. Effect size, on the other hand, is a measure of the magnitude of the relation between the variables. Something can be statistically significant and yet have a small effect size. Suppose, for example, other-race identifications were only 1% less accurate than are within-race identifications. This result might be statistically signifi-

---

43. Thomas E. O'Rourke et al., *The External Validity of Eyewitness Identification Research: Generalizing Across Subject Populations,* 13 LAW & HUM. BEHAV. 385 (1989).

44. *See* CHILDREN'S EYEWITNESS MEMORY (Stephen J. Ceci et al. eds., 1987); CHILDREN AS WITNESSES (Helen Dent & Rhonda Flin eds., 1992); THE SUGGESTIBILITY OF CHILDREN'S RECOLLECTIONS (John Doris ed., 1991); A. Daniel Yar-

mey, *Age as a Factor in Eyewitness Memory, in* EYEWITNESS TESTIMONY: PSYCHOLOGICAL PERSPECTIVES 142–154 (Gary L. Wells & Elizabeth F. Loftus eds., 1984).

45. *See, e.g.,* Rogers Elliott, *Expert Testimony About Eyewitness Identification: A Critique,* 17 LAW & HUM. BEHAV. 423 (1993).

cant but the effect size would be small. Suppose, however, the difference was 15%–20% between the accuracy of own-race and other-race identifications. This result would be considered a moderate effect size or, by some definitions, a large effect size. Unfortunately, there are some difficulties with what seems like a straightforward issue. First, percentage differences between two groups is not a statistically appropriate way to estimate effect sizes because it does not reflect within-group variance and because the size of the difference is dependent on base rates for accuracy. As a result, effect sizes are measured in standard deviation units, which reflect the differences between the groups in units related to the variance within the groups. Those who have not received statistical training in these issues are unlikely to fully understand the statistical concepts here. Suffice to note at this point that effect size measures from experiments are not necessarily applicable to actual cases (even when measured as standard deviation units), because experiments tend to hold constant and ensure the independence of other variables that could influence eyewitness accuracy. The result of this is that most eyewitness experts are reluctant to make firm statements regarding effect sizes. This makes some experts resistant to the idea of giving expert testimony whereas other experts feel comfortable relying on the fact that the effect is statistically significant.

Related to disagreement about the importance of effect sizes is the question of the size of the relation between certainty and accuracy. The estimated size of the relation between certainty and accuracy varies from one study to the next, sometimes not reaching statistical significance and sometimes being highly significant,[46] which is what would be expected if the true relation is not a powerful one. In recent years, the volume of studies on this issue has reached a point where it can be subjected to meta-analytic statistics, which combine the results of a large number of studies. The results of these meta-analyses indicate that the relation is statistically significant and positive, which indicates that eyewitnesses in these studies who made accurate identifications were more certain of their identifications on average than were those who made false identifications.[47] The potential disagreement on the issue of the certainty/accuracy relation is not whether these average differences in certainty were due to chance; the statistical significance of the meta-analysis indicates that this certainty/accuracy relation is not due to chance alone. Instead, the potential disagreement among eyewitness experts is over the issue of how large the difference is between accurate and inaccurate eyewitness. This is an important issue because the size of this difference is an index of the extent to which there are highly certain eyewitnesses who are nevertheless mistaken in their identification. Although the meta-analyses provide estimates of effect size, these effect sizes are calculated from relatively "clean" experimental conditions that are unlikely to exist in actual cases. Consider that the experiments on which the analyses of the certainty/accuracy relation were based were carefully constructed to hold constant certain factors that might in fact strengthen the certainty/accuracy relation. For example, these experiments were careful to measure eyewitness certainty immediately

46. *See* Wells & Murray, *supra* note 38.

47. *See* Robert K. Bothwell et al., *Correlation of Eyewitness Accuracy and Confidence: Optimality Hypothesis Revisited*, 72 J. APPLIED PSYCHOL. 691 (1987); Sigfried Sporer et al.,

Gaining Confidence in Confidence: A New Meta–Analysis on the Confidence–Accuracy Relationship in Eyewitness Identification Studies, unpublished paper, Aberdeen University (1994).

after the identification, use standardized measurement techniques, and withhold any hint as to the status of the identified person until after the eyewitness had responded to the certainty measure. Contrast this with police practices in which a question about certainty may be leading (e.g., "You're sure aren't you?") and, more importantly, may not be asked or recorded until after the investigators have briefed the eyewitness as to the status of the identified person (e.g., "That is the same guy we suspected; he has a record of this type of offense."). This is a dramatic illustration of the difficulty with using experiment-based estimates of effect size for making statements about the size of the effect in other environments. Experts can agree that there is some potential utility to eyewitness certainty based on the experimental data and yet be reluctant to make the argument that the relation between certainty and accuracy is meaningful in actual cases owing to the way that the system allows certainty-inflating contaminants to operate in the handling of eyewitnesses.

Assisting the argument of eyewitness scientists as to the generalizability of the gist of the experimental findings are recent analyses describing the pattern underlying the DNA exonerations of previously-convicted persons. Over 80% of these wrongful convictions were cases in which the principal evidence against the person was eyewitness identification. These DNA exonerations do not constitute data regarding the generalizability of conclusions about specific variables (e.g., weapon focus). Nevertheless they support the gist of what eyewitness scientists have been arguing: false identifications are not uncommon; identification evidence can be persuasive to juries even when it is mistaken; mistaken eyewitnesses are often very certain; even when more than one eyewitness has identified the suspect, the identification might be mistaken.[48]

§ 8–2.3.2 Effects of Expert Testimony

Related to the issue of generalizability is the question of what effects can be expected from expert testimony. The scientific literature contains disparate views on the question of whether eyewitness experts who share their knowledge through opinion testimony benefits judges and juries.[49] This is related in part to the effect-size concern described earlier because one can question whether it is particularly useful simply to note that a particular variable is related to eyewitness accuracy (or inaccuracy) without also being able to specify precisely how strong is that relation. But the question of whether eyewitness experts can aid a jury goes well beyond the question of effect sizes *per se*. Some argue that convincing proof still does not exist that judges and jurors are overly willing to believe eyewitnesses or that judges and jurors do not already understand how critical variables combine to increase or decrease the accuracy of eyewitnesses.[50]

These concerns have spawned a number of studies designed to address the question of whether jurors are over-believing of eyewitnesses or are otherwise in need of help in assessing eyewitness issues. Scientists approach

48. Connors et al., *supra* note 16; Gary Wells et al., *Eyewitness Identification Procedures: Recommendations for Lineups and Photospreads*, 22 LAW & HUM. BEHAV. 603 (1998); SCHECK, ET AL., *supra* note 18.

49. *See* 1 & 2 LAW & HUMAN BEHAVIOR (1986) (providing a detailed discussion of many of the issues discussed here).

50. *See* Elliott, *supra* note 45.

this issue in a variety of ways. Some involve questionnaires designed to assess people's knowledge of the factors that influence eyewitness accuracy.[51] One of these instruments, called the Knowledge of Eyewitness Behavior Questionnaire, has been administered to American, British, and Australian samples. Six of the items are designed to measure people's beliefs about the factors that affect eyewitness identification accuracy and the results are quite consistent across the diverse samples of respondents. For example, American, British, and Australian respondents seem to appreciate the problem of other-racial identification but not the influence of age or retention interval.[52] Some argue, however, that results from questionnaires such as this are not particularly meaningful because the way that the question is asked is quite likely to affect the results; moreover, critics argue that hypothetical responses of this type may not reflect how people would actually respond to eyewitness testimony at trial.[53]

A second approach attempts to answer the question of whether eyewitness research results are just a matter of common sense. In these "prediction" studies, people try to predict the outcomes of eyewitness experiments based on a description of the experiment. For example, people might be told of an experiment in which the lineup administrator either gave the instruction emphasizing that the culprit might not be in the lineup or gave instructions that did not include the warning. People would then be asked to predict how this affected the likelihood of a false identification. Studies of this sort typically show that people have a limited ability to predict the actual outcomes of the experiments.[54] Again, however, studies of this sort fail to be totally convincing regarding whether jurors need help because they fail to simulate trial testimony by the eyewitnesses. The question remains as to how adequately people would deal with testimony as it would be presented at trial. Courts seem to assume, for instance, that useful information is contained in the demeanor of eyewitnesses that triers of fact can use to make good decisions regarding the validity of the eyewitnesses' sworn testimony.

A third approach to assessing whether jurors need help in assessing eyewitness accuracy involves the use of mock juror studies in which the mock jurors view such testimony and make judgments about the credibility of the eyewitnesses. In some of these studies, eyewitness evidence is manipulated systematically to test jurors' sensitivity to factors that are known to affect the accuracy of eyewitness testimony. The idea behind this work is that jurors ought to be able to discount such testimony when the variables associated with low accuracy are present and augment their belief of the testimony when the variables associated with high accuracy are present. Results from these studies indicate that jurors are insensitive to most of the factors that influ-

51. Kenneth A. Deffenbacher & Elizabeth F. Loftus, *Do Jurors Share a Common Understanding Concerning Eyewitness Behavior?* 6 LAW & HUM. BEHAV. 15 (1982); Kevin M. McConkey & Suzanne M. Roche, *Knowledge of Eyewitness Memory,* 24 AUSTRALIAN PSYCHOLOG. 377 (1989); Elizabeth Roche & Clive Hollin, *Lay Knowledge of Eyewitness Behaviour: A British Survey,* 1 APPLIED COGNITIVE PSYCHOL. 143 (1987).

52. *Id.*

53. Gary L. Wells, *How Adequate is Human Intuition For Judging Eyewitness Testimony? in* EYEWITNESS TESTIMONY: PSYCHOLOGICAL PERSPECTIVES (Gary L. Wells & Elizabeth F. Loftus eds., 1984).

54. John C. Brigham & Robert K. Bothwell, *The Ability of Prospective Jurors to Estimate the Accuracy of Eyewitness Identifications,* 7 LAW & HUM. BEHAV. 19 (1983); Gary L. Wells, *supra* note 53.

ence eyewitness accuracy.[55] Another method has used a "two phase" procedure developed by Gary Wells, Roderick Lindsay, & Tamara Ferguson. In the two-phase procedure, eyewitnesses to staged crimes attempt to make an identification of the culprit and are later cross-examined. Mock jurors, who view this cross examination, are given the task of trying to determine whether or not the central issue of the testimony (i.e., the identification evidence) was accurate or inaccurate. Based on a series of such studies, it is clear that people are unable to discriminate between accurate and inaccurate eyewitness identification testimony.[56] Some of this work with the two-phase procedure has been described in the eyewitness literature as evidence that people are overbelieving of eyewitness identification evidence because the percentage of mock jurors believing the eyewitnesses exceeds the percentage of accurate eyewitnesses.[57] Caution should be exercised in making this conclusion, however, because comparing rates of juror belief to rates of eyewitness accuracy has an uncertain conceptual status.

Taken together, this work implies that jurors need some help in assessing the factors that govern eyewitness identification accuracy. Concluding that jurors could use help in assessing eyewitness identification accuracy, however, is somewhat less controversial than the question of whether expert testimony is an effective aid to the juror. Eyewitness researchers disagree on this question. One line of work responding to this question used trial simulations to see how people react to expert opinion testimony on eyewitness identification. A consistent finding that emerges from this work is that reduced belief of eyewitness testimony and fewer convictions are obtained when expert testimony is presented than when it is not presented.[58] Hence, to the extent that jurors are overbelieving of eyewitnesses, these are positive outcomes. As was noted earlier, however, the question of whether jurors are overbelieving of eyewitness identification testimony is difficult to answer definitively. Therefore, this increased skepticism of eyewitness identification testimony in the face of expert testimony cannot be clearly labeled as a positive effect. It is possible that such testimony makes jurors too skeptical of eyewitnesses. In light of this possibility, it is important to note that some research indicates

---

55. *See* Brad E. Bell & Elizabeth F. Loftus, *Trivial Persuasion in the Courtroom: The Power of (A Few) Minor Details*, 56 J. PERSONALITY & SOC. PSYCHOL. 669 (1989); Brian L. Cutler et al., *The Eyewitness, The Expert Psychologist, and the Jury*, 13 LAW & HUM. BEHAV. 311 (1989); Brian L. Cutler et al., *Jury Decision Making in Eyewitness Identification Cases*, 12 LAW & HUM. BEHAV. 41 (1988); R. C. L. Lindsay et al., *Mock Juror Evaluations of Eyewitness Testimony: A Test of Metamemory Hypotheses*, 16 J. APPLIED SOC. PSYCHOL. 447 (1986).

56. R. C. L. Lindsay et al., *Mock Juror Belief of Accurate and Inaccurate Eyewitnesses: A Replication*, 13 LAW & HUM. BEHAV. 333 (1989); R. C. L. Lindsay et al., *Can People Detect Eyewitness Identification Accuracy Within and Between Situations?* 66 J. APPLIED PSYCHOL. 79 (1981); Gary L. Wells & Michael R. Leippe, *How Do Triers of Fact Infer the Accuracy of Eyewitness Identifications? Memory for Peripheral Detail Can Be Misleading*, 66 J. APPLIED PSYCHOL. 682 (1981); Wells et al., *supra* note 19.

57. Michael R. Leippe, *The Appraisal of Eyewitness Testimony*, in ADULT EYEWITNESS TESTIMONY 385–418 (David F. Ross et al. eds., 1994).

58. *See* Steven G. Fox & H. A. Walters, *The Impact of General Versus Specific Expert Testimony and Eyewitness Confidence Upon Mock Juror Judgment*, 10 LAW & HUM. BEHAV. 215 (1986); Harmon M. Hosch et al., *Influence of Expert Testimony Regarding Eyewitness Accuracy on Jury Decisions*, 4 LAW & HUM. BEHAV. 287 (1980); Elizabeth F. Loftus, *Impact of Expert Psychological Testimony on the Unreliability of Eyewitness Identification*, 65 J. APPLIED PSYCHOL. 6 (1980); Anne Maass et al., *Testifying on Eyewitness Reliability: Expert Advice is Not Always Persuasive*, 15 J. APPLIED SOC. PSYCHOL. 207 (1985); Gary L. Wells et al., *Effects of Expert Psychological Advice on Juror Judgments in Eyewitness Testimony*, 4 LAW & HUM. BEHAV. 275 (1980).

that expert testimony that emphasizes the problems with using eyewitness certainty and that stresses the importance of eyewitnessing conditions can lead people to pay attention to other, more diagnostic, information and can lead them to an improved ability to make discriminating judgments of the likelihood of accurate versus false identification.[59]

In summary, issues of disagreement among eyewitness experts pertain less to disagreement over the scientific findings in the research and more to the question of how these findings can be generalized to actual cases facing the courts and the question of whether expert opinion testimony is beneficial to the trier of fact.

§ 8–2.3.3 Pretrial Motions to Suppress Identification Evidence

Eyewitness experts sometimes testify at pretrial hearings in relation to motions to suppress the identification evidence. At suppression hearings, the issue usually involves the suggestiveness of the procedures. For instance, a lineup that uses fillers who do not fit the description of the culprit (whereas the suspect fits the description), or the failure of police to warn the eyewitness prior to viewing the lineup that the culprit might not be any of the lineup members, or police reinforcing the eyewitness's choice of lineup member would each be considered a suggestive procedure. Eyewitness experts have found that these suggestive procedures increase the chances of mistaken identification and can induce false certainty in the eyewitness. Usually, however, these motions to suppress are denied because courts rely on two-pronged admissibility tests of the type laid out in *Neil v. Biggers*.

The scientific literature on eyewitnesses is at odds with the two-pronged tests that dominate the behaviors of United States courts in suppression hearings. In these two-pronged tests, the first test is whether the procedure was suggestive. If it was not suggestive, then the identification is not suppressed. If the procedure was suggestive, then the second prong is considered. The issue in the second prong concerns whether the identification was reliable (accurate) nevertheless. In order to determine this, *Biggers* noted that five criteria should be applied: (1) Did the witness get a reasonable <u>view</u> of the perpetrator? (2) Did the witness give sufficient <u>attention</u> to the perpetrator? (3) Did the witness give a good <u>description</u> of the perpetrator? (4) Did the identification occur within a reasonable <u>time</u> after the witnesses event? (5) Was the witness <u>certain</u> in the identification? If the eyewitness has a reasonable standing on these criteria (e.g., witness says she had a view of the perpetrator, says she attended to the face, gave a description that more or less fits the suspect, made the identification without an inordinate amount of time passing, and is certain), then the suggestiveness of the procedure is "trumped" and the identification evidence is allowed.

Eyewitness experts have three major concerns with the two-pronged tests used in suppression hearings. First, the second-prong criteria (e.g., certainty, description) have not received good empirical support as indicators of the reliability (accuracy) of the identification.[60] Second, recent research shows that

59. Brian L. Cutler et. al., *supra* note 55; Gary L. Wells, *Expert Psychological Testimony: Empirical and Conceptual Analyses of Effects,* 10 LAW & HUM. BEHAV. 83 (1986); Wells, et al., *supra* note 58.

60. Gary L. Wells & Donna M. Murray, *What Can Psychology Say About the* Neil vs.

the use of suggestive identification procedures not only increases the chances of mistaken identification but also serves to distort witnesses' reports of their standing on the second-prong variables. For instance, suggestive procedures can lead eyewitnesses to inflate the certainty they express in their identifications, claim to have had a better view than they did, and report having attended more closely to the face of the culprit.[61] In other words, the very criteria that are used by courts to decide whether the suggestive procedure was problematic are themselves distorted by the use of the suggestive procedure. Because suggestive procedures artificially enhance the witness's standing on the second-prong criteria, identification evidence from suggestive procedures is rarely suppressed. A third concern that eyewitness experts have with the failure of the courts to suppress identifications resulting from suggestive procedures is that the situation creates an incentive for law enforcement to continue the use of suggestive procedures. In general, eyewitness scientists believe that the courts have underestimated the power of suggestive procedures to produce mistaken identifications and have failed to appreciate that suggestive procedures distort other important aspects of the witness's testimony (e.g., certainty). To the extent that trial judges do not appear to understand how suggestive procedures affect the reliability of eyewitness identification evidence, it rings hollow to eyewitness scientists when the courts deny expert testimony because jurors are presumed to already understand these things.

§ 8–2.3.4 Guidelines for Conducting Lineups

Somewhat in contrast to various court's reluctance to learn from and try to use eyewitness research findings, the United States Justice Department under Attorney General Janet Reno took very seriously the findings of eyewitness researchers and created a Technical Working Group on Eyewitness Evidence in April 1998. This action represents an acknowledgment in the Department of Justice that an eyewitness evidence problem exists. The working group of police, prosecutors, defense attorneys, and eyewitness scientists identified various problems with eyewitness evidence and made extensive use of the scientific eyewitness literature to develop recommendations regarding the collection and preservation of eyewitness evidence.[62]

The results of the Technical Working Group deliberations were published in November 1999 by the U.S. Department of Justice in the form of guidelines for the collection and preservation of eyewitness evidence.[63] These recommendations for the collection and preservation of eyewitness evidence are a valuable resource for defense lawyers in eyewitness identification cases. The Guide covers such important matters as how eyewitnesses should be instructed prior to viewing a lineup, how members of the lineup should be selected, and other details that can affect the reliability of eyewitness identifications.

Biggers *Criteria for Judging Eyewitness Identification Accuracy?* 68 J. APPLIED PSYCHOL. 347 (1983).

61. Wells & Bradfield, *supra* note 27.

62. Gary L. Wells et al., *From the Lab to the Police Station: A Successful Application of Eyewitness Research*, 55 AM. PSYCHOLOG. 581 (2000).

63. U.S. DEPARTMENT OF JUSTICE, OFFICE OF JUSTICE PROGRAMS, EYEWITNESS EVIDENCE: A GUIDE FOR LAW ENFORCEMENT (1999), available at http://www.ncjrs.org/txtfiles1/nij/178240.txt (also availably by calling 1–800–851–3420 and asking for a copy of the Guide).

The recommendations in the Department of Justice Guide largely parallel the recommendations of eyewitness experts and lawyers might find the Guide to be a useful tool for motions to suppress identification evidence and for cross examining law enforcement on the procedures that they used in a particular case.

The Department of Justice guidelines on recommended procedures for collecting eyewitness evidence are the first national guidelines on eyewitness evidence. As such, the Guide is likely to enhance the ability of defense lawyers to effectively criticize live lineups and photo lineups that use suggestive procedures. In addition, because the Guide relies heavily on the eyewitness research literature written by eyewitness experts, it is likely to increase the tendencies of judges to admit expert testimony in cases where the procedures used for collecting eyewitness evidence deviate significantly from the recommendations of experts.

§ 8–2.4 Future Directions

There is an enhanced awareness among eyewitness scientists that eyewitness certainty is both the most influential variable affecting jurors' perceptions of eyewitness accuracy and is also readily manipulable as a function of information that an eyewitness encounters after the identification and before trial. As a result, we can expect new studies to be conducted directed at uncovering the system variables that muddy the relation between certainty and accuracy, especially those variables that cause inflation in the certainty of eyewitnesses and thereby render certainty a misleading cue to the accuracy of the eyewitness's memory. In part, the emphasis on certainty-inflating variables is seen by eyewitness experts to be important because there are remedies that can be imposed by the system. Standardization and videotaping of lineup and photospread procedures, which should include a clear non-leading question of the eyewitness's certainty, is the most obvious safeguard against later manipulations of the eyewitness's certainty. Discrepancies between the certainty that the eyewitness expressed at the initial identification and later in-court testimony could then be used to suggest that the eyewitness is basing his certainty on something other than the strength of his recollection because memory does not improve over time. This seems like a straightforward lesson that the courts ought to readily appreciate without additional data. Nevertheless, courts are not critical of the failure of police investigators to ask eyewitnesses objectively about their identification certainty or their failure to record the eyewitness's certainty at the time of initial identification. This suggests to eyewitness researchers that the courts are not yet convinced that these post-identification factors can lead inaccurate eyewitnesses to be highly certain. For these reasons, more studies are likely to be directed at the problem of certainty malleability. Along with this research will come an increasingly clear message that the person who administers a lineup or photospread to an eyewitness should not know which person is the suspect in the case so as to avoid the potential for the lineup administrator to bias the eyewitness toward the suspect.

Eyewitness researchers are likely to continue to examine the question of whether expert testimony on eyewitness issues will assist the jury. Current data using simulations with mock jurors indicate that jurors might become more discerning decision makers with the provision of expert testimony. But this research has not clearly confronted the question of whether this same level of "assistance" could be offered by counsel through arguments pitched to the common sense of the jury. What is needed is a series of studies that show whether this same knowledge can be effectively communicated to the jury through means already in place that do not require specialized scientific knowledge.

Future research efforts are likely to be directed at the continuing problem of the role that police investigators themselves play in enhancing the likelihood of false identification. The resistance of police investigators to change their lineup and photospread procedures in light of research findings is perhaps understandable because courts have tended to tolerate procedures that are not standardized and are not externally recorded. What is less understood by eyewitness scientists is why courts are so tolerant, why they rarely show concern for the lax standards for conducting lineups and photospreads, and why they do not call for videotaping of the critical juncture in which an eyewitness is instructed, shown a lineup or photospread, and makes an identification decision. Eyewitness researchers can only assume that courts are not yet persuaded of something that eyewitness researchers are now convinced about, namely that the context, behaviors, and micro-events that surround the conducting of a lineup or photospread can have strong effects on the likelihood of a false identification. Hence, future research efforts are likely to continue to document the powerful influence that certain procedures, to which the courts have not objected, are contributing unnecessarily to the risk of false identification testimony from eyewitnesses who are certain in spite of their mistake.

Finally, future research is likely to focus more heavily on the many ways in which police can influence witnesses while administering photo lineups. Researchers involved in the development of the Department of Justice Guide pressed for double-blind testing for photo lineups, which would mean that the person administering a photo-lineup does not know which person is the suspect in the lineup. The researchers were disappointed to have this important idea rejected by the Working Group. The absence of counsel at photo lineups, coupled with the fact that the lineup is run by the case detective who is motivated to secure an identification of the suspect, creates a dynamic setting in which verbal and non-verbal cues to witnesses can be rampant.

CHAPTER 9

HYPNOSIS

Table of Sections

A. LEGAL ISSUES

Westlaw Electronic Research

See Westlaw Electronic Research Guide preceding the Summary of Contents.

A. LEGAL ISSUES

§ 9–1.0 THE LEGAL RELEVANCE OF RESEARCH ON HYPNOSIS

§ 9–1.1 Introduction

Unlike most of the topics in this book, hypnosis does not fall squarely into the general category of scientific evidence.[1] Specifically, hypnosis occurs prior to trial and the product of this technique, hypnotically refreshed recall, is introduced at trial through the witness himself, rather than through expert testimony.[2] Nonetheless, despite some ambiguity regarding which rules apply to hypnotically refreshed testimony, there is surprising consensus among courts about the dangers associated with this evidence. The consensus regarding the dangers of hypnosis, however, has not led to consensus about the admissibility of hypnotically refreshed recall. Indeed, hypnosis illustrates well how courts approach controversial science, since courts range from a *per se* admissible test, which leaves the matter entirely to the discretion of the jury, to a *per se* inadmissible test, which takes the matter entirely away from the jury.

In general, courts uniformly identify a host of dangers associated with hypnotically refreshed testimony.[3] First, courts worry that hypnosis leads to the subject's loss of the ability to critically assess memories. After hypnosis, the subject has difficulty distinguishing "true" memories from those created or expanded under hypnosis. Second, courts fear the influence the hypnotist might have on the subject, both inadvertently and intentionally. The hypnotist might, through subtle or not so subtle cues, impart information to the subject. Third, courts find that subjects "confabulate," or fill in details, while under hypnosis in order to satisfy the hypnotist's demands. Fourth, and particularly troubling for courts, hypnosis leads to increased, but misplaced, confidence on the part of subjects regarding their memory of events. Courts refer to this phenomenon as "memory hardening" and fear it especially because it increases the persuasiveness of the witness in the eyes of the jury. Finally, and also of considerable concern for courts, is the fear that jurors will be awed by an aura of infallibility that might attach to memories recalled under hypnosis. Hypnosis, as with all ostensibly scientific techniques, might defy critical assessment by a lay jury.

Some commentators, however, argue that when used for therapeutic purposes, such as recovery of repressed memories of traumatic events, hypnosis should be viewed more favorably than when it is used to buttress memories of events to which the subject was an eyewitness.[4] They claim that greater danger attends forensic use of hypnosis than therapeutic use.[5] Courts,

---

§ 9–1.0

1. Hypnosis, however, is not unique in creating an important admissibility issue surrounding a scientific technique that does not fit squarely into the standard expert testimony category. Predictions of violence, for instance, also lie at the periphery of the scientific evidence rules. *See* Chapter 2.

2. What qualifies as "hypnosis" has itself been a question that several courts have struggled with. *See, e.g.,* Franklin v. Stevenson, 987 P.2d 22 (Utah 1999) (The court rejected the trial court's conclusion that a therapist's "communicating with one's inner child" was "hypnosis-like" in nature. However, the court nonetheless found that such communications were inadmissible because they had not been shown to be reliable.); *cf.* Wall v. Fairview Hospital and Healthcare Services, 584 N.W.2d 395, 409–

11 (Minn.1998) (The court considered the similarities between dissociative identity disorder (DID), or multiple personality disorder, and hypnosis for purposes of admissibility of certain statements. It found some similarities, and held that "district courts are in the best position to determine how to handle witnesses with DID and whether their testimony is admissible.").

3. *See* State v. Fertig, 143 N.J. 115, 668 A.2d 1076, 1078 (N.J.1996) (providing a summary of the dangers associated with hypnosis as identified by courts through the years).

4. *See, e.g.,* Jacqueline Kanovitz, *Hypnotic Memories and Civil Sexual Abuse Trials,* 45 VAND. L. REV. 1185 (1992).

5. *Id.* at 1243–52.

however, have yet to be convinced of this argument and they treat hypnosis similarly in the two contexts. In *Borawick v. Shay*,[6] for example, the court observed as follows:

> [E]ven though there may be important distinctions between the use of hypnosis to enhance memories of witnessed events and the use of hypnosis to retrieve repressed memories, given the lack of empirical studies as to the latter and the complicated nature of hypnotically-induced recall, we are not willing to assume that the risks of suggestability, confabulation, and memory hardening are significantly reduced when the hypnosis that triggers the testimony is used for therapeutic purposes.[7]

In fact, use of hypnosis to retrieve repressed memories poses a more complicated and challenging situation to courts than forensic use. First, the concept of repressed memory itself is not well understood and today is quite controversial.[8] Second, unlike forensic use, there is slight opportunity to impose checks on the hypnotic sessions before they begin in order to avoid the therapist's influence on the memories "recovered." Third, in therapy, drugs or other manipulations might be used to buttress the therapeutic outcome, but at the possible expense of accuracy. Finally, as with the many other clinical techniques being introduced in the courtroom, those acceptable for therapy might not be appropriate for forensic use.[9] After all, although hypnotically un-repressed memories might begin as therapeutic, in the courtroom they are being introduced to prove the truth of the matter asserted.[10]

§ 9–1.2 By What Rule Should Hypnosis Be Evaluated?

A significant threshold question presented in these cases concerns the selection of a rule by which to evaluate the admissibility of hypnotically refreshed testimony. Courts settle on a variety of alternatives, including the expert testimony rules, competency of witness standards and general statements of probative value and possible unfair prejudice.

Many courts question the applicability of the expert testimony rules because the proponent of hypnotically refreshed recall does not proffer "expert opinion." Under this view, *Frye* and *Daubert* do not apply to this evidence.[11] For example, in *Borawick v. Shay*,[12] the court declined to rely on *Daubert*:

> We do not believe that *Daubert* is directly applicable to the issue here since *Daubert* concerns the admissibility of data derived from scientific techniques or expert opinions. The issue before us is whether [the

---

6. 68 F.3d 597 (2d Cir.1995).

7. *Id.* at 607.

8. *See* Chapter 10.

9. *See* People v. Wilson, 116 Ill.2d 29, 106 Ill.Dec. 771, 506 N.E.2d 571, 577 (Ill.1987); State v. Mack, 292 N.W.2d 764 (Minn.1980).

10. *See generally* Zani v. State, 758 S.W.2d 233, 237 (Tex.Cr.App.1988) ("In the therapeutic setting, however, the value of hypnosis is in no way contingent upon the historical accuracy of the memory that may come to light thereunder."); *cf.* Franklin v. Fox, 107 F.Supp.2d 1154,

1158–60 (N.D.Cal.2000) (In a civil suit for damages arising out of the recovery of "repressed memories," the plaintiff claimed that the arresting officer's knowledge that the alleged victim's recall was hypnotically induced should have alerted him that he did not have probable cause to arrest.).

11. *See* State v. Brown, 337 N.W.2d 138 (N.D.1983) (rejecting applicability of the *Frye* test to hypnotically refreshed testimony).

12. 68 F.3d 597 (2d Cir.1995).

plaintiff] is a competent witness or whether her lay testimony is admissible.[13]

Other courts, however, disagree and find that hypnotically refreshed testimony "is the product of scientific intervention."[14] The hypnosis procedure, according to this view, changes the content and presentation of the evidence and thus is, effectively, present in the courtroom.[15] Indeed, the fact that the expert's participation occurs behind-the-scenes and is not directly observable by the trier of fact, makes it more imperative that the judge screen the product of the technique. In fact, courts that eschew reliance on the expert testimony rules typically note that the conclusion they reached through another avenue is consistent with those rules.[16]

Although, in practice, the rule employed to assess hypnotically refreshed testimony appears to matter little, in theory it should be a significant factor. Under the Federal Rules of Evidence and most state codes, if a court relies on either general relevancy concepts or rules regarding the competency of witnesses, a strong presumption of admissibility should attach to hypnotically refreshed testimony.[17] In contrast, the standards for expert testimony, whether in line with *Frye* or *Daubert,* are somewhat less accommodating. For example, despite the *Daubert* Court's recognition of the liberal thrust of the Federal Rules, the Court found that Rule 702 appoints judges as gatekeepers to screen scientific evidence. Moreover, pursuant to that role, judges can only admit scientific evidence that the court has preliminarily determined to be more likely than not valid. Under the Federal Rules, therefore, Rule 702 (which is joined by Rule 403) appears to be a more substantial barrier than Rule 601 or a general relevancy analysis.[18]

§ 9–1.3 Admissibility of Hypnotically Refreshed Testimony

§ 9–1.3.1 per se Admissible

A small group of states deem hypnotically refreshed testimony to be generally admissible.[19] These courts expressly reject assertions that hypnosis

13. *Id.* at 610. *See also* State v. Wren, 425 So.2d 756, 759 (La.1983) ("[T]he testimony of a witness who had his or her memory refreshed through hypnosis should be treated as other 'recollection refreshed' testimony, because the hypnosis affects the credibility, and not the admissibility, of the evidence.").

14. State v. Tuttle, 780 P.2d 1203, 1211 (Utah 1989); *see also* Contreras v. State, 718 P.2d 129 (Alaska 1986); Zani v. State, 758 S.W.2d 233 (Tex.Cr.App.1988).

15. *See* People v. Hughes, 59 N.Y.2d 523, 466 N.Y.S.2d 255, 453 N.E.2d 484 (N.Y.1983) (noting that "hypnosis is a scientific process and the recollections it generates must be considered as scientific results").

16. *See, e.g.,* Borawick v. Shay, 68 F.3d 597, 610 (2d Cir.1995) (noting that the underlying principle of *Daubert* is consistent with the "totality of the circumstances" test adopted by the court); State v. Armstrong, 110 Wis.2d 555, 329 N.W.2d 386, 393 n. 14 (Wis.1983)(noting that if *Frye* did apply, "there

is a strong argument" it would be met, since "hypnosis has been accepted by the appropriate scientific discipline").

17. Rule 601 states broadly that "[e]very person is competent to be a witness except as otherwise provided in these rules." The Advisory Committee's Note adds the following, for emphasis: "A witness wholly without capacity is difficult to imagine. The question is one particularly suited to the jury as one of weight and credibility." Adv. Committee's Note, Fed. R.Evid. 601. The general relevancy rules, Rules 401, 402 and 403, also strongly presume admissibility, as indicated by Rule 403's injunction that relevant evidence should be excluded only when its unfair prejudicial effect *substantially* outweighs its probative value.

18. *But see* Peterson v. State, 448 N.E.2d 673 (Ind.1983), *appeal after remand,* 514 N.E.2d 265 (1987) (finding that hypnotically refreshed testimony has no probative value).

19. *See* State v. Brown, 337 N.W.2d 138, 151 (N.D.1983); State v. Jorgensen, 8 Or.App.

renders a witness "incompetent" and find that the trier of fact should determine the value of the testimony. As the court in *State v. Brown* succinctly stated, "We believe that an attack on credibility is the proper method of determining the value of hypnotically induced testimony."[20] Indeed, these courts find that mandatory procedural safeguards may be counterproductive, finding that they unduly restrict the utilization of the technique and offer misleading benchmarks for evaluating the reliability of post-hypnotic testimony.[21] Instead, courts embracing a test of general admissibility express confidence that triers of fact can critically assess hypnotically refreshed testimony and thus distinguish memories previously held and those that might have been suggested to the witness during hypnosis.[22]

§ 9–1.3.2 Totality of the Circumstances

Many courts, especially federal courts, evaluate hypnotically refreshed testimony on an ad hoc basis by considering the totality of the circumstances surrounding the hypnosis session.[23] These courts begin with the premise that a *per se* rule of exclusion would prohibit too much reliable evidence.[24] Thereafter, courts considering the totality of the circumstances examine a wide variety of factors. In *Borawick v. Shay*,[25] for example, the court suggested eight factors that should go into the admissibility determination. These include the following: (1) "the purpose of the hypnosis," with special concern for forensic uses as compared to therapeutic uses, (2) "whether the witness received any suggestions from the hypnotist or others prior to or during hypnosis," (3) "the presence or absence of a permanent record" [e.g., a videotape], (4) the qualifications of the hypnotist, (5) "whether corroborating evidence exists to support the reliability of the hypnotically-refreshed memories," (6) the susceptibility of the subject to hypnosis and hence his "prone[ness] to confabulate," (7) expert testimony concerning "the reliability of the procedures used in the case," and (8) the testimony deduced at a pretrial hearing.[26] Finally, according to the court, "the party attempting to admit the hypnotically-enhanced testimony bears the burden of persuading the district court that the balance tips in favor of admissibility."[27]

1, 492 P.2d 312, 315 (Or.App.1971); State v. Glebock, 616 S.W.2d 897, 903–04 (Tenn.Crim. App.1981); Prime v. State, 767 P.2d 149, 153 (Wyo.1989).

20. *Brown,* 337 N.W.2d at 151. It should be noted that the *Brown* court believed itself to be aligning "with the majority of jurisdictions which have held that hypnosis affects credibility but not admissibility." *Id.* If this ever was the majority rule, it is no longer so today. *See* § 9–1.3.4, *infra.*

21. *See infra* § 9–1.3.3.

22. *See* Chapman v. State, 638 P.2d 1280 (Wyo.1982).

23. *See* Mersch v. City of Dallas, 207 F.3d 732, 735 (5th Cir.2000); Borawick v. Shay, 68 F.3d 597, 607 (2d Cir.1995); Bundy v. Dugger, 850 F.2d 1402, 1415 (11th Cir.1988); McQueen v. Garrison, 814 F.2d 951, 958 (4th Cir.1987); United States v. Kimberlin, 805 F.2d 210, 219 (7th Cir.1986); Sprynczynatyk v. General Mo-

tors Corp., 771 F.2d 1112, 1122–23 (8th Cir. 1985); United States v. Valdez, 722 F.2d 1196, 1203 (5th Cir.1984); *see also* State v. Iwakiri, 106 Idaho 618, 682 P.2d 571 (Idaho 1984); State v. Johnston, 39 Ohio St.3d 48, 529 N.E.2d 898, 906 (Ohio 1988); Walters v. State, 680 S.W.2d 60, 63 (Tex.App.1984).

24. *See Valdez,* 722 F.2d at 1203.

25. 68 F.3d 597 (2d Cir.1995).

26. *Id.* at 608.

27. *Id.* at 608–09. In *Mersch v. City of Dallas,* 207 F.3d 732 (5th Cir.2000), the court identified the following five factors that bear on the reliability of hypnotically refreshed testimony:

1) the hypnosis is done by a psychologist or psychiatrist trained in its use and independent of either party; 2) the hypnosis is done in a neutral setting with only the hypnotist and the subject present; 3) an audio or vid-

§ 9–1.3.3 Admissible With Safeguards

A number of courts have approached hypnotically refreshed testimony with caution and, citing the significant dangers associated with it, adopt a compromise.[28] Courts that admit with safeguards recognize the dangers associated with hypnosis, but also caution that other forms of testimony suffer from similar reliability problems. In particular, eyewitness identifications are routinely relied upon despite the weaknesses associated with them. Hence, the issue for these courts is the reliability of hypnotically refreshed testimony as compared to other kinds of testimony.[29] These courts determine that post-hypnotic testimony is acceptable only if an array of procedural guidelines have been followed. The procedural safeguard approach was first articulated in *State v. Hurd*.[30] Relying on the views of Dr. Martin Orne, the court listed six criteria for hypnotically refreshed testimony:

> "First, a psychiatrist or psychologist experienced in the use of hypnosis must conduct the session. This professional should also be able to qualify as an expert in order to aid the court in evaluating the procedures followed....
>
> Second, the professional conducting the hypnotic session should be independent of and not regularly employed by the prosecutor, investigator or defense. This condition will safeguard against any bias on the part of the hypnotist that might translate into leading questions, unintentional cues, or other suggestive conduct.
>
> Third, any information given to the hypnotist by law enforcement personnel or the defense prior to the hypnotic session must be recorded, either in writing or another suitable form....
>
> Fourth, before inducing hypnosis the hypnotist should obtain from the subject a detailed description of the facts as the subject remembers them. The hypnotist should carefully avoid influencing the description by asking structured questions or adding new details.
>
> Fifth, all contacts between the hypnotist and the subject must be recorded. This will establish a record of the pre-induction interview, the hypnotic session, and the post-hypnotic period, enabling a court to determine what information or suggestions the witness may have received during the session and what recall was first elicited through hypnosis....
>
> Sixth, only the hypnotist and the subject should be present during any phase of the hypnotic session, including the pre-hypnotic testing and the post-hypnotic interview."[31]

In addition to these procedural requirements, *Hurd* "also requires that 'the party seeking to introduce the hypnotically refreshed testimony has the burden of establishing admissibility by clear and convincing evidence.' "[32] This

eo recording is made of all interrogations before, during and after hypnosis; 4) corroborating evidence exists; and 5) the pre-hypnosis and post-hypnosis statements substantially correspond.

Id. at 735.

28. *See, e.g.*, Rowland v. Commonwealth, 901 S.W.2d 871, 873 (Ky.1995).

29. *See* State v. Hurd, 86 N.J. 525, 432 A.2d 86 (N.J.1981).

30. 86 N.J. 525, 432 A.2d 86 (N.J.1981).

31. State v. Fertig, 143 N.J. 115, 668 A.2d 1076, 1078–79 (N.J.1996)(*quoting* State v. Hurd, 86 N.J. 525, 432 A.2d 86 (N.J.1981)).

32. *Id.* at 1079 (*quoting Hurd,* 432 A.2d at 97).

relatively high burden is justified, according to the *Hurd* court, "by the potential for abuse of hypnosis, the genuine likelihood of suggestiveness and error, and the consequent risk of injustice."[33] Moreover, the New Jersey Supreme Court subsequently buttressed the *Hurd* requirements by holding that trial judges must instruct jurors regarding the dangers of hypnotically refreshed testimony.[34]

In *State v. Dreher*,[35] a New Jersey intermediate appellate court considered the admissibility of pre-hypnotic recall when the hypnotic session violated the *Hurd* procedural requirements. As the court described the issue, "[does] a suggestive hypnosis procedure . . . so taint[] a witness's pre-hypnotic recollection as to render his testimony inadmissible at trial."

The court concluded that this determination must be made on a case by case basis. Even memory not tainted by hypnosis, the court argued, is inexact and subject to confabulation and inaccuracies introduced throughout the process. In general, then, the court stated, " 'we depend on the adversary system to inform the jury of the inherent weaknesses of the evidence.' "[36] In deciding whether suggestive hypnosis procedures render pre-hypnotic recollection too unreliable to be admitted, the court suggested that judges consider

> the extent to which the pre-hypnotic recollections have been recorded; the degree to which the witness had confidence in his pre-hypnotic recollection; the extent of the witness's belief that hypnosis will yield the truth; the type of questioning employed; and "any other factor relevant to determining whether hypnosis so enhanced the witness's confidence in his original recollection as to substantially impair the opposing party's right to cross-examination."[37]

In the case at hand, the court concluded that the judge below had adequately employed these factors in permitting the witness' pre-hypnotic recall.

Many courts and commentators, however, challenge the usefulness of the *Hurd* guidelines, and some find them counterproductive. It is worth noting, in particular, that the intellectual progenitor of the guidelines, Dr. Martin Orne, stated shortly after *Hurd* that he no longer believed that they can protect against the many dangers associated with hypnosis.[38] Courts that adopt a general admissibility standard attack the guidelines as unwise and counterproductive; courts that adopt a *per se* rule of exclusion attack the guidelines as unwise and ineffective.

---

33. *Hurd,* 432 A.2d at 97.

34. *Fertig,* 668 A.2d at 1082. *See also* Mersch v. City of Dallas, 207 F.3d 732, 736 (5th Cir.2000) ("If requested, the district court should hold a hearing when a case presents a significant issue concerning hypnotically-enhanced testimony.").

35. 302 N.J.Super. 408, 695 A.2d 672 (1997).

36. *Id.* at 715 (*quoting Hurd*, 432 A.2d at 95).

37. *Id.* at 714 (*quoting* State v. Dreher (I), 251 N.J.Super. 300, 598 A.2d 216, 221 (App. Div.1991)). *See also* Commonwealth v. Young, 561 Pa. 34, 748 A.2d 166 (Pa.1999) ("[T]he trial court admitted [the formerly hypnotized witness's] testimony without requiring the Commonwealth to prove that it was independent of hypnosis or that the hypnotist was neutral, and the court did not issue a cautionary instruction. This was clearly erroneous.").

38. Martin T. Orne, et al., *Hypnotically Induced Testimony in* EYEWITNESS TESTIMONY: PSYCHOLOGICAL PERSPECTIVES, 171, 205 (Gary L. Wells & Elizabeth F. Loftus eds. 1984) ("[H]ypnosis should not be used to prepare a witness to testify in court, such as in an attempt to improve the recall of a previously unreliable or uncertain witness.").

Courts that generally admit hypnotically refreshed testimony raise a wide variety of objections to the use of the six *Hurd* factors. Contrary to offering a prophylactic against unreliable testimony, the court in *People v. Gonzales*[39] concluded that applying *Hurd* would have an "affirmatively detrimental effect."[40] The *Gonzales* court asserted that testimony refreshed according to the *Hurd* guidelines would possess "an aura of reliability which, in actuality, it does not possess."[41] Other courts have criticized the *Hurd* factors for creating "a fertile new field for litigation," producing inconsistent results across cases[42] and operating as too great a barrier to hypnotically refreshed recall.[43] Moreover, the *need* for hypnosis as an investigatory tool is cited by some courts that fear that placing concrete requirements on the practice will handcuff the police or lead to suspension of its use. The *Hurd* procedures do not capture the complexity of the hypnosis context and these courts prefer to allow juries to hear the matter in full and decide it according to their common sense.[44]

Courts on the other side of the issue reject the *Hurd* guidelines as being insufficiently effective to guarantee reliable evidence. These courts point out that safeguards can lessen the dangers but they cannot eliminate them.[45] The concern lies in the fact that even experts cannot distinguish between "real" memories and those that are the product of suggestion. Further, courts voice a substantial concern with the time and resources wasted under the *Hurd* approach.[46]

§ 9–1.3.4 *per se* Inadmissible, but With Two Caveats

The majority of courts employ a *per se* rule of inadmissibility for hypnotically refreshed testimony.[47] Foremost, courts justify *per se* exclusion by citing

39. 108 Mich App 145, 310 N.W.2d 306 (Mich App 1981).

40. *Id.* at 313

41. *Id.*

42. State v. Brown, 337 N.W.2d 138, 150–51 (N.D.1983).

43. State ex rel. Collins v. Superior Court, 132 Ariz. 180, 644 P.2d 1266, 1294 (Ariz.1982); *Brown*, 337 N.W.2d at 151.

44. *See* Chapman v. State, 638 P.2d 1280, 1283 (Wyo.1982).

45. *See* Contreras v. State, 718 P.2d 129 (Alaska 1986); *see also* People v. Hughes, 59 N.Y.2d 523, 466 N.Y.S.2d 255, 453 N.E.2d 484 (N.Y.1983) (noting that safeguards apply to police and therapist, but do not contribute to confidence in the accuracy of what is recalled or dispel the artificial confidence boost instilled by hypnosis).

46. *See, e.g.,* People v. Shirley, 31 Cal.3d 18, 181 Cal.Rptr. 243, 723 P.2d 1354 (Cal. 1982); State v. Collins, 296 Md. 670, 464 A.2d 1028 (Md.1983).

47. *See* Contreras v. State, 718 P.2d 129 (Alaska 1986); *see also* State ex rel. Collins v. Superior Court, 132 Ariz. 180, 644 P.2d 1266 (Ariz.1982); Rock v. State, 288 Ark. 566, 708 S.W.2d 78 (Ark.1986), *vacated and remanded,*

483 U.S. 44, 107 S.Ct. 2704, 97 L.Ed.2d 37 (1987); People v. Shirley, 31 Cal.3d 18, 181 Cal.Rptr. 243, 723 P.2d 1354 (Cal.1982); State v. Atwood, 39 Conn.Sup. 273, 479 A.2d 258 (Conn.1984); State v. Davis, 490 A.2d 601 (Del.Super.1985); Bundy v. State, 471 So.2d 9 (Fla.1985); Walraven v. State, 255 Ga. 276, 336 S.E.2d 798 (Ga.1985) State v. Moreno, 68 Haw. 233, 709 P.2d 103 (Haw.1985); People v. Zayas, 131 Ill.2d 284, 137 Ill.Dec. 568, 546 N.E.2d 513 (Ill.1989); Clark v. State, 447 N.E.2d 1076 (Ind. 1983); State v. Haislip, 237 Kan. 461, 701 P.2d 909 (Kan.1985); State v. Culpepper, 434 So.2d 76 (La.App.1982); State v. Collins, 296 Md. 670, 464 A.2d 1028 (Md.1983); Commonwealth v. Kater, 388 Mass. 519, 447 N.E.2d 1190 (Mass.1983); People v. Gonzales, 415 Mich. 615, 329 N.W.2d 743 (Mich.1982); State v. Mack, 292 N.W.2d 764 (Minn.1980); Alsbach v. Bader, 700 S.W.2d 823 (Mo.1985); State v. Palmer, 210 Neb. 206, 313 N.W.2d 648 (Neb. 1981); People v. Hughes, 59 N.Y.2d 523, 466 N.Y.S.2d 255, 453 N.E.2d 484 (N.Y.1983); State v. Peoples, 311 N.C. 515, 319 S.E.2d 177 (N.C.1984); Harmon v. State, 700 P.2d 212 (Okla.Crim.App.1985); Commonwealth v. Smoyer, 505 Pa. 83, 476 A.2d 1304 (Pa.1984); State v. Mitchell, 779 P.2d 1116 (Utah 1989); Hall v. Commonwealth, 12 Va.App. 198, 403 S.E.2d 362 (Va.App.1991); State v. Martin, 101 Wash.2d 713, 684 P.2d 651 (Wash.1984).

the substantial dangers associated with, and the unreliability of, hypnotically refreshed testimony. In addition, these courts find that a *per se* rule avoids the need for judges to become experts on hypnosis, undue waste of time,[48] and the risk of inconsistent results. It is noteworthy that several jurisdictions that once applied a rule of general admissibility, now employ a *per se* inadmissible rule.[49]

Although highly critical of hypnotically refreshed testimony, courts applying a *per se* rule of exclusion tend to find that the prior hypnosis does not render witnesses incompetent to testify. Specifically, courts often permit witnesses to testify to those facts known prior to the hypnosis session.[50] This caveat on the rule of *per se* exclusion requires that the fourth *Hurd* factor, memorializing the facts known by the witness before the session, be followed.

The decision to permit witnesses to testify about facts known prior to the hypnosis session rests largely on the principle of necessity. A rule that renders these witnesses incompetent to testify would effectively remove hypnosis as an investigatory tool.[51] Courts are reluctant to take this step and, instead, seek a viable compromise position. The Arizona Supreme Court's struggle with this issue is instructive. In *Collins II*,[52] the court concluded "that any person hypnotized ... is incompetent to testify."[53] After granting the state's petition for rehearing, however, the court reconsidered this conclusion: "we modify our previous decision and hold that a witness will not be rendered incompetent merely because he or she was hypnotized during the investigatory phase of the case."[54]

The great danger associated with permitting a witness who has undergone hypnosis to testify is that the procedure will affect the later testimony. If hypnosis shores up a witness' confidence and makes it more difficult for even the witness himself to determine "real" memories from "created" ones, subsequent cross-examination might not be effective. Moreover, the principal safeguard of recording pre-hypnotic knowledge provides little real protection. These recordings are themselves hearsay and, like all hearsay, are introduced without the benefit of cross-examination. It is little solace to the opponent of a witness who has undergone hypnosis to be informed that the principal protection against the admittedly unreliable hypnotically refreshed testimony is the pre-hypnotic recorded statements of the adverse witness, made out of

---

48. *See Collins*, 464 A.2d at 1044; *see also Shirley*, 723 P.2d at 1366.

49. *See, e.g.*, State v. Peoples, 311 N.C. 515, 319 S.E.2d 177 (N.C.1984) *overruling* State v. McQueen, 295 N.C. 96, 244 S.E.2d 414 (N.C. 1978); State v. Collins, 296 Md. 670, 464 A.2d 1028 (Md.1983) *overruling* Harding v. State, 5 Md.App. 230, 246 A.2d 302 (Md.App.1968).

50. *See, e.g.*, State v. Lopez, 181 Ariz. 8, 887 P.2d 538 (Ariz.1994) (The court "held that 'a witness will not be rendered incompetent merely because he or she was hypnotized during the investigatory phase of the case. That witness will be permitted to testify with regard to those matters which he or she was able to recall and relate prior to hypnosis.'") (*quoting* Collins v. Superior Court, 132 Ariz. 180, 644 P.2d 1266, 1295 (Ariz.1982) (*Collins II*)).

51. *See Collins II*, 644 P.2d at 1296 ("We are persuaded ... that with respect to investigatory use of hypnosis, the benefit does outweigh the danger.").

52. 132 Ariz. 180, 644 P.2d 1266 (Ariz. 1982).

53. *Id.* at 1276.

54. *Collins II*, 644 P.2d at 1295; for similar holdings, *see, e.g.*, Commonwealth v. Kater, 432 Mass. 404, 734 N.E.2d 1164, 1177 (Mass. 2000); Rowland v. Commonwealth, 901 S.W.2d 871 (Ky.1995); State v. Peoples, 311 N.C. 515, 319 S.E.2d 177 (N.C.1984); Commonwealth v. Taylor, 294 Pa.Super. 171, 439 A.2d 805 (Pa.Super.1982); State v. Palmer, 210 Neb. 206, 313 N.W.2d 648, 655 (Neb.1981); State v. Wallach, 110 Mich.App. 37, 312 N.W.2d 387 (Mich.App.1981).

court and not under oath. Under most codes of evidence, such statements are excluded under the hearsay rule, and this is true even when the declarant is available and may be subjected to an effective cross-examination. Courts should proceed with extreme caution in permitting these statements when the cross-examination of the declarant is rendered less effective, or ineffective, by hypnosis.[55] Indeed, the issues surrounding the admissibility of both the prerecorded statements, if any, and hypnotically refreshed testimony, raise confrontation clause and due process concerns.[56]

On the reverse side of this issue, the constitutional standards surrounding a defendants' proffer of hypnotically refreshed testimony, the United States Supreme Court has rejected the use of a *per se* rule of exclusion. In *Rock v. Arkansas*,[57] the petitioner was convicted of manslaughter in the shooting death of her husband. The petitioner and her husband had fought on the night in question and after the fight turned violent, the petitioner picked up a gun.[58] After her husband hit her, the gun went off; the husband died from a bullet wound to the chest.[59] After the incident, the petitioner could not remember any details of the event, so her counsel suggested the use of hypnosis to refresh her recollection. During the hypnosis she did not recall any new details; shortly afterward, however, she remembered that she did not have her finger on the trigger.[60] This recollection led to the hiring of a handgun specialist who later testified that the gun was defective and would fire when hit or dropped.[61] At trial, the court permitted the testimony of the handgun specialist, but limited the petitioner to a description of the facts as she recalled them prior to the hypnosis.[62]

Citing the Fifth, Sixth, and Fourteenth Amendments, the Court held that the Constitution provides "[t]he right to testify on one's own behalf at a criminal trial."[63] Although this right is not absolute, the Court found that it was sufficiently great that a *per se* rule disabling a defendant from testifying was invalid. In reaching this conclusion, the Court surveyed courts' responses to this evidence and the benefits and dangers associated with it.[64] The Court was persuaded that, despite its weaknesses, hypnosis could lead to reliable

55. The *Collins II* court appreciated the potential costs associated with a witness who has been previously hypnotized, but concluded that, on balance, these dangers did not render such a witness incompetent to testify to facts previously known. The court concluded as follows:

> We recognize ... that there is danger in allowing testimony of facts recalled prior to hypnosis, because the subsequent hypnosis does have an effect upon the witness' confidence of those facts.... We are persuaded, however, that with investigatory use of hypnosis, the benefit does outweigh the danger.

Collins II, 644 P.2d at 1296.

56. Several courts have rejected the argument that the admission of hypnotically refreshed testimony violates the defendant's confrontation clause rights. *See, e.g.*, State v. Evans, 316 S.C. 303, 450 S.E.2d 47, 50–51 (S.C.1994); *see also* State v. Armstrong, 110 Wis.2d 555, 329 N.W.2d 386, 393–94 (Wis. 1983); Clay v. Vose, 771 F.2d 1, 4 (1st Cir.

1985). Although the in-court testimony of a hypnotically refreshed witness has been found to meet Sixth Amendment requirements, state use of prerecorded statements might fail such an analysis. To date, however, there appear to be no cases presenting this issue, since defendants are most likely to rely on these statements at trial in order to rebut hypnotically refreshed testimony.

57. 483 U.S. 44, 107 S.Ct. 2704, 97 L.Ed.2d 37 (1987).

58. *Id.* at 45.

59. *Id.*

60. *Id.* at 47.

61. *Id.*

62. *Id.* at 48.

63. *Id.* at 51; *see also* Harris v. New York, 401 U.S. 222, 91 S.Ct. 643, 28 L.Ed.2d 1 (1971) ("Every criminal defendant is privileged to testify in his own defense, or to refuse to do so.").

64. *Rock,* 483 U.S. at 58–60.

evidence, especially when procedural safeguards such as those articulated in *Hurd* are employed. In addition, confidence in the evidence is increased when other evidence corroborates the facts refreshed through hypnosis.[65] The *Rock* Court concluded as follows:

> The State would be well within its powers if it established guidelines to aid trial courts in the evaluation of posthypnosis testimony and it may be able to show that testimony in a particular case is so unreliable that exclusion is justified. But it has not shown that hypnotically enhanced testimony is always so untrustworthy and so immune to the traditional means of evaluating credibility that it should disable a defendant from presenting her version of the events for which she is on trial.[66]

Although *Rock* merely carved an exception into the majority rule of *per se* exclusion for the defendant's own hypnotically refreshed recollection, this holding has reverberated more broadly. For example, in *Zani v. State*,[67] the court considered the admissibility of hypnotically refreshed testimony in a case in which the prosecutor's only witness selected the defendant's picture from a photo spread after a hypnosis session. After fully reviewing the case authority in this area, the court expressed the desire to follow the majority view of *per se* exclusion: "Were we writing on an entirely clean slate we would be inclined to hold that it has not been shown that hypnosis is a generally accepted means of refreshing memory that is *either* historically accurate *or* comparable in accuracy to pristine recollection."[68] However, in light of *Rock,* the court felt constrained from reaching this conclusion. The court appreciated that the United States Constitution would allow a one-way exclusionary rule.[69] Nonetheless, the court concluded that "we are unwilling to impose such a rule of exclusion unilaterally against the State."[70]

---

65. *Id.* at 60.

66. *Id.* at 61. *See also* State v. Woodfin, 539 So.2d 645 (La.App.1989) (holding that, under *Rock,* the defendant must still demonstrate that the hypnosis session adhered to the *Hurd* guidelines).

67. 758 S.W.2d 233 (Tex.Cr.App.1988).

68. *Id.* at 242 (emphasis in original).

69. *Id.* at 243.

70. *Id.* The *Zani* court held that "because of the uncertainties inherent in posthypnotic testimony it is appropriate to require the proponent of such testimony to demonstrate to the satisfaction of the trial court, outside the jury's presence, by clear and convincing evidence, that such testimony is trustworthy." *Id.*

In *Pruett v. Norris,* 959 F.Supp. 1066 (E.D.Ark.1997), *reversed on other grounds,* 153 F.3d 579 (8th Cir.1998), the defendant had been convicted for capital murder and sentenced to death. Among other claims of error, the defendant argued that the use of hypnotically refreshed recall at the sentencing phase violated his constitutional right of confrontation. The defendant had not been notified that the witness had undergone hypnosis. The district court agreed "that the admission of the hypnotically induced testimony violated [the defendant's] rights under the Confrontation Clause." *Id.* at 1081. Moreover, the lower court found that this error "was not harmless beyond a reasonable doubt." *Id.* at 1082. On appeal, however, the Eighth Circuit reversed, finding that any error committed here was harmless. Pruett v. Norris, 153 F.3d 579, 590 (8th Cir.1998). The district court in *Pruett* found that the prosecutor did not know that the witness had been hypnotized and was not to blame for failing to inform the defendant. *Pruett,* 959 F.Supp. at 1081. The court held that because the hypnosis had been conducted without procedural safeguards, it was "inherently unreliable." *Id.* at 1083. The court cited and quoted the procedural safeguards described in *Sprynczynatyk v. General Motors Corp.,* 771 F.2d 1112, 1123 n. 14 (8th Cir. 1985):

(1) The hypnotic session should be conducted by an impartial licensed psychiatrist or psychologist trained in the use of hypnosis and thus aware of its possible effects on memory; (2) information given to the hypnotist by either party concerning the case should be noted; (3) before hypnosis, the hypnotist should obtain a detailed description of the facts from the subject; (4) the session should be recorded so a permanent record is available; (5) preferably only the hypnotist and subject should be present.

In another post-*Rock* constitutional analysis, the court in *Burral v. State*[71] was presented with the question whether the "reasoning of the Court is equally applicable to a defendant's Sixth Amendment right to present other witnesses in his own defense."[72] The court concluded that the answer was no, finding "no language in Rock, or in any subsequent Supreme Court decision, to support [this] argument."[73] The *Burral* court's conclusion appears to be supported by *United States v. Scheffer*.[74] In *Scheffer*, the Court held that a *per se* rule excluding polygraph evidence did not violate a defendant's Sixth Amendment rights. This holding was largely premised on the reasonableness of the government's conclusion that polygraph evidence was insufficiently reliable to be admitted.[75] The Court, moreover, distinguished *Rock*, since there the *per se* rule excluded the only witness who had first-hand knowledge, a witness who also happened to be the defendant. Hypnosis shares similar reliability problems to that of polygraphs and might suffer the same fate. *Scheffer*, however, can be distinguished on the basis that polygraph testimony provides evidence about the credibility of other evidence whereas hypnotically refreshed recall sometimes might be the only evidence available. Hypnotically refreshed testimony is more likely to survive a necessity analysis than polygraphs.

§ 9–1.4   Conclusion

Hypnotically refreshed testimony presents formidable difficulties for courts. One immediate concern is what rules of evidence regulate this kind of evidence. Courts have varied in their responses to this matter, with some viewing admissibility as a matter of the competency of witnesses and general standards of relevancy and unfair prejudice, while other courts subject this testimony to rules controlling expert testimony. The former strategy results in a somewhat more lenient response to the evidence, though courts typically

---

Pruett, 959 F.Supp. at 1083 n.18 (*citing Sprynczynatyk*, 771 F.2d at 1123 n.14). In addition, the court found substantial inconsistencies between the witness's statements before and after hypnosis. *Id.* at 1082. The Eighth Circuit, however, disagreed. It stated that "[t]he admission of hypnotically refreshed testimony does not invariably result in constitutional error." *Pruett*, 153 F.3d at 589. The appellate court assumed, without deciding, that an error had occurred, but concluded that under the circumstances presented in this case any such error was harmless. In particular, the court pointed to the basic similarity between the witness's pre-and post-hypnotic statements. *Id.* at 590. Accordingly, "any error resulting from the post-hypnotic testimony was harmless beyond a reasonable doubt." *Id.*

71. 118 Md.App. 288, 702 A.2d 781 (Md. App.1997). On appeal, the Maryland Court of Appeals affirmed the conclusion and the reasoning of the lower court:

> *Rock v. Arkansas* obviously stands as a Constitutionally-based exception to the predominant rule that testimony based on hypnotically enhanced recollections is not admissible, but we find no Constitutional

requirement to extend that exception to other defense witnesses. . . .

> The *Rock* Court's reference to the right of compulsory process can be given proper effect without extending it beyond what we believe was intended. That reference . . . was only one of three sources cited by the Court as establishing the right of a defendant to testify in his or her own defense. The other two—the due process right to be heard in one's own defense and the Fifth Amendment right to testify or not—are peculiar to defendants. No other court in the country has so extended the *Rock* holding on a constitutional basis, and in light of the Supreme Court's own expressed limitation, we shall not be the first to do so.

Burral v. State, 352 Md. 707, 724 A.2d 65, 81–82 (Md.1999).

72. *Id.* at 786.

73. *Id.*

74. 523 U.S. 303, 118 S.Ct. 1261, 140 L.Ed.2d 413 (1998).

75. *Id.* at 1265.

insist that the admissibility determination does not depend on the rule under which the evidence is evaluated.

Courts have divided into four camps regarding the admissibility of hypnotically refreshed testimony. A small group of states holds that this testimony is generally admissible and leave it to the jury to determine what weight, if any, it should receive. Many courts, including most federal courts, apply a flexible, case-by-case, standard, and determine admissibility on the basis of the totality of the circumstances surrounding the proffered evidence. A third group allows hypnotically refreshed testimony only if a stringent set of guidelines were followed in conducting the hypnosis session, with the proponent further bearing the burden of demonstrating admissibility by clear and convincing evidence. Finally, the majority of states apply a *per se* rule of exclusion for hypnotically refreshed testimony. Two important exceptions, however, attach to this exclusionary approach. First, these courts typically permit formerly hypnotized witnesses to testify to facts known and recorded prior to the hypnosis session. Second, the United States Supreme Court held in *Rock v. Arkansas* that the Constitution prohibits courts from applying a *per se* rule to exclude criminal defendants from testifying in their own defense; the Court, however, did find that specific circumstances might mandate exclusion and observed that states might still establish guidelines to regulate hypnosis sessions intended to produce evidence for trial.

B.   SCIENTIFIC STATUS

by

Michael Nash* & Robert Nadon**

§ 9–2.0 THE SCIENTIFIC STATUS OF RESEARCH ON HYPNOSIS

§ 9–2.1 Introductory Discussion of the Science

§ 9–2.1.1 The Scientific Questions

For over two centuries scientists and clinicians have noted that some people, when exposed to a variety of procedures that involve suggestion, undergo sometimes dramatic and rapid transformations in behavior, percep-

* Michael Nash, Ph.D., is Associate Professor at the University of Tennessee and is actively engaged in clinical training, research, and teaching. He is Editor in Chief of the INTERNATIONAL JOURNAL OF CLINICAL AND EXPERIMENTAL HYPNOSIS, Past President of Division 30 of the American Psychological Association, Fellow of both the Society for Clinical and Experimental Hypnosis and the American Psychological Association, and is a Diplomate of the American Board of Professional Psychology. Dr. Nash has published extensively on the effects of sexual abuse, short-term psychotherapy, and hypnosis. Dr. Nash is Co–Editor with Dr. Fromm of the classic text on experimental hypnosis, CONTEMPORARY HYPNOSIS RESEARCH, and his re-

search and writing have earned him numerous awards.

** Robert Nadon, Ph.D., is Associate Professor of Psychology at Brock University in St. Catharines, Ontario, Canada. Actively engaged in both research and teaching, Dr. Nadon has published extensively on hypnosis, with particular interest in personality and methodological issues. He is a Fellow of the Society for Clinical and Experimental Hypnosis, a past Research Fellow of the Canadian Social Sciences and Humanities Research Council, an Advisory Editor for the INTERNATIONAL JOURNAL OF CLINICAL AND EXPERIMENTAL HYPNOSIS, and a Consultant Editor, for CONTEMPORARY HYPNOSIS.

tion, and cognition. The scientific community has defined a subset of these changes as hypnosis. Our understanding of the nature of these changes has evolved over decades of empirical work to the point where there is now a considerable amount of consensus within the scientific community as to the nature of hypnosis, the determinants of hypnotic response, and the psychological mechanisms which define hypnotic responsiveness. Although areas of disagreement exist, the general descriptive domain of hypnosis has remained relatively consistent. When a subject responds successfully to hypnosis he can elicit a host of experiences and behaviors including: motor anomalies, the creation of hallucinations, absence of pain (anesthesia), age regression, posthypnotic amnesia, and posthypnotic suggestion. For the most part subjects experience these events as compellingly genuine, taking place without their conscious participation. The domain of hypnosis is further enriched by the clinical application of hypnotic technique with medical and psychological problems including major burns, anxiety disorders, phobias, psychophysiological disorders, stress disorders, and childbirth, to name just a few.

For the purposes of scientific study it is important to move from a general familiarity with hypnosis to a more precise definition of what it is, and what it is not.

[1] What Is Hypnosis?

A concise, integrative definition of hypnosis, is derived from the work of Nadon, Laurence, and Perry (1991). Simply put, hypnosis is a situation in which subjects attempt to rally (usually with the encouragement of a therapist or experimenter) certain cognitive abilities in order to successfully alter normal cognitive functioning in accordance with the given suggestions [1] The degree to which the subjects are successful depends on the implicit and explicit demands of the hypnotic context, their beliefs and attitudes toward hypnosis, and toward the hypnotist, and the degree to which they utilize certain relevant cognitive skills. It is important to note here that Nadon et al. first define a "situation," not a product. According to this definition, whether (and to what extent) a person actually becomes hypnotized is dependent upon the subject's relative capacity to rally relevant cognitive abilities.

[2] When Is a Person Hypnotized?

Earlier researchers argued that a subject is hypnotized after the hypnotic "induction" (i.e., a set of instructions administered by the hypnotist which invites the subject to become "hypnotized" and to experience suggestions fully).[2] According to this view, the subject's subjective experiences in response to the induction and to the suggestions are irrelevant to determining whether he was hypnotized. Though use of a hypnotic induction is the traditional practice, and though there is some merit in this definition, it is clear now that a formal hypnotic induction is not a sufficient condition for a person to be

§ 9–2.0

1. Robert Nadon, Jean–Roch Laurence & Campbell Perry, *The Two Disciplines of Scientific Hypnosis: A Synergistic Model, in* THEORIES OF HYPNOSIS: CURRENT MODELS AND PERSPECTIVES 485–519 (Steven J. Lynn & Judith W. Rhue eds., 1991).

2. THEODORE X. BARBER, HYPNOSIS: A SCIENTIFIC APPROACH (1969).

hypnotized. For instance, no matter what induction procedures might be employed, hypnosis does not take place if 1) the subject does not wish to be hypnotized or 2) the subject does not possess the ability to experience hypnosis. As we will discuss later, hypnotizability (or hypnotic responsiveness) is a fairly enduring characteristic of an individual, which does not change significantly over time. It is agreed among scientists that subjects of differing hypnotic ability report dramatically different experiences following a hypnotic induction. Individuals who are low hypnotizables report few, if any, of the cognitive, perceptual, and personal experiences commonly associated with being hypnotized. In contrast, highly hypnotizable subjects respond to induction in sometimes dramatic ways, easily identifiable as falling within the domain of hypnosis. For investigative purposes then, hypnosis can be conveniently operationalized as what takes place after a hypnotic induction with a willing and responsive subject. Outside of the laboratory, however, the situation can be complicated by the fact that *de facto* hypnotic inductions may be presented under different labels, such as "guided imagery" or "relaxation therapy." For these techniques to be considered "hypnotic," an induction of some type, usually but not necessarily including suggestions for relaxation, would be followed by other suggestions.

But if a hypnotic induction is not a sufficient condition for hypnosis, neither is it necessary.[3] People who are very high in hypnotic responsiveness sometimes require no formal induction to become hypnotized. This is especially true for highly responsive subjects who have been hypnotized before and who have practiced a number of times. At the same time, it is important to stress that as a matter of definition most scientists agree that for hypnosis to occur without a formal induction the context must be defined as hypnotic. This nuance distinguishes the views of most scientists from those of clinicians, many of whom argue that individuals can be in a "hypnotic trance" virtually at will if the situation calls for it to be used as a "defense mechanism" (e.g., during physical or sexual abuse). This belief led one prominent practitioner to argue publicly that an abuser's threat to kill the victim if he reports the abuse is a hypnotic suggestion for posthypnotic amnesia. This type of musing presented as fact by fiat is not only impossible to investigate empirically, it reflects a definition of hypnosis so broad that it can encompass virtually any idea that strikes the clinician's fancy. Spontaneously occurring mental states (both pathological and non-pathological) may superficially resemble hypnosis, but it is the convention within the scientific community to delimit hypnosis to interactions which are defined by the participants (or at least by the subject) as hypnosis.

Thus, the hypnotic situation involves an attempt to alter usual cognitive functioning, it does not insure it. There is consensus among researchers that for investigative purposes hypnosis can be conveniently operationalized in part as what takes place after a hypnotic induction with a willing and hypnotizable subject. But at the same time, the field recognizes that the essence of what it means to be "in hypnosis" is more precisely understood in terms of changes in behavior, cognition, and experience rather than as mere

---

3. Kenneth S. Bowers & Paul Kelly, *Stress, Disease, Psychotherapy, and Hypnosis,* 88 J.   ABNORMAL PSYCHOL. 490 (1979).

antecedent event. The utility of the Nadon, Laurence, and Perry definition is in its recognition of this fact.

[3] The Research Foundation in Hypnosis

Hypnosis has been the topic of a robust research literature for over 100 years, dating back to the very inception of neurology, psychiatry, and psychology.[4] Over the last 30 years there has been more than 4,500 articles on hypnosis in the professional and scientific literatures. About half of these are treatises on the specifics of treatment application and the other half are controlled laboratory and clinical research studies.[5] These articles appear in a host of different medical journals, psychological journals, and interdisciplinary journals, including the most prestigious scientific journals in the world. Thus, each year about 150 hypnosis articles appear in the mainstream medical science, psychological science, and general science journals. When compared to many other sub-areas in psychiatry and psychology (psychotherapy, psychoanalysis, family therapy) the hypnosis literature is characterized by a much higher percentage of articles devoted to controlled empirical investigation, and a broader dissemination across the scientific literature.[6] One result of this activity has been the formal recognition of hypnosis as a viable medical and psychological treatment by the American Medical Association[7] and the American Psychological Association among others.

[4] The Scientific Questions

Almost all general theorists in psychiatry and psychology have attempted to explain hypnosis according to their own model of the mind. Without going into the sometimes arcane nuances differentiating various contemporary approaches to this problem, it is possible to discern two broadly competing theoretical perspectives which nonetheless converge on several important points. There are those theorists who posit that there is a discernible shift in cognitive functioning among some subjects during hypnosis which accounts for the altered behavior and experience produced by suggestion.[8] These theorists also stress the importance of innate hypnotic ability as the primary determinant of what a subject does and experiences during hypnosis. On the other hand, there are theorists who view hypnotic responding as fundamentally similar to other social interactions which involve role playing and self-

---

4. HENRI F. ELLENBERGER, THE DISCOVERY OF THE UNCONSCIOUS (1970).

5. Michael R. Nash et al., *Twenty Years of Scientific Hypnosis in Dentistry, Medicine, and Psychology: A Brief Communication*, 36 INT'L J. CLINICAL & EXPERIMENTAL HYPNOSIS (1988).

6. Michael R. Nash, The Scientific Status of Hypnosis (Aug. 1994) (unpublished manuscript presented at the meeting of the American Psychological Association, Los Angeles, on file with the author).

7. American Medical Association, *Medical Use of Hypnosis*, 168 J. AM. MED. ASS'N. 186 (1958).

8. *See, e.g.*, Eric Z. Woody & Kenneth S. Bowers, *A Frontal Assault on Dissociated Control, in* DISSOCIATION: CLINICAL, THEORETICAL AND RESEARCH PERSPECTIVES 52 (Steven J. Lynn & Judith W. Rhue eds., 1994); HERBERT SPIEGEL & DAVID SPEIGEL, TRANCE AND TREATMENT: CLINICAL USES OF HYPNOSIS (1978); Earnest R. Hilgard, *Dissociation and Theories of Personality, in* CONTEMPORARY HYPNOSIS RESEARCH 69 (Erika Fromm & Michael Nash eds., 1992); Erika Fromm, *An Ego–Psychological Theory of Hypnosis, in* CONTEMPORARY HYPNOSIS RESEARCH 131 (Erika Fromm & Michael Nash eds., 1992).

deception.[9] These theorists acknowledge that innate ability may play some modest role in determining hypnotic response, but contend that immediate social cues are far more important. Of course, there is a great deal of conceptual "middle ground" between these two positions, a middle ground which is indeed occupied by most scientists.

For the purposes of this chapter, we have defined four classes of hypnosis research questions which we believe capture the general focus of the field. Within each class we enumerate questions for which there is consensual agreement within the scientific community (Section II) and questions for which there is substantial and important disagreement (Section III).

[a] Personality and Hypnosis

The single most important breakthrough in hypnosis research occurred in the late 1950's and early 1960's at Stanford University. Ernest Hilgard and André Weitzenhoffer developed, standardized and normed the Stanford Hypnotic Susceptibility Scales.[10] As a result, there was an explosion of research activity, much of it addressing the trait of hypnotic susceptibility and its relationship to personality as a whole. An enduring research tradition emerged which examined the following questions:

i.   Is hypnotic responsiveness stable? (substantial agreement).

ii. What accounts for an individual's responsiveness to hypnosis? (substantial agreement).

iii. What kind of people respond well (and what kind respond poorly) to hypnosis? (substantial agreement).

iv. Does the stability of hypnotic responsiveness reflect primarily an enduring personality trait or does it reflect primarily stability of the testing context? (substantial disagreement).

v.   Are personality, social, and cognitive factors implicated in hypnotic responsiveness best understood in additive terms or do their respective weights depend on the person's level of hypnotic responsiveness? (substantial disagreement).

[b] The Effects of Hypnosis on Behavior, Physiology, and Experience

Once armed with more precisely refined indices of hypnotic responsiveness, researchers were better able to pursue the nature and limits of hypnotic response. Turn-of-the-century medical speculation and media-generated sensationalism had led to some grossly excessive beliefs about hypnosis among the lay and professional communities alike. As contemporary researchers began to very carefully "dissect" the hypnotic situation (to discern what

9. *See, e.g.*, Nicholas P. Spanos & William C. Coe, *A Social–Psychological Approach to Hypnosis, in* CONTEMPORARY HYPNOSIS RESEARCH 102 (Erika Fromm & Michael Nash eds., 1992); Irving Kirsch & James R. Council, *Situational and Personality Correlates of Hypnotic Responsiveness, in* CONTEMPORARY HYPNOSIS RESEARCH 267 (Erika Fromm & Michael Nash eds., 1992);

Steven J. Lynn & Harry Sivec, *The Hypnotizable Subject as Creative Problem–Solving Agent, in* CONTEMPORARY HYPNOSIS RESEARCH 292 (Erika Fromm & Michael Nash eds., 1992).

10. ANDRÉ M. WEITZENHOFFER & ERNEST R. HILGARD, STANFORD HYPNOTIC SUSCEPTIBILITY SCALE, FORMS A AND B (1959).

actually does, and does not, happen during hypnosis) the wheat came to be separated from the chaff. The three domains across which some effect for hypnosis might be found are behavior, physiology, and subjective experience.

  i. Does hypnosis have a neurophysiological signature? (substantial agreement).

  ii. Are hypnotic subjects passive or active participants? (substantial agreement).

  iii. Does hypnosis enable subjects to transcend volitional capacity? (substantial agreement).

  iv. To what extent do increases in hypnotic responsiveness induced by laboratory procedures reflect temporary behavioral compliance as opposed to more enduring changes in level of responsiveness? (substantial disagreement).

  v. Do behaviors and reports of subjective experience that phenotypically resemble those found in hypnosis, but which were not preceded by a hypnotic induction, reflect hypnotic or nonhypnotic processes? (substantial disagreement).

  vi. Is there a causal link between early trauma, dissociative pathology, and high hypnotizability? (substantial disagreement).

[c] Memory, Responsibility, and Certainty

For well over a century hypnosis had been believed to engender dramatic changes in memory and responsibility which were of particular relevance in the courtroom as well as in the psychiatric consulting room.[11] A very active research literature has developed to empirically address these vital issues, with questions falling into two broad areas:

  i. Does hypnotizing a subject increase accuracy of memory? How does hypnosis affect the subject's ability to distinguish fantasy from fact? How does it affect the subject's confidence? (substantial agreement).

  ii. Are hypnotized subjects in control of their behavior during and after hypnosis? Can they be made to do things against their will? (substantial agreement).

[d] Clinical Efficacy

There is a final domain of research activity which addresses the purported effectiveness of hypnosis in the treatment of a host of medical and psychological problems. With changes in the health care environment, a premium has been placed on accountability as mental health professionals attempt to understand what treatments work best, for what type of patients, with what types of problems. There has been a great deal of clinical research addressing the following questions:

  i. When used properly, is hypnosis an effective intervention with medically and/or psychologically disordered patients? When is hypnosis indicated? When is it not indicated? (substantial agreement).

11. *See, e.g.,* JEAN-ROCH LAURENCE & CAMPBELL PERRY, HYPNOSIS, WILL, AND MEMORY: A PSY-CHO-LEGAL HISTORY (1988).

ii. When employed clinically, are there negative side-effects of hypnosis? (substantial agreement).

§ 9–2.1.2 The Scientific Methods Applied in the Research

Scientific study of hypnosis has been conducted exclusively with human subjects; so-called "animal hypnosis" is an entirely different phenomenon. There is a rich tradition of carefully designed and controlled laboratory and field research in hypnosis which meets the exacting standards of scientific rigor. Because anecdotal and single case studies of hypnotic phenomena have failed to meet these same standards we base our analysis on the research literature only.

[1] Scientifically Reliable and Valid Measurement of Hypnotic Response

Observations that people differ in their general level of responsiveness to hypnotic procedures date back to the 18th century. Systematic attempts to measure hypnotic responsiveness began in the 19th century with Braid (1843) and Bernheim (1889) leading the way.[12] The single most important breakthrough in modern hypnosis research, however, occurred in the late 1950's and early 1960's at Stanford University where the Stanford Hypnotic Susceptibility Scales, Forms A, B, and C (SHSS: A,B,C) were developed, standardized, and normed.[13]

The Stanford scales are administered to individual subjects and involve rigorously standardized hypnotic induction procedures (a set of instructions administered by the hypnotist that invites the subject to become hypnotized and which typically includes suggestions for relaxation and for full experience of suggestions during the session). The induction is followed by a series of 12 suggestions to which the subject either responds behaviorally or not. If the subject responds behaviorally to the suggestion, he passes that item. If the subject does not respond to the suggestion, he fails that item. The subject's score is the total number of items (or suggestions) passed. Thus scores on these test can range from 0 (no items passed) to 12 (all items passed) with individuals scoring on the lower end of the spectrum being less "hypnotizable", and those at the upper end being more hypnotizable. More people score in the mid range (5–7) than in the low (0–4) or high (8–12) ranges. Most people (95%) can experience hypnosis to some extent. The scientific importance of the development of the Stanford scales was immense. As noted by Perry, Nadon, and Button (1992), "at last the field had a uniform yardstick, against which experimental studies from different investigators could be gauged."[14]

Although the hypnotic suggestions present in the Stanford (and other) scales have defied precise statistical categorization, researchers have found it useful to distinguish among ideomotor suggestions (e.g., an extended arm that

12. LAURENCE & PERRY, HYPNOSIS, WILL, & MEMORY, *supra* note 11.

13. WEITZENHOFFER & HILGARD, Stanford Hypnotic Scale, *supra* note 10; ANDRÉ M. WEITZENHOFFER & ERNEST R. HILGARD, STANFORD HYPNOTIC SUSCEPTIBILITY SCALE, FORM C (1962).

14. Campbell Perry et al., *The Measurement of Hypnotic Ability, in* CONTEMPORARY HYPNOSIS RESEARCH 459, 460 (Erika Fromm & Michael Nash eds., 1992).

becomes unbearably heavy and moves down); challenge suggestions (e.g., hands that become so tightly interlocked that they can not be separated, despite being "challenged" to do so); cognitive suggestions (e.g., amnesia), and perceptual suggestions (e.g., visual or auditory hallucinations). Almost everyone can respond positively to at least some ideomotor suggestions. Challenge suggestions are more difficult. Cognitive and perceptual suggestions are the most difficult suggestions to pass; depending on the suggestion, no more than approximately 15% of the population is capable of passing this type of suggestion. Typically, a person who responds to at least some of the cognitive or perceptual suggestions will respond to the less difficult ideomotor and challenge suggestions; similarly, a person who responds to the challenge suggestions (but not to the cognitive or perceptual ones) will generally respond to ideomotor suggestions.

While the Stanford Scales (especially Form C) remain somewhat of a "gold standard" in hypnosis research, numerous other scales have been developed for various practical and theoretical reasons (see Table 1).[15] For example, two scales have been developed specifically to facilitate hypnosis of groups of people: the Harvard Group Scale of Hypnotic Susceptibility, Form A (HGSHS: A; based on SHSS: A and SHSS: B)[16] and the Waterloo–Stanford Group C Scale of Hypnotic Susceptibility (WSGC; based on SHSS: C)[17]. The Stanford Hypnotic Clinical Scale for Adults (SHCS: Adult)[18] and the Hypnotic Induction Profile (HIP)[19] were developed for administration in clinical contexts. The Computer Assisted Hypnosis Scale[20] was developed for computer-aided administration. Based on more theoretical grounds, the induction of the group-administered seven-item Carleton University Responsiveness to Suggestion Scale (CURSS)[21] informs subjects that "Your ability to be hypnotized depends entirely on your willingness to cooperate" in contrast to the Stanford Scales which represent hypnosis as involving both ability and willingness to cooperate.[22]

15. For overviews of the available scales, see PERRY et al., Hypnotic Ability, *supra* note 14, at 459; PETER W. SHEEHAN & KEVIN M. MCCONKEY, HYPNOSIS AND EXPERIENCE: THE EXPLORATION OF PHENOMENA AND PROCESS (1982).

16. RONALD E. SHOR & EMILY C. ORNE, HARVARD GROUP SCALE OF HYPNOTIC SUSCEPTIBILITY, FORM A (1962)

17. Kenneth S. Bowers, *The Waterloo–Stanford group C Scale of Hypnotic Susceptibility: Normative and Comparative Data*, 41 INT'L J. CLINICAL & EXPERIMENTAL HYPNOSIS 35 (1993); *see also*, WEITZENHOFFER & HILGARD, FORM C, *supra* note 13.

18. Arlene H. Morgan & Josephine R. Hilgard, *The Stanford Hypnotic Clinical Scale For Adults and Children*, 21 AM. J. CLINICAL HYPNOSIS 134 (1978–79).

19. HERBERT SPIEGEL & A.A. BRIDGER, MANUAL FOR THE HYPNOTIC INDUCTION PROFILE (1970); Herbert Spiegel, *The Grade 5 Syndrome: The Highly Hypnotizable Person*, 22 INTERNATIONAL J. CLINICAL & EXPERIMENTAL HYPNOSIS, 303–319 (1974).

20. Carol D. Grant & Michael R. Nash, *The Computer Assisted Hypnosis Scale: Standardization and Norming of a Computer–Administered Measure of Hypnotic Ability*, 7 PSYCHOL. ASSESSMENT 49 (1995).

21. Nicholas P. Spanos et al., *The Carelton University Responsiveness to Suggestion Scale: Normative and Psychometric Properties*, 53 PSYCHOL. REPORTS 523 (1983).

22. Nicholas P. Spanos, *The Carleton University Responsiveness to Suggestion Scale (Group Administration)*, unpublished manuscript, Carleton University, Ottawa, Ontario, Canada.

TABLE 1

SCALE NAME	MODALITY	# OF ITEMS	DURATION	TYPICAL USES
The Stanford Hypnotic Susceptibility Scale (Forms A and B) Weitzenhoffer, A. M., & Hilgard, E. R. (1959). Stanford Hypnotic Susceptibility Scale. Forms A and B. Palo Alto, CA: Consulting Psychologists Press.	ADULT INDIVIDUAL	12	1 hr. 15 min	Used primarily in research as a preliminary screening devise to serve as a nonthreatening initial estimate of hypnotic responsivity. Sometimes used clinically for assessment.
The Stanford Hypnotic Susceptibility Scale (Form C) Weitzenhoffer, A. M., & Hilgard, E. R. (1962). Stanford Hypnotic Susceptibility Scale. Form C. Palo Alto, CA: Consulting Psychologists Press.	ADULT INDIVIDUAL	12	1 hr. 15 min	Generally used in research, and considered the touchstone against which all other measures of susceptibility are gauged. Some demanding items which give it more "top". More regressive items.
Stanford Profile Scales of Hypnotic Susceptibility (Forms I and II) Weitzenhoffer, A. M., & Hilgard, E. R. (1967). Revised Stanford Profile Scales of Hypnotic Susceptibility. Forms I and II. Palo Alto, CA: Consulting Psychologists Press.	ADULT INDIVIDUAL	12	1 hr. 30 min	The most thorough hypnotizability test yielding a profile of abilities for each subject. Some exceedingly difficult items. Rarely used in either research or clinical settings.
Stanford Clinical Hypnosis Scale (Adult and Child Forms). Morgan, A. H. & Hilgard, J. R. (1978-79). The Stanford Hypnotic Clinical Scale fro adults and children. American Journal of Clinical Hypnosis, 21, 134-169.	CHILD AND ADULT INDIVIDUAL	5	20min.	Brief 5-item versions of the Stanford Scales designed for clinical use. There is a form for children (ages 3-16) and adults.
Harvard Group Scale of Hypnotic Susceptibility (Forms A and B) Shor, R. E., & Orne, E. C. (1962). Harvard Group Scale of Hypnotic Susceptibility, Form A. Palo Alto, CA: Consulting Psychologists Press.	ADULT GROUP	12	1 hr. 15 min	Used in research as a preliminary screening device designed to serve as a nonthreatening initial estimate of hypnotic responsivity. A Relatively "easy" scales.
The Waterloo-Stanford Group C Scale of Hypnotic Susceptibility Bowers, K. S. (1993). The Waterloo-Stanford Group C Scale of Hypnotic Susceptibility: Normative and comparative data. International Journal of Clinical and Experimental Hypnosis. 41. 35-46.	ADULT INDIVIDUAL	12	1 hr. 15 min	Developed as a substitute for the Stanford C. Contains more difficult items than other group scales. Used exclusively for research.

Scale	Population	No.	Time	Description
The Computer Assisted Hypnosis Scale Grant, C. D. & Nash, M. R. (in press). The Computer Assisted Hypnosis Scale: Standardization and norming of a computer-administered measure of hypnotic ability. Psychological Assessment	ADULT INDIVIDUAL	12	1 hr. 15 min	Interactive computer software (for both MAC and DOS for Windows) which utilizes graphics and digital voice technology to administer and score a hypnotizability test. The items are similar to the Stanford C scale in content and difficulty. Research and clinical screening uses.
The Children's Hypnotic Susceptibility Scale London, P. (1963). The Children's Hypnotic Susceptibility Scale. Palo Alto, CA: Consulting Psychologists Press.	CHILD INDIVIDUAL	12	1 hr. 15 min	A modification of the Stanford A scale but modified for the understanding and behavior of children
Hypnotic Induction Profile Spiegel, H. & Bridger, A. A. (1970). Manual for the Hypnotic Induction Profile. New York: Soni Medica.	ADULT INDIVIDUAL	5	10 min	A scale using extent of eye roll, arm levitation, involuntariness, dissociation, and ability to terminate hypnosis. A relatively easy scale employed clinically and in some research settings.
The Carleton University Responsiveness to Suggestion Scale Spanos, N. P., Radtke, H. L., Hodgins, D. C., Stam, H. J., & Bertrand, L. D. (1983). The Carleton University Responsiveness to Suggestion Scale: Normative data and psychometric properties. Psychological Reports, 53, 523-535.	ADULT GROUP OR INDIVIDUAL	7	30 min	A scale that yields four responsiveness subscores: behavioral, subjective, involuntariness, and compliance. Used almost exclusively in research settings.

Differences aside, all scales operate from the basic premise that hypnotic responsiveness is best measured by hypnotizing a subject, administering a series of suggestions which are either passed or failed, and adding the number of "passed" items to obtain a score. For these reasons, the various scales all appear to be tapping hypnotic phenomena to some degree. As with all measurement scales used in science and medicine, a person's score on a hypnosis scale reflects error to some degree. Nonetheless, all hypnosis scales currently in use by scientists meet accepted reliability and validity standards for scientific indices.

Other aspects of current scales are worth mentioning. Many contemporary scientists have altered in minor ways the exact wording of the inductions and suggestions of the older scales (like the Stanford scales) while nonetheless preserving the same intent conveyed in the original versions. For the most part, these wording changes reflect changing social sensibilities. For example, a phrase like "You will not wake up until I tell you to" from the original SHSS: C induction may be changed to "You will not wake up until I *ask* you to" (italics added).[23] Also, the original scoring criterion for the amnesia suggestions on the Stanford and other scales was the simple non-reporting of a specific number of suggestions that were administered during the session; most researchers, however, require that a subject first fails to report a specific number of suggestions when asked but then does so once the amnesia has been cancelled by a pre-arranged cue (e.g., the statement "Now you can remember everything.")[24] Finally, "tailored versions" of SHSS: C, in which one or two suggestions are replaced by other suggestions, are often used by researchers.[25] When the suggestions are replaced by other standardized and normed suggestions of equivalent difficulty, it is unlikely that there is any great threat to either the reliability or the validity of the total hypnotic response score. As Sheehan and McConkey caution, however, the adequacy of the measurement is uncertain when non-equivalent or non-standardized suggestions are used.[26]

The various aspects of hypnosis measurement outlined above reflect scientists' attempts to come to terms with the not always complementary theoretical tasks of (1) amalgamating laboratory and clinical concerns; (2) standardizing measurement while avoiding the perceived limitations of others' theoretical views; and (3) reconciling the need for measurement of overall hypnotic response with theoretical interest in responses to particular individual suggestions. For all these reasons, hypnotic scales are not entirely interchangeable: when a person's global hypnotic score is at issue, at least two assessments are recommended.

[2] The Simulation (Faking) of Hypnosis

What renders hypnotically suggested behavior so fascinating and instructive, is that it is not experienced by the subject as something actively achieved. To the contrary, its enactment is typically experienced by the subject as nonvolitional or effortless—as something that happens *to* the

---

23. WEITZENHOFFER & HILGARD, Form C, *supra* note 13, at 15.

24. John F. Kihlstrom & Patricia A. Register, *Optimal Scoring of Amnesia on the Harvard Group Scale of Hypnotic Susceptibility, Form A*, 32 INT'L J. CLINICAL & EXPERIMENTAL HYPNOSIS, 51–57 (1984).

25. Ernest R. Hilgard, Helen J. Crawford, Kenneth S. Bowers & John F. Kihlstrom, *A Tailored SHSS:C, Permitting User Modification for Special Purposes*, 27 INT'L. J. CLINICAL & EXPERIMENTAL HYPNOSIS 125 (1979).

26. SHEENAN & MCCONKEY, *supra* note 15.

subject (e.g. "my hand became heavy and moved down by itself"; "suddenly I found myself feeling no pain", "I can't bend my arm no matter how hard I try", or "I can't remember what happened just a moment ago"). Once established, an experimenter's attempts to challenge these impasses are typically unsuccessful, and there is ample empirical evidence using standard physiological indices of deception to rule out willful faking.[27]

Nevertheless, numerous studies from different laboratories have shown that properly motivated undergraduate college students with no formal training can successfully fake being the behavior of hypnotized subjects.[28] These studies, which incorporated what is known as the real/simulator design, have found that hypnosis researchers of varying expertise are equally unsuccessful at detecting simulating subjects, even when they know the proportion of simulators and genuine subjects that are in the study.[29]

Because determinations of whether a person is simulating hypnosis are necessarily based on reports from the subject and on other overt behaviors, a successful simulating performance merely requires that the subject either know in advance, or more typically be able to determine from the ongoing hypnotic session, what is the "correct" thing to do or say. Unfortunately, although the plethora of popular books on hypnosis convey a myriad of misconceptions about the underlying mechanisms of hypnosis, they do as a rule convey accurately how highly responsive hypnotized persons behave during hypnosis. Doubly unfortunate is the fact that what is expected of a hypnotized subject is invariably obvious (e.g., an arm lowering item of a hypnotic susceptibility scale typically includes wording like: "your arm is becoming heavy.... so heavy, that soon it will begin to move down.... heavier and heavier, moving down more and more"). All hypnosis—whether in a laboratory, clinical, or forensic context—requires that the hypnotist's suggestions be conveyed to the subject. Notwithstanding the theoretical difficulty of discerning the underlying psychological mechanisms implicated in results of these studies (indeed, proponents of various theories each claim support for their respective positions based on the same data), researchers agree that faking hypnotic responses well is a relatively straightforward matter, even for the uninitiated. There is currently no definitive way to discern if a subject being administered a hypnotic procedure is "really" hypnotized or if he is faking. Those who are faking can sometimes be identified because, like the bulk of malingerers, they "over-play" the role. An example is the notorious Hillside Strangler case.[30]

Kenneth Bianchi, who was eventually convicted of brutal serial killings, initially convinced a series of psychiatrists that he had a dual personality and that it was his "other personality" who had committed the murders. In a series of clever hypothesis testing procedures, Martin Orne was able to make

---

27. Kinnunen,-Taru; Zamansky,-Harold–S; Block,-Martin L, *Is the Hypnotic Subject Lying?* J. ABNORMAL PSYCHOL. 103, 184–192

28. Nicholas P. Spanos et al., *"Trance Logic" Duality and Hidden Observer Responding in Hypnotic, Imagination Control, and Simulating Subjects*, 94 J. ABNORMAL PSYCHOL. 611 (1985).

29. Martin T. Orne, *On the Simulating Subject as a Quasi–Control Group in Hypnosis*

Research: What, Why, and How, in HYPNOSIS: RESEARCH DEVELOPMENTS AND PERSPECTIVES 519–565 (Erika Fromm & R.E. Shor eds., 1972).

30. Martin T. Orne et al., *On the Differential Diagnosis of Multiple Personality in the Forensic Context* 32 INTERNATIONAL J. CLINICAL & EXPERIMENTAL HYPNOSIS, 118 (1984); State v. Bianchi, No. 79 10116 (Wash. Super. Ct. October 19, 1979).

a reasonable deduction that Bianchi was faking. Two examples will suffice to illustrate the approach.

In an early encounter, Orne told Bianchi that it was unusual to have only one additional "personality" in this type of case. Orne reasoned that if Bianchi was faking, an additional "personality" should soon appear, which indeed occurred. In another instance, Orne gave Bianchi the hypnotic suggestion to hallucinate his lawyer. Upon opening his eyes, Bianchi reported that he saw his lawyer standing close to him. At this point, it was impossible to know whether Bianchi was faking the hallucination or not. Bianchi, however, "over-acted" and went to shake the hallucinated lawyer's hand. It is typical of hallucinating subjects to remain passive. Indeed, this is likely typical behavior of individuals who experience any type of non-disease related hallucination.[31] These two instances were consistent with other indications that Bianchi was grossly over-playing a role, a behavioral pattern typical of people who feign medical and psychological disorders. Orne was thus able to make the reasonable deduction that Bianchi was feigning both multiple personality and hypnosis so that he might avoid the death penalty for his crimes.

More formally, using what has been called the Experiential Analysis Technique (EAT),[32] McConkey and his colleagues have conducted extensive research that suggests promising methods for the detection of simulation that go beyond assessment of over-acting. For example, simulating and genuinely highly responsive subjects in two studies received a suggestion for posthypnotic amnesia (that is, that they would experience amnesia for events that occurred during the hypnosis session once hypnosis was terminated). After hypnosis but while the amnesia suggestion was still in effect, the subjects were then shown a videotape of the hypnotic session. One striking finding of the studies is that genuine hypnotic subjects at times reported that they could recall the behaviors being shown on the video but not the subjective experiences they felt during those behaviors. In one study, thirty-seven percent[33] and in another 31 percent[34] of genuine highly responsiveness subjects who showed amnesia by standardized criteria made this behavior/experience distinction. By contrast, none of the simulating subjects in either study made that distinction.

[3] Research Design and Methodology

Scientists have used correlational and experimental research designs in laboratory and clinical contexts. As with most psychological research, laboratory studies are typically conducted with university undergraduate students. Not surprisingly, clinical studies have more diversified subject populations, although many clinical studies are also conducted with university undergraduate students. Historically, however, the distribution of hypnotic responsiveness among the general population has been remarkably consistent, despite major differences in the measurement of hypnosis and despite extensive

31. DANIEL C. DENNETT, CONSCIOUSNESS EXPLAINED (1991).

32. SHEENAN & MCCONKEY, HYPNOSIS AND EXPERIENCE, *supra* note 15.

33. Kevin M. McConkey, Peter W. Sheehan, Darryl G. Cross, *Posthypnotic Amnesia:*

Seeing Is Not Remembering, 19 BRIT. J. SOC. & CLINICAL PSYCHOL. 99 (1980).

34. Kevin M. McConkey & Peter W. Sheehan, *The Impact of Videotape Playback of Hypnotic Events on Posthypnotic Amnesia,* 90 J. ABNORMAL PSYCHOL. 46 (1981).

cultural and geographical differences in the populations.[35] Accordingly, there is little reason to think that hypnosis research with university students does not generalize to the general population, although how "general population" is defined depends on the particular area of study. It would be difficult, for example, to argue that the results of a study on hypnosis and memory conducted with university students would generalize to people of retirement age because of the known effects of aging on memory.

It is an axiom of research methodology that "correlation does not imply causation." What is often not appreciated is that the axiom refers to research designs and not to the particular statistical test conducted on the data. Regardless of the statistical test used, a correlational design is one in which the quantitative relationship between at least two variables that have not been subjected to manipulation by the researcher is assessed. By contrast, an experimental design is one in which the relationship between at least one manipulated variable and another variable is assessed. Researchers can infer causality with more certainty with an experimental design.

Most modern hypnosis research combines correlational and experimental methodologies,[36] what Cronbach called the two disciplines of scientific psychology.[37] Because a person's score on a standardized hypnosis scale is what it is and is not manipulated by the experimenter, it forms the correlational part of most hypnosis studies. From a scientific stance, it becomes difficult to say that a person's global hypnotic responsiveness caused a particular response to a new hypnotic suggestion. It may be that a person's ability to respond to the new suggestion may actually be the cause of their overall responsiveness. Another possibility is that a third variable (e.g., a particular gene or gene pattern) may cause them both.

While technically it is less difficult to infer cause from experimental components of hypnosis studies (e.g., different effects of suggestions when two groups of randomly assigned subjects are given different sets of instructions), the psychological mechanisms underlying experimental effects may be anything but obvious. Indeed, it is in the interpretation of experimental effects where there is most disagreement among hypnosis scientists.

As already discussed, part of the difficulty is that for the most part the intent of hypnotic suggestions is obvious. As discussed by Orne,[38] even when what is required is not patently obvious, subjects are often able to discern the intent from various factors, including subtle cues (known as demand characteristics) from the experimenter and the experimental context. It is possible to separate two testing contexts (one in which hypnosis is assessed and one in which some other psychological or physiological phenomenon of interest is assessed) as far as the subjects are concerned and thereby minimize demand characteristic influences. This type of study, however, is limited to making

35. C. Perry, R. Nadon & J. Button, *The Measurement of Hypnotic Ability, in* CONTEMPORARY HYPNOSIS RESEARCH (E. Fromm & M.R. Nash eds. 1992).

36. Robert Nadon, *Individual Differences and Hypnosis.* Manuscript submitted for publication (1995). Brock University, St. Catharines, Ontario, Canada.

37. Lee J. Cronbach, *The Two Disciplines of Scientific Psychology,* 12 AM. PSYCHOLOGIST 671 (1957).

38. Martin T. Orne, *On the Social Psychology of the Psychological Experiment: With Particular Reference to Demand Characteristics and Their Implications,* 17 AM. PSYCHOLOGIST 776 (1962).

generalizations about hypnotic responsiveness as an individual characteristic. Minimizing demands when hypnosis *per se* is investigated is more difficult because subjects of necessity are aware that the relation between hypnosis and some other phenomenon (e.g., memory) is being studied. Because of these difficulties inherent in much of hypnosis research, control and quasi-control procedures unique to hypnosis have been developed (real/simulator design[39] and task motivation design).[40] Other approaches to avoid this potential difficulty include obtaining measures in hypnosis other than mere self-report (such as a physiological index or performance on a cognitive task). Regardless of the care in which a single study is done, results in hypnosis research are often subject to different theoretical spins.

In sum, since the advent of reliable and valid scientific indices of hypnotic responsiveness in the late 1950's, the empirical work on hypnosis has, as a literature, conformed to scientific standards of careful control and observation. As a result, hypnosis research has come to be carried-out at scientific and medical research facilities around the world and scientific research reports are published in the most rigorously selective and influential journals in basic and applied science.

§ 9–2.2   Areas of Scientific Agreement

As is the case with any vital research area, there are some points about hypnosis on which scientists simply do not agree. Nevertheless, empirical study over many decades has yielded an extensive record of discoveries which have withstood the test of scientific scrutiny. On these fundamental principles of hypnosis there is broad agreement even among scientists from highly divergent theoretical perspectives and methodological orientations. Though some of the principles outlined below have not been embraced unanimously, they represent fairly non-controversial facts about which the overwhelming majority of informed scientists agree.

We must quickly note however that psychiatrists, psychologists, and other mental health professionals can be notoriously uninformed about scientific developments in their own fields. Thus, erroneous, even atavistic, opinions about psychotherapy in general, and hypnosis in particular, are occasionally espoused by these individuals in spite of sometimes incontrovertible scientific evidence to the contrary.

For example, a number of clinicians draw a distinction between "clinical hypnosis" and "experimental hypnosis."[41] While it is true that different contextual and inter-and intra-personal factors are at play during hypnosis conducted in the laboratory and hypnosis conducted in the clinic, scientists agree that effects of hypnosis *per se* can be and have been isolated. While the terms "clinical" versus "scientific" hypnosis serve at times as useful shorthand among professionals, scientists agree that hypnosis is the same basic phenomenon in both the laboratory and the clinic. Further, a substantial

---

39. Martin T. Orne, *On the Simulating Subject as a Quasi–Control Group in Hypnosis Research: What, Why, and How, in* HYPNOSIS: RESEARCH DEVELOPMENTS AND PERSPECTIVES 519–565 (E. Fromm & R.E. Shor eds., 1972).

40. BARBER, A SCIENTIFIC APPROACH, *supra* note 2.

41. For a discussion, *see* William C. Coe, *Hypnosis: Wherefore art thou?* 40 INTERNATIONAL J. CLINICAL & EXPERIMENTAL HYPNOSIS 219 (1992); John F. Kihlstrom, *Hypnosis: A Sesquicentennial Essay: Comment,* 40 INTERNATIONAL J. CLINICAL & EXPERIMENTAL HYPNOSIS 301 (1992).

proportion of hypnosis research is conducted in the clinical setting, with patients in hospitals, medical schools, and outpatient settings. The issue is then not "experimental versus clinical", but scientifically sound control versus casual anecdote. When we speak of broad areas of agreement, then, we are speaking of agreement within the scientific community.

§ 9–2.2.1 Principles Relating Hypnosis to Personality

[1] Hypnotic Responsiveness Is Stable

A person's ability to respond to hypnosis (termed hypnotic responsivity, hypnotizability, or hypnotic susceptibility) is remarkably stable over time. Perhaps the most compelling illustration of the stability of hypnotic susceptibility is the long term follow-up study on subjects first tested 10–25 years before the second test was administered.[42] Table 2 summarizes the results for 10–year, 15–year, and 25–year test intervals. Overall the test-retest reliability for the Stanford Hypnotic Susceptibility Scale, Form A is .71 across these three periods. In addition, the group averages change little over time. These combined results mean that a person's hypnotic susceptibility does not change much even over very extended periods. This kind of stability compares quite well with test-retest reliabilities for IQ tests. A 13 year test-retest reliability for the WAIS IQ test is reported as .73.[43] Further, there is strong evidence that hypnotic susceptibility may have an hereditary component, as indicated by substantial correlations of the scores of monozygotic twins as compared with dizygotic twins, with a resultant heritability index (h^2). of .62.[44] Nonetheless, as we discuss below, there is disagreement in the field about whether the stability of hypnotic responsiveness is due to personality traits or to more transient situational factors, and about the related (though not redundant question) of whether hypnotic responsiveness can be increased by laboratory training procedures.[45] Despite these theoretical disagreements, researchers agree that without any intrusive procedures to support change, hypnotic responsiveness scores are remarkably stable across time.

42. Carlos Piccione et al., *On the Degree of Stability of Measured Hypnotizability Over a 25–year Period,* 56 J. Personality & Soc. Psychol. 56 (1989).

43. J. Kangas & K. Bradway, *Intelligence at Middle Age: A Thirty–Eight Year Follow-up,* 5 Developmental Psychol. 333 (1971).

44. Arlene H. Morgan, *The Heritability of Hypnotic Susceptibility in Twins,* 82 J. Abnor-

mal Psychol. 55 (1973); Arlene H. Morgan et al., *EEG Alpha: Lateral Asymmetry Related to Task, and Hypnotizability,* 11 Psychophysiology 275 (1974).

45. Donald R. Gorassini & Nicholas P. Spanos, *A Social–Cognitive Skills Approach to the Successful Modification of Hypnotic Susceptibility,* 50 J. Personality & Soc. Psychol. 1004 (1986).

TABLE 2

TEST-RELATED CORRELATION COEFFICIENTS OF MEASURED HYPNOTIZABILITY (STANFORD HYPNOTIC SUSCEPTIBILITY SCALE, FORM A), FOR TOTAL SAMPLE AND BY SEX

Retest	Total (n = 50)	Male (n = 24)	Female (n = 26)
25 years (1960-1985)	.71	.69	.73
15 years (1970-1985)	.82	.82	.81
10 years (1960-1970)	.64	.62	.67

Note: All correlations are statistically significant, p less than .01, but no one correlation differs significantly from another, p greater than .05, two-tailed. From "On the Degree of Stability of Measured Hypnotizability over a 25-Year Period" (p. 291) by C. Piccione, E. R. Hilgard and P. G. Zimbardo, 1989, Journal of Personality and Social Psychology. 56, 289-295. Copyright 1989 by the American Psychological Association. Reprinted by permission.

[2] Hypnotic Responsiveness Depends More on the Efforts and Abilities of the Subject Than on the Skill of the Person Administering Hypnosis

The principal factor determining how fully a patient experiences hypnosis has almost nothing to do with therapist or experimenter technique, or any other hypnotist-related factor for that matter. Instead, how fully a patient or subject experiences hypnosis is predicted by his hypnotic ability which, as stated earlier, is fairly immutable over time. A highly responsive subject will become hypnotized under a host of experimental conditions and therapeutic settings. A low hypnotizable person will not. For all patients and subjects then, the extent to which they become hypnotized has more to do with what they bring to the session (e.g., ability, attitude, expectation) than with what the therapist does or says.

Learning to hypnotize someone is fairly easy. It is an elementary skill which can be learned through brief instruction, or simply reading sample inductions from a book.[46] Many clinicians (notably those who associate themselves with the teachings of Milton Erickson)[47] believe that suggestibility can be enhanced through special, and sometimes arcane induction techniques which purportedly "tap the unconscious" and thus increase suggestibility. There is no scientific evidence to support this claim. When these procedures have been studied in a controlled setting they have been found to have no effect on suggestibility beyond that which would be obtained through use of traditional inductions.[48]

Though learning to hypnotize someone is rather simple, learning to do hypnosis *therapeutically* is another matter. Here the therapist must marshal all of his clinical abilities. Empathy, conceptual rigor, theoretical sophistication, and technical savvy, are all necessary to maximally utilize the special aspects of hypnosis in service of the therapeutic goal—whether it be symptom removal or insight. Use of hypnosis does not, and cannot, make a poor therapist better. Its use in no way compensates for personal and professional limitations that the therapist brings to the consulting room. If anything, therapist limitations may be greater in sessions when hypnosis is used precisely because the pace and emotional intensity of the interaction can be so accelerated. The analogy to surgery seems apt; anyone can wield a scalpel so as to cut, but cutting *therapeutically* involves years of training and experience.

[3] The Ability to Experience Hypnosis Is Not Meaningfully Related to Personality

The idea that hypnotizability is related to some pattern of personality characteristics has been exhaustively examined over the past 30 years.[49] The results are clear. Hypnotizability is essentially unrelated to general personality characteristics including such things as gullibility, hysteria, general psychopathology, trust, aggressiveness, submissiveness, and religiosity. Nor is being hypnotically responsive the same thing as being suggestible in a global sense. Social suggestibility, often labeled conformity, is entirely unrelated to a person's ability to experience hypnosis.[50] Nor is hypnosis a species of placebo

---

46. Kirsch & Council, *supra* note 9.

47. STEPHEN LANKTON & CAROL LANKTON, THE ANSWER WITHIN: A CLINICAL FRAMEWORK OF ERICKSONIAN THERAPY (1983); E.L. ROSSI, THE PSYCHOBIOLOGY OF MIND-BODY HEALING: NEW CONCEPTS OF THERAPEUTIC HYPNOSIS (1986); MILTON H. ERICKSON, E.L. ROSSI, & S. ROSSI, HYPNOTIC REALITIES (1976).

48. Kirsch & Council, *supra* note 9.

49. ERNEST R. HILGARD, HYPNOTIC SUSCEPTIBILITY (1965); Kirsch & Council, *Hypnotic Responsiveness*, *supra* note 9.

50. Alisa Burns & Gordon Hammer, Hypnotizability and Amenability to Social Influence (Oct. 1970) (unpublished manuscript presented at the meeting for Clinical and Ex-

responding. McGlashan, Evans, and Orne convincingly demonstrated that placebo response is different from hypnotic response in nature and extent.[51] The correlations between hypnotic responsiveness and personality characteristics that do emerge in the literature are either not replicated or are of very meager explanatory value. An example of the latter case is the observation that a person's capacity for hypnotic responsiveness is related to the personality characteristic labeled variously as "absorption"[52] or "fantasy proneness"[53] and to other related psychological constructs.[54] The relation between hypnotic responsiveness and these personality characteristics, however, is primarily of theoretical interest because the correlations are so small. There is some new evidence that prediction of hypnotic responsiveness may be improved by combining the subject's scores on a number of personality measures.[55] Scientists agree however that the best way to discover a person's capacity for hypnosis is to hypnotize him and that an adequate theory of hypnosis must consider other factors.

It has been an enduring notion that good hypnotic subjects must be extraordinary good imagers: able to generate such compelling images that they sometimes mistake them for reality, or can become so engrossed in these images that they do not "process" events that might otherwise impinge on consciousness (e.g. pain). Two recent studies suggest that this is not the case. First, Glisky and his colleagues employed state-of-the-art measures of imaging ability, to test whether this ability is in any way (linearly or non-linearly) related to hypnotic response.[56] They found no relationship whatsoever. They did however leave open the possibility that better imagery instruments that tap a broader range of imagery abilities would allow a stronger correlation of those measures with hypnotizability. In order to pursue this possibility, Kogan and her colleagues correlated computer-generated imagery tasks which assess the ability to generate, maintain and transform images with hypnotizability to explore further the relationship between imagery ability and hypnotizability.[57] They hypothesized that these tasks would be better predictors of hypnotizability because they are more objective, repeatable and less prone to interpretation than self-report measures. This hypothesis was not borne-out by the data. Their null findings were similar to those of Glisky and his colleagues.

perimental Hypnosis, Philadelphia, on file with the author); R. K. Moore, *Susceptibility to Hypnosis and Susceptibility to Social Influence,* 68 J. ABNORMAL PSYCHOL. 55 (1964).

51. Thomas H. McGlashan et al., *The Nature of Hypnotic Analgesia and Placebo Response to Experimental Pain,* 31 PSYCHOSOMATIC MED. 227 (1969).

52. Auke Tellegen & Gilbert Atkinson, *Openness to Absorbing and Self—Altering Experiences ("Absorption"), a Trait Related to Hypnotic Susceptibility,* 83 J. ABNORMAL PSYCHOL. 268 (1974).

53. Steven J. Lynn & Judith W. Rhue, *Fantasy Proneness: Hypnosis, Developmental Antecedents, and Psychopathology,* 43 AM. PSYCHOLOGIST 35 (1988).

54. Robert Nadon et al., *Absorption and Hypnotizability: Context Effects Reexamined,* 60 J. PERSONALITY & SOC. PSYCHOL. 144 (1991); Suzanne M. Roche, & Kevin M. McConkey, *Absorption: Nature, Assessment, and Correlates,* 59 J. PERSONALITY & SOC. PSYCHOL. 91 (1990).

55. Robert Nadon et al., *Multiple Predictors of Hypnotic Susceptibility,* 53 J. PERSONALITY & SOC. PSYCHOL. 948 (1987).

56. M.L. Glisky, D.J. Tataryn, J.F. Kihlstrom, *Hypnotizability and Mental Imagery,* 43 INTERNATIONAL J. CLINICAL & EXPERIMENTAL HYPNOSIS 34 (1995).

57. M. Kogan et al., *Imagery and Hypnotizability Revisited,* 46 INTERNATIONAL J. CLINICAL & EXPERIMENTAL HYPNOSIS 363 (1998).

What is probable is that good imagery ability may to a degree be related to hypnotizability, but it is not sufficient. Rather, it is the good imager's ability to experience the image in an *effortless, nonvolitional manner* (e.g., as a visitation), which may be related to hypnotizability. That is, hypnotic imaging involves *both* a good imagery ability *and* an ability to experience images as "happening by themselves." Though these two studies yielded null findings, they inform future work as to where and how to look for the associations between imagination and hypnotic response.

§ 9–2.2.2 Hypnosis and Its Effect on Behavior, Physiology, and Experience

A great deal of scientific effort has been directed at defining what effects hypnosis does, and does not, have on behavior, physiology, and experience.

[1] **When neurological activity is monitored, administration of an hypnotic induction alone is associated with no unique or discernable alteration in brain functioning. However, when highly hypnotizable subjects are selected and when they are given very specific suggestions for altered experience (e.g. hallucination, altered pain perception, motor anomalies) there is now emerging evidence that meaningful and measurable shifts in brain activity occur—shifts which make sense in terms of the suggestion given and the brain area activated.**

Most serious hypnosis researchers, even those most disinclined to explain behavior in terms of physiology, agree that examination of how the brain functions in regards to hypnosis is a worthwhile endeavor. The question is really two-fold.[58] First, during the normal day-to-day waking state, do the brains of highly hypnotizable individuals "work differently" than those of low hypnotizables? Second, are there changes in the brain that occur during hypnosis?

Twenty years ago there was a great deal of excitement about hemispheric differences in alpha brain wave production among hypnotized and nonhypnotized individuals. Researchers thought that a relative preponderance of alpha in the left hemisphere indicated greater activity in the right during hypnosis,[59] but this has not been borne out in subsequent research[60] either for hypnotized versus nonhypnotized subjects, or for high hypnotizables versus low hypnotizables in baseline condition. The excitement right now is in bands other than alpha. The most solid finding to date is that hypnotizability might be related to electrocortical activity in the range of theta (4–8 Hz). In general, EEG activity in the theta range is associated with a lowering of systemic excitation, along with enhancement of selective attention to some particular event. Researchers in this area posit that this accounts for the highly hypnotizable

58. N. Graffin et al., *EEG Concomitants of Hypnosis and Hypnotizability,* 104 J. Abnormal Psychol. 123 (1995).

59. Arlene H. Morgan et al., *EEG Alpha: Lateral Asymmetry Related to Task, and Hypnotizability,* 11 Psychophysiology 275 (1974).

60. William E. Edmonston & Harry C. Moscovitz, *Hypnosis and Lateralized Brain Functions,* 38 Int'l J. Clinical & Experimental Hypnosis 70 (1990).

subject's ability to narrowly focus attention and ignore competing stimuli.[61] In all, with extensive effort, researchers have teased-out some intriguing findings. But nothing even close to a certifiable EEG signature for either the condition of hypnosis or the trait of high hypnotizability has surfaced.

A second research approach to this problem is to examine cortical event-related potentials or ERPs. The idea here is that perceptual alteration (for instance, after suggestion for a positive hallucination) should correspond to ERP changes in amplitude. About 20 studies find this effect, and an equal number do not.[62] One laboratory, David Spiegel's, reports some promising findings in regards to P300 and P100 components of ERP which suggest early filtering of somatosensory signals during hypnotic hallucinations.[63] But again these findings have not been sufficiently replicated.

A third approach scientists use is to work with brain imaging and blood flow analyses. Over the past five years this has led to a number of intriguing findings which document that when hypnotic subjects successfully respond to suggestions for alteration of pain experience (e.g. analgesia), for auditory hallucinations, for visual hallucinations and for motor paralysis the areas of the brain which mediate these functions undergo a change which reflects the suggested experience. These shifts in brain functioning can not be explained by mere compliance or imagination. Four important recent studies are illustrative.

In a positron emission tomography study published in *The Procedures of the National Academy of Sciences*, researchers examined changes in the grain associated with hypnotically suggested auditory hallucinations.[64] An auditory hallucination shares with imagined hearing the property of being self-generated. It shares with *real* hearing the experience of the stimulus as coming from an external source (happening by itself). By monitoring regional cerebral blood flow via positron emission tomography (PET) in areas activated during both hearing and hallucination, but *not* during simple imagining, the investigators sought to determine where in the brain an hallucinated auditory event is "tagged" as originating in the outside world. Analysis revealed that during hypnotic hallucination a region of the right anterior cingulate was activated at levels over baseline to the same extent as during actual hearing, whereas during the imagining condition this was not the case. Individuals who could not hallucinate, despite being presented with exactly the same task demands, showed no such pattern of activity in this region. Further, the extent of activation in this area correlated significantly with subjects' self ratings of stimulus externality and clarity.

A second PET imaging study published in *Science* by Pierre Rainville and his colleagues attempted to locate the cortical structures associated with the suffering (as distinct from the sensory) component of the pain experience.[65]

61. Graffin et al., *EEG Concomitants, supra* note 58.

62. David Spiegel & Arreed F. Barabasz, *Effects of Hypnotic Instructions on P300 Event–Related–Potential Amplitudes: Research and Clinical Applications,* 31 AM. J. CLINICAL HYPNOSIS 11 (1988).

63. David Spiegel et al., *Hypnotic Alteration of Somatosensory Perception,* 146 AM. J. PSYCHI-

ATRY 749 (1989); David Speigel et al., *Hypnotic Hallucination Alters Evoked Potentials,* 94 J. ABNORMAL PSYCHOL. 249 (1985).

64. H. Szechtman et al., 95 PROCEDURES OF THE NAT'L. ACAD. SCIENCES 1956 (1998).

65. P.Rainville et al., *Pain Affect Encoded in Human Anterior Cingulate But Not Somatosensory Cortex.* 277 SCIENCE 968 (1997).

Tracking regional cerebral blood flow during hypnosis revealed that perceived suffering was associated with activation levels within the anterior cingulate cortex (ACC). Hypnotic suggestions for reduced suffering was associated with reduced activation in the ACC. Further, subject ratings of reductions in suffering was linked to reductions in ACC activity. This research helps support the notion that the anterior cingulate gyrus is involved in pain and emotions, and this may explain where and how hypnotic analgesia can sometimes secure dramatic relief in suffering.

A third PET imaging study published in the *American Journal of Psychiatry* examined how hypnotic suggestions for alterations in visual experience of color (or no-color) are associated with changes in blood flow in those portions of the brain that process perception of color and hue.[66] Results indicated that highly hypnotizable subjects evidenced changes in neural functioning in the lingual/fusiform gyrus consistent with suggestions to enhance or diminish color perception. Interestingly the left hemisphere color area reflected color enhance/diminish suggestions only when the subject was formally hypnotized.

A fourth imaging study published in *Lancet* revisited the classic and venerable notion in psychiatry that motor conversion disorders and hypnotically induced motor paralyses share common brain patterns.[67] The authors replicated a positron emission tomography protocol originally carried out with a patient who had longstanding conversion hysteria (leg paralysis). In that original protocol it was found that the patient had two distinct areas of prefrontal cortex activated. The investigators posited that the brain regions activated when lower limb paralysis was hypnotically suggested in a *normal* high hypnotizable subject would be similar to those activated in hysterical paralysis. They found this to be the case, with shifts in brain flow during hypnosis occurring in the same cytoarchitectural regions as the shifts noted in the case of conversion paralysis.

In sum, recent state-of-the-art brain imaging studies appear to document that when individuals who are highly responsive to hypnosis are administered specific suggestions during hypnosis, portions of the brain relevant to the suggested alteration are activated in ways that differ from controls who are not hypnotized. It seems that simply hypnotizing someone and monitoring the brain in the absence of specific suggestions garners little meaningful data. However, when highly hypnotizable subjects are selected and when they are given very specific suggestions for altered experience (e.g. hallucination, pain perception, motor anomalies) there is now evidence that meaningful and measurable shifts in brain activity occur—-shifts which make sense in terms of what we know about how the brain works in general. This suggests that the dramatic alterations in the hypnotic subject's experience and behavior which have been observed for decades are in fact reflected not just behaviorally but neurologically as well, at least for some individuals under some circumstances.

[2] Hypnotic Subjects Typically Report Effortless Nonvolitional Experience but in Fact Remain Active Participants

Good hypnotic subjects almost always report that their hypnotic responses were nonvolitional, that their experience happened *to* them (e.g., "my

66. S. M., Kosslyn et al., *Hypnotic Visual Illusion Alters Color Processing in the Brain.* Am. J. Psychiatry 157, 1279–1284 (2000).

67. P.W. Halligan et al., *Imaging Hypnotic Paralysis: Implications for Conversion Hysteria* 355 Lancet 986–987 (2000).

hand became heavy and moved down by itself"; "suddenly I found myself feeling three years old again", or "I can't bend my arm no matter how hard I try"). In fact, hypnotic subjects are not passive automatons, mechanically responding to the immutable imperatives of an altered state of consciousness or the explicit demands embodied in the hypnotist's suggestions. Instead, there is ample evidence from laboratories operating from a variety of theoretical perspectives that hypnotic subjects are cognitively active problem solvers who are, albeit unconsciously, incorporating cultural ideas about hypnosis into their response, and responding to implicit expectations inherent in the immediate interpersonal matrix.[68]

Consider, for example, a suggestion to a hypnotized person that his outstretched arm is too rigid to bend. The person is then asked to try to bend the arm. If the person does not bend the arm simply because he was so instructed, failure to bend the arm is uninteresting from a scientific or any other perspective. But when highly hypnotizable persons report that they *can not* bend the arm, despite their best efforts, curious and interesting psychological factors are afoot.

Hypnotized individuals, however, are clearly in error when they report that they cannot bend the arm. They have lost none of the motor skills or brain mechanisms needed to do so. All that is necessary to bend the arm is the cancellation of the suggestion, ostensibly by the hypnotist but in actuality by the hypnotized person. Because suggestions must be accepted and enacted upon by hypnotized individuals themselves, all hypnotic suggestions are in effect self-suggestions and all hypnosis is in effect self-hypnosis.[69] What then are we to make of hypnotized persons' reports that they cannot bend the arm?

Following Sutcliffe, there is general agreement that hypnotized individuals are not lying, but are genuinely self-deceiving when they report that their hypnotic responses are involuntary.[70] By this, Sutcliffe meant that hypnotized persons are temporarily unaware that they can act otherwise. Shor made a similar argument when he characterized hypnotized subjects' as limiting reality testing.[71]

This is not the extraordinary process that it might appear to be at first blush. In everyday life, we all remain ignorant of many of the forces that shape our experiences and behavior. To take one example, subtle social manipulations can lead to profound changes in attitudes concerning a host of

68. Patricia G. Bowers, *Understanding Reports of Nonvolition,* 9 BEHAVIORAL & BRAIN SCI. 469 (1986); ERNEST R. HILGARD, DIVIDED CONSCIOUSNESS: MULTIPLE CONTROLS IN HUMAN THOUGHT AND ACTION (1977); PETER SHEENAN & KEVIN McCONKEY, HYPNOSIS AND EXPERIENCE, *supra* note 15; Nicholas P. Spanos & John F. Chaves, *The Cognitive–Behavioral Alternative in Hypnosis Research, in* HYPNOSIS: THE COGNITIVE-BEHAVIORAL PERSPECTIVE 9 (Nicholas P. Spanos & John F. Chaves eds., 1989).

69. Irving Kirsch, *Defining Hypnosis: A Core of Agreement in the Apple of Discord,* 11 CONTEMPORARY HYPNOSIS 160 (1994); John F. Kihlstrom, *Exhumed Memory, in* TRUTH IN MEMORY (Steven J. Lynn & Nicholas P. Spanos eds., 1994).

70. John P. Sutcliffe, *"Credulous" and Skeptical Views of Hypnotic Phenomena: Experiments on Esthesia, Hallucination and Delusion,* 62 J. ABNORMAL & SOCIAL PSYCHOL. 189 (1961).

71. Ronald E. Shor, *Hypnosis and the Concept of the Generalized Reality–Orientation,* 13 AM. J. PSYCHOTHERAPY 582 (1959).

issues, including firmly held beliefs. For the most part, however, people often are unaware that their attitudes have changed at all and when they do realize the change they most often attribute it to irrelevant factors.[72] Thus, the seeming paradox that highly hypnotizable subjects are the agents of their own experiences while remaining unaware of this basic fact is at the root of modern scientific understanding of hypnosis. This apparent paradox was perhaps put most aptly by Bowers and Davidson: "... one of the most striking features of hypnotically suggested behavior is that its enactment is typically experienced as nonvolitional or effortless—as something that happens to the person, rather than something actively achieved (the so-called 'classic suggestion effect'),"[73] that is, "... hypnotic responses can be purposeful without being enacted on purpose."[74] Similarly, Kirsch has stated:

> If hypnotic responses were simply voluntary acts, their probability of occurrence would be identical to people's intention to bring them about. But it is not. People can intend to experience a hypnotic response. They can try their best to make it occur. And they can fail! The fact that people often fail to emit intended hypnotic responses indicates that those responses are not fully under their voluntary control.[75]

Other theorists have tried to capture this characteristic of hypnosis by stating that " ... the construction of hypnotic responses involves a shift in the way that subjects process information, and that this shift occurs because of both the facilitative social features of the hypnotic setting and the essential cognitive skills of the subjects."[76] These social features are seen as engendering a "motivated cognitive commitment" on the part of both hypnotist and subject.[77] What is remarkable about hypnosis, when properly conducted and given sufficient skill on the part of the subject, is that after an induction of 15 or fewer minutes, it can create a situation that taps " ... the general human capacity for creating psychological situations that engender desired experiences."[78]

From the above depictions, it is clear that being hypnotized is not the same thing as being suggestible in a global sense. Social suggestibility, often labeled as gullibility or conformity, are entirely unrelated to a person's ability to experience hypnosis.[79] Nor is hypnosis a species of placebo responding. McGlashan, Evans, and Orne[80] have demonstrated that placebo response is different from hypnotic response in nature and extent.

72. Philip Zimbardo & M. Leippe, Psychology of Social Influence and Attitude Change (1991).

73. Kenneth S. Bowers & Thomas M. Davidson, *A Neodissociative Critique of Spanos's Social–Psychological Model of Hypnosis, in* Theories of Hypnosis: Current Models and Perspectives 105, 131 (Steven J. Lynn & Judith W. Rhue eds., 1991).

74. *Id.* at 134.

75. Irving Kirsch, *The Social Learning Theory of Hypnosis, in* Theories of Hypnosis: Current Models and Perspectives 439 (S.J. Lynn & J.W. Rhue eds., 1991).

76. Kevin M. McConkey, *The Construction and Resolution of Experience and Behavior in Hypnosis, in* Theories of Hypnosis: Current Models and Perspectives 542, 547 (S.J. Lynn & J.W. Rhue eds., 1991).

77. Peter W. Sheehan, *Hypnosis, Context, and Commitment, in* Theories of Hypnosis: Current Models and Perspectives 520, 526 (S.J. Lynn & J.W. Rhue eds., 1991).

78. Steven Jay Lynn & Judith W. Rhue, *An Integrative Model of Hypnosis*, Theories of Hypnosis: Current Models and Perspectives 397, 401 (S.J. Lynn & J.W. Rhue eds., 1991).

79. Burns & Hammer, *supra* note 49; Moore, *supra* note 50.

80. McGlashan et al., *supra* note 51.

In sum, the evidence is quite clear on whether hypnotic subjects are active or passive. Hypnotic subjects are alertly, and sometimes uncannily, attuned to the interpersonal, physical, and social surround. They are not "mindless automatons"; they are not in a sleep or coma-like state, they are not "under the hypnotist's control." Hypnotic subjects typically know what is going on around them during hypnosis and, when hypnosis is discontinued, subjects routinely remember everything that happened during the session.[81]

[3] Hypnosis Does Not Enable Subjects to Transcend Volitional Capacity

For many years it was widely believed that hypnotized subjects can do miraculous things with their body and mind, things that would be impossible outside of hypnosis. Examples include board-like muscle rigidity, heightened physical performance, and dramatic feats of cognition. Further, phenomena like hypnotically induced amnesia, analgesia, deafness, color blindness, and dreaming, were all considered the physiological equivalent of their naturally occurring counterpart. For example, hypnotic suggestions for color blindness were thought to actually produce a neurological/ocular aberration or that hypnotic suggestions for not remembering produce a physiological condition identical to that of organic amnesia. There is in fact little or no evidence for such claims.[82] First, many of the seemingly remarkable behaviors evidenced in some hypnosis demonstrations do not require hypnosis at all. Second, there is no evidence that under normal circumstances simply suggesting increased physical performance enables subjects to transcend what they could do if they were otherwise fully motivated. Third, although there is a phenotypic similarity between certain hypnotically induced phenomena (e.g., analgesia, amnesia, dreaming, deafness, and catalepsy), and their naturally occurring counterparts, they in fact involve radically different cognitive and physiological mechanisms.[83] For instance, hypnotic deafness is not the same thing as literally not hearing; hypnotic amnesia is not the same thing as literally forgetting; hypnotic age regression does not involve the literal reinstatement of childhood psychological functioning. Instead, the hypnotic performances of deafness, amnesia, and age regression are more akin to believed-in role play. Behavior corresponds to the subject's *understanding* of the condition, not the condition itself. Nevertheless (and this is important for forensic purposes), good hypnotic subjects report these experiences as compellingly authentic, genuinely real, and literally true.

§ 9–2.2.3 Memory, Responsibility, and Certainty

[1] Hypnotizing a Subject Does Not Increase Accuracy of Memory

A great deal of public attention has focused on the advisability of using hypnosis to "enhance recall" for recent and remote events. There are still many clinicians willing to testify to the effectiveness of hypnosis in this

81. THEODORE X. BARBER, HYPNOSIS: A SCIENTIFIC APPROACH (1979).

82. *Id.*

83. Michael R. Nash, *Hypnosis and Psychopathology: Is There An Underlying Shared Process, in* CONTEMPORARY HYPNOSIS RESEARCH 149 (Erika Fromm & Michael Nash eds., 1992).

regard. Nevertheless, there is consensus within the scientific community on six points.[84] First, hypnotizing a person and giving suggestions for improved memory is no more effective than are other nonhypnotic interrogation techniques. Second, any increase in accurate memories during hypnosis is accompanied by an increase in inaccurate memories. Third, use of hypnotic age regression techniques does not enable adults to respond like children; nor does it enable them to remember events more accurately. Fourth, because hypnosis involves explicit suggestion, subjects are at increased risk to leading questions on the part of the interrogator. Fifth, hypnosis may compromise the subject's ability to distinguish memory of an actual event from cognitive residue of the fantasy and imaginative process inherent in the hypnotic experience (and often directly suggested by clinicians. Sixth, when hypnotic (as opposed to nonhypnotic) techniques are used to interrogate, subjects tend to emerge from hypnosis being more certain of the content, even when it is inaccurate. Thus, confidence levels of the witness are artificially inflated, which can then prejudice a jury. For these reasons the American Medical Association and the Society for Clinical and Experimental Hypnosis advise extreme caution in its use.[85] Many courts follow suit.[86]

There is ample evidence that hypnosis contributes to the problem of false positive memories (that is, remembering things that did not in fact happen). The evidence from the research laboratory and the field is clear. No responsible clinician or researcher can simply ignore the possibility of this form of memory error. For the purpose of *therapeutic progress*, hypnosis and other psychotherapy techniques may be indicated. But, for the quite distinct purpose of investigation (for finding out the historical truth) these techniques can obscure rather than clarify what actually happened in the past; and hypnosis can be part of that problem. It seems incumbent on therapists, therefore, to remain abreast of scientific developments in this area, and to inform patients that introduction of hypnosis into the therapeutic mix may be exceedingly problematic, legally and emotionally.

In a sense, however, hypnosis has been unfairly singled-out by the media and the courts on this issue. Of the hundreds of expressive therapeutic techniques now extant, hypnosis is the only one for which there are substantial data on memory and its accuracy. For various historical reasons, no other therapy technique has been so scrupulously examined as to its effect on memory. Because of this, hypnosis has become a kind of whipping boy for the

84. For reviews of this extensive literature, see M.H. Erdelyi, *Hypermnesia: The Effect of Hypnosis, Fantasy, and Concentration, in* HYPNOSIS AND MEMORY 64 (H.M. Pettinati ed., 1988); Kihlstrom, *supra* note 69; J.F. Kihlstrom & T.M. Barnhardt, *The Self–Regulation of Memory For Better and For Worse, With and Without Hypnosis, in* HANDBOOK OF MENTAL CONTROL 88 (D.M. Wegner & J.W. Pennebaker eds., 1993); Kevin M. McConkey, *The Effects of Hypnotic Procedures on Remembering: The Experimental Findings and Their Implications for Forensic Hypnosis, in* CONTEMPORARY HYPNOSIS RESEARCH 405 (Erika Fromm & Michael R. Nash eds., 1992); Michael R. Nash, *What, If Anything, Is Regressed About Hypnotic Age Regression? A Review of the Empirical Literature,* 102 PSYCHOL. BULL. 42 (1987).

85. Council on Scientific Affairs, American Medical Association, *Scientific Status of Refreshing by the Use of Hypnosis,* 253 J. AM. MED. ASSOC. 1918 (1985); Society for Clinical and Experimental Hypnosis, *Scientific Status of Refreshing Recollection by the Use of Hypnosis,* 34 INT'L J. CLINICAL & EXPERIMENTAL HYPNOSIS 1 (1986).

86. LAURENCE & PERRY, *supra* note 11; Martin T. Orne et al., *Reconstructing Memory Through Hypnosis: Forensic and Clinical Implications, in* HYPNOSIS AND MEMORY, THE GUILFORD CLINICAL AND EXPERIMENTAL HYPNOSIS SERIES 21, 63 (Helen M. Pettinati ed., 1988).

sins of psychotherapy in general. The media and the courts focus on the memory-distorting effects of hypnosis precisely because hypnosis researchers are the ones who have most rigorously documented how plastic memory is in treatment. They have thoroughly documented the role of expectation, suggestion, imagination, and fantasy as co-determinants of what people report remembering, in treatment and outside of it. It is not that these factors are absent in other expressive therapies, it is just that if one wants to find out what science has to say about how memories can be distorted in therapy, one is going to encounter hypnosis, and not much of anything else. Hypnosis research has delivered an important and disturbing message to society at large: Passionately believed-in recollections about the past are not always what they appear to be. This message is so profoundly upsetting to cherished conventional notions of memory that courts, and some elements of the mental health community, yearn to "kill the messenger." The issue is much more complex than this. The problem is not just the nature of hypnosis *per se*, but the nature of memory as it emerges in the context of any psychotherapy.

When we are faced with patients who experience themselves as suddenly and agonizingly remembering a previously forgotten trauma, either in the course of hypnosis or in spontaneous flashback states, we should indeed consider that these reports might represent memory traces of an historical event (in this sense an undoing of a false negative error). But we owe it to ourselves, the patients, the patients' family, and society at large, to be mindful that a literal re-living of an historical event is not humanly possible. Memories do not literally "return" in pristine form, unsullied by contemporary factors like suggestion, transference, values, social context, and fantasies. In short, false memories can and do occur. Further, it is the special responsibility of clinicians to be mindful that getting better in therapy does not bestow upon the patient a mantle of infallibility. Indeed what we call insight may be more a process of creation than a process of discovery.

[2] Hypnotized Subjects Are Able to Control Their Behavior

Though the popular print, video, and film media abound in fictional accounts of sinister characters employing hypnosis to "make" others do things they would ordinarily not do, there is no scientific evidence that this is possible. Despite sometimes ingenious attempts by researchers to deceive or induce hypnotic subjects into immoral or self-injurious behavior, investigators have failed to demonstrate that hypnosis exerts any special influence on the value-based or safety-based decisions made by subjects.[87]

§ 9–2.2.4 Clinical Efficacy

[1] When Used Properly, Hypnosis Is an Effective Intervention With Some Medically and Psychologically Disordered Patients

In evaluating the scientific literature on the clinical effectiveness of hypnotic interventions one immediately encounters a problem. Rarely, if ever, is hypnosis the sole form of treatment with a patient. Unlike psychoanalytic,

---

87. LAURENCE & PERRY, *supra* note 11.

cognitive-behavioral, and client-centered therapies, hypnosis is not a therapy unto itself, it is a technique. Indeed, it can be, and at times is, incorporated into all of the above models of psychotherapy. The position of the Society for Clinical and Experimental Hypnosis and the American Society for Clinical Hypnosis is that hypnosis can not, and should not, stand alone as the sole intervention in any comprehensive form of psychotherapy. Hypnosis is an adjunctive technique. Of course, this renders evaluation of its effectiveness quite complex, though not impossible.

Fortunately there is a research literature which examines the impact of relatively brief and pristine hypnotic interventions in the treatment of circumscribed disorders including pain disorders, asthma, gastrointestinal disorders, skin disorders, insomnia, and post-traumatic stress disorder. In 1982, Wadden and Anderton comprehensively reviewed the empirical literature on the effectiveness of hypnotic interventions with these types of disorders.[88] They concluded that there was sufficient research evidence to support the contention that hypnosis is effective in the treatment of pain disorders, asthma, and skin disorders. Further, they noted that when measured at the onset of treatment, hypnotizability scores (on standard measures such as the Stanford scales) positively correlated with treatment outcome, but not for self-initiated conditions such as smoking, obesity, or drug addictions. The correlation issue is immensely important in helping us be certain that the therapeutic effect in hypnotic treatment of some disorders is due to hypnosis rather than to various nonspecific effects of treatment in general. When patients had little or no hypnotic ability, outcome for treatment of some disorders suffered accordingly.

Since the Wadden and Anderson review,[89] a number of controlled studies have been reported which support the contention that hypnosis is effective with a host of other behavioral, psychophysiological, and immune related disorders.[90]

Another reason for confidence in the efficacy of hypnosis is meta-analytic studies examining the effects of hypnosis across outcome investigations. Table 3 summarizes the results of the classic Smith, Glass, and Miller meta-analysis relevant to hypnosis.[91]

Three very recent developments in the clinical research literature further define how clinical hypnosis has emerged as a mainstream treatment approach to specific medical and psychological disorders.

88. Thomas A. Wadden & Charles H. Anderton, *The Clinical Use of Hypnosis*, 91 Psychological Bull. 215 (1982).

89. *Id.*

90. Arreed F. Barabasz & Marianne Barabasz, *Effects of Restricted Environmental Stimulation: Enhancement of Hypnotizability for Experimental and Chronic Pain Control*, 37 Int'l J. Clinical & Experimental Hypnosis 217 (1989); Daniel Brom, Rolf Kleber, P.B. Defargs, *Brief Psychotherapy for Posttraumatic Stress Disorders*, 57(5) J. Consulting & Clinical Psychol. 607 (1989); Gordon Cochrane & John Friesen, *Hypnotherapy in Weight Loss Treatment*, 54 J. Consulting & Clinical Psychol. 489 (1986); T.C. Ewer & D.E. Stewart, *Improvement in Bronchial Hyper–Responsiveness in Patients With Moderate Asthma After Treatment With A Hypnotic Technique*, 1 Br. Med. J. 1129 (1986); Nicholas P. Spanos et al., *Hypnosis, Placebo and Suggestion in the Treatment of Warts*, 50 Psychosomatic Med. 245 (1988); D.J. Tosi et al., *The Effects of A Cognitive Experiential Therapy Utilizing Hypnosis, Cognitive Restructuring, and Developmental Staging on Psychological Factors Associated With Duodenal Ulcer Disease: A Multivariate Experimental Study*, 3 J. Cognitive Psychotherapy 273 (1989).

91. Mark L. Smith, Gene V. Glass, T.I. Miller, The Benefits of Psychotherapy (1980).

First, in 1996 the *Journal of the American Medical Association* published the National Institute of Health Technology Assessment Panel Report on treatments for insomnia and chronic pain.[92] The Panel judged hypnosis to be a viable and effective intervention for alleviating pain with cancer, and other chronic pain conditions. This, in addition to a voluminous clinical literature and an increasingly robust research literature, leaves no doubt that patients undergoing burn wound debridement, or children repeatedly undergoing bone marrow aspirations, or mothers in the delivery room, can sometimes achieve a dramatic reduction in pain through hypnosis. In some cases the degree of analgesia matches or exceeds that derived from morphine.

Second, in 1998 a report of the American Psychological Association designated hypnosis as used in conjunction with cognitive-behavioral treatment to be among the efficacious and possibly efficacious treatments.[93] In part, this judgment was based on a meta-analysis of studies comparing clinical outcome in cognitive behavioral therapies with, and without, hypnosis. In this meta-analysis, Kirsch, Montgomery, & Sapirstein[94] examined 18 studies (1974 to 1993) that compared a cognitive-behavioral treatment with the same treatment supplemented by hypnosis. The mean effect size for the difference between hypnotic and non-hypnotic treatments was 0.87 standard deviations, indicating that hypnotherapy was significantly superior to non-hypnotic treatment. Studies of obesity, which had by far the largest effects, were eliminated from the calculation of the overall effect size, in order to produce a more conservative estimate. A value of 0.53 was obtained, indicating that clients receiving hypnotic therapy were better off at the end of treatment than 70% of clients who received only cognitive-behavioral therapy.

In April 2000 a long overdue, tough-mined, review of all the research literature to date on the efficacy of hypnotic interventions across medicine and psychotherapy was published in *The International Journal of Clinical and Experimental Hypnosis*. This landmark document, with six independent articles and a frank summary assessment of where the field is vis a vis empirical validation, provides a definitive rendering of what we now know about the efficacy of hypnosis interventions, and supplies direction for future work on clinical efficacy. The articles assess the evidence for efficacy using the Chamblis & Hollon standards in six arenas: pediatrics,[95] relief of pain,[96] adjunctive use with cognitive-behavioral psychotherapy,[97] medicine,[98] smoking cessation,[99]

92. *NIH Technology Assessment Panel on Integration of Behavioral and Relaxation Approaches into Treatment of Chronic Pain and Insomnia*, 276 JAMA 313 (1996).

93. Chamblis, D. L., & Hollon, S. D., *Defining Empirically Supported Therapies*, 60 J. CONSULTING & CLINICAL PSYCHOL. 7 (1998).

94. I. Kirsch et al., *Hypnosis as an Adjunct to Cognitive–Behavioral Psychotherapy: A Meta–Analysis*, 63 J. CONSULTING & CLINICAL PSYCHOL. 214 (1995).

95. L. S Milling & C. A. Costantino, *Clinical Hypnosis with Children: First Steps Toward Empirical Support*, 48 INTERNATIONAL J. CLINICAL & EXPERIMENTAL HYPNOSIS 113 (2000).

96. G. H. Montgomery et al., *A Meta–Analysis of Hypnotically Induced Analgesia: How Effective is Hypnosis*, 48 INTERNATIONAL J. CLINICAL & EXPERIMENTAL HYPNOSIS 138 (2000).

97. N. E. Schoenberger, *Research on Hypnosis as an Adjunct to Cognitive–Behavioral Psychotherapy* 48 INTERNATIONAL J. CLINICAL & EXPERIMENTAL HYPNOSIS 154 (2000).

98. C. M. Pinnell & N. A. Covino, *Empirical Findings on the Use of Hypnosis in Medicine: A Critical Review*, 48 INTERNATIONAL J. CLINICAL & EXPERIMENTAL HYPNOSIS 170 (2000).

99. J. P. Green & S. J. Lynn, *Hypnosis and Suggestion–Based Approaches to Smoking Cessation: An Examination of the Evidence*, 48 INTERNATIONAL J. CLINICAL & EXPERIMENTAL HYPNOSIS 195 (2000).

and trauma-related disorders.[100] The summary article concludes that though there is much empirical work yet to be accomplished, there is ample empirical evidence that hypnosis can ameliorate a number of medical and psychological conditions.[101]

EFFECT SIZES FOR DIFFERENT FORMS OF PSYCHOTHERAPY AS DERIVED FROM THE SMITH, GLASS, AND MILLER (1980) DATA[1]

TYPE OF THERAPY	EFFECT SIZE
HYPNOTHERAPY	1.82
COGNITIVE THERAPY	1.58
BEHAVIOR THERAPY	1.02
PSYCHODYNAMIC THERAPY	0.76

[1]Kirsch, I. (1990). Changing expectations: A key to effective psychotherapy. Pacific Grove, CA: Brooks/Cole Publishing Co.

In sum, there is credible scientific evidence supporting the contention that hypnotic interventions can be effective when used properly.

100. E. Cardeña, *Hypnosis in the Treatment of Trauma: A Promising, But Not Fully Supported Efficacious Intervention*, 48 INTERNATIONAL J. CLINICAL & EXPERIMENTAL HYPNOSIS 225 (2000).

101. S. J. Lynn et al., *Hypnosis as an Empirically Supported Clinical Intervention: The State of the Evidence and a Look into the Future*, 48 INTERNATIONAL J. CLINICAL & EXPERIMENTAL HYPNOSIS 239 (2000).

[2] The Risk for Negative Side–Effects Associated With Hypnotic Treatment Appears Comparable to That Associated With Other Forms of Psychological Intervention

As for negative side effects of hypnosis when conducted in a professional research setting, measurement of hypnotizability has been shown to involve no more risk for negative side effects than does listening to a college lecture or taking a test.[102]

For patients, it is a different matter. It is now abundantly clear that for the most part psychotherapy is beneficial.[103] But it is equally clear that in a small percentage of cases psychotherapy in general is associated with the patient getting "worse." In the review by Smith, Glass, and Miller nine percent of effect size measures were negative (i.e., nine percent of psychotherapy patients got worse during the index period.)[104] Jacobson and Edinger reported that five percent of patients were adversely effected by relaxation training.[105] It is within this context that the negative effects of therapeutic applications of hypnosis should be assessed. As Frauman, Lynn, and Brentar point out: "These statistics (regarding psychotherapy in general) are a reasonable estimate of the frequency of negative effects during and after (clinical) hypnosis. Hypnosis is neither more nor less hazardous than other psychotherapeutic procedures that are used because of their potential to influence and treat clients."[106] Nevertheless, it is important for the therapist to understand and appreciate the conditions under which negative effects may occur when using hypnosis. Prudence dictates that when patients seek a professional who might use hypnosis, they choose one who is thoroughly and broadly credentialed in his field. Patients should thus select someone who would also be competent and trained to treat the problem *without* hypnosis.

§ 9–2.3 Areas of Scientific Disagreement

§ 9–2.3.1 Principles Relating Hypnosis to Personality

[1] Does the Stability of Hypnotic Responsiveness Reflect Primarily a Stable Personality Trait or Does it Reflect Primarily Stability of the Testing Context?

Hypnosis scientists disagree on the mechanisms that underlie the stability of hypnotic responsiveness as measured by standardized scales. Some scientists argue that the ability to experience hypnotic suggestions is trait-like.[107] What this means is that hypnotic responsiveness is stable across time because of an enduring personal characteristic that a person carries with him

---

102. William C. Coe & K. Ryken, *Hypnosis and Risks to Human Subjects*, 34 Am. Psychologist 673 (1979).

103. Larry, E. Beutler et al., *The Status of Programmatic Research*, in Psychotherapy Research 325 (L.E. Beutler & M. Crago eds., 1991).

104. Mark L. Smith, et al., The Benefits of Psychotherapy (1980).

105. R. Jacobson & J.D. Edinger, *Side Effects of Relaxation Training*, 139 Am. J. Psychiatry 952 (1982).

106. David C. Frauman et al., *Prevention and Therapeutic Management of "Negative Effects" in Hypnotherapy*, in Handbook of Clinical Hypnosis 95 (Judith Rhue et al. eds., 1994).

107. Kenneth S. Bowers, Hypnosis for the Seriously Curious (1983); Ernest R. Hilgard, *Dissociation and Theories of Personality*, in Contemporary Hypnosis Research (E. Fromm & M.R. Nash eds. 1992); Herbert Spiegel & David Spiegel, Trance and Treatment: Clinical Uses of Hypnosis (1978).

throughout adult life. This is not to say that a person will respond stereotypically to hypnotic situations or suggestions solely according to his level of hypnotic responsiveness. According to the trait view, situations can and do determine in part how a person will respond to any situation. For example, a highly hypnotizable person with chronic pain may not respond to a hypnotic treatment to alleviate the pain (despite extensive evidence that hypnosis is an effective treatment for pain alleviation, particularly among high hypnotizable persons) if he achieves secondary gain from maintaining the pain (e.g., affection from a previously inattentive spouse, workers compensation). Rather, these researchers conceptualize a person's hypnotic capacity as an enduring upper limit for hypnotic performance. Although a person may choose to not use his hypnotic skill to its full extent or may not recognize the potential utility of that skill in a particular situation, a low hypnotizable person cannot experience hypnosis extensively no matter how motivated. According to this conceptualization, a trait is a relatively stable tendency to act and experience in a particular way given particular circumstances.[108] Accordingly, these scientists argue that given that a trusting relationship between hypnotist and subject in a non-threatening environment is established, a person will respond to hypnosis in essentially the same way throughout adult life.

Other scientists argue that the trait-like stability of hypnotic responsiveness is an illusion. Rather than reflect a characteristic of the person, they argue that stability of hypnotic responsiveness reflects the stability of the hypnosis testing context. Of necessity, hypnosis scales are standardized and are administered to subjects in essentially the same manner at each testing. It is this stability, according to these scientists, that produces the high test-retest correlations between hypnotizability scores determined at different times.

This latter interpretation, however, does not do justice either to the complexity of hypnotic responsiveness or to human behavior in general. For example, it is clear from the general social psychology literature that it is a person's understanding of a particular context rather than its external characteristics that determines in part how a person will behave in a given situation.[109] In order for the stability of hypnotizability scores to be contextually-determined, one would have to argue that the middle-aged former Stanford students in the Piccione et al. study interpreted the hypnosis testing context the second time in the same manner as they did when they were students, a seemingly unlikely event.[110]

It is impossible from the Piccione data, however, to determine which of the two theoretical positions is correct. As with much correlational psychological research, the data are consistent with more than one theoretical view. Nonetheless, the bulk of psychological evidence favors the ontological status of traits, which has prompted Walter Mischel, the first and most forceful proponent of the anti-trait view, to observe that psychological researchers are

108. Auke Tellegen, *Practicing the Two Disciplines for Relaxation and Enlightenment: Comment on "Role of the Feedback Signal in Electromyograph Biofeedback: The Relevance of Attention" by Qualls and Sheehan*, 110 J. Experimental Psychol.: General 217 (1981).

109. Philip Zimbardo & M. Leippe, Psychology of Social Influence and Attitude Change (1991).

110. Piccione et al., *supra* note 42.

spending less time arguing the existence of traits and instead are exploring their structure and function within human experience and behavior.[111]

[2] Are Personality, Social, and Cognitive Factors Implicated in Hypnotic Responsiveness Best Understood in Additive Terms or Do Their Respective Weights Depend on the Person's Level of Hypnotic Responsiveness?

Another area of disagreement involves the optimal statistical combination of the various personality, social psychological, and cognitive factors that underlie hypnotic response. Should they be understood in additive or multiplicative terms? Under an additive model, various predictor variables have equal weight across subjects in the prediction of hypnotic response. By contrast, under a multiplicative (interactionist) model, predictors have different weights, depending on other predictors.

For example, hypnotic behavior is known to predict reports of "hypnotic depth." On standardized scales, the more hypnotic suggestions a person "passes" behaviorally, the "deeper" they report being hypnotized. These reports, however, are also influenced by the wording of the question aimed at eliciting the depth reports. Consideration of the additive effect of both these factors (behavioral hypnotic response and scale wording) provides better prediction of depth reports than either factor alone. Additional consideration of their combined multiplicative effect, however, improves prediction over the additive model. Subjects in middle range of hypnotic response are more influenced by scale wording than those of low or high hypnotizability.[112]

Some scientists have argued explicitly for multiplicative models of one form or another.[113] It is presently unclear, however, how generalizable these types of models will be, that is, whether they will apply to a wide or narrow range of hypnotic responses.

§ 9–2.3.2 The Effects of Hypnosis on Behavior, Physiology, and Experience.

[1] To What Extent Do Increases in Hypnotic Responsiveness Induced by Laboratory Procedures Reflect Temporary Behavioral Compliance as Opposed to More Enduring Changes in Level of Responsiveness?

An earlier debate on this issue[114] resurfaced with the introduction of a series of studies about the effectiveness of a multi-faceted training program

111. J.C. Wright & Walter Mischel, *A Conditional Approach to Dispositional Constructs: The Local Predictability of Social Behavior*, 53 J. PERSONALITY & SOC. PSYCHOL. 1159 (1987).

112. H. Lorraine Radtke, & Nicholas P. Spanos, *The Effect of Rating Scale Descriptors on Hypnotic Depth Reports*, 111 J. PSYCHOL. 235 (1982); Jean–Roch Laurence & Robert Nadon, *Reports of Hypnotic Depth: Are They More Than Mere Words?* 34 INTERNATIONAL J. CLINICAL & EXPERIMENTAL HYPNOSIS 215 (1986).

113. Steven Jay Lynn, & Judith W. Rhue, *An Integrative Model of Hypnosis, in* THEORIES

OF HYPNOSIS: CURRENT MODELS AND PERSPECTIVES 397 (S.J. Lynn & J.W. Rhue eds., 1991a); Kevin M. McConkey, *The Construction and Resolution of Experience and Behavior in Hypnosis, in* THEORIES OF HYPNOSIS: CURRENT MODELS AND PERSPECTIVES 563 (S.J. Lynn & J.W. Rhue eds., 1991); Nadon, et al., *supra* note 1; Peter W. Sheehan, *Hypnosis, Context and Commitment, in* THEORIES OF HYPNOSIS: CURRENT MODELS AND PERSPECTIVES 541 (S.J. Lynn & J.W. Rhue eds., 1991).

114. Michael J. Diamond, *Hypnotizability is Modifiable: An Alternative Approach*, 25 IN-

that was developed by Spanos and colleagues.[115] Initial studies showed average increases in hypnotizability scores; indeed, some subjects who scored initially in the low range increased their scores after training into the high range. These studies have been criticized on various grounds. Bates, for example, argues that most of the increase in hypnotizability scores was due to the compliance component of the training program.[116] Increases in scores from baseline to post-training, he maintains, reflected subjects' desire to conform to instructions rather than to their learning how to experience suggested effects. More recently, however, researchers have found that equivalent increases in hypnotizability scores could be produced with or without compliance instructions. The question of the underlying nature of trained increases in hypnotic response remains open.

[2] Do Behaviors and Reports of Subjective Experience That Phenotypically Resemble Those Found in Hypnosis, But Which Were Not Preceded by a Hypnotic Induction, Reflect Hypnotic or Nonhypnotic Processes?

It is clear that behaviors identical to those found after a hypnotic induction can be reproduced by non-hypnotic instructions. Spanos has used the logic of equivalence to argue that identical behaviors produced in hypnotic and non-hypnotic contexts reflect the same underlying psychological mechanisms.[117] Based on consensus among scientists, however, this argument is valid only to the extent that the same subjective experiences accompany both the hypnotically and the nonhypnotically-induced behaviors. Because the same types of nonhypnotic instructions that elicit hypnotic-like behaviors can also elicit hypnotic-like reports of mental state changes, it becomes difficult to know whether the latter reports reflect genuine subjective experiences or mere compliance. Even if the reports reflect genuine subjective experiences, they may be produced by psychological processes that are different in kind from those produced in hypnosis.[118] As Bowers stated, "One must not assume that because a person with a headache becomes headache-free after taking aspirin ... headache-free people secretly take aspirin."[119] Ultimately, studies that use the logic of equivalence can only suggest possible identical mecha-

TERNATIONAL JOURNAL OF CLINICAL AND EXPERIMENTAL HYPNOSIS 147 (1977); Campbell Perry, *Is Hypnotizability Modifiable?* 25 INTERNATIONAL J. CLINICAL & EXPERIMENTAL HYPNOSIS 125 (1977).

115. Donald Gorassini & Nicholas Spanos, *supra* note 45; Nicholas P. Spanos et al., *The Carleton University Responsiveness to Suggestion Scale: Normative Data and Psychometric Properties*, 53 PSYCHOL. REP. 523 (1983).

116. Brad L. Bates, *Compliance and the Carleton Skill Training Program*, 7 BRIT. J. EXPERIMENTAL & CLINICAL HYPNOSIS 159 (1990).

117. Nicholas P. Spanos, *Hypnotic Behavior: A Social Psychological Interpretation of Amnesia, Analgesia, and "Trance Logic"* 9 BEHAVIORAL & BRAIN SCIENCES 449 (1986b).

118. M.E. Miller & Kenneth S. Bowers, *Hypnotic Analgesia and Stress Inoculation in the Reduction of Pain*, 56 J. PERSONALITY & SOC. PSYCHOL. 182 (1986); *but see* Nicholas P. Spanos & J. Katsanis, *Effects of Instructional Set on Attributions of Nonvolition During Hypnotic and Nonhypnotic Analgesia*, 56 J. PERSONALITY & SOC. PSYCHOL. 182 (1989).

119. Bowers, *supra* note 68, at 469; *see also*, Michael Dixon & Jean–Roch Laurence, *Hypnotic Susceptibility and Verbal Automaticity: Automatic and Strategic Processing Differences in the Stroop Color Naming Task*, 101 J. ABNORMAL PSYCHOL. 344 (1992).

nisms; they cannot demonstrate them unequivocally. Further, a distinguishing characteristic of hypnotic phenomena is that their onset and termination rapidly follow a pre-arranged cue from the hypnotist; these phenomena are, in short, reversible (e.g., an hallucination appears and goes away on cue; a hand becomes numb when the experimenter says the word "ice" and returns to normal when the experimenter says the word "normal"). This is usually not the case in mental conditions or disorders which may superficially resemble hypnosis. Nonetheless, because the body of existing data is consistent with both theoretical views, the issue remains unresolved.

[3] Is There a Causal Link Between Early Trauma, Dissociative Pathology, and High Hypnotizability?

Some clinical theorists and researchers contend that early trauma engenders the repeated use of dissociative techniques, resulting in dramatic alterations in experiences of self and environment, experiences that are at least phenotypically similar to hypnotic experiences.[120] Indeed, Frischholz, Bliss, and Spiegel, among others, argue that hypnotizability levels are sensitive indices of dissociation and, thus, reliable markers of pathology presumably rooted in trauma.[121]

From this theoretical perspective, the logic of a hypnosis-dissociation link is persuasive. Dissociative psychopathology (e.g., multiple personality disorder, fugue disorder, and psychogenic amnesias) is characterized by intense absorption, amnesias, fantasy proneness, automatism, depersonalization, and cognitive inconsistencies. Since these same phenomena figure so prominently in hypnosis, a propensity for spontaneous self-hypnosis may underlie dissociative disorders. If true, then patients suffering from these disorders should test as more hypnotizable than control individuals.

Clinical observation and theoretical formulations strongly suggest a relationship between hypnosis and dissociation. If hypnosis and dissociative disorders do indeed share important underlying psychic mechanisms, three core findings should be found across clinical and non-clinical samples. First, if the trait of dissociativity captures something essential about the trait of hypnotizability, then these two abilities should be positively correlated, with highly hypnotizables also being highly dissociative (overlapping traits). Second, if hypnosis and dissociativity share common developmental pathways involving trauma, then a history of trauma should be associated with increased hypnotizability, and increased dissociativity (common etiology). Third, if hypnosis captures some essential pathological feature of dissociative disor-

---

120. Edward J. Frischholz, *The Relationship Among Dissociation, Hypnosis, and Child Abuse in the Development of Multiple Personality, in* Childhood Antecedents of Multiple Personality 99 (R.P. Kluft ed. 1985); Richard P. Kluft, *An Update on Multiple Personality Disorder,* 38 Hosp. & Community Psychiatry 363 (1987); Frank W. Putnam, *Dissociation as A Response to Extreme Trauma, in* Childhood Antecedents of Multiple Personality 65 (R.P. Kluft ed., 1985); David Spiegel, T. Hunt & H.F. Dondershine, *Dissociation and Hypnotizability*

in Posttraumatic Stress Disorder, 145(3) Am J. Psychiatry 301 (1988).

121. Edward J. Frischholz, *The Relationship Among Dissociation, Hypnosis, and Child Abuse in the Development of Multiple Personality, in* Childhood antecedents of multiple personality 99 (R.P. Kluft ed. 1985); E.L. Bliss, *Spontaneous Self–Hypnosis in Multiple Personality Disorder,* 7 Psychiatric Clinics N. Am. 135 (1984); David Speigel, *Dissociating Damage,* 29 Am. J. Clinical Hypnosis 123 (1986).

ders, it may be especially effective in the treatment of these disorders (clinical efficacy).[122]

Evidence for the common etiology hypothesis, that early trauma exaggerates an individual's hypnotizability and dissociativity, is scant. First, trauma does not appear to be an important feature in the development of high hypnotizability. The overwhelming preponderance of high hypnotizables have not been traumatized; and those subjects who have been traumatized are no more hypnotizable than non-traumatized controls. Though there may be some possibility for an association between trauma and hypnotizability within narrow diagnostic categories, there is, at best, mixed evidence as to whether a history of early trauma is associated with high hypnotizability. Second, there is a fairly extensive research literature which finds an association between trauma and dissociation. There is some evidence that trauma and dissociation may be linked, although methodological and definitional issues make these studies difficult to interpret.[123] Moreover, it seems probable that any link is not a linear cause-effect relationship. Indeed, given the confounding of dissociation measures with measures of gross pathology, and the neglect of other pathogenic factors, what dissociation researchers may be finding is simply that people who have had horribly troubling and chaotic home environments are more grossly pathological than those who had reasonably stable childhood home environments. But even if we accept the premise that dissociativity is directly associated with trauma, hypnosis is not. Therefore, experiences of early trauma do not exaggerate both an individual's dissociativity and hypnotizability. In this sense, then, hypnotizability and dissociativity are not "fellow travelers," following parallel trajectories in response to early trauma. There is good reason to reject the conclusion that these phenomena involve shared psychic mechanisms.

If there is any relationship between the constructs of dissociation and hypnosis it is complex and indirect. The three propositions, rooted in the assumption of a hypnosis-dissociation link, are not fully supported empirically. The overlapping trait proposition has been thoroughly tested. Hypnotizability and dissociativity do not covary and positive correlations between these measures are rare and non-replicable. The common traumagenic etiology proposition also has not been confirmed empirically. No definitive developmental pathway conjoining trauma, dissociativity, and hypnotizability has emerged from the data.

§ 9–2.4　Future Directions

The tradition of empirical study of hypnosis remains a robust component of the mainstream psychological and medical research literatures. There are six areas of current research interest in which we can expect some advances over the next few years.

---

122. For reviews, see Jonathan E. Whalen & Michael R. Nash, *Hypnosis and Dissociation: Theoretical, Empirical, and Clinical Perspectives, in* HANDBOOK OF DISSOCIATION: THEORETICAL, EMPIRICAL, AND CLINICAL PERSPECTIVES (Larry Michelson & William Ray eds., 1995); Jane G. Tillman, Michael R. Nash & P.M. Lerner, *Does Trauma Cause Dissociative Pathology? in* DISSOCIATION: CLINICAL AND THEORETICAL PERSPECTIVES 395 (S. Lynn & J. Rhue eds., 1994).

123. Nash, *supra* note 83.

§ 9–2.4.1 Hypnosis and the Brain

As noted earlier, recently developed brain imaging and blood flow analyses enable scientists to develop a much more fine-grained "picture" of what is happening in specific parts of the brain. We anticipate that over the next five years these sophisticated technologies will be applied to the study of hypnosis, yielding a clearer understanding of what happens in the brain during hypnosis.

§ 9–2.4.2 Hypnosis and Cognition

We expect that some strides will soon be made in our understanding of how information is processed during hypnosis. Various claims have been made about how information might be processed differently during hypnosis. These claims include more automatically,[124] more holistically,[125] more effortlessly,[126] or more regressively.[127] Because these theories generate testable hypotheses, they are well-suited for empirical research in the laboratory.

§ 9–2.4.3 Dissecting Hypnotic Response

For over 30 years now the assumption has been that hypnotic susceptibility is a single ability that is more-or-less normally distributed across the population. Groundbreaking work by Woody, Bowers, and Oakman at the University of Waterloo has challenged this idea. They posit that the ability to experience hypnosis may actually be two abilities. One ability having to do with compliance, the other having to do with altering cognitive processing.[128] This would be similar to the idea that intellectual ability can be parsed into its two constituent components: verbal ability, and spatial/motor ability. If hypnotizability is similarly bi-dimensional, our understanding of the nature of hypnosis will be transformed.

§ 9–2.4.4 Hypnosis and Clinical Outcome

We can expect new, more sophisticated clinical trials of hypnotic interventions in the fields of behavioral medicine, pain, psychophysiological disorders, and psychiatric disorders. This should enable us to make more precise treatment plans in regards to the use of hypnosis in these types of situations. Of particular importance is our ability to gauge the extent to which hypnosis *per se* was the active agent in the therapy, as opposed to the non-specific aspects of any kind of treatment. If treatment outcome is positively correlated to hypnotizability, then we can be fairly certain that the mutative factor in the therapy involved suggestion. If, on the other hand, treatment outcome is not correlated with hypnotizability, then getting better may have had little or

124. Michael Dixon & Jean–Roch Laurence, *Hypnotic Susceptibility and Verbal Automaticity: Automatic and Strategic Processing Differences in the Stroop Color Naming Task,* 101 J. Abnormal Psychol. 344 (1992).

125. Helen J. Crawford, *Cognitive and Physiological Flexibility: Multiple Pathways to Hypnotic Responsiveness, in* Suggestion and Suggestibility: Theory and Research 155 (V. Ghorghui et al. eds., 1989).

126. Bowers & Davidson, *supra* note 73.

127. Nash, *supra* note 83.

128. Emil Z. Woody et al., *A Conceptual Analysis of Hypnotic Responsiveness: Experience, Individual Differences, and Context, in* Contemporary Hypnosis Research 3 (Erika Fromm & Michael R. Nash eds., 1992).

nothing to do with the hypnotic procedures themselves, but some other aspect of the treatment (e.g., therapist's attention, reassurance, hope).

§ 9–2.4.5 Hypnosis, Trauma, and Dissociation

We can expect that there will be a great deal of attention given to the relationship between early trauma, the development of dissociative disorders, and high hypnotizability. Longitudinal clinical research should clarify whether dissociative disordered patients really are more hypnotizable than controls; whether trauma is figural in the etiology of dissociative disorders; and whether traumatized patients are prone to experiencing "spontaneous hypnotic states."

§ 9–2.4.6 Hypnosis and the Immune System

A heralded study was conducted at Stanford Medical School by David Spiegel and colleagues which documented that metastatic breast cancer patients who participated in group therapy (with a substantial hypnosis component) survived longer than control subjects matched on a host of diagnostic, prognostic and demographic variables.[129] We expect that more studies examining hypnosis' possible effects on the human immune system will be conducted. This research will test the replicability of the Spiegel findings and should suggest possible underlying mechanisms of this type of effect if it proves to be reliable.

129. David Spiegel et al., *Effect of Psychosocial Treatment on Survival of Patients With Metastic Breast Cancer,* ii LANCET 888 (1989).

CHAPTER 10

REPRESSED MEMORIES

Table of Sections

A. LEGAL ISSUES

Westlaw Electronic Research

See Westlaw Electronic Research Guide preceding the Summary of Contents.

A. LEGAL ISSUES

§ 10–1.0 THE LEGAL RELEVANCE OF RESEARCH ON REPRESSED MEMORIES

§ 10–1.1 Introduction

Expert testimony on repressed memories is relevant at several levels of the legal process.[1] Foremost, it has been employed to toll statutes of limitations that would otherwise bar actions arising out of alleged incidents of child sexual abuse that purportedly occurred years before the actions were commenced, but the memories of which were "repressed" until more recently. If

---

§ 10–1.0

1. Courts and commentators sometimes refer to the phenomenon as "recovered memories."

successful in overcoming limitation bars to the action, proponents of this form of expert testimony would also seek to introduce it at trial to support the testimony of the alleged victim of the abuse. In this latter form, the expert testimony might have two purposes. First, it has a non-evidentiary use that permits judges to evaluate the competency of the complaining witness.[2] Typically, the abuse is "recovered" through therapy, a process that might involve hypnosis, drugs or other techniques possibly affecting the reliability of the recall. Second, the expert testimony might be offered to support the credibility of the witness, or otherwise assist the trier of fact to assess the evidence. To date, most court opinions center on the use of repressed memory to toll the limitations period, and we begin with this issue. In addition, this section considers the evidentiary issues that have arisen, and also considers briefly the more recent phenomenon of alleged abusers suing the therapists who "discovered" the abuse leading to the allegations against them.

§ 10–1.2   Tolling the Statute of Limitations

All states place limitations periods on the time within which a person can bring a civil cause of action.[3] Although state practices vary, they typically involve a set period for most claimants, such as two to four years, with special provisions tolling the period during minority, mental illness, or other disability. In cases of children, state statutes typically toll the limitations period until the alleged victim reaches the age of majority, whereupon it runs for a set period of time.[4] The essential purposes supporting limitations periods are to promote timely litigation in order to protect defendants from having to fight against old and possibly fraudulent claims.[5]

2. *See, e.g.,* Borawick v. Shay, 68 F.3d 597, 610 (2d Cir.1995) (The court outlined a totality of circumstances test for purposes of evaluating hypnotically refreshed recall of child sexual abuse; the court also noted that *Daubert* does not apply because the issue was the competence of the witness, not the admissibility of research studies or expert opinion.); *see also* Daubert v. Merrell Dow Pharmaceuticals, Inc., 509 U.S. 579, 113 S.Ct. 2786, 125 L.Ed.2d 469 (1993); *see generally* Chapter 9.

More commonly, however, courts expect that testimony of recovered memories will be accompanied by expert testimony. *See, e.g.,* Moriarty v. Garden Sanctuary Church of God, 341 S.C. 320, 534 S.E.2d 672 (S.C.2000) ("[E]xpert testimony is required to prove both the abuse and the repressed memory."); Doe v. Shults–Lewis Child and Family Services, Inc., 718 N.E.2d 738, 748 (Ind.1999) (Same).

3. This introduction focuses on the use of expert testimony on repressed memories in the civil context, because that is the domain in which most cases will be found. The criminal context generally presents similar issues, so most of the discussion here is relevant to that context as well. In murder cases, however, there is no statute of limitations, so the issue surrounding use of repressed memories is one of due process more generally. *See, e.g.,* Franklin v. Duncan, 884 F.Supp. 1435 (N.D.Cal.

1995) (The defendant was convicted based, in part, on testimony of his daughter who claimed that twenty years before, as a child, she saw her father kill a young girl, but had repressed the memory ever since.).

4. *See, e.g.,* K.G. v. R.T.R., 918 S.W.2d 795 (Mo.1996) (applying two year limitation period that begins running at the age of majority (there 21)).

In *Fager v. Hundt,* 610 N.E.2d 246 (Ind. 1993), the court noted that Indiana requires that tort claims that are incurred while the plaintiff is a minor must be brought within two years after reaching the age of majority. In ordinary cases, however, parents have the responsibility to alert their children to any tortious actions that were committed against them. Recognizing the extreme unlikelihood that a child abuser would alert his victim to the legal implications of abuse, the court decided that "the doctrine of fraudulent concealment should be available to estop a defendant from asserting the statute of limitations" when he concealed material facts about abuse from the plaintiff. *Id.* at 251. Thus, a parent who concealed abuse would be estopped from asserting a statute of limitations defense.

5. *See* Farris v. Compton, 652 A.2d 49, 58 (D.C.Ct.App.1994) ("To permit a plaintiff to avoid the statute of limitations ... might re-

Recently, however, courts have begun to apply the "delayed discovery rule" in child sex abuse cases. This rule allows tolling of the statute of limitations until an injury is, or, in some cases, reasonably should have been, discovered. Historically, the discovery rule frequently has been applied in medical malpractice cases. A simple example is when a surgeon accidentally leaves a sponge or other instrument inside a patient, and it takes the patient substantial time to determine the source of his discomfort.[6] In the context of sex abuse, the point of discovery is when the victim becomes aware of either the injury or the link between the injury and his or her psychological distress. Although the vast majority of states now permit use of the discovery rule in child sexual abuse cases, either by court decision or legislation, courts' enthusiasm for employing this exception varies widely.[7]

Lemmerman v. Fealk,[8] a Michigan Supreme Court decision, offers a good illustration of the issues surrounding application of the discovery rule, as well as the typical factual circumstances presented in repressed memory cases. *Lemmerman* consolidated two different causes of action. In the first, the plaintiff brought suit in 1990 against her father's estate, her mother, and her aunt, alleging childhood sexual abuse beginning in 1939 and lasting ten years. The plaintiff contended that she developed a second personality "who took her place during the abusive episodes."[9] Consequently, she had no active memory of the abuse until it was revealed to her in a conversation with her

---

quire the defendant to go to trial with his ability to defend himself severely curtailed, if not completely eviscerated, by the passage of time.").

6. *See e.g.*, Gaddis v. Smith, 417 S.W.2d 577, 580 (Tex.1967) (discovery rule applied where surgeon left sponge in plaintiff's body). *See also* McCollum v. D'Arcy, 138 N.H. 285, 638 A.2d 797, 798 (N.H.1994) (discussing the common law roots of the discovery rule, and applying it to a civil sexual assault case). The discovery rule was first applied in *Urie v. Thompson*, 337 U.S. 163, 69 S.Ct. 1018, 93 L.Ed. 1282 (1949), in which the plaintiff's cause of action was held to accrue at discovery of silicosis (brown lung disease) rather than at the most recent exposure.

7. Many of these cases, however, do not specifically consider the soundness of the psychological theory surrounding repressed memories. Because most of them come to appellate courts from orders granting motions for summary judgment, these courts, following procedural conventions, accept the factual pleadings of the party against whom summary judgment was ordered. But courts do not always follow their own admonition that they should only assume, but not decide, the validity of the phenomenon of repressed memories. For example, in *Doe v. Roe*, 191 Ariz. 313, 955 P.2d 951 (Ariz.1998), the Arizona Supreme Court explicitly declined to reach the question of the scientific validity of the theory of repressed memories. *Id.* at 956. Nonetheless, they conducted an extensive literature review and offered substantive conclusions on this very issue:

From a review of the literature, we must conclude that repressed memories of childhood abuse can exist and can be triggered and recovered. We also conclude that such memories can be inaccurate, may be implanted, and may be attributable to poorly trained therapists or use of improper therapeutic techniques. On the record before us, it is impossible to say which is the case here. Suffice it to say at this stage of the proceedings—summary judgment—we must assume the truth of Plaintiff's submission and that it would be for the jury to decide the question of repressed memory recovery or false memory syndrome.

Id. at 959. This conclusion seems to assume that the phenomenon is admissible in the first place, an issue the court had earlier stated plainly that it would not reach. This *obiter dicta* sparked the ire of Justice Martone who criticized the majority for discussing "legitimacy of a scientific theory in a case in which the scientific issue is not even presented." *Id.* at 969 (Martone, J., concurring). He found this especially objectionable since "[n]othing that appears in the court's opinion on this issue came from the parties." *Id.*

The Arizona Supreme Court reached the issue of the admissibility of repressed memories (but not the validity of the research supporting their existence) in a later case, *Logerquist v. McVey*, 196 Ariz. 470, 1 P.3d 113 (Ariz.2000), discussed *infra* § 10–1.3.1.

8. 449 Mich. 56, 534 N.W.2d 695 (Mich. 1995).

9. *Id.* at 696.

father in 1989. The second case involved a daughter's 1993 suit against her father, alleging that he sexually abused her and forced her into prostitution from the time she was five (in 1942) until her adolescence. She claimed that she had repressed all memories of the abuse until therapy uncovered them in 1992.[10]

The Michigan Supreme Court began by noting that the plaintiffs' claims were barred by the statute of limitations unless either the discovery rule or the "insanity disability grace period" operated to extend the limitations period.[11] The court explained that the policies behind statutes of limitations were to "encourage plaintiffs to pursue claims diligently" and "protect defendants from having to defend against stale and fraudulent claims."[12]

The court responded to the plaintiffs' discovery rule claim by observing that, despite the discovery rule, Michigan law allows a cause of action to move forward if "a plaintiff would otherwise be denied a reasonable opportunity to bring suit because of the latent nature of the injury or the inability to discover the causal connection between the injury and the defendant's breach of duty owed to the plaintiff."[13] Michigan courts are to weigh "the benefit of application of the discovery rule to the plaintiff against the harm this exception would visit on the defendant" before allowing the plaintiff to bring suit.[14] According to the *Lemmerman* court, the discovery rule extends the statute of limitations only when "the dispute between [the] parties [can be] based on evaluation of a factual, tangible consequence of action by the defendant, measured against an objective standard."[15] If the trier of fact is unable to measure the defendant's actions "against an objective standard of care," then the claim is barred.[16] In these cases, because liability could only be "determined solely by reference to one person's version of what happened as against another's," the discovery rule did not apply.[17] The court concluded by asserting that "we cannot conclude with any reasonable degree of confidence that factfinders could fairly and reliably resolve the questions before them, given

---

10. *Id*. at 697.

11. *Id*. at 698.

12. *Id*. Many other states struggle with the task of reconciling fairness for the plaintiff and due process for the defendant. Noting that, as time passes, memories fade and witnesses die, Illinois allows plaintiffs to file claims based on recovered memory until only age thirty. *See* Boggs v. Adams, 45 F.3d 1056, 1059–60 (7th Cir.1995) (interpreting Illinois law, S.H.A. 735 ILCS 5/13–202.2(6)). As one court said in dismissing a claim made against a retired couple living on a pension in Florida by their daughters who alleged abuse from 18 to 24 years earlier:

If such an open-ended discovery rule were applied, suits could be maintained against defendants who would be not only much older, and more infirm, than plaintiffs, but also are more likely to be dead. In a case like this, where over two decades have passed since the alleged misconduct began, it is easy to imagine how witnesses could be deceased or become unavailable, memories could fade

to black, or tangible evidence simply disappear.

Messina v. Bonner, 813 F.Supp. 346, 349 (E.D.Pa.1993).

13. *Lemmerman*, 534 N.W.2d at 698.

14. *Id*. at 699.

15. *Id*.

16. *Id*.

17. *Id*. The court also dismissed the plaintiffs' claims that the insanity disability exception applied to these suits. Under Michigan law, a plaintiff who is insane when a claim accrues is given a one-year grace period after sanity is restored to file suit. Again, the court determined that the critical issue that courts must assess in deciding whether to allow a suit is "whether the overarching policy goals normally protected by the statute of limitations remain inviolate." *Id*. at 702. Because these policy goals would be endangered by applying the insanity disability provision, the court held that this avenue was also closed to the plaintiffs. *Id*.

the state of the art regarding repressed memory and the absence of objective verification."[18]

The Texas Supreme Court also concluded that the discovery rule cannot be appropriately applied in child sexual assault cases. In *S.V. v. R.V.*,[19] in a long and careful opinion, the court noted that the discovery rule is typically employed when either there is fraudulent concealment of the wrong or when the nature of the injury is inherently undiscoverable and the evidence of the injury is objectively verifiable.[20] The court accepted that, given the special relationship involved in these cases, undiscoverability of the injury could be assumed. However, these cases do not offer enough objective verification of the wrong and the injury to apply the discovery rule.[21] The only proof in many of these cases that abuse occurred and caused the psychological trauma of repressed memories are the memories themselves. After extensively surveying the psychological literature on repressed memories, the court found little agreement on the existence of the phenomenon or the credibility of memories claimed to have been uncovered through therapy.[22] The court concluded that "[o]pinions in this area simply cannot meet the 'objective verifiability' element for extending the discovery rule."[23]

Courts also have struggled with several questions surrounding the interpretation of the discovery rule. In general, "discovery occurs when the party knows of facts sufficient to put a person of ordinary intelligence and prudence on inquiry which, if pursued, would lead to the discovery of facts constituting the basis of the cause of action."[24] Some courts, however, have found that repression cannot toll a limitations period when the repression occurs after a time when the claimant had already "discovered" the basis of the cause of action.[25] The plaintiff ordinarily bears the burden of proof to demonstrate lack of knowledge during the relevant period.[26]

A related concern regards the question of what sort of disability, if any, the phenomenon of repressed memories qualifies under for purposes of tolling

18. *Id.* at 703. The *Lemmerman* court also expressed the view that it must "defer to the legislature to consider the appropriateness of extending the limitation period ... in such situations." *Id.* at 704.

19. 933 S.W.2d 1 (Tex.1996).

20. *Id.* at 4.

21. *Id.*

22. *Id. See also* Dalrymple v. Brown, 549 Pa. 217, 701 A.2d 164, 170 (Pa.1997) ("Under application of the objective standard it would be absurd to argue that a reasonable person, even assuming for the sake of argument, a reasonable six-year old, would repress the memory of a touching so that no amount of diligence would enable the person to know of the injury.").

23. *Id.* In *Demeyer v. Archdiocese of Detroit*, 233 Mich.App. 409, 593 N.W.2d 560, 563 (Mich.App.1999), the court noted that the importance of the discovery rule lies in the need to "be assured of reliable fact finding." Accordingly, where there is independent corroborative evidence of the underlying claim of abuse, such

as an admission by the alleged perpetrator, there is less concern that the cause of action involves "stale and unverifiable claims" which are the target of limitations periods. *Id. See also* Moriarty v. Garden Sanctuary Church of God, 341 S.C. 320, 534 S.E.2d 672 (S.C.2000) ("[A] plaintiff must present independently verifiable, objective evidence that corroborates a repressed memory claim in order to assert the discovery rule.").

24. Teater v. State, 252 Neb. 20, 559 N.W.2d 758, 761 (Neb.1997).

25. *See, e.g., Burkholz*, 972 P.2d at 1237 ("[T]he discovery rule simply does not apply where the plaintiff, at some point during the limitations period, has knowledge of the facts underlying his claim.").

26. *See* Martinelli v. Bridgeport Roman Catholic Diocesan Corp., 196 F.3d 409, 427 (2d Cir.1999) (Interpreting Connecticut law, court found that the "plaintiff's ignorance of the facts is a necessary element of tolling under [the] statute."); Bonilla–Aviles v. Southmark San Juan, Inc., 992 F.2d 391, 393 (1st Cir. 1993).

a statute of limitations period. For example, in *Smith v. O'Connell*,[27] a federal district court was confronted with the issue whether repressed memories constituted an "unsound mind," a classification that would have tolled the limitations period. After carefully examining the statutory language and history, the court concluded that the legislature intended that "unsound mind" refers "only to incompetency or an inability to manage one's everyday affairs."[28] It did not, therefore, encompass repressed memories.

§ 10–1.3 Evidentiary Issues

Courts have increasingly considered the issue of the evidentiary value of repressed memories under both *Daubert* and *Frye*.[29] As would be expected, state courts have had greater numbers of repressed memory cases and have supplied a preponderance of the case law on the subject. In the federal arena, there are relatively few cases on the matter and a general dearth of carefully reasoned authority. This is mainly because the evidentiary issues seem to be most plainly presented in criminal cases which primarily arise in state courts. The few federal cases that have squarely considered this question have not distinguished themselves in evaluating the basis for recovered memory testimony.[30] We begin our analysis with the states, where courts have taken diametrically opposed positions on the subject. We then consider the few federal cases that have addressed repressed memories under *Daubert* and Rule 702.

§ 10–1.3.1 State Case Law

On the issue of the evidentiary value of recovered memories, the New Hampshire Supreme Court has offered a careful analysis of the underlying science. In *State v. Hungerford*[31] and *State v. Walters*,[32] the court evaluated the admissibility of testimony that was based on memories once repressed and now claimed to be recovered. Because *Hungerford* was decided first, we shall

27.   997 F.Supp. 226 (D.R.I.1998).

28.   *Id.* at 235.

29.   California generally exempts medical and psychological expert testimony from its admissibility requirements for scientific evidence. For "traditional" scientific evidence, California courts apply a general acceptance standard associated with the former *Frye* test which was incorporated into California law through *People v. Kelly*, 17 Cal.3d 24, 130 Cal.Rptr. 144, 549 P.2d 1240 (Cal.1976); *see* Frye v. United States, 293 F. 1013 (D.C.Cir. 1923). The California Supreme Court explained that the *Kelly* test "is intended to forestall the jury's uncritical acceptance of scientific evidence or technology that is so foreign to everyday experience as to be unusually difficult for laypersons to evaluate." People v. Venegas, 18 Cal.4th 47, 74 Cal.Rptr.2d 262, 954 P.2d 525 (Cal.1998). According to California courts, expert medical and psychiatric opinion does not present a danger of overwhelming jurors with the aura of certainty associated with the "harder" sciences. *See* People v. McDonald, 37 Cal.3d 351, 208 Cal.Rptr. 236, 690 P.2d 709 (Cal.1984). Consequently, in *Wilson v. Phillips*,

73 Cal.App 4th 250, 86 Cal.Rptr.2d 204 (Cal. App.1999), the court held that *Kelly* does not apply to the theory of repressed memories. The court explained that the expert's "testimony on her findings amounted to little more than run-of-the-mill expert medical opinion," *Id.* at 255. At least one other California court, however, has observed that "it appears highly unlikely that [repressed memory theory] commands anything close to the necessary general acceptance within the relevant scientific community to pass *Kelly*." Trear v. Sills, 69 Cal.App.4th 1341, 82 Cal.Rptr.2d 281, 285 n. 14 (Cal.App. 1999).

What might be termed the California rule— no substantive review of expert opinion testimony that is a product of experience—is considered later in this section in our discussion of an Arizona case, *Logerquist v. McVey*, 196 Ariz. 470, 1 P.3d 113 (Ariz.2000).

30.   *See infra* § 10–1.3.2.

31.   142 N.H. 110, 697 A.2d 916 (N.H.1997).

32.   142 N.H. 239, 698 A.2d 1244 (N.H. 1997).

focus our attention there. Both, however, offer excellent yardsticks by which this kind of evidence can be measured.

New Hampshire applies a validity test based on *Daubert*.[33] The *Hungerford* court noted, however, that the inquiry in repressed memory cases is not the usual evaluation of the scientific basis for an expert's opinion. Instead, since the evidence being offered is a lay witness who would testify to the witness' own recovered memories, courts essentially are engaged in an evaluation of witness competency in these cases.[34] Nonetheless, the court found that reliability of recovered memories could not be separated from the validity of the psychology of repressed memories. Therefore, "when challenged, testimony that relies on memories which previously have been partially or fully repressed must satisfy a pretrial reliability determination."[35] Recovered memories, like hypnotically refreshed recall, raise substantial questions concerning the trustworthiness of the memories.[36] This determination requires courts to consider expert testimony on the phenomenon.[37]

In order to assess the reliability of recovered memories, the New Hampshire court listed eight factors that trial courts should consider:

> (1) the level of peer review and publication of the phenomenon of repression and recovery of memories; (2) whether the phenomenon has been generally accepted in the psychological community; (3) whether the phenomenon may be and has been empirically tested; (4) the potential or known rate of recovered memories that are false; (5) the age of the witness at the time the event or events occurred; (6) the length of time between the event and the recovery of the memory; (7) the presence or absence of objective, verifiable, corroborative evidence of the event; and (8) the circumstances attendant to the witness's recovery of the memory, i.e., whether the witness was engaged in therapy or some other process seeking to recover memories or likely to result in recovered memories.[38]

It is worth noting that the first four factors are based specifically on *Daubert* and concern the validity of the underlying science, and the remaining four are helpful guideposts for evaluating a particular witness' testimony. Applying these factors to the case before it, the court concluded that "[t]he phenomenon of recovery or repressed memories has not yet reached the point where we may perceive these particular recovered memories as reliable."[39] Still, individual cases might present circumstances compelling the conclusion that the memories recovered are sufficiently reliable. Also, someday, research might develop sufficiently to support the phenomenon more broadly. But, " '[t]hat day is not here.' "[40]

---

33. *Hungerford*, 697 A.2d at 919.

34. *Id.* at 920.

35. *Id.*

36. *Id.* at 922–23; *see also* Chapter 9, § 9–1.1.

37. *Id.* at 922.

38. *Id.* at 925 (citations omitted); *see also* State v. Walters, 142 N.H. 239, 698 A.2d 1244, 1246–47 (N.H.1997).

39. *Hungerford*, 697 A.2d at 929.

40. *Id.* (*quoting* Ault v. Jasko, 70 Ohio St.3d 114, 637 N.E.2d 870, 874–75 (Ohio 1994)

(Moyer, J., dissenting)). *See also* Franklin v. Stevenson, 987 P.2d 22 (Utah 1999); State v. Quattrocchi, 1999 WL 284882 *13 (R.I.1999), affirmed. However, the court in *Moriarty v. Garden Sanctuary Church of God*, 334 S.C. 150, 511 S.E.2d 699 (S.C.Ct.App.1999), found the theory of repressed memory to be more than sufficiently reliable to survive summary judgment. In an extended discussion of the phenomenon, the court concluded that "repressed memories of childhood sexual abuse can exist and can be triggered and recovered." *Id.* at 705. Relying on Freudian conceptions of

Courts in some states, however, apply no substantive review of psychological opinion testimony such as that on repressed memories. This approach might be termed the "California rule," since it appears to trace its origins there. Under the California rule, courts apply a restrictive *Frye*-styled general acceptance test to testimony based on a "new scientific technique." The primary concern with this kind of evidence, according to the California Supreme Court in *People v. Kelly*,[41] was the possibly overwhelming influence complex scientific evidence might have on jurors. The court observed that "[l]ay jurors tend to give considerable weight to 'scientific' evidence when presented by 'experts' with impressive credentials."[42] Therefore, "[t]he primary advantage ... of the *Frye* test lies in its essentially conservative nature."[43] However, under California law, expert opinion not based on complex science receives no substantive scrutiny. The main reason given for this gaping exception to the *Kelly-Frye* test is that jurors are less likely to be overwhelmed by an "aura of infallibility." The California Supreme Court explained:

> When a witness gives his personal opinion on the stand—even if he qualifies as an expert—the jurors may temper their acceptance of his testimony with a healthy skepticism born of their knowledge that all human beings are fallible.[44]

It is not entirely obvious where the line sits between "expert opinion evidence" and "expert scientific opinion evidence."[45] In fact, California case law appears confused on the issue.[46] In the context of repressed memories, the best example of the confused state of the California rule comes from Arizona.

In *Logerquist v. McVey*,[47] the Arizona Supreme Court rejected the adoption of the *Daubert* validity test preferring to retain the more easily applied

---

the brain from the nineteenth century and numerous law review articles, the court accepted that sometimes "an event occurs which is so traumatic that, in a desperate effort to cope, one's mind dissociates itself and shuts the memory out." *Id.* at 703 (*citing* Rola J. Yamini, Note, *Repressed and Recovered Memories of Child Sexual Abuse: The Accused as "Direct Victim,"* 47 HASTINGS L.J. 551 (1996)). According to the court, "[m]any, if not most, survivors of child sexual abuse develop amnesia that is so complete they simply do not remember they were abused at all." *Id.* at 705 (*citing* Jocelyn B. Lamm, Note, *Easing Access to the Courts for Incest Victims: Toward and Equitable Application of the Delayed Discovery Rule*, 100 YALE L.J. 2189 (1991)). Given that the *Moriarty* court cited no scientific research done after 1900, and relied exclusively on law review commentary and the compendium of psychological diagnoses compiled by the American Psychiatric Association, its quoting of the following statement borders on high comedy: " 'Rules of law are not petrified in the past but flow with the current of expanding knowledge.' " *Id.* at 705 (*quoting* Shahzade v. Gregory, 923 F.Supp. 286, 290 (D.Mass.1996)).

41. 17 Cal.3d 24, 130 Cal.Rptr. 144, 549 P.2d 1240, 1244 (Cal.1976).

42. *Id.* at 1245.

43. *Id.*

44. People v. McDonald, 37 Cal.3d 351, 208 Cal.Rptr. 236, 690 P.2d 709, 724 (Cal.1984).

45. The United States Supreme Court rejected a similar distinction, between scientific and non-scientific evidence, in *Kumho Tire*.

46. California courts *not* applying *Kelly-Frye:* People v. McDonald, 37 Cal.3d 351, 208 Cal.Rptr. 236, 690 P.2d 709 (Cal.1984) (eyewitness identification expert); Wilson v. Phillips, 73 Cal.App.4th 250, 86 Cal.Rptr.2d 204 (1999) (repressed memories); People v. Ward, 71 Cal. App.4th 368, 83 Cal.Rptr.2d 828 (1999) (sexually violent predator); People v. Mendibles, 199 Cal.App.3d 1277, 245 Cal.Rptr. 553 (1988) (child sexual abuse); *In re* Amber B., 191 Cal. App.3d 682, 236 Cal.Rptr. 623 (1987) (child sexual abuse). California courts applying *Kelly-Frye:* People v. Shirley, 31 Cal.3d 18, 181 Cal. Rptr. 243, 723 P.2d 1354 (Cal.1982) (hypnotically refreshed testimony); People v. Bledsoe, 36 Cal.3d 236, 203 Cal.Rptr. 450, 681 P.2d 291 (Cal.1984) (rape trauma syndrome).

47. 196 Ariz. 470, 1 P.3d 113 (Ariz.2000).

Frye test.[48] The court held, however, that *Frye's* general acceptance test does not apply to experience-based testimony on the phenomenon of repressed memories.[49] It opted explicitly to follow the California rule. The court explained that *"Frye* is applicable when an expert witness reaches a conclusion by deduction from the application of novel scientific principles, formulae, or procedures developed by others." But, the court argued, *Frye* "is inapplicable when a witness reaches a conclusion by inductive reasoning based on his or her own experience, observation, or research." The reasoning of the *Logerquist* holding was severely criticized by two dissenting justices,[50] and has been the subject of an intensive critical barrage from scholars.[51]

Unlike California courts, and to its credit, the *Logerquist* court sought to define the boundary between "scientific opinion" testimony and "expert opinion" testimony. As noted, the court explained that the former is a product of deductive reasoning and the latter comes from inductive reasoning. The court explained the consequences of its analysis as follows:

> Our decision … does not turn on an attempt to determine whether repressed memory is "scientific" or "unscientific." Plaintiff does not claim her memories are proved true as a matter of scientific fact. *Frye* is applicable when an expert witness reaches a conclusion by deduction from the application of novel scientific principles, formulae, or procedures developed by others. It is inapplicable when a witness reaches a conclusion by inductive reasoning based on his or her own experience, observation, or research. In the latter case, the validity of the premise is tested by interrogation of the witness; in the former case, it is tested by inquiring into general acceptance.[52]

Although much can be, and undoubtedly will be, said about the Arizona court's analysis, we limit our comments here to the proposed distinction between science and non-science as determined by whether the opinion is the product of inductive or deductive reasoning. The court stated that a principal reason for distinguishing inductive and deductive reasoning was to avoid having to decide "whether repressed memory is 'scientific' or 'unscientific.'" But it is clear from the decision that the court actually made this determination, since it agreed that " '[r]epression … has not yet been appropriately tested.' "[53] Thus, repression is not science. The court believed, nonetheless, that an expert's experience with the phenomenon still makes the testimony probative, because the "[p]laintiff does not claim her memories are proved true as a matter of scientific fact."[54]

---

48. The Logerquist court's primary reason for not adopting *Daubert* was its concern that judges do not have the competence to employ it well. "[M]ost judges, like most jurors, have little or no technical training 'and are not known for expertise in science.' " *Id.* at 129 (*quoting* 1 DAVID L. FAIGMAN, DAVID H. KAYE, MICHAEL J. SAKS & JOSEPH SANDERS, MODERN SCIENTIFIC EVIDENCE: THE LAW AND SCIENCE OF EXPERT TESTIMONY vii (1997)).

49. *Id.* at 133 ("This case turns on a non-scientific issue.").

50. *Logerquist*, 1 P.3d at 136 (Martone, J., dissenting) ("[T]here are almost no views or opinions expressed in the majority opinion that

I share."); *Id.* at 140 (McGregor, J., dissenting) (asserting that the distinction the majority draws between scientific and non-scientific expert testimony does not "rest[] on a firm basis").

51. *See* Symposium: *Logerquist v. McVey*, 33 ARIZ. ST. L.J. 40 (2001).

52. *Logerquist*, 1 P.3d at 133.

53. *Id.* at 134 (*quoting* MODERN SCIENTIFIC EVIDENCE, *supra* note 48, § 10–2.4 at 150 (Supp.1999)).

54. *Id.* at 133.

The error the Arizona court made was believing that scientific knowledge is discrete or categorical. It is not. The scientific method is a process. This process employs both inductive and deductive reasoning and by no means privileges simple experience. Certainly, scientists invariably begin the process with experience (or observation). A medical doctor, for example, might observe that blood-letting relieves his patient's headaches and thus develops a hypothesis regarding both the mechanism and effectiveness of this therapy. This experience might be multiplied by additional cases from the doctor's, and possibly other doctors', clinics. Of course, it is to be expected that not all patients benefit from this therapy, but experience well demonstrated that many did. Does inductive reasoning thus demonstrate the effectiveness of blood-letting? For many centuries it did. In Arizona, it still might.

A good scientist tests theories using both inductive and deductive reasoning, together with a surfeit of possible methodologies. For example, in the context of repressed memories, a doctor might have examined one or more people who claimed to have begun remembering things of a disturbing nature that they had previously not known about. A scientist's approach to this phenomenon would be at least two-fold. On the one hand, employing inductive reasoning, he might look for further instances of this phenomenon. This initial observation could have been an anomaly or not accurate for a variety of reasons. In seeking confirmation, the wise researcher would want to ensure that the underlying traumas occurred, that the amnesias were not explainable by other factors—such as biological amnesia—and that the reports of repression were not spurious products of expectations of either the subjects or the researchers.[55] At the same time, using deductive reasoning, the scientist would seek to integrate his observations into what is generally known about human memory and the brain.

In time, we expect, the California rule will prove to be unworkable. Its main defect lies in that it cannot be consistently applied. Arizona's attempt to discern a dividing line based on the distinction between inductive and deductive reasoning is destined to fail. It simply does not pertain to the reality of knowledge acquisition in the twenty-first century. Expert opinion, whether labeled science or non-science, is inevitably a product of both types of reasoning.

§ 10–1.3.2   Federal Case Law

Very few federal cases have considered the admissibility of expert testimony regarding repressed memories. The few that have reached the question have not provided deep or cogent analysis of the matter. In *Hoult v. Hoult*,[56] the First Circuit applied a very deferential standard of review because the case came to it on appeal from a denial of relief from judgment under Rule 60(b) of the Federal Rules of Civil Procedure.[57] In *Isely v. Capuchin Province*,[58]

55. *See* discussion *infra* § 10–2.1.2.

56. 57 F.3d 1 (1st Cir.1995).

57. *Id.* at 2. The *Hoult* court explained that "district courts enjoy broad discretion in deciding motions brought under Rule 60(b), and [appellate courts] review such rulings only for abuse of discretion." *Id.* at 3. Moreover, appel-

late "review is limited to the denial of the motion itself. [Appellate courts] may not consider the merits of the underlying judgment." *Id.*

58. 877 F.Supp. 1055 (E.D.Mich.1995).

the district court applied Rule 702 incorrectly.[59]

Although the *Hoult* court could not provide relief for mistakes of law under Rule 60(b), the court did not refrain from stating that it had serious doubts about the lower court's relaxed standard for admitting expert testimony on repressed memories. First of all, the court explained that *Daubert* requires "district courts to conduct a preliminary assessment of the reliability of expert testimony, even in the absence of an objection."[60] Since failure to provide this preliminary assessment would be a mistake of law, however, it did not constitute "grounds for relief under Rule 60(b)."[61] The *Hoult* court also reviewed the expert's testimony which, according to the defendant, " 'usurped the function of the jury' by opining on the plaintiff's credibility."[62] The court found that her testimony "came perilously close to testifying that this particular victim/witness could be believed."[63] But since the defendant did not object to this testimony or appeal its admission, the court could not conclude that it was "a 'plain usurpation of the jury's function constituting a violation of due process.' "[64]

In *Isely v. Capuchin Province*,[65] the court was squarely presented with the question whether "there is a sufficient scientific basis of support for the theory [of repressed memories] . . . to permit the issue to go to the jury."[66] The court, however, misconstrued its role in evaluating this evidence under *Daubert*. The court "perceive[d] its role with respect to the admissibility of expert testimony as being a 'screener' of expert testimony, similar to its role under Fed.R.Evid. 104(b) of screening conditionally relevant evidence."[67] This is plainly wrong. Under *Daubert,* the district court judge is not a "screener" under Rule 104(b), he is a "gatekeeper" under Rule 104(a).[68] In fact, the *Isely* court did little more than check the expert's credentials, and provided absolutely no review of the validity of the scientific basis—even under the avowed screening function of Rule 104(b).[69]

---

59. In a third federal case squarely presented with the validity of repressed memories under *Daubert, Shahzade v. Gregory,* 923 F.Supp. 286 (D.Mass.1996), the court followed *Isely v. Capuchin,* 877 F.Supp. 1055 (E.D.Mich. 1995), a case which had applied *Daubert* incorrectly. This is especially surprising, since the *Shahzade* court is in the First Circuit, which had decided *Hoult v. Hoult,* 57 F.3d 1 (1st Cir.1995), probably the best reasoned federal decision. The *Shahzade* court ignored *Hoult* and agreed with *Isely* that the theory of repressed memories was sufficiently valid to admit the testimony.

60. *Id.* at 5. The court noted, however, that this does not mean district courts must, "sua sponte, . . . make explicit on-the-record rulings regarding the admissibility of expert testimony." *Id. See also* United States v. Locascio, 6 F.3d 924 (2d Cir.1993).

61. *Hoult,* 57 F.3d at 5.

62. *Id.* at 6.

63. *Id.* at 7.

64. *Id.*

65. 877 F.Supp. 1055 (E.D.Mich.1995).

66. *Id.* at 1066.

67. *Id.*

68. *Daubert,* 509 U.S. at 591 & 592 n. 10; *see also* Bourjaily v. United States, 483 U.S. 171, 175–76, 107 S.Ct. 2775, 97 L.Ed.2d 144 (1987).

69. *Isely,* 877 F.Supp. at 1066. The *Isely* court more successfully responded to the conventional question of the permissible scope of the proposed expert testimony. The court concluded that the expert could testify that the plaintiff's "behavior is consistent with someone who is suffering repressed memory." However, the expert "should not be permitted to testify that she either believes [the plaintiff] or believes that the incidents he alleges occurred. . . . Thus, [the expert] may testify concerning repressed memory, give her opinions about it, and she can testify as to whether [the plaintiff], in [the expert's] belief, has experienced or suffers from repressed memory." *Id.* at 1067.

In addition, many courts voice substantial concerns regarding the "therapeutic techniques" that are used to "recover" repressed memories. These courts cite the danger that highly suggestive, and possibly coercive, techniques produce "memories" that have little or no foundation in fact.[70] In *S.V. v. R.V.*,[71] for example, the court observed as follows:

> Therapists who expect to find abuse often do. And because the therapist occupies a position of authority and trust with the patient, this "confirmatory bias" can lead to leading questions and other forms of suggestion . . . . Therapists also may interpret certain symptoms as indicating childhood sexual abuse, but those symptoms may be so general that they do not eliminate other possible ills.

> In short, the preconceptions of the therapist, the suggestibility of the patient, the aleatory nature of memory recall, and the need to find a clear culprit for a diffuse set of symptoms may lead to false memories.[72]

§ 10–1.4   Civil Suits Brought by the Alleged Abusers Against Therapists

A backlash has developed in response to lawsuits involving repressed memories of long past alleged sexual abuse, resulting in several novel strains of litigation. These "backlash" suits reflect the view that therapists and other proponents of memory repression therapy owe a duty of care to those whose reputations, families, careers, finances, or emotional health may be destroyed by allegations of abuse that arise from therapy. Jurors are asked to decide whether the therapist elicited a true memory or created a false one through suggestion or coercion.[73]

In *Sullivan v. Cheshier*,[74] parents sued their daughter's psychologist. At age twenty-three, the daughter accused her older brother of sexually abusing her when she was a child.[75] She claimed to have recovered memories of the abuse while under hypnosis in Cheshier's care in 1990. She refused contact with her parents, explaining that Dr. Cheshier had advised her not to discuss her memories with anyone who did not accept them. The parents claimed loss of their daughter's society, intentional and reckless infliction of emotional distress, and injury to the family relationship.

The psychologist filed a motion for summary judgment, asserting that the statute of limitations had run on the parents' claims. The parents argued that under a catch-all provision, the period was five years, which had not expired. The court, looking to the nature of the damage and whether the injury was tangible,[76] granted summary judgment on two claims. The court, however, denied the motion for summary judgment on the claims of malpractice and

---

70. *See id.* ("[T]here is considerable doubt about the reliability of memories that are recalled with the assistance of a therapist or psychoanalyst."); State v. Hungerford, 1995 WL 378571 *14 (N.H.1995) (noting that the psychotherapy used in that case showed "complete disregard of the basic standards.").

71. 933 S.W.2d 1 (Tex.1996).

72. *Id.* at 18.

73. *See generally* Lindgren v. Moore, 907 F.Supp. 1183 (N.D.Ill.1995); Shanley v. Braun,

1997 WL 779112 (N.D.Ill.1997). *Cf.* Franklin v. Terr, 201 F.3d 1098 (9th Cir.2000) (Court dismissed § 1983 suit against therapist and others for conspiracy to commit perjury in earlier criminal prosecution on the basis that witnesses enjoy absolute immunity.).

74. 846 F.Supp. 654 (N.D.Ill.1994).

75. *Id.* at 656.

76. *Id.* at 659–60.

loss of society and companionship. In reaching its conclusion, the court stated as follows:

> Parents may not sue generally for damages caused by malpractice against a child, but the summary record here can be read to say that Dr. Cheshier specifically directed his actions, in part, against the parents and their interests, that he imposed a false memory in Kathleen Sullivan, instructed her to break contact with her parents if they dissented from her memory and prevented the parents from taking reasonable steps to inquire into the validity of the memory.[77]

Although therapists clearly owe a duty of care to their patients,[78] courts are reluctant to extend this duty to third parties.[79] In *Doe v. McKay*,[80] for example, the Illinois Supreme Court refused to extend a therapist's duty of care to a third party hurt by false suggestions allegedly made to the patient regarding past sexual assaults. The court extolled the value of psychotherapy to society and thought imposing such a duty would undermine its effectiveness.[81] "Hoping to avoid liability to third parties," the court observed, "a therapist might . . . find it necessary to deviate from the treatment the therapist would normally provide, to the patient's ultimate detriment."[82] The court concluded, "[t]his would exact an intolerably high price from the patient-therapist relationship and would be destructive of that relationship."[83]

A subsidiary issue which has yet to receive substantial judicial attention involves the empirical question whether research supports the conclusion that false memories can be implanted. Referred to as False Memory Syndrome, psychologists are engaged in a significant debate whether it is itself a real phenomenon.[84] Courts will likely have to confront questions surrounding false memory syndrome in time.

§ 10–1.5 Conclusion

In many respects, the phenomenon of repressed memory, whatever its validity, presents a classic problem for the law and science relationship. As the next section indicates, it remains woefully short of being empirically verified and, indeed, heralds from a non-rigorous school of psychology in which empirical validation is not a core tenet. The theory of repressed memories has its roots in clinical therapy, a domain in which validity is not a factor of

---

77. *Id.* at 660.

78. *See* Lujan v. Mansmann, 1997 WL 634499 (E.D.Pa.1997); Shanley v. Braun, 1997 WL 779112 (N.D.Ill.1997).

79. Where the defendant is in a special relationship with either the victim or tortfeasor, an exception might apply. *See, e.g.,* Funkhouser v. Wilson, 89 Wash.App. 644, 950 P.2d 501 (Wash.App.1998). For an excellent discussion of the public policy considerations associated with extending the duty of care to third parties, *see* J.A.H. v. Wadle & Assoc., 589 N.W.2d 256, 257–63 (Iowa 1999). *But see* Sawyer v. Midelfort, 227 Wis.2d 124, 595 N.W.2d 423, 431 (Wis.1999) (holding that public policy sometimes allows third parties to maintain suits against therapists).

80. 183 Ill.2d 272, 233 Ill.Dec. 310, 700 N.E.2d 1018 (Ill.1998).

81. *Id.* at 1024 (*citing* Jaffee v. Redmond, 518 U.S. 1, 116 S.Ct. 1923, 135 L.Ed.2d 337 (1996)); *see also* Strom v. C.C., 1997 WL 118253 (Minn.App.1997).

82. *Id.*

83. *Id.*

84. *See* RECOVERED MEMORIES AND FALSE MEMORIES (Martin A. Conway ed. 1997); *see also* Kenneth S. Pope, *Memory, Abuse, and Science: Questioning Claims About the False Memory Syndrome Epidemic*, 51 AMER. PSYCHOLOGIST 957 (1996); *but see Comments* (re Pope (1996)), 52 AMER. PSYCHOLOGIST 987 (1997).

overriding concern. In therapy, support and improved mental health are the predominant outcome measures.

The law, too, does not approach the issues raised by the theory of repressed memory only concerned about the theory's "truth." The law must also balance justice, fairness, efficiency and other factors related to its special role in American society. But these factors cannot be achieved, or at least not achieved well, without a sound understanding of the empirical validity of the phenomenon of interest. Although fairness, for instance, might or might not support allowing expert testimony on repressed memories, and the litigations in which they play a central role, it cannot be adequately determined without knowing the depth and quality of the research on which that expert testimony is based. These cases present profound and heart rending problems for the courts concerning policy and justice between parties; but which course will lead to just outcomes must be based on judgments about the soundness of the science.

B. SCIENTIFIC STATUS

by

Harrison G. Pope, Jr.,* Paul S. Oliva,** & James I. Hudson.***

§ 10–2.0 THE SCIENTIFIC STATUS OF RESEARCH ON RE-PRESSED MEMORIES

§ 10–2.1 Introductory Discussion of the Science

Traumatic events are memorable. Even years later, we can recall terrible and frightening experiences in vivid detail. That the brain works in this way seems logical: if one developed amnesia after being bitten by a snake or attacked by another person, one might place oneself in the same jeopardy over and over again.

Despite this general impression, however, various writers have hypothesized that individuals can sometimes develop amnesia for seemingly unforgettable traumatic events. In this postulated process, variously described as "repression,"[1] "dissociation,"[2] or "psychogenic amnesia,"[3] the memory of the

* Harrison G. Pope, Jr., M D is a Professor of Psychiatry at Harvard Medical School and Chief of the Biological Psychiatry Laboratory at the McLean Hospital Alcohol and Drug Abuse Research Center in Belmont, Massachusetts. He is an author of more than 300 published papers on a range of topics in psychiatry, including eating disorders, mood disorders, psychiatric diagnosis, substance abuse, psychopharmacology, and the current debate about trauma and memory. Dr. Pope currently devotes most of his time to research and teaching. Correspondence should be addressed to Dr. Pope at McLean Hospital, 115 Mill Street, Belmont, MA 02478; Telephone: (617) 855–2911; Fax: (617) 855–3585.

** Paul Oliva, B.A., M.A. is a former senior clinical research technician in the Biological Psychiatry Laboratory at McLean Hospital.

*** James I. Hudson, M.D. is an Associate Professor of Psychiatry at Harvard Medical School and an Associate Psychiatrist at McLean Hospital, Belmont, Massachusetts. He is an author of more than 150 articles in the areas of eating disorders, fibromyalgia, psychopharmacology, the neurophysiology of sleep, and the issues of trauma and memory. He is currently engaged in studies of the genetic epidemiology of affective spectrum disorder, and of new medications for mood, anxiety and eating disorders.

§ 10–2.0

1. S. FREUD, THE STANDARD EDITION OF THE COMPLETE PSYCHOLOGICAL WORKS OF SIGMUND

trauma is presumed to become inaccessible to consciousness—though under certain conditions it may sometimes be "recovered." In particular, some recent scholarly[4] and popular works[5] have argued that such amnesia may occur frequently in victims of childhood sexual abuse. For the sake of simplicity, we will use the term "repression" to refer to this process, while acknowledging that alternative proposed terms and proposed mechanisms exist.

In this chapter, we review the evidence for repression of memories of trauma in general and of sexual abuse in particular. We begin by examining general psychiatric studies of trauma survivors, to assess the validity of our original proposition that trauma is generally well remembered. Second, we propose methodologic criteria for an adequate demonstration to show that some individuals can repress the memory of a trauma. Third, we review studies cited as evidence that repression occurs in response to various traumas, such as wartime situations; prisoner-of-war, torture and concentration camp experiences; natural and man-made disasters; and after committing murder. Fourth, we look specifically at studies assessing whether individuals can repress memories of childhood sexual abuse. We conclude with suggestions for designing subsequent, more rigorous investigations.

§ 10–2.1.1 The Scientific Questions

To provide a foundation for our review, we performed a non-selective literature search for examples of studies between 1960 and 1999 where the investigators performed psychological assessments on groups of survivors of specific, historically documented traumatic events. There is no shortage of such studies; the 77 studies summarized in table 1 and referenced in Appendix A, assessing victims of all manner of traumatic events, are merely representative of a larger literature.

TABLE 1. Studies of Psychological Symptoms in Trauma Survivors

Study	Event	No. of Subjects	Data Collection Method	Amnesia?	Remarks
Adler, 1943	Cocoanut Grove Fire	46	Questionnaire	Yes	29 subjects lost consciousness. Several subjects had

FREUD 1–24 (Strachey J. London ed. & trans., Hogarth Press, 1953) (1974); M. H. Erdelyi & B. Goldberg, *Let's Not Sweep Repression Under the Rug: Toward a Cognitive Psychology of Repression*, in FUNCTIONAL DISORDERS OF MEMORY (F. J. Kihlstrom ed., 1979).

2. P. JANET, L'AUTOMATISME PSYCHOLOGIQUE (Flix Alcan, Paris, 1889); B.A. van der Kolk & R. Fisler, *Dissociation and the Fragmentary Nature of Traumatic Memories: Overview and Exploratory Study*, 8 J. TRAUMATIC STRESS 505–25 (1995).

3. D. J. Siegel, *Memory, Trauma, and Psychotherapy: A Cognitive Science View*, 4 J. PSYCHOTHERAPY PRAC. RES. 93–122 (1995).

4. D. Gelinas, *The Persisting Negative Effects of Incest*, 46 PSYCHIATRY 313–32 (1983); L. Berliner & J. R. Wheeler, *Treating the Effects of Sexual Abuse in Children*, 2 J. INTERPERSONAL VIOLENCE 415–34 (1987); J. HERMAN, TRAUMA AND RECOVERY (1992); C. L. WHITFIELD, MEMORY AND ABUSE: REMEMBERING AND HEALING THE EFFECTS OF TRAUMA (1995); A.W. Scheflin and D. Brown, *Repressed Memory or Dissociative Amnesia: What the Science Says*, 24 J. PSYCHIATRY & L 143 (1996); D.F. BROWN, A.W. SCHEFLIN & D.C. HAMMOND, MEMORY, TRAUMA TREATMENT, AND THE LAW (1998); D.F Brown, A.W. Scheflin, & C.L. Whitfield, *Recovered Memories: The Current Weight of the Evidence in Science and in the Courts* 27 J. PSYCHIATRY & L. 5–156 (1999).

5. E. S. BLUME, SECRET SURVIVORS (1990); R. FREDRICKSON, REPRESSED MEMORIES: A JOURNEY TO RECOVERY FROM SEXUAL ABUSE (1992); R. ARNOLD, MY LIVES (1994); E. BASS & L. DAVIS, THE COURAGE TO HEAL: A GUIDE FOR WOMEN SURVIVORS OF CHILD SEXUAL ABUSE (3d ed. 1994).

Study	Event	No. of Subjects	Data Collection Method	Amnesia?	Remarks
					blood carbon monoxide levels "sufficient to kill"; all subjects who did not lose consciousness remembered seeing flames
Levy, 1944	Children in surgery	124	Review of records	No	
Strom et al., 1961	Holocaust	100	Interviews	No	
Chodoff 1963	Holocaust	23	Psychiatric Interview	No	Subjects reported their experiences with "a vivid immediacy and wealth of detail"
Lepold et al. 1963	Marine explosion	34	Interviews	No	Authors note that "repression does not appear possible"
Terr, (1979, 1983)	Chowchilla bus kidnapping	26	Interviews	No	
Eaton et al., 1982	Holocaust	135	Interview	No	Although 20 (15%) of the 135 survivors had memory problems, so did 15 (11%) of the 133 non-traumatized controls; none reported to have amnesia
Wilkinson, 1983	Hyatt skywalk collapse	102	Questionnaire, interviews	No	
Hoiberg et al., 1984	Collision at sea	336	Extracted records from Naval Health Research Ctr.	No	11% were hospitalized for various psychiatric difficulties following the collision. None suffered from amnesia
Dollinger, 1985	Lightning strike disaster	38	Interviews	Yes (2 cases)	The 2 children that had amnesia were side flash victims
Malmquist 1986	Children who witnessed parental murder	16	Questionnaire (Impact of Events Scale)	No	"Recollection of vivid memories of the event were present in all 16 of the children"
Kinzie et al., 1986, 1989; Sack et al., 1993	Cambodian concentration camp victims	40	Interviews	No	
Shore et al., 1987	Mt. St. Helens explosion	548	Interviews	No	
Aveline et al., 1987	Ejection from military aircraft	175	Questionnaire	No	
Goldfeld et al, 1988	Torture victims	294	Review of several case series	Yes	No description of amnesia in the absence of head injury
McFarlane (series) 1988	Australian brush fires	469	Questionnaire, interviews	No	After 11 months, firefighters with PTSD actually displayed better memory than those without PTSD
Pynoos, 1988	Children who witnessed sexual assault of their mothers	10	Interviews	No	
Pynoos, 1989	Sniper attack at elementary school	133	Interviews	No	Some children "remembered" the sniper although they were not actually at the scene. None reported amnesia
England et al., 1989	Oil rig disaster	134	Questionnaire	No	
Nadler and Ben–Shushan 1989	Holocaust	34	Interview	No	
Stoddard et al., 1989	Burned children	30	Interview, review of records	No	

Study	Event	No. of Subjects	Data Collection Method	Amnesia?	Remarks
Robinson et al., 1990	Holocaust	86	Questionnaire	No	82% of subjects reported hyperamnesia continuously since World War II
Wagenaar and Groeneweg 1990	Holocaust	78	Review of testimony in De Rijke case	No	Almost all witnesses remembered Camp Erika in "great detail," even after 40 years
Green et al., 1991	Buffalo Creek Disaster (children)	179	Interview	Yes	7% unable to recall part of event, but 43 (25%) subjects were aged 2–7 at time of flood
Realmuto et al., 1991	Williams Pipeline Disaster	24	Interview	?	Amnesia only briefly mentioned; no cases presented
Stuber et al., 1991	Pediatric bone marrow transplant patients	6	Interview and assessment through scales	No	
Weissberg and Katz 1991	Crash of Continental 1713	15	Questionnaire, interview	No	Study of hospital-based personnel who worked with crash victims
Rothbaum et al., 1992	Rape victims	95	Questionnaire, interview	No	Many subjects had impaired concentration and memory, but none described as having amnesia
Cardena and Spiegel, 1993	Earthquake	100	Questionnaire, interview	No	"Dissociative symptoms" described, but no subject had amnesia for the earthquake
Krell, 1993	Holocaust	35	Interview and therapy	No	Results largely non-quantitative
Lee et al., 1995	World War II combat	107	Questionnaire	No	Cohort assembled in 1938 at college students and studied prospectively
Ursano et al., 1995	Explosion on USS Iowa	54	Questionnaire	No	Study of body handlers
Weine et al., 1995	"Ethnic cleansing" in Bosnia	20	Interviews, Questionnaire	No	

Upon examining the table, it is striking that none of the more than 11,000 victims is reported to have repressed the memory of the traumatic event. Admittedly, some of the survivors in some of the studies did exhibit amnesia for the trauma—but in all cases, the amnesia appears explainable for ordinary reasons, such as loss of consciousness or early childhood amnesia—phenomena which we will discuss further below. Only two fragmentary case reports in two of the studies[6] suggest even partial amnesia in individuals over the age of three who did not lose consciousness. Some of the studies in the table report "memory disturbances" among some trauma survivors. However, "memory disturbances" should not be misinterpreted as evidence that the subjects forgot the trauma itself. In fact, disturbances of memory and concentration are ubiquitous in mood and anxiety disorders, regardless of whether these disorders occur in the wake of trauma.[7] Indeed, impairment of concentration is one of the criteria in DSM–IV for the diagnosis of major depressive disorder.[8] It is illustrative, in this respect, to note the study of Eaton et al.,

6. R. Krell, *Child Survivors of the Holocaust—Strategies of Adaptation*, 38 CAN. J. PSYCHIATRY 384–89 (1993); S. M. Weine, D. F. Becker, T. H. McGlashan, D. Laub, S. Lazrove, D. Vojvoda, & L. Hyman, *Psychiatric Consequences of "Ethnic Cleansing:" Clinical Assessments and Trauma Testimonies of Newly Resettled Bosnian Refugees*, 152 AM. J. PSYCHIATRY 536–42 (1995).

7. J. P. Mialet, H. G. Pope, Jr., & D. Yurgelun–Todd, *Impaired Attention in Depressive States: A Non-specific Deficit?*, 26 PSYCHOL. MED. 1009–20 (1996).

8. AMERICAN PSYCHIATRIC ASSOCIATION, DIAGNOSTIC AND STATISTICAL MANUAL OF MENTAL DISORDERS (4th ed. 1994) (DSM–IV).

who found "memory problems" in 15% of trauma survivors, but also found similar memory disturbances in 11% of control subjects.[9]

In short, therefore, the findings from our preliminary survey would suggest, as a working hypothesis, that although people experience many adverse psychological consequences from trauma, they generally do not develop amnesia for what happened. But is it possible that some cases of repression were missed in these studies? After all, if someone had complete amnesia for a traumatic event, he or she might never be identified by researchers in the first place. Or perhaps subjects with repression were seen in some of these studies, but the investigators simply failed to comment on it. Certainly one must acknowledge these possibilities, but if so, it would seem unusual that none of the 77 studies would have presented, even in passing, a clear description of subjects who had repressed the memory.

Still, even granting that most survivors do remember trauma, one might argue that certain individuals possess a particular ability to repress memories, perhaps by learning to dissociate after repeated "practice" in recurrent traumatic situations. Even this possibility, however, is called into question by a recent study of victims of sickle cell anemia, a disease that causes periodic unpredictable, painful vaso-occlusive "crises."[10] In this study, a group of investigators attempted to train 78 young subjects with sickle cell anemia to perform self-hypnosis, i.e., to deliberately dissociate, in order to reduce their sensitivity to pain during the "crises." However, in an analysis of 37 subjects who had completed the full year of training, the subjects reported only a modest decrease in their need for pain medications, and actually rated their pain episodes as significantly longer and more intense. Certainly no subject appeared to have learned to develop amnesia for the crises.

Given the above observations, then, an analysis of the concept of repression must logically start with the working hypothesis that individuals normally do *not* develop amnesia for traumatic events. In other words, the burden of proof must rest on those who theorize that it is possible to repress a memory. The reverse hypothesis—that repression does exist unless it is proven impossible—would be inherently untestable.

§ 10–2.1.2 The Scientific Methods Applied in the Research

What observations would satisfy the "burden of proof"? As we have discussed in previous papers,[11] the requirements for a satisfactory demonstration of repression are straightforward. First, a study must show that its subjects experienced a documented trauma. It is not sufficient to trust the subjects' memories in the absence of external corroboration: for many years,

9. W. W. Eaton, J. J. Sigal, & M. Weinfeld, *Impairment in Holocaust Survivors After 33 Years: Data from an Unbiased Community Sample*, 139 Am. J. Psychiatry 773–77 (1982).

10. D. F. Dinges, W. G. Whitehouse, E. C. Orne, et al., *Self-hypnosis Training as an Adjunctive Treatment in the Management of Pain Associated with Sickle-cell Disease*, 45 Int'l J. Clinical Experimental Hypnosis 417–32 (1997).

11. H. G. Pope, Jr. & J. I. Hudson, *Can Memories of Childhood Sexual Abuse Be Repressed?*, 25 Psychol. Med. 121–26 (1995); H.

G. Pope, Jr. & J. I. Hudson, *Can Individuals "Repress" Memories of Childhood Sexual Abuse?: An Examination of the Evidence*, 25 Psychiatric Annals 715–19 (1995); H.G. Pope Jr., J.I. Hudson, J.A. Bodkin, P. Oliva, *Questionable Validity of "Dissociative Amnesia" in Trauma Victims. Evidence from Prospective Studies*, 172 Br. J Psychiatry 210–215 (1998); A Piper Jr ,H G Pope, Jr, J. J. Borowiecki III, *Custer's Last Stand: Brown, Scheflin, and Whitfield's Latest Attempt to Salvage "Dissociative Amnesia."* J Psychiatry & L. (in press).

investigators have noted that some "remembered" events may be entirely false.[12] Therefore, adequate documentation of a traumatic event should include either reports from independent witnesses, or physical evidence of the event, such as photographs, police reports, or medical records.

Second, a study must show that subjects truly developed amnesia for the trauma, and that this amnesia cannot be explained by any of four more ordinary, already-established phenomena. These are: a) amnesia due to biological factors, such as loss of consciousness, intoxication with alcohol or other substances, or other neurological insults;[13] b) early childhood amnesia, which is the normal and well-documented amnesia that children experience for most events prior to the age of two or three;[14] c) ordinary forgetfulness, as a result of normal memory decay for events not perceived by the subjects as particularly memorable at the time that they occurred;[15] and d) allegations of "amnesia" for secondary gain, in which a subject merely claims to have forgotten an event in order to avoid pain or embarrassment, or to toll a statute of limitations.[16]

These criteria, summarized in table 2, are all that need be met for a demonstration of repression. For our present exercise, it is not necessary, nor even relevant, to speculate about the intrapsychic mechanism by which repression is presumed to occur. It does not matter, for the purposes of demonstration, whether the memory is claimed to be lost via "repression," "dissociation," or "psychogenic amnesia." It is sufficient simply to show that subjects experienced a documented trauma and developed amnesia that cannot be explained by one of the four alternative processes enumerated above. Equally irrelevant to our analysis are discussions of the biological mechanisms proposed to cause repression. Studies of the neurotransmitters involved in

12. JANET P, LES MÉDICATIONS PSYCHOLOGIQUES (Félix Alcan, Paris, 1919–1925); K. JASPERS, GENERAL PSYCHOPATHOLOGY (Henig & Hamilton trans., 1963); J. PIAGET, PLAY, DREAMS, AND IMITATION IN CHILDHOOD (Gattegno & Hodgson trans., 1951); E. Loftus, *The Reality of Repressed Memories*, 48 AM. PSYCHOLOGIST 518–37 (1993); E. Loftus, *When a Lie Becomes Memory's Truth: Memory Distortion After Exposure to Misinformation*, 1 CURRENT DIRECTIONS IN PSYCHOL. SCI. 121–23 (1992); R. J. Ofshe, *Inadvertent Hypnosis During Interrogation: False Confession Due to Dissociative State; Mis-identified Multiple Personality and the Satanic Cult Hypothesis*, 40 INT'L J. CLINICAL EXPERIMENTAL HYPNOSIS 125–56 (1992); E. F. Loftus & J. E. Pickrell, *The Formation of False Memories*, 25 PSYCHIATRIC ANNALS 720–25 (1995); I. E. Hyman, T. H. Husband, & F. J. Billings, *False Memories of Childhood Experiences*, 9 APPLIED COGNITIVE PSYCHOL. 181–95 (1995); P. Mayer & H. G. Pope, Jr., *Unusual Flashbacks in a Vietnam Veteran*, 154 AM. J. PSYCHIATRY 713 (1997); B. Gonsalves, K.A. Paller. *Memories Can Deceive: Brain Potentials Distinguish Between True and False Memories*. J. COGNITIVE NEUROSCIENCE 138 (S 2000).

13. D. BLUMER, PSYCHIATRIC ASPECTS OF EPILEPSY (1984); L. R. SQUIRE, MEMORY AND BRAIN (1987); A. Stracciari, E. Ghidoni, M. Guarino, M. Polette, & P. Pazzaglia, *Post-traumatic Retrograde Amnesia with Selective Impairment of Autobiographical Memory*, 30 CORTEX 459–68 (1994); G. Forrester, J. Encel, & G. Geffen, *Measuring Post-traumatic Amnesia (PTA): An Historical Review*, 8 BRAIN INJURY 175–84 (1994).

14. J. F. Kihlstrom & J. M. Harackiewicz, *The Earliest Recollection: A New Survey*, 50 J. PERSONALITY 134–48 (1982); M. L. Howe & M. L. Courage, *On Resolving the Enigma of Infantile Amnesia*, 113 PSYCHOL. BULL. 305–26 (1993); R. FIVUSH & J. A. HUDSON, KNOWING AND REMEMBERING IN YOUNG CHILDREN (1990); J. A. Usher & V. Neisser, *Childhood Amnesia and the Beginnings of Memory for Four Early Life Events*, 122 J. EXPERIMENTAL PSYCHOL. 155–65 (1993).

15. F. C. BARTLETT, REMEMBERING: A STUDY IN EXPERIMENTAL AND SOCIAL PSYCHOLOGY (1977); H. G. Pope, Jr., B. Mangweth, A. B. Negrão, et al., *Childhood Sexual Abuse and Bulimia Nervosa: A Comparison of American, Austrian, and Brazilian Women*, 151 AM. J. PSYCHIATRY 732–37 (1994); and D. L. SCHACTER, SEARCHING FOR MEMORY: THE BRAIN, THE MIND, AND THE PAST (1996).

16. H. MERSKEY, THE ANALYSIS OF HYSTERIA (1979).

memory,[17] or neuroendocrine and imaging studies of trauma victims,[18] although certainly of interest, do not provide specific evidence for or against our specific, operational question of whether individuals are capable of repressing a memory. In other words, these biological findings suggest only how repression theoretically *could* occur in the brain[19] but do not demonstrate whether it actually *does* occur.

Table 2

Criteria for a Satisfactory Demonstration of Repression

I.   Documentation that the traumatic event actually occurred (historical accounts, police reports, medical records, reliable independent witnesses).

II.   Evidence that subjects developed amnesia for the trauma, *not* explainable by:

> A.   Biological amnesia (head injury, seizures, other neurological insults);
>
> B.   Early childhood amnesia (most events prior to age three and many prior to age six);
>
> C.   Ordinary forgetfulness (event not perceived as memorable at the time);
>
> D.   Allegations of amnesia for secondary gain (to avoid embarrassment, toll a statute of limitations, etc.)

III.   Demonstration of amnesia in a group of subjects from a larger unselected cohort (individual case reports or retrospective case series are inadequate, since they may represent false-positives due to "measurement error," as discussed in the text).

To illustrate this point, consider an example. Biological studies of the animal kingdom have shown that species with larger brains tend to be more intelligent than those with smaller brains: sparrows are more intelligent than insects, and dogs are more intelligent than sparrows. Studies have also shown that in humans, average brain size is larger in men than in women. Yet it

17. B. A. van der Kolk & J. Saporta, *The Biological Response to Psychic Trauma: Mechanisms and Treatment of Intrusion and Numbing*, 4 ANXIETY RES. 199–212 (1991); R. K. Pitman, *Post-traumatic Stress Disorder, Hormones, and Memory*, 26 BIOLOGICAL PSYCHIATRY 221–23 (1989).

18. B. A. van der Kolk, *The Body Keeps the Score: Memory and the Evolving Psychobiology of Posttraumatic Stress*, 1 HARV. REV. PSYCHIATRY 253–65 (1994); Y. Ito, M. H. Teicher, C. A. Glod, D. Harper, E. Magnus, H. A. Gelbard, *Increased Prevalence of Electrophysiological Abnormalities in Children with Psychological, Physical, and Sexual Abuse*, 5 J. NEUROPSYCHIATRY CLINICAL NEUROSCIENCE 401–08 (1993); R.E. O'Carroll, E. Drysdale, L. Cahill, P. Shajahan, K.P. Ebmeier, *Stimulation of the Noradrenergic System Enhances and Blockade Reduces Memory for Emotional Material in Man*, 29

PSYCHOLOGICAL MED. 1083–88 (1999); J. D. Bremner, P. Randall, T. M. Scott, R. A. Bronen, J. P. Seibyl, S. M. Southwick, R. C. Delany, G. McCarthy, D. S. Charney, & R. B. Innis, *MRI-based Measurement of Hippocampal Volume in Patients with Combat-related Posttraumatic Stress Disorder*, 152 AM. J. PSYCHIATRY 973–81 (1995); S. L. Rauch, B. A. van der Kolk, R. E. Fisler, N. M. Alpert, S. P. Sorr, C. R. Savage, A. J. Fishman, M. A. Jenike, & R. K. Pitman, *A Symptom Provocation Study of Posttraumatic Stress Disorder Using Positron Emission Tomography and Script-driven Imagery*, 53 ARCHIVES GEN. PSYCHIATRY 380–87 (1996).

19. J. D. Bremner, J. H. Krystal, D. S. Charney, & S. M. Southwick, *Neural Mechanisms in Dissociative Amnesia for Childhood Abuse: Relevance to the Current Controversy Surrounding the "False Memory Syndrome,"* 153 AM. J. PSYCHIATRY 71–82 (1996).

would be fallacious to infer from these biological observations that men are more intelligent than women. To test this hypothesis, one would need to assess actual men and women for intelligence. By analogy, studies of repression must demonstrate that it actually does occur, rather than illustrate how it theoretically might occur in the brain.

One other *caveat* remains: one cannot base a demonstration of repression on individual case reports. The basis for this assertion is easily illustrated by example. In Florida, a test using police radar clocked a grove of trees moving at 86 miles per hour and a house moving at a more leisurely 28 miles per hour.[20] But we cannot conclude from this "case report" that trees can exceed the speed limit. The reason for our skepticism, scientifically speaking, is "measurement error." Given a large number of observations, occasional false-positive results are bound to occur, and some of these will find their way into the literature. For the case of repression, when it is considered that hundreds of thousands of clinicians have observed millions of patients throughout this century, then occasional false-positive reports, just like the 86–mph trees, are inevitable. Therefore, case reports, or even collections of the individual case reports, however well-validated they may seem to be,[21] do not provide a satisfactory scientific test of repression. Stated differently, such reports are useful and welcome as "hypothesis-generating" material, but they are almost valueless as "hypothesis-testing" material. Thus, a satisfactory demonstration of repression must exhibit this phenomenon in some percentage of a cohort of patients, rather than in scattered individual cases where no denominator is provided.

An example of the hazards of the case-report method can be found by reading a recent paper by Cheit and a subsequent reply to that paper by Piper.[22] Cheit's paper describes a series of case reports of individual instances of repressed and subsequently recovered memories that were allegedly corroborated. However, upon analysis by Piper, many of these putative cases prove to be of questionable validity. Further, even if we grant that some of Cheit's cases would survive an initial inspection, they still fail to confirm the existence of repression because of the problem of measurement error discussed above. To cite an analogy used by Piper, thousands of Elvis sightings have been reported since the time of Elvis Presley's death.[23] Many of these sightings are quite obviously invalid, but some might seem fairly plausible. Nevertheless, even a collection of 10 or 20 of the most rigorously documented sightings, assembled as series of the "case reports," would not constitute

---

20. D. Smith & J. Tomerlin, Beating the Radar Rap (1990).

21. *See, eg.,* D. L. Corwin & E. Olefson, *Videotaped Discovery of a Reportedly Unrecallable Memory of Child Sexual Abuse: Comparison with a Childhood Interview Videotaped 11 Years Before,* 2 Child Maltreatment 91–112; *see also* commentary on this report by various authors in 2 Child Maltreatment 113–33; the Recovered Memory Project (1998) http://www.brown.edu/Departments/Taubman_Center/Recovmem/Archive.html; and S. Duggal and L.A. Srofe, *Recovered memory of childhood sexual trauma: A documented case*

from a longitudinal study 11 J Traumatic Stress 301 (1998).

22. R.E. Cheit, *Consider This, Skeptics of Recovered Memory,* 8 Ethics & Behavior 141 (1998). *See also* Recovered Memory Project *supra* note 21; A. Piper, *A Skeptic Considers, then Responds to Cheit's "Consider This, Skeptics of Recovered Memory,"* 9 Ethics & Behavior 277 (1999); R.E. Cheit, *Junk Skepticism and Recovered Memory: a reply to Piper,* 9 Ethics & Behavior 295–318 (1999).

23. See online: http://www.deadelvis.com/sighting/seedead.html.

evidence that Elvis still lives; a more sophisticated study would be required to prove this assertion.

[1] Studies of Amnesia for Various Traumatic Events

Wartime situations: Perhaps the most extensive literature describing possible repression of memories of trauma has arisen from studies of individuals in combat situations. This literature, however, is quite varied. Many well-known studies of "war neurosis"[24] or combat-induced "stress reactions"[25] do not describe individuals with amnesia for traumatic events at all. However, some studies have described amnesia in wartime situations, spanning from World War I to the present.[26] Upon analysis of these, however, none approaches meeting our basic criteria for a demonstration of repression. First, and most commonly, many individuals in these studies experienced amnesia for biological reasons, such as loss of consciousness, grand mal seizures, and other neurological insults. Most wartime studies acknowledge these factors, but fail to assess neurological insults in a quantitative fashion. Perhaps the most systematic attempt to control for biological factors was the study of Sargant and Slater, who reported that they excluded cases of "interference with memory due to disease of the brain, and of transient loss of consciousness after head injury."[27] But only three paragraphs later, these authors state that head injury was a "causative factor" in 10 of their 144 cases, and note that many other patients had experienced severe sleep deprivation, profound fatigue and weight loss, and other biological stress from heavy enemy action surrounding the evacuation from Dunkirk. It is important to note, in this connection, that many biological insults can cause amnesia, even in the individuals who do not actually lose consciousness. One study, for example, described retrograde amnesia for as much as a year in individuals who

24. L. B. Kalinowsky, *Problems of War Neuroses in the Light of Experiences in Other Countries*, 107 Am. J. Psychiatry 340–46 (1950); S. Futterman & E. Pumpian–Mindlin, *Traumatic War Neuroses Five Years Later*, 108 Am. J. Psychiatry 401–08 (1951); D. Dobbs & W. P. Wilson, *Observations on Persistence of War Neurosis*, 21 Diseases of the Nervous System 686–91 (1960).

25. H. C. Archibald, D. M. Long, C. Miller, & R. D. Tuddenham, *Gross Stress Reaction in Combat—A 15-year Follow-up*, 119 Am. J. Psychiatry 317–22 (1962); H. C. Archibald & R. D. Tuddenham, *Persistent Stress Reaction After Combat a 20-year Follow-up*, 12 Archives Gen. Psychiatry 475–81 (1965); L. C. Kolb, *The Post-traumatic Stress Disorders of Combat: A Subgroup with a Conditioned Emotional Response*, 149 Mil. Med. 237–43 (1984).

26. C. S. Myers, *A Contribution to the Study of Shell-shock*, 1 Lancet 316–20 (1915); E. E. Southard, Shell-shock and Other Neuropsychiatric Problems (1919); D. A. Thom & N. Fenton, *Amnesias in War Cases*, 76 Am. J. Insanity 437–48 (1920); A. Kardiner, The Traumatic Neuroses of War (1941); W. Sargant & E. Slater, *Amnesic Syndromes in War*, 34 Proc.

Royal Soc. Med. 757–64 (1941); L. S. Kubie, *Manual of Emergency Treatment for Acute War Neuroses*, 4 War Med. 582–99 (1943); J. L. Henderson & M. Moore, *The Psychoneuroses of War*, 230 New Eng. J. Med. 273–78 (1944); R. R. Grinker & J. P. Spiegel, Men Under Stress (1945); C. Fisher, *Amnesic States in War Neuroses: The Psychogenesis of Fugues*, 14 Psychoanalytic Q. 437–68 (1945); J. O. Cavenar & J. L. Nash, *The Effects of Combat on the Normal Personality: War Neurosis in Vietnam Returnees*, 17 Comp. Psychiatry 647–53 (1976); G. Kalman, *On Combat-neurosis (Psychiatric Experience During the Recent Middle–East War)*, 23 J. Soc. Psychiatry 195–203 (1977); H. Hendin, A. P. Haas, P. Singer, W. Houghton, M. Schwartz, & V. Wallen, *The Reliving Experience in Vietnam Veterans with Posttraumatic Stress Disorder*, 25 Comp. Psychiatry 165–73 (1984); S. M. Sonnenberg, A. S. Blank, & J. A. Talbott, The Trauma of War: Stress and Recovery in Vietnam Veterans (1985); D. K. Roszell, M. E. McFall, & K. L. Malas, *Frequency of Symptoms and Concurrent Psychiatric Disorder in Vietnam Veterans with Chronic PTSD*, 42 Hosp. Community Psychiatry 293–96 (1991).

27. Sargant & Slater, *supra* note 26.

sustained modest head injuries without loss of consciousness.[28] This finding emphasizes the need for caution in interpreting any wartime study in which victims sustained severe biological stress.

Second, several of the wartime studies employed either hypnosis or barbiturates (Amytal or Pentothal) to "reconstruct" memories of combat situations. However, both hypnosis[29] and barbiturates[30] can stimulate confabulation. Thus, any "memory" described in such studies, without independent documentation of the traumatic event, becomes suspect. An example of such a "memory" is presented by Grinker and Spiegel, who treated an airman after a bombing raid.[31] With Pentothal treatment, the patient recalled seeing an old man, dressed in brown, come out of a building just as the bombs were dropped. The authors point out that, because of the speed of low-flying aircraft, it was unlikely that the patient could have actually identified an isolated man, much less distinguished his age and clothes. Instead they speculate that the man represented the patient's father.

Third, a number of investigators suspected malingering among their "amnestic" subjects. For example, Kalman, describing veterans of the 1967 Middle–East War, suggests that most cases of combat-neurosis and amnesia involved exaggeration or malingering, although he is careful to acknowledge that the terror and anxiety were genuine.[32] Sargant and Slater, mentioned above, also noted malingering in their cohort. Clearly, many sorts of secondary gain might accrue from professing amnesia for a combat situation.

Fourth, some studies describe amnesia reported by soldiers in the absence of any known wartime trauma at all. For example, Fisher describes several individuals who developed amnesia for long periods of time, including amnesia for their personal identities, even in the absence of a specific combat experience.[33] While accounts of such "fugue states" are intriguing, they do not provide evidence that specific traumatic events cause repression.

Fifth, few studies provide documentation that the traumatic events occurred as described. Admittedly, there is little question that most of the soldiers studied were involved in genuine combat situations. However, the details of the traumatic event itself were often not documented by independent witnesses.

Sixth, many of the studies, including even those of monograph length, offer only a collection of case reports.[34] Interesting and detailed as these

28. Stracciari et al., *supra* note 13.

29. H. BERNHEIM, HYPNOSIS AND SUGGESTIONS IN PSYCHOTHERAPY (Aronson 1973) (1888); M. T. Orne, *The Use and Misuse of Hypnosis in Court*, 27 INT'L J. CLINICAL EXPERIMENTAL HYPNOSIS 311–41 (1979); J. R. Laurence & C. Perry, *Hypnotically Created Memory Among Highly Hypnotizable Subjects*, 222 SCI. 523–24 (1983); and American Medical Association Council of Scientific Affairs, *Scientific Status of Refreshing Recollection by the Use of Hypnosis*, 253 JAMA 1918–23 (1985). *See generally* Chapter 16 (Hypnosis).

30. M. J. Gerson & F. M. Victoroff, *Experimental Investigation into the Validity of Con-* *fessions Obtained Under Sodium Amytal Narcosis*, 9 J. CLINICAL PSYCHOPATHOLOGY 359–75 (1948); E. A. Weinstein & S. Malitz, *Changes in Symbolic Expression with Amytal Sodium*, 111 AM. J. PSYCHIATRY 198–206 (1954); A. Piper, Jr., *"Truth Serum" and "Recovered Memories" of Sexual Abuse: A Review of the Evidence*, J. PSYCHIATRY & L., Winter 1993, 447–71.

31. GRINKER & SPIEGEL, *supra* note 26, at 404–05.

32. Kalman, *supra* note 26.

33. Fisher, *supra* note 26.

34. SOUTHARD, *supra* note 26; KARDINER, *supra* note 26; GRINKER & SPIEGEL, *supra* note 26.

reports may be, they remain subject to the risk of false-positive findings due to measurement error, as exemplified by our case of the 86–mph trees.

In one recent report Karon and Widener describe a single case of "repressed memories" and World War II.[35] However, a recent critique of this paper[36] has noted that there is no proof that the World War II airman described in this case had actually forgotten the traumatic incident, let alone repressed it. The same critique notes many inaccuracies in Karon and Widener's interpretation of the wartime literature.

Another recent demonstration of the fallibility of wartime case reports arose from the report of a Korean War veteran, Edward Daily, who recalled committing atrocities at No gun Ri. Subsequently, a number of other veterans recovered memories that Mr. Daily was with them at the No gun Ri massacre more than 40 years earlier.[37] However, United States military records indicated that Daily was never present at No gun Ri, and instead had been working as a clerk and a mechanic in the prosaic 27th Ordnance Maintenance Company, well behind the front lines.

In summary, then, no study of wartime trauma, to our knowledge, exhibits a cohort of victims who displayed documented amnesia, not explained by biological factors or malingering, for a documented trauma. Of course, one cannot exclude the possibility that at least some of the subjects in some of the studies might nevertheless have experienced repression. But, as discussed in the introduction, such speculation is insufficient to demonstrate repression— since we must logically begin with the working hypothesis that people remember traumas until specifically proved otherwise.

Prisoners of war, torture victims, and concentration camp survivors: Even lacking evidence for repression of wartime traumas, one might perhaps expect to find cases of repression among victims of torture or imprisonment, who experienced repeated traumas over a prolonged period. This prediction might be based, for example, on the theory of Terr, who has suggested that memories for single traumas (so-called "type I" traumas) are usually retained vividly, whereas repeated ("type II") traumas are more often repressed.[38] Although the sickle cell anemia study, described above, would seem to weigh against Terr's theory, it is still critical to study extraordinary, repeated, human-induced traumas, to see whether repression might operate there.

Upon examining studies of prisoners of war and Holocaust survivors, however, we have been unable to find clear evidence for repression, meeting our criteria in table 2. Note first that several such studies were reviewed in our original survey of trauma research above.[39] Although many of these

---

35. B.P. Karon & A.J. Widener, *Repressed Memories and World War II: Lest we Forget*, 28 PROFESSIONAL PSYCHOLOGY: RESEARCH AND PRACTICE 338 (1997).

36. A. Piper, *Repressed Memories from World War II: Nothing to Forget. Examining Karon and Widener's Claim to have Discovered Evidence for Repression*, 29 PROFESSIONAL PSYCHOLOGY: RESEARCH AND PRACTICE 476 (1998).

37. M. Moss, *The Story Behind a Soldier's Story*. NEW YORK TIMES May 31, 2000, Section A, p. 1.

38. L. C. TERR, TOO SCARED TO CRY (1990); L. C. Terr, *Childhood Traumas: An Outline and Overview*, 148 AM. J. PSYCHIATRY 10–20 (1991);L. C. TERR, UNCHAINED MEMORIES (1994).

39. A. Strom, S. B. Refsum, L. Eitenger, O. Gronvik, A. Lonnum, A. Engeset, K. Osvik, & B. Rogan, *Examination of Norwegian Ex-con-centration Camp Prisoners*, 4 J. NEUROPSYCHIA-TRY 43–62 (1961); P. Chodoff, *Late Effects of the Concentration Camp Syndrome*, 8 ARCHIVES OF GEN. PSYCHIATRY 323–33 (1963); Eaton et al., *supra* note 9; J. D. Kinzie, W. Sack, R. H. Angell, S. Manson, & R. Ben, *The Psychiatric*

studies describe the usual disturbances of concentration and memory typically seen in depressed and anxious individuals, none reports patients who repressed the memory of their trauma. For example, in Wagenaar and Groeneweg's study of survivors of Camp Erika, sometimes cited as evidence favoring repression, all subjects remembered the camp very well even upon interview 40 years later.[40] Not surprisingly, these survivors had forgotten various details of the experience after four decades, but this forgetfulness was random, and not confined to the traumatic events only. Thus, the study would actually seem to argue against the possibility of repression. The reader is referred to our recent review for a more detailed analysis of this study.[41]

Several other studies of concentration camp survivors have also been cited as evidence of repression.[42] Upon inspection, however, these studies again provide no cases meeting our methodologic criteria, for several reasons. First, many cases of amnesia appear due to biological problems, such as loss of consciousness from head injury or other neurological insults. Second, prisoners with a history of months or years of repeated traumas would not be expected to remember every traumatic event individually. This forgetfulness is not repression; rather, it is the well-known "serial position effect"—the normal human tendency to forget individual events from a series of many similar events.[43] Third, survivors of concentration camps are often reluctant to describe gruesome memories. A possible illustration of this last phenomenon appears in the monograph of Krystal, where a survivor of the Chelmno concentration camp claimed on interview that the camp was merely a "farm."[44] When pressed to describe her experiences at Chelmno, she became "very anxious, cringing with every motion or question of Dr. Krystal's . . ." This behavior does not establish that she had repressed her painful memories; instead she may not have wanted to describe them in front of multiple observers. Similar evidence for non-disclosure comes from another study of 23 Holocaust survivors,[45] in which most "reported that they completely avoided

Effects of Massive Trauma on Cambodian Children: I. The Children, 25 J. Am. Acad. Child Adolesc. Psychiatry 370–76 (1986); J. D. Kinzie, W. Sack, R. H. Angell, G. Clarke, & R. Ben, *A Three-year Follow-up of Cambodian Young People Traumatized as Children*, 28 J. Am. Acad. Child Adolesc. Psychiatry 501–04 (1989); W. H. Sack, G. Clarke, C. Him, D. Dickason, B. Goff, K. Lanham, J. D. Kinzie, *A 6–year Follow-up Study of Cambodian Refugee Adolescents traumatized as children*, 32 J. Am. Acad. Child Adolesc. Psychiatry 431–37 (1993); A. Nadler & D. Ben–Shushan, *Forty Years Later: Long-term Consequences of Massive Traumatization as Manifested by Holocaust Survivors from the City and the Kibbutz*, 57 J. Consulting & Clinical Psychol. 287–93 (1989); W. A. Wagenaar & J. Groeneweg, *The Memory of Concentration Camp Survivors*, 4 Applied Cognitive Psychol. 77–87 (1990); Krell, *supra* note 6.

40. Wagenaar & Groeneweg, *supra* note 39.

41. H. G. Pope, Jr., J. I. Hudson, J. A. Bodkin, & A. Oliva, *supra* note 11; *see also* commentary by C. R. Brewin in 172 Brit. J. Psychiatry 216–17 (1998).

42. R. Jaffe, *Dissociative Phenomena in Former Concentration Camp Inmates*, 49 Int'l J. Psychoanalysis 310–12 (1968); W. G. Niederland, *Clinical Observations on the "Survivor Syndrome,"* 49 Int'l J. Psychoanalysis 313–15 (1968); H. Krystal, Massive Psychic Trauma (1968); N. K. Dor–Shav, *On the Long-range Effects of Concentration Camp Internment of Nazi Victims: 25 Years Later*, 46 J. Consulting & Clinical Psychol. 1–11 (1978); K. Kuch & B. J. Cox, *Symptoms of PTSD in 124 Survivors of the Holocaust*, 149 Am. J. Psychiatry 337–40 (1992).

43. J. W. McCrary & W. S. Hunter, *Serial Position Curves in Verbal Learning*, 117 Sci. 131–34 (1953); E. A. Feigenbaum & H. A. Simon, *A Theory of the Serial Position Effect*, 53 Brit. J. Psychol. 307–20 (1962).

44. Krystal, *supra* note 42, at 43.

45. H. Kaminer & P. Lavie, *Sleep and Dreaming in Holocaust Survivors: Dramatic Decrease in Dream Recall in Well-adjusted Survivors*, 179 J. Nervous Mental Disease 664–69 (1991).

talking about the Holocaust, even though they emphasized that they had never forgotten what they had undergone."[46]

Similar considerations apply to studies of torture victims. Several of these studies, comprising 294 subjects, are reviewed by Goldfeld et al.[47] These authors note that head injury was common in torture victims; no case of amnesia in the absence of head injury is described.

Studies of disaster victims: Various studies of victims of natural and manmade disasters are also sometimes cited as evidence of repression. Upon inspection, however, these studies are subject to the same considerations discussed in previous sections. For example, one study of victims of a tornado in North Carolina describes the familiar phenomena of "memory impairment" and "concentration difficulty," but provides no evidence that any of the 279 victims repressed the memory of the tornado.[48] Another study describes a woman who reportedly forgot the Cocoanut Grove fire of 1942.[49] But upon reading a contemporaneous study of 46 survivors of the fire, one finds that more than half had lost consciousness, and that some had blood levels of carbon monoxide "sufficient to kill."[50] Thus, the profound biological traumas of the fire could easily account for the amnesia observed. Similar considerations apply to the study of Dollinger,[51] who examined 38 schoolchildren who were victims of a lightning strike disaster. Two children displayed amnesia for the incident. But both of these amnestic children were "side flash" victims who were knocked unconscious by the large dose of electricity—and when electric current is delivered to the brain, as during electroconvulsive therapy, amnesia is a normal side effect.[52] Thus, victims of naturally induced shock treatment hardly provide evidence for repression.

Many other disaster studies are summarized in table 1. Throughout these studies, victims remembered the events vividly. Of particular note is McFarlane's finding that firefighters who appeared more traumatized remembered events even better than those traumatized less.[53]

46. Anonymous, *Repressing Memories of the Past Helps Holocaust Survivors—Could Freud Have Been Wrong?* 75 S. Afr. Med. J. xii (1989).

47. A. E. Goldfeld, R. F. Mollica, B. H. Pescacento, & S. V. Faraone, *The Physical and Psychological Sequelae of Torture: Symptomatology and Diagnosis*, 259 JAMA 2725–29 (1988).

48. S. Madakasira & K. O'Brien, *Acute Posttraumatic Stress Disorder in Victims of a Natural Disaster*, 175 J. Nervous Mental Disease 286–90 (1987).

49. B. A. van der Kolk & W. Kadish, *Amnesia, Dissociation, and the Return of the Repressed*, in Psychological Trauma 173–90 (B. A. van der Kolk ed., 1987).

50. A. Adler, *Neuropsychiatric Complications in Victims of Boston's Cocoanut Grove Disaster*, 149 JAMA 1098–1101 (1943).

51. S. J. Dollinger, *Lightning-strike Disaster Among Children*, 58 Brit. J. Med. Psychol.

375–83 (1985). For details on the children's medical symptoms, *see* S. Kotagal, C.A. Rawlings, S. Chen, G. Burris, & S. Nouri, *Neurologic, Psychiatric, and Cardiovascular Complications In Children Struck by Lightning*, 70 PEDIATRICS 190–2 (1982).

52. L. R. Squire & P. C. Slater, *Electroconvulsive Therapy and Complaints of Memory Dysfunction: A Prospective Three-year Follow-up Study*, 142 Brit. J. Psychiatry 1–8 (1983); C. D. Frith, M. Stevens, E. C. Johnstone, J. F. W. Deakin, P. Lawler, & T. J. Crow, *Effects of ECT and Depression on Various Aspects of Memory*, 142 Brit. J. Psychiatry 610–17 (1983).

53. A. C. McFarlane, *The Phenomenology of Posttraumatic Stress Disorders Following a Natural Disaster*, 176 J. Nervous Mental Disease 22–29 (1988); A. C. McFarlane, *The Longitudinal Course of Posttraumatic Morbidity: The Range of Outcomes and Their Predictors*, 176 J. Nervous Mental Disease 30–39 (1988); A. C. McFarlane, *Relationship Between Psychiatric Impairment and a Natural Disaster: The Role of Distress*, 18 Psychol. Med. 129–39 (1988).

Amnesia After Committing Murder: Another body of literature, also sometimes cited as evidence for repression, involves murderers who report amnesia for their act. These studies are reviewed in detail by Schacter.[54] There is no doubt that many murderers profess amnesia for the moment of their crime, but it is also clear that a large percentage of them were intoxicated with alcohol or other substances at the time. For example, in the study of Gudjonsson et al., published since Schacter's review, 9 of 16 murderers reported amnesia for their act—but all of these nine admitted that they were intoxicated at the time.[55] In addition, murderers might derive considerable secondary gain by professing amnesia, leading to a high rate of malingering. Thus, it would seem unwise to base a demonstration of repression on the testimony of murderers.

[2] Studies of Memories of Childhood Sexual Abuse

The above review finds no study providing evidence of repression that meets the basic criteria presented in table 2. But it might be argued that childhood sexual abuse is very different from the trauma of war, imprisonment, natural disaster, or murder. It is typically secret, and the victim is pressured never to reveal its existence.[56] And often it is a trauma perpetrated by a loved one, rather than an identified adversary. Thus, it might be much harder to integrate into memory than a fire or tornado.[57] Indeed it has recently been suggested that such "betrayal trauma" would be the type of trauma most likely to foster repression.[58] Therefore, repression might be found among survivors of sexual abuse, even if it were not documented elsewhere.

Moreover, if repression of childhood sexual abuse does occur, it should be common. Childhood sexual abuse, regrettably, is frequent in every society where it has been studied.[59] In the United States, depending upon the criteria used, between 10% and 40% of women and 5% to 15% of men have experienced significant sexual abuse, prior to the age of 18, involving physical

54. D. L. Schacter, *Amnesia and Crime: How Much Do We Really Know?*, 41 AM. PSYCHOLOGIST 286–95 (1986).

55. G. H. Gudjonsson, H. Petursson, S. Skulasson, & H. Siguroardöttir, *Psychiatric Evidence: A Study of Psychological Issues*, 80 ACTA PSYCHIATRICA SCANDINAVICA 165–69 (1989).

56. Gelinas, *supra* note 4; Berliner & Wheeler, *supra* note 4; HERMAN, *supra* note 4; Whitfield, *supra* note 4; BLUME, supra note 5; FREDRICKSON, *supra* note 5; R. ARNOLD, *supra* note 5; BASS & DAVIS, *supra* note 5; M. Van Debur Atler, *Say "Incest" Out Loud*, MCCALL'S, Sept. 1991, at 78ff; L. ARMSTRONG, ROCKING THE CRADLE OF SEXUAL POLITICS: WHAT HAPPENED WHEN WOMEN SAID INCEST (1994); D. E. H. RUSSELL, THE SECRET TRAUMA: INCEST IN THE LIVES OF GIRLS AND WOMEN (1986).

57. van der Kolk & Fisler, *supra* note 2; HERMAN, *supra* note 4; and TERR (1994), *supra* note 38.

58. J. J. FREYD, BETRAYAL TRAUMA: THE LOGIC OF FORGETTING CHILDHOOD ABUSE (1996).

59. RUSSELL, *supra* note 56; C. L. Nash & D. J. West, *Sexual Molestation of Young Girls: A Retrospective Survey*, in SEXUAL VICTIMIZATION, Part 1, 1–92 (D. J. West ed. 1985); G. Wyatt, *The Sexual Abuse of Afro–American and White American Women in Childhood*, 9 CHILD ABUSE & NEGLECT 507–19 (1985); C. Bagley & R. Ramsay, *Sexual Abuse in Childhood: Psychosocial Outcomes and Implications for Social Work Practice*, 4 J. SOC. WORK & HUMAN SEXUALITY 33–47 (1986); D. Finkelhor, G. Hotaling, I. A. Lewis, & C. Smith, *Sexual Abuse in a National Survey of Adult Men and Women: Prevalence, Characteristics, and Risk Factors*, 14 CHILD ABUSE & NEGLECT 19–28 (1990); J. Anderson, J. Martin, P. Mullen, S. Romans, & P. Herbison, *Prevalence of Childhood Sexual Experiences in a Community Sample of Women*, 32 J. AM. ACAD. CHILD ADOLESC. PSYCHIATRY 911–19 (1993); D. Finkelhor, *The International Epidemiology of Child Sexual Abuse*, 18 CHILD ABUSE & NEGLECT 409–17 (1994).

contact.[60] Even taking the lowest figures from these ranges, and multiplying by the number of Americans presently over the age of 18, one obtains a figure of 14 million Americans who are former victims. If repression operates in only 10% of these individuals, then 1,400,000 Americans presently harbor repressed memories of sexual abuse. If there is such a large pool of cases, one might expect a substantial number of rigorous studies, using well-controlled prospective designs, describing cohorts of patients with repressed memories of childhood sexual abuse. It is perhaps surprising, then, to find that most of the available studies are retrospective studies of limited methodological utility, and that only five prospective studies, to our knowledge, have appeared.

[a]   Retrospective studies

More than 40 retrospective studies have now attempted to demonstrate repression in individuals believed to be victims of childhood sexual or physical abuse.[61] By "retrospective," we mean that both the putative traumatic event

60. RUSSELL, *supra* note 56; Wyatt, *supra* note 59; Finkelhor et al. (1990), *supra* note 59; Anderson et al, *supra* note 59.

61. van der Kolk & Fisler, *supra* note 2; J. L. Herman & E. Schatzow, *Recovery and Verification of Memories of Childhood Sexual Trauma*, 4 PSYCHOANALYTIC PSYCHOL. 1–14 (1987); N. DRAIJER, SEKSUELE TRAUMATISERING IN DE JEUGD: GOVOLGEN OPLANGE TERMIJN VAN SEKSUEEL MISBRUIK VAN MEISJES DOOR VERWANTEN (1990); R. J. ENSINK, CONFUSING REALITIES: A STUDY OF CHILD SEXUAL ABUSE AND PSYCHIATRIC SYMPTOMS (1992); J. Briere & J. Conte, *Self-reported Amnesia for Abuse in Adults Molested as Children*, 6 J. TRAUMATIC STRESS 21–31 (1993); C. Z. Bernet, R. Doutscher, R. E. Ingram et al., *Differential Factors in the Repression of Memories of Childhood Sexual Abuse*, a poster presented at the Annual Convention of the Association for the Advancement of Behavioral Therapy (Atlanta, Ga.) (Nov. 1993); E. F. Loftus, S. Polonsky, M. T. Fullilove, *Memories of Childhood Sexual Abuse: Remembering and Repressing*, 18 PSYCHOL. WOMEN Q. 67–84 (1994); S. Feldman–Summers & K. S. Pope, *The Experience of "Forgetting" Childhood Abuse: A National Survey of Psychologists*, 62 J. CONSULTING & CLINICAL PSYCHOL. 636–39 (1994); S. N. Gold, D. Hughes, & L. Hohnecker, *Degrees of Repression of Sexual Abuse Memories*, 49 AM. PSYCHOLOGIST 441–42 (1994); C. Cameron, *Women Survivors Confronting Their Abusers: Issues, Decisions and Outcomes*, 3 J. CHILD SEX ABUSE 7–35 (1994); D. M. Elliott & B. Fox, *Child Abuse and Amnesia: Prevalence and Triggers to Memory Recovery*, a paper presented at the annual meeting of the International Society of Traumatic Stress Studies (Chicago, Ill.) (Nov. 1994); T. A. Roesler & T. W. Wind, *Telling the Secret: Adult Women Describe Their Disclosures of Incest*, 9 J. INTERPERSONAL VIOLENCE 327–38 (1994); D. M. Elliott & J. Briere, *Posttraumatic Stress Associated with the Delayed Recall of Sexual Abuse: A General Population Study*, 8 J. TRAUMATIC STRESS 629–47 (1995); L. M. Williams, *Recovered Memories of Abuse in Women with Documented Child Sexual Victimization Histories*, 8 J. TRAUMATIC STRESS 649–73 (1995); J. Pomerantz, *Memories of Abuse: Women Sexually Traumatized in Childhood*, a poster presented at 12th Annual Meeting of the International Society for Traumatic Stress Studies, Trauma and Controversy (S.F., Cal.) (Nov. 9–13, 1995); B. Andrews, J. Morton, D. A. Bekerian, C. R. Brewin, G. M. Davies & P. Mollon, *The Recovery of Memories in Clinical Practice: Experiences and Beliefs of the British Psychological Society Practitioners*, 8 THE PSYCHOLOGIST 209–14 (1995); W. E. Hovdestad & C. M. Kristiansen, *A Field Study of "False Memory Syndrome:" Construct Validity and Incidence*, J. PSYCHIATRY & L., Summer 1996, at 299–338; C. M. Roe & M. F. Schwartz, *Characteristics of Previously Forgotten Memories of Sexual Abuse: A Descriptive Study*, J PSYCHIATRY & L. 189–206 Summer 1996 0; J. M. Golding, R. P. Sanchez, & S. A. Sego, *Do You Believe in Repressed Memories?*, 27 PROF. PSY. CHOL., RES. & PRAC. 429–32 (1996); C. J. Dalenberg, *Accuracy, Timing and Circumstances of Disclosure in Therapy of Recovered and Continuous Memories of Abuse*, J. PSYCHIATRY & L. 229–75 (Summer 1996); M. A. Polusny & V. M. Follette, *Remembering Childhood Sexual Abuse: a National Survey of Psychologists' Clinical Practices, Beliefs, and Personal Experiences*, 27 PROF. PSYCHOL., RES. & PRAC. 41–52 (1996); J. L. Herman & M. R. Harvey, *Adult Memories of Childhood Trauma: A Naturalistic Clinical Study*, 2 J. TRAUMATIC STRESS 557–71 (1997); R. P. Kluft, *The Confirmation and Disconfirmation of Memories of Abuse in DID Patients: A Naturalistic Clinical Study*, 8 DISSOCIATION 253–58 (1995); C. L. Whitfield & W. E. Stock, *Traumatic Memories in 50 Adult Survivors of Child Sexual Abuse*, a paper presented at Trauma and Memory: An International Research Conference (Durham, N.H.) (July 26–

and the period of amnesia for that event occurred prior to the time point at which the subject was evaluated in the study. Although there are variations in the exact methodology of these studies, they are relatively similar in design. First, a group of individuals presumed to include victims of childhood sexual

28, 1996); S. Grassian & D. Holtzen, *Memory of Sexual Abuse by a Parish Priest*, a paper presented at Trauma and Memory: An International Research Conference (Durham, N.H.) (July 26–28, 1996); D. M. Elliott, *Traumatic Events: Prevalence and Delayed Recall in the General Population*, 65 J. CONSULTING & CLINICAL PSYCHOL. 811–20 (1997); J.A. Sheiman, *I've Always Wondered if Something Happened to Me: Assessment of Child Sexual Abuse Survivors with Amnesia* 2 J CHILD SEXUAL ABUSE 13 (1993); R.L. Binder, D.E. McNeil, & R.L. Goldstone, *Patterns of Recall of Childhood Sexual Abuse as Described by Adult Survivors* 22 BULLETIN OF THE AMERICAN ACADEMY OF PSYCHIATRY & L. 357 (1994); G. Goodman, J. Qin, B.L. Bottoms & P.R. Shaver, *Characteristics and Sources of Allegations of Ritualistic Child Abuse* Final Report to the National Center of Child Abuse and Neglect (1995); F. Albach, P.P. Moormann & B. Bermond, *Memory Recovery of Childhood Sexual Abuse* 9 DISSOCIATION 261 (1996); J.A. Chu, J. Matthews, L.M. Frey & B. Ganzel, *The Nature of Traumatic Memories of Childhood Abuse* 9 DISSOCIATION 2 (1996); P.M. Coons, E.S. Bowman & V. Milstein, *Repressed Memories in Patients with Dissociative Disorder: Literature Review, Controlled Study, and Treatment Recommendations* 16 REVIEW OF PSYCHIATRY 153 (1997); S. Joslyn, L. Carlin & E.F. Loftus, *Remembering and Forgetting Childhood Sexual Abuse* 5 MEMORY 703 (1997); C. Koopman, C. Gore–Felton & D. Spiegel, *Acute Stress Disorder Symptoms Among Female Sexual Abuse Survivors Seeking Treatment* 6 J CHILD SEXUAL ABUSE 65 (1997); N. Rodriquez, S.W. Ryan, H. van de Kemp & G.W. Foy, *Posttraumatic Stress Disorder in Adult Female Survivors of Childhood Sexual Abuse: A Comparison Study*, J CONSULTING AND CLINICAL PSYCHOLOGY 53–59 (1997); J.W. Schooler, Z. Ambadar & M. Bendiksen, *A Cognitive Corroborative Case Study Approach for Investigating Discovered Memories of Sexual Abuse*, in J.D. Read and D. Stephen Lindsay (eds.), RECOLLECTIONS OF TRAUMA: SCIENTIFIC EVIDENCE AND CLINICAL PRACTICE 379–387 (1997); P. Dale & J. Allen, *On Memories of Childhood Abuse: A Phenomenological Study*, 22 CHILD ABUSE AND NEGLECT 799–812 (1998); M.A. Epstein & B.L. Bottoms, *Memories of Childhood Sexual Abuse: A Survey of Young Adults*, 22 CHILD ABUSE AND NEGLECT 1217–1238 (1998); S.P. Orr, N.B. Lasko, L.J. Metzger, N.J. Berry, C.E. Ahern & Roger Pitman, *Psychophysiologic Assessment of Women with Posttraumatic Stress Disorder Resulting from Childhood Abuse*, 66 J CONSULTING AND CLINICAL PSYCHOLOGY 906–913 (1998); C. Cameron, *Comparing Amnesic and Nonamnesic Survivors of Childhood Sexual Abuse: A Longitudinal Study* 41–68 *in* K. Pezdek & W.,P. Banks

(eds.), THE RECOVERED MEMORY/FALSE MEMORY DEBATE (1996); B Andrews, *Forms of Memory Recovery Among Adults in Therapy: Preliminary Results From an In–Depth Survey* 455–460, *in* J.D. Read and D. Stephen Lindsay (eds.), RECOLLECTIONS OF TRAUMA: SCIENTIFIC EVIDENCE AND CLINICAL PRACTICE (1997); E. Carlson, *Sex Differences in Amnesia for Childhood Physical and Sexual Abuse in Inpatients*, paper presented at Trauma and Memory: An International Research conference, University of New Hampshire, Durham, NH July 26–28, 1996; R. Kluft, *The Argument for the Reality of the Delayed Recall of Trauma*, *in* TRAUMA AND MEMORY: CLINICAL AND LEGAL CONTROVERSIES 25–57 (P.S. Appelbaum, L. Uyehara & M. Elin eds. 1997); A.S. Dorado, *Remembering and Coming to Terms with Sexual Abuse for Incest Survivors*, paper presented at Trauma and Memory: An International Research Conference, University of New Hampshire, Durham, NH July 26–28, 1996; R. Cheit, *supra* note 22; C.L. Whitfield, *Traumatic Amnesia: The Evolution of Our Understanding From a Clinical and Legal Perspective*, 4 SEXUAL ADDICTION & COMPULSIVITY 107–135 (1997); D.S. Lindsay and J.D. Read, *"Memory Work" and Recovered Memories of Childhood Sexual Abuse: Scientific Evidence and Public, Professional, and Personal Issues*, 1 PSYCHOLOGY, PUBLIC POLICY AND LAW 846–908 (1995); J.D. Read, *Memory Issues in the Diagnosis of Unreported Trauma*, *in* RECOLLECTIONS OF TRAUMA: SCIENTIFIC EVIDENCE AND CLINICAL PRACTICE 79–108 (J.D. Read & D. Stephen Lindsay eds. 1997); B.A. van der Kolk, S. Roth, D. Pelcovitz, & F. Mandel, *Disorders of Extreme Stress: Results of the DSM–IV Field Trials for PTSD* (Washington, DC: American Psychiatric Association, 1993); F.K. GROSSMAN, A.B. COOK, S.K. KEPKEP AND K.C. KOENEN, WITH THE PHOENIX RISING: LESSONS FROM TEN RESILIENT WOMEN WHO OVERCAME THE TRAUMA OF CHILDHOOD SEXUAL ABUSE (1999); V. Fish & C. G. Scott, *Childhood Abuse Recollections in a Nonclinical Population: Forgetting and Secrecy.* 23 CHILD ABUSE & NEGLECT 791–802 (1999); T. P. Melchert, *Childhood Memory and a History of Different Forms of Abuse*, 27 PROF. PSYCHOL., RES. & PRAC. 438–46 (1996); T. P. Melchert & R. L. Parker, *Different Forms of Childhood Abuse and Memory*, 21 CHILD ABUSE & NEGLECT 125–35 (1997); T.P. Melchert, *Relations Among Childhood Memory, a History of Abuse, Dissociation, and Repression*, 14 J. INTERPERSONAL VIOLENCE 1172 (1999); T.D. Brewerton, B.S. Dansky, D.G. Kilpatrick and P.M. O'Neil, *Bulimia nervosa, PTSD, and Forgetting: Results From the National Women's Survey*, *in* TRAUMA AND MEMORY 127–138 (L.M. Williams & V.L. Banyard eds. 1999). *See also* several unpublished studies cited in Brown et al. 1999, *supra* note 4.

or physical abuse was recruited. These victims may have been recruited from among patients entering or engaged in therapy,[62] by newspaper or other advertisement,[63] from among respondents to questionnaires sent to a given population,[64] or by some other method designed to locate a cohort of victims.[65] Then, these subjects were asked whether they forgot the presumed episode of abuse at some earlier time during their lives. Subjects' reports about forgetting were typically obtained either from their answers to questionnaire items, from the experience of their therapists, or by a personal interview in which the subject was asked whether he or she could recall a period of having forgotten the trauma. Third, in some of the subjects in some of the studies, an attempt was made to obtain corroboration that the trauma had actually occurred. Since these studies have employed similar methodology, we will not attempt to summarize the details of each individual study here. Instead, we give examples of two of the most widely cited studies and then discuss the methodological limitations of retrospective studies of this type in general.

In the first and perhaps best known retrospective investigation, Herman and Schatzow described 53 women drawn from therapy groups for "incest survivors."[66] The selection criteria for the subjects were not presented in further detail. Fourteen (26%) of the 53 women were reported to have had "severe" amnesia for the presumed incest. Also, 21 (40%) of the 53 patients were described as having obtained "corroborating evidence" for their abuse. Another 18 (34%) were said to have discovered that another child had been abused by the same perpetrator. However, the authors did not specify whether any of the 21 individuals with direct corroboration of their trauma overlapped with the 14 cases of "severe amnesia." Thus, the study did not provide evidence of a specific group of individuals with both amnesia and corroboration. Admittedly, the authors provide one case example involving at least some reported amnesia, with good confirmation. But even this case, it turns out, was not a real person, since the authors state that all cases presented are "composites of several cases."[67] It is also interesting to note that in a book by Herman, *Father Daughter Incest*,[68] published only six years earlier, all of the 40 victims appeared to have had clear and continuous memories of their abuse.

Another widely cited retrospective study is that of Briere and Conte,[69] who analyzed questionnaires from 450 therapy patients reporting a history of sexual abuse. The questionnaire contained a single question regarding possible repression: "During the period of time between when the first forced sexual experience happened and your eighteenth birthday was there ever a time when you could not remember the forced sexual experience?" Nearly 60% of respondents answered "yes" to this question. However, no confirmation of the trauma was obtained in any of the cases. More importantly, no

---

62. Herman & Schatzow, *supra* note 61; Ensink, *supra* note 61; Briere & Conte, *supra* note 61; Bernet et al., supra note 61; Loftus et al., *supra* note 61; Gold et al., *supra* note 61; Cameron, *supra* note 61; Dalenberg, *supra* note 61; Kluft, *supra* note 61.

63. van der Kolk & Fisler, *supra* note 2.

64. Draijer, *supra* note 61; Feldman–Summers & Pope, *supra* note 61; Elliott & Fox, *supra* note 61; Elliott & Briere, *supra* note 61;

Andrews et al., *supra* note 61; Elliott, *supra* note 61.

65. Roesler & Wind, *supra* note 61; Williams, *supra* note 61.

66. Herman & Schatzow, *supra* note 61.

67. *Id.* at 6.

68. J. L. Herman, Father-Daughter Incest (1981).

69. Briere & Conte, *supra* note 61.

evidence was offered to *validate* the meaning of a "yes" answer on this question. In other words, the authors did not provide evidence that a "yes" on this particular question actually corresponded to a period of frank amnesia for the event. We will return to this methodological issue below.

Most other retrospective studies have used similar methods. For example, Loftus and associates asked similar questions of 52 substance-abusing women who reported a history of sexual abuse; 10 (19%) reported that they had "forgotten" the experience at some time.[70] In a questionnaire survey, Feldman–Summers and her colleague, Kenneth Pope, similarly found a 40% rate of reported "forgetting" among psychologists who themselves claimed to have been sexually abused.[71] Gold and colleagues found that 31 (30%) of 105 subjects entering or engaged in therapy claimed that they had "completely blocked out any recollection of the abuse" for at least a year.[72] Roe and Schwartz reported that 40 (77%) of 52 patients hospitalized for treatment of sexual trauma claimed that they had not always remembered their abuse.[73] Elliott and Briere found that of 107 individuals reporting sexual abuse on a questionnaire, 24 (22%) answered that they had "no memory" of the experience at some time prior to data collection.[74] Bernet and colleagues reported that among 129 college undergraduates claiming a history of sexual abuse, 46 (36%) reported having had no memory for at least one such experience.[75] van der Kolk and Fisler reported that 15 (43%) of 35 subjects with childhood trauma reported "total amnesia" for the trauma at some time in their lives.[76] Williams found that among 75 women who recalled an episode of sexual abuse, 12 (16%) claimed on interview that there was a time when they "did not remember that this had happened."[77]

Do these various retrospective studies provide evidence meeting the criteria in table 2 for a demonstration of repression? Looking first at the criterion of documentation of the traumatic event, most of the retrospective studies falter at the outset. Many investigations did not attempt to assess whether the traumatic event had actually occurred, but simply accepted that the "memory" was true. Of course, most memories in everyday life *are* true; if someone recalls where he or she went to college, one does not insist on a certified copy of the diploma for corroboration. However, as discussed earlier, a substantial literature has shown that individuals can sometimes develop "memories" for events that never actually happened.[78] Thus, a rigorous scientific study, attempting to test an as yet unproven hypothesis such as that of repression, would require a high standard of documentation of trauma, rather than just the subject's report that he or she remembered it.

Some of the available retrospective studies do suggest that corroboration was obtained in a portion of the cases. However, the details of this "corroboration" are often sketchy. For example, in the Herman and Schatzow study described above, the authors stated that some subjects "corroborated" their

---

70. Loftus et al., *supra* note 61.

71. Feldman–Summers & Pope, *supra* note 61.

72. Gold et al., *supra* note 61.

73. Cameron, *supra* note 61.

74. Elliott & Briere, *supra* note 61.

75. Bernet et al., *supra* note 61.

76. van der Kolk & Fisler, *supra* note 2.

77. Williams, *supra* note 61.

78. JANET, *supra* note 12; JASPERS, *supra* note 12; PIAGET, *supra* note 12; Loftus (1993), *supra* note 12; Loftus (1992), *supra* note 12; Ofshe, *supra* note 12; Loftus & Pickrell, *supra* note 12; Hyman et al., *supra* note 12; Mayer & Pope, *supra* note 12; Moss *supra* note 37.

memories of childhood sexual abuse by discovering that another child, such as a sibling, had been abused.[79] But this sort of "corroboration" is open to question for several reasons. First, is there concrete evidence that the other child was actually abused? Second, even assuming such evidence, does it therefore follow that the study subject was abused also? Suppose, hypothetically, that a patient, suffering from severe depression, has a vague sense that someone may have abused her. She recalls that her uncle used to behave in an inappropriately sexual manner with young girls. Thus, she comes to believe that her uncle must have abused her. Later, at a family reunion, she learns that this uncle was recently arrested for abusing another child. Is her "memory" now corroborated? No. She has known since her childhood that the uncle was a bad actor; the fact that he has now been caught merely confirms something that she already had known before she ever formed her own "memory."

The study with probably the best historical documentation of trauma is that of Williams, described above.[80] But even here, it is unclear whether all of the cases would fully meet the criterion of confirmation of the traumatic event. For example, consider one case presented by Williams, in which an uncle allegedly put his penis in the vagina of a subject when she was age four. In girls under the age of 10, such genitogenital contact has been shown to produce positive findings on unaided medical examination in 96% of cases.[81] But in this girl, no medical findings were noted, and the uncle claimed that the event did not occur. Thus, it seems hazardous to classify cases such as this as confirmed.

In summary, therefore, it does not appear that any of the available retrospective studies of childhood sexual abuse fully meet the first criterion of confirmation of the traumatic event. But even setting aside this problem, the retrospective studies also encounter serious difficulties on our second criterion, namely exclusion of other possible causes of amnesia. First, many of the studies fail to exclude cases of early childhood amnesia, as illustrated for example by the Herman and Schatzow study,[82] described earlier, where the mean ($\pm$ SD) age of onset of abuse in the cases of "severe amnesia" was 4.9 ± 2.4 years. Such cases suggest a problem: an individual might sustain a genuine trauma at age two or three, then forget it as a natural effect of early childhood amnesia. Then, at a later date, others might remind the victim of the event, perhaps asking, "don't you remember when that happened to you?" Gradually, the victim may come to believe that the "memory" is his or her own, even though it was actually created from the accounts of others. Thus, the victim may genuinely believe that he or she forgot and later remembered the event, when in fact the memory was merely constructed from external information.

Second, biological causes of amnesia may sometimes represent a confounding variable. For example one man, describing longstanding amnesia for childhood sexual abuse by a priest,[83] recalled that the priest had apparently

79. Herman & Schatzow, *supra* note 61; Moss, *supra* note 37.

80. Williams, *supra* note 61.

81. D. Muram, *Child Sexual Abuse—Genital Tract Findings in Prepubertal Girls: I. The*

Unaided Medical Examination, 160 Am. J. Obstetrics & Gynecology 328–33 (1989).

82. Herman & Schatzow, *supra* note 61.

83. P. A. Chernoff, J. A. Bodkin, J. A. Chu, E. J. Collins, F. L. Fitzpatrick, A. M. Markham, J. C. Moriarty, & C. Rudnick, *Repressed*

put some drug in his food, causing him to feel sick, lie down, and pass out. Thus, he might have experienced genuine biological amnesia for much of the abuse, and only many years later attempted to reconstruct what happened. As in the example of childhood amnesia described above, he may have come to regard the memory as his own, when in fact he had filled in a "blank" spot with a contemporary reconstruction of the events.

Third, virtually none of the retrospective studies provides thorough *validation* for its questions regarding prior periods of "forgetting." The importance of validation may be illustrated by example: suppose that one asked 100 college women the question, "did you ever suffer from bulimia while in high school?" If 10% answered "yes," would one be justified in assuming that any of the respondents had actually met DSM–IV diagnostic criteria for bulimia nervosa while in high school? No. One must first validate such a questionnaire by demonstrating that individuals answering "yes" actually had bulimia nervosa, as assessed by some more detailed, independent evaluation. Otherwise, a "yes" answer may simply represent a false-positive response. By analogy, if one asks an individual whether he or she remembers having forgotten something at some previous time, it is hazardous to assume that a "yes" answer is actually valid evidence of amnesia. In other words, suppose that a 30–year-old woman currently remembers an experience of childhood sexual abuse, but claims to have "forgotten" it as a teenager. But if we could go back in time, meet that individual at age 17, and ask her directly about that abuse experience, would she express no knowledge of it? Such a conclusion cannot be drawn.

Striking evidence of the need for validation emerges from three recent studies examining college students who reported memories of sexual, physical, or emotional abuse in childhood.[84] As in other retrospective studies discussed above, a certain percentage of these students reported periods of having "forgotten" their abuse. In one study, among 111 students reporting a history of childhood sexual abuse, 22 (19.8%) answered "yes" to the question, "has there ever been a time when you could not remember the sexual/physical/emotional abuse that happened to you?"[85] However, rather than assuming that these cases represented repression, the authors asked a further question: "If there was a time when you could not remember the abuse, why do you think you couldn't remember it?" The students were given various optional answers to this question. The answer that seemed to correspond best to true repression was, "because I simply had no memories of it ever happening." Interestingly, none of the 22 students endorsed this response. Instead, they chose responses such as, "if I remembered, I would feel terrible, so I pushed it out," or "because I didn't want to think about it." Similarly, of 9 students who claimed to have forgotten physical abuse and 15 who claimed to have forgotten emotional abuse for some period of time, none endorsed the item stating that "I simply had no memories." These findings would seem to suggest that when subjects report having "forgotten" a traumatic event for some period of

Memory Syndrome Roundtable Discussion, 4 Mass. L. Rev. 1–20 (Winter 1996–1997).

84. Melchert (1996), *supra* note 61; Melchert & Parker, *supra* note 61; Melchert (1999), *supra* note 61.

85. Melchert & Parker, *supra* note 61.

their lives, they do not mean that the memory was completely lost from consciousness—as would be predicted if repression actually occurred.

By contrast, in another recent retrospective study,[86] a minority of respondents replied that there was a period during which they would not have remembered the abuse event even if asked about it directly. However, as in most of the other retrospective studies, there was no validation that the event had actually occurred, nor of course was there any way to demonstrate that these respondents would in fact have displayed amnesia if they actually had been asked directly about the abuse event at some earlier point in their lives. Indeed, the investigators did not actually interview any of these respondents; the data is based entirely on anonymous questionnaire responses.

Fourth, retrospective studies rarely discuss the possibility of allegations of amnesia for secondary gain. Yet there are many reasons why individuals might claim to have forgotten a traumatic event, even though they in fact had always remembered it. For example, a man abused as a teenager by a priest might make an effort not to think about this experience in subsequent years. If the event later came to light (for example, when other victims of the same priest stepped forward), it might be easier for him to say that he had repressed the memory, rather than to admit that he had simply withheld the information all along. Also, in legal cases, an individual may actually remember a long-past episode of childhood sexual abuse, but allege repression in order to toll a statute of limitations.

In summary, retrospective studies are subject to many inherent methodologic limitations that compromise their ability to test the hypothesis of repression. Thus, even though there are more than 40 such studies, their cumulative number does not help us greatly. Now of course it might still be argued (as discussed earlier with regard to wartime studies) that with so many subjects in so many studies, at least some must have "escaped" all of the methodologic pitfalls listed above, and hence represented *bona fide* cases of repression. But once again, such speculation is inadequate to demonstrate that repression actually occurs.

In the above analysis, we do not mean to appear unduly disparaging of retrospective reports. Recently, for example, careful and systematic accounts have appeared from individual psychotherapists, describing groups of patients from their private practice who apparently had forgotten at least some of the details of experiences of childhood sexual abuse.[87] In both series, some of the patients reportedly recovered memories of these events, and corroboration of various types was obtained. Even though these cases were not prospectively ascertained by specific operational criteria, the authors have attempted to provide as much quantitative analysis of the results as possible. Certainly, these studies represent responsible attempts to validate instances of repression in the clinical experience of the therapist.

Nevertheless, as with all retrospective accounts, especially those representing the experience of a single practitioner, these studies must be regarded with caution. In the past, for example, one classic monograph, presenting a case series of children with infantile autism, reported that 17 could "for all

---

86. S. Joslyn, L. Carlin, & E. F. Loftus, *supra* note 61.

87. Dalenberg, *supra* note 61; Kluft, *supra* note 61.

practical purposes be considered 'cured'" with psychoanalytic psychothera-py.[88] Yet subsequent prospective studies have failed to confirm that infantile autism actually responds to psychoanalytic psychotherapy, and now this belief has faded from the psychiatric literature.[89] Similarly, a careful retrospective case series reported that the vitamins nicotinamide and nicotinic acid (niacin) were highly effective for schizophrenia.[90] Yet this treatment has also been discredited.[91] By analogy, it seems prudent to regard even the best retrospective studies of repression with appropriate skepticism, while awaiting the findings of prospective designs. Therefore, we now present the five available prospective studies known to us that have been cited as evidence for repression of memories of childhood sexual abuse.

[b] Prospective Studies

We begin with the most widely cited of the five prospective studies, because an examination of its methodological limitations may subsequently be applied to the others. In this investigation, Williams studied 129 women who had been seen at a city hospital emergency department in 1973–1975, when they were 10 months to 12 years of age, for evaluation of reported sexual abuse.[92] Apparently the severity of abuse varied: Williams notes that in about one third of cases, the alleged abuse involved only touching and fondling.[93]

Seventeen years later, when the subjects were 18 to 31 years old, they were contacted and interviewed. The interviewers did not reveal the purpose of the study; subjects were merely told that they had been "selected from the records of people who went to the city hospital in 1973–1975" for an "important follow-up study of the lives and health of women." The interview included detailed questions about history of sexual abuse, including even questions about events which the subject did not consider to be abuse, but which others had. However—and this fact is critical–subjects were asked only about experiences of sexual abuse in general; they were *not* specifically asked about their known visit to the hospital to see whether they remembered it.

Forty-nine (38%) of the 129 women failed to mention their recorded episode of sexual abuse on interview. Williams, and many subsequent writers citing her study, imply that many of these 49 individuals did not recall the memory of the experience. Indeed, this finding is often considered the strong-

---

88. B. BETTELHEIM, THE EMPTY FORTRESS 415 (1967).

89. M. Campbell & E. Schopler, *Pervasive Developmental Disorders, in* 1 TREATMENTS OF PSYCHIATRIC DISORDERS: A TASK FORCE REPORT OF THE AMERICAN PSYCHIATRIC ASSOCIATION 179 (T. B. Karasu ed., 1989).

90. A. HOFFER, NIACIN THERAPY IN PSYCHIATRY (1962).

91. M. Deutsch, J. V. Ananth, & A. Bant, *Nicotinic Acid in the Treatment of Chronic Hospitalized Schizophrenics: A Placebo-controlled Clinical Study,* 13 PSYCHOPHARMACOLOGY BULL. 21–23 (1977).

92. L. M. Williams, *Recall of Childhood Trauma: A Prospective Study of Women's Memories of Child Sexual Abuse,* 62 J. CONSULTING &

CLINICAL PSYCHOL. 1167–76 (1994). Note that Williams has also performed a similar follow-up study of men's memories of childhood sexual abuse, but to our knowledge, this study has appeared only as a poster session, L.M. Williams & V.L. Banyard. *Gender and Recall of Child Sexual Abuse: A Prospective Study* Poster session abstracts *in* J.D. Read and D. Stephen Lindsay (eds.), RECOLLECTIONS OF TRAUMA: SCIENTIFIC EVIDENCE AND CLINICAL PRACTICE 371–377 (1997).

93. L. M. Williams, *Adult Memories of Child Sexual Abuse: Preliminary Findings from a Longitudinal Study,* 5 AM. SOC. PREVENTION OF CHILD ABUSE ADVISOR 19–20 (1992).

est evidence that individuals can repress the memory of childhood sexual abuse.

But does this conclusion withstand scientific scrutiny? The study would initially seem to meet our first criterion of adequate documentation of the traumatic event. But an inspection of the data raises questions. Only 37 (28%) of the 129 women were reported to display evidence of genital trauma at the time of their index hospital evaluation. By contrast, as mentioned earlier, gynecological studies have shown that as many as 96% of young girls subjected to genitogenital contact display genital tract abnormalities, even on an unaided medical examination.[94] Similar questions emerge upon reading an earlier publication describing this same sample of women when they were girls in the 1970's. In this monograph, Williams (then publishing under the name of Meyer), together with two co-authors, implies that for many of the girls, the experience of sexual abuse was not particularly traumatic or even memorable:

> Whereas the event [*the index episode*] is disturbing to the victim, it is perhaps no more disturbing than so many other aspects of a child's life. In the first year following the rape [*in the broad, statutory definition of the term, which includes simple fondling*], the victim's family may deliberately maintain an "everything-is-normal" posture. These efforts, combined with the child's natural tendencies to forget and to replace bad feelings with good feelings, usually result in the appearance of few adjustment problems. . . .[95]

Thus, Williams' own description, coupled with the low prevalence of medical findings, suggests that many of the women, even though they were evaluated at the hospital, may not have undergone a seriously traumatic experience of childhood sexual abuse which they would always be expected to remember.

Furthermore, even if we assume that the majority of women did experience serious trauma, can we conclude that the 49 non-reporters actually repressed their memory of their abuse? First, one must eliminate cases of ordinary childhood amnesia: 12 (24%) of the 49 non-reporting subjects had experienced their index episode of sexual abuse at age 4 or earlier, and one was as young as 10 months old. Indeed, the only subject described in detail experienced her abuse (of unspecified severity) at the age of 4. Of course, some individuals might recall severe abuse occurring at the age of four or even earlier, but the total of 49 must clearly be reduced to account for childhood amnesia.

Next, one must eliminate cases of ordinary forgetfulness. Given that many of the cases may have involved exclusively touching and fondling, it seems possible that some experiences were not perceived by young children as particularly memorable (as Williams herself seems to suggest in the quote above). Furthermore, an individual who has made many other visits to the same emergency ward throughout her childhood—for illnesses, injuries, and perhaps even other episodes of physical or sexual abuse—might easily forget one specific index episode of sexual abuse 17 years later. This is the "serial

94. Muram, *supra* note 81.

95. T. W. McCahill, L. C. Meyer, & A. Fischman, The Aftermath of Rape (1979).

position effect" described earlier: individuals characteristically forget individual events in a series of many.[96]

But even after eliminating these two groups of cases, it would still seem that at least some of the non-reporting subjects must have experienced abuse severe enough to be memorable, at an age when they were old enough to remember it. Can these remaining cases be assumed to represent repression? No. We must recall that these individuals *were never actually asked whether they remembered the abuse episode*. In other words, they may have remembered the experience clearly, but failed to report it on interview.

Williams argues that such non-disclosure is unlikely. She notes that many subjects revealed sensitive or embarrassing information, including even episodes of sexual abuse other than the index episode, during the course of their interviews. Such observations, she suggests, indicate that subjects were candid with the interviewers.

But this interpretation is called into serious question when we examine the literature on non-disclosure. For example, in a second prospective study, Femina and colleagues interviewed 69 adults whose abuse histories had been documented years earlier when they were adolescents.[97] Interestingly, 26 (38%) of the subjects gave interview responses discrepant with their previously recorded histories. Specifically, 18 of these 26 subjects, each of whom was known to have experienced severe physical or sexual abuse in childhood, denied or minimized any such history on interview. Unlike Williams, Femina and colleagues contacted and re-interviewed 8 of these 18 "non-disclosers." In this second interview, called the "clarification interview," the authors asked the subjects directly about their known abuse histories. When confronted, all 8 subjects admitted that they had actually remembered these experiences, but had merely chosen not to reveal them during the initial interview.

One of Femina's subjects, for example, when asked why she had failed to disclose her known history of physical and sexual abuse on the initial interview, replied "I didn't say it 'cuz I wanted to forget. I wanted it to be private." Similarly, a man, who had initially failed to disclose physical abuse by his father, admitted to the abuse on the clarification interview and explained "my father is doing well now. If I told now, I think he would kill himself." On the basis of such responses, Femina and colleagues explain reasons for non-disclosure of abuse as "embarrassment, a wish to protect parents, a sense of having deserved the abuse, a conscious wish to forget the past, and a lack of rapport with the interviewer." In no case, however, did these authors find that the non-disclosure was attributable to repression of the memory.

Similar evidence for non-disclosure arises from a study of Pelcovitz et al., who examined 22 school children, ranging in age from six to 10 years old, all of whom were sexually abused by the same perpetrator over a two-year period.[98] These children were enrolled in a school-based sexual abuse preven-

96. McCrary & Hunter, *supra* note 43; Feigenbaum & Simon, *supra* note 43.

97. D. D. Femina, C. A. Yeager, & D. O. Lewis, *Child Abuse: Adolescent Records vs. Adult Recall*, 145 Child Abuse & Neglect 227–31 (1990).

98. D. Pelcovitz, N. A. Adler, S. Kaplan, L. Packman, R. Krieger, *The Failure of a School-based Child Sexual Abuse Prevention Program*, 31 J. Am. Acad. Child Adolesc. Psychiatry 887–92 (1992).

tion program, and had seen "Too Smart for Strangers," a film designed to teach children to protect themselves against physical and sexual abuse. Yet none of the 22 children disclosed the abuse to an adult until it was accidentally discovered.

Non-disclosure of other known life events on interview has been noted in studies for decades. For example, a long series of studies, undertaken by the United States Department of Health, Education, and Welfare, has specifically addressed the question of whether individuals will correctly report past life events to interviewers. These studies have consistently produced substantial rates of underreporting. In one study, for example, 28% of individuals, when interviewed by trained researchers, failed to report a one-day hospitalization which they were known to have undergone during the previous year.[99] In another, 35% of respondents failed to report a doctor's visit which they were known to have made during the past two weeks.[100] In another, 54% failed to report a hospital admission which they were known to have experienced 10–11 months prior to the date of interview.[101] Furthermore, rates of non-disclosure in these studies were greater among subjects with lower incomes than among subjects with higher incomes, and greater among non-White subjects than among White subjects.[102] Williams' subjects were mostly non-White, lower-income women.[103]

Non-disclosure has been documented in numerous other settings in which people are interviewed about sensitive or embarrassing information. Such underreporting has been documented with respect to alcohol consumption,[104] cigarette smoking,[105] drug use,[106] history of drunk driving charges,[107] arrest records,[108] HIV infection,[109] epilepsy,[110] history of psychiatric disorders,[111] and

99. *National Center for Health Statistics, Reporting of Hospitalization in the Health Interview Survey: A Methodological Study of Several Factors Affecting the Reporting of Hospital Episodes,* pub. no. 584–D4 (Dep't Public Health, Education, & Welfare, May 1961).

100. National Center for Health Statistics, Health Interview Responses Compared with Medical Records: Vital and Health Statistics, PHS pub. no. 1000–2–7 (Public Health Service, July 1965).

101. National Center for Health Statistics, *supra* note 99.

102. Health Resources Administration, A Summary of Studies of Interviewing Methodology, DHEW pub. no. HRA0 77–1343 (Dep't Health, Education, & Welfare 1977).

103. Williams, *supra* note 92; and McCa-HILL et al., *supra* note 95.

104. J. M. POLICH, D. ARMOR, & H. B. BRAIKER, THE COURSE OF ALCOHOLISM: FOUR YEARS AFTER TREATMENT (1979); D. J. Cooke & C. A. Allan, *Self-reported Alcohol Consumption and Dissimulation in a Scottish Urban Sample,* 4 J. STUDY ALCOHOL 617–29 (1983); L. T. Midanic, *Validity of Self-reported Alcohol Use: A Literature Review and Assessment,* 83 BRIT. J. ADDICTION 1019–29 (1988).

105. S. M. Blynn, C. L. Gruder, & J. A. Jegerski, *Effects of Biochemical Validation of Self-reported Cigarette Smoking on Treatment Success and on Misreporting Abstinence,* 5 HEALTH PSYCHOL. 125–36 (1986).

106. N. R. Swerdlow, M. A. Geyer, W. Perry, K. Cadenhead, & D. L. Braff, *Drug Screening in "Normal" Controls,* 38 BIOLOGICAL PSYCHIATRY 123–24 (1995).

107. W. Locander, S. Sudman, N. Bradburn, *An Investigation of Interview Method, Threat and Response Distortion,* 71 J. AM. STAT. ASS'N 269–75 (1971).

108. P. E. Tracy & J. A. Fox, *The Validity of Randomized Response for Sensitive Measurements,* 46 AM. SOCIOLOGICAL REV. 187–200 (1981).

109. G. Marks, N. I. Bundek, J. L. Richardson, M. S. Ruiz, N. Maldonado, H. R. Mason, *Self-disclosure of HIV Infection: Preliminary Results from a Sample of Hispanic Men,* 11 HEALTH PSYCHOL. 300–06 (1992); and G. M. McCarthy, F. S. Haji, & I. D. Mackie, *HIV-infected Patients and Dental Care: Nondisclosure of HIV Status and Rejection for Treatment,* 80 ORAL SURGERY, ORAL MED., ORAL PATHOLOGY, ORAL RADIOLOGY ENDOD. 655–59 (1995).

110. M. C. Salinsky, K. Wegener, F. Sinnema, *Epilepsy, Driving Laws, and Patient Dis-*

history of having been a victim of a crime.[112] For example, in the National Crime Survey, known crime victims underreported burglaries by 14%, robberies by 24%, and assaults by 64%.[113] Also, several studies, in addition to the Femina et al. study just described,[114] have documented non-disclosure of childhood sexual abuse.[115] In one of these studies, in fact, 85 (72%) of 116 self-acknowledged victims of childhood sexual abuse reported that they had elected not to disclose their history of abuse when interviewed initially—a figure even more remarkable than the 38% non-disclosure rate documented by Femina and associates.[116]

Given these many findings, it appears that Williams may have rediscovered a phenomenon already well-documented: interviewees will frequently not report known events in their life histories, particularly if they are not questioned directly about the known event. If 35% of interviewees do not report a doctor's appointment from the past two weeks, 64% of assault victims do not reveal that they were assaulted, and 72% of sexual abuse victims admit that they did not disclose their history on an initial interview, then it hardly seems surprising that 38% of Williams' subjects might withhold information about an episode of sexual abuse 17 years earlier, especially when they were not specifically asked about this episode. It would thus be hazardous to conclude that the women in the Williams study had repressed their memory.

Further, data presented by Williams in her own study would actually seem to argue against the repression hypothesis.[117] If repression occurs, one would expect that traumatic events would more likely be repressed than benign events. At first, Williams' findings seem consistent with this theory, when she writes, "There is a tendency for the women who were subjected to more force to not recall the abuse."[118] However, upon inspecting her data, this statement appears to represent an error in the text, which apparently she has since acknowledged.[119] Specifically, as shown in table 2 of her paper, degree of force was *higher* in women who "remembered" than in women with "no recall"—a difference which approaches statistical significance (p=.059). Similarly, in table 4, there is a negative correlation between degree of force and "no recall" (i.e., with greater force, "memory" gets better). Thus, the trend of the data appears opposite to that which would be predicted if repression occurred.

closure to Physicians, 33 EPILEPSIA 469–72 (1992).

111. M. H. Sacks, J. H. Gunn, & W. A. Frosch, *Withholding of Information by Psychiatric Inpatients*, 32 HOSP. COMM. PSYCHIATRY 424–25 (1981); M. Bennett, J. Rutledge, *Self-disclosure in a Clinical Context by Asian and British Psychiatric Outpatients*, 28 BRIT. J. CLINICAL PSYCHOL. 155–63 (1989).

112. R. G. Lehnen & W. G. Skogan, The National Crime Survey: Working Papers: I: Current and Historical Perspectives, NCJ-75374 (Dep't Just. Bureau Just. Statistics, Dec. 1981).

113. *Id.*

114. Femina et al., *supra* note 97.

115. L. R. Farrell, *Factors That Affect a Victim's Self-disclosure in Father-daughter Incest*, 67 CHILD WELFARE LEAGUE AM. 462–68 (1988); N. Faulkner, *Sexual Abuse Recognition and Non-disclosure Inventory of Young Adolescents* (1996) (Ph.D. dissertation, Indiana State University) (on file with the Indiana State University Library); T. Sorensen & B. Snow, *How Children Tell: The Process of Disclosure in Child Sexual Abuse*, 70 CHILD WELFARE LEAGUE AM. 3–15 (1991).

116. Sorensen & Snow, *supra* note 115.

117. E. Harrington, *Research Note*, FALSE MEMORY SYNDROME FOUND. NEWSL. 9 (Feb. 1995).

118. Williams, *supra* note 92, at 1172.

119. Harrington, *supra* note 117.

Finally, it should be noted that Williams has also co-authored a review article which seems to argue against the repression hypothesis.[120] In this review, the authors examine the sequelae of childhood sexual abuse documented in 45 published studies examining a total of 3369 victims. None of the victims in any of these studies, as far as can be judged from the review, was described as having repressed the memory of the abuse experience.

Thus the Williams study, though widely quoted, provides no acceptable evidence that any subjects repressed the memory of their sexual abuse experiences. The combination of childhood amnesia, ordinary forgetting, and—most importantly—elective non-disclosure can more than explain a 38% non-reporting rate, without the need to postulate repression.

Similar methodology considerations affect all of the other three prospective studies that have examined memory in victims of childhood sexual abuse. The first of these three studies assessed 20 women in London who had been removed from their homes, at a mean age of 12.3 years, by social service agencies.[121] Sexual abuse had been confirmed in these subjects both from their own reports as children and by the report of at least one adult familiar with the home at the time. The age of the victims at the time of the abuse was not specified. Follow-up interviews were performed when these women were between 18 and 24 years old. Three (15%) did not give a positive response to the question, "were you sexually abused as a child?" However, as in the Williams study above, the author did not ask the subjects specifically about their known sexual abuse history. Since this non-reporting rate of 15% is well below the 38% to 72% rates of deliberate non-disclosure found in the Femina et al. and Sorensen and Snow[122] studies described above, it appears explainable on the basis of non-disclosure alone, without a need to postulate repression.

In the second study, a group of investigators performed follow-up interviews with 22 children who had reportedly been abused in day care centers.[123] Three (14%) of these children were said to display no memory of their abuse when interviewed, and others were described as showing only partial memory. However, confirmation of the original traumatic event was not satisfactory; the principal documentation for the abuse was that the day care centers in question had been engaged in legal proceedings resulting in civil settlements. Further, the study indicates that many of the children had been very young, well within the period of normal early childhood amnesia, at the time of the alleged abuse. Indeed, the median age of the children at the time of abuse was 2½ years; at least one was less than 12 months of age, and another was 21 months old. Thus, early childhood amnesia would appear to explain much, if not all, of the memory deficits in this sample. Furthermore, the possibility of deliberate non-disclosure is not discussed.

120. K. A. Kendall–Tackett, L. M. Williams, & D. Finkelhor, *Impact of Sexual Abuse on Children: A Review and Synthesis of Recent Empirical Studies*, 113 PSYCHOL. BULL. 164–80 (1993).

121. C. BAGLEY, CHILD SEXUAL ABUSE AND MENTAL HEALTH IN ADOLESCENTS AND ADULTS: BRITISH AND CANADIAN PERSPECTIVES (1995).

122. Femina et al., *supra* note 97; Sorenson & Snow, *supra* note 115.

123. A. W. Burgess, C. R. Hartman, & T. Baker, *Memory Presentations of Childhood Sexual Abuse*, 33 J. PSYCHOSOCIAL NURSING 9–16 (1995).

In the most recent prospective study, Widom and Morris report on follow-up interviews conducted with 1,181 individuals, of whom 94 were known from court records to have been sexually abused before the age of 12.[124] The documentation of trauma appears quite good in this study, in that cases were chosen only where the perpetrator had actually been convicted of the abuse crime. As in the Williams study, the subjects were not asked specifically about the episode that had precipitated the court case, but were merely asked in general terms about a list of sexual experiences that they might have had before the age of 12. Then they were asked whether they considered any of these experiences to represent sex abuse, whether they had ever had sex with a person more than 10 years older than themselves, and whether they had been subjected to sex against their will. Among the 94 interviewees with a known history of childhood sexual abuse, 59 (63%) acknowledged one or more of the items on the list of sexual experiences before age 12, but only 54% of the interviewees considered their experiences to represent sex abuse, and 47% of the subjects reported that they had experienced sex against their will. Subjects who did not describe their known abuse episode on this general questioning were not specifically asked about it later. In other words, no "clarification interviews" were administered in the manner of the Femina et al. study described above.[125]

Unlike Williams, who implies that her subjects did not recall their index episode of abuse, Widom and Morris do not equate non-reporting with forgetfulness, much less repression. Instead, they note that non-reporting of crimes is common, and cite the National Crime Survey, which we have mentioned above.[126] It will be recalled that as many as 64% of adults in this survey did not report a recent assault which they were known to have experienced. Therefore, Widom and Morris do not appear surprised at the rate of non-reporting in their own study:

> Although this lack of reporting is significant, it may not be surprising when viewed in a somewhat different context. Nonreporting by crime victims in the context of victimization surveys has been studied for a number of years ... and problems with respondent embarrassment about the incident or "protective mechanisms," or simply memory decay or forgetting have been described.[127]

In other words, Widom and Morris do not present their study as evidence for repression, but rather as a demonstration of the general problem of underreporting. Indeed, in a companion paper, Widom and Shepard[128] describe similar underreporting for physical abuse, and cite a large and venerable literature on the general unreliability of adults' reports of their childhood experiences.[129] If this unreliability were due to repression, one would expect

---

124. C. S. Widom & S. Morris, *Accuracy of Adult Recollections of Childhood Victimization: Part 2. Childhood Sexual Abuse*, 9 PSYCHOL. ASSESSMENT 34–46 (1997).

125. Femina et al *supra* note 97.

126. Lehnen & Skogan, *supra* note 112.

127. Widom & Morris, *supra* note 124, at 143.

128. C. S. Widom & R. L. Shepard, *Accuracy of Adult Recollections of Childhood Victim-*

ization: Part 1. Childhood Physical Abuse, 8 PSYCHOL. ASSESSMENT 412–21 (1996).

129. L. N. ROBINS, DEVIANT CHILDREN GROWN UP (1966); M. R. Yarrow, J. D. Campbell, & R. V. Burton, *Recollections of Childhood: A Study of the Retrospective Method*, 5 MONOGRAPHS SOC. RES. CHILD DEV. 135, 138 (1970); J. C. Schwarz, M. L. Barton–Henry, & T. Pruzinsky, *Assessing Child-rearing Behaviors: A Comparison of Ratings Made by Mother, Father, Child, and Sibling on the CRPBI*, 56 CHILD DEV. 462–79

that adults would recall benign childhood experiences accurately and traumatic events poorly. But in fact, all types of childhood events are inaccurately reported. For example, in a recent study from New Zealand, interview data from 1,008 18–year-olds were compared with data obtained earlier from these same subjects as they grew up.[130] Substantial inaccuracies—usually in the direction of underreporting—were found for items as varied as number of changes of residence, history of bone fractures and other physical injuries, hyperactivity as a child, and having shoplifted prior to age 13. In another recent study,[131] 73 14–year-old males were studied in 1962. Sixty-seven of these subjects were reinterviewed in person at age 48. In both interviews, the subjects were asked about family relationships, home environment, sexuality, dating, religion, parental discipline, and general activities. The investigators found large differences between the adults' memories of their adolescence and what they had actually reported in their adolescence. Indeed, accurate memory in these individuals proved no better than expected by chance.

Returning, then, to the five available prospective studies of memory of childhood sexual abuse, four found that some percentage of interviewees did not report an experience of abuse they were known to have undergone many years previously.[132] However, in all four of these studies, the interviewees were never specifically asked about the known incident of abuse; instead, they were simply asked about experiences of sexual abuse in general. Thus, the rates of non-reporting found in these four studies appear well within the range previously documented for non-reporting of numerous life events,[133] without any need to postulate repression. It is telling, in this connection, that the fifth prospective study[134] found that all non-reporters, when asked directly about

(1985); N. M. Bradburn, L. J. Rips, & S. K. Shevell, *Answering Autobiographical Questions: The Impact of Memory and Inference on Surveys*, 236 SCI. 157–61 (1987); A. M. Berger, J. F. Knutson, J. G. Mehm, & K. A. Perkins, *The Self-report of Punitive Childhood Experiences of Young Adults and Adolescents*, 12 CHILD ABUSE & NEGLECT 251–62 (1988); D. O. Lewis, C. Mallouh, & V. Webb, *Child Abuse, Delinquency, and Violent Criminality*, in CHILD MALTREATMENT 707–21 (D. Cicchetti & V. Carlson eds., 1989); M. Ross, *Relation of Implicit Theories to the Construction of Personal Histories*, 96 PSYCHOL. REV. 341–57 (1989); C. Kruttschnitt & M. Dornfeld, *Will They Tell?*, 29 J. RES. IN CRIME & DELINQ. 136–47 (1992); B. Henry, E. G. Moffitt, A. Caspi, J. Langley, & P. A. Silva, *On the "Remembrance of Things Past": A Longitudinal Evaluation of the Retrospective Method*, 6 PSYCHOL. ASSESSMENT 92–101 (1994); D. Finkel & M. McGue, *Twenty-five Year Follow-up of Child-rearing Practices: Reliability of Retrospective Data*, 15 PERSONALITY & INDIVIDUAL DIFFERENCES 147–54 (1993); *see also* reviews in C. R. Brewin, B. Andrews, I. H. Gotlib, *Psychopathology and Early Experience: A Review of Retrospective Reports*, 113 PSYCHOL. BULL. 82–98 (1993).

130. Henry et al., *supra* note 129.

131. D. Offer, M. Kaiz, K.I. Howard, & E.S. Bennett, *The Altering of Reported Experiences*

J AMER ACAD. CHILD ADOLESCENT PSYCHIATRY 735–42 (2000).

132. Williams, *supra* note 92; BAGLEY, *supra* note 121; Burgess et al., *supra* note 123; Widom & Morris, *supra* note 124.

133. Femina et al., *supra* note 97; Pelcovitz et al., *supra* note 98; National Center for Health Statistics, supra note 99; National Center for Health Statistics, *supra* note 100; Health Resources Administration, *supra* note 102; POLICH, *supra* note 104, Cooke & Allan, *supra* note 104; Midanic, *supra* note 104; Blynn et al., *supra* note 105; Swerdlow et al., *supra* note 106; Locander et al., *supra* note 107; Tracy & Fox, *supra* note 108; Marks et al., *supra* note 109; McCarthy et al., *supra* note 109; Salinsky et al., *supra* note 110; Sacks et al., *supra* note 111; Bennett & Rutledge, *supra* note 111; Lehnen & Skogan, *supra* note 112; Farrell, *supra* note 115; Faulkner, *supra* note 115; Sorensen & Snow, *supra* note 115; ROBINS, *supra* note 129; Yarrow et al., *supra* note 129; Schwarz et al., *supra* note 129; Bradburn et al., *supra* note 129; Berger et al., *supra* note 129; Lewis et al., *supra* note 129; Ross et al., *supra* note 129; Kruttschnitt & Dornfeld, *supra* note 129; Henry et al., *supra* note 129; Finkel & McGue, *supra* note 129; Brewin et al., *supra* note 129.

134. Femina et al., *supra* note 97.

their known abuse history in a "clarification interview," acknowledged that they remembered the events, and had deliberately withheld the information initially.

Two other recent case reports have been cited as examples of "prospective studies" documenting repression.[135] These do not deserve extensive review here, since individual case reports are of little value to our present exercise, for reasons discussed above. Further, both have been criticized as unsatisfactory examples of unequivocal repression in the first place.[136]

The failure of these prospective studies to provide satisfactory evidence of repression accords with the findings of prospective studies of other types of trauma, as we have discussed earlier.[137] In summary, looking at the entire literature of prospective studies, examining victims of all types of trauma including childhood sexual abuse, we are unable to find any investigations in which victims displayed unexplained amnesia for the events when asked directly about these events on a follow-up interview.

Various other authors have analyzed the literature on repression of memories of childhood sexual abuse, and reached conclusions similar to ours. These analyses may be found both in the scientific literature[138] and in popular works.[139] However, at least three other recent reviews have argued the

135. D.L. Corwin and E. Olafson, *supra* note 21; Duggal & Srofe, *supra* note 21.

136. Piper et al., *supra* note 11.

137. *See especially* R. L. Leopold & H. Dillon, *Psycho-anatomy of a Disaster: A Long Term Study of Post-traumatic Neuroses in Survivors of a Marine Explosion*, 119 Am. J. Psychiatry 913–21 (1963); L. C. Terr, *Children of Chowchilla: A Study of Psychic Trauma*, 34 Psychoanalytic Study Child 552–623 (1979); L. C. Terr, *Chowchilla Revisited: The Effects of Psychic Trauma Four Years After a School-bus Kidnaping*, 140 Am. J. Psychol. 1543–50 (1983); U. Malt, *The Long-term Psychiatric Consequences of Accidental Injury: A Longitudinal Study of 107 Adults*, 153 Brit. J. Psychiatry 810–18 (1988); Wagenaar & Groeneweg, *supra* note 39; and L. C. Terr, D. A. Bloch, B. A. Michel, H. Shi, J. A. Reinhardt, & S. Metayer, *Children's Memories in the Wake of Challenger*, 153 Am. J. Psychiatry 618–25 (1996).

138. Loftus (1993), *supra* note 12; S. Lindsay & J. D. Read, *Psychotherapy and Memories of Childhood Abuse: A Cognitive Perspective*, 8 Applied Cognitive Psychol. 281–338 (1994); F. H. Frankel, *Adult Reconstruction of Childhood Events in the Multiple Personality Literature*, 150 Am. J. Psychiatry 954–58 (1993); R. J. Ofshe & M. T. Singer, *Recovered-memory Therapy and Robust Repression: Influence and Pseudomemories*, 42 Int'l J. Clinical Experimental Hypnosis 391–410 (1994); T. W. Campbell, *Repressed Memories and Statutes of Limitations: Examining the Data and Weighing the Consequences*, 16 Am. J. Forensic Psychiatry 25–51 (1995); F. H. Frankel, *Discovering New Memories in Psychotherapy—Childhood Revis-*

ited, Fantasy, or Both?, 333 New Eng. J. Med. 591–94 (1995); D. S. Lindsay & J. D. Read, *"Memory Work" and Recovered Memories of Childhood Sexual Abuse: Scientific Evidence and Public, Professional, and Personal Issues*, 1 Psychol. Pub. Pol'y L. 846–908 (1995); J. Boakes, *False Memory Syndrome*, 346 Lancet 1048–1109 (1995); H. Merskey, *Ethical Issues in the Search for Repressed Memories*, 50 Am. J. Psychotherapy 323–35 (1996); J. Paris, *A Critical Review of Recovered Memories in Psychotherapy: Part I—Trauma and Memory & Part II—Trauma and Therapy*, 41 Can. J. Psychiatry 201–10 (1996); J. F. Kihlstrom, *Suffering from Reminiscences: Exhumed Memory, Implicit Memory, and the Return of the Repressed*, in Recovered Memories and False Memories 100–17 (M. A. Conway ed., 1997); E. F. Loftus, E. Milo, & J. R. Paddock, *The Accidental Executioner: Why Psychotherapy Must Be Informed by Science*, 23 Counseling Psychologist 300–09 (1995); J. G. Tillman, M. R. Nash, & P. M. Lerner, *Does Trauma Cause Dissociative Pathology?*, in Dissociation: Clinical, Theoretical and Research Perspectives (S. Lynn & J. Rhue eds., 1994); A. Piper, *What Science Says—and Doesn't Say–About Repressed Memories: A Critique of Sheflin and Brown*, J. Psychiatry & L. 615–36 (Winter 1997); and S. Brandon, J. Boakes, D. Glaser, & R. Green, *Recovered Memories of Childhood Sexual Abuse: Implications for Clinical Practice*, 172 Brit. J. Psychiatry 296–307 (1998).

139. H.G. Pope Jr. Psychology Astray (1998); E. Loftus & K. Ketcham, The Myth of Repressed Memory: False Memories and Allegations of Sexual Abuse (1994); R. J. Ofshe & E. Waters, Making Monsters: False Memories, Psy-

conclusion that repression may occur.[140]

§ 10–2.4 Future Directions

The analysis in this chapter rests on four initial assumptions. First, rather than review the entire literature on all aspects of trauma and memory, we have focused on one specific operational question: can human beings develop amnesia for seemingly unforgettable traumatic events? This hypothesized process has been variously termed "repression," "dissociative amnesia," or "psychogenic amnesia,"—depending in part on the intrapsychic process believed to underlie it. For simplicity, we have used the term "repression" throughout this section, since our question remains the same regardless of the particular terminology used, or the particular mechanisms postulated to occur within the brain.

Second, we have surveyed general studies of victims of known traumas. Upon examining 73 studies of more than 11,000 victims of various traumas (table 1), together with a review of 45 additional studies of 3369 victims of childhood sexual abuse,[141] we find that in general, human beings remember traumatic events clearly, barring such factors as loss of consciousness or early childhood amnesia. Therefore, we have concluded that, as a working hypothesis, we must begin with the assumption that people generally do remember traumatic events, and that the burden of proof therefore falls on investigators to demonstrate that some people can instead develop amnesia for such events.

This second assumption reflects a fundamental principle of science, namely that when a new hypothesis of causality is proposed, it remains unproven until other, already established causes have been excluded. This concept was well expressed by Sir Isaac Newton when he wrote, "we are to admit to no more causes of natural things than such as are both true and sufficient to explain their appearances."[142] To give an example of this principle, the theory of relativity in physics carried the burden of demonstrating that classical mechanics were violated at speeds approaching the speed of light. Similarly, an epidemiologist who claims to have recognized a new infectious disease assumes the burden of demonstrating that the patients' illness cannot be explained by an already recognized microorganism.

This burden of proof, furthermore, must not be shifted merely because a concept enjoys widespread cultural acceptance. For example, many Americans believe that chicken soup is effective for the common cold. But this does not mean that scientists now bear the burden of proving that chicken soup is *not* effective. Similarly, the notion of amnesia for traumatic events began to appear in romantic novels and poetry in the mid-nineteenth century[143]—long

CHOTHERAPY AND SEXUAL HYSTERIA (1994); H. WAKEFIELD & R. UNDERWAGER, RETURN OF THE FURIES: AN INVESTIGATION INTO RECOVERED MEMORY THERAPY (1994); R. M. DAWES, HOUSE OF CARDS: PSYCHOLOGY AND PSYCHOTHERAPY BUILT ON MYTH (1994); F. CREWS, THE MEMORY WARS: FREUD'S LEGACY IN DISPUTE (1995); M. PENDERGRAST, VICTIMS OF MEMORY (2d ed., 1996); M. A. HAGEN, WHORES OF THE COURT: THE FRAUD OF PSYCHIATRIC TESTIMONY AND THE RAPE OF AMERICAN JUSTICE (1997); Anonymous, *Remind Me One More Time*, THE ECONOMIST 75–77, Jan. 18, 1997.

140. Sheflin & Brown, *supra* note 4; K. S. Pope, *Memory, Abuse, and Science: Questioning Claims About the False Memory Syndrome Epidemic*, 51 AM. PSYCHOLOGIST 957–74 (1996); Brown et al., 1999, *supra* note 4.

141. Kendall–Tackett et al., *supra* note 120.

142. I. NEWTON, MATHEMATICAL PRINCIPLES OF NATURAL PHILOSOPHY 398 (Andrew Florian Motte trans., revised by Cajori) (1934).

143. POPE, *supra* note 139.

before Freud or Janet proposed the scientific concepts of "repression" or "dissociation"—and it continues in contemporary culture in movies, magazines, and television. But the fact that repression is widely endorsed in our culture does not render it an established fact of science. Therefore, the burden of proof still rests on investigators to "reject the null hypothesis"—namely to prove that, although most people remember traumas, certain people, under certain circumstances, do not.

Third, we have proposed minimum criteria (table 2, supra § 10–2.1.2) necessary for a study to reject the "null hypothesis." These include 1) documentation that the traumatic event actually occurred and 2) demonstration that a group of individuals developed amnesia for the event, not explainable by known processes such as early childhood amnesia, biological insults, ordinary forgetfulness, or deliberate allegation of amnesia for secondary gain. We have also noted that individual case reports, or even retrospective anecdotal case series, are insufficient to reject the null hypothesis.

Fourth, we have applied these methodologic criteria to available studies where groups of individuals were reported to have developed amnesia for traumatic events, including all of the studies known to us that have been cited as evidence for repression of memories of childhood sexual abuse. Upon analysis of these studies, we have been unable to find evidence of repression that satisfies our minimum criteria. We conclude that, at present, there is insufficient evidence to permit the conclusion that individuals can "repress" such memories.

Several criticisms of our analysis must be considered. First, it might be argued that absence of evidence is not evidence of absence. In other words, although none of the above studies presents clear evidence of repression, one is not justified in concluding that repression cannot occur. This reasoning is correct, but with several reservations. First, as just noted, the burden of proof must fall on those who argue that repression of memories can occur: until a methodologically sound demonstration of repression is presented, we cannot, *a priori*, posit its existence. Second, if repression did occur, we might reasonably expect to see some evidence of it in laboratory studies, even if it had not been demonstrated unequivocally in real life. Yet more than 60 years of laboratory research have failed to produce a study providing clear evidence of repression.[144] Thus, it is even more imperative that a clear clinical demonstration of repression be provided before we accept the concept. Third, if repression does occur, even rarely, we should expect to see many reported cases, as noted above in our calculations of the number of Americans who might be predicted to harbor repressed memories of childhood sexual abuse. Therefore the absence of evidence here is, to some degree, evidence of absence. Fourth, there are already many well-documented reasons why people may fail to report past life events, including biological amnesia, early childhood amnesia, ordinary forgetfulness, allegations of forgetfulness for secondary gain, and elective non-disclosure. In science, when simple explanations of a phenomenon are already available, it is inappropriate to postulate another, more complex explanation without adequate evidence. This "principle of parsimony," often

144. D. Holmes, *The Evidence for Repression: An Examination of Sixty Years of Research, in* REPRESSION AND DISSOCIATION: IMPLICA-TIONS FOR PERSONALITY, THEORY, PSYCHOPATHOLOGY AND HEALTH 85–102 (J. Singer ed., 1990).

known as "Ockham's razor" after the 14th century monk, William of Ockham,[145] states that entities are not to be multiplied beyond necessity (*non sunt multiplicanda entia praeter necessitatem*). Ockham's razor would dictate that we not assume the existence of repression in any case until we have ruled out other, simpler possibilities.

A second criticism of our analysis might be that we have proposed impossibly rigorous criteria for a satisfactory demonstration of repression. First, we have insisted on clear documentation of the traumatic event. Yet childhood sexual abuse is often a secret trauma, known only to the victim and perpetrator, and hence difficult to document.[146] To make matters even more difficult, our exclusion criteria for causes of amnesia have fluid boundaries. One can argue at length about the age threshold for "early childhood amnesia," the degree of forgetting that can be reasonably ascribed to biological factors such as head injury, or the limits of what can be explained by ordinary forgetfulness. But these problems are not insuperable: if repression occurs, one might reasonably expect to see cases in which the trauma was unequivocally documented, and where it occurred indisputably beyond the age for childhood amnesia, in the absence of any biological factors, and was too pronounced to be lost to ordinary forgetfulness. Admittedly, these requirements make a demonstration of repression even more difficult. But simply because a hypothesis is difficult to prove does not require that we relax our standards for accepting it. Furthermore, if repression of childhood sexual abuse afflicts hundreds of thousands of individuals, as discussed above, one might reasonably expect rigorous demonstrations of this phenomenon, even if only a small fraction of the available cases fully met our methodologic criteria.

Another possible criticism of our discussion is that we might have selectively omitted relevant data that would contradict our reasoning. Several points should be made in response to this criticism. First, we have included every published peer-reviewed study, to our knowledge, which even approaches addressing our operational question about repression of memory in victims of childhood sexual abuse, and have even included many as yet unpublished studies in this area. To ensure completeness in this respect, we have examined recent reviews favoring the repression hypothesis,[147] and have included all of the studies cited in these reviews.

Second, we should acknowledge that *DSM-IV* and its more recent text revision, *DSM–IV–TR*[148] recognize the category of "dissociative amnesia" as a diagnostic entity.[149] However, we have not included a discussion of *DSM–IV* in the text of this chapter, since *DSM–IV* does not represent an actual study, but

---

145. William of Ockham: Dialogus, Latin text and English translation, edited by R.W. Dyson, J. Kilcullen, G. Knysh, V. Leppin and J. Scott under the auspices of the Medieval Texts Editorial Committee of the British Academy (London: The British Academy, 1999) available online at: http://britac3.britac.ac.uk/pubs/dialogus/ockdial.html.

146. Herman, *supra* note 4; Terr (1990), *supra* note 38; Terr (1994), *supra* note 38; Van Debur Atler, *supra* note 56; Armstrong, *supra* note 56; Russell, *supra* note 56; Freyd, *supra* note 58; Nash & West, *supra* note 59; Wyatt, *supra* note 59; Bagley & Ramsay, *supra* note 59; Finkelhor et al. (1990), *supra* note 59; Anderson et al., *supra* note 59; Finkelhor (1994), *supra* note 59.

147. Sheflin & Brown, *supra* note 4; and Pope, *supra* note 137; Brown et al. (1998), *supra* note 4; Brown et al. (1999), *supra* note 4.

148. American Psychiatric Association, *supra* note 8; American Psychiatric Association, Diagnostic and Statistical Manual of Mental Disorders (4th ed., text revision 2000) (DSM–IV–TR); Brown et al., *supra* note 4.

149. American Psychiatric Association (2000) *supra* note 148, at 520.

rather the recommendations of a "work group" formed to propose diagnostic criteria and associated text. In other words, no actual data are presented in the *DSM–IV* discussion of "dissociative amnesia." Furthermore, the work group notes that there are "very different interpretations" of this phenomenon, with some authorities feeling that it is underdiagnosed, and others believing that "the syndrome has been overdiagnosed in individuals who are highly suggestible."[150] Therefore, *DSM–IV* should not be seen as providing concrete scientific evidence for or against repression, but merely as proposing criteria for a concept that it acknowledges to be controversial. Indeed, evidence from other areas in psychiatry has shown that the inclusion of a diagnosis in DSM–IV is no guarantee of its validity: as we have noted elsewhere, the DSM–IV entity, "cannabis-induced psychotic disorder" is almost completely devoid of support in the published scientific literature.[151]

We would also note, parenthetically, that the DSM–IV concept of "dissociative amnesia" does not enjoy general acceptance among board-certified American psychiatrists in any event. In a recent study,[152] we mailed a one-page questionnaire to a representative national sample of 367 board-certified American psychiatrists, asking their opinions of the diagnostic status and scientific validity of the DSM–IV categories of "dissociative amnesia" and "dissociative identity disorder." Of the 301 respondents (an 82% response rate), only 35 percent replied that "dissociative amnesia" should be included without reservation in DSM–IV; a larger number felt that this entity should be included only as a "proposed" (that is, unofficial) diagnosis. Only 23 percent of the respondents felt that there was "strong evidence" for the validity of dissociative amnesia. A similar study of Canadian psychiatrists found even lower rates of acceptance of these concepts.[153]

Next, it might be argued that we should have provided more references and more discussion regarding biological and neurological studies of memory,[154] studies of the effects of anxiety on memory function,[155] psychodynamic theories of repression and related defense mechanisms,[156] studies of fugue

150. *Id.* at 521.

151. A. J. Gruber & H. G. Pope, Jr., *Cannabis Psychotic Disorder: Does It Exist?*, 3 Am. J. Addictions 72–83 (1994); American Psychiatric Association (2000), *supra* note 148

152. H. G. Pope, Jr., P. S. Oliva, J. I. Hudson, J. A. Bodkin, & A. J. Gruber, *Attitudes Towards DSM–IV Dissociative Disorders Diagnoses Among Board-certified American Psychiatrists*, 156 Am. J. Psychiatry 321–323 (1999).

153. J.K. Lalonde, J.I. Hudson, R.A. Gigante, & H.G. Pope Jr., *Attitudes of American and Canadian Psychiatrists Towards DSM–IV Dissociative Disorders Diagnoses*, 49th Annual Meeting of the Canadian Psychiatric Association, Toronto, September, 1999.

154. B. S. McEwen, *Adrenal Steroid Actions on Brain: Dissecting the Fine Line Between Protection and Damage*, in Neurobiological and Clinical Consequences of Stress: From Normal Adaptation to Posttraumatic Stress Disorder (M. J. Friedman, D. S. Charney, & A. Y.

Deutch eds., 1995); B. A. van der Kolk, A. C. McFarlane, & L. Weisaeth, Traumatic Stress: The Effects of Overwhelming Experience on Mind, Body, and Society (1996); D. S. Charney, A. Y. Deutch, J. H. Krystal, S. M. Soutwick, & M. Davis, *Psychobiological Mechanisms of Posttraumatic Stress Disorder*, 50 Archives Gen. Psychiatry 294–305 (1993).

155. M. W. Eysenck, *Anxiety, Learning, and Memory: A Reconceptualization*, 13 J. Res. Pers. 363–85 (1979); M. W. Eysenck, Anxiety: The Cognitive Perspective (1992); R. A. Cohen & B. F. O'Donnell, *Neuropsychological Models of Attentional Dysfunction*, in The Neuropsychol. Attention 329–49 (R. A. Cohen ed., 1993); J. P. Mialet, J. C. Bisserbe, A. Jacobs, & H. G. Pope, Jr., *Two-dimensional Anxiety: A Confirmation Using Computerized Neuropsychological Testing of Attentional Performance*, 11 Eur. Psychiatry 344–52 (1996).

156. M. H. Erdleyi, *Repression, Reconstruction, and Defense: History and Integration of the Psychoanalytic and Experimental Frameworks*, in Repression and Dissociation: Implica-

states[157] and so forth. Although there is a rich literature in all of these areas, discussion of these topics falls outside of the scope of this chapter, since we have focused only on the specific operational question of whether human beings have been shown to develop complete amnesia for a seemingly unforgettable traumatic event.

Certainly, further biological studies, laboratory studies, and psychodynamic studies are welcome. But to answer our specific question, the most valuable study at this point would be a rigorous prospective investigation of whether individuals can repress the memory of childhood sexual abuse. It would not be extraordinarily difficult to design such a study, fully meeting all of the methodologic criteria spelled out in this chapter. One would begin with a cohort of individuals documented to have been abused. For example, one could use medical records, as Williams did,[158] or one could locate all of the victims identified by reliable evidence in some forensic setting as did Widom and Morris.[159] Then, one would select all individuals who were over the age of five at the time of the abuse (to exclude normal childhood amnesia), and who experienced abuse of sufficient magnitude that they would not reasonably be expected to have forgotten it (to exclude ordinary forgetfulness). One would of course also exclude any individuals with a possible biological cause for amnesia such as head injury or drug intoxication. One would then follow up all remaining individuals and interview them at a later time (with suitable psychological and ethical precautions) to ascertain whether they remembered their experiences of sexual abuse. Individuals denying abuse upon the initial interview would then be administered a "clarification interview" in the manner of Femina and associates, as described above, in which they would be presented with the fact of their known abuse experience and asked directly if they remembered it.[160] If a significant percentage of subjects continued to report amnesia for the abuse despite direct questioning—and they derived no obvious secondary gain by doing so—then one would have a satisfactory demonstration that repression of traumatic memories can occur.

Repression, in short, is a testable hypothesis, but it has not yet been appropriately tested. Pending satisfactory studies, therefore, the most reasonable scientific position is to maintain skepticism.

TIONS FOR PERSONALITY, THEORY, PSYCHOPATHOLOGY AND HEALTH 1–31 (J. Singer ed., 1990); D. Spiegel, *Dissociative Disorders*, in 10 REV. PSYCHIATRY 143–280 (A. Tasman ed., 1991); and S. J. Lynn & J. Rhue, DISSOCIATION: CLINICAL, THEORETICAL AND RESEARCH PERSPECTIVES (1994).

157. N. Kapur, *Amnesia in Relation to Fugue States—Distinguishing a Neurological from a Psychogenic Basis*, 159 BRIT. J. PSYCHIATRY 872–77 (1991); A. M. Riether & A. Stoudemire, *Psychogenic Fugue States: A Review*, 81 S. MED. J. 568–71 (1988).

158. Williams, *supra* note 92.

159. Widom & Morris, *supra* note 124.

160. Femina et al., *supra* note 97.

Appendix A

1. A. Strom, S. B. Refsum, L. Eitenger, O. Gronvik, A. Lonnum, A. Engeset, K. Osvik, & B. Rogan, *Examination of Norwegian Ex-concentration Camp Prisoners*, 4 J. NEUROPSYCHIATRY 43–62 (1961);

2. P. Chodoff, *Late Effects of the Concentration Camp Syndrome*, 8 ARCHIVES OF GEN. PSYCHIATRY 323–33 (1963);

3. R. L. Leopold & H. Dillon, *Psycho-anatomy of a Disaster: A Long Term Study of Post-traumatic Neuroses in Survivors of a Marine Explosion*, 119 AM. J. PSYCHIATRY 913–21 (1963);

4. L. C. Terr, *Children of Chowchilla: A Study of Psychic Trauma*, 34 PSYCHOANALYTIC STUDY CHILD 552–623 (1979);

5. L. C. Terr, *Chowchilla Revisited: The Effects of Psychic Trauma Four Years After a School-bus Kidnaping*, 140 AM. J. PSYCHIATRY 1543–50 (1983);

6. W. W. Eaton, J. J. Sigal, & M. Weinfeld, *Impairment in Holocaust Survivors After 33 Years: Data from an Unbiased Community Sample*, 139 AM. J. PSYCHIATRY 773–77 (1982);

7. C. B. Wilkinson, *Aftermath of a Disaster: The Collapse of the Hyatt Regency Hotel Skywalks*, 140 AM. J. PSYCHIATRY 1134–39 (1983);

8. A. Hoiberg & B. G. McCaugher, *The Traumatic Aftereffects of Collision at Sea*, 141 AM. J. PSYCHIATRY 70–73 (1984);

9. S. J. Dollinger, *Lightning-strike Disaster Among Children*, 58 BRIT. J. MED. PSYCHOL. 375–83 (1985);

10. C. P. Malmquist, *Children Who Witness Parental Murder: Posttraumatic Aspects*, 25 J. AM. ACAD. CHILD PSYCHIATRY 320–25 (1986);

11. J. D. Kinzie, W. Sack, R. H. Angell, S. Manson, & R. Ben, *The Psychiatric Effects of Massive Trauma on Cambodian Children: I. The Children*, 25 J. AM. ACAD. CHILD PSYCHIATRY 370–76 (1986);

12. J. D. Kinzie, W. Sack, R. H. Angell, G. Clarke, & R. Ben, *A Three-year Follow-up of Cambodian Young People Traumatized as Children*, 28 J. AM. ACAD. CHILD ADOLESC. PSYCHIATRY 501–04 (1989);

13. W. H. Sack, G. Clarke, C. Him, D. Dickason, B. Goff, K. Lanham, J. D. Kinzie, *A 6-year Follow-up Study of Cambodian Refugee Adolescents Traumatized as Children*, 32 J. AM. ACAD. CHILD ADOLESC. PSYCHIATRY 431–37 (1993);

14. J. H. Shore, E. L. Tatum, W. M. Vollmer, *Psychiatric Reaction to Disaster: The Mount St. Helens Experience*, 143 AM. J. PSYCHIATRY 590–95 (1986);

15. M. O. Aveline, D. G. Fowlie, *Surviving Ejection from Military Aircraft: Psychological Reactions, Modifying Factors and Intervention*, 3 STRESS MED. 15–20 (1987);

16. F. Earls, E. Smith, W. Reich, K. G. Jung, *Investigating Psychopathological Consequences of a Disaster in Children: A Pilot Study Incorporating a Structured Diagnostic Interview*, 27 J. AM. ACAD. CHILD ADOLESC. PSYCHIATRY 90–95 (1988);

17.   U. Malt, *The Long-term Psychiatric Consequences of Accidental Injury: A Longitudinal Study of 107 Adults*, 153 BRIT. J. PSYCHIATRY 810–18 (1988);

18.   A. C. McFarlane, *The Phenomenology of Posttraumatic Stress Disorders Following a Natural Disaster*, 176 J. NERVOUS & MENTAL DISEASE 22–29 (1988);

19.   A. C. McFarlane, *The Longitudinal Course of Posttraumatic Morbidity: The Range of Outcomes and Their Predictors*, 176 J. NERVOUS & MENTAL DISEASE 30–39 (1988);

20.   A. C. McFarlane, *Relationship Between Psychiatric Impairment and a Natural Disaster: The Role of Distress*, 18 PSYCHOL. MED. 129–39 (1988);

21.   R. S. Pynoos & K. Nader, *Children Who Witness the Sexual Assaults of Their Mothers*, 27 J. AM. ACAD. CHILD ADOLESC. PSYCHIATRY 567–72 (1988);

22.   S. Dahl, *Acute Response to Rape—A PTSD Variant*, 80 ACTA PSYCHIATRICA SCANDINAVICA SUPP. 355, 56–62 (1989);

23.   S. Ersland, L. Weisaeth, & A. Sund, *The Stress upon Rescuers Involved in an Oil Rig Disaster, "Alexander L. Kielland" 1980*, 80 ACTA PSYCHIATRICA SCANDINAVICA SUPPL. 355, 38–49 (1989);

24.   A. Feinstein, *Posttraumatic Stress Disorder: A Descriptive Study Supporting DSM–III–R Criteria*, 146 AM. J. PSYCHIATRY 665–66 (1989);

25.   K. Hytten & A. Hasle, *Fire Fighters: A Study of Stress and Coping*, 80 ACTA PSYCHIATRICA SCANDINAVICA SUPP. 355, 50–55 (1989);

26.   M. Maj, F. Starace, P. Crepet, S. Lobrace, F. Veltro, F. DeMarco, & D. Kemali, *Prevalence of Psychiatric Disorders Among Subjects Exposed to a Natural Disaster*, 79 ACTA PSYCHIATRICA SCANDINAVICA 544–549 (1989);

27.   A. Nadler & D. Ben–Shushan, *Forty Years Later: Long-term Consequences of Massive Traumatization as Manifested by Holocaust Survivors from the City and the Kibbutz*, 57 J. CONSULTING & CLINICAL PSYCHOL. 287–93 (1989);

28.   R. S. Pynoos, K. Nader, *Children's Memory and Proximity to Violence*, 28 J. AM. ACAD. CHILD ADOLESC. PSYCHIATRY 236–41 (1989);

29.   F. J. Stoddard, D. K. Norman, J. M. Murphy, & W. R. Beardslee, *Psychiatric Outcome of Burned Children and Adolescents*, 28 J. AM. ACAD. CHILD ADOLESC. PSYCHIATRY 589–95 (1989);

30.   L. Weisaeth, *Torture of a Norwegian Ship's Crew: The Torture, Stress Reactions and Psychiatric After-effects*, 80 ACTA PSYCHIATRICA SCANDINAVICA SUPP. 355, 63–72 (1989);

31.   L. Weisaeth, *A Study of Behavioural Responses to an Industrial Disaster*, 80 ACTA PSYCHIATRICA SCANDINAVICA SUPPL. 355, 13–24 (1989);

32.   L. Weisaeth, *The Stressors and the Post-traumatic Stress Syndrome After an Industrial Disaster*, 80 ACTA PSYCHIATRICA SCANDINAVICA SUPP. 355, 25–37 (1989);

33.   S. Robinson, J. Rapaport, R. Durst, M. Rapaport, P. Rosca, S. Metzer, & L. Zilberman, *The Late Effects of Nazi Persecution Among Elderly Holocaust Survivors*, 82 ACTA PSYCHIATRICA SCANDINAVICA 311–15 (1990);

34. W. A. Wagenaar & J. Groeneweg, *The Memory of Concentration Camp Survivors*, 4 APPLIED COGNITIVE PSYCHOL. 77–87 (1990);

35. B. L. Green, M. Korol, M. C. Grace, M. G. Vary, A. C. Leonard, G. C. Gleser, & S. Smitson–Cohen, *Children and Disaster: Age, Gender, and Parental Effects on PTSD Symptoms*, 30 J. AM. ACAD. CHILD ADOLESC. PSYCHIATRY 945–50 (1991);

36. S. Nolen–Hoeksema & J. Morrow, *A Prospective Study of Depression and Posttraumatic Stress Symptoms After a Natural Disaster: The 1989 Loma Prieta Earthquake*, 61 J. PERS. SOC. PSYCHOL. 115–21 (1991);

37. G. M. Realmuto, N. Wagner, & J. Bartholow, *The Williams Pipeline Disaster: A Controlled Study of a Technological Accident*, 4 J. TRAUMATIC STRESS 469–79 (1991);

38. M. L. Stuber, K. Nader, P. Yasuda, R. S. Pynoos, & S. Cohen, *Stress Responses After Pediatric Bone Marrow Transplantation: Preliminary Results of a Prospective Longitudinal Study*, 30 J. AM. ACAD. CHILD ADOLESC. PSYCHIATRY 952–57 (1991);

39. M. P. Weissberg, T. A. Katz, *The Crash of Continental 1713: The Impact on Hospital-based Personnel*, 9 J. EMERGENCY MED. 459–63 (1991);

40. N. Brooks & W. McKinlay, *Mental Health Consequences of the Lockerbie Disaster*, 5 J. TRAUMATIC STRESS 527–43 (1992);

41. J. J. Breton, J. P. Valla, J. Lambert, *Industrial Disaster and Mental Health of Children and Their Parents*, 32 J. AM. ACAD. CHILD ADOLESC. PSYCHIATRY 438–45 (1993);

42. R. B. Scott, N. Brooks, & W. McKinlay, *Post-traumatic Morbidity in a Civilian Community of Litigants: A Follow-up at 3 Years*, 8 J. TRAUMATIC STRESS 403–17 (1995);

43. J. I. Escobar, G. Canino, M. Rubio–Stipec, & M. Bravo, *Somatic symptoms after a natural disaster: a prospective study*, 149 AM. J. PSYCHIATRY 965–67 (1992);

44. G. M. Realmuto, A. Masten, L. F. Carole, J. Hubbard, A. Groteluschen, & B. Chhun, *Adolescent Survivors of Massive Childhood Trauma in Cambodia: Life Events and Current Symptoms*, 5 J. TRAUMATIC STRESS 589–99 (1992);

45. B. O. Rothbaum, E. B. Foa, D. S. Riggs, T. Murdock, & W. Walsh, *A Prospective Examination of Post-traumatic Stress Disorder in Rape Victims*, 5 J. TRAUMATIC STRESS 455–75 (1992);

46. E. Cardeña & D. Spiegel, *Dissociative Reactions to the San Francisco Bay Area Earthquake of 1989*, 150 AM. J. PSYCHIATRY 474–78 (1993);

47. R. Krell, *Child Survivors of the Holocaust—Strategies of Adaptation*, 38 CAN. J. PSYCHIATRY 384–89 (1993);

48. T. Lundin & M. Bodegard, *The Psychological Impact of an Earthquake on Rescue Workers: A Follow-up Study of the Swedish Group of Rescue Workers in Armenia*, 6 J. TRAUMATIC STRESS 129–39 (1993);

49. R. M. Bowler, D. Mergler, G. Huel, & J. E. Cone, *Psychological, Psychosocial, and Psychophysiological Sequelae in a Community Affected by a Railroad Chemical Disaster*, 7 J. TRAUMATIC STRESS 601–24 (1994);

50. S. B. Hardin, M. Weinrich, S. Weinrich, T. L. Hardin, & C. Garrison, *Psychological Distress of Adolescents Exposed to Hurricane Hugo*, 7 J. TRAUMATIC STRESS 427–40 (1994);

51. R. T. Jones, D. P. Ribbe, & P. Cunningham, *Psychosocial Correlates of Fire Disaster Among Children and Adolescents*, 7 J. TRAUMATIC STRESS 117–22 (1994);

52. C. Koopman, C. Classen, & D. Spiegel, *Predictors of Posttraumatic Stress Symptoms Among Survivors of the Oakland/Berkeley, California Firestorm*, 151 AM. J. PSYCHIATRY 888–94 (1994);

53. V. J. Carr, T. J. Lewin, R. A. Webster, P. L. Hazell, J. A. Kenardy, & G. L. Carter, *Psychosocial Sequelae of the 1989 Newcastle Earthquake: I. Community Disaster Experiences and Psychological Morbidity 6 Months Post-disaster*, 25 PSYCHOL. MED. 539–55 (1995);

54. R. Hagström, *The Acute Psychological Impact on Survivors Following a Train Accident*, 8 J. TRAUMATIC STRESS 391–402 (1995);

55. S. W. Turner, J. Thompson, & R. M. Rosser, *The King's Cross Fire: Psychological Reactions*, 8 J. TRAUMATIC STRESS 419–27 (1995);

56. K. A. Lee, G. E. Vaillant, W. C. Torrey, & G. H. Elder, *A 50-year Prospective Study of the Psychological Sequelae of World War II Combat*, 152 AM. J. PSYCHIATRY 516–22 (1995);

57. R. J. Ursano, C. S. Fullerton, T. Kao, & V. R. Bhartiya, *Longitudinal Assessment of Posttraumatic Stress Disorder and Depression After Exposure to Traumatic Death*, 183 J. NERVOUS & MENTAL DISEASE 36–42 (1995);

58. S. M. Weine, D. F. Becker, T. H. McGlashan, D. Laub, S. Lazrove, D. Vojvoda, & L. Hyman, *Psychiatric Consequences of "Ethnic Cleansing:" Clinical Assessments and Trauma Testimonies of Newly Resettled Bosnian Refugees*, 152 AM. J. PSYCHIATRY 536–42 (1995);

59. L. M. Najarian, A. K. Goenjian, D. Pelcovitz, F. Mandel, & B. Najarian, *Relocation After a Disaster: Posttraumatic Stress Disorder in Armenia After the Earthquake*, 35 J. AM. ACAD. CHILD ADOLESC. PSYCHIATRY 384–91 (1996);

60. D. Savin, W. H. Sack, G. N. Clarke, N. Meas, & I. M. L. Richart, *The Khmer Adolescent Project: III. A Study of Trauma from Thailand's Site II Refugee Camp*, 35 J. AM. ACAD. CHILD ADOLESC. PSYCHIATRY 384–91 (1996);

61. J. A. Shaw, B. Applegate, & C. Schorr, *Twenty-one Month Follow-up Study of School-age Children Exposed to Hurricane Andrew*, 35 J. AM. ACAD. CHILD ADOLESC. PSYCHIATRY 359–64 (1996);

62. S. Tyano, I. Iancu, Z. Solomon, J. Sever, I. Goldstein, Y. Touviani, & A. Bleich, *Seven-year Follow-up of Child Survivors of a Bus–Train Collision*, 35 J. AM. ACAD. CHILD ADOLESC. PSYCHIATRY 365–72 (1996);

63. L. C. Terr, D. A. Bloch, B. A. Michel, H. Shi, J. A. Reinhardt, & S. Metayer, *Children's Memories in the Wake of Challenger*, 153 AM. J. PSYCHIATRY 618–25 (1996);

64. A.M. LaGreca, W.K. Silverman, E.M. Vernberg, M.J. Prinstein, *Symptoms of Posttraumatic Stress in Children after Hurricane Andrew: A Prospective Study*, 64 J. CONSULTING CLIN. PSYCHOLOGY 712–23 (1996);

65. I.V.E. Carlier, B.P.R. Gersons, *Stress Reactions in Disaster Victims Following the Bijlmermeer Plane Crash*, 10 J. TRAUMATIC STRESS 329–335 (1997);

66. A.K. Goenjian, I. Karayan, R.S. Pynoos, D. Minassian, L.M. Najarian, A.M. Steinberg, L.A. Fairbanks, *Outcome of Psychotherapy Among Early Adolescents After Trauma*, 154 AM. J. PSYCHIATRY 536–42 (1997);

67. A. DiGallo, J. Barton, W.LI. Parry–Jones, *Road Traffic Accidents: Early Psychological Consequences in Children and Adolescents*, 170 BR. J PSYCHIATRY 358–62 (1997);

68. S.M. Southwick, C.A. Morgan, A.L. Nicolaou, D.S. Charney, *Consistency of Memory for Combat–Related Traumatic Events in Veterans of Operation Desert Storm*, 154 AM. J. PSYCHIATRY 173–77 (1997);

69. B. Engdahl, T.N. Dikel, R. Eberly, A. Blank, Jr., *Posttraumatic Stress Disorder in a Community Group of Former Prisoners of War: A Normative Response to Severe Trauma*, 154 AM. J. PSYCHIATRY 1576–81 (1997);

70. R.F. Mollica, M.A.R., C. Poole, L. Son, C.C. Murray, S. Tor, *Effects of War Trauma on Cambodian Refugee Adolescents' Functional Health and Mental Health Status*, 36 J. AM ACAD. CHILD ADOLESC. PSYCHIATRY 1098–1106 (1997);

71. C.S. North, E.M. Smith, E. L. Spitznagel, *One-Year Follow–Up of Survivors of a Mass Shooting*, 154 AM. J. PSYCHIATRY 1696–1702 (1997);

72. M.A. Jenkins, P.J. Langlais, D. Delis, R. Cohen, *Learning and Memory in Rape Victims with Posttraumatic Stress Disorder*, 155 AM. J. PSYCHIATRY 278–9 (1998);

73. J. Asarnow, S. Glynn, R.S. Pynoos, J. Nahum, D. Guthrie, D.P. Cantwell, B. Franklin, *When the Earth Stops Shaking: Earthquake Sequelae Among Children Diagnosed for Pre–Earthquake Psychopathology*, 38 J. AM ACAD. CHILD ADOLESC. PSYCHIATRY 1016–23 (1999);

74. D. Koren, I. Arnon, E. Klein, *Acute Stress Response and Posttraumatic Stress Disorder in Traffic Accident Victims: A One–Year Prospective, Follow–Up Study*, 156 AM. J. PSYCHIATRY 367–73 (1999);

75. D.F. Becker, S.N. Weine, D. Vojvoda, T.H. McGlashan, Case Series: PTSD *Symptoms in Adolescent Survivors of "Ethnic Cleansing." Results From a 1–Year Follow-up Study*, 38 J. AM. ACAD. CHILD ADOLESC. PSYCHIATRY 775–781 (1999);

76. A. Favaro, F.C. Rodella, G. Colombo, P. Santonastaso, *Post-traumatic Stress Disorder and Major Depression Among Italian Nazi Concentration Camp Survivors: A Controlled Study 50 Years Later*, 29 PSYCHOL. MEDICINE 87–95 (1999);

77. W.S. Sack, C. Him, D. Dickason, *Twelve-Year Follow-up Study of Khmer Youths Who Suffered Massive War Trauma as Children*, 38 J. AM. ACAD. CHILD ADOLESC. PSYCHIATRY 1173–9 (1999).

CHAPTER 11

GENDER STEREOTYPING

Table of Sections

Westlaw Electronic Research

See Westlaw Electronic Research Guide preceding the Summary of Contents.

A.   LEGAL ISSUES

§ 11–1.0   THE LEGAL RELEVANCE OF RESEARCH ON GENDER STEREOTYPING

§ 11–1.1   Introduction

One significant value of much social science research is that it makes clearer what we only dimly perceive, if we perceive it at all. It is not surprising to hear people say about many psychological findings that, "of course, we knew this all along." Yet, very often, what we thought we knew all along is not quite correct or, more importantly, not quite correct in substantial detail. Perhaps the paradigmatic example of this is research on eyewitness identification. Many courts continue to insist that research on the reliability of eyewitness identifications simply confirms common sense.[1] The number of eyewitness identification cases that have led to mistaken convictions, as demonstrated by subsequent DNA testing, belies this sanguine attitude.[2] Although not as well researched as eyewitness identifications, the work on gender stereotyping roughly fits this model. Gender stereotyping research offers insights about gender relations—a subject with which we all have first-hand knowledge—beyond what experience alone can provide.

This is not to say, however, that expert testimony on gender stereotyping should be admitted in all cases, or admitted on all issues for which a proponent might offer it. This is an admissibility determination that depends on the circumstances of the case, the qualifications of the expert, and whether the research is sufficiently valid for the proposition for which it is offered. Moreover, like eyewitness identification research, the primary value of work on gender stereotyping might be to educate the fact finder regarding the nature of the phenomenon, rather than to offer an opinion about the specific case before the court. Hence, courts might very well determine that the state of the art of the science is good enough to be admitted for some purposes, but not for all purposes.

---

§ 11–1.0

1. *See generally* Chapter 15.

2. *See* BARRY SCHECK, PETER NEUFELDT & JAMES DWYER, ACTUAL INNOCENCE (2000).

§ 11–1.2   The Statutory Background

Title VII of the Civil Rights Act of 1964 makes it "an unlawful employment practice for an employer . . . to discriminate against any individual with respect to his compensation, terms, conditions, or privileges of employment, because of such individual's . . . sex. . . ."[3] This seemingly straightforward injunction has proved to contain substantial ambiguity when applied to concrete cases. For example, does Title VII prohibit discrimination when the employer and employee are the same sex? Does the law extend to discrimination that targets gender generally, as opposed to the sort that is associated with sexual relations?[4] The Supreme Court has answered these two questions affirmatively. Title VII applies quite generally to discrimination that, at its root, is associated with gender roles and the social expectations that surround them. Research on gender stereotyping has already influenced this doctrine and it has the potential to have a deep impact on its continuing development.

§ 11–1.2.1   Same–Sex Discrimination

In *Oncale v. Sundowner Offshore Services, Inc.*,[5] the Supreme Court held that Title VII's prohibition of discrimination "because of . . . sex" applied to sexual harassment between a supervisor and an employee of the same sex. Title VII's provision extends beyond the simple terms and conditions of employment and includes "the entire spectrum of disparate treatment of men and women in employment."[6] As the Court has explained,

> When the workplace is permeated with discriminatory intimidation, ridicule, and insult that is sufficiently severe or pervasive to alter the conditions of the victim's employment and create an abusive working environment, Title VII is violated.[7]

A persistent concern among courts, however, has been distinguishing between simple teasing between members of the same sex and conduct that is so abusive that it violates Title VII.[8] The *Oncale* Court recognized this concern, but found it no more intractable in the same sex context as it is when the alleged harasser is a different sex than the employee. The Court observed as follows:

> Title VII does not prohibit all verbal or physical harassment in the workplace; it is directed at "discriminat[ion] . . . because of . . . sex." We have never held that workplace harassment, even harassment between men and women, is automatically discrimination because of sex merely because the words used have sexual content or connotations. "The critical issue, Title VII's text indicates, is whether members of one sex are

---

3. 42 U.S.C.A. § 2000e–2(a)(1).

4. A third question raised early on was whether the discriminatory ground was actionable only when it constituted a but-for cause of the action. In *Price Waterhouse*, the Court held that the defendant could show it had other—non-discriminatory—grounds for the action. Subsequently, this holding was statutorily overruled so that a plaintiff can prevail in a Title VII action if the illicit criterion was a "motivating factor" in the adverse treatment. 42 U.S.C.A. § 2000e–2(m).

5. 523 U.S. 75, 118 S.Ct. 998, 140 L.Ed.2d 201 (1998).

6. Meritor Savings Bank, FSB v. Vinson, 477 U.S. 57, 64, 106 S.Ct. 2399, 91 L.Ed.2d 49 (1986).

7. Harris v. Forklift Systems, Inc., 510 U.S. 17, 21, 114 S.Ct. 367, 126 L.Ed.2d 295 (citations and internal quotation marks omitted).

8. *See, e.g.*, Goluszek v. H.P. Smith, 697 F.Supp. 1452 (N.D.Ill.1988).

exposed to disadvantageous terms or conditions of employment to which members of the other sex are not exposed."[9]

Social context and the specific circumstances surrounding the complained of conduct thus determine whether a violation of Title VII has occurred. "The real social impact of workplace behavior often depends on a constellation of surrounding circumstances, expectations, and relationships which are not fully captured by a simple recitation of the words used or the physical acts performed."[10] In practice, the *Oncale* Court believed, "[c]ommon sense, and an appropriate sensitivity to social context, will enable courts and juries to distinguish between simple teasing or roughhousing among members of the same sex, and conduct which a reasonable person in the plaintiff's position would find severely hostile or abusive."[11]

§ 11–1.2.2 Defining "because of . . . sex" Under Title VII

Both before and after *Oncale*, courts struggled with the question of how to define "sex" for purposes of setting the scope of Title VII protection. Courts generally agree that the prohibition reaches beyond discrimination that has a sexual component. The word "sex" in Title VII reaches sex as an adjective, not merely a verb. Hence, so long as the discrimination is directed at a person "as a woman" or "as a man," Title VII applies. Title VII thus reaches *gender* discrimination.

The basic principle supporting this interpretation of the law comes from *Price Waterhouse v. Hopkins*.[12] In *Price Waterhouse*, the plaintiff was denied a partnership because she failed to meet the firm's expectations about how a woman ought to act. For instance, as the Court put it, the *coup de grace* was one partner's advice that she "walk more femininely, talk more femininely, dress more femininely, wear make-up, have her hair styled, and wear jewelry."[13] In *Price Waterhouse*, the discrimination was based on social perceptions and perceived gender role stereotypes and not on sexuality. In *Schwenk v. Hartford*,[14] the Ninth Circuit summarized the legal scope of Title VII:

> In *Price Waterhouse*, . . . the Supreme Court held that Title VII barred not just discrimination based on the fact that Hopkins was a woman, but also discrimination based on the fact that she failed "to act like a woman"—that is, to conform to socially-constructed gender expectations. . . . Thus, under *Price Waterhouse*, "sex" under Title VII encompasses both sex—that is, the biological differences between men and women—and gender.[15]

But defining "gender" for Title VII purposes has not been a straightforward matter. In *Shwenk*, for instance, the plaintiff was a prisoner who described herself as a "pre-operative male to female transsexual who plans someday to obtain sex reassignment surgery."[16] The plaintiff was incarcerated in an all male prison in Washington State. She complained that a guard at the prison "subjected her to an escalating series of unwelcome sexual advances

9. *Oncale*, 523 U.S. at 80 (quoting *Harris*, 510 U.S. at 25 (Ginsburg, J., concurring)).

10. *Id.* at 81–82.

11. *Id.* at 82.

12. 490 U.S. 228, 109 S.Ct. 1775, 104 L.Ed.2d 268 (1989).

13. *Id.* at 235.

14. 204 F.3d 1187 (9th Cir.2000).

15. *Id.* at 1201–02.

16. *Id.* at 1193.

and harassment that culminated in a sexual assault."[17] According to the defendant, Title VII did not apply because the alleged attacks were premised on the plaintiff's transsexuality, a condition which "is not an element of gender, but rather constitutes gender dysphoria, a psychiatric illness."[18]

The Ninth Circuit disagreed. It found that the plaintiff alleged facts that squarely placed her complaint into the gender-discrimination box. The court summarized some of the relevant allegations as follows:

[She] testified that [the guard's] demands for sex began only after he discovered that she considered herself female and that they escalated and included commentary about her transsexuality.... [The guard] offered to bring her make-up and other "girl stuff" from outside the prison in order to enhance the femininity of her appearance. Thus, the evidence offered by [the plaintiff] tends to show that [the guard's] actions were motivated, at least in part, by [her] gender—in this case, by her assumption of a feminine rather than a typically masculine appearance or demeanor.[19]

The Ninth Circuit concluded, therefore, that the terms "sex" and "gender" encompassed discrimination motivated by bias toward a person's violation of sex-role stereotypes. Legal protection extends to those "who do not conform to socially prescribed gender expectations."[20]

Closely related to gender expectations is the issue whether Title VII reaches discrimination on the basis of sexual orientation. In the muddied gray of the real world, bias is often directed at a constellation of behaviors and superficial characteristics. Separating discrimination based on sex stereotypes from that based on sexual orientation might prove to be a lesson in futility.

In *Spearman v. Ford Motor Co.*,[21] for instance, the plaintiff claimed he suffered sexual harassment because he was homosexual. He argued that the sexually explicit insults were directed at him because "his coworkers perceived him to be too feminine to fit the male image at Ford."[22] The Seventh Circuit observed, however, that the language of Title VII "means that 'it is unlawful to discriminate against women because they are women and against men because they are men.' "[23] The court continued by stating that, "[i]n other words, Congress intended the term 'sex' to mean 'biological male or biological female,' and not one's sexuality or sexual orientation."[24] Therefore, " '[t]he plaintiff must show that the employer actually relied on [the plaintiff's] gender in making its decision.' "[25]

The *Spearman* court found that the evidence proffered on summary judgment showed that the plaintiff's "coworkers maligned him because of his apparent homosexuality, and not because of his sex."[26] This was true, according to the Seventh Circuit, even though many of the comments were directed

17. *Id.* The legal claim in *Schwenk* arose under the Gender–Motivated Violence Act (GMVA). The GMVA's gender provision was modeled after Title VII. "[B]oth statutes prohibit discrimination based on gender as well as sex. Indeed, for purposes of these two acts, the terms 'sex' and 'gender' have become interchangeable." *Id.* at 1202.

18. *Id.* at 1200.

19. *Id.* at 1202.

20. *Id.*

21. 231 F.3d 1080 (7th Cir.2000).

22. *Id.* at 1085.

23. *Id.* at 1084 (quoting Ulane v. Eastern Airlines, Inc., 742 F.2d 1081, 1085 (7th Cir. 1984)).

24. *Id.*

25. *Id.* at 1085 (quoting *Price Waterhouse*, 490 U.S. at 251).

26. *Id.*

at his non-conventional demeanor and his coworkers' belief that he violated sex-role expectations. The court believed that the plaintiff's "coworkers directed stereotypical statements at him to express their hostility to his perceived homosexuality, and not to harass him because he is a man."[27]

The Seventh Circuit's distinction between, on the one hand, harassment involving sexual stereotypes and sexually charged epithets based on "perceived homosexuality" and, on the other hand, harassment involving identical stereotypes and epithets based on the plaintiff not acting "man enough" is, at best, ephemeral. Indeed, the Seventh Circuit itself observed that the plaintiff suffered discrimination because of his *perceived* homosexuality, not because he was homosexual. The Seventh Circuit appears to draw a distinction between harassment targeting someone who acts in an effeminate way and someone who fails to act like a man. This is a distinction without a difference. It is also inconsistent with the Ninth Circuit's ruling in *Schwenk, supra*, which found that Title VII applied when "the perpetrator's actions stem from the fact that he believed that the victim was a man who 'failed to act like' one."[28]

In *Higgins v. New Balance Athletic Shoe, Inc.*,[29] the First Circuit resolved the distinction between "sex stereotyping" and "sexual orientation" essentially by making it a matter of a pleading requirement. In *Higgins*, the plaintiff claimed that he suffered same-sex harassment because of his homosexuality. Although the plaintiff was the victim of stereotyped views because of his effeminate behavior, he had alleged only that the discrimination was premised on his sexual orientation. The district court had granted the defendant's motion for summary judgment because it found that Title VII did not extend to sexual orientation discrimination.[30] The First Circuit agreed, finding that the plaintiff "did not mention gender stereotyping below and he did not present any considered argumentation along that line."[31] However, the First Circuit made it clear that if the plaintiff had asserted that the harassment of his "effeminate characteristics ... was based on sexual stereotypes," he would have a claim under Title VII.[32] The court explained:

> *Oncale* confirms that the standards of liability under Title VII, as they have been refined and explicated over time, apply to same-sex plaintiffs just as they do to opposite-sex plaintiffs. In other words, just as a woman can ground an action on a claim that men discriminated against her because she did not meet stereotyped expectations of femininity, a man can ground a claim on evidence that other men discriminated against him because he did not meet stereotyped expectations of masculinity.[33]

Under the First Circuit's approach, then, someone who suffers discrimination because they act effeminately and "like a homosexual," can bring a cause of action so long as he phrases his complaint in terms of sex stereotyping and not sexual orientation. Presumably, under *Oncale*, this strategy should work even in the Seventh Circuit. In fact, it is hard to imagine a case of sexual orientation discrimination that could not be recast in this way. After all, discrimination in the workplace against gays and lesbians typically in-

27. *Id.* at 1085–86.

28. *Schwenk*, 204 F.3d at 1202.

29. 194 F.3d 252 (1st Cir.1999).

30. Higgins v. New Balance Athletic Shoe, Inc., 21 F.Supp.2d 66, 75 (D.Me.1998).

31. *Higgins*, 194 F.3d at 261.

32. *Id.*

33. *Id.* at 261 n.4.

volves the way they *behave*, and not who they *are*.[34] Like the transsexual in *Schwenk*, putting the right spin on an old package can be liberating, transforming and, legally, quite effective.

§ 11–1.3 Proving Gender Stereotyping

In *Price Waterhouse*, the Court found an abundance of evidence indicating that some of the partners perceived the plaintiff as failing to reflect the feminine ideal in behavior. One partner described her as "macho," while another thought she might benefit from "a course at charm school."[35] Some in the partnership apparently felt, and one said, that she could find success at the firm if she only would "walk more femininely, talk more femininely, dress more femininely, wear make-up, have her hair styled, and wear jewelry."[36] In addition to this proof, the plaintiff introduced the expert testimony of Dr. Susan Fiske, who was allowed to testify "that the partnership selection process at Price Waterhouse was likely influenced by sex stereotyping."[37]

The Court noted that Fiske's testimony went beyond the "overtly sex-based comments of partners."[38] She also testified regarding the relevance of "gender-neutral remarks, made by partners who knew Hopkins only slightly, that were intensely critical of her."[39] The Court explained further as follows:

> According to Fiske, Hopkins' uniqueness (as the only woman in the pool of candidates) and the subjectivity of the evaluations made it likely that sharply critical remarks such as these were the product of sex stereotyping although Fiske admitted that she could not say with certainty whether any particular comment was the result of stereotyping. Fiske based her opinion on a review of the submitted comments, explaining that it was commonly accepted practice for social psychologists to reach this kind of conclusion without having met any of the people involved in the decisionmaking process.[40]

Although the defendant failed to object to Fiske at trial, it complained on appeal that her testimony constituted "gossamer evidence," and was a product of "intuitive hunches" and was "intuitively divined."[41] The Court, however, ruled that these objections had come too late.[42] By failing to object to Fiske at trial, Price Waterhouse had waived any claim of error on appeal. The dissent agreed that the defendant had waived any objection to Fiske by failing

---

34. An unlikely source of support for the blurring of the distinction between conduct and status comes from Justice Scalia's dissent in *Romer v. Evans*, 517 U.S. 620, 116 S.Ct. 1620, 134 L.Ed.2d 855 (1996). In *Romer*, Justice Scalia argued that Colorado's Amendment 2, which denied the benefit of anti-discrimination laws to homosexuals, did not violate the Equal Protection Clause. In reaching this conclusion, Justice Scalia relied on *Bowers v. Hardwick*, in which the Court upheld a criminal sanction against homosexual conduct. Since Colorado's Amendment 2 spoke in terms of status as a homosexual, Justice Scalia had to explain why the *Bowers'* principle of criminalizing conduct permitted discriminatory treatment on the basis of status. Justice Scalia discounted the status-conduct distinction, observing that "where criminal sanctions are not involved, homosexual 'orientation' is an acceptable stand-in for homosexual conduct." *Id.* at 642 (Scalia, J., dissenting). Although Justice Scalia might not entirely agree with the logic, it follows that discrimination against a perceived homosexual for not being "man enough," is an acceptable stand-in for discrimination "because of ... sex" under Title VII.

35. *Price Waterhouse*, 490 U.S. at 235.

36. *Id.*

37. *Id.*

38. *Id.*

39. *Id.*

40. *Id.* at 235–36.

41. *Id.* at 255.

42. *Id.*

to raise it below, but it was more sympathetic to the argument that Fiske's testimony had little probative force.[43] In particular, the dissent asserted that any expert testimony concluding that the partners had erroneously stereotyped Hopkins on the basis of gender neutral statements describing her as "overbearing, arrogant and abrasive" should have established that she in fact was not overbearing, arrogant and abrasive. The dissent complained that "Fiske purported to discern stereotyping in comments that were gender neutral—e.g., 'overbearing and abrasive'—without any knowledge of the comments' basis in reality and without having met the speaker or subject."[44] In effect, then, the dissent argued that expert testimony would not be necessary when the statements are not gender neutral, since the jury can discern on its own the fact that calling a woman "macho," for instance, is evidence of sex stereotyping. Moreover, according to the dissent, expert testimony is not reliable if it is based on gender neutral statements that might reflect either a stereotype or reality, where the expert cannot say which is the case.

The majority opinion did not entirely disagree with the dissent on this point, though it did chastize "the dissent's dismissive attitude toward Dr. Fiske's field of study and toward her own professional integrity."[45] But ultimately the Court found the gender-charged statements made by some partners to be sufficient to indicate sex stereotyping. The Court explained that it was "tempted to say that Dr. Fiske's expert testimony was merely icing on Hopkins' cake."[46] It continued as follows:

> It takes no special training to discern sex stereotyping in a description of an aggressive female employee as requiring "a course at charm school." Nor ... does it require expertise in psychology to know that, if an employee's flawed "interpersonal skills" can be corrected by a soft-hued suit or a new shade of lipstick, perhaps it is the employee's sex and not her interpersonal skills that has drawn the criticism.[47]

To the extent that interpersonal skills are a relevant consideration for advancement, as they often are, it would appear that ground truth is relevant to the probative value of gender stereotyping expert testimony in particular cases. Describing a woman negatively as abrasive and overbearing might indeed reflect a gender stereotype rejecting "unladylike behavior," but it might also simply be accurate. Just as it would not be actionable to fail to promote a male employee for being abrasive or overbearing, it is not actionable to treat a female employee similarly. In fact, it might be actionable otherwise. This analysis leads naturally to our considering the question of the relevance and fit of research on gender stereotyping.

§ 11–1.4 The Relevance or "Fit" of Research on Gender Stereotyping

As we have discussed numerous times in these volumes, scientific evidence typically comes to the courts at two levels of abstraction, general and specific.[48] The general refers to research on the phenomenon of interest as it

---

43. *Id.* at 293–94 (Kennedy, J., dissenting).

44. *Id.* at 294 n.5 (Kennedy, J., dissenting).

45. *Id.* at 255.

46. *Id.* at 256.

47. *Id.*

48. For a full discussion of this subject, see Science in the Law: Standards, Statistics and Research Issues, Chapter 1, § 3.4.1.

transcends particular contexts. Questions such as whether memory repression occurs, or silicone implants cause atypical connective tissue disorder are general in scope. The law, of course, is usually interested in applying the science to specific cases. Thus, experts are often offered to testify that a general proposition, such as asbestos causes lung cancer, is true for a particular plaintiff's lung cancer. Courts have increasingly become more sophisticated regarding these separate levels of science. For example, when medical causation is in issue, such as in toxic tort cases, courts demand proof of both general causation and specific causation; thus, a plaintiff claiming that smoking caused his cancer must produce proof both that tobacco can cause the kind of cancer he has and that the defendant's cigarettes caused his cancer.[49]

Sometimes, however, scientists have considerable research on general matters, but cannot offer an opinion better than a layperson about a particular case. This does not undermine the value of the science that is available; it only means that there are certain opinions that the expert cannot forward because there is no empirical basis demonstrating that they are reliable. Perhaps the quintessential example of this is research on the reliability (or unreliability) of eyewitnesses. Experts on this subject testify to general factors or circumstances that interfere with accurate eyewitness identifications. They do not offer an opinion regarding whether a particular witness is accurate. The science does not support such inferences, and experts on eyewitnesses, to their great credit, do not offer such "clinical assessments." Unfortunately, many other experts, with less basic research supporting their general theories, are far less reticent.

Although courts have yet to seriously examine research on gender stereotyping, they would be well advised to keep the distinction between general theories and specific applications in mind. As § 2.0, *infra*, illustrates, psychologists have conducted a substantial amount of rigorous research on the subject. However, just as in the context of toxic torts, where high quality research indicates that asbestos causes lung cancer, courts should not allow experts to testify if one of two situations is present. (1) If the case does not present facts to which the general research applies, then the expert should be excluded altogether; and (2) if the expert cannot demonstrate a reliable basis for opining that the plaintiff's case is an instance of the general phenomenon, then case-specific testimony should be excluded. In this latter situation, testimony regarding general research results should still be admissible to provide a framework in which to place the plaintiff's claim.

In *Butler v. Home Depot, Inc.*,[50] the court considered the admissibility of expert testimony on gender stereotyping under Rule 702 and *Daubert*. Dr. Susan Fiske, the same expert that appeared in *Price Waterhouse*, was one of four experts proffered by the plaintiffs. Although several of the experts offered testimony relevant to the plaintiff's discrimination claims—based on, among other things, gender stereotyping—we will limit our discussion to the court's analysis of Dr. Fiske's proffered testimony. Dr. Fiske offered to testify regarding five propositions, as follows:

49. *See generally* DAVID L. FAIGMAN, DAVID H. KAYE, MICHAEL J. SAKS & JOSEPH SANDERS, MODERN SCIENTIFIC EVIDENCE: THE LAW AND SCIENCE OF EXPERT TESTIMONY, Chapter 20 (2d ed. 2002).

50. 984 F.Supp. 1257 (N.D.Cal.1997).

(1) that gender stereotyping plays a major role in Home Depot's hiring, placement, and promotion patterns, (2) that much of this stereotyping is automatic and not fully conscious at the individual level, (3) that stereotyping is nevertheless convenient for individual decision-makers, so they do not examine it, (4) that organizations can control these effects of stereotyping through proper information and motivation, and (5) that Home Depot has not taken adequate steps to control these biased individual practices.[51]

Home Depot objected to Dr. Fiske's testimony on both Rule 702 and 403 grounds. However, the gravamen of the defendant's objection was that she had little basis for opining that the general research literature on stereotyping applied to the circumstances of the particular case. The court, after itself determining that the general "theories underlying Professor Fiske's testimony have been tested in the laboratory and in the field," observed that the defendant did not contest this issue.[52] The court stated that, for Home Depot, "the issue is not so much the reliability of social psychological theories generally; rather, the issue is Professor Fiske's methodology in arriving at the 'facts' to which she applies her theories."[53] The court explained further that

> Home Depot critiques Professor Fiske's findings on the grounds that she has prejudged this matter without reviewing all of the relevant facts and deposition testimony and that she has resolved material facts underlying her opinion in favor of the plaintiffs, despite her lack of expertise to make such credibility determinations.[54]

The court rejected these objections, but unfortunately without substantively examining them. Instead, the court stated that it "views the objections raised by Home Depot as issues of weight, rather than the admissibility of Professor Fiske's testimony."[55] The court's failure to evaluate the methods by which Dr. Fiske applied the general theories to the specific case was error under *Daubert*. This failure was analogous to a court's not determining that a medical doctor employed differential diagnosis correctly in reaching the conclusion that a particular toxin caused a specific ailment. Under *Daubert*, the question whether Dr. Fiske properly applied the general theories to the facts of the case is a matter of admissibility, not weight. Indeed, whether such clinical assessments are even within the purview of expertise of social psychologists should be determined by the court.

If there was any doubt after *Daubert* that Rule 702 made trial court judges gatekeepers regarding both general theories and specific applications, it was removed with the 2000 amendment to Rule 702. New Rule 702 specifically requires that judges determine whether "the witness has applied the principles and methods reliably to the facts of the case."[56] In the future, experts on gender stereotyping should be expected to show that they can reliably apply the general lessons of the research to specific cases. It is not clear, however, that this research has yet been done.

51. *Id.* at 1262.
52. *Id.* at 1263.
53. *Id.*
54. *Id.*

55. *Id.*
56. Fed.R.Evid. 702.

§ 11–1.5   Conclusion

Title VII makes it "an unlawful employment practice for an employer . . . to discriminate . . . because of . . . sex."[57] This injunction extends to "the entire spectrum of disparate treatment of men and women in employment."[58] It includes same-sex harassment, and discrimination targeting a person who fails to act according to certain sex-role stereotypes. Research on gender stereotyping offers courts and fact finders considerable information regarding gender stereotyping biases, and can assist the decision-making process in these cases. Courts, however, have failed to closely examine the scope of the research and the parameters of proffered expertise on gender stereotypes. Under *Daubert* and Rule 702, courts are obligated to evaluate both the bases for the general theories upon which experts rely as well as their ability to provide valid case-specific opinions on the subject. Courts so far have found the general research on gender stereotypes to be uncontroversial, but have yet to determine whether social psychologists can reliably provide clinical assessments in specific cases.

57. 42 U.S.C.A. § 2000e–2(a)(1).

58. *Meritor Savings Bank*, 477 U.S. at 64.

B.   SCIENTIFIC STATUS

by

Jennifer S. Hunt,* Eugene Borgida,** Kristina M. Kelly,*** & Diana Burgess****

§ 11–2.0 THE SCIENTIFIC STATUS OF RESEARCH ON GENDER STEREOTYPING

§ 11–2.1 Introductory Discussion of the Science

Stereotyping has been the subject of considerable psychological research and theorizing for most of the twentieth century, and it is an important subject of psychological inquiry at the beginning of the twenty-first century. Early research on stereotyping tended to focus on people's beliefs about different racial and religious groups, especially Black Americans and Jewish individuals. This early work focused on the attributes associated with different social groups,[1] as well as on psychodynamic accounts of the types of individuals who were likely to be prejudiced.[2]

Psychologists became interested in gender stereotyping in the late 1960s.[3] Although initial interest was fueled by the women's movement, psychologists soon realized that there are important scientific reasons to focus on stereotypes about gender. Gender stereotypes are similar to other kinds of stereo-

* Jennifer S. Hunt, Ph.D. is an Assistant Professor of Psychology at the University of Nebraska–Lincoln. Her research investigates the ways that pre-existing expectations, including stereotypes, influence people's thoughts and behavior. Her current work is examining the effects of stereotypes on health judgments, as well as the influence of individuating information on stereotype activation. In addition, she is investigating how cultural variations in beliefs about the justice system affect legal participation.

The writing of this chapter was supported in part by a National Science Foundation Graduate Research Fellowship awarded to the first author while she was at the University of Minnesota.

** Eugene Borgida, Ph.D. is Professor of Psychology and Law at the University of Minnesota, Twin Cities. He is also a Morse–Alumni Distinguished Teaching Professor of Psychology. In addition, Borgida is Adjunct Professor of Political Science and serves as Co-Director of the University's Center for the Study of Political Psychology. He has served as Associate Dean of the College of Liberal Arts and as chair of the Psychology Department. Borgida is a Fellow of the APA and APS, and on the Board of Directors for APS and the Social Science Research Council. He has published on a variety of research issues in psychology and law and in social psychology, and his work has been funded by NIMH, NIH, and NSF.

*** Kristina Kelly is a doctoral candidate at the University of Minnesota, Twin Cities. Her research interests include the psychology of gender and the study of health judgment and decision-making. She is currently investigating how social and cultural factors affect women's behaviors and cognitions, and in particular, how these factors influence the ways that women explain their own behavior in health and non-health domains.

**** Diana Burgess, Ph.D. is a senior research associate in Strategic Growth Initiatives in the Consumer Insights division of General Mills. She has conducted research on sexual harassment, gender stereotyping and political participation. Currently, she is conducting organizational research on knowledge sharing and knowledge seeking within General Mills. She also is conducting pro bono research for the National Campaign to Prevent Teen Pregnancy.

§ 11–2.0

1. D. Katz & K.W. Braly, *Racial Stereotypes of 100 College Students*, 28 J. ABNORMAL AND SOC. PSYCHOL. 280 (1933).

2. *See, e.g.*, THE AUTHORITARIAN PERSONALITY (T. W. Adorno et al., eds., 1950).

3. K. Deaux, *How Basic Can You Be?: The Evolution of Research on Gender Stereotypes*, 51 J. SOC. ISSUES 11 (1995).

types in many ways; however, they also have some distinguishing characteristics.[4] For example, most group-based stereotypes are descriptive in nature, that is, they summarize the attributes that are associated with particular groups. In contrast, gender stereotypes have both descriptive and prescriptive components; they specify the characteristics men and women do possess as well as the characteristics they should possess. Another distinguishing characteristic involves complexity. Unlike most social groups, men and women interact with each other frequently and intimately; as a result, gender stereotypes tend to be more complex than are other kinds of stereotypes.

Following more than two decades of study, research on gender stereotyping came before the courts in the form of psychological expert testimony in *Hopkins v. Price Waterhouse.*[5] Since *Hopkins,* social scientific research on

4. S. T. Fiske & L. E. Stevens, *What's So Special About Sex? Gender Stereotyping and Discrimination, in* GENDER ISSUES IN CONTEMPORARY SOCIETY: APPLIED SOC. PSYCHOL. ANNUAL 173 (S. Oskamp & M. Costanzo eds., 1990).

5. The case, which involved charges that the Price Waterhouse accounting firm discriminated against manager Ann Hopkins, on the basis of gender, eventually was appealed to the United States Supreme Court. Price Waterhouse v. Hopkins, 490 U.S. 228, 109 S.Ct. 1775, 104 L.Ed.2d 268 (1989); *see also Hopkins v. Price Waterhouse,* 618 F.Supp. 1109 (D.D.C. 1985). One of the documents submitted to the Court was an amicus curiae brief provided by the American Psychological Association, which described psychological research about gender stereotyping and the ways in which it might lead to employment discrimination. Brief of Amici Curiae American Psychological Association et al. Price Waterhouse v. Hopkins 490 U.S. 228, 109 S.Ct. 1775, 104 L.Ed.2d 268 (1989).

The APA *Hopkins* brief contained four arguments about gender stereotyping in general, as well as the role it might have played in the case at hand. The first argument was that psychologists had been conducting empirical research on gender stereotyping for several decades, and that such research was well established as a scientific area of study in the social scientific community. The authors explained that, over the preceding fifty years, a large body of research had accumulated detailing the cognitive structure of stereotypes, the psychological processes involved in stereotype use, and the influence that stereotypes can exert on expectations, judgments, and behavior. They asserted that this body of literature met scientific standards for both internal and external validity, showed breadth of knowledge, and was able to withstand peer review.

The brief's second argument was that, in certain situations, stereotyping can result in discrimination against groups such as women. The authors explained that stereotypes are formed from the normal cognitive processes of categorization and generalization. However, because stereotypes are overgeneralizations about groups, they can be misapplied to specific individuals, resulting in faulty judgments and discriminatory treatment. Because biological sex is one of the most common means of categorization for people, stereotypes about gender shape people's expectations about what women are like, as well as what they should be like. Women who violate these expectations by engaging in gender-incongruent behavior therefore may be sanctioned.

The third and fourth arguments related research on gender stereotyping to the *Hopkins* case. In the third argument, the authors asserted that three conditions that promote stereotyping were present at Price Waterhouse. First, because few women were employed at the firm, those women were highly salient and thus more likely to be seen in a stereotypical manner. Second, the firm's use of ambiguous evaluative criteria allowed promotion decisions to be influenced by subjective, stereotypical judgments. Third, because individuals who did not have adequate information about Hopkins provided input into decisions about her promotion, those decisions might have been affected by gender stereotypes.

The final argument in the brief was that, although the use of stereotypes cannot be eliminated, it can be controlled by providing clear and relevant information about an individual, increasing the time and attention allotted for decision-making, and instilling motivation to be accurate (for example, by increasing accountability for decisions or actively discouraging the use of stereotypes). The brief asserted that Price Waterhouse did not employ any of those methods.

The Supreme Court held that gender stereotyping impermissibly influenced decisions about Hopkins' promotion. The Court's opinion dismissed Price Waterhouse's attacks on the validity of psychological research on gender stereotyping. However, the Court also suggested that, in this case, the evidence of gender stereotyping was strong enough to make psychological research "icing on Hopkins' cake." *Id.* at 256.

gender stereotyping and gender prejudice has continued to expand and mature.[6] The focus of the present chapter is to review psychological research and theory on gender stereotyping, with a particular emphasis on research published since *Hopkins*. Our goal is to identify and highlight major issues and themes rather than to provide a comprehensive review of the literature. We begin by outlining the types of questions that psychologists ask about gender stereotyping and the methods that have been used to address those questions. We then discuss the scientific literature on gender stereotyping. Finally, we highlight particular areas of agreement and disagreement within the psychological community and suggest directions that research on gender stereotyping may take within the next several years.

§ 11–2.2 Scientific Questions about Gender Stereotyping

Legal cases involving alleged gender discrimination and sexual harassment attempt to determine whether gender impermissibly influenced the treatment of a particular person or group of people. In deciding such cases, courts also have addressed related issues, such as the evidentiary standards for proving discrimination[7] and the appropriateness of using gender-specific standards for sexual harassment.[8]

The questions addressed by psychological research on gender stereotyping (as well as other kinds of stereotyping) differ from legal considerations in several important ways. Psychological research on gender stereotyping does not examine individual cases to determine whether discrimination or harassment occurred. Instead, this research attempts to discern psychological processes related to the overall use of stereotypes. Notably, in the course of searching for these general processes, psychologists have investigated a broad array of questions related to gender stereotyping. For example, research has examined cognitive processes involved in group categorization and stereotyping, contextual variables that promote and discourage stereotyping, and characteristics of individuals that lead to both stereotyping and being stereotyped. However, in all of these areas, psychological questions about gender stereotyping are limited to inquiries that can be framed as hypotheses (i.e., statements about the predicted relationships between different variables) that

For commentary about the brief, see G. V. Barrett & S. B. Morris, *The American Psychological Association's Amicus Curiae Brief in Price Waterhouse v. Hopkins: The Values of Science Versus the Values of the Law*, 17 LAW & HUM. BEHAV. 201 (1993); S. T. Fiske et al., *Social Science Research on Trial: Use of Sex Stereotyping Research in Price Waterhouse v. Hopkins*, 46 AM. PSYCHOL. 1049 (1991); S. T. Fiske et al., *What Constitutes a Scientific Review?: A Majority Retort to Barrett and Morris*, 17 LAW & HUM. BEHAV. 217 (1993).

In the decade following the *Hopkins* decision, expert psychological testimony on gender stereotyping research has informed several additional cases involving gender discrimination and sexual harassment. *See, e.g.*, Butler v. Home Depot, 1997 WL 605754 (N.D.Cal.1997); Jenson v. Eveleth Taconite Co., 824 F.Supp. 847 (D.Minn.1993); Robinson v. Jacksonville Shipyards, Inc., 760 F.Supp. 1486 (M.D.Fla. 1991).

6. *See, e.g.*, E. Borgida & S. T. Fiske, *By Way of Introduction*, 51 J. Soc. ISSUES 1 (1995); D. Burgess & E. Borgida, *Who Women Are, Who Women Should Be: Descriptive and Prescriptive Gender Stereotyping, in Sex Discrimination*, 5 PSYCHOL., PUB. POL'Y & L., 665 (1999); Deaux, *supra* note 3; K. Deaux & M. E. Kite, *Gender Stereotypes, in* HANDBOOK ON THE PSYCHOLOGY OF WOMEN 107 (F. Denmark & M. Paludi eds., 1993); K. Deaux & M. LaFrance, *Gender, in* HANDBOOK OF SOCIAL PSYCHOLOGY 788 (D.T. Gilbert, S.T. Fiske, & G. Lindzey eds., 4th ed. 1998).

7. *See, e.g.*, Price Waterhouse v. Hopkins, 490 U.S. 228, 109 S.Ct. 1775, 104 L.Ed.2d 268 (1989).

8. Ellison v. Brady, 924 F.2d 872 (9th Cir. 1991).

can be tested and potentially disproven through the use of established scientific techniques. Thus, in comparison to legal questions, scientific questions about gender stereotyping are in some respects more broad (i.e., in looking for general processes and examining numerous factors related to stereotyping), but in other respects more narrow (i.e., limiting questions to testable, falsifiable hypotheses).

Psychological questions about gender stereotyping can be divided into five general categories. First, psychologists have studied the content of gender stereotypes, that is, the traits and characteristics that are associated with women and men. Stereotype content has been assessed for the genders as a whole, as well as for specific subcategories of men and women (e.g., business women). The second set of questions investigated by psychologists involves the application of gender stereotypes. This research, which most closely relates to legal questions about gender discrimination and sexual harassment, investigates how gender stereotypes affect judgments of and behavior toward men and women. The third category of questions relates to the psychological processes that underlie the use of stereotypes. This research attempts to describe the cognitive mechanisms governing the use of gender stereotypes. Fourth, psychologists have investigated individual differences related to the use of gender stereotypes. They have studied characteristics that make certain people more or less likely than others to engage in stereotyping. Finally, some psychologists have begun to conduct research that investigates the accuracy of gender stereotypes, that is, the extent to which gender stereotypes conform to pre-determined standards of appropriateness.

These questions are discussed in the sections below. Before describing the research, however, it is necessary to discuss some methodological issues related to the study of gender stereotyping.

§ 11–2.3 Methodological Issues

In this section, we provide an overview of the methodologies used in research on gender stereotyping. We describe two recent methodological developments, response latency measures and meta-analysis, in some depth. Finally, we discuss criticisms that have been made about the usefulness of research on gender stereotyping for understanding actual cases of alleged gender discrimination and sexual harassment.

§ 11–2.3.1 Traditional Research Methodologies

Research on gender stereotyping employs a number of scientific methodologies. The use of several methodologies is a strength of the field, as it creates converging evidence about the existence, use, and effects of gender stereotypes. In other words, using multiple methods allows scientists to have more confidence that gender stereotypes function in a certain manner, independent of any particular research method.

Traditionally, three types of research methods have been used to investigate various aspects of gender stereotyping. First, researchers have used surveys (i.e., structured sets of questions that participants must answer) in order to determine the nature of gender stereotypes. For example, surveys are used to document the content of gender stereotypes (i.e., the characteristics that are associated with women and men). Surveys also are used to assess the extent to which people openly show gender prejudice (e.g., expressing negative attitudes about women or the belief that only women are suited for certain occupations).

Second, a number of judgment tasks are used to investigate the effects of stereotypes on decisions and evaluations about other people. For example, in a classic judgment task known as the Goldberg paradigm, research participants are presented with information about a target individual (e.g., an essay or a job resume).[9] Some participants are told that the individual is a man, and other participants are told that the individual is a woman. The actual information presented, however, is exactly the same for all participants. Participants read the information about the individual, then render some kind of judgment about it (e.g., the quality of the essay or the suitability of that individual for a certain job). Because the information given to participants is held constant, gender stereotyping is inferred from differences in judgments made for male and female target individuals.

A third set of methodologies commonly used consists of analog or simulation paradigms. In these studies, participants engage in simulated workplace interactions, such as job interviews. One or more aspects of their behavior are measured in order to assess gender stereotyping. For example, Rudman and Borgida conducted a study in which male participants interviewed female job applicants.[10] The researchers collected data on the types of questions the participants asked, the physical distance between the participants and the applicants, the information the participants remembered about the applicants' qualifications, and the applicants' impressions of the interview process. Frequently, analog studies manipulate certain aspects of workplace interactions in order to determine the effects of contextual factors on gender stereotyping. For example, Rudman and Borgida's study manipulated the male participants' exposure to commercials that depicted women as sexual objects in order to investigate whether exposure to such material affects men's treatment of female job applicants.

§ 11–2.3.2 Response Latency Measures

In recent years, an increasing number of scientists have started to use a new research methodology to assess gender as well as other forms of stereotyping. The three traditional methodologies discussed above all involve explicit measures of gender stereotyping. Participants in these studies consciously choose their responses to questions or analog situations. Although such explicit measures are extremely useful for conducting research about stereotyping, they have an important limitation. Because most individuals do not want to appear prejudiced, they may alter their responses or behavior in order to appear unbiased. These social desirability concerns may affect the results of studies relying on explicit measures.

Thus, scientists have developed implicit measures of gender stereotyping in order to measure the use of gender stereotypes in a non-reactive manner (i.e., without participants knowing that stereotypes are being assessed). The

9. P. Goldberg, *Are Women Prejudiced Against Women?*, 5 TRANSACTION 316 (1968).

10. L.A. Rudman & E. Borgida, *The Afterglow of Construct Accessibility: The Cognitive and Behavioral Consequences of Priming Men to View Women as Sexual Objects*, 31 J. EXPERIMENTAL SOC. PSYCHOL. 493 (1995).

most common implicit measure involves the use of response latencies, that is, the amount of time (measured in milliseconds) that participants take to respond to certain stimuli. Conceptually, the length of time participants take to respond to a stimulus is related to the accessibility of the stimulus in the participants' minds. More accessible concepts can be recognized more quickly than less accessible concepts. Response latencies also can show how closely related two concepts are to each other. Concepts that are associated ("linked") in a person's mind should facilitate each other, so that activating one of the concepts should decrease the length of time needed to activate the other. Conversely, concepts that are not associated should inhibit each other. In other words, activating one concept should increase the length of time required to recognize the other. Therefore, stereotyping can be inferred from the overall accessibility of certain concepts (e.g., sexist words), as well as from certain patterns of facilitation (e.g., responding more quickly to women's names after exposure to traditionally feminine characteristics) and inhibition (e.g., taking longer to respond to feminine pronouns after exposure to stereotypically masculine occupations).

Response latency measures usually are collected through the use of specially created computer programs. In one common paradigm, called a lexical decision task, participants are exposed to a prime (e.g., a word or picture) that is expected to activate a certain concept (e.g., women or men). Primes can be presented supraliminally (i.e., when participants consciously process the prime) or subliminally (i.e., below the threshold for consciously processing a prime). Following the prime, participants are exposed to a target about which they have to make a judgment (e.g., whether it is a word or a non-word). In another paradigm, known as the Implicit Associations Test (IAT), participants simultaneously categorize words that fall along two separate, but related dimensions.[11] For example, a person may categorize names as "male" or "female" while simultaneously categorizing other words as "agentic" or "communal."[12] In both paradigms, the time participants take to make their judgments is the response latency. Participants respond to dozens or even hundreds of prime-target pairs in order to produce reliable measures of response latency.

Response latency methodologies are useful because they allow scientists to measure gender stereotyping in situations in which participants do not know that stereotypes are being studied and therefore cannot control their responses. Researchers therefore can assess the extent to which stereotyping occurs, as well as the effects that stereotyping has on later judgments and behavior. In addition, the use of these methodologies allows comparisons between responses to different types of stimuli (e.g., gender and race groups; sexist and non-sexist words) that would not be possible using explicit measures. As a result, response latency methodologies have contributed significantly to scientific knowledge about gender stereotyping, making them an important and complementary addition to traditional gender stereotyping methodologies.

11. A. G. Greenwald, D. McGhee, & J. L. K. Schwartz, *Measuring Individual Differences in Implicit Cognition: The Implicit Associations Test*, 74 J. PERSONALITY SOC. PSYCHOL. 1464 (1998).

12. L. A. Rudman & S. E. Kilianski, *Implicit and Explicit Attitudes Toward Female Authority*, 26 PERSONALITY SOC. PSYCHOL. BULL. 1315 (2000).

The primary criticism of response latency methodologies involves the interpretation of differences in response latencies. Because differences in response latencies frequently involve differences of only a few milliseconds, the practical importance of these differences has been questioned. The criticism points to the real need for researchers to continue to document the relationship between implicit measures of stereotyping and explicit responses and behavior.[13] However, given the firm grounding of the methodologies in cognitive psychology as well as the consistency of response patterns found across numerous studies, there is no serious question within the psychological community about whether response latency methodologies are a useful means of studying stereotyping.

§ 11–2.3.3   Meta–Analysis

Another important methodological development in the gender stereotyping literature involves a statistical procedure known as meta-analysis. Over the past 25 years, literally hundreds of studies on gender stereotypes have been published.[14] As a result, there is a need for reviews that organize the literature, identify important themes, and draw conclusions about the state of the science. Traditionally, researchers have used qualitative techniques to review large scientific literatures. In a qualitative literature review, researchers examine the results of statistical significance tests across several studies and declare that the literature provides "consistent" or "inconsistent" support for a phenomenon based on the number of "significant" or "non-significant" results among the studies. Qualitative reviews can be extremely useful and important. However, because statistical significance tests are heavily dependent on sample size, qualitative reviews that merely code studies as "significant" or "non-significant" may draw incorrect inferences about a phenomenon when studies do not have sample sizes that are large enough to detect significant differences. Some commentators assert that such low statistical power frequently occurs in experimental studies.[15]

Researchers have developed meta-analysis as a quantitative method for integrating existing studies. In meta-analysis, statistical procedures are used to assess the magnitude of a phenomenon across different studies, independent of the studies' sample sizes. As a result, meta-analysis protects against dismissing large effects that are "non-significant" because of small sample sizes, as well as overemphasizing small effects that are "significant" because of large sample sizes.[16]

In conducting a meta-analysis, researchers first locate as many studies as possible that investigate the question of interest. Next, researchers compute an effect size (d)[17] reflecting the size of the results obtained in each individual study. The general formula for effect size involves subtracting the mean score for one group from the mean score for another group, then dividing the

13. *See, e.g.,* Rudman & Borgida, *supra* note 10; L. A. Rudman & P. Glick, *Prescriptive Gender Stereotypes and Backlash Toward Agentic Women*, J. Soc. Issues (forthcoming 2001).

14. Deaux, *supra* note 3, at 20.

15. J. E. Hunter & F. L. Schmidt, *Cumulative Research Knowledge and Social Policy For-* *mulation: The Critical Role of Meta–Analysis*, 2 Psychol., Pub. Pol'y & L. 324 (1996).

16. J.S. Hyde, *Can Meta–Analysis Make Feminist Transformations in Psychology?*, 18 Psychol. Women Q. 451 (1994).

17. Effect sizes also can be computed with an r statistic. The conversion between the two statistics is approximately $d = 2r$.

difference by the combined variability within the groups (i.e., the pooled standard deviation). For example, if researchers are attempting to determine whether job resumes are more favorably evaluated when the applicant was depicted as a man as opposed to a woman, the effect size d would be computed by subtracting the mean score for female applicants from the mean score for male applicants and dividing the difference by the combined within-gender standard deviation. The d effect size thus indicates the difference in men and women's ratings in standard deviation units.[18]

After computing effect sizes for individual studies, researchers average the d values, often weighting the individual studies based upon the number of subjects in each study[19] or the error variance of each study.[20] The resulting mean d enables researchers to make a judgment about the relative size of a particular effect. Cohen suggested that, as a general guideline, a d of .20 is small, .50 is moderate, and .80 is large.[21] However, the importance of a given effect size depends on the nature of the phenomenon. Researchers also can examine whether certain factors influence (moderate) the size of the effects found in individual studies. Such analyses are conducted by coding studies on theoretically important variables (e.g., whether a task is stereotypically masculine or feminine), then computing separate effect sizes for studies containing each type of variable. Such analyses can show, for example, that bias in the evaluation of women's task performance is stronger when the tasks are masculine rather than feminine in nature.[22]

Like other scientific methodologies, it is important to evaluate meta-analyses in terms of their methodological rigor. Meta-analyses should be evaluated according to several criteria. First, evaluators must examine the breadth of the literature search. In general, meta-analyses that are based on a larger number of studies are more reliable than meta-analyses based on fewer studies. Second, it is important to be aware of methodological decisions made by the researchers that can affect conclusions about the magnitude of effects. For example, failing to correct effect sizes for statistical artifacts (e.g., for the unreliability of measures) reduces observed effect sizes. The decision to treat effect sizes that are not reported or are reported as "non-significant" as effect sizes of zero also reduces observed effect size. In contrast, relying only on published studies, which are more likely than non-published studies to have significant results, may increase the observed effect size.

Well-conducted meta-analyses are important ways to evaluate the results of an accumulated body of studies, as well as determine areas in which future research is needed. As a result, in this chapter, we report the findings of meta-analyses whenever appropriate.

§ 11–2.3.4 Criticisms of These Research Paradigms

An important characteristic of research on gender stereotyping is that it primarily has studied two different populations: college students and employees in various workplace environments. College students frequently are used

---

18. Hyde, *supra* note 16.

19. METHODS OF META-ANALYSIS (J. E. Hunter & F. L. Schmidt eds., 1990).

20. STATISTICAL METHODS FOR META-ANALYSIS (L. Hedges & I. Olkin eds., 1985).

21. STATISTICAL POWER FOR THE BEHAVIORAL SCIENCES (J. Cohen ed., 1969).

22. J. Swim et al., *Joan McKay Versus John McKay: Do Gender Stereotypes Bias Evaluations?*, 105 PSYCHOL. BULL. 409 (1989).

in research because of their availability to researchers who work in university settings. College students also tend to be used in research that utilizes methodologies that are difficult to import into workplace settings (e.g., elaborate simulations, response latency paradigms).

However, the use of college student participants and experimental, laboratory-based studies has been one of the primary criticisms of the applicability of research on gender stereotyping to litigation on gender discrimination and sexual harassment. Specifically, some scholars assert that laboratory research using students has minimal generalizability to the actual workplace environments where discrimination and harassment occur.[23]

This criticism is tempered by a considerable number of non-laboratory studies involving different participant populations that provide empirical evidence consistent with the findings reported in laboratory studies.[24] Moreover, the use of meta-analyses allows researchers to investigate whether effects that are found in laboratory settings or with student participants are found in research conducted in workplace settings. The use of meta-analysis has revealed that gender stereotyping effects tend to be consistent across student and employee participant samples. When differences do emerge, they tend to show that individuals in workplace environments show more evidence of bias than do college students.[25] Thus, the accumulated body of research suggests that weak external validity is not an important problem with laboratory research on gender stereotyping.

The other general criticism involving the applicability of scientific research on gender stereotypes to legal cases involving alleged gender discrimination and sexual harassment is the argument that conclusions aggregated from the existing research literature cannot be applied to individual cases involving specific work or organizational settings.[26] Scholars making this argument assert that it is more appropriate to conduct contract research within the actual organization involved in litigation. In this research, employees are asked directly whether they believe, for example, that gender stereotypes play a role in performance appraisals. Researchers also may ask attitude questions to determine whether men in the workplace generally view their female colleagues in gender stereotypic ways.

The law, however, regularly relies on findings from the accumulated body of scientifically valid, peer-reviewed literature in an area to inform the fact-finder in a particular case. In addition, the argument that contract research is the appropriate method of determining whether gender stereotyping occurred ignores several important limitations of conducting such research. One serious problem with the contract approach is that there is no way of determining

23. G.V. Barrett & C. A. Lees, *Stereotyping and Sexual Harassment: Is There a Way to Eliminate the Problem at Work?*, 3 EMP. TESTING 154 (1994).

24. *See, e.g.*, P.R. Sackett et al., *Tokenism in Performance Evaluations: The Effects of Work Group Representation on Male–Female and White–Black Differences in Performance Ratings*, 76 J. APPLIED PSYCHOL. 263 (1991); *see generally*, M. E. Heilman, *Sex Stereotypes and Their Effects in the Workplace: What We Know and What We Don't Know*, 10 J. SOC. BEHAV.

PERSONALITY 3 (1995); V. F. Nieva & B. A. Gutek, *Sex Effects on Evaluation*, 5 ACAD. MGMT. REV. 267 (1980).

25. A. H. Eagly et al., *Gender and the Evaluation of Leaders: A Meta–Analysis*, 111 PSYCHOL. BULL. 3 (1992).

26. Barrett & Lees, *supra* note 23; *see also* S. T. Fiske & E. Borgida, *Social Framework Analysis as Expert Testimony in Sexual Harassment Suits*, in SEXUAL HARASSMENT IN THE WORKPLACE 575 (S. Estreicher ed., 2000).

the extent to which employees' responses will be tainted by knowledge of the litigation underway, the sponsors of the survey, or the potential ramifications of their responses.[27] It is likely that employees will try to give unbiased responses, even if they are not accurate. Moreover, research indicates that gender stereotyping often occurs outside of conscious awareness, so even if employees are completely honest, their responses may not reveal the actual occurrence of gender stereotyping.[28] Therefore, relying on the conclusions of scientifically valid, peer-reviewed social science research to make inferences about a case represents a more scientifically informed approach to assisting fact finders.

§ 11–2.4   Summary of the Scientific Research

Our review of the scientific research on gender stereotyping is organized around the five general categories of research described earlier. First, we discuss research on the content of gender stereotypes (i.e., the information contained within those stereotypes). Second, we discuss the application of gender stereotypes (i.e., how gender stereotypes are used). Third, we review the psychological processes that underlie the use of stereotypes. Fourth, we describe some individual differences in the use of gender stereotypes. Finally, we discuss the debate over the accuracy of gender stereotypes.

§ 11–2.4.1   Content

[1]   Introduction

Stereotypes are "a set of attributes ascribed to a group and imputed to its individual members simply because they belong to that group."[29] Gender stereotypes have both descriptive and prescriptive components.[30] The descriptive component of gender stereotypes refers to specific beliefs about the characteristics of men and women, whereas the prescriptive component sets expectations for appropriate behavior for men and women. Research indicates that people believe that men are agentic or achievement-oriented (e.g., competent, independent, active, competitive) and women are communal or affiliation-oriented (e.g., nurturing, dependent, passive, non-competitive). The communal stereotype associated with women undermines perceptions of their competence within the workplace.

People tend to believe that there is little variability within members of a group. In other words, people believe that women tend to be similar to other women, and men tend to be similar to other men. This psychological process makes it more difficult for people to notice and use individuating information, such as a particular man or woman's job-related skills. However, there are subcategories within the overall categories of "men" and "women." For

---

27. Barrett & Lees, *supra* note 23.

28. S. T. Fiske, *Stereotyping, Prejudice, and Discrimination, in* 2 HANDBOOK OF SOCIAL PSYCHOLOGY 357 (D. T. Gilbert et al. eds., 4th ed. 1998).

29. M. E. Heilman, *Sex Bias in Work Settings: The Lack of Fit Model, in* 5 RESEARCH IN ORGANIZATIONAL BEHAVIOR 269, 271 (L. L. Cummings & B. M. Staw eds., 1983).

30. In the APA *Hopkins* brief, the prescriptive component is referred to as the normative component. These two terms are interchangeable; however, more recent research and theory has tended to use the former term.

example, career-oriented women may be assigned to the subcategory of "Iron Maidens."

[2] Overall Gender Stereotypes

More recent research supports the conclusion that women are seen as communal and men are seen as agentic. There is, however, some evidence that people are seeing women as increasingly agentic. In a study by Diekman and Eagly, college and community participants rated various characteristics of women and men at three points in time (1950, present day, projecting to 2050).[31] Consistent with past and expected changes in women's social roles, ratings of women's agency increased at each time point. Notably, ratings of men's communality were not consistently affected.

In addition, recent research has challenged the conclusion that the characteristics stereotypically ascribed to men are considered more positive than are the characteristics stereotypically ascribed to women. Eagly and Mladinic have demonstrated a strong positive bias toward women, a phenomenon known as the "women are wonderful" effect.[32] Both male and female respondents rate women more favorably than men on general attitude measures. In addition, the stereotypical characteristics associated with women are evaluated more positively than are the stereotypical characteristics associated with men.

However, closer examination reveals that there is an important qualification to the "women are wonderful" effect. Eagly and Mladinic determined that people evaluate women more positively than men largely because the positive qualities associated with nurturance and a communal orientation are assigned to women much more frequently than to men.[33] Thus, people evaluate women positively because they think about them in traditional ways (i.e., as homemaker and nurturer). In contrast, men are associated with agentic qualities that, although less favorably evaluated, are associated with success in the domain of paid employment. As a result, women are considered nice but incompetent, whereas men are considered less nice but competent, a pattern with distinct implications for workplace judgments.

[3] The Relationship between Gender and Occupational Stereotypes

Several studies have demonstrated that the agentic gender stereotype associated with men is more closely related to people's expectations for certain occupations than is the communal gender stereotype associated with women. For example, Glick had a sample of community members indicate the importance of stereotypically masculine and feminine traits for a variety of occupa-

31. A. Diekman & A.H. Eagly, *Stereotypes as Dynamic Constructs: Women and Men of the Past, Present, and Future*, 26 PERSONALITY & SOC. PSYCHOL. BULL. 1171 (2000).

32. A. H. Eagly & A. Mladinic, *Gender Stereotypes and Attitudes Toward Women and Men*, 15 PERSONALITY & SOC. PSYCHOL. BULL. 543 (1989); A. H. Eagly & A. Mladinic, *Are People Prejudiced Against Women?: Some Answers From Research on Attitudes, Gender Stereotypes, and Judgments of Competence*, in 5 EUR. REV. SOC. PSYCHOL. 1 (W. Stroebe & M. Hewstone eds., 1994); A. H. Eagly, A. Mladinic, & S. Otto, *Are Women Evaluated More Favorably Than Men? An Analysis of Attitudes, Beliefs, and Emotions*, 15 PSYCHOL. WOMEN Q. 203 (1991).

33. Eagly & Mladinic, *supra* note 32.

tions.[34] He found that, overall, people consider stereotypically masculine traits to be more valuable than stereotypically feminine traits in occupational settings.[35] Other research has shown that masculine traits are associated with male-dominated and prestigious jobs, whereas feminine traits are associated with female-dominated jobs.[36]

These findings are consistent with research showing that the characteristics associated with women are not the same as the characteristics associated with successful managers.[37] For example, Heilman et al. conducted a survey in which 268 managers rated numerous characteristics of "successful managers," "men in general," "women in general," "men managers," "women managers," "successful men managers," and "successful women managers."[38] The researchers found a strong positive correlation between the ratings of "men in general" and "successful managers." However, the characteristics of "women in general" and "successful managers" were unrelated. The correlation between ratings of women and "successful managers" increased when the women were described as managers or successful managers. Still, those correlations were significantly smaller than the corresponding correlations between men and "successful managers." Moreover, women described as managers or successful managers were increasingly likely to receive negative ratings on interpersonal skills (e.g., they were considered bitter and quarrelsome).[39]

A more recent study by Martell et al. examined gender stereotyping in perceptions of characteristics associated with successful executives (i.e., those characteristics that are most likely to affect whether managers are promoted).[40] Martell et al. surveyed a large number of male managers to determine the primary characteristics of successful executives. They then had another group of 132 male middle-to senior-level managers evaluate "women middle managers," "men middle managers," "successful women middle managers," and "successful men middle managers" with respect to those characteristics. Regardless of whether they were described as successful, women managers were rated less favorably than men managers on two out of the four characteristics (i.e., agent of change, managerial courage). On a third characteristic, leadership, there was a difference between women and men managers, but not between successful women and successful men managers. Only one characteristic, results-oriented, did not show any gender differences.

---

34. P. Glick, *Trait-Based and Sex–Based Discrimination in Occupational Prestige, Occupational Salary, and Hiring*, 25 Sex Roles 351 (1991) (Study 1).

35. Specifically, Glick found that, compared to stereotypically feminine traits, people believe that stereotypically masculine traits are more important for stereotypically masculine jobs and equally important for gender-neutral and stereotypically feminine jobs.

36. M. A. Cejka & A.H. Eagly, *Gender Stereotypic Images of Occupations Correspond to Sex Segregation of Employment*, 25 Personality & Soc. Psychol. Bull. 413 (1999); P. Glick et al., *Images of Occupations: Components of Gender and Status in Occupational Stereotypes*, 32 Sex Roles 565 (1995).

37. M. E. Heilman et al., *Sex Stereotypes: Do They Influence Perceptions of Managers?*, 10 J. Soc. Behav. & Personality 237 (1995); M. E. Heilman et al., *Has Anything Changed?: Current Characterizations of Men, Women, and Managers*, 74 J. Applied Psychol. 935 (1989); R. F. Martell et al., *Sex Stereotyping in the Executive Suite: "Much Ado About Something,"* 13 J. Soc. Behav. & Personality 127 (1998).

38. Heilman et al. (1989), *supra* note 37.

39. Heilman et al. (1989), *supra* note 37. Heilman et al. (1995), *supra* note 37.

40. Martell et. al., *supra* note 37.

Taken together, this body of research indicates that both community members and professionals believe that women possess fewer of the qualities associated with occupational success and advancement than do men. The implications of that stereotype for employment decisions will be discussed in the section on Applications.

[4] Subtypes and Subgroups

People do not always use the global stereotypes for women or men when they evaluate specific women or men. Instead, they may use a more specific stereotype, such as a stereotype for a subcategory of women or men that seems relevant to a particular individual. For example, a sexy woman at a bar may be stereotyped as a "vamp" rather than as a "woman" per se. Recent research has explored both the content and the process of using stereotypes about subcategories. The former topic will be discussed in this section, and the latter issue will be covered in the section on psychological processes.

Researchers have proposed that people use two different kinds of subcategories to distinguish superordinate group members.[41] Subtypes are sets of individuals who appear to belong to a group yet possess characteristics that contradict the overall group stereotype. Separating such individuals into subtypes maintains the existing group stereotype by casting those individuals as deviants.[42] For example, because lesbians tend to violate the overall stereotype for women, they often are considered separate from other women. In contrast, subgroups are sets of individuals in a group who share some but not all of the characteristics of the larger group. Subgroup members continue to be categorized within the larger group, adding variability to the overall group stereotype. Notably, the subtype-subgroup distinction is blurred in much of the gender stereotype literature.

Although people recognize numerous subtypes of women and men, research has demonstrated that there are a few dominant themes in gender subtypes.[43] In a representative study, Six and Eckes had a group of West German undergraduates list the characteristics of "the most common types of men and women."[44] They then had a second group of participants sort those lists into groups based on similarity. Statistical analyses revealed three dominant clusters of subtypes of women: 1) Non-traditional women (e.g., feminists, career women), 2) Sex objects (e.g., vamps, tarts), and 3) Traditional women (e.g., housewives, mothers). Six and Eckes found that the subtypes of men were less distinct than were the subtypes of women, but they seemed to involve two primary dimensions: 1) whether the man was "hard" (e.g., macho) or "soft" (e.g., gay), and 2) whether the man was "reliable" (e.g., a manager) or "unreliable" (e.g., a playboy).

41. Fiske, *supra* note 28.

42. Z. Kunda & K. C. Olesen, *Maintaining Stereotypes in the Face of Disconfirmation: Constructing Grounds for Subtyping Deviants*, 68 J. PERSONALITY & SOC. PSYCHOL. 565 (1995).

43. A. K. Clifton et al., *Stereotypes of Woman: A Single Category?*, 2 SEX ROLES 135 (1976); K. Deaux et al., *Level of Categorization and Content of Gender Stereotypes*, 3 SOC. COGNITION 145 (1985); T. Eckes, *Features of Men, Features of Women: Assessing Stereotypic Beliefs About Gender Subtypes*, 33 BRITISH J. SOC. PSYCHOL. 107 (1994); C. M. Noseworthy & A. J. Lott, *The Cognitive Organization of Gender–Stereotypic Categories*, 10 PERSONALITY & SOC. PSYCHOL. BULL. 474 (1985); B. Six & T. Eckes, *A Closer Look at the Complex Structure of Gender Stereotypes*, 24 SEX ROLES 57 (1991).

44. Six & Eckes, *supra* note 43.

A subsequent study by Eckes incorporated both subtypes and related trait descriptions into a similar statistical analysis.[45] The richer set of data revealed the same three clusters for women found by Six and Eckes, though other clusters (e.g., wallflower, hippie/punk) also emerged.[46] Notably, Eckes included the phrases "typical woman" and "typical man" in the relevant analyses. He found that "typical woman" (i.e., the global stereotype of women) was related to the housewife subtype, but not the non-traditional or sex object subtypes; "typical man" (i.e., the global stereotype of men) was not included in any cluster of male subtypes. Eckes also found that the subtypes of women were more distinct (i.e., they overlapped less) than were the subtypes of men. These patterns suggest that women are divided into clearly defined groups based on their characteristics and behaviors, with only one set of features (i.e., those characteristic of a housewife) being seen as typical of women as a whole.[47] In contrast, subtypes of men often have overlapping features, with no one subtype being considered representative of men as a whole.

Other studies have investigated the content of subgroups. Landrine conducted a study that assessed stereotypes of subgroups of women based on race and socioeconomic status.[48] Landrine had participants rate middle-and lower-class White and Black women on numerous attributes. Analyses of those ratings revealed significant effects for both race and class. Middle class women were rated significantly higher than lower-class women on qualities such as ambition, competence, happiness, and intelligence. In contrast, they were rated significantly lower on characteristics such as dirtiness, hostility, and impulsiveness. Black women were rated significantly higher than White women on dirtiness, hostility, and superstitiousness, but significantly lower than White women on characteristics such as competence, intelligence, and passivity. Landrine concluded that the stereotype for subgroup of middle-class White women is closest to the global stereotype for "women." However, all of the targets were perceived in a stereotypically feminine manner, regardless of race or socioeconomic status.

A more extensive study, conducted by Niemann et al., compared stereotypes for eight combinations of gender and race.[49] The researchers found that people have complex stereotypes that vary by both the gender and the ethnic background of a target person. For example, whereas both male and female Anglo–Americans were seen as achievement-oriented, racist, and upper-class, Anglo–American women also were seen as caring, friendly, attractive, egotistical, and socially active. African–Americans and Mexican–Americans generally were seen as ambitionless, not college educated, unmannered, and lower-class. However, the stereotype for African–American men also included athleticism and criminal behavior, whereas the stereotype for Mexican–American women included bad-temper, promiscuity, passivity, and religiosity. Thus, the study

45. Eckes, *supra* note 43.

46. Six & Eckes, *supra* note 43.

47. *See also*, G. Haddock & M. P. Zanna, *Preferring "Housewives" to "Feminists:" Categorization and the Favorability of Attitudes Toward Women*, 18 PSYCHOL. WOMEN Q. 25 (1994); J. E. Riedle, *Exploring the Subcategories of Stereotypes: Not All Mothers Are the Same*, 24 SEX ROLES 711 (1991).

48. H. Landrine, *Race X Class Stereotypes of Women*, 13 SEX ROLES 65 (1985).

49. Y. F. Niemann et al., *Use of Free Responses and Cluster Analysis to Determine Stereotypes of Eight Groups*, 20 PERSONALITY & SOC. PSYCHOL. BULL. 379 (1994).

demonstrated that stereotypes vary both between and within ethnic backgrounds and genders.

Taken together, these studies demonstrate the need to look at differences in stereotypes that occur when people are categorized in terms of subtypes or subgroups. The overall stereotype for "women" may reflect some subtypes (i.e., housewives) and subgroups (i.e., White, middle-class women), but it may not include stereotypes about other subtypes (e.g., non-traditional women) or subgroups (e.g., minority or lower-class women). Because the specific stereotypes associated with different subtypes and subgroups may have different positive and negative components, they may lead to different outcomes, both compared to each other and compared to the global "woman" stereotype.

§ 11–2.4.2   The Application of Gender Stereotypes

[1]   Introduction

In certain situations, gender stereotyping can lead to discrimination against women. First, when forming impressions of individual women, people frequently rely on generalizations about women as a whole rather than considering individuating information about the specific person. This process can result in faulty expectations and judgments, as well as discriminatory treatment. For example, empirical studies indicate that people's explanations for an individual's success or failure often depend on the gender of the individual. Women's successes are more likely to be explained by unstable causes, such as good luck or hard work, rather than stable causes, such as ability and competence.

Second, the prescriptive component of gender stereotypes sets expectations for appropriate behavior for men and women. Men are expected to engage in masculine behavior, and women are expected to engage in feminine behavior. Sanctions may be imposed on individuals who engage in gender-incongruent behavior (i.e., gender non-conformists). For example, research demonstrates that women who violate prescriptive expectations for their gender often receive poor work evaluations.

Stereotypic patterns can create a double bind for women in management. Specifically, the stereotype for women is considered incompatible with the characteristics of a manager. Thus, a woman may be passed over for promotions because she is considered unable to manage, regardless of her actual abilities. On the other hand, if a woman does succeed in proving herself as an effective manager, she has violated prescriptive expectations for feminine behavior (e.g., by acting competitively) and therefore may be sanctioned. Either way, a woman may experience considerable gender-related difficulties in the workplace.

[2]   Evaluations and Attributions

In recent years, social scientists have continued to investigate the effects of gender stereotypes on judgments that people make about women and men. Two major questions addressed by this research include: 1) Do people make the same evaluations for men and women's accomplishments?, and 2) Do people make the same attributions (i.e., causal explanations) for women and men's behaviors?

[a] Evaluations

Swim et al. conducted a meta-analysis to examine whether gender stereotypes bias people's evaluations of men and women's performance.[50] The researchers collected 123 studies using the Goldberg paradigm. Recall that, in this paradigm, participants are provided with identical information about a target person's performance on a task, but are told that the target person is either male or female. Participants then are asked to evaluate the target person's performance, and analyses are conducted to determine whether people's evaluations differ as a function of the target's gender.

Swim et al.'s meta-analysis found a very small overall effect (d = .05), indicating that there is only a slight tendency for people to evaluate men more positively than equally-performing women. The size of this effect was similar for both male and female evaluators, although the evaluations made by men were more variable than were the evaluations made by women. Although still quite small, the effect sizes were larger when the tasks being evaluated were stereotypically masculine (d = .12) or gender-neutral (d = .13) rather than stereotypically feminine (d = .01). This pattern of results is consistent with the gender-role congruency hypothesis, which posits that women are more likely to be negatively evaluated when they fulfill traditionally male roles or behave in ways that are incongruent with the female gender role.

Another area in which men and women may be evaluated involves leadership ability. Because of stereotypes about men's superior leadership ability, men may be evaluated more favorably than women for the same leadership behavior. To determine whether people are biased against female leaders, Eagly et al. conducted a meta-analysis of 61 studies involving evaluations of male and female leaders.[51] The meta-analysis included studies in which participants read written descriptions of managerial behavior by either male or female managers, as well as analog studies in which participants were "supervised" by trained research confederates. Although the majority of the studies used college students, some studies included managers and non-managerial employees.

Consistent with Swim et al.'s results, the overall effect size in Eagly et al.'s meta-analysis was extremely small (d = .05), demonstrating only a slight tendency to favor male leaders.[52] However, the researchers identified several factors moderating that effect. The tendency to favor men was larger when the leadership style was autocratic (i.e., highly controlling; d = .30) or masculine (d = .15), when the situation traditionally involved male leadership (d = .09), and when the situation involved athletics (d = 1.03). Again, this pattern of results supports the gender-role congruency hypothesis, showing that female leaders are more likely to be devalued when they lead in ways and situations that are stereotypically masculine.[53] Notably, in contrast to female

50. Swim et al., *supra* note 22.

51. Eagly, *supra* note 25.

52. *Id.*

53. Notably, a meta-analysis by Eagly et al., on the actual effectiveness of male and female leaders produced consistent results. A.H. Eagly et al., *Gender and the Effectiveness*

leaders, male leaders were not devalued when they led in a stereotypically feminine style or when they occupied stereotypically female leadership roles. Also notable was the finding that evaluations of female leaders did not differ as a function of leadership success, suggesting that women who led in a stereotypically masculine manner were being evaluated in terms of femininity rather than skill.

When Eagly et al. examined demographic characteristics, they found that male subjects ($d = .15$) favored male leaders somewhat more than did female subjects ($d = .04$).[54] Particularly noteworthy was the fact that non-managerial employees favored male leaders ($d = .43$) to a much greater extent than did college students ($d = .01$) or a pure sample of managers ($d = .01$). Because the majority of studies included college students, it may be that the level of bias against female leaders in the workplace is greater than the overall effect size this meta-analysis suggests.

[b] Attributions

In addition to affecting evaluations of men and women's work, gender stereotypes may influence the explanations people give for other individuals' behaviors. Swim and Sanna conducted a meta-analysis of 58 studies examining attributions for women's and men's successes and failures.[55] In each of the studies, participants read a scenario in which a man or a woman experienced success or failure at a task, then made attributions about the cause of that performance. Most of the studies used college-aged students as participants, although some of the studies used older participants.

The meta-analysis showed that, compared with men's successes, women's successes on masculine tasks were less likely to be attributed to ability ($d = .08$) and more likely to be attributed to effort ($d = .17$). This pattern of effects was reversed for failures, such that women's failures on masculine tasks were attributed to task difficulty ($d = .28$), whereas men's failures on the same tasks were explained by low effort ($d = .16$) and bad luck ($d = .13$). As with the Swim et al. and Eagly et al. meta-analyses, these effect sizes tended to be small.[56] However, the researchers used a conservative method of estimating effect studies for studies that did not provide enough statistical information.

of Leaders: A Meta–Analysis, 117 PSYCHOLOGICAL BULL. 125 (1995). The overall mean weighted effect size of the 96 studies indicated that gender differences in leadership effectiveness did not differ significantly from zero. However, as the gender congeniality hypothesis would predict, male leaders were considered more effective when leadership roles were male-dominated and when subordinates were male. The level of leadership also influenced gender differences in effectiveness; men were judged as more effective in first-level (or line) positions; women were judged as more effective in second-level (or middle-management) positions. This may be due to the fact that first-level positions involve more technical supervision, whereas second-level positions generally require a greater degree of human relations skills, an explanation that is consistent with the gender congruency hypothesis.

54. A recent study by Rudman and Kilianski used the IAT to demonstrate that bias against female leaders is found even at the implicit level. Notably, Rudman and Kilianski did not find gender differences, suggesting that women may view female leaders as negatively as men do, but adjust their explicit evaluations in a positive direction. L.A. Rudman & S.E. Kilianski, Implicit and Explicit Attitudes Toward Female Authority, 26 PERSONALITY & SOCIAL PSYCHOL. BULL. 1315 (2000).

55. J. K. Swim & L. J. Sanna, He's Skilled, She's Lucky: A Meta–Analysis of Observers' Attributions for Women's and Men's Successes and Failures, 22 PERSONALITY & SOC. PSYCHOL. BULL. 507 (1996).

56. Swim et. al., supra note 50; Eagly et al., supra note 25.

Thus, the computed effect sizes are likely to underestimate the actual effect sizes. Moreover, because the differences in attributions were strongest for effort-related explanations and for stereotypically masculine tasks, the meta-analysis provided additional support for the gender-role congruency hypothesis.

Notably, a study by Greenhaus and Parasuraman demonstrated gender-biased attributions in the workplace. The researchers asked 748 supervisors to make attributions about the job performance of subordinate managers.[57] They found a small effect in which male managers' successes were more likely than female managers' successes to be attributed to ability. The effect was strongest when the supervisors had little experience with the managers.

[c]   Practical Significance of Evaluations and Attributions

Before leaving the topic of biased evaluations and attributions, it is important to discuss the practical significance of small effect sizes. The meta-analyses discussed in this section consistently found small effect sizes for gender biases in evaluations and attributions. However, it is important to note that the small magnitudes of those effects should not lead policy makers to discount the importance of the phenomena. For example, a computer simulation by Martell et al. demonstrated that even biases of 1–5% can have important practical consequences in workplace settings.[58] Martell et al. simulated an organizational structure with eight levels of employees from entry level to executive. They placed 500 employees, half male and half female, at the entry level. Those employees were given initial distributions of performance ratings that were identical except that a 1% or 5% bias score was added to men's ratings. The researchers then compared the proportion of men and women who reached the highest level of the organization after 20 rounds of simulated promotion decisions. In the 1% bias condition, 65% of the employees at the highest level were men and 35% were women; in the 5% bias condition, 71% were men and 29% were women. This simulation thus demonstrates that even small amounts of bias related to gender stereotypes can lead to major workplace discrimination.

[3]   Standards for Evaluation

An important question when considering gender bias in evaluations is whether people use the same standards when they evaluate women and men. Biernat and her colleagues have described a shifting standards model in which the criteria used to evaluate members of one social group differ from the criteria used to evaluate members of another social group, even if the evaluations involve the same dimension (e.g., intelligence).[59] Specifically, peo-

---

57. J. H. Greenhaus & S. Parasuraman, *Job Performance Attributions and Career Advancement Prospects: An Examination of Gender and Race Effects*, 55 ORGANIZATIONAL BEHAV. & HUM. DECISION PROCESSES 273 (1993).

58. R. F. Martell et al., *Male-Female Differences: A Computer Simulation*, 51 AMERICAN PSYCHOL. 157 (1996).

59. M. Biernat & D. Kobrynowicz, *A Shifting Standards Perspective on the Complexity of Gender Stereotypes and Gender Stereotyping*, in SEXISM AND STEREOTYPES IN MODERN SOCIETY: THE GENDER SCIENCE OF JANET TAYLOR SPENCE 75 (W.B. Swann, Jr., J.H. Langlois, & L.A. Gilbert eds. 1999). M. Biernat & D. Kobrynowicz, *Gender- and Race–Based Standards of Competence: Lower Minimum Standards but Higher Ability*

ple use within-group standards to judge individual group members. With respect to gender, women are compared against other women, whereas men are compared against other men. Because within-group standards are used, judgments are affected by gender stereotypes. For example, because women are expected to be passive, a woman engaging in somewhat aggressive behavior would be considered more aggressive than would a man engaging in identical behavior.[60]

One implication of the shifting standards model is that ratings made on subjective scales (e.g., scales going from "not at all successful" to "extremely successful") should differ from ratings made on objective scales (e.g., ratings of height in inches and dollars earned per year). Because subjective scales do not have precise anchors for measurement, ratings are based on gender-specific criteria. In contrast, objective scales are used similarly across groups. Consistent with this prediction, Biernat et al. found that differences in judgments of men and women's height and weight were smaller when ratings were made on subjective rather than objective scales. A woman and a man both considered "tall" on subjective scales were described as 5'9" and 6'3", respectively, on objective scales.[61] Likewise, Biernat and Manis found that, consistent with stereotypes about men and women's verbal abilities, women were perceived as having higher verbal ability than men when objective scales were used, but not when subjective scales were used.[62]

The shifting standards model also has been applied to employment-relevant judgments. Biernat and Kobrynowicz provided participants with resumes of female and male job applicants.[63] Participants then answered questions about the standards that should be used to evaluate those applicants. When participants used subjective scales, standards for minimum competence and ability to succeed did not differ for the female and male job applicants. However, when participants used objective scales, participants who read about the female applicant specified lower standards for minimum competence and higher standards for ability to succeed. Thus, although the female applicant was given the benefit of the doubt for minimal competence, she was expected to demonstrate a greater level of achievement in order to prove her ability to succeed.[64] In another study, Biernat et al. examined perceptions of men's and women's job earnings.[65] Subjective and objective ratings diverged such that women were subjectively considered to be more financially successful than men when they objectively earned several thousand dollars less per year.

The finding that subjective scales mask the use of gender stereotypes suggests that the effect sizes found for gender biases in evaluations and attributions may be artificially reduced by the use of subjective ratings.[66] Consistent with that analysis, Biernat and Kobrynowicz found that, when

Standards for Devalued Groups, 72 J. Person-ality & Soc. Psychol. 544 (1997); M. Biernat & M. Manis, *Shifting Standards and Stereotype–Based Judgments*, 66 J. Personality & Soc. Psychol. 5 (1994); M. Biernat et al., *Stereotypes and Standards of Judgment*, 60 J. Personality & Soc. Psychol. 485 (1991).

60.   Biernat & Manis, *supra* note 59.

61.   M. Biernat et al., *supra* note 59.

62.   Biernat & Manis, *supra* note 59.

63.   Biernat & Kobrynowicz, *supra* note 59.

64.   *See also*, R. F. Martell, *What Mediates Gender Bias in Work Behavior Ratings?*, 35 Sex Roles 153 (1996).

65.   Biernat & Manis, *supra* note 59.

66.   Eagly et. al., *supra* note 25; Swim et. al., *supra* note 22; Swim & Sanna, *supra* note 55.

objective ratings were made, female applicants were given more positive evaluations for stereotypically feminine jobs, whereas male applicants were given more positive evaluations for stereotypically masculine jobs.[67] The reverse pattern was found for subjective ratings. Thus, the small effect sizes found in the Swim and Sanna meta-analysis may reflect judgments that a target's performance is either "good–for a woman" or "good–for a man."[68]

[4]　Employment Decisions

In addition to affecting attributions and evaluations, gender stereotypes may influence employment decisions. This claim is supported by numerous studies conducted in organizational settings as well as in research laboratories. It also is consistent with the perceptions of working women, including managers. For example, when Ragins et al. surveyed a sample of female managers about barriers to their advancement, they found that 52% of the women considered gender stereotypes held by men at work to be their primary barrier.[69]

Previously, we discussed several studies indicating that people believe that women possess fewer of the characteristics associated with occupational success and advancement than do men.[70] From a theoretical standpoint, these gender stereotypes are likely to affect numerous occupational decisions, including the initial decision about whether to hire a person for a particular job. Heilman proposed a lack of fit model, which asserts that male-dominated jobs become associated with masculine characteristics (e.g., masculine skills, abilities, and personality traits).[71] Those characteristics eventually become seen as predictors of success in those occupations. Thus, stereotypes about women conflict with beliefs about important employee characteristics, leading employers to believe that women are unqualified for or unlikely to succeed at stereotypically masculine occupations. Heilman's model therefore suggests that gender stereotypes lead to an increased likelihood of hiring men, especially for traditionally masculine jobs.

Two meta-analyses are relevant to Heilman's predictions. Both meta-analyses included studies in which students, employment recruiters, and other participants made employment decisions based on information (usually hypothetical resumes) describing applicants for specific jobs. A meta-analysis of 20 studies, conducted by Olian, Schwab, and Haberfield, assessed the effects of gender and job qualifications on hiring decisions.[72] They found that gender had a small-to-moderate effect ($d = .41$) on hiring decisions, with participants preferring to hire male applicants. However, job qualifications had a much larger effect ($d = 1.64$), with participants preferring to hire more highly qualified applicants. Another meta-analysis of 49 studies, conducted by Davi-

67.　Biernat & Manis, *supra* note 59; *see also* Biernat & Kobrynowicz, *supra* note 59.

68.　Swim & Sanna, *supra* note 55.

69.　B. R. Ragins et al., *Gender Gap in the Executive Suite: CEOs and Female Executives Report on Breaking the Glass Ceiling*, 12 ACAD. MGMT. EXECUTIVE 28 (1998).

70.　Glick, *supra* note 34; Heilman et al., *supra* note 37; Martell et al., *supra* note 37.

71.　Heilman, *supra* note 29; *see, e.g.*, Cejka & Eagly, *supra* note 36; Glick et al., *supra* note 36.

72.　J. D. Olian. et al., *The Impact of Applicant Gender Compared to Qualifications on Hiring Recommendations: A Meta–Analysis of Experimental Studies*, 41 ORGANIZATIONAL BEHAV. & HUM. DECISION PROCESSES 180 (1988).

son and Burke, evaluated the effect of job type (masculine, feminine) on employment decisions for male and female applicants.[73] The researchers found that employment decisions were more favorable when male candidates applied for stereotypically masculine jobs (d = .34) and when female candidates applied for stereotypically feminine jobs (d = .26). They also found some evidence that bias against female applicants was stronger when less information about the job candidates was available. Notably, none of these effects differed as a function of participant occupation (i.e., student v. employment recruiter) or gender.[74] Thus, taken together, the Olian et al. and Davison and Burke meta-analyses provide support for Heilman's lack of fit model, indicating that although there is some overall gender bias in employment decisions, discrimination is strongest when those decisions involve jobs stereotypically associated with the opposite gender or when little information about applicant qualifications is known.

The Olian et al. and Davison and Burke meta-analyses investigated the overall effects of gender, job qualifications, and job type on employment decisions. Additional studies have expanded this work by testing more nuanced predictions and by investigating the effects of specific kinds of gender stereotypes on hiring decisions.

Glick refined predictions about the effects of gender on hiring decisions by differentiating between gender-typed and sex-typed discrimination.[75] Gender-typed discrimination involves the use of gender stereotypes. It occurs when employers try to match people with masculine and feminine personality traits to stereotypically masculine and feminine jobs. In contrast, sex-typed discrimination refers to the effects of sex over and above stereotypes about personality traits. It occurs when employers hire men for jobs with high male:female sex ratios and women for jobs with high female:male sex ratios. Glick tested these two forms of discrimination by having business and career placement professionals rate the suitability of fictitious job applicants for a variety of jobs.[76] Evidence of both gender-typed and sex-typed discrimination was found in the professionals' hiring decisions. The professionals were more likely to recommend masculine applicants for masculine jobs and feminine applicants for feminine jobs, thus demonstrating gender-typed discrimination. However, there were additional effects of sex-typed discrimination in that the professionals were more likely to recommend men for jobs that were stereotypically masculine or had high male:female sex ratios and women for jobs that were stereotypically feminine or had high female:male sex ratios. Thus, Glick's work suggests that women may be doubly penalized when they apply for stereotypically masculine jobs.[77] They are less likely to be hired because of stereotypical assumptions about their personality traits, as well as their sex itself.

73. H. K. Davison & M. J. Burke, *Sex Discrimination in Simulated Employment Contexts: A Meta–Analytic Investigation*, 56 J. VOCATIONAL BEHAV. 225 (2000).

74. Olian et.al., *supra* note 72; Davison & Burke, *supra* note 73.

75. Glick, *supra* note 34; P. Glick et al., *What Mediates Sex Discrimination in Hiring Decisions?*, 55 J. PERSONALITY & SOC. PSYCHOL. 178 (1988).

76. Glick, *supra* note 34 (Study 2); Glick et. al., *supra* note 75.

77. Stereotypically masculine jobs are considered more prestigious; they also have higher salaries. Cejka & Eagly *supra* note 36; Glick, *supra* note 34 (Study 1); Glick et al., *supra* note 36.

Thus far, we have discussed research indicating that hiring decisions are influenced by common stereotypes about the general characteristics of women and men. Pratto et al. demonstrated that hiring decisions also can be influenced by less obvious gender stereotypes, such as stereotypes about the relative Social Dominance Orientation (SDO) of women and men.[78] SDO is an individual difference assessing the extent to which people accept the dominance of certain groups in society. People who are high in SDO believe in ideologies and practices that legitimize group inequalities, whereas people who are low in SDO believe that group inequalities should be eliminated. Notably, occupations vary along a dimension similar to SDO. Some occupations (e.g., corporate law) are hierarchy-enhancing, that is, they serve the interests of elite groups. Other occupations (e.g., public interest law) are hierarchy-attenuating, that is, they serve the needs of oppressed groups.

Pratto et al. demonstrated that hiring decisions are influenced by gender stereotypes suggesting that men are higher than women in SDO.[79] Participants read fictitious resumes and job descriptions, then matched the candidates with suitable jobs. The resumes varied on two dimensions. First, half of the applicants were male, and half of the applicants were female. Second, the applicants had qualifications that implied different levels of SDO (e.g., president of "Capital Operations" v. "Life Savers"). The job descriptions also were varied such that some jobs were hierarchy-enhancing and some jobs were hierarchy-attenuating. Pratto et al. found that both applicant gender and implied SDO influenced hiring decisions. Regardless of their own genders or levels of SDO, participants preferred to hire high SDO people for hierarchy enhancing jobs and low SDO people for hierarchy-attenuating jobs. In addition, about 50% more women than men were chosen for hierarchy-attenuating jobs, and about 50% more men than women were chosen for hierarchy-enhancing jobs. Thus, gender stereotypes about SDO affected hiring decisions over and above the apparent interests of the job candidates.

Research on the effects of gender stereotypes on hiring decisions seems to suggest that women who are seeking stereotypically masculine jobs, such as managerial positions, should try to show employers that they have stereotypically masculine characteristics (i.e., that they are agentic). However, this strategy carries some risks. Recent research suggests a backlash effect in which agentic women are penalized for violating the prescriptive stereotype that women should be communal.[80] Because women are expected to be nice, the social skills of agentic women are evaluated harshly. As a result, agentic women are less likely than equally agentic men to be hired for "feminized" managerial jobs (i.e., managerial positions requiring social skills).[81] Women applying for management positions therefore may find themselves in a bind with important career implications. To be seen as competent, they must portray themselves as agentic, yet to be seen as socially skilled, they cannot portray themselves as agentic.

---

78. F. Pratto et al., *The Gender Gap in Occupational Attainment: A Social Dominance Approach,* 72 J. PERSONALITY & SOC. PSYCHOL. 37 (1997).

79. *Id.* (Study 2).

80. L. A. Rudman, *Self-Promotion as a Risk Factor for Women: The Costs and Benefits of Counterstereotypical Impression Manage-* *ment,* 74 J. PERSONALITY & SOC. PSYCHOL. 629 (1998); L. A. Rudman & P. Glick, *Feminized Management and Backlash Toward Agentic Women: The Hidden Costs to Women of a Kinder, Gentler Image of Middle–Managers,* 77 J. PERSONALITY & SOC. PSYCHOL. 1004 (1999).

81. Rudman & Glick, *supra* note 80.

Finally, gender stereotypes may continue to affect employment decisions even after a person has been hired. A study by Larwood et al. showed that gender stereotypes affect decisions about job assignments, with male employees being more likely than female employees to be chosen for important assignments unless there is a clear "signal" that assigning the task to a woman would be beneficial (e.g., the client is a woman or is known for speaking out against discrimination).[82] This research implies that stereotypes about women's work abilities may be perpetuated because women are not given ample opportunities to demonstrate their skills in important contexts. Gender stereotypes also can affect the likelihood that women who allege to have been sexually harassed are believed. Burgess and Borgida presented students with hypothetical harassment scenarios that varied by type of harassment (i.e., unwanted sexual attention, gender harassment, sexual coercion), as well as the occupation of the woman who was harassed.[83] They found that people were more likely to believe that women with traditional (e.g., secretary) rather than non-traditional (e.g., steel worker) jobs had been sexually coerced. A subsequent study suggested that this effect was due to a mismatch between the stereotypes of non-traditional women and sexual harassment victims. Because the non-traditional women were considered stronger and less vulnerable, their claims of sexual coercion were less likely to be believed.[84]

[5] Descriptive vs. Prescriptive Stereotyping in the Workplace

A recent review by Burgess and Borgida suggested that descriptive and prescriptive gender stereotypes may have different effects on women in the workplace.[85] According to their analysis, descriptive stereotyping leads to gender discrimination when women are not hired or promoted because their stereotypical attributes do not match (usually masculine) employment criteria. Several of the studies discussed in the previous section support these findings of descriptive stereotyping.[86] Descriptive stereotyping in the workplace thus generally lead to legal claims of disparate impact (i.e., the use of practices that systematically disadvantage one class of people). In contrast, prescriptive stereotyping causes gender discrimination when female employees are sanctioned for violating expectations about how women should act (i.e., traditional gender roles). Notably, because success in many occupations is associated with agentic (hence masculine) behaviors, successful female employees may experience the effects of prescriptive stereotyping. In contrast to descriptive stereotyping, prescriptive stereotyping in the workplace generally leads to claims of disparate treatment (e.g., hostile environment harassment).

There are several important distinctions between workplace-relevant descriptive and prescriptive gender stereotyping. First, different groups of

82. L. Larwood et al., *Sex and Race Discrimination Resulting From Manager–Client Relationships: Applying the Rational Bias Theory of Managerial Discrimination*, 18 SEX ROLES 9 (1988).

83. D. Burgess & E. Borgida, *Sexual Harassment: An Experimental Test of Sex–Role Spillover Theory*, 23 PERSONALITY & SOC. PSYCHOL. BULL. 63 (1997).

84. D. Burgess & E. Borgida, *Refining Sex–Role Spillover Theory: The Role of Gender Subtypes and Harasser Attributions*, 15 SOC. COGNITION 291 (1998).

85. Burgess & Borgida, *supra* note 6.

86. Glick, *supra* note 34 (Study 2); Glick et al., *supra* note 75; Olian et al., *supra* note 72; Pratto et. al., *supra* note 78.

women may experience the two forms of stereotyping. Women who are stereotype-consistent are more likely to experience descriptive stereotyping because they are more likely to be considered poor fits for masculine-typed jobs.[87] In contrast, women who are stereotype-inconsistent are more likely to experience prescriptive stereotyping. Even though they may have proven themselves effective at their jobs, they still may be sanctioned for being "unfeminine."[88] Second, with respect to evaluations, descriptive stereotyping tends to lower judgments about a woman's competence, whereas prescriptive stereotyping often results in poor ratings on interpersonal skills (or simply general dislike).[89] Finally, descriptive stereotyping does not need to be conscious, nor does it require bias against or hostility to women. For example, judgments made by people with egalitarian beliefs still can be affected by cultural stereotypes about women's abilities. On the other hand, prescriptive stereotyping tends to be more conscious and bias-driven (e.g., designed to "keep women in their place").

[6]   Under What Circumstances are Gender Stereotypes Applied?

Decision-makers are more likely to rely on gender stereotypes when gender is salient, when they have little information on which to base a decision, when they are asked to evaluate individuals using subjective criteria, and when they work in a sexualized environment in which gender stereotypes are considered acceptable. In contrast, decision-makers are less likely to use gender stereotypes when they have adequate information, when they have ample time to make judgments, and when they are held accountable for their decisions (i.e., when they are motivated to be accurate).[90] Recent research also has examined the roles that individuating information and power play in determining the use of gender stereotypes.

[a]   The Role of Individuating Information in Gender Stereotyping

An important issue related to gender stereotyping involves the use of individuating information, that is, information about personal characteristics, such as background, personality traits, interests, and preferences. Early studies suggested that knowledge of individuating information could reduce or even eliminate the influence of gender stereotypes on judgments about that individual.[91] These studies have been misinterpreted as evidence that perceiv-

87.   Heilman, *supra* note 29.

88.   Burgess & Borgida, *supra* note 6 (suggesting that this distinction may help identify the most relevant parts of the gender stereotyping literature with respect to a particular gender discrimination or sexual harassment case).

89.   P. Glick et al., *The Two Faces of Adam: Ambivalent Sexism and Polarized Attitudes Toward Women*, 23 PERSONALITY & SOC. PSYCHOL. BULL. 1232 (1997); Heilman et. al., *supra* note 37; Rudman, *supra* note 80; Rudman & Glick, *supra* note 80.

90.   *See, e.g.,* S. L. Neuberg & S. T. Fiske, *Motivational Influences on Impression Forma-* tion: *Outcome Dependency, Accuracy–Driven Attention, and Individuating Processes*, 53 J. PERSONALITY & SOC. PSYCHOL. 431 (1987); R. F. Martell, *Sex Bias at Work: The Effects of Attentional and Memory Demands on Performance Ratings of Men and Women*, 21 J. APPLIED SOC. PSYCHOL. 1939 (1991); Martell, *supra* note 64; L. F. Pendry & C. N. Macrae, *What the Disinterested Perceiver Overlooks: Goal–Directed Social Categorization*, 22 PERSONALITY & SOC. PSYCHOL. BULL. 249 (1996).

91.   *See, e.g.,* A. Locksley et al., *Sex Stereotypes and Social Judgment*, 39 J. PERSONALITY & SOC. PSYCHOL. 821 (1980); A. Locksley et al., *Social Stereotypes and Judgments of Individuals: An Instance of the Base–Rate Fallacy*, 18 J.

ers will not use stereotypes as long as they have any form of individuating information about a person.[92] However, additional research and theory indicate that the effects of individuating information are considerably more complex.

Several cognitive processes work against the use of individuating information. Newer models of impression formation emphasize the primacy of category-based inferences.[93] When forming impressions, perceivers automatically assign individuals to existing social groups, such as women and men. The individuals' characteristics then are compared with the stereotypes associated with those groups. Individuating information is considered only if the individuals' characteristics are inconsistent with group stereotypes. Moreover, inconsistent individuating information still may be ignored if perceivers are not motivated or do not have the cognitive resources necessary to form an individualized impression of the person.[94] The mere process of trying to suppress a stereotype consumes cognitive resources, making it harder to process individuating information.[95]

Even when individuating information is considered, it might be processed in a biased manner. Without necessarily realizing it, perceivers tend to selectively process information about individuals that is consistent with group stereotypes,[96] while inhibiting information that is inconsistent with stereotypes.[97] Perceivers also use stereotypes when they interpret individuating information. For example, Kunda and Sherman–Williams found that participants who read about a housewife "hitting someone who annoyed her" imagined a mother spanking her child, whereas participants who read about a construction worker engaging in the same behavior imagined a man punching a co-worker.[98] Thus, people tend to interpret ambiguous or internally contradictory (i.e., mixed) individuating information in stereotype-consistent ways. Only individuating information that is truly unambiguous is seen as stereotype-disconfirming.[99] This process of biased information-processing is particularly insidious because people believe that they are judging others on the basis of personal characteristics, often unaware of the influence that stereotypes have on the interpretation of those characteristics.

EXPERIMENTAL SOC. PSYCHOL. 23 (1982); R. E. Nisbett et al., *The Dilution Effect: Non–Diagnostic Information Weakens the Implications of Diagnostic Information*, 13 COGNITIVE PSYCHOL. 248 (1981).

92. E. Borgida et al., *On the Courtroom Use and Misuse of Gender Stereotyping Research*, 51 J. SOC. ISSUES 181 (1995).

93. M. B. Brewer, *A Dual Process Model of Impression Formation, in* ADVANCES IN SOCIAL COGNITION 1 (R. Wyer & T. Srull eds., vol. 1, 1988); S. T. Fiske & S. L. Neuberg, *A Continuum of Impression Formation, From Category–Based to Individuating Processes: Influences of Information and Motivation on Attention and Interpretation, in* ADVANCES IN EXPERIMENTAL SOCIAL PSYCHOLOGY 1 (M. P. Zanna ed., vol. 23, 1990); *but see*, Z. Kunda & P. Thagard, *Forming Impressions From Stereotypes, Traits, and Behaviors: A Parallel–Constraint–Satisfaction Theory*, 103 PSYCHOL. REV. 284 (1996).

94. Martell, *supra* note 90.

95. C. N. Macrae et al., *On Resisting the Temptation for Simplification: Counterintentional Consequences of Stereotype Suppression for Social Memory*, 14 SOC. COGNITION 1 (1996).

96. G. V. Bodenhausen, *Stereotypic Biases in Social Decision Making and Memory: Testing Process Models of Stereotype Use*, 55 J. PERSONALITY & SOC. PSYCHOL. 726 (1988).

97. A. Dijksterhuis & A. van Knippenberg, *The Knife That Cuts Both Ways: Facilitated and Inhibited Access to Traits as a Result of Stereotype Activation*, 32 J. EXPERIMENTAL SOC. PSYCHOL. 271 (1996).

98. Z. Kunda & B. Sherman–Williams, *Stereotypes and the Construal of Individuating Information*, 19 PERSONALITY & SOC. PSYCHOL. BULL. 90 (1993).

99. *Id.*

Notably, even information that initially appears unambiguous may be construed as stereotype-consistent. Research has demonstrated that, when motivated to do so, people are able to employ a number of biased reasoning strategies in order to reach particular conclusions.[100] Thus, people who hear about a woman's quick rise to executive status may attribute her success to unstable or derogatory factors (e.g., that she slept her way to the top).[101]

Individuating information is most likely to influence a judgment when it is diagnostic (i.e., relevant to the decision). Thus, individuating information about previous job performance is more likely to influence employment decisions than is information about personal hobbies. Notably, gender also varies in perceived diagnosticity. Gender may be considered diagnostic for certain decisions (e.g., hiring for traditionally masculine or feminine jobs), but not for other decisions (e.g., hiring for gender-neutral jobs). The relative influence that gender stereotypes and individuating information have on decisions, therefore, depends on the perceived diagnosticity of each type of information to the judgment at hand.[102] For example, Heilman had MBA students evaluate applications for managerial positions that ostensibly were submitted by male or female applicants.[103] The applications contained job-relevant individuating information (i.e., business major, economics minor), job-irrelevant individuating information (i.e., biology major, political science minor), or no individuating information. Results indicated that the male and female candidates were seen as equally qualified when job-relevant individuating information was provided. The male candidate was preferred, however, when participants read job-irrelevant or no individuating information.

Non-diagnostic individuating information still may affect judgments, but through a different process, such as altering the degree to which an individual is seen as a representative member of a particular social group. To the extent that individuating information, regardless of its diagnosticity to a judgment, makes an individual seem less like a typical man or woman (e.g., finding out that a woman has worked in a sporting goods store), the information should decrease the use of global gender stereotypes in judgments about that person.[104] However, if non-diagnostic individuating information makes a person seem more like a typical man or woman (e.g., finding out that a woman was on the pep squad), it actually can increase use of gender stereotypes.[105]

Finally, recent evidence demonstrates that, even when individuating information eliminates the effects of stereotypes on judgments about a person's traits, it may not eliminate stereotypical expectations about that person's future behavior.[106] For example, information about a woman's job

---

100. For a review see, Z. Kunda, *The Case for Motivated Reasoning*, 108 Psychol. Bull. 480 (1990).

101. Borgida et. al., *supra* note 92.

102. J. Krueger & M. Rothbart, *Use of Categorical and Individuating Information in Making Inferences About Personality*, 55 J. Personality & Soc. Psychol. 187 (1988).

103. M. E. Heilman, *Information as a Deterrent Against Sex Discrimination: The Effects of Applicant Sex and Information Type on Preliminary Employment Decisions*, 33 Organizational Behav. & Hum. Performance 174 (1984).

104. Glick et. al., *supra* note 75; Nisbett et. al., *supra* note 91; E. Peters & M. Rothbart, *Typicality Can Create, Eliminate, and Reverse the Dilution Effect*, 26 Personality & Soc. Psychol. Bull. 177 (2000).

105. Glick et. al., *supra* note 77; Peters & Rothbart, *supra* note 104.

106. Z. Kunda et al., *Equal Ratings But Separate Meanings: Stereotypes and the Construal of Traits*, 72 J. Personality & Soc. Psychol. 720 (1997).

performance may lead evaluators to think she is assertive, but not change their expectation that she will act in a deferential manner in the future. Thus, the relationship between knowledge of individuating information and stereotype use is complex, depending on elements of the target, the perceiver, the individuating information, the relationship between the information and the group stereotype, and the particular decision being made.

[b]   The Role of Power in Gender Stereotyping

Fiske proposed a model asserting that people in high power positions are more likely to stereotype people in low power positions than vice versa. By definition, powerful individuals control the outcomes of less powerful individuals.[107] Because of their lack of control, low power individuals are motivated to pay careful attention to high power individuals. By forming accurate impressions of powerful people, low power individuals are better able to predict and control their own outcomes. In contrast, high power individuals do not need to pay as much attention to less powerful people. When they are in control, high power individuals can rely on stereotypes to guide their interactions. This model predicts that, when women occupy low power positions in organizations, they are likely to be perceived in a stereotypical manner by their male supervisors.

Support for this model has been demonstrated for both gender and non-gender stereotypes. Goodwin et al. assigned participants to either high power or low power positions, then had them read stereotype-consistent and inconsistent information about several men and women.[108] Results indicated participants assigned to low-power positions paid more attention to stereotype-inconsistent information than to stereotype-consistent information. However, participants in powerful positions attended more to stereotype-consistent information than to stereotype-inconsistent information. These findings suggest powerful individuals are likely to perceive less powerful individuals as stereotypical, even if they have stereotype-inconsistent characteristics or behaviors.

Another way in which power can affect impressions of women involves the relationship between power and sex. Recent research by Bargh et al. has demonstrated that some men have an automatic (i.e., non-conscious) cognitive association between power and sex.[109] For these men, being in a position of power automatically leads to thoughts about sex, which in turn might lead to sexually harassing behavior.

Bargh et al. used a priming paradigm to demonstrate that power could invoke thoughts about sex.[110] Participants were subliminally primed with words related to power, ambiguously sexual words, and neutral words. Following each prime, participants were shown a target word taken from the same

107. S.T. Fiske, *Controlling Other People: The Impact of Power on Stereotyping*, 48 AM. PSYCHOLOGIST, 621 (1993).

108. S. A. Goodwin et al., *Power and Motivated Impression Formation: How Powerholders Stereotype by Default and by Design* (1995) (unpublished manuscript, on file with University of Massachusetts at Amherst).

109. J. A. Bargh et al., *Attractiveness of the Underling: An Automatic Power–Sex Association and its Consequences for Sexual Harassment and Aggression*, 68 J. PERSONALITY & SOC. PSYCHOL. 768 (1995).

110. *Id.*

groups. The researchers found that men who scored high on the Likelihood to Sexually Harass (LSH) and the Attractiveness of Sexual Aggression (ASA) scales responded more quickly to the ambiguously sexual target words when they were preceded by power primes than when they were preceded with neutral primes.[111] Thus, for these men, there was an automatic association between power and sex. In a second study, the researchers found that power caused men who were high in ASA to interpret ambiguous aspects of the environment in a sexualized manner. These men reported greater attraction to a female confederate when they were primed with power words than when they were primed with neutral words. Notably, when asked to report the reasons for their attraction to the woman, the men were unaware of the influence of the power primes on their ratings.

Another study by Rudman and Borgida manipulated the power of male participants interviewing a female job candidate.[112] Half of the men interviewed the candidate under high power conditions (i.e., they were told that they would have the power to make a hiring decision). The other half of the men interviewed her under low power conditions (i.e., they were asked to help her with a practice interview). The researchers found that the men in the high power condition were more likely to make stereotypical judgments about the woman's qualifications and to treat her in a sexual manner than were the men in the low power condition.

These findings have important implications for the workplace. Specifically, for some men, simply occupying positions of power may activate sexual thoughts, leading them to interpret their environment in a sexualized way and apply sexually-oriented gender stereotypes to female coworkers. Such cognitions could lead to unwelcome sexual advances and harassment.

§ 11–2.4.3 Psychological Processes Related to Stereotyping

[1] Introduction

Stereotypes are formed from two normal cognitive processes: categorization and generalization. In order to simplify their complex environments, humans automatically categorize objects (including other people) into groups. Categorization leads to two types of biases. First, people show in-group favoritism, that is, they are positively biased toward members of their own groups when making evaluations and allocating resources. Second, members of social categories are assumed to share certain characteristics, which are cognitively represented as stereotypes. Because of its salience, biological sex is one of the most common means of categorizing people. As a result, gender stereotypes frequently are formed as cognitive mechanisms for storing and applying generalized information about women and men.

Over the last decade, psychological processes related to stereotyping have received considerable theoretical and empirical attention. Researchers have continued to investigate the process of categorization. In addition, research

---

111. J. B. Pryor, *Sexual Proclivities in Men*, 17 Sex Roles 269 (1987); N. M. Malamuth, *The Attraction to Sexual Aggression Scale: Part One*, 26 J. Sex Res. 26 (1989a); N.M. Malamuth, *The Attraction to Sexual Ag-*gression Scale: Part Two*, 26 J. Sex Res. 324 (1989b).

112. Rudman & Borgida, *supra* note 10.

has expanded to consider two complementary processes: stereotype activation and stereotype inhibition. Stereotype activation is the process by which information related to stereotypes is "turned on" in the brain, that is, the process by which stereotypes that are stored in the brain become capable of influencing thought and behavior. In contrast, stereotype inhibition is a control process through which the brain attempts to suppress or counteract the use stereotypes. Research in all of these areas will be discussed in this section.

[2] Categorization

It is well-established that people routinely categorize other individuals into various social groups, such as race, gender, age, and occupation. Recent research, therefore, has focused on understanding more complex categorization processes. Two of these issues are discussed in this section: 1) How likely are people to categorize women and men according to gender?, and 2) When do people use broad categories (e.g., women) versus more specific categories (e.g., subtypes, such as businesswomen)?

[a] Likelihood of Categorization

Given that categorization is a necessary precursor to stereotyping, it is important to know whether certain individuals are more likely to be categorized (and therefore stereotyped) than are others. Recent evidence suggests that certain social groups function as cognitive "defaults" or assumptions. In the domain of gender, "male" is the default assumption for "person." When people are given information about an unknown individual (e.g., Professor Smith), they tend to assume that the person is a man. Groups that differ from defaults are "marked" because of their distinctiveness. As a result, their group membership takes on enhanced importance. For example, some people emphasize the gender of women, referring to female internists as "lady doctors" instead of simply doctors.[113]

A research paradigm known as the social verification task compares the time it takes people to categorize individuals according to different social groupings (e.g., gender, race). Research using this paradigm has provided evidence that gender is considered more important for women than for men. Because "female" is a marked (i.e., distinctive) category, people are able to make gender categorizations more quickly for female targets than for male targets.[114]

A recent study by Zárate and Sandoval used an expanded version of the social verification task to investigate the effects of occupational context on categorizations of men and women.[115] Participants in the study categorized male and female targets pictured in traditionally male (e.g., mechanic, judge) and traditionally female (e.g., hairdresser, teacher) professions according to gender and occupation. The study found that, in the presence of occupational

---

113. Fiske, *supra* note 28.

114. M. A. Zárate & P. Sandoval, *The Effects of Contextual Cues on Making Occupational and Gender Categorizations*, 34 Brit. J. Soc. Psychol. 353 (1995); M. A. Zárate & E. R.

Smith, *Person Categorization and Stereotyping*, 8 Soc. Cognition 161 (1990).

115. Zárate & Sandoval, *supra* note 114.

information, people are equally quick to categorize male and female targets according to gender. However, gender differences emerge for occupational categorizations. Male targets are more quickly categorized as workers when they are shown in traditionally male occupations. In contrast, female targets are more quickly categorized as workers when they are shown in traditionally female occupations.

In sum, categorization processes may make women both more likely than men to be the target of negative stereotyping and less likely than men to be the target of positive stereotyping. Research suggests that, in the absence of contextual information, women are categorized according to gender more quickly than are men. Therefore, women generally are more likely than men to be perceived in a stereotypical manner (i.e., as communal rather than agentic). Moreover, in comparison to men, women are more quickly categorized as workers in traditionally feminine roles, but less quickly categorized as workers in traditionally masculine roles. As a result, even when women work in non-stereotypical professions, people are slower to assign them to those categories and thus less likely to perceive them as agentic.[116]

[b]   Broad versus Specific Categories

As discussed earlier, subtypes are clusters of individuals within a broader social group who possess non-stereotypical characteristics. Because the communal characteristics associated with women are different from the more agentic characteristics associated with good workers, women in the workplace may benefit from categorization at the subtype level.[117] The subtype for non-traditional (business) women includes many of the characteristics associated with occupational success, such as intelligence and confidence.[118] Thus, women in workplace settings who are categorized as businesswomen may be less likely to be the target of gender stereotyping.

A recent study by Pendry and Macrae demonstrated the importance that accountability plays in motivating such non-stereotypical perceptions of a businesswoman.[119] In their study, college student participants watched a short videotape that depicted a woman at work. In an accountable condition, participants were instructed to form an impression of the woman that they later could justify to a third party. In two unaccountable conditions, participants were told to focus on either the woman's physical characteristics or on

116. A related body of research on crossed categorization has examined how people categorize and evaluate individuals who are members of multiple social groups (e.g., someone who is a woman, a Latina, a mother, and a partner at a law firm). Several crossed categorization studies have been interpreted as evidence that the use of multiple social categories may lead to reduced stereotyping and bias. M. J. Migdal et al., *The Effects of Crossed Categorization on Intergroup Evaluations: A Meta-Analysis*, 37 BRIT. J. SOC. PSYCHOL. 303 (1998); L. M. Urban & N. Miller, *A Theoretical Analysis of Crossed Categorization Effects: A Meta-Analysis*, 74 J. PERSONALITY & SOC. PSYCHOL. 894 (1998); *but see* T. K. Vescio et al., *Perceiving and Responding to Multiple Categorizable Indi-*

viduals: Cognitive Processes and Affective Intergroup Bias, in SOCIAL IDENTITY AND SOCIAL COGNITION 111 (M. Hogg & D. Abrams eds., 1999). Although crossed categorization is relevant to the use of gender stereotypes in the workplace, we do not review it further because most of the relevant studies have focused on social groups other than gender. Interested readers are referred to the articles cited above.

117. Glick, *supra* note 34; Heilman et al., *supra* note 38; Heilman et al., *supra* note 37; Martell et al., *supra* note 37.

118. Deaux et al., *supra* note 43; Six & Eckes, *supra* note 43.

119. Pendry & Macrae, *supra* note 90.

the clarity of the video. After viewing the video, the participants completed an ostensibly unrelated second experiment involving a computerized response latency measure. The words used in the task were words that previous research participants had rated as characteristic of either "women" (e.g., caring, nurturing) or "businesswomen" (e.g., independent, competitive), but not both. Pendry and Macrae found that accountable participants had significantly shorter latencies for "businesswomen" words than for "women" words, whereas participants in the non-accountable conditions displayed the reverse pattern. These results indicate that the accountable participants categorized the woman as a businesswoman, but the unaccountable participants categorized her as simply a woman. Notably, even the accountable participants showed some facilitation for words related to "women" (as compared to a no video control condition). Thus, even though accountability can promote subtyping, it does not completely eliminate categorization at the broader level.

[3] Stereotype Activation

As discussed earlier, research has shown that people associate communal characteristics with women and agentic characteristics with men. These stereotypes are stored in memory and can be retrieved when necessary (e.g., when directly asked). However, many instances of stereotyping and discrimination may occur outside of conscious awareness. For example, a supervisor may rely on gender stereotypes during a promotion decision without being aware of doing so. As a result, it is necessary to understand stereotype activation, that is, the process by which stereotypes stored in memory become capable of influencing thought and behavior. In addition, it is important to understand implicit (also known as automatic) stereotyping processes, that is, the ways in which stereotypes can affect judgments and behavior without conscious awareness.

Research on stereotype activation and implicit stereotyping frequently uses response latency measures. These measures are used because they allow researchers to assess the speed with which individuals respond to different types of stimuli (e.g., stereotypically feminine and masculine words) after exposure to various primes. Faster response times to stereotype-relevant words reveal stereotype activation and usage. Moreover, because the judgments have no overt connection to stereotypes (e.g., deciding whether strings of letters form words), participants remain unaware that stereotypes may be influencing their responses.

This body of research provides considerable evidence that stereotypes are automatically activated when people are exposed to group-relevant cues.[120] For example, Rudman and Borgida conducted a study in which male students completed three separate tasks.[121] First, the men participated in a "market research" task during which they evaluated a series of television commercials. In the experimental condition, the commercials included stereotypical images

120. *See* J. A. Bargh, *The Automaticity of Everyday Life, in* Advances in Social Cognition 1 (R.S. Wyer, Jr. ed., vol. 10, 1997); G. V. Bodenhausen & C. N. Macrae, *Stereotype Activation and Inhibition, in* Advances in Social Cognition 1 (R. S. Wyer, Jr. ed., vol. 11, 1998);

Fiske, *supra* note 28; J. L. Hilton & W. von Hippel, *Stereotypes*, 47 Ann. Rev. Psychol. 237 (1996).

121. Rudman & Borgida, *supra* note 10.

of women as sexual objects (e.g., the Swedish Bikini Team). In the control condition, the commercials had stereotype-neutral portrayals of women. The second component of the study involved a response latency task in which the men made word/non-word judgments about words that either were sexist (e.g., bimbo, playboy), non-sexist (e.g., mother, sister), ambiguously sexual (e.g., cherry, strip), or neutral (e.g., book). In the third task, the men were asked to interview a female job applicant. The results of the response latency task indicated that watching the sexist commercials activated the men's stereotypes about women as sexual objects. Specifically, the men who saw the sexist commercials responded more quickly to the sexist words than to the non-sexist or neutral words. Moreover, they were more likely than the men who saw the non-sexist commercials to make sexual interpretations of the ambiguously sexual words.

The automatic activation of gender stereotypes can lead people to use those stereotypes without being aware of it. Research by Rudman used the IAT to demonstrate that people can categorize names and traits more quickly when they are gender stereotype-consistent (e.g., female names and traits related to warmth; male names and traits related to potency) than when they are gender stereotype-inconsistent (e.g., male names and traits related to warmth).[122] This pattern indicates that, even at an implicit level, people associate women with communal traits and men with agentic traits. In a similar vein, research by Banaji and Hardin used a lexical decision task in which participants were primed with words that were stereotypically associated with either women or men (e.g., stereotypically feminine or masculine jobs), then asked to make judgments about pronouns (e.g., whether the pronoun was masculine or feminine or whether a word actually was a pronoun).[123] Results indicated that participants made those judgments more quickly when the gender of the prime matched the gender of the pronoun (e.g., nurse-she) than when the genders of the prime and the pronoun were mismatched (e.g., mechanic-she). Again, this pattern indicates that people automatically use gender stereotypes when making judgments, even when those judgments are not gender-relevant (e.g., pronoun/non-pronoun judgments).

Additional research suggests that the applicability of an activated stereotype to a given judgment is an important determinant of its usage.[124] When stereotypes are applicable to a given decision, they are likely to affect that judgment. For example, if a person is primed with words related to the trait, such as dependence, before evaluating a woman, the woman is likely to be seen as more dependent than she otherwise would be. However, if activated stereotypes are not applicable to a judgment, they are unlikely to affect it. Thus, because women are not expected to be aggressive, primes related to

122. Rudman & Glick, *supra* note 13; L. A. Rudman et al., *Implicit Self–Concept and Evaluative Implicit Gender Stereotypes: Self and Ingroup Share Desirable Traits*, PERSONALITY & SOC. PSYCHOL. BULL. (forthcoming 2001); Rudman & Kilianski, *supra* note 12.

123. M. R. Banaji & C. Hardin, *Automatic Stereotyping*, 7 PSYCHOL. SCI. 136 (1996); *see also* M. R. Banaji & A. G. Greenwald, *Implicit Gen-der Stereotyping in Judgments of Fame*, 68 J. PERSONALITY & SOC. PSYCHOL. 181 (1995).

124. M. R. Banaji et al., *Implicit Stereotyping in Person Judgment*, 65 J. PERSONALITY & SOC. PSYCHOL. 272 (1993); C. D. Hardin & A. J. Rothman, *Rendering Accessible Information Relevant: The Applicability of Everyday Life*, in ADVANCES IN SOCIAL COGNITION 143 (R.S. Wyer, Jr. ed., vol. 10, 1997).

aggressiveness are unlikely to affect evaluations of a woman.[125] This pattern suggests that exposure to gender stereotypes about women are likely to affect judgments about women on stereotype-relevant dimensions (e.g., kindness, job-related competence), but not on stereotype-irrelevant dimensions (e.g., musical ability).

Notably, automatically activated stereotypes can affect judgments about and behavior toward women in job-relevant contexts. In the previously described study by Rudman and Borgida, male participants interviewed a female job candidate, then made judgments about her suitability for the job.[126] Analyses of the men's behavior during the interviews showed that the stereotype-primed men sat significantly closer to the female job candidate during the interview and also asked her more sexist questions than did the men whose stereotypes were not primed. Moreover, when asked to evaluate the woman, the stereotype-primed men judged the woman to be more friendly but less competent (i.e., more stereotypical) than did the other men. They also remembered more about the woman's appearance than about her qualifications. The study therefore demonstrated that gender stereotypes that are automatically activated by situational factors such as sexist materials in the workplace can affect the way women are perceived and treated in occupational settings.

[4] Stereotype Inhibition

A question that inevitably arises when considering research on stereotype activation involves the suppression of stereotypes. Given the abundance of research showing that stereotypes that are automatically activated in response to relevant cues affect our judgments and behaviors, is it possible for individuals to control their use of stereotypes? Currently, a considerable amount of research attention is being focused on processes related to the stereotype inhibition.[127] This research has focused primarily upon two related issues: 1) when are stereotypes unintentionally inhibited (i.e., what are the conditions under which stereotypes are not activated)?, and 2) how can individuals control their own use of stereotypes?

[a] Unintentional Stereotype Inhibition

With respect to the first question, research suggests that there are a few conditions under which stereotypes are not activated. Macrae et al. propose a single category dominance model, which asserts that two or more categories cannot be activated simultaneously.[128] When an individual belongs to two or more social groups, he or she is categorized according to the group that is most salient in the given situation. For example, Macrae et al. found that a

---

125. Banaji et al., *supra* note 124.

126. Rudman & Borgida, *supra* note 10.

127. Stereotypes can be inhibited at the cognitive level (e.g., trying to eliminate the influence of gender stereotypes on performance evaluations), as well as at the behavioral level (e.g., avoiding sexist remarks). Both types of inhibition can be affected by egalitarian social norms and personal motivation to be unbiased.

See Bodenhausen & Macrae, *supra* note 120. Consistent with the chapter's emphasis on judgmental processes, we focus here on stereotype inhibition at the cognitive level.

128. C. N. Macrae et al., *The Dissection of Selection in Person Perception: Inhibitory Processes in Social Stereotyping*, 69 J. PERSONALITY & SOC. PSYCHOL. 397 (1995); *see also*, Bodenhausen & Macrae, *supra* note 120.

Chinese woman is categorized as a Chinese person if she is using chopsticks, but as a woman if she is applying lipstick. An important implication of this model is that the unused category is actively inhibited. Thus, after categorizing a Chinese woman as a woman, participants actually became slower to respond to words related to Chinese individuals.

Macrae et al.'s model implies that women will not be subjected to gender stereotypes as long as they are categorized along non-gender dimensions.[129] However, other evidence suggests that this outcome may not be inevitable. Earlier, we discussed research showing that there are established subtypes and subgroups for the broad categories of men and women. For example, people consistently associate traits with the subtype of "business women" that they do not associate with women as a whole.[130] To the extent that people can categorize women into subtypes or subgroups, like "business women," that account for their multiple group memberships, they may not completely inhibit the gender stereotype.[131]

Another circumstance under which stereotypes may not be activated involves cognitive load. Although people are more likely to use stereotypes when their cognitive resources are taxed (e.g., when they are trying to solve a complex problem), it appears that at least some cognitive resources may be required to activate stereotypes.[132] Thus, cognitively busy individuals may not be able to activate a stereotype in response to a relevant cue. However, recent research by Spencer et al. suggests that when a person feels threatened (e.g., by negative feedback), stereotypes can be activated even under conditions of cognitive load.[133] This finding suggests that busy decision-makers still may activate gender stereotypes when they have reason to do so (e.g., when making judgments about women whose success they find threatening).

[b]   Intentional Stereotype Suppression

A related issue involves the ability of individuals to control their own use of gender (and other) stereotypes. Research suggests that the intentional stereotype suppression is a difficult process that can occur only under certain circumstances. Further, recent research has documented a rebound effect, in which stereotype use actually increases when a person ceases active efforts to inhibit stereotypes.

Recent theories emphasize that the use of stereotypes can be reduced or eliminated through controlled processing, that is, careful, deliberative thought.[134] However, two elements are required for controlled processing to occur. First, a person needs enough cognitive resources (i.e., mental energy) to be able to engage in deliberative processing. Second, a person must be

---

129. Macrae et al., *supra* note 128; Bodenhausen & Macrae, *supra* note 120.

130. Deaux et. al., *supra* note 43; Six & Eckes, *supra* note 43.

131. Bodenhausen & Macrae, *supra* note 120; Pendry & Macrae, *supra* note 90.

132. D. T. Gilbert & J. G. Hixon, *The Trouble of Thinking: Activation and Application of Stereotypic Beliefs*, 60 J. PERSONALITY & SOC. PSYCHOL. 509 (1991).

133. S. J. Spencer et al., *Automatic Activation of Stereotypes: The Role of Self–Image Threat*, 24 PERSONALITY & SOC. PSYCHOL. BULL. 1139 (1998).

134. *See, e.g.*, Brewer, *supra* note 95; P. G. Devine, *Stereotypes and Prejudice: Their Automatic and Controlled Components*, 56 J. PERSONALITY & SOC. PSYCHOL. 5 (1989); Fiske & Neuberg, *supra* note 93.

motivated to undertake this more effortful processing. Thus, stereotype suppression requires both cognitive ability and motivation. Consistent with this analysis, a series of response latency experiments conducted by Blair and Banaji found that gender stereotypes consistently were activated in situations where participants had high cognitive loads and little motivation to avoid the use of stereotypes.[135] Stereotype activation was reduced, though not eliminated, when participants were motivated to avoid stereotyping, but had high cognitive loads. Finally, the activation of gender stereotypes was eliminated when participants were motivated to avoid the use of stereotypes and had light cognitive loads. This research therefore indicates that the activation of gender stereotypes can be controlled, but doing so requires cognitive resources and motivation that may not be present in many situations.

Moreover, recent evidence suggests that attempts to suppress stereotypes often lead to rebound effects in which stereotype use increases once active suppression efforts stop.[136] For example, Wegner et al. asked participants to complete sentences that could be finished in either sexist or non-sexist ways (e.g., "Women who go out with lots of men are . . .").[137] One group of participants was instructed to suppress the use of sexist responses, while another group was not. In addition, the participants completed the task either with or without time pressure. When the sentences were rated for sexist content, the researchers found that the participants who were instructed to suppress sexist responses were able to do so when there was no time pressure. However, when time pressure was imposed, undermining suppression efforts, participants who were trying to inhibit sexist responses actually made more sexist sentence completions than did the control participants who were not trying to inhibit sexist comments. Thus, the act of stereotype suppression can backfire, leading to increased use of stereotypes when active suppression efforts are interrupted.

As a whole, the research on stereotype inhibition and suppression suggests that, although stereotypes may be unintentionally inhibited under certain circumstances (e.g., multiple group memberships), the more likely path to reduced stereotype use involves personal control efforts. Fortunately, under certain circumstances, individuals are able to reduce or even eliminate their use of gender (and other) stereotypes. However, many people may lack either the motivation or the cognitive resources needed to effectively inhibit stereotypes. Moreover, even when stereotype suppression initially is successful, a backlash can occur, actually increasing the use of stereotypes after active inhibition efforts end. This research therefore suggests that controlling the use of gender stereotypes in busy workplace environments may be very difficult, indeed.

§ 11–2.4.4 Individual Differences in the Use of Gender Stereotypes

Another important issue related to gender stereotyping involves individual differences in usage. Specifically, research suggests that some types of

135. I. V. Blair & M. R. Banaji, *Automatic and Controlled Processes in Stereotype Priming*, 70 J. PERSONALITY & SOC. PSYCHOL. 1126 (1996).

136. *See,* D. M. Wegner & J. A. Bargh, *Control and Automaticity in Social Life, in* HANDBOOK OF SOCIAL PSYCHOLOGY 446 (D.T. Gil-

bert, S.T. Fiske, & G. Lindzey eds., 4th ed. vol. 1, 1998).

137. D.M. Wegner et al., On Trying Not to be Sexist (1996) (unpublished manuscript, on file with authors).

people are more likely than others to use gender stereotypes or show gender bias. This section discusses two individual differences that are related to gender stereotyping and bias: Right Wing Authoritarianism and Ambivalent Sexism.

[1] Right Wing Authoritarianism

An individual difference known as Right Wing Authoritarianism (RWA) is characterized by three qualities: Conventionalism (i.e., endorsement of traditional norms and values), authoritarian submission (i.e., submission to authority), and authoritarian aggression (i.e., the tendency to aggress against non-conventional individuals).[138] Accordingly, people who are high in RWA should endorse traditional gender roles (conventionalism) and therefore disapprove of non-traditional women (authoritarian aggression).

A study by Haddock and Zanna found that people who were low and high in RWA did not differ in their evaluations of either women as a whole or housewives.[139] However, men who were high in RWA rated feminists significantly less favorably than they rated housewives. Moreover, the ratings of feminists given by high RWA men were significantly lower than the evaluations of feminists given by any other group of participants. The denigration of feminists by men who were high in RWA may have been partially due to two factors. First, in men, high RWA was associated with less favorable symbolic beliefs about feminists. For example, men who were high in RWA believed that feminists do not promote equality or freedom and that they violate traditional family values. Second, high RWA men believed that feminists hold values different from their own, a belief that is threatening to the conventionalism of people who are high in RWA.

[2] Ambivalent Sexism

Traditionally, sexism (i.e., bias against women) has been viewed as a unitary construct. However, a recent theoretical model known as Ambivalent Sexism Theory identifies three separate motivations underlying sexism.[140] Paternalism refers to a tendency to deal with women as if they were children, gender differentiation pertains to a motivation to make distinctions between men and women, and heterosexuality refers to the tendency to view relationships between men and women as different from other relationships. Importantly, each of these three sexist motivations can be either hostile or benevolent. Paternalism can result from either a desire to dominate or a desire to protect, gender differentiation can reflect either a competitive orientation or a view that men and women are complementary to each other, and heterosexuality can be viewed either with hostility or as a source of intimacy.[141]

---

138. B. ALTEMEYER, RIGHT-WING AUTHORITARIANISM (1981); B. ALTEMEYER, ENEMIES OF FREEDOM: UNDERSTANDING RIGHT-WING AUTHORITARIANISM (1988).

139. Haddock & Zanna, *supra* note 47.

140. S. T. Fiske & P. Glick, *Ambivalence and Stereotypes Cause Sexual Harassment: A Theory With Implications for Organizational Change*, 51 J. SOC. ISSUES 97 (1995); P. Glick &

S. T. Fiske, *The Ambivalent Sexism Inventory: Differentiating Hostile and Benevolent Sexism*, 70 J. PERSONALITY & SOC. PSYCHOL. 491 (1996).

141. Fiske & Glick, *supra* note 140, suggested that different subtypes of women may be subjected to different sexist motivations. Non-traditional women may experience bias that is based on competitive gender differentiation and domination-oriented paternalism. In

As a result, Glick and Fiske assert that sexism actually consists of two separate components. Hostile sexism involves "sexist antipathy toward women based on an ideology of male dominance, male superiority, and a hostile form of sexuality (in which women are treated merely as sexual objects)."[142] In contrast, benevolent sexism involves "subjectively positive, though sexist, attitudes that include protectiveness toward women, positively valenced stereotypes of women (e.g., nurturance), and a desire for heterosexual intimacy."[143] Notably, people can have both hostile and benevolent motives for sexism, creating ambivalent forms of sexism. For example, men can desire sexual intimacy with women (benevolent heterosexuality) while still considering them to be unwelcome competitors in the workplace (hostile gender differentiation).

Ambivalent sexism theory has been validated in numerous cultures around the world.[144] Notably, Glick and his colleagues have demonstrated that men's levels of ambivalent sexism are associated with their stereotypes and attitudes about women.[145] Men who are high in ambivalent sexism spontaneously classify women into extremely positive (e.g., sex object) and negative (e.g., "bitch") subtypes.[146] Breaking down ambivalent sexism, hostile sexism is correlated with negative stereotypes and attitudes about women (especially non-traditional women), whereas benevolent sexism is correlated with positive stereotypes and attitudes about women (especially traditional women).[147] However, it is important to note that the positive stereotypes associated with benevolent sexism reflect women's supposedly communal nature, not their workplace competence.[148] Thus, men who are high on either type of ambivalent sexism are likely to subscribe to stereotypes that are detrimental to women.

§ 11–2.4.5 Accuracy of Gender Stereotypes

The final issue that we will address in our research summary involves the accuracy of gender stereotypes, specifically, the frequent claim that gender stereotypes reflect actual differences between women and men. Although gender stereotypes are overgeneralized beliefs about women and men, their content does not, by definition, need to be inaccurate. However, there is little research evidence demonstrating that the stereotypes that men are agentic and women are communal are accurate. In fact, substantial research indicates that the differences between women and men in cognitive abilities, personality traits, and vocational interests and abilities are much smaller than are the differences within each gender on those characteristics.[149]

contrast, traditional women may be subjected to protective paternalism. Finally, bias against sex objects may be based upon benevolent or hostile heterosexual motives.

142. Fiske & Glick, *supra* note 140, at 96.

143. *Id.*

144. P. Glick et. al., *Beyond Prejudice as Simple Antipathy: Hostile and Benevolent Sexism Across Cultures*, 79 J. PERSONALITY & SOC. PSYCHOL. 473 (2000).

145. Glick et al., *supra* note 89; Glick & Fiske, *supra* note 140.

146. Glick et al., *supra* note 89.

147. *Id*; Glick & Fiske, *supra* note 140.

148. *See also* Eagly & Mladinic, *supra* note 32.

149. *See* J. S. Hyde & L. A. Frost, *Meta-Analysis in the Psychology of Women, in* HANDBOOK ON THE PSYCHOLOGY OF WOMEN 67 (F. Denmark & M. Paludi eds.,1993).

In recent years, there has been a resurgence in interest about the accuracy of stereotypes.[150] Some social scientists have asserted that stereotypes (both gender-relevant and non-gender-relevant) may be more accurate than previously assumed.[151] This assertion is supported by research comparing people's beliefs about men and women with objective indicators of the characteristics that men and women actually possess. For example, Swim conducted two studies comparing people's perceptions of gender differences with meta-analytic findings about gender differences on 17 characteristics, representing a number of cognitive abilities, traits, and social behaviors (e.g., math ability, aggression).[152] For each characteristic, participants estimated the magnitude and direction of the average difference between men and women. In both studies, perceived and actual differences were highly correlated. Moreover, when participants' beliefs were erroneous, they tended to underestimate actual gender differences and also to favor women rather than men.[153]

There is, however, an important limitation to the conclusions that can be drawn from this research. Stereotype accuracy can be conceptualized in several ways.[154] Research comparing people's beliefs about women and men with documented gender differences addresses a particular question about stereotype accuracy: Whether the content of stereotypes reflects overall differences between men and women. It does not address a second question related to stereotype accuracy: Whether people are able to apply stereotypes to specific individuals who may or may not have average characteristics. Some theorists believe that application accuracy is more important than content accuracy.[155] Strictly speaking, there are no negative consequences to simply having inaccurate beliefs (content) about the average differences between women and men. Rather, it is the use of stereotypes in judgments about specific individuals that has the potential to harm members of stereotyped groups. Because of individual variability, a given stereotype cannot be true for all members of a group. As a result, the use of any stereotype in relation to specific individuals inevitably leads to unfair (i.e., inaccurate) outcomes. As seen throughout this review, gender stereotypes frequently influence the way women are judged and treated, even when those women have non-stereotypical characteristics.[156] Thus, "the primary source of inaccuracy in gender

150. STEREOTYPE ACCURACY: TOWARD APPRECIATING GROUP DIFFERENCES (Y. Lee, L. Jussim, & C.R. McCauley eds., 1995).

151. L. Jussim et al., *Why Study Stereotype Accuracy and Inaccuracy?*, in STEREOTYPE ACCURACY 3 (Y. Lee, L. Jussim, & C.R. McCauley eds., 1995); V. Ottati & Y. Lee, *Accuracy: A Neglected Component of Stereotype Research, in* STEREOTYPE ACCURACY: TOWARD APPRECIATING GROUP DIFFERENCES 29 (Y. Lee, L. Jussim, & C.R. McCauley eds., 1995); C. R. McCauley, *Are Stereotypes Exaggerated?: A Sampling of Racial, Gender, Academic, Occupational, and Political Stereotypes, in* STEREOTYPE ACCURACY: TOWARD APPRECIATING GROUP DIFFERENCES 215 (Y. Lee, L. Jussim, & C.R. McCauley eds., 1995).

152. J. Swim, *Perceived Versus Meta–Analytic Effect Sizes: An Assessment of the Accuracy of Gender Stereotypes*, 66 J. PERSONALITY & SOC. PSYCHOL. 21 (1994).

153. See also, J. A. Hall & J. D. Carter, *Gender-Stereotype Accuracy as an Individual Difference*, 77 J. PERSONALITY & SOC. PSYCHOL. 350 (1999); C. L. Martin, *A Ratio Measure of Sex Stereotyping*, 52 J. PERSONALITY & SOC. PSYCHOL. 489 (1987); McCauley, *supra* note 151.

154. See, e.g., C. M. Judd & B. Park, *Definition and Assessment of Accuracy in Social Stereotypes*, 100 PSYCHOL. REV. 109 (1993); C. Stangor, *Content and Application Inaccuracy in Social Stereotyping, in* STEREOTYPE ACCURACY: TOWARD APPRECIATING GROUP DIFFERENCES 275 (Y. Lee, L. Jussim, & C.R. McCauley eds., 1995).

155. Stangor, *supra* note 154.

156. See, e.g., Eagly et al., *supra* note 25; Glick, *supra* note 34; Glick et al., *supra* note 75; Olian et al., *supra* note 72; Pratto et. al., *supra* note 78; Swim et. al., *supra* note 50; Swim & Sanna, *supra* note 55.

stereotyping may result from inappropriate application of stereotypes to particular individuals ... rather than from overestimating average differences between women and men."[157]

§ 11–2.5 Areas of Agreement and Disagreement

In the previous section, we reviewed a considerable amount of research addressing five major issues related to gender stereotypes: Content, application, psychological processes, individual differences, and accuracy. In this section, we will highlight the areas of that research that we believe are generally agreed upon by the social science community, as well as indicate the areas that are considered less conclusive.

§ 11–2.5.1 Areas of Agreement

There is considerable agreement[158] in the social science community about the content of gender stereotypes (i.e., that women are seen as communal and men are seen as agentic), as well as the existence of subtypes and subgroups. There also is substantial agreement that these gender stereotypes have small but consistent effects on judgments of women and men (including evaluations, attributions, and employment decisions), particularly when women and men act in stereotype-inconsistent ways. Moreover, there is agreement that gender stereotypes are more likely to be used in certain circumstances, such as when gender is salient and when decision-makers are not motivated to make accurate judgments. Social scientists agree on several psychological processes related to gender stereotyping, in particular, that people automatically categorize others according to social group, that gender is a fundamental dimension of categorization, and that categorization can lead to stereotype activation, of which individuals may be unaware. Finally, there is consensus that certain individual differences influence the use of gender stereotypes.

§ 11–2.5.2 Areas of Disagreement

Despite the considerable amount of consensus, there are several issues related to the use of gender stereotypes on which there is disagreement. As noted in the section on methodology, some scholars believe that laboratory research on gender stereotyping is not able to inform our understanding of the ways that women and men are treated in organizations. However, as mentioned earlier, this view is not common among social scientists. Most researchers believe that laboratory studies are relevant to "real world" contexts. This position is supported by research indicating that the patterns of results found in laboratory studies also are seen in organizational contexts.

More substantial disagreements about gender stereotyping tend to involve the specifics of the psychological processes that are involved in the use of stereotypes. First, there is disagreement about the processes involved in categorizing and stereotyping individuals who are members of multiple social groups. Additional research is needed to determine whether certain categories are given priority in categorization, whether the use of certain categories

---

157. Swim, *supra* note 152, at 33.

158. Agreement is assessed on the basis of factors such as consistency of findings, articles published in peer reviewed journals, and the conclusions of qualitative literature reviews and meta-analyses.

inhibits the use of other categories, and whether the use of multiple categories reduces stereotyping and bias. Second, although researchers agree that prejudiced individuals are more likely to use stereotypes when consciously making judgments, there is a lack of agreement about the relationship between overt prejudice (i.e., sexism) and automatic stereotype activation. Further research is needed to make definitive conclusions about whether prejudiced individuals are more likely to automatically activate group stereotypes in response to relevant cues.[159] Third, more research on stereotype inhibition and suppression is needed to further our understanding of the ways in which stereotype use can be reduced. Finally, there still is no consensus within the social science community about the way(s) in which stereotype accuracy should be conceptualized and measured.

It is important to note that the existence of these disagreements is indicative of the fact that research on gender (and other forms of) stereotyping is a thriving field in which theoretical advances continue to be made. The disagreements among gender stereotyping researchers are a normal and healthy part of scientific progress, not indications of an immature or inconclusive literature.

§ 11–2.6 Future Directions

To conclude our review, we offer some educated guesses about the directions that research on gender stereotyping will take in the next 5–10 years. In our opinion, future research in this area is likely to focus on the following issues: 1) refining our understanding of the psychological processes involved in stereotype activation and inhibition, 2) increasing our understanding of the ways in which targets who belong to two or more social groups are categorized, 3) continuing to study the effects of stereotyping on members of stigmatized groups, 4) continuing to develop interventions for reducing stereotype use, 5) examining the ways in which gender stereotypes affect judgments of and treatment toward men, and 6) developing integrative theories of stereotype use.

First, as discussed earlier, there recently has been an explosion of interest in automatic stereotype activation and inhibition. We predict that this area will continue to be the subject of considerable research in years to come. In particular, we expect researchers to continue exploring the conditions under which gender (and other) stereotypes are and are not automatically activated, as well as the behavioral consequences of automatic stereotype activation.[160] We also expect researchers to further explore the effects that individual differences such as overt prejudice and motivation to appear unprejudiced have on stereotype activation and inhibition.[161]

159. *See, e.g.,* Devine, *supra* note 134; Greenwald et al., *supra* note 11; L. Lepore & R. Brown, *Category and Stereotype Activation: Is Prejudice Inevitable?*, 72 J. PERSONALITY & SOC. PSYCHOL. 275 (1997); Rudman & Glick, *supra* note 122; Rudman et al., *supra* note 122; Rudman & Kilianski, *supra* note 12; B. Wittenbrink et al., *Evidence for Racial Prejudice at the Implicit Level and its Relationship With Questionnaire Measures*, 72 J. PERSONALITY & SOC. PSYCHOL. 262 (1997).

160. *See, e.g.,* J. A. Bargh et al., *Automaticity of Social Behavior: Direct Effects of Trait Construct and Stereotype Activation on Action*, 71 J. PERSONALITY & SOC. PSYCHOL. 230 (1996); Rudman & Borgida, *supra* note 10; Rudman & Glick, *supra* note 122.

161. Devine, *supra* note 134; Greenwald et al., *supra* note 11; Lepore & Brown, *supra* note 159; Rudman & Glick, *supra* note 122; Rudman et al., *supra* note 122; Rudman & Kilianski, *supra* note 12; Wittenbrink et al., *supra*

Second, we predict that issues related to multiple categorization will continue to be the focus of considerable research and theorizing. As mentioned earlier, there are competing predictions in the literature about the processes involved in categorizing individuals who belong to multiple social groups, as well as whether the use of multiple social categories reduces stereotyping and bias.[162] We expect this issue to be clarified considerably in the next few years.

Third, we expect a continuation of the recent scholarly interest in the effects of being the target of stereotyping, prejudice, and discrimination.[163] For example, recent research by Steele demonstrates that the fear of confirming an unfavorable group stereotype (i.e., stereotype threat) negatively impacts the performance of members of stereotyped groups (e.g., women perform more poorly on tests when they are framed as stereotype-relevant assessments of math ability).[164] This shift in focus from the stereotyper to the stereotyped individual holds great promise for understanding the full consequences of stereotyping in academic, business, and other contexts.

Fourth, we predict that researchers will continue to investigate both organizational interventions and personal control strategies for reducing the use of gender stereotypes.[165] In addition, there may be increased focus on strategies that the targets of stereotyping can use to undermine stereotypes directed at themselves. Eberhardt and Fiske proposed several target-initiated strategies, such as trying to motivate stereotypers to recategorize them along stereotype-neutral dimensions (e.g., as fellow college educated individuals) or appealing to the interests of stereotypers (e.g., emphasizing interdependence or accountability to a third party).[166] Currently, these strategies have not been systematically evaluated, so it is unclear whether they are successful in promoting unbiased treatment. We expect that future research will evaluate the efficacy of these and other target interventions, as well as other institutional and personal control strategies for the reduction of stereotype use.

Fifth, we expect that future research will investigate the effects of gender stereotyping on men, particularly men who are gender non-conformists (e.g., gay or effeminate men). This research has particular relevance to legal cases

note 159; B. C. Dunton & R. H. Fazio, *An Individual Difference Measure of Motivation to Control Prejudiced Reactions*, 23 PERSONALITY & SOC. PSYCHOL. BULL. 316 (1997); E. A. Plant & P. G. Devine, *Internal and External Motivation to Respond Without Prejudice*, 75 J. PERSONALITY & SOC. PSYCHOL. 811 (1998).

162. *See, e.g.*, Macrae et al., *supra* note 128; Migdal et al., *supra* note 116; Pendry & Macrae, *supra* note 90; Urban & Miller, *supra* note 116; Vescio et al., *supra* note 116; Zárate & Sandoval, *supra* note 114; Zárate & Smith, *supra* note 114.

163. *See* J. Crocker et al., *Social Stigma, in* HANDBOOK OF SOCIAL PSYCHOLOGY 504 (D.T. Gilbert, S.T. Fiske, & G. Lindzey eds., 4th ed. Vol. 1, 1998); PREJUDICE: THE TARGET'S PERSPECTIVE (J. K. Swim & C. Stangor eds., 1998).

164. C. M. Steele, *A Threat is in the Air: How Stereotypes Shape Intellectual Identity*

and Performance, 52 AMER. PSYCHOLOGIST 613 (1997); S. J. Spencer et al., *Stereotype Threat and Women's Math Performance*, 35 J. EXPERIMENTAL SOC. PSYCHOL. 4 (1999).

165. J. F. Dovidio & S. L. Gaertner, *Reducing Prejudice: Combating Intergroup Biases*, 8 CURRENT DIRECTIONS PSYCHOL. SCI. 101 (1999); M. Hewstone, *Contact and Categorization: Social Psychological Interventions to Change Intergroup Relations, in* STEREOTYPES & STEREOTYPING 323 (C.N. Macrae, C. Stangor, & M. Hewstone eds., 1996); T. F. Pettigrew, *Intergroup Contact Theory*, 49 ANN. REV. PSYCHOL. 65 (1998).

166. J. L. Eberhardt & S. T. Fiske, *Motivating Individuals to Change: What is a Target To Do?, in* STEREOTYPES & STEREOTYPING 369 (C.N. Macrae, C. Stangor, & M. Hewstone eds., 1996).

involving allegations of sexual harassment against men.[167]

Finally, we predict that, as the literature on gender stereotypes continues to expand, there will be continued emphasis on the development of integrative theories that tie together different areas of empirical research in order to provide comprehensive explanations of stereotype use. Research in the last decade was greatly aided by the development of such models, and we expect the need for such models to continue as our understanding of stereotyping processes grows more comprehensive and refined.[168]

---

167. Oncale v. Sundowner Offshore Ser vices, Inc., 523 U.S. 75, 118 S.Ct. 998, 140 L.Ed.2d 201 (1998).

168. *See, e.g.,* Bargh, *supra* note 120; Bodenhausen & Macrae, *supra* note 120; Fiske & Neuberg, *supra* note 93.; Kunda & Thagard, *supra* note 93.

CHAPTER 12

POLYGRAPH TESTS

Analysis

A. LEGAL ISSUES

Sec.

Westlaw Electronic Research

See Westlaw Electronic Research Guide preceding the Summary of Contents.

A. LEGAL ISSUES

§ 12–1.0 THE LEGAL RELEVANCE OF SCIENTIFIC RESEARCH ON POLYGRAPH TESTS

§ 12–1.1 Introduction

In 1923, in *Frye v. United States*,[1] the United States Court of Appeals for the District of Columbia excluded the defendant's proffer of the results of an early form of the polygraph test because it was not "sufficiently established to have gained general acceptance in the particular field in which it belongs."[2] Seventy years later, in *Daubert v. Merrell Dow Pharmaceuticals*,[3] the United States Supreme Court ruled that *Frye's* "general acceptance" criterion is only one among many factors that federal courts should consider in deciding the determinative question of scientific validity.[4] Following *Daubert*, federal and state courts were asked in case after case to reconsider their approach to polygraphs. In particular, polygraph proponents argued that the *Daubert* standard was inconsistent with excluding this kind of testimony.[5] Some courts agreed with this argument, but most did not. In addition, the United States Supreme Court in 1998 considered the claim that a *per se* rule excluding polygraph testimony in criminal cases violated the Sixth Amendment.[6] The Court rejected the constitutional claim,[7] but five members of the Court noted "some tension" between *Daubert* and a *per se* rule of exclusion of scientific evidence.[8]

Polygraphy, as indicated by its being the subject behind the *Frye* rule, has had a long and mostly troubled history in American courts. Throughout the twentieth century, courts have been, at best, skeptical of polygraph tests and, at worst and more usual, hostile to them.[9] Courts remain wary of the technique. It must be emphasized, however, that polygraphs are used in a wide variety of contexts and under different legal circumstances. Modern courts have begun to consider the value of polygraphs in light of the complex and specific circumstances in which they are offered.[10]

§ 12–1.0

1. 293 F. 1013 (D.C.Cir.1923).

2. *Id.* at 1014.

3. 509 U.S. 579, 113 S.Ct. 2786, 125 L.Ed.2d 469 (1993).

4. *Cf.* United States v. Microtek Int'l Develop. Systems, Inc., 2000 WL 274091 *6 (D.Ore. 2000) (Court concluded that although "[p]olygraphs have come a long way," they are still not reliable enough to admit.). *See generally* Chapter 1.

5. Commonwealth v. Duguay, 430 Mass. 397, 720 N.E.2d 458, 463 (Mass.1999) (Court rejected defendant's argument that Massachusetts' decision adopting *Daubert* test meant that polygraphs were admissible.).

6. United States v. Scheffer, 523 U.S. 303, 118 S.Ct. 1261, 140 L.Ed.2d 413 (1998).

7. *See infra* § 1.4.

8. *Scheffer*, 523 U.S. at 317 (Kennedy, J., concurring in part and concurring in the judgment) (Three Justices, O'Connor, Ginsburg and Breyer, joined Kennedy's opinion that noted this tension. Justice Stevens, the fifth who joined this view, dissented. *Id.* at 319 (Stevens, J., dissenting)).

9. *See* CHARLES A. WRIGHT & KENNETH W. GRAHAM, 22 FEDERAL PRACTICE & PROCEDURE § 5169 n.67 (Supp.1995); *see generally* Charles Robert Honts & Bruce D. Quick, *The Polygraph in 1995: Progress in Science and the Law,* 71 N. DAKOTA L. REV. 987 (1995); Roberta A. Morris, *The Admissibility of Evidence Derived From Hypnosis and Polygraph, in* PSYCHOLOGICAL METHODS IN CRIMINAL INVESTIGATION AND EVIDENCE (David C. Raskin ed., 1989).

10. *See, e.g.,* Ulmer v. State Farm Fire & Cas. Co., 897 F.Supp. 299 (W.D.La.1995) (admitting polygraph evidence after conducting Rule 702—Rule 403 evaluation under *Daubert*);

§ 12–1.2 Admissibility

In general, courts divide into three camps regarding the admissibility of polygraph evidence. First, many courts apply a *per se* rule of exclusion for polygraph evidence. Second, some jurisdictions view polygraph evidence more favorably, and permit it subject to the discretion of the trial court and sometimes only for limited purposes.[11] Third, a significant proportion of jurisdictions permit the parties to stipulate, prior to the test's administration, to the admissibility of the examiner's opinion concerning the results. These three approaches generally describe the division of opinion among courts whether they apply *Frye* or *Daubert* to the evidence. Because courts applying *Daubert* roughly parallel the outcomes of courts applying *Frye*, this section considers the several approaches courts use irrespective of the rule of admissibility they employ. Nonetheless, since the rule of admissibility inevitably affects the *reasons* courts give for their decisions, we explicitly examine these reasons along the way.

§ 12–1.2.1 per se Exclusion

Many courts, especially state courts, maintain a *per se* rule excluding polygraphs.[12] Courts adopting a *per se* rule excluding the use of polygraph evidence base this determination on a variety of reasons. These concerns can be roughly categorized into three principal objections. First, many courts find that polygraphs have not yet been shown to be sufficiently valid or reliable. Second, many courts applying the *Frye* test conclude that polygraph evidence is not generally accepted. And third, a large number of courts believe that the dangers associated with polygraphs are too great.

Although decided long before *Daubert,* the Illinois Supreme Court voiced doubt that polygraphs could meet a scientific validity test: "Almost all courts refuse to admit unstipulated polygraph evidence because there remain serious doubts about the reliability and scientific recognition of the tests."[13] More recently, a federal district court applying the scientific validity test excluded polygraph evidence on the basis of its unreliability.[14] In general, these courts find the subjective nature of the examination,[15] and the slight requirements

State v. Travis, 125 Idaho 1, 867 P.2d 234, 237 (Idaho 1994) (permitting polygraph in Child Protective Act proceedings where sexual abuse is alleged and most of the evidence is second-hand).

11. For example, in *United States v. Piccinonna*, 885 F.2d 1529 (11th Cir.1989) (*en banc*), the Eleventh Circuit held that polygraphs could be admitted for impeachment or corroboration purposes, but any other use had to be the subject of a stipulation. *See infra* § 1.2.4.

12. *See,. e.g.*, State v. Porter, 241 Conn. 57, 698 A.2d 739 (Conn.1997); State v. Shively, 268 Kan. 573, 999 P.2d 952 (Kan.2000); State v. Robertson, 712 So.2d 8 (La.1998); Tavares v. State, 725 So.2d 803, 810 (Miss.1998) (*en banc.*); State v. Hall, 955 S.W.2d 198, 207 (Mo. 1997); State v. Allen, 252 Neb. 187, 560 N.W.2d 829, 833 (Neb.1997); People v. Clarence, 175 Misc.2d 273, 669 N.Y.S.2d 161

(1997); Matthews v. State, 953 P.2d 336 (Okla. Cr.App.1998); State v. Sullivan, 152 Or.App. 75, 952 P.2d 100 (Or.App. 1998); Commonwealth v. Marinelli, 547 Pa. 294, 690 A.2d 203 (Pa.1997); Hall v. State, 970 S.W.2d 137 (Tex. App.1998).

13. People v. Baynes, 88 Ill.2d 225, 58 Ill. Dec. 819, 430 N.E.2d 1070, 1077 (Ill.1981).

14. United States v. Black, 831 F.Supp. 120, 123 (D.N.Y.1993).

15. *See, e.g.*, People v. Anderson, 637 P.2d 354, 360 (Colo.1981) (describing polygraph techniques as "art"); People v. Monigan, 72 Ill.App.3d 87, 28 Ill.Dec. 395, 390 N.E.2d 562, 569 (1979) (objecting to the subjectiveness surrounding the use of the polygraph and the "interpretation of the results"); State v. Frazier, 162 W.Va. 602, 252 S.E.2d 39, 48 (1979) (same).

for qualifying polygraph examiners,[16] to be factors that undermine the value of the test.

Courts also find that polygraph techniques remain highly controversial among "scientific experts" and therefore have yet to achieve "general acceptance." Courts, however, disagree concerning the scope of the "pertinent field" in which polygraphs must gain acceptance in order to be admitted. According to *Frye* itself, the fields of psychology and physiology should be surveyed for general acceptance.[17] Some courts also include polygraph examiners in this field.[18] But other courts specifically reject any reliance on polygraph examiners, because of the examiners' general lack of training and their interest in the outcome.[19]

Relevant to both *Frye* and *Daubert* evaluations of polygraph evidence, the National Academies of Science (NAS) organized a committee to review the scientific evidence on the polygraph in January, 2001. The Committee's report should be available in the Summer of 2002. Committee members' fields of expertise range widely, from biostatistics to psychophysiology.[20] From a *Frye* perspective, NAS's decision to include such a wide spectrum suggests that the "particular field" which should evaluate polygraph validity ranges far beyond polygraph operators or experimental psychologists.[21] This is a lesson worth considering in other scientific evidence contexts. From a *Daubert* perspective, the NAS report will evaluate the scientific basis for polygraphs, a core issue under Rule 702.[22]

Finally, courts express great concern about the effect polygraph evidence has on the trial process. These concerns range from the opinion that polygraphs usurp the jury's traditional role of evaluating credibility[23] to the belief

16. *See, e.g., Anderson,* 637 P.2d at 360 ("The absence of adequate qualification standards for the polygraph profession heighten[s] the possibility for grave abuse.")

17. *Frye v. U.S.,* 293 F. 1013, 1014 (D.C.Cir.1923).

18. *See, e.g.,* United States v. DeBetham, 348 F.Supp. 1377, 1388 (S.D.Cal.1972).

19. *See, e.g., U.S. v. Alexander,* 526 F.2d 161, 164 n. 6 (8th Cir.1975) ("Experts in neurology, and physiology may offer needed enlightenment upon the basic premise of polygraphy. Polygraphists often lack extensive training in these specialized sciences."); *but see* United States v. Oliver, 525 F.2d 731, 736 (8th Cir.1975) ("We believe the necessary foundation can be constructed through testimony showing a sufficient degree of acceptance of the science of polygraphy by experienced practitioners in polygraphy and other related experts.").

20. The complete list of expertises includes social psychology, statistics, neuroscience, psychophysiology, biostatistics, systems engineering, memory and cognition, signal detection theory, industrial and organizational psychology, economics, and law.

21. Strictly speaking, the NAS report will not answer the *Frye* question whether polygraph validity is "generally accepted." However, failure of the NAS committee to accept polygraph validity would undoubtedly affect courts' conclusions on this matter.

22. The NAS Polygraph Committee's mandate is to review the use of polygraphs in the area of personnel security. The polygraph is used in this context in two ways. The first is as a screening device, in which the examinee is not specifically accused of anything, and the examiner canvasses broad areas of past conduct that might raise concerns for the respective government agency, such as engaging in acts of terrorism, espionage or spying. Screening is an essentially non-forensic use of the polygraph. However, the polygraph is also used in personnel security to uncover specific acts, such as when a computer disc is missing or a screening test uncovers specific concerns that then narrow the examiner's scope of inquiry. This specific incident form of polygraph examination is essentially the same as occurs when polygraphs are used forensically. The NAS report is expected to examine polygraphs both when used for screening purposes and when employed to investigate specific incidents.

23. *See, e.g.,* State v. Beachman, 189 Mont. 400, 616 P.2d 337, 339 (Mont.1980) ("It is distinctly the jury's province to determine whether a witness is being truthful."); State v. Miller, 258 Neb. 181, 602 N.W.2d 486, 499

that this evidence will overwhelm the jury.[24]

§ 12–1.2.2 Discretionary Admission

Courts agree that *Daubert* applies to polygraph evidence.[25] The biggest change in form, if not in substance, since *Daubert* in regard to polygraphs is the increased number of federal courts that articulate a discretionary standard for this evidence.[26] Several states using a *Daubert*-based validity test have also moved to a standard that leaves polygraph admission within the discretion of trial courts.[27] Leaving discretion to trial courts rather than prescribing a *per se* rule does not seem to have changed practice substantially, however.

For example, in *Cordoba*, the Ninth Circuit held that *Daubert* requires trial courts to evaluate polygraph evidence with particularity in each case.[28] However, district courts applying *Cordoba* usually exclude polygraph evidence.[29] Indeed, courts generally are not sympathetic to proffers of polygraph evidence. They point to high error rates and the lack of standards for administering polygraphs. Moreover, Rule 403 has played a prominent part in courts' particularized analyses of polygraph evidence. Courts cite concerns

(Neb.1999) (noting that polygraphs duplicate purpose of trial).

24. *See, e.g., Alexander,* 526 F.2d at 168 ("When polygraph evidence is offered . . . , it is likely to be shrouded with an aura of near infallibility, akin to the ancient oracle of Delphi."); *Shively,* 999 P.2d at 958 (Court noted that it had long voiced "concern about the weight a jury might place on such evidence."). When the polygraph is proffered in a bench trial, courts may be less concerned with its prejudicial effect. *See, e.g.,* Gibbs v. Gibbs, 210 F.3d 491 (5th Cir.2000) ("Most of the safeguards provided for in *Daubert* are not as essential in a case such as this where a district judge sits as the trier of fact in place of a jury.").

25. *See, e.g.,* United States v. Galbreth, 908 F.Supp. 877, 881 (D.N.M.1995) (analyzing in some detail the application of *Daubert* to polygraph tests); *see also* United States v. Lee, 25 F.3d 997, 998 (11th Cir.1994) (extending *Daubert* to specialized technical equipment). *See generally* James R. McCall, *Misconceptions and Reevaluation—Polygraph Admissibility After* Rock *and* Daubert, 1996 U.ILL.L.REV. 363.

26. *See* United States v. Posado, 57 F.3d 428, 434 (5th Cir.1995); United States v. Beyer, 106 F.3d 175, 178 (7th Cir.1997); United States v. Williams, 95 F.3d 723, 728–30 (8th Cir.1996); United States v. Cordoba, 104 F.3d 225 (9th Cir.1997); United States v. Call, 129 F.3d 1402 (10th Cir.1997); United States v. Gilliard, 133 F.3d 809 (11th Cir.1998); United States v. Saldarriaga, 179 F.R.D. 140, 1998 WL 324582 (S.D.N.Y.1998); United States v. Marshall, 986 F.Supp. 747 (E.D.N.Y.1997); Meyers v. Arcudi, 947 F.Supp. 581 (D.Conn.1996); United States v. Redschlag, 971 F.Supp. 1371 (D.Colo.1997).

27. *See, e.g.,* State v. Brown, 948 P.2d 337 (Utah 1997); State v. Crosby, 927 P.2d 638 (Utah 1996); State v. Porter, 241 Conn. 57, 698 A.2d 739 (Conn.1997).

28. *Cordoba,* 104 F.3d at 229. *See also* Mars v. United States, 25 F.3d 1383, 1384 (7th Cir.1994) ("[W]e have . . . decided to leave the issue of the admissibility of lie-detector evidence up to the individual trial judge, rather than formulate a circuit-wide rule.").

29. In *Cordoba* itself, after the Ninth Circuit remanded the case to the district court for a particularized evaluation, the lower court again excluded the evidence. On appeal, the Ninth Circuit affirmed. United States v. Cordoba, 194 F.3d 1053 (9th Cir.1999). In its opinion, the court reviewed the scientific premises of the polygraph in some detail. The appellate court noted that the district court had found that the polygraph had been subject to testing, albeit with mixed results. *Id.* at 1058. Also, polygraph research had been published in peer reviewed journals. *Id.* The remaining two *Daubert* factors, however, proved the polygraph's undoing. The district court determined that there was no error rate for polygraphs in various contexts, and that the field was badly divided regarding their basic validity. *Id.* at 1059–61. These conclusions, the appellate court found, were well supported. Finally, the district court also concluded that the polygraph exam administered here ran afoul of Rule 403. The Ninth Circuit agreed with this judgment. *Id.* at 1063. *See also* United States v. Microtek Int'l Develop. Systems Div., 2000 WL 274091 (D.Or.2000); United States v. Orians, 9 F.Supp.2d 1168 (D.Ariz.1998); United States v. Cordoba, 991 F.Supp. 1199 (C.D.Cal.1998); United States v. Pitner, 969 F.Supp. 1246, 1252 (W.D.Wash.1997).

about infringing on the role of the jury in making credibility assessments,[30] confusion of issues and waste of time,[31] and the problems created if the opposing party does not have a reasonable opportunity to replicate the exam or to have been present when it was given.[32] Courts seem to agree with the Ninth Circuit's conclusion that "[polygraph evidence] still has grave potential for interfering with the deliberative process."[33]

The Fifth Circuit similarly found that its *"per se* rule against admitting polygraph evidence did not survive *Daubert."*[34] The Court explained that *Daubert* changed the evidentiary standard under which the *per se* rule was crafted and, thus, polygraphs would now have to be reevaluated. The court noted "that tremendous advances have been made in polygraph instrumentation and technique in the years since *Frye"* and discussed some of these "advances."[35] Therefore, the court observed, "[w]hat remains is the issue of whether polygraph techniques can be said to have made sufficient technological advance in the seventy years since *Frye* to constitute the type of 'scientific, technical, or other specialized knowledge' envisioned by Rule 702 and *Daubert.* We cannot say without a fully developed record that it has not."[36] The court remanded to the trial court to hold a preliminary hearing to determine this matter.[37]

Several courts find that *Daubert* has not changed their approach to

30. *Orians,* 9 F.Supp.2d at 1175; *Cordoba,* 991 F.Supp. at 1208; *Pitner,* 969 F.Supp. at 1252.

31. *Gilliard,* 133 F.3d at 815 16; *Pitner,* 969 F.Supp. at 1252.

32. *See Croft,* 124 F.3d at 1120.

33. *Cordoba,* 104 F.3d at 228.

34. *Posado,* 57 F.3d at 429.

Another federal court similarly found that *Daubert* permits a more flexible approach to polygraph evidence than that permitted under the *Frye* test. In United States v. Crumby, 895 F.Supp. 1354 (D.Ariz.1995), the court observed that the historical concern with polygraph evidence has been two-fold, reliability of the test and the prejudicial effect on the jury of admitting it. *Id.* at 1356. The court also noted that good reasons now existed for reconsidering the admissibility of polygraph evidence. These included (1) the fact that in this case the defendant has consistently maintained his innocence and passed a polygraph, (2) *Daubert,* (3) the increase in reliability in the test itself and (4) an alternative vision of the polygraph sketched out in United States v. Piccinonna, 885 F.2d 1529 (11th Cir.1989) (en banc). *Id.* at 1357–58. The court then embarked on an in-depth analysis of the polygraph and found that polygraphy now met the four factors identified in *Daubert. Id.* at 1361. The court placed particular reliance on the scientific research of Dr. David Raskin in reaching its conclusions; the court, however, did not cite or even mention the substantial literature that challenges the validity of polygraph tests. Finally, the court evaluated polygraph evidence under Rule 403,

finding that its probative value was not outweighed by unfair prejudice. *Id.* The court stressed several factors as being important in its determination, including in particular that the defendant not the state offered it here and that it would be permitted for a limited purpose. *Id.* at 1363. The court concluded that the defendant could introduce evidence that he took and passed the polygraph if (1) he gave notice to the government, (2) made himself available to a polygraph exam administered by the government, (3) introduced the evidence only to support credibility, if attacked, under Rule 608(a), and (4) the specific questions and physiological data are not introduced into evidence, though the general science of polygraphy may be discussed under Rule 702. *Id.* at 1365. *See also* United States v. Galbreth, 908 F.Supp. 877 (D.N.M.1995) (offering a similar analysis of the issue to that of *Crumby).*

35. *Posado,* 57 F.3d at 434.

36. *Id.* at 433.

37. *Id.* at 436. Lower courts in the Fifth Circuit appear to have embraced their new responsibility to evaluate the admissibility of polygraphs under the specific facts of particular cases. *See, e.g.,* Ulmer v. State Farm Fire & Casualty Co., 897 F.Supp. 299 (W.D.La.1995) (Applying *Posado,* the court permitted the introduction of polygraph results in a civil action in which the defendant insurance company had prompted a Fire Marshall to investigate the plaintiffs for arson; the plaintiffs passed the test administered by a certified, and neutral, examiner.).

polygraph evidence. In *United States v. Black*,[38] for example, the court stated that "nothing in *Daubert* changes the rationale excluding evidence because of reliability concerns."[39] The court concluded that "[a]fter evaluating the standard set forth in the *Daubert* case, premised on Rule 702 of the Federal Rules of Evidence, the Court believes that nothing in *Daubert* would disturb the settled precedent that polygraph evidence is neither reliable nor admissible."[40]

[1]   Rule 403

Although not a major part of *Daubert* itself, Rule 403 figures prominently in federal courts' *Daubert* evaluations of polygraph evidence.[41] There is good reason for this, since research indicates that polygraphs are somewhat reliable, but courts are reluctant to find them reliable enough.[42] Since *Daubert's* focus is primarily on relevance, reliability and fit, polygraphs might be thought to meet the basic test. But concerns with this evidence range from friendly and thus invalid tests to invasion of the province of the jury.[43] Rule 403 has permitted courts a more discriminating tool than that permitted by Rule 702 alone. In *Posado,* for example, the court observed that "the presumption in favor of admissibility established by Rules 401 and 402, together with *Daubert's* 'flexible' approach, may well mandate an enhanced role for Rule 403 in the context of the *Daubert* analysis, particularly when the scientific or technical knowledge proffered is novel or controversial."[44] The Sixth Circuit took a similar approach in *Conti v. Commissioner of Internal Revenue*.[45] In *Conti,* the court upheld the lower court's use of Rule 403 to exclude polygraph tests taken unilaterally. The court observed that "the prejudicial effect of [unilateral] polygraph test results outweighs their probative value under Federal Rule of Evidence 403, because the party offering them did not have an adverse interest at stake while taking the test."[46]

Courts, however, have not always used the Rule 403 tool in a discriminating manner. In *United States v. Waters*,[47] the defendant appealed from his conviction for child abuse. The defendant complained on appeal, among other things, that the trial court had erred in refusing to hold a *Daubert* hearing to consider the admissibility of the defendant's polygraph results. At the government's request, the defendant had taken a polygraph, administered by a special agent of the FBI, and had "passed" when asked whether he had ever touched the alleged victim's "private areas in a sexual way."[48]

---

38. 831 F.Supp. 120 (D.N.Y.1993).

39. *Id.* at 123 (*citing Rea,* 958 F.2d at 1224).

40. *Id.*; *see also* State v. Fain, 116 Idaho 82, 774 P.2d 252, 256 (Idaho 1989) (stating general rule of exclusion, because polygraphs lack validity and reliability).

41. Rule 403 also played a prominent role in admissibility determinations prior to *Daubert. See, e.g., Piccinonna,* 885 F.2d at 1536; Wolfel v. Holbrook, 823 F.2d 970, 972 (6th Cir.1987); United States v. Miller, 874 F.2d 1255 (9th Cir.1989).

42. *See, e.g.,* United States v. Benavidez–Benavidez, 217 F.3d 720 (9th Cir.2000) (District court excluded polygraph evidence for fail-

ing one *Daubert* factor—general acceptance—as well as under Rule 403. Circuit Court ruled that the evidence could pass *Daubert* scrutiny, but be wholly excluded under Rule 403 alone.).

43. *See, e.g.,* United States v. Wright, 22 F.Supp.2d 751, 755 (W.D.Tenn.1998) (noting concern that polygraphs might "supplant the fact-finding function of the jury").

44. *Posado,* 57 F.3d at 435.

45. 39 F.3d 658 (6th Cir.1994).

46. *Id.* at 663; *see also* United States v. Harris, 9 F.3d 493, 502 (6th Cir.1993).

47. 194 F.3d 926 (8th Cir.1999).

48. *Id.* at 928.

In a cursory analysis, the Eighth Circuit concluded that it did not even have to reach the *Daubert* issue, since "the district court independently excluded the evidence under Fed.R.Evid. 403, which provides for exclusion of evidence 'if its probative value is substantially outweighed by the danger of unfair prejudice, confusion of the issues, or misleading the jury, or by consideration of undue delay, waste of time....' "[49] It is not clear how a *Daubert* analysis can be avoided when balancing probative value against prejudicial effect, since the amount of probative value expert testimony has depends necessarily on the reliability of the evidence. The court cited *United States v. Scheffer*[50] for the proposition that there is substantial disagreement regarding the reliability of polygraphs. But *Scheffer* is not particularly good authority in this case. *Scheffer* was a constitutional challenge in which the Court ruled that it was not unreasonable for the military to adopt a *per se* rule excluding polygraph evidence. Rule 403, in contrast, calls upon courts to conduct a case-by-case evaluation. In *Waters*, there were several factors supporting the polygraph results, at least against government challenges. First, the government had sponsored the test and a government examiner had interpreted it. Second, in a child abuse case such as this, there is little evidence other than the child's statements, evidence not usually deemed the most dependable. The trial court refused even to hold a *Daubert* hearing, and thus never even considered the reliability (and thus the probative value) of the evidence. Without knowing the probative value of the evidence, it is impossible to say that the unfair prejudice is greater.

Rule 403 gives courts the flexibility by which they can manage scientific evidence. Rule 702, among other things, queries the scientific validity of the basis for proffered expert testimony. Yet, in reality, science does not come packaged neatly into "valid" and "invalid" containers. Sometimes, substantial testing will give courts great confidence in the validity of relevant scientific evidence; more usually, however, the testing will leave courts less sure. Rule 403 allows courts to take into account the dangers associated with a particular type of expert testimony as compared to the benefits it offers. Polygraph tests present a particularly appropriate example of the importance of Rule 403 in managing scientific evidence. As the *Posado* court noted, "the traditional objection to polygraph evidence is that the testimony will have an unusually prejudicial effect which is not justified by its probative value, precisely the inquiry required of the district court by Rule 403."[51] At the same time, the *Posado* court noted that polygraphs might possess significant probative value.[52] Hence, courts must now judge the polygraph through the Rule 702 and 403 lenses.

[2] Other Approaches to Discretionary Admittance

In Massachusetts, a *Daubert* state, polygraph evidence is admissible only after the proponent introduces results of proficiency exams that indicate that the examiner can reliably discern truth-telling.[53] The Supreme Judicial Court explained the rule as follows:

---

49. *Id.* at 930.

50. 523 U.S. 303, 118 S.Ct. 1261, 140 L.Ed.2d 413 (1998).

51. *Posado,* 57 F.3d at 435.

52. *Id.*

53. *Duguay,* 720 N.E.2d at 463.

"If polygraph evidence is to be admissible in a given case, it seems likely that its reliability will be established by proof in a given case that a qualified tester who conducted the test, had in similar circumstances demonstrated, in a statistically valid number of independently verified and controlled tests, the high level of accuracy of the conclusions that the tester reached in those tests."[54]

This requirement, in practice, almost certainly results in the exclusion of most polygraph evidence. Outside of the federal government, polygraph examiners do not undergo routine proficiency tests. Even inside government laboratories, it is somewhat unclear what levels of quality control exist, or whether government records would be readily forthcoming if requested.

Probably the most permissive approach to polygraph evidence occurs in New Mexico. A New Mexico statute "entrusts the admissibility of polygraph evidence to the sound discretion of the trial court."[55] The court in *Tafoya v. Baca*[56] explained the operation of the rule:

"Under [Evidence] Rule 707(d), any party intending to use polygraph evidence at trial must give written notice to the opposing party of his intention. Under Rule 707(g), once such notice has been given, the court may compel ... a witness who has previously voluntarily taken a polygraph test to submit to another polygraph test by an examiner of the other party's choice. If such witness refuses to submit, no polygraph test evidence is admissible at trial. Under [Criminal Procedure] Rule 28(a)(2), a defendant must disclose only those results of a polygraph test which the defendant intends to use at trial."[57]

In addition, New Mexico courts must determine that (1) the polygraph examiner is qualified, (2) the procedures employed were reliable, and (3) the test administered to the subject was valid.[58]

§ 12–1.2.3   Admissibility by Stipulation

By far the most unusual aspect of polygraph evidence is the large part the parties often play in controlling admissibility through stipulation.[59] Although, theoretically, stipulation could be a factor in a wide variety of evidentiary contexts, as a practical matter it is not. This device adds an interesting wrinkle to the problem of the admissibility of scientific evidence.[60]

Although the vast majority of courts routinely exclude the results of polygraph tests, many of these courts qualify this ruling by permitting polygraph results when the parties stipulate to their admissibility prior to the administration of the test.[61] Courts typically premise the decision to permit

---

54. *Id.* (*quoting* Commonwealth v. Stewart, 422 Mass. 385, 663 N.E.2d 255 (1996)).

55. B & W Construction Co. v. N.C. Ribble Co., 105 N.M. 448, 734 P.2d 226 (N.M.1987).

56. 103 N.M. 56, 702 P.2d 1001 (N.M. 1985).

57. *Id.* at 1005.

58. *Id.* at 1003.

59. *See generally* Note, *Admissibility of Polygraph Test Results Upon Stipulation of the Parties,* 30 Mercer L. Rev. 357 (1978).

60. *See also* David Katz, *Dilemmas of Polygraph Stipulations,* 14 Seton Hall L. Rev. 285 (1984).

61. *See, e.g., Piccinonna,* 885 F.2d at 1536 ("Polygraph expert testimony will be admissible in this circuit when both parties stipulate in advance as to the circumstances of the test and as to the scope of its admissibility."); *see also* United States v. Gordon, 688 F.2d 42, 44 (8th Cir.1982); Ex Parte Hinton, 548 So.2d 562, 569 (Ala.1989); People v. Fudge, 7 Cal.4th

polygraph results through prior stipulation on principles of estoppel.[62] Some courts also believe that prior stipulations increase the validity of the procedure.[63] Many courts, however, insist that stipulations cannot cure the defects associated with polygraphy.[64] Moreover, absent stipulation, courts uniformly exclude evidence indicating the defendant's willingness[65] or unwillingness[66] to take a polygraph examination.

Most of the courts which permit polygraph results by stipulation require that certain conditions be met. For example, in the widely followed case of *State v. Valdez*,[67] the Arizona Supreme Court established the following four conditions:

(1) That ... counsel all sign a written stipulation providing for defendant's submission to the test and for the subsequent admission at trial of the graphs and the examiner's opinion. . . .

(2) That notwithstanding the stipulation the admissibility of the test results is subject to the discretion of the trial judge. . . .

(3) That if the graphs and examiner's opinion are offered in evidence the opposing party shall have the right to cross-examine the examiner respecting

    a. the examiner's qualifications and training;

    b. the conditions under which the test was administered;

    c. the limitations of and possibilities for error in the technique of polygraphic interrogation; and

    d. at the discretion of the trial judge, any other matter deemed pertinent to the inquiry;

(4) That if such evidence is admitted the trial judge should instruct the jury that the examiner's testimony does not tend to prove or disprove any element of the crime with which a defendant is charged but at most tends only to indicate that at the time of the examination defendant was not telling the truth. Further, the jury members should be instructed that it is for them to determine what corroborative weight and effect such testimony should be given.[68]

1075, 31 Cal.Rptr.2d 321, 875 P.2d 36 (Cal. 1994).

62. *See, e.g.*, Herman v. Eagle Star Ins. Co., 396 F.2d 427 (9th Cir.1968); State v. Olmstead, 261 N.W.2d 880 (N.D.1978); State v. Rebeterano, 681 P.2d 1265 (Utah 1984); McGhee v. State, 253 Ga. 278, 319 S.E.2d 836 (Ga.1984).

63. *See infra* notes 73–74 and accompanying text.

64. *See* United States v. A & S Council Oil Co., 947 F.2d 1128, 1133–34 (4th Cir.1991); United States v. Hunter, 672 F.2d 815, 817 (10th Cir.1982); United States v. Skeens, 494 F.2d 1050, 1053 (D.C.Cir.1974); Pulakis v. State, 476 P.2d 474, 478 (Alaska 1970); Carr v. State, 655 So.2d 824, 836 (Miss.1995); State v. Biddle, 599 S.W.2d 182, 185 (Mo.1980).

65. *See, e.g.*, People v. Espinoza, 3 Cal.4th 806, 12 Cal.Rptr.2d 682, 838 P.2d 204 (Cal.

1992); People v. Mann, 646 P.2d 352, 361 (Colo.1982).

66. *See, e.g.*, Houser v. State, 234 Ga. 209, 214 S.E.2d 893 (Ga.1975).

67. 91 Ariz. 274, 371 P.2d 894 (Ariz.1962).

68. *Id.* at 900–901. *See also* State v. Souel, 53 Ohio St.2d 123, 372 N.E.2d 1318, 1323–24 (Ohio 1978) (adopting *Valdez* rule); Cullin v. State, 565 P.2d 445, 457 (Wyo.1977) (adopting *Valdez* rule and providing, in cases of stipulation, cross-examination before admitting polygraph evidence); State v. Rebeterano, 681 P.2d 1265, 1268 (Utah 1984) (adopting *Valdez* rule and requiring that the defendant's participation be voluntary). *See generally* Wynn v. State, 423 So.2d 294 (Ala.Crim.App.1982); State v. Milano, 297 N.C. 485, 256 S.E.2d 154 (N.C.1979).

The generous reliance on stipulations to manage polygraph evidence raises substantial analytical difficulties that courts applying *Daubert* and analogous standards of admissibility should consider. Although a factual question, the validity and reliability of polygraph evidence under *Daubert* is, at heart, a legal determination under Rule 104(a).[69] Under the federal rules, judges determine the existence of preliminary facts that are necessary to the application of a particular rule under the preponderance of the evidence standard of Rule 104(a). The admissibility of polygraph evidence thus depends on a judge's preliminary determination that the technique is sufficiently valid to support expert testimony. The fact that the parties are willing to stipulate to polygraph evidence should not free the judge from making this preliminary determination of validity.[70] To be sure, parties regularly stipulate to evidence. But polygraphy is unique, in that the stipulation occurs before the real evidence—the polygraph result—exists. If polygraph results contain too large a margin of error, then a party who stipulates to their admission is playing roulette with his juristic fate. Courts might be reluctant to endorse stipulations that amount to little more than a calculated gamble.

The Illinois Supreme Court asserted that there is an "inconsistency [in] admitting polygraph evidence on the basis of a stipulation since the stipulation does little if anything to enhance the reliability of polygraph evidence."[71] The Illinois court refused to permit the parties to stipulate to the admissibility of results derived from a process that it considered little better than flipping a coin.[72] Other courts, however, find that the stipulation device increases the reliability of the test sufficiently to make it acceptable.[73] According to this view, the stipulation raises the subject's apprehension and leads to the selection of more impartial polygraphers, both factors leading to more accurate results.[74] Whatever the case, notwithstanding the parties' willingness to stipulate, Rules 702 and 403 probably require some preliminary determination that the polygraph test is sufficiently valid and that the agreement to admit the results does not produce excessive unfair prejudice or waste of time.

§ 12–1.2.4   Corroboration and Impeachment Purposes

Many courts do not permit polygraph results as substantive evidence (at least absent stipulation), but permit them for corroboration or impeachment purposes.[75] Several courts allow polygraphs to be used on credibility matters

---

69. *Daubert*, 509 U.S. at 592 n. 10.

70. *See, e.g.*, Hoult v. Hoult, 57 F.3d 1, 4 (1st Cir.1995) ("We think *Daubert* does instruct district courts to conduct a preliminary assessment of the reliability of expert testimony, even in the absence of an objection.").

71. People v. Baynes, 88 Ill.2d 225, 58 Ill. Dec. 819, 430 N.E.2d 1070, 1078 (Ill.1981) (citing State v. Dean, 103 Wis.2d 228, 307 N.W.2d 628 (Wis.1981)).

72. *See generally Piccinonna*, 885 F.2d at 1537 (Johnson, J., concurring in part and dissenting in part) ("Because the polygraph can predict whether a person is lying with accuracy that is only slightly greater than chance, it will be of little help to the trier of fact.").

73. *See, e.g., Id.* at 1536; Anderson v. United States, 788 F.2d 517, 519 (8th Cir.1986); *Oliver*, 525 F.2d at 737 ; Ex Parte Clements, 447 So.2d 695, 698 (Ala.1984); State v. Montes, 136 Ariz. 491, 667 P.2d 191, 199 (Ariz.1983); *Valdez*, 371 P.2d at 900.

74. *See* United States v. Wilson, 361 F.Supp. 510, 514 (D.Md.1973) (noting that without stipulation the defendant is secure in knowing that unwelcome results can be buried; "[t]his sense of security diminishes the fear of discovered deception, upon which an effective examination depends"); McMorris v. Israel, 643 F.2d 458, 463 (7th Cir.1981) (same).

75. *See, e.g., Piccinonna*, 885 F.2d at 1536.

only when the parties stipulated to this use prior to the examination.[76] Other courts, as noted above, do not allow polygraph results for any purpose, including credibility.[77]

The suitability of employing polygraph evidence for impeachment and corroboration purposes under the federal rules and similar state codes is not obvious. In *Piccinonna,* for example, the court held that polygraph evidence may be introduced "to impeach or corroborate the testimony of a witness at trial."[78] The court established three criteria for such use: (1) notice to the opposing party; (2) reasonable opportunity for the opponent to administer a polygraph to the witness using his own expert; and (3) adherence to Federal Rule 608, which governs evidence proffered to impeach or corroborate a witness.[79]

Rule 608, however, is not well-tailored to this use of polygraph examinations. Rule 608 identifies two kinds of evidence permitted for impeachment and corroboration purposes, as provided under subsections (a) and (b) of the rule.[80] Rule 608(a) allows "opinion and reputation evidence of character." This appears to provide authority, since the proponent of the evidence seeks to introduce "expert *opinion*" on the witness' veracity. Rule 608(a) is ambiguous, however, because it limits opinion evidence to the witness' *"character* for truthfulness or untruthfulness."[81] It is not clear whether polygraph experts

---

76. *See, e.g., State v. Souel,* 53 Ohio St.2d 123, 372 N.E.2d 1318 (Ohio 1978).

77. *See, e.g., United States v. Sanchez,* 118 F.3d 192, 195 (4th Cir.1997) ("[P]olygraph evidence is never admissible to impeach the credibility of a witness."); Robinson v. Commonwealth, 231 Va. 142, 341 S.E.2d 159 (Va.1986); State v. Muetze, 368 N.W.2d 575 (S.D.1985).

78. *Piccononna,* 885 F.2d at 1536.

79. *Id.* Specifically, the court noted as follows:

Rule 608 limits the use of opinion or reputation evidence to establish the credibility of a witness in the following way: "[E]vidence of truthful character of the witness is admissible only after the character of the witness for truthfulness has been attacked by opinion or reputation evidence or otherwise." Thus, evidence that a witness passed a polygraph examination, used to corroborate that witness's in-court testimony, would not be admissible under Rule 608 unless or until the credibility of that witness were first attacked.

Id.

80. Rule 608 provides, in pertinent part, as follows:

(a) **Opinion and reputation evidence of character.** The credibility of a witness may be attacked or supported by evidence in the form of opinion or reputation, but subject to these limitations: (1) the evidence may refer only to character for truthfulness or untruthfulness, and (2) evidence of truthful character is admissible only after the character of the witness for truthfulness has

been attacked by opinion or reputation evidence or otherwise.

(b) **Specific instances of conduct.** Specific instances of the conduct of a witness, for the purpose of attacking or supporting the witness' credibility, other than conviction of crime as provided in rule 609, may not be proved by extrinsic evidence. They may, however, in the discretion of the court, if probative of truthfulness or untruthfulness, be inquired into on cross-examination of the witness (1) concerning the witness' character for truthfulness or untruthfulness, or (2) concerning the character for truthfulness or untruthfulness of another witness as to which character the witness being cross-examined has testified.

FED. R. EVID. 608.

81. FED. R. EVID. 608(a), emphasis added. The Rule 608(a) language closely tracks the "reputation and opinion provision of Rule 405(a)." In fact, the Advisory Committee's Note to Rule 608 refers back to the Note accompanying Rule 405. The Rule 405 Note explains the expansion of the rule from the common law practice of limiting character evidence to reputation to the modern approach that allows opinion. The Advisory Committee Note indicates that the word "opinion" was intended to include expert opinion:

If character is defined as the kind of person one is, then account must be taken of varying ways of arriving at the estimate. These may range from the opinion of the employer who has found the man honest to the opinion of the psychiatrist based upon examina-

testify to subjects' characters or, rather, as the much-cited *Valdez* court remarked, only to whether the witness was or was not telling the truth "at the time of the examination."[82] Rule 608 thus does not obviously apply to the situation in which the witness states "X" on the witness stand and the polygrapher testifies as to whether the witness was truthful in saying "X" during the polygraph test. Alternatively, passing or failing a polygraph might be considered a "specific instance of conduct" that indicates the subject's character for truthfulness or untruthfulness. Rule 608(b) regulates the admission of such evidence. But subsection (b) specifically provides that "specific instances of conduct" *cannot* be introduced to support or attack credibility. Specific instances of conduct only can be inquired into on cross-examination. Under Rule 608(b), therefore, a polygraph expert would not be permitted to testify, though the opponent may be permitted to question the witness about the results of the polygraph examination on cross-examination.

§ 12–1.3 Confessions Before, During and After Polygraph Examinations

Courts generally do not exclude confessions made in anticipation of taking, or as a consequence of failing, a polygraph test.[83] Courts do not find the circumstances surrounding polygraph examinations themselves to be unreasonably coercive.[84] However, the circumstances of the polygraph examination might implicate constitutional guarantees[85] and require specific waivers of the right to counsel.[86] In addition, mental incapacity of the subject or extreme and unusual conditions imposed by the examiners, can lead to exclusion of the confession.[87] Even jurisdictions that apply a *per se* rule of inadmissibility allow the use of statements elicited during a polygraph examination, so long as no mention of the polygraph examination is made.[88]

tion and testing. No effective dividing line exists between character and mental capacity, and the latter traditionally has been provable by opinion.

ADVISORY COMMITTEE NOTE TO FED. R. EVID. 405. The kind of expert opinion contemplated by this Note, however, probably does not extend to polygraph testimony, since polygraph experts do not give opinions on "the kind of person" the subject is. Instead, they offer an opinion on whether the subject was or was not lying in response to specific questions.

82. *Valdez,* 371 P.2d at 901.

83. *See, e.g.,* Johnson v. State, 660 So.2d 637 (Fla.1995); Smith v. State,265 Ga. 570, 459 S.E.2d 420 (Ga.1995); State v. Blosser, 221 Kan. 59, 558 P.2d 105 (Kan.1976).

84. *See, e.g.,* People v. Madison, 135 A.D.2d 655, 522 N.Y.S.2d 230 (1987).

85. In *People v. Storm*, 94 Cal.Rptr.2d 805 (2000), the court found that a reasonable person would have believed himself to be in custody "when the polygraph operator told him he had badly flunked the examination." *Id.* at 813. The court of appeal explained that "when appellant was told he had abysmally failed the

polygraph test and therefore was lying when he denied he killed his wife, the only reasonable conclusion appellant could reach was that he was then no longer free to leave." *Id.* at 814.

86. United States v. Leon–Delfis, 203 F.3d 103, 109–112 (1st Cir.2000).

87. *See* People v. Zimmer, 68 Misc.2d 1067, 329 N.Y.S.2d 17 (1972) (subject was emotionally upset, coerced, never read his *Miranda* rights, and was told the polygraph results could be used against him in court); People v. Brown, 96 Misc.2d 244, 408 N.Y.S.2d 1007 (1978) (subject was deprived of sleep and questioned for an excessive length of time); *but see* Keiper v. Cupp, 509 F.2d 238 (9th Cir.1975) (Although the test was conducted in the early morning and the subject was upset and crying, the court held that the test was not "involuntary.").

88. *See* Edwards v. Commonwealth, 573 S.W.2d 640, 642 (Ky.1978); *see also* People v. Ray, 431 Mich. 260, 430 N.W.2d 626 (Mich. 1988) (allowing admissions made before, during or after a polygraph test if the admissions are voluntary); State v. Marini, 638 A.2d 507, 512 (R.I.1994) (same).

§ 12–1.4 Polygraph Evidence and Constitutional Guarantees

Two issues in particular arise concerning the use of polygraph tests under the United States Constitution.[89] Some defendants claim that exclusion of exculpatory polygraph results violates a defendant's Sixth Amendment right to present evidence; other defendants claim that admission of inculpatory polygraph results violates a defendant's Fifth and Fourteenth Amendment rights to due process.[90] In general, courts uniformly hold that the Constitution does not erect *per se* barriers or mandate *per se* admission of polygraph evidence. Instead, courts find that reservations regarding polygraphs are evidentiary concerns that generally do not rise to constitutional dimensions.[91]

In *Scheffer*, the Supreme Court held that a *per se* rule excluding polygraph evidence does not violate the Sixth Amendment right of the accused to present a defense. The Court found that "state and federal lawmakers have 'broad latitude under the Constitution to establish rules excluding evidence from criminal trials.' " Exclusionary rules "do not infringe the rights of the accused to present a defense as long as they are not 'arbitrary' or 'disproportionate to the purposes they are designed to serve.' "[92] The Court held that the rule was not arbitrary in that it was designed to ensure "that only reliable evidence is introduced at trial, [to] preserve[ ] the jury's role in determining credibility, and [to] avoid[ ] litigation that is collateral to the primary purpose of the trial."[93] The rule, the Court concluded, was not "disproportionate in promoting these ends."[94]

According to the Court, the *per se* rule of exclusion had the aim of keeping unreliable evidence from the jury. This "is a principal objective of

---

89. This section does not address constitutional issues raised by the use of polygraphs in non-evidentiary contexts, such as procedural due process concerns surrounding the use of these tests in the employment context. Under federal law, the Employee Polygraph Protection Act (EPPA), private employers are prohibited from using polygraphs (or any kind of lie detector test), except under certain highly circumscribed circumstances. 29 U.S.C.A. § 2001 et seq. The EPPA, however, does not apply to governmental employers or certain private companies that contract with particular agencies of the government. 29 U.S.C.A. § 2006. *See generally* Veazey v. Communications & Cable of Chicago, 194 F.3d 850, 859 (7th Cir. 1999) ("Congress intended the prohibition on the use of lie detectors to be interpreted broadly."). In addition, many states have anti-polygraph statutes. *See, e.g.*, West's Ann.Cal.Labor Code § 432.2. To the extent state regulations conflict with federal law, the former are preempted by the latter. Stehney v. Perry, 101 F.3d 925, 938 (3d Cir.1996) (finding New Jersey anti-polygraph law preempted by EPPA to the extent the state law prohibited the National Security Agency from administering a polygraph).

90. *See generally* Note, *Compulsory Process and Polygraph Evidence: Does Exclusion Violate a Criminal Defendant's Due Process Rights?*, 12 CONN. L. REV. 324 (1980); Note,

Admission of Polygraph Results: A Due Process Perspective, 55 IND. L.J. 157 (1979).

91. *See, e.g.*, Middleton v. Cupp, 768 F.2d 1083, 1086 (9th Cir.1985) ("We have never held that the Constitution prevents the admission of testimony concerning polygraph verification, although we have expressed an 'inhospitable' leaning against the admission of such evidence as a matter of the federal rules of evidence.").

In *Watkins v. Miller*, 92 F.Supp.2d 824 (S.D.Ind.2000), the court held that "the prosecutor's suppression of the fact that another suspect failed a polygraph test is . . . a Brady violation that is also sufficient by itself to warrant habeas relief." *Id.* at 852. The court explained that "even where exculpatory information is not directly admissible, such as a polygraph result, it may still qualify as Brady material." *Id.* at 851.

92. *Scheffer*, 523 U.S. at 307, (*quoting* Rock v. Arkansas, 483 U.S. 44, 55, 107 S.Ct. 2704, 97 L.Ed.2d 37 (1987)). *But see* Paxton v. Ward, 199 F.3d 1197, 1215–16 (10th Cir.1999) (Court found that the state's *per se* rule excluding polygraphs, applied mechanistically, violated a capital defendant's right to present mitigating evidence at the sentencing phase of the trial.).

93. *Sheffer*, at 307–09.

94. *Id.* at 309.

many evidentiary rules."[95] The government's conclusion that polygraphs were not sufficiently reliable was supported by the fact that "[t]o this day, the scientific community remains extremely polarized about reliability of polygraph techniques."[96]

Justice Kennedy, joined by Justices O'Connor, Ginsburg and Breyer, wrote in concurrence, stating that he would have rested the holding exclusively on "[t]he continuing, good faith disagreement among experts and courts on the subject of polygraph reliability."[97] Justice Kennedy, however, did not agree that the argument that polygraphs usurp the jury's function was especially credible.[98] This argument "demeans and mistakes the role and competence of jurors in deciding the factual question of guilt or innocence."[99] It also, according to Justice Kennedy, relies on the "tired argument," that a jury should not "hear 'a conclusion about the ultimate issue in the trial.' "[100]

Justice Stevens dissented. He began by arguing that the majority's conclusion was inconsistent with *Daubert* which, as lower courts had also read it, gave district judges "broad discretion when evaluating the admissibility of scientific evidence."[101] The core of Stevens' dissent concerned his view that the Court had "all but ignor[ed] the strength of the defendant's interest in having polygraph evidence admitted in certain cases."[102] This interest lay in the defendant's desire to introduce expert opinion that would "bolster his own credibility."[103]

Finally, Justice Stevens argued that polygraph unreliability was greatly exaggerated and that "even the studies cited by the critics place polygraph accuracy at 70%."[104] Moreover, polygraphs compare favorably to many other kinds of evidence that courts routinely admit, including handwriting, fingerprinting and eyewitness identifications. Justice Stevens concluded, "[v]igorous cross-examination, presentation of contrary evidence, and careful instruction on the burden of proof are the traditional and appropriate means of attacking shaky but admissible evidence."[105]

Although *per se* exclusion of polygraph evidence does not violate constitutional guarantees, the Seventh Circuit has held that in jurisdictions in which polygraphs are admissible following stipulation of the parties, prosecutors must provide valid reasons for refusing to stipulate.[106] According to this view, a prosecutor's purely tactical decision to refuse a stipulation concerning polygraph evidence violates due process.[107] In addition, courts hold that due

---

95. *Id.*

96. *Id.* (*citing* Modern Scientific Evidence 565, § 12–2.0, and § 12–3.0 (1997)).

97. *Id.* at 317 (Kennedy, J., concurring in part and concurring in the judgment).

98. *Id.*

99. *Id.*

100. *Id.* (*quoting Id.* at 313, 118 S.Ct. at 1267).

101. *Id.* at 321 (*citing* United States v. Cordoba, 104 F.3d 225, 227 (9th Cir.1997)). Justice Kennedy also agreed that the majority's decision was "in tension" with *Daubert*. *Id.* at 1269 (Kennedy, J., concurring in part and concurring in the judgment).

102. *Id.* at 330 (Stevens, J., dissenting).

103. *Id.*

104. *Id.* at 331 (*citing* Iacono & Lykken, *The Case Against Polygraph Tests*, Modern Scientific Evidence, at 608).

105. *Id.* at 334.

106. McMorris v. Israel, 643 F.2d 458, 466 (7th Cir.1981).

107. *Id. But see* Israel v. McMorris, 455 U.S. 967, 970, 102 S.Ct. 1479, 71 L.Ed.2d 684 (1982) (Rehnquist, J., dissenting from denial of certiorari) (finding the lower court's decision to be a "dubious constitutional holding"); Jones v. Weldon, 690 F.2d 835, 838 (11th Cir.1982) (rejecting *McMorris* holding). Given the

process might also permit defense use of exculpatory polygraph results at the sentencing phase of capital cases. For example, in *State v. Bartholomew*,[108] the Washington Supreme Court held "that polygraph examination results are admissible by the defense at the sentencing phase of capital cases, subject to certain restrictions."[109] These restrictions include, first, that the test be "conducted under proper conditions," and, second, that the examiner be subject to thorough cross-examination by the state.[110]

Constitutional questions also arise when defendants claim that admission of inculpatory polygraph results violate principles of due process. Once again, in general, courts find that the evidentiary standards for polygraph examinations meet constitutional requirements. They hold, however, that the Fifth Amendment privilege against self-incrimination applies to the taking of a polygraph.[111] Thus, courts carefully evaluate a defendant's waiver of right to counsel or right to remain silent in regard to stipulation agreements concerning polygraph examinations.[112] Moreover, under the Fifth Amendment, a defendant's refusal to take a polygraph examination cannot be used against him.[113]

§ 12–1.5 Conclusion

More than most areas of scientific evidence, polygraphs present courts with substantial challenges under the rules of evidence, and implicate most of the panoply of considerations raised by testimony on ostensibly scientifically derived opinion. From the start, given its role in the formulation of the *Frye* test itself, polygraphs have been viewed with suspicion and concern by courts. A principal concern for courts has been defining the "particular field" in which polygraphs belong, especially since they have not been a subject of intense interest among scientists generally. Clearly, polygraphers cannot be the defined field, since they have a peculiar interest in accepting the validity of the trade they ply. Yet, few scientists have studied polygraphs carefully,

---

Court's holding in *Scheffer*, *McMorris* is unlikely to have much practical effect. Any prosecutor paying the least bit of attention could simply cite the Supreme Court's statement that there is a substantial split in authority over the validity of polygraphs to support a decision not to stipulate to a polygraph examination. *See* Jackson v. State, 997 P.2d 121, 122 (Nev.2000) ("[A]ny party to any criminal or civil action may refuse to agree to the stipulation of a polygraph test for any reason, or no reason at all.").

108. 101 Wash.2d 631, 683 P.2d 1079 (Wash.1984).

109. *Id.* at 1089.

110. *Id.* These two factors come from the *Valdez* test, *infra* note 67 and accompanying text, as adopted in Washington in *State v. Renfro*, 96 Wash.2d 902, 639 P.2d 737 (Wash. 1982).

111. *See* Schmerber v. California, 384 U.S. 757, 764, 86 S.Ct. 1826, 16 L.Ed.2d 908 (1966); *see also* Commonwealth v. Juvenile, 365 Mass. 421, 313 N.E.2d 120, 127 (Mass.1974) ("The polygraph results are essentially testimonial in

nature and therefore a defendant could not be compelled initially to take such an examination on the Commonwealth's motion.").

112. *See, e.g.*, People v. Leonard, 421 Mich. 207, 364 N.W.2d 625, 633–35 (Mich.1984) (finding that defendant did not make a knowing waiver of right to counsel at the polygraph examination to which he stipulated); *see also* Patterson v. State, 212 Ga.App. 257, 441 S.E.2d 414, 416 (1994) ("It is not required that the accused have counsel present or act only upon the advice of counsel in order to render a stipulation to the admissibility of the results of a polygraph examination valid and binding upon the accused."); Bowen v. Eyman, 324 F.Supp. 339, 341 (D.Ariz.1970).

113. *See* Melvin v. State, 606 A.2d 69, 71 (Del.1992) ("The trial judge's reliance on [the defendant's] refusal to submit to a polygraph examination violates [his] constitutional right against self-incrimination as guaranteed by the Fifth Amendment to the United States Constitution.").

and some fields in which we would expect interest, such as neuroscience, have ignored the matter entirely.

Under *Daubert*, polygraphs present special challenges. Unlike much expert opinion struggling under *Daubert's* expectations for data, many peer reviewed studies have been conducted testing the validity of polygraphs. As the next two sections make clear, the research completed so far has possibly raised more dust than it has settled. In addition, under Rule 403, courts are particularly concerned with possible prejudice that might accompany expert opinion, ranging from invading the province of the jury to overwhelming it.

Courts are likely to continue to struggle with the issue of polygraphs for some time to come. With the expected publication of an extensive evaluation of polygraphs by a NAS panel, the courts might expect some objective light to be cast on this subject. In addition, the NAS report will hopefully lead to greater interest in polygraphs and other techniques among scientists, prompting the development of psychophysiological or neurological tests that might offer much more powerful techniques than are available given the state of the art today. Almost certainly, the lessons courts learn in this struggle will serve them well in their dealings with other kinds of scientific evidence.

B. SCIENTIFIC STATUS[†]

by

Charles R. Honts*, David C. Raskin**, & John C. Kircher***

§ 12–2.0 THE SCIENTIFIC STATUS OF RESEARCH ON POLYGRAPH TECHNIQUES: THE CASE FOR POLYGRAPH TESTS

§ 12–2.1 Introductory Discussion of the Science

§ 12–2.1.1 Background

Polygraph techniques for the detection of deception and verification of truthfulness have a long history of scientific research, and many prominent

---

† Scientific opinion about the validity of polygraph techniques is extremely polarized. Therefore, the editors invited scientists from the "two camps" on this issue to present their views. Consistent with classical principles of debate, we have placed the affirmative argument in favor of polygraph tests first. The argument against polygraph techniques, written by Professors Iacono and Lykken, begins at § 12–3.0, infra.

* Professor Honts is the Department Head and a Professor of Psychology at Boise State University and Editor of The Journal of Credibility Assessment and Witness Psychology. He is the recipient of grants from the U.S. Office of Naval Research and from the Royal Canadian Mounted Police to conduct research on the psychophysiological detection of deception. He is a Forensic Psychological Consultant to nu-

merous public agencies in the United States in Canada. He has been a licensed polygraph examiner for 25 years.

** Professor Raskin is Professor Emeritus, University of Utah and Editor of Psychological Methods in Criminal Investigation and Evidence and Co–Editor of Electrodermal Activity in Psychological Research. He has been the recipient of numerous grants and contracts from the National Institute of Justice, U.S. Department of Defense, U.S. Secret Service, and U.S. Army Research and Development Command to conduct research and development on psychophysiological detection of deception. He was the Co–Developer of the first computerized polygraph system. He was Past President Rocky Mountain Psychological Association and is an Elected Fellow in the American Psychological Association, American Psy-

psychologists and other scientists have contributed to the existing literature. Following World War II, polygraph testing grew rapidly in its applications within the law enforcement, government, and commercial sectors of our society. This was soon followed by increased scientific research and intense debate within the scientific, legal, and political communities.

Critics as well as supporters of polygraph techniques have pointed out many limitations and misapplications of polygraph techniques.[1] However, we believe that the most vocal critics[2] have grossly overstated the case against the polygraph, in part because of their lack of direct research or experience with the techniques and their applications.[3] Since the fundamental scientific question is the extent to which a psychophysiological test can differentiate truthful from deceptive individuals, much of this section is devoted to that issue and other factors that may affect the various types of polygraph tests in use today.

Scientific research clearly demonstrates that properly conducted polygraph tests have sufficient reliability and validity to be of considerable value to individuals, the criminal justice process, and society. In this chapter, we briefly review the historical development of the polygraph test along with current scientific knowledge concerning the reliability and validity of various polygraph techniques. We discuss the strengths and weaknesses of various approaches and techniques and when their application may or may not be justified on the basis of scientific research. In so doing, we comment on various problems that arise in the field, describe what has been accomplished toward correcting the problems that have plagued attempts to use psychophysiological methods to assess credibility, and suggest ways to improve their accuracy and applications.

Polygraphy is one of the oldest areas of research in applied psychology, and its history is distinguished by the stature of those who have worked in the

---

chological Society, American Association for Applied and Preventive Psychology. He has served as a Forensic Psychological Consultant to numerous federal and local agencies and legislative bodies in the United States, Canada, Israel, United Kingdom, and Norway. He has been a licensed polygraph examiner for 27 years.

*** Professor Kircher is an Associate Professor of Educational Psychology, University of Utah. He specializes in the use of computer, psychometric, and decision theoretic methods for assessing truth and deception from physiological recordings. He pioneered the development of the first computerized polygraph system and has collaborated with David C. Raskin and Charles R. Honts since 1977 on research and development of methods for the physiological detection of deception.

§ 12–2.0

1. *See, e.g.,* Charles R. Honts, *The Psychophysiological Detection of Deception*, 3 CURRENT DIRECTIONS IN PSYCHOL. SCI. 77 (1994); William G. Iacono & Christopher J. Patrick, *Assessing Deception: Polygraph Techniques, in* CLINICAL ASSESSMENT OF MALINGERING AND DECEPTION 205

(Richard Rogers ed., 1988); David C. Raskin, *The Polygraph in 1986: Scientific, Professional, and Legal Issues Surrounding Applications and Acceptance of Polygraph Evidence*, 1986 UTAH L. REV. 29 (1986); David C. Raskin, *Does Science Support Polygraph Testing, in* THE POLYGRAPH TEST: LIES, TRUTH AND SCIENCE 90 (Anthony Gale ed., 1988).

2. *See, e.g.,* GERSHON BEN-SHAKAR & JOHN J. FUREDY, THEORIES AND APPLICATIONS IN THE DETECTION OF DECEPTION (1990); DAVID T. LYKKEN, A TREMOR IN THE BLOOD (1981); Leonard Saxe, *Detection of Deception: Polygraph and Integrity Tests*, 3 CURRENT DIRECTIONS IN PSYCHOLOGICAL SCIENCE 69 (1994).

3. *See, e.g.,* Charles R. Honts, *Heat Without Light: A Review of Theories and Applications in the Detection of Deception*, 30 PSYCHOPHYSIOLOGY 317 (1993); David C. Raskin & John C. Kircher, *The Validity of Lykken's Criticisms: Fact or Fancy?* 27 JURIMETRICS 271 (1988); David C. Raskin & John C. Kircher, *Comments on Furedy and Heslegrave: Misconceptions, Misdescriptions, and Misdirections, in* ADVANCES IN PSYCHOPHYSIOLOGY 215 (Patrick K. Ackles et. al. eds., vol. 4, 1991).

area.[4] Modern physiological methods for assessing truth and deception began in Italy near the end of the 19th century.[5] In the United States, polygraph techniques were developed as an investigative tool for the law enforcement community, and the early work by Marston[6] and subsequent improvements by Larson[7] and Keeler[8] resulted in a portable polygraph instrument and a general method known as the relevant-irrelevant technique.

§ 12–2.1.2 Psychophysiological Detection of Deception Techniques

[1] The Relevant–Irrelevant Test (RIT)

In the RIT, two types of questions are presented to the subject. Relevant questions directly address the matter under investigation (e.g., "Did you take that $10,000 from the safe?"), whereas irrelevant questions concern neutral topics, such as the subject's name, place of birth or residence, or simple statements of fact (e.g., "Are you sitting down?"). As in all polygraph deception tests, questions must be answered "Yes" or "No." Respiration, electrodermal, and blood pressure responses to the relevant questions are compared to those produced by the irrelevant questions. If the reactions to the relevant questions are generally stronger, the subject is judged to be deceptive to the relevant questions. Conversely, if reactions to the relevant and irrelevant questions are similar in magnitude, the subject is considered truthful to the relevant questions.

The RIT gained widespread use in law enforcement, government, and the private sector in the absence of any credible evidence that it can be used to distinguish truthful and deceptive answers with a reasonable degree of accuracy.[9] Fundamental flaws in the RIT argue strongly against its use in criminal investigations.[10] Most serious is the naive and implausible rationale underlying the test. Although deceptive individuals are likely to produce relatively strong physiological reactions to the relevant questions and be diagnosed as deceptive, many truthful individuals are likely to perceive the relevant questions as more threatening, causing them to react more strongly

4. *See, e.g.*, Roland C. Davis, *Physiological Responses as a Means of Evaluating Information, in* THE MANIPULATION OF HUMAN BEHAVIOR 142 (Albert D. Biderman & Herbert Zimmer eds., 1961); David B. Lindsley, *The Psychology of Lie Detection, in* PSYCHOLOGY FOR LAW ENFORCEMENT OFFICERS 89 (George J. Dudycha ed., 1955); ALEKSANDR R. LURIA, THE NATURE OF HUMAN CONFLICTS (1932); HUGO MUNSTERBERG, ON THE WITNESS STAND (1908); Max Wertheimer & Julius Klein, *Psychologische Tatbestandsdiagnostick*, 15 ARCHIV FUR KRIMINAL-ANTHROPOLGIE UND KRIMINALISTIK 72 (1904). *See also* Paul V. Trovillo, *A History of Lie Detection*, 29 J. CRIM. L. CRIMINOLOGY & POLICE SCI. 848 (1939); Paul V. Trovillo, *A History of Lie Detection*, 30 J. CRIM. L. CRIMINOLOGY & POLICE SCI. 104 (1939) (a two part detailed review of the early history of lie detection).

5. *See, e.g.*, CESARE LOMBROSO, L'HOMME CRIMINEL (2d ed.1895).

6. *See* William M. Marston, *Systolic Blood Pressure Symptoms of Deception*, 2 J. EXPERIMENTAL PSYCHOL. 117 (1917).

7. JOHN A. LARSON, LYING AND ITS DETECTION (1932).

8. Leonarde Keeler, *Scientific Methods of Criminal Detection With the Polygraph*, 2 KAN. B. ASS'N 22 (1933).

9. *See, e.g.*, David C. Raskin et al., *Recent Laboratory and Field Research on Polygraph Techniques, in* CREDIBILITY ASSESSMENT 1 (John C. Yuille ed., 1989).

10. *See, e.g.*, RASKIN (1986), *supra* note 1; David C. Raskin, *Polygraph Techniques for the Detection of Deception, in* PSYCHOLOGICAL METHODS IN CRIMINAL INVESTIGATION AND EVIDENCE 247 (David C. Raskin ed., 1989).

to them. As a result, the RIT can be expected to produce highly accurate decisions on deceptive subjects (true positives) and a large percentage of incorrect decisions on truthful subjects (false positives). Recent research has demonstrated that these predictions are correct. Horowitz, Raskin, Honts, & Kircher reported that only 22% of the innocent subjects in their experiment were able to produce truthful outcomes with the RIT.[11] Another study reported that none of the innocent subjects was able to pass the RIT.[12]

Use of the RIT has declined substantially in recent years, and in most jurisdictions it has fallen into disuse for forensic applications.[13] The Polygraph Protection Act of 1988 essentially eliminated its widespread use by commercial polygraph examiners. Although it offers little protection against false positive errors and the available scientific research argues against its use, the RIT is still employed by polygraph examiners in some federal programs (e.g., Federal Bureau of Investigation and National Security Agency). However, some jurisdictions have recognized the limitations of the RIT and either prohibit its use as evidence[14] or its use for any purpose.[15]

[2] The Control Question Test (CQT)

To overcome the weaknesses of the RIT, Reid devised the control question test (CQT).[16] The CQT differs from the RIT in that physiological reactions to relevant questions are compared to those produced by control (probable-lie) questions. Since control questions are designed to arouse the concern of innocent subjects, it is expected that innocent subjects will react more strongly to them than to the relevant questions. For example, if the subject were suspected of a theft, a control question might be, "During the first 22 years of your life, did you ever take something that did not belong to you?" Control questions are intentionally vague, cover a long period of the subject's life, and include acts that most individuals have committed but are embarrassed or reluctant to admit during a properly conducted polygraph examination. During the pretest review of the questions to be asked on the test, control questions are introduced by the polygraph examiner in such a way that the subject will initially or eventually answer "No" to each of them.

Innocent subjects answer the relevant questions truthfully but are likely to be deceptive or uncertain about their truthfulness when answering the control questions. Therefore, innocent subjects are expected to react more strongly to the control questions than to the relevant questions. In contrast, guilty subjects are expected to be concerned about failing the test because their answers to the relevant questions are deceptive, and they are likely to show stronger reactions to the relevant questions.[17]

11. Steven W. Horowitz et al., *The Role of Comparison Questions in the Physiological Detection of Deception,* 34 PSYCHOPHYSIOLOGY 118 (1997).

12. Frank S. Horvath, *The Utility of Control Questions and the Effects of Two Control Question Types in Field Polygraph Techniques,* 16 J. POLICE SCI. & ADMIN. 198 (1988).

13. OFFICE OF TECHNOLOGY ASSESSMENT, SCIENTIFIC VALIDITY OF POLYGRAPH TESTING: A RESEARCH REVIEW AND EVALUATION (1983).

14. N.M. R. EVID. 707.

15. UTAH CODE ANN. § 34–37–1 (1974).

16. John E. Reid, *A Revised Questioning Technique in Lie Detection Tests,* 37 J. CRIM. L., CRIMINOLOGY & POLICE SCI. 542 (1947).

17. For a more detailed description of the CQT, *see* Raskin, *supra* note 10.

Recently, the term "control question" has been the subject of controversy and confusion in the scientific literature.[18] Control questions are misnamed because they do not function as controls in the strict scientific sense of the term, i.e., they do not elicit reactions that indicate how subjects would react if their answers to the relevant questions were truthful. Rather, they provide an estimate of how innocent subjects would react if their answers to relevant questions were actually deceptive. The fundamental issue is not whether control questions function as controls in the usual scientific sense, but whether they elicit larger reactions than relevant questions from innocent subjects and thereby reduce the risk of false positive errors.

[3] The Directed Lie Test (DLT)

New question structures and examination procedures have been developed to overcome some of the problems that have plagued traditional comparison question techniques. The most promising of these is the directed lie test (DLT) developed at the University of Utah.[19] The traditional CQT relies on the effectiveness of probable-lie comparison questions that are formulated and chosen by the polygraph examiner to suit each case. Such questions vary considerably and may also be intrusive and ineffective with some subjects. In contrast, the DLT employs a straightforward approach that has clear face validity and uses a relatively small set of simple comparison questions that are much easier to standardize.

The DLT includes questions to which the subject is instructed to lie, e.g., "Before 1998, did you ever make even one mistake?" or "Before 1998, did you ever do something that you later regretted?" The directed-lie questions are introduced during the review of all questions that follows the administration of a number test in which the subject had been instructed to choose a number and lie about the number that was chosen. The subject is told that the number test enables the examiner to determine when the subject is lying and when the subject is answering truthfully. The examiner then explains that the directed-lie questions will ensure that the subject will be correctly classified as truthful or deceptive on the subsequent polygraph test. These procedures reduce the number of false positive errors[20] and increase the standardization and ease of administration of polygraph examinations.[21]

[4] Guilty Knowledge Tests (GKT)

The concealed knowledge or guilty knowledge test (GKT) is another method for detecting deception.[22] In contrast to the RIT and CQT, the GKT

18. *See, e.g.,* John J. Furedy & Ronald J. Heslegrave, *The Forensic Use of the Polygraph: A Psychophysiological Analysis of Current Trends and Future Prospects, in* ADVANCES IN PSYCHOPHYSIOLOGY (Patrick K. Ackles et. al., eds. 1991); David T. Lykken, *The Detection of Deception,* 86 PSYCHOL. BULL. 47 (1979); Raskin & Kircher, *supra* note 7; David C. Raskin & John A. Podlesny, *Truth and Deception: A Reply to Lykken,* 86 PSYCHOL. BULL. 54 (1979).

19. Charles R. Honts & David C. Raskin, *A Field Study of the Validity of the Directed Lie*

Control Question, 16 J. POLICE SCI. ADMIN. 56 (1988); Horowitz et al., *supra* note 11; Raskin, *supra* note 10; Raskin et al., *supra* note 9.

20. Honts & Raskin, *supra* note 19; Horowitz et al., *supra* note 11.

21. Honts, *supra* note 1; Raskin, *supra* note 10.

22. David T. Lykken, *The GSR in the Detection of Guilt,* 43 J. APPLIED PSYCHOL. 385 (1959); Raskin, *supra* note 10.

does not attempt to directly assess the veracity of a person's statements concerning knowledge or involvement in a crime. Instead, this technique is used to determine if the subject is concealing knowledge of details of the crime that would be known only to a guilty person.

The GKT consists of a series of multiple-choice questions, each of which addresses a different aspect of the crime. For example, if the subject is suspected of stealing a ring, a question on the test might be, "Regarding the type of ring that was stolen, do you know if it was: (1) a ruby ring, (2) a gold wedding ring, (3) a pearl ring, (4) a diamond ring, (5) a sapphire ring, (6) a silver and turquoise ring?"[23] A guilty subject who knows the correct alternative is expected to show a relatively strong physiological reaction to that item. However, an innocent subject who has no specific knowledge is not expected to respond differentially to correct and incorrect alternatives.

Typically, only electrodermal responses to the questions are scored, and reactions to the first alternatives are not evaluated because the first item in a series typically produces a large orienting reaction that is independent of any specific knowledge that may be possessed by the subject. Thus, for one multiple-choice question, the probability that the subject's strongest electrodermal response will occur by chance to the correct alternative is 1 in 5, or 20%. With several multiple-choice questions, the chance probability that a subject who has no concealed knowledge will consistently react most strongly to the correct alternatives is exceedingly small.[24]

§ 12–2.2 Areas of Scientific Agreement and Disagreement

§ 12–2.2.1 Survey of the Accuracy of Polygraph Tests

Prior to 1970, virtually no scientific research on the reliability and validity of the CQT in criminal investigation had been conducted. The first scientific study was performed in our laboratory at the University of Utah.[25] By 1983, the Office of Technology Assessment [OTA] had identified 14 analog studies and 10 field studies of the CQT, some of which can reasonably be used to make inferences about the accuracy of control question tests in the field.[26] Lykken reported the first laboratory research on the accuracy of the GKT,[27] and Elaad reported the first field study of the GKT in 1990.[28]

When scientists attempt to assess the usefulness of techniques such as polygraph tests, they are concerned with reliability and validity. In its scientific sense, reliability refers to the consistency of a technique. In studies of polygraph tests, reliability focuses on the consistency of the scoring of the physiological data. Establishing this inter-rater reliability is an important first step in evaluating any test. Reliability and validity are related in that reliability is necessary, but is not sufficient for validity. That is, if a test

---

23. John A. Podlesny & David C. Raskin, *Effectiveness of Techniques and Physiological Measures in the Detection of Deception*, 15 Psychophysiology 344 (1978).

24. For a detailed description of the GKT, see Raskin, *supra* note 10.

25. Gordon H. Barland & David C. Raskin, *An Evaluation of Field Techniques in Detection of Deception*, 12 Psychophysiology 321 (1975).

26. OTA, *supra* note 13.

27. Lykken, *supra* note 22.

28. Eitan Elaad, *Detection of Guilty Knowledge in Real–Life Criminal Investigations*, 75 J. Applied Psychol. 521 (1990).

cannot be scored consistently (reliably), then the scores cannot be valid. The scientific issues surrounding the concept of validity are complex and scientists use the term in several different ways. However, in this context, validity may be considered simply as the accuracy of the polygraph techniques.

The reliability of scoring of the CQT has been studied extensively. Research has clearly indicated that when the performance of competent evaluators is assessed, the reliability of numerical scoring is very high. It is not unusual for agreement on decisions by independent evaluators to approach 100%, and correlational assessments of the reliability of numerical scoring are usually greater than 0.90.[29] The reliability of the GKT has not been reported in the literature, but the simplicity of scoring this test would be expected to produce very high inter-rater reliability. Computer-based statistical decision-making with the CQT is perfectly reliable as long as the computers are functioning properly.[30]

Assessing the validity of polygraph tests is considerably more complex than assessing their reliability. Science has generally approached such problems with different research methodologies that involve conducting research in the laboratory and in the field. Each of these approaches has strengths and weaknesses. The strength of the laboratory approach is that the scientist has control over the situation. Subjects can be randomly assigned to conditions and the scientist knows with certainty who is, and who is not, telling the truth during the polygraph examination. Variables can be manipulated with precision and strong inferential statements can often be made. However, laboratory approaches can be weak in that they may lack realism when compared to the field situation they model.[31]

The main strength of field research is that the scientist can study the phenomenon of interest in real-life settings where realism is not an issue. However, scientific control in field studies can be very difficult. A central issue for field studies is the quality of the criterion of guilt and innocence. This raises questions about how the researchers determined who was truthful and who was deceptive, which is not an easy task. If there had been strong proof of guilt or innocence in the actual cases, polygraph tests would probably not have been conducted.

Neither the laboratory nor the field approach is perfect, so the best strategy is to use both methodologies. To the extent that laboratory studies and field studies converge on the same results, they reinforce and complement each other in determining the true state of the world. The techniques scientists use to overcome the relative weakness of these two methodologies are discussed in the following sections.

29. *See* David C. Raskin, *The Scientific Basis of Polygraph Techniques and Their Uses in the Judicial Process, in* RECONSTRUCTING THE PAST: THE ROLE OF PSYCHOLOGISTS IN CRIMINAL TRIALS (Arne Trankell ed., 1982).

30. John C. Kircher & David C. Raskin, *Human Versus Computerized Evaluations of Polygraph Data in Laboratory Setting,* 73 J. APPLIED PSYCHOL. 291 (1988); Charles R. Honts & Mary K. Devitt, *Bootstrap Decision Making*

for Polygraph Examinations: Final Report of DOD/PERSEC Grant No. N00014–92–J–1794, [available from the Defense Technical Information Center, Building 5 Cameron Station, Alexandria, VA 22304–6145].

31. John A. Podlesny & David C. Raskin, *Physiological Measures and the Detection of Deception,* 84 PSYCHOL. BULL. 782 (1977).

[1] Laboratory Studies

[a] Control Question Test

Laboratory research has traditionally been an attractive alternative because the scientist can control the environment. By randomly assigning subjects to conditions, the scientist can know with certainty who is telling the truth and who is lying. Laboratory research on credibility assessment has typically made some subjects "guilty" by having them commit a mock crime (e.g. "steal" a watch from an office), and then instructing them to lie about it during a subsequent test. From a scientific viewpoint, random assignment to conditions is highly desirable because it controls for the influence of extraneous variables that might confound the results of the experiment.[32] The most accepted type of laboratory study realistically simulates a crime in which some subjects commit an overt transaction, such as a theft.[33] While the guilty subjects enact a realistic crime, the innocent subjects are merely told about the nature of the crime and do not enact it. All subjects are motivated to produce a truthful outcome, usually by a cash bonus for passing the test. For example, one such study used prison inmates who were offered a bonus equal to one month's wages if they could produce a truthful outcome.[34]

The advantages of careful laboratory simulations include total control over the issues that are investigated and the types of tests that are used, consistency in test administration and interpretation, specification of the subject populations that are studied, control over the skill and training of the examiners, and absolute verification of the accuracy of test results. Carefully designed and conducted studies that closely approximate the methods and conditions characteristic of high quality practice by polygraph professionals and use subjects similar to the target population, such as convicted felons or a cross-section of the general community, provide the most generalizable results.[35] Laboratory research in general, and credibility assessment in particular, is sometimes criticized for lack of realism, which may limit the ability of the scientist to apply the results of the laboratory to real-world settings. However, a recent analysis reported in the flagship journal of the American Psychological Society examined a broad range of laboratory-based psychological research.[36] The authors concluded, "correspondence between lab-and field-based effect sizes of conceptually similar independent and dependent variables was considerable. In brief, the psychological laboratory has generally produced truths, rather than trivialities."[37] Our position with regard to the high quality studies of the CQT and DLT is similar. We believe that these studies produce important information about the validity of such tests that is not trivial and ungeneralizable, as some critics have claimed. As described below, a recent scientific survey of psychological scientists who work on applied problems in psychology and the law indicates that the vast majority of them share our belief in the value of laboratory studies of the validity of the polygraph.

32. Thomas D. Cook & Donald T. Campbell, Quasi-experimentation: Design & analysis issues for Field Settings (1979).

33. Raskin, *supra* note 29.

34. David C. Raskin & Robert D. Hare, *Psychopathy and Detection of Deception in a Prison Population*, 15 Psychophysiology 126.

35. John C. Kircher et al., *Meta-analysis of Mock Crime Studies of the Control Question Polygraph Technique*, 12 L. & Hum. Behav. 79 (1988).

36. C. A. Anderson et al., *Research in the Psychological Laboratory: Truth or Triviality?*, 8 Curr. Dir. Psychological Sci. 3 (1999).

37. *Id.*

In 1997, a Committee of Concerned Social Scientists filed a Brief for Amicus Curiae[38] with the Supreme Court of the United States in the case of *United States v. Scheffer*.[39] They identified eight high quality laboratory studies of the CQT,[40] the results of which are illustrated in Table 1. These high quality laboratory studies indicate that the CQT is a very accurate discriminator of truthful and deceptive subjects. Overall, these studies correctly classified 91% of the subjects and produced approximately equal numbers of false positive and false negative errors.

Table 1
Results of High Quality Laboratory Studies

Study	n	% correct	% wrong	% Inc.	n	% correct	% wrong	% Inc.
		Guilty				Innocent		
Control Question Tests								
Glinton, et al. (1984)	2	100	0	0	13	85	15	0
Honts, et al. (1994)[a]	20	70	20	10	20	75	10	15
Horowitz, et al. (1994)[b]	15	53	20	27	15	80	13	7
Kircher & Raskin (1988)	50	88	6	6	50	86	6	8
Podlesny & Raskin (1978)	20	70	15	15	20	90	5	5
Podlesny & Truslow (1993)	72	69	13	18	24	75	4	21
Raskin & Hare (1978)	24	88	0	12	24	88	8	4
Rovner, et al. (1979)[c]	24	88	0	12	24	88	8	4
Weighted Means	227	77	10	13	190	84	8	8
Directed Lie Control[d]								
Traditional Control Questions	15	53	20	27	15	80	13	7
Personally Relevant Directed Lie	15	73	13	13	15	87	0	13
Trivial Directed Lie	15	54	20	26	15	67	13	20
Relevant/Irrelevant	15	100	0	0	15	20	73	7
Concealed Knowledge Tests								
Davidson (1968)	12	92	8		36	100	0	
Honts, et al. (1994)[e]	10	80	20		10	90	10	
Lykken (1959)	37	86	14		12	100	0	
Podlesny & Raskin (1978)	10	90	10		10	100	0	
Steller, et al. (1987)	47	85	15		40	100	0	
Weighted Means	116	86	14		108	99	1	

a.   Countermeasure Subjects Excluded.
b.   Traditional Control Question Subjects Only.
c.   Countermeasure Subjects Excluded.
d.   Data from Horowitz et al. (1994).
e.   Countermeasure Subjects Excluded.

[b]   Directed Lie Test

Since the DLT is relatively new, there are fewer studies of its validity. Seven laboratory studies have been conducted, but they are not all of high

38.   Charles R. Honts & Charles F. Peterson, Brief of the Committee of Concerned Social Scientists as Amicus Curiae, United States v. Scheffer, in the Supreme Court of the United States (1997). The Amicus was co-signed by 17 individuals holding advanced scientific degrees.

39.   523 U.S. 303, 118 S.Ct. 1261, 140 L.Ed.2d 413 (1998).

40.   *See* Avital Ginton et al., *A Method for Evaluating the Use of the Polygraph in a Real–Life Situation*, 67 J. APPLIED PSYCHOL. 131 (1982); Charles R. Honts et al., *Mental and Physical Countermeasures Reduce the Accuracy of Polygraph Tests*, 79 J. APPLIED PSYCH. 252 (1994); Horowitz et al., *supra* note 11; Kircher & Raskin, *supra* note 30; Podlesny & Raskin, *supra* note 31; John A. Podlesny & Connie M. Truslow, *Validity of an Expanded–Issue (Modified General Question) Polygraph Technique in a Simulated Distributed–Crime–Roles Context*, 78 J. APPLIED PSYCHOL. 788 (1993); David C. Raskin & Robert D. Hare, *Psychopathy and Detection of Deception in a Prison Population*, 15 PSYCHOPHYSIOLOGY 126 (1978); Louis I. Rovner et al., *Effects of Information and Practice on Detection of Deception*, 16 PSYCHOPHYSIOLOGY 197 (1979).

quality.[41] The Horowitz et al. study is the most carefully designed and conducted.[42] It used a mock crime that closely approximated the field situation, similar to those described for the CQT in the previous section. The Horowitz study compared the effectiveness of the DLT with the CQT and RIT. Different groups received one of two types of directed lies, personally-relevant directed lies using the procedures previously described or simple directed lies to three of the neutral questions that were used in the RIT. The results indicated that the personal directed lie produced the highest accuracy, except for the RIT with guilty subjects. The outcomes for the four types of tests are presented in Table 2. Among all question structures, the personal directed-lie produced the highest number of correct decisions on innocent subjects and among the three tests that employed comparison questions, it produced the highest number of correct decisions on guilty subjects.

Table 2
Test outcomes of the Horowitz et al. (1997) study

Experimental Groups	Test Outcomes (%)			% Correct Decisions
	Correct	Wrong	Inconclusive	
Guilty				
Relevant-irrelevant	100	0	0	100
Trivial Directed Lie	53	20	27	73
Personal Directed Lie	73	14	13	84
Probable Lie Comparison	53	20	27	73
Innocent				
Relevant-irrelevant	20	73	7	22
Trivial Directed Lie	67	13	20	84
Personal Directed Lie	87	13	0	87
Probable Lie Comparison	80	13	7	86

n = 15 for each of the experimental groups.
The percentage of correct decisions was calculated by excluding inconclusive outcomes.

The U. S. Department of Defense has conducted three sets of studies concerning the validity of the DLT. Barland examined the validity of the Military Intelligence version of the DLT in a mock screening setting with 26 truthful subjects and 30 subjects who attempted deception.[43] All subjects were tested with the DLT; no other techniques were examined. Excluding inconclusive outcomes, Barland's evaluators correctly classified 79% of the subjects. Although this performance appears modest compared to that obtained in

41. Gordon H. Barland, *A Validity and Reliability Study of Counterintelligence Screening Tests*, Unpublished manuscript, Security Support Battalion, 902nd Military Intelligence Group, Fort George G. Meade, Maryland (1981); Department of Defense Polygraph Institute Research Division Staff, *A Comparison of Psychophysiological Detection of Deception Accuracy Rates Obtained Using the Counterintelligence Scope Polygraph (CSP) and The Test for Espionage and Sabotage (TES) question formats* 26 POLYGRAPH 79 (1997); Department of Defense Polygraph Institute Research Division Staff, *Psychophysiological Detection of Deception Accuracy Rates Obtained Using the Test for Espionage and Sabotage (TES)*, 27 POLYGRAPH 68 (1998); Horowitz et al., *supra* note 11; Sheila Reed, *A New Psychophysiological Detection of Deception Examination for Security Screening*, 31 PSYCHOPHYSIOLOGY S80 (1994).

42. Horowitz et al., *supra* note 11.

43. Barland, *supra* note 41.

Horowitz et al. and the studies reported above for the CQT, it should be pointed out that Barland's study was conducted in a screening setting. By comparison, other mock-screening studies produced near chance performance with probable-lie tests.[44] Therefore, the performance of the directed lie in the Barland study was actually quite strong.

The other two sets of studies on the DLT concern a new test, the test of espionage and sabotage (TES) developed by DODPI for use in national security screening tests. Reed reported three laboratory mock screening studies of the DLT.[45] Following a series of studies that indicated that the national security screening tests of the time were making an unacceptably high number of false negative errors,[46] DODPI attempted to develop a more accurate screening test. It should be noted that the primary concern in conducting national security screening tests is a desire to avoid false negative errors. Following a series of studies that are not publicly available, Reed described the product of DODPI's efforts.

In the first study, the TES test format with only directed-lie comparison questions was tested against two versions of the counterintelligence scope polygraph (CSP) test. One version of the CSP used probable-lie comparison questions (the type of comparison question used in the standard CQT) while the other used directed-lie comparison questions. The TES outperformed both of the CSP formats in terms of correctly identifying guilty subjects. The CSP with directed-lie comparisons was slightly, but not significantly, better at identifying guilty subjects than was the CSP with probable-lie comparisons. The second study produced even higher accuracy for the TES, a directed-lie comparison test format. Little information is provided about the third study, but it also appears to show considerable accuracy for the directed-lie TES. Most recently, DODPI reported a mock espionage/sabotage study that involved 82 subjects.[47] All subjects were tested with the TES. Excluding one inconclusive outcome, the examiners correctly identified 98% of the innocent subjects and 83.3% of the guilty subjects. This study also indicates that the directed-lie TES is extremely successful in discriminating between innocent and guilty subjects.

Abrams reported the only other study of the DLT. Unfortunately that study was so poorly designed and so methodologically flawed that the data are meaningless.[48] Although Abrams and Matte have become outspoken critics of the DLT, their criticisms lack merit and their attacks on the DLT are baseless.[49] Interested readers are referred to the research and commentary by Honts and his colleagues.[50]

44. Gordon H. Barland et al., *Studies of the Accuracy of Security Screening Polygraph Examinations*. Department of Defense Polygraph Institute, Fort McClellan, Alabama. Available *at* http://truth.boisestate.edu/raredocuments/bhb.html (1989); Charles R. Honts, *Counterintelligence Scope Polygraph (CSP) Test Found to be a Poor Discriminator*, 5 FORENSIC REPORTS 215 (1992).

45. Reed, *supra* note 41; also published as Department of Defense Polygraph Institute Research Staff, (1997), *supra* note 41.

46. Gordon H. Barland et al., *supra* note 44; Charles R. Honts, *The Emperor's New Clothes: Application of Polygraph Tests in the American Workplace*, 4 FORENSIC REPORTS 91 (1991); Charles R. Honts, *supra* note 44;

Charles R. Honts, *The Psychophysiological Detection of Deception*, 3 CURRENT DIRECTIONS IN PSYCHOLOGICAL SCI. 77 (1994).

47. Department of Defense Polygraph Institute Research Staff (1998), *supra* note 41.

48. Stanley Abrams, *The Directed Lie Control Question*, 20 POLYGRAPH 26 (1991).

49. *See* Stanley Abrams, *A Response To Honts On The Issue Of The Discussion Of Questions Between Charts* 28 POLYGRAPH 223 (1999); John A. Matte, *An Analysis Of The Psychodynamics Of The Directed Lie Control Questions In The Control Question Technique*, 27 POLYGRAPH 56 (1998).

50. Charles R. Honts, *The Discussion of Comparison Questions Between List Repeti-*

[c] Guilty Knowledge Test

There are many published laboratory studies of the GKT, but many of these studies used artificial and unrealistic methods that render the studies useless for providing estimates of accuracy in the field. However, a review of the scientific literature reveals five laboratory studies of the GKT that appear to have methodology realistic enough to allow some generalization to the field.[51] The results of these studies are summarized in Table 3. As with the CQT, the quality laboratory studies of the GKT indicate a high level of accuracy for the technique, but the GKT consistently produces more false negative than false positive errors. This is disturbing because the conditions for the detection of concealed knowledge with the GKT are optimized in the laboratory as compared to the field. In GKT lab studies, the experimenters usually pretest potential items for their salience and memorability by guilty subjects and for their transparency to innocent subjects, i.e., can innocent subjects guess the correct response? Although it might be possible to test the transparency of GKT items in the field, it is not possible to test the memorability of key items. Moreover, there is no clear theoretical basis for judgments about what a guilty person is likely to remember about a crime scene. Those factors likely result in an under-estimation of the field rate of false negative errors when generalizing from laboratory studies of the GKT.

Table 3
The results of studies of the GKT

	Guilty			Innocent		
	n	% Correct	% Wrong	n	% Correct	% Wrong
Laboratory Studies						
Davidson (1968)	12	92	8	36	100	0
Honts et al. (1994)[a]	10	80	20	10	90	10
Lykken (1959)	37	86	14	12	100	0
Podlesny & Raskin (1978)	10	90	10	10	100	0
Steller et al. (1987)	47	85	15	40	100	0
Weighted Means	**116**	**86**	**14**	**108**	**99**	**1**
Field Studies						
Elaad (1990)	48	42	58	50	98	2
Elaad, et al., (1992)	40	53	47	40	97	3
Weighted Means	**88**	**47**	**53**	**90**	**98**	**2**

[a] Countermeasure subjects excluded.

tions (Charts) is Associated With Increased Test Accuracy. 28 POLYGRAPH 117 (1999); Charles R. Honts, A Brief Note on the Misleading and the Inaccurate: A Rejoinder to Matte (2000) With Critical Comments on Matte and Reuss (1999), 29 POLYGRAPH 321 (2000); Charles R. Honts & Anne Gordon, A Critical Analysis Of The Directed Lie, 27 POLYGRAPH 241 (1998); Charles R. Honts et al., The Hybrid Directed Lie Test, The Overemphasized Comparison Question, Chimeras And Other Inventions: A Rejoinder To Abrams (1999), 29 POLYGRAPH 156 (2000).

51. See Park O. Davidson, Validity of the Guilty–Knowledge Technique: The Effects of Motivation, 53 J. APPLIED PSYCHOL. 62 (1968); Charles R. Honts, et al., Mental and Physical Countermeasures Reduce the Accuracy of the Concealed Knowledge Test, 33 PSYCHOPHYSIOLOGY 84 (1994); Lykken, supra note 22; Podlesny & Raskin, supra note 23; Max Steller et al., Extraversion and the Detection of Information, 21 J. RES. IN PERSONALITY 334 (1987).

[2] Field Studies

As noted earlier, the greatest problems in conducting field polygraph studies are the development of criteria for determining who was actually telling the truth and who was lying and the lack of control that the experimenter has over the testing situation. There is a consensus among researchers that field studies should have the following characteristics:

1. Subjects should be sampled from the actual population of subjects in which the scientist is interested. If the objective is to determine the accuracy of a polygraph examination on criminal suspects, then the subjects of the study should be criminal suspects.

2. Subjects should be sampled by some type of random process, and cases must be included independent of the accuracy of the original examiner's decision or the quality of the polygraph charts.

3. The physiological data should be evaluated independently by persons trained and experienced in the evaluation of polygraph tests who employ scoring techniques that are representative of those used in the field. The evaluations should be based only on the physiological data, and the evaluators should not have access to other case information. This provides an estimate of the accuracy of the decisions based solely on the physiological information. However, decisions rendered by the original examiner probably provide a better estimate of the accuracy of polygraph techniques as they are actually employed in the field setting by criminal investigators.

4. The credibility of the subject should be determined by information independent of the polygraph test. Confession substantiated by physical evidence is the best criterion for use in these studies.

[a] Control Question Test

The 1983 OTA review of the scientific literature on polygraph tests identified 10 field studies in the scientific literature that met minimal standards for acceptability.[52] However, none of the 10 studies meets all four of the

---

52. OTA, supra note 13; the 10 studies included by the OTA were: Gordon H. Barland & David C. Raskin, Validity and Reliability of Polygraph Examinations of Criminal Suspects 1 U.S. Department of Justice Report No. 76–1, Contract No. 75–NI–99–0001 (1976); Philip J. Bersh, A Validation Study of Polygraph Examiner Judgments, 53 J. Applied Psychol. 399 (1969); William A. Davidson, Validity and Reliability of the Cardio Activity Monitor, 8 Polygraph 104 (1979); Frank S. Horvath, The Effect of Selected Variables on Interpretation of Polygraph Records, 62 J. Applied Psychol. 127 (1977); Frank S. Horvath & John E. Reid, The Reliability of Polygraph Examiner Diagnosis of Truth and Deception, 62 J. Crim. L., Criminology & Police Sci. 276 (1971); Fred L. Hunter & Phillip Ash, The Accuracy and Consistency of Polygraph Examiners' Diagnoses, 1 J. Police Sci. & Admin. 370 (1973); Benjamin Kleinmuntz & Julian Szucko, A Field Study of the Fallibility of Polygraphic Lie Detection, 308 Nature 449 (1984); David C. Raskin, 1 Reliability of Chart Interpretation and Sources of Errors in Polygraph Examinations, U.S. Department of Justice, Report No. 76–3, Contract No. 75–NI–0001. (1976); Stanley M. Slowik & Joseph P. Buckley, Relative Accuracy of Polygraph Examiner Diagnosis of Respiration, Blood Pressure, and GSR Recordings, 3 J. Police Sci. & Admin. 305 (1975); Douglas E. Wicklander & Fred L. Hunter, The Influence of Auxiliary Sources of Information in Polygraph Diagnoses, 3 J. Police Sci. & Admin. 405 (1975).

above criteria for an adequate field study. The overall accuracy of the polygraph decisions in the OTA review was 90% on criterion-guilty suspects and 80% on criterion-innocent suspects. In spite of the inclusion of studies with serious methodological problems, accuracy in field cases was higher than is claimed by some of the most vocal critics.[53]

Subsequent to the OTA study, four field studies of the CQT that meet the criteria for an adequate field study have been reported.[54] As shown in Table 4, they produced a combined estimate of 90.5% accuracy, which is higher than that developed by OTA on the basis of the 10 less rigorous early studies.

Table 4. The Accuracy of Independent Evaluations in High Quality Field Studies of the CQT

Study	Guilty				Innocent			
	n	% Correct	% Wrong	% Inc	n	% Correct	% Wrong	% Inc
Honts (1996)a	7	100	0	0	6	83	0	17
Honts & Raskin (1988)b	12	92	0	8	13	62	15	23
Patrick & Iacono (1991)c	52	92	2	6	37	30	24	46
Raskin et al. (1989)d	37	73	0	27	26	61	8	31
Means	108	89	1	10	82	59	12	29
Percent Decisions		**98**	**2**			**75**	**25**	

a Subgroup of subjects confirmed by confession and evidence.

b Decision based only on comparisons to traditional comparison questions.

c.Results from mean blind rescoring of the cases "verified with maximum certainty" p. 235.

d. There results are from an independent evaluation fo the "pure verification" cases.

It is interesting to note that only in the Patrick and Iacono study did the original examiners perform at a much higher level than the independent evaluators.[55] Patrick and Iacono's original examiners correctly classified 100% of their guilty subjects and 90% of the innocent subjects,[56] which was similar to the performance of the original examiners in the Honts[57] study that used examiners from the same law enforcement agency. Given the general performance of independent evaluators across these high quality field studies, it appears that the performance of the blind evaluators in Patrick and Iacono could be viewed as an outlying data point. Honts provides a discussion of this and other potential problems with the Patrick & Iacono study.[58] If the Patrick & Iacono study is excluded, the remaining three field studies produce an estimate of accuracy of 96%.

53. David T. Lykken, *A Tremor In The Blood: Uses And Abuses Of The Lie Detector* (1998).

54. Charles R. Honts, *Criterion Development and Validity of the Control Question Test in Field Application* 123 J. GENERAL PSYCHOL. 309. (1996); Honts & Raskin, *supra* note 19; Christopher J. Patrick & William G. Iacono, *Validity of the Control Question Polygraph Test: The Problem of Sampling Bias*, 76 J. APPLIED PSYCHOL. 229 (1991); David C. Raskin et al., *A Study of the Validity of Polygraph Examinations in Criminal Investigation*, 1 NAT'L INST. OF JUST. (1988).

55. Patrick & Iacono, *supra* note 54.

56. *Id.*

57. Honts, *supra* note 1.

58. *Id.*

Although the better quality field studies indicate a high accuracy rate for the CQT, all of the data presented in Table 4 were obtained from independent evaluations of the physiological data. That method is desirable for scientific purposes because it eliminates possible contamination (e.g., knowledge of the case facts and the overt behaviors of the subject during the examination) that might have influenced the decisions of the original examiners. Such contamination could distort research designed to determine how much discriminative information was contained in the physiological recordings. However, independent evaluators rarely testify in legal proceedings, nor do they make decisions in most applied settings.

The original examiner renders the diagnosis of truthfulness or deception in an actual case and would testify in court. Thus, accuracy of decisions by independent evaluators is not the true figure of merit for legal proceedings and most other applications. The Committee of Concerned Social Scientists[59] presented the data from the original examiners in the studies reported in Table 4 along with two additional studies that are often cited by critics of the CQT,[60] as shown in Table 5. Those data indicate that the original examiners achieved accuracy rates of 98% on verified innocent suspects and 97% on verified guilty suspects, which are higher than the results from the independent evaluators.

59. Honts & Peterson *supra* note 38.

60. Those two studies are, Benjamin Kleinmuntz & Julian J. Szucko, *A Field Study of the Fallibility of Polygraphic Lie Detection*, 308 NATURE 449 (1984), Frank Horvath, *The Effects of Selected Variables on Interpretation of Polygraph Records*, 62, J. APPLIED PSYCHOL. 127 (1977). Neither of these studies meets the generally accepted requirements for useful field studies but nevertheless they are frequently cited by critics of the CQT as evidence that the CQT is not accurate. The study reported by Benjamin Kleinmuntz and Julian J. Szucko fails to meet the criteria for a useful field study because (1) the subjects were employees who were forced to take tests as part of their employment, not criminal suspects (2) the case selection method was not specified, and (3) the data were evaluated by students at a polygraph school that does not teach blind chart evaluation. Moreover, those students were given only one ninth of the usual amount of data collected in a polygraph examination and were forced to use a rating scale with which they were not familiar. The Horvath study also fails to meet the criteria for a useful study because (1) about half of the innocent subjects were victims of violent crime, not suspects, (2) virtually all of the false positive errors in that study were with innocent victims, not innocent suspects, (3) the independent evaluators were all trained at a polygraph school that does not teach numerical chart evaluation, and (4) cases were not selected at random. Some cases were excluded from the study because of the nature of the charts. An interesting fact that critics almost never mention is that the decisions by the original examiners in the Horvath Study were 100% correct. Also see the discussion in David C. Raskin, *Methodological Issues in Estimating Polygraph Accuracy in Field Applications*, 19, CANADIAN J. BEHAVIOUR. SCI. 389 (1987).

Table 5. Percent Correct Decisions by Original Examiners in Field Cases Using the CQT		
Study	**Innocent**	**Guilty**
Horvath (1977)	100	100
Honts and Raskin (1988)	100	92
Kleinmuntz and Szucko (1984)	100	100
Raskin, Kircher, Honts, & Horowitz (1988)a	96	95
Patrick and Iacono (1991)	90	100
Honts (1996)b	100	94
Means	**98**	**97**
a Cases where all questions were confirmed.		
b Includes all cases with some confirmation.		

[b]   Directed Lie Test

To date, Honts and Raskin have reported the only field study of the DLT. They conducted polygraph tests of criminal suspects over a 4–year period and obtained 25 confirmed tests in which one personal directed lie was included along with typical probable-lie comparison questions.[61] Each author then performed blind interpretations of the charts obtained by the other author, scoring them with and without the use of the directed-lie question. The results of the Honts and Raskin study indicated that inclusion of the directed-lie question in the numerical evaluation of the charts had a noticeable effect on the confirmed innocent suspects, reducing the false positive rate from 20% to 0%. For the confirmed guilty suspects, it had the slight effect of changing one inconclusive outcome to a false negative. The effects of the directed-lie question on the total numerical scores were more dramatic. Inclusion of the directed-lie comparisons almost doubled the size of the total numerical scores for the confirmed innocent suspects, raising the mean score from +4.7 to +9.0. It had a lesser effect on the scores of the confirmed guilty suspects, lowering them from –13.8 to –11.5. Thus, the directed-lie question raised the mean score for innocent suspects from the inconclusive range into the definite truthful area, while the mean score for guilty suspects remained clearly in the deceptive area. The main impact of the directed-lie question was a reduction in false positive errors.

[c]   Guilty Knowledge Test

The only two field studies of the GKT were published in 1990 and 1992.[62] Both are high in quality and meet the four requirements for an adequate field study of polygraph tests described above. The results of those studies are presented in Table 3. Those studies show that the GKT has a very high false

61. Honts & Raskin, *supra* note 19.

62. Elaad (1990), *supra* note 28; Eitan Elaad et al., *Detection Measures in Real–Life* *Criminal Guilty Knowledge Tests,* 77 J. APPLIED PSYCHOL. 757 (1992).

negative rate (53%) in field applications. In both studies, more than half of the guilty criminal suspects passed their GKT examinations, appearing to lack knowledge of the crimes that they had actually committed. In light of the data from laboratory studies and the difficulties in developing good GKT tests as described above, the results of the field studies of the GKT are not at all surprising. Given the extensive literature on the fallibility of eyewitness memory, especially when witnesses are aroused or under stress, it is not surprising that criminals have poor memory for the details of crimes they have committed.[63]

Another factor to consider when evaluating the potential of the GKT as a field polygraph technique is the applicability of the technique to actual cases. In order to conduct a GKT, the examiner must have a number of key items of information from the crime scene to develop the test. Podlesny examined the applicability of the GKT by studying the information available in FBI case files.[64] He estimated that a meaningful GKT could be developed in only 13%–18% of the cases examined. This study suggests that the field applicability of the GKT is extremely limited, even if it had an acceptable level of validity. Given this limitation, demonstrably low accuracy, and strong theoretical reasons why the GKT cannot work properly in the field, it is clear that the GKT is useful only as a vehicle for laboratory research.

§ 12–2.2.2   Countermeasures

Countermeasures are behaviors that an individual may use to attempt to defeat or distort a polygraph test. Countermeasures might be employed either by guilty subjects who are trying to beat the test by appearing truthful or innocent subjects who do not trust the test and want to hedge their bets. Conceptually, countermeasures fall into two major categories, general-state countermeasures that are designed to affect the general mental or physical state of the subject, and specific-point countermeasures that are used to produce physiological changes at specific points during the test. General-state countermeasures include ingestion of drugs, relaxation, and a variety of mental strategies, such as dissociation, self-deception, and rationalization. Specific-point countermeasures include physical and mental maneuvers during and following specific questions in order to increase or decrease physiological reactions to those questions.

Scientists have addressed the problem of polygraph countermeasures, primarily in the laboratory setting. The research clearly indicates that all general-state countermeasures (including drugs) and specific-point counter-measures designed to reduce reactions to relevant questions fail to produce inconclusive or false positive outcomes.[65] However, studies in which subjects have been carefully trained to use specific-point countermeasures to enhance their reactions to control questions have increased false negative rates with both the CQT and the GKT.

63. ELIZABETH F. LOFTUS & K. KETCHAM, WITNESS FOR THE DEFENSE (1991).

64. John A. Podlesny, *Is the Guilty Knowledge Polygraph Technique Applicable in Criminal Investigations? A Review of FBI Case Records*, 20 CRIME LABORATORY DIG. 59 (1993).

65. *See, e.g.*, Charles R. Honts, *Interpreting Research on Countermeasures and the Physiological Detection of Deception*, 15 J. POLICE SCI. & ADMIN. 204 (1987); Raskin, *supra* note 10.

An initial study of the spontaneous use of countermeasures by subjects in mock crime experiments found that countermeasure usage by guilty subjects was high (61% attempted one or more countermeasures), but no guilty subject defeated the test and no innocent subject reported attempting a countermeasure.[66] That study was recently replicated by Honts and his colleagues.[67] In the context of a laboratory study of the CQT, they found that 90% of the guilty and 46% of the innocent subjects reported attempting at least one countermeasure. The spontaneous countermeasures had no significant effects with the guilty subjects, but they did produce a significant effect with innocent subjects. Innocent subjects who attempted a spontaneous countermeasure significantly shifted their scores in the deceptive direction, making it more likely that they would fail the test. It is important to note that providing the subjects with detailed information about the rationale of the control question test and suggestions concerning countermeasures that might be used did not enable them to defeat the test.[68]

[1] Countermeasures and the CQT

A series of studies by Honts and his colleagues examined the effects of specific-point mental and physical countermeasures with the CQT.[69] In these studies, guilty subjects in realistic mock-crime experiments were trained for approximately 30 minutes in the use of one or more of the following countermeasures: biting the tongue, pressing the toes to the floor, mentally subtracting 7s from a number larger than 200. They were fully informed about the nature of the CQT and told that to pass the test they would have to produce larger physiological reactions to the control questions than to the relevant questions. They were instructed to begin their countermeasure as soon as they recognized any control question, stop the countermeasure long enough to answer the question, and resume and continue their countermeasure until the next question began. All subjects were motivated by the promise of a cash bonus if they were successful in producing a truthful outcome.

Across this series of studies, approximately half of the decisions with trained countermeasure subjects were incorrect. There was no significant difference between mental and physical countermeasures, and experienced examiners were unable to detect the use of countermeasures either by inspecting the polygraph charts or by observing the subjects' overt behavior. However, computerized scoring of the polygraph charts outperformed the human evaluators and was more robust in the face of countermeasures. When the discriminant analysis classification model of Kircher & Raskin was applied to these data,[70] the false negative rate was reduced by half.[71] It seems likely that statistical models can be developed to discriminate countermeasure users

---

66. Charles R. Honts et al., *Effects of Spontaneous Countermeasures on the Physiological Detection of Deception,* 16 J. POLICE SCI. & ADMIN. 91 (1988).

67. Charles R. Honts et al., *Effects Of Spontaneous Countermeasures Used Against The Comparison Question Test,* POLYGRAPH (forthcoming 2001).

68. Rovner et al., *supra* note 40.

69. Charles R. Honts et al., *Effects of Physical Countermeasures on the Physiological Detection of Deception,* 70 J. APPLIED PSYCHOL. 177 (1985); Charles R. Honts et al., *Effects of Physical Countermeasures and Their Electromyographic Detection During Polygraph Tests for Deception,* 1 J. PSYCHOPHYSIOLOGY 241 (1987); Honts et al., *supra* note 40.

70. Kircher & Raskin, *supra* note 30.

71. Honts et al., *supra* note 40.

from innocent subjects and improve this performance. Moreover, it should be noted that all of the countermeasure research data are from laboratory studies because it would be unethical and possibly illegal to train criminal suspects to apply countermeasures in order to defeat law enforcement or defense polygraph examinations in actual criminal cases.[72] Since the task of a countermeasure subject should be easier in the laboratory than in a field setting where the relevant questions are more powerful, the findings of laboratory studies of countermeasures are likely to represent a worst case scenario with regard to the effectiveness of countermeasures.

There is no published research on the effects of countermeasures on the DLT. However, the dynamics and scoring of the DLT are very similar to the CQT, and there is no reason to expect that the DLT is more or less susceptible to countermeasures than the CQT.

[2] Countermeasures and the GKT

In 1960, Lykken made an effort to train a group of psychologists, psychiatrists, and medical students to beat a GKT.[73] He informed his subjects about the nature of the GKT and instructed them about various maneuvers designed to augment their responses to the incorrect items. Despite the sophistication of the subjects and Lykken's efforts, he failed to produce any effects of countermeasure training. However, subsequent research and analysis discovered a serious methodological flaw in Lykken's research.[74] Elaad's research was somewhat more successful.[75] Significant effects were obtained by having subjects mentally count sheep during the presentation of all of the items on a GKT, but the countermeasure effects were not dramatic.

These results and others that indicate a lack of effects of drugs on the GKT have led some proponents of the GKT to conclude that the GKT is immune to the effects of countermeasures.[76] However, a study by Honts and

72. Lykken attacks polygraph evidence favorable to a defendant by repeatedly reporting the alleged results of an unpublished countermeasures field study that he designed and conducted with the aid of Floyd Fay, an Ohio prison inmate who had failed two polygraphs and was convicted of murder. *See* David C. Raskin, *Science, Competence and Polygraph Techniques*, 8 CRIM. DEF. 11 (1981). Lykken provided Fay with information to train other prison inmates to defeat polygraph tests administered during criminal investigations in the prison and claimed that he and Fay were successful in assisting 23 of 27 guilty prisoners to fool the polygraph. However, they presented no data other than Fay's claims that all of the prisoners he trained according to Lykken's instructions told him that they were guilty and that they took polygraph tests administered by the prison authorities. Fay reported that 23 of his fellow inmates told him they had used the Lykken countermeasure techniques to fool the polygraph. This claim was based on nothing more than undocumented and unsubstantiated claims by a prison inmate about what he claims other admitted felons told him about polygraph tests they claimed to have taken and

beaten. Aside from the ethical issues raised by such a "study," Lykken's report violates all of the requirements for a scientific study put forward by Iacono, Lykken, and everyone else. As one of us told Floyd Fay, "If you can't trust the reports made by a convicted felon, who can you trust?" Interestingly, Fay admitted to one of us that he unsuccessfully used countermeasures on one of the tests that he failed.

73. David T. Lykken, *The Validity of the Guilty Knowledge Technique: The Effects of Faking*, 44 J. APPLIED PSYCHOL. 258 (1960).

74. Honts et al., *supra* note 51; Charles R. Honts & John C. Kircher, *Legends Of The Concealed Knowledge Test: Lykken's Distributional Scoring System Fails To Detect Countermeasures*, 32 PSYCHOPHYSIOLOGY S41 (1995).

75. Eitan Elaad & Gershon Ben–Shakkar, *Effects of Mental Countermeasures on Psychophysiological Detection in the Guilty Knowledge Test*, 11 INT'L J. PSYCHOPHYSIOLOGY 99 (1991).

76. BEN–SHAKAR & FUREDY, *supra* note 2.

his colleagues has shown that conclusion to be incorrect. They examined the effects of pressing the toes to the floor and mentally subtracting 7s on the accuracy of the GKT.[77] Using methods similar to those previously described in studies of countermeasures and the CQT, they informed mock-crime subjects about the nature of the GKT. They told them that in order to pass the GKT they would have to produce larger physiological responses to the non-critical items than to the key items. Subjects were offered a monetary bonus if they could pass their GKT. Ninety percent of the subjects trained in a physical countermeasure and 60% of the subjects trained in a mental countermeasure were able to beat the GKT. The results of this study clearly demonstrate that the accuracy of the GKT is substantially reduced by countermeasures and that the GKT may be even more susceptible than the CQT to the effects of physical countermeasures. However, as with the CQT, the application of the Kircher and Raskin discriminant classification model[78] to these data dramatically improved performance.[79]

§ 12–2.2.3 The Polygraph in Practice

[1] Application of Comparison Question Tests

Comparison question tests are the most widely used techniques in criminal investigations and judicial proceedings.[80] Almost every major federal, state, and local law enforcement agency employs such tests to reduce the number of suspects so that limited resources can be focused on likely suspects, that is, those who have failed polygraph examinations. Comparison question tests are also used to examine prime suspects and persons formally charged with criminal acts.

In many jurisdictions, prosecutors and defense attorneys make informal agreements that if the suspect or defendant passes a polygraph examination from a competent and well-qualified examiner, the prosecutor will seriously consider dismissing the charges. Alternatively, prior to the conduct of a polygraph examination, prosecutors and defense attorneys may enter into formal stipulations that the results will be admissible as evidence at trial. Under these arrangements, costly trials are often avoided by guilty pleas or dismissals based in part on the results of polygraph tests. Polygraph tests are sometimes used by prosecutors to assess the veracity of individuals involved in the crime who may testify for the prosecution in exchange for immunity or reduced charges if they demonstrate their truthfulness on the polygraph test. Also, some courts use polygraph evidence in post-conviction proceedings, such as sentencing and motions for new trials. A comprehensive compilation and discussion of the federal and state case law and legislation concerning the admissibility of polygraph evidence and the polygraph examiner licensing regulations in the United States was provided by Morris.[81] Honts and Perry and others have provided a summary of the arguments in support of the use

---

77. Honts et al., *supra* note 51.

78. Kircher & Raskin, *supra* note 30.

79. Honts et al., *supra* note 51.

80. Raskin (1986), *supra* note 1.

81. Roberta A. Morris, *The Admissibility of Evidence Derived From Hypnosis and Polygraph, in* PSYCHOLOGICAL METHODS IN CRIMINAL INVESTIGATION AND EVIDENCE 333 (David C. Raskin ed., 1989).

of polygraph tests in legal proceedings.[82]

[2] Application of the Guilty Knowledge Test

Several practical problems prevent widespread use of the GKT, some of which concern the circumstances surrounding many crimes. Consistently choosing details of a crime that are likely to be recognized by the guilty suspect during the test is an insurmountably difficult task for investigators and polygraph examiners. Details of a crime that may seem quite distinctive and memorable to an investigator or polygraph examiner may be unnoticed or forgotten by the perpetrator because of emotional stress, confusion, inattention, or intoxication during the commission of the crime. Thus, the false negative rate of the GKT in criminal investigation is likely to be high.

The utility of the GKT is also limited because innocent subjects frequently are informed about the details of the crime prior to taking a polygraph test. It is common practice for police investigators to disclose details of crimes to suspects in the process of interrogation, for news media to publicize the details of many crimes, and for defense attorneys to discuss the details of police reports and allegations with their clients. Thus, the majority of innocent and guilty criminal suspects obtain knowledge of the critical crime information after the crime was committed, which renders them unsuitable for a GKT.

Many criminal investigations do not lend themselves to the GKT because certain types of crimes characteristically have no special information that is unknown to potential polygraph subjects. Such situations include allegations of forcible sexual assault when the accused claims that the sexual acts were consensual, claims of self-defense in physical assault and homicide cases, and crimes in which the suspect admits having been present at the scene but denies any criminal participation. Because of its high rate of false negative errors and inapplicability in most investigative situations, the GKT is not likely to become a substitute for comparison question tests.

§ 12–2.2.4 General Acceptance of Polygraph Testing by the Scientific Community

Several sources of evidence demonstrate that the validity of polygraph tests is generally accepted in the relevant scientific community. Two valid surveys of the Society for Psychophysiological Research (SPR) directly addressed the general acceptance issue.[83] The SPR is a professional society of scientists who study how the mind and body interact, which makes it an appropriate scientific organization for assessing general acceptance. The Gallup Organization survey was replicated and extended in 1994 by Amato at the

82. Charles R. Honts & Mary V. Perry, *Polygraph Admissibility: Changes and Challenges*, 16 L. & HUM. BEHAV. 357 (1992); James R. McCall, *Misconceptions and Reevaluation—Polygraph Admissibility After* Rock *and* Daubert, 1996 U.ILL.L.REV. 363; Edward J. Imwinkelreid & James R. McCall, *Issues Once Moot: The Other Evidentiary Objections to the Admission of Exculpatory Polygraph Examinations*, 32 WAKE FOREST L. REV. 1045 (1997).

83. The Gallup Organization, *Survey of the Members of the Society for Psychophysiological Research Concerning Their Opinions of Polygraph Test Interpretations,* 13, POLYGRAPH, 153 (1984); Susan L. Amato, A Survey of The Members of the Society for Psycholphsiological Research Regarding The Polygraphs: Opinions and Implications (1993) (Unpublished Master's Thesis, University of North Dakota, Grand Forks) (on file with authors).

University of North Dakota. The results of those surveys were very consistent. Approximately two-thirds of the doctoral-level members of the SPR who were surveyed stated that polygraph tests are a valuable diagnostic tool when considered with other available information.[84] When only those respondents who described themselves as highly informed about the scientific polygraph literature are considered, the percentage who indicated that polygraph tests are a useful diagnostic tool rose to 83%. Since fewer than 10% reported being involved in conducting polygraph examinations professionally, the results were not influenced by financial interests of the respondents. These findings indicate that there is a great deal of acceptance of polygraph techniques by members of the SPR.[85]

84. Respondents in both surveys gave responses to the following question: Which one of these four statements best describes your own opinion of polygraph test interpretations by those who have received systematic training in the technique, when they are called upon to interpret whether a subject is or is not telling the truth? A) It is a sufficiently reliable method to be the sole determinant, B) It is a useful diagnostic tool when considered with other available information, C) It is of questionable usefulness, entitled to little weight against other available information, D) It is of no usefulness.

85. A third survey of the members of the SPR was reported by Iacono and Lykken in *The Scientific Status of Research on Polygraph Techniques: The Case Against Polygraph Tests*, MODERN SCIENTIFIC EVIDENCE: THE LAW AND SCIENCE OF EXPERT TESTIMONY, (David L. Faigman, David Kaye, Michael J. Saks, & Joseph Sanders eds. 1997); also partially available at William Iacono & David Lykken, *The Validity of the Lie Detector: Two Surveys of Scientific Opinion*, 87 J. APPLIED PSYCH. 426 (1997). Iacono and Lykken are two of the most outspoken critics of polygraph testing. However, the present authors believe that the Iacono and Lykken survey is so flawed and suspect that it cannot be used for any substantive purpose. Problems with the Iacono and Lykken study include: 1) The cover letter for the Iacono and Lykken survey described it as answering questions regarding the admissibility of polygraph evidence in court, rather than the scientific validity of the technique. They inappropriately asked the respondents to make a political and legal judgment rather than a scientific one. Few, if any, SPR members have the legal background to offer an opinion about admissibility. In contrast, Amato and Honts presented the issues in the context of whether or not the SPR should have a formal scientific policy regarding the validity of polygraph testing. 2) Court-ordered discovery and cross-examination in the cases of *State of Washington v. Daniel Gallegos*, 95–1–02749–7 (1996) and *Steve Griffith v. Muscle Improvement, Inc.*, Superior Court of California, sworn deposition 21 April 1998, forced Iacono to reveal that the sample of respondents to the Iacono and Lykken survey described themselves as very uninformed about the topic of polygraph examinations. Iacono and Lykken's respondents were asked, "About how many empirical studies, literature reviews, commentaries, or presentations at scientific meetings dealing with the validity of the CQT have you read or attended?" Unfortunately, subjects were asked to respond on an unusual non-linear scale. Conversion of the scale units to numbers of items indicates that the average respondent had contact with only 3 items dealing with the validity of the polygraph. Since the responses on this non-linear scale are positively skewed, this means that many more than 50% of the subjects responded that they had contact with fewer than 3 items. In light of the large volume of scientific articles and presentations on this topic (we have either authored or co-authored over 300 such papers and presentations ourselves), these data demonstrate that the Iacono and Lykken sample was relatively ignorant about the science relating to the polygraph; therefore, the subjects were not qualified to offer an opinion about its scientific validity. This information, which Iacono and Lykken chose not to include in either of their publications, would remain hidden were it not for compulsory discovery and cross-examination. 3) Another anomaly in the Iacono and Lykken data analysis makes it impossible to compare some of their results to the other surveys in any meaningful way. In defining their "highly informed" group, Iacono and Lykken included those who chose 4 or higher on their 7–point scale of polygraph knowledge, whereas Amato and Honts included only those who chose 5 and above. This difference in cutting scores makes it impossible to compare these results across the two surveys. Because Iacono and Lykken included relatively ignorant respondents in their highly informed group, their entire analysis is suspect. 4) In their 1997 chapter in this volume, Iacono and Lykken described their survey as a "random sample." However, in their publication Iacono and Lykken revealed that their sampling was not random. They deliberately excluded the authors of this chapter, and possibly other scientific supporters of the polygraph. 5) Because of Iacono and Lykken's unusual and suspicious data analyses and their misrepresentation of the

In November of 2000, Honts, Thurber, and their students conducted a telephone survey of the at-large members of the American Psychology–Law Society (AP–LS). The AP–LS is a particularly relevant scientific group because the members are highly familiar with the nature and difficulty of applied psychology-law research and because they are generally familiar with the legal requirements for the admissibility of scientific evidence. The AP–LS members were asked about a variety of issues concerning polygraph research, general acceptance, and relative validity of the polygraph. The survey required about 10 minutes, and 72% of those contacted agreed to respond. Subjects were told that their responses should take into consideration the use of the comparison question test in forensic situations.

The AP–LS respondents reported having read an average of 14 articles from peer-reviewed publications concerning the polygraph, which is nearly five times the number indicated by the SPR respondents in the Iacono and Lykken survey.[86] The AP–LS members indicated a generally favorable attitude toward the use of laboratory data for estimating the validity of the polygraph in the real world. The majority of the respondents (89%) indicated that laboratory studies should be given at least some weight by policy makers and the courts, and a large number (49%) stated that moderate to considerable weight should be given to laboratory results.[87] This finding strikingly contrasts to the position espoused by Iacono and Lykken, who dismiss such studies. The opinions of the members of the AP–LS about laboratory research are particularly persuasive since they routinely apply the results of science to real-world problems, a process relatively unfamiliar to SPR members whose research is typically theoretically oriented. The vast majority of the AP–LS respondents (91%) believe that it is possible to conduct useful field studies of the polygraph.[88] Nearly all of them (96%) stated that the publication of polygraph studies in peer-reviewed psychology journals is indicative of a

survey in a publication intended for the legal profession, Amato and Honts were concerned that there might be other undisclosed problems with the Iacono and Lykken survey. Under the ethical standards of the American Psychological Association, scientists are required to make their data available for reanalysis by qualified scientists. On March 10, 1997 and subsequent occasions, Amato and Honts wrote Iacono and then Lykken requesting the data from their survey for the purpose of performing an independent reanalysis. To date, they have refused to provide their data. However, Iacono subsequently requested copies of the data from the Amato and Honts survey, which were provided to Iacono within two weeks of the receipt of their request. Iacono and Lykken have said they offered to share their data with Amato and Honts, which is misleading. They offered to provide only the summary data upon which their published analyses were based and would allow Amato and Honts simply to check their calculations. Since they would not permit discovery of other possible irregularities in their analyses and reports nor permit a reanalysis that would allow the results to be compared to the findings of the Amato and Honts survey,

their offer was rejected. Iacono and Lykken's claim that they offered access to their data is simply disingenuous.

86. *See supra* note 85.

87. Respondents were asked the following question: Laboratory mock-crime studies are often used to study polygraph tests. Consider a properly designed and conducted study that employed a realistic mock-crime paradigm (for example a guilty subject goes to an unfamiliar place and takes money from a cash box) and used techniques that are as similar as possible to actual field practice. How much weight should policy makers and courts give to the results of such studies in estimating the validity the polygraph in real world tests? Please choose one of the following: a. No weight, b. Little weight, c. Some weight, d. Moderate weight, e. Considerable weight.

88. Respondents were asked the following question: Do you believe that it is possible to conduct a scientific field validity study of polygraph testing that can yield a useful estimate of the validity of the comparison question test? Yes or No.

general acceptance of the scientific methodology used in those studies.[89]

The AP–LS respondents were also asked about the validity of the CQT. Two approaches were taken to that issue. Respondents were first asked to compare the usefulness of a properly-conducted CQT to seven other types of frequently admitted evidence. The majority of respondents indicated that polygraph results are at least as useful as, or more useful than, psychological opinions about parental fitness, psychological opinions regarding malingering, eyewitness identification, psychological assessments of dangerousness, and psychological assessment of temporary insanity, but are less useful than fingerprint and DNA evidence. They were also asked their opinion of the impact that CQT polygraph evidence would have on the accuracy of judicial verdicts about guilt and innocence. The majority (52%) reported that judicial decision accuracy would be improved by allowing polygraph evidence, while 20% stated that polygraph evidence would have no impact on judicial accuracy. Only 28% indicated that the accuracy of verdicts would decrease if polygraph experts were allowed to testify.

The results of the AP–LS survey present an overall picture that strongly supports the usefulness of polygraph evidence in court. This relevant and knowledgeable scientific community, which is highly experienced with applied research and the requirements of the legal profession, believes that polygraph tests are at least as accurate as many types of evidence currently admitted in court. Moreover, the majority stated that introduction of polygraph evidence would improve the accuracy of judicial decision-making. These results replicate and extend the results reported by Gallup[90] and Amato.[91] They also underscore concerns about the findings reported by Iacono and Lykken.[92]

Another important indicator of the acceptance of the psychophysiological detection of deception in the scientific community is provided by the large number of original scientific studies published in peer-reviewed scientific journals. Studies reporting positive results for the validity of polygraph examinations have appeared in the *Journal of Applied Psychology, Journal of General Psychology, Psychophysiology, Journal of Police Science and Administration, Current Directions in Psychological Science, Psychological Bulletin, Journal of Research in Personality, Law and Human Behavior,* and many others. The review and acceptance process for these journals is lengthy and difficult. The journal editor first sends a submitted article for review by two or three independent scientists who are knowledgeable about the topic and research methods but are not personally involved with the article under consideration. These peer-reviewers comment on the quality of the literature review, the research design, the statistical analyses, the reasonableness of the conclusions drawn, and the appropriateness of the article for publication in the journal. The editor also reviews the article and incorporates the comments and recommendations of the reviewers to make a decision about publication. Minor or extensive revisions are usually required before publication. Manu-

---

89. Respondents were asked the following question: In general, do you believe that studies of the polygraph published in peer-reviewed scientific journals (e.g. PSYCHOPHYSIOLOGY, JOURNAL OF APPLIED PSYCHOLOGY, THE JOURNAL OF GENERAL PSYCHOLOGY) are based on generally accepted scientific methodology? Yes or No.

90. Gallup, *supra* note 83.

91. *Id.*

92. Iacono & Lykken, *supra* note 85.

scripts with unacceptable scientific methods, statistics, or insupportable conclusions are not published (assuming that the methods and data have been honestly and completely reported). For example, the Journal of Applied Psychology has published numerous articles on the psychophysiological detection of deception,[93] even though it rejects 85% of the manuscripts submitted for publication. The publication of numerous articles in mainstream journals of scientific psychology clearly demonstrates that the psychophysiological detection of deception is generally accepted by the community of scientific psychologists. This conclusion was supported by 96% of the AP–LS respondents in the survey described above.

§ 12–2.3   Major Developments and Future Prospects

Major beneficial effects have been produced by improvements in physiological measures and examination procedures and the development and implementation of computer techniques through federally funded research that began at the University of Utah in 1970. By applying the methods and principles of human psychology and psychophysiology, Raskin, Kircher, Honts, and their colleagues refined the pretest interview, improved and developed new test methods, developed better techniques for recording and analyzing the physiological reactions, improved the reliability and accuracy of the numerical scoring system, and developed the first computerized polygraph. The latest version, the Computerized Polygraph System (CPS), is based on the methods and findings of their 30 years of scientific research on the physiological detection of deception.[94] The resulting examination procedures and computer methodology have simplified and improved the standardization of the polygraph examination, enhanced the quality of the polygraph recordings, increased the reliability and accuracy of the polygraph results, and provided higher quality printouts and documentation of the entire procedure. These improvements have generally raised the quality of training and practice of polygraph examiners in agencies such as the US Secret Service, Royal Canadian Mounted Police, other federal, state, provincial, and local law enforcement agencies, and private examiners in the United States, Canada, and many other countries.

93. Some of the articles on the polygraph published in the JOURNAL OF APPLIED PSYCHOLOGY are as follows: P. J. Bersh, *A Validation Study of Polygraph Examiner Judgments*, 53 J. APPLIED PSYCHOL. 399 (1969); P.O. Davidson, *Validity of the Guilty Knowledge Technique: The Effects of Motivation*, 52 J. APPLIED PSYCHOL. 62–65 (1968); E. Elaad, *Detection of Guilty Knowledge in Real–Life Criminal Investigations*, 75 J. APPLIED PSYCHOL. 521–529 (1990); E. Elaad et al., *Detection Measures in Real–Life Criminal Guilty Knowledge Tests*, 77 J. APPLIED PSYCHOL. 757–767 (1992); A. Ginton et al., *A Method for Evaluating the Use of the Polygraph in a Real–Life Situation*, 67 J. APPLIED PSYCHOL. 131–137 (1982); C. R. Honts et al., *Effects of Physical Countermeasures on the Physiological Detection of Deception*, 70 J. APPLIED PSYCHOL. 177–187 (1985); C. R. Honts et al., *Mental and Physical Countermeasures Reduce the Accuracy*

of Polygraph Tests, 79 J. APPLIED PSYCHOL. 252–259 (1994); F. S. Horvath, *The Effect of Selected Variables on Interpretation of Polygraph Records*, 62 J. APPLIED PSYCHOL. 127–136 (1977); J, C, Kircher, & D. C. Raskin, *Human Versus Computerized Evaluations of Polygraph Data in a Laboratory Setting*, 73 J. APPLIED PSYCHOL. 291–302 (1988); C. J. Patrick, & W. G. Iacono, *Validity of the Control Question Polygraph Test: The Problem of Sampling Bias*, 76 J. APPLIED PSYCHOL. 229–238 (1991); J. A. Podlesny & C. Truslow, *Validity of an Expanded–Issue (Modified General Question) Polygraph Technique in a Simulated Distributed–Crimes–Roles Context*, 78 J. APPLIED PSYCHOL. 5 (1993).

94. Information about the CPS can be obtained from the Stoelting Company, 620 Wheat Lane, Wood Dale, IL 60191, *at* http://www.stoeltingco.com.

As a result of efforts by scientists and policy makers, many of the most objectionable applications of polygraph tests have been eliminated or severely curtailed by recent legislation and administrative decisions.[95] Along with the reduction in undesirable applications, a large number of the least competent polygraph practitioners were forced to leave the profession. This raised the level of competence and practice in the field and also fostered an increase in research funds and growth of research programs in universities and government agencies. These programs have also served to improve the training and competence of government, law enforcement, and private polygraph examiners.

Automated Test Administration. In an effort to reduce problems that may be associated with examinations performed by human polygraph examiners, Honts and Amato designed a completely automated polygraph test.[96] In the context of a pre-employment screening polygraph examination, they compared the accuracy of polygraph tests conducted by an experienced human polygraph examiner to a standardized examination conducted by tape recording. Automated examination outcomes were significantly more accurate than human-administered examinations. Although these results were obtained from pre-employment type polygraph examinations that are not directly generalizable to forensic settings, they suggest a promising area of research. If similar results can be obtained with forensic polygraph examinations, then a major source of variability and possible bias in polygraph examinations (the examiner) can be greatly reduced. The resulting increase in standardization and decrease in variability would be highly desirable.

The Impact of Outside Issues. Polygraph examiners have long been concerned that outside issues may reduce the accuracy of a polygraph examination. Consider a subject taking a polygraph test for the theft of a small amount of money from a convenience market. The subject had taken the money but is also guilty of a more serious, undiscovered crime of armed robbery and shooting. Many in the polygraph profession believe that the subject's secret concern about the more serious crime might overshadow the relatively minor issue of theft of money and result in a false negative outcome (a guilty person producing a truthful outcome). These examiners attempt to counter the potential effects of outside issues by asking outside-issue questions, e.g., "Is there something else you are afraid I will ask you a question about even though I told you I would not?" Until recently, neither the effects

---

95. The most important development was the passage of the Employee Polygraph Protection Act of 1988, 29 U.S.C.A. §§ 2001–09 (1991). The regulations promulgated by the Department of Labor [29 C.F.R. § 801; 56 Fed. Reg. 9046 (1991)] resulted in the elimination of more than 1 million tests that were conducted each year on applicants for jobs in the private sector and the consequent reduction in the number of polygraph examiners whose primary income was derived from such undesirable and abusive practices. One of us (Raskin) served as the expert for the US Senate Committee on Labor and Human Resources in drafting the legislation and testifying at the Senate hearings.

96. Charles R. Honts & Susan L. Amato, THE AUTOMATED POLYGRAPH EXAMINATION: FINAL REPORT OF U. S. GOVERNMENT CONTRACT No. 110224–1998–MO. Boise State University (1999). Also reported as: Charles R. Honts & Susan L. Amato, *Human V. Machine: Research Examining The Automation Of Polygraph Testing.* Paper presented at the annual meeting of the Rocky Mountain Psychological Association, Fort Collins Colorado (April, 1999), and Susan L. Amato & Charles R. Honts, *Automated Polygraph Examination Outperforms Human In Employment Screening Context.* Paper presented at the annual meeting of the Midwestern Psychological Association, Chicago, Illinois (May, 1999).

of outside issues nor the effectiveness of outside issue questions had been studied scientifically.

Honts and his colleagues examined the effects of outside issues in a laboratory mock-crime experiment.[97] Half of the subjects stole $1.00 and half did not. Half of the innocent subjects and half of the guilty subjects then committed another crime, the theft of $20.00. All subjects were given a standard CQT concerning only the theft of $1.00. Half of the polygraph tests included two outside issue questions and half contained none. Subjects were told that if they passed their polygraph test, they could keep the money they had stolen. Subjects who stole neither the $1.00, nor the $20.00, were offered a $1.00 bonus if they could pass their polygraph test. Performance was very high for subjects tested with a standard CQT and who did not have the outside issue. With innocent subjects, 91.7% were correctly classified and there were 8.3% false positive errors. With guilty subjects, 91.7% were correctly classified and 8.3% of the outcomes were inconclusive. There were no false negative errors.

The presence or absence of an outside issue produced results that failed to support the traditional beliefs of the polygraph profession. In contrast to the concerns of the polygraph profession, the outside issue manipulation had a minimal and non-significant impact on subjects who stole the $1 (the actual topic of the examination). However, the presence of an outside issue had a major impact on subjects who were innocent of stealing the $1. For those subjects, correct classification rates dropped from 91.7% to 25.0%, a highly significant and powerful result. Furthermore, the outside issue questions were ineffective for detecting the presence of outside issues. These findings might explain some of the variability in false positive errors in field studies of polygraph validity. If the subject population of an agency includes many subjects who have outside issues, then the false positive rate would be expected to be higher and vice versa. The laboratory findings further support the notion that greater confidence can be placed in truthful outcomes of polygraph examinations, whereas failed polygraph examinations should be viewed more cautiously. Finally, the results of the outside issue study suggest that the exact wording of relevant questions is not critical for the detection of subjects who are attempting deception. These results suggest that even if specific details included in a relevant question were incorrect (for example, dates, amounts of money, or specific sexual acts), a subject attempting deception in the matter under investigation would still respond to those relevant questions and would very likely fail the examination. The results are consistent with, and extend the similar findings of Podlesny and Truslow.[98]

§ 12–2.4 Misconceptions About Control (Comparison) Questions

Iacono and Lykken have provided numerous and lengthy arguments attacking the CQT and the DLT while they promote the GKT. Their arguments and analyses rely on a combination of 1) incorrect assumptions and misunderstandings of the conceptual bases of the CQT and DLT, 2) selective

---

97. Charles R. Honts et al., *Outside Issues Dramatically Reduce The Accuracy Of Polygraph Tests Given To Innocent Individuals,* presented at the American Psychology–Law Society Biennial Meeting, New Orleans, Louisiana (March 2000).

98. Podlesny and Truslow, *supra* note 40.

presentation of the available scientific and professional literature, 3) flawed theoretical speculation based on an incomplete understanding of actual applications of polygraph techniques and other critical aspects of law enforcement investigations and the criminal justice process, and 4) inaccurate and misleading descriptions of virtually all of the research they selected to present (including their own).

The Iacono and Lykken attack on CQT theory centers on the so-called control questions, which they claim "do not serve as strict controls in the scientific sense of this term; the subject's responses to the CQT's control questions do not predict how this subject should respond to the relevant questions if he is answering truthfully."[99] In fact, the control (comparison) questions are designed to predict how the subject would respond to the relevant questions if he were answering *deceptively*.[100] This is the very heart of the CQT and the DLT, and Iacono and Lykken's failure to understand this fundamental principle renders their entire analysis moot. The problem is compounded by their apparent failure to understand how control questions are actually formulated. Rather than demanding great examiner skill, as Iacono and Lykken claim, control questions require only basic knowledge to formulate and properly present to the subject. They also speculate that guilty subjects may react more strongly to the control questions because they encompass other criminal activity that they have not disclosed, thereby beating the test. However, for many laboratory subjects, their lies to the control questions encompass prior criminal acts far more serious than the mock crime, yet they routinely fail the CQT even though there is only a few dollars at stake when they lie to the relevant questions.[101]

§ 12–2.4.1 Inconsistency, Selectivity, and Misrepresentations

Iacono and Lykken change their requirements for valid research studies to fit the current circumstance. When it suits their purpose, they dismiss laboratory studies as useless for estimating polygraph accuracy in real life, stating that only field studies published in peer-reviewed scientific journals are useful. Their position is not supported by the science[102] nor by the opinions of the members of the American Psychology–Law Society as was described above. Furthermore, they ignore a powerful structural analysis demonstrating the fundamental correspondence between the psychophysiological processes underlying laboratory and field polygraphs,[103] as well as a meta-analysis[104] that indicated similar high levels of accuracy of well-executed field studies and laboratory studies that realistically simulate the field polygraph situation. On the other hand, when laboratory findings suit their immediate purposes, Iacono and Lykken frequently rely on carefully selected studies, presentations at scientific meetings, published abstracts, and unpublished studies to support their current argument.

99. Iacono & Lykken, *supra* note 85, at 597

100. See the discussion in John A. Podlesny & David C. Raskin, *Physiological Measures and the Detection of Deception*, 84 PSYCHOLOGICAL BULL. 782 (1977).

101. See the review in John C. Kircher et al., *Meta-analysis of Mock Crime Studies of the Control Question Polygraph Technique*, 12 LAW & HUM. BEHAV. 79 (1988).

102. Anderson et al., *supra* note 36.

103. *See* Raskin, et al., *supra* note 9. *See also* Charles R. Honts et al., *supra* note 51 (reaching a similar conclusion through a different analysis).

104. *See* Kircher et al., *supra* note 101.

When they are unable to find any basis for dismissing studies that contradict their position, Iacono and Lykken resort to more extreme solutions. Lykken testified that studies reporting higher accuracy rates than he claims are possible must have flaws in their research designs or analyses, even though he is unable to identify any flaws.[105] This unsupported backward inference defies science and simple logic. When confronted with the publication of the Honts field study,[106] which contradicted their major arguments against the CQT, they did not re-examine their position. Instead, they resorted to a series of baseless attacks against the editor and the editorial board of a respected peer-reviewed scientific journal that has been published for more than 70 years.[107]

In the 1997 edition of this volume, Iacono and Lykken presented misdescriptions of criminal investigative processes, how polygraphs are used, and the typical circumstances of confessions to create a basis for their argument that it is impossible to accurately assess the accuracy of field polygraph tests. Neither of them has any training or experience in these areas (collectively, we have more than 50 years of such experience), and they employed false assumptions that formed the basis for their erroneous analysis. They claimed that polygraphs are used by police when "there is no hard evidence against a suspect and no arrest has been made" and by defense attorneys when their clients have already "been arrested and there is sufficient evidence to warrant a trial. The rate of guilt thus must be higher for those who are defendants rather than suspects."[108] In reality, the opposites are true. Polygraphs are frequently used by police when they have reason to believe that the suspect is guilty and may confess, and by defense attorneys whose clients may or may have not been arrested or facing trial. Since most criminal cases are resolved by guilty pleas, a large proportion of those who demand a trial are actually innocent. Neither the failure to obtain a confession following a deceptive polygraph nor the suspect passing a polygraph is an automatic end to the investigation of that suspect or any other suspect. The police must continue to pursue investigations in spite of these factors, and many such suspects confess later in the investigation.

Iacono and Lykken used their erroneous assumptions to argue that field studies include only those cases where "a guilty suspect failed a CQT and subsequently confessed . . . [but] all polygraph errors in which an innocent person failed a test are omitted . . . [and] all cases in which a guilty subject erroneously passed a test would also be excluded. Thus, confession studies rely on a biased set of cases . . . where the original examiner was shown to be correct."[109] On the contrary, the field studies presented above in Table 4 included both types of cases where the original examiner was shown to be incorrect. Moreover, their argument inescapably leads to the conclusion that all field studies must show 100% accuracy on guilty and innocent subjects alike. Instead of examining the facts and data related to their assumptions,

---

105. California v. Parrison and Parrison, San Diego Superior Court, August 20, 1982.

106. Honts, *supra* note 1.

107. William G. Iacono & David T. Lykken, *supra* note 85, at 227 (Pocket Part 2000). Lykken even went so far as to write one of Professor Honts' undergraduate students and suggest there was impropriety in the peer-

review process that allowed publication of the Honts study. A copy of this letter is available from Dr. Honts on request.

108. Iacono & Lykken, *supra* note 85, at 599.

109. *Id.* at 602.

Iacono and Lykken then proposed a totally impractical study in which no suspect would be given any test results, none would be interrogated after failing the test, investigators would be deprived of any polygraph outcomes that would help them investigate or solve their cases, and innocent people would be forced to continue as suspects even after passing the polygraph. Such a study raises serious ethical and legal questions.

The above arguments are a variant of an illusory analysis that Iacono invented to attack the field studies based on confessions.[110] He suggested that a sampling anomaly allows a technique with only chance accuracy to produce an estimate that the technique is 90% accurate. Iacono invented a set of circumstances to illustrate this possibility without any data to support his speculation. Although it cannot be tested empirically, Iacono and Lykken have treated this creation as if it were fact. Armed with this unsupported and misleading argument, they confuse triers of fact and lead them to question the value of all field studies of polygraphs. Therefore, Iacono's formulation requires a detailed analysis to expose its fundamental flaws.

Iacono made the following assumptions for his illusory analysis:

1. 400 innocent and 400 guilty criminal suspects are tested.

2. The polygraph is not better than chance in identifying innocent or guilty subjects.

3. Each crime has only two suspects.

4. A guilty suspect is tested first in half of the cases.

5. If the first suspect fails the test, the second suspect will not be tested.

6. Neither innocent suspects nor guilty suspects who pass the test will ever confess.

7. Only 20% of the guilty who are interrogated will confess.

For the illusory analysis to produce the desired result, the following implicit assumptions are required:

8. The polygraph is the only source of information about who is guilty.

9. Guilty people confess only after failing a polygraph test.

Careful examination of Iacono's assumptions yields the following conclusions:

1. A base rate of 50% is statistically neutral, but may not be representative of field conditions. The base rate of guilt in criminal cases varies widely depending upon how and when the polygraph is used. If it is used early in an investigation, there are likely to be many more innocent than guilty subjects; if it is used late in an investigation, there may be many more guilty than innocent subjects. Changes in the base rate will dramatically alter the outcome of the thought experiment.

2. Chance accuracy was assumed for the sake of argument and is contrary to research findings.

110. William J. Iacono, *Can We Determine the Accuracy of Polygraph Tests? in* 4 Advances in Psychophysiology (J. Richard Jennings et al. eds., 1991).

3. Iacono's assertion that this assumption can be made without a loss of generality is obviously incorrect.

4. This assumption is tenable only if the base rate is 50%, and then only if the order of testing subjects in forensic cases is random. Law enforcement typically tests subjects who are most likely guilty before they test those more likely to be innocent. They never select subjects by a formally random process.

5. This assumption is not in accord with common police practices. If the first suspect fails and does not confess, it is likely that other suspects will be tested. If other suspects pass their tests, more pressure will be brought to bear on the suspect who failed. Further investigation and interrogation often produce a confession from this suspect. Investigations continue until the cases are solved or found to be unsolvable.

6. This assumption is not in accord with standard police practice and forensic experience. The guilty individual may not confess after the polygraph (passed or failed), but may decide to confess later. This often occurs as the result of additional investigation revealing further evidence or as part of an agreement to resolve the case. Recent research suggests that false confessions by innocent people may be a significant problem.[111]

7. This assumption grossly underestimates the confession rate. The Department of Defense reported a confession rate higher than 70% following failed polygraph tests,[112] the Federal Bureau of Investigation reported 56% confessions by deceptive suspects, the U.S. Secret Service reported that 70% of deceptive results were confirmed by admissions and confessions and more than 90% of polygraph examiners' decisions were later confirmed, and the Drug Enforcement Administration reported that 65% confess following a deceptive polygraph result and 85% of those found truthful are later confirmed by investigations.[113]

8. This assumption is also incorrect. There are many other sources of information available to police. Honts and Raskin[114] and Raskin and his colleagues reported field studies in which evidence other than confessions was used to confirm polygraph results,[115] and Honts explored the use of that information in confirming polygraph test outcomes.[116] He found that approximately 80% of case files contained inculpatory information independent of confessions. The assumption that cases are solved only through polygraph tests is clearly not correct, but it is necessary for Iacono's thought experiment to work as described.

111. Saul M. Kassin & Katherine L. Kiechel, *The Social Psychology of False Confessions: Compliance, Internalization, and Confabulation*, 7 PSYCHOLOLOGICAL SCI. 125 (1996).

112. Charles R. Honts, *The Emperor's New Clothes: Application of Polygraph Tests in the American Workplace*, 4 FORENSIC REPORTS, 91 (1991) and the sources cited therein.

113. SCIENTIFIC VALIDITY OF POLYGRAPH TESTING: A RESEARCH REVIEW AND EVALUATION—TECHNICAL MEMORANDUM, 111 (Washington, DC: U.S. Congress, Office of Technology Assessment, OTA–TM–H–15, November 1983).

114. *Supra* note 54.

115. *Id.*

116. *Id.*

9. This assumption is contradicted by data. In the Honts field study,[117] *none* of the confessions that confirmed the innocent subjects was obtained from polygraph testing situations. This analysis clearly reveals that the Iacono illusory analysis is a post-hoc formulation designed specifically to support Iacono's unscientific hypothesis.[118]

In summary, the Iacono analysis lacks logic and contradicts established facts and produces a misleading conclusion. This is sophistry, not science.

§ 12–2.4.2   The Friendly Polygrapher

In discussing law enforcement and privileged polygraph tests, Iacono and Lykken stated, "The more usual case for an evidentiary hearing is one where the defense counsel arranges a privately administered or 'friendly' polygraph test ... there is not a single study demonstrating that friendly tests are valid."[119] This argument was developed by Orne,[120] who speculated that a guilty suspect who takes a non-law enforcement polygraph examination on a confidential basis might beat the test because of a lack of fear that an adverse result will be disclosed to the authorities. This speculation was based solely on the results of an unrealistic laboratory study in which college students were given only card tests and not a CQT.[121] Orne argued that a suspect who expects that only favorable results will be reported has little at stake and is more confident, the examiner is more supportive, and the lack of fear of failure and subsequent disclosure will enable a guilty person to pass the test. However, Raskin demonstrated that the scientific literature provides no support for the friendly examiner hypothesis and generally contradicts it.[122]

As noted above, laboratory studies where there is little at stake routinely produce detection rates of approximately 90%, and laboratory studies using placebos and other procedures designed to make guilty subjects believe they can pass the polygraph test showed no reduction in detection rates even for the GKT, which is easier to beat than the CQT.[123] If Orne's hypothesis were

---

117. *Id.*

118. Iacono's hypothesis is literally "unscientific" in the sense that it cannot be falsified. There is no way to prove that any field study was not the result of processes similar to those invented by Iacono.

119. Iacono & Lykken, *supra* note 85, at 599. Unfortunately, Iacono and Lykken's lack of consistency is not restricted to academic arguments. Although they argue against the CQT and its use by defense attorneys, they themselves devised and performed a CQT on Wounded Knee criminal defendant Russell Means to be presented as evidence for the defense at Means' federal trial in Sioux Falls, South Dakota. This came to light after Lykken testified for the prosecution against the validity of polygraph techniques and the admission of such evidence on behalf of defendant William Wong (*Regina v. Wong*, 33 C.C.C.2d 511 [B.C.S.Ct.1976]. During cross-examination, Lykken admitted under oath that he had never received training in the administration of polygraph tests and he did not believe in them. He admitted that he believed Defendant Means

was "guilty of the specific allegations against him ... and was probably lying," but he was prepared to testify on his behalf in court because "in my opinion the application of the standard polygraphic inference rules would lead to the conclusion that he [Means] was telling the truth." Lykken justified his actions by stating, "I felt that Mr. Means deserved and needed all the help he could get ... the test interpreted in the usual way would come out in his favor. It seemed to me possible that it would come out that way precisely because I don't much believe in the test."

120. Martin Orne, *Implications of Laboratory Research for the Detection of Deception, in* Legal Admissibility of the Polygraph 94 (N. Ansley ed. 1975).

121. For a complete description and analysis, see Raskin (1986), *supra* note 1.

122. *Id.*

123. Howard Timm, *Effect of Altered Outcome Expectancies Stemming from Placebo and Feedback Treatments on the Validity of the Guilty Knowledge Technique,* 67 J. Applied Psychol. 391 (1982).

correct, laboratory studies of the CQT would produce relatively more false negative than false positive errors, which is contrary to the data. Honts reviewed 20 laboratory studies of the CQT with a total of 567 guilty subjects and 490 innocent subjects.[124] The false negative rate was 12% and the false positive rate was 16%. This outcome is opposite to the prediction generated by the friendly examiner hypothesis. Notably, 6 of the 20 studies reported no errors with guilty subjects, even though they had no fear of any negative sanctions associated with failing the test.

Criminal suspects have no assurance that adverse results will remain confidential since most examiners advise them of their rights and obtain a written waiver prior to the test.[125] However, suspects have a great deal at stake. A favorable test may help to obtain a dismissal or acquittal on the charges, and an unfavorable outcome may result in increased legal costs, personal stress, and disruption of their relationship with their defense counsel. These are far greater motivations than the small amount of money guilty subjects have at stake when they routinely fail laboratory polygraph tests. Furthermore, in order to pass a CQT, the guilty suspect must show stronger physiological reactions to comparison (control) questions than to the relevant questions about the allegations. There is no known mechanism or logical argument that explains how a low level of fear or concern about the test outcome can selectively reduce the reactions to the relevant questions so as to produce the pattern of stronger reactions to the comparison questions that is indicative of truthfulness. In fact, fear is not a necessary part of any modern scientific polygraph theory.[126] The laboratory data and logical analysis contradict the "friendly examiner" hypothesis.

There are two published sets of data from tests of criminal suspects that strongly contradict the friendly examiner hypothesis. Raskin presented complete data from 12 years of his confidential CQT examinations for defense attorneys and non-confidential tests for law enforcement, courts, and stipulated situations.[127] He reported that 58% of suspects who agreed in advance that the results would be provided to the prosecution passed their tests, but only 34% of those who took confidential defense tests were able to pass. In addition, the numerical scores were significantly more negative (in the deceptive direction) for confidential tests compared to the more positive scores (in the truthful direction) for non-confidential tests. Honts recently presented a similar, complete set of data from 14 years of confidential and non-confidential examinations.[128] He reported that 70% of the non-confidential tests were passed, while only 44% of the confidential tests were passed. These data also contradict the predictions of the friendly examiner hypothesis. The friendly examiner hypothesis fails on all counts. It is illogical, unsupported by laboratory studies, and contradicted by data from actual field cases.

124. Charles R. Honts, *Is It Time to Reject the Friendly Polygraph Examiner Hypothesis (FEPH)?*, A paper presented at the annual meeting of the American Psychological Society, Washington, D.C (1997, May). Available at: http://truth.idbsu.edu/polygraph/fpeh.html.

125. David C. Raskin, *Polygraph Techniques for the Detection of Deception, in* Psychological Methods in Criminal Investigation and Evidence 255 (D. Raskin ed. 1989).

126. *See* John A. Podlesny & David C. Raskin, *Physiological Measures and the Detection of Deception*, 84 Psychological Bull. 783 (1977); J. Peter Rosenfeld, *Alternative Views of Bashore and Rapp's (1993) Alternatives to Traditional Polygraphy: A Critique*, 117 Psychological Bull. 159 (1995).

127. Raskin (1986), *supra* note 1, at 62.

128. *See Honts supra* note 124.

§ 12–2.4.3 The Polygraph and Juries

One of the major issues addressed by the Court in *Scheffer*[129] concerned the potential impact of expert polygraph testimony on jury decisions. Opponents of the admission of polygraph evidence have long argued that such evidence will have an undue influence on jury decision processes, usurp the jury function, confuse the issues, and mislead the jury.[130] However, the majority of justices rejected those arguments in *Scheffer*. Their position is consistent with courtroom experiences in actual cases and the published scientific evidence. Numerous scientific studies have been performed on this topic using mock juries, post-trial interviews with jurors who were presented with expert polygraph testimony, and surveys of prosecutors and defense attorneys in cases where polygraph evidence was presented at trial.[131] The results consistently demonstrate that jurors are cautious with polygraph evidence, and they do not give it undue weight. Also consistent with the majority of the *Scheffer* court, the results show that polygraph testimony does not unduly prolong trials or jury deliberations. Prosecutors and defense attorneys who tried cases with polygraph evidence were highly satisfied with polygraph testimony and they did not believe that it had a disruptive impact on the trials or that the judge or jury disregarded significant evidence because of the polygraph testimony. Like other types of evidence, in some cases juries reached decisions that were contrary to the polygraph evidence. Thus, there are no scientific data to support the claims of critics that polygraph evidence is disruptive to the trial process, and the evidence and our own extensive experience in actual cases supports the usefulness of competent polygraph evidence at trial. More detailed analyses of these studies can be found in Raskin[132] and the Amicus Curiae Brief of the Committee of Concerned Social Scientists submitted in *Scheffer*.[133]

§ 12–2.5 Conclusions

We have spent much of our scientific careers conducting scientific research and development on polygraph techniques for the physiological detection of deception.[134] We have received numerous grants and contracts from

129. *Supra* note 38.

130. *See* M. Abbell, *Polygraph Evidence: the Case Against Admissibility in Federal Criminal Trials*, 15 AM. CRIM. L. REV. 29, 38 (1977).

131. F. Barnett, *How Does a Jury View Polygraph Examination Results?*, 2 POLYGRAPH 275 (1973); Nancy J. Brekke, et al., *The Impact of Nonadversarial Versus Adversarial Expert Testimony*, 15 LAW & HUM. BEHAV. 451 (1991); S.C. Carlson et al., *The Effect of Lie Detector Evidence on Jury Deliberations: An Empirical Study*, 5 POLICE SCI. & ADMIN. 148 (1977); A. Cavoukian & R. J. Heslegrave, *The Admissibility of Polygraph Evidence in Court: Some Empirical Findings*, 4 LAW & HUM. BEHAV. 117 (1980); A. Markwart, & B. Lynch, *The Effect of Polygraph Evidence on Mock Jury Decision–Making*, 7 POLICE SCI. & ADMIN. 324 (1979); Bryan Meyers & Jack Arbuthnot, *Polygraph Testimony and Juror Judgments: A Comparison of the Guilty Knowledge Test and the Control Question Test*, 27 J. APPLIED SOC. PSYCHOL. 1421 (1997); R. Peters, *A Survey of Polygraph Evidence in Criminal Trials*, 68 A.B.A. J. 161 (1982); L. Vondergeest et al., *Effects of Juror and Expert Witness Gender on Jurors' Perceptions of an Expert Witness*, MODERN PSYCHOLOGICAL STUDIES 1 (1993).

132. Raskin (1986), *supra* note 1.

133. Available through *Polygraph Law Resource Pages* at http://truth.idbsu.edu.

134. In is of interest to note that Raskin initiated the research program at the University of Utah after being asked to testify in 1970 in a capital case in which he criticized prosecution polygraph evidence based on police administration of an RIT. Raskin embarked on a scientific program that he expected would demonstrate that polygraph tests were not accurate. However, results of the first laboratory study of the accuracy of the CQT (see Barland & Raskin, *supra* note 25) contradicted the com-

federal agencies and universities in the United States and Canada for this research, and we have authored hundreds of scientific articles, chapters, books, and scientific presentations on these topics. Two of us have conducted polygraph examinations in more than 2,000 criminal and civil cases, including many of the most celebrated cases of the past three decades, and we have provided expert testimony hundreds of times in federal and state courts. On the basis of the extensive scientific evidence and our personal experiences in actual cases, we firmly believe that polygraph techniques and evidence are of great value to the criminal justice system and the courts. However, general acceptance by our legal system has lagged far behind the science and its applications.

Although virtually all federal, state, and local law enforcement agencies and prosecutors rely heavily on polygraph results, they have routinely opposed the admissibility of polygraph evidence at trial. This has been a major determiner of the long history of rejection by our courts. After the *Daubert* decision, it appeared that there was a new opportunity for the courts to correctly recognize the scientific basis for polygraph techniques.[135] Some influential law review articles argued for admissibility, but a flurry of attempts to admit polygraph evidence met with only limited success.[136] In spite of the strong scientific basis for admitting polygraph evidence at trial, the current status of polygraph evidence in our courts remains relatively unchanged. We believe this is the result of ingrained institutional impediments to the admission of such evidence.

Our judicial system is founded on the premise that jurors have both the ability and sole responsibility to judge the credibility of the testimony of witnesses who appear before them. However, a large and compelling body of scientific literature demonstrates the inability of people, including jurors, to make accurate judgments of credibility.[137] In spite of this evidence, law schools continue to train students in the outmoded, traditional belief, and many courts continue to use it as a basis for excluding polygraph evidence.

Courts often raise the old specter of the "scientific aura" of polygraph evidence overwhelming the jurors and preventing them from properly considering other evidence. The jury research evidence previously described demonstrates the error of that thinking. After considering the available scientific evidence, the majority of the *Scheffer* court rejected the argument that jurors would be unable to give proper weight to polygraph evidence.[138] This has not prevented most courts from continuing to use the old excuse for rejecting polygraph evidence. If there were merit in this argument for exclusion, then all courts should uniformly exclude DNA and fingerprint evidence. This inconsistency is highlighted by the Supreme Court decision in *Barefoot*.[139] Although the Court acknowledged that two-thirds of psychiatric predictions of future dangerous behavior are incorrect, they ignored the opposition of the

monly-held belief about polygraph inaccuracy, and he was obliged by the ethics and principles of science to revise his beliefs to be consistent with the data. Unfortunately, many of today's vocal critics of polygraph maintain their positions in spite of the large body of scientific data to the contrary.

135. *See infra* § 12–1.0.

136. *See* McCall, *supra* note 82; Imwinkelreid & McCall, *supra* note 82.

137. Aldert Vrij Detecting Lies and Deceit (2000).

138. *See supra* note 38.

139. *Barefoot v. Estelle*, 463 U.S. 880, 103 S.Ct. 3383, 77 L.Ed.2d 1090 (1983).

American Psychiatric Association to such testimony and affirmed the admission of a psychiatrist's prediction of future dangerous behavior that resulted in defendant Barefoot being executed. When we compare the handling of polygraph evidence with the routine admission of more influential and sometimes erroneous evidence, it is clear that the courts are biased against polygraph evidence.

Another major impediment for polygraph evidence is the fact that polygraph evidence is almost always proffered by the defendant. Many prosecutors oppose it for this reason and their desire to totally control its use in the criminal justice system, especially when the results of polygraphs they have secretly conducted on prosecution witnesses would be helpful to the defendant. This generally hostile attitude of prosecutors is met with sympathy from the majority of judges who have been drawn from the ranks of former prosecutors.

When all else fails, many courts take refuge in the fact that one party (usually the prosecution) has presented expert testimony that attacks the polygraph. The mere appearance of one inflexible, well-known and well-paid critic of the polygraph provides the excuse for the court to exclude the proffered evidence. Sometimes the expert does not have any scientific credentials to testify in a *Daubert* hearing, but hostile courts will admit and rely on testimony in spite of a record that fails to rebut the scientific basis of the evidence presented by a highly qualified scientific expert.[140] They also may accept an argument that a dispute about the polygraph evidence will become a trial of collateral issues and will consume too much time, even though that argument was also rejected by the *Scheffer*[141] Court. It is time that the courts recognize the legitimate scientific evidence and reject the specious arguments put forth by polygraph critics for personal gain and furtherance of their political agendas.[142]

It is instructive to note that only the New Mexico courts have extensive experience with polygraph evidence. Since 1975, polygraph evidence has been admissible at trial in New Mexico.[143] After eight years of generally positive experience with such evidence in trials, in 1983 the Supreme Court of New Mexico adopted a comprehensive rule that specifies the requirements for admitting polygraph evidence at trial.[144] Although polygraph admissibility has been vigorously challenged by prosecutors numerous times in the 18 years since its adoption, the New Mexico Supreme Court has not reversed its stance. We wonder why almost all other state and federal courts have chosen to ignore the 25 years of positive experience of the New Mexico courts while they continue to exploit all legal devices to exclude polygraph evidence. Clearly, the well-regulated approach to the admission of polygraph evidence has been of

140. *See United States v. Cordoba,* 991 F.Supp. 1199 (C.D.Cal.1998). The court admitted the testimony of two FBI agents in a *Daubert* hearing. Neither witness had any scientific credentials or training. However, the judge relied on their testimony and openly attacked the uncontradicted scientific testimony of the defendant's expert, whom the judge himself described as "a pioneer psychophysiologist, nationally known scholar in forensic polygraphy, and generally acknowledged as the nation's foremost polygraph expert." We found the court's rulings, to say the least, disheartening.

141. *Supra* note 38.

142. *Supra* note 125.

143. *State v. Dorsey,* 88 N.M. 184, 539 P.2d 204 (1975). Polygraph evidence was admitted by the New Mexico Supreme Court under the constitutional right for a defendant to present a defense.

144. N. M. R. Evid. 707.

benefit to the judicial process in New Mexico courts. There is no logical or practical reason that the situation should be any different in the rest of the United States.

In conclusion, we note that during the summer of 1997 a group of scientists formed the ad hoc Committee of Concerned Social Scientists and submitted a Brief for Amicus Curiae[145] to the United States Supreme Court in *United States v. Scheffer*.[146] That Amicus was signed by 17 professionals with advanced degrees (15 doctoral level). They concluded as follows:

> For the foregoing reasons, the members of the Committee of Concerned Social Scientists respectfully submit that polygraph testing is a valid application of psychological science and that it is generally accepted by the majority of the informed scientific community of psychological scientists as such. Polygraph testing has a known but acceptable error rate that has been well defined by scientific research. Furthermore, there is no scientific evidence that suggests the admission of the results of a polygraph examination before lay jurors will overwhelm their ability to use and value other evidence. Overwhelming the trier of fact is particularly unlikely when the quality and training of the members of a court martial are considered. Many of the traditional objections to the polygraph have been shown by science to be without merit. Although there are problems with the quality of practice in the polygraph profession, such problems are not unique to polygraph tests. They are likely to occur in any situation where a human evaluator is needed to interpret data. In any event, the problems of examiner practice are easily remedied by the traditional means of cross-examination and evidentiary rule.

It is our sincere hope that eventually the courts will recognize the merits and wisdom of this position and accord polygraph evidence its rightful place in the judicial process.

§ 12–3.0 THE SCIENTIFIC STATUS OF RESEARCH ON POLYGRAPH TECHNIQUES: THE CASE AGAINST POLYGRAPH TESTS

by

William G. Iacono* & David T. Lykken**

§ 12–3.1 Introductory Discussion of the Science

Psychophysiological interrogation is based on the plausible assumption that various involuntary physiological reactions to salient questions might

---

145. *Supra* note 133.

146. *Supra* note 38.

* *Distinguished McKnight University Professor*, Professor of Psychology, University of Minnesota, Director, Clinical Science and Psychopathology Research Training Program, recipient of the American Psychological Association's *Distinguished Scientific Award for an Early Career Contribution to Psychology*, the Society for Psychophysiological Research's *Distinguished Scientific Award for an Early Ca-*

reer Contribution to Psychophysiology, Past-President of the Society for Psychophysiological Research (1996–97) and former Member, Department of Defense Polygraph Institute's Curriculum and Research Guidance Committee.

** Professor of Psychology, University of Minnesota, author of A TREMOR IN THE BLOOD: USES AND ABUSES OF THE LIE DETECTOR, (2d ed. 1998), recipient of the American Psychological Association's Award for a *Distinguished Con-*

reveal truths that the person being questioned is attempting to conceal. Psychophysiological Detection of Deception (PDD) is based on assumptions regarding how guilty and innocent individuals respond differentially to accusatory questions about their involvement in a crime and their character. We shall demonstrate that the assumptions of PDD are in fact implausible, unsupported by credible scientific evidence, and rejected by most members of the relevant scientific community. PDD is widely used in the U.S. both in criminal investigation and for pre- and post-employment screening, mainly by federal police and security agencies. Although claims about its accuracy are unfounded, we shall show that PDD has been embraced by law enforcement agencies because it has utility as an interrogation tool, eliciting confessions or damaging admissions from naïve but guilty suspects. On the other hand, however, we shall show that unjustifiable faith in conclusions based on PDD has permitted sophisticated guilty suspects to escape detection while unsophisticated innocents have been condemned and punished.

Another method of psychophysiological interrogation is for the purpose of detecting the presence of guilty knowledge as opposed to the detection of lying. The Guilty Knowledge Test is used in criminal investigation in Japan and in Israel but is, so far, seldom used in the United States. We shall demonstrate that the assumptions of the Guilty Knowledge Test are quite plausible and that the limited research concerning its validity has so far been encouraging.

§ 12–3.1.1 Background

[1] Instrumentation

The polygraph instrument consists typically of four pens recording physiological responses on a moving paper chart. Two "pneumo" pens, driven by pneumatic belts fastened around the subject's chest and abdomen, record thoracic and abdominal breathing movements. A third pen is connected to a blood pressure cuff or sphygmomanometer around one upper arm. During questioning, this cuff is inflated to partially occlude the flow of blood to the lower arm. Each heart beat then causes this "cardio" pen to briefly deflect while changes in blood pressure cause the entire tracing to move up or down on the chart. The fourth, the GSR or "electrodermal" pen, is connected to two metal electrodes attached to the fingerprint area of two fingers of one hand. This pen records changes in the electrical resistance of the palmar skin, which are caused in turn by sweat gland activity. Thus, the polygraph provides continuous recordings of breathing movements, blood pressure changes, and the sweating of the palms.

The restriction of blood flow in the arm produces ischemic pain after several minutes, which limits the number of questions that can be asked during one "chart" to about ten, after which the cuff pressure must be released. Depending on the polygraph procedure used, a typical test involves

tribution to *Psychology in the Public Interest* (1991) and for *Distinguished Scientific Contributions for Applications of Psychology* (2001), Past–President of the Society for Psychophysi-   ological Research (1980–81), and recipient of that Society's *Award for Distinguished Scientific Contributions to Psychophysiology* (1998).

several "charts," usually with the same questions repeated in the same or different order, with a rest of several minutes between charts.

At the present time, nearly all polygraphic interrogation is intended to determine whether the respondent is answering a specific question or questions deceptively. Contrary to popular belief, however, the polygraph is not a "lie detector." Although some practitioners claim that certain patterns of physiological response recorded on the polygraph chart are specifically indicative of lying,[1] there is no serious scientific support for this view.

Most polygraph examiners, therefore, employ a technique that provides an opportunity to compare physiological responses to different kinds of questions, including questions directly relevant to the issue at hand.

[2] The Control Question Technique (CQT)

For most forensic applications, a procedure known as the "control question test" is used to evaluate a subject's truthfulness. The CQT is actually a collection of procedures which, although differing from one another slightly in format, all involve the comparison of a subject's responses to relevant questions with responses to interspersed "control" or comparison questions. The CQT is a descendant of the relevant-irrelevant test (RIT), a technique that although widely discredited for criminal applications is still used for employee screening.

The criminal application of the RIT involved two types of questions. The relevant questions focused on the matter of interest and were presented as implicit accusations. In a criminal investigation, the relevant questions usually dealt with a single issue and asked about involvement in an alleged crime, e.g., "Did you rob the First National Bank?" or "Were you involved in any way in the robbery of that bank?" Interposed among these relevant questions were irrelevant questions dealing with innocuous issues unlikely to be of much concern to anyone. Sample irrelevant questions include, "Are you sitting down?" and "Is today Wednesday?" Subjects were expected to answer these questions truthfully, so the physiological responses they elicit served as a baseline against which to compare the responses to the relevant questions. If the responses to the relevant questions were larger than those to the irrelevant queries, then the subject would be deemed deceptive. A truthful verdict required the two types of questions to yield reactions of similar size. The major criticism of this technique is that the irrelevant questions provide no "control" for the psychological impact of being asked the relevant question. The relevant question differs from the irrelevant question both in that it conveys an emotionally loaded accusation and the subject may be lying in response to it. There is no way to determine that a larger response to the relevant question is not due simply to the subject's nervousness about being asked this question. Because of this serious shortcoming, innocent criminal suspects were likely to fail the RIT.

The CQT attempts to improve on the RIT format by keeping the relevant questions and replacing the irrelevant questions with so-called control ques-

§ 12–3.0

1. John E. Reid & Fred E. Inbau, Truth and Deception 61–71 (2d ed. 1977).

tions. The control questions refer in a deliberately vague or general way to possible misdeeds from the subject's past, misdeeds that may be chosen so that they deal with a theme similar to that covered by the relevant question. Typically, qualifying phrasing is added to the control question so that it does not involve the same period of time covered by the relevant question. Examples of control questions used with relevant questions dealing with theft and sexual abuse might be: "Prior to last year, did you ever take something of value from someone who trusted you?" and "Before age 25, did you ever engage in an unusual sex act?"

[a]　Theory of the CQT

Critical to the outcome of the CQT is the manner in which the control questions are introduced. After the relevant questions have been formulated and reviewed, the control questions are presented to the subject with the explanation that they are intended to assess the subject's basic character with regard to honesty and trustworthiness in order to make sure that the subject has never done anything in the past similar to what the subject currently stands accused of doing.[2] The subject is actually told by the examiner that the expectation is that the subject will answer the control questions with a denial. If he or she answers such a question "yes," the examiner responds in a way that suggests disapproval. Thus, the examiner creates a dilemma for the subject by simultaneously creating the expectation that the subject will be honest and yet answer the control questions "no." As Raskin observes, this manipulation "leads the subject to believe that admissions [to the control questions] will cause the examiner to form the opinion that the subject is dishonest and is therefore guilty. This discourages [further] admissions and maximizes the likelihood that the negative answer [to the control question] is untruthful."[3] Raskin goes on to explain that it is important to get the subject to believe that deceptive answers to the control questions "will result in strong physiological reactions during the test and will lead the examiner to conclude that the subject was deceptive with respect to the relevant issues" concerning the alleged crime. However, he acknowledges, "in fact, the converse is true."[4]

CQT theory, therefore, is based on the premise that stronger responses to the control than to the relevant questions indicates that the latter have been answered truthfully. The theory assumes that the guilty person, who must answer the relevant questions deceptively, will be more disturbed by those questions than by the control questions and that his physiological responses will be stronger to the relevant than to the control questions. The theory also assumes that an innocent person, answering the relevant questions truthfully, will be relatively more disturbed by the control questions, because only the answers to these questions involve deception or significant concern.

2.　David C. Raskin, *Polygraph Techniques for the Detection of Deception, in* Psychological Methods in Criminal Investigation and Evidence 247, 254 (David C. Raskin ed., 1989).

3.　*Id.* at 255.

4.　*Id.*

[b]   Scoring the CQT

Some polygraphers use a "global" procedure to help decide the outcome of the examination. With this approach, the examiner takes into account the relative size of the responses to the relevant and control questions as well as all other available information, including the case facts, the subject's explanation of the facts, and his or her demeanor during the examination. Most contemporary practitioners eschew the global approach, preferring instead a semi-objective quantitative method, referred to as "numerical scoring," to decide truthfulness. Each relevant response is compared with the response to an adjacent control question; each such comparison yields a score of –3 if the relevant response is much larger than the control response, a score of +3 if the control response is the much larger of the two, a score of zero if the two responses are about equal, with scores of 1 or 2 for intermediate values. For a typical CQT, the total score might range from +30 to –30 with positive scores interpreted as indicating truthfulness and negative scores indicating deception. Scores in some narrow range about zero, typically between +5 and –5, are interpreted as inconclusive. An increasingly common practice is to feed the polygraph data into a computer that is programmed to score the responses according to some standard algorithm.[5]

[c]   The "Stimulation" Test

As part of the CQT, examiners commonly employ a stimulation ("stim") test, the purpose of which is to convince subjects that their physiological responses do in fact give them away when they lie. This procedure is typically administered either prior to asking the first set of CQT questions or after the list of CQT questions has been presented once (i.e., after the first "chart"). Some examiners have the subject select a card from a covertly-marked deck and then instruct him or her to answer "No" to questions of the form: "Is it the 10 of spades?" Because the examiner knows in advance which card was selected, he can ensure that he identifies the correct card irrespective of the subject's polygraphic reaction. Other examiners have the subject choose a number between, say, 1 and 7, and then openly tell the examiner which number was chosen. The subject then is told: "Now when you answer 'No' to the number you selected, I will be able to determine what your polygraphic response looks like when you lie." Some examiners will show subjects the physiological tracings that gave them away in order to prove that they can be detected, perhaps mechanically manipulating the deflection of the pens when the critical item is presented so the subject can easily identify the response. In fact, because people do not show distinctive or characteristic physiological responses when they lie, this form of stim test is also deceptive, falsely suggesting that the examiner has somehow calibrated the test to work optimally on this particular subject.

[d]   The Directed Lie Test (DLT): A Variant of the CQT

The DLT is a form of the CQT in which the subject is *instructed* to

5. *Id.* at 260–261; *see also* John C. Kircher & David C. Raskin, *Human versus Computerized Evaluations of Polygraph Data in a Labo-* *ratory Setting*, 44 J. APPLIED PSYCHOL. 291, 291–302 (1988).

answer each control question deceptively.[6] "You've told a lie sometime in the past, haven't you? Well, I'm going to ask you about that on the test and I want you to answer 'No.' Then you and I will both know that that answer was a lie and the tracings on the polygraph will show me how you react when you're lying." The DLT is scored in the same way as a standard CQT. Advocates believe that the DLT is an improvement because there is greater certainty that the subject's answers to control questions are false. The DLT involves a slightly different assumption, namely, that innocent persons will be more disturbed while giving—on instruction—a false answer to a question about their past than they will while truthfully denying a false accusation about a crime of which they are currently suspected.

§ 12–3.1.2 The Scientific Questions and Methods

[1] What Branch of Science Is Relevant to the Evaluation of CQT Theory and Application?

Polygraphy is unusual in that it has evolved without formal ties to any scientific discipline. Practitioners are graduates of polygraph trade schools. The faculty at these schools are usually polygraphers or law enforcement professionals. Few are trained as scientists and few have the background necessary to be able to provide competent evaluations of their discipline. As we shall see, even examiners with long experience have no way of knowing how often their decisions are correct. What feedback they do receive is limited to confessions obtained from suspects whom they have diagnosed as deceptive and then interrogated. These events necessarily confirm the examiner's conclusion and, thus, provide the examiner with a grossly misleading impression of consistent accuracy. Because polygraph testing is used for making psychological inferences or diagnoses, we conclude that psychology is the branch of science that is relevant to its evaluation.

[2] Is the CQT a Test?

Standardization and *objectivity* are essential to the definition of a psychological test. A test is considered standardized when its administration and scoring is uniform across examiners and situations. If the outcome of polygraph tests is to be trusted for different subjects and examiners, it is essential that the procedure is always the same. As Anastasi points out, this requirement is "only a special application of the need for controlled conditions in all scientific applications."[7] A technique that is not standardized cannot easily be evaluated; each of its variants would have to be evaluated separately to determine if, as it is generally applied, it is accurate. A test is objective insofar as its administration, scoring, and interpretation are independent of the subjective judgment of a particular examiner.[8] The validity of a test that was not objective would be undermined by individual differences in judgment that varied from one examiner to the next. We conclude that the CQT is neither standardized nor objective and therefore fails to meet the scientific definition

---

6. Raskin (1989), *supra* note 2, at 271.

7. Anne Anastasi, Psychological Testing 25 (6th ed. 1988).

8. *Id*. at 27.

of a psychological test.[9]

[3] Does the CQT Produce Consistent (Reliable) Results?

In psychological science, reliability refers to the likelihood that the test yields results that are consistent and reproducible. Would another examiner score the charts in the same way? Would another test administered to the same subject yield the same results? A test can be reliable and yet inaccurate but a test that is not reliable cannot be accurate.

There are two ways to evaluate the reliability of a polygraph test. *Test-retest* reliability refers to whether the test produces the same result when it is repeated on a second occasion. The other form of reliability, *inter-scorer* reliability, asks whether two examiners can obtain the same result when they independently score the same set of charts. We conclude that inter-scorer reliability can be high (but is not always high in practice) and that test-retest reliability has not been (and probably cannot be) validly assessed.

[4] Is CQT Theory Scientifically Sound?

It is generally agreed that the accusatory relevant questions used in the CQT will tend to produce emotional responses (and associated physiological reactions) in both truthful and innocent suspects. The theory of the CQT is that a truthful suspect will react still more strongly to the comparison questions that refer with deliberate vagueness to possible past misdeeds. We conclude that these "control" questions are not controls in the scientific sense and that the theory of the CQT is not scientifically plausible.[10]

[5] Can CQT Theory Be Tested?

The scientific method requires that hypotheses be testable empirically. In the case of the CQT, these hypotheses are that guilty suspects will consistently display stronger physiological reactions to the relevant (than to the control) questions, and that innocent suspects will consistently be more disturbed by the control questions. We conclude that existing data permit a reasonably fair test of the second hypothesis but that the first hypothesis, concerning the validity of the CQT in detecting deception in guilty suspects, cannot be adequately tested with the available data.

[6] What Scientific Standards Must a Study Satisfy to Provide a Meaningful Appraisal of CQT Accuracy?

There are hundreds of studies on polygraphy, many of which are controversial because of the way they were conducted and the results they obtained. Some of these reports are unpublished, many have been published in polygraph and police trade publications, and many have appeared in scientific journals. Conclusions about polygraphy will depend in part on which of these

---

9. Polygraph examiners, in recognition of this fact, often refer to the CQT as the control question "technique" rather than "test."

10. Faced with this valid criticism, proponents now often refer to the CQT as the "comparison question technique."

reports are accepted as scientifically credible. Among this array of papers, how do we decide which to use to evaluate polygraph testing? We conclude that the only studies worth consideration are those that have appeared in peer-reviewed scientific journals.

[7] Is the CQT Accurate (Valid)?

Validity is a synonym for accuracy. Determining the degree to which the examiner's decisions about the truthfulness of subjects agree with ground truth assesses validity. We conclude that the validity of the CQT in detecting truthfulness is negligible and that no acceptable method has yet been implemented for assessing the validity of the CQT in detecting deception.

[8] Can Guilty Persons Be Trained to Use "Countermeasures" to Defeat a CQT?

Countermeasures are deliberately adopted strategies used to manipulate the outcome of a polygraph test. Effective countermeasures should be aimed at enhancing one's response to control questions. This might be accomplished by unobtrusive self-stimulation such as biting one's tongue or thinking stressful thoughts when confronted with this material on a polygraph test. The effectiveness of countermeasures can be determined by instructing guilty subjects on polygraph theory and encouraging them to use these strategies with the appropriate questions as they arise during the examination. By subsequently determining how many of these individuals escaped detection, it is possible to evaluate the effectiveness of different countermeasure maneuvers. We conclude that effective countermeasures against the CQT are easily learned and that no effective means of defeating such tactics have as yet been demonstrated.

[9] Has the Computerization of the CQT Improved its Accuracy?

An increasingly common practice in polygraphy is to use a computer to record the physiological responses of subjects. With some computer systems, software is included to score the physiological data and even interpret it. We conclude that computerization of the CQT lends an aura of objectivity and accuracy that is almost entirely specious.

[10] Why Do Law Enforcement Agencies Use the CQT?

A question that frequently arises concerns why the CQT is used so pervasively if its accuracy is questionable. The simple answer is that under the pressure of taking the CQT, many guilty people confess, thus resolving a case that often could not be resolved through any other means. We conclude that the CQT can be very useful as a tool for inducing confessions (i.e., it has utility) even though its accuracy as a test is negligible.

[11] What Is the Prevailing Scientific Opinion About CQT Theory and Testing?

As will become apparent, it is difficult to provide straightforward answers to many of these questions by conducting scientific investigations. However, polygraph testing, as it is currently practiced, has been around for over forty years, providing ample opportunity for scientists to consider the questions posed here. The views of the relevant scientific community can be surveyed to determine whether there is a consensus of expert opinion regarding the major questions about polygraphy. We provide data showing that the prevailing opinion of the relevant scientific community is that the CQT is not based on sound scientific principles and that the results of CQT should not be relied upon.

[12] Is Polygraph Screening of Federal Employees and Job Applicants Scientifically Justified?

PDD is often used to determine if a job applicant or employee is of good character and would represent a reasonable security risk. There are no credible scientific demonstrations of the accuracy of this PDD application. However, often employees, pressured by polygraphers to divulge everything in their background relevant to such an assessment, make damaging admissions concerning past misbehaviors. We conclude that these tests are used only because employers have found them to be an effective tool for eliciting such information.

[13] Is There an Accurate Psychophysiological Test for Identifying Criminals?

Often scientists are criticized for undermining PDD, thus hampering law enforcement efforts, without offering any workable alternative procedure for identifying criminals. The implication is that scientists find deception detection procedures inherently objectionable and hold a philosophical objection to PDD. In fact there is an alternative to traditional PDD that has a solid scientific foundation, is broadly embraced by scientists, but is ignored by the polygraph profession. We conclude that this alternative, known as the guilty knowledge test, appears to have great promise as a forensic investigative aid.

§ 12–3.2 Areas of Scientific Agreement and Disagreement

§ 12–3.2.1 The Relevant Scientific Community

[1] Scientists at Arms Length

Polygraph tests are psychological tests that use physiological reactions to psychological stimuli (questions) as a basis for inferring a psychological process or state (e.g., deception or guilty knowledge). This means that polygraphic interrogation is a form of applied psychology and, hence, that psychologists constitute the scientific community relevant to polygraph testing. Because polygraphy involves psychophysiological recordings, members of the premier organization composed of psychophysiologists, the Society for

Psychophysiological Research, constitute an important part of the relevant scientific community. Members of this organization have been repeatedly surveyed to determine their opinions about polygraph testing.

There is little scientific controversy surrounding the physiological aspects of polygraphy. That is, there is no debate about the adequacy of the instrumentation or the physiological measurements. The controversy about polygraphy concerns its psychological and psychometric aspects, i.e., its properties (e.g., reliability, validity) as a diagnostic technique. Most psychologists are capable of evaluating the psychological principles on which a procedure is based and are knowledgeable about the problems of psychological measurement and should be capable of understanding the scientific questions at issue in this area. Psychologists recognized for distinguished achievement by election as Fellows to the American Psychological Association have recently been surveyed regarding their opinions of polygraph testing. We will review the results of these various surveys near the end of this chapter, after we have completed our analysis of polygraph theory and practices.

[2]   Polygraph Examiners Are Not Scientists

It must be stressed that professional polygraph examiners do *not* constitute the relevant scientific community. Few polygraph examiners have any psychological or scientific training. Polygraph schools provide a curriculum lasting from 7 to 12 weeks and the only admission requirement is, in some cases, law enforcement experience. Moreover, even the most experienced polygraph examiner has been systematically misled by the peculiarities of his trade. He seldom discovers for certain whether any given test result is right or wrong. The only certain feedback he does get is when a suspect, whom he interrogates because that suspect "failed" the test, is induced to confess.[11] But these confessions necessarily confirm the test just given. Since suspects are either lying (guilty) or not (innocent), a test as invalid as a coin toss would fail guilty suspects about half the time and some of these would confess after interrogation. Since their experience is thus selectively misleading, polygraph examiners are perhaps the group whose opinions concerning the technique are, paradoxically, of the least value.

§ 12–3.2.2   Why the CQT is Not a Test

[1]   Question Construction and Administration Are Not Standardized

As we noted in our description of the CQT, it is not a uniformly applied technique but rather a collection of related procedures. These procedures differ in what kinds of questions, other than relevant and control questions, appear on a test, how questions are ordered and grouped, how best to word relevant and control questions, how to conduct oneself during the interview phases of the interrogation, and how to score and interpret charts. The actual structure of a given CQT depends on what polygraph school a polygrapher attended and the examiner's own preferred practices. The only feature all

---

11. William G. Iacono, *Can We Determine the Accuracy of Polygraph Tests?, in* 4 AD-   VANCES IN PSYCHOPHYSIOLOGY (J. Richard Jennings et al. eds., 1991).

CQTs have in common is the inclusion of control and relevant questions. Because there is no single CQT format, the CQT is clearly not a standardized procedure.

In order to conduct a CQT, the examiner must review the case facts, consider the subject's account of the case, and decide how best to formulate relevant questions that clearly cover the issue at hand. What is required under these circumstances is a series of subjective assessments regarding question development. Different examiners reach different conclusions about what questions to ask; this fact again demonstrates the lack of standardization of the CQT.

The examiner also must succeed in deceiving the subject regarding the purpose and function of the control questions. In the case of the CQT, the subject must be led to believe that his being disturbed by these questions might result in his failing the test when, in fact, the reverse is true. In the case of the DLT, he must be led to believe that his directed lie responses will show the examiner what his responses to the relevant questions will be like if he answers the latter questions deceptively; this claim is of course untrue. Failure to adequately deceive the subject in these ways invalidates a basic assumption of the test. Because some examiners are better deceivers than others, and some examinees are more easily deceived than others, this problem represents a serious failure of standardization.

[2] Subjectivity of Chart Interpretation

The interpretation of the polygraph charts is also problematic. Those employing the global scoring approach are by design using a non-objective, non-standardized procedure. Although numerical scoring is supposed to be based solely on the physiological data, the examiner scoring the chart, just like those adopting the global approach, is aware of the case facts and the subject's behavior during the examination. Patrick and Iacono showed that this information can compromise the examiner's objectivity.[12] Working with real-life cases from a major police agency, the Royal Canadian Mounted Police (RCMP), these investigators found that the examiners often ignored their own numerical scoring when interpreting charts. For instance, when the numerical scoring indicated deception, 18% of the time examiners concluded the test outcome was either inconclusive or truthful. When the scoring fell in the inconclusive range, the examiners actually classified subjects as guilty or truthful 49% of the time.[13]

[3] Absence of Controlling Standards

In *United States v. Scheffer*,[14] the Supreme Court noted that "there is simply no way to know in a particular case whether a polygraph examiner's conclusion is accurate, because certain doubts and uncertainties plague even the best polygraph exams." We would add that there is no standard in the field regarding what constitutes the "best polygraph exams." The accuracy of

12. Christopher J. Patrick & William G. Iacono, *Validity of the Control Question Polygraph Test: The Problem of Sampling Bias*, 76 J. APPLIED PSYCHOL. 229, 229–238 (1991).

13. *Id.* at 233.

14. 523 U.S. 303, 312, 118 S.Ct. 1261, 140 L.Ed.2d 413 (1998).

a test that is administered with no controlling standards cannot be determined. This is in effect what the court ruled in a *Daubert* hearing in *United States v. Cordoba.*[15] The court, after reviewing manuals and practice codes from various professional polygraph organizations and agencies, and after hearing the testimony of Dr. David Raskin, noted that particular polygraph practices are followed more out of custom or habit than because examiners follow a prescribed set of standards.[16]

§ 12–3.2.3   The CQT Has Unknown Reliability

[1]   Inter–Scorer Agreement

The only systematic studies of polygraph reliability have focused on the CQT. There is general agreement that examiners trained in numerical scoring can produce reasonably consistent numerical scores. The Patrick and Iacono findings cited above, however, show that the original examiner, influenced by his knowledge of the case facts, will sometimes disregard the physiological data when reaching a decision. In addition, Patrick and Iacono showed that when another examiner blindly scored the same charts, he would sometimes reach a decision that differed from that of the original examiner. For example, of the 72 charts that the original examiner both scored truthful and judged to be from a truthful person, only 51(71%) were scored truthful by the blind examiner. Because the blind examiner who rescored the charts based his

---

15. U.S. v. Cordoba, 104 F.3d 225 (9th Cir. 1997).

16. For instance, the court noted that the Department of Defense Polygraph Institute, which is the most prestigious training facility for polygraphers, "teaches that if a subject fails one relevant question, the subject fails the entire test. Dr. Raskin, however, follows a standard where a subject who fails one relevant question may still pass the test." The court recognized Dr. Raskin as "probably the strongest and best informed advocate of polygraph admissibility" yet expressed the following opinion regarding his testimony about the adequacy of the CQT administered in this particular instance:

> The evidence shows, and the court finds, Defendant's test contained many factors which would be considered defects under various versions of industry "standards." The duration and substance of the pre-test interview was not preserved. No tape or video was made of the pre-test interview or the polygraph exam. The examiner didn't calibrate the machine at the prison test site. Although the examiner asked four supposedly "relevant questions," only one was really relevant: two involved undisputed facts, one was marginally relevant, and the wording of the truly relevant question was arguably too ambiguous to be helpful. The examiner found deception in the marginally-relevant question's answer (while Dr. Raskin did not), but the examiner scored it as truthful after

obtaining Defendant's explanation for the answer. The examiner's report was filled with errors and defects: the report was drafted before the test, it did not include a fingertip test, according to Dr. Raskin it lacked attention to detail, it omitted Defendant's response to whether he was under drugs or medication, it misstated the machine used, and it says the stimulation test was done after the first test when it was obviously done first. Although there was movement on a response, the examiner scored the response. The examiner did not record a significant breath. The examiner did not ask if defendant had proper sleep before the exam. The examiner acknowledged the exam was conducted in a poor setting with many distractions. Although each of these occurrences is a defect under various expressions of the industry's standards, Dr. Raskin declined to criticize the test in any meaningful way, and found the test to be entirely acceptable. Confronted with each defect, Dr. Raskin staunchly stuck to his view that the test was reliable and acceptable ... If pro-polygraph's best expert declines to find any fault with an obviously faulty examination, that is strong evidence that there are insufficient controlling standards ... The court finds there are no *controlling* standards to ensure proper protocol or provide a court with a yardstick by which a defendant's examination can be measured. *Id.* at 1207–08 (emphasis added).

decision solely on the physiological data, the discrepancy in the number of subjects scored truthful by the two examiners roughly reflects the extent to which the original examiner's chart scoring was influenced by his knowledge of the case facts. That is, for the original examiner to score many more charts truthful than the blind examiner who relied exclusively on the physiological data, the original examiner's chart scoring was likely affected by his knowledge of the case facts and therefore was not entirely objective.

The case of the Los Alamos Laboratory scientist accused of mishandling nuclear bomb secrets is illustrative. According to three Department of Energy polygraphers, Dr. Wen Ho Lee passed a polygraph test administered December 23, 1999, but, after suspicions grew that he had passed secrets to China, FBI polygraphers rescored those original charts and concluded that they indicated deception. Nevertheless, when Richard Keifer of the American Polygraph Association examined Lee's polygraph charts, he said "he had never been able to score anyone so high on the non-deceptive scale."[17]

[2] Test–Retest Agreement

No good scientific data are available that can be used to evaluate the consistency of results when separate CQTs are administered to the same subject by different examiners. A different choice of control questions, a different wording of the relevant questions, even a different manner displayed by the examiner, might influence the emotional responses to the questions and thus change the test outcome, whether computer-scoring is in use or not. Moreover, the CQT relies on the subject's confidence in the accuracy of the procedure; an innocent suspect who has lost confidence in the test may react more strongly to the relevant questions in consequence while a guilty suspect, who has avoided detection on the first test, might be still less disturbed by the relevant questions on the second test. Thus, mistakes on the first test may be likely to be repeated on the second due to their effect on the suspect's confidence. Finally, the psychophysiological phenomenon of habituation could impact repeated testing. Habituation refers to the fact that physiological reactions diminish with repeated exposure to stimuli. It is reasonable to expect that a subject would be less responsive to the questions asked in a second polygraph test, and that such habituated responding might influence the outcome.

In real life, it is not uncommon for a second polygraph to be administered in order to confirm or check the results of the first test. In our experience, these retests provide no useful data about reliability because the polygrapher conducting the second test is always aware of the results of the first test. This knowledge is likely to affect how the examiner conducts and scores the second test; the results of the second test are thus not independent of the results of the first. Under the circumstances, obtaining the same outcome on two polygraph examinations should not be taken as convincing evidence of innocence or guilt.

17. *Wen Ho Lee's Problematic Polygraph,* Sharyl Attkisson, http://www.cbsnews.com/ now/story10,1597,157220–41200.shtml (last visited March 27, 2001).

§ 12–3.3.4 Implausibility of CQT Theory

The scientific plausibility of the CQT can be determined by appraising the psychological assumptions on which it is based. These assumptions, analyzed below, concern what causes the response to relevant questions to be larger or smaller than the response to the "control" or comparison questions.

[1] Control Questions Do Not Work for the Innocent

At the heart of the CQT is the assumption that truthful subjects will respond more strongly to the control than the relevant questions. For this to occur, it must indeed be the case, as the proponents of the CQT assert, that innocent subjects will be more disturbed by this question than by the relevant question. As we noted in our discussion of the RIT, it is important that the comparison question that is paired with the relevant question should control for the emotional impact of simply being confronted with an accusatory question. For that to happen, the answer to the comparison question should be just as important to the subject as the answer to the relevant question.

Being asked the relevant questions is likely to evoke large physiological reactions regardless of one's guilt. The theory of the CQT is implausible because the so-called control questions actually used do not serve as strict controls in the scientific sense of this term; the subject's responses to the CQT's control questions do not predict how this subject should respond to the relevant questions if he is answering truthfully.

[2] A Genuine Control Question

How might we design a polygraph test in which the comparison question would provide a true control for the relevant question? One approach would be to lead subjects to believe that they are plausible suspects in two different crimes, both of which bear similar consequences if guilty. However, unknown to the subject, one of the crimes never occurred, so the examiner is certain the suspect did not commit it. A polygraph test containing a true control question could be derived from this scenario by using as the comparison question the "relevant" question pertaining to the nonexistent crime. From the suspect's vantage point, the test would now contain two types of equally threatening relevant questions. The only reason for a stronger response to be elicited by the real relevant question would be because it was answered with a lie. Such genuine control questions are not employed in real life, however.

[3] Polygraphers Cannot Protect the Innocent from Failing the CQT

Proponents of the CQT argue that the apparent imbalance in the emotional impact of the relevant and control questions fails to take into account the subtle manner in which examiners manipulate subjects into believing that the control questions are just as important as the relevant questions to the outcome of the test. Recall from Raskin's characterization of how control questions are introduced to the subject that the examiner attempts to convince the subject that the test will be failed if the control question is answered deceptively and that the subject is manipulated to hold back admissions about material covered by these questions so that he is likely to be answering them deceptively.[18] The assumption is that this manipulation will protect innocent subjects from failing a CQT.

There are several problems with this assumption:

(1) Regardless of how skilled the examiner is, subjects may not be concerned about their responses to the control questions. Subjects might feel comfortable with their denials to them or, perhaps, because they cannot recall an instance indicating that their response would be untruthful.

(2) Even when the manipulation works exactly as CQT theory requires, it is still the case that the relevant question deals with the material that is of greatest significance, the only material that could directly link the subject to the crime. Given its perceived significance, it is likely to arouse stronger responses than control questions.

(3) The manipulation is obviously difficult to accomplish. It may be impossible to achieve the desired result in many instances, either because the examiner is not skilled enough to deceive subjects in this way or because sophisticated subjects see through the deception.

(4) Finally, any procedure that is predicated on the examiner's ability to deceive the subject in this fashion is vulnerable to the possibility that the suspect may have learned prior to the testing how the procedure is supposed to work and therefore be immune to the requisite deceptions. It is noteworthy that a trained polygraph examiner, who finds himself suspected of some crime, could not be expected to generate a valid CQT, whether innocent or guilty, since he could not be deceived in the required ways.

[4] How Over–Reacting to Control Questions Makes Guilty Suspects Appear Truthful

Another basic assumption of the CQT is that the deceptive subject will respond more strongly to the relevant than the control question. This assumption requires that suspects not use physical or mental strategies to augment their responses to the control questions. However, as we have already noted, given an explanation of CQT test structure plus coaching on how to willfully enhance physiological reactivity, guilty subjects *can* defeat a CQT. Another problem with this assumption arises from the examiner's attempt, when control questions are introduced, to discourage admissions concerning the topics covered in these questions. If a guilty subject had, for example, a history of undetected criminal activity and kept this secret during the examination, he may indeed be lying in response to the control questions, causing larger responses to these than to the relevant questions. It is important to note that anyone familiar with CQT theory would understand that they should not make admissions to the examiner concerning the content of control questions, and that they should in fact think of the worst transgressions when asked these questions. This simple strategy can be used by anyone to help insure a truthful outcome on a CQT.

18. Raskin (1989), *supra* note 2, at 254–255.

[5]   Adversarial vs. "Friendly" CQTs

The notion that a deceptive response to the relevant question will provide a stronger reaction than that to a control question is, according to CQT theory, dependent on the subject's fear of the consequences of detection. If the subject has little to fear, the significance of lying to the relevant question would be diminished and the strength of the physiological reaction to this lie would be reduced. When the police give a CQT, the results of which are public (at least they would be known to the police), the consequences of detection are serious, and the physiological reactivity associated with lying would be expected to be substantial. But such CQTs, administered under adversarial circumstances, seldom become the basis of an evidentiary hearing in court. The more usual case for an evidentiary hearing is one where the defense counsel arranges a privately administered or "friendly" polygraph test. If the subject fails, he has little to lose because the results, protected by attorney-client privilege, will remain secret. If the test is passed, defense counsel releases the results and attempts to get them into evidence in court. Under these "friendly" conditions, the fear of detection assumption is largely violated, responsivity to relevant questions can be expected to be diminished, and guilty suspects are more likely to be scored truthful. There are other reasons why friendly tests have reduced probative value. The fact that there is no assurance that the suspect would not "shop around," taking several tests from different examiners, before achieving a favorable result, indicates further that friendly tests cannot be safely relied upon. When a test is taken under "friendly" circumstances, the examiner knows that he can earn witness fees only if the results are favorable. Without necessarily impugning the integrity of polygraph examiners, this factor would skew the results of such tests.

Despite the fact that the results of friendly, rather than adversarial, tests are likely to be the subject of *Daubert* hearings, research on the validity of polygraph tests has focused on adversarial tests. There is not a single study demonstrating that friendly polygraph tests are valid. Proponents of the polygraph defend the admissibility of friendly tests by claiming that examiners in private practice who conduct tests for both the police and defense attorneys fail about the same proportion of subjects referred from both sources. Besides the fact that polygraph examiners seldom back up such assertions with an independent audit of their own records, thus leaving open the possibility that their claims are inaccurate, to make sense of a finding of equal proportions of failed tests from these two sources requires consideration of the likelihood that subjects from these two settings are guilty. When the police conduct a polygraph test, usually there is no hard evidence against a suspect and no arrest has been made. When a defense attorney offers his client for a polygraph, usually the suspect has been arrested and there is sufficient evidence to warrant a trial. The rate of guilt thus must be higher for those who are defendants rather than mere suspects, and these defendants should be expected to fail CQTs at a rate that is substantially higher than that for suspects tested by the police. For both groups of suspects to fail CQTs at the same rate, a substantial number of guilty suspects would have to pass friendly tests.

[6] The Implausibility of the Directed Lie Test (DLT)

The only differences between the DLT and the standard CQT are as follows: (1) for the CQT, the examiner assumes the control answer is deceptive while, for the DLT, both the examiner and the suspect know that these answers are false; and (2) the subject answers the control questions deceptively on instruction rather than by choice. The DLT assumes that, when instructed to answer falsely a question about some past and trivial misdeed, an innocent suspect will be more disturbed than while truthfully denying his guilt in crime of which he stands accused. Just as for the CQT, the "control" questions are not controls in the scientific sense and there is no discernible reason for supposing that innocent persons will be reliably more disturbed while lying on instruction about some past event than while telling the truth about a recent and serious event that poses a genuine threat.

Proponents of the conventional CQT argue that one of its strengths derives from the fact that control questions are never identified as such to subjects.[19] Indeed, they are deliberately misled to believe that lying to the control questions will generate a deceptive verdict. To the extent that this deception is successful, an advantage of this approach is that unsophisticated guilty subjects may not figure out that it is to their advantage to try to augment their responses to these questions. However, it *is* obvious that even unsophisticated guilty suspects would be able to identify and understand the significance of the directed lie questions. They could easily self-stimulate (e.g., bite their tongues) after each directed lie answer in order to augment reactions to these control questions and thus defeat the test.

§ 12–3.3.5 Intractable Problems Inherent to the Evaluation of CQT Theory

Determining if polygraph theory is testable requires evaluation of the methods that have been used to test it. Two types of studies have been used to determine whether polygraph tests work. In laboratory or analog studies, volunteer subjects, often college students, commit or do not commit mock crimes and are then subjected to polygraph tests. These tests are scored and the percentage of subjects assigned to the innocent and guilty conditions is determined. The great advantage of the analog method is that one has certain knowledge of "ground truth," of which subjects are lying and which are being truthful.

[1] Disadvantages of Laboratory Studies

The disadvantages of laboratory studies include the following:

(1) The volunteer subjects are unlikely to be representative of criminal suspects in real life.

(2) The volunteers may not feel a life-like concern about mock crimes that they have been instructed to commit and about telling lies that they are instructed to tell.

(3) The CQT is an attempt to assess emotions by measuring the physiological reactions associated with lying. Laboratory studies have no

19. Raskin (1989), *supra* note 2, at 254.

way of reproducing the emotional state of a criminal suspect facing possible prosecution for a crime. Compared to criminal suspects, the volunteers are unlikely to be as apprehensive about being tested with respect to mock crimes for which they will not be punished, irrespective of the test's outcome.

(4) The administration of the polygraph tests tends not to resemble the procedures followed in real life. For example, unlike real-life tests, which are most often conducted well after the crime took place, laboratory subjects are typically tested immediately after they commit the mock crime. Moreover, in laboratory research, to make the study scientifically acceptable, there is an attempt to standardize the procedure (e.g., all subjects are asked identical questions), a factor that distinguishes these from real-life tests.

The many problems with laboratory studies indicate that their results are not generalizable to real-life applications of polygraph testing. Consequently, these studies cannot be used to determine the accuracy of polygraph tests.

[2] Field Studies

Another approach to evaluating the validity of polygraph tests is to rely on data collected from field or real life settings. Since the original examiner possesses knowledge of the case facts and can observe the demeanor of the suspect during interrogation, this extraneous information might influence his scoring or interpretation of the test. Therefore, field studies have used a design in which different examiners, ignorant of the case facts, "blindly" rescore polygraph charts produced by suspects later determined to have been either truthful or deceptive.

Although free of the disadvantages of the analog design, real life studies must confront the problem of determining ground truth. Most commonly, confessions have been used as the criterion, either establishing that the person tested was lying, because he subsequently confessed, or that some alternative suspect in the same crime, cleared by another's confession, was telling the truth during his polygraph test. Unfortunately, relying on confessions to establish ground truth has serious drawbacks that may not be apparent at first glance. The problem is not with the confession *per se*, but with the consequences of the method used to get the confession.

[a] How Confessions Are Obtained

In CQT studies that have used the confession method to try to estimate polygraph accuracy, confessions are obtained when the examiner interrogates a suspect whom he has scored as deceptive on a just-completed CQT. As indicated above, being told that one has "failed the lie detector" often leads a guilty suspect to conclude that continued denials will be futile and that he may as well confess and make the best deal possible. Because they are obtained pursuant to interrogation after "failing" the CQT, these confessions invariably verify *that* test as accurate. In cases with more than one suspect, such a confession may also clear other suspects; if another suspect has "passed" a CQT prior to the confession, that prior test will also be verified as accurate.

[b]   Problems With the Confession Criterion

Because field studies must rely on confessions to determine ground truth, the only cases selected for study are those involving a guilty suspect who failed a CQT and subsequently confessed. All the polygraph errors in which an innocent person failed a test are omitted from the study because, absent a confession, none of these cases would qualify for inclusion. Similarly, because there would be no confession, all the cases in which a guilty subject erroneously passed a test would also be excluded. Thus, confession studies rely on a biased set of cases by systematically eliminating those containing errors and including only those where the original examiner was shown to be correct.

As we noted previously, polygraph scoring is reasonably consistent from one polygrapher to another. Consequently, when this biased set of confession-verified cases, all chosen in such a manner as to guarantee that the original examiner was correct, is rescored blindly by another examiner, it should be no surprise that the second examiner is also correct. Nothing can be concluded about the accuracy of the CQT from a study like this. The consequence of reliance on the confession criterion is that such studies *must* over-estimate the validity of the CQT both in the case of truthful and of deceptive suspects.

[c]   Independent Criteria of Guilt

This problem with confession studies is caused by the fact that the confession obtained following a failed CQT is not independent of the outcome of the CQT. That is, the only way to get a confession is first for the subject to have failed the polygraph. To determine if they could overcome this problem, Patrick and Iacono carried out a field study with the RCMP in Vancouver, British Columbia.[20] These investigators began with 402 polygraph cases representing all of the cases from a designated metropolitan area during a five-year period. Rather than rely on confessions that were dependent on failing a polygraph test to determine ground truth, they searched police investigative files for ground truth information uncovered after the polygraph test was given, such as non-polygraph-related confessions or statements indicating no crime was committed (e.g., something reported stolen was really lost and subsequently recovered by the owner). These authors found only one case out of over 400 that independently established the guilt of someone who took a polygraph test.

It is interesting to consider why it was not possible to establish independent evidence of ground truth for guilty persons in this study. The reason lies in how law enforcement agencies use polygraph tests. Typically, a lie detector test is not introduced into a case until all the leads have been exhausted and the investigation is near a dead end. If one of the suspects fails the test, it is hoped that the subsequent interrogation will lead to a confession, thereby resolving the issue at hand. However, if the test is failed and there is no confession, there will be no new leads to follow, so the police, assuming that the person who failed the polygraph is guilty, do not investigate the case further. Hence, there is almost no opportunity for additional evidence estab-

20.   Patrick & Iacono, *supra* note 12.

lishing ground truth to emerge. This disappointing finding indicates that, as polygraphy is now employed in law enforcement, it is virtually impossible to establish ground truth in a manner that is independent of polygraph test outcome. Consequently, the accuracy of the CQT for guilty subjects cannot be reliably determined from the research thus far reported.

[d]   Independent Criteria of Innocence

Interestingly, if all the suspects in a case pass a polygraph, because the guilty person could potentially still be identified through further police work, the file is kept active and additional leads are investigated if they arise. Hence, Patrick and Iacono were able to identify 25 cases where no suspect failed a test but where, for example, subsequent police work led to confessions from suspects who never took a polygraph test but whose confession established as innocent those who had.[21] Because these confessions were not dependent on someone having failed a CQT, they could be used to establish the accuracy of the CQT for innocent people by having the physiological charts blindly rescored. The results of this rescoring are presented in the validity section below.

[e]   Summary

Laboratory studies, because they do a poor job of simulating the emotionally-laden scenario that exists in real-life criminal investigations, cannot be relied on to estimate polygraph accuracy. Field studies that employ confessions following a failed polygraph also cannot be relied on for this purpose. Credible field studies would be possible, but difficult to implement. To date, no scientifically credible field study of the validity of the CQT in detecting guilty suspects has been accomplished. On the other hand, as Patrick and Iacono showed, because police practices differ between cases that yield at least one failed test and those that yield only passed tests, it is possible to collect data that bears on the accuracy of the CQT for innocent subjects.[22]

§ 12–3.3.6 How to Identify Scientifically Credible Studies

Because the theory of the CQT is so implausible, a heavy burden of proof rests on those who would claim that this procedure can validly distinguish truth from falsehood in the interrogation of criminal suspects. In spite of decades of extensive use in the United States, by federal agencies and local law enforcement, as we have seen, no scientifically acceptable assessment of CQT validity has yet been published. This is due in part to the fact that the real value of the polygraph in criminal investigation is as an interrogation tool, an inducer of confessions, rather than as a decision-making tool or test. Post-test interrogations that elicit a confession necessarily confirm the CQT result that prompted the interrogation. In the absence of systematic evidence concerning the accuracy of CQT results that do *not* lead to confessions, examiners have been able to sustain the belief that all their diagnoses are extremely accurate.

21. *Id.* at 234.   **22.** *Id.*

[1] Criteria for a Credible Validity Study

It will be useful to consider the minimum requirements for an acceptable study of CQT validity. These include the following:

(a) Subjects should be a representative sample of suspects tested in the course of criminal investigation.

(b) Since one wishes to estimate with reasonable precision both the CQT's validity in detecting truthful responding and its validity in detecting deception, test results from at least 100 guilty (deceptive) and 100 innocent (truthful) suspects should be available for the assessment.

(c) For reasons reviewed earlier in discussing the problems of the confession criterion, the innocence or guilt of these study subjects must be determined subsequent to the CQT procedure by investigative methods that are wholly independent of the outcome of the CQT.

(d) Finally, to permit generalizability of the findings, the study would be replicated in a different context (e.g., by a different investigative agency using different examiners).

[2] Plan for a Credible Validity Study

A scientifically credible study of CQT validity might be accomplished by an investigative agency such as the FBI in the following manner:

(1) For a period of months or years, until the necessary number of verified cases had accumulated, *all* suspects under investigation would be given a CQT without post-test interrogation by the examiners.

(2) The test results would be filed separately and not revealed to anyone, including criminal investigators so as not to bias their investigative decisions.

(3) As cases were resolved, the CQT results would be validated against the independent investigative findings.

(4) Should the results prove favorable enough to warrant further study, the project would be replicated by a different investigative agency.

[3] Example of a Non-credible Validity Study

In contrast to this systematic and unbiased research design, we might consider the study by Raskin, Kircher, Honts, and Horowitz of CQT results selected from the files of the US Secret Service.[23] Despite this study's having been completed in 1988, it has not been published in or even reviewed by a scientific journal. Instead, what the authors did must be pieced together from unpublished reports and book chapters in which the procedures and results are selectively presented.

A complication of this study that makes it difficult to compare to others is that it was not possible to verify subjects as truthful or deceptive to all of the

---

23. David C. Raskin et al., *A Study of the Validity of Polygraph Examinations in Criminal Investigations* (May 1988) (unpublished manuscript, on file with the University of Utah, Department of Psychology).

questions they were asked on the CQT. Instead, they were classified as "verified deceptive" if at least one CQT question elicited a confession and the answer to no other question could be confirmed truthful. Likewise, they were "verified truthful" if an alternative suspect admitted guilt to the issue covered by a single question and the subject did not admit to guilt on the issues covered by the other questions. Hence, for many subjects, only partial verification of guilt or innocence was obtained.

From a total of 2,522 CQTs administered, 66 or about 3% resulted in post-test confessions which verified at least one question on the test that prompted the interrogation, and 39 confessions verified the truthfulness of other suspects regarding their response to at least one test question. The 39 verified-truthful CQTs were administered to persons in multiple-suspect cases who were tested prior to some alternative suspect who later confessed. Thus, in this study, only about 4% of the CQTs administered were "verified" as indicating guilt or innocence, and this verification was incomplete, pertaining only to a single relevant question for many of the subjects. The representativeness of these partially verified cases is obviously open to question.

However, a more serious concern is that the method of verification virtually guaranteed that the original examiners' diagnosis would have been correct. That is, the 66 verified deceptive CQTs were verified because the examiner diagnosed deception, interrogated on that basis, and obtained a confession. Similarly, we know that the 39 CQTs verified as truthful by the confession of an alternative suspect would have been classified as truthful by the original examiner, else he would have had little reason to test the alternative suspect who later confessed.

We can therefore conclude that at least 4% of the suspects tested by the Secret Service produced CQT results like those predicted by the theory (deceptive suspects more disturbed by relevant than by control questions, truthful suspects more disturbed by the control questions). We can also conclude that other examiners, asked to score these same polygraph charts, were likely to get results similar to those obtained by the original examiners. But these results are entirely compatible with the assumption that there is no relationship whatever between the veracity of the suspect and his score on the CQT!

Let us suppose that 50% (1,261) of the 2,522 suspects tested were in fact guilty. Let us assume further that the CQT identified deception in these individuals with only chance accuracy. This would result, by chance alone, in 630 of the guilty suspects being classified as deceptive. All or most of these 630 would be interrogated and, as in this case, some 66 of them might confess their guilt. Since some of these 66 would be involved in cases with multiple suspects, their confessions would exculpate the alternative suspects. These alternative suspects were most likely tested and diagnosed truthful prior to the testing of the guilty suspect who confessed, otherwise the suspect who confessed would most likely not have been tested because the guilty party would already have been identified. Note that under these circumstances, the testing of these subjects would be correct 100% of the time even though the test itself has only chance accuracy. If we now take the charts from these cases and have them blindly rescored, because scoring is reliable, we are likely to obtain nearly the same results that the original examiners obtained.

However, these results, suggesting near infallibility, are totally misleading and tell us nothing about CQT accuracy.

Raskin et al. emphasize a unique feature of their study as though it represents a significant methodological refinement over other reports. In addition to requiring a confession to substantiate guilt, they also required the presence of "independent corroboration" of the confession in the form of some type of physical evidence. Although this requirement would appear to eliminate the occasional false confession, it does not deal with the fundamental problem inherent in using confessions to establish ground truth. The problem with this requirement is that the corroborating physical evidence is not independent of test outcome. Had the suspect not failed the CQT, there would be no confession, and had there been no confession, there would have been no opportunity to recover the physical evidence. Hence, there is nothing "independent" about the corroborating evidence. Just like the confession, it too is dependent on having failed the polygraph test.

In short, although much has been made of the Secret Service study, as if it had demonstrated a high degree of accuracy for the CQT, when properly analyzed it can be seen to be wholly without probative value. The fact that this study has not been accepted for publication in a peer-reviewed scientific journal illustrates the utility of impartial peer review as a minimum criterion for consideration of scientific claims.

§ 12–3.3.7 CQT Accuracy: Claims of CQT Proponents Are Not Supported

[1] Laboratory Studies

The studies that have achieved publication, although none of them meets the criteria set out above for an adequate validity assessment, do permit certain limited conclusions to be drawn. First, there are a number of studies in which volunteer subjects, usually college students, are required to commit a mock crime and then to lie about it during a CQT examination.[24] Control subjects do not commit the crime and are truthful on the CQT.[25] Instead of fear that failing the CQT will lead to punishment (such as criminal prosecution), subjects in these studies were motivated by a promise of a money prize if they were able to be classified as truthful on the CQT.[26] In these highly artificial circumstances, CQT scores successfully discriminated between the two groups.

When the circumstances are made somewhat more realistic, however, even this mock crime design produces results similar to those reported in the better field studies (discussed below). Patrick and Iacono, for example, using prison inmate volunteers, led their subjects to suppose that their failing the CQT might result in the loss to the entire group of a promised reward and

---

24.   Gordon H. Barland & David C. Raskin, *An Evaluation of Field Techniques in Detection of Deception,* 12 Psychophysiology 321, 321–330 (1975); David C. Raskin & Robert D. Hare, *Psychopathy and Detection of Deception in a Prison Population,* 15 Psychophysiology 126, 126–136 (1978).

25.   Barland & Raskin, *supra* note 24; Raskin & Hare, *supra* note 24.

26.   Barland & Raskin, *supra* note 24; Raskin & Hare, *supra* note 24.

thus incur the enmity of their potentially violent and dangerous comrades.[27] Under these circumstances, nearly half of the truthful subjects were classified erroneously as deceptive.[28] In another study, Foreman and McCauley permitted their volunteer subjects to choose for themselves whether to be "guilty" and deceptive or "innocent" and truthful.[29] Those who elected to be truthful knew that their reward would be smaller but presumably more certain.[30] This manipulation is analogous to crime situations where an individual is confronted with an opportunity to commit a crime with little likelihood of getting caught, e.g., an unlocked car with a valuable item in sight, or a poorly watched-over purse or briefcase, and must decide whether to take advantage of the opportunity. By thus increasing the realism of the test conditions, Foreman and McCauley probably also obtained a more realistic result, with about half of their truthful subjects being erroneously classified as deceptive.

Thus, although mock crime studies with volunteer subjects clearly do not permit any confident extrapolation to the real life conditions of criminal investigation, it does appear that the designs with the greater verisimilitude, which threaten punishment or which merely permit subjects to decide for themselves whether to be truthful or deceptive, demonstrate that the CQT identifies truthful respondents with only chance accuracy.[31]

[2] Field Studies

All reputable scientists acknowledge the importance of the peer-review process as a first line of defense against spurious claims. Studies published in archival scientific journals will have passed the scrutiny of independent scientists knowledgeable in the given area of investigation. No one believes that this process is infallible. Spurious results and dubious conclusions can and do find their way into the scientific literature from time to time. Most scientists consider publication in a peer-reviewed scientific journal to be a necessary but not sufficient basis for the serious consideration of a scientific finding or interpretation. This requirement applies as well to polygraph research as it does to other types of scientific inquiry.

Appearance in a peer-reviewed journal, however, is no guarantee of scientific quality. For example, Honts[32] undertook to evaluate the validity of CQTs administered by the RCMP, using extra-polygraphic criteria of ground truth. The plan was to obtain 75 criminal cases with extra-polygraphic confirmation of guilt and 75 cases in which the suspects had been confirmed to be innocent, also independently of polygraph results. Yet only 13 (rather than the proposed 150) tests were rated as having been strongly confirmed

---

27. Christopher J. Patrick & William G. Iacono, *Psychopathy, Threat, and Polygraph Test Accuracy*, 74 J. APPLIED PSYCHOL. 347, 348–349 (1989).

28. *Id.* at 350.

29. Robert F. Forman & Clark McCauley, *Validity of the Positive Control Test Using the Field Practice Model*, 71 J. APPLIED PSYCHOL. 691, 691–698 (1986).

30. *Id.* at 693.

31. Raskin et al. do not include these more ecologically valid studies by Patrick and Iacono

and Forman and McCauley in their lists of "high quality" laboratory studies (first edition). All but one of the studies they cite is the work of Raskin and his students. The one study not from their laboratory [Ginton et al., 1984] included only two guilty subjects and thus has no bearing on their calculation of CQT accuracy with guilty subjects in laboratory investigations.

32. Charles R. Honts, *Criterion Development and Validity of the CQT in Field Application*, 123 J. GEN. PSYCHOL. 309–324. (1997).

and in all of these cases polygraph-induced confessions of the perpetrator determined ground truth. All of the 7 guilty suspects were scored as deceptive and the 6 innocent suspects were scored either truthful or inconclusive. Apart from these very small and unrepresentative samples, this study failed utterly to assess CQT validity with criteria of ground truth that were independent of the polygraph results, thus guaranteeing a misleading, high accuracy rate. Because this study adds nothing to the sum of our knowledge about the real accuracy of the CQT in criminal investigation, we were surprised that it would be accepted for publication in an archival scientific journal, even the journal edited by a colleague of Honts' at Boise State University. The quality of the peer review that the Honts paper received may be suggested by the following facts: 1) errata were subsequently published to correct obvious arithmetical mistakes pointed out by a reader, 2) the number of subjects in the various groups studied by Honts is inconsistently reported between the published version of this work and the technical report from which the publication was derived,[33] and 3) the *Journal of General Psychology* was ranked 82nd in "impact" among the 97 general psychology journals analyzed by the Institute for Scientific Information.[34]

Four other studies have been published in scientific journals.[35] All four include cases where the verification of guilt and innocence was not entirely dependent on polygraph-induced confessions. In one of these studies, Bersh determined ground truth by relying on the consensus of a panel of attorneys who evaluated the available evidence on each case.[36] Since this evidence included reports of polygraph-induced confessions where they occurred, this criterion is contaminated and, moreover, the evidence did not always permit a confident verdict. In addition, this study, which relied on global chart scoring, did not employ blind chart review. Because the polygraph operators in this study adopted the global approach to chart scoring, their decisions regarding guilt and innocence were based on the same information the panel was given. Given these serious methodological flaws, it is not surprising that the panel and the polygraph operators agreed with each other.

Although not published in a peer-reviewed journal, Barland and Raskin extended the Bersh study using the same research design except that numeri-

33. Although this problem was been pointed out to Dr. Honts in a letter of 15 May 1998, in his reply of 24 May 1998, he refused to explain the discrepancies across these different versions of his work. Dr. Honts refused a request for the data on which this report was based. Letter from Charles Honts to William Iacono (May 24, 1998) (on file with author).

34. Social Sciences Citation Index, 1993, *Journal Citation Reports*. Philadelphia: Institute of Scientific Information. "Impact factor" is a measure of the frequency with which articles published in a journal are actually cited by other authors. For the *Journal of General Psychology*, the average paper was cited only about 0.1 times, indicating that for every 10 articles published by this journal, only one is cited. Hence, scientists ignore most articles in this publication. Competitive peer review occurs in journals that reject most submissions made to them. The field studies that we have identified as the best (which can be found in footnote 1 source, Table 1, p. 608) are published in the *Journal of Applied Psychology* and *Nature*, journals that reject 85% or more of the submissions made to them and whose impact factors rank them as among the very best scientific journals.

35. Philip Bersh, *A Validation Study of Polygraph Examiner Judgments*, 53 J. APPLIED PSYCHOL. 399, 399–403 (1969); Frank Horvath, *The Effect of Selected Variables on Interpretation of Polygraph Records*, 62 J. APPLIED PSYCHOL. 127, 127–136 (1977); Benjamin Kleinmuntz & J.J. Szucko, *A Field Study of the Fallibility of Polygraphic Lie Detection*, 308 NATURE 449, 449–450 (1984); Patrick & Iacono, *supra* note 27; Honts, *supra* note 32.

36. Bersh, *supra* note 35.

cal scoring and blind chart review were used.[37] The importance of this study, which its authors have repudiated, is that it reveals that the principal scientific advocate of the CQT, Dr. Raskin, who independently scored all the charts, classified more than half of the innocent suspects as deceptive.[38]

The studies by Horvath and by Kleinmuntz and Szucko both used confession-verified CQT charts obtained respectively from a police agency and the Reid polygraph firm in Chicago.[39] The original examiners in these cases did not rely only on the polygraph results in reaching their diagnoses but also employed the case facts and their clinical appraisal of the subject's behavior during testing.[40] Therefore, some suspects who failed the CQT and confessed were likely to have been judged deceptive and interrogated based primarily on the case facts and their demeanor during the polygraph examination, leaving open the possibility that their charts may or may not by themselves have indicated deception. Moreover, some other suspects were cleared by confessions of others, even though the cleared suspects, judged truthful using global criteria, could have produced charts indicative of deception. That is, the original examiners in these cases were led to doubt these suspects' guilt despite the evidence in the charts and proceeded to interrogate an alternative suspect in the same case who thereupon confessed. For these reasons, some undetermined number of the confessions in these two studies were likely to be relatively independent of the polygraph results, revealing some of the guilty suspects who "failed" it. The hit rates obtained in these studies are indicated in Table I.

Table I

Summary of Studies of Lie Test Validity that Were Published in Scientific Journals and that Used Confessions to Establish Ground Truth

	Horvath (1977)	Kleinmuntz & Szucko (1984)	Patrick & Iacono (1991)	Mean
Guilty Correctly Classified	77%	76%	98%	84%
Innocent Correctly Classified	51%	63%	57%	57%
Mean of Above:	64%	70%	77%	70%

In a study by Patrick and Iacono, 65% of the innocent suspects were confirmed as such independently of polygraph results (e.g., the complainant later discovered the mislaid item originally thought to have been stolen).[41] As

37. GORDON H. BARLAND & DAVID C. RASKIN, U.S. DEP'T OF JUSTICE, VALIDITY AND RELIABILITY OF POLYGRAPH EXAMINATIONS OF CRIMINAL SUSPECTS (1976).

38. *Id.*

39. Horvath, *supra* note 35; Kleinmuntz & Szucko, *supra* note 35.

40. Horvath, *supra* note 35, at 129–130; Kleinmuntz & Szucko, *supra* note 35, at 449.

41. Patrick & Iacono, *supra* note 12, at 234.

can be seen in Table I, 43% of these innocent suspects were wrongly classified as deceptive by the CQT. Only one guilty suspect could be confirmed as such from file data independent of CQT-induced confessions; his charts were classified as inconclusive by the CQT. The remaining guilty suspects in the Patrick and Iacono study were all classified solely on the basis of having been scored as deceptive on the polygraph and then interrogated to produce a confession.[42] Understandably, when examiners trained in the same method of scoring independently rescored these charts, they agreed with the original examiners in 98% of cases.[43] This 98% figure is inflated because only charts that the original examiner decided indicated deception were used in its calculation.[44]

[3] Conclusions

While none of the available studies meet the criteria listed earlier, certain useful conclusions can be drawn. First, the accuracy estimates shown in Table I must all be over-estimates of the real accuracy of the CQT since there was at least some reliance in each study on polygraph-induced confessions as the criterion for ground truth. (Where there is total reliance on the confession criterion, as in the Secret Service study reviewed above, then the apparent accuracy achieved by the examiners who independently rescore the charts is really just a measure of the inter-scorer reliability—an impressively high value but wholly uninformative regarding actual CQT validity.)

Because all the validity estimates are overestimates, a second conclusion permitted by the studies in Table I is that an innocent suspect has little more than a 50% chance of being classified as truthful by an adversarially administered CQT. Thus, had the prosecution offered to drop charges if these suspects passed the polygraph, on the stipulation that adverse results would be admitted as evidence at trial, at least half of these innocent suspects would have heard a polygraph examiner testify before a jury that they had been deceptive in denying their guilt.

Finally, it must be recalled that the polygraph tests involved in these three studies were all administered prior to about 1985, before the existence of an easily-learned method of beating the CQT was widely known.[45] It is a safe assumption that few, if any, of the guilty suspects involved in these four studies employed these effective countermeasures. We know that the 84% average success in detecting deception, shown on the right of Table I, is already an overestimate due to criterion contamination. In the future, as the method to "beat the lie detector" becomes more widely known within the

---

42. *Id.* at 234.

43. *Id.*

44. Raskin et al., in DAVID L. FAIGMAN, DAVID H. KAYE, MICHAEL J. SAKS & JOSEPH SANDERS, MODERN SCIENTIFIC EVIDENCE: THE LAW AND SCIENCE OF EXPERT TESTIMONY, 627 (1997), argued that it is the accuracy of the original examiner in these studies summarized in Table I that "is the true figure of merit" when evaluating CQT accuracy because it is the original examiner's decision that would be presented in court. However, when confessions are used to select cases, because a confession can only follow a

test scored deceptive by the original examiner, the only cases of the original examiner selected for study will be the ones where he is correct. Citing such figures as legitimate accuracy estimates is thus grossly misleading.

45. Charles R. Honts et al., *Effects of Physical Countermeasures on the Physiological Detection of Deception*, 70 J. APPLIED PSYCHOL. 177, 177–187 (1985); Charles R. Honts et al., *Mental and Physical Countermeasures Reduce the Accuracy of Polygraph Tests*, 79 J. APPLIED PSYCHOL. 252, 252–259 (1994).

criminal community (instructions on how to beat the polygraph are now available in any public library and also on the internet), we can expect further deflation of the CQT's success in detecting deception.

The burden of proof remains on the advocates of the control question polygraph technique to demonstrate empirically that a method based on such implausible assumptions can have useful accuracy. That proof has not appeared and what relevant data are available, data that permit us at least to set an upper limit on CQT validity, indicate clearly that the accuracy of the CQT is too low for it to qualify as a courtroom aid.

§ 12–3.2.8 How Guilty Persons Can Learn to Produce Truthful CQT Outcomes

Drugs that act to decrease responding in a general way will not normally affect the accuracy of polygraph tests because the CQT is scored by comparing the subject's response to two types of questions. Therefore, successful countermeasures rely on the subject's efforts to artificially augment his response to the control questions. Certain techniques of covert self-stimulation, such as biting the tongue, flexing the toes, or performing mentally stressful arithmetic exercises, can augment the physiological response to a question. To employ such countermeasures, the subject must understand the principle on which the test is based and be able to identify which are the control questions.

Research, as well as a consensus among scientists, supports the view that persons with rather brief training or explanation can covertly self-stimulate so as to augment their responses to CQT control questions, that even experienced examiners cannot detect these countermeasures, and that they may be successful in preventing a guilty suspect from being classified as deceptive on the CQT.[46] There is no good evidence as to how well these countermeasures work under real life conditions and no evidence at all concerning how frequently such countermeasures are successfully employed in real life by sophisticated subjects.

§ 12–3.3.9 Why Computerization Does Not Boost CQT Accuracy

In this increasingly common practice, the physiological responses of the suspect to the questions of a CQT are measured by a computer which then scores the result and compares that score to a table of scores from known truthful or deceptive subjects, stored in the computer's memory. The result of this comparison is a computer-generated statement indicating the probability of truthfulness or deception. For instance, Dr. Raskin testified in *United States v. Clayton and Dalley*, based on a computer determination, that the probability that the defendant was truthful was .993.[47]

Substantial scientific controversy surrounds three assumptions underlying computer scoring:

46. Honts et al. 1985, *supra* note 45; Honts et al. 1994, *supra* note 45.

47. United States v. Clayton, U.S. District Court, Phoenix, Arizona, March 22, 1994, No.

92–374–PCT–RCB at 109 (trial transcript of the direct examination of Dr. David Raskin).

(1) that the probability of truth or deception in real-world situations can be determined from the score on a CQT (this is the basic assumption of lie detection);

(2) that the scores stored in the computer accurately represent the scores to be expected from truthful or deceptive subjects obtained under circumstances similar to those obtaining in the instant test;

(3) that 50 percent of those who are tested with this instrument are deceptive.

To satisfy the second assumption of computer scoring, the database stored in the machine would have to contain the results of polygraph tests administered under real-life conditions to a representative sample of criminal suspects who had been subsequently proven to be innocent, and also a representative sample of suspects later proven to be guilty. Because of the problems of the confession criterion, outlined above, these tests would have to have been verified by some means other than by polygraph-induced confessions. The results of tests administered in the mock crime conditions of laboratory experiments, or tests administered privately to criminal suspects, would not be appropriate to use in this application because such differences in the conditions of testing will yield differences in the distribution and meaning of the scores. It should be emphasized that *no such database currently exists* and that, absent this necessary basis for comparison, the attachment of probability values to results of polygraph tests, whether calculated by a computer or in any other way, is necessarily spurious and misleading. With regard to the third assumption, there is no way of knowing that 50% of those tested will be in fact guilty, nor is it likely that this number does not vary across jurisdictions, settings, and applications. To the extent that considerably fewer or more than 50% of subjects are actually guilty, computer determined probabilities of truthfulness can be quite misleading.

This marriage of the myth of the "lie detector" to the mystique of the computer is a particularly insidious development. When an alleged expert testifies that a defendant's denials of guilt have been scientifically assessed by a computer, which has reported a high probability that these denials are not truthful, one must expect the average juror to give considerable weight to such evidence. However, there does not exist (and may never exist) the database required to yield accurate estimates for computerized chart interpretation. These requirements cannot now be met for criminal suspects tested either under adversarial conditions or privately by an examiner engaged by the defense.

§ 12–3.3.10   The Limited Research on the Directed Lie Version of the CQT

Only two studies are available that examine the accuracy of the DLT. Horowitz et al.[48] conducted a laboratory investigation, which like other laboratory studies, produces results that cannot be generalized to real life because the testing circumstances are too artificial. This leaves a field study by Honts and Raskin[49] as the only investigation that can be used to support

---

48. Steven W. Horowitz et al., *The Role of Comparison Questions in Physiological Detection of Deception*, 34 PSYCHOPHYSIOLOGY 108–115 (1997).

49. Charles R. Honts & David C. Raskin, *A Field Study of the Directed Lie Control Question*, 16 J. POLICE SCI. & ADMIN. 56–61 (1988).

the forensic use of the DLT. This study has several important shortcomings. The most serious concerns the use of confessions to establish ground truth. As we have pointed out before, those real-life studies in which tests given to criminal suspects are confirmed by polygraph-induced confessions, and the polygraph charts are later scored blindly by different examiners, must overestimate polygraph accuracy. The other serious shortcomings of this study are that only 12 guilty subjects were included (too small a sample for thorough evaluation of the effectiveness of a new technique) and that the test administered was not a DLT. Instead it was a CQT with one directed lie control question. We can only agree with Honts and Raskin when they concluded their paper with the following remarks: "It is not known whether an examination with only [directed lie control questions] would be valid."[50]

§ 12–3.3.11 Why Law Enforcement Agencies Use Polygraph Tests Despite Their Limitations

Given all of the controversy that exists surrounding polygraph testing, why is it that law enforcement and national security agencies make extensive use of polygraph tests? The answer to this question lies with the fact that they have been found to have considerable utility because of the admissions that some subjects make under the stress of these procedures.

[1] The Polygraph as an Inducer of Confessions

There is no doubt that being told that one has "failed the polygraph" or "seems to be having difficulty with certain questions" is a powerful inducement to confessions or damaging admissions, especially among unsophisticated criminal suspects. Since even innocent suspects have been known to confess in this situation, unsubstantiated confessions pursuant to polygraph testing should be treated with great caution. Examiners often tell suspects that anything they feel guilty about may produce an adverse outcome and, in this way, damaging admissions are often elicited that do not specifically acknowledge guilt in the matter under investigation. Such damaging admissions are sometimes counted as verifications of the polygraph test that produced them; this is, of course, erroneous and may have led to overconfidence in the validity of the CQT. Even if a polygraph technique had only chance accuracy, 50% of the truly guilty would be expected to fail the test and, upon being interrogated, the more unsophisticated of these guilty persons may confess. Those who believe that the utility of polygraphy justifies its use should recognize that the CQT's utility would be even greater if *all* subjects were interrogated as if they had "failed" the test. Guilty suspects who pass the CQT would then not escape interrogation and some of them would respond by confessing.

[2] The Polygraph Test as an Interrogation Tool

The polygraph can also be a useful aid to criminal investigation. Should a suspect exhibit an unusual emotional and physiological response to questions that would not be expected to disturb him if his story is a true one,

---

50. *Id.* at 61.

investigators can be led to look for evidence in new directions. It must be emphasized, however, that the utility of the polygraph in criminal investigation or interrogation does not imply nor depend on the accuracy of the procedure. By the same token, endorsement by scientists that the polygraph might be useful in these ways does not imply that these scientists believe the CQT to be accurate as a test for truth.

An example of a government agency that finds that polygraph testing has utility even though its validity is unproven is the FBI. Despite the FBI's extensive use of polygraph testing, according to James K. Murphy, former Chief of the FBI Laboratory's Polygraph Unit in Washington, D.C., "The United States Department of Justice and the FBI oppose any attempt to enter the results of polygraph examinations into evidence at trial because the polygraph technique has not reached a level of acceptance within the scientific community and there is no existing standard for training or conducting examinations under which all polygraph examiners must conform."[51]

§ 12–3.3.12 Scientists Are Skeptical of the CQT

We have already stressed that, in the absence of wholly adequate empirical studies of the validity of either the CQT or the GKT, decisions about when and whether to rely on the results of these techniques must be based largely on the scientific plausibility of the respective assumptions on which they are based. For this reason, accurate assessments of the opinions of members of the relevant scientific community, concerning the plausibility of these two techniques, would seem to be of special importance.

In 1994, Amato and Honts reported findings from a survey of the opinions about lie detection of members of the Society for Psychophysiological Research (SPR). This report, based on a response rate of only 30%, was published as an abstract that did not undergo scientific peer review. It followed on the heels of another survey of the members of SPR that also was not published in a scientific journal. Because of these (and other) inadequacies, we conducted new and more extensive surveys of SPR members and also of general psychologists distinguished by election as Fellows of Division 1 of the American Psychological Association (APA1). The results of these surveys, which achieved return-rates of 91% (SPR) and 74% (APA1), were published as a peer-reviewed article in a first-rank journal. These findings show that the vast majority of both groups surveyed expressed grave doubts about the validity of polygraphic lie detection and therefore opposed the introduction of lie test results as evidence in courts. Another recent study found that psychology textbooks express a "strongly negative" opinion of the scientific status of the lie detector. Finally, in September 1999, a panel of senior scientists and engineers from the Department of Energy's weapons laboratories published a detailed appraisal of the scientific status of polygraphy, especially as used in the screening of federal employees. In this section, we review these several sets of data.

51. Affidavit of James K. Murphy, Chief of Polygraph, Federal Bureau of Investigation (March 3, 1995) (on file with the authors).

[1] Methodologically Flawed Surveys of Scientists

Two prior surveys of members of the Society for Psychophysiological Research (SPR) have been conducted. The first was a 1982 telephone survey of 155 members by the Gallup Organization on behalf of a litigant who wished to introduce into evidence the results of a polygraph test.[52] The unpublished results of this survey are difficult to evaluate because few details have been provided about how the survey was conducted. In particular, there was no indication how many SPR members could not be contacted or refused the telephone poll, information that is essential to evaluating the generalizability of the results.

The second survey, by Amato and Honts,[53] was sent by mail to 450 members of SPR. Only 30% responded. Both surveys asked a single question requiring an appraisal of the "usefulness" of polygraph testing in which respondents were asked to choose one of four statements that best described their "opinion of polygraph test interpretations" to determine "whether a subject is or is not telling the truth." The responses this question received in both surveys is reproduced in Table II.

Proponents of polygraph testing have drawn special attention to the fact that about 60% of respondents in both surveys endorsed alternative "B" indicating that polygraph interpretation "is a useful diagnostic tool." This finding led Amato and Honts to conclude that the membership of SPR consider polygraph tests "useful for legal proceedings,"[54] even though the question does not ask for an opinion concerning the use of polygraph results in court. In fact, the meaning of the response is ambiguous.[55] We have already noted that there is general agreement that polygraph testing has utility as an investigative aid, and there is no reason to suppose that respondents who chose option B considered their response to refer to anything more than investigative applications. Since these surveys made no distinction between the CQT, which most scientists consider to be based on implausible assumptions, and the guilty knowledge test (GKT), which many consider to be scientifically credible, there is also no way of knowing to what type of polygraph test the question refers. Because of the many ambiguities associated with the interpretation of responses to this question coupled with concerns about the representativeness of survey respondents, we undertook our own

52. The Gallup Organization, Survey of Members of the American Society for Psychophysiological Research Concerning Their Opinion of Polygraph Test Interpretation (1982).

53. Susan L. Amato, *A Survey of the Society for Psychophysiological Research Regarding the Polygraph: Opinions and Implications* (1993) (unpublished Master's thesis, University of North Dakota); Susan L. Amato & Charles R. Honts, *What Do Psychophysiologists Think About Polygraph Tests? A Survey of the Membership of the Society for Psychophysiological Research* (1994) (poster presented at the Society for Psychophysiological Research's Annual Meeting).

54. *Id.*

55. Another question on the Amato and Honts survey is less ambiguous in its intent and obtained results indicating substantial doubt about CQT accuracy. It asked: "How accurate is the control question test when administered to a guilty suspect during a criminal investigation?" Subjects answered on a 1–5 scale anchored with "no better than chance" (i.e., 50%) at the low end and "nearly perfect (100%)" at the high end. The mean response was 3.08, at the approximate midpoint of the scale, corresponding to about 75% accuracy. This accuracy estimate is much lower than the 95% claimed by Raskin, Honts and Kircher, and similar to the upper-bound accuracy estimate we made for criterion guilty subjects in the best field studies on CQT validity (see Table I).

independent surveys to determine the views of the scientific community concerning deception detection.[56]

Table II

Opinions of Members of the Society for Psychophysiological Research Regarding the "Usefulness" of Polygraph Test Interpretation in Three Surveys

Response Options:	Gallup (1982)	Amato & Honts (1993)	Iacono & Lykken (1995)
A. Sufficiently reliable method to be the sole determinant	1%	1%	0%
B. Useful diagnostic tool when considered with other available information	61%	60%	44%
*Between "B" and "C"	2%	–	2%
C. Questionable usefulness, entitled to little weight against other available information	32%	37%	53%
D. No usefulness	3%	2%	2%

*Note: Although not offered as an option, in two of the surveys respondents indicated a choice that fell between alternatives B and C.

[2] An Accurate Survey of Society for Psychophysiological Research Members

We conducted a mail survey of a random sample of 50% of the nonstudent members of SPR who had United States addresses according to a SPR membership list provided to us by the Society in October, 1994.[57] To insure anonymity and encourage responsiveness, respondents were asked to return, under separate cover from their questionnaire, a postage-paid post card indicating that they had returned the survey. Those who did not return the postcard received up to three subsequent mailed prompts in an effort to obtain as complete a sample as possible.[58]

Of the 214 SPR members surveyed, 91% returned questionnaires. According to the former US Office of Statistical Standards, response rates of 90% or

56. William G. Iacono & David T. Lykken, *The Validity of the Lie Detector: Two Surveys of Scientific Opinion*, 82 J. APPLIED PSYCHOL. 426–433 (1997).

57. Because we conducted the surveys so we could include the results in the MODERN SCIENTIFIC EVIDENCE (1st ed.) chapter to which Raskin, Honts, and Kircher were co-contributors, we did not consider it appropriate to include either them or ourselves in the surveys. In addition, to avoid the possibility that our surveys would be unduly influenced by the inclusion of respondents from our own department (who agree with our views), we eliminated members of our department from both the SPR and APA surveys. The most likely effect of these exclusions was to reduce the overall negativity of the survey results. Because Ras-

kin, Honts, and Kircher are not members of APA, this would be especially true of the APA survey results.

58. A difference between our survey and that of Amato and Honts was that they did not prompt SPR members in an effort to obtain a representative sample. It is possible that had we not prompted our survey subjects, we would have obtained a sample that was more supportive of polygraph testing. To test this possibility, we contrasted the responses of those who responded early to our survey with those who responded late (after prompting). There were no statistically significant differences between these two groups in their opinions to survey questions.

more can generally be treated as random samples of the overall population and response rates above 75% usually yield reliable results.[59] Significant caution is recommended when response rates drop below 50% as they did in the Amato and Honts survey.[60]

Included with each questionnaire was a letter explaining that the survey was prompted in part by *Daubert* and the likelihood that Federal courts might hold hearings to determine the admissibility of polygraph evidence, hearings that would consider in part the general acceptance of the technique by the scientific community. Because *Daubert* hearings are most likely to consider the admissibility of CQT results, respondents were told that all but a few of the survey questions dealt specifically with the CQT.[61]

An abbreviated listing of other key questionnaire items is presented in Table III.[62] The first item asked if respondents would agree that the CQT "is based on scientifically sound psychological principles or theory." Sixty-four percent of SPR members denied that the CQT is based on sound principles. The next two questions inquired separately whether respondents would "advocate that courts admit into evidence the outcome of control question polygraph tests, that is, permit the polygraph examiner to testify that in his/her opinion, either the defendant was deceptive when denying guilt" or

59. *See* Modern Scientific Evidence, *supra* note 44, at § 5–1.0 (1st ed.).

60. *Id.*

61. Raskin, Honts and Kircher have incorrectly asserted that we have refused to share our survey data, implying that we have something to hide. See Brief of the Committee of Concerned Social Scientists as *Amicus Curiae* in Support of the Respondent, filed in the Supreme Court of the United States, October term 1996 (No. 96–1133), United States v. Scheffer (Raskin, Honts, Kircher and their colleagues prepared this brief.) In fact, when we offered to share our data with Drs. Honts and Amato in 1997, they rejected the terms of our offer. They then contacted the editor of the journal in which the survey was published, asking him to mediate a data sharing arrangement that satisfied the ethical guidelines of the American Psychological Association. Guided by the journal editor, who characterized our data-sharing proposal as a good-faith effort that he found acceptable, we once again offered to share our data with Honts and Amato. They once again rejected our offer. In April 1998, we requested the data from the Amato and Honts survey. Although they sent copies of the questionnaires completed by those participating in their survey, 22 of the questionnaires were reproduced with such poor quality that the responses to questions on them were illegible. This problem was brought to Dr. Amato's attention in a letter on 4 June 1998. Although she apologized for and promised to correct this problem, despite follow-up phone and mail requests for better reproductions of these questionnaires, we have not yet received them. Consequently, what we received from them is useless because it is not possible to analyze the complete data set to check it for accuracy.

62. Our surveys provided respondents with information about the methods and assumptions of polygraph testing, quoting directly from the work of Raskin, Honts and Kircher when appropriate. We defined each type of polygraph test and gave the rationale underlying each by quoting verbatim Dr. Raskin's characterization of the CQT and the DLT from his past writings. We also provided examples of what hypothetical questions might look like using information from the O.J. Simpson and Unabomber (Ted Kaczynski) cases which were in the news at the time the surveys were done, although in neither case had the trials for these individuals begun. Unfortunately, the Gallup and Amato and Honts surveys did not similarly make unambiguous the terminology used in their polls. Scientists knowledgeable about the methods and problems of psychological testing can evaluate the plausibility and probable accuracy of lie detection, but only if they are clear about the procedures employed and the rationale supporting the use of these tests. The 30% of SPR members who replied to the Amato and Honts survey doubtless included all of the professional polygraphers who belong to that organization (e.g., Raskin, Honts and Kircher themselves) and it is their small and unrepresentative survey that in fact was biased by their failure to describe lie detection techniques so that SPR members who are not polygraphers could offer an informed opinion. An advantage of our survey of APA Fellows was that this distinguished group, none of whom were polygraphers, was able to provide an evaluation of polygraph techniques unmotivated by self-interest.

"truthful when denying guilt." Over 70% of SPR members would oppose the use of CQT results as evidence in court under either circumstance. Question 5 revealed that respondents were in overwhelming agreement with the "notion that the CQT can be 'beaten' by augmenting one's response to the control questions." For this question, respondents were divided into two groups based on their familiarity with the publication of Honts et al.[63] on countermeasures. Those responding to this question in both groups were almost unanimous in their opinion that the CQT could be beaten in this manner.

Proponents of polygraphy typically assert that the CQT is better than 90% accurate. For example, in *United States v. Clayton and Dalley*,[64] David Raskin testified that an experienced examiner could be expected to identify correctly "about 95% of the deceptive" and "about 90% of the truthful people." As the responses to Question 6 indicate, the SPR membership disagrees with this claim: Only about 25% agree that the CQT is accurate as often as 85% of the time.

For the next item, survey subjects were asked whether, all things being equal, it was more likely that a defendant awaiting trial would pass a friendly test arranged by defense counsel or a test administered by a police examiner. Three fourths of respondents thought a friendly test would be more likely to be passed. The final CQT item results showed that SPR members found it unreasonable for judicial proceedings to give substantial weight to the classification hit rates obtained in mock crime studies.

Table III

Opinions of Members of the Society for Psychophysiological Research about Polygraphy

Questionnaire Item	Percent Agree	Percent Disagree
1. CQT is scientifically sound	36	64
2. GKT is scientifically sound	77	23
3. Would admit failed tests as evidence in court	24	76
4. Would admit passed tests as evidence in court	27	73
5. CQT can be beaten	99	1
6. CQT is at least 85% accurate		
a. for guilty	27	73
b. for innocent	22	78
7. Friendly test more likely to be passed than adversarial test	75	25
8. Reasonable to use laboratory studies to estimate CQT validity	17	83

We also asked the same question that the Gallup poll and Amato and Honts asked. The results are summarized in the third column of Table II. Compared to the earlier surveys, a substantially smaller fraction endorsed

63. Charles R. Honts et al., *Mental and Physical Countermeasures Reduce the Accuracy of Polygraph Tests*, 79 J. APPLIED PSYCHOL. 252, 252–259 (1994).

64. *Supra* note 47.

option B in our sample and a substantially larger proportion felt that polygraph test interpretations have "questionable usefulness." Possible explanations for these different endorsement frequencies lie with our having made clear that our survey dealt primarily with the CQT (although we did not alter the wording of this question from that of the previous surveys) and our having a representative sample of the SPR membership. Even the minority of SPR members who thought the CQT might be a "useful tool" was unenthusiastic about the CQT. When this selected subset's responses to other questions were examined, fewer than 40% were found to believe that the CQT's validity was as high as 85% and 51% opposed admitting CQTs as evidence in court. Seventy-three percent thought a friendly test was more likely than an adversarial test to be passed.[65]

[3] A Survey of Distinguished Psychologists

Not all SPR members are psychologists and, indeed, not all of them are scientists. A number of practicing polygraph examiners, including the editor of the trade journal *Polygraph*, for example, hold membership in SPR. To more clearly characterize the opinions of psychological scientists, we thought it appropriate to conduct a similar survey of an elite group of psychologists, persons who had been elected Fellows of the General Psychology Division of the American Psychological Association. Of the 226 Fellows surveyed with addresses in the United States who were still professionally active, 74% responded. This response rate, although quite high for mail survey research,[66] was lower than that in our SPR survey, most likely because this group, honored for their accomplishments by election to the status of Fellow, was less likely to respond because of the demands their careers place on their time.

Table IV

Opinions of Distinguished Members of the American Psychological Association about CQT Polygraphy

Questionnaire Item	Percent Agree	Percent Disagree
1. CQT is scientifically sound	30	70
2. Would admit failed tests as evidence in court	20	80
3. Would admit passed tests as evidence in court	24	76
4. Confident could learn to beat the CQT	75	25
5. CQT is standardized	20	80
6. CQT is objective	10	90

65. Raskin et al. have implied that our obtaining results to the question in Table II that differed from those of the other surveys may be due to our inclusion of illustrative CQT questions that hypothetically could have been used in the O.J. Simpson case. They assert that somehow the mention of Simpson led otherwise rational scientists to instantly develop a negative view of polygraphy as they completed their surveys. Because polygraph testing was not a part of the Simpson trial, it is difficult to see how the mention of Simpson is connected to one's views on polygraphy, and if they were connected, why they would be any more likely to lead to negative than positive views about the polygraph.

66. *See* MODERN SCIENTIFIC EVIDENCE, *supra* note 44, at § 5–4.7.3 (1st Ed.).

Questionnaire Item	Percent Agree	Percent Disagree
7. If innocent, would take an adversarial test	35	65
8. If guilty, would take a friendly test	73	27
9. DLT is scientifically sound*	22	78

* Asked of half of the APA members.

Abbreviated results of this survey are presented in Table IV. The first three questions were repeated from our SPR survey and replicated the results of that survey by yielding almost identical endorsement frequencies. The fourth question from the Table asked how confident respondents were that they could personally learn to use physical or mental countermeasures to defeat a CQT. Over 70% felt they could do so with moderate to high confidence. The next two questions dealt with whether the administration of the CQT could accurately be considered standardized and was independent of differences among examiners in skill and subjective judgment. The CQT came up short on both counts.

Questions 7 and 8 dealt with the subjects' confidence in the CQT and the friendly polygrapher issue. Subjects were first asked if they personally would take a CQT administered by a police officer if they were *"wholly innocent"* and "the results would be admitted into evidence" before a jury. Only about a third of respondents would be inclined to take such a test, indicating that their confidence that the CQT can be used to fairly assess the truthfulness of innocent individuals is low. The second question required respondents to assume they were *"guilty"* and that their defense attorney arranged a private test by an examiner with expertise equal to that of the police examiner in the preceding question. Would they take this friendly test? Almost three quarters would, indicating that they felt they were risking little under the circumstances.[67] The final question dealt with the scientific justification for the DLT.

67. To determine if those with greater expertise about polygraphy had opinions that differed from those less well informed in our two surveys, we divided our SPR and APA respondents into two groups based on their own appraisal of how informed they were about CQT validity. The results of these analyses are summarized in detail in our journal article. W.G. Iacono & D.T. Lykken, *The Validity of the Lie Detector: Two Surveys of Scientific Opinion*, 82 J. APPLIED PSYCHOL. 426–433 (1997). Briefly, these two groups did not differ in any important respect regarding how they endorsed responses to the questions in Tables II–IV. We also examined the respondents who might be judged as most informed because they reported reading/attending at least six articles/presentations specifically about the accuracy of CQT polygraphy. Even among those in this select group (which made up 23% of the total respondents), there was little enthusiasm for the CQT. For instance, 66% believe the CQT is not based on sound scientific principles and 62% believe that passed CQTs should not be admissible in court. In this regard, it is important to note that the number of papers a scientist has read on CQT validity does not measure the value of his or her opinion about the accuracy of the technique. It would be a mistake to restrict the analysis of scientific opinion to just those few scientists who practice polygraphy or are otherwise involved in this profession. Such individuals, who are likely to consider themselves highly informed and would thus be disproportionately represented in any group selected for familiarity with this topic, are not capable of dispassionate evaluation of polygraph techniques because their livelihood depends on the use of these procedures. Finally, polygraph techniques are based on very simple principles that the vast majority of psychologists are capable of evaluating provided they know what they are. As previously noted, a strength of our surveys is that these principles were presented to respondents by directly quoting from the work of Raskin, Honts and Kircher so there could be no argument regarding whether they were fairly characterized. Our survey results showed that regardless of how well informed respondents were about this topic, most hold decidedly negative views about CQT polygraphy. The Gallup survey of SPR members also failed to find any difference between SPR members who were more versus those who were less informed

The APA fellows were overwhelmingly of the opinion that the DLT was not scientifically sound.[68]

[4] Further Evidence of Scientific Opinion: Attitudes toward Polygraphy in Psychology Textbooks

Honts and colleagues at Boise State University have established a website called the *Journal of Credibility Assessment and Witness Psychology*. One of the few essays to appear on this site was an analysis by Devitt et al. of the treatment of polygraphic detection of deception (PDD) in 37 different introductory psychology textbooks published between 1987 and 1994. This essay reports that "PDD received strongly negative treatment in the texts."[69] Only 16% of the texts provided any positive citations to polygraphy, with the ratio of negative to positive citations exceeding 15 to 1. The authors complain that textbook writers tend to cite mainly critics of the lie detector (including us) and various factual errors are commented upon. The one error cited in the text concerns one author's discussion of the demonstration by Honts et al.[70] that college students can be easily taught to beat the lie detector. That author mistakenly reported that the method taught for producing augmented responses to the control questions involved pressing on a tack in one's shoe. In fact, Honts et al.'s subjects were instructed to press their toes on the floor after answering the control questions.

The tack-in-the-shoe method would undoubtedly work as well or better than the methods employed by Honts et al.[71] Floyd Fay used this technique while serving two years of a life sentence for aggravated murder prior to the discovery of the real killers, which led to his release.[72] Fay's false conviction resulted from testimony that he had failed two stipulated polygraph tests and this led him to make a study of polygraphy while in prison. The institution in which he was incarcerated used the lie detector to adjudicate charges against inmates of violating prison rules. Before his release, Fay managed to train a number of inmates to beat the lie test by pressing on a tack in their shoe after each control question. These and other examples have been reviewed by Lykken.[73]

about polygraph testing. Our findings thus confirm that highly knowledgeable as well as less informed scientists were equally skeptical about the CQT.

68. We have been informed that Honts has been conducting a telephone survey of opinions about polygraphy of the members of the American Psychology and Law Society, a group whose membership includes non-scientists (our informant was a surveyed attorney with no scientific training).

69. Mary K. Devitt, et al., *Truth or Just Bias: The Treatment of the Psychophysiological Detection of Deception in Introductory Psychology Textbooks*, as 1 J. Credibility Assessment, 9–32 (1997) (This journal is a publication of Charles Honts' website.)

70. Charles R. Honts, et al., *Effects of Physical Countermeasures on the Physiological De-tection of Deception*, 70 J. Applied Psychol. 177–187 (1985).

71. This line of research has shown that various techniques can be used to defeat the CQT. In addition to toe pressing, biting the tongue and mentally counting backwards when presented with a control question have been identified as effective covert methods that enable guilty persons to pass a CQT. Honts et al., *supra* note 70; Charles R. Honts, David C. Raskin, & John C. Kircher, *Mental and Physical Countermeasures Reduce the Accuracy of Polygraph Tests*, 79 J. Applied Psychol. 252–259 (1994).

72. Adrian Cimerman, "They'll Let Me Go Tomorrow," The Fay Case, 8(3) Criminal Defense 7–10 (1981).

73. David T. Lykken, A Tremor in the Blood: Uses and Abuses of the Lie Detector (1981); David T. Lykken, A Tremor in the Blood: Uses and Abuses of the Lie Detector (2nd ed. 1998).

The main impression left by this review of Devitt et al. is that the authors of psychology textbooks were nearly unanimous in concluding that the lie detector has poor scientific credentials and negligible forensic utility except, perhaps, as an inducer of confessions. As such, this review corroborates the findings from our SPR and APA1 surveys by illustrating that another group of broadly informed psychologists are overwhelmingly negative in their appraisal of polygraph testing.

[5] Summary of Scientific Opinion

These findings make it clear that the scientific community regards the CQT to be an unstandardized, nonobjective technique, based on implausible assumptions, a technique that can be easily defeated by sophisticated guilty suspects, and which is unlikely to achieve good accuracy in detecting either truthfulness or deception. Scientists do not believe that either inculpatory or exculpatory CQT results have sufficient probative value to be introduced as evidence in court and they are especially skeptical about the validity of friendly tests. They do not believe that laboratory studies should be used to estimate CQT accuracy. Further, they do not believe that the recent CQT variant, the Directed Lie Test, provides a credible solution to the defects of the CQT. These same scientists believe that the GKT, in contrast, is scientifically credible.

§ 12–3.3.13 Scientifically Based Forensic Psychophysiology: The Guilty Knowledge Test (GKT)

The major problem with conventional psychophysiological detection of deception (PDD) techniques is that their validity depends on being able to measure complex human emotions to determine if a person is guilty or innocent. Because individual differences in the expression of emotion are substantial, causing the same stimulus to elicit quite different emotions in different people, and specific emotions produce similar physiological reactions, it may never be possible to develop a PDD technique with high accuracy. It is primarily because PDD is an emotion-based assessment that it is not possible to use laboratory studies to gauge accuracy because real life emotion cannot be reproduced adequately in laboratory simulations.

An alternative to PDD involves developing procedures that are not emotion-based. One such technique, the guilty knowledge test (GKT) provides a measure of the cognitive processing associated with memory, something that can be determined using psychophysiological procedures. The GKT answers the question: What does this person know about the crime? Laboratory studies can be used to show how well certain memories can be detected because the assessment of memory in the laboratory does not differ in any important way from the assessment of memory in the field. Two types of measures have been used to assess recognition memory with the GKT. The traditional GKT has involved the measurement of autonomic nervous system responses, especially the galvanic skin response (GSR). More recently, a version of the GKT has been introduced that relies on the monitoring of brain electrical activity.

[1]   Rationale Behind the Traditional GKT

The GKT provides an assessment of an individual's memory about crime relevant information, i.e., knowledge about the crime that the perpetrator would be expected to have. Such "guilty knowledge" can only be assessed in situations in which the examiner knows certain facts about the crime that would also be known to a guilty—but not to an innocent—suspect. These facts or "keys" can be presented in the form of multiple-choice questions: "If you killed Mr. Jones, then you will know where in the house we found his body. Did we find him: In the kitchen? In the basement? In the living room? On the stairway? In the bedroom?" A traditional GKT might involve 5–10 such multiple choice questions, each with keys and foils covering a different memory about the crime.

The GKT assumes that the guilty person's recognition of the correct alternative will cause him to produce a stronger physiological response to that alternative. The incorrect alternatives provide an estimate of what the response to the correct alternative would look like if the subject did not know which alternative was correct; thus, unlike the comparison questions used in the CQT or DLT, the incorrect alternatives of the GKT questions provide genuine controls.

An innocent suspect would have about one chance in five of giving the largest response to the correct alternative in such a five-choice question; thus, the probability of false detection (a false-positive error) on a single GKT item would be 0.20. This probability of error decreases rapidly, however, for each additional GKT item that can be devised; an innocent person would have about 4 chances in 100 of "hitting" on both of two items, 8 chances in 1000 of giving the largest response to the correct alternative on three consecutive items, and so on.

[2]   Measuring Brainwaves with the GKT: "Brain Fingerprinting"

In the last decade, scientists have refined the GKT by measuring brain electrical activity rather than the galvanic skin response to assess recognition memory. This GKT application, referred to as "brain fingerprinting" in the popular press, involves attaching electrodes to the scalp and measuring event-related potentials (ERP). An ERP is a brainwave generated every time a person is presented with a discrete stimulus. This complex wave has multiple components, but one aspect of the signal, called the P300 or P3 wave (because it has a latency of over 300 milliseconds and is the third positive component of the ERP), is especially useful for assessing recognition memory. A P300 wave arises every time a stimulus stands out as different from other stimuli a person is presented with. In the context of the GKT, the key alternatives will stand out to the guilty person because they are recognized as guilty knowledge. For the innocent person, none of the alternatives has distinct meaning, so none will evoke a P300 wave.

For the typical adult, the P300 wave has an amplitude of only about 15 microvolts, far smaller than the background electrical activity that is continuously present in the brain. In order to measure P300, the same stimulus must be repeatedly presented, each time recording the brain's electrical response.

All the responses to this stimulus are eventually averaged together. The background electrical activity of the brain varies randomly around the time a stimulus is presented. Averaging this random activity causes it to disappear from the averaged signal. Because the ERP is "time locked" to the stimulus (i.e., its shape and latency is the same to every stimulus presentation beginning the moment the stimulus is presented), averaging enhances the ERP signal. Hence, averaging makes it possible to measure accurately this tiny response by strengthening the representation of the ERP while causing the brain's random background electrical activity to fade away. The implications of this for the GKT are several. First, the stimuli must be presented with precise timing and for very short durations. Typically, a computer is used to present them, and they only appear on a computer monitor for about 50 milliseconds. Second, to facilitate averaging, the same stimuli must be presented repeatedly, perhaps 20 or more times. Because a stimulus can be presented every few seconds, this requirement poses few logistical problems because hundreds of stimuli can be presented in a 15–minute recording session.

Because the shape of ERPs vary from person to person, it is important to know what a P300 wave looks like for the given individual. It is also important to make certain that individuals being tested pay attention to the stimuli. Hence, the ERP–GKT includes some special stimuli that the person being tested admits knowledge of and must respond to. Assume, for instance, that one ERP–GKT item deals with knowledge of the weapon used to kill someone. The examiner and the person being tested agree that the item used was not a gun. The actual crime weapon was a hammer. These words, *gun* (the target) and *hammer* (the probe) are flashed every two seconds or so on a computer screen, randomly interspersed with the irrelevant words *knife*, *rope*, and *poison*. The subject is told to press a red response key every time *gun* appears on the screen and a green response key every time another word is presented. This manual response requirement forces the person to pay attention because it compels cognitive processing of each word in order to be able to press the correct key. Because the word *gun* stands out as memorable, when the ERPs to this word are averaged, a distinct P300 wave will be seen. *Knife*, *rope* and *poison* have no special meaning, so ERPs averaged to these words will not contain a distinct P300 wave. The important question concerns whether the probe word *hammer* produces an ERP with a P300 wave that resembles that produced by the target word *gun* or a wave that looks indistinguishable to that of the irrelevant foils. If it resembles *gun*, the subject is attaching special meaning to the presentation of the word representing the murder weapon, i.e., the subject has guilty knowledge. If the ERP resembles that of the foils, there is no evidence of guilty knowledge for the murder weapon. Statistical procedures have been developed to determine the degree to which the ERP to the probe word more closely resembles that of the target or the irrelevant foils. Just as with the regular GKT, the ERP–GKT involves the presentation of multiple items that may include as stimuli words, phrases, and visual displays such as pictures of the crime scene, victim, weapon, etc.

The ERP–GKT has several advantages over the traditional GKT. First, because of the inclusion of the target word, it is possible to determine that the test was properly administered to the subject. We can make this determination by a) showing that the proper button was pressed in response to this word, and b) showing that this word elicits an ERP that is distinctly different from that to the irrelevant foils. If either of these features is absent, the test of the particular subject would not be valid. Second, a built-in control for individual differences in how a person's brain responds to memorable information is included in the test. It would be possible to drop the target condition from the test and simply determine if the probe ERP differs from the irrelevant ERPs. However, we would not know how different it would have to be to signal the typical recognition response of this person's brain. By including the target condition, we know what a given person's recognition response should look like. Third, the ERP–GKT is not dependent on the measurement of autonomic nervous system responses like the GSR. These responses are not always reliably produced and they can be generated by extraneous factors like unintentional movements or provocative thoughts. The ERP is an involuntary response that is always present if the subject is paying attention. Fourth, the ERP–GKT is unlikely to be easily defeated by employing countermeasures. Because ERPs are derived from brain signals that occur only a few hundred milliseconds after the GKT alternatives are presented, and because as yet no one has shown that humans can selectively alter these brain potentials at will, it is unlikely that countermeasures could be used successfully to defeat a GKT derived from the recording of cerebral signals.

[3] Evidence Supporting GKT Accuracy

There are two distinct questions to ask concerning GKT accuracy. The first concerns whether this technique can be used to determine whether someone has recognition memory for an item or event. This question can be answered with laboratory research. The second concerns what items and events it is reasonable to expect a person who has committed a crime to remember. This question is best addressed from field studies that determine what criminals pay attention to and remember as aspects of a crime they commit. As we show below, studies of the GKT are clear in demonstrating that this is a highly accurate technique for determining if an individual recognizes information. However, at present there are no field studies demonstrating what people who commit a crime are likely to remember.[74] Consequently, we can confidently determine whether a subject has recognition memory, but we cannot determine scientifically whether someone who committed a crime should necessarily have certain memories.

[a] Traditional GKT

A virtue of the GKT is that its validity with innocent suspects can be estimated *a priori*. With 5 equally plausible alternatives in each GKT ques-

---

74. Although they were not studies designed to determine what criminals remember from a crime scene, Elaad et al. have carried out field studies using the traditional GKT. Eitan Elaad et al., *Detection Measures in Real–Life Guilty Knowledge Tests*, 77 J. Applied Psychol. 757, 757–767 (1992); Eitan Elaad, *Detection of Guilty Knowledge in Real–Life Criminal Investigations*, 75 J. Applied Psychol. 521, 521–529 (1990). These studies, carried out in Israel, showed that innocent suspects responded to GKT items as predicted by theory. Guilty suspects seemed to remember about 70% of the guilty knowledge facts used for GKT items, as compared with about 88% for subjects involved in the mock crimes of laboratory studies where the details of the crime scene were still fresh in their minds. The Israeli field studies achieved 97% detection of innocent suspects but only 76% detection of guilty suspects, which has been cited as indicating a defect of the GKT. But this is an erroneous conclusion. Elaad et al. used GKTs with only 1 to 6 items (mean = 1.8), each repeated typically 3 times, so that their detection efficiencies were predictably less than would be expected with GKTs constructed from 6 to 10 different guilty knowledge facts.

tion, an innocent person would have a 20% chance of giving his strongest response to the correct alternative on one question, a 4% chance of appearing guilty on both of two questions, and so on. With a 10–question GKT, if we require five items to be "failed" to classify a person as guilty, more than 99% of innocent suspects can be expected to be correctly classified. The GKT's validity with guilty suspects cannot be predicted with such confidence because we cannot be certain that each suspect will have noticed and remembered all 10 of the items of guilty knowledge.

The ability of the GKT to detect both innocence and guilt decreases when there are fewer items and also when there are fewer alternatives per item. The validity estimates that have been obtained in the laboratory studies of the GKT that have been published to date have been close to those predicted from the numbers of items and alternatives-per-item used in each study. For instance, a review of eight GKT laboratory studies revealed that the GKT had an accuracy of 88% with guilty study subjects and 97% with innocent subjects.[75]

The GKT is unlikely to be suitable for the investigation of all crimes. Its results will be dependent on what the perpetrator pays attention to and remembers and how well the examiner is able to determine what that may be.[76] Premeditated crimes and those for which it can be determined what exactly the perpetrator did would make good GKT cases. These would include a planned murder, a theft involving unrecovered items, and a sex crime where the victim can give a good account of what happened.[77]

[b]   ERP–GKT

The ERP–GKT received its impetus from the work of Dr. Lawrence Farwell. In an initial report by Farwell and Donchin,[78] 20 laboratory subjects were exposed to guilty knowledge about one of two espionage cases. Hence, each subject possessed guilty knowledge regarding one case and not the other. Excluding inconclusive test outcomes, the ERP–GKT was 100% accurate. That is, it was possible to determine for every subject which espionage

75. LYKKEN, *supra* note 73.

76. Just as fingerprint evidence, when absent at a crime scene, is not exculpating, a passed GKT indicating no recognition of crime scene information also cannot establish innocence. A failed GKT, on the other hand, indicating the presence of knowledge a suspect claims not to have, is potentially as incriminating as fingerprints found at a crime scene.

77. Podlesny et al. have concluded, after a review of FBI files, that only a small fraction of cases would be suitable for GKTs [John A. Podlesny, *Is the Guilty Knowledge Applicable in Criminal Investigations? A Review of FBI Case Records*, 20 CRIME LABORATORY DIG. 59 (1993); John A. Podlesny et al., *A Lack of Operable Case Facts Restricts Applicability of the Guilty Knowledge Deception Detection Method in FBI Criminal Investigations: A*

Technical Report, U.S. DEPT. OF JUSTICE, FBI, FORENSIC SCIENCE RESEARCH AND TRAINING CENTER, QUANTICO, VIRGINIA (1995)]. We expect that a search of Scotland Yard files prior to 1900, when the Galton–Henry system of fingerprint classification was established, would also have failed to find many instances where this powerful forensic tool could be employed retrospectively. When police investigators are trained to search crime scenes for items on which GKT questions might be based, they will in many cases find them.

78. Lawrence A. Farwell & Emanuel Donchin, *The Truth Will Out: Interrogative Polygraphy ("Lie Detection") with Event Related Potentials*, 28 PSYCHOPHYSIOLOGY 531, 531–547 (1991).

scenario he was familiar with and which scenario he had no knowledge of by showing that guilty knowledge probes produced ERPs that closely resembled targets when individuals were guilty and that closely resembled irrelevant foils when individuals were innocent. Allen, Danielson, and Iacono[79] carried out three studies of the ERP–GKT using a different method to determine whether a probe ERP better resembled the target or the irrelevant foil ERPs, a method that did not allow for the possibility of inconclusive outcomes. Examining a total of 60 subjects across three studies, they obtained an overall classification accuracy of 96%. Allen and Iacono[80] later re-analyzed their data using the scoring method of Farwell and Donchin. Excluding inconclusives, they obtained 100% accuracy. Allen and Iacono varied the motivation their subjects had to try to conceal their guilty knowledge and avoid being detected by giving them varying degrees of incentive to try to "beat the test." They found that as incentive was increased, fewer subjects were classified as inconclusive. These results suggest that in real life, the ERP–GKT may work even better than in the laboratory.

Other studies also suggest that the ERP–GKT is likely to work well in the real world. Several clinical studies have been carried out to determine the validity of amnesia claims made by different types of study participants. In one study, four patients with multiple personality disorder (also called dissociative identity disorder) were assessed to determine if the memories of one personality can be recognized by an alter personality that claims amnesia for them.[81] This study involved presenting to the alter personality memorized information learned by the other personality. This memorized information provided the material for the GKT's probe stimuli, while information memorized by the alter personality served as the source of target stimuli. Other meaningless stimuli served as irrelevant foils. The results showed that the alter personalities generated probe ERPs resembling the target ERPs, indicating recognition memory for the alleged amnesic information in all four cases. A similar study evaluated hypnotized individuals with profound recognition memory amnesia. Again, the ERPs to the memory probes closely resembled those of targets, not irrelevant foils.[82]

Farwell and colleagues have also shown the ERP–GKT is likely to be effective in field applications.[83] In one study, subjects admitted to arrests for minor crimes like public drunkenness. They were queried about the details of the event (e.g., who they were with, where they were) and GKT probes, targets, and irrelevant foils were developed. Each subject was tested for guilty knowledge related to his crime and also for guilty knowledge related to a crime of one of the other participants. Again, no errors of classification were evident. In another investigation, individuals reported to a laboratory with a

79. John J. Allen et al., *The Identification of Concealed Memories Using the Event–Related Potential and Implicit Behavioral Measures: A Methodology for Prediction in the Face of Individual Differences*, 29 PSYCHOPHYSIOLOGY 504, 504–522 (1992).

80. John J.B. Allen & William G. Iacono, *A Comparison of Methods for the Analysis of Event–Related Potentials in Deception Detection*, 34 PSYCHOPHYSIOLOGY 234, 234–240 (1997).

81. John J.B. Allen & Hallam L. Movius III, *The Objective Assessment of Amnesia in Dissociative Identity Disorder Using Event–Related Potentials*, 38 INT'L. J. PSYCHOPHYSIOLOGY 21, 21–41 (2000).

82. John J. Allen et al., *An Event–Related Potential Investigation of Posthypnotic Recognition Amnesia*, 104 J. ABNORMAL PSYCHOL. 421, 421–430 (1995).

83. Farwell & Donchin, *supra* note 78, at 531–547.

close friend.[84] The friend was interviewed regarding the details of an important event in the life of the study subject, and this information was used to develop memory probes. When subjects were tested, their ERPs to the probe material provided by their friends matched the target ERPs, not those of irrelevant foils. Again, there were no classification errors.

In *Iowa v. Harrington*,[85] the results of an ERP–GKT were introduced in court for the first time as part of an evidentiary hearing. Dr. Farwell administered two separate tests to Terry Harrington, a man who, although steadfastly maintaining his innocence, was convicted of murder over 20 years ago. Farwell thoroughly investigated the nature of the crime scene, paying particular attention to unusual obstacles the perpetrator would have been confronted by during his flight from the murder scene. This information was not presented at trial, and Harrington claimed no knowledge of these details. Dr. Farwell was able to demonstrate that Harrington's ERP to probe words characterizing these crime facts resembled his ERPs to irrelevant phrases. The target word phrases produced an ERP with a distinct P300 wave, making it distinctly different form the ERPs associated with the other two types of words. Dr. Farwell also tested Harrington on the details of his alibi on the night of the crime. The probe words, representing information Harrington should have remembered about the events surrounding his alibi, evoked an ERP that matched the ERP of the target words and not the ERP of the irrelevant foils. Taken in combination, these results show that Harrington did not have memories related to the commission of the crime but he did recognize information associated with his alibi. The fact that his brain response showed recognition of alibi-relevant information clearly demonstrated that he was able to remember details of the night in question. Judge O'Grady, who held an evidentiary hearing to review the science supporting the ERP–GKT ruled that while the P300 evidence was "arguably merely cumulative or impeaching, it may be material to the issues in the case," but that Harrington "failed to meet his burden to prove that the P300 evidence probably would have changed the result of the trial."[86]

[4] Scientific Opinion

In the surveys conducted by Iacono and Lykken of members of SPR and APA, respondents were asked their opinions regarding the GKT. The results are summarized in Table V. The members of both organizations clearly believed the GKT to have a solid scientific foundation. They also believed that GKT results have probative value. When asked if it was reasonable to believe that a person who failed 8 of 10 GKT items was guilty, the vast majority of both organizations agreed that it was. Finally, asked what was more believable, a failed GKT or a passed CQT administered through a defendant's attorney, respondents found the GKT to offer the more credible result. These results establish two important points. First, scientists find the GKT to be a theoretically sound forensic tool with great potential. Second, scientists are able to distinguish between different forensic uses of psychophysiological

84. Lawrence A. Farwell & Sharon S. Smith, *Using Brain MERMER Testing to Detect Knowledge Despite Efforts to Conceal*, 46 J. Forensic Sci. 1, 1–9 (2001).

85. Terry Harrington v. State of Iowa, PCCV073247, 5 March 2001.

86. *Id.*

procedures. It is not the case that they are opposed in principle to forensic applications of psychophysiology, they are only opposed to those that have a weak scientific basis.

Table V

Opinions of Members of the Society for Psychophysiological Research (SPR) and Fellows of the American Psychological Association (APA) about the GKT

Questionnaire Item	Percent Agree	Percent Disagree
1. GKT is scientifically sound.		
SPR	77	23
APA*	72	28
2. Reasonable to believe a suspect is guilty if 8 out of 10 GKT items were failed.		
SPR	72	28
APA*	75	25
3. If a suspect failed a GKT but passed a CQT dealing with the same crime, which result would be more believable?		
GKT result more believable**	73	27

Note: * Asked of half of APA members; ** Asked of SPR members only

§ 12–3.3.14 Polygraph Screening of Federal Employees and Job Applicants

[1] National Security Screening

In view of the federal Employee Polygraph Protection Act of 1988,[87] which prohibits requiring employees or job applicants in the private sector to submit to polygraph testing, it is ironic that the federal government is the principal employer of polygraph examiners. Applicants for positions with the FBI, CIA, NSA, Secret Service, and similar agencies are required to undergo lie detector tests intended to supplement or substitute for background investigations. Current employees of some of these agencies, military personnel who hold high security clearances, and civil employees of defense contractors doing classified work may be required to undergo periodic tests for screening purposes. The Department of Defense conducted some 17,970 such tests in 1993.[88] Most of these tests, which are based on the relevant/irrelevant polygraph technique, are referred to as counterintelligence scope polygraph tests by the government.

87. 29 U.S.C.A. § 2001 et seq. (2000).

88. DEPT. OF DEFENSE POLYGRAPH INSTITUTE, *A Comparison of Psychophysiological Detection of Deception Accuracy Rates Obtained Using the Counterintelligence Scope Polygraph and the Test for Espionage and Sabotage Question Formats*, 26 POLYGRAPH 79–80 (1997) (hereafter DoDPI Study 1).

As a consequence of Public Law 106–65 (S. 1059) passed as part of the National Defense Authorization Act of 2000, potentially thousands of scientists and security personnel employed at U.S. weapons labs at Lawrence Livermore, Sandia, or Los Alamos must submit to polygraph tests as part of an effort to improve nuclear security. A relatively new procedure, the Test for Espionage and Sabotage (TES), or a nearly identical variant of this procedure, the Test for Espionage, Sabotage, and Terrorism (TEST), is used.

As outlined in the recently promulgated Department of Energy (DOE) Rule 709 these counterintelligence polygraph examinations are to be limited to coverage of six topics:[89]

1) espionage,

2) sabotage,

3) terrorism,

4) intentional unauthorized disclosure of classified information,

5) intentional unauthorized foreign contacts, and

6) deliberate damage or malicious use of a U.S. government or defense system.

Rule 709 has a number of interesting features that are similar to those governing the use of polygraph tests by other federal agencies and that are likely to stimulate law suits.[90] These include the following:

- Prospective employees of the DOE or its contractors who refuse to take a polygraph cannot be hired and incumbent employees must be denied access to secret information.

- Using the results of a polygraph test as an "investigative lead" can result in an administrative decision that denies or revokes an employee's access to classified information and may lead DOE to "reassign the individual or realign the individual's duties within the local commuting area or take other actions consistent with the denial of access."

- These tests will be conducted at least every five years and also on an aperiodic basis.

- Public comment on the proposed regulations revealed widespread opinion that "that polygraph examinations have no theoretical foundation or validity." DOE decided, however, that "as a matter of law," the agency is mandated to conduct polygraph examinations, and "is no longer free to act favorably on comments arguing against establishment of a counterintelligence scope polygraph examination program because of information and claims about deficiencies in polygraph reliability."

The TES[91] is a type of DLT that includes four irrelevant questions (e.g., "Do you sometimes drink water?" "Is today ____?") and the following four relevant questions: "Have you committed espionage?" "Have you given classi-

---

89. Part 709 "Polygraph Examination Regulations' " in Chapter III of Title 10 of the Code of Federal Regulations.

90. In anticipation of the DOE regulations, attorneys representing government employees and employee prospects have indicated a desire to sue the government based on adverse em-

ployee decisions made as a result of polygraph examinations.

91. Because the government has published information only on the TES, we will refer to this procedure in the remainder of this section.

fied information to any unauthorized person?" "Have you failed to notify, as required, any contact with citizens of sensitive countries including China?" "Have you been involved in sabotage?" The responses to the relevant questions are compared to the responses to four "directed lie" questions that serve as "controls" or comparisons by providing an example of a response to a known lie. The directed lies are questions that both the examiner and the examinee know will be answered falsely. These four questions are chosen from a list of acceptable alternatives, but may include any of the following, which the examinee is directed to answer "No": "Did you ever violate a traffic law?" "Did you ever say something that you later regretted?" "Did you ever lie to a co-worker about anything at all?" Examinees who show greater autonomic disturbance following the questions about espionage and sabotage, than they show following these directed lies, are classified as deceptive.

The field validity of counterintelligence scope polygraph examinations, including the TES, is unknown. However, the Department of Defense Polygraph Institute (DoDPI) has reported two laboratory studies of the validity of the TES.[92] These both employed paid volunteers, 115 of whom were innocent while 60 others were each required to enact simulated acts of espionage or sabotage. Of the innocent subjects, 14 or 12.5% responded in the deceptive direction. Of the "guilty" subjects, 10 or 17% were misclassified as innocent.

It is obviously likely that innocent scientists or other persons with high security clearances would be more disturbed by the TES relevant questions asked during an official screening test than were these volunteers for whom the test carried no threat to their reputations or careers. The disturbance produced by the directed-lie questions, on the other hand, might be expected to be no greater in real-life than in simulated conditions of testing. Therefore, when innocent, loyal government employees with top secret classifications are subjected to the TES, one might expect many more to be classified as deceptive than the 12.5% suggested by the DoDPI studies. The actual rate of false-positive diagnoses is probably close to the 44% level indicated by the real-life studies summarized in Table I.

When DOE scientists are subjected to the planned TES (or TEST), these data indicate that large numbers of innocent employees would be classified as deceptive if the test scores were relied upon. DOE's polygraph examiners avoid any such disastrous result because they know that the base rate of spying (the proportion likely to be spies) among such a highly screened and dedicated group is likely to be tiny. Consequently, they cannot fail 44% or even 12.5% of scientists without undermining their own credibility, creating a personnel management nightmare, and wreaking havoc on employee morale.

Therefore, subjects who are more troubled by "Have you committed espionage?" than by "Did you ever say something that you later regretted?" are invited by the examiner to explain why they might have responded in this way. If the respondent's answer and demeanor satisfy the examiner, his "fail" is converted to a "pass." Thus, by permitting the polygraph operator to be the ultimate arbiter, relying on whatever clinical skills or intuitions the examiner may (or may not) possess, the frequency of false-positive diagnoses is kept to a

---

92. DoDPI Study 1, *supra* note 88; DEPT. OF DEFENSE POLYGRAPH INSTITUTE, *Psychophysiological Detection of Deception Accuracy Rates Ob-* *tained using the Test for Espionage and Sabotage*, 27 POLYGRAPH 68–73 (1998).

low value. Nevertheless, if as few as 2% of the 10,000 workers potentially covered by Rule 709 receive final diagnoses of "deception indicated," 200 highly trained but probably innocent scientists would be implicated as spies in the first round of testing.[93]

Although the controversy surrounding the DOE polygraph screening program has focused on the high likelihood that innocent individuals will be judged to be spies, there is little evidence that the program will actually catch spies. The laboratory studies of the TES, which reported only 83% accuracy in identifying persons "guilty" of committing mock-espionage, overestimate accuracy for the real-life guilty in two important ways.

First, consistent with real life screening test practices that help to keep the number failing these tests low, these studies did not conclude that deceptive polygraph tests were in fact failed if, during a post-test interview, an examinee offered information that reasonably justified why the test might be a false positive outcome. However, the design of the studies allowed only innocent test subjects this opportunity to "talk their way out of" a failed test because guilty people were instructed to confess as soon as the examiner confronted them with their deceptive test results. We do not know how many guilty individuals would have been mistakenly judged "false positives" had they been allowed to try to "explain away" the outcome of their examinations.

Second, these DoDPI studies did not account for the likelihood that real spies would use countermeasures to defeat the TES. DOE scientists are not simpletons: if one or two are in fact spies, surely both they and their foreign handlers would have sense enough to be prepared to bite their tongues after each directed-lie question. Thus it is to be expected that the *only* weapons-lab scientists, with their highly specialized skills, who fail the projected DOE polygraph screens, will be truthful, honorable people who cannot offer a plausible excuse for failing their polygraphs. The most likely result of Rule 709 will be their ruined reputations and the government's loss of skilled, dedicated employees.

Besides the facts that these tests are not justified on scientific grounds and that they are clearly biased against truthful employees, there is no evidence that personnel screening tests have any true utility.[94] No spy has

---

93. The Department of Defense Polygraph Program report to Congress for Fiscal Year 2000 illustrates how polygraphers adjust the outcomes of their tests to minimize failing anyone. *Department of Defense Polygraph Program Annual Report to Congress, Fiscal Year 2000, Office of the Assistant Secretary of Defense* (2000); available at http://www.fas.org/sgp/othergov/polygraph/dod-2000.html. For fiscal year 2000, 7,688 individuals were given counterintelligence scope polygraph tests but demonstrated "no significant physiological response to the relevant questions and provided no substantive information." In other words, some undetermined number provided a substantial physiological response but passed because they did not make incriminating revelations. An additional 202 individuals produced significant physiological reactions and provided "substantive informa-

tion." Of these, 194 received "favorable adjudication" with the remaining 8 cases still pending decisions, with no one receiving "adverse action denying or withholding access" to classified information. These data confirm that the government goes to extreme lengths to ensure no one fails these tests, but they also demonstrate that the tests have no utility.

94. In the Clinton Administration's Joint Security Commission Report ["Redefining Security," A Report to the Secretary of Defense and the Director of Central Intelligence, February 28, 1994, Joint Security Commission, Washington, D.C. 20505; available at http://www.fas.org/sgp/library/jsc/index.html], it is noted that "the most important product of the polygraph process is more likely to be an admission made during the interview than a chart interpretation ... While senior officials at the CIA and the NSA acknowledge the con-

ever been uncovered because of a failed polygraph test. Although the government has argued that the admissions individuals make when undergoing these tests provide valuable information, there is no evidence documenting that vital or even important information has been uncovered as a result of polygraph tests. It is possible that employee screening has a deterrent effect in that knowledge that one must pass such tests may discourage would be spies from seeking employment, and it may discourage the currently employed from entertaining thoughts about becoming a spy. However, there is no evidence to support such an assertion. Given the ease with which individuals can learn to defeat these tests coupled with the fact that almost no one is judged to have failed them, it is unlikely that they have any serious deterrent effect.[95]

[2] Opinions of DOE National Laboratory Senior Scientists Regarding Employee Screening

Concerned by the requirement that national laboratory employees submit to periodic lie detector tests, a panel of the more senior national laboratory scientists and engineers undertook a detailed appraisal of the existing literature relating to the nature and validity of polygraph screening methods. Sandia's Senior Scientists and Engineers ("Seniors") provide a service to the Laboratories as independent, experienced, corporate evaluators of technical issues. They are available as a group to assist Sandia management with technical reviews of particularly significant issues and programs. Implementation uses subpanels of the Seniors (helped as necessary by other Sandia staff) to conduct the initial, detailed review of issues or programs. The reports of the subpanels are then made available for review by all other Seniors prior to submission to management. The report of the subpanel studying polygraphs and security at Sandia was circulated in the fall of 1999.[96]

These Seniors, whose expertise is in physics, chemistry, or mathematics, do not pretend to be psychologists, psychophysiologists, or psychometricians. But they do know how to read research reports and to evaluate statistical evidence and probabilities. In their Executive Summary, they concluded that

1) There were no adequate studies to support polygraph screening

2) It is impossible to predict what error rates to expect

3) Polygraph testing could drive away existing innocent, talented workers who have provided value to national security programs, and it would deter prospective, talented employment candidates from considering a career in the national laboratories

4) Because few spies are likely to be detected, real subversives may be more likely to become insiders—particularly if over-reliance on polygraph testing leads to reduced emphasis on other security and counterintelligence methods.

troversial nature of the polygraph process, they also strongly endorse it as the most effective information gathering technique available in their personnel security systems."

95. *See* footnote 93 summarizing the DoD Fiscal year 2000 report.

96. Polygraphs and Security, A Study by a Subpanel of Sandia's Senior Scientists and Engineers, October 21, 1999, Sandia, NM; available at http://www.fas.org/sgp/othergov/polygraph/sandia.html.

§ 12–3.4 Summary of Areas of Agreement: Topics for Future Research

The concept of the "lie detector" is so deeply entrenched in American mythology that it has proved difficult to eradicate. This aspect of American culture has never caught on in European countries although polygraphy is used by law enforcement in Canada, Israel, and Japan. However, CQT results are not admissible in the courts of these countries and, at least in Israel and Japan, police polygraphers seem to prefer to use the GKT where possible, in place of the discredited methods of "lie detection." However, because it is effective, as a "bloodless 3rd degree," in inducing confessions, the polygraph is likely to continue to be valued in police work.

There is general agreement on a number of scientific issues relevant to the use of polygraph tests.

The polygraph machines used to monitor physiological responses, provided they are in good working order, provide adequate recordings.[97]

1) When these physiological signals are computerized, a properly programmed computer can provide an adequate representation of the signals. However, computerized polygraph testing does nothing to resolve any of the controversies surrounding polygraph accuracy because these controversies concern the lack of scientific support for PDD theory and the fact that the results depend on how questions are formulated and asked, unpredictable individual differences in how a person responds emotionally to control and relevant questions, and the likelihood that a guilty person will use undetected countermeasures.

2) PDD procedures are not standardized or objective. This is true about their administration and scoring.

3) The proper administration of a CQT requires the examiner to deceive the examinee by leading the examinee to believe that "failing" the control questions will lead to an deceptive verdict when in fact the opposite is true. Unless innocent people have great concern about failing the control questions, they will inadvertently respond more strongly to the relevant questions and be judged deceptive. Left unresolved is how the test can be valid for an innocent person who is unconvinced by this deception.

4) The comparison or control questions on a CQT or DLT are not controls in the scientific sense in that there is no reason to assume that relevant and control questions have equivalent psychological significance.

5) Basic questions about the reliability or consistency with which polygraph tests produce the same result remain unanswered. In particular, it is not known how likely it is that two different examiners testing the same person would obtain the same result (referred to as test-retest reliability).

6) There are no field studies of CQT accuracy with unambiguous criteria for ground truth that have overcome the confession bias problem.

97. Christopher J. Patrick & William G. Iacono, *A Comparison of Field and Laboratory* *Polygraphs in the Detection of Deception*, 28 PSYCHOPHYSIOLOGY 632–638 (1991).

Consequently, there are no studies that both proponents and opponents of polygraph testing can point to as providing a valid estimate of CQT accuracy.

7) Countermeasures can be employed successfully by guilty individuals to pass a polygraph test, and the use of these countermeasures is not detectable.

8) The GKT is a scientifically sound alternative to PDD. Whether based on the measure of autonomic nervous system responses like the GSR or on brain potentials, this technique can accurately determine if someone has recognition memory for information they claim to have no knowledge of.

9) Polygraphers are not scientists, and their opinions regarding polygraph testing are not relevant to how scientists appraise polygraphy. Psychologists, especially those trained in psychophysiology, have the requisite knowledge to evaluate these psychologically based PDD techniques.

10) Personnel screening cannot be scientifically justified. These PDD procedures are biased against the innocent, and have not even been shown to have the kind of utility that the CQT has.

§ 12–3.4.1 The Future of the "Lie Detector"

Because the CQT and its progeny are based on such implausible assumptions, it is unlikely that future research will do more than confirm the present view of the scientific community that these techniques have negligible validity.[98] As we have seen, the fatal defects of the CQT are: (1) innocent suspects are likely to be more disturbed by the relevant questions than by the comparison questions, while (2) sophisticated guilty suspects can easily (and without being detected) self-stimulate so as to augment their responses to the comparison questions and thus to beat the test. Whether scientifically supportable alternative lie detection techniques can be developed remains to be seen. It is well established that cognitive effort produces pupillary dilation and that the greater the effort, the larger the pupillary change. Building on this fact, it has recently been shown that giving a narrative (rather than a Yes or No) answer to a question produces greater pupillary dilation when the answer is deceptive rather than truthful.[99] Although such work requires replication and study in real-life applications, it illustrates that it may be possible to develop instrumental lie detection techniques that circumvent the weaknesses of CQT polygraphy.

§ 12–3.4.2 The Future of the Guilty Knowledge Test

The detection of guilty knowledge, on the other hand, is entirely feasible from a scientific point of view and the limited research so far conducted with the GKT indicates that this technique works just as the theory would predict. The GKT cannot be employed in many situations where lie detection is now

98. A recent analysis of CQT polygraphy in light of *Daubert* has reached a similar conclusion. Leonard Saxe & Gershon Ben–Shakar, *Admissibility of Polygraph Tests: The Application of Scientific Standards Post–Daubert*, 5 PSYCHOL., L., & PUB. POL'Y., 203 (1999).

99. Daphne P. Dionisio et al., *Differentiation of Deception Using Pupillary Responses as an Index of Cognitive Processing*, 38 PSYCHOPHYSIOLOGY 205–211 (2001).

used. Its utility is limited to those instances in which the investigator can identify a number of facts about the crime scene that are likely to be recognized by a guilty suspect but not by one without guilty knowledge. But it is important to realize that many celebrated criminal cases, including those involving espionage, could have been solved with dispatch and a high level of statistical confidence had the defendant been administered a GKT.

One example is the case of the missing computer hard drives at the Los Alamos nuclear facility.[100] These laptop drives, about the size of a deck of playing cards, contained nuclear secrets and were missing for as long as six months. They reappeared in a package behind a photocopying machine in one of the nuclear facility buildings. The members of the Los Alamos "X Division" that was entrusted with the security of the drives were flown to Albuquerque for a day and polygraphed, but the mystery regarding who placed the drives behind the photocopier remains unsolved. Had the FBI not publicized the recovery of the drives, the information regarding their whereabouts could have been used to develop a GKT which then could have been administered to X Division personnel. For instance, only the guilty individual would know in what building and room the drive was deposited, that it was placed behind a photocopier, and that it was in a certain type of packaging. The GKT also has screening applications. For instance, notorious FBI spy Robert Hanssen reportedly hacked into a secure computer to access secrets.[101] Hanson and any agent could be routinely asked to take a ERP–GKT where various words and pictures would be flashed, including those associated with information the tested person should not have memory for. Probe words in such a test might include the classified computer password that was last in effect, file names, pictures of computer screens that would have to be processed to access information, and other items that would be salient to someone who gathered information from the computer. To an innocent person, all of these stimuli, mixed in with foils, would evoke no memories or P3 wave. A guilty person, by contrast, would show a P3 recognition response to the probe items.

The GKT has not been used by US law enforcement for two reasons. First, there remains a strong, albeit unjustified, faith in "lie detection" which is so much easier to employ. Secondly, use of the GKT requires that the person who will identify the facts to be used in GKT items must visit the crime scene with the original investigative team. Polygraph examiners do not visit crime scenes and criminalists are not yet being trained to develop GKT items that might later be used by polygraph examiners. It is possible, however, that the apparent possibilities of this technique will come to be exploited in the future. If that time does come, the courts may have occasion to consider such questions as the admissibility of GKT results or whether requiring a suspect to undergo a GKT examination is equivalent to requiring him to permit a photograph or a blood sample to be taken.

§ 12–3.4.3 To Accept the Pro–Polygraph Arguments, One Must Believe

Scientists have often noted that extraordinary claims demand extraordinary supporting evidence. With no solid scientific foundation and a lack of

100. *FBI Ends Inquiry in Los Alamos*, NEW YORK TIMES, January 19, 2001.

101. *A Search for Answers: The Suspect; FBI Never Gave Lie Test to Agent Charged as Spy*, NEW YORK TIMES, February 22, 2001.

methodologically sound supporting research, the claims that polygraph tests are up to 95% accurate demand close scrutiny. As a convenience to the reader, we conclude by summarizing what would be required to accept the proponents' conclusions about lie detector tests in preference to ours, as follows:

[1] Regarding Surveys of the Scientific Community:

That two surveys, one by Amato and Honts and the other by the Gallup organization, neither of which was published in a scientific journal, and neither of which asks directly about the scientific soundness of the CQT or the desirability of using it in legal proceedings, are to be preferred over our surveys of two different scientific organizations, each yielding very similar and overwhelmingly negative results, a study that was published in a scientific journal that regularly rejects over 85% of submitted papers.

That the SPR survey of Amato and Honts, which obtained a response rate of only 30%, did a fairer job capturing the opinions of the relevant scientific community than our survey to which 91% responded.

[2] Regarding Countermeasures:

That, in real life, subjects cannot be expected to learn how to employ countermeasures despite the widespread availability of information, in the library or on the internet, on how to accomplish this objective and Raskin, Honts and Kircher's published work showing that guilty subjects can successfully employ countermeasures with no more than a half-hour of instruction[102]

[3] Regarding the Directed Lie Test:

That the results of the directed lie test, a procedure that has received little systematic scientific study and that is not even generally accepted by the professional polygraph community,[103] meets the *Daubert* standards for credible scientific evidence.

[4] Regarding Friendly Polygraph Tests:

That polygraph tests arranged by a suspect's defense counsel, the results of which are protected by attorney-client privilege, involve the same degree of fear of detection as adversarial tests administered by the police, the results of which are available to the prosecution.

That friendly tests meet the *Daubert* standard despite the absence of even one empirical study attesting to the accuracy of these tests.

102. Besides countermeasure information being available in university libraries, in texts such as this, it is also available in public libraries and bookstores in Lykken's books (cited in footnote 73), and on the worldwide web under www.polygraph.com, www.antipolygraph.org, and www.nopolygraph.com.

103. Responding to a request for information made under the Freedom of Information Act, the Department of Defense Polygraph Institute's Dr. Gordon Barland noted in October of 1996 that "we do not teach, nor do we advocate, [the directed lie test's] use in criminal testing."

[5] Regarding Laboratory Studies:

That laboratory studies in which participants are passive recipients of instructions to carry out mock crimes, and which are without the fear of detection that exists in real-life polygraph tests, can be used to accurately estimate the validity of lie detector tests in real life.

[6] Regarding Field Studies:

That those field studies, in which polygraph-induced confessions are the basis for determining ground truth, can be used to estimate CQT accuracy when the only cases selected for study are likely to be the ones that were scored correctly by the original examiner.

[7] Regarding Industry Standards:

That polygraph testing is standardized enough to constitute a scientific test when in fact there are no standards as to what constitutes an acceptable test and the nature of individually administered CQTs varies substantially from one examiner to another.

[8] Regarding Personnel Screening:

That government use of screening tests is justified despite their being strongly biased against the innocent and a complete lack of evidence that they either catch or deter spies.

Index

References Are to Sections, Segmented by Chapter

You might also consult this work's table of contents as a finding device. The table of contents lists every section included in the work and the page number where each topical section is to be found. This is most useful when you know within what chapter or for what subject heading you are searching. The summary of contents that precedes the table of contents may be similarly used.

†